About The National Gardens Scheme

Welcome to The Yellow Book and to the thousands of gardens inside, just waiting to be discovered.

The National Gardens Scheme has been opening gardens to raise money for nursing and caring charities since 1927. So by visiting an NGS garden this year you will be following in a great British tradition and making a vital contribution to the charities the NGS supports.

Funds are donated to our beneficiaries annually. How much we are able to give away is driven by the number of visitors that go to the gardens. So by visiting a garden that opens on behalf of the National Gardens Scheme you can really make a difference and help raise much needed money.

Thanks to the generosity and hard work of garden owners, volunteers and visitors, in 2014 the NGS gave away £2.5 million to our beneficiaries. You can find out more about them on Page 7.

Most of the gardens that open for the National Gardens Scheme are privately owned and offer visitors a unique opportunity to enjoy the garden owners' individual creations. The variety is breathtaking: from village openings to roof gardens; tiny cottage gardens to rolling acres; allotments to barges; you will find gardens to inform and inspire. Your donation, as well as the tea you drink, the cake you eat and the plants you buy, will make a real difference to the life of someone who needs care or support at a critical time in their life.

Enjoy your garden visiting in 2015.

Thank you.
Your visit to a garden really counts.

D0242991

Image: Parsonage Farm, Su

One of the great strengths of the National Gardens Scheme is the fact that every year, amongst the thousands of gardens which open to raise money for charity, there will be hundreds of new ones for visitors to unearth. Many are opening for the first time, others are returning after a break. Either way, they ensure that the wonderful kaleidoscope of gardens is constantly changing and refreshed from one year to the next.

This is important because it gives visitors a sense of expectation. For the N.G.S.'s regular supporters it means they can open their crisp copies of *The Yellow Book 2015* and discover those beguiling 'NEW' labels. I know from my own visits to gardens that I enjoy returning to favourite, familiar places, but equally I look forward to being introduced to unknown treasures.

For the garden owners their first opening in aid of the N.G.S. can be daunting. They are proud of their garden and they want visitors to be admiring and complimentary. Additionally, there are the uncertainties of the British weather and the question of tea; have they baked enough cakes!

Once the first opening is over, however, I am sure that these new recruits soon come to realise that they have joined a remarkable organisation. They will have been welcomed into one of the happiest fundraising operations this country has known - one which spreads its rewards generously to a wide audience; to its volunteers who work so hard to organise the scheme; to those who open their gardens; to the visitors and, not least, to the nursing charities that are the beneficiaries.

So whether you are looking to return to some special favourites, enjoy pastures new, or to explore the N.G.S. for the first time, I can only encourage you to visit the National Gardens Scheme's breathtaking array of gardens and help support this vibrant charity, of which I am proud to be Patron.

Image: 19 Barnwood Road, Hants © Leigh Clapp

229

Image: Hestercombe, Somerset © Jason Ingram

488

Image: Trentham, Staffordshire © Joe Wainwright

513

Contents

ngs gardens open for charity

The National Gardens Scheme
A company limited by guarantee. Registered in England & Wales.
Charity No. 1112664. Company No. 5631421

Registered & Head Office: Hatchlands Park, East Clandon,
Guildford, Surrey, GU4 7RT

T 01483 211535
Web www.ngs.org.uk

© The National Gardens Scheme 2015

Published by Constable, an imprint of Constable & Robinson Ltd,
100 Victoria Embankment, London EC4Y 0DY
An Hachette UK Company
www.hachette.co.uk
www.constablerobinson.com

Front cover image: Rock Farm, Kent
Photographer: Leigh Clapp

Chairman's Message

Last November I took over as Chairman of the National Gardens Scheme from Penny Snell who gave the charity unstinting commitment during her six years in office. She set the bar very high, but I aspire to follow her superb example. Top of my priorities is to make this remarkable organisation better known. Greater awareness of who we are and what we do: our volunteers; the quality of our gardens; our charitable activities; will lead to more visitors to our gardens and more support in various guises. Together they will enable us to increase the amounts of our annual grants to our beneficiaries in nursing and caring and our contribution to health and wellbeing in this country.

A few months ago, one of the last things Penny Snell did as chairman was to open a brand new cancer wellbeing centre at the main NHS hospital in Bristol. We funded the centre in partnership with Macmillan Cancer Support and it is called the NGS Macmillan Wellbeing Centre. The building and its work are a tangible example of the NGS's significant contribution which is only made possible by our garden owners and the visitors to their gardens.

A. Martin McMillan OBE

Image: Hill House, Hampshire © Leigh Clapp

BEAUTIFUL TREES MAKE A HOUSE A HOME.

We're Bartlett Tree Experts, a 100+ year old tree and shrub care company with global reach and local roots. We provide expert, attentive service, a safety-first record and a range of services that includes:

- Tree & Shrub Pruning
- Cabling & Bracing
- Fertilisation & Soil Care
- Insect & Disease Management

BARTLETT

BARTLETT TREE EXPERTS

SCIENTIFIC TREE CARE SINCE 1907

Our Charitable Heritage

The National Gardens Scheme is one of the most significant charitable funders of nursing and caring in the UK. It was founded in 1927 by the Queen's Nursing Institute to raise funds to support district nurses, for whom the QNI was responsible until the introduction of the National Health Service in 1948. At that time the Scheme had become so successful and popular that the QNI continued it as an annual fundraising project. In 1980 the QNI created an independent charity with the foundation of the National Gardens Scheme Charitable Trust and this charitable body has continued ever since.

Since our foundation we have donated over £42 million to nominated beneficiaries (see opposite). Our continuing support means that for all of our beneficiaries we are the largest cumulative donor in their histories; this is the case with our founder the QNI, and with our two largest beneficiaries, Macmillan and Marie Curie.

The physical and mental health benefits of visiting gardens and, indeed, of actual gardening are very real and form an increasingly significant link between the National Gardens Scheme and its beneficiaries. In a sense it is integral to our charitable heritage and the element that we are actively developing in partnership with our beneficiaries.

Above: Penny Snell opening the new NGS Macmillan Wellbeing Centre at Bristol's NHS Southmead Hospital in September 2014

The Trustees of The National Gardens Scheme regularly review the charity's beneficiary policy and in addition to annual donations to major beneficiaries they oversee other donations. The Elspeth Thompson Bursary Fund is a partnership with the Royal Horticultural Society with the NGS providing the funds and the RHS administering the bursaries.

In addition to the core beneficiary policy of funding nursing and caring, the NGS continues to support the training of new gardeners. Currently this includes supporting the National Trust's Careership scheme, funding trainees at the Royal Horticultural Society and funding a trainee at the Garden Museum.

Since 2010 a different 'guest' charity has been chosen from recommendations from NGS volunteers. In 2013 the decision was taken to extend the period for a guest charity from one to two or three years and the current guest charity is Parkinson's UK.

The National Gardens Scheme's commitment to nursing and caring remains constant and we are working increasingly closely with our beneficiaries to maximise the amounts we are able to give and the effect that the funds have. Every visitor to an NGS garden is making an essential contribution to the care of others, in particular care at home and for those with chronic or life-threatening illness.

Our Beneficiaries

WE ARE MACMILLAN. CANCER SUPPORT

The NGS has been a partner of Macmillan Cancer Support since 1985 and is proud to be the charity's largest single donor. Having donated a total in excess of £14.7 million, in 2014 for the first time the NGS grant was used to help fund a new NGS Macmillan Wellbeing Centre, at Bristol's main NHS Southmead Hospital. This and the NGS's previous funding of Macmillan services has helped Macmillan ensure that no one has to face cancer alone.

The NGS has supported Marie Curie Cancer Care since 1996, raising a staggering £6 million during this time. This money enables the charity to continue to provide high quality nursing, totally free, to give people with terminal cancer and other illnesses the choice of dying at home, supported by their families.

Qni The Queen's Nursing Institute

The Queen's Nursing Institute works to improve nursing services for patients in their own homes and communities. We believe that skilled and compassionate nursing should be available to everyone, where and when they need it. We achieve this through our network of Queen's Nurses who are experts in delivering care, benefiting the patients and communities they serve.

carerstrust
action · help · advice

Carers Trust works to improve support, services and recognition for anyone living with the challenges of caring, unpaid, for a family member or friend who is ill, frail, disabled or has mental health or addiction problems. Ongoing support from the NGS has meant so much to carers over the years, and countless individuals have benefited as a direct result of its donations.

hospice UK

Hospice UK is the national charity for hospice care, supporting over 200 UK hospices. Our aim is that everyone with a life limiting condition gets the very best care. Hospices care for around 360,000 people every year, and we support them in their vital work. We are very grateful for the NGS's support, which has raised over £3 million for hospice care since 1996. Over the years, their generous funding has supported a variety of our programmes.

PERENNIAL
GARDENERS' ROYAL BENEVOLENT SOCIETY
Helping Horticulturists In Need Since 1839

Through Perennial, the NGS helps horticulturists who are facing difficulties. The NGS donation is invaluable to the charity's on-going work to help individuals and families. The annual donation to Perennial for gardeners' children also enables on-going support for families when one or both parents have died, and for children who are disadvantaged by other circumstances.

Guest charity

PARKINSON'S UK
CHANGE ATTITUDES.
FIND A CURE.
JOIN US.

Parkinson's UK is the research and support charity for anyone affected by the condition. We are privileged to be the first guest charity to be supported for three years by the NGS, who are helping to fund specialist Parkinson's nurses. Not everyone with Parkinson's in the UK has access to this vital service so, together with the NGS, we're working to ensure that no one faces Parkinson's alone.

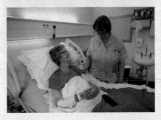

"This is the 21st anniversary of our sponsorship of the National Gardens Scheme and we're confident it's also going to be a very special year for the charity and garden owners."

Jonathan Wragg
Chief Executive, Investec Wealth & Investment

Individuals \ International \ Financial Advisers \ Charities \ Court of Protection

Offices at: Bath Belfast Birmingham Bournemouth Cheltenham Edinburgh Exeter Glasgow Guildford Leeds Liverpool London Manchester Reigate Sheffield

Gardening for Britain

Robin Lane Fox, doyen of garden columnists, salutes
the NGS and the Yellow Book

This article first appeared in full in the Financial Times

**Like English cricket, English garden visiting is highly susceptible to weather.
There is more than ever to be seen, visited and appreciated but owners had to fix
the dates of their open days last year. The stars of their open gardens may not be
those they have publicised in advance.**

As ever, the essential guide is the National Gardens Scheme's *The Yellow Book*. In the 2014 edition the Prince of Wales, the scheme's patron, wrote justly in his annual preface that it exemplifies 'volunteering and community service' and 'constantly strikes [him] with its outstanding model for such forms of selfless service'. In short, garden openers and the NGS were representing the Big Society in action, long before that concept baffled some of us during Conservative canvassing at the last general election. Last year £2.5m was given to the NGS's chosen charities. The Big Society, meanwhile, has gone off the front page but the NGS has continued to grow. It now offers us about 3,800 gardens for visiting, teas and, sometimes, taking dogs on leads. No other country can begin to equal this scope and number. The NGS and its openers are an enduring, golden part of Team GB. Here is what I mean by 'enduring'. The scheme began in 1927 with the Queen's Nursing Institute. It wished to raise

funds for district nurses in the days before any NHS. Regular openers and visitors still talk of opening for 'the nurses' but the range of charities helped by the NGS has widened over the years. District nurses were absorbed into the NHS but, outside it, the privately funded Macmillan cancer nurses sprang up and the privately funded hospice movement was soon accompanying them. Since 1985, Macmillan nurses have received more than £14m from the NGS, enabling them to fund about 150 specialised services and accompanying posts. Also outside the NHS, Marie Curie Cancer Care has received about £6m since 1996. When my back aches ominously in the late evening after a long bank holiday in the garden, I am reassured

that one day I could, perhaps, be looked after by one of these privately funded services, relying on FT readers who have put their own backs into visiting so many gardens so much better than my own. The NGS has now also begun to help Parkinson's UK, a private charity that provides visiting nurses for those with the disease. I much like the sound, too, of its help for the charity Perennial, which 'helps horticulturalists who are facing difficulties'. We all are.

Fashions have always been pushed at keen gardeners. Historians can trace them neatly through past *Yellow Books*. My 1970 edition, when I started to write for the FT, says zero about ornamental grass gardens and is not in the least soppy about 'wildlife'. Nobody made much

of their vegetable gardens or rebranded them as 'potagers'. Although there were 'wild areas', there was not a hint of the slippery term 'sustainable'. Nobody was offering unmown areas of grass with much pride. There may have been 'locally sourced' food in the tea room but nobody made a fuss about it. Gardens were mostly more formal unless they were havens of camellias and rhododendrons or had resorted to rampant 'ground cover'.

Since 1970, openings of London gardens have proliferated, extending outwards to Treetops in Northwood whose photograph looks dreamy, depicting a 'vibrant vision'. On a wider front, *The Yellow Book* is an invitation to visit so many of the loveliest parts of Britain, places where the 'vibrancy' is not just noise and mess. Since 1970, there are so many more media prizes for competing gardens that it is fascinating to see what wins.

Top: Treetops in North London

Left: The famous fritillaries in the meadow garden of Magdalene College, one of a number of Oxford University colleges who generously open their gardens for the NGS. Image: Andrew Lawson

Above: 2 Manvers Street, Derby. Image: Fiona Lea

At 2 Manvers Street in Ripley, Derbyshire, the owners describe their garden of 10 borders, 26 clematis and much else as an 'awe-inspiring oasis'. I note the exact counting. The garden won the Daily Mirror cup for most inspiring garden. I have not seen it but it represents a class that anyone interested in planting and layout is strongly advised to see. The single best training for a discerning gardener and garden maker is to go round the country with *The Yellow Book* and see the gardens marked with a floral symbol. Even if they are a let-down, they have lessons in them. The biggest problem, I find, for new 'designers' is that they simply have not seen enough in situ.

The most inspiring gardens do not have to be big. Not far from London, Benington Lordship, near Stevenage, Hertfordshire, is a seven-acre garden with a hidden double border that has long been one of my favourites. Up beside the famous gardens at Hidcote, the superb privately owned gardens at Kiftsgate Court, Gloucestershire remain among Britain's great gardens. They open otherwise throughout most of the year (visit kiftsgate.co.uk). On a smaller scale, gardens such as 5 Beckett Drive in Northwick, Worcester, look from the photos to be well worth the attention of any gardener with a smallish space and a love of flowers. I tend to find the mass openings of gardens in one village or small town are less rewarding than a single garden with a floral symbol to mark floral distinction. However, there are ideas everywhere, and it was during a collective opening that I first saw the beauty of pure white Dierama, or Venus's Fishing Rod,

growing on its own in a blank expanse of dug soil.

When visiting, please remember that the visit is not all about yourself and your own garden back home. It is a visit, not a shopping trip, although museums, exhibitions and even some gardens try so hard to make us blur the line. It is fun to go with our notebooks and jot down plants or ideas that appeal to us. The bigger question, however, is not 'What is here for me, me, me?' but 'If I had owned this site, what would I have done with it? Has the owner been rather good at it, perhaps without fully thinking why?' Even if the answers are 'not much' and 'no', there are always the teas, the home-made cakes and a wondrous diversity of dogs, in car parks, or on controlling leads.

Below: The borders at Benington Lordship, Hertfordshire

Image: Foxcombe Hall, Oxfordshire

For the Love of Gardens

Have you enjoyed visiting our gardens? Or perhaps you have enjoyed opening your garden, welcoming visitors and raising money for the National Gardens Scheme? If you have, then it is likely you know that the money we raise goes to a group of nursing and caring charities. Alternatively, perhaps you are a garden lover who might like to support us.

We make the link between people's love of gardens and the vital work our beneficiaries do. We need all the help we can get to ensure we give them as much as possible.

If you would like to help us extend the support we give to our beneficiaries, you might consider making a gift in your will to the National Gardens Scheme. Any gift, large or small, is of great significance. To find out more please call Kali Masure on 01483 213907, or have a look at our website: **www.ngs.org.uk/leaveagift**

Tresco's Abbey Gardens

Malvern style

Ilnacullin

Japanese tradition

RHS Harlow Carr

Quality Garden Tours
The Brightwater Collection

No-one has a wider selection of well-paced, well-planned, quality garden tours than Brightwater Holidays. In our new portfolio we have a wonderful range of escorted tours to the best gardens throughout the gardening world.

Famous and grand gardens mix with small and private gardens in all regions of the UK; from private gardens in **Shetland** to hidden gardens in **Cornwall,** and most points in between.

In continental Europe we visit **Holland's magnificent spring bulbfields; Monet's Garden, Menton** and the **Loire Valley** in France, alongside classic **Italian gardens** like **Ninfa** and the famous Alhambra Palace and Generalife Gardens in **Andalucia.**

Further afield we offer exotic holidays of a lifetime to colourful lands such as **India, Japan, South Africa, Ecuador, Yunnan Province** and **Costa Rica.**

Order your copy of our new 2015 brochure today.

www.brightwaterholidays.com

brightwater
holidays

Brightwater Holidays Ltd
Eden Park House, Cupar, Fife KY15 4HS
info@brightwaterholidays.com
+44 (0) 1334 657155

Forty Years On

George Plumptre, Chief Executive of the NGS, celebrates the longevity of some garden owners support

Loyalty runs deep in the National Gardens Scheme, certainly amongst our volunteers but also amongst our garden owners. In 2015 there will be 170 gardens all of which will have opened for 40 years or more. Together they have opened in aid of the NGS for a remarkable total of 9,700 years and raised a total of £4.5 million.

Many of the gardens have been opened by successive owners or generations of the same family, but there is a select group of individuals who have themselves been opening for 40 or more years.

John Berkeley at Spetchley Park in Worcestershire is a perfect example. In 1969, on the death of his father (who had opened the garden ever since the NGS's first year in 1927), he took over the management of Spetchley. He and his wife Gina carried out careful regeneration of the garden, celebrating the Edwardian glories of his grandmother and her sister, the famous plantswoman, Ellen Willmott. 45 years later, they are still managing the gardens alongside their son and daughter-in-law.

In spring, with its expanses of lawn scattered with daffodils that lead to a woodland garden, Spetchley is a special place to visit; in July when it has a second NGS day, the Willmott inspired treasures of the walled gardens and main borders can be discovered.

A few years ago the Old Rectory, Farnborough, high on the Berkshire Downs, was voted Britain's most beautiful Old Rectory by Country Life magazine. In the mid-1960s it was bought by Michael and Caroline Todhunter and in 1971, they first opened for the NGS. From the outset the garden quickly gained a special reputation – helped by the fact that previously it had been the home of Sir John Betjeman. Forty five years later they are still welcoming visitors to their magical garden.

Top: Spetchley Park in Spring.
Image: Clive Crump

Left: Caroline and Michael Todhunter in the garden at the Old Rectory.
Image: Nicola Stocken Tomkins

Their memories are typical as Caroline described:

"We have always been amazed by the loyalty of visitors, many of whom come again and again, year after year. The challenge with the teas is a bit like dealing with a funeral – you never know how many are going to come and when there are too many it is lovely but can get tricky! Over the years I have made so many friends from just striking up conversations with strangers as they walk round or ask a question."

Another much loved garden belongs to Victoria Wakefield and her husband at Bramdean House in Hampshire and here the NGS lineage is a distinguished one. Victoria's parents bought Bramdean in 1944 and opened in 1947; her mother was the NGS county organiser from 1946 to 1976 and as a child during post-war austerity when paper was scarce, Victoria remembers learning to write on the back of Hampshire Yellow Book proofs! Victoria and her husband took over in 1976 since when she has enhanced this superlative plantsman's garden. 2015 will be her 40th consecutive year of opening and visitors old and new continue to discover its horticultural treasures and be thrilled by the unforgettable view up mirror borders.

One of our most venerable garden owners is the distinguished statesman Lord Carrington. When the garden at the Manor House, Bledlow in Buckinghamshire first opened in 1968 it was mainly the domain of his wife, Iona. But it quickly

became the creation of their partnership and since Lady Carrington's death in 2009 Lord Carrington has forged ahead with new projects and ideas. In 2013 for the first NGS Festival Weekend, Anneka Rice dropped in by helicopter at the end of a day-long tour for the NGS. Constantly asking "are you sure you're not getting tired" her nonagenarian host led her enthusiastically from one immaculate enclosure to the next, proudly pointing out his sculpture garden and new William Pye water feature.

In his article on page 10, Robin Lane Fox applauds the 'enduring' qualities of NGS garden owners. We at the National Gardens Scheme are indeed fortunate to be given such continuous commitment and dedication and we are eternally grateful to all of our garden owners.

Above: Lord Carrington and Anneka Rice at the Manor House

Top: Herbaceous borders at Bramdean House

National Trust

Gardens are for sharing

From intimate walled gardens to wisteria walks, the places we look after play a big part in supporting the National Gardens Scheme.

To find a garden near you, please visit ngs.org.uk/nationaltrust

Working together for over 70 years

ngs gardens open for charity

Our supporters

Griffin Glasshouses

Griffin Glasshouses is proud to support
The National Gardens Scheme as its partner. Griffin
Glasshouses creates beautiful bespoke glasshouses,
greenhouses and orangeries for discerning gardeners,
featuring The National Gardens Scheme (NGS)
Collection. This exclusive collection includes five
popular designs which can be personalised with
a range of accessories and finished in any colour.
Griffin's glasshouses are individually designed to
be perfect for you, offering many gardener-friendly
features, virtually no maintenance and with a lifetime
structural guarantee.

GRIFFIN GLASSHOUSES
GLASSHOUSES OF DISTINCTION

Dobies of Devon

Discover the NGS Online Garden Centre! Find all the
best value seeds, plants and gardening equipment in
one convenient website, whilst raising valuable funds
for the charities the NGS supports. Plus, don't forget
to claim your £2 off any NGS plant collection today at
www.ngsdobies.co.uk.

Dobies of Devon, alongside our customers, are proud
to support The National Gardens Scheme by raising
funds through our gardening catalogues and the new
NGS Online Garden Centre, and hope to do so for
many years to come.

of Devon

Quality Garden Tours

Brightwater Holidays are delighted to continue partnering
with the National Gardens Scheme to offer exclusive
holidays based on stunning NGS gardens. For each
place booked on these tours Brightwater Holidays will
make a donation from the total booking cost to the NGS.

Similarly, for any other Brightwater holiday, either in the
UK or abroad, booked through the NGS Brightwater
will again make a donation to the NGS.

For full details contact Brightwater Holidays
01334 657155 or ngs@brightwaterholidays.com

brightwater
holidays

Buy a Woodmansterne greeting card and spread the word

Woodmansterne's greeting cards have been bringing awareness of the NGS brand to the High Street since 2006 and helping to contribute to the wonderful work of the charities the NGS supports.

Look out for the ever-changing photography being added every year (around 25 designs across different shapes and sizes this year alone). Ever popular are favourite themes such as making fun in the garden, relaxing, admiring flowers and cheeky garden animals. A range of small square cards are the latest innovation.

Cards are available from all good independent card and gift shops, garden centres and WHSmith, Waitrose, and John Lewis.

Woodmansterne
Top-notch British greeting cards
for thoughts that count

The NGS Posh Shed

The Posh Shed Company is the latest member of our partnership scheme and has designed and built the very first NGS Posh Shed (see photograph) which is available now. The cost is £4,995 which includes delivery and installation as well as a contribution to our funds.

The NGS Posh Shed has a 8ft by 7ft footprint which includes the veranda, and is constructed from FSC certified tanalised timber that has been pressure treated. It also comes with a two year guarantee for complete peace of mind.

The Posh Shed Company produces a standard range of sheds, as well creating bespoke, one-off creations – and this Posh Shed has been specifically designed for the NGS and its members. For more information visit www.theposhshedcompany.co.uk

THE
POSHSHED
COMPANY

NFU MUTUAL BESPOKE

HOME INSURANCE

TAILORED COVER WITH A REAL FOCUS ON THE FINER DETAILS

Take a closer look at NFU Mutual Bespoke – tailored home insurance rated
5 Star by independent financial research company Defaqto. Designed for those
with higher value homes and contents worth over £100,000 including fine art and
collections, our expert team work closely with you to tailor cover that meets your
specific requirements. We are dedicated to providing you with a great service and
peace of mind, every step of the way.

To find out more and to arrange a meeting with one of our expert team,
we'll put you in touch with your local branch.

nfumutual.co.uk | 0800 197 1283

NFU **Mutual**

INSURANCE | PENSIONS | INVESTMENTS

It's about time®

Rhinefield House Hotel
The New Forest, Hampshire

Wood Hall Hotel & Spa
Wetherby, West Yorkshire

Fawsley Hall Hotel & Spa
Fawsley, Northamptonshire

Ettington Park Hotel
Stratford-upon-Avon, Warwickshire

OUTSTANDING NATURAL BEAUTY...

Hand Picked Hotels is the UK's leading collection of architecturally splendid country house hotels – built for pleasure and continuing a centuries-old tradition of offering guests an indulgent yet attainable country house experience. The award-winning hotels are renowned for exquisite food, fine wines and bespoke service in stylish rural settings.

Combine a visit to a National Gardens Scheme garden with a stay at one of the 17 Hand Picked Hotels in England and Wales. Explore the gardens and extensive parkland landscaped by Capability Brown at Fawsley Hall in Northamptonshire. Wood Hall is perched high on a hill among 100 acres, with fine views of the surrounding area in West Yorkshire. Rhinefield House is set deep in the New Forest National Park, among tall conifers and scented pines.

Stay the night with our special National Gardens Scheme offer of dinner, bed and breakfast plus a bottle of Villa Saletta Spumante from £175 midweek and £189 weekends per room per night.

Visit handpickedhotels.co.uk/nationalgardens to view offers, terms and conditions or call 01642 706 606 and quote promotion code PNGS15.

Hand PICKED
HOTELS
BUILT FOR PLEASURE

01642 706 606   handpickedhotels.co.uk

How to use your Yellow Book

This book lists all gardens opening for the NGS between January 2015 and early 2016. It is divided up into county sections, each including a calendar of opening dates and details of each garden, listed alphabetically.

There are three simple ways to find gardens to visit:

If you are looking for a specific garden, you can look it up in the index at the back, or if you know which county it is in, you can go straight to the relevant county section.

If you want to find out more about gardens near you or in a specific location, go to the relevant county map (at the front of each section) and look for the numbered markers. Use those numbers to look up further information in the county listings.

3 If you are looking to see what is open near you on a specific date, go straight to the relevant county. There is a calendar of opening dates after each county map.

Images and longer descriptions of nearly 3,800 gardens that will open this year on behalf of the National Gardens Scheme can be found by visiting: **www.ngs.org.uk**

County name
Gardens in England are listed first, followed by gardens in Wales.

Directions
A simple set of directions to each garden. Most gardens also list postcodes for use with computer or satellite navigation systems.

Description
A short description of each garden covers the main features. This is written by the garden owner.

Group opening information
Showing gardens that open together on the same day or days.

Admission price
The admission price applies to all visitors unless exceptions are noted e.g. child free.

Sample listing excerpt:

202 ESSEX

37 UNDERHILL ROAD
Benfleet SS7 1EP, Mr Allan & Mrs Diane Downey, 01268 565291, allan.downey@yahoo.co.uk. *Approx 2m from Sadlers Farm r'about on A13. Towards Southend, take R turn at Tarpots Harvester continue to South Benfleet School turn L opp. in to Thundersley Park Rd, continue to Underhill Rd 500yds on R. Home-made teas.* Adm £3.50, chd free. Suns 28 June, 26 July, 23 Aug, 6 Sept (1-6). Visitors also welcome by arrangement June to Sept weekdays only min 10.

A ¼ acre garden offering a relaxing visit featuring topiary shrubs and climbers incl campsis, clematis, honeysuckle and jasmine. Over 40 heucheras in beds with sedums, rudbeckias and hydrangeas. Lovely views from all areas. Undercover Bonsai area, many colourful baskets and containers. Several cast iron and stone sculptures. Patio area to enjoy refreshments.

GROUP OPENING

WALTHAM ABBEY
Waltham Abbey EN9 1LG. *8m W of Epping Town, M25, J26 to Waltham Abbey. At Tarpots by McD turn R to r'about. Take 2nd exit to next r'about. Take 3rd exit (A112) to Tylers. L to Monkswood Av. Home-made teas at Silver Birches, Quendon Drive.* Combined adm £5, chd free. Sun 7 June, Sun 6 Sept (12-6).

62 EASTBROOK ROAD
Caroline Cassell.
not open Sept. No Parking in Eastbrook Rd. Off Honey Lane. walking distance from Halfhides & The Glade Way approx 7mins

39 HALFHIDES
Chris Hamer

76 MONKSWOOD AVENUE
Cathy & Dan Gallagher

SILVER BIRCHES
Quendon Drive. Linda & Frank Jewson

Historic Waltham Abbey is near Epping Forest. The Abbey is purported to be last resting place of King Harold. Lee Valley Regional Park is nearby. Silver Birches boasts 3 lawns on 3 levels. This surprisingly secluded garden has many mixed borders packed with all year interest.

Mature shrubs and trees create a short woodland walk. Crystal clear water flows through a shady area of the garden. At 39 Halfhides the garden has evolved over 45yrs. It features mixed shrubs and perennial borders on 2 levels. Waterfall linking two ponds leads to shade garden. Alpines thrive on scree and in troughs. Beautiful autumn colour. 76 Monkswood Ave is a plantswoman's garden. Mixed borders filled with specimen trees, shrubs and perennials incl asters, dahlias and late-flowering anemones. Wildlife pond. 62 Eastbrook Rd is a small cottage garden, traditional perennial planting, topiary and circular themed hard landscaping. Reclaimed chimney pots for sale as planters. 62 Eastbrook Rd not suitable for wheelchairs.

WASHLANDS
Prayors Hill, Sible Hedingham CO9 3LE. Tony & Sarah Frost, 01787 460702, tony@washlands.co.uk. *½ m NW of Sible Hedingham Church. At former Sugar Loaves PH on A1017 turn SW into Rectory Rd. At former White Horse PH, pass St Peters Church on RH-side. ½ m NW on Prayors Hill.* Home-made teas. Adm £3.50, chd free. Sun 21 June (2-6). Evening Opening, wine, Wed 24 June (5.30-8.30). Sun 28 June (2-6). Visitors also welcome by arrangement June to Aug, groups of 10+.

Informal, tranquil garden approx 1 acre with good views over rolling countryside. Features incl a horse pond. Wide herbaceous, shrub and woodland borders incl roses and peonies. Many young and mature

trees enhance the garden. A developing retirement project. Pond has steep banks. Woodland walk unsuitable for wheelchairs.

GROUP OPENING

WENDENS AMBO GARDENS
Saffron Walden CB11 4UJ. *Parking at village hall nr Church & Colonial Barn signed on day.* Home-made teas at Crossways. Combined adm £5, chd free. Sun 7 June (2-6).

2 CHURCH PATH
Mr Rupert Fulford

3 CHURCH PATH
Ms Liz Hartley

COURTLANDS HOUSE
Dr & Mrs C Glazebrook

CROSSWAYS
Rookery Lane. Mrs Andrea Reynolds.
Leave Newport on B1383 towards Cambridge over 1st r'about then immed L - 250 yds on R between main rd & level crossing

KATIE'S MILLENNIUM WOOD
Duck Street. Dr Katie Petty-Saphon.
Turn off B1039 into Duck St at phone box just E of The Bell PH. After 400yds Duck St bends sharp L but continue straight ahead. Wood is to L & R before tunnel under M11

Wendens Ambo is a meandering historic village. 3 Church Path, quintessential cottage garden adjacent to historic church set behind a chocolate box thatched cottage. Terraced garden with mixed shrubs, perennials, beautiful clematis and roses. Hidden vegetable garden and fruit trees. 2 Church Path, sweeping lawn and orchard area complement cottage. Garden affords wonderful views of historic village. Courtlands House, low maintenance, minimalistic garden with interesting topiary, varieties of hostas, seasonal pots. Ferns and gunnera in shady areas. Crossways, 5 acre informal 'family' garden with mixed planting. Sweeping lawn and wild flowers. Wildlife areas and large pond, a haven for frogs! Specimen trees. Katie's Millennium Wood,10,000 trees planted as whips in 2000 - 2001.

NGS National Gardens Festival Weekend – 6 & 7 June

Symbols explained

NEW Gardens opening for the first time this year or re-opening after a long break.

◆ Garden also opens on non-NGS days. (Gardens which carry this symbol contribute to the NGS either by opening on a specific day(s) and/or by giving a guaranteed contribution.)

♿ Wheelchair access to at least the main features of the garden.

🐕 Dogs on short leads welcome.

✿ Plants usually for sale.

NCH Plant Heritage National Plant Collection.

🛏 Gardens that offer accommodation.

☕ Refreshments are available, normally at a charge.

D Garden designed by a Fellow, Member or Pre-registered Member of The Society of Garden Designers.

🚌 Garden accessible to coaches. Coach sizes vary so please contact garden owner or County Organiser in advance to check details.

Group Visits Group Organisers may contact the County Organiser or a garden owner direct to organise a group visit to a particular county or garden. See the front of each county section for County Organiser contact details, or visit www.ngs.org.uk

Children must be accompanied by an adult

Photography is at the discretion of the garden owner; please check first. Photographs must not be used for sale or reproduction without prior permission of the owner.

Share To indicates that a proportion of the money collected will be given to the nominated charity.

Toilets are not usually available at private gardens

If you cannot find the information you require from a garden or County Organiser, call the NGS office on 01483 211535

Geographical area map

The areas shown on this map are specific to the organisation of The National Gardens Scheme. The Gardens of Wales, listed by area, follow the Gardens of England.

Discover wonderful gardens near you

In 2015 there will be nearly 3,800 gardens across England and Wales opening on behalf of The National Gardens Scheme. In the last 10 years the NGS has donated more than £26 million to nursing, caring and gardening charities.

How you can help support the NGS:

Visit a garden – All our gardens offer something special, and with so many uniquely different gardens to visit you could be spoilt for choice. A visit typically offers the chance to meet the garden owner, with tea and home-made cake in lovely surroundings. Go home inspired with ideas and perhaps a plant from the plant stall - then spread the word to your family and friends!

Open your garden – Joe Swift says: 'It's the sense of community, sharing and fun which makes the gardens which open for the NGS so special'. Opening your garden is a rewarding way to share your passion and hard work while raising money for charity. Size is not critical; many NGS gardens are no larger than typical back gardens. Visitors are looking for interesting design, a good range of plants and gardens which have been tended with love and care. Why not talk to our friendly County Volunteers (details at the front of each county)?

Volunteer – **Lend a hand** and join your local team! The NGS is run by volunteers based in each county and over 400 people share the fun and work involved in organising thousands of open garden events. A range of roles is available, so you don't need to be a gardening expert, but should enjoy being part of a team and working with and meeting new people.

Make a donation – support this wonderful tradition by making a donation online at **www.justgiving.com/ngs/donate**

To find out more or to receive our newsletter please visit www.ngs.org.uk or phone 01483 211535

Image: The Mill at Gordleton, Hampshire © Leigh Clapp

Bedfordshire

Bedfordshire may be one of England's smallest counties, but it has a lot to be proud of.

The county town of Bedford was named the most generous town in the UK by JustGiving in 2014. Bedford can also boast of having one of the finest riverside settings in the country, with stunning panoramic views of the River Great Ouse from the restored Castle Mound – the last remnant of Bedford Castle which was destroyed in 1224.

The county of Bedfordshire is steeped in history; many kings and queens held court and hunted in its forests over the centuries. The impressive country house of Luton Hoo (now a luxury spa hotel) has enjoyed many famous visitors over the years, including Samuel Johnson in 1771 and Winston Churchill.

The grounds of Luton Hoo and the Luton Hoo Walled Garden, which was designed by Capability Brown and established by Lord Bute in the late 1760s, are open for the NGS today.

Bedfordshire offers a variety of stunning NGS gardens, perfect for those seeking a special day out.

Below: Luton Hoo Hotel Golf & Spa

Bedfordshire Volunteers

County Organiser
Judy Stewart
01234 708629
jug.stewart@gmail.com

County Treasurer
Colin Davies
01525 712721
colin.davies@which.net

Publicity
Gill Smith
01525 404121
smith201@btinternet.com

Booklet Coordinator
Edwina Robarts
01279 842422
edwina.robarts@gmail.com

Assistant County Organisers
Geoff & Davina Barrett
01908 585329
geoffanddean@gmail.com

Victoria Coubrough
01234 822371
victoria@coubrough.co.uk

Victoria Diggle
01767 627247
victoria@diggledesign.com

Opening Dates

All entries subject to change.
For latest information check www.ngs.org.uk

January

Sunday 25
8 King's Arms Garden

February

Sunday 15
12 The Manor House, Stevington

March

Sunday 29
14 The Old Vicarage

April

Sunday 26
16 Secret garden

May

Saturday 2
16 Secret garden
Sunday 10
5 Flaxbourne Farm
Saturday 23
13 The Old Rectory

Sunday 24
13 The Old Rectory
Sunday 31
1 NEW Ampthill Grange

June

Festival Weekend

Sunday 7
2 Dragons Glen
5 Flaxbourne Farm
14 The Old Vicarage
17 Southill Park
Saturday 13
7 The Hyde Walled Garden
19 The Swiss Garden
Sunday 21
11 The Manor House, Barton-le-Clay
18 NEW Speeds Dairy Farmhouse
21 Wayside Cottage
Sunday 28
4 The Firs

July

Sunday 5
7 The Hyde Walled Garden
Sunday 12
6 How End Cottage

Saturday 18
20 Walnut Cottage
Sunday 19
20 Walnut Cottage
Saturday 25
15 NEW 1a St Augustine's Road
Sunday 26
9 Luton Hoo Hotel Golf & Spa

August

Wednesday 5
10 Luton Hoo Walled Garden
Sunday 9
5 Flaxbourne Farm

Beautiful and entertaining fun garden of 3 acres, lovingly developed with numerous water features . . .

September

Sunday 6
2 Dragons Glen

October

Sunday 25
8 King's Arms Garden

January 2016

Sunday 31
8 King's Arms Garden

Gardens open to the public

8 King's Arms Garden
10 Luton Hoo Walled Garden
12 The Manor House, Stevington

By arrangement only

3 22 Elmsdale Road

Also open by arrangement

2 Dragons Glen
4 The Firs
5 Flaxbourne Farm
6 How End Cottage
16 Secret garden
20 Walnut Cottage

The Gardens

1 NEW **AMPTHILL GRANGE**
Flitwick Road, Ampthill, Bedford MK45 2NY. Martin & Kath Tidd.
Ampthill Grange is situated on Flitwick Road, on the S edge of town directly opp Redbourne School. The house is accessed via wrought iron gates with two lions on the Gate Pillars. There is no parking on site but there is ample parking across the way in the service rd/bus laybys for Redbourne School. Parking for disabled badge holders at house. Tea. **Adm £4, chd £2. Sun 31 May (2-5.30).**
Ampthill Grange was built circa 1820 and the house was recently sympathetically restored retaining much of the existing character by the current owners. The house sits in 5 acres of grounds that incl a Victorian Walled Garden, Victorian secret garden, orchards, lawns, ornamental ponds and fountains and a significant number of specimen trees and a

Rhododendron Walk. Restoration of the grounds and gardens has been very much work in progress over the past 2 years as we continue to get it back to its former glory.
&. 🐝 ☕

2 **DRAGONS GLEN**
17 Great Lane, Clophill, Bedford MK45 4BQ. Kate Gardner, 07725 307803, kgardner287@gmail.com. *Clophill is situated approx midway between Bedford & Luton on the A6.* Home-made teas. Gluten and dairy free as standard. **Adm £3.50, chd free. Sun 7 June, Sun 6 Sept (2-5.30). Visitors also welcome by arrangement June to Sept.**
This contemporary garden takes full advantage of the sloped landscape and dry conditions of its Greensand Ridge location to great effect. Dry woodland, herbaceous borders, waterfall and wildlife pond create distinct spaces that are linked together by the oriental influences

that run throughout the garden. Partial wheelchair access due to steep slopes and steps around the garden.
&. 🐝 ☕

3 **22 ELMSDALE ROAD**
Wootton, Bedford MK43 9JN. Roy & Dianne Richards, 07733 222495, roy.richards60@ntlworld.com. *4m from J13 M1. Join old A421 towards Bedford, follow signs to Wootton. Turn R at The Cock PH follow rd to Elmsdale Rd on R.* Tea and coffee available. **Adm £3.50, chd free. Visitors welcome by arrangement for groups 8+.**
Topiary garden greets visitors before they enter a genuine Japanese Feng Shui garden incl bonsais, every plant is strictly Japanese, large Koi pond with bridge and Tea House. The garden was created from scratch by the owners and has many interesting features. Large koi pond, Japanese lanterns and a large collection of

Japanese plants and bonsai. From China the Kneeling Archer terracotta soldier.

4 ▶ THE FIRS
33 Bedford Road, Sandy SG19 1EP. Mr & Mrs D Sutton, 01767 227589, d.sutton7@ntlworld.com. *7m E of Bedford. On B1042 between Sandy town centre & A1. On-road parking.* Home-made teas. **Adm £3.50, chd free. Sun 28 June (2-5). Visitors also welcome by arrangement June to Sept refreshments for groups of 10+, by request.**
¼-acre town garden with many garden features reflecting the different conditions from full sun to shade. Designed and created from scratch since 2000 this garden has matured and is productive in fruit, flowers, vegetables and wildlife. Run organically, this garden has everything from shrubs, trees, alpines, perennials, to water features, sculpture and railway memorabilia. Money raised from the refreshments will go to the Need Project, providing food parcels in Bedfordshire. Some gravel paths.

5 ▶ FLAXBOURNE FARM
Salford Road, Aspley Guise MK17 8HZ. Geoff & Davina Barrett, 01908 585329, geoffanddean@gmail.com. *5m W of Ampthill. 1m S of J13 of M1. Turn R in village centre, 1m over railway line.* Home-made teas. **Adm £5, chd free. Sun 10 May, Sun 7 June, Sun 9 Aug (2-6). Visitors also welcome by arrangement May to Sept, conducted tours for groups 12+.**
Beautiful and entertaining fun garden of 3 acres, lovingly developed with numerous water features, windmill, modern arches and bridges, small moated castle, lily pond, herbaceous borders, Greek temple ruin. Recently established three way bridge, planted up with Japanese acers, tree ferns, echiums, bananas and zinnia creating a tropical full of the Wow Factor! New for 2011 Japanese garden with flyover walkway, inspirational woodland setting. Crow's nest, crocodiles, tree house with zip wire for children. Huge Roman stone arched gateway as recently featured in ITV's This Morning programme and BBC One Show. An ideal garden for coach tours lasting at least 3 hours, if teas and conducted tour requested.

The Manor House, Stevington

Wheelchair access is available to all the main parts of the garden.

GREYWALLS
See Northamptonshire.

6 ▶ HOW END COTTAGE
How End Road, Houghton Conquest MK45 3JT. Jeremy & Gill Smith, 0151 540 4121, smith201@btinternet.com. *1m N of Ampthill. Turn R 1m from Ampthill off B530 towards Houghton Conquest. How End Rd 300yds on R. Garden at end of rd, approx ½ m.* Home-made teas. **Adm £4, chd free. Sun 12 July (2.30-5.30). Visitors also welcome by arrangement Mar to Aug, groups of 10+.**
Approx 1 acre garden with 2 ponds, large vegetable garden, greenhouse and orchard. Large lawn gives an uninterrupted view of Houghton House. The garden contains mature trees and beds with many types of slow growing fir trees. Flower beds contain home grown bedding plants and roses. 3 acres of paddocks, wood and further pond. Many spring bulbs.

7 ▶ THE HYDE WALLED GARDEN
East Hyde, Luton LU2 9PS. D J J Hambro Will Trust. *2m S of Luton. M1 exit J10/10a.* Home-made teas.

Adm £3.50, chd free. Sat 13 June, Sun 5 July (2-5).
Walled garden adjoins the grounds of The Hyde (not open). Extends to approx 1 acre and features rose garden, seasonal beds and herbaceous borders, imaginatively interspersed with hidden areas of formal lawn. An interesting group of Victorian greenhouses, coldframes and cucumber house are serviced from the potting shed in the adjoining vegetable garden. Gravel paths.

8 ▶ ♦ KING'S ARMS GARDEN
Ampthill MK45 2PP. Ampthill Town Council, 01525 755648, bryden.k@ntlworld.com. *8m S of Bedford. Free parking in town centre. Entrance opp old Market Place, down King's Arms Yard.* Light refreshments. **Adm £2, chd free. For NGS: Sun 25 Jan, Sun 25 Oct (2-4), Sun 31 Jan 2016. For other opening times and information, please phone or see garden website.**
Small woodland garden of about 1½ acres created by plantsman the late William Nourish. Trees, shrubs, bulbs and many interesting collections throughout the yr. Maintained since 1987 by 'The Friends of the Garden' on behalf of Ampthill Town Council. Wheelchair access to most of the garden.

The Firs

magnificent wisteria thrives at the rear of the house. Children under supervision as there is a water hazard. Partial wheelchair access, 2ft wide bridges.

12 ◆ THE MANOR HOUSE, STEVINGTON

Church Road, Stevington, nr Bedford MK43 7QB. Kathy Brown, 01234 822064, www.kathybrownsgarden.com. *5m NW of Bedford. Off A428 through Bromham.* Home-made teas. **Adm £4, chd free. For NGS: Sun 15 Feb (11-4). For other opening times and information, please phone or see garden website.**

Savour a Winter Walk through the Grasses, Barks, Stems, Seedheads and Bulbs of the Manor House Garden. An avenue of white stemmed birch Betula utilis var jacquemontii Grayswood Ghost looks wonderful backed by creamy Pampass and Calamagrostis. Salmon pink cornus stems vie for attention in the winding winter walk under a canopy of weeping birches, with aconites and arums on the ground. Elsewhere there are major naturalistic borders and the formal garden with its clipped jury scene. Coaches by arrangement only. Featured in The Garden (RHS). Partial wheelchair access. Disabled WC.

13 THE OLD RECTORY

Church Lane, Wrestlingworth, Sandy SG19 2EU. Mrs Josephine Hoy. *5m E of Sandy, 5m NE of Biggleswade. Wrestlingworth is situated on B1042. 5m from Sandy & 6m from Biggleswade.* Home-made teas. **Adm £4, chd free. Sat 23, Sun 24 May (2-6).**

4 acre garden full of colour and interest. The owner has a free style of gardening sensitive to wildlife. Beds overflowing with tulips, alliums, bearded iris, peonies, poppies, geraniums and much more. Beautiful mature trees and many more planted in the last 30 years. Incl a large selection of betulas. Gravel gardens, box hedging, woodland garden and wild flower meadows. Wheelchair access maybe limited on grass paths.

14 THE OLD VICARAGE

Church Road, Westoning MK45 5JW. Ann & Colin Davies. *2m S of Flitwick. Off A5120, 2m N of M1*

9 LUTON HOO HOTEL GOLF & SPA

The Mansion House, Luton Hoo, Luton LU1 3TQ. Luton Hoo Hotel Golf & Spa, www.lutonhoo.co.uk. *Approx 1m from J10 M1, take London Rd A1081 signed Harpenden for approx ½ m - entrance on L for Luton Hoo Hotel Golf & Spa.* Light refreshments. **Adm £5, chd free. Sun 26, Sun 26 July (11-4).**

The gardens and parkland designed by Capability Brown are of national historic significance and lie in a conservation area. Main features - lakes, woodland and pleasure grounds, Victorian grass tennis court and late C19 sunken rockery. Italianate garden with herbaceous borders and topiary garden. Gravel paths.

10 ◆ LUTON HOO WALLED GARDEN

Luton Hoo Estate, Luton LU1 4LF. Exors of N H Phillips, 01582 879089, www.lhwg.org.uk. *Luton Hoo Estate. Take A1081. Turn at sign for Newmill End. After approx. 100 metres turn L through black gates. Follow red signs to Walled Garden.* Home-made teas. **Adm £3, chd free. For NGS: Wed 5 Aug (11-3). For other opening times and information, please phone or see garden website.**

The 5 acre Luton Hoo Walled Garden was designed by Capability Brown and established by Lord Bute in the late 1760s. Successive owners of the estate adapted the garden to match changing horticultural fashions, only for it to fall into decline in the 1980s. The garden is now being restored. Guided tours. Illustrated talks. Exhibition of old tools. Children's trail. Disabled parking next to Walled Garden Entrance. A hard path goes through and around the garden.

11 THE MANOR HOUSE, BARTON-LE-CLAY

87 Manor Road, Barton-le-Clay MK45 4NR. Mrs Veronica Pilcher. *Off A6 between Bedford & Luton. Take old A6 (Bedford Rd) through Barton-le-Clay Village (not the by-pass) and Manor Rd is off Bedford Rd. Parking in paddock.* Home-made teas and cakes. **Combined adm with Wayside Cottage £4, chd free. Sun 21 June (2-5).**

The garden was beautifully landscaped during the 1930s and much interest is created by picturesque stream which incorporates a series of waterfalls and ponds. Colourful streamside planting incl an abundance of arum lilies. Sunken garden with lily pond and a

J12. ¼ m up Church Rd, next to church. Cream teas at C14 church next door. **Adm £4, chd free. Sun 29 Mar, Sun 7 June (2-5.30).** A traditional 2-acre vicarage garden on sandy soil with box and laurel hedges, a formal lawn and many mature shrubs and trees. More recent additions incl colour co-ordinated herbaceous beds, an enlarged cornfield meadow, an English rose garden, pond, rockery and small vegetable plot. There should be a good show of hellebores and daffodils in spring. Wheelchair access generally good.

& ✿ ☕

---

15 NEW 1A ST AUGUSTINE'S ROAD
Bedford MK40 2NB. Chris Damp. *St. Augustine's Rd on L off Kimbolton Rd as you leave the centre of Bedford.* Home-made teas. **Adm £2.50, chd free. Sat 25 July (12-4).** A small but colourful suburban garden, comprising mainly of flower beds and a few vegetables. Path from street is level, but there is a two inch step from the path onto the lawn.

& ✿ ☕

---

16 SECRET GARDEN
4 George Street, Clapham, Bedford MK41 6AZ. Graham Bolton, 07746 864247, bolton_graham@hotmail.com. *3m N of Bedford (not the bypass). Clapham Village High St. R into Mount Pleasant Rd then L into George St. 1st white Bungalow on R.* Tea. **Adm £2, chd free. Sun 26 Apr, Sat 2 May (2-5.30). Visitors also welcome by arrangement, 9 to 16 Apr, 27 Apr to 16 May.** Alpine lovers can see a wide variety of alpines in two small scree gardens, front and back of bungalow plus pans, tubs with dwarf Salix, rhododendron, daphne's. Dwarf acers conifers and pines hellebores epimediums. Two small mixed borders of herbaceous salvias, lavenders and potentillas. Two small greenhouses and cold frames with plants for sale. Partial wheelchair access. No access at the rear of property due to narrow gravel paths but garden can be viewed from the patio.

& ✿ ☕

---

17 SOUTHILL PARK
Southill, nr Biggleswade SG18 9LL. Mr & Mrs Charles Whitbread. *3m W*

---

of Biggleswade. In the village of Southill. 3m from A1 junction at Biggleswade. Cream teas. **Adm £4, chd free. Sun 7 June (2-5).** Large garden, with mature trees and flowering shrubs, herbaceous borders, rose garden and wild garden. Large conservatory with tropical plants. The parkland was designed by Lancelot 'Capability' Brown in 1777.

& ✿ ☕

WE ARE MACMILLAN. CANCER SUPPORT

The NGS has funded 147 different Macmillan projects

---

18 NEW SPEEDS DAIRY FARMHOUSE
Beadlow, Shefford, Bedfordshire SG17 5PL. Martin & Sarah Hind, 01525 860437, sarah.hind1@btinternet.com. *Off the A507 between Clophil & Shefford.* Tea. coffee and cakes. **Adm £4, chd free. Sun 21 June (2-5.30).** The front garden is laid mainly to mature trees, a pond and fruit trees. The back garden was landscaped 4 yrs ago and comprises of a gravel path meandering through borders with a mixture of shrubs and perennials. At the bottom of the rear garden is a vegetable patch and wooden framed greenhouse. Access via a gravel driveway.

& 🍴 ✿ ☕

---

19 THE SWISS GARDEN
Old Warden Aerodrome, Old Warden, Biggleswade SG18 9ER. Shuttleworth Trust in Partnership with Central Beds Council, www.shuttleworth.org/swiss-garden/. *2m W of Biggleswade. Signed from A1 & A600.* The Shuttleworth Collection's restaurant open all day. **Adm £8, chd free. Sat 13 June (9.30-5).** This enchanting garden was created in the 'Swiss Picturesque' style for the 3rd Lord Ongley in the early C19

---

and reopened in July 2014 after a major HLF-funded restoration. Serpentine paths lead to cleverly contrived vistas, many of which focus on the thatched Swiss Cottage. Beautiful wrought-iron bridges, ponds, sweeping lawns and the magnificent Pulhamite-lined Grotto Fernery have all been given a new lease of life by this landmark restoration. A new Woodland Sculpture Trail is now available - themed to represent the stories of the garden and the family who created it. The pathways in the Swiss Garden are firm and even, with minimal gradients, and most are suitable for access by wheelchair users.

& ✿ 🛒 ☕

---

20 WALNUT COTTAGE
8 Great North Road, Chawston MK44 3BD. D G Parker, 0778 4792975. *2m S of St Neots. Between Wyboston & Blackcat r'about on S-bound lane of A1. Turn off at McDonalds, at end of filling station forecourt turn L. Off rd parking.* Home-made teas. **Adm £4, chd free. Sat 18, Sun 19 July (2-6). Visitors also welcome by arrangement Mar to Nov refreshments on request.** Once a land settlement. Ass. 4 acre smallholding. 1 acre cottage garden. Over 2000 species give year round interest. Bulbs, herbaceous, water, bog plants, ferns, grasses, shrubs, trees, coppiced paulownias. Rare, exotic and unusual plants abound. Large pond, level grass paths. 1 acre young trees and shrubs. 2500sq metre glasshouse growing Chinese vegetable. 1½ -acre picnic and party zone. Level grass paths.

& 🍴 ✿ 🛒 ☕

---

21 WAYSIDE COTTAGE
74 Manor Road, Barton-le-Clay MK45 4NR. Nigel Barrett. *1m off A6. Take old A6 (Bedford Rd) through Barton-le-Clay Village (not the by-pass), Manor Rd is off Bedford Rd. Parking in paddock at the Manor House.* Tea at The Manor House. **Combined adm with The Manor House, Barton-le-Clay £4, chd free. Sun 21 June (2-5).** The garden is sited on a ½ -acre plot. Developed over 50yrs it has mature trees, shrubs and flower borders. A well-stocked pond with fountain and waterfalls. A variety of attractive outbuildings nestle within the old walled garden for a tranquil scene with plenty of hidden corners.

& 🍴 ✿ ☕

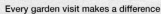

BERKSHIRE

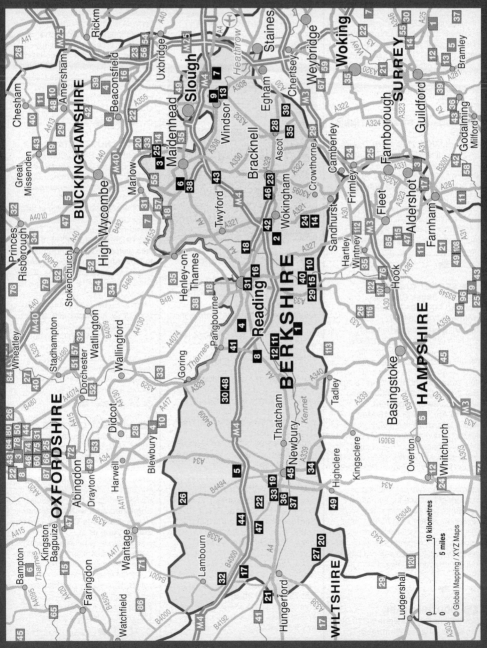

Berkshire

Hello from the NGS team in Berkshire, and thank you for helping us raise over £65,000 for our beneficiary charities last year!

In 2015, special thanks go to Caroline & Michael Todhunter, who have opened their lovely garden at The Old Rectory, Farnborough, for 45 years – a marvellous achievement.

Amongst our new gardens, two in Woolton Hill are owned by artists who will be opening their studios for visitors over the NGS Festival Weekend on the 6th and 7th June.

Also, if you saw the Eton College gardens on BBC Gardener's World, they will be open again on Saturday 13th June.

Many gardens such as Old Waterfield sell plants, and most offer home-made teas and cakes. Baking fans will be excited to know that from March onwards, groups can support the NGS by visiting Welford Park, the stunning setting for the BBC's Great British Bake-Off in 2014.

If you are organising group visits, please see 'Gardens Open By Arrangement' or contact us via angela.oconnell@icloud.com.

Our garden owners work hard in all weather to make NGS days really enjoyable. Whether you are a regular supporter or first-time visitor, we look forward to seeing you soon.

Berkshire Volunteers

County Organiser
Heather Skinner
01189 737197
heatheraskinner@aol.com

County Treasurer
Hugh Priestley
01189 744349 Fri – Mon
hughpriestley@aol.com

Publicity
Heather Skinner
(as above)

Booklet Coordinator
Heather Skinner
(as above)

Assistant County Organisers
Gill Cheetham
01344 423440
gillcheetham@btopenworld.com

Ron Cummings
01488 608124
ron@roncummings.co.uk

Carolyn Foster
01628 624635
candrfoster@btinternet.com

Angela & Graham O'Connell
01252 668645
angela.oconnell@icloud.com

Nikki Sketch
07768 934030
Nikki@sketch.cc

Yvonne Sonsino
07557 133140
yvonnesonsino@gmail.com

Charlotte Stacey
07785 308109
charlotte_stacey@hotmail.co.uk

Left: Eton College Gardens

Since our foundation we have donated more than £42.5 million to charity

Opening Dates

All entries subject to change. For latest information check www.ngs.org.uk

February

Sunday 22
24 Oak Cottage

March

Saturday 28
38 Stubbings House
Sunday 29
7 Ditton Manor
38 Stubbings House

April

Sunday 12
26 The Old Rectory Farnborough
Sunday 26
3 2 Belle Vue Cottages
25 Odney Club
37 Stockcross House
Wednesday 29
17 Inholmes
32 Rooksnest

May

Sunday 3
14 Glenmere
24 Oak Cottage
Saturday 9
31 The RISC Roof Garden, Reading
38 Stubbings House

Sunday 10
26 The Old Rectory Farnborough
38 Stubbings House
Sunday 17
2 Bearwood College
Wednesday 27
39 Sunningdale Park
Sunday 31
33 Rookwood Farm House
36 Springfield Cottage

June

Tuesday 2
13 Frogmore House Garden

Festival Weekend

Saturday 6
49 NEW Woolton Hill Gardens
Sunday 7
4 80 Chapel Hill
37 Stockcross House
41 The Tithe Barn
47 Wickham House
49 NEW Woolton Hill Gardens
Saturday 13
9 Eton College Gardens
19 Jannaways
Sunday 14
5 Chieveley Manor
15 NEW Handpost
26 The Old Rectory Farnborough
46 Whitehouse Farm Cottage
Sunday 21
6 Deepwood Stud Farm

33 Rookwood Farm House
36 Springfield Cottage
Monday 22
6 Deepwood Stud Farm
Wednesday 24
17 Inholmes
32 Rooksnest
Sunday 28
20 Kirby House
21 Littlecote House Hotel
27 The Old Rectory Inkpen
30 Pyt House
35 Southgate
40 Swallowfield Horticultural Society
45 NEW West Mills Allotments & Island Cottage
48 Willow Tree Cottage

July

Saturday 4
31 The RISC Roof Garden, Reading
Sunday 12
16 The Harris Garden
Sunday 19
10 Farley Hill Place Gardens
Sunday 26
18 Ivydene
21 Littlecote House Hotel

August

Saturday 8
31 The RISC Roof Garden, Reading
Sunday 23
21 Littlecote House Hotel

Sunday 30
28 Old Waterfield

September

Sunday 6
7 Ditton Manor

Gardens open to the public

8 Englefield House

By arrangement only

1 Barnwood
11 Field Farm Cottage
12 Folly Farm
22 The Mill House, Boxford
23 Moor Close Gardens
29 The Priory
34 Sandleford Place
42 Twigs
43 Waltham Place Gardens
44 Welford Park

Also open by arrangement

2 Bearwood College
5 Chieveley Manor
6 Deepwood Stud Farm
10 Farley Hill Place Gardens
14 Glenmere
18 Ivydene
32 Rooksnest
37 Stockcross House
38 Stubbings House
46 Whitehouse Farm Cottage
47 Wickham House

The Gardens

1 BARNWOOD
Burghfield Common RG7 3DS. Mrs Wanda Ayres, 01189 831274, wanda.ayres@gmail.com. *6m SW of Reading. Directions available by email or phone*. Home-made teas. **Adm £3.50, chd free. Visitors welcome by arrangement from Mon 1 June to Fri 10 July.**
1/2 acre terraced plantswoman's garden. This natural garden has a lovely woodland backdrop and consists of many interesting perennials, shrubs, spring bulbs and annuals. With areas of sun and shade

the garden combines multiple environments for yr-round interest. Incl greenhouse, fruit cage and raised vegetable beds. Particularly pretty in early summer.
❀ ☕

2 BEARWOOD COLLEGE
Winnersh RG41 5BG. Richard Ryall, 01189 7874300, rpr@bearwoodcollege.co.uk. *5m SE of Reading. Off B3030, 1m S of A329/B3030 intersection at Winnersh, between Reading & Wokingham. Look for Bearwood Rd & College sign*. Home-made teas. **Adm £4, chd free. Sun 17 May (2-5).**

Visitors also welcome by arrangement May to June. Visits subject to school activities.
Late C19 mansion and parkland once owned by the last private owner of The Times newspaper, now an independent school. Azaleas, rhododendrons, walks through mature woodland. Pinetum, lake, natural margins, and icehouse. Extensive hidden Pulham rock and water garden under restoration. Visits incl access to some of the mansion rooms. Features incl specialist plants and charcoal making (subject to weather). Wildlife information stalls on-site.

---

3 ▸ 2 BELLE VUE COTTAGES

The Pound, Cookham SL6 9QF.
Liz & William Wells. *3¹/₂ m N of Maidenhead. On B4447 in Cookham. Car parking best at The Odney Club (¹/₂ m) for both gardens, or at NT Cookham Moor or street parking.* **Adm £2.50. Sun 26 Apr (2-6). Also open Odney Club (10 mins walk).**
This small, stunning modern garden shows just what can be achieved within a narrow space. Cleverly designed and planted, a curving walkway weaves through arbours bordered by lush exotic and native evergreen planting; punctured by dabs of intense colour. Sorry garden is not suitable for children or dogs. Featured in Garden Answers & Détente Jardin.

4 ▸ 80 CHAPEL HILL

Tilehurst, Reading RG31 5DQ. Mrs Iris Geater. *4m S of Reading. M4 J12, exit A4 to Reading. Go over 2 r'abouts, then L at T-lights up Langley Hill onto Park Lane, 1m over 2 r'abouts. At 3rd r'about turn L into Chapel Hill.* **Adm £2.50, chd free. Sun 7 June (2-5). Also open The Tithe Barn (2¹/₂ miles west).**
This may be a small town garden, but it is a little oasis with lots of ideas for the keen gardener. Both front and back areas have colour for yr-round interest. The back garden has been creatively developed with lush deep borders, ferns, acers, roses, heucheras and many shrubs.

♿ ❀

Kirby House

5 ▸ CHIEVELEY MANOR

Chieveley, Nr Newbury RG20 8UT. Mr & Mrs CJ Spence, 01635 248208, spence@chieveleymanor.fsworld.co.uk. *5m N of Newbury. Take A34 N, pass under M4, then L to Chieveley. After ¹/₂ m L up Manor Lane.* Home-made teas. **Adm £4, chd free. Share to St Mary's Church, Chieveley. Sun 14 June (2-5.30). Visitors also welcome by arrangement June to July for groups of 20 max.**
Large garden surrounding listed house (not open) in the heart of Chieveley village. Attractive setting with fine views over stud farm. Walled garden containing lovely borders, shrubs and rose garden, evolving every yr. Box parterre, filled with alliums, white geraniums and lavender. Many viticella clematis growing through shrubs.

♿ ❀ ☕

6 ▸ DEEPWOOD STUD FARM

Henley Road, Stubbings, Nr Maidenhead SL6 6QW. Mr & Mrs E Goodwin, 01628 822684, deepwood@dsl.pipex.com. *2m W of Maidenhead. M4 J8/9 take A404M N. 2nd exit for A4 to Maidenhead. L at 1st r'about on A4130 Henley, approx 1m on R.* Home-made teas on lawn or in conservatory. **Adm £3.50, chd free. Sun 21, Mon 22 June (2-5). Visitors also welcome by arrangement May to Aug for groups of 10-20.**
4 acres of formal and informal gardens within a stud farm, so great roses! Small lake with Monet style bridge and 3 further water features. Several neo-classical follies and statues. Walled garden with windows cut in to admire the views and horses. Woodland walk and enough hanging baskets to decorate a pub! Partial wheelchair access.

♿ ☕

7 ▸ DITTON MANOR

Riding Court Road, Datchet, Slough SL3 9LL. CA Technologies. *Leave M4 J5, follow signs for Langley. At T-lights (Marriott Hotel is on the L) turn L. Crossover r'about then next turning on the R, entrance on the L.* Home-made teas. **Adm £3.50, chd free. Sun 29 Mar, Sun 6 Sept (11-5).**
Ditton Manor sits on a 14 acre moated island at the centre of a fine 208 acre estate created in the traditional English landscape style, originally designed by Lancelot Capability Brown. The Manor enjoys fine views over parkland, woodland and lakes. Formal lawns, walled garden, kitchen garden and cutting garden. Delicious home-made cakes, preserves and honey. Featured in The Telegraph (9 Aug 2014).

♿ ❀ ☕

8 ◆ ENGLEFIELD HOUSE
Englefield, Reading RG7 5EN.
Mr & Mrs Richard Benyon,
01189 302504,
www.englefieldestate.co.uk. *6m W
of Reading. M4 J12. Take A4 towards
Theale. 2nd r'about take A340 to
Pangbourne. After ⅛ m entrance on
L.* **For opening times and
information, please phone or see
garden website.**
The 12 acre garden descends
dramatically from the hill above the
historic house through woodland
where mature native trees mix with
Victorian conifers. Drifts of spring and
summer planting are followed by
striking autumn colour. Stone
balustrades enclose the lower
terrace, with wide lawns, roses,
mixed borders and topiary. A
children's garden with hidden jets of
water provides fun for younger
visitors. Open every Mon throughout
the year (10-6). Group bookings only:
Tues-Thur from 4 March - 30
October. Light refreshments at the
house for group visits only. Featured
in Country Life articles written by
Gervase Jackson-Stops, Arthur
Hellyer and more recently Kathryn
Bradley-Hole. Viewing points and
parts of the garden are accessible for
wheelchairs.

9 ETON COLLEGE GARDENS
Eton SL4 6DB. Eton College.
*½ m N of Windsor. Parking signed off
B3022, Slough Rd, entering Eton.
Walk across fields to entry. Cars with
disabled badges will be directed
closer. Tickets & maps sold at
entrance to Head Master's garden.*
Cream teas. **Adm £5, chd free.
Sat 13 June (2-5).**
A rare chance to visit a group of
central College gardens surrounded
by historic school buildings, incl
Luxmoore's garden on an island in
the Thames reached across two
attractive bridges. Also an
opportunity to explore the fascinating
Eton College Natural History Museum
and a small group of other private
gardens. Featured on BBC
Gardener's World and in The
Telegraph. Wheelchair access limited
to 3 central gardens and over grass
to Luxmoores, with no access to the
Museum or further gardens in Eton
town.

10 FARLEY HILL PLACE GARDENS
Church Road, Farley Hill, Reading
RG7 1TZ. Tony & Margaret Finch,
01189 762544,
tony.finch7@btinternet.com. *From
M4 J11, take A33 S to Basingstoke.
At T-lights turn L for Spencers Wood,
B3349. Go 2m turn L, through
Swallowfield towards Farley Hill.
Garden ½ m on R.* Home-made teas.
**Adm £4, chd free. Sun 19 July
(2-5). Visitors also welcome by
arrangement Mar to Sept for
groups of 15+. Please mention
NGS.**
A 4 acre, C18 cottage garden.
1½ acre walled garden with yr-round
interest and colour. Well stocked
herbaceous borders, large productive
vegetable areas with new herb
garden, dahlia and cutting flower
beds. Victorian glasshouse recently
renovated and small nursery. Garden
featured on Waitrose Garden website
with Alan Titchmarsh and Matt
James, filming tips in the walled
garden. Partial wheelchair access.

11 FIELD FARM COTTAGE
Sulhamstead Hill, Sulhamstead
RG7 4DA. Mrs Anne Froom, 01189
302735, annefroom@knowall.co.uk,
www.bandbwestberkshire.co.uk.
*From A4 take lane by The Spring Inn
for 1m. Garden on L 150yds past 2
LH turns.* **Adm £3, chd free. Visitors
welcome by arrangement May to
Sept for groups of 10+.
Refreshments on request.**
A pretty ¾ acre cottage garden
planted with a wide variety of
herbaceous perennials, set in a series
of garden rooms. Lovely borders spill
over the lawn and there is a large
pond which is fed by a natural spring.
Wild garden, small white garden and
a variety of trees planted by the
owner. Small vegetable garden and
greenhouse.

12 FOLLY FARM
Sulhamstead Hill, Sulhamstead
RG7 4DG. *7m SW of Reading. From
A4 between Reading & Newbury (2m
W of M4 J12) take road marked
Sulhamstead at The Spring Inn.
Restricted car parking.* Tea & home-
made pastries. **Adm £25 (all adm to
the NGS, and matched by an
identical donation from the Garden
Owners). Private tours for groups
of 12 only on Wed 27 May, Wed 10
June, Wed 1 July.** Pre-booking

essential due to limited availability.
For tickets please phone 01483
211535 or visit www.ngs.org.uk.
Gardens laid out in 1912 by Sir Edwin
Lutyens and Gertrude Jekyll. Garden
designs evolved during culmination of
their partnership and considered one
of their most complex. Extensively
restored and replanted by current
owners assisted by Dan Pearson.
Recently reopened for private group
visits which include 1½ hour guided
tour and refreshments. Please note
paths are uneven and there are many
sets of steps between areas of the
garden. Sorry no dogs.

13 ◆ FROGMORE HOUSE GARDEN
Windsor SL4 1LB. Her Majesty The
Queen. *1m SE of Windsor. Entrance
via Park St gate into Long Walk.* Light
refreshments available & picnics
welcome. **For NGS: Tue 2 June.
For advance tickets, please phone
NGS 01483 211535 or visit
www.ngs.org.uk.**
The private royal garden at Frogmore
House on the Crown Estate at
Windsor. This landscaped garden set
in 30 acres with notable trees, lawns,
flowering shrubs and C18 lake, is rich
in history. It is largely the creation of
Queen Charlotte, who in the 1790s
introduced over 4,000 trees and
shrubs to create a model picturesque
landscape. The historic plantings, incl
tulip trees and redwoods, along with
Queen Victoria's Tea House, remain
key features of the garden today.
Please note the Royal Mausoleum is
closed due to long term restoration.
Optional garden history tours (approx
45 mins) with limited availability.
Please phone NGS 01483 211535 for
tickets.

14 GLENMERE

246 Nine Mile Ride,
Finchampstead RG40 3PA. Heather
Bradly & John Kenney, 01189
733274. *2¹/₂ m S of Wokingham. On
B3430, ¹/₄ m E of California
Crossroads r'about*. Home-made
teas at Oak Cottage. **Adm £3.50,
chd free. Sun 3 May (2-5).
Combined adm with Oak Cottage
£4.50, chd free, 3 May only. Visitors
also welcome by arrangement Apr
to Aug for 12 max, with teas on
request.**
Japanese style garden with waiting
arbour, raked gravel area, teahouse,
Torii gate, dry stream bed with bridge
and pond. Vegetable garden,
greenhouse and soft fruit area.

15 NEW HANDPOST

Basingstoke Road, Swallowfield,
Reading RG7 1PU. Faith Ramsay.
*From M4 J11, take A33 S. At 1st
T-lights turn L on B3349 Basingstoke
Rd. Follow road for 2³/₄ m, garden on
L.* Tea. **Adm £4, chd free. Sun 14
June (2-5).**
4 acre designer's garden with many
areas of interest. Features incl two
lovely long borders attractively and
densely planted in six colour sections,
a formal rose garden, old orchard
with a grass meadow, pretty pond
and peaceful wooded area. Large
variety of plants, trees and a
productive fruit and vegetable patch.

16 THE HARRIS GARDEN

Whiteknights, Reading RG6 6UR.
The University of Reading,
www.friendsoftheharrisgarden.org.
uk. *1¹/₂ m S of Reading. Off A327,
Shinfield Rd. Turn R inside Pepper
Lane entrance to campus*. Light
refreshments. **Adm £3.50, chd free.
Sun 12 July (2-5).**
Interesting and spacious 12 acre
amenity, research and teaching
garden. Lots of areas to enjoy incl
floral meadows, herbaceous borders,
stream garden and pond, notable
trees and shrubs, some are very rare.
National Plant Heritage collection of
Digitalis.

♿ NCH

17 INHOLMES

Woodlands St Mary RG17 7SY. *3m
SE Lambourn. M4 J14, take A338 N
(Wantage Rd), then 1st L onto B4000
towards Lambourn. After 1¹/₆ m,
Inholmes signed on L*. Light
refreshments.

**Adm £4.50, chd free. Wed 29 Apr,
Wed 24 June (11-4). Combined
adm with Rooksnest £6.50, chd
free.**
Set in 10 acres with wonderful views
over parkland. A wide variety of
different areas to enjoy incl walled
gardens with formal planting and
inspirational herbaceous borders,
rose beds, cutting and sunken
garden. Walks to the lake and
through the meadow. In spring the
woods are carpeted with bluebells
and in summer the borders are
bursting with colour.

> Reflecting
> pond with
> fountain, lake,
> walled garden and
> contemporary
> sculptures . . .

18 IVYDENE

283 Loddon Bridge Road,
Woodley, Reading RG5 4BE. Janet
& Bill Bonney, 01189 697591,
billabonney@aol.com. *3¹/₂ m E of
Reading. Loddon Bridge Rd is main
road through Woodley. Garden
approx 100yds S of Just Tiles
r'about. Parking in adjacent roads*.
Home-made teas. **Adm £3.50, chd
free. Sun 26 July (2-5). Visitors also
welcome by arrangement June to
Aug for groups of 10-15.**
Small urban gardeners' garden, with
mature tree fern walkway and many
unusual hostas, ornamental grasses
and plants. Overflowing herbaceous
borders and rose bed, using mainly
patio roses. New and developing are
the vertical garden and the Heuchera
Tapestry bed. The garden also
features stained glass and ceramic
art to complete the picture. Owner is
a previous BBC Gardener of the Year
finalist. Featured in Garden News,
Garden of the Week.

19 JANNAWAYS

Bagnor, Newbury RG20 8AH. Mr &
Mrs Sharples. *3m W of Newbury.
From M4 J15, S on A34. Take A4 exit
towards Newbury. 1st L to Station*

---

*Rd. Turn L to Lambourn Rd. 1st R to
Bagnor then follow NGS signs*. Tea.
**Adm £4, chd free. Sat 13 June
(2-5.30).**
This 5 acre garden encompasses a
lake naturally fed by springs. A
circular walk from formal beds near
the house, leads along a woodland
path, crossing a weir to wild flowers
and specimen trees. A pitch perfect
lawn, fishpond, pagodas and many
hidden gems provide visitors with a
rich panoply of vistas round every
corner.

20 KIRBY HOUSE

Upper Green, Inkpen RG17 9ED.
Mr & Mrs R Astor. *5m SE of
Hungerford. A4 to Kintbury. At Xrds in
Kintbury, take Inkpen Rd. Follow road
into Inkpen. Pass common on L. Just
past Crown & Garter PH, turn L (to
Combe & Faccombe). Downhill, at
T-junction turn L, house on R*. **Adm
£4, chd free. Sun 28 June (2-5).
Combined adm with The Old
Rectory, Inkpen (2 miles) £5.00,
chd free.**
7 acres in beautiful setting with views
of S Berkshire Downs and historical
Combe Gibbet, across lawn with ha-
ha and parkland. C18 Queen Anne
House (not open). Formal rose
borders, double herbaceous border,
colour themed border between yew
buttress hedges. Lily pond garden
and terraces laid out by Harold Peto.
Reflecting pond with fountain, lake,
walled garden and contemporary
sculptures. Featured in Country Life
magazine. Some uneven paths.

21 LITTLECOTE HOUSE HOTEL

Hungerford RG17 0SU. Warner
Leisure Hotels, 01488 682509,
www.warnerleisurehotels.co.uk.
*2m W of Hungerford. From A4 turn
R onto B4192 signed Swindon. After
1¹/₂ m exit L & follow signs*. Cream
teas. **Adm £4. Sun 28 June, Sun 26
July, Sun 23 Aug (11-4).**
Beautiful setting around Grade I listed
house with views of the Kennet Valley
over lawns and parkland. Formal
areas incl herbaceous borders, rose
and herb garden, clipped yew, box
hedging, and fruit trees. Don't miss
the stumpery and the courtyard with
large planters. Attractive selection of
hanging baskets. Sorry, no children.
Plants and garden gifts for sale in
Potting Shed Shop. Gravel paths,
some slopes.

Inholmes

22 **THE MILL HOUSE, BOXFORD**

Boxford, Newbury RG20 8DP. Mrs Heather Luff, 01488 608385, H4luff@gmail.com. *5m W of Newbury. Take B4000 to Stockcross. 2m on, turn R to Boxford. At T-junction turn R & then L. Over bridge, The Mill House is 1st on L.* Tea. **Adm £5, chd free. Visitors welcome by arrangement Apr to Oct for groups of 4-20.**

Very attractive large mature garden surrounding Grade II listed Mill House (not open) with R Lambourn running through. Herbaceous borders, rose garden, espalier fruit trees, lawns and vegetables. Good spring colour with daffodils, tulips and alliums. Riverside walk overlooking water meadows. Lovely autumn garden with sedum, echinacea and clipped box. Featured in Country Homes & Interiors and Period Living.

23 **MOOR CLOSE GARDENS**

Popeswood Road, Binfield RG42 4AH. Newbold College, 01344 452424, avtm96@ntlworld.com. *2m W of Bracknell. M4 J10, A329M S to Bracknell. Take 1st exit, then L on B3408 to Bracknell. At 2nd T-lights, L into St Marks Rd, go ⅓ m to entrance at Popeswood Rd.* **Adm £3, chd free. Visitors welcome by arrangement Apr to Sept for groups of 25 max. Refreshments on request.**

Small Grade II listed garden designed 1911-13 by Oliver Hill and a rare example of his early work. Lavender garden, water parterre, remains of Italianate garden. Undergoing long-term restoration, it currently offers most interest in its historical architecture rather than planting. We hope you enjoy learning about its history from tours with our knowledgable volunteers.

24 **OAK COTTAGE**

99B Kiln Ride, Finchampstead, Wokingham RG40 3PD. Ms Liz Ince, www.facebook.com/oakcottagegarden. *2½ m S of Wokingham. Off B3430 Nine Mile Ride between A321 Sandhurst Rd & B3016 Finchampstead Rd.* Home-made teas. **Adm £3.50, chd free. Sun 22 Feb (2-4.30); Sun 3 May (2-5). Combined adm with Glenmere £4.50, chd free, 3 May only.**

¼ acre garden with woodland feel. Mature trees underplanted with snowdrops and other spring flowering bulbs. Several unusual winter flowering plants incl an Edgeworthia chrysantha, Chrysosplenium macrophyllum and many hellebores. Pine pergola with various climbers, greenhouse, island beds and eclectic planting. Small vegetable patch with fruit trees. Featured in Amateur Gardening magazine. Main paths offer partial wheelchair access, but others are gravel and unsuitable.

Visit a garden in your own time – look for by arrangement gardens

25 ODNEY CLUB

Odney Lane, Cookham SL6 9SR. John Lewis Partnership. *3m N of Maidenhead. Off A4094 S of Cookham Bridge. Signs to car park in grounds.* Light refreshments. **Adm £4.50, chd free. Share to Thames Valley Adventure Playground. Sun 26 Apr (2-6). Also open 2 Belle Vue Cottages** (½ mile west).

This 120 acre site beside the Thames is continuously developing, and with lovely riverside walks, can take a full afternoon to visit. A favourite with Stanley Spencer who featured our magnolia in his work. Magnificent wisteria, specimen trees, herbaceous borders, side gardens, spring bedding and ornamental lake. Some gravel paths.

THE OLD MILL

See Wiltshire.

26 THE OLD RECTORY FARNBOROUGH

Wantage, Oxon OX12 8NX. Mr & Mrs Michael Todhunter. *4m SE of Wantage. Take B4494 Wantage-Newbury road, after 4m turn E at sign for Farnborough. Approx 1m to village, Old Rectory on L.* Home-made teas. **Adm £5, chd free. Share to Farnborough PCC. Sun 12 Apr, Sun 10 May, Sun 14 June (2-5.30).**

In a series of immaculately tended garden rooms, incl herbaceous borders, arboretum, boules, rose, pool and vegetables. There is an explosion of rare and interesting plants, beautifully combined for colour and texture. With stunning views across the countryside, it is the perfect setting for the 1749 rectory (not open), once home of John Betjeman, in memory of whom John Piper created a window in the local church. Awarded Finest Parsonage in England by Country Life and the Rectory Society. Plants and preserves for sale. Featured in Country Life magazine. Some steep slopes and gravel paths.

27 THE OLD RECTORY INKPEN

Lower Green, Inkpen RG17 9DS. Mrs C McKeon. *4m SE of Hungerford. From centre of Kintbury at the Xrds, take Inkpen Rd. After ½ m turn R, then go approx 3m (passing Crown & Garter PH then Inkpen Village Hall on L). Near St. Michaels Church, follow car park signs.*

Adm £3.50, chd free. Sun 28 June (2-5). Combined adm with Kirby House (2 miles) £5.00, chd free.
On a gentle hillside with lovely countryside views, the Old Rectory offers a peaceful setting for this pretty 2 acre garden. Enjoy strolling through the formal and walled gardens, herbaceous borders, pleached lime walk and wild flower meadow (some slopes).

A haven
for bees and
butterflies . . .

28 OLD WATERFIELD

Winkfield Road, Ascot SL5 7LJ. Hugh & Catherine Stevenson. *6m SW of Windsor to E of Ascot Racecourse. On A330 midway between A329 & A332. Parking by kind permission of Royal Ascot Golf Club. Access near entrance to Golf Club.* Home-made teas. **Adm £4, chd free. Sun 30 Aug (2-5).**
Set in 4 acres between Ascot Heath and Windsor Great Park, the original cottage garden has been developed and extended over the past few yrs. Herbaceous borders, meadow with specimen trees, large productive vegetable garden, orchard, and mixed hedging. Plants and dried flowers for sale incl unusual varieties grown from seed. Home-made jams and chutneys also for sale.

29 THE PRIORY

Beech Hill RG7 2BJ. Mr & Mrs C Carter, 01189 883146, tita@getcarter.org.uk. *5m S of Reading. M4 J11, A33 S to Basingstoke. At T-lights, L to Spencers Wood. After 1½ m turn R for Beech Hill. After approx 1½ m, L into Wood Lane, R down Priory Drive.* **Adm £4, chd free.**

Visitors welcome by arrangement June to Aug for groups of 6+. Light refreshments on request.
Extensive gardens in grounds of former C12 Benedictine Priory (not open), rebuilt 1648. The mature gardens are in a very attractive setting beside the R Loddon. Large formal walled garden with espalier fruit trees, lawns, mixed and replanted herbaceous borders, vegetables and roses. Woodland, fine trees, lake and Italian style water garden.

30 PYT HOUSE

Ashampstead RG8 8RA. Hans & Virginia von Celsing. *4m W of Pangbourne. From Yattendon head towards Reading. Road forks L into a beech wood towards Ashampstead. Keep L & join lower road. ½ m turn L just before houses.* Home-made teas. **Combined adm with Willow Tree Cottage £5, chd free. Sun 28 June (2-5).**
A 4 acre garden planted over the last 9 yrs by designer owner, around C18 house (not open). Mature trees, yew, hornbeam and beech hedges, pleached limes, modern perennial borders, pond, orchard and vegetable garden. New iris beds. Broadly organic, a haven for bees and butterflies, and we also have chickens.

31 THE RISC ROOF GARDEN, READING

35-39 London Street, Reading RG1 4PS. Reading International Solidarity Centre, www.risc.org.uk/garden. *Central Reading. 5 mins walk from Oracle Shopping Centre. 10 mins from station. Park in Queens Rd or Oracle car parks.* Refreshments at RISC Global Cafe. **Adm £3, chd free. Share to RISC. Sat 9 May, Sat 4 July, Sat 8 Aug (12-4).**
Small edible roof forest garden developed to demonstrate sustainability and our dependence on plants. All plants in the garden have an economic use for food, clothing, medicine etc, and come from all over the world. Demonstration of renewable energy, water harvesting and irrigation systems. Garden accessed by external staircase. Regular tours of garden. Featured in The Daily Telegraph by Mark Diacono (9 Aug 2014).

32 ROOKSNEST
Ermin Street, Lambourn Woodlands RG17 7SB. Dame Theresa Sackler, 01488 71678, garden@rooksnest.net. *2m S of Lambourn on B4000. From M4 J14, take A338 Wantage Rd, turn 1st L onto B4000 (Ermin St) to Lambourn. Rooksnest signed after 3m.* Light refreshments. **Adm £4.50, chd free. Wed 29 Apr, Wed 24 June (11-4). Combined adm with Inholmes £6.50, chd free. Visitors also welcome by arrangement Apr to June for groups of 10+.**
Approx 10 acre exceptionally fine traditional English garden. Rose and herbaceous garden, newly redesigned and planted pond area, herb garden, vegetables and glasshouses. Many specimen trees and fine shrubs, orchard and terraces renovated and recently replanted. Garden mostly designed by Arabella Lennox-Boyd since 1980. Light refreshments incl teas, coffees, home-made cakes and light lunches. Plants sale at June opening only. Mostly grass, some patio and gravel. Happy to provide assistance to wheelchair users.

 ♿ ⚘ ❁ ⛟ Ⓓ ☕

33 ROOKWOOD FARM HOUSE
Stockcross RG20 8JX. The Hon Rupert & Charlotte Digby, www.rookwoodfarmhouse.co.uk. *3m W of Newbury. M4 J13, A34(S). After 3m exit for A4(W) to Hungerford. At 2nd r'about take B4000 towards Stockcross, after approx 3/4 m R then L into Rookwood.* Home-made teas. **Combined adm with Springfield Cottage £5, chd free. Sun 31 May, Sun 21 June (1-5).**
This exciting valley garden, a work in progress, has elements all visitors can enjoy. A rose covered pergola, fabulous tulips, giant alliums, a kitchen garden featuring a parterre of raised beds, as well as bog gardens and colour themed herbaceous planting, all make Rookwood well worth a visit. Please see website for B&B details. Gravel paths, some steep slopes.

 ❁ ⇋ ☕

34 SANDLEFORD PLACE
Newtown, Newbury RG20 9AY. Mel Gatward, 01635 40726, melgatward@btinternet.com. *1 1/2 m S of Newbury on A339. House on NW side of Swan r'about at Newtown on A339.* Light refreshments. **Visitors welcome by arrangement Feb to Oct.**

A plantswoman's 4 acres, more exuberant than manicured with R Enborne flowing through. Various areas of shrub and mixed borders create a romantic, naturalistic effect. Wonderful old walled garden. Long herbaceous border flanks wild flower meadow. Yr-round interest from early carpets of snowdrops and daffodils, crocus covered lawn, to autumn berries and leaf colour. Wheelchair access to most areas. Guide dogs only.

 ♿ ☕

35 SOUTHGATE
Hurstwood, South Ascot SL5 9SP. Mr & Mrs Tony & Judy Bryant, www.jplot.co.uk. *7m SW of Windsor. Off A330 1/2 m S of Ascot Racecourse turn R into Coronation Rd, 2nd R into Woodlands Ride, 1st L into Hurstwood. Turn R at T-junction, follow road to L up slight hill, garden on L.* Home-made teas. **Adm £4, chd free. Sun 28 June (2-5).**
Unusual 1 acre woodland garden on poor acid soil with much dry shade planting under mature trees. Steeply banked and planted rockery water feature and pond, cottage border, woodland walk, vegetable garden and greenhouse. Owner is a hosta enthusiast.

 Ⓓ ☕

36 SPRINGFIELD COTTAGE
Stockcross RG20 8LJ. Anne & Ron Cummings. *3m W of Newbury. M4 J13, A34(S). After 3m exit for A4(W) to Hungerford. At 2nd r'about take B4000 towards Stockcross, after approx 3/4 m first cottage on L.* **Combined adm with Rookwood Farm House £5, chd free. Sun 31 May, Sun 21 June (1-5).**
Pretty cottage garden attached to a C16 listed thatched property (not open) and terraced on three levels. Lovingly designed and created by the owner over the last 8 yrs with mixed shrub and herbaceous borders, rose garden and lawns with seating areas, small pond and laburnum arbour.

 ❁ ☕

37 STOCKCROSS HOUSE
Church Road, Stockcross, Nr Newbury RG20 8LP. Susan & Edward Vandyk, 07765 674863, dragonflygardens@btinternet.com. *3m W of Newbury. M4 J13, A34(S). After 3m exit A4(W) to Hungerford. At 2nd r'about take B4000, 1m to Stockcross, 2nd L into Church Rd.* Home-made teas. **Adm £4.50,**

chd free. **Sun 26 Apr, Sun 7 June (11-5). Visitors also welcome by arrangement May to June for groups of 10+.**
A lovely 2 acre garden set around a Grade II Listed former Vicarage (not open) with an emphasis on plant partnerships, colour combinations and naturalistic planting. Long wisteria and clematis covered pergola, reflecting pool with folly, cascade with pond and duck house, rich variety of roses, vegetable and cutting garden. Sculptural elements by local artists. New for 2015 a small stumpery and fernery. Partial wheelchair access with some gravelled areas.

 ♿ ❁ ☕

hospiceUK

Visit a garden and support hospice care

38 STUBBINGS HOUSE
Henley Road, Maidenhead SL6 6QL. Mr & Mrs D Good, 01628 825454, www.stubbingsnursery.co.uk. *2m W of Maidenhead. From A4130 Henley Rd follow signed private access road opp Stubbings Church. See website for further directions.* Cream teas in Nursery Café. **Adm £3.50, chd free. Sat 28, Sun 29 Mar, Sat 9, Sun 10 May (10.30-4). Visitors also welcome by arrangement Mar to Oct for groups of 10+.**
Parkland garden accessed via adjacent retail nursery. Set around C18 house (not open), home to Queen Wilhelmina of Netherlands in WW2. Large lawn with ha-ha and woodland walks. Notable trees incl historic cedars and araucaria. March brings an abundance of daffodils, and in May a 60 metre wall of wisteria. Attractions incl a C18 icehouse, and access to adjacent NT woodland. A level site, with firm gravel paths.

 ♿ ⚘ ❁ ☕

39 SUNNINGDALE PARK
Larch Avenue, Ascot SL5 0QE. De Vere Group, 01344 634000, sunningdale@deverevenues.co.uk. *6m S of Windsor. On A30 at Sunningdale take Broomhall Lane.*

After ¹/₂ m, R into Larch Ave. From A329 turn into Silwood Rd towards Sunningdale. Home-made teas. **Adm £4, chd free. Wed 27 May (2-5).** Over 20 acres of beautifully landscaped gardens in Capability Brown style. Terrace garden and Victorian rockery designed by Pulham incl cave and water features. Lake area with paved walks, extensive lawns with specimen trees and flower beds, and early rhododendrons. Lovely 1m woodland walk. Grade II listed building (not open). Free garden history tour at 3pm. There are steps down to the lake.

GROUP OPENING

40 SWALLOWFIELD HORTICULTURAL SOCIETY

Swallowfield RG7 1QX. *5m S of Reading. M4 J11 & A33/B3349 signed Swallowfield NGS Opening. Tickets from Doctors Surgery car park, The Street RG7 1QY.* Light refreshments. **Combined adm £6, chd free. Sun 28 June (11-5).**

THE ALLOTMENTS
Pam Wright

APRIL COTTAGE
Linda & Bill Kirkpatrick

5 BEEHIVE COTTAGES
Ray Tormey

BORDER COTTAGE
David & Caroline Cotton

BRAMBLES
Sarah & Martyn Dadds

GREENWINGS
Liz & Ray Jones

LODDON LOWER FARM
Mr & Mrs J Bayliss

NORKETT COTTAGE
Jenny Spencer

PRIMROSE COTTAGE
Mr & Mrs Hilda & Eddie Phillips

THREE GABLES
Sue & Keith Steptoe

WESSEX HOUSE
Val Payne

Swallowfield a real village enhanced by a C12 church, nestled amongst rural countryside, by the Whitewater, Blackwater and Loddon rivers, creating an abundance of wildlife and lovely views. We are proud to offer a variety of beautiful well stocked gardens of all shapes and sizes, incl a model train at Wessex House. Some gardens are within walking distance of each other, but transport is required to see the gardens that are not in the village centre. April Cottage featured in Amateur Gardening and Border Cottage featured in The Kitchen Gardener.

41 THE TITHE BARN

Tidmarsh RG8 8ER. Fran Wakefield. *1m S of Pangbourne, off A340. In Tidmarsh, turn by side of Greyhound PH, over bridge, R into Mill Corner field for car park. Short walk over field to garden.* Home-made teas at adjacent Norman church. **Adm £3.50, chd free. Sun 7 June (2-5). Also open 80 Chapel Hill (2¹/₂ miles east).**
This is a delightful ¹/₄ acre village garden within high brick walls around The Tithe Barn (not open) dating from 1760. Formally laid out with parterres of box and yew. There are roses, hostas, delphiniums and lavender as well as interesting vintage pots and containers. Working beehives. Winner of the English Garden magazine Gardener's Garden competition.

Emphasis on plant partnerships, colour combinations and naturalistic planting . . .

42 TWIGS

Old Forest Road, Winnersh, Wokingham RG41 1JA. Jenny & Gerry Winterbourne, 01189 018249, gerry.winterbourne@ntlworld.com, www.pbase.com/gerrywinterbourne/garden_intro. *1¹/₂ m NW of Wokingham. From Winnersh A329/B3030 junction (Sainsburys) S for approx ³/₄ m towards Wokingham. Turn L into Old Forest Rd, over bridge, ¹/₃ m on L.* **Adm £4, chd free. Visitors welcome by arrangement Apr to Sept for groups of 4+. Light refreshments on request.**
A ¹/₂ acre semiformal garden with two lily ponds at the top, a small vegetable garden to one side and gravel paths that lead down to a more natural woodland area. Planting is mainly trees and shrubs, under planted with drifts of bulbs and perennials. There are no lawns, the whole garden is given over to a large number of interesting plants.

43 ◆ WALTHAM PLACE GARDENS

Church Hill, White Waltham SL6 3JH. Mr & Mrs N Oppenheimer, 01628 825517, www.walthamplace.com. *3¹/₂ m W of Maidenhead. From M4 J8/9 take A404. Follow signs to White Waltham. Pass airfield on R. Turn L to Windsor/Paley Rd. Uphill 550 metres, entrance on L by post box.* Home-made cakes, organic soup and salads made from produce from the garden available in our tearoom. **Adm £5, chd £1. For NGS: Visitors welcome by arrangement for tours with a gardener at 11am & 2pm every Weds from 20 May to 30 Sept. Please phone to book.**
Influenced by Henk Gerritsen, who collaborated with Strilli Oppenheimer to embrace a naturalistic philosophy combining forces with nature. A haven for insects, animals, fungi and indigenous flora. Naturalistic planting, woodland and meadows. Organic and bio-dynamic kitchen garden and farm.

44 ◆ WELFORD PARK

Welford, Newbury RG20 8HU. Mrs J H Puxley, 01488 608203, dpuxley@welfordpark.co.uk. *6m NW of Newbury. M4 J13, A34(S). After 3m exit for A4(W) to Hungerford. At 2nd r'about take B4000, after 4m turn R signed Welford. Entrance on Newbury-Lambourn road.* Light refreshments on request. **Adm £5, chd free. For NGS: Visitors welcome by arrangement from March for groups of 6-40. Please phone or email to book, mentioning NGS.**
An NGS 1927 pioneer garden on the R Lambourn. Queen Anne House with mature trees and formal garden with fabulous peony border and extensive lawns. Emphasis on wildlife habitat, naturalistic and healing planting. Stunning setting for BBC Great British Bake Off 2014.

GROUP OPENING

45 NEW WEST MILLS ALLOTMENTS & ISLAND COTTAGE

West Mills, Newbury RG14 5HT. *In centre of Newbury near the canal. From M4 J13, A339 S. At 3rd r'about, R to Kennet Centre, road winds. After multi-storey, L at T-lights, then 1st R Craven Rd, 1st R Oddfellows Rd, L at end. Street parking or public car parks close by.* Light refreshments at Island Cottage (weather permitting). **Combined adm £4.50, chd free. Sun 28 June (2-5).**

> **NEW ISLAND COTTAGE**
> Mr & Mrs Swaffield

> **NEW WEST MILLS ALLOTMENTS**
> Susan Millington

Allotments and small town garden in the centre of Newbury. You are welcome to visit a small selection of allotments on our 120 plot site, and the opportunity to talk to some of the plot holders about their methods. A variety of fruit, vegetables and flowers to see, some in greenhouses and polytunnels. Island Cottage is a small town garden set between a backwater of the R Kennet and the Kennet and Avon Canal. You will find a mismatch of colour and texture to look at rather than walk through, although you can do that too. A deck overlooks a sluiceway towards a lawn and border. Started from scratch in 2005, and mostly again after the floods of 2014! Featues incl a studio with a small art display of local artists at Island Cottage and plants for sale at both sites.

46 WHITEHOUSE FARM COTTAGE

Murrell Hill Lane, Binfield RG42 4BY. Keir & Louise Lusby, 01344 423688, garden.cottages@ntlworld.com. *Between Bracknell & Wokingham. For SatNav use RG42 4EE. From A329 take B3408. At 2nd set of T-lights turn L into St Marks Rd, 2nd L (opp Roebuck PH) into Foxley Lane. L into Murrell Hill Lane.* Home-made teas. **Adm £3.50, chd free. Share to Sam Beare Hospice. Sun 14 June (11-5). Visitors also welcome by arrangement May to July.** Atmospheric cottage garden of rooms with brick, china and decorative pebble areas. Riotously planted with roses, herbs, ferns and other favourites. The courtyard with pot and lily ponds leads to terrace with circular domed seating area. Pond garden contains a pretty summerhouse and glasshouse with potting shed. Look out for Florence and Fergus the scarecrow couple. Featured on ITV's Love Your Garden.

Enjoy the views across the meadows with home-made tea and cake . . .

47 WICKHAM HOUSE

Wickham, Newbury RG20 8HD. Mr & Mrs James D'Arcy, philippa@darcy3.com. *7m NW of Newbury or 6m NE of Hungerford. From M4 J14, take A338(N) signed Wantage. Approx ³/₄ m turn R onto B4000 for Wickham & Shefford Woodlands. Through Wickham village, entrance 100yds on R.* Home-made teas & home cooked gammon baps. **Adm £4.50, chd free. Sun 7 June (11-4). Visitors also welcome by arrangement May to Sept for groups of 10+.** In a beautiful country house setting, this exceptional ¹/₂ acre walled garden was created from scratch 5 yrs ago. Designed by Robin Templar-Williams, the different rooms have distinct themes and colour schemes. Delightful arched clematis and rose walkway. Wide variety of trees, planting, pots brimming with colour and places to sit and enjoy the views. Separate cutting and vegetable garden. Gravel paths.

D

48 WILLOW TREE COTTAGE

Ashampstead RG8 8RA. Katy & David Weston. *4m W of Pangbourne. From Yattendon head towards Reading. L fork in beech wood to Ashampstead, keep L, join lower road, ¹/₂ m turn L before houses.* Home-made teas at Pyt House. **Combined adm with Pyt House £5, chd free. Sun 28 June (2-5).** Small pretty cottage garden surrounding the house that was originally built for the gardener of Pyt House. Substantially redesigned and replanted in recent yrs. Perennial borders, vegetable garden, pond with ducks and chickens.

GROUP OPENING

49 NEW WOOLTON HILL GARDENS

Nr Newbury RG20 9XQ. *12 mins S of M4 J13, follow A34 to Winchester. A34 exit for Highclere & Wash Common A343. At end of sliproad go R onto A343. Approx ¹/₂ m turn R at Xrds. Take 3rd L onto Church Rd with NGS signs.* Home-made teas. **Combined adm £4.50, chd free. Sat 6, Sun 7 June (1-5).**

> **NEW CANJE GROVE**
> Yvonne & Simon Sonsino

> **NEW ROOKERY FARM**
> Mr & Mrs Perris

Two quite different neighbouring gardens in a rural setting. Both sets of gardeners share a passion for art and the outdoors and this is reflected in the planting combinations and the use of space. Canje Grove is an artist and flower arrangers garden, just over ¹/₃ acre. The garden features multiple colour and plant themed areas, courtyard, a wooden Shepherd's hut, and lots more. Rookery Farm has a rural garden created in the old farmyard. There is a natural pond, formal areas, large rose clad pergola and raised slate bed. Enjoy the views across the meadows with home-made tea and cake. Both owner's art studios open on NGS days and plants for sale.

Whitehouse Farm Cottage

Treat yourself to a plant from the plant stall ✿

BUCKINGHAMSHIRE

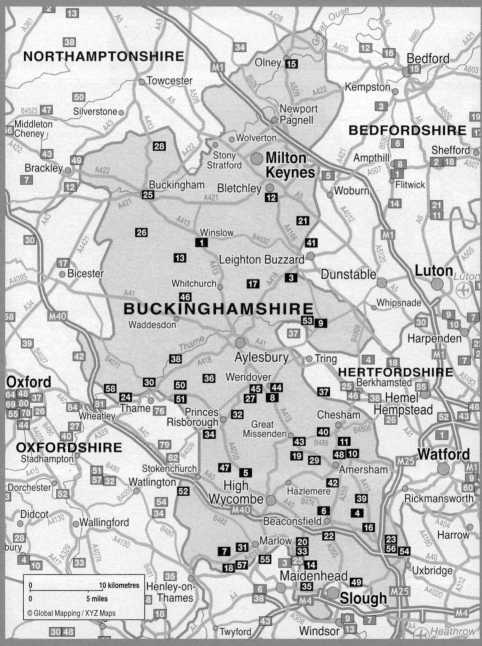

Buckinghamshire

Buckinghamshire has a beautiful varied landscape; edged by the River Thames to the south, crossed by the Chiltern Hills, and with the Vale of Aylesbury stretching to the north.

Many of our group openings can be found in villages of thatched or brick and flint cottages. We boast many historical gardens, including Ascott, Stoke Poges Memorial Gardens (Grade 1 listed), Cliveden and Cowper and Newton Museum Gardens.

So many Buckinghamshire gardens have been used as locations for films and television, with the Pinewood Studios nearby and excellent proximity to London.

Visitors looking for a really interesting afternoon out are encouraged to visit the Cheddington Combined School Sensory Garden, which was created in 2007 by a Year 5 class based on the senses of sight, sound, taste and smell.

The Cheddington Allotments are also well worth a visit, and offer fine vegetable plots, soft fruit trees and beautiful wide views of the Chilterns.

Buckinghamshire Volunteers

County Organiser
Maggie Bateson
01494 866265
maggiebateson@gmail.com

County Treasurer
Tim Hart
01494 837328
tim.hart@virgin.net

Publicity
Sandra Wetherall
01494 862264
sandracwetherall@gmail.com

Booklet Coordinator
Maggie Bateson
(as above)

Assistant County Organisers
Rosemary Brown
01296 429605
grahama.brown@virgin.net

Janice Cross
01494 728291
gwendalice@aol.com

Judy Hart
01494 837328
judy.hart@virgin.net

Margaret Higgins
01844 347072
jhiggins816@btinternet.com

Mhairi Sharpley
01494 782870
mhairisharpley@btinternet.com

Left: Wind in the Willows, Higher Denham Gardens

Since our foundation we have donated more than £42.5 million to charity

Opening Dates

All entries subject to change.
For latest information check www.ngs.org.uk

February
Sunday 22
46 Quainton Gardens

March
Sunday 1
33 Magnolia House
Sunday 15
56 Wind in the Willows
Sunday 29
10 Chesham Bois House

April
Sunday 5
43 Overstroud Cottage
Monday 6
48 Rivendell
Sunday 12
53 Westend House
Saturday 25
14 Cliveden
Sunday 26
30 Long Crendon Gardens
49 Stoke Poges Memorial Gardens
55 Whitewalls

May
Sunday 3
43 Overstroud Cottage
Monday 4
3 Ascott
45 The Plough
50 Turn End
Sunday 10
10 Chesham Bois House
34 The Manor House
Sunday 17
19 Fressingwood
45 The Plough
Tuesday 19
47 Red Kites
Saturday 23
35 Maryfield
Sunday 24
11 NEW Chesham Old Town Gardens
23 Higher Denham Gardens
35 Maryfield

Monday 25
38 Nether Winchendon House
Sunday 31
13 The Claydons
20 Grange Drive Wooburn
40 The Old Sun House

June
Wednesday 3
20 Grange Drive Wooburn

Festival Weekend
Saturday 6
15 Cowper & Newton Museum Gardens
Sunday 7
1 Abbots House
15 Cowper & Newton Museum Gardens
17 Cublington Gardens
43 Overstroud Cottage
54 The White House
Sunday 14
6 18 Brownswood Road
9 Cheddington Gardens
12 126 Church Green Road
21 Great Brickhill Gardens
26 Hillesden House
28 NEW Lillingstone Lovell Gardens
41 NEW One South Lodge
46 Quainton Gardens
Tuesday 16
12 126 Church Green Road
Thursday 18
31 Lords Wood
Saturday 20
44 11 The Paddocks
Sunday 21
7 Burrow Farm
44 11 The Paddocks
51 Tythrop Park
Wednesday 24
42 NEW Orchard House
58 Worminghall Gardens
Sunday 28
5 Bradenham Manor
34 The Manor House

July
Saturday 4
44 11 The Paddocks
Sunday 5
24 NEW Hill House
29 Little Missenden Gardens
44 11 The Paddocks

Tuesday 7
47 Red Kites
Sunday 12
7 Burrow Farm
10 Chesham Bois House
32 NEW Lowthorpe
57 Wittington Estate
Sunday 19
52 The Walled Garden
55 Whitewalls

August
Sunday 2
53 Westend House
Wednesday 12
18 Danesfield House
Monday 31
3 Ascott

September
Sunday 6
55 Whitewalls
Thursday 10
31 Lords Wood

February 2016
Sunday 21
46 Quainton Gardens

Gardens open to the public
3 Ascott
14 Cliveden
15 Cowper & Newton Museum Gardens
38 Nether Winchendon House
49 Stoke Poges Memorial Gardens

By arrangement only
4 Beech House
8 Cedar House
16 Craiglea House
22 Hall Barn
25 Hill House, Buckingham
27 Homelands
36 Moat Farm
37 Montana
39 North Down

Also open by arrangement
1 Abbots House
6 18 Brownswood Road
9 Bridge Cottage, Cheddington Gardens
10 Chesham Bois House
18 Danesfield House
26 Hillesden House
31 Lords Wood
33 Magnolia House
35 Maryfield
42 NEW Orchard House
43 Overstroud Cottage
44 11 The Paddocks
45 The Plough
46 Thorngumbald, Quainton Gardens
47 Red Kites
55 Whitewalls
56 Wind in the Willows

A strong focus on home grown food with an idyllic organic kitchen garden, small orchard . . .

Hill House

The Gardens

1 ABBOTS HOUSE

10 Church Street, Winslow
MK18 3AN. Mrs Jane Rennie,
01296 712326,
jane@renniemail.com. *9m N of
Aylesbury. A413 into Winslow. From
town centre take Horn St & R into
Church St, L fork at top. Entrance 20
metres on L. Parking in town centre &
adjacent streets.* Home-made teas.
Adm £3, chd free. Sun 7 June
(12.30-5.30). Visitors also welcome
by arrangement May to Aug for
groups of 20 max.
Garden on different levels divided into
four. Courtyard near house with
arbour, pond and pots, woodland
garden with rose gazebo, swimming
pool garden with grasses. Walled
Victorian kitchen garden with glass
houses, potager, fruit pergola, wall
trained fruit, many Mediterranean
plants and recent meadow planting.
Partial wheelchair access, garden
levels accessed by steps only.

3 ◆ ASCOTT

Ascott, Wing, Leighton Buzzard
LU7 0PR. Sir Evelyn de Rothschild,
National Trust, 01296 688242,
www.nationaltrust.org.uk/ascott.
*2m SW of Leighton Buzzard, 8m NE
of Aylesbury. Via A418. Buses: 150
Aylesbury - Milton Keynes, 100
Aylesbury & Milton Keynes.* Adm £5,
chd £2.50 (NT members are
required to pay to enter the
gardens on NGS days). For NGS:
Mon 4 May, Mon 31 Aug (2-6). For
other opening times and
information, please phone or see
garden website.
Combining Victorian formality with
early C20 natural style and recent
plantings to lead it into the C21, with
a recently completed garden
designed by Jacques and Peter Wirtz
who designed the gardens at Alnwick
Castle, and also a Richard Long
Sculpture. Terraced lawns with
specimen and ornamental trees,
panoramic views to the Chilterns.
Naturalised bulbs, mirror image
herbaceous borders, impressive
topiary incl box and yew sundial.
Entry into Ascott House is free to NT
members, non-members will be

required to pay. Outdoor wheelchairs
available from car park. Indoor
wheelchairs available in the house.
Mobility buggy, prior booking advised.

4 BEECH HOUSE

Long Wood Drive, Jordans,
Beaconsfield HP9 2SS. Sue & Ray
Edwards, raybc@tiscali.co.uk. *From
A40, L to Seer Green & Jordans for
approx 1m. Turn into Jordans Way on
L. Longwood Drive 1st L. From A413
turn into Chalfont St Giles. Straight
ahead until L signed Jordans. 1st L
Jordans Way.* Adm £3, chd free.
Visitors welcome by arrangement
Mar to Nov.
2 acre plantsman's garden built up
over the last 27 yrs, with a wide range
of plants aimed at providing yr-round
interest. Many shrubs, roses,
grasses, ferns, perennials and trees
planted for their ornamental bark and
autumnal foliage. A particular feature
is the meadow in the back garden
with numerous bulbs and wild flowers
in spring and early summer.
Wheelchair access dependent upon
weather conditions.

Bring a bag for plants – help us give more to charity

5 BRADENHAM MANOR

Bradenham, High Wycombe
HP14 4HF. National Trust & Grant
Thornton UK,
www.nationaltrust.org.uk. *2¹/₂ m
NW of High Wycombe, 5m S of
Princes Risborough. On A4010, turn
by Red Lion PH, car park signed on
village green.* Home-made teas in the
cricket pavillion on the village green.
Adm £3.50, chd free. Sun 28 June
(12-4.30).

C17 yew trees line a unique
wilderness garden cut into steep hill,
offering stunning views. NT
restoration reinstated Victorian
parterres, summer borders, and
rejuvenated 100 yr old orchard. New
guardianship aims to restore Kitchen
Garden, cut flower borders, the
Gardeners Cottage Garden, and a
Secret Garden overlooking Medieval
church rarely open to the public.
Share our plans and progress in our
maiden year, chat with our beekeeper
and try Bradenham Manors' own
apple juice in the orchard. St
Botolph's Church is opening
especially for NGS, offering guided
tours (incl in adm). Gravel paths,
steep grass slopes, cobbled paths,
some narrow entrances.

6 18 BROWNSWOOD ROAD

Beaconsfield HP9 2NU. John &
Bernadette Thompson, 01494
689959, tbernadette60@gmail.com.
*Beaconsfield New Town. From New
Town turn R into Ledborough Lane, L
into Sandleswood Rd, 2nd R into
Brownswood Rd.* Home-made teas
with gluten free options. **Adm £3,
chd free.** Sun 14 June (1.30-5.30).
Visitors also welcome by
arrangement Mar to Aug for
individuals and groups of 36 max.
A plant filled garden designed by
Barbara Hunt. A harmonious
arrangement of arcs and circles
introduces a rhythm that leads
through the garden. Sweeping box
curves, gravel beds, brick edging and
lush planting. A restrained use of
purples and reds dazzle against a
grey and green background. A
beautiful new auricula theatre is at its
best in late spring.

7 BURROW FARM

Hambleden RG9 6LT. David Palmer.
*1m SE of Hambleden. On A4155
between Henley & Marlow, turn N at
Mill End. After 300yds, R onto Rotten
Row. After ¹/₂ m, Burrow Farm
entrance on R.* Home-made teas.
Adm £5, chd free. Sun 21 June,
Sun 12 July (2-5).
Burrow Farm and the adjacent
cottages (not open) are part Tudor
and part Elizabethan, set in the
Chilterns above Hambleden Valley
where it meets the Thames. Views of
pasture and woodlands across the
ha-ha greatly enhance the setting.
Special features are the parterre,
arboretum and C15 barn, where
home-made teas will be served.

8 CEDAR HOUSE

Bacombe Lane, Wendover
HP22 6EQ. Sarah Nicholson,
01296 622131,
jeremynicholson@btinternet.com.
*5m SE Aylesbury. From Gt
Missenden take A413 into Wendover.
Take 1st L before row of cottages,
house at top of lane.* Tea. **Adm
£3.50, chd free.** Visitors welcome
by arrangement May to Sept for
groups of 10+.
A chalk garden in the Chiltern Hills
with a steep sloping lawn leading to a
natural swimming pond with aquatic
plants. Wild flowers with native
orchids. Shaped borders hold a great
variety of trees, shrubs and
perennials. A lodge greenhouse and a
good collection of half hardy plants in
pots. Steep, sloping lawn.

GROUP OPENING

9 CHEDDINGTON GARDENS

nr Leighton Buzzard LU7 0RQ. *7m
E of Aylesbury, 5m S of Leighton
Buzzard, 5m W of Dunstable. Turn off
B489 at Pitstone. Turn off B488 at
Cheddington Station.* Home-made
teas in Methodist Hall by the green,
St Giles Church & Bridge Cottage.
Combined adm £5, chd free. Share
to Methodist Church, St Giles
Church & Village School. Sun 14
June (1.30-5.30).

BRIDGE COTTAGE
Mr & Mrs B Hicks
Visitors also welcome by
arrangement Apr to Sept.
01296 660313
georgeous1@gmail.com

**CHEDDINGTON
ALLOTMENTS**
Church Lane. Cheddington
Parish Council

**CHEDDINGTON COMBINED
SCHOOL SENSORY GARDEN**
Cheddington Combined School

THE OLD POST OFFICE
27 High Street. Alan & Wendy
Tipple

**NEW THE OLD READING
ROOM**
48 High Street. Mrs Kim
Goldhagen

WOODSTOCK COTTAGE
42 High Street. Mr & Mrs D
Bradford

Mentioned in Domesday Book
Cheddington is a friendly active
village, winner of the DeFraine Cup in
the Bucks Best Kept Village Awards
2014. We have six gardens to view in
2015 which vary in size, aspect and
content reflecting their owners style
and passions. The School was the
first in the UK to join an NGS Group.
We invite you to enjoy a relaxed and
pleasant stroll from garden to garden,
visiting St Giles by taking the footpath
through old orchards (or car to
Church Path). Situated in the Vale of
Aylesbury at the northern end of the
Chilterns, Cheddington has an
interesting church dating back to
C12; existing building is C14/C15
(open). Cheddington is home to the
world's first branch railway line (1830-
1964) and The Great Train Robbery of
1963. Partial wheelchair access.

10 CHESHAM BOIS HOUSE

85 Bois Lane, Chesham Bois
HP6 6DF. Julia Plaistowe,
01494 726476,
julia.plaistowe@yahoo.co.uk. *1m N
of Amersham-on-the-Hill. Follow
Sycamore Rd (main shopping centre*

road of Amersham) which becomes Bois Lane. Do not use SatNav once in lane as you will be led astray. Home-made teas. **Adm £3.50, chd free.** Sun 29 Mar (2-5); Sun 10 May, Sun 12 July (2-5.30). Visitors also welcome by arrangement Mar to Sept.

3 acre plantswoman's garden with primroses, daffodils and hellebores in early spring. Interesting for most of the yr with lovely herbaceous borders, rill with small ornamental canal, walled garden, old orchard with wildlife pond, and handsome trees of which some are topiaried. It is a peaceful oasis. Featured in RHS The Garden magazine. Gravel at front of the house.

GROUP OPENING

11 NEW CHESHAM OLD TOWN GARDENS
Chesham HP5 1HY. Church St, Chesham Old Town on B485 Missenden Rd. About ¹/₂ m SW of Chesham Underground Station & follow signs to Church St. Park in Watermeadow car park (free parking) where maps showing location of gardens will be available. Home-made teas in the Old School House garden. **Combined adm £4, chd free.** Sun 24 May (2.30-5.30).

NEW 30 CHURCH STREET
Mrs Angela Bishop

NEW 68 CHURCH STREET
Mr & Mrs R Payne

NEW 1 GERMAIN CLOSE
Mrs Colette Littley

NEW OLD SCHOOL HOUSE
Mrs Geraldine Berry

Four very different gardens in terms of size, design and planting within easy walking distance of each other in a conservation area. 30 and 68 Church Street are hidden behind town houses. No 30 is packed with plants, has cottage garden planting, small trees, a small pond, and flowers and pots in abundance. No 68 in contrast is slightly more formal with an auricula theatre, pleached hornbeam above lavender and a yew hedge leads onto a chamomile lawn bordered by a 30cm high box hedge. No 1 Germain Close reflects the owner's interest in mirrors and other interesting artefacts; it has a wild flower front garden and many terracotta pots. The Old School House is a riverside

garden on the R Chess with a large open lawn and borders with mature shrubs and trees. The river is on the boundary of the property and is well planted. There is also an enclosed garden planted with perennials, most of which have been given from friends as cuttings.

---

12 126 CHURCH GREEN ROAD
Bletchley, Milton Keynes MK3 6DD. David & Janice Hale. 13m E of Buckingham, 11m N of Leighton Buzzard. Off B4034 into Church Green Rd, take L turn at mini-r'about. Home-made teas. **Adm £3, chd free.** Sun 14 June (2-6); Tue 16 June (2-5).

A gentle sloping mature garden of ¹/₂ acre is a plant lover's delight, which incl a small formal garden, shady areas and mixed borders of shrubs, perennials and roses. Features incl a thatched wendy house, pergola, formal pond, wildlife pond, productive fruit and vegetable garden, two greenhouses and patio.

GROUP OPENING

13 THE CLAYDONS
East Claydon MK18 2ND. 1¹/₂ m SW Winslow. In Winslow turn R off High St, follow NT signs to Claydon House. The Old Rectory, Middle Claydon is close to the entrance to Claydon House (NT). Home-made teas in the village hall. **Combined adm £5, chd free.** Sun 31 May (2-6).

ASHTON
Mr & Mrs G Wylie

NEW CLAYDON COTTAGE
Mr & Mrs Tony Evans

INGLENOOKS
Mr & Mrs David Polhill

THE OLD RECTORY
Mrs Jane Meisl

THE OLD VICARAGE
Nigel & Esther Turnbull

Three small villages, originally part of the Claydon Estate, with typical N Buckinghamshire cottages, and 2 C13 churches. Inglenooks is an informal cottage garden with different areas of interest, many roses, surrounding C17 timber framed thatched cottage (not open). The Old Vicarage, a large garden on clay.

Mixed borders, scented garden, dell, shrub roses, vegetables and a natural clay pond. Small meadow area and planting to encourage wildlife. Access via gravel drive. Ashton has lovely views, pots and containers, a vegetable patch and hidden corners, Claydon Cottage has many quirky features and surprises. The Old Rectory is a large garden with a wild flower meadow, herbaceous borders, a woodland walk and cloud hedging. Partial wheelchair access.

Secret Garden overlooking Medieval church rarely open to the public . . .

---

14 ◆ CLIVEDEN
Taplow, Maidenhead SL6 0JA. National Trust, 01628 605069, www.nationaltrust.org.uk/cliveden. 2m N of Taplow. Leave M4 at J7, take A4 towards Maidenhead or M40 at J4, take A404 S & follow brown tourism signs. Cream teas. **Adm £10.50, chd £5.25. For NGS: Sat 25 Apr (10-5).** For other opening times and information, please phone or see garden website.

Set high above the R Thames, discover a garden that delights throughout the seasons with a colourful planting scheme for the famous parterre, impressive floral displays, distinctive topiary and an outstanding sculpture collection. Garden highlights incl spring and summer floral displays on the parterre and in the long garden, autumn colour in the water garden and a new rose garden. Features incl a children's storybook themed play area, yew tree maze, woodland play trail and a shop. Step free route map available from information centre. Wheelchairs available to borrow.

Hollydyke House, Little Missenden Gardens

15 ◆ COWPER & NEWTON MUSEUM GARDENS

Market Place, Olney MK46 4AJ. Mrs E Knight, 01234 711516, www.cowperandnewtonmuseum.org.uk. 5m N of Newport Pagnell. 12m S of Wellingborough. On A509. Please park in public car park in East St. Home-made teas. Adm £2.50, chd free. For NGS: Sat 6, Sun 7 June (10.30-4.30). For other opening times and information, please phone or see garden website.
Restored walled flower garden with plants pre 1800, many mentioned by C18 poet, William Cowper, who said of himself 'Gardening was, of all employments, that in which I succeeded best'. Also summerhouse garden in Victorian kitchen style with organic, new and old vegetable varieties. Herb and medicinal plant borders in memory of the garden's original use by an apothecary. Features incl lacemaking demonstrations and local artists painting live art.

&. ⊕ ☕

16 ◆ CRAIGLEA HOUSE

Austenwood Lane, Chalfont St Peter, Gerrards Cross SL9 9DA. Jeff & Sue Medlock, 01753 884852, suemedlock@msn.com, www.craigleahouse.com. 6m SE Amersham. From Gerrards Cross take B416 to Amersham. Take L fork after ¹/₂ m into Austenwood Lane, garden is ¹/₃ m on R. Park at St Joseph's Church or Priory Rd. Home-made teas. Adm £4, chd free.
Visitors welcome by arrangement Apr to Aug.
Delightful 1 acre garden complements the Arts and Crafts House which it surrounds. The planting ranges from the formal rose garden, lawns, herbaceous borders and pergola, to the natural planting around wildlife ponds, apple trees and along a fairy inhabited fern walk. Garden contains a wide range of plants, incl many hostas, a vegetable garden and many seats affording lovely views of garden.

&. ⊕ ☕

GROUP OPENING

17 CUBLINGTON GARDENS

Cublington, Leighton Buzzard LU7 0LF. 5m SE Winslow, 5m NE Aylesbury. From Aylesbury take A413 Buckingham Rd. After 4m, at Whitchurch, turn R to Cublington. Tea at the village hall, an old Victorian school. Combined adm £5, chd free. Sun 7 June (2-5.30).

> **NEW** CEDAR COTTAGE, 4 THE WALLED GARDENS
> April Curnow

> **NEW** CHERRY COTTAGE, 3 THE WALLED GARDENS
> Gwyneira Waters

> **LARKSPUR HOUSE**
> Mr & Mrs S Jenkins

> **OLD MANOR COTTAGE**
> Dr J Higgins

> **THE OLD STABLES**
> Mr & Mrs S George

> **1 STEWKLEY ROAD**
> Tom & Helen Gadsby

A group of diverse gardens in this attractive Buckinghamshire village listed as a conservation area. The Old Stables is a large established garden divided into areas of different character both formal and informal. Larkspur House is a beautifully maintained modern garden with hostas and alliums being firm favourites. It has a large, newly planted orchard and meadow. Old Manor Cottage is a listed, timber framed property with cottage garden giving yr-round colour, water features and courtyard for outside dining. 1 Stewkley Road has a strong focus on home grown food with an idyllic organic kitchen garden, small orchard and courtyard garden. New for 2015

are the cottages of The Walled Gardens that are accessed via a private tree lined drive, and demonstrate how small gardens can be full of interest and accommodate the lifestyle of the owners. Some gravel paths.

& ⬤ ☕

---

18 DANESFIELD HOUSE
Henley Road, Marlow SL7 2EY. Danesfield House Hotel, 01628 891010, www.danesfieldhouse.co.uk. *3m from Marlow. On the A4155 between Marlow & Henley-on-Thames. Signs on the LH-side Danesfield House Hotel and Spa.* Pre-booking essential for lunch and afternoon tea. **Adm £4, chd free. Wed 12 Aug (10-4.30).** Visitors also welcome by arrangement in Aug.
The gardens at Danesfield were completed in 1901 by Robert Hudson, the Sunlight Soap magnate who built the house. Since the house opened as a hotel in 1991, the gardens have been admired by several thousand guests each yr. However, in 2009 it was discovered that the gardens contained outstanding examples of pulhamite in both the formal gardens and the waterfall areas. The 100 yr old topiary is also outstanding. Part of the grounds incl an Iron Age fort. Guided tours welcome on NGS open days. Pre-booking essential. Restricted wheelchair access to the gardens due to gravel paths.

& ⬤ ☕

19 FRESSINGWOOD
Hare Lane, Little Kingshill, Great Missenden HP16 0EF. John & Maggie Bateson. *1m S of Gt Missenden, 4m W of Amersham. From the A413 at Chiltern Hospital, turn L signed Gt & Lt Kingshill. Take 1st L into Nags Head Lane. Turn R under railway bridge, then L into New Rd & continue to Hare Lane.* Home-made teas. **Adm £3.50, chd free. Sun 17 May (2-5.30).**
Thoughtfully designed garden with yr-round colour and many interesting features. Shrubbery with ferns, grasses and hellebores. Small formal garden, herb garden, pergolas with wisteria, roses and clematis. Topiary and landscaped terrace. Newly developed area incorporating water with grasses. Herbaceous borders and bonsai collection.

⚙ ☕

Jams for sale made with fruits from the garden . . .

GROUP OPENING

20 GRANGE DRIVE WOOBURN
Wooburn Green HP10 0QD. *On A4094, 2m SW of A40, between Bourne End & Wooburn. From Wooburn Church, direction Maidenhead, Grange Drive is on L before r'about. From Bourne End, L at 2 mini-r'abouts, then 1st R.* Tea. **Combined adm £3.50, chd free. Sun 31 May (11-2); Wed 3 June (2-5).**

MAGNOLIA HOUSE ⬒
Alan & Elaine Ford
(See separate entry)

THE SHADES
Pauline & Maurice Kirkpatrick

2 diverse gardens in a private tree lined drive which formed the entrance to a country house now demolished. Magnolia House is a 1/2 acre garden with many mature trees incl magnificent copper beech and magnolia reaching the rooftop, a small cactus bed, fernery, stream leading to pond and greenhouses with 2 small aviaries. Front garden now has natural pond and bees. The Shades drive is approached through mature trees and beds of herbaceous plants and 60 various roses. A natural well is surrounded by shrubs and acers. The garden was developed in 2010 to incl a natural stone lawn terrace and changes made to the existing flower beds. A green slate water feature with alpine plants completes the garden. Partial wheelchair access.

& ⚙ ☕

GROUP OPENING

21 GREAT BRICKHILL GARDENS
Milton Keynes MK17 9AS. *6m S of Milton Keynes. At Old Red Lion PH go up Pound Hill. No 2 is R opp the PH, No 28 is further up on RH-side.* **Combined adm £4, chd free. Sun 14 June (1-6).** Also open One South Lodge.

2 POUND HILL
Mr Ivan Mears

28 POUND HILL
Ms Beata Baker

2 village gardens in the picturesque hilltop village of Great Brickhill. 2 Pound Hill is a small terraced cottage garden full of unusual perennials and a huge collection of heucheras and hostas. 28 Pound Hill is a mature, 1/2 acre garden. Extensive deep borders densely filled with shrubs and perennials in contrasting colours and textures. Many unusual plants, with over 50 different varieties of mostly English roses. Other features incl lily and aquatic plants' pond surrounded by naturalistic borders, fruit and vegetable plot and many exotic plants in pots. 28 Pound Hill featured in Amateur Gardener magazine (2014).

⚙ ☕

22 HALL BARN
Windsor End, Beaconsfield HP9 2SG. The Hon Mrs Farncombe, jenefer@farncombe01.demon.co.uk. *Lodge gate 300yds S of St Mary & All Saints' Church in Old Town centre. Please do not use SatNavs.* **Adm £4, chd free. Visitors welcome by arrangement Feb to Sept for groups of 10+.** Home-made teas and tour on request.
Historical landscaped garden laid out between 1680-1730 for the poet Edmund Waller and his descendants. Features 300 yr old cloud formation yew hedges, formal lake and vistas ending with classical buildings and statues. Wooded walks around the grove offer respite from the heat on sunny days. One of the original NGS garden openings of 1927. Open-air Shakespeare Festival for the mid 2 weeks in June. Gravel paths.

& ⬤ ☕

A natural garden
in harmony with
its setting . . .

GROUP OPENING

23 HIGHER DENHAM GARDENS

Higher Denham UB9 5EA. *6m E of Beaconsfield. Turn off the A412 about 1/2 m N of junction with A40 into Old Rectory Lane. After 1m enter Higher Denham straight ahead. Tickets for all gardens available at the community hall.* Home-made teas in community hall. **Combined adm £5, chd free. Share to Higher Denham Community Association.** Sun 24 May (1-5).

LOWER ROAD

NEW 9 LOWER ROAD
Ms Patricia Davidson

30 LOWER ROAD
Mr & Mrs Mike Macgowan

19 MIDDLE ROAD
Sonia Harris

WIND IN THE WILLOWS
Ron James
(See separate entry)

5 gardens, incl 1 new, in the delightful chalk stream Misbourne Valley. Wind in the Willows has over 350 shrubs and trees, informal, woodland and wild gardens incl riverside and bog plantings and a collection of 80 hostas. 'Really different' and 'stunning' are typical visitor comments. 19 Middle Road has a terrace overlooking a garden crowded with as many plants as possible with some fruit bushes and vegetables. The 3 gardens in Lower Road are medium size, one a work in progress with raised beds perennials and shrubs incl roses, ceanothus and clematis and patio pots, the second a wildlife friendly garden with interesting shrubs, pond, vegetables and ferns and a new garden backing onto the river and recently professionally redesigned. Compare the design with

the outcome and see how existing shrubs and trees have been integrated into the design. The owner of Wind in the Willows will lead guided tours of the garden starting at 2pm and 4pm. Tours last approx 1 hour. Partial wheelchair access to some gardens.

24 NEW HILL HOUSE

Mill Road, Shabbington, Aylesbury HP18 9HQ. Professor Richard Mayou. *2m from Thame between Oxford & Aylesbury. From A418 Wheatley to Thame/Aylesbury road, follow sign to Shabbington. Hill House is on the L 300yds beyond The Old Fisherman & next to the church. Parking in road or in field opp.* Home-made teas. **Adm £4, chd free.** Sun 5 July (2-5.30).
Garden created over 22 yrs around a C18 and C19 Vicarage next to C11 church. 1 acre with 10 compartments incl parterre, herbaceous border, new perennial garden, pool garden and orchard. Walk around 1 1/2 acre field with views of church, house and countryside. Home-made teas and exhibition of village photographs in St Mary Magdalene Church (next door).

25 HILL HOUSE, BUCKINGHAM

Castle Street, Buckingham MK18 1BS. Leonie & Peter Thorogood, 07860 714758, leonie@pjtassociates.com. *By parish church in Buckingham town centre. Signed off bypass at Tingewick Rd Industry turn off.* **Adm £3, chd free. Visitors welcome by arrangement** May to Sept with home-made teas on request.
1/3 acre town garden on old castle walls by parish church in Buckingham conservation area. Aiming for ease of maintenance, yr-round interest and colour, incl good roses, hostas, and herbaceous. Slight slopes to some areas of the garden.

26 HILLESDEN HOUSE

Church End, Hillesden MK18 4DB. Mr & Mrs R M Faccenda, 01296 730451, suefaccenda@aol.com. *3m S of Buckingham through Gawcott. Next to church in Hillesden.* Home-made teas. **Adm £5, chd free.** Sun 14 June (2-5). Visitors also welcome by arrangement June to July for groups of 20+.

By superb church Cathedral in the Fields. Carp lakes, fountains and waterfalls with mature trees. Rose, alpine and herbaceous borders, 5 acres of formal gardens with 80 acres of deer park and parkland. Wild flower areas and extensive lakes developed by the owner. Lovely walks and plenty of wildlife. Also a newly created woodland and vegetable garden. A new conservatory has been added recently. No wheelchair access to lakes.

27 HOMELANDS

Springs Lane, Ellesborough, Aylesbury HP17 0XD. Jean & Tony Young, 01296 622306, young@ellesborough.fsnet.co.uk. *6m SE of Aylesbury. On the B4010 between Wendover & Princes Risborough. Springs Lane is between village hall at Butlers Cross & the church. Narrow lane with an uneven surface.* Light refreshments. **Adm £3.50, chd free. Visitors welcome by arrangement** May to Aug.
Secluded 3/4 acre garden on difficult chalk, adjoining open countryside. Designed to be enjoyed from many seating positions. Progress from semi formal to wild flower meadow and wildlife pond. Deep borders with all season interest and gravel beds with exotic late summer and autumn planting.

GROUP OPENING

28 NEW LILLINGSTONE LOVELL GARDENS

Lillingstone Lovell, Buckingham MK18 5BD. *5m E Buckingham. From Old Gaol in centre of Buckingham take A413 towards Towcester for 5m. Turn R, on a bend, when you see signs to Lillingstone Lovell.* Home-made teas in village hall. **Combined adm £3.50, chd free.** Sun 14 June (12-5).

NEW 9 BROOKSIDE
Mrs Jane Scott
01280 860014
jane@thatchedholidaycottage.co.uk

NEW GLEBE FARM
Mr David Hilliard
01280 860384
thehilliards@talk21.com

Two lovely gardens in the pretty conservation village of Lillingstone

Lovell. The enthusiastic keen gardeners have an abundance of colourful planting and creative ideas, beds of perennials, ponds, vegetables, sculptural elements and everything you would expect from true cottage gardens. Partial wheelchair access to both gardens with some steps and narrow pathways.

♿ 🐕 ⚗ ☕

GROUP OPENING

 LITTLE MISSENDEN GARDENS
Amersham HP7 0RD. *2¹/₂ m NW of Old Amersham. On A413 between Great Missenden & Old Amersham.* Home-made teas. **Combined adm £5, chd free.** Sun 5 July (2-6).

HOLLYDYKE HOUSE
Bob & Sandra Wetherall

KINGS BARN
Mr & Mrs A Playle

MANOR FARM HOUSE
Evan Bazzard

MILL HOUSE
Terry & Eleanor Payne

NEW MISSENDEN LODGE
Rob & Carol Kimber

TOWN FARM COTTAGE
Mr & Mrs Tim Garnham

NEW THE WHITE HOUSE
Mr & Mrs Harris

A variety of gardens set in this attractive Chiltern village in an area of outstanding natural beauty. You can start off at one end of the village and wander through stopping off halfway for tea at the beautiful Anglo-Saxon church built in 975. The gardens reflect different style houses including several old cottages, a Mill House and a more modern house. There are herbaceous borders, shrubs, trees, old fashioned roses, hostas, topiary, koi and lily ponds, kitchen gardens, play areas for children and the R Misbourne runs through a few. Some gardens are highly colourful and others just green and peaceful. Beekeeper at Hollydyke House. Partial wheelchair access to some gardens due to gravel paths and some steps.

♿ 🐕 ⚗ ☕

GROUP OPENING

30 LONG CRENDON GARDENS
Long Crendon HP18 9AN. *2m N of Thame. Long Crendon Village is situated on the B4011 Thame-Bicester road. Maps showing the location of the gardens will be available on the day.* Home-made teas at Church House, High St. **Combined adm £6, chd free. Share to Long Crendon Day Centre & Community Library.** Sun 26 Apr (2-6).

BAKER'S CLOSE
Mr & Mrs Peter Vaines

BARRY'S CLOSE
Mr & Mrs Richard Salmon

48 CHILTON ROAD
Mr & Mrs M Charnock

25 ELM TREES
Carol & Mike Price

MANOR HOUSE
Mr & Mrs West

MULBERRY HOUSE
Ken Pandolfi & James Anderson

TOMPSONS FARM
Mr & Mrs T Moynihan

7 gardens to visit, 3 along the High St; Tompsons Farm a large woodland garden with mature trees and lawns sweeping down to an ornamental lake; Mulberry House a restored, old vicarage garden which incl a formal knot garden, a wooded walkway, pond and Zen style area; Manor House a large garden with 2 ornamental lakes and fine views towards the Chilterns and a large variety of spring flowering bulbs and shrubs. Along the Bicester Road, 2 large gardens; Baker's Close partly walled with terraced lawns, rockery, shrubs and a wild area, a spring planting of thousands of daffodils, narcissi and tulips; Barry's Close has a collection of spring flowering trees forming a backdrop to borders, pools and a water garden. Then 2 cottage gardens; 25 Elm Trees with a terrace, small orchard area, wildlife pond, rockery and deep borders; and 48 Chilton Road with spring bulbs, shrubs, perennial borders and a summerhouse area. Partial wheelchair access to some gardens.

♿ 🐕 ⚗ ☕

2015 sees the NGS total to Macmillan pass £15 million

31 LORDS WOOD
Frieth Road, Marlow Common SL7 2QS. Mr & Mrs Messum, millie-messum@messums.com. *1¹/₂ m NW Marlow. From Marlow turn off the A4155 at Platts Garage into Oxford Rd, towards Frieth for 1¹/₂ m. Garden is 100yds past the Marlow Common turn, on the L.* Home-made teas. **Adm £4, chd free.** Thur 18 June, Thur 10 Sept (11-4.30). **Visitors also welcome by arrangement June to Sept for groups of 15+.**
Lords Wood was built in 1899 and has been the Messums family home since 1974. The 5 acres of garden feature extensive borders in widely varying styles. From vegetable, flower and herb gardens, to large water gardens and rockery, orchard, woodland, and meadow with fantastic views over the Chilterns. We are always bringing new ideas to Lords Wood, you will find something different to enjoy with every visit. Partial wheelchair access; gravel paths and steep slopes.

♿ ☕

32 NEW LOWTHORPE
Crowbrook Road, Askett, Princes Risborough HP27 9LS. Margaret & John Higgins. *100 metres down Crowbrook Rd (north end) on LH-side.* Home-made teas. **Adm £3, chd free.** Sun 12 July (2-5.30).
Set in the conservation area of Askett, the garden has been extensively altered and replanted by the current owners since 2012. A S-facing garden with features incl; herbaceous border, shrub border, roses, fruit cage, and ferns. Wheelchair access to all areas over grass, gravel drive.

♿ 🐕 ☕

33 MAGNOLIA HOUSE

Wooburn HP10 0QD. Alan & Elaine Ford, 01628 525818, landforddesigns@gmail.com, www.lanford.co.uk/events. *On A4094 2m SW of A40 between Bourne End & Wooburn. From Wooburn Church, direction Maidenhead, Grange Drive is on L before r'about. From Bourne End, L at 2 mini-r'abouts, then 1st R.* Light refreshments. **Adm £3, chd free.** Sun 1 Mar (11-2). Visitors also welcome by arrangement Feb to Sept.

¹/₂ acre, many mature trees incl magnificent copper beech and large magnolia. Wollemi pine, cactus, fernery, stream, 2 ponds, 2 greenhouses. 2 small aviaries, beehives, 10,000 snowdrops and hellebores in spring. Collection of over 60 different hostas. Stay in our self-catering accommodation and enjoy the garden. It is constantly being updated and new features added. Partial wheelchair access. Small well behaved dogs allowed by arrangement.

34 THE MANOR HOUSE

Church End, Bledlow, Nr Princes Risborough HP27 9PB. The Lord Carrington. *9m NW of High Wycombe, 3m SW of Princes Risborough. ¹/₂ m off B4009 in middle of Bledlow Village. SatNav directions HP27 9PA.* Tea. **Adm £5, chd free.** Sun 10 May, Sun 28 June (2-5). Paved garden, parterres, shrub borders, old roses and walled kitchen garden. Water garden with paths, bridges and walkways, fed by 14 chalk springs. Also 2 acres with sculptures and landscaped planting. Partial wheelchair access to some parts of the gardens.

35 MARYFIELD

High Street, Taplow SL6 0EX. Jacqueline & Roger Andrews, 01628 667246, japrivate@btinternet.com. *1m S Cliveden. 1/2 m E Maidenhead. From M4 J7 or M40 J4 follow signs for Taplow. Drive past church & up High St. Maryfield is on bend of High St. Please enter through iron gates.* Home-made teas. **Adm £4.50, chd free.** Sat 23, Sun 24 May (2-5). Visitors also welcome by arrangement Apr to Oct for groups of 12+.

A 5 acre garden wrapped around our

Victorian home in the heart of Taplow Village. A series of rooms influenced by Gertrude Jekyll, Christopher Lloyd, Mien Ruys, and many others. Planting incl a prairie garden, white garden, exotic garden and walled vegetable garden. Transitioning from formal to woodland; from classic borders to highly contemporary. Lovely to explore or just sit and have tea, and ask for our delicious signature rhubarb & sour cream cake. Partial wheelchair access. Some narrow paths.

An abundance of colourful planting and creative ideas . . .

36 MOAT FARM

Water Lane, Ford, Aylesbury HP17 8XD. Mr & Mrs P Bergqvist, 01296 748560, patricia@quintadelarosa.com. *Turn up Water Lane by Dinton Hermit in the middle of Ford Village, after approx 200yds turn L over cattle grid between beech hedges into Moat Farm.* Home-made teas. **Adm £4, chd free.** Visitors welcome by arrangement Apr to Sept.

A country garden with herbaceous borders, roses, hostas, trees and water. A moat that flows through the garden and a blind moat through the arboretum. Small walled garden and some vegetables.

37 MONTANA

Shire Lane, Cholesbury HP23 6NA. John & Diana Garner, 01494 758347, montana@cholesbury.net. *3m NW of Chesham. Leave A41 at A4251 North Church. Go through Wigginton Village, R after Champneys. 2nd R is Shire Lane. From Chesham pass Full Moon PH on your L, take 1st R, 1st L is Shire Lane. Montana ¹/₂ m on L.* Home-made teas. **Adm £3.50, chd free.** Visitors welcome by arrangement Mar to June.

A 4 acre garden for all seasons, comprising herbaceous borders, unusual flowering trees and shrubs, meandering paths through woodland which has been planted with

thousands of daffodils. The garden has evolved from virtually nothing since 1995. Plenty of seats to enjoy the peace. Features incl spring bulbs, vegetables, ponds, greenhouses, chickens and bees. An unmanicured but happy garden.

38 ◆ NETHER WINCHENDON HOUSE

Nether Winchendon, Near Thame, Aylesbury HP18 0DY. Mr Robert Spencer Bernard, 01844 290101, www.netherwinchendonhouse.com. *6m SW of Aylesbury, 6m from Thame. Approx 4m from Thame on A418 turn 1st L to Cuddington, turn L at Xrds, downhill, turn R, & R again to parking by house* (2.30-5). **Adm £4, chd free. For NGS: Mon 25 May (2-5.30).** For other opening times and information, please phone or see garden website.

Nether Winchendon House is set in 7 acres of garden with fine and rare trees and surrounded by parkland. A Founder Garden (1927). Medieval and Tudor house set in stunning landscape. The South Lawn runs down to the R Thame. Picturesque village with interesting church. Conducted tours of the house (additional adm, not to NGS).

39 NORTH DOWN

Dodds Lane, Chalfont St Giles HP8 4EL. Merida Saunders, 01494 872928. *4m SE of Amersham, 4m NE of Beaconsfield. Opp the green in centre of village, at Crown Inn turn into UpCorner onto Silver Hill. At top of hill fork R into Dodds Lane. North Down is 7th on L.* Light refreshments. **Adm £3.50, chd free.** Visitors welcome by arrangement May to Sept for groups of 4-30.

A passion for gardening is evident in this plantswomans lovely ³/₄ acre garden which has evolved over the yrs with scenic effect in mind. Colourful and interesting throughout the yr. Large grassed areas with island beds of mixed perennials, shrubs and some unusual plants. Variety of rhododendrons, azaleas, acers, clematis and a huge Kiftsgate rose. Displays of sempervivum varieties, alpines, grasses and ferns. Small patio and water feature, greenhouse and an Italianate front patio to owner's design.

Lemon drizzle cake, Victoria sponge ... yummy!

40 THE OLD SUN HOUSE
Pednor, Chesham HP5 2SZ. Mr & Mrs M Sharpley. *3m E of Gt Missenden, 2m W of Chesham. From Gt Missenden take B485 to Chesham, 1st L & follow signs approx 2m. From Chesham Church St (B485) follow signs approx 1½ m.* Home-made teas. **Adm £4, chd free.** Sun 31 May (2-5.30).
5 acre garden on a Chiltern ridge giving superb views over organic farmland. Mature native trees surround the garden with inner planting of unusual trees and shrubs. Large ornamental pond with water loving marginal plants. Other features incl herbaceous beds, vegetable and herb garden, woodland walk, pheasants and chickens. A natural garden in harmony with its setting. Gravel drive.
♿ 🐾 ✺ ☕

41 NEW ONE SOUTH LODGE
Linslade Road, Heath and Reach, Leighton Buzzard LU7 0EB. David Foley & Stephen Milne. *1m Leighton Buzzard town centre, end of Plantation Rd, junction with Bragenham Lane. From M1 J13, 7m through Woburn to Heath & Reach, take R onto Linslade Rd, past Rushmere Park entrance on R. The house is 1st R on the next bend.* Light refreshments. **Adm £3, chd free.** Sun 14 June (1-6). Also open Great Brickhill Gardens.
One of two Lutyens style lodges bordering Rushmere Park, the garden of One South Lodge has been extensively renovated over the last 3 yrs to create a French inspired Villandry formal garden, and an informal secret garden bordering one of Rushmere's lakes. Although small scale, many features have been introduced; bespoke ironworks complement abundant planting. Visitors can walk with their dogs through the adjacent 450 acre Rushmere Park. Light refreshments incl wood fired pizza slices, tea, coffee & home-made cakes.
♿ 🐾 ☕

42 NEW ORCHARD HOUSE
Tower Road, Coleshill, Amersham HP7 0LB. Mr & Mrs Douglas Livesey, 01494 432278, jane.livesey@virgin.net. *From Amersham Old Town take the A355 to Beaconsfield. Appox ¾ m along this road at top of hill take the 1st R into Tower Rd. Parking in cricket club grounds.* Home-made teas in the barn.

9 Brookside, Lillingstone Lovell Gardens

Adm £4.50, chd free. Wed 24 June (2-5). Visitors also welcome by arrangement June to July.
The 5 acre garden is made up of two wooded areas with eco hedges for wildlife, two ponds with wild flower planting. Large avenues of silver birches, a bog garden with board walk running through. A wild flower meadow. There is a raised garden area with numerous raised beds used as a cutting garden for flowers and some vegetables. Bees. Rear garden lawn slopes down.
♿ 🐾 ☕

43 OVERSTROUD COTTAGE
The Dell, Frith Hill, Gt Missenden HP16 9QE. Mr & Mrs Jonathan Brooke, 01494 862701, susie@jandsbrooke.co.uk. *½ m E Gt Missenden. Turn E off A413 at Gt Missenden onto B485 Frith Hill to Chesham Rd. White Gothic cottage set back in lay-by 100yds uphill on L. Parking on R at church.* Cream teas at parish church. **Adm £3.50, chd £0.50.** Sun 5 Apr, Sun 3 May, Sun 7 June (2-5). Visitors also welcome by arrangement Apr to June for groups of 15+.
Artistic chalk garden on 2 levels. Collection of C17 and C18 plants. Potager/herb garden, spring bulbs, hellebores, succulents, auricula, pulmonaria, geraniums, species and old fashioned roses and lily pond.

Cottage was once C17 fever house for Missenden Abbey. Features incl a garden studio with painting exhibition (share of flower painting proceeds to NGS).
✺ ☕

44 11 THE PADDOCKS
Wendover HP22 6HE. Mr & Mrs E Rye, 01296 623870, pam.rye@talktalk.net. *5m from Aylesbury, on A413. From Aylesbury turn L at mini-r'about onto Wharf Rd. From Gt Missenden turn L at the Clock Tower, then R at mini-r'about onto Wharf Rd.* **Adm £2.50, chd free. Share to Bonnie People in South Africa.** Sat 20, Sun 21 June, Sat 4, Sun 5 July (2-5.30). Visitors also welcome by arrangement June to July for groups of 30 max.
Small peaceful garden with mixed borders of colourful herbaceous perennials and a special show of David Austin roses and a large variety of spectacular named Blackmore and Langdon delphiniums. A tremendous variety of colour in a small area. The White Garden with a peaceful arbour, The Magic of Moonlight created for the BBC. Featured as Garden of the Week in Garden News magazine (June 2014). Most of the garden can be viewed from the lawn.
♿ ✺

Look out for exciting Designer Gardens [D]

THE PLOUGH
Chalkshire Road, Terrick,
Aylesbury HP17 0TJ. John & Sue
Stewart, 01296 612477,
johngooldstewart@gmail.com. *2m
W of Wendover. Entrance to garden
& car park signed off B4009 Nash
Lee Rd. 200yds E of Terrick r'about.
Access to garden from field car park.*
Home-made teas. **Adm £3, chd free.**
Mon 4, Sun 17 May (1-5). Visitors
also welcome by arrangement May
to Sept for groups of 12+.
Formal garden with open views to the
Chiltern countryside. Designed as a
series of outdoor rooms around a
listed former C18 inn, incl border,
parterre, vegetable and fruit gardens,
and a newly planted orchard. Jams
for sale made with fruits from the
garden.

GROUP OPENING

 QUAINTON GARDENS
Quainton HP22 4AY. *7m W of
Aylesbury, 2m N of Waddesdon A41.
Nr Waddesdon turn off A41.* Home-
made teas at The Vine (Feb) & at
Banner Farmhouse (June) or at parish
church if wet. **Combined adm £4
(Feb) & £5 (June), chd free.** Sun 22
Feb (12-4); Sun 14 June (2-6);
Sun 21 Feb 2016 (12-4).

CAPRICORNER
Mrs Davis

HOPE HOUSE
4 Station Road. Jane & Jeff.
Open June date only

MILL VIEW
Upper Street. Jane & Nigel
Jackson
www.millviewquainton.com

135A STATION ROAD
Mr & Mrs Carter.
Open June date only

THORNGUMBALD
Jane Lydall
Visitors also welcome by
arrangement Feb to Oct for
groups of 6+.
01296 655356
janelydall@gmail.com

THE VINE
10 Upper Street. Mr & Mrs D A
Campbell

The village lies at foot of Quainton
Hills with fine views over Vale of
Aylesbury to Chiltern Hills. There is a
C14 church with outstanding

monuments, a C19 working windmill
milling Quainton flour (open Sundays
am), and a steam railway centre.
Heavy clay but well watered from the
hills. The gardens are varied in their
styles and content and also incl part
of the allotments. No wheelchair
access at The Vine or rear garden at
Mill View.

RED KITES
46 Haw Lane, Bledlow Ridge
HP14 4JJ. Mag & Les Terry, 01494
481474, les.terry@lineone.net. *4m
S of Princes Risborough. Off A4010
¹/₂ way between Princes Risborough
& West Wycombe. At Hearing Dogs
sign in Saunderton turn into Haw
Lane, then ³/₄ m on L.* Home-made
teas. **Adm £3.50, chd free.** Tue 19
May, Tue 7 July (2-5). Visitors also
welcome by arrangement Apr to
Sept for groups of 15+.
Chiltern hillside garden with terracing,
slopes and superb views. The 1¹/₂
acres are planted for yr-round interest
and lovingly maintained, with mixed
and herbaceous borders, wild flower
orchard, established pond, vegetable
garden, managed woodland area and
hidden garden. Wide use of climbers
and clematis throughout.

RIVENDELL
13 The Leys, Amersham HP6 5NP.
Janice & Mike Cross. *Off A416.
Take A416 N towards Chesham. The
Leys is on L ¹/₂ m after Boot & Slipper
PH. Park at Beacon School, 100yds
N.* Home-made teas. **Adm £3, chd
free.** Mon 6 Apr (2-5).
S-facing garden featuring a series of
different areas, incl a raised woodland
bed under mature trees, bog garden,
gravel area with grasses and pond,
auricula theatre, raised alpine bed,
bug hotel, box edged herbaceous
beds surrounding a circular lawn with
a rose and clematis arbour and
containing a wide variety of shrubs,
bulbs and perennials.

**◆ STOKE POGES
MEMORIAL GARDENS**
Church Lane, Stoke Poges, Slough
SL2 4NZ. South Bucks District
Council, 01753 523744,
memorial.gardens@southbucks.
gov.uk. *1m N of Slough, 4m S of
Gerrards Cross, follow signs to Stoke
Poges & then to Memorial Gardens.
The car park for the Memorial*

*Gardens is opp the gardens
entrance. Disabled visitor parking in
the gardens.* Home-made teas. **Adm
£4, chd free.** For NGS: Sun 26 Apr
(2-5). For other opening times and
information, please phone or email.
Unique 20 acre Grade I registered
garden constructed 1934-9. Rock
and water gardens, sunken
colonnade, rose garden incl 500
individual gated gardens. Spring
garden, bulbs, wisteria,
rhododendrons. Beautiful autumn
colours. Guided tours on the hour.
Guide dogs only.

> Extensively
> renovated over the
> last 3 years to
> create a French
> inspired Villandry
> formal garden . . .

 TURN END
Townside, Haddenham, Aylesbury
HP17 8BG. Peter Aldington,
www.turnend.org.uk. *3m NE of
Thame, 5m SW of Aylesbury. Turn off
A418 to Haddenham. Turn at Rising
Sun to Townside. Please park at a
distance with consideration for
neighbours.* Home-made teas. **Adm
£4, chd free.** Mon 4 May (2-5.30).
Intriguing series of garden rooms
enveloping architect's own post war
2* listed house (not open). Sunken
gardens, raised beds, formal box
garden, richly planted borders,
curving lawn and glades, framed by
ancient walls and mature trees.
Spring bulbs, irises, wisteria, roses
and climbers. Courtyards with pools,
secluded seating and Victorian Coach
House. Open studios, displays and
demonstrations by creative artists.
Gravel and stone paths, narrow
archways, some steps.

TYTHROP PARK
Kingsey HP17 8LT. Nick & Chrissie
Wheeler. *2m E of Thame, 4m NW of
Princes Risborough. Via A4129, at
T-junction in Kingsey turn towards
Haddenham, take L turn on bend.
Parking in field on L.* Home-made
teas. **Adm £6, chd free.** Share to St
Nicholas Church, Kingsey. Sun 21
June (2-5.30).

10 acres of gardens surrounding C17 Grade I listed manor house. In the past 7 yrs the grounds at Tythrop have undergone some major changes, and now blend traditional styles with more contemporary planting. Features incl large intricate parterre, deep mixed borders, water features, large greenhouse, kitchen and cut flower garden, wild flower meadow, many old trees and shrubs.

52 THE WALLED GARDEN
Wormsley, Stokenchurch, High Wycombe HP14 3YE. Wormsley Estate. *Leave M40 at J5. Turn towards Ibstone. Entrance to estate is ¼ m on R. NB: 20mph speed limit on estate. Please do not drive on grass verges.* Adm £7 incl teas, chd free. Sun 19 July. Pre-booking essential. For timed tickets from 2.00pm, please phone 01483 211535 or visit www.ngs.org.uk.
The Walled Garden at Wormsley Estate is a 2 acre garden providing flowers, vegetables and tranquil contemplative space for the occupiers of the main house. For many years the garden was neglected until Sir Paul Getty purchased the estate in the mid 1980s. In 1991 the garden was redesigned by the renowned garden designer Penelope Hobhouse. Wheelchair ramp available for garden access. Please ensure the requirement is mentioned upon booking.

53 WESTEND HOUSE
Cheddington, Leighton Buzzard LU7 0RP. His Honour Judge & Mrs Richard Foster, 01296 661332, westend.house@hotmail.com, www.westendhousecheddington. co.uk. *5m N of Tring. From double mini-r'about in Cheddington take turn to Long Marston. Take 1st L & Westend House is on your R.* Home-made teas. Adm £3, chd free. Sun 12 Apr, Sun 2 Aug (2-5.30).
2 acre garden restored, extended and developed during the last 10 yrs featuring herbaceous and shrub borders, formal rose garden, wild flowers, natural pond newly planted in 2014 for late summer colour, potager with vegetables and flowers for picking. More spring bulbs planted for 2015. Wood sculptures created from old tree stumps. Orchard and adjoining paddock with rare breed hens, sheep and pigs. Some

bespoke sculptures for sale. Seasonal vegetables for sale. Wildlife pond with dragonflies, butterflies and much more. Wheelchair access to wild flower garden and pond limited to one side.

54 THE WHITE HOUSE
Village Road, Denham Village UB9 5BE. Mr & Mrs P G Courtenay-Luck. *3m NW of Uxbridge, 7m E of Beaconsfield. Signed from A40 or A412. Parking in village road. The White House is in centre of village.* Cream teas. Adm £4.50, chd free. Sun 7 June (2-5).
Well established 6 acre formal garden in picturesque setting. Mature trees and hedges, with R Misbourne meandering through lawns. Shrubberies, flower beds, rockery, rose garden and orchard. Large walled garden with Italian garden and developing laburnum walk. Herb garden, vegetable plot and Victorian greenhouses. Gravel entrance and path to gardens.

55 WHITEWALLS
Quarry Wood Road, Marlow SL7 1RE. Mr W H Williams, 01628 482573. *½ m S Marlow. From Marlow crossover bridge. 1st L, 3rd house on L with white garden wall.* Adm £2.50, chd free. Sun 26 Apr, Sun 19 July, Sun 6 Sept (2-5). Visitors also welcome by arrangement Apr to Sept.
Thames side garden approx ½ acre with spectacular view of weir. Large wildlife pond, interesting planting of trees, shrubs, herbaceous perennials and bedding, and a large conservatory. Many chairs to sit by river and view weir.

56 WIND IN THE WILLOWS
Moorhouse Farm Lane, Off Lower Road, Higher Denham UB9 5EN. Ron James, 07740 177038, r.james@company-doc.co.uk. *Moorhouse Farm Lane, off Lower Rd, Higher Denham. Take lane next to the community centre & Wind in the Willows is the 1st house on L.* Home-made teas. Adm £4, chd free. Sun 15 Mar (2-5). Visitors also welcome by arrangement Feb to Sept for groups of 10+.
3 acre wildlife friendly yr-round garden comprising informal, woodland and wild gardens, separated by streams lined by iris and primulas. Over 350

shrubs and trees, many variegated or uncommon, marginal and bog plantings incl a collection of 80 hostas. 'Stunning' was the word most often used by visitors last year. 'Best private garden I have visited in 20 yrs of NGS visits' said one visitor. Gravel paths.

57 WITTINGTON ESTATE
Henley Road, Medmenham, Marlow SL7 2EB. SAS Institute, www.sas.com. *The Wittington Estate is located off r'about approx 1½ m from Marlow on the A4155 Henley Rd.* Light refreshments in stables. Adm £5, chd free. Sun 12 July (10.30-4.30).
Situated on the banks of the Thames, between Marlow and Henley is SASUK and the Wittington Estate. Built in 1898 for Hudson Ewbank Kearley, later Viscount Devonport. Stunning viewpoints, rose garden, court garden, herbaceous borders, flash-lock capstan wheel, boathouse and arboretum (under restoration). Wood tree sculpture.

GROUP OPENING

58 WORMINGHALL GARDENS
Worminghall HP18 9LE. *3m NE of Wheatley. 3m NW of Thame. From the A418 follow signs for Worminghall. Turn L into village, follow NGS signs. Follow signs to church parking area at end of the avenue.* Tea at Rose Tree Cottage. Combined adm £4, chd free. Wed 24 June (2-5.30).

LAPPINGFORD FARM
Mrs Toby Gawith

ROSE TREE COTTAGE
Roger & Penny Rowe

Two contrasting gardens set either side of C11 church. One a formal terrace garden with lawns opening onto an extensive meadow grass and woodland pasture with cut pathways. The other a mature traditional cottage garden, with spring and summer interest with approx ½ acre of roses, clematis, shrubs, fruit, and a vegetable and herb garden, set around a cottage. Features incl Lappingford Farm meadow walk. Partial wheelchair access at both gardens.

CAMBRIDGESHIRE

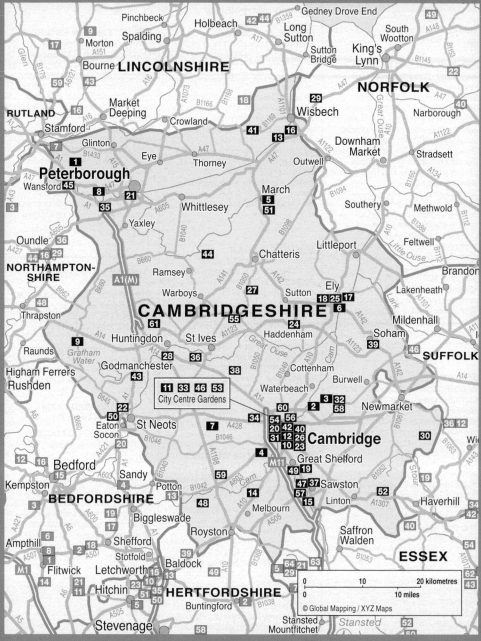

Cambridgeshire

The low-lying flat lands of Cambridgeshire offer many diverse and interesting gardens.

The Cambridge University gardens, which open for the NGS, are well worth a visit; these include Fitzwilliam College, Trinity College, King's College, Corpus Christi College, Robinson College, Clare College and Madingley Hall.

Those interested in urban gardens can find plenty in the city of Cambridge – these smaller gardens are ideal for giving inspiration for back garden planting and design.

Countywide, there are two National Trust properties – Anglesey Abbey and Wimpole Estate.

Ely has a delightful group of gardens in this historic Cathedral City, and Peterborough has a fascinating collection of town gardens.

The whole county embraces many delightful gardens, from former rectory gardens to very small urban gardens. There are many surprises waiting to be discovered in Cambridgeshire, and our generous garden owners invite you to come and take a closer look.

Cambridgeshire Volunteers

County Organiser
George Stevenson
01733 262698
ChrisGeorge1a@aol.com

County Treasurer
Nicholas Kyberd
01954 200568
n.kyberd@ntlworld.com

Publicity
Angie Jones
01733 222367
janda.salix@gmail.com

Booklet Coordinator
Robert Marshall
01733 555978
robfmarshall@btinternet.com

Assistant County Organisers
Pam Bullivant
01353 667355
pbu1@hotmail.co.uk

Patsy Glazebrook
01799 541180
glazebrc@doctors.org.uk

Nicholas Kyberd
(as above)

Mike Tuplin
01353 612029
miketuplin@yahoo.co.uk

Annette White
01638 730876
annette323@btinternet.com

Left: Leckhampton

Currently the NGS donates around £2.5 million every year

Opening Dates

All entries subject to change.
For latest information check www.ngs.org.uk

January

45 Robinson College (daily)

February

45 Robinson College (daily)
Sunday 22
44 6 Robins Wood

March

45 Robinson College (every weekday)
Sunday 29
30 Kirtling Tower

April

45 Robinson College (daily until April 17)
Sunday 5
39 Netherhall Manor
Sunday 12
4 Barton Gardens
11 Churchill College
20 Fitzwilliam College
30 Kirtling Tower
53 Trinity College, Fellows' Garden
54 Trinity Hall - Wychfield
Tuesday 14
48 South Farm & Brook Cottage
Sunday 19
30 Leckhampton
Saturday 25
42 The Old Vicarage
Sunday 26
6 Bishop Woodford House
14 Docwra's Manor
25 Hazeldene
42 The Old Vicarage

May

Sunday 3
10 Chaucer Road Gardens
33 Lucy Cavendish College
39 Netherhall Manor

Monday 4
10 Chaucer Road Gardens
Sunday 10
32 Lode Gardens
Tuesday 12
48 South Farm & Brook Cottage
Saturday 30
13 Clear View
22 Great Staughton & Hail Weston Gardens
50 Staploe Gardens
Sunday 31
7 Cambourne Gardens
13 Clear View
15 NEW Duxford Gardens
22 Great Staughton & Hail Weston Gardens
28 Island Hall
29 Kenilworth Smallholding
34 Madingley Hall
50 Staploe Gardens

June

46 Robinson College (daily from June 15)

Festival Weekend

Saturday 6
51 Steeple View
Sunday 7
4 Barton Gardens
17 Ely Gardens 1
41 The Old Rectory
51 Steeple View
52 Streetly End Gardens
Sunday 14
9 Catworth, Molesworth, Brington & Spaldwick Gardens
18 Ely Gardens 2
24 Haddenham Gardens
26 Highsett Cambridge
44 Ramsey Forty Foot
Tuesday 16
3 Anglesey Abbey, Gardens & Lode Mill
Saturday 20
1 Abbot's Barn
Sunday 21
1 Abbot's Barn
2 Abbots Way
30 Kirtling Tower
57 Whittlesford Gardens
61 Wytchwood
Saturday 27
5 45 Beaver Lodge

8 Castor House (Evening)
56 West Chesterton
Sunday 28
5 45 Beaver Lodge
49 Stapleford Gardens
56 West Chesterton

July

46 Robinson College (daily)
Sunday 5
12 Clare College Fellows' Garden
47 Sawston Gardens
Saturday 11
55 Twin Tarns
Sunday 12
37 Mary Challis Garden
55 Twin Tarns
Tuesday 14
48 South Farm & Brook Cottage
Saturday 18
19 6 Finch's Close
Sunday 19
19 6 Finch's Close
32 Lode Gardens
Wednesday 22
59 Wimpole Estate (Evening)
Saturday 25
19 6 Finch's Close
Sunday 26
19 6 Finch's Close
40 Norfolk Terrace Garden
Wednesday 29
59 Wimpole Estate (Evening)

August

46 Robinson College (daily)
Saturday 1
19 6 Finch's Close
Sunday 2
16 Elgood's Brewery Gardens
19 6 Finch's Close
39 Netherhall Manor
Sunday 9
39 Netherhall Manor
Saturday 15
51 Steeple View
Sunday 16
51 Steeple View
Sunday 23
8 Castor House
Saturday 29
5 45 Beaver Lodge

Sunday 30
5 45 Beaver Lodge

September

46 Robinson College (daily)
Tuesday 15
48 South Farm & Brook Cottage

February 2016

Sunday 28
45 6 Robins Wood

Gardens open to the public

3 Anglesey Abbey, Gardens & Lode Mill
14 Docwra's Manor
16 Elgood's Brewery Gardens
36 The Manor, Hemingford Grey
59 Wimpole Estate

By arrangement only

21 39 Foster Road
23 NEW Greenglade
27 NEW Horseshoe Farm
35 Manor House, Alwalton
38 5 Moat Way
43 23a Perry Road
58 Wild Rose Cottage
60 The Windmill

Also open by arrangement

5 45 Beaver Lodge
9 32 High Street, Catworth, Molesworth, Brington & Spaldwick Gardens
9 7 Thrapston Road, Catworth, Molesworth, Brington & Spaldwick Gardens
10 Upwater Lodge, Chaucer Road Gardens
13 Clear View
44 The Elms, Ramsey Forty Foot
45 6 Robins Wood
52 Clover Cottage, Streetly End Gardens
55 Twin Tarns

Find a garden near you – download our free Android app

The Gardens

1 ▶ ABBOT'S BARN
Southorpe, Stamford PE9 3BX.
Mr & Mrs Carl & Vanessa Brown.
*5m SE of Stamford, 8m W of
Peterborough. On entering Southorpe
Village from A47, 1st house on L.*
Home-made teas. **Adm £4, chd free.
Sat 20, Sun 21 June (2-5.30).**
2-acre garden surrounding converted
Georgian barn. Large 'family' garden
with herbaceous borders and wild
flower meadow, allotment-sized
vegetable plot, orchard, woodland
area with mown grass paths, small
woodland garden, beach garden with
decking, wildlife pond, large courtyard
garden with garden-sized croquet
lawn, cutting flower garden,
gravel/pergola walkways. We
maintain the garden using organic
methods, providing a rich wildlife
habitat. Free range Pekin bantams so
chicken-friendly dogs on leads
welcome!

2 ▶ ABBOTS WAY
Horningsea CB25 9JN. Sally & Don
Edwards, 01223 861234. *4m NE of
Cambridge. ¹/₂ m from A14. No
access from Abbots Way. Follow
signs in Horningsea to car park &
garden.* Home-made teas. **Adm £4,
chd free. Share to St Peters
Church Horningsea.** Sun 21 June
(2-5.30).
1¹/₄ acre sloping garden, with many
herbaceous beds. Views to church
and over the R Cam and its water
meadows. Interesting plants and use
of colour. 180ft double herbaceous
borders; 116ft pergola with large
collection of roses, clematis and other
climbers. Natural pond with bridge.
Access for wheelchair users may be
difficult from car park. Please phone
ahead for alternative access from
front of house.

3 ▶ ♦ ANGLESEY ABBEY,
GARDENS & LODE MILL
Quy Road, Lode, Cambridge
CB25 9EJ. National Trust,
01223 810080,
www.nationaltrust.org.uk/anglesey
abbey. *6m NE of Cambridge. From
A14 J35, on B1102 through Stow-
cum-Quy.* Light refreshments in
Visitor Centre. **Adm £7.85, chd
£4.20. For NGS: Tue 16 June
(10-5.30). For other opening times
and information, please phone or**

South Farm & Brook Cottage

© Ria Mishaal

see garden website.
Anglesey is one of England's great
gardens, with captivating views,
vibrant colour and delicious fragrance
for every season. Delight in the
sweeping avenues, classical statuary
and beautiful flower borders. June
favourites include the colourful
herbaceous borders, rose garden and
wildlife rich wildflower meadows. Take
a tour with a garden guide and be
inspired by the seasonal highlights.
Large proportion of gardens fully
accessible for wheelchair users with
hard surfaced paths.

GROUP OPENING

4 ▶ BARTON GARDENS
High Street, Barton, Cambridge
CB23 7BG. *3¹/₂ m SW of Cambridge.
Barton is on A603 Cambridge to
Sandy Rd, ¹/₂ m for J12 M11.* Home-
made teas in Barton Village Hall. The
White Horse Inn serves meals.
**Combined adm £4 (Apr), £5 (June),
chd free. Sun 12 Apr, Sun 7 June
(2-5).**

FARM COTTAGE
18 High Street. Dr R M Belbin

114 HIGH STREET
Meta & Hugh Greenfield

31 NEW ROAD
Dr & Mrs D Macdonald.
Not open 12th April

THE SIX HOUSES
33-45 Comberton Road.
Perennial (GRBS)

Varied group of large and small
gardens reflecting different
approaches to gardening.
Farm Cottage: landscaped cottage
garden with herbaceous beds and
themed woodland walk. 114 High
Street: small cottage garden with an
unusual layout comprising several
areas incl vegetables, fruit and a
secret garden. 31 New Road: large,
wildlife friendly cottage garden with a
good show of spring flowers, mature
shrubs, trees and a kitchen garden.
The Six Houses: recently renovated
gardens, incl winter and dry gardens,
lovely spring bulbs and a small wood.
Some gardens have gravel paths.

5 45 BEAVER LODGE

Henson Road, March PE15 8BA.
Mr & Mrs Maria & Paul Nielsen
Bom, 01354 656185,
beaverbom@gmail.com. *A141 to*
Wisbech rd into March, turn L into
Westwood Ave, follow rd leading to
Henson Rd, turn R. Property opp
school playground. Home-made teas.
Adm £2.50, chd free. Sat 27, Sun
28 June, Sat 29, Sun 30 Aug
(10.30-4). Visitors also welcome by
arrangement June to Sept small
groups welcome.
A delightful town garden divided into
several rooms. A pergola leads to an
ornamental pond with koi carp,
surrounded by borders with a large
variety of plants and ornamental
trees. Fern area with ornamental
waterfall. The whole garden has an
Oriental theme with bonsais and
statues. Also a corner with a fountain
that has a Mediterranean feel.
Featured in Cambridgeshire Times.

6 BISHOP WOODFORD HOUSE

Barton Road, Ely CB7 4DX. Miss
Michelle Collins. *14m N of*
Cambridge. Enter Ely from A10,
south. Parking at Barton rd car park,
R off Cambridge Rd. (NGS sign) Both
gardens are very close. Home-made
teas at Hazeldene. Combined adm
with Hazeldene 36 Barton Road,
£4, chd free. Sun 26 Apr (2-5.30).
This garden displays a passion for
plants. In April the late spring garden
is in full bloom: speciality tulips,
hyacinth and early flowering shrubs,
incl magnolia and malus can be seen.

GROUP OPENING

7 CAMBOURNE GARDENS

Great Cambourne CB23 6AH. *8m*
W of Cambridge on A428. From
A428 Cambourne junction into Great
Cambourne. Follow NGS signs to
start at any garden. Home-made
teas. Combined adm £5, chd free.
Sun 31 May (11-5).

NEW 16 APLEY WAY
Lower Cambourne. Mr & Mrs
Sean & Tina Grainger.
Enter lower Cambourne on
School Lane, from great
Cambourne, take 2nd R into
Apley Way. Property 200 meters
on R, with driveway

NEW 65 BROOKFIELD WAY
Lower Cambourne. Jan &
Campbell Macqueen

14 GRANARY WAY
Great Cambourne. Mrs Jackie
Hutchinson.
Exit A428 Cambourne, 2nd exit
on next two r'abouts. At
Morrisons turn L onto High St
then Monkfield Lane. R
Greenhaze Lane

128 GREENHAZE LANE
Great Cambourne. Fran & John
Panrucker.
At the end of Greenhaze Lane, up
a short drive between nos. 126 &
130

22 JEAVONS LANE
Great Cambourne. Mr
Sheppard.
Entry via Chervil Way

5 MAYFIELD WAY
Great Cambourne. Debbie &
Mike Perry.
S on Cambourne Rd at r'about
take 2nd exit onto Broad St L
onto High St, R onto Monkfield
Lane R onto Jeavons Lane

43 MONKFIELD LANE
Great Cambourne. Tony &
Penny Miles

6 ST JOHN'S WAY
Lower Cambourne. Greg
Barnes

A unique and inspiring modern group,
all created from new build in just a
few years. This selection of eight,
including two new entries for 2015,
demonstrates how imagination and
gardening skill can be combined in a
short time to create great effects from
unpromising and awkward
beginnings. The grouping includes a

garden inspired by the French Riviera
complete with a miniature meadow, a
foliage garden, two stunning modern
treatments featuring Astroturf along
with several more showing their
owners' creativity and love of growing
fine plants well. Cambourne is one of
Cambridgeshire's newest
communities, and this grouping
showcases the happy, vibrant place it
has become. No garden is more than
14 years old. and most are much
younger.

8 CASTOR HOUSE

Peterborough Road, Castor,
Peterborough PE5 7AX. Ian &
Claire Winfrey,
www.castorhousegardens.co.uk.
4m W of Peterborough. House on
main Peterborough rd in Castor.
Parking in paddock off Water Lane.
Home-made teas. Adm £4, chd free.
Evening Opening, wine, Sat 27
June (5.30-9). Sun 23 Aug (2-5).
12 acres of gardens and woodland,
redesigned 2010. Italianate spring fed
pond and stream gardens.
Ornamental potager with greenhouse.
Annual meadow and willow arbour.
Woodland garden. Peony and prunus
walk. Rose and cottage gardens,
'Hot' double border. New stumpery
2015. Planted for yr round interest.
Late C17 house (closed). TR20s jazz
band, picnics welcome on 27 June.
No dogs. Coaches welcome. For
more information and openings by
appt please see garden website.

GROUP OPENING

9 CATWORTH, MOLESWORTH, BRINGTON & SPALDWICK GARDENS

nr Huntingdon PE28 0PF. *10m W of*
Huntingdon. A14 W for Catworth,
Molesworth & Brington exit at J16
onto B660. For Spaldwick exit A14 at
J18. Home-made teas at Molesworth
House, Yew Tree Cottage & 7
Thrapston Road. Combined adm £4,
chd free. Sun 14 June (2-6).

32 HIGH STREET
Colin Small
Visitors also welcome by
arrangement June evening &
weekends.
01832 710269
sheila.small@btinternet.com

MOLESWORTH HOUSE
Molesworth. John Prentis.
Next to the church in Molesworth

7 THRAPSTON ROAD
Spaldwick. Stewart & Mary Barnard.
Take J18 off A14 to centre of village, garden approx 50 metres from George PH
Visitors also welcome by arrangement May to July.
01480 890060
mnbarnard@btinternet.com

YEW TREE COTTAGE
Brington. Christine & Don Eggleston.
Leave A14 at B660 to Brington past school, garden is 200yds up hill

4 varied gardens showing the best of planting, design and creativity representing classic tradition but with a modern twist. 32 High Street is a long narrow garden with many rare plants including ferns, herbaceous borders, woodland area and wildlife pond. Molesworth House is a Victorian Rectory garden with a bit of everything, old fashioned and proud of it but with a groovy tropical house. Yew Tree Cottage comprises flower beds, lawn, vegetable patch, boggy area, copse and orchard. Plants in pots and hanging baskets.
7 Thrapston Road comprises mature trees under planted with mixed borders of shrubs, bulbs, herbaceous plants and fish pond. A pleasant outlook to the rear over the village church. Partial wheelchair access.

GROUP OPENING

10 CHAUCER ROAD GARDENS
Cambridge CB2 7EB. *1m S of Cambridge. Off Trumpington Rd (A1309), nr Brooklands Ave junction. Parking available at MRC Psychology Dept on Chaucer Rd.* Home-made teas at Upwater Lodge. **Combined adm £5, chd free. Sun 3, Mon 4 May (2-5).**

16 CHAUCER ROAD
Mrs V Albutt

UPWATER LODGE
Cambridge. Mr & Mrs George Pearson
Visitors also welcome by arrangement Apr to July parking for 8-10 cars available.
07890 080303
jmp@pearson.co.uk

16 Chaucer Road ½-acre garden, divided by arches and hedges into separate areas, each with its own character. The garden is more open this year with some hedges removed. Spring flowering shrubs and trees, bulbs in borders and wildlife area. Waterproof footwear advised. Upwater Lodge 6 acres with mature trees, fine lawns, old wisterias, and colourful borders. Small, pretty potager and newly planted vineyard. A network of paths through a bluebell wood leads down to water meadows and small flock of rare breed sheep by R Cam. Enjoy a walk by the river and watch the punts go by. Cakes made with garden fruit where possible. Swings and climbing ropes. Stalls selling plants, cards, prints and fabric crafts. Some gravel areas and grassy paths with fairly gentle slopes.

The River Cam flows gently through the 3½ acre rural garden enclosed with mature box hedges . . .

11 CHURCHILL COLLEGE
Storey's Way, Cambridge CB3 0DS. University of Cambridge, www.chu.cam.ac.uk. *1m from M11 J13. 1m NW of Cambridge city centre. Turn into Storeys Way from Madingley Rd (A1303), or from Huntingdon Rd (A1307). Parking on site.* Home-made teas. **Combined adm with Fitzwilliam College £5, chd free. Sun 12 Apr (2-5).**
42-acre site designed in 1960s for foliage and form, to provide year round interest in peaceful and relaxing surrounds with courtyards, large open spaces and specimen trees. 5m 2 orchid greenhouse, herbaceous plantings. Beautiful grouping of Prunus Tai Haku (great white cherry) trees forming striking canopy and drifts of naturalised bulbs in grass around the site. The planting provides a setting for the impressive collection of modern sculpture. Orchid house, Sculptures.

12 CLARE COLLEGE FELLOWS' GARDEN
Trinity Lane, Cambridge CB2 1TL. The Master & Fellows, www.clare.cam.ac.uk. *Central to city. From Queens Rd or city centre via Senate House Passage, Old Court & Clare Bridge.* Home-made teas, with coffee and soft drinks. **Adm £3.50, chd free. Sun 5 July (2-6).**
2 acres. One of the most famous gardens on the Cambridge Backs. Herbaceous borders; sunken pond garden, fine specimen trees and tropical garden. Gravel paths.

13 CLEAR VIEW
Cross Lane, Wisbech St Mary PE13 4TX. Margaret & Graham Rickard, 01945 410724, magsrick@hotmail.com. *3m SW of Wisbech. Approach village via Barton Rd from Wisbech; Leverington Common into Station Rd or Sandbank & from Guyhirn. Yellow signs at most junctions.* Home-made teas. **Adm £3, chd free. Sat 30, Sun 31 May (10.30-5.30). Visitors also welcome by arrangement Apr to July.**
Approx 1½-acre with lake incorporating large wildlife area, and wildlife meadow. Secluded cottage garden with many old fashioned plants, herbaceous border, gravel garden with raised bed and pond. Allotments and small orchard. Plenty of secluded seating. Gravel paths in cottage garden are too narrow but garden can be viewed from the picket fencing and the grass.

14 ◆ DOCWRA'S MANOR
2 Meldreth Road, Shepreth, Royston SG8 6PS. Mrs Faith Raven, 01763 260677, www.docwrasmanorgarden.co.uk. *8m S of Cambridge. ½ m W of A10. Garden is opp the War Memorial in Shepreth. King's Cross-Cambridge train stop 5 min walk.* Teas. **Adm £5, chd free. For NGS: Sun 26 Apr (2-5). For other opening times and information, please phone or see garden website.**
2½ acres of choice plants in a series of enclosed gardens. Tulips and Judas trees. Opened for the NGS for more than 40yrs. The garden is featured in great detail in a book published 2013 'The Gardens of England' edited by George Plumptre. Wheelchair access to most parts of the garden, gravel paths.

21 Lode Road, Lode Gardens

GROUP OPENING

15 NEW DUXFORD GARDENS
Cambridge CB22 4PT. *M11 leave at J10, A505. ¹/₂ m signed Duxford. St Peter's St gardens close to Londis shop. The Biggen is a cul de sac off Hinxton Rd, which starts at the trianglular War Memorial at end of St Peter's St. The entrance to Mill Lane is opp The John Barleycorn PH. Garden is at the end of Mill Lane with white gates and white sign Parking at Temple Farm House.* Home-made teas. at Temple Farmhouse.
Combined adm £5, chd free.
Sun 31 May (2-6).

> **NEW 2 THE BIGGEN**
> Mr & Mrs Derek & Judy Chamberlain.
> *The Biggen is a Cul de Sac off Hinxton Rd, which starts at the triangular war memorial at end of St Peter's St*

> **NEW 6 THE BIGGEN**
> Mrs Bettye Reynolds

> **NEW BUSTLERS COTTAGE**
> 26 St Peter's Street. Mr John Marks

> **NEW 31 ST PETER'S STREET**
> Mr David Baker

> **NEW TEMPLE FARMHOUSE**
> Mill Lane. Peter & Jenny Shaw

These are all new garden and are an extremely interesting mix, ranging from very large to very small. The gardens are all examples of what can be easily grown in Duxford.
2 The Biggen created in 9yrs from an overgrown plot of greenery, has mixed borders, small stumpery and alpine area. 6 The Biggen a ¹/₄ acre plants women's garden with unusual perennials, charming places to sit and enjoy. 31 St Peter's Street the garden slopes down to a rockery and circular stone steps leading to a secluded patio. Bustlers Cottage is a traditional Cambridgeshire cottage garden extending over 1 acre with old roses, herbaceous borders, vegetables and an old fig tree. Temple Farmhouse the R Cam flows gently through the 3¹/₂ acre rural garden with majestic trees, informal flowerbeds, vegetable garden enclosed with mature box hedges.
&♿ ☕

16 ♦ ELGOOD'S BREWERY GARDENS
North Brink, Wisbech PE13 1LW. Elgood & Sons Ltd, 01945 583160, www.elgoods-brewery.co.uk. *1m W of town centre. Leave A47 towards Wisbech Centre. Cross river to North Brink. Follow river & brown signs to brewery & car park beyond.* Light refreshments. Adm £3.50, chd free.
For NGS: Sun 2 Aug (11.30-4.30).

For other opening times and information, please phone or see garden website.
Approx 4 acres of peaceful garden featuring 250yr old specimen trees providing a framework to lawns, lake, rockery, herb garden, dipping pool and maze. Wheelchair access to Visitor Centre and most areas of the garden.
♿ ❀ ☕

GROUP OPENING

17 ELY GARDENS 1
CB7 4TX. *14m N of Cambridge. Parking at Rosewell House off B1382 N of Ely, Council office car park, or Barton Rd car park. Map given at first garden visited.* Tea at Rosewell House. Combined adm £5, chd free. Sun 7 June (2-6).

> **THE BISHOPS HOUSE**
> The Bishop of Ely

> **12 & 26 CHAPEL STREET**
> Ken & Linda Ellis

> **50A PRICKWILLOW ROAD**
> Mr & Ms Hunter

> **ROSEWELL HOUSE**
> 60 Prickwillow Road. Mr & Mrs A Bullivant.
> *On edge of Ely on B1382, turn R into Environment Agency office on Prickwillow Rd, 150 metres after mini r'about*

A delightful and varied group of gardens in an historic Cathedral city. Take a leisurely circular walk of about 1m to access all gardens. Rosewell House has splendid views of Cathedral and surrounding fenland. Herbaceous borders, roses, small pond and kitchen garden. Meadow with area of cornfield planting. Also ' Rhobile' moving sculptures by Andrew Jones. Close by, 50A Prickwillow Rd is an enthusiast's small walled garden with shade border, succulents and vegetable plot, the emphasis being on foliage. The Bishop's garden adjoining Ely Cathedral has mixed planting with roses, wisteria and more. 12 & 26 Chapel Street: the former a small town garden reflecting the owners eclectic outlook, from alpine to herbaceous, all linked with a model railway! The latter a surprisingly long garden with shrubs and developing areas of herbaceous planting. An oasis of peace in the city. Wheelchair access to areas of most gardens.

GROUP OPENING

18 ELY GARDENS 2

CB7 4HZ. *A10 from Cambridge (14m). Easy walking distance from Barton Rd car park. Hazeldene at 36 Barton Rd is within sight of the car park. The other gardens are within easy walking distance. Home-made teas at Hazeldene.* **Combined adm £5, chd free.** Sun 14 June (2-5.30).

> **NEW 32B DOWNHAM ROAD**
> Ely. Mrs P Carrott

> **42 CAMBRIDGE ROAD**
> Ely. Mr & Mrs J & C Switsur.
> *On corner of Cambridge Rd & Tower Rd*

> **HAZELDENE**
> Mike & Juliette Tuplin
> (See separate entry)

Hazeldene is a wild life friendly Organic garden and includes plenty of interest. Cambridge Road is a Victorian house with lots of summer colour and interesting features, set in the garden of a Victorian house. Downham Road is a deceptive and unusual garden for a bungalow and has quality paving with interesting planting. Hazeldene was featured in Amateur Gardening.

19 6 FINCH'S CLOSE

CB22 5BL. Prof & Mrs S Sutton. *4m S of Cambridge on A1301. Cul-de-sac off Bar Lane.* Tea. **Adm £3, chd free.** Sat 18, Sun 19, Sat 25, Sun 26 July, Sat 1, Sun 2 Aug (1-6). Small Spanish-styled patio leads to the fruit and vegetable garden and greenhouse. The borders around the lawn and wildlife pond are well-stocked with shrubs and mature trees whilst gentle musical chimes can be heard in the breeze. gravel paths, large lawn area.

20 FITZWILLIAM COLLEGE

Storeys Way, Cambridge CB3 0DG. Master & Fellows, www.fitz.cam.ac.uk. *1m NW of Cambridge city centre. Turn into Storeys Way from Madingley Rd (A1303) or from Huntingdon Rd (A1307). Free parking.* On-site coffee shop for drinks and snacks. **Combined adm with Churchill College £5, chd free.** Sun 12 Apr (2-5).

Traditional topiary, borders, woodland walk, lawns from the Edwardian period and specimen trees are complemented by modern planting and wild meadow. The avenue of limes, underplanted with spring bulbs, leads to The Grove, the 1813 house once belonging to the Darwin Family (not open). Some ramped pathways.

21 39 FOSTER ROAD

Campaign Ave, Sugar Way, Woodston, Peterborough PE2 9RS. Robert Marshall & Richard Handscombe, 01733 555978, robfmarshall@btinternet.com. *1m SW of Peterborough City Centre. A605 Oundle Rd, N into Sugar Way. Cross r'about, L at 2nd r'about to Campaign Ave. R at next r'about on C. Ave. 2nd R to Foster Rd. L into cul-de-sac.* Light refreshments in garden pergola or indoor lounge, weather depending. **Adm £3.50, chd free. Visitors welcome by arrangement** Feb to Sept, weekends & week days possible, groups very welcome. Teas incl in adm.

Plantsman's garden in small, new estate plot. Mixed borders; woodland/shade; 'vestibule' garden; exotics and ferns; espaliered fruit; pergola; patio; pond; parterre; many pots; octagonal greenhouse; seating and sculpture. Uncommon

snowdrops, over 200 hostas, plus daphnes, acers and other choice/unusual cultivars. Trees and hedges create enclosure and intimacy. 4 British Shorthair cats. Featured on & in BBC Radio Cambridgeshire, Local Magazines, Newspapers & Saturday Mail Magazine. All viewings accompanied by garden owner(s). Adm also incl tea/coffee/biscuits. Main garden and WC accessible by wheelchair.

Climbing jasmine supported by steel towers provide a summer scented walk . . .

GROUP OPENING

22 GREAT STAUGHTON & HAIL WESTON GARDENS

St. Neots PE19 5JS. *From A1 take B645 in direction of Kimbolton & High Ferrers.* Home-made teas. **Combined adm £3, chd free.** Sat 30, Sun 31 May (1-5).

> **109 HIGH STREET** D
> Hail Weston. Dawn Isaac.
> *Take 1st R signed Hail Weston & follow High St round. 109 is opp church & village hall*
> www.dawn-isaac.com

> **THE OLD VICARAGE**
> Causeway, Great Staughton.
> Mr & Mrs Richard Edmunds

109 High Street set in 1/3 acre, this space has been designed to show that a practical family garden can still be beautiful. There is a large lawn with a sunken trampoline surrounded by mixed borders, ornamental vegetable garden, children's play area and greenhouse. The Old Vicarage a good Old Vicarage garden, redesigned in 2008/9 to enhance original plan.

23 NEW GREENGLADE

64 Glebe Road, Cambridge CB1 7SZ. Alison Howat, aph@greenglade.co.uk. *Off Hills Road, Cambridge. Aim for Hills Rd A1307. Turn into Glebe Rd from Hills Rd. 1/2 way along Glebe Rd & opp Baldock Way is entrance to garden. Entrance down drive, through gate. Free parking on rd. Bikes can be brought in.* Tea. **Adm £4, chd free. Visitors & groups welcome by arrangement Apr to Sept.**
Glowing coloured grasses, evergreen shrubs and trees give yr round interest in this 15yr old garden. The two lawn areas, and the multicoloured lavenders and roses shaded by lovely variegated acres give summer/autumn new interest. Evergreen and perennial ferns, and abutilons grace shaded areas. Climbing jasmine supported by steel towers provide a summer scented walk. Steel structures continue elsewhere. Small bog garden and pond support the newts and frogs. Adjoins fruit growing allotment.

♿ ☕

GROUP OPENING

24 HADDENHAM GARDENS

Station Road, Haddenham CB6 3XD. *5m SW of Ely Cambs. From A142, take A1421 S to Haddenham. Gardens are on & off Station Rd, on the R, on entry to village from the N, before the road rises sharply.* **Combined adm £5, chd free. Sun 14 June (1-5).**

COLLEGE FARM
Station Road, Haddenham. Mr & Mrs J & S Waller.
At the Xrds in Haddenham, from Stretham & Wilburton, turn R, past the church. At bottom of the hill, turn L down a narrow drive with a mill wheel on R
www.primaveragallery.co.uk

53 STATION ROAD
Jo Pooley.
Entering Haddenham village from N 200 metres on R

Two very different gardens, very close to each other. Jo's garden, 53 Station Road, is an intimate organic cottage garden with a very special collection of flowers, scrubs and trees. Winding paths and clever planting mask many hidden gems. Ponds, a bug hotel and chickens, a fernery and an iris emporium are only

some of them! Just three minutes walk away, where you can park off the road to visit both gardens, Sheila and Jeremy's garden at College Farm is a complete contrast. Originally a working farm with no garden and few trees. Now Sheila and Jeremy have created paths, which cross large ponds and ancient pasture land. They have planted many interesting trees and special areas with wild flowers, wildlife habitats and roses. Water plants provide the perfect home for abundant wildlife. Roses and borders intermingle between the lovely old farm buildings. Sculptures and interesting objects are to be found, and the inside gallery explored.

> A haven for children and wildlife. Architect Eric Lyons planned the whole estate in the late 1950's the very ethos of tranquil living space for all generations . . .

25 HAZELDENE

36 Barton Road. CB7 4HZ. Mike & Juliette Tuplin. *Close to Barton Road car park. On entering Ely from South on A10, turn R at car park / ngs sign to Barton Rd car park.* Home-made teas. **Combined adm with Bishop Woodford House £4, chd free. Sun 26 Apr (2-5.30).**
Organic garden reflecting an interest in wildlife. Interesting planting and structures including kitchen garden with raised beds, living roof, courtyard garden and small ponds. Small area with chickens The Spring garden is entered via a courtyard with Camelias. There are lots of bulbs and hellebores to be found as the garden emerges from Winter. Small sculptures enhance the garden. There is a shaded area with a large walnut tree.

❀ ☕

GROUP OPENING

26 HIGHSETT CAMBRIDGE

Cambridge CB2 1NZ. *Centre of Cambridge. Via Station Rd, Tenison Rd, 1st L Tenison Ave, entrance ahead. SatNav CB1 2DX.* Light refreshments at 82 & 83 Highsett. **Combined adm £5, chd free. Sun 14 June (2-5).**

NEW 38 HIGHSETT
Mr Michael Welch

NEW 49 HIGHSETT
Mrs Elizabeth Newlands

NEW 50 HIGHSETT
Mrs Victoria Woodward

NEW 52 HIGHSETT
Mrs Madelaine Watt.
Reached from estate path at Tenison Ave gate. Back garden reached from behind terrace. Signed

54 HIGHSETT
Dr L Bernal.
Small wooden gate on W side of Tenison Ave, just N of Highsett entrance

59 HIGHSETT
Mr & Mrs Griffiths.
Entrance via Tenison Ave, garden at rear of 59

NEW 69 HIGHSETT
Mrs Liz Bingham

73 HIGHSETT D
Mrs P Caldwell

82 HIGHSETT
Mrs A Fleet

NEW 85 HIGHSETT
Mrs Shirley Foulsham

10 delightful town gardens within Central Cambridge. Set in large communal grounds with fine specimen trees and lawns. A haven for children and wildlife. Architect Eric Lyons planned the whole estate in the late 1950's with a mixture of flats, small houses and large town houses, the very ethos of tranquil living space for all generations. Several of the Open Gardens have been skilfully modernised by garden designers.

♿ ☕

27 NEW HORSESHOE FARM

Chatteris Road, Somersham, Huntingdon PE28 3DR. Neil & Claire Callan, 01354 693546, nccallan@yahoo.co.uk. *9m NE of St Ives, Cambs. Easy access from the*

A14. Situated on E side of B1050, 4m N of Somersham Village. Parking for 8 cars in the drive. Home-made teas. **Adm £4, chd free. Visitors welcome by arrangement Feb to Sept groups up to 30.**
This ³/₄ acre plant-lovers' garden not only has lots of spring interest, but has a large pond with summer-house and decking, bog garden, alpine troughs, more than 25 varieties of irises, mixed rainbow island beds, water features, a small hazel woodland area and a wildlife meadow. Planned for 2015 is a lookout tower, for wide fenland views and bird watching.

28 ISLAND HALL
Godmanchester PE29 2BA. Mr Christopher & Lady Linda Vane Percy, www.islandhall.com. 1m S of Huntingdon (A1). 15m NW of Cambridge (A14). In centre of Godmanchester next to free car park. Home-made teas. **Adm £4, chd free. Sun 31 May (11-5).**
3-acre grounds. Mid C18 mansion (not open). Tranquil riverside setting with mature trees. Chinese bridge over Saxon mill race to an embowered island with wild flowers. Garden restored in 1983 to mid C18 formal design, with box hedging, clipped hornbeams, parterres, topiary and good vistas over borrowed landscape, punctuated with C18 wrought iron and stone urns. The ornamental island has been replanted with Princeton elms (ulmus americana).

29 KENILWORTH SMALLHOLDING
West Drove North, Walton Highway PE14 7DP. John & Marilyn Clarke, 07884 491105, bookings@kenilworthhouse.co.uk, www.kenilworthhouse.co.uk. 6m E of Wisbech. Off A47 through Walton Highway, at E end of village turn N towards Walpole St Peter, on 2nd sharp bend turn R into Farm Lane. Light refreshments. **Adm £4, chd free. Sun 31 May (11-5). Visitors also welcome by arrangement Mar to Oct.**
Varied country garden set around 100yr-old Bramleys. Beds, large ponds, fern greenhouse, shade garden and herb bed. Working smallholding with goats and sheep. Tree lined path past paddocks to secluded mixed dessert apple

orchard and copse. Japanese Garden. Teas served in outbuilding housing exhibition of the development of the smallholding and archaeology. Two awards Wisbech in Bloom - Wildlife friendly garden and Large out of town gardens (Highly Commended).

NGS support helps to boost our profile

30 KIRTLING TOWER
Newmarket Road, Kirtling, nr Newmarket CB8 9PA. The Lord & Lady Fairhaven. 6m SE of Newmarket. From Newmarket head towards village of Saxon Street, through village to Kirtling, turn L at war memorial, signed to Upend, entrance is signed on L. Light refreshments. Selection of hot and cold food, sandwiches and cakes, tea and coffee. **Adm £5, chd free. Sun 29 Mar, Sun 12 Apr, Sun 21 June (11-4).**
Surrounded by a moat, formal gardens and parkland. In the spring swathes of daffodils, narcissi, crocus, muscari, chionodoxa and tulips. Closer to the house vast lawn areas, Secret and Cutting Gardens. In the summer the Walled Garden has superb herbaceous borders with anthemis, hemerocalis, geraniums and delphiniums. The Victorian Garden is filled with peonies. Views of surrounding countryside. Display and demonstrations of stonemasonry from Lady Fairhaven's stone yard, and the chance to have a go yourself. Collection of Classic Cars on display. Many of the paths and routes around the garden are grass - they are accessible by wheelchairs, but can be hard work if wet.

31 LECKHAMPTON
37 Grange Road, Cambridge CB3 9BJ. Corpus Christi College. Runs N to S between Madingley Rd (A1303) & A603. Entrance opp Selwyn College. No parking available on site. Home-made teas. **Adm £4, chd free. Sun 19 Apr (2-6).**
10 acres comprising formal lawns and extensive wild gardens, featuring walkways and tree-lined avenues, fine specimen trees under-planted with spring bulbs, cowslips, anemones, fritillaries and a large area of lupins. Gravel and grass paths.

GROUP OPENING

32 LODE GARDENS
Cambridgeshire CB25 9FW. 10m NE of Cambridge. Take B1102 from Stow-cum-Quy r'about, NE of Cambridge at junction with A14, Lode is 2m from r'about. Home-made teas at Carpenter's End. **Combined adm £5, chd free. Sun 10 May, Sun 19 July (12-5).**

CARPENTERS END
Mr & Mrs Paul Webb

21 LODE ROAD
Mr Richard P Ayres

2 contrasting gardens set in a picturesque village to E of Anglesey Abbey Garden. 21 Lode Road is planted with bold groups of herbaceous plants creating an element of mystery and delight. Carpenters End displays shrubs, trees, herbaceous plants and a fine lawn.

33 LUCY CAVENDISH COLLEGE
Lady Margaret Road, Cambridge CB3 0BU. Lucy Cavendish College. 1m NW of Gt St Mary. College situated on corner of Lady Margaret Rd & Madingley Rd (A1303). Entrance off Lady Margaret Rd. **Adm £3.50, chd free. Sun 3 May (2-5).**
The gardens of 4 late Victorian houses have been combined and developed over past 25yrs into an informal 3 acre garden. Fine mature trees shade densely planted borders. An Anglo Saxon herb garden is situated in one corner. The garden provides a rich wildlife habitat.

34 MADINGLEY HALL

nr Cambridge CB23 8AQ. University of Cambridge, 01223 746222, reservations@madingleyhall.co.uk, www.madingleyhall.co.uk. *4m W of Cambridge. 1m from M11 J13.* Home-made teas at St Mary Magdalene Church adjacent to Madingley Hall Drive. **Adm £5, chd free. Sun 31 May** (2.30-5.30).
C16 Hall (not open) set in 8 acres of attractive grounds. Features incl landscaped walled garden with hazel walk, alpine bed, medicinal border and rose pergola. Meadow, topiary, mature trees and wide variety of hardy plants. St Mary Magdalene Church open throughout the event.

🏵 ⊨ ☕

Planted to attract bees and wildlife, through which meandering paths have created hidden vistas . . .

35 MANOR HOUSE, ALWALTON

Church Street, Alwalton, Peterborough PE7 3UU. Malcolm & Jane Holmes, 01733 233435. *Alwalton Village. Turn into centre of old village, after church take R fork & continue for 100 metres.* Light refreshments. **Visitors welcome by arrangement** June to July groups up to 20.
Walled garden divided into rooms. Wild garden overlooking Nene Valley. Topiary and mixed borders.

☕

36 ◆ THE MANOR, HEMINGFORD GREY

nr Huntingdon PE28 9BN. Mrs D S Boston, 01480 463134, www.greenknowe.co.uk. *4m E of Huntingdon. Off A14. Entrance to garden by small gate off river*

towpath. Very limited parking on verge half way up drive, parking near house for disabled. Otherwise park in village. **For opening times and information, please phone or see garden website.**
Garden designed and planted by author Lucy Boston, surrounds C12 manor house on which Green Knowe books based (house open by appt). 4 acres with topiary; over 200 old roses, extensive collection of irises incl Cedric Morris varieties and herbaceous borders with mainly scented plants. Meadow with mown paths. Enclosed by river, moat and wilderness. Late May splendid show of Irises followed by the old roses. Care is taken with the planting to start the year with a large variety of snowdrops and to extend the flowering season right through to the first frosts. The garden is interesting even in winter with the topiary. Gravel paths but wheel chairs are encouraged to go on the lawns.

♿ 🏵

37 MARY CHALLIS GARDEN

High Street, Sawston CB22 3BG. A M Challis Trust Ltd. *7m SE of Cambridge. Entrance via lane between 60 High St & 66 High St (Billsons Opticians).* Home-made teas. **Adm £3, chd free. Sun 12 July** (2-5.30).
Given to Sawston in 2006 this 2 acre garden is being restored by volunteers: formal flower garden, vegetable beds with vine house, meadow and woodland, with concern for the flora and fauna - and the village children. Paths and lawns should be accessible from car-park.

♿ 🎋 🏵 ☕

38 5 MOAT WAY

Swavesey CB24 4TR. Mr & Mrs N Kyberd, 01954 200568, n.kyberd@ntlworld.com. *Off A14, 2m beyond Bar Hill. Look for School Lane/Fen Drayton Rd, at mini r'about turn into Moat Way, no.5 is approx 100 metres on L.* **Adm £3, chd free. Visitors welcome by arrangement** May to July.
Colourful garden filled with collection of trees, shrubs and perennials. Large patio area displaying many specimen foliage plants in planters, incl pines, hostas and acers.

39 NETHERHALL MANOR

Tanners Lane, Soham CB7 5AB. Timothy Clark. *6m Ely, 6m Newmarket. Enter Soham from*

Newmarket, Tanners Lane 2nd R 100yds after cemetery. Enter Soham from Ely, Tanners Lane 2nd L after War Memorial. Home-made teas. **Adm £2, chd free. Suns 5 Apr, 3 May, 2, 9 Aug** (2-5).
An elegant garden 'touched with antiquity' Good Gardens Guide. An unusual garden appealing to those with an historical interest in the individual collections of genera and plant groups: March - old primroses, daffodils and Victorian double flowered hyacinths. May - old English tulips. Crown Imperials. Aug - Victorian pelargonium, heliotrope, calceolaria, dahlias. Author of Margery Fish's Country Gardening and Mary McMurtrie's Country Garden Flowers. Historic Plants 1500-1900. Double flowered Hyacinths,.Tudor type primroses. Victorian Pelargoniums. The only bed of English tulips on display in the country. Author's books for sale. Featured on Radio Cambridgeshire.

♿ ☕

40 NORFOLK TERRACE GARDEN

38 Norfolk Terrace, Cambridge CB1 2NG. John Tordoff & Maurice Reeve. *Central Cambridge. A603 East Rd turn R into St Matthews St to Norfolk St, L into Blossom St & Norfolk Terrace is at the end.* Tea. **Adm £2, chd free. Sun 26 July** (12-6).
A small, paved courtyard garden in Moroccan style. Masses of colour in raised beds and pots, backed by oriental arches. An ornamental pool done in patterned tiles offers the soothing splash of water. The owners' previous, London garden, was named by BBC Gardeners' World as 'Best Small Garden in Britain'.

☕

41 THE OLD RECTORY

Main Road, Parson Drove, Wisbech PE13 4LF. Helen Roberts. *SW of Wisbech. From Peterborough on A47 follow signs to Parson Drove L after Thorney Toll. From Wisbech follow the B1166 through Levrington Common.* Home-made teas. **Adm £3.50, chd free. Sun 7 June** (11-4).
Walled Georgian cottage garden of 1 acre, opening into wild flower meadow and paddocks. Long herbaceous border, 2 ponds and unusual weeping ash tree. Terraced areas and outdoor kitchen! No hills but lovely open Fen views.

♿ 🏵 ☕

Treat yourself to a plant from the plant stall 🏵

Abbot's Barn

42 ▶ THE OLD VICARAGE
Thompsons Lane, Cambridge
CB5 8AQ. Christa Pleasants. *St
Clements Church Gardens,
Cambridge. Enter Thompson's Lane
from Bridge St. Old Vicarage is 1st
house on R. Enter garden through
iron gate, up two steps to path &
lawn.* Adm £2.50, chd free. Sat 25,
Sun 26 Apr (2-5).
The garden to this distinctive historic
house has been transformed since
2012 by designer Michael C Wood.
Set within the churchyard of St
Clement. The garden is enclosed by a
curving, swooping fence of woven
willow. New stone paving, structures
and richly-textured planting have
been worked around mature trees to
create a delightful, calm oasis in this
busy part of the city.

43 ▶ 23A PERRY ROAD
Buckden, St. Neots PE19 5XG.
David & Valerie Bunnage,
01480 810553,
d.bunnage@btinternet.com. *5m S
of Huntingdon on A1. From A1
Buckden r'about take B661, Perry Rd
approx 300yds on L.* Adm £3.50,
chd free. Visitors welcome by
arrangement Mar to Oct.
Approx 1 acre garden consisting of
many garden designs incl Japanese
interlinked by gravel paths. Large
selection of acers, pines, rare and
unusual shrubs. Also interesting

features, a quirky garden. Plantsmans
garden for all seasons new wildlife
pond with small stumpery and
woodland plus small seaside garden
with beach hut. WC. Coaches
welcome.

GROUP OPENING

44 ▶ RAMSEY FORTY FOOT
nr Ramsey PE26 2YA. *3m N of
Ramsey. From Ramsey (B1096) travel
through Ramsey Forty Foot, just
before bridge over drain, turn into
Hollow Rd at The George PH, First
Cottage 300yds on R, next door to
The Elms. Home-made teas at First
Cottage.* Combined adm £3, chd
free. Sun 14 June (2-6).

THE ELMS
Mr R Shotbolt
Visitors also welcome by
arrangement May to Aug.
01487 812601
richard@shotbolt.freeserve.
co.uk

FIRST COTTAGE
Hollow Road. Mr & Mrs Fort

THE WILLOWS
Jane & Andrew Sills

3 interesting and contrasting gardens
in the village of Ramsey Forty Foot.
The Elms 1½-acre water garden
around C19 clay pit backed by

massive elms. Large collection of
shrubs, perennials, bog and aquatic
plants. Woodland and arid plantings.
First Cottage 150ft x 40ft garden with
herbaceous borders, shrub beds,
natural pond. Miniature steam railway.
The Willows is a cottage garden with
riverside location filled with old roses,
herbaceous beds; shrubs, ferns,
pond and vegetable garden. Some
wheelchair access.

45 ▶ 6 ROBINS WOOD
Wansford, Peterborough PE8 6JQ.
Carole & Forbes Smith, 01780
783094,
caroleannsmith@tiscali.co.uk. *7m
W of Peterborough on A1/A47
junction. From A47 turn towards
Wansford. At Xrds by church turn W
onto Old Leicester Rd. Approx
500yds turn R into Robins Field,
follow on to Robins Wood.* Home-
made teas. and soup. Adm £3, chd
free. Sun 22 Feb (11-4) 2015, Sun
28 Feb 2016. Visitors also welcome
by arrangement Jan to May.
Small woodland garden with a
collection of 300+ varieties of
snowdrops. Various hellebore and
corydalis followed by other spring
woodland plants and bulbs. Small
alpine plant house. Still creating beds
in any spare corner to accommodate
new varieties.

46 ROBINSON COLLEGE

Grange Road, Cambridge
CB3 9AN. Warden and Fellows,
01223 339100,
www.robinson.cam.ac.uk/about/
gardens/ngs.php. *Garden at main
Robinson College site, report to
Porters' Lodge. There is only on-
street parking.* **Adm by donation.
Every Mon to Fri 1 Jan to 17 Apr &
15 June to 31 Dec (10-4). Every
Sat & Sun 1 Jan to 17 Apr & 15
June to 31 Dec (2-4).**
10 original Edwardian gardens are
linked to central wild woodland water
garden focusing on Bin Brook with
small lake at heart of site. This gives a
feeling of park and informal
woodland, while at the same time
keeping the sense of older more
formal gardens beyond. Central area
has a wide lawn running down to the
lake framed by many mature stately
trees with much of the original
planting intact. More recent planting
incl herbaceous borders and
commemorative trees. Partial
closures due to building works till
summer 2015. Please report to
Porters' Lodge on arrival to make
donation and for guidebook. No
picnics. Children must be
accompanied at all times. For any
further enquiries please ring Porters
Lodge. Ask at Porters' Lodge for
wheelchair access.

& ☕

GROUP OPENING

47 SAWSTON GARDENS

Sawston, nr Cambridge CB22 3HY.
*5m SE of Cambridge. Halfway
between Saffron Walden &
Cambridge on A1301 close to A505
'McDonalds' r'about.* Light
refreshments at Sweet Tea, High St.
**Combined adm £5, chd free. Sun 5
July (1-6).**

BROOK HOUSE
Mr & Mrs Ian & Mia Devereux.
*Short walk S from the village
centre; opp Hutchings & Harding
chamois leather works*

DRIFT HOUSE
19a Babraham Road. Mr Alan &
Mrs Jean Osborne

11 MILL LANE
Tim & Rosie Phillips.
*Close to village centre. Approx
200yds W along Mill Lane from its
junction with the High Street (Post
Office corner)*

35 MILL LANE
Doreen Butler.
*Next to fire station. Approx
halfway between the village
centre and western by-pass*

THE NEW VICARAGE
Revd Alan Partridge.
*Behind the Church Hall. Enter
through the Church Hall car park*

22 ST MARY'S ROAD
Ann & Mike Redshaw.
*Enter Church Lane at the War
Memorial. 1st R onto St Mary's
Rd*

VINE COTTAGE
Dr & Mrs Tim Wreghitt

7 delightful gardens. Brook House
has many lovely recently designed
and planted features set in 1½ acres.
One of the many highlights is a
stunning large walled garden not to
be missed. Drift House has ⅓ acre of
mature mixed planting in a 1960s
garden, also featuring cloud pruned
Junipers. 35 Mill Lane has colourful
massed annual and perennial floral
displays and fascinating water
features. Find immaculate lush lawns,
delightful mature mixed borders and
large fruit cage at 11 Mill Lane. The
New Vicarage is a developing garden
with interestingly designed and
planted borders. 22 St Mary's Road
has views over SSS1 meadows,
wildlife friendly planting and charming
colour-themed contemporary
borders. Vine Cottage's large mature
garden has an intriguing secret
Japanese courtyard. Many other
features to be found something for
everyone. Great value seven gardens
for £5. Enjoy a cream tea at 'Sweet
Tea', or take up the exclusive
discount offer for garden visitors at
the Jade Fountain. With such a
variety of gardens, clearly wheelchair
access is variable.

& 🐾 ✿ ☕

---

*An elegant pergola
accessed via a
bridge over the
main pond
stretches the
full length of the
garden . . .*

48 SOUTH FARM & BROOK COTTAGE

Shingay-cum-Wendy, Royston
SG8 0HR. Philip Paxman, 01223
207581, info@south-farm.co.uk,
www.southfarming.co.uk. *12m W of
Cambridge. 500 metres S of
A603/A1198. 5m N of Royston turn L
to Wendy, then L again at sign to
South Farm.* Cream teas at South
farm. Pre-booked cream teas are
available for £4.50. Please telephone
South Farm to book 01223 207581.
**Adm £3.50, chd free. Tue 14 Apr,
Tue 12 May (2-6); Tue 14 July (2-8);
Tue 15 Sept (2-6).**
Transformed by Philip Paxman over
40yrs South Farm is a diverse country
garden and smallholding. The formal
garden has planting schemes with
colour, structure and creative bursts
throughout the yr. Smallholding
provides 190 types of fruit,
vegetables and herbs. In 2013, a
formal herb and kitchen garden was
created. In 2011 a 5 acre British
Hardwood arboretum and heritage
meadow established. Restored listed
barnyard (open). Private Nature
Reserve with lake, otters, dragonfiles,
native crayfish and wild flowers.
Neighbouring **Brook Cottage** (Mr &
Mrs Charville) Countryman's cottage
garden.

& 🐾 🚐 ☕

GROUP OPENING

49 STAPLEFORD GARDENS

Cambridge CB22 5DG. *4m S of
Cambridge on A1301. In London
Road next to Church Street. Parking
available on site.* Tea at 6 Finch's
Close and 59-61 London Rd. Jam &
Chutney sale at 59-61 London Rd.
**Combined adm £5, chd free.
Sun 28 June (10.30-6).**

6 FINCH'S CLOSE
Prof & Mrs S Sutton
(See separate entry)

59-61 LONDON ROAD
Dr & Mrs S Jones

5 PRIAMS WAY
Tony Smith

Contrasting gardens showing a range
of size, planting and atmosphere in
this village just S of Cambridge. The
London Road and Priam's Way
gardens form an interlocking series of
garden rooms incl herbaceous beds,
kitchen garden, pit and summer
houses with sculptures set around. At
6 Finch's Close small Spanish-styled

patio leads to the fruit and vegetable garden and greenhouse. The borders around the lawn and wildlife pond are well-stocked with shrubs and mature trees whilst gentle musical chimes can be heard in the breeze.

 ♿ ☕

GROUP OPENING

50 STAPLOE GARDENS
Staploe, St. Neots PE19 5JA. *Great North Rd in western part of St Neots. At r'about just N of the Coop store, exit westwards on Duloe Rd. Follow this under the A1, through the village of Duloe & on to Staploe.* Home-made teas. **Combined adm £3.50, chd free.** Sat 30, Sun 31 May (1-5).

NEW ▶ **FALLING WATER HOUSE**
Caroline Kent

OLD FARM COTTAGE
Sir Graham & Lady Fry

Old Farm Cottage: flower garden surrounding thatched house (not open), with 3 acres of orchard, grassland, young woodland and pond maintained for wildlife. Falling Water House: a mature woodland garden, partly reclaimed from farmland 10yrs ago, it is constructed around several century old trees incl three Wellingtonia. Kitchen garden potager, courtyard and herbaceous borders, planted to attract bees and wildlife, through which meandering paths have created hidden vistas.

♿ 🐕 ❀ ☕

51 STEEPLE VIEW
20 Steeple View, March PE15 9QH. Mr & Mrs Allan & April Hammond. *1m S of March town centre. Steeple View is a turning off Knights End Rd which is situated off the A141 March bypass. Limited parking at garden. Therefore please park in the rd leading up to St Wendreda's Church.* Home-made teas. **Adm £3, chd free.** Sat 6, Sun 7 June (10-4); Sat 15, Sun 16 Aug (10-5).
Enter the main garden through a neat pebbled side walkway. The garden overlooks meadows and comprises of a mixture of well stocked beds and borders. An elegant pergola accessed via a bridge over the main pond stretches the full length of the garden. Exit via a small orchard area and cottage garden. Twice winners of

Overall Best Garden in March. Champion of Champion winners in the March garden competition. Narrow pebbled path not suitable for wheelchair access.

❀ ☕

PARKINSON'Sᵁᴷ

Thank you to the NGS for supporting Parkinson's nurses

GROUP OPENING

52 STREETLY END GARDENS
West Wickham CB21 4RP, 01223 893122. *3m from Haverhill & 3m from Linton. On A1307 between Linton & Haverhill. Turn N at Horseheath towards West Wickham, from Horseheath turn L at triangle of grass & trees, well signed.* Home-made teas at Chequer Cottage. **Combined adm £3.50, chd free.** Sun 7 June (12-5).

CHEQUER COTTAGE 🛏
43 Streetly End. Mr & Mrs D Sills.
After triangle on R bend, cottage on R, look for B&B sign
01223 891522
stay@chequercottage.com
www.chequercottage.com

CLOVER COTTAGE
Mr Paul & Mrs Shirley Shadford.
At triangle of grass & trees turn L, cottage on R next to old windmill, signed
Visitors also welcome by arrangement May to July adm incl tea or coffee & biscuits.
01223 893122
shirleyshadford@live.co.uk

Find arches of roses and clematis at Clover Cottage and many varieties of hardy geraniums, and raised fruit/vegetable beds. Delightful pond and borders of English roses, climbers and herbaceous plants. Also ferns and shade plants and views over open countryside from summerhouse in sunken garden. At

Chequer Cottage enjoy mixed cottage and contemporary planting of Monet style rose arch, perennial beds with many iris, delphiniums, roses. Unusual trees, pond, bog garden, art studio. Long vegetable garden, interesting walls, paths and rockery. In walled garden evergreen shrubs, damp shade and hot dry borders. Art studio open, art work and home-made teas for sale at Chequer Cottage. Plants and greetings cards for sale at Clover Cottage featuring photos of the garden and cottage. **NO WHEELCHAIRS, NO PUSHCHAIRS & NO DOG ACCESS TO GARDENS AT ALL.**

❀ 🚐 🛏 ☕

53 TRINITY COLLEGE, FELLOWS' GARDEN
Queens Road, Cambridge CB3 9AQ. Master and Fellows' of Trinity College. *Short walk from city Centre. At the Northampton St/Madingley Rd end of Queens Rd close to Garrett Hostel Lane.* Home-made teas. **Adm £3.50, chd free.** Sun 12 Apr (1-4).
Garden of 8 acres, originally laid out in the 1870s by W B Thomas. Lawns with mixed borders, shrubs and specimen trees. Drifts of spring bulbs. Recent extension of landscaped area among new college buildings to West of main garden. Some gravel paths.

♿ ❀ ☕

54 TRINITY HALL - WYCHFIELD
Storeys Way, Cambridge CB3 0DZ. The Master & Fellows, www.trinhall.cam.ac.uk/about/gardens/wychfield.asp. *1m NW of city centre. Turn into Storeys Way from Madingley Rd (A1303).* Home-made teas. **Adm £4.50, chd free. Share to Royal National Lifeboat Institution.** Sun 12 Apr (11.30-3.30).
A beautiful large garden that complements the interesting and varied architecture. The Edwardian Wychfield House and its associated garden areas contrast with the recent contemporary development located off Storeys Way. Majestic trees, a wide array of spring flowering bulbs, shady under storey woodland planting and established lawns, work together to provide a inspiring garden. Plant Sale. Home-made tea and cakes. Some gravel paths.

♿ 🐕 ❀ ☕

55 TWIN TARNS

6 Pinfold Lane, Somersham
PE28 3EQ. Michael & Frances
Robinson, 01487 843376,
mikerobinson987@btinternet.com.
*Easy access from the A14. 4m NE of
St Ives. Turn onto Church St. Pinfold
Lane is next to the church.* Cream
teas. Adm £4, chd free. Sat 11,
Sun 12 July (1-5). Visitors also
welcome by arrangement May to
Sept any size group.
One-acre wildlife garden with formal
borders, kitchen garden and ponds,
large rockery, mini woodland, wild
flower meadow (June/July). Topiary,
rose walk, willow sculptures.
Character oak bridge. Hammock.
Adjacent to C13 village church.
Featured on Gardeners' World BBC2,
Love Your Garden ITV, and in
Cambridgeshire Journal, Garden
News and Landscape.

GROUP OPENING

56 WEST CHESTERTON

Cambridge CB4 2AQ. *Accessed
from Milton Rd (A10 to Ely) between
Gilbert Rd & Elizabeth Way. Some
designated parking in Milton Rd; easy
parking in nearby side streets.* Home-
made teas at 16 & 18 Chesterton Hall
Crescent. Combined adm £5, chd
free. Sat 27, Sun 28 June (2-6).

16 CHESTERTON HALL CRESCENT

Eve Corder.
*Accessed either from Chesterton
Rd or on foot from Milton Rd.
Parking limited*

18 CHESTERTON HALL CRESCENT

Hazel & Julian Bland.
*From Milton Rd or Chesterton Rd.
Limited parking in the Crescent &
surrounding streets*

10 GURNEY WAY

Gillian Perkins.
Off Gilbert Rd

55 MILTON ROAD

Richard & Pauline Freeman.
*No 55 lies approx 1/2 way
between Gilbert Rd & Ascham Rd*

Four town gardens varying in size and
design. 16 Chesterton Hall Crescent
is a sculptor's garden with workshop,
work area and sculpture set around a
wildlife pond and informal planting.
Next door, 18 Chesterton Hall
Crescent has herbaceous borders,
pond, mature trees and particularly
fine roses. 10 Gurney Way is planted
by a self-confessed plantaholic with
herbaceous borders, pond and large
productive vegetable garden.
55 Milton Road is subdivided by a
mature beech hedge and is full of
herbaceous plants, shrubs and roses.
Partial wheelchair access, some small
steps and narrow paths.

Find a great variety
of country, formal,
modern and wildlife
friendly gardens
here . . . .

GROUP OPENING

57 WHITTLESFORD GARDENS

Whittlesford CB22 4NR. *7m S of
Cambridge. 1m NE of J10 M11 &
A505. Parking nr church, additional
parking will be signed.* Light
refreshments at the church.
Combined adm £4, chd free.
Sun 21 June (2-6).

NEW 1 CHURCH LANE

Mr & Mrs Peter & Frances
Dumbleton.
*In centre of Whittlesford, adjacent
to telephone box. At top of
Church Lane*

MARKINGS FARM

32 West End. Mr & Mrs A
Jennings.
Parking space

5 PARSONAGE COURT

Mrs L Button.
Please park on rd

RYECROFT

1 Middlemoor Road. Mr & Mrs
Paul Goodman.
*From village centre, past 'Tickell
Arms' and 'Bees in the wall', L
into Middlemoor Road, L turn and
driveway 1st on L*

11 SCOTTS GARDENS

Mr & Mrs M Walker

31 WEST END

Mr & Mrs Neil & Betty Barber

WHITBY COTTAGE

20 West End. Mrs Laura
Latham

Find a great variety of country, formal,
modern and wildlife friendly gardens
here. 2 new gardens this year,
1 Church Lane is a stunning new
small modern courtyard garden,
enhanced by interesting planting and
the borrowed landscape of the old
Guildhall. 31 West End is a sizeable
wildlife friendly garden, with extensive
charming herbaceous borders, and
fruit and vegetables. Whitby Cottage
is a small claybat walled pretty
cottage garden with interesting water
features and large koi carp. Ryecroft
is a large elegant garden with trees,
shrubs and fruitful patio area.
Markings Farm is a lovely old
fashioned country garden with a
variety of shrubs and fabulous
vegetable patch. Parsonage Court
has an arched walkway, shrubs,
raised fish pond and delightful seating
area around an old tree. 11 Scotts
Gardens is a shady small walled
cottage garden with chickens and a
variety of shrubs and perennials.

58 WILD ROSE COTTAGE

Church Walk, Lode, Cambridge
CB25 9EX. Mrs Joy Martin,
01223 811132,
joymartin123@btinternet.com.
*From A14 take the rd towards
Burwell turn L in to Lode & park on L.
Walk straight on between cottages to
the archway of Wild Rose Cottage.*
Adm by donation. Visitors
welcome by arrangement Mar to
Oct please email or phone.
A real cottage garden overflowing
with plants. Gardens within gardens
of abundant vegetation, roses
climbing through trees, laburnum
tunnel, a daffodil spiral which
becomes a daisy spiral in the
summer. Circular vegetable garden
and wildlife pond. Described by one
visitor as a garden to write poetry in!
Chickens ducks and dog, circular
vegetable garden, wild life pond, and
wild romantic garden! Featured on
Love My Gardens and in Homes and
Gardens.

59 ◆ WIMPOLE ESTATE

Arrington SG8 0BW. National Trust,
0844 249 1895,
www.nationaltrust.org.uk/wimpole-
estate. *7m N of Royston (A1198). 8m
SW of Cambridge (A603). J12 off
M11, 30 mins from A1(M).* Entry by
ticket only. To pre-book the tour adm
£8 incl a drink. Contact Wimpole box
office on 0844-249 1895. Max 35..

For NGS: Evening Openings £8, chd free, wine/coffee, Wed 22, Wed 29 July (7-9). For other opening times and information, please phone or see garden website.

For the guided tour we meet at the stable block and take in the formal gardens, the pleasure grounds and finishing in the walled garden with a close look at our back sheds containing the mushroom house and apple store along with our gardens bothy. We will also be looking at the progress with our garden vision which is to open up many new areas and historic routes for our visitors. The evening will finish with a glass of wine or coffee in the Soane glasshouse, first built in 1790 destroyed by a WW11 bomb and re-built in 2000 with financial assistance from the NGS.. Contact Wimpole box office on 0844-249 1895. Electric buggies available, please book before arrival.

60 THE WINDMILL

Cambridge Road, Impington CB24 9NU. Pippa & Steve Temple, 07775 446443, mill.impington@ntlworld.com, www.impingtonmill.org. *2¹/₂ m N of Cambridge. Off A14 at J32, B1049 to Histon, L into Cambridge Rd at T-lights, follow Cambridge Rd round to R, the Windmill is approx 400yds on L.* Light refreshments. **Adm £3, chd free. Visitors welcome by arrangement** Apr to Oct.

A previously romantic wilderness of 1¹/₂ acres surrounding windmill, now filled with bulbs, perennial beds, pergolas, bog gardens, grass bed and herb bank. Secret paths and wild areas with thuggish roses maintain the romance. Millstone seating area in smouldering borders contrasts with the pastel colours of the remainder of the garden. Also 'Pond Life' seat, 'Tree God' and amazing compost area! The Windmill - an C18 smock on C19 tower on C17 base on C16 foundations - is being restored. Featured in Daily Mail, local press and on Radio Cambridgeshire.

61 WYTCHWOOD

7 Owl End, Great Stukeley, Huntingdon PE28 4AQ. Mr David Cox. *2m N of Huntingdon on B1043. Parking available at Great Stukeley Village Hall in Owl End.* Home-made teas. **Adm £3.50, chd free. Sun 21 June (1.30-5.30).**

A 2 acre garden with borders of perennials, annuals and shrubs, lawns, fish pond and a larger wildlife pond. The garden includes 1 acre for wildlife with grasses set among rowan, birch, maple and field maple trees, foxgloves, ferns and bulbs. Roses are a special feature in June. Enjoy home made and cream teas, plenty of seats. Parking at the village hall is a approx 100 metres from the garden. Short gravel drive at the garden entrance.

23a Perry Road

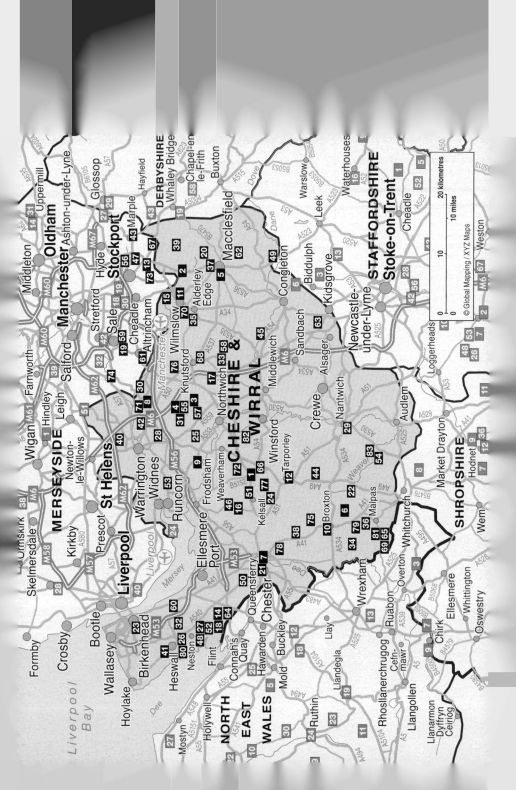

Cheshire & Wirral

The NGS 'county' of 'Cheshire and Wirral' comprises what are now the four administrative regions of west Cheshire and Chester, east Cheshire, Warrington and Wirral, together with gardens in the south of Greater Manchester and Trafford.

The perception of the area is that of a fertile county dominated by the Cheshire Plain, but to the extreme west it enjoys a mild maritime climate, with gardens often sitting on sandstone and sandy soils and enjoying mildly acidic conditions.

A large sandstone ridge also rises out of the landscape, running some 30-odd miles from north to south. Many gardens grow ericaceous-loving plants, although in some areas, the slightly acidic soil is quite clayey. But the soil is rarely too extreme to prevent the growing of a wide range of plants, both woody and herbaceous.

As one travels east and the region rises up the foothills of the Pennine range, the seasons become somewhat harsher, with spring starting a few weeks later than in the coastal region.

As well as being home to one of the RHS's major shows, the region's gardens include two NGS 'founder' gardens in Arley Hall and Peover Hall, as well as the University of Liverpool Botanic Garden at Ness.

Cheshire & Wirral Volunteers

County Organiser
John Hinde
01513 530032
john.hinde@maylands.com

County Treasurer
Andrew Collin
01513 393614
andrewcollin@btinternet.com

Publicity
Graham Beech
01625 402946
gb.ngs@talktalk.net

Booklet Coordinator
John Hinde
(as above)

Assistant County Organisers
Janet Bashforth
01925 349895
janbash43@sky.com

Sue Bryant
01619 283819
suewestlakebryant@btinternet.com

Jean Davies
01606 892383
mrsjeandavies@gmail.com

Sandra Fairclough
01513 424645
sandra.fairclough@tiscali.co.uk

Juliet Hill
01829 732804
t.hill573@btinternet.com

Romy Holmes
01829 732053
romy@holmes-email.co.uk

Left: Cogshall Grange © Marianne Majerus

Since our foundation we have donated more than £42.5 million to charity

Opening Dates

All entries subject to change.
For latest information check **www.ngs.org.uk**

February

Sunday 22
17 Bucklow Farm

March

Sunday 1
30 Dunham Massey
Sunday 29
57 Parm Place

April

Friday 3
3 NEW All Fours Farm
Saturday 18
61 NEW Racefield
Sunday 19
14 Briarfield
61 NEW Racefield
Saturday 25
6 Bank House
60 Poulton Hall
61 NEW Racefield
Sunday 26
6 Bank House
44 Long Acre
60 Poulton Hall
61 NEW Racefield

May

Saturday 2
36 Hannets Cottage
Sunday 3
1 Abbeywood Gardens
36 Hannets Cottage
51 Mount Pleasant
80 69 Well Lane

The back garden has colourful informal herbaceous borders packed with a variety of plants . . .

Monday 4
3 NEW All Fours Farm
51 Mount Pleasant
80 69 Well Lane
Sunday 10
77 Tirley Garth
Wednesday 13
76 Tatton Park
Thursday 14
22 Cholmondeley Castle Garden
Saturday 16
41 Inglewood
43 Leawood
Sunday 17
29 Dorfold Hall
41 Inglewood
43 Leawood
72 Stonyford Cottage
75 Tattenhall Hall
77 Tirley Garth
Saturday 23
21 Chester Cathedral
Sunday 24
46 Manley Knoll
Monday 25
27 Delfan
48 Millheyes
Saturday 30
55 The Old Parsonage
58 Peover Hall Gardens
73 Sun House
74 Sycamore Cottage
Sunday 31
23 28 Christchurch Road
55 The Old Parsonage
58 Peover Hall Gardens
73 Sun House
74 Sycamore Cottage
77 Tirley Garth

June

Festival Weekend

Saturday 6
3 NEW All Fours Farm
6 Bank House
34 Grafton Lodge
38 Hatton House Gardens
Sunday 7
2 Adlington Hall
6 Bank House
16 Brooklands
34 Grafton Lodge
38 Hatton House Gardens
53 Norton Priory Museum & Gardens
Wednesday 10
76 Tatton Park

Saturday 13
19 NEW 5 Carnforth Drive
59 17 Poplar Grove
Sunday 14
17 Bucklow Farm
19 NEW 5 Carnforth Drive
25 Cogshall Grange
59 17 Poplar Grove
66 Sandymere
71 NEW 10 Statham Avenue
Thursday 18
78 NEW Touchstone
Friday 19
78 NEW Touchstone
Saturday 20
5 Ashmead
49 Millpool
69 Somerset House
71 NEW 10 Statham Avenue
81 The White Cottage
Sunday 21
5 Ashmead
12 Bowmere Cottage
26 29 Dee Park Road
30 Dunham Massey
46 Manley Knoll
49 Millpool
52 Ness Botanic Gardens
62 Ridgehill
69 Somerset House
81 The White Cottage
Wednesday 24
54 Oakfield Villa
83 Wren's Nest
Saturday 27
36 Hannets Cottage
Sunday 28
18 Burton Village Gardens
24 NEW Clemley House
31 The East Garden
36 Hannets Cottage
40 Holly Mere
57 Parm Place

July

Saturday 4
3 NEW All Fours Farm
7 150 Barrel Well Hill
9 Bluebell Cottage Gardens
Sunday 5
7 150 Barrel Well Hill
9 Bluebell Cottage Gardens
33 Free Green Farm
47 NEW 218 Marple Road
Friday 10
68 Somerford (Evening)

Saturday 11
50 NEW Mollington Village Gardens
65 The Rowans
70 68 South Oak Lane
Sunday 12
50 NEW Mollington Village Gardens
65 The Rowans
70 68 South Oak Lane
Saturday 18
13 NEW 167 Bramhall Moor Lane
15 Brooke Cottage
28 Dingle Farm
37 Hathaway
Sunday 19
8 Beechwood Cottage
13 NEW 167 Bramhall Moor Lane
15 Brooke Cottage
28 Dingle Farm
32 Fieldcrest
37 Hathaway
Saturday 25
28 Dingle Farm
Sunday 26
28 Dingle Farm

August

Saturday 1
28 Dingle Farm
67 21 Scafell Close
Sunday 2
1 Abbeywood Gardens
4 Arley Hall & Gardens
28 Dingle Farm
47 NEW 218 Marple Road
67 21 Scafell Close
68 Somerford
72 Stonyford Cottage
Saturday 15
36 Hannets Cottage
42 Laskey Farm
Sunday 16
36 Hannets Cottage
42 Laskey Farm

September

Saturday 5
51 Mount Pleasant
56 39 Osborne Street
Sunday 6
51 Mount Pleasant
56 39 Osborne Street
Sunday 20
30 Dunham Massey

October

Sunday 4
45 The Lovell Quinta Arboretum

Over 400 Volunteers help run the NGS – why not become one too?

The Gardens

1 ◆ ABBEYWOOD GARDENS
Chester Road, Delamere, Northwich CW8 2HS. The Rowlinson Family, 01606 889477, www.abbeywoodgardenscheshire. co.uk. *11m E of Chester. On the A556 facing Delamere Church.* Restaurant in garden. **Adm £5.50, chd free. For NGS: Sun 3 May, Sun 2 Aug (9-5). For other opening times and information, please phone or see garden website.**
Superb setting near Delamere Forest. Total area 45 acres incl mature woodland, new woodland and new arboretum all with connecting pathways. Approx 4½ acres of gardens surrounding large Edwardian House. Vegetable garden, exotic garden, chapel garden, pool garden, woodland garden, lawned area with beds. Featured in The English Garden.

2 ◆ ADLINGTON HALL
Macclesfield SK10 4LF. Mrs Camilla Legh, 01625 827595, www.adlingtonhall.com. *4m N of Macclesfield, situated between Wilmslow & Prestbury. Well signed off A523 at Adlington.* Light refreshments. **Adm £3, chd free. For NGS: Sun 7 June (2-5). For other opening times and information, please phone or see garden website.**
Adlington Hall and Gardens consists of a formal garden area with the Rose Garden and Yew maze. Beyond the South Front sits the Wilderness, a woodland with follies and a river winding through it. The trees and features date back centuries with some rare specimens having been planted by various members of the Legh family. There is often an abundance of wildlife within this area too. Recently restored Shell Cottage. Our gardening team were part of the RHS Tatton Show 2014 Garden that was Highly Commended. We designed a half-scale replica of our T'ing House. The original can be seen in the Gardens. Partial wheelchair access.

3 NEW ALL FOURS FARM
Colliers Lane, Aston by Budworth, Northwich CW9 6NF. Mrs Hazel Evans, 01565 733243. *M6 J19, take A556 towards Northwich, turn immed R, past The Windmill PH. Turn R after approx 1m, follow road, garden on L after approx 2m.* Home-made teas. **Adm £4, chd free. Fri 3 Apr, Mon 4 May, Sat 6 June, Sat 4 July (10-4). Visitors also welcome by arrangement Apr to July.**
A traditional and well established country garden with a wide range of roses, hardy shrubs, bulbs, perennials and annuals. You will also find a small vegetable garden, pond and greenhouse as well as vintage machinery and original features from its days as a working farm. The majority of the garden is accessible by wheelchair, we're happy to allow direct access for drop off and collection for those with limited mobility.

Poulton Hall

Bring a bag for plants – help us give more to charity

4 ◆ ARLEY HALL & GARDENS

nr Northwich CW9 6NA. The Viscount Ashbrook, 01565 777353, www.arleyhallandgardens.com. *5m from Knutsford, Warrington & Northwich. Well signed from M6 J19 & 20, & M56 J9 & 10.* Adm £7.50, chd £3. For NGS: Sun 2 Aug (11-5). For other opening times and information, please phone or see garden website.

One of Britain's finest gardens, Arley has been lovingly created by the same family over 250yrs and is famous for its yew buttressed herbaceous border, avenue of ilex columns, walled garden, pleached lime avenue and Victorian Rootree. A garden of great atmosphere, interest and vitality throughout the seasons. Specialist nursery adjacent.

  ♿ 🐕 ❀ 🚌 ☕

Marie Curie Cancer Care

Marie Curie's hospice gardens provide tranquillity for patients

5 ▶ ASHMEAD

2 Bramhall Way, off Gritstone Drive, Macclesfield SK10 3SH. Peter & Penelope McDermott. *1m W of Macclesfield. Along Victoria Rd, 1st L after Macclesfield Hospital complex into Pavilion Way. L onto Gritstone Dr. Turn R into Bramhall Way, corner house. Travelling from Knutsford on A537 Chelford Rd turn L at Broken Cross r'about, straight across next r'about at 'The Villas' down hill passing the clock tower on R, Pavilion Way is 1st R, then Gritstone Dr first L & Ashmead first R on corner.* Home-made teas. Adm £3, chd free. Sat 20, Sun 21 June (1-5).

1/8 acre suburban cottage garden, featuring plant packed mixed borders, rock gardens, kitchen garden, island beds, water feature. The garden demonstrates how small spaces can be planted to maximum

effect to create all round interest. Extensive range of plants favoured for colours, texture and scent. Pots used in a creative way to extend and enhance borders.

  ♿ ❀ ☕

6 ▶ BANK HOUSE

Goldford Lane, Bickerton SY14 8LL. Dr & Mrs M A Voisey, 01829 782287, voisey598@btinternet.com. *4m NE of Malpas. 11m S of Chester on A41 turn L at Broxton r'about to Nantwich on A534. Take 5th R (1³/₄ m) to Bickerton. Take 2nd R into Goldford Lane. Bank House is approx 1m on L. Field parking.* Teas and homemade cakes. Adm £4, chd free. Sat 25, Sun 26 Apr, Sat 6, Sun 7 June (1.30-5). Visitors also welcome by arrangement Apr to July.

1³/₄ -acre garden at the foot of Bickerton Hill, in area of outstanding beauty, with extensive views to the East and South. Sheltered, terraced borders stocked with a wide range of shrubs, trees and herbaceous plants; established wild garden, Millennium garden with water features and productive vegetable garden. Unfenced swimming pool and ponds. Partial wheelchair access.

  ♿ 🐕 ❀ ☕

7 ▶ 150 BARREL WELL HILL

Boughton, Chester CH3 5BR. Dr & Mrs John Browne. *On riverside ³/₄ m E of Chester off A5115. No parking at garden. Preferred access via Chester Boats, on the hour from the Groves, central Chester. Cost £3.50 one way. Or bus to St Pauls Church. Public car park adjacent to Bill Smiths Motors.* Home-made teas. Adm £4, chd £2. Sat 4, Sun 5 July (11-5).

Spectacular terraced garden with views over the R Dee to the Meadows and Clwyd Hills. Uniquely, preferred method of arrival is by leisurely river cruiser from Chester. Informal cottage style garden on historic site by the Martyrs Memorial. Lawns running down to the river, prolific shrub and flower beds, productive vegetable patch and soft and hard fruit areas, springs, stream and lily pond. River cruisers leave the centre of Chester regularly and arrangements have been made that they will drop off and pick up garden visitors on their way up river. Not suitable for wheelchairs or children under eight due to unprotected drop into river.

  ☕

8 ▶ BEECHWOOD COTTAGE

64 Crouchley Lane, Lymm WA13 0AT. Ian & Amber Webb. *8m S of Altrincham. 4m from J7 or 2m J21 M6 onto A56 turn into Crouchley Ln past Lymm Rugby Club on R, 300yds on R (opp Crouchley Mews).* Home-made teas. Adm £4, chd free. Sun 19 July (11-5).

2 acre garden looking out to fields. Large lawn with herbaceous borders. Formal walkway with rose arches, topiary garden and orchard. Wild flower meadow - shaded area with tree ferns, hellebores and ferns. The grandest chicken shed outside Highgrove. Under cover tea room. Some gravel paths.

  ♿ ☕

9 ◆ BLUEBELL COTTAGE GARDENS

Lodge Lane, Dutton WA4 4HP. Sue & Dave Beesley, 01928 713718, www.bluebellcottage.co.uk. *5m NW of Northwich. From M56 (J10) take A49 to Whitchurch. After 3m turn R at T-lights towards Runcorn/Dutton. Then 1st turning L.* Home-made teas. Adm £4, chd free. For NGS: Sat 4, Sun 5 July (10-5). For other opening times and information, please phone or see garden website.

1¹/₂ -acre south facing garden on a quiet rural lane in the heart of Cheshire. Packed with thousands of rare and familiar hardy herbaceous perennials, shrubs and trees. Unusual plants available at adjacent nursery. The July opening dates coincide with the peak of flowering in the herbaceous borders. Featured in House and Garden magazine. Some gravel paths. Wheelchair access to 90% of garden. WC is not fully wheelchair accessible.

  ♿ ❀ 🚌 ☕

10 ▶ BOLESWORTH CASTLE

Tattenhall CH3 9HQ. Mrs Anthony Barbour, 01829 782210, dcb@bolesworth.com. *8m S of Chester on A41. Enter by Lodge on A41.* Light Refreshments can be arranged. There are plenty of nice places to have lunch or tea in and around Tattenhall. Adm £5, chd free. Visitors welcome by arrangement Apr to May groups of 10+.

Rock Walk above castle with one of the finest collections of rhododendrons, camellias and acers in any private garden in the NW. Set

on a steep hillside accessed by a gently rising woodland walk and overlooking spectacular view of the Cheshire plain. Formal lawns beside and below castle with well stocked shrub borders.

11 BOLLIN HOUSE
Hollies Lane, Wilmslow SK9 2BW. Angela Ferguson & Gerry Lemon, 07828 207492, fergusonang@doctors.org.uk. *Hollies Lane is off Adlington Rd 2nd exit on R coming from Wilmslow. Proceed to turning circle at end of lane, take 2nd exit off to Bollin House.* Home-made teas. **Adm £4, chd free. Visitors welcome by arrangement May to July groups 8-25. If more than 10 cars please phone.**
There are two components to this garden, the formal garden and the wild flower meadow. The garden contains richly planted, deep, herbaceous borders with a wide plant variety. Also an orchard, wild flower area and vegetable garden. The meadow contains both cornfield annuals and perennial wild flower areas which are easily accessible with meandering mown paths. Ramps to gravel lined paths to most of the garden. Some narrow paths through borders. Mown pathways in the meadow.

12 BOWMERE COTTAGE
Bowmere Road, Tarporley CW6 0BS. Romy & Tom Holmes, 01829 732053, romy@holmes-email.co.uk. *10m E of Chester. From Tarporley High St (old A49) take Eaton Rd signed Eaton. After 100 metres take R fork into Bowmere Rd, Garden 100 metres on LH-side.* Home-made teas. **Adm £4, chd free. Sun 21 June (1.30-5.30). Visitors also welcome by arrangement June to Aug.**
Mature 1-acre country style garden around a Grade II listed house (not open). Mixed shrub and herbaceous borders, pergolas, 2 plant filled courtyard gardens and small kitchen garden. Shrub and rambling roses, clematis, hardy geraniums and a wide and colourful range of plants make this a very traditional English garden. Cobbled drive and courtyard. Gravel paths. Featured in Concept For Living Magazine.

13 NEW 167 BRAMHALL MOOR LANE
Hazel Grove, Stockport SK7 5BB. David & Angela Brannan, 0161 483 2704, mail@angela8brannan-99.co.uk. *4m S of Stockport. From Bramhall take A5102. Turn R at Bramhall Hall up Bridge Lane A5143 at r'about take 2nd exit Bramhall Moor Lane. From A6 take rd opp Sainsbury's.* Home-made teas. **Adm £3, chd free. Sat 18, Sun 19 July (12-5). Visitors also welcome by arrangement May to Sept.**
The overall garden has a theme of light and dark. The front garden is a formal garden with box hedging and Indian bean trees with a background of shrubs chosen for texture and foliage. The back garden has colourful informal herbaceous borders packed with a variety of plants and standard trees and a small nursery and vegetable plot at the side. Unusual trees in containers, small nursery.

14 BRIARFIELD
The Rake, Burton, Neston CH64 5TL. Liz Carter, 0151 336 2304, carter.burton@virgin.net. *9m NW of Chester. Turn off A540 at Willaston-Burton Xrds T-lights & follow rd for 1m to Burton village centre.* Home-made teas in St Nicholas' Church, close to the garden. **Adm £4, chd free. Sun 19 Apr (2-5). Visitors also welcome by arrangement Mar to Oct.**
Tucked under the S-facing side of Burton Wood the garden is home to many specialist and unusual plants, some available in plant sale. This 2-acre garden is on two sites, a couple of minutes along an unmade lane. Shrubs, bulbs, alpines and several water features compete for attention as you wander through four distinctly different gardens. Always changing, Liz can't resist a new plant! Plants sold (60% to NGS) in Neston Market each Friday morning and from the house.

15 BROOKE COTTAGE
Church Road, Handforth SK9 3LT. Barry & Melanie Davy, 01625 536511, barry.davy@ntlworld.com. *1m N of Wilmslow. Centre of Handforth, behind Health Centre. Turn off Wilmslow Rd at St Chads, follow Church Rd round to R. Garden last on L. Parking in Health Centre car*

park. Home-made teas. **Adm £3.50, chd free. Sat 18, Sun 19 July (12-5). Visitors also welcome by arrangement May to July.**
Garden designer's plant-filled garden surrounded by trees and shrubs. 3 distinct areas and planting styles. Woodland garden: unusual water feature, 20+ fern varieties incl tree ferns, astrantias, hydrangeas, foxgloves, shade-loving plants. Container garden: huge variety of hostas, ligularias, dahlias, bamboo, daylilies, pond. Colourful naturalistic style herbaceous borders, island beds, grasses, late flowering perennials. Featured in Garden News and House Beautiful.

Vintage machinery and original features from its days as a working farm . . .

16 BROOKLANDS
Smithy Lane, Mouldsworth CH3 8AR. Barbara & Brian Russell-Moore, ngsmouldsworth@aol.co.uk. *1½ m N of Tarvin. 5½ m S of Frodsham. Smithy Lane is off B5393 via A54 Tarvin/Kelsall rd or the A56 Frodsham/Helsby rd.* Home-made teas. **Adm £4, chd free. Sun 7 June (2-5). Visitors also welcome by arrangement May to July for groups of 10+.**
Lovely country style, ¾ -acre garden with backdrop of mature trees and shrubs. The planting is based around azaleas, rhododendrons, mixed shrub and herbaceous borders. Small vegetable garden, supported by a greenhouse.

Tatton Park

17 ▸ **BUCKLOW FARM**
Pinfold Lane, Plumley, Knutsford
WA16 9RP. Dawn & Peter Freeman.
*2m S of Knutsford. M6 J19, A556
Chester. L at 2nd set of T-lights. In
1¼ m, L at concealed Xrds. 1st R.
From Knutsford A5033, L at Sudlow
Lane. becomes Pinfold Lane.* Home-
made teas. **Adm £3 £4, chd free.
Share to Knutsford Methodist
Church. Sun 22 Feb (1.30-3); Sun
14 June (2-5).**
Country garden with shrubs,
perennial borders, rambling roses,
herb garden, vegetable patch, wildlife
pond/water feature and alpines.
Landscaped and planted over the last
26yrs with recorded changes. Free
range hens. Carpet of snowdrops
and spring bulbs. Leaf, stem and
berries to show colour in autumn and
winter. Cobbled yard from car park,
but wheelchairs can be dropped off
near gate.
&♿ ❀ ☕

GROUP OPENING

18 ▸ **BURTON VILLAGE
GARDENS**
Neston, Cheshire CH64 5SJ. *9m
NW of Chester. Turn off A540 at
Willaston-Burton Xrds T-lights &
follow rd for 1m to Burton. Maps
given to visitors. Buy your ticket at
first garden.* Home-made teas in
Village Hall. Home made cakes.
**Combined adm £5, chd free.
Sun 28 June (11-5).**

> **BRIARFIELD**
> Liz Carter
> (See separate entry)

> ◆ **BURTON MANOR WALLED
> GARDEN**
> Burton Manor Gardens Ltd
> For other opening times and
> information, please see garden
> website.
> www.burtonmanorgardens.org.
> uk

LYNWOOD
Pauline Wright.
*Through Burton village centre
towards Ness Gardens*
Visitors also welcome by
arrangement May to July.
0151 336 2311

Burton is a medieval village built on
sandstone overlooking the Dee
estuary, about a mile from Ness
Gardens. Three gardens are open,
each with its own unique character.
Lynwood, a half-acre plantswoman's
garden, has a superb view across the
Dee to the Clwydian hills. Set on an
extensive sandstone outcrop
enclosing a sunken pond, the garden
is divided into 'rooms', each with its
own collection of colourful
herbaceous plants. Briarfield's
sheltered site, nestling under the
south side of Burton Wood (National
Trust), is home to many specialist and
unusual plants, some available in the
plant sale at the house. The intricate
layout of the 1½ acre main Briarfield
garden invites exploration not only for

its huge variety of plants but also for the imaginative use of ceramic sculptures. Period planting with a splendid vegetable garden surrounds the restored Edwardian glasshouse in Burton Manor's walled garden. All gardens have a plant sale. Well signed car parks. Maps available. Burton Manor only.

&♿ ⊛ ☕

---

19 **NEW** **5 CARNFORTH DRIVE**
Sale M33 4BF. Anne Earnshaw. *A56 from Altrincham turn R into Marsland Rd then 200yds turn R on to Walton Rd before Sale Cemetry & Brooklands Stn & Carnforth Drive is 2nd turning on R. Home-made teas.* **Combined adm with 17 Poplar Grove £6, chd free. Sat 13, Sun 14 June (2-5).**
It is a suburban mature garden with secret paths, hidden corners, partly lawned and a small pond. A large magnolia tree captures your attention. Also with mature shrubs and trees with colour, texture line and form. A delightful herbaceous border with healing colours of blues, pinks and purples. People have commented how beautiful and calm it is with its restful sitting areas.

☕

20 **4 CHESHIRE VIEW**
Kerridge, Macclesfield SK10 5AU. Peter & Georgie Everson, 01625 572445, pandg@uwclub.net. *3m from Macclesfield. A523 from Macclesfield. A5090 turn 1st R to Kerridge. After 1¹/₂ m pass Bulls Head on R & park on rd. Garden is 5 mins walk over stone stile & 2 fields. Owner will meet you in village. Ignore satnav.* Tea. **Adm £3, chd free. Visitors welcome by arrangement** July to Aug, only suitable for active and able visitors.
A magical ²/₃ acre hillside garden at 650ft with W facing views over the Cheshire plain to Alderley Edge and Mersey estuary. Magnificent sunsets. Landscaped on several levels using old railway sleepers with shrubs, late herbaceous perennials and a background of wooded slopes. Visitors must be able bodied and wear stout footwear. Spectacular view across Cheshire Plain. Please phone for viewing times and candlelit openings. Featured in Amateur Gardening and local press.

♿ ☕

---

21 **CHESTER CATHEDRAL**
Chester CH1 2HU. Dean of Chester Cathedral. *Centre of Chester. Admission at SW entrance on St Werburgh St, Chester.* **Adm £3, chd free. Sat 23 May (1-4).**
Cloister Garth 2004, haven of peace and tranquillity surrounded by ancient architecture, sculpture fountain and exotic plants. 2012 Jubilee Garden with abundance of herbaceous and rare trees, fern border and new developments in Abbey Street, Abbey Square and Cathedral Green. Gardens designed by botanist and maintained by volunteers. Open day followed by (horticultural) Choral Evensong at 4.15pm in iconic C14 quire, sung by Cathedral Nave Choir. The Bishop's and Deanery Gardens will also be open.

♿ ☕

22 ◆ **CHOLMONDELEY CASTLE GARDEN**
Cholmondeley, nr Malpas SY14 8AH. Lavinia, Dowager Marchioness of Cholmondeley, 01829 720383, www.cholmondeleycastle.com. *4m NE of Malpas. Signed from A41 Chester-Whitchurch rd & A49 Whitchurch-Tarporley rd.* Light lunches, homemade teas. **Adm £6, chd £3. For NGS: Thur 14 May (11-4.30).** For other opening times and information, please phone or see garden website.
Over 20 acres of romantically landscaped gardens with fine views and eye-catching water features, but still manages to retain its intimacy. Beautiful mature trees form a background to spring bulbs, exotic plants in season incl magnolias, rhododendrons, azaleas and camellias and many other, particularly *Davidia Involucrata* which will be in flower in late May. Magnificent magnolias. Partial wheelchair access.

♿ 🐕 ⊛ 🚐 ☕

23 **28 CHRISTCHURCH ROAD**
Oxton CH43 5SF. Tom & Ruth Foster. *1m SW of Birkenhead. At M53 J3 take A552 to Birkenhead. Cross junction at T-lights after Sainsbury's. At next T-lights bear L. Take 2nd L. Christchurch R is after church.* Home-made teas. **Adm £4, chd free. Sun 31 May (1-5).**
Grade II listed Victorian Folly with crenellated towers forms a unique feature in this ¹/₄ -acre plot. The garden is on different levels with many seating areas, terraced banks,

---

planted sandstone walls, water features, herbaceous borders, lawns, trees (many acers) and a Japanese style garden. All areas are connected by a series of tunnels, pathways and steps.

🐕 ☕

Delightful herbaceous border with healing colours of blues, pinks and purples . . .

24 **NEW** **CLEMLEY HOUSE**
Well Lane, Duddon Common, Duddon, Tarporley CW6 0HG. Sue & Tom Makin, 07790 610586, s_makingardens@yahoo.co.uk. *8m S.E of Chester, 3m W of Tarporley. Take A51 from Chester towards Tarporley. 1m after Tarvin turnoff, at bus shelter, turn L into Willington Rd. After 1m turn L into Well Lane.* Home-made teas. Home grown organic fruits used in jams & cakes. **Adm £4, chd free. Sun 28 June (12-5). Visitors also welcome by arrangement** June to Aug for groups of 10+.
2 acre organic, wildlife friendly, gold award winning cottage garden. Features orchard, wildlife ponds, wildflower meadow, fruit and veg areas, badger sett, rose pergola, gazebo, summer house, barn owl and many other nest boxes, gravel and shade gardens, shepherd's hut and poly tunnel. Year round interest. Its development features regularly in the N.W. Cottage Garden Society newsletter. 'Frogwatch' charity volunteers transport migrating amphibians to the safety of these ponds when they are found on the roads in early spring. Regularly features in the Lancashire and North West Area Cottage Garden Society newsletter. Gravel paths may be difficult to use but most areas are flat and comprise grass paths or lawn.

♿ ⊛ ☕

---

25 COGSHALL GRANGE
Hall Lane, Antrobus, Northwich
CW9 6BJ. Anthony & Margaret
Preston. *3m NW of Northwich. Take
A559 Northwich to Warrington. Turn
into Wheatsheaf Lane or Well Lane.
Head S on Sandiway Lane to grass
triangle & then R into Hall Lane.* Tea.
**Adm £6, chd free. Sun 14 June
(11-5).**
Set in the historic landscape of a late
Georgian country house this is a
contemporary garden, designed by
the internationally renowned garden
designer, Tom Stuart-Smith. The
gardens contain a mixture of both
informal and formal elements,
modern herbaceous plantings, a
walled garden, wild flower meadows,
an orchard and woodland borders
with views to parkland and the
surrounding countryside.

26 29 DEE PARK ROAD
Gayton CH60 3RG. E Lewis,
0151 342 5893,
eileen.lewis29@tiscali.co.uk. *7m S
of Birkenhead. From Devon
Doorway/Glegg Arms r'about at
Heswall travel towards Chester on
A540 for approx ¼ m. R into Gayton
Lane, then 5th L.* Home-made teas.
**Adm £3, chd free. Sun 21 June
(1-5).** Visitors also welcome by
arrangement June to Aug.
A redesigned secret garden. A white
border. A new border leading to a
small summer house. Rose and
clematis covered trellis and pergolas.
An arbour conceals further 'room'.
Many cottage garden perennials.
Gravel garden, alpines and thymes.
Featured in Amateur Gardening.
Partial wheelchair access.

27 DELFAN
Burton Road, Little Neston, Neston
CH64 4AF. Chris Sullivan. *10m NW
of Chester situated between Neston
& Ness Gardens. M53 J4, follow
signs M56 & A5117 (signed N Wales).
Turn onto A540 follow signs for
Hoylake. Garden is 1m past Ness
Gardens. Garden is near to
Marshlands Rd. Parking at St
Michael's Church.* Light refreshments
at St Michael's Church. **Combined
adm with Millheyes £4, chd free.
Mon 25 May (1-5).**
The garden is surrounded by mature
trees. Spring borders with camellias
and rhododendrons, followed by
herbaceous borders offering colour
and variety of planting. The borders

provide fragrance with roses climbing
up obelisks. A tender plant area and
fern bed sit amongst the cottage
garden plants. Late summer colour is
provided by echinaceas, heleniums
and dahlias.

28 DINGLE FARM
Dingle Lane, Appleton, Warrington
WA4 3HR. Robert Bilton,
www.dinglefarmonline.co.uk. *2m N
from M56 J10. A49 towards
Warrington, R at T-lights onto Stretton
Rd, 1m turn L at The Thorn PH, after
1m turn L into Dingle Lane. Plenty of
parking.* **Adm £3, chd
free. Sat 18, Sun 19, Sat 25, Sun
26 July, Sat 1, Sun 2 Aug (10-5).**
The garden is only 4yrs old but gives
the impression of being more
established. Features include a large
pond, wild flower garden, vegetable
patch with chicken run and a wooded
area. The garden is overlooked by the
world famous Dingle Farm Tea
Rooms, Art Studio & Gift Shop set in
the beautiful Cheshire countryside.
Woodland walks adjacent to the site.

29 DORFOLD HALL
Nantwich CW5 8LD. Mr & Mrs
Richard Roundell. *1m W of
Nantwich. On A534 between
Nantwich & Acton.* Tea. **Adm £6, chd
£2.50. Sun 17 May (2-5.30).**
18-acre garden surrounding C17
house (not open) with formal
approach; lawns and herbaceous
borders; spectacular spring woodland
garden with rhododendrons, azaleas,
magnolias and bulbs.

30 ◆ DUNHAM MASSEY
Altrincham WA14 4SJ. National
Trust, 0161 941 1025,
www.nationaltrust.org.uk/dunham
massey. *3m SW of Altrincham. Off
A56; M6 exit J19; M56 exit J7. Foot:
close to Trans-Pennine Trail &
Bridgewater Canal. Bus: Nos 38 & 5.*
**Adm £8.40, chd £4.20. For NGS:
Sun 1 Mar, Sun 21 June, Sun 20
Sept (11-5.30). For other opening
times and information, please
phone or see garden website.**
Enjoy the elegance of this vibrant
Edwardian garden. Richly planted
borders packed with colour and
texture, sweeping lawns, majestic
trees and shady woodland all await
your discovery. Explore the largest
Winter Garden in Britain and marvel
at the colourful, scent-filled Rose

Garden. Water features. C18
Orangery, rare Victorian Bark House.
Visitors to the garden, incl NT
members, should collect ticket from
Ticket Office at Visitor Reception.

31 ▶ THE EAST GARDEN
Arley Hall, Northwich CW9 6LZ.
Mrs Jane Foster & Mrs Tessa
Holmes, 01565 777231,
jmefoster@btinternet.com. *6m W of
Knutsford. Follow brown signs for
Arley Hall from M6 Junc 19 & 20 &
M56 J9 & 10. Park in Arley Hall car
park. Entry via Gift Shop.* Light
refreshments. **Adm £4.50, chd free.
Sun 28 June (11-5). Combined
adm with Arley Hall Gardens £10.
Visitors also welcome by
arrangement June to Aug.**
Two modern, very attractive gardens
made since 1992 on the site of the
C19 East Garden by the owners of
Arley Hall Nursery and the East
House, Arley Hall. Old shrub roses,
early summer perennials and circular
herbaceous borders enclosed by yew
hedges. Many varieties of hardy
herbaceous perennials - the speciality
of the nursery. Refreshments
provided. Wheelchair access
throughout.

32 ▶ ◆ FIELDCREST
Thornton Common Road, Thornton
Hough, Wirral CH63 0LT. Paul &
Christine Davies, 0151 334 8878,
www.fieldcrestgarden.com. *5m S of
Birkenhead, 4m SE of Heswall. Exit
J4 M53, follow B5151
Clatterbridge/Willaston for 1m. Follow
tourist sign for Merebrook House,
turning L at r'about signed Raby*

Mere & Wirral RFC. Garden ½ m on R. Home-made teas served under cover. **Adm £4, chd free. Sun 19 July (1-4). For other opening times and information, please phone or see garden website.**
Country garden in 1¼ acres, planted for year round colour and interest. Cottage garden divided into 'rooms', shrub borders, potager with fruit and and vegetables. Specialised herb and cut flower beds. Country lane walk, wild flower area with young fruit trees. Wide variety of summer perennials. 'Chocolate' border. Featured in Cheshire Life and Garden Answers magazine. Gravel in drive area and some paths. Winner Britain's Best Lawn.

33 FREE GREEN FARM
Free Green Lane, Lower Peover WA16 9QX. Sir Philip & Lady Haworth. *3m S of Knutsford. Near A50 between Knutsford & Holmes Chapel. Off Free Green Lane.* Home-made teas. **Adm £5, chd free. Sun 5 July (2-5.30).**
2-acre garden with pleached limes, herbaceous borders, ponds, parterre, garden of the senses, British woodland with fernery, quasi jungle area with Saracenia. Topiary. Assortment of trees, and ten different forms of hedging. Wheelchair access not easy in the wood.

34 GRAFTON LODGE
Stretton, Tilston, Malpas SY14 7JE. Simon Carter & Derren Gilhooley, 01829 250670, simoncar@aol.com. *For Sat Nav please use SY14 7JA NOT 7JE. 12m S of Chester. A41 S from Chester toward Wrexham on A534 at Broxton r'about. Pass Carden Park hotel - turn L at Cocko Barton PH to Stretton & Tilston.* Tea. **Adm £4, chd free. Sat 6, Sun 7 June (12-5.30). Visitors also welcome by arrangement June.**
Vibrantly colourful garden of 2 acres crammed with herbaceous plants, shrubs and roses. There are lawns, natural and formal ponds, specimen trees, mixed hedges and garden rooms incl cottage garden, rose circle, large pergola with sprawling roses and climbers, herbaceous beds, perfumed gazebo, roof terrace with far reaching views.

35 GREENWAYS
82 Knutsford Road, Alderley Edge SK9 7SF. Jenny & Roger Lloyd, 01625 583488, jenny.plants@btinternet.com. *1m W of Alderley Edge. 1m from Alderley Edge & Wilmslow on B5085 to Knutsford. Close to Chorley Village Hall.* Home-made teas. **Adm £4, chd free. Visitors welcome by arrangement May to Aug max group 50.**
Even more plants now in this obsessive collector's garden with interest throughout Spring and Summer. Over 400 named varieties and much more. Plant maps available. A personal collection of unusual and familiar perennials and shrubs set in 1½ acres, displaying a diversity of planting styles in a range of growing conditions. Unfenced pools. Wheelchair access possible throughout garden.

36 HANNETS COTTAGE
Tilston Road, Kidnal, Malpas SY14 7DH. Doris Bamforth, 01948 860979, deabamforth@aol.com. *Approx 1 mile NW of Malpas town centre. From Malpas town centre up High St towards Tilston. You are now on Tilston Rd. Continue for ¾ m. Do not use sat-nav.* Cream teas. **Adm £4, chd free. Sat 2, Sun 3 May, Sat 27, Sun 28 June, Sat 15, Sun 16 Aug (12-5.30). Visitors also welcome by arrangement May to Aug groups of 10 - 30.**
This ½ acre cottage garden surrounds a typical Cheshire, grade 2 listed, cottage (not open). Different rooms for sun and shade lovers will show you how to create interest and movement. Unusual plants (plus good plant stall), various water features, cosy seats and lovely views will make your visit to this quirky and much loved garden one to remember. Partial wheelchair access.

37 HATHAWAY
1 Pool End Road, Tytherington, Macclesfield SK10 2LB. Mr & Mrs Cordingley. *2m N of Macclesfield, ½ m from The Tytherington Club. Stockport: follow A523 to Butley Ash, R on A538 Tytherington. Knutsford: follow A537 at A538, L for Tytherington. Leek: follow A523 at A537 L & 1st R A53.* Home-made teas. **Adm £3.50, chd free. Sat 18, Sun 19 July (10.30-4.30).**

Garden of approx ⅓ acre. SW facing. Garden laid out in two parts. Large lawn area surrounded by mature, colourful perennial borders. Rose arbour, small pond with koi, patio, raised fruit and cut flower bed. Small mature wooded area with winding paths on a lower level. Front, laid to lawn with two main borders separated by a small grass area. Good wheelchair access to most of garden except wood area.

Quirky features including original gasometer rediscovered in 2006, converted into sunken eating area . . .

38 HATTON HOUSE GARDENS
Hatton Heath, Chester CH3 9AP. Judy Halewood, basebotanics@hotmail.com. *4m SE of Chester. From Chester on A41 2km past The Black Dog PH. From Whitchurch on A41 7km past the Broxton r'about.* **Adm £5, chd free. Sat 6, Sun 7 June (12-4.30). Visitors also welcome by arrangement Apr to Sept for groups of 5+.**
Approx 8 acres of beautifully landscaped gardens both formal and natural. Pathways leading through extensive herbaceous borders and rose garden give way to lawns, azalea rock gardens, waterfalls and wild flowers. The 2 acre lake is rich in wildlife and flanked by woodland, wild flowers, bulbs, bridges and follies. All of the gardens are wheelchair friendly apart from the Sunken Garden.

39 ▶ HILLSIDE COTTAGE

Shrigley Road, Pott Shrigley
SK10 5SG. Anne & Phil
Geoghegan, 01625 572214,
annegeoghegan@btinternet.com.
*6m N of Macclesfield. On A523 at
Legh Arms T-lights turn to Pott
Shrigley. Take 3rd. L after approx
1¹/₂ m. After 1m at Green Close
Methodist Church turn R to garden.*
Light refreshments. Tea, coffee and
home made cakes are incl in the adm
and wine with nibbles for evening
visits. **Adm £6, chd free. Visitors
welcome by arrangement June to
Aug groups of 10+.**
A ¹/₄ -acre garden with panoramic
views over the treetops. Packed with
colourful perennials, roses, clematis,
shrubs and small trees. Landscaped
on several discreet levels with various
places to sit and enjoy the garden incl
a summerhouse, conservatory and
rose covered arbour. Small walled
patio with a water feature and
container planting. Partial wheelchair
access.

 ♿ ❀ 🚌 ☕

40 ▶ HOLLY MERE

4 Radley Lane, Houghton Green,
Warrington WA2 0SY. Angela &
Graham Harrop. *2m N of
Warrington. M6 J22 to Newton.
250yds L into Highfield Lane. At T-
junction L into Middleton Lane. 1st R
into Delph Lane. Over M62, R into
Mill Lane. Park at 'The Plough' (WA2
0SU). 50 metre walk into Radley
Lane.* Home-made teas and coffee.
**Adm £3.50, chd free. Sun 28 June
(11-5).**
¹/₂ acre garden. Some specimen trees
and shrubs. Wide borders of
interesting herbaceous perennials
(some colour themed), roses and
grasses, around extensive lawns.
Most plants are labelled. Many AGM
plants. Several seating areas. Small
kitchen garden.

❀ ☕

41 ▶ INGLEWOOD

4 Birchmere, Heswall CH60 6TN.
Colin & Sandra Fairclough,
0151 3424645,
sandra.fairclough@tiscali.co.uk,
www.inglewood-
birchmere.blogspot.co.uk. *6m S of
Birkenhead. From A540 Devon
Doorway/Clegg Arms r'about go
through Heswall. ¹/₄ m after Tesco, R
into Quarry Rd East, 2nd L into Tower
Rd North & L into Birchmere.* Home-
made teas. **Adm £4, chd free. Sat
16, Sun 17 May (1.30-5). Visitors**

also welcome by arrangement May
to July min 12, max 30.
Beautiful ¹/₂ acre garden with stream,
large koi pond, 'beach' with grasses,
wildlife pond and bog area. Brimming
with shrubs, bulbs, acers, conifers,
rhododendrons, herbaceous plants
and new hosta border and scree
garden. Interesting features incl hand
cart, antique mangle, wood carvings,
bug hotel and Indian dog gates
leading to a secret garden. Lots of
seating to enjoy refreshments.

 ♿ 🐕 ❀ ☕

Predominately a woodland garden with lovely herbaceous borders . . .

42 ▶ LASKEY FARM

Laskey Lane, Thelwall, Warrington
WA4 2TF. Howard & Wendy Platt,
07740 804825,
wendy.platt1@gmail.com,
www.laskeyfarm.com. *3m From
M6/M56. From M56/M6 follow
directions to Lymm. At T-junction turn
L onto Booths Lane in Warrington
direction. Turn R onto Lymm Rd. Turn
R onto Laskey Lane.* Home-made
teas. **Adm £5, chd free. Sat 15,
Sun 16 Aug (11-5). Visitors also
welcome by arrangement June to
Aug groups of 10+.**
1-acre garden packed with late
summer colour which incls
herbaceous and rose borders,
vegetable area and parterre, while the
greenhouse contains a collection of
pelargonium and tropical plants.
Interconnected pools for wildlife, fish
and terrapins form an unusual water
garden. In addition, a new maze was
created in 2014 featuring prairie style
planting. Large, attractive
greenhouse; extensive water garden;
large maze featuring prairie style
planting. Most areas of the garden
may be accessed by wheelchair.

 ♿ 🐕 ❀ 🚌 ☕

43 ▶ LEAWOOD

off Longhurst Lane, Marple Bridge
SK6 5AE. John & Mary Hartley,
0161 427 1882,
mary.hartleycat@talktalk.net. *4m E
of Stockport. A626 to Marple -
Marple Bridge, through village, signed*

*Mellor. 100yds on L from car park in
Marple Bridge, down the side of 21
Longhurst Ln.* Light refreshments.
**Adm £3.50, chd free. Sat 16, Sun
17 May (11-4). Visitors also
welcome by arrangement May to
June.**
³/₄ -acre hidden woodland garden
facing E-W surrounded by trout
stream. Large lawns and flower beds
of mixed planting giving rise to
panoramic view of hillside with
rhododendrons, azaleas and
camellias. Terraced paths pass small
spring fed ponds and wildlife areas of
bluebells and unusual shade loving
plants. Bird box cameras - Owl, Blue
Tit, Gt Tit. Ducks, badgers and fox
(special wildlife interest). Steep paths
and steps.

❀ ☕

44 ▶ LONG ACRE

Wyche Lane, Bunbury CW6 9PS.
Margaret & Michael Bourne,
01829 260944,
mjbourne249@tiscali.co.uk. *3¹/₂ m
SE of Tarporley. In Bunbury village,
turn into Wyche Lane by Nags Head
PH car park, garden 400yds on L.
Disabled parking in lane adjacent to
garden.* Home-made teas. **Adm £4,
chd free.** Share to St Boniface
Church Flower Fund. **Sun 26 Apr
(2-5).** Visitors also welcome by
arrangement Apr to June groups of
10+.
Plantswoman's garden of approx
1 acre with unusual plants and trees,
pool gardens, exotic conservatory,
herbaceous, specialise in proteas,
S African bulbs and clivia. Spring
garden with camellias, magnolias,
bulbs. Wheelchair access to most
areas.

 ♿ ❀ ☕ ☕

45 ▶ ◆ THE LOVELL QUINTA ARBORETUM

Swettenham CW12 2LD. Tatton
Garden Society, 01477 537698,
www.tattongardensociety.co.uk.
*4m NW of Congleton. Turn off A54 N
2m W of Congleton or turn E off A535
at Twemlow Green, NE of Holmes
Chapel. Follow signs to Swettenham.
Park at Swettenham Arms PH.* **Adm
£5, chd free. For NGS: Sun 4 Oct
(12-4).** For other opening times and
information, please phone or see
garden website.
The 28-acre arboretum has been
established since 1960s and contains
around 10,000 trees and shrubs of
over 2,000 species, some very rare.
Incl National Collections of Pinus and

Lemon drizzle cake, Victoria sponge … yummy!

Fraxinus, large collection of oak, a collection of hebes and autumn flowering shrubs. A lake and way-marked walks. A guided tour at 2.30pm is incl. Care required but wheelchairs can access much of the arboretum on the mown paths.

 NCH

46 **MANLEY KNOLL**
Manley Road, Manley WA6 9DX. Mr & Mrs James Timpson, 01928 740458, james@timpson.com, www.manleyknoll.com. *3m N of Tarvin. On B5393, via Ashton & Mouldsworth. 3m S of Frodsham, via Alvanley.* Home-made teas. **Adm £3.50, chd free. Sun 24 May, Sun 21 June (12-5). Visitors also welcome by arrangement May to July.**
Arts and Crafts garden created early 1900s. Covering 6 acres, divided into different rooms encompassing parterres, clipped yew hedging and ornamental ponds. Banks of rhododendron and azaleas frame a far-reaching view of the Cheshire Plain. Also a magical quarry/folly garden with waterfall.

47 NEW **218 MARPLE ROAD**
Stockport SK2 5HE. Barry & Pat Hadfield. *3¹/₂ m E of Stockport leave M60 J27 at the r'about take 5th exit onto A626 signed for Marple, follow the A626, parking on L at Offerton Sand & Gravel. Disabled parking at house.* Home-made teas. **Adm £4, chd free. Sun 5 July, Sun 2 Aug (11-4.30).**
This secret south facing garden approx 1 acre, full of herbaceous plants, vegetable plot, plant growing area, topiary, unfenced ponds/water features, fun areas/features, developed from paddock to garden over 20yrs by current owners. Wheelchair access to most areas.

48 **MILLHEYES**
Little Neston, Neston CH64 4AF. Mr & Mrs Clive & Jane Harding. *10m NW of Chester. M53 J4, follow signs M56 and A5117. Turn onto A540 & follow signs for Hoylake. Garden is 1m further along from Ness Gardens (signed locally). Parking at St Michael's Church.* Home-made teas at St Michael's Church. **Combined adm with Delfan £4, chd free. Mon 25 May (1-5).**
Hedge enclosed front garden with circular lawn and deep

Brooke Cottage

herbaceous/perennial border and vegetable plot. Sandstone terraced back garden with wildlife pond, wisteria pergola, azaleas, perennial borders and seating areas. Views over to the Welsh hills. Front garden wheelchair accessible. Restricted access in back garden.

49 **MILLPOOL**
Smithy Lane, Bosley SK11 0NZ. Joe & Barbara Fray, 01260 226581. *5m S of Macclesfield. Just off A523 at Bosley. Turn L 1m S of A54 T-lights. From Leek, turn R, 2¹/₂ m N of The Royal Oak PH at Rushton. Please follow direction to parking areas. No*

parking at garden. Home-made teas. **Adm £3.50, chd free. Sat 20, Sun 21 June (1-5). Visitors also welcome by arrangement May to Sept for groups 10-40 max.**
Garden designed to extend the seasons with colour, texture and scent. Lush herbaceous borders and areas of deep shade. Small stream, pond and bog garden. Gravel plantings, containers and a fine collection of bonsai trees. An ever increasing collection of modern ceramics and a most productive vegetable garden in tubs and baskets. Children's interest trail and craft activities and large plant sale.

Developed from paddock to garden over 20 years by current owners . . .

GROUP OPENING

50 NEW MOLLINGTON VILLAGE GARDENS
Townfield Lane, Mollington, Chester CH1 6NJ. *Satnav use postcode. 3m N of Chester. From the Wirral take A540 to Chester, off A540 Parkgate Rd as signed. Cross A55 at r'about contintue past Wheatsheaf PH, turn L into Overwood Lane. At T-junction turn R into Townfield Lane. Parking will be signed.* Tea at Home Farm. **Combined adm £5, chd free. Sat 11, Sun 12 July (1-5).**

NEW ADSWOOD
Ken & Helen Black
Visitors also welcome by arrangement Apr to Sept groups of 10 plus preferred.
01244 851327
ken@potentialsolutions.org.uk

BEECHWOOD
Meadow Court, off Townfield Lane. Mr Dave & Mrs Sue Colegate

NEW HOME FARM
Townfield Lane. Christine & Roger Jones

Mollington is a picturesque village in a rural setting 3m from Chester. Beechwood: Set in ²/₃ acre walled gardens originally part of the Mollington Hall estate. Summerhouse overlooking natural pond with rose covered pergola, hostas, ferns, grasses and gunnera, wild life area, rockery, quirky features incl Mollington Hall's original gasometer rediscovered in 2006, converted into sunken eating area, new features for 2015. Home Farm House: Small walled garden with densely packed borders provides the setting for this C17 farm house Established wisteria, climbing roses, range of shrubs/herbaceous plants designed to attract wildlife and provide all year round interest while being low maintenance. Adswood: A cottage garden with side borders and island beds packed with a wide range of bulbs, perennials, climbers and traditional roses. The garden is home to over 50 varieties of clematis. There is a raised ornamental fish pond and several seating areas incl a garden pavilion.

51 ◆ MOUNT PLEASANT
Yeld Lane, Kelsall CW6 0TB. Dave Darlington & Louise Worthington, 01829 751592, www.mountpleasantgardens.co.uk. *8m E of Chester. Off A54 at T-lights into Kelsall. Turn into Yeld Lane opp Farmers Arms PH, 200yds on L. Do not follow SatNav directions.* Tea. **Adm £5, chd £1. For NGS: Sun 3, Mon 4 May, Sat 5, Sun 6 Sept (12-5). For other opening times and information, please phone or see garden website.**
10 acres of landscaped garden and woodland started in 1994 with impressive views over the Cheshire countryside. Steeply terraced in places. Specimen trees, rhododendrons, azaleas, conifers, mixed and herbaceous borders; 4 ponds, formal and wildlife. Vegetable garden, stumpery with tree ferns, sculptures, wild flower meadow and Japanese garden. Bog garden, tropical garden. September Sculpture Exhibition. Please ring prior to visit for wheelchair access.

52 ◆ NESS BOTANIC GARDENS
Ness, Neston CH64 4AY. The University of Liverpool, 0845 030 4063, www.nessgardens.org.uk. *10 NW of Chester. Off A540. M53 J4, follow signs M56 & A5117 (signed N Wales). Turn onto A540 follow signs for Hoylake. Ness Gardens is signed locally.* Light refreshments. **Adm by donation. For NGS: Sun 21 June (10-5). For other opening times and information, please phone or see garden website.**
Gardens cover some 64 acres, having a distinctly maritime feel and housing The National Collection of Mountain Ash (Sorbus). Among some of the significant specimens that still flourish in the gardens are Pieris Forrestii which was collected for Bulley by George Forrest in Yunnan. Herbaceous borders, Potager and WilderNESS conservation area. Mobility scooters and wheelchairs available free - advance booking recommended.

53 ◆ NORTON PRIORY MUSEUM & GARDENS
Tudor Road, Manor Park, Runcorn WA7 1SX. Norton Priory Museum Trust, 01928 569895, www.nortonpriory.org. *2m SE of Runcorn. If using Sat-Nav try WA7 1BD and follow the brown Norton Priory signs.* Light refreshments. **Adm £3.50, chd £2.70. For NGS: Sun 7 June (10-5). For other opening times and information, please phone or see garden website.**
Beautiful 2¹/₂ -acre Georgian Walled Garden, with fruit trees, herb garden, colour borders and rose walk. Home to the National Collection of Tree Quince (Cydonia Oblonga) and surrounded by historic pear orchard and wildflower meadow. Tea room and plant sales in the courtyard. Museum re-opening 2016.

54 OAKFIELD VILLA
Nantwich Road, Wrenbury, Nantwich CW5 8EL. Carolyn & Jack Kennedy. *6m S of Nantwich & 6m N of Whitchurch. Garden on main rd through village next to Dairy Farm. Parking in field between Oak Villas & School 1min walk to garden.* Home-made teas. **Combined adm with Wren's Nest £5, chd free. Wed 24 June (10.30-5).**
Romantic S-facing garden of densely planted borders and creative planting in containers, incl climbing roses, clematis and hydrangeas. Divided by screens into rooms, the garden incl a small fishpond and water feature. Pergola clothed in beautiful climbers provides relaxed sheltered seating area. Small front garden, mainly hydrangeas and clematis. 50+ clematis and many hydrangeas. Some gravelled areas.

55 THE OLD PARSONAGE
Arley Green, via Arley Hall & Gardens CW9 6LZ. The Viscount & Viscountess Ashbrook, 01565 777277, www.arleyhallandgardens.com. *5m NNE of Northwich. 3m NNE of Great Budworth. M6 J19 & 20 & M56 J10. Follow signs to Arley Hall & Gardens. From Arley Hall notices to Old Parsonage which lies across park at Arley Green.* Home-made teas. **Adm £4.50, chd free. Share to Save The Children Fund. Sat 30, Sun 31 May (2-5.30). Visitors also welcome by arrangement May to June groups of 10+.**

2-acre garden in attractive and secretive rural setting in secluded part of Arley Estate, with ancient yew hedges, herbaceous and mixed borders, shrub roses, climbers, leading to woodland garden and unfenced pond with gunnera and water plants. Rhododendrons, azaleas, meconopsis, cardiocrinum, some interesting and unusual trees. Wheelchair access over mown grass.

 ♿ 🐕 🌸 ☕ 🍴

56 ▶ 39 OSBORNE STREET
Bredbury, Stockport SK6 2DA. Geoff & Heather Hoyle, geoff.hoyle@btinternet.com, www.youtube.com/user/ Dahliaholic. *1¹/₂ m E of Stockport, just off B6104. Follow signs for Lower Bredbury/Bredbury Hall. Leave M60 J27 (from S & W) or J25 (from N & E). Osborne St is adjacent to pelican crossing on B6104.* Light refreshments. Teas, coffees, and cakes. **Adm £3.50, chd free. Sat 5, Sun 6 Sept (1-5).** Visitors also welcome by arrangement Sept.
This dahliaholic's garden contains over 350 dahlias in 150+ varieties, mostly of exhibition standard. Shapely lawns are surrounded by deep flower beds that are crammed with dahlias of all shapes, sizes and colours, and complemented by climbers, soft perennials and bedding plants. An absolute riot of early autumn colour. The garden comprises two separate areas, both crammed with very colourful flowers. The dahlias range in height from 18 inches to 8 feet tall, and are in a wide variety of shapes and colours. They are interspersed with salvias, fuchsias, argyranthemums, and bedding plants. The garden is on YouTube: search for Dahliaholic. Featured in Landscape, Amateur Gardener, Daily Mail, and on BBC Gardeners World.

☕

57 ▶ PARM PLACE
High Street, Great Budworth CW9 6HF. Peter & Jane Fairclough, 01606 891131, janefair@btinternet.com. *3m N of Northwich. Great Budworth on E side of A559 between Northwich & Warrington, 4m from J10 M56, also 4m from J19 M6. Parm Place is W of village on S side of High St.* Home-made teas. **Adm £4, chd free. Share to Great Ormond Street Hospital. Sun 29 Mar, Sun 28 June (1-5).** Visitors also welcome by arrangement Apr to Aug between 10 and 40.

Well-stocked ¹/₂-acre plantswoman's garden with stunning views towards S Cheshire. Curving lawns, shrubs, colour co-ordinated herbaceous borders, roses, water features, rockery, gravel bed with grasses. Fruit and vegetable plots. In spring large collection of bulbs and flowers, camellias, hellebores and blossom. Parterre new.

 ♿ 🌸 🚌 ☕

58 ▶ ◆ PEOVER HALL GARDENS
Over Peover, Knutsford WA16 9HW. Randle Brooks, 01565 724220, www.peoverhall.com. *4m S of Knutsford. A50/Holmes Chapel Rd/Whipping Stocks PH turn onto Stocks Lane. Approx 0.9m turn onto Grotto Lane. ¹/₄ m turn onto Goostrey Lane. Main entrance on bend.* Home-made teas in Park House Tea Room & Paddock. **Adm £4, chd free. For NGS: Sat 30, Sun 31 May (2-5).** For other opening times and information, please phone or see garden website.
Set in 15 acres, 'garden rooms' filled with clipped box, topiary, lily ponds, herb, walled gardens, Romanesque loggia, C19 dell, rhododendrons, pleached limes. Grade I Carolean Stables - more architecturally important than the house itself. Partial wheelchair access to garden.

🚌 ☕

59 ▶ 17 POPLAR GROVE
Sale M33 3AX. Mr Gordon Cooke. *3m N of Altrincham. From the A6144 at Brooklands Stn turn into Hope Rd. Poplar Grove 3rd on R.* Home-made teas. **Combined adm with 5 Carnforth Drive £6, chd free. Sat 13, Sun 14 June (2-5).**
This S-facing suburban garden is on many levels. Its strongly diagonal design features a pebble mosaic 'cave', topiary, sculpture garden, living roof and exotic planting. A mix of formality and dense planting in the contemporary 'English' style. Exhibition of Garden Ceramics. Featured in RHS magazine,The Garden, and in many books and magazines over the years.

🌸 ☕

60 ▶ POULTON HALL
Poulton Lancelyn, Bebington CH63 9LN. The Lancelyn Green Family, 0151 3342057, jlgpoulton@talktalk.net, www.poultonhall.co.uk. *2m S of Bebington. From M53, J4 towards Bebington; at T-lights R along Poulton*

Rd; house 1m on R. Cream teas. **Adm £4, chd free. Sat 25, Sun 26 Apr (2-5.30).** Visitors also welcome by arrangement Apr to Aug teas by arrangement.
3 acres; lawns fronting house, wild flower meadow. A surprising approach to the walled garden, with reminders of Roger Lancelyn Green's retellings, Excalibur, Robin Hood and Jabberwocky. Scented sundial garden for the visually impaired. Memorial sculpture for Richard Lancelyn Green by Sue Sharples. Rose, nursery rhyme, witch, herb and oriental gardens. Organ Music at 4pm in the music room of the Hall. There are often choirs or orchestral music in the garden. Level gravel paths. Separate access (not across parking field) for wheelchairs.

 ♿ 🌸 ☕

61 ▶ NEW ▶ RACEFIELD
St. Margarets Road, Bowdon, Altrincham WA14 2AR. Paul N di C Willan, 0161 941 7411, jeanniewillan@btinternet.com. *Bowdon, Altrincham. Turn off A56 (Dunham Rd) on to St Margaret's Rd (at the large church). Racefield is 3rd house on L, a semi-detached Victorian villa with curved sandstone gateposts.* Light refreshments. **Adm £4, chd free. Sat 18, Sun 19, Sat 25, Sun 26 Apr (12-4.30).** Visitors also welcome by arrangement Mar to June groups of 10+.
The front garden is semi formal, with tree peonies (esp. Rockii forms) and herbaceous peonies, edged with lavender. This central beds are surrounded by mature beds of Rhodos, Azaleas, Camellias and acers which also characterise the entrance drive. The side garden has a large rockery with semi dwarf conifers and climbers (Rosa Kiftsgate) growing into trees. Rear garden incl a cactus collection. All areas accessible on the level save the front terrace and raised swimming pool area.

 ♿ 🐕 🌸 ☕

Arley Hall and Gardens

© Joe Wainwright

Rhododendrons in April/May and unusual flowering trees from March to June. Autumn Cyclamen in quantity from Aug to Nov. Perhaps the greatest delight to owners is a large Cornus capitata, flowering in June. Bees kept in the garden. Honey sometimes available.

♿ ❀ 🚐 ☕

65 THE ROWANS
Oldcastle Lane, Threapwood, nr Malpas SY14 7AY. Paul Philpotts & Alan Bourne, 01948 770522, alanandpaul@btinternet.com. *3m SW of Malpas. Leave Malpas on B5069 for Wrexham, after 3m, take 1st L after Threapwood Shop/PO into Chapel Lane, L into Oldcastle Lane, garden 1st Bungalow on R.* Home-made teas. Adm £4, chd free. Sat 11, Sun 12 July (1-5.30). Visitors also welcome by arrangement June to Aug groups of 15+, refreshments by arrangement.
This 1-acre multi-award winning garden, has an Italianate theme. Divided into numerous formal and natural areas, in which to sit and enjoy the views and feature statuary. Many mature and unusual trees, several ponds, herbaceous borders, vegetable plots, greenhouse, extensive Hosta collection and a tranquil secret garden. Something of interest for every visitor and an exquisite sanctuary. Featured in Garden News and Amateur Gardening.

❀ 🚐 ☕

62 RIDGEHILL
Ridge Hill, Sutton, Macclesfield SK11 0LU. Mr & Mrs Martin McMillan, Pat@normanshall.co.uk. *2m SE of Macclesfield. From Macclesfield take A523 to Leek. After Silk Rd look for T-lights signed Langley, Wincle & Sutton. Turn L into Byron's Lane, under canal bridge, 1st L to Langley at junction Church House PH. Ridge Hill Rd is opp turn up Ridge Hill Rd, garden on R..* Home-made teas. Adm £5, chd free. Sun 21 June (10-4.30). Visitors also welcome by arrangement May to July 12+.
4 acre garden set in the hills above Macclesfield overlooking the Cheshire plain. Herbaceous borders, old Rose garden, shrubbery with rhododendron, azaleas, water features, topiary, plus a new Victorian greenhouse and potager in its seconded year and is fully organic. Raffle. Garden accessories, teas/coffee, home made cakes, plants, wine and soft drinks.

❀ ☕

63 ◆ RODE HALL
Church Lane, Scholar Green ST7 3QP. Sir Richard & Lady Baker Wilbraham, 01270 873237, www.rodehall.co.uk. *5m SW of Congleton. Between Scholar Green*

(A34) & Rode Heath (A50). **For opening times and information, please phone or see garden website.**
Nesfield's terrace and rose garden with view over Humphry Repton's landscape is a feature of Rode gardens, as is the woodland garden with terraced rock garden and grotto. Other attractions incl the walk to the lake, restored ice house, working walled kitchen garden and Italian garden. Fine display of snowdrops in Feb. Daily for Snowdrop Walks 7 Feb - 8 March 11-4pm Closed Mons. Partial wheelchair access, gravel and woodchip paths, but WC and tearooms accessed easily.

♿ ⛳ ❀ 🚐 ☕

64 ROSEWOOD
Old Hall Lane, Puddington, Neston CH64 5SP. Mr & Mrs C E J Brabin, 0151 353 1193, angela.brabin@btinternet.com. *6m N of Chester. From A540 turn down Puddington Lane, 1½ m. Park by village green. Walk 30yds to Old Hall Lane, turn L through archway into garden.* wine. Adm £3, chd free. Visitors welcome by arrangement individuals, medium or large groups.
All yr garden; thousands of snowdrops in Feb, Camellias in autumn, winter and spring.

66 SANDYMERE
Middlewich Road, Cotebrook CW6 9EH. John & Alex Timpson, 07900 567944, rme2000@aol.com. *5m N of Tarporley. On A54 approx 300yds W of T-lights at Xrds of A49/A54.* Home-made teas. Adm £4, chd free. Sun 14 June (2-5.30). Visitors also welcome by arrangement Apr to Aug.
16 landscaped acres of beautiful Cheshire countryside with terraces, walled garden and amazing hosta garden. Long views, native wildlife and tranquillity of 3 lakes. Elegant planting schemes, shady seats and sun-splashed borders, mature pine woods and rolling lawns accented by graceful wooden structures. Different every year. Kitchen garden with organically grown vegetables, fruit cage and small orchard, also extensive range of penstemon plants. Partial wheelchair access.

♿ ☕

67 ▶ 21 SCAFELL CLOSE
High Lane, Stockport SK6 8JA.
Lesley & Dean Stafford, 01663
763015, lesley.stafford@live.co.uk.
*High Lane is on the A6 SE of
Stockport towards Buxton.* Cream
teas. **Adm £3, chd free. Sat 1, Sun
2 Aug (1-4.30). Visitors also
welcome by arrangement Aug.**
¹/₃ acre landscaped suburban garden.
Colour themed annuals border the
lawn featuring the Kinder Ram statue
in a heather garden, passing into
vegetables, soft fruits and fruit trees.
Returning perennial pathway leads to
the fishpond and secret terraced
garden with modern water feature
and patio planting. Finally visit the
blue front garden. Partial wheelchair
access.

68 ▶ SOMERFORD
19 Leycester Road, Knutsford
WA16 8QR. Emma Dearman & Joe
Morris, 01565 621095,
emmadearman1@gmail.com.
*1m from centre of Knutsford. From
Knutsford town centre, take Toft Rd
(A50) direction Holmes Chapel (S).
After approx 1m, turn sharp L into
Leycester Rd, immed after Esso
garage. Cross Legh Rd. Somerford is
found on your L opp Leycester Close.
Park on Leycester Rd or Legh Rd
with consideration to residents.*
Home-made teas. **Adm £4, chd free.
Evening Opening £5, chd free,
wine, Fri 10 July (6-8.30). Sun 2
Aug (1-6). Visitors also welcome by
arrangement June to Aug groups
of 10+.**
Majestic trees surround this 1¹/₂ acre
garden which has been completely
re-designed and planted. Hard
landscaping and sculptures
complement lush herbaceous and
perennial borders. Croquet and pond
lawns are separated by a magnificent
oak pergola. Cube-headed
hornbeams lead into the snail-trail
walk and informal lawn and fernery.
Stable courtyard with box parterres.
The garden featured as an inspiration
garden in 2014 for ITV's Love Your
Garden with Alan Titchmarsh. Most of
the garden is accessible by
wheelchair. Ring for further
information.

69 ▶ SOMERSET HOUSE
Sarn Road, Threapwood, Malpas
SY14 7AW. Sir Jonathan & Lady
Clark. *Just off B5069 3¹/₄ m W of
Malpas. From East leave A41 at*

*Hampton for Malpas 1¹/₂ m turn 1st L
past church 3m B5069. W from A525
go Bangor on Dee take B5069 4m to
Threapwood on Sarn Rd.* Cream
teas. **Combined adm with The
White Cottage £5, chd free. Sat 20,
Sun 21 June (1-5).**
A cottage garden that has evolved
over 30yrs. An old orchard is set
behind a trellis dividing it from the
front lawn surrounded by beds
containing herbaceous plants, shrubs
and roses. Surrounded by more beds
pond and rockery with a large rose
bed and bank with mature trees
beyond. Separated by the drive is an
extensive vegetable garden, large
pond with shade plants and new
orchard.

70 ▶ 68 SOUTH OAK LANE
Wilmslow SK9 6AT. Caroline &
David Melliar-Smith, 01625 528147,
caroline.ms@btinternet.com. *³/₄ m
SW of Wilmslow. From M56 (J6) take
A538 (Wilmslow) R into Buckingham
Rd. From centre of Wilmslow turn R
onto B5086, 1st R into Gravel Ln, 4th
R into South Oak Ln.* **Adm £3.50,
chd free. Sat 11, Sun 12 July (11-
4.30). Visitors also welcome by
arrangement May to Aug max
group 30.**
With year-round colour, scent and
interest, this attractive, narrow,
hedged cottage garden has evolved
over the years into 5 natural 'rooms'.
These Hardy Plant Society members
passion for plants, is reflected in the
variety of shrubs, trees, flower
borders and pond, creating havens
for wildlife. Share this garden with its'
varied history from the 1890's. Some
rare and unusual hardy and shade
loving plants.

71 ▶ NEW 10 STATHAM AVENUE
Lymm WA13 9NH. Mike & Gail
Porter. *Approx 1m from J20 M6
/M56 interchange. Take the B5158
signed Lymm. Take A56 Booth's Hill
Rd, towards Warrington, turn R on to
Bars Bank Lane after passing under
the Bridgwater canal turn R (50m)
onto Statham Ave. No 10 is 100
metres on R.* Home-made teas.
Home-made cakes and meringues
with fresh fruit. **Adm £4, chd free.
Sun 14, Sat 20 June (11-5).**
Beautifully structured and planned, a
¹/₄ acre south facing plot, carefully
terraced as it rises to the Bridgewater
tow path. Hazel arch entrance to

formal paved patio area with
cordoned fruit trees and raised salad
plot. Brick pathway passing working
greenhouse into several well stocked
herbaceous beds, shaded area with
variety of azaleas and rhododendrons
and formal lawn. Interesting
outhouses. Short gravel driveway and
some steps to access the rear
garden.The rear garden is sloping.

> ¹/₃ acre south
> facing plot,
> carefully terraced
> as it rises to
> the Bridgewater
> tow path . . .

72 ▶ ◆ STONYFORD COTTAGE
Stonyford Lane, Oakmere
CW8 2TF. Janet & Tony Overland,
01606 888970,
www.stonyfordcottagegardens.co.
uk. *5m SW of Northwich. From
Northwich take A556 towards
Chester. ³/₄ m past A49 junction turn
R into Stonyford Lane. Entrance ¹/₂ m
on L.* Home-made teas. lunches also
available. **Adm £4.50, chd free. For
NGS: Sun 17 May, Sun 2 Aug
(11.30-4.30). For other opening
times and information, please
phone or see garden website.**
Set around a tranquil pool this Monet
style landscape has a wealth of
moisture loving plants, incl iris and
candelabra primulas. Drier areas
feature unusual perennials and rarer
trees and shrubs. Woodland paths
meander through shade and bog
plantings, along boarded walks,
across wild natural areas with views
over the pool to the cottage gardens.
Unusual plants available at the
adjacent nursery. Open Tues - Sun &
BH Mons Apr - Sept 10-5. Some
gravel paths.

73 SUN HOUSE
66 Bridge Lane, Bramhall, Stockport SK7 3AW. Peter & Susan Hale. *3½ m S of Stockport. Sun House is on Bridge Lane (A5143) between junction with A5102 at the Bramall Hall r'about & Bramhall Moor Lane.* Home-made teas. **Adm £3.50, chd free. Sat 30, Sun 31 May (1.30-5.30).**

Sun House garden is quirky and romantic, full of interest and colour all year round. The garden is surrounded by mature trees with dry, shady, acid soil addressed by building numerous ponds and bog areas which are at their best in Spring. It has a wide range of herbaceous plants, mosaic and ceramic decorations, gravel garden, vegetable plot, chickens and two life-sized terracotta warriors. Display and sale of ceramics and crafts. New exploration trail for children each year. Featured in Amateur Gardener and local gardening magazines and due to appear in the BBC2's Great British Garden Revival episode on bog gardens. Some paths need care, unfenced ponds.

74 SYCAMORE COTTAGE
Manchester Road, Carrington, Manchester M31 4AY. Mrs C Newton. *From M60 J8 take Carrington turn (A6144) through 2 sets of lights. Garden approx 1m after 2nd set of lights on R. From M6 J20 follow signs for Partington/Carrington garden approx 1m on L.* Light refreshments. **Adm £3.50, chd free. Sat 30, Sun 31 May (1-5).**

Approx ⅕ acre cottage garden split into distinct areas, with woodland banking, natural spring, well and ponds. Also features decking with two seating areas and summer house. Garden featured on Cupranols TV advert.

75 TATTENHALL HALL
High Street, Tattenhall CH3 9PX. Jen & Nick Benefield, Chris Evered & Jannie Hollins, 01829 770654, janniehollins@gmail.com. *8m S of Chester on A41. Turn L to Tattenhall, through village, turn R at Letters PH, past war memorial on L through Sandstone pillared gates. Park on rd or in village car park.* Home-made teas. **Adm £4.50, chd free. Sun 17 May (2-5.30).** Visitors also welcome by arrangement Mar to Oct, limited parking facilities.

Plant enthusiasts garden around Jacobean house (not open). 4½ acres, wild flower meadows, interesting trees, large pond, stream, walled garden, colour themed borders, succession planting, spinney walk with shade plants, yew terrace overlooking meadow, views to hills. Glasshouse and vegetable garden. Wildlife friendly sometimes untidy garden, interest throughout the year, continuing to develop. Gravel paths, cobbles and some steps.

carerstrust
action · help · advice

NGS funding helps us support more carers

76 ◆ TATTON PARK
Knutsford WA16 6QN. National Trust, leased to Cheshire East Council, 01625 374400, www.tattonpark.org.uk. *2½ m N of Knutsford. Well signed on M56 J7 & from M6 J19. in gardeners cottage.* **Adm £6, chd £4. For NGS: Wed 13 May, Wed 10 June (10-5).** For other opening times and information, please phone or see garden website.

Features incl orangery by Wyatt, fernery by Paxton, restored Japanese garden, Italian and rose gardens. Greek monument and African hut. Hybrid azaleas and rhododendrons; swamp cypresses, tree ferns, tall redwoods, bamboos and pines. Fully restored productive walled gardens. everywhere apart from Rose Garden and Japanese Gareden.

77 ◆ TIRLEY GARTH
Mallows Way, Willington, nr Tarporley CW6 0RQ. *2m N of Tarporley. 2m S of Kelsall. Entrance 500yds from village of Utkinton. At N of Tarporley take Utkinton rd.* Home-made teas. **Adm £5, chd free. Sun 10, Sun 17, Sun 31 May (1-5).**

40-acre garden, terraced and landscaped, designed by Thomas

Mawson (considered the leading exponent of garden design in early C20), it is the only Grade II* Arts and Crafts garden in Cheshire that remains complete and in excellent condition. The gardens are an important example of an early C20 garden laid out in both formal and informal styles. By early May the garden is bursting into flower with almost 3000 Rhododendron and Azalea many 100 years old. Exhibition by local Artists.

78 NEW TOUCHSTONE
Greenfields Lane, Rowton, Chester CH3 6AU. Simon & Jacqui Maudslay. *1st house on R next to village green. Please park in Rowton Hall car park which is 50 metres from the garden. It is not possible to park outside the garden due to the narrow lane.* Morning coffee, cream teas, scones and cakes. **Adm £4, chd free. Thur 18, Fri 19 June (10-5).**

Touchstone is predominately a woodland garden with lovely herbaceous borders. The garden is 0.7 of an acre, presented at its best in June, the focus point is a delightful range of herbaceous borders, with an emphasis on the look of a cottage garden. This is a practical, colourful family garden.

79 THE WELL HOUSE
Wet Lane, Tilston, Malpas SY14 7DP. Mrs S H French-Greenslade, 01829 250332. *3m NW of Malpas. On A41, 1st R after Broxton r'about, L on Malpas Rd through Tilston. House & antique shop on L.* **Adm £5, chd free. Visitors welcome by arrangement Feb to Oct, not open in Aug.** Refreshments by appt.

1-acre cottage garden, bridge over natural stream, spring bulbs, perennials, herbs and shrubs. Triple ponds. Adjoining ¾ -acre field made into wild flower meadow; first seeding late 2003. Large bog area of kingcups and ragged robin. Febuary for snowdrop walk. Coach parties welcome.

80 69 WELL LANE
Gayton CH60 8NH. Angus & Sally Clark. *7m S of Birkenhead. 20yds past Shell Garage (opp Devon Doorway/Glegg Arms) bear L into Well Lane; 250yds on bear L again (narrow). Garden seen on L as rd*

widens. Light refreshments. **Adm £3.50, chd free. Sun 3, Mon 4 May (2-5).**

After an absence of two years this 1 acre garden returns with its outstanding gently sloping rear garden set against natural woodland. There are wild areas and old farm buildings. Rhododendrons, azaleas and many other spring shrubs with surprises at every corner. Wheelchair access to most of the garden.

81 THE WHITE COTTAGE
Threapwood, Malpas SY14 7AL. Chris & Carol Bennion. *3m SW of Malpas. From Malpas take Wrexham Rd B5069 W for 3m. From Bangor on Dee take B5069 E to Threapwood. Car Park in field opp shop & garage.* Refreshments at Somerset House and WC. **Combined adm with Somerset House £5, chd free. Sat 20, Sun 21 June (1-5).**

Lots to see and experience in this pretty, half acre cottage garden, containing a mixture of mature trees, shrubs, herbaceous plants and bulbs. Open spaces and secluded areas merge to provide new interest at every corner. Flower beds meander along the drive with roses, astrantias, geraniums, foxgloves, violas and other summer flowering plants. A brick built greenhouse, various arches, pergola and dovecote. Several mature trees and a variety of hedging. Superb views over Cheshire countryside. NB this garden sits alongside a Nature Conservation Zone. There is a long gravel drive. Narrow pathways and steps surround the cottage.

82 WOOD END COTTAGE
Grange Lane, Whitegate, Northwich CW8 2BQ. Mr & Mrs M R Everett, 01606 888236, woodendct@supanet.com. *4m SW of Northwich. Turn S off A556 (Northwich bypass) at Sandiway PO T-lights; after 1³/₄ m, turn L to Whitegate village; opp school follow Grange Lane for 300yds.* Home-made teas. **Adm £4, chd free. Visitors welcome by arrangement May to July.**

Plantsman's ¹/₂ acre garden in attractive setting, sloping to a natural stream bordered by shade and moisture-loving plants. Background of mature trees. Well stocked herbaceous borders, trellis with roses and clematis, magnificent

delphiniums, many phlox and choice perennials. Interesting shrubs and flowering trees. Vegetable garden.

83 WREN'S NEST
Wrenbury Heath Road, Wrenbury, Nantwich CW5 8EQ. Sue Clarke, 01270 780704, wrenburysue@gmail.com. *Nantwich 12m from M6 J16. From Nantwich signs for A530 to Whitchurch, reaching Sound school turn 1st R Wrenbury Heath Rd, across the Xrds and bungalow is on L, telegraph pole right outside.* at Oakfield Villa. **Combined adm with Oakfield Villa £5. Wed 24 June (10.30-5).** Visitors also welcome by arrangement May & June, phone or email. Refreshments can be arranged if required.

Set in a semi-rural area, this bungalow has a Cottage Garden Style of lush planting and is 80ft x 45ft. The garden is packed with unusual and traditional perennials and shrubs incl over 100 hardy geraniums, campanulas, crocosmias, hostas, iris, geums, herbs and pots and alpine troughs. National Collection of Hardy Geraniums syvaticum and renardii types. With gravel paths.

Ness Botanic Gardens

© Joe Wainwright

Recycle – bring a bag for your plant purchases

CORNWALL

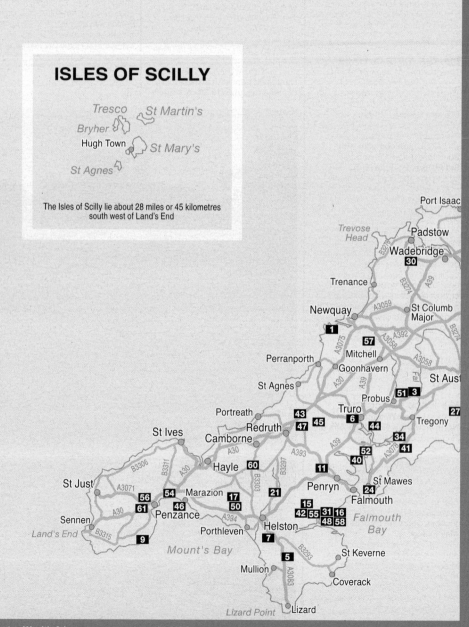

ISLES OF SCILLY

Tresco
Bryher
St Martin's
Hugh Town
St Mary's
St Agnes

The Isles of Scilly lie about 28 miles or 45 kilometres
south west of Land's End

Port Isaac
Trevose Head
Padstow
Wadebridge
30

Trenance

Newquay
St Columb Major
1
57
Mitchell
Perranporth
Goonhavern
St Agnes
St Aust
Probus
51 **3**
Truro
27
Portreath
43
Redruth
47 **45**
6
44
Tregony
Camborne
34
St Ives
52 **41**
Hayle
60
40
St Just
11
Marazion
Penryn
St Mawes
56 **54**
17
24
61 **46**
50
21
Falmouth
Penzance
15
16
Sennen
42 **55** **31**
Porthleven
48 **58**
Falmouth Bay
Land's End
9
Helston
7
Mount's Bay
5
St Keverne
Mullion
Coverack
Lizard Point
Lizard

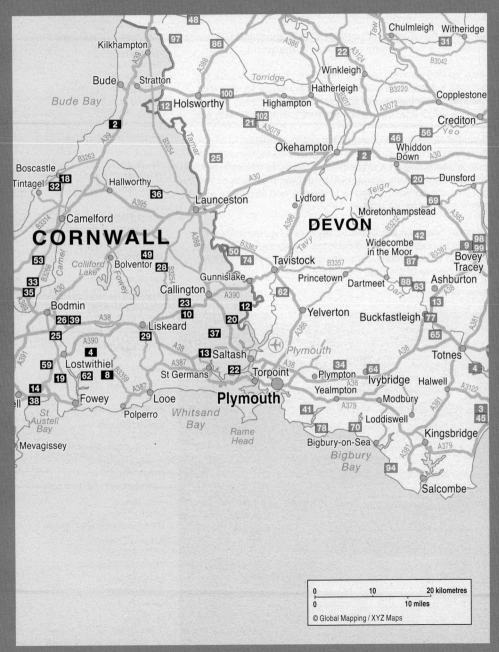

Kilkhampton
48
97
86
Bude
Stratton
A39
Bude Bay
B3263
2
Boscastle
Tintagel 32 18
Camelford
CORNWALL
53
33
35
Bodmin
26 39
25
59
19 62 8
14
38
St Austell Bay
Mevagissey
Fowey
Looe
Polperro
Lostwithiel
Liskeard
29
37
13 Saltash
St Germans
22
Torpoint
Whitsand Bay
Rame Head
Plymouth
Colliford Lake
Bolventor 28
Callington
23
10
20
Gunnislake
12
Hallworthy
36
Launceston
50
74
Holsworthy
12
100
Highampton
21 102
25
Okehampton
Lydford
Tavistock
Princetown
Dartmeet
Yelverton
Buckfastleigh
Plympton
Yealmpton
Modbury
Loddiswell
Bigbury-on-Sea
Bigbury Bay
94
Salcombe
Kingsbridge
3 45
Totnes
4
Halwell
Ivybridge
64
34
88 63
13
65
77
Ashburton
Bovey Tracey
9 98 99
87
42
Widecombe in the Moor
Moretonhampstead
69
Dunsford
20
Whiddon Down
2
46 56
Crediton
Yeo
Copplestone
Hatherleigh
Winkleigh
22
31
Witheridge
Chulmleigh
Taw
DEVON

0   10   20 kilometres
0   10 miles
© Global Mapping / XYZ Maps

Investec Wealth & Investment supports the NGS

Cornwall

Cornwall has some of the most beautiful natural landscapes to be found anywhere in the world.

Here, you will discover some of the country's most extraordinary gardens, a spectacular coastline, internationally famous surfing beaches, windswept moors and countless historic sites. Cornish gardens reflect this huge variety of environments particularly well.

A host of National Collections of magnolias, camellias, rhododendrons and azaleas, as well as exotic Mediterranean semi-tropical plants and an abundance of other plants flourish in our acid soils and mild climate. Surrounded by the warm currents of the Gulf Stream, with our warm damp air in summer and mild moist winters, germination continues all year.

Cornwall boasts an impressive variety of NGS gardens. These range from coastal-protected positions to exposed cliff-top sites, moorland water gardens, Japanese gardens and the world famous tropical biomes of the Eden Project.

Below: Trebah

Currently the NGS donates around £2.5 million every year

Cornwall Volunteers

County Organiser
Bryan Coode
01726 882488
bhcoode@btconnect.com

County Treasurer
Andrew Flint
01726 879336
flints@elizaholidays.co.uk

Publicity
Sue Bradbury
01872 863863
sue@suebradburypr.com

Nutty Lim
01726 815247
christianne.gf.lim@gmail.com

Booklet Coordinator
Peter Stanley
01326 565868
stanley.m2@sky.com

Assistant County Organisers
Ginnie Clotworthy
01208 872612
giles.clotworthy@btopenworld.com

William Croggon
01872 530499
wrcroggon@btinternet.com

Sarah Gordon
01579 362076
sar.gordon@virgin.net

Cecilia Hodgson
01566 772880
cecilia.hodgson@hotmail.com

Caroline Latham
01566 782970
carolineattrebartha@gmail.com

Katie Nichols
01872 275786
katherinemlambert@gmail.com

Alison O'Connor
01726 882460
tregoose@tregoose.co.uk

Marion Stanley
01326 565868
stanley.m2@sky.com

Ian Wright
07884 425899
ian.wright@nationaltrust.org.uk

Opening Dates

All entries subject to change.
For latest information check www.ngs.org.uk

February

Sunday 1
51 Tregoose

Sunday 8
51 Tregoose

Saturday 14
38 Pinetum Park & Pine Lodge Gardens

Sunday 15
10 Coombegate Cottage

Sunday 22
10 Coombegate Cottage
22 Ince Castle

March

Sunday 1
6 Bosvigo House
10 Coombegate Cottage

Sunday 8
10 Coombegate Cottage
22 Ince Castle

Sunday 15
10 Coombegate Cottage

Sunday 22
22 Ince Castle

Tuesday 24
12 Cotehele

Sunday 29
61 Trewidden Garden

April

Sunday 12
15 Ethnevas Cottage
22 Ince Castle
44 Riverside Cottage

Saturday 18
19 Hidden Valley Gardens

Sunday 19
7 Carminowe Valley Garden
19 Hidden Valley Gardens
47 Scorrier House

Wednesday 22
35 Pencarrow

Saturday 25
9 Chygurno

Sunday 26
8 Casa Laguna
9 Chygurno
22 Ince Castle
40 Polgwynne
53 NEW Tremeer
56 Trengwainton

May

Friday 1
16 Glendurgan
52 Trelissick

Sunday 3
4 Boconnoc
15 Ethnevas Cottage
24 Lamorran House

Monday 4
29 Moyclare

Tuesday 5
25 Lanhydrock House & Gardens

Wednesday 6
5 Bonython Manor

Thursday 7
57 Trerice

Sunday 10
17 Godolphin

Sunday 17
31 Navas Hill House
33 NEW The Old Watermill
36 NEW Penheale Manor
44 Riverside Cottage
49 Trebartha
55 Trenarth (Evening)

Sunday 31
2 The Barn House
13 Cutlinwith Farm

June

Festival Weekend

Saturday 6
38 Pinetum Park & Pine Lodge Gardens

Sunday 7
46 St Michael's Mount
56 Trengwainton

Saturday 13
18 Half Acre
39 Pinsla Garden & Nursery

Sunday 14
18 Half Acre
39 Pinsla Garden & Nursery
59 Trethew

Thursday 18
9 Chygurno

Friday 19
9 Chygurno

Saturday 20
45 Roseland House

Sunday 21
1 Arundell
7 Carminowe Valley Garden
37 Pillaton Parish Gardens
45 Roseland House

Sunday 28
3 Benallack Barn
21 The Homestead Woodland Garden
42 NEW Potager Gardeh (Evening)
58 NEW Trerose Manor

July

Sunday 12
55 Trenarth

Thursday 16
25 Lanhydrock House & Gardens

Sunday 19
1 Arundell

Saturday 25
45 Roseland House

Sunday 26
45 Roseland House

August

Sunday 2
20 Highcroft Gardens

Saturday 8
39 Pinsla Garden & Nursery

There are games to play, hammocks to laze in and boule and badminton to enjoy . . .

Sunday 9
39 Pinsla Garden & Nursery

Saturday 15
34 Parc-Lamp
41 Poppy Cottage Garden

Sunday 16
20 Highcroft Gardens
34 Parc-Lamp
41 Poppy Cottage Garden

Sunday 23
6 Bosvigo House

September

Sunday 6
50 NEW Tregonning

Saturday 12
11 Cosawes Barton

Wednesday 23
12 Cotehele

October

Sunday 4
54 Tremenheere Sculpture Garden

Sunday 11
49 Trebartha

Gardens open to the public

4 Boconnoc
5 Bonython Manor
6 Bosvigo House
9 Chygurno
12 Cotehele
14 Eden Project
16 Glendurgan
17 Godolphin
19 Hidden Valley Gardens
21 The Homestead Woodland Garden
23 Ken Caro
24 Lamorran House
25 Lanhydrock House & Gardens
27 The Lost Gardens of Heligan
29 Moyclare
35 Pencarrow
38 Pinetum Park & Pine Lodge Gardens
39 Pinsla Garden & Nursery
41 Poppy Cottage Garden
42 NEW Potager Garden
45 Roseland House
46 St Michael's Mount
48 Trebah
52 Trelissick

Visit a garden on National Gardens Festival Weekend 6 & 7 June

© Carole Drake

Trewidden Garden

54	Tremenheere Sculpture Garden
56	Trengwainton
57	Trerice
61	Trewidden Garden

By arrangement only

26	**NEW** The Lodge
28	Middlewood House
30	Nanfenten
32	The Old Rectory
43	Primrose Farm
60	Trevoole Farm
62	Waye Cottage

Also open by arrangement

1	Arundell
2	The Barn House
7	Carminowe Valley Garden
10	Coombegate Cottage
15	Ethnevas Cottage
18	Half Acre
20	Highcroft Gardens
37	Pillaton Parish Gardens
55	Trenarth

The Gardens

1 ARUNDELL
West Pentire, Crantock TR8 5SE. Brenda & David Eyles, 01637 831916, david@davideyles.com. *1m W of Crantock. From A3075 take signs to Crantock. At junction in village keep straight on to West Pentire (1m). Park in field (signed) or public car parks at W Pentire.* Cream teas. Homemade biscuits. **Adm £5, chd free. Sun 21 June, Sun 19 July (1-5).** Visitors also welcome by arrangement May to Aug on Thursdays.
A garden where no garden should be! - on windswept NT headland between 2 fantastic beaches. 1 acre around original farm cottage. Front: cottage garden. Side: small Mediterranean courtyard. Rear: rockery and shrubbery leading up to a 'stumpery' and fernery and on to a stream and pond, a 'Cornish Corner', herbaceous borders, Beth Chatto dry garden, a small pinetum and spectacular 'jungle' garden. Featured on Gardeners World and in Coast, Cornwall Today and Cornwall Life. Wheelchair access from public car

park with entrance via rear gate. 14 shallow steps in centre of garden useable with care.
& ⚘ ✿ ☕

2 THE BARN HOUSE
Higher Penhalt, Poundstock, Bude EX23 0DG. Tim & Sandy Dingle, 01288 361356, timdingle237@btinternet. com. *5m S of Bude. 1m off A39 to Widemouth Bay. Take Millook rd by Widemouth Manor Hotel. Follow rd for 1m, signed L at top of hill.* Home-made teas. **Adm £3.50, chd free. Sun 31 May (11-5).** Visitors also welcome by arrangement Apr to Sept access limited to cars only.
Garden that shows you can battle with the elements above dramatic cliffs of N Cornish coast and win. ½ - acre garden designed for yr-round interest with many colourful and unusual plants. Divided and enclosed by sheltering hedges. Herbaceous borders, prairie bed, pond, kitchen garden and patio. A walk through fields and wooded valley often gives glimpses of abundant wildlife and wild flowers. Partial wheelchair access.
& ⚘ ✿ 🛏 ☕

3 BENALLACK BARN
Grampound Road, Truro TR2 4BY. Linda Pelham, 01726 883618, info@benallack.net, www.benallack.net. *Between Grampound & Grampound Rd. From Truro, L to Grampound Road, 1st R. From A30, exit Fraddon to Grampound Rd, 1st L after village. From St Austell, R at pet shop in Grampound.* Home-made teas. **Adm £4, chd free. Sun 28 June (1-5).**
3-acre garden surrounding 400 yr-old converted barn, sloping towards R Fal. S-facing courtyard with climbers and planted granite troughs; sculptured cotoneaster hedges and colour-themed herbaceous borders; bog garden; small orchard; vegetable garden, greenhouse; wildflower borders in meadow leading to small lake with island and summerhouse surrounded by giant gunneras, grasses and perennials. Lawn access to most areas of the garden.
& ⚘ ✿ 🛏 ☕

4 ◆ **BOCONNOC**
Lostwithiel PL22 0RG. Anthony
Fortescue, 01208 872507,
info@boconnoc.com. *Off A390
between Liskeard & Lostwithiel. From
East Taphouse follow signs to
Boconnoc. (Sat Nav does not work
well in this area).* Home-made teas in
Stable Yard. **Adm £5, chd £2. For
NGS: Sun 3 May (2-5). For other
opening times and information,
please phone or email.**
20 acre gardens surrounded by
parkland and woods with magnificent
trees, flowering shrubs and stunning
views. The gardens are set amongst
mature trees which provide the
backcloth for exotic spring flowering
shrubs, woodland plants, with newly-
planted magnolias and a fine
collection of hydrangeas.

5 ◆ **BONYTHON MANOR**
Cury Cross Lanes, Helston
TR12 7BA. Mr & Mrs Richard
Nathan, 01326 240550,
www.bonythonmanor.co.uk. *5m
S of Helston. On main A3083 Helston
to Lizard Rd. Turn L at Cury Cross
Lanes (Wheel Inn). Entrance 300yds
on R.* Home-made teas. **Adm £7,
chd £2. For NGS: Wed 6 May
(2-4.30). For other opening times
and information, please phone or
see garden website.**
Magnificent 20-acre colour garden
incl sweeping hydrangea drive to
Georgian manor (not open).
Herbaceous walled garden, potager
with vegetables and picking flowers;
3 lakes in valley planted with
ornamental grasses, perennials and
South African flowers. A 'must see'
for all seasons colour.

6 ◆ **BOSVIGO HOUSE**
Bosvigo Lane, Truro TR1 3NH.
Wendy Perry, 01872 275774,
www.bosvigo.com/. *Truro City
Centre. At Highertown, nr Sainsbury
r'about, turn down Dobbs Lane. After
500yds, entrance to house is on L,
after sharp LH-bend.* Home-made
teas in servants hall. **Adm £5, chd
free. For NGS: Sun 1 Mar, Sun 23
Aug (2-5.30). For other opening
times and information, please
phone or see garden website.**
The 3 acre garden surrounding the
Georgian house (not open) and
Victorian conservatory includes a
woodland garden. A sinuous path
winds between heavily planted areas
in the woodland. In spring, before the

leaves open on the beech and
sycamore, the area is carpeted with
drifts of snowdrops, hellebores, wood
anemones, epimediums,
erythroniums and scented narcissus.
For the Aug opening the hot garden,
featured several times on television,
will be a blaze of colour.

7 ◆ **CARMINOWE VALLEY
GARDEN**
Tangies, Gunwalloe TR12 7PU.
Mr & Mrs Peter Stanley,
01326 565868,
stanley.m2@sky.com,
www.carminowevalleygarden.
co.uk. *3m SW of Helston. A3083
Helston-Lizard rd. R opp main gate to
Culdrose. 1m downhill, garden on R.*
Home-made teas. **Adm £4, chd free.
Sun 19 Apr, Sun 21 June (12-5).
Visitors also welcome by
arrangement Apr to Aug.**
Overlooking the beautiful Carminowe
Valley towards Loopool this abundant
garden combines native oak
woodland, babbling brook and large
natural pond with more formal areas.
Wild flower meadow, mown
pathways, shrubberies, orchard,
nectar beds, cutting garden, kitchen
garden, summerhouse. Enclosed
cottage garden, tulips in spring and
roses early summer provide huge
contrast. Featured in Cornwall Today
and Cornwall Life. Gravel paths,
slopes.

8 ◆ **CASA LAGUNA**
School Rd, Lanreath, Looe
PL13 2NX. Ivor & Margaret Dungey.
*5m SW of East Taphouse. From A390
take B3359 signed Looe Lanreath.
Lanreath village 5m. Garden 150yds*

*from village hall car park where
parking available.* Home-made teas.
**Adm £4, chd free. Sun 26 Apr
(11-4).**
Drive with shrubs leading to colourful
spring garden, approx 1/2 acre.
Azaleas, camellias and
rhododendrons in arrangement of
beds. Assortment of conifers, all
intermingled with seasonal bulbs and
small plants. Disabled parking at
house. Reasonably level garden, no
steps.

9 ◆ **CHYGURNO**
Lamorna TR19 6XH. Dr & Mrs
Robert Moule, 01736 732153,
rmoule010@btinternet.com. *4m
S of Penzance. Off B3315. Follow
signs for The Lamorna Cove Hotel.
Garden is at top of hill, past Hotel on
L.* **Adm £5, chd free. For NGS: Sat
25, Sun 26 Apr, Thur 18, Fri 19
June (2-5). For other opening times
and information, please phone or
email.**
Beautiful, unique, 3-acre cliffside
garden overlooking Lamorna Cove.
Planting started in 1998, mainly
S-hemisphere shrubs and exotics
with hydrangeas, camellias and
rhododendrons. Woodland area with
tree ferns set against large granite
outcrops. Garden terraced with steep
steps and paths. Plenty of benches
so you can take a rest and enjoy the
wonderful views. Featured in Gardens
Illustrated.

10 ◆ **COOMBEGATE COTTAGE**
St Ive, Liskeard PL14 3LZ.
Michael Stephens, 01579 383520,
mike@coombegate.wanadoo.co.uk.
*4m E of Liskeard. From A390 at St
Ive take turning signed Blunts. After
100 metres turn L & continue to
bottom of hill.* Home-made teas in
village hall. **Adm £3.50, chd free.
Every Sun 15 Feb to 15 Mar incl
(1-4). Visitors also welcome by
arrangement Feb & Mar.**
Prepare to be entranced by how
colourful, fragrant and interesting a
garden can be in winter and early
spring. See what use has been made
of a beautiful one acre steep valley
site. All the winter favourites including
drifts of snowdrops. Also more
unusual seasonal plants, many
available in the excellent plant sale.
Open unless ice/snow - phone to
check if in doubt.

11 ◆ COSAWES BARTON

Ponsanooth, nr Truro TR3 7EJ.
Louise Bishop, 01872 864026,
info@cosawesbarton.co.uk,
www.cosawesbarton.co.uk. 8½ m
W of Truro. A39 Truro - Falmouth rd.
At Treluswell r'about take A393
Redruth/Ponsanooth rd. After Burnt
House 1st L. ¾ m nr 30mph sign,
house on R. Light refreshments. **Adm
£4, chd free. Sat 12 Sept (2-5).**
An idyllic spot. Gardens surround
C18 farmhouse, cottage and
courtyard. Inner courtyard garden, a
formal, very well-established area and
extensive wooded walks covering 14
acres. There are gorgeous views over
the Kennal Valley and to the North
beyond.

Many mature and
unusual shrubs
to enjoy . . .

12 ◆ COTEHELE

Saltash PL12 6TA. National Trust,
01579 351346,
www.nationaltrust.org.uk. 2m E of
St Dominick. 4m from Gunnislake.
(Turn at St Annís Chapel); 8m SW of
Tavistock; 14m from Plymouth via
Tamar Bridge. Light refreshments in
Barn Restaurant & The Edgcumbe.
**Adm £7, chd £3.50. For NGS: Tue
24 Mar, Wed 23 Sept (11-4). For
other opening times and
information, please phone or see
garden website.**
Formal garden, orchards and
meadow. Terrace garden falling to
sheltered valley with ponds, stream
and unusual shrubs. Historic
collection of daffodils. Fine Tudor
house (one of the least altered in the
country); armour, tapestries, furniture.
Gravel paths, some steep slopes in
Valley Garden.

13 CUTLINWITH FARM

Tideford, Saltash PL12 5HX.
Peter & Mary Hamilton. 1½ m N of
Tideford, 5m W of Saltash. Tideford is
on the A38 between Liskeard &
Landrake. Yellow signs from Tideford
& Landrake. Home-made teas.
Cream teas. **Adm £4, chd free.
Sun 31 May (2-5.30).**
3-acre garden in small valley. Begun
14yrs ago and now beginning to
mature. The design aim is to have all
yr round interest. Features trees,
borders, water garden incl stream
and ponds. Developing acer,
magnolia and bluebell walk leading to
woodland paths. Music in the garden
incl local brass band. Other country
type attractions, such as beekeeping,
sometimes available. Featured on
Radio Cornwall.

14 ◆ EDEN PROJECT

Bodelva PL24 2SG. The Eden
Trust, 01726 811911,
www.edenproject.com. 4m E of St
Austell. Brown signs from A30 &
A390. **For opening times and
information, please phone or see
garden website.**
Described as the eighth wonder of
the world, the Eden Project is a global
garden for the C21. Discover the
story of plants that have changed the
world and which could change your
future. The Eden Project is an exciting
attraction where you can explore your
relationship with nature, learn new
things and get inspiration about the
world around you. Year-round
programme of talks, events and
workshops. Wheelchairs available -
booking of powered wheelchairs is
essential; please call 01726 818895
in advance.

15 ETHNEVAS COTTAGE

Constantine, Falmouth TR11 5PY.
Lyn Watson, 01326 340076. 6m SW
of Falmouth. Nearest main rds A39,
A394. Follow signs to Constantine. At
lower village sign, at bottom of
winding hill, turn off on private lane.
Garden ¾ m up hill. Home-made
teas. **Adm £4, chd free. Sun 12 Apr,
Sun 3 May (1-4.30). Visitors also
welcome by arrangement Mar to
Sept for groups of 20 max.**
Isolated granite cottage in 2 acres.
Intimate flower and vegetable garden.
Bridge over stream to large pond and
primrose path through semi-wild bog
area. Hillside with grass paths among
native and exotic trees. Many
camellias and rhododendrons. Mixed
shrubs and herbaceous beds, wild
flower glade, spring bulbs. A garden
of discovery of hidden delights.
Featured in Cornwall Life.

16 ◆ GLENDURGAN

Mawnan Smith, Falmouth
TR11 5JZ. National Trust,
01326 252020,
www.nationaltrust.org.uk/
glendurgan. 5m SW of Falmouth.
Follow rd out of Mawnan Smith to
Helford Passage. Brown signs to
Glendurgan. **Adm £8, chd £4.
For NGS: Fri 1 May (10.30-5.30).
For other opening times and
information, please phone or see
garden website.**
Three valleys of natural beauty and
amazing plants. Discover lush tender
plantings in the jungle-like lower valley
and spiky arid plants basking on
sunny upper slopes. Wander down to
hamlet of Durgan on R Helford.
Banks of wild flowers teeming with
wildlife - and 180 yr-old maze!

17 ◆ GODOLPHIN

Godolphin Cross, Helston
TR13 9RE. National Trust,
01736 763194,
www.nationaltrust.org.uk/
godolphin. 5m NW of Helston.
From Helston take A394 to Sithney
Common, turn R B3302 to
Leedstown, turn L, follow signs. From
Hayle B3302 Leedstown, turn R,
follow signs. Light refreshments.
**Adm £6, chd £3. For NGS: Sun 10
May (10-5). For other opening
times and information, please
phone or see garden website.**
A garden layout which is a rare
survival from the C16, unchanged by
garden fashions through the
centuries. The planting is informal and
wild around the ancient layout. There
are medieval stew ponds, a walled
privy garden and raised wall walks
over looking sunken lawns and
orchards. The stone walls and ancient
trees display the ghost of a formal
garden. Acquired by the National
Trust in 2007. Limited wheelchair
access, gravel paths, steep slopes,
uneven surfaces and steps.

18 HALF ACRE

Mount Pleasant, Boscastle
PL35 0BJ. Carole Vincent, 01840
250263, www.carolevincent.org.
5m N of Camelford. Park at doctors'
surgery at top of village (clearly
signed). Limited parking for disabled
at Half Acre. Home-made teas. **Adm
£3.50, chd free. Sat 13, Sun 14
June (1.30-5.30). Visitors also
welcome by arrangement.**

Sculpture in one and a half acres of 3 gardens; cottage, small wood and Blue Circle garden (RHS Chelsea 2001), constructed in coloured concrete with coastal planting. Studio open. Painting exhibition.

❀ ☕

19 ◆ HIDDEN VALLEY GARDENS

Treesmill, Par PL24 2TU. Tricia Howard, 01208 873225, www.hiddenvalleygardens.co.uk. *2m SW of Lostwithiel. Yellow sign directions on A390 between Lostwithiel (2m) & St Austell (5m), directing onto B3269 towards Fowey, followed by a R turn.* Cream teas. **Adm £4.50, chd free. For NGS: Sat 18, Sun 19 Apr (10-5). For other opening times and information, please phone or see garden website.**
Award-winning 3-acre colourful garden in 'hidden' valley with nursery. Cottage-style planting with herbaceous beds and borders, grasses, ferns and fruit. Gazebo with country views. Iris fairy well and vegetable potager. April opening for special displays ferns, spring bulbs and many varieties of old and new primroses grown from seed from the famous Barnhaven strains. Children's quiz. Special drop off parking for wheelchair access directly into garden area. Some gentle sloping ground.

♿ 🐕 ❀ 🛏 ☕

20 HIGHCROFT GARDENS

Cargreen, Saltash PL12 6PA. Mr & Mrs B J Richards, 01752 848048, gardens@bjrichardsflowers.co.uk, www.bjrichardsflowers.com. *5m NW of Saltash. 5m from Callington on A388 take Landulph Cargreen turning. 2m on, turn L at Landulph Xrds. Park at Methodist Church.* Cream teas in Methodist Church. **Adm £4, chd free. Sun 2, Sun 16 Aug (1.30-5). Visitors also welcome by arrangement July to Sept for garden clubs and groups of 10+.**
3-acre garden in beautiful Tamar Valley. Japanese-style garden, hot border, pastel border, grasses, arboretum with hemerocallis and new blue borders. Prairie planting containing 2,500 plants of herbaceous and grasses. Buddleia and shrub rose bank. Pond. All at their best in July, Aug and Sept. Collection of hydrangeas and agapanthus.

❀ ☕

The Homestead Woodland Garden

21 ◆ THE HOMESTEAD WOODLAND GARDEN

Crelly, Trenear, Wendron TR13 0EU. Shirley Williams & Chris Tredinnick, 01326 562808, www.the-homestead-woodland-garden.com. *3m N of Helston. From Helston B3297 towards Redruth, 3m. Entrance 3rd on R 200 metres past Crelly/Bodilly sign & bus shelter.* Light refreshments. **Adm £4, chd free. For NGS: Sun 28 June (1-4.30). For other opening times and information, please phone or see garden website.**
3 acres of divided gardens giving all-yr round interest and 3 acres of wildlife habitat and deciduous woodland with primroses in spring. Cornish variety apple orchard where chickens, ducks and geese roam free. Vegetable garden, mature garden with pond and mixed borders. Archways, pergolas, seating, water features, hot and shady areas, walled garden, Japanese and Moroccan area. Sculptures sited throughout. Featured in Cornwall Life. Unfenced pond, uneven paths (which can be slippery) and steps.

♿ ❀ 🚐 🛏 ☕

22 INCE CASTLE

Saltash PL12 4RA. Lord & Lady Boyd, www.incecastle.co.uk. *3m SW of Saltash. From A38 at Stoketon Cross take turn signed Trematon, then Elmgate. No large coaches.* Home-made teas. **Adm £4, chd free. Sun 22 Feb (11-3); Sun 8, Sun 22 Mar, Sun 12, Sun 26 Apr (2-5).**
Romantic garden at the end of winding lanes, surrounding C17 pink brick castle on a peninsula in the R Lynher. Old apple trees with bulbs, woodland garden with fritillaries, camellias and rhododendrons. Extraordinary 1960s shell house on edge of formal garden. Partial wheelchair access.

♿ 🐕 ❀ ☕

23 ◆ KEN CARO

Bicton, nr Liskeard PL14 5RF. Mr & Mrs K R Willcock, 01579 362446. *5m NE of Liskeard. From A390 to Callington turn off N at St Ive. Take Pensilva Rd, follow brown tourist signs, approx 1m off main rd. Plenty of parking.* Tea/coffee with shortbread. **For information, please phone.**
Connoisseurs garden full of interest all yr round. Lily ponds, panoramic views, plenty of seating, picnic area, in all 10 acres. Garden started in 1970, recently rejuvenated. Woodland walk, which has one of the largest beech trees. Good collection of yellow magnolias and herbaceous plants. Daily 22 Mar to 30 Sept (10-5), adm £5. Partial wheelchair access.

♿ 🐕 🚐 ☕

Visit a garden in your own time – look for by arrangement gardens

24 ◆ **LAMORRAN HOUSE**
Upper Castle Road, St Mawes, Truro TR2 5BZ. Robert Dudley-Cooke, 01326 270800, www.lamorrangarden.co.uk. *A3078, R past garage at entrance to St Mawes. ³/₄ m on L. ¹/₄ m from castle if using passenger ferry service.* Adm £7, chd free. For NGS: Sun 3 May (11-4). For other opening times and information, please phone or see garden website.
4-acre subtropical garden overlooking Falmouth bay. Designed by owner in an Italianate/Cote d'Azur style. Extensive collection of Mediterranean and subtropical plants incl large collection of palms Butia capitata/Butia yatay and tree ferns. Reflects both design and remarkable micro-climate. Beautiful collection of Japanese azaleas and tender rhododendrons. Large collection of S-hemisphere plants. Italianate garden with many water features. Champion trees.

🏠 🚐

25 ◆ **LANHYDROCK HOUSE & GARDENS**
Bodmin PL30 5AD. National Trust, 01208 265950, www.lanhydrock@nationaltrust.org.uk. *2¹/₂ m SE of Bodmin. 2¹/₂ m on B3268. Stn: Bodmin Parkway 1³/₄ m walk.* Cream teas. Adm £7.20, chd £3.60. For NGS: Tue 5 May, Thur 16 July (10-5.30). For other opening times and information, please phone or see garden website.
Large formal garden laid out in 1857. Ornamental parterres. Many fine specimens of camellias, rhododendrons and magnolias. Good summer colour with herbaceous borders, roses and parterres with seasonal planting. Woodland walks. Lovely views. Mainly Victorian country house, though some parts date back to C17, with over 50 rooms open to the public. Formal and woodland gardens. Garden tours most weekdays. Wheelchair access route around formal garden. Gravel paths and slopes to higher woodland garden.

♿ 🌼 🚐 ☕

26 NEW **THE LODGE**
Fletchers Bridge, Bodmin PL30 4AN. Mr Tony Ryde, 01208 821431. *2m E of Bodmin. From A38 at Glynn Crematorium r'about take road towards Cardinham, 1st R over*

river at Fletchersbridge. Limited off-road parking must be reserved by phone in advance. Cream teas. Adm £3.50, chd free. Sun 5, Tue 14, Sun 26 Apr, Mon 4, Sun 17, Mon 25 May, Tue 9, Sun 21 June (2-6). NB because of limited off-road parking, visitors must phone in advance to book.
3-acre riverside garden some 15 yrs old specialising in trees and shrubs chosen for their flowers, foliage and form. Magnolias and camellias start the spring show, yielding to prunus and pieris, azaleas and rhododendrons, paulownias and viburnums, with cornus, davidias and stewartia starring in summer. Informal setting complemented by ponds, waterfalls, spring bulbs and herbaceous flowers, surrounding a Gothic former lodge by the Glynn estate. Only open by prior arrangement on dates specified. Wheelchair access to gravelled areas around house and along two sides of garden.

♿ ☕

27 ◆ **THE LOST GARDENS OF HELIGAN**
Pentewan, St Austell PL26 6EN. Heligan Gardens Ltd, 01726 845100, www.heligan.com. *5m S of St Austell. From St Austell take B3273 signed Mevagissey, follow signs.* For opening times and information, please phone or see garden website.
Lose yourself in the mysterious world of The Lost Gardens where an exotic sub-tropical jungle, atmospheric Victorian pleasure grounds, an interactive wildlife project and the finest productive gardens in Britain all await your discovery. Wheelchair access to Northern gardens. Armchair tour shows video of unreachable areas. Wheelchairs available at reception.

♿ 🏠 🌼 🚐 NCH ☕

28 **MIDDLEWOOD HOUSE**
Middlewood, North Hill, Launceston PL15 7NN. Brian & Cathy Toole, 01566 782118, cathy.toole@btinternet.com. *On B3254, 7m S of Launceston, 7m N of Liskeard. North of village on B3254, lay-by with parking for up to 6 cars or coach, 16-seater max.* Home-made teas. Adm £3.50, chd free. Visitors welcome by arrangement Apr to July.
Beautiful, tranquil 1¹/₄ -acre garden nestling in Lynher valley. In a series of

semi-formal destinations, spring shrubs and flowers are complemented by extensive herbaceous beds. Fernery, raised beds, water features, wooden and other architectural structures. Garden is sloped but good paths allow wheelchair access to most of it.

♿ 🏠 🚐 ☕

Blue Circle garden (RHS Chelsea 2001), constructed in coloured concrete with coastal planting . . .

29 ◆ **MOYCLARE**
Lodge Hill, Liskeard PL14 4EH. Elizabeth & Philip Henslowe, 01579 343114, www.moyclare.co.uk. *1m S of Liskeard centre. Approx 300yds S of Liskeard railway stn on St Keyne-Duloe rd (B3254).* Home-made teas. Adm £3.50, chd free. For NGS: Mon 4 May (2-5). For other opening times and information, please phone or see garden website.
Gardened by one family for over 80yrs; mature trees, shrubs and plants (many unusual, many variegated). Once most televised Cornish garden. Now revived and rejuvenated and still a plantsman's delight, full of character. Camellia, brachyglottis and astrantia (all 'Moira Reid') and cytisus 'Moyclare Pink' originated here. Meandering paths through fascinating shrubberies, herbacious borders and sunny corners. Wellstocked pond. Wildlife habitat area. Most of the garden can be enjoyed by wheelchair users.

♿ 🌼 🚐 ☕

30 **NANFENTEN**
Little Petherick, Wadebridge PL27 7QT. Trevor & Jackie Bould, 01841 540480, nanfentensgarden@hotmail.co.uk, www.nanfentensgarden.com. *3m W of Wadebridge, A389 to Little Petherick. Turn into lane next to white cottage almost opp church, Nanfenten 150 metres on L. Limited parking, larger groups please use village hall car park.* Home-made teas. Adm £3.50, chd free. Visitors

welcome by arrangement May to Aug single visitors or groups all welcome.

$^2/_3$ -acre plantsman's garden on side of valley. Views of Petherick Creek to Padstow. Cottage-style planting on difficult terrain. Many beautiful roses. Steep sloping aspect to rear garden with wide variety of shrubs and plants. Unusual sloping water feature. Pergola and summerhouse. A surprise around every corner with beautiful views. Many seating areas.

31 ▶ NAVAS HILL HOUSE

Bosanath Valley, Mawnan Smith, Falmouth TR11 5LL. Aline & Richard Turner, 01326 251233, alineturner@btinternet.com. *1$^1/_2$ m from Trebah & Glendurgan Gdns. Head for Mawnan Smith, pass Trebah and Glendurgan Gdns then follow yellow signs.* Cream teas. **Adm £3.50, chd free. Sun 17 May (2-5.30). Also open Trenarth Garden (5-8).**

8$^1/_2$ -acre garden divided into various zones; kitchen garden with greenhouses, potting shed, fruit cages, orchard; 2 plantsman areas with specialist trees and shrubs; walled rose garden; ornamental garden with water features and rockery; wooded areas with bluebells and young large leafed rhododendrons. Seating areas with views across wooded valley, no car in sight! Partial wheelchair access, some gravel and grass paths.

32 ▶ THE OLD RECTORY

Trevalga, Boscastle PL35 0EA. Jacqueline M A Jarvis, 01840 250512, jacqueline@jacquelinejarvis.co.uk. *Coastal road between Tintagel & Boscastle. At Trevalga Xrds turn inland away from hamlet. Garden $^1/_2$ m up narrow, steep hill. Limited parking.* Light refreshments. **Adm by donation. Visitors welcome by arrangement** Apr to Sept.

On North Cornish coast, a challenging, exposed, NW-facing garden with panoramic sea views, $^1/_2$ m inland, elevation 500ft. 'From Field to Garden' a 25 yr project by artist owner. Informal incl woodland, perennial borders, sunken and walled areas. Lookout at front of garden (4 step spiral stair access) with stunning views across circa 50m of coastline - Hartland Point to Pentire Point. Featured in Cornish Guardian and

Parc-Lamp

Amateur Gardening. Gravel drive and partial wheelchair access to garden.

33 NEW ▶ THE OLD WATERMILL

St. Mabyn, Bodmin PL30 3BX. Mr & Mrs ER Maunsell. *SE edge of St Mabyn on road to Helland. Approx 1m from B3266, 2m from A39.* Cream teas. **Adm £4, chd free. Sun 17 May (1.30-5.30).**

A 2-acre garden in the making - started approx 4 years ago, creating a new garden out of wilderness. Two ponds, one stream, several springs. Ancient Cornish hedges and mature trees. Characterful woodland beds, interlinking paths and bridges. Orchard, lawns and sitting areas. Plentiful wildlife. Gravel paths.

34 ▶ PARC-LAMP

Ruan Lanihorne, Truro TR2 5NX. Kathleen Ward. *2$^1/_2$ m W of Tregony. Truro to Tregony: A390 E to St Austell. Turn R on A3078 to St Mawes Rd. In Tregony cross bridge then 1st R to Ruan Lanihorne. Garden 1st L after bend.* **Adm £3.50, chd free. Sat 15, Sun 16 Aug (2-5.30). Also open Poppy Cottage Garden.**

Small, intensively-planted, terraced

Mediterranean style garden with travertine paving and gravelled areas. The sheltered site has a micro-climate which allows many unusual tender trees and plants to thrive. Enjoy the garden from various seating places. Entry is by steep steps.

35 ▶ ◆ PENCARROW

Washaway, Bodmin PL30 3AG. Molesworth-St Aubyn family, 01208 841369, www.pencarrow.co.uk. *4m NW of Bodmin. Signed off A389 & B3266.* Light refreshments. **Adm £5.50, chd £2.50. For NGS: Wed 22 Apr (10-5.30). For other opening times and information, please phone or see garden website.**

50 acres of tranquil, family-owned Grade II* listed gardens. Superb specimen conifers, azaleas, magnolias and camellias galore. 700 varieties of rhododendron give a blaze of spring colour; blue hydrangeas line the mile-long carriage drive throughout the summer. Discover the Iron Age hill fort, lake, Italian gardens and granite rockery. Free parking, dogs welcome, cafe and children's play area. Gravel paths, some steep slopes.

36 NEW ▶ PENHEALE MANOR

Egloskerry, Launceston PL15 8RX.
Mr & Mrs James Colville. *Penheale Manor SX26 88; 3¹/₂ m NW of Launceston. Take rd from St Stephen's, Launceston, to Egloskerry. From centre of village to Penheale entrance is ¹/₂ m on R.* Home-made teas. **Adm £6, chd £2. Sun 17 May (2-5).**
A rare opportunity to enjoy the listed walled gardens which surround a C17 Jacobean manor house incl impressive yew hedges, with enclosures and surprises, herbaceous borders and rose gardens. In addition there are beautiful woodland areas with streams, pools and ponds. Wheelchair users will be given help and guidance.

GROUP OPENING

37 ▶ PILLATON PARISH GARDENS

Pillaton, Saltash PL12 6QS, 01579 350629, tony@laurillard.eclipse.co.uk. *4m S of Callington. Signs from r'abouts on A388 at St Mellion & Hatt or on A38 at Landrake. 1st garden in centre of village opp Weary Friar PH. Roadside parking. No parking in PH car park.* Home-made teas. **Combined adm £4, chd free. Sun 21 June (12-5).**
Visitors also welcome by arrangement for coach parties or club groups.

NORTH SILLATON FARMHOUSE
Linda Mavin

SOUTH LEA
Viv & Tony Laurillard
Pillaton is a quiet village in SE Cornwall with C12 church and thriving village pub, set in farmland above the R Lynher valley. Two gardens are open this year. South Lea, a colourful, cottage style garden in the village centre has extensive views across the valley. About 0.3 acre, it presents a tropical theme to the front, and steps up to a newly planted dry/arid area. The S-facing rear garden has sun terraces, greenhouse, garden room, sloping and level lawns, herbaceous borders, good sized pond and shady woodland area. Seating is provided in all areas. North Sillaton Farmhouse, 1¹/₂ m away, has about 1 acre. The property was bought at Duchy auction 27 years ago. Apart from a

privet hedge, everything has since been added. This mixed garden, on a S-facing slope, has a pond, herbaceous border, vegetable beds and fruit trees with poly tunnel, small poultry house and several outbuildings. To the north is a Cornish hedge. There are several areas to sit with protection from the weather. Sloping lawns, soft paths. Wheelchair access at South Lea only to rear terrace overlooking main garden.

38 ▶ ♦ PINETUM PARK & PINE LODGE GARDENS

Holmbush, St Austell PL25 3RQ.
Mr Chang Li, 01726 73500, www.pinetumpark.com. *1m E of St Austell. On A390 between Holmbush & St Blazey at junction of A391.* Light refreshments. Hot and cold food and cream teas. **Adm £7.50, chd free. For NGS: Sat 14 Feb, Sat 6 June (10-5). For other opening times and information, please phone or see garden website.**
30-acre estate comprises gardens within a garden. Some 6,000 plants, all labelled, have been thoughtfully laid out using original designs and colour combinations to provide maximum interest. Rhododendrons, magnolias, camellias, herbaceous borders with many rare and tender plants, marsh gardens, tranquil lily ponds, lake with black swans within the park, pinetum. Japanese garden and arboretum. 3-acre winter garden. Winter Garden Festival in Feb. Featured in Discover Britain's Gardens. No wheelchair access to Japanese garden.

39 ▶ ♦ PINSLA GARDEN & NURSERY

Cardinham PL30 4AY. Mark & Claire Woodbine, 01208 821339, www.pinslagarden.net. *3¹/₂ m E of Bodmin. From A30 or Bodmin take A38 towards Plymouth, 1st L to Cardinham & Fletchers Bridge, 2m on R.* Home-made teas. **Adm £3, chd free. For NGS: Sat 13, Sun 14 June, Sat 8, Sun 9 Aug (9-5.30). For other opening times and information, please phone or see garden website.**
Romantic 1¹/₂ -acre artist's garden set in tranquil woodland. Naturalistic cottage garden planting surrounds our C18 fairytale cottage. Imaginative design, intense colour and scent, bees and butterflies. Unusual shade

plants, acers and ferns. Fantastic range of plants and statues on display and for sale. Friendly advice in nursery. Some paths are narrow and bumpy.

Characterful woodland beds, interlinking paths and bridges . . .

40 ▶ POLGWYNNE

Feock TR3 6SG. Amanda & Graham Piercy. *5m SW of Truro. Take A39 out of Truro signed Falmouth. At Playing Place turn L onto B3289. After 2m look for NGS signs.* Home-made teas. **Adm £4, chd free. Sun 26 Apr (2-5.30).**
Wonderful 4-acre garden looking out over the sea. Walled formal and cottage gardens, terraced lawns, formal pond and woodland. Vegetable and picking gardens, with greenhouses whose mechanisms were described in The Journal of the RHS in 1852. Many unusual plants and what is believed to be the largest female Ginkgo biloba in Britain. Partial wheelchair access, gravel paths, some slopes.

41 ▶ ♦ POPPY COTTAGE GARDEN

Ruan High Lanes, Truro TR2 5JR.
Tina & David Primmer, 01872 501411, www.poppycottagegarden.co.uk. *On Roseland Peninsula. Turn off A390 Truro - St Austell rd onto A3078 to St Mawes. Garden 4m out of Tregony.* Home-made teas. **Adm £3.50, chd free. For NGS: Sat 15, Sun 16 Aug (2-5.30). For other opening times and information, please phone or see garden website.**
Situated on the beautiful Roseland peninsula, this 1-acre garden is a plantsman's paradise. Planted for yr-round interest and divided into rooms, its intense planting of shrubs and

herbaceous under-planted with bulbs provides colourful and intriguing surprises around every corner. Small orchard with ornamental ducks and chickens. Featured in Garden News.

♿ 🏠 ⊛ 🚐 ☕

42 NEW ◆ POTAGER GARDEN
High Cross, Constantine, Falmouth TR11 5RF. Mr Mark Harris, 01326 341258, www.potagergarden.org. *5m SW of Falmouth. From Falmouth, follow signs to Constantine. From Helston, drive through Constantine and continue towards Famouth.* **For NGS: Evening Opening by donation, wine, Sun 28 June (5-9). Also open Trerose Manor (1-5). For other opening times and information, please phone or see garden website.**
Potager has emerged from the bramble choked wilderness of an abandoned plant nursery. With mature trees which were once nursery stock and lush herbaceous planting interspersed with fruit and vegetables Potager aims to demonstrate the beauty of productive organic gardening. There are games to play, hammocks to laze in and boule and badminton to enjoy.

♿ 🏠 ⊛ ☕

43 PRIMROSE FARM
Skinners Bottom, Redruth TR16 5EA. Barbara & Peter Simmons, 01209 890350, babss@me.com, www.primrosefarmgarden. blogspot.com. *6m N of Truro. At Chiverton Cross r'about on A30 take Blackwater turn. Down hill, R by Red Lion PH up North Hill, 1st L (mini Xrd), garden approx 1/2 m on L.* Light refreshments. **Adm £3.50, chd free. Visitors welcome by arrangement** Apr to Sept groups welcome.
Rambling informal cottage-style garden with woodland glade. Mature trees and shrubs, herbaceous and mixed borders. Patio area with exotic plants. Gravel path to pergola with scented climbers and summerhouse. Vegetable patch and wildlife pond. New secret garden. A plantsman's garden.

♿ ⊛ 🚐 ☕

44 RIVERSIDE COTTAGE
St. Clement, Truro TR1 1SZ. Billa & Nick Jeans. *11/2 m SE of Truro. From Trafalgar r'about on A39 in Truro, follow signs for St Clement, up St Clement Hill. R at top of hill, continue to car park by river.* Cream teas. **Adm**

£3.50, chd free. **Sun 12 Apr, Sun 17 May (2-5).**
Small garden on beautiful St Clement Estuary. Small Victorian orchard and nut walk with wild flower areas, borders and vegetable patch. Steep paths and steps but plenty of seats. Walk through to C13 St Clement Church and 'living churchyard'. Featured in Cornish Life.

☕

45 ◆ ROSELAND HOUSE
Chacewater TR4 8QB. Mr & Mrs Pridham, 01872 560451, www.roselandhouse.co.uk. *4m W of Truro. At Truro end of main st. Park in village car park (100yds) or on surrounding rds.* Home-made teas. **Adm £4, chd free. For NGS: Sat 20, Sun 21 June, Sat 25, Sun 26 July (1-5). For other opening times and information, please phone or see garden website.**
The 1-acre garden is a mass of rambling roses and clematis. Ponds and borders alike are filled with plants, many rarely seen in gardens. National Collection of clematis viticella cvs can be seen in garden and display tunnel, along with a huge range of other climbing plants. Featured on Gardeners World. Some slopes.

♿ 🏠 ⊛ NCH ☕

46 ◆ ST MICHAEL'S MOUNT
Marazion TR17 0HS. James & Mary St Levan, 01736 710507, www.stmichaelsmount.co.uk. *21/2 m E of Penzance. 1/2 m from shore at Marazion by Causeway; otherwise by motor boat.* Cream teas in Island Cafe & Sail Loft Restaurant. **Adm £5.50, chd £2.50. For NGS: Sun 7 June (10.30-5). For other opening times and information, please phone or see garden website.**
Infuse your senses with colour and scent in the unique sub-tropical gardens basking in the mild climate and salty breeze. Clinging to granite slopes the terraced beds tier steeply to the ocean's edge, boasting tender exotics from places such as Mexico, the Canary Islands and South Africa. The Laundry Lawn, Mackerel Bank, Pill Box, Gun Emplacement, Tiered Terraces, The Well, Tortoise Lawn. Walled Gardens, Seagull Seat. The garden lawn can be accessed with wheelchairs although further exploration is limited due to steps and steepness.

⊛ 🚐 ☕

47 SCORRIER HOUSE
Scorrier, Redruth TR16 5AU. Richard & Caroline Williams, www.scorrierhouse.co.uk. *21/2 m E of Redruth. Signed from B3207 and Redruth Truro rd B3287.* Home-made teas. **Adm £4, chd free. Sun 19 Apr (1.30-5).**
Scorrier House and gardens have been in the Williams family for 7 generations. The gardens are set in parkland with a new conservatory, formal garden with herbaceous borders and walled garden with camellias, magnolias and rare trees, some collected by the famous plant collector William Lobb. Unfenced swimming pool.

🏠 🚐 ☕

48 ◆ TREBAH
Mawnan Smith TR11 5JZ. Trebah Garden Trust, 01326 252200, www.trebah-garden.co.uk. *4m SW of Falmouth. Follow tourist signs from Hillhead r'about on A39 approach to Falmouth or Treliever Cross r'about on junction of A39-A394. Parking for coaches.* **For opening times and information, please phone or see garden website.**
26-acre S-facing ravine garden, planted in 1830s. Extensive collection rare/mature trees/shrubs incl glades; huge tree ferns 100yrs old, subtropical exotics. Hydrangea collection covers 21/2 acres. Water garden, waterfalls, rock pool stocked with mature koi carp. Enchanted garden for plantsman/artist/family. Play area/trails for children. Use of private beach. Steep paths in places. 2 motorised vehicles available, please book in advance.

♿ 🏠 ⊛ 🚐 ☕

49 **TREBARTHA**
nr Launceston PL15 7PE. The
Latham Family. *6m SW of
Launceston. North Hill, SW of
Launceston nr junction of B3254 &
B3257. No coaches.* Home-made
teas. Adm £5, chd free. Sun 17
May, Sun 11 Oct (2-5).
Wooded area with lake surrounded
by walks of flowering shrubs;
woodland trail through fine woods
with cascades and waterfalls;
American glade with fine trees. Major
but exciting clearance and replanting
is underway in these fine
landscape/woodland gardens which
will not interfere with your walk but
we do request that visitors keep to
the signed paths and other directions.

50 NEW **TREGONNING**
Carleen, Breage, Helston
TR13 9QU. Andrew & Kathryn
Eaton. *1m S of Godolphin Cross.
From Xrds in centre of Godolphin
Cross head S towards Carleen. In
¹/₂ m at fork signed Breage 1¹/₄ turn R
up narrow lane marked no through
road. After ¹/₂ m parking on L opp
Tregonning Farm.* Home-made teas.
Adm £3.50, chd free. Sun 6 Sept
(11-4).
Located 300ft up NE side of
Tregonning Hill this small (less than 1
acre) developing garden will hopefully
inspire those thinking of making a
garden from nothing more than a
pond and copse of trees (in 2009).
With the ever present challenge of
storm force winds, garden offers yr
round interest and a self-sufficient
vegetable and soft fruit paddock.
Sculpted grass meadow, with
panoramic views from Carn Brea to
Helston.

51 **TREGOOSE**
Grampound TR2 4DB. Mr & Mrs
Anthony O'Connor, 01726 882460,
tregoose@tregoose.co.uk. *7m E of
Truro, 1m W of Grampound. Off
A390. Lane entrance is 100yds W of
New Stables Xrds & ¹/₂ m E of
Trewithen r'about.* Home-made teas.
Adm £4, chd free. Sun 1, Sun 8
Feb (1-4.30).
2-acre garden. Woodland area with
early spring shrubs underplanted with
snowdrops, erythroniums, hellebores
and small narcissus cultivars.
Summer and autumn flowering areas
incl walled garden overtopped by
Acacia baileyana purpurea, scarlet
blue and yellow border and potager

full of herbs and cutting beds with
arches covered with gourds, roses
and honeysuckle. Snowdrop
collection. Most of the summer
flowering area can take a wheelchair.

Small developing
garden from
nothing more
than a pond and
copse of trees . . .

52 ♦ **TRELISSICK**
Feock TR3 6QL. National Trust,
01872 862090,
www.nationaltrust.org.uk/trelissick.
*4m S of Truro. From A39 Truro to
Falmouth, turn onto B3289 at Playing
Place. Follow signs to Trelissick &
King Harry Ferry.* Adm £9.50, chd
£4.75. For NGS: Fri 1 May
(10.30-5). For other opening times
and information, please phone or
see garden website.
Woodland garden with fantastic views
out to water on 3 sides. Contrasts
between light and shade and
inspiration from gardening in a variety
of woodland environments. Mixed
borders designed for long term
interest with a mixture of popular
hardy favourites and tender exotics
with foliage interest. With the house
now open and the terrace boasting
one of Cornwall's finest views. Guided
tour of garden to learn about
woodland gardening and mixed
borders for lasting impact 2.30pm.
Partial wheelchair access, map
provided. Wheelchairs and mobility
vehicles available, ring to book in
advance.

53 NEW **TREMEER**
St Tudy, Nr Bodmin PL30 3NL.
Lady George. *8m N of Bodmin; W of
B3266. ¹/₄ m from centre of St Tudy
on Wadebridge road (just past
community shop). Signed from A39
and B3266.* Tea. Adm £5, chd free.
Sun 26 Apr (12-5).
5 acre garden was laid out in 1945 by
General Harrison, encouraged by
Walter Magor of Lamellen. Both were

distinguished collectors and
propagators of azaleas and
rhododendrons and as a result there
are now many mature and unusual
shrubs to enjoy. Paths lead from
expansive lawn in front of house
through woodland to small lake. It is
believed the first blood transfusion in
the history of medicine was
conducted by Dr Richard Lower in
1667 in the basement of Tremeer.
Partial wheelchair access, woodland
area difficult.

54 ♦ **TREMENHEERE**
SCULPTURE GARDEN
Penzance TR20 8YL. Drs Neil
Armstrong & Jane Martin, 01736
448089, www.tremenheere.co.uk.
*1m E of Penzance. From Gulval
church proceed ³/₄ m due E. L at sign
Entrance, gates straight ahead.* Light
refreshments. Adm £6.50, chd £3.
For NGS: Sun 4 Oct (10-5). For
other opening times and
information, please phone or see
garden website.
Spectacular valley setting overlooking
St Michael's Mount provides
microclimate for large scale
subtropical planting. Habitats from
ponds to hot slopes provide wide
variety of landscaping styles. High
quality contemporary sculpture by
internationally-renowned artists.

55 **TRENARTH**
High Cross, Constantine TR11 5JN.
Lucie Nottingham, 01326 340444,
lmnottingham@tiscali.co.uk,
www.trenarthgardens.co.uk. *6m
SW of Falmouth. Main rd A39/A394
Truro to Helston, follow Constantine
signs. High X garage turn L for
Mawnan, 30yds on R down dead end
lane, Trenarth is ¹/₂ m at end.* Home-
made teas. Adm £4, chd free.
Evening Opening £4, chd free,
wine, Sun 17 May (5-8). Sun 12
July (2-5). Also open Navas Hill
House Sun 17 May (2-5.30).
Visitors also welcome by
arrangement Mar to Oct please
contact before visiting. Guided
tours.
4-acres round C17 farmhouse in
peaceful pastoral setting. Yr-round
interest. Emphasis on tender, unusual
plants, structure and form. C16
courtyard, listed garden walls, yew
rooms, vegetable garden, traditional
potting shed, orchard, new woodland
area with childrens interest, palm and
gravel garden. Circular walk down

ancient green lane via little lake to Trenarth Bridge, and on to Navas Hill House, or returning through bluebell woods. Abundant wildlife. Bees in tree bole, lesser horseshoe bat colony, swallows and house martins nesting, wild flowers and butterflies.

56 ◆ **TRENGWAINTON**
Madron, Penzance TR20 8RZ. National Trust, 01736 363148, www.nationaltrust.org.uk/trengwai nton. *2m NW of Penzance. ¹/₂ m W of Heamoor. On Penzance-Morvah rd (B3312), ¹/₂ m off St Just rd (A3071). Signed from A30.* Light refreshments. **Adm £8, chd £4. For NGS: Sun 26 Apr, Sun 7 June (10.30-5). For other opening times and information, please phone or see garden website.**
Glorious spring displays of magnolias, rhododendrons, azaleas and camellias; walled kitchen garden built to dimensions of Noahs Ark and breathtaking views across Mounts Bay. Lose yourself amongst winding, wooded paths, picnic by the stream or simply find a quiet corner to sit within Trengwainton's peaceful 25 acres. WW2 'Dig for Victory' allotment, complete with reproduction Anderson shelter. Free guided tour 11.30am. Wheelchairs available, booking essential. Gravel paths and slope, assistance may be needed.

57 ◆ **TRERICE**
Kestle Mill, Newquay TR8 4PG. National Trust, 01637 875404, www.nationaltrust.org.uk/trerice. *3m SE of Newquay. From Newquay via A392 & A3058; turn R at Kestle Mill (NT signs) or signed from A30 at Summercourt via A3058.* Light refreshments in The Barn restaurant. **Adm £8.50, chd £4.25. For NGS: Thur 7 May (10.30-4.30). For other opening times and information, please phone or see garden website.**
Small intimate romantic house and garden set in unspoilt countryside. The garden has interest throughout the year incl spring flowering bulbs, summer annuals, borders, cut flowers, herbs and fruit. The magnificent newly planted Knot Garden was opened in 2014. Due to historic nature of property only partial wheelchair access.

58 **NEW** ◆ **TREROSE MANOR**
Old Church Road, Mawnan Smith, Falmouth TR11 5HX. Mr & Mrs Piers & Tessa Phipps, 01326 250784, info@trerosemanor.co.uk, www.trerosemanor.co.uk. *Some parking at house, otherwise on road or field if signed. From Mawnan Smith bear L at Red Lion. ¹/₂ m turn R into Old Church Rd. After ¹/₂ m garden is immed after Trerose Farm.* Cream teas. **Adm £4, chd free. Sun 28 June (1-5). Also open Potager Garden (5-9).**
Old Cornish Manor House. An acre of garden planned for all seasons. Various rare and tender plants. Camelias in winter. Akebia, pink wisteria, cassia in spring. Poppies, alstroemerias, hollyhocks, echiums, cornus giving way to agapanthus, purple and pink passion flowers, salvias, campsis, tibouchinas, clerodendrums and dahlias including dahlia imperialis.

59 **TRETHEW**
Lanlivery, Nr Bodmin PL30 5BZ. Ginnie & Giles Clotworthy. *3 m W of Lostwithiel. On rd between Lanlivery and Luxulyan. Signed from both villages and A390.* Home-made teas. **Adm £4, chd free. Sun 14 June (12-6).**
Series of profusely planted and colourful areas surrounding an ancient Cornish farmhouse. Features incl terracing with pergola, parterre, gazebo and herbaceous borders within yew hedges, all overlooking orchard and pond. Magnificent views.

60 **TREVOOLE FARM**
Trevoole, Praze-an-Beeble, Camborne TR14 0RN. Mr & Mrs Stevens, 01209 831243, beth@trevoolefarm.co.uk, www.trevoolefarm.co.uk. *3m SSW of Camborne. From Camborne on B3303 towards Helston. Past Pendarves Nature Reserve, L into lane just after 2 mine chimneys.* Light refreshments. **Visitors welcome by arrangement Mar to Oct.**
The gardens are nestled around C18 smallholding. Old farmhouse and shade garden, charming courtyard of restored granite buildings. Old orchard and herb garden. Patchwork potager. Bog garden, shepherd's hut, cottage garden and rose walk. Gravel paths.

61 ◆ **TREWIDDEN GARDEN**
Buryas Bridge, Penzance TR20 8TT. Mr. Alverne Bolitho - Richard Morton, Head Gardener, 01736 351979/363021, www.trewiddengarden.co.uk. *2m W of Penzance. Entry on A30 just before Buryas Bridge. Sat nav TR19 6AU.* Cream teas. **Adm £6.50, chd free. For NGS: Sun 29 Mar (10.30-5.30). For other opening times and information, please phone or see garden website.**
Historic Victorian garden with magnolias, camellias and magnificent tree ferns planted within ancient tin workings. Tender, rare and unusual exotic plantings create a riot of colour thoughout the season. Water features, specimen trees and artefacts from Cornwall's tin industry provide a wide range of interest for all.

Series of profusely planted and colourful areas surrounding an ancient Cornish farmhouse . . .

62 **WAYE COTTAGE**
Lerryn, nr Lostwithiel PL22 0QQ. Malcolm & Jennifer Bell, 01208 872119. *4m S of Lostwithiel. Village parking, garden 10min, level stroll along riverbank/stepping stones.* Home-made teas. **Adm £3.50, chd free. Visitors welcome by arrangement** Apr to Sept with garden clubs at reduced rate.
Never immaculate but abundantly-planted, this 1-acre cottage garden has a large and interesting collection of plants, some rare and unusual, together with delightful bonsai theatre. Wander along the meandering paths, sit on the many benches and enjoy stunning river views. Steep and sadly only for those sound in wind and limb. Attractive riverside village with pub and shop which supplies picnics to eat on trestle tables on the village green.

Share your passion: open your garden

CUMBRIA

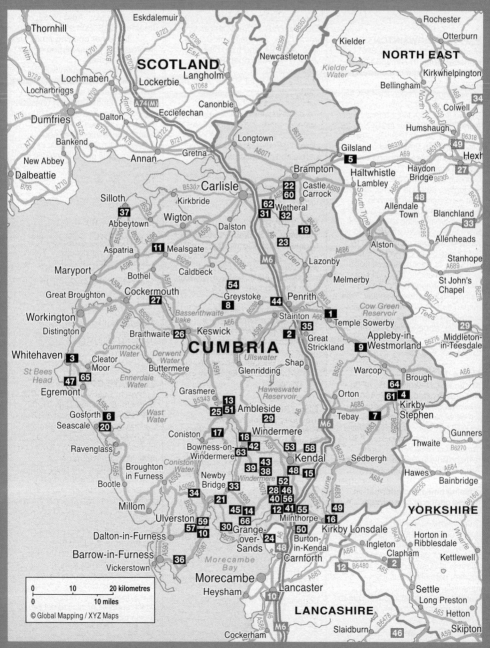

Cumbria

For over 300 years, Cumberland and Westmoreland (now Cumbria) have provided England with gardens and scenery second to none.

From Rydal Hall's 17th century Picturesque 'Viewing Room', through Dora's Field (Wordsworth's beautiful remembrance of his daughter), to gardens created by Chelsea Gold Medal winners – Cumbria is still the county to visit for gardens that encompass all gardening traditions.

All can be found in the far north-west of England, from real cottage gardens providing produce for the family, to the set-piece gardens of the great estates.

Venture into Defoe's 'county eminent only for being the wildest, most barren and frightful of any that I have passed over in England, or even in Wales itself', and you will be amazed by the gardens and horticultural excellence that Cumbria can offer.

Cumbria Volunteers

County Organiser
Diane Hewitt
01539 446238
dhewitt.kinsman@gmail.com

County Treasurer
Derek Farman
01539 444893
derek@derejam.myzen.co.uk

**Publicity –
Gardens & Special Interest**
Carole Berryman
01539 443649
Carole.Berryman@student.sac.ac.uk

Publicity – Twitter
Gráinne Jakobson
01946 813017
gmjakobson22@gmail.com

Booklet Production
Diane Hewitt
(as above)

Assistant County Organisers

Central
Carole Berryman
(as above)

North
Alannah Rylands
01697 320413
alannah.rylands@me.com

North East
Cate Bowman
01228 573903
catebowman@icloud.com

South East
Linda & Alec Greening
01524 781624
linda.greening@virgin.net

West
Gráinne Jakobson
(as above)

Borders Liaison
Sue Clapperton
01387 381004
charlieclapperton@hotmail.com

Left: Chapelside

Since our foundation we have donated more than £42.5 million to charity

Opening Dates

All entries subject to change.
For latest information check www.ngs.org.uk

February

Sunday 15
55 Summerdale House

March

55 Summerdale House (every Friday)
Sunday 22
2 Askham Hall
Sunday 29
1 Acorn Bank
13 Dora's Field
25 NEW High Close Estate
26 High Moss
29 Holehird Gardens
39 Low Fell West
51 Rydal Hall

April

55 Summerdale House (every Friday)
Sunday 19
60 West Garth Cottage
Saturday 25
10 Conishead Priory & Buddhist Temple
Sunday 26
10 Conishead Priory & Buddhist Temple

May

55 Summerdale House (every Friday)
Friday 1
8 Chapelside
Saturday 2
8 Chapelside
Sunday 3
8 Chapelside
39 Low Fell West
55 Summerdale House
63 Windy Hall
Monday 4
39 Low Fell West
Saturday 9
18 Gatesbield
Sunday 10
12 Dallam Tower
23 Hazel Cottage

37 Lilac Cottage Garden
60 West Garth Cottage
65 Woodend House
Thursday 14
51 Rydal Hall
Saturday 16
34 Langholme Mill
Sunday 17
1 Acorn Bank
34 Langholme Mill
42 Matson Ground
45 The Old Vicarage & Fell Cottage
Friday 22
8 Chapelside
Saturday 23
8 Chapelside
Sunday 24
8 Chapelside
16 Fell Yeat
17 Field Head
Wednesday 27
35 Larch Cottage Nurseries
Sunday 31
11 Crookdake Farm

June

55 Summerdale House (every Friday)

Festival Weekend

Sunday 7
23 Hazel Cottage
27 Higham Hall
63 Windy Hall
66 Yewbarrow House
Friday 12
8 Chapelside
Saturday 13
8 Chapelside
Sunday 14
1 Acorn Bank
2 Askham Hall
8 Chapelside
24 Hazelwood Farm
36 Leece & Dendron Village Gardens
62 NEW Wetheral Gardens
Tuesday 16
44 Newton Rigg College Gardens
Wednesday 17
9 Church View
Thursday 18
51 Rydal Hall
Saturday 20
7 NEW The Chantry

49 Park House
Sunday 21
5 NEW Braeside
7 NEW The Chantry
28 NEW Hillside
32 Ivy House
40 4 Low Pastures
49 Park House
53 Sprint Mill
55 Summerdale House
Thursday 25
21 Haverthwaite Lodge
33 Lakeside Hotel & Rocky Bank
Sunday 28
4 Boxwood House
15 Ewebank Farm
54 Stewart Hill Cottage
59 NEW Ulverston Gardens

July

55 Summerdale House (every Friday)
Friday 3
8 Chapelside
Saturday 4
8 Chapelside
Sunday 5
8 Chapelside
19 NEW Greenfield House
47 Orchard House
66 Yewbarrow House
Thursday 9
51 Rydal Hall
Sunday 12
61 Westview
64 Winton Park
Wednesday 15
9 Church View
Thursday 16
29 Holehird Gardens
Saturday 18
52 Sizergh Castle

Small stumpery, wild flower area, bog garden . . .

Sunday 19
17 Field Head
22 Hayton Village Gardens
45 The Old Vicarage & Fell Cottage
58 Tenter End Barn
Sunday 26
31 Holme Meadow
38 NEW Low Blakebank
39 Low Fell West
43 Middle Blakebank

August

55 Summerdale House (every Friday)
Sunday 2
16 Fell Yeat
66 Yewbarrow House
Sunday 9
4 Boxwood House
Wednesday 19
9 Church View
Thursday 20
21 Haverthwaite Lodge
33 Lakeside Hotel & Rocky Bank
Sunday 23
3 Berriedale
Thursday 27
30 Holker Hall Gardens
Saturday 29
56 Sunnyside
Sunday 30
48 8 Oxenholme Road
56 Sunnyside

September

Sunday 6
66 Yewbarrow House
Wednesday 16
9 Church View
Sunday 20
2 Askham Hall

October

Wednesday 7
44 Newton Rigg College Gardens
Sunday 11
35 Larch Cottage Nurseries
Wednesday 21
9 Church View

November

Sunday 15
2 Askham Hall

Over 400 Volunteers help run the NGS – why not become one too?

The Gardens

1 ◆ ACORN BANK
Temple Sowerby CA10 1SP.
National Trust, 017683 61893,
www.nationaltrust.org.uk. *6m E of Penrith. Off A66; ¹/₂ m N of Temple Sowerby. Bus: Penrith-Appleby or Carlisle-Darlington; alight Culgaith Rd end.* Light refreshments. **Adm £6.30, chd £3.15. For NGS: Sun 29 Mar, Sun 17 May, Sun 14 June (10-5).**
For other opening times and information, please phone or see garden website.
Sheltered and tranquil, walled gardens contain a herb garden with more than 250 medicinal and culinary plants. Traditional apple orchards and mixed borders. Beyond the walls lie woodland walks with a wonderful display of snowdrops, daffodils and wild flowers in spring. Dogs welcome on leads on woodland walks.
29 March, NGS Cumbria 'Wordsworth's Daffodil Legacy'. Walled gardens accessible with grass and firm gravel paths, woodland paths have steep gradients and some steps. Access map and information available.

2 ASKHAM HALL
Askham, Penrith CA10 2PF.
Countess of Lonsdale,
www.askhamhall.co.uk. *5m S of Penrith. Turn off A6 for Lowther & Askham.* Home-made teas. **Adm £4, chd free. Share to Askham and Lowther Churches. Suns 22 Mar, 14 June, 20 Sept, 15 Nov (11-4).**
Askham Hall is a Pele Tower incorporating C14, C16 and early C18 elements in a courtyard plan. Recently opened with luxury accommodation, a restaurant and spa. Splendid formal garden with terraces of herbaceous borders and topiary, dating back to C17. Meadow area with trees and pond. Combined with country market and car boot sale.

3 BERRIEDALE
15 Loop Road South, Whitehaven CA28 7TN. Enid & John Stanborough, 01946 695467. *From S, A595 through T-lights onto Loop Rd approx 150yds on R. From N, A595 onto Loop Rd at Pelican Garage, garden approx 1¹/₂ m on L.* Home-made teas. **Adm £3, chd free.**

Crookdake Farm
© Val Corbett

Sun 23 Aug (2-5). Visitors also welcome by arrangement, teas must be ordered in advance.
Large cottage style garden divided into several areas incl Japanese style, wildlife, patio, large vegetable garden with fruit trees, show class vegetables and flowers. Large front garden, 2 lawns surrounded by flower borders and small pond. Large pond with seating area leading to greenhouse of fuchsias and plants for sale. Oil paintings by local artist. Partial wheelchair access to most of flower garden. Vegetable garden can be accessed by separate entrance.

4 BOXWOOD HOUSE

Hartley, Kirkby Stephen CA17 4JH. Colin & Joyce Dirom, 01768 371306, boxwoodhouse@hotmail.co.uk. *In the centre of Hartley approx. 1m from Kirkby Stephen. Exit M6 J38. Follow A685, R in Kirkby Stephen for Hartley. From A66 exit at Brough onto A685, 1st L in Kirkby St for Hartley.* Adm £3.50, chd free. Sun 28 June, Sun 9 Aug (11-5). Visitors also welcome by arrangement June to Aug for groups of 10-30.

Take a walk through this peaceful natural garden. Packed herbaceous borders, herb, hosta and heuchera beds plus the tranquil pond are designed to be wildlife friendly. The summer house provides one of the many seating areas around the garden overlooking productive vegetable plot and fruit trees, whilst a meadow walk leads to a stunning view of the whole garden. Fenced off chicken area. Featured in Amateur Gardening.

🏵 ❀ ☕

5 NEW BRAESIDE

Bank Top, Greenhead in Northumberland, Brampton CA8 7HA. Mrs Shelagh Potts, 016977 47443, smpotts@ymail.com. *18m E of Carlisle on A69, 3m W of Haltwhistle. Turn off A69 to Greenhead & Hadrian's Wall. At T-junction turn L. Go up hill thro 'No Through road' sign 400 metres. Braeside at top of hill.* Home-made teas. Adm £3, chd free. Sun 21 June (1-4.30). Visitors also welcome by arrangement June max 20.

Cottage -style garden approx 1/4 acre with wonderful views towards Hadrian's Wall. Roman Army Museum and Walltown Crag minutes away. Herbaceous borders with interesting and varied plants - hostas, primulas, meconopsis, grasses and ferns. Small stumpery, wild flower area, bog garden. Added interest of metal garden ornaments with some for sale.

❀ 🛏 ☕

6 BUCKBARROW HOUSE

Denton Park Court, Gosforth CA20 1BN. John Maddison, 019467 25431, jhnmaddison@gmail.com. *13m S of Whitehaven. E off A595 into Gosforth, after village centre, L at fork. Next L into Denton Park, keep bearing R into Denton Park Court to number 8.* Light refreshments. Adm £5, chd free.

Visitors welcome by arrangement May to June max 16.

Small densely-planted garden with a number of compartments incl wildlife pond, shrub area, cottage garden borders, and natural stream. Also Japanese style garden area, including small gravel garden. Decking area. Decorative stone front garden. Favourite plant acers. A visitor said 'A small garden which appears to be much larger than it is!'. Increasing Japanese Garden influence.

☕

WE ARE MACMILLAN. CANCER SUPPORT

The NGS has funded 147 different Macmillan projects

7 NEW THE CHANTRY

Ravenstonedale, Kirkby Stephen CA17 4NQ. Joan & John Houston. *8m E J38 M6 (Tebay), 4m W Kirkby Stephen. From A685, follow signs for Ravenstonedale, into village.* Home-made teas. Adm £3.50, chd free. Sat 20 June (11-4.30); Sun 21 June (11-3.30).

In 'one of Westmorland's loveliest villages' (Wainwright), set around a Victorian house, with panoramic views of the Howgill Fells (very exposed windy site) mostly newly established. Formal areas around house contrast with informal areas, incl a large wildlife pond. Various seating areas and features using reclaimed materials. Garden - and gardener! - still very much 'work in progress'.

☕

8 CHAPELSIDE

Mungrisdale, Penrith CA11 0XR. Tricia & Robin Acland, 017687 79672. *12m W of Penrith. On A66 take minor rd N signed Mungrisdale. After 2m, sharp bends, garden on L immed after tiny church on R. Park at foot of our short drive.* Adm £3, chd free. Share to Mungrisdale Parish Church. Fris, Sats, Suns 1, 2, 3, 22,

23, 24 May, 12, 13, 14 June, 3, 4, 5 July (1-5). Visitors also welcome by arrangement Apr to Sept refreshments for groups by arrangement.

1-acre organic windy garden below fell, around C18 farmhouse and outbuildings, latter mainly open. Fine views. Tiny stream, large pond. Alpine, herbaceous, raised, gravel, damp and shade beds, bulbs in grass. Extensive range of plants, many unusual. Art constructions in and out, local stone used creatively. Experimental planting within clear overall design is proving exciting. Featured in Cumbria Life.

🏵 ❀

9 CHURCH VIEW

Bongate, Appleby-in-Westmorland CA16 6UN. Mrs H Holmes, 017683 51397, engcougars@btinternet.com, www.engcougars.co.uk/church-view. *0.4 miles S Appleby town centre. A66 N take B6542 for 2m St Michael's Church on L garden opp. A66 S take B6542 & continue to Royal Oak Inn, garden next door, opp church.* Adm £3.50, chd free. Weds 17 June, 15 July, 19 Aug, 16 Sept, 21 Oct (12-4). Visitors also welcome by arrangement.

A modern cottage garden with coherent layers of colour, texture and interest. From spring bulbs, through the lushness of summer roses and herbaceous plants galore, to the inherent richness of late perennials and graceful grasses well into late autumn. Plants occupy every inch of this garden for all seasons! Also vegetables in a raised bed system. Approx 2/5 acre. Part of the garden is readily accessible in a wheelchair, but the main garden is on a sloping site with gravel paths.

❀ 🚐

10 ◆ CONISHEAD PRIORY & BUDDHIST TEMPLE

A5087 Coast Road, Ulverston LA12 9QQ. Manjushri Kadampa Meditation Centre, 01229 584029, www.manjushri.org. *2m S of Ulverston on A5087 Coast Rd. 30 mins from M6 J36, follow A590 to Ulverston then L onto A5087 Coast Rd signed Bardsea & 'Coastal route to Barrow'.* Light refreshments. Adm £3.80, chd free. For NGS: Sat 25, Sun 26 Apr (11-5). For other opening times and information, please phone or see garden website.

70 acres of gardens and woodland surrounding Temple and Romantic Gothic mansion. Temple garden an oasis of peace, wildlife and cottage gardens, arboretum. Free map with woodland walks to beach on Morecambe Bay. Free guided tours of Temple and part of the mansion. Cafe and gift shop. 'It is an amazing house, one of the most spectacular in Cumbria', Hunter Davies in 'Best of Lakeland'.

11 CROOKDAKE FARM
Aspatria, Wigton CA7 3SH. Kirk & Alannah Rylands, 016973 20413, alannah.rylands@me.com. *3m NE of Aspatria. Between A595 & A596. From A595 take B5299 at Mealsgate signed Aspatria. After 2m turn sharp R in Watch Hill signed Crookdake. House 1m on L.* Home-made teas. **Adm £3.50, chd free. Sun 31 May (1-5).** Visitors also welcome by arrangement June to July 10+.
Windswept informal farmhouse (not open) garden with a careful colour combination of planting sympathetic to the landscape incl various different areas with densely planted herbaceous borders, vegetable patch, wild meadow and large pond area home to moisture-loving plants, tame hens and wild moorhens. Opening supported by old vehicle enthusiasts. All types of old vehicles encouraged to attend.

12 DALLAM TOWER
Milnthorpe LA7 7AG. Mr & Mrs R T Villiers-Smith. *7m S of Kendal. 7m N of Carnforth. Nr J36 off M6. A6 & B5282. Stn: Arnside, 4m; Lancaster, 15m.* Cream teas. **Adm £3.50, chd free. Sun 10 May (2-5).**
Large garden; natural rock garden, water garden; wood walks, lawns, shrubs. C19 cast iron orangery. limited wheelchair access deep gravel paths.

13 ◆ DORA'S FIELD
Rydal, Ambleside LA22 9LX. National Trust, www.nationaltrust.org.uk. *1½ m N of Ambleside. Follow A591 from Ambleside to Rydal. Dora's Field is next to St Mary's Church.* **Adm by donation. For NGS: Sun 29 Mar (11-4).** For other opening times and information, please phone or see garden website.
Named for Dora, the daughter of the

poet William Wordsworth. Wordsworth planned to build a house on the land but, after her early death, he planted the area with daffodils in her memory. Now known as Dora's field the area is renowned for its spring display of daffodils. 29 March; Wordsworth's Daffodil Legacy.

> Various seating areas and features using reclaimed materials. Garden - and gardener! - still very much 'work in progress' . . .

14 ELLER HOW HOUSE
Lindale, Grange-Over-Sands LA11 6NA. John & Helen Churchill, 015395 32479, ellerhowhouse@hotmail.co.uk. *Off A590 above Lindale. East of the A590 on the Lindale by-pass. Gateposts with large pieces limestone & avenue of trees. Can send detailed directions by email.* **Adm £3.50, chd free.**
Visitors welcome by arrangement Jan to Oct for groups of 2 - 12.
A romantic Regency house and grounds with 12 acres of steep fellside garden, designed by the architect George Webster as his family home. Wild daffodils abound in the woods and on the hillside. Eleven acres of Repton style landscaped woodland with meandering pathways, a lake with bridge and cascade, ruined folly, reposoir, sea view and rocky outcrops. Snowdrops from mid February. Daffodils from mid March. Bluebells from mid April. Autumn colours during October.

15 EWEBANK FARM
Old Hutton, Kendal LA8 0NS. Sue & Barry Sharkey. *3m NE of Kendal. Oxenholme Stn - B6254 - Old Hutton. 3rd turning on L. R turns at next 2 junctions. M6 take J37 A684 Sedbergh. 1st R & R again. After 3m turn L. Ewebank.* Home-made teas. **Adm £3.50, chd free. Sun 28 June (1-5).**

Relaxing, rural, flower arrangers garden, friendly hens and suggestions of music. Large lawn sloping down to a stream where curved decking follows the gentle contours of the land. Planting mostly formal with areas of shade for ferns, hostas and other moisture-loving plants. Mixed borders, statues, topiary, orchard and espaliered apples. Visitor from the Owl Sanctuary.

16 FELL YEAT
Casterton, nr Kirkby Lonsdale LA6 2JW. Mrs A E Benson, 01524 271340. *1m E of Casterton Village. On the rd to Bull Pot. Leave A65 at Devils Bridge, follow A683 for 1m, take the R fork to High Casterton at golf course, straight across at two sets of Xrds, house on L, ¼ m from no-through-rd sign.* Home-made teas. **Adm £4, chd free. Sun 24 May, Sun 2 Aug (1-5).** Visitors also welcome by arrangement May to Aug groups of 15-30. No coaches.
1-acre country garden with mixed planting, incl unusual trees, shrubs and some topiary. Small woodland garden and woodland glades. 2 ponds which encourage dragonflies. Several arbours where you can sit and relax. New paved topiary garden. Many ferns in a designated area; old roses in mixed borders and a large collection of hydrangeas. A garden to explore. Adjoining nursery specialising in ferns, hostas, hydrangeas and many unusual plants. Slight rises between areas.

17 FIELD HEAD
Outgate, Ambleside LA22 0PY. Moira & Kirsty Rowlinson. *3m S of Ambleside, 1m N of Hawkshead. Off B5286 Ambleside to Hawkshead Rd on lane signed Field Head & Knipe Fold, 300yds on R after Outgate Inn.* Home-made teas. **Adm £3.50, chd free. Sun 24 May, Sun 19 July (11-5).**
A 1½ acre country garden 1m North of Hawkshead with lovely views South to Esthwaite Water and surrounding countryside and hills. Herbaceous, mixed and shrub beds, lawns, rockeries, hosta bed, vegetable garden and two ponds. Partial wheelchair access possible though there are several steep paths.

Hall Senna

© Val Corbett

18 GATESBIELD

New Road, Windermere LA23 2LA. Gatesbield Quaker Housing Assoc, www.gatesbield.org.uk. *¹/₂ m from Windermere Rail/Bus stn. From Windermere take New Rd southward (direction Bowness). Gatesbield is on R shortly after the Ellerthwaite Hotel.* Home-made teas. **Adm £3.50, chd free. Sat 9 May (2-5).**
Extensive gardens with fine collection of rhododendrons, azaleas, and specimen trees in rocky dells. Former home of Stanley Davies, distinguished Arts and Crafts furniture maker, and Emily Davies, now sheltered housing. Exhibition. Refreshments served in Arts and Crafts House, where you can view the Stanley Davies exhibition. Some gravel paths and steep slopes. Level access to Gatesbield House.

19 NEW GREENFIELD HOUSE

Newbiggin, Heads Nook, Brampton CA8 9DH. Emma & Chris Gray. *8m S of Brampton. Located between the villages of Cumrew & Croglin off B6413.* Home-made teas. **Adm £3.50, chd free. Sun 5 July (1-5).**
A village garden set on the edge of the Pennines comprising of a series of garden rooms and lawn areas divided by beech and yew hedges. Contained within are richly planted shrub and herbaceous borders in colour themed planting schemes, roses, a box parterre, an orchard area with espalier apple trees and a

productive vegetable garden. Approx 1 acre of gardens and grounds. The garden is mainly level, however there are some steps which make smaller parts of the garden inaccessible by wheelchair.

20 HALL SENNA

Hallsenna, Gosforth, Holmrook CA19 1YB. Chris & Helen Steele, 01946 725436, helen.steele5@btinternet.com. *2m SW of Gosforth. Follow main A595 either N or S. 1m S of Gosforth turn down lane opp Seven Acres Caravan Park, proceed for approx 1m.* Home-made teas. **Adm £5, chd free.**
Visitors welcome by arrangement June to Aug access via bridleway, no coaches.
Tucked away within the hamlet of Hallsenna close to the West Cumbrian coast this garden provides the visitor with many different aspects of gardening. The 1.3 acre site includes borders fully planted for year round colour and many delightful structures built to provide interest, and punctuate your journey through the garden. Plant sales, home made teas. Partial wheelchair access due to steep slopes on entry into the garden.

21 HAVERTHWAITE LODGE

Haverthwaite LA12 8AJ. David Snowdon, 015395 39841, sheena.taylforth@lakesidehotel.co. uk. *100yds off A590 at Haverthwaite.*

Turn S off A590 opp Haverthwaite railway stn. Light refreshments at Lakeside Hotel. 20% discount from Hotel Conservatory Menu on the Open Day. **Adm £3, chd free. Thur 25 June, Thur 20 Aug (11-4).**
Combined adm with Lakeside & Rocky Bank £6. Visitors also welcome by arrangement Jan to Sept.
Traditional Lake District garden that has been redesigned and replanted. Gardens on a series of terraces leading down to the R Leven and incl: rose garden, cutting garden, dell area, rock terrace, herbaceous borders and many interesting mature shrubs. In a stunning setting the garden is surrounded by oak woodland and was once a place of C18 and C19 industry.

GROUP OPENING

22 HAYTON VILLAGE GARDENS

Hayton, Brampton CA8 9HR. *7m E of Carlisle. 5m E of M6 J43. ¹/₂ m S of A69, 3m E of Brampton signed to Hayton. Maps of gardens with tickets, Park on one side of road only please.* Home-made teas at Hayton Village Primary School. Usually Pimms/Cava (+ non alcoholic equivalent) too, by an outside fireplace under a honeysuckle laden pergola - if weather suitable! **Combined adm £3.50, chd free. Share to Hayton**

Every garden visit makes a difference

Village Primary School. **Sun 19 July (12-5).**

BRACKENHOW
Susan & Jonny Tranter

THE CEDARS
Mrs Lynda Hayward

CHESTNUT COTTAGE
Mr Barry Bryan

HAYTON C OF E PRIMARY SCHOOL
Hayton C of E Primary School

KINRARA
Tim & Alison Brown. *Immed W of the village green* Visitors also welcome by arrangement Apr to Sept. 01228 670067 (ashton design) tim@tjbgallery.com

LITTLE GARTH
Dugald Campbell

Easily accessible attractive village with a green growing one of the oldest walnut trees in the country, church and Inn (weekend meals and WCs). Not far from Hadrian's Wall, Talkin Tarn, N. Pennine fells, Eden Valley and small market town of Brampton with particular attractions such as a Philip Webb church (Burne Jones stained glass). Gardens of varied size and styles all within ¹/₂ m, mostly of old stone cottages. Smaller and larger cottage gardens, courtyards and containers, steep wooded slopes, sweeping lawns, exuberant borders, frogs, pools and poultry, colour and texture throughout. Homemade Teas at the school. Pimms or similar depending on weather! Often an informal treasure hunt for children young and old. Gardens additional to those listed also generally open (eleven in 2014) and views into numerous others. Varying degrees of access from full to minimal.

 ♿ ✿ ☕

23 HAZEL COTTAGE
Armathwaite CA4 9PG. Mr D Ryland & Mr J Thexton. *8m SE of Carlisle. Turn off A6 just S of High Hesket signed Armathwaite, after 2m house facing you at T-junction.* Home-made teas. **Adm £3.50, chd free. Sun 10 May, Sun 7 June (12-5).**
Developing flower arrangers and plantsmans garden. Extending to approx 5 acres. Incls herbaceous borders, pergola, ponds and planting of disused railway siding providing

home to wildlife. Many variegated and unusual plants. Varied areas, planted for all seasons, S-facing, some gentle slopes.

✿ ☕

The vista from the top of the garden looks towards Morecambe Bay . . .

24 HAZELWOOD FARM
Hollins Lane, Silverdale, Carnforth LA5 0UB. Glenn & Dan Shapiro, www.hazelwoodfarm.co.uk. *4m NW of M6 J35. From Carnforth follow signs to Silverdale, after 1m turn L signed Silverdale, after level Xing turn L then 1st L into Hollins Lane. Farm on R.* Home-made teas. **Adm £4, chd free. Sun 14 June (11-5).**
A theatre of light curtained by backdrops of woodland. Steep paths winding up and through natural limestone cliff, intersected by a tumbling rill joining ponds, provide staging for alpine gems and drifts of herbaceous, prairie and woodland planting. Old and English roses, bulbs and the National Collection of Hepatica. Wildlife friendly garden surrounded by NT access land. New bird, bee and butterfly garden. Featured on and in BBC Gardeners' World TV and Magazine, Lancashire Magazine.

✿ NCH ☕

25 NEW ◆ HIGH CLOSE ESTATE
Loughrigg, Ambleside LA22 9HH. National Trust, 015394 37623, neil.winder@nationaltrust.org.uk. *10 min NW from Ambleside. Ambleside (A593) to Skelwith Bridge signed for High Close, turn R & head up hill until you see a white painted stone sign to 'Langdale', turn L, High Close on L.* Light refreshments. Small cafe in house part of the YHA. **Adm by donation. Sun 29 Mar (11-4). For other opening times and information, please phone or see garden website.**

Originally planted in 1866 by Edward Wheatley-Balme, High Close was designed in the fashion of the day using many of the recently discovered 'exotic' conifers and evergreen shrubs coming into Britain from America. Today the garden contains a variety of tree species many of which are the remains of the original Victorian plantings. Tree trail.

🏰 ☕

26 HIGH MOSS
Portinscale, Keswick CA12 5TX. Christine & Peter Hughes, christine_hug25@hotmail.com. *1m W of Keswick. Enter village off A66, take 1st turning R through white gates, on R of rd after ¹/₃ m.* **Adm £3, chd free. Share to Hospice at Home. Sun 29 Mar (11-4). Visitors also welcome by arrangement Apr to Sept.**
Lakeland Arts and Craft house (not open) and garden (mentioned in Pevsner). Restored over six years with help from Tom Attwood (Halecat Nurseries) and returned to the Scheme in 2010 after many years' absence. 4¹/₂ acres of formal and informal S-facing terraced gardens. Magnificent views of the fells. Many fine trees, rhododendrons and azaleas. Old tennis court converted into vegetable/flower parterre for the Diamond Jubilee. Open as part of Cumbria Daffodil Day. Photographed by Val Corbett. Featured in Arts and Craft Houses in the Lake District (Frances Lincoln), and articles in Cumbria Life.

✿

27 HIGHAM HALL
Bassenthwaite Lake, Cockermouth CA13 9SH. Higham Hall College, www.highamhall.com. *Northern edge of Lake District, between Cockermouth & Keswick. From Penrith (M6,J40) or Keswick, follow the A66, after Bassenthwaite Lake turn R. From Cockermouth, follow A66 for 3m, turn L at B5291.* Home-made teas. **Adm £3.50, chd free. Sun 7 June (11-4).**
C19 Gothic mansion (not open) set in approximately 6 acres of mature garden with wonderful open views of Skiddaw and surrounding fells. Many interesting trees and perennials, stream with wildlife pond, large lawn, raised bed cut flower and vegetable area. Woodland walks with many wild birds and a chance to see red squirrels. Plant sales.

🏰 ✿ ☕

28 NEW HILLSIDE

Hutton Lane, Levens, Kendal LA8 8PA. Miss Rosalie Sullivan & Mrs Rachel Sullivan. *6m S of Kendal. Turn off A590 into Levens village. At Methodist Church Xrds follow the rd down Hutton Lane for approx 500 metres. Hillside on L. Parking in the village, disabled parking only at Hillside.* Lemon squash on the Lawn, Pimms on the Patio, Gin & Tonic on the Terrace. **Adm £3, chd free. Sun 21 June (1-5). Combined adm with 4 Low Pastures £5.**

Hillside is a work in progress. A garden of about ⅓ acre on several levels, some of which are wheelchair accessible. Long herbaceous borders planted in an informal cottage garden style full of fragrance, colour and unusual perennials. Special emphasis on attracting butterflies and pollinators. Beautiful views across the Lythe Valley to the Coniston fells. Main garden accessible. Dogs on leads and helper dogs welcome.

Full of fragrance, colour and unusual perennials. Special emphasis on attracting butterflies and pollinators . . .

29 ◆ HOLEHIRD GARDENS

Patterdale Road, Windermere LA23 1NP. Lakeland Horticultural Society, 015394 46008, www.holehirdgardens.org.uk. *1m N of Windermere. On A592, Windermere to Patterdale rd.* Self-service hot drinks available. **Adm £4, chd free. For NGS: Sun 29 Mar, Thur 16 July (10-5). For other opening times and information, please phone or see garden website.**

Run by volunteers with the aim of promoting knowledge of the cultivation of plants particularly suited to Lakeland conditions. One of the best labelled gardens in the UK. National Collections of *astilbe*, *polystichum* (ferns) and meconopsis. Set on the fellside with stunning views over Windermere. The walled garden gives protection to mixed borders whilst alpine houses display an always colourful array of tiny gems. Consistently voted among the top gardens in Britain and Europe. Featured in BBC programme 'Glorious Gardens from Above'. Wheelchair access limited to walled garden and beds accessible from drive.

30 ◆ HOLKER HALL GARDENS

Cark-in-Cartmel, Grange-over-Sands LA11 7PL. The Cavendish Family, www.holker.co.uk. *4m W of Grange-over-Sands. 12m W of M6 (J36) Follow brown tourist signs.* Light refreshments in Courtyard Cafe. **Adm £8, chd free. For NGS: Thur 27 Aug (10.30-5). For other opening times and information, please phone or see garden website.**

25 acres of romantic gardens, with peaceful arboretum, inspirational formal gardens, flowering meadow and Labyrinth. Spring sees thousands of bulbs and flowers. Summer brings voluptuous mixed borders and bedding. Discover unusually large rhododendrons, magnolias and azaleas, and the National Collection of Styracaceae. Discover our latest garden feature - The Pagan Grove, designed by Kim Wilkie. Guided tour of the gardens, take the opportunity to tour the gardens with our experienced guide. Donation required.

31 HOLME MEADOW

1 Holme Meadow, Cumwhinton, Carlisle CA4 8DR. John & Anne Mallinson, 01228 560330, jwai.mallinson@btinternet.com. *2m S of Carlisle. From M6 J42 take B6263 to Cumwhinton, in village take 1st L then bear R at Lowther Arms, Holme Meadow is immed on R.* Tea. **Adm £3, chd free. Sun 26 July (11-5). Visitors also welcome by arrangement June to Aug.**

Village garden developed and landscaped from scratch by owners. Incl shrubbery, perennial beds supplemented by annuals, gazebo, pergola and trellis with climbers, slate beds and water feature, ornamental copse, pond, wild flower meadow and kitchen garden. Designed, planted and maintained to be wildlife friendly.

32 IVY HOUSE

Cumwhitton, Brampton CA8 9EX. Martin Johns & Ian Forrest. *6m E of Carlisle. At the bridge at Warwick Bridge on A69 take turning to Great Corby & Cumwhitton. Through Great Corby & woodland until you reach a T-junction Turn R.* Home-made teas in Cumwhitton village hall. **Adm £3.50, chd free. Sun 21 June (1-5).**

Approx 2 acres of sloping fell-side garden with meandering paths leading to a series of 'rooms': pond, fern garden, gravel garden with assorted grasses, vegetable and herb garden. Copse with meadow leading down to beck. Trees, shrubs, bamboos and herbaceous perennials planted with emphasis on variety of texture and colour. Featured in Cumbria Life. Steep slopes.

33 LAKESIDE HOTEL & ROCKY BANK

Lake Windermere, Newby Bridge, Ulverston LA12 8AT. Mr N Talbot, 015395 39841, sheena.taylforth@lakesidehotel.co.uk, www.lakesidehotel.co.uk. *1m N of Newby Bridge. Turn N off A590 across R Leven at Newby Bridge along W side of Windermere.* Light refreshments. 20% discount from Hotel Conservatory menu on Open Day. **Adm £5, chd free. Thur 25 June, Thur 20 Aug (11-4). Combined adm with Haverthwaite Lodge £6. Visitors also welcome by arrangement Apr to Sept.**

Two diverse gardens on the shores of Lake Windermere. Lakeside has been created for year round interest, packed with choice plants, incl some unusual varieties. Main garden area with herbaceous borders and foliage shrubs, scented and winter interest plants and seasonal bedding. Roof garden with lawn, espaliered local heritage apple varieties and culinary herbs. Lawn art on front lawn. Rocky Bank is a traditional garden with rock outcrops. Planted with unusual specimen alpines. Herbaceous borders, shrubs and ornamental trees. Woodland area with species rhododendrons. Working greenhouse and polytunnels. Wild flower garden and cut flower garden. Wheelchair access not available at Rocky Bank.

34 LANGHOLME MILL

Woodgate, Lowick Green LA12 8ES. Judith & Graham Sanderson, judith@themill.biz. *7m NW of Ulverston. Take A590 towards*

Ulverston. At Greenodd turn R on to A5902 towards Broughton. Langholme Mill is approx. 3m along this rd on L. Tea. **Adm £3, chd free. Sat 16, Sun 17 May (12-6).** Visitors also welcome by arrangement Apr to Aug please phone Judith on 01229 885215 to arrange.

Approx 1 acre of mature woodland garden with meandering lakeland stone paths surrounding the mill race stream which can be crossed by a variety of bridges. The garden hosts well established bamboo, rhododendrons, hostas, acers and astilbes and a large variety of country flowers. Featured in Westmorland Gazette.

35 LARCH COTTAGE NURSERIES
Melkinthorpe, Penrith CA10 2DR. Peter Stott, www.larchcottage.co.uk. From N leave M6 J40 take A6 S. From S leave M6 J39 take A6 N signed off A6. **Adm £3.50, chd free. Wed 27 May, Sun 11 Oct (1-4).**
For 2 days only Larch Cottage Nurseries are opening the new lower gardens and chapel for NGS visitors. The gardens incl lawns, flowing perennial borders, rare and unusual shrubs, trees, small orchard and kitchen garden. A natural stream runs into a small lake - a haven for wildlife and birds. At the head of the lake stands a chapel, designed and built by Peter for family use only. Larch Cottage has a Japanese Dry garden, ponds and Italianesque columned garden specifically for shade plants, the Italianesque tumbled down walls are draped in greenery acting as a backdrop for the borders filled with stock plants. Newly designed and constructed lower gardens and chapel. The gardens are accessible to wheelchair users although the paths are rocky in places.

GROUP OPENING

36 LEECE & DENDRON VILLAGE GARDENS
Cumbria LA12 0QP. 2m E of Barrow-in-Furness. J36 on M6 onto A590 to Ulverston. Take A5087 Coast Rd to Barrow. Approx 8m (opp sea wall), turn R for Leece, & a further 1/2 m for Dendron. Light refreshments at Leece Village Hall. **Combined adm £3.50, chd free. Sun 14 June (11-5).**

BRIAR HOUSE
Jeff & Gill Lowden

BROW EDGE
Mrs Lynn Furzeland-Ridgway

THE DIN DRUM, DENDRON
Adrian & Julie Newnham.
Dendron is a small village, just off the main rd between Gleaston & Leece

3 PEAR TREE COTTAGE
Jane & Rob Phizacklea

ST MARGARETS, LEECE
Lyn & Sabine Dixon

WINANDER
Mrs Enid Cockshott

Two small close villages on the Furness Peninsula 1 1/2 m from Morecambe Bay, rural but not remote, with working farms centred around a small tarn. Gardens of varying size and individual styles, all of which enjoy wonderful views. Features incl exciting and varied vegetable gardens, a willow yurt, green roof, a white garden, hay meadow with maze, mature trees, herbaceous borders, wildlife ponds and streams, bees, cottage garden, alpines, perennials, shrubs, water features, climbers... and much much more!.

37 LILAC COTTAGE GARDEN
Blitterlees, Silloth CA7 4JJ. Jeff & Lynn Downham, 0169 7332171, lilaccottage@tiscali.co.uk. 1m S of Silloth. On B5300 Maryport to Silloth rd. Home-made teas. **Adm £3, chd free. Sun 10 May (11-4).** Visitors also welcome by arrangement Apr to Aug groups welcome.
Approx 1-acre garden set in compartments in a coastal setting. Featuring raised and ornamental gardens, herbaceous borders, large lawned areas and a recently

converted sandstone gazebo into a superb garden room. Each garden has an individual theme, well stocked with plants and shrubs and seasonal vegetables.with colour and interest in early spring which continues throughout summer and into autumn. The raised garden is the only area not accessible by wheelchair users.

38 NEW LOW BLAKEBANK
Underbarrow, Kendal LA8 8BN.
Mrs Catherine Chamberlain. Lyth Valley between Underbarrow & Crosthwaite. The garden is 1st drive on R off Broom Lane, a turning off the main rd between Crosthwaite & Underbarrow. Signed Red Scar & Broom Farm. Home-made teas at Middle Blakebank. **Combined adm with Middle Blakebank £5, chd free. Sun 26 July (10.30-4.30).** Charming and secluded 3 acre garden surrounding a C17 Lakeland farmhouse (not open) and bank barn. Plenty of seating to enjoy the beautiful views of the Lyth Valley and Scout Scar. Garden under development. Mixed borders, ponds, lawned areas, topiary, small bluebell wood and vegetable garden.

39 LOW FELL WEST
Crosthwaite, Kendal LA8 8JG.
Barbie & John Handley, 015395 68297, barbie@handleyfamily.co.uk. 4 1/2 m S of Bowness. Off A5074, turn W just S of Damson Dene Hotel. Follow lane for 1/2 m. Home-made teas. **Adm £3.50, chd free. Sun 29 Mar (11-4); Sun 3 May (1.30-5.30); Mon 4 May (10.30-1.30); Sun 26 July (10.30-5).** Visitors also welcome by arrangement Mar to Nov.
This 2 acre woodland garden in the tranquil Winster Valley has extensive views to the Pennines. The four season garden, restored since 2003, incl expanses of rock planted sympathetically with grasses, unusual trees and shrubs, climaxing for autumn colour. There are areas of plant rich meadows and native hedges. A woodland area houses a gypsy caravan and there is direct access to Cumbria Wildlife Trust's Barkbooth Reserve of Oak woodland, blue bells and open fellside. Wheelchair access to much of the garden, but some rough paths, steep slopes.

Plenty of seating to enjoy the beautiful views of the Lyth Valley and Scout Scar . . .

40 4 LOW PASTURES
Lowgate, Levens, Kendal LA8 8QH. Peter & Pam Martin, 015395 60441, pammartin47@gmail.com. *5m S of Kendal. From A590 take 3rd R going W from Brettargh Holt r'about - signed to Levens Village & Brigsteer. Continue up the hill passing the Hare & Hounds on R. 4 Low Pastures is 600yds on L.* Home-made teas. **Adm £3, chd free.** Sun 21 June (1-5). **Combined adm with Hillside £5. Visitors also welcome by arrangement May to Aug groups of 10+.**
Set on the limestone scar overlooking the Lyth Valley, with magnificent views to the Langdales, this sustainable garden for wildlife, offers varied planting styles and habitats. Single, perennial flowers and mixed, preferably flowering evergreens provide food and cover for insects and birds. Totally organic and peat free. Wildlife pond. Ornamental kitchen garden. Growing collection of succulents. File of articles on wildlife gardening and sustainabile gardening available to browse through plus a range of books on the same topics. Bee conservation expert Julia Pigott will show visitors how to identify the bee species commonly seen in Cumbrian gardens. Featured in: The Lakeland Gardener, Amateur Gardening and Westmorland Gazette. No wheelchair access. Ornamental garden may be viewed from a balcony on request. Kitchen garden may be viewed from bottom path. Dogs on leads welcome.

41 LOWER ROWELL FARM & COTTAGE
Milnthorpe LA7 7LU. John & Mavis Robinson & Julie & Andy Welton, 015395 62270. *Approx 2m from Milnthorpe, 2m from Crooklands. Signed to Rowell off B6385. Garden 1/2 m up lane on L.* **Adm £4, chd free. Visitors welcome by arrangement Feb to July groups of 15+, refreshments by arrangement.**
Approx 1 1/4 acre garden with views to

Farleton Knott and Lakeland hills. Unusual trees and shrubs, plus perennial borders; architectural pruning; retro greenhouse; polytunnel with tropical plants; cottage gravel garden and vegetable plot. Fabulous display of snowdrops in spring followed by other spring flowers, with colour most of the year. Featured in the Westmorland Gazette for snowdrops.

42 MATSON GROUND
Windermere LA23 2NH. Matson Ground Estate Co Ltd, 015394 47892, info@matsonground.co.uk. *2/3 m E of Bowness. Turn N off B5284 signed Heathwaite. From E 400yds after Windermere Golf Club, from W 100yds after Windy Hall Rd.* Home-made teas. **Adm £3.50, chd free.** Sun 17 May (1-5). **Visitors also welcome by arrangement.**
2 acre formal garden with a mix of established borders, wild flower areas and stream leading to a large pond and developing aboretum. Rose garden, rockery and topiary terrace borders; white garden. Walled kitchen garden with raised beds, fruit trees and greenhouse. The garden is constantly developing and regular visitors will see changes each year.

43 MIDDLE BLAKEBANK
Underbarrow, Kendal LA8 8HP. Mrs Hilary Crowe. *Lyth Valley between Underbarrow & Crosthwaite. East off the A5074 to Crosthwaite. The garden is on Broom Lane, a turning between Crosthwaite & Underbarrow signed Red Scar & Broom Farm.* Home-made teas. **Adm £4, chd free.** Sun 26 July (10.30-4.30). **Combined adm with Low Blakebank £5.**
The garden overlooks the Lyth Valley with extensive views south to Morecambe Bay and east to the Howgills. It comprises 4 acres of orchard, wild flower meadow and plantings that take the garden through to early autumn.

44 NEWTON RIGG COLLEGE GARDENS
Newton Rigg, Penrith CA11 0AH. Newton Rigg College part of Askam Bryan College, www.newtonrigg.ac.uk. *1m W of Penrith. 3m W from J40 & J41 off M6. 1/2 m off the B5288 W of Penrith.* Tea. **Adm £4, chd free.** Tue 16 June

(3-8); Wed 7 Oct (3-6). **Visitors also welcome by arrangement Apr to Oct 15+.**
The Educational Gardens and Grounds have much of horticultural interest incl herbaceous borders, nine ponds, expanded organic garden with fruit cage and display of composting techniques, woodland walk, scented garden, 2 arboretums, annual Pictorial Meadows, Pleached Hornbeam Walkway and extensive range of ornamental trees and shrubs. Guided tour of the gardens by the horticultural team at Newton Rigg, incl the organic garden, ornamental garden, the aboretum and herbaceous borders. Expert staff available for information on courses in horticulture, garden design and floristry as well as an extensive range of land based subjects.

45 THE OLD VICARAGE & FELL COTTAGE
Field Broughton, Grange-Over-Sands LA11 6HW. Louise Shrapnel & Malcolm Slater. *1 1/2 m N of Cartmel. In the centre of Field Broughton village, next to Parish Rooms. Parking on village 'green' near to church, 5min walk to gardens.* Light refreshments. **Adm £4, chd free.** Sun 17 May, Sun 19 July (11-5).
The Old Vicarage is a small, cottage style walled garden on two levels, planted for spring and summer colour and to give year round interest. Greenhouse, vegetable area, fish pond, deep borders, lots of sunny and sheltered seating areas. Combined with the gardens of Fell Cottage and Broughton Grove, new areas of the garden are open this year to enjoy splendid spring colours and structural planting.

46 ORCHARD COTTAGE
Hutton Lane, Levens, Kendal LA8 8PB. Shirley & Chris Band, 015395 61005, chrisband67@gmail.com. *6m S of Kendal. Turn N off A590 or A6 signed Levens. From Xrds by Methodist Church, 300 metres down Hutton Lane. Park near this Xrds. Garden access via 'The Orchard'.* **Adm £4, chd free. Visitors welcome by arrangement Mar to Oct any size group from 1 to 60.**
3/4 acre sloping garden in old orchard. Plantsperson's paradise with winding paths, diverse habitats, secret vistas,

hidden places. All yr round interest and colour. Collections of ferns (100+), hellebores (70+), grasses, cottage plants, geraniums. Auricula theatres, 'imaginary' stream, bog garden. Trees support clematis, roses and honeysuckle. Wildlife friendly.

47 ORCHARD HOUSE

115 Main Street, St. Bees CA27 0AA. Dr Juliet Rhodes, 01946 824510, juliet.rhodes3@virgin.net. *From railway stn approx 500yds up hill (towards Egremont). Free parking at stn, limited on street parking. From Main St, wooden gates to gravel drive.* Home-made teas. **Adm £3, chd free. Sun 5 July (10.30-5.30). Visitors also welcome by arrangement Mar to Aug.** Surprisingly generous secluded cottage style garden behind Georgian house on village main street sheltered from coastal winds by tall trees. Designed and developed by owner since 2005 it's varied planting is enhanced by local red sandstone in walls and paving. Features incl a well, woodland area, stumpery, greenhouse, vegetable plot, espaliered fruit trees, gravel garden, bees and hens.

48 8 OXENHOLME ROAD

Kendal LA9 7NJ. Mr & Mrs John & Frances Davenport, 01539 720934, frandav8@btinternet.com. *SE Kendal. From A65 (Burton Rd, Kendal/Kirkby Lonsdale) take B6254 (Oxenholme Rd). No.8 is 1st house on L beyond red post box.* Light refreshments. **Adm £3.50, chd free. Sun 30 Aug (10-4). Visitors also welcome by arrangement May to July for groups of 10 - 25.** Artist and potters garden of approx ½ acre of mixed planting designed for year-round interest, incl two small ponds. The garden runs all round the house with a gravel garden at the front, as well as a number of woodland plant areas. Garden essentially level, but access to WC is up steps.

49 PARK HOUSE

Barbon, Kirkby Lonsdale LA6 2LG. Mr & Mrs P Pattison, 015242 76346, philip@ppattison.co.uk. *2½ m N of Kirkby Lonsdale. Off A683 Kirkby Lonsdale to Sedburgh rd. Follow signs into Barbon Village.* Home-made teas. **Adm £5, chd free.**

Sat 20 June (10.30-4.30); Sun 21 June (11-4). Visitors also welcome by arrangement May to Sept groups of 10+. Romantic Manor house. Extensive vistas. Formal tranquil pond encased in yew hedging. Meadow with meandering pathways, water garden filled with bulbs and ferns. Formal lawn gravel pathways, cottage borders with hues of soft pinks and purples. shady border, kitchen garden. An evolving garden to follow.

50 PEAR TREE COTTAGE

Dalton, Burton-in-Kendal LA6 1NN. Linda & Alec Greening, 01524 781624, linda.greening@virgin.net, www.peartreecottagecumbria. co.uk. *5m from J35 & J36 of M6. From northern end of Burton-in-Kendal (A6070) turn E into Vicarage Lane & continue approx 1m.* **Visitors welcome by arrangement June to July groups of 15+. Refreshments by arrangement.** ⅓ acre cottage garden in a delightful rural setting. A peaceful and relaxing garden, harmonising with its environment and incorporating many different planting areas, from packed herbaceous borders and rambling

roses, to wildlife pond, bog garden, rock garden and gravel garden. A plantsperson's delight, incl over 200 different ferns, and many other rare and unusual plants.

51 ◆ RYDAL HALL

Ambleside LA22 9LX. Diocese of Carlisle, 01539 432050, www.rydalhall.org. *2m N of Ambleside. E from A591 at Rydal signed Rydal Hall.* Light refreshments in tea shop on site. **Adm by donation. For NGS: Sun 29 Mar, Thur 14 May, Thur 18 June, Thur 9 July (11-4). For other opening times and information, please phone or see garden website.** Formal Italianate gardens designed by Thomas Mawson in 1911 set in 34 acres. The gardens have recently been restored over a 2yr period returning to their former glory. Informal woodland garden, leading to C17 viewing station/summerhouse, fine herbaceous planting, community vegetable garden, orchard and apiary. Opening for Wordsworth's Daffodil Legacy - 29 March.

Woodend House

© Linda Greening

Hazelwood Farm

52 ◆ **SIZERGH CASTLE**
nr Kendal LA8 8DZ. National Trust,
015395 60951,
www.nationaltrust.org.uk. *3m S of
Kendal. Approach rd leaves A590
close to & S of A590/A591
interchange.* **Adm £6.80, chd £3.40.
For NGS: Sat 18 July (10-5).** For
other opening times and
information, please phone or see
garden website.
²/₃ acre limestone rock garden, largest
owned by National Trust; collection of
Japanese maples, dwarf conifers,
hardy ferns; hot wall border with
fruiting trees. Wild flower areas,
herbaceous borders, 'Dutch' garden.
Terraced garden and lake; kitchen
garden; fruit orchard with spring
bulbs. National Collection of
*Asplenium scolopendrium,
Cystopteris, Dryopteris, Osmunda.*
Also open on **29 March Daffodil Day
& 10 Oct** for Acers, donations to
NGS.

♿ ❀ 🚐 NCH ☕

53 **SPRINT MILL**
Burneside LA8 9AQ. Edward &
Romola Acland, 01539 725168,
edwardacland@freeuk.com. *2m N
of Kendal. From Burneside follow
signs to Skelsmergh for ¹/₂ m then L
into drive of Sprint Mill.* Light lunches

and home-made teas all day. **Adm
£3, chd free. Sun 21 June (11-5).**
Visitors also welcome by
arrangement May to Sept.
Unorthodox organically run garden
combining the wild and natural
alongside provision of owners' fruit,
vegetables and firewood. Idyllic
riverside setting, 5 acres to explore
including wooded riverbank with
hand-crafted seats. Large vegetable
and soft fruit area, following no-dig
and permaculture principles. Hand-
tools prevail. Historic water mill with
original turbine.The 3-storey building
houses owner's art studio and
personal museum, incl collection of
many old hand tools associated with
rural crafts. Green woodworking
demonstrations. Goats, hens, ducks,
rope swing, family-friendly. Access for
wheelchairs to some parts of both
garden and mill.

♿ 🐴 ❀ ☕

54 **STEWART HILL COTTAGE**
nr Hesket Newmarket CA7 8HX. Mr
& Mrs D Scott. *7m W of Penrith.
From S leave A66 at Sportsman's Inn
- drive 5m Haltcliffe Bridge. Turn
before Haltcliffe Bridge signed
Newsham 2m garden 200yds on R.*
Home-made teas. **Adm £3.50, chd
free. Share to Community Action**

Nepal. **Sun 28 June (2-4.30).**
Visitors also welcome by
arrangement June.
6yr old garden comprising mainly
roses, courtyard newly designed,
organic vegetable garden incl walled
kitchen garden, potager, ornamental
pool and croquet lawn.

❀ ☕

55 **SUMMERDALE HOUSE**
Nook, nr Lupton LA6 1PE.
David & Gail Sheals,
www.summerdalegardenplants.
co.uk. *7m S of Kendal, 5m W of
Kirkby Lonsdale. From J36 M6 take
A65 towards Kirkby Lonsdale, at
Nook take R turn Farleton. Location
not always signed on highway.
Detailed directions available on our
website.* Home-made teas.
Refreshments on Suns only. Home-
made soups & bread (Feb only).
**Adm £4, chd free. Sun 15 Feb
(11.30-4). Every Fri 6 Mar to 28
Aug (11-4.30). Sun 3 May, Sun 21
June (11.30-4). Sun 21 Feb 2016.**
1¹/₂ -acre part-walled country garden
set around C18 former vicarage.
Several defined areas have been
created by hedges, each with its own
theme and linked by intricate cobbled
pathways. Beautiful setting with fine
views across to Farleton Fell.

Traditional herbaceous borders, ponds, woodland and meadow planting provide year round interest. Large collections of auricula, primulas and snowdrops. Adjoining specialist nursery growing a wide range of interesting and unusual herbaceous perennials. Home made jams and chutneys for sale. Featured in Cumbria Life.

56 SUNNYSIDE
Woodhouse Lane, Heversham, Milnthorpe LA7 7EW. Bill & Anita Gott, 015395 63249, willgottatsunnyside@hotmail.co.uk. *1¹/₂ m N of Milnthorpe. From A6 turn into Heversham, then R at church signed Crooklands. In ¹/₂ m turn L down lane.* Home-made teas. **Adm £3.50, chd free. Sat 29, Sun 30 Aug** (1-5). Visitors also welcome by arrangement June to July groups of 10-25. Refreshments by arrangement.
¹/₂ -acre country cottage garden with a well at the bottom, 3 greenhouses, pond, mixed borders and a stunning display of dahlias in August. Large, immaculate vegetable garden. Orchard with hens and we usually have chicks. Area to attract bees and butterflies. Winner of local garden competition. Featured in the Westmorland Gazette.

57 ◆ SWARTHMOOR HALL
Swarthmoor Hall Lane, Ulverston LA12 0JQ. Jane Pearson, 01229 583204, www.swarthmoor.co.uk. *1¹/₂ m SW of Ulverston. A590 to Ulverston. Turn off to Ulverston railway stn. Brown tourist signs to Hall, R into Urswick Rd, then R into Swarthmoor Hall Lane.* **For opening times and information, please phone or see garden website.**
Wild purple crocus meadow in early spring: late February or early March depending on weather, earlier if mild winter later if cold and frosty. Also, good displays of snowdrops, daffodils and tulips.

58 TENTER END BARN
Docker, Kendal LA8 0DB. Mrs Hazel Terry, 01539 824447, hnterry@btinternet.com. *3m N Kendal. From Kendal take A685 Appleby rd. Then 2nd on R to Docker. At the junction bear L.* Home-made teas. **Adm £3.50, chd free. Sun 19**

July (11-4.30). Visitors also welcome by arrangement June to Sept for groups of 4+.
3 acres of cultivated and natural areas, in a secretive rural setting. A patio garden, large lawns, herbaceous borders and a small vegetable patch. Walks on the wild side around a mere and woodlands. Many birds can be seen at various feeding stations, also waterfowl on the mere. All managed by one OAP. Rather uneven around the woodland paths. Could be difficult around mere in wet weather.

GROUP OPENING

59 NEW ULVERSTON GARDENS
Oubas Hill, Ulverston LA12 7LA. *A590 to Ulverston, parking available at Booths Supermarket. Maps available at gardens.* **Combined adm £4, chd free. Sun 28 June** (10.30-5).

NEW 1 GRASMERE ROAD
Ulverston. Wayne & Jude Evans.
From A5087 turn onto Watery Lane, take 2nd R turn onto Rydal Rd, Grasmere Rd is next L

NEW HAMILTON GROVE
Helen & Martin Cooper

NEW 11 OUBAS HILL
David & Janet Parratt.
On A590 opp Booths Supermarket

NEW 14 OUBAS HILL
Pat & Barry Bentley.
On A590 opp Booths Supermarket

NEW ULVERSTON PERMACULTURE PROJECT
Urswick Road. The Community.
From T-lights on A590 in Ulverston turn into Prince's St, following signs for Scales. Pass stn on R, High School on L, then R into Urswick Rd after dip in rd www.ulverstonpermaculturepro ject.co.uk

NEW WREAY
North Lonsdale Road. Jeniffer & Maurice Snell.
S of A590 into North Lonsdale Rd. Garden on R immed under railway bridge

Diverse gardens in and around Ulverston; town, permaculture and hillside gardens. 1 Grasmere Road small low maintenance garden with a Mediterranean feel. It features decking, paving, gravel areas, pergolas, rockeries, ponds, a bridge and several water features. Hamilton Grove the garden slopes down from a large terrace, through beds planted with herbaceous perennials, to a now dry feeder stream for the Ulverston canal. A large collection of scented-leaved pelargoniums.11 Oubas Hill is a hillside garden. The flower beds around the lawn have mixed planting and small orchard. A walk leads to the summerhouse and greenhouse with various types of fruit and vegetables. The vista from the top of the garden looks towards Morecambe Bay in the distance. A working potter. 14 Oubas hillside garden with steep meandering paths, densely planted beds, ponds, patio and summer house. Bees and rescue chickens. Terraced front garden with vegetable, fruit and herbaceous areas. Ulverston Permaculture is all about establishing a self-sustaining community that cares for the earth, cares for other people and shares the surplus. There are about 15-20 regulars that come to the project to help develop this land into a permaculture site and others who dip in and out. People contribute their skills and spare resources and share the produce. Wreay mature garden with dwarf conifers, rhododendrons and hidden surprise. Garden landscaped around a 32mm and 45mm model railway featuring live steam locomotives and rolling stock. Also a small collection of antique horse drawn vehicles As well as a potter, model railway, horse drawn vehicles and children's quizzes.

Look out for the NGS yellow arrows …

60 WEST GARTH COTTAGE
Hayton, Brampton CA8 9HL.
Debbie Jenkins, www.westgarth-cottage-gardens.co.uk. *5m E of Carlisle. M6 J43 E A69 5m E of Carlisle, 3m W of Brampton. Turn for Hayton. Park in central village, cottage 2 mins walk.* **Adm £3.50, chd free.** Sun 19 Apr, Sun 10 May (1-5).
An Artist's garden. A canvas of colours and textures. An acre of hidden walled gardens to capture and delight the senses. Parterres, stream, sculptures, sundial garden, leading to a relaxing wild garden with beautiful plantings for every season, many tulips, fragrant old roses and white perennials.. Garden studio/gift shop, Cottage perennials. Artists garden, with many metal sculptures. For further information please see garden website. Featured in Cumbria Life magazine. Wheelchair access is easier by back gates (by prior arrangement).
&. 🐕 ❀ 🍵

61 WESTVIEW
Fletcher Hill, Kirkby Stephen CA17 4QQ. Reg & Irene Metcalfe. *Kirkby Stephen town centre, T-lights opp Antiques & Collectables.* **Combined adm with Winton Park £5, chd free.** Sun 12 July (11-5).
Tucked away behind the town centre, this secret walled cottage garden is a little haven. The main garden is filled with perennials, shrubs and large collection of hostas, with small wildlife pond. The adjacent prairie-style nursery beds are at their best in July.
&. ❀ 🍵

GROUP OPENING

62 NEW WETHERAL GARDENS
Carlisle CA4 8JG. *4m E of Carlisle. Situated 2m from both J42 & J43 off the M6 motorway or approx 1m off the A69 Carlisle to Newcastle rd.* Home-made teas in Wetheral Community Hall. **Combined adm £3.50, chd free.** Sun 14 June (12-5).

NEW ACORN BANK
Isabel Ferguson

NEW BOWLING GREEN LODGE
Mr & Mrs J Kendall

NEW EDEN CROFT
Jack & Ali Spedding.
Opp Wetheral Church

NEW EDENSIDE HOUSE
Mary Beresford-Jones

NEW 5 GOOSE GARTH
Paul & Celia Diggle

NEW GREEN FARM
The Green. June Swinhoe

NEW HIGH CROFT
Sheila Clarke

NEW HIGH CROFT HOUSE
Rosemary & Peter Harman

NEW HILLCREST
Joyce Johnston

NEW HOWARD COTTAGE
Pat Howe.
100yds N of Viaduct Bridge, on R of riverside rd. Approaching from Warwick Bridge end it is 1st house

NEW ROTHAY
Plains Road. John & Heather Park

NEW STATION MASTER HOUSE
Judith Jansen.
Past Crown Hotel & leave vehicle in parking area. Garden is over the railway footbridge

NEW WHITEGATE
Anne & Trevor Dearnley.
Centre of Wetheral Village - 100 metres W of shop/cafe

A trail of village gardens around Wetheral incl village, alpine, herbaceous, kitchen, vegetable, and allotments both large and small. Acorn Bank a medium sized garden with herbaceous borders, gravel garden, orchard and vegetable patch. Bowling Green Lodge is a private garden in the Eden valley. Eden Croft a large children friendly garden with sweeping lawns and fantastic views. Edenside House is beside the R Eden. A natural garden dominated by the rear sandstone rock face, combining hard landscaping, raised beds and lawn. 5 Goose Garth an average sized family garden on two levels with herbaceous border, lawn, fruit beds, rockery and small water feature. High Croft a large cottage garden with vegetable plot. High Croft House is a relatively new garden with raised beds and interesting planting. Hillcrest small garden with open views clipped shrubs and trees, stone toughs, small pond and interesting plants. Howard Cottage a 'cottage garden' which slopes down towards the river bank. It has a pond with tench and goldfish, many shrubs and a small terrace garden at the front of the house. Many of the plants grown are enjoyed by those with a love of flower arranging. Rothay traditional country garden with lawns and mixed borders comprising colour and textured planting with an assortment of container plants. Station Master House is a perennial cottage style planting, vegetable plots and small orchard. Walled patio area, stone steps. Whitegate mixed garden - vegetables and fruit - lawn with flower beds. Partial wheelchair access for some areas..
🍵

A trail of village gardens around Wetheral including cottage, alpine, herbaceous, kitchen, vegetable, and allotments . . .

63 WINDY HALL
Crook Road, Windermere LA23 3JA. Diane & David Kinsman, 015394 46238, dhewitt.kinsman@gmail.com. *¹/₂ m S of Bowness-on-Windermere. On western end of B5284 (Crook Rd) up Linthwaite House Hotel driveway.* Home-made teas. **Adm £4.50, chd free.** Sun 3 May, Sun 7 June (10-5). Visitors also welcome by arrangement Apr to Aug guided tours for group of 8+.
2 people, 4-acres, 6ft rain, 30+ gardening years. Fellside woodland with rhododendrons, camellias, magnolias, hydrangeas, bluebells and foxgloves. Pond, kitchen, 'privy' and 'Best' gardens, Japanese influenced quarry garden. Waterfowl garden with stewartias and large gunneras, alpine area with little gunneras. Moss path and wild flower meadow. Abundant wildlife, many native birds nesting in the garden. Exotic waterfowl and pheasants. National Collections of *Aruncus* and *Filipendula*. Black, multi-horned Hebridean sheep. Featured in Sunday Telegraph.
❀ 🚐 🛏 🍵

64 WINTON PARK

Appleby Road, Kirkby Stephen CA17 4PG. Mr Anthony Kilvington. *2m N of Kirkby Stephen. On A685 turn L signed Gt Musgrave/Warcop (B6259). After approx 1m turn L as signed.* Light refreshments. **Combined adm with Westview £5, chd free. Sun 12 July (11-5).**
3-acre country garden bordered by the Banks of the R Eden with stunning views. Many fine conifers, acers and rhododendrons, herbaceous borders, hostas, ferns, grasses and several hundred roses. Four formal ponds plus rock pool. Partial wheelchair access.

  ♿ ☕

65 WOODEND HOUSE

Woodend, Egremont CA22 2TA. Grainne & Richard Jakobson, 01946 813017, gmjakobson22@gmail.com. *2m S of Whitehaven. Take the A595 from Whitehaven towards Egremont. On leaving Bigrigg take 1st turn L. Go down hill, garden at bottom on R opp Woodend Farm.* Home-made teas. **Adm £3, chd free. Sun 10 May (11-5.30). Visitors also welcome by arrangement Feb to Oct max 12.**
Secluded garden in quiet location set against background of mature trees. Relaxed style of planting, colour themed with unusual plants. The garden, mainly on a slope, surrounds an attractive Georgian house with meandering gravel paths. A wildlife friendly garden incl small wildlife pond, summer wild flower meadow and mini native woodland and shady walk. Plants sale, homemade teas, mini-quiz for children.

  ❀ ☕

66 YEWBARROW HOUSE

Hampsfell Road, Grange-over-Sands LA11 6BE. Jonathan & Margaret Denby, 015395 32469, jonathan@bestlakesbreaks.co.uk, www.yewbarrowhouse.co.uk. *¼ m from town centre. Proceed along Hampsfell Rd passing a house called Yewbarrow to brow of hill then turn L onto a lane signed 'Charney Wood/Yewbarrow Wood' & sharp L again.* Cream teas. **Adm £4, chd free. Suns 7 June, 5 July, 2 Aug, 6 Sept (11-4). Visitors also welcome by arrangement May to Oct.** Morning coffee, tea with biscuits for groups £2 a head.
Mediterranean style garden on 4½ -acre elevated site with magnificent views over Morecambe Bay. The garden features a restored walled Victorian kitchen garden; Italianate terrace garden; exotic gravel garden; fern garden, Japanese Hot Spring pool. Dahlia trial beds, Orangery, Sculpture and Sensory gardens. A starred garden in the Good Gardens Guide.

   ❀ ☕

Holehird Gardens

© Joe Wainwright

DERBYSHIRE

Derbyshire

Derbyshire is the county where the Midlands meet the North, and visitors are attracted to the rugged hills of the High Peak, the high moorlands near Sheffield and the unspoilt countryside of the Dales.

Above: 10 Chestnut Way

There are many stately homes in the county with world famous gardens, delightful private country gardens, and interesting small cottage and town gardens.

Some of the northern gardens have spectacular views across the Peak District; their planting reflecting the rigours of the climate and long, cold winters. In the Derbyshire Dales, stone walls give way to hedges and the countryside is hilly with many trees, good agricultural land and very pretty villages.

South of Derby the land is much flatter, the architecture has a Midlands look with red brick replacing stone and softer planting in the gardens.

The east side of Derbyshire is different again, reflecting the recent past with small pit villages, and looking towards the rolling countryside of Nottinghamshire. There are fast road links with other parts of the country via the M1 and M6, making a day trip to Derbyshire an easy choice.

Derbyshire Volunteers

County Organiser
Irene Dougan
01335 370958
emily.dougan@btinternet.com

County Treasurer
Robert Little
01283 702267
rlittleq@gmail.com

Publicity
Irene Dougan
(as above)

Booklet Coordinator
Dave Darwent
01142 665881
dave@poptasticdave.co.uk

Assistant County Organisers
Dave Darwent
(as above)

Gill and Colin Hancock
01159 301061
gillandcolin@tiscali.co.uk

Jane Lennox
01663 732381
jane@lennoxonline.net

Pauline Little
01283 702267
plittle@hotmail.co.uk

Christine Sanderson
01246 570830
christine.r.sanderson@uwclub.net

Peter & Kate Spencer
01629 822499
pandkspencer@yahoo.co.uk

Opening Dates

All entries subject to change.
For latest information check www.ngs.org.uk

March

Sunday 15
- 6 Bluebell Arboretum and Nursery

Sunday 29
- 6 Bluebell Arboretum and Nursery
- 14 Chevin Brae
- 24 Dove Cottage
- 30 37 High Street, Repton

April

Monday 6
- 8 The Burrows Gardens

Saturday 11
- 35 The Leylands

Sunday 12
- 4 334 Belper Road
- 6 Bluebell Arboretum and Nursery

Saturday 18
- 45 Old English Walled Garden, Elvaston Castle Country Park

Sunday 19
- 13 10 Chestnut Way

Sunday 26
- 6 Bluebell Arboretum and Nursery

May

Sunday 3
- 42 Moorfields

Monday 4
- 1 12 Ansell Road
- 8 The Burrows Gardens

Tuesday 5
- 50 Renishaw Hall & Gardens

Sunday 10
- 18 Coxbench Hall
- 53 Tilford House

Sunday 17
- 4 334 Belper Road
- 6 Bluebell Arboretum and Nursery
- 27 Gamesley Fold Cottage
- 46 The Paddock
- 63 Windward

Saturday 23
- 23 NEW 77 Devonshire Road

- 24 Dove Cottage
- 44 9 Newfield Crescent

Sunday 24
- 1 12 Ansell Road
- 23 NEW 77 Devonshire Road
- 24 Dove Cottage
- 44 9 Newfield Crescent
- 55 NEW 12 Water Lane

Monday 25
- 1 12 Ansell Road
- 8 The Burrows Gardens
- 13 10 Chestnut Way
- 54 Tissington Hall
- 55 NEW 12 Water Lane

Saturday 30
- 40 Melbourne Hall Gardens
- 49 Rectory House

Sunday 31
- 2 Askew Cottage
- 6 Bluebell Arboretum and Nursery
- 15 13 Chiltern Drive
- 27 Gamesley Fold Cottage
- 40 Melbourne Hall Gardens
- 58 Westgate

June

Festival Weekend

Sunday 7
- 4 334 Belper Road
- 11 Cascades Gardens
- 57 13 Westfield Road

Saturday 13
- 51 Rosebank

Sunday 14
- 6 Bluebell Arboretum and Nursery
- 8 The Burrows Gardens
- 26 Fir Croft
- 37 Locko Park
- 60 24 Wheeldon Avenue
- 61 26 Wheeldon Avenue

Wednesday 17
- 53 Tilford House

Friday 19
- 19 Craigside

Saturday 20
- 19 Craigside
- 33 NEW Hollies Farm Plant Centre

Sunday 21
- 1 12 Ansell Road
- 12 Cherry Hill
- 19 Craigside

- 33 NEW Hollies Farm Plant Centre
- 41 Meynell Langley Trials Garden

Saturday 27
- 25 Elmton Gardens

Sunday 28
- 6 Bluebell Arboretum and Nursery
- 16 Clovermead
- 25 Elmton Gardens
- 29 High Roost
- 30 37 High Street, Repton
- 36 The Lilies
- 42 Moorfields
- 58 Westgate
- 59 Wharfedale

WE ARE MACMILLAN.
CANCER SUPPORT

2015 sees the NGS total to Macmillan pass £15 million

July

Saturday 4
- 62 26 Windmill Rise

Sunday 5
- 62 26 Windmill Rise

Tuesday 7
- 50 Renishaw Hall & Gardens

Saturday 11
- 39 2 Manvers Street
- 43 New Mills School

Sunday 12
- 6 Bluebell Arboretum and Nursery
- 8 The Burrows Gardens
- 11 Cascades Gardens
- 39 2 Manvers Street
- 43 New Mills School
- 56 NEW Weleda Herb Garden
- 64 Woodend Cottage

Saturday 18
- 3 Barlborough Gardens
- 10 Calke Abbey

Sunday 19
- 3 Barlborough Gardens
- 21 8 Curzon Lane
- 41 Meynell Langley Trials Garden

Sunday 26
- 2 Askew Cottage
- 6 Bluebell Arboretum and Nursery
- 9 Byways
- 17 The Cottage
- 21 8 Curzon Lane
- 59 Wharfedale

August

Saturday 1
- 38 9 Main Street

Sunday 2
- 17 The Cottage
- 38 9 Main Street
- 57 13 Westfield Road

Sunday 9
- 46 The Paddock

Monday 10
- 10 Calke Abbey

Saturday 15
- 45 Old English Walled Garden, Elvaston Castle Country Park

Sunday 16
- 6 Bluebell Arboretum and Nursery
- 17 The Cottage
- 52 Thornbridge Hall

Sunday 23
- 41 Meynell Langley Trials Garden
- 64 Woodend Cottage

Sunday 30
- 6 Bluebell Arboretum and Nursery
- 17 The Cottage
- 55 NEW 12 Water Lane
- 59 Wharfedale

Monday 31
- 1 12 Ansell Road
- 8 The Burrows Gardens
- 17 The Cottage
- 54 Tissington Hall
- 55 NEW 12 Water Lane

September

Sunday 6
- 36 The Lilies

Sunday 13
- 2 Askew Cottage
- 6 Bluebell Arboretum and Nursery
- 8 The Burrows Gardens
- 13 10 Chestnut Way
- 18 Coxbench Hall
- 48 22 Pinfold Close

Currently the NGS donates around £2.5 million every year

Sunday 20
- **1** 12 Ansell Road
- **41** Meynell Langley Trials Garden

Sunday 27
- **6** Bluebell Arboretum and Nursery

October

Sunday 11
- **6** Bluebell Arboretum and Nursery
- **41** Meynell Langley Trials Garden

November

Sunday 1
- **6** Bluebell Arboretum and Nursery

Sunday 22
- **6** Bluebell Arboretum and Nursery

Gardens open to the public

- **6** Bluebell Arboretum and Nursery
- **8** The Burrows Gardens
- **10** Calke Abbey
- **11** Cascades Gardens
- **34** Lea Gardens
- **40** Melbourne Hall Gardens
- **41** Meynell Langley Trials Garden
- **45** Old English Walled Garden, Elvaston Castle Country Park
- **50** Renishaw Hall & Gardens
- **54** Tissington Hall

By arrangement only

- **5** Birchfield

- **7** Brick Kiln Farm
- **20** Cuckoostone Cottage
- **22** Dam Stead
- **28** Green Meadows
- **31** Highfield House
- **32** Hillside
- **47** Park Hall

Also open by arrangement

- **1** 12 Ansell Road
- **2** Askew Cottage
- **4** 334 Belper Road
- **9** Byways
- **12** Cherry Hill
- **13** 10 Chestnut Way
- **14** Chevin Brae
- **17** The Cottage
- **19** Craigside
- **21** 8 Curzon Lane
- **23** NEW ▶ 77 Devonshire Road
- **24** Dove Cottage
- **27** Gamesley Fold Cottage
- **29** High Roost
- **35** The Leylands
- **38** 9 Main Street
- **39** 2 Manvers Street
- **42** Moorfields
- **44** 9 Newfield Crescent
- **46** The Paddock
- **48** 22 Pinfold Close
- **51** Rosebank
- **53** Tilford House
- **55** NEW ▶ 12 Water Lane
- **56** NEW ▶ Weleda Herb Garden
- **57** 13 Westfield Road
- **58** Westgate
- **59** Wharfedale
- **61** 26 Wheeldon Avenue
- **63** Windward
- **64** Woodend Cottage

The Gardens

1 ▶ 12 ANSELL ROAD
Ecclesall, Sheffield S11 7PE. Dave Darwent, 01142 665881, dave@poptasticdave.co.uk, www.poptasticdave.co.uk/_/Horticulture.html. *Approx 3m SW of City Centre. Travel to Ringinglow Rd (88 bus), then Edale Rd (opp Ecclesall C of E Primary School). 3rd R - Ansell Rd. No 12 on L ¾ way down, solar panel on roof.* Light refreshments. Gluten free options and savoury items available. **Adm £2.50, chd free. Mon 4, Sun 24, Mon 25 May (12-6); Sun 21 June (2-8); Mon 31 Aug, Sun 20 Sept (1-7). Visitors also welcome by arrangement Apr to Aug. Groups 20 max. No parking for large coaches.**
Established 1930s, the garden contains many original plants maintained in the original style. Traditional rustic pergola and dwarf wall greenhouse. Owner (grandson of first owner) aims to keep the garden as a living example of how inter-war gardens were cultivated to provide decoration and produce. More detail online. Openings which extend to sunset will incl fairy lights and candles. Featured in Sunday Mirror gardening supplement; Sheffield Star; Sheffield Telegraph; Dronfield Eye; Active8; My Kind Of Town (Local History book).
❀ ☕

2 ▶ ASKEW COTTAGE
23 Milton Road, Repton, Derby DE65 6FZ. Louise Hardwick, 01283 701608, louise.hardwick@hotmail.co.uk, www.hardwickgardendesign.co.uk. *6m S of Derby. From A38/A50 junction S of Derby. Follow signs to Willington then Repton.on B5008. In Repton turn 1st L then bear sharp R into Milton Rd.* **Adm £3, chd free. Sun 31 May, Sun 26 July, Sun 13 Sept (2-5.30). Combined with 10 Chestnut Way and 22 Pinfold Close, single garden adm £3, combined adm £6 (Sun 13 Sep).**

Visitors also welcome by arrangement May to Oct. Adm £6 incl refreshments.
The rear garden comprises several different areas, all connected with flowing curved paths. Formal beech, box and yew hedges give structure and the garden features incl a circle of meadow grass set within a cloud box hedge, trained apple trees, a small wildlife pool and bog garden, a kitchen garden with raised beds, and plenty of interesting shrubs and perennials.

8 Curzon Lane

© Louise Jolley

Find a garden near you – download our free Android app

GROUP OPENING

BARLBOROUGH GARDENS

Barlborough, Chesterfield S43 4ER. Christine Sanderson, 07956 203184, christine.r.sanderson@uwclub.net. *7m NE of Chesterfield. Off A619 midway between Chesterfield & Worksop. ¹/₂ m E M1, J30. Follow signs for Barlborough then yellow NGS signs. Parking available in village centre. Coach parking available at Royal Oak PH in village centre. Map detailing all gardens issued with admission ticket.* Home-made teas at Church Institute. Cream teas at Stone Croft. **Combined adm £6, chd free. Sat 18, Sun 19 July (1-6).**

CLARENDON
Neil & Lorraine Jones

GOOSE COTTAGE
Mick & Barbara Housley

NEW GREYSTONES BARN
Jenny & Ernie Stamp

THE HOLLIES
Vernon Sanderson

LINDWAY
Thomas & Margaret Pettinger

ROSE COTTAGE
Kathy & Steve Thomson

WOODSIDE HOUSE
Tricia & Adrian Murray-Leslie

Barlborough is an attractive historic village and a range of interesting buildings can be seen all around the village centre. The village is situated close to Renishaw Hall for possible combined visit. Opening coincides with the village well dressing and St James's Church Flower Festival - free entry but donations welcome. Featured in the Daily Telegraph's NGS Gardens to visit. Partial wheelchair access at Rose Cottage and The Hollies. Access to rear of Clarendon via stone slabs.

4 334 BELPER ROAD

Stanley Common DE7 6FY. Gill & Colin Hancock, 01159 301061, www.hamescovert.com. *7m W of Derby. 3m W of Ilkeston. On A609, ³/₄ m from Rose & Crown Xrds (A608). Please park in field up farm drive or Working Men's Club rear car park if wet.* Home-made teas. April highlight - home-made soup and bread as well as cakes. **Adm £3, chd**

free. **Sun 12 Apr, Sun 17 May, Sun 7 June (12-5).** Visitors also welcome by arrangement Apr to July, **adm £6 incl tea/coffee/cake and our personal attention.**
Relax in our constantly evolving country garden with informal planting and features. Plenty of seating to enjoy our highly recommended home-made cakes. Take a scenic walk to a 10 acre wood with glades and ¹/₂ acre lake. April: hellebores and cowslips. May: laburnum tunnel and wisteria. June: wild flowers, hostas, ferns and roses. Children welcome with plenty of activities to keep them entertained. Paths round wood and lake not suitable for wheelchairs.

NGS support makes a vital difference to our patient care

5 BIRCHFIELD

Dukes Drive, Ashford in the Water, Bakewell DE45 1QQ. Brian Parker, 01629 813800. *2m NW of Bakewell. On A6 to Buxton between New Bridge & Sheepwash Bridge.* **Share to Thornhill Memorial Trust. Visitors welcome by arrangement, adm £3 April - Sept and £2 Oct - March.**
Beautifully situated ³/₄ acre part terraced garden with pond and a 1¹/₄ acre arboretum and wild flower meadow. An extremely varied collection of trees, shrubs, climbers, colourful perennials, bulbs, grasses and bamboos, all designed to give yr-round colour and interest. No refreshments at garden, but available at Ashford in the Water or Bakewell.

6 ◆ BLUEBELL ARBORETUM AND NURSERY

Annwell Lane, Smisby, Ashby de la Zouch LE65 2TA. Robert & Suzette Vernon, 01530 413700, www.bluebellnursery.com. *1m NW of Ashby-de-la-Zouch. Arboretum is clearly signed in Annwell Lane, ¹/₄ m S, through village of Smisby off B5006, between Ticknall & Ashby-de-la-Zouch. Free parking.* **Adm £5, chd free. For NGS: Suns 15, 29 Mar, 12, 26 Apr, 17, 31 May, 14, 28 June, 12, 26 July, 16, 30 Aug, 13, 27 Sept, 11 Oct, 1, 22 Nov (10.30-4). For other opening times and information, please phone or see garden website.**
Beautiful 9 acre woodland garden with a large collection of rare trees and shrubs. Interest throughout the yr with spring flowers, cool leafy areas in summer and sensational autumn colour. Many information posters describing the more obscure plants. Bring wellingtons in wet weather. Adjacent specialist tree and shrub nursery. Please be aware this is not a wood full of bluebells, despite the name. The woodland garden is fully labelled and the staff can answer questions or talk at length about any of the trees or shrubs on display. Please wear sturdy, waterproof footwear during wet weather! Tea/coffee on request (no food). Full wheelchair access in dry, warm weather however grass paths can become wet and inaccessible in snow or after rain.

7 BRICK KILN FARM

Hulland Ward, Ashbourne DE6 3EJ. Mrs Jan Hutchinson, 01335 370440, robert.hutchinson123@btinternet.com, www.youtube.com/watch?v=G-nk3hZ6Pmo. *4m E of Ashbourne (A517). 1m S of Carsington Water. From Hulland Ward take Dog Lane past church 2nd L. 100yds on R. From Ashbourne A517 Bradley Corner turn L follow sign for Carsington Water 1m on L.* Light refreshments. **Adm £3.50, chd free. Share to Great Dane Adoption Society. Visitors welcome by arrangement May to Aug (am, pm and evening visits acceptable).**
A small country garden which wraps around an old red brick farmhouse accessed through a courtyard with original well. Irregularly shaped lawn bounded by wide herbaceous borders leading to duck pond and

pet's memorial garden. A description that did not disappoint - Ashbourne Telegraph. Garden can be viewed online on Peak District TV. Level garden, some uneven flagstones, gravel drive.

8 ◆ THE BURROWS GARDENS
Burrows Lane, Brailsford DE6 3BU. Mr B C Dalton, 01335 360745, www.burrowsgardens.com. *5m SE of Ashbourne; 5m NW of Derby. Look for yellow AA signs. A52 from Derby: turn L opp sign for Wild Park Leisure 1m before village of Brailsford. ¹/₄ m.* Home-made teas. **Adm £5, chd free. For NGS: Mon 6 Apr, Mon 4, Mon 25 May, Sun 14 June, Sun 12 July, Mon 31 Aug, Sun 13 Sept (10.30-4.30). For other opening times and information, please phone or see garden website.** 5 acres of stunning garden set in beautiful countryside where immaculate lawns show off exotic rare plants and trees, mixing with old favourites in this outstanding garden. A huge variety of styles from temple to Cornish, Italian and English, gloriously designed and displayed. This is a must-see garden. Open every Tues, Fri, and Sun from April - September incl. Look out for Special events such as Shakespeare productions and Wine tasting. Refreshments can be provided for pre booked groups. Featured in The Derbyshire magazine, Derby evening telegraph, on Radio Derby and other publications. Most of garden accessible to wheelchairs.

9 BYWAYS
7A Brookfield Avenue, Brookside, Chesterfield S40 3NX. Terry & Eileen Kelly, 01246 566376, telkel1@aol.com. *1¹/₂ m W of Chesterfield. Follow A619 from Chesterfield towards Baslow. Brookfield Av is 2nd R after Brookfield Sch. Please park on Chatsworth Rd (A619).* Home-made teas. **Adm £3, chd free. Share to Ashgate Hospice. Sun 26 July (12.30-5).** Visitors also welcome by arrangement July to Aug, adm £5.50, chd free. Chesterfield in Bloom results: Previous winners of the Best Back Garden over 80sq m, and Best Container Garden and Best Hanging Basket. Well established perennial borders incl helenium, monardas,

phlox, penstenom, grasses, acers (30+), giving a very colourful display. Rock and alpine gardens and planters containing hostas 42, Fuchsia 40, ferns and roses. 5 seating areas. Featured in Garden News, Garden of the Week and Derbyshire Reflections.

A huge variety of styles from temple to Cornish, Italian and English, gloriously displayed . . .

10 ◆ CALKE ABBEY
Ticknall DE73 7LE. National Trust, 01332 865587, www.nationaltrust.org.uk. *10m S of Derby.* On A514 at Ticknall between Swadlincote & Melbourne. Light refreshments. **Adm £8, chd £4 (incl parking, entrance to park and stable). For NGS: Sat 18 July, Mon 10 Aug (10-5). For other opening times and information, please phone or see garden website.** Late C18 walled gardens gradually repaired over the last 25yrs. Flower garden with summer bedding, herbaceous borders and the unique auricula theatre. Georgian orangery, impressive collection of glasshouses and garden buildings. Icehouse and recently repaired grotto. Vegetable garden growing heirloom varieties of fruit and vegetables, often on sale to visitors. Restaurant at main visitor facilities for light refreshments and locally sourced food. Kiosk in gardens serving teas, coffees, ice cream and cake. Electric buggy available for those with mobility problems.

11 ◆ CASCADES GARDENS
Clatterway, Bonsall, Matlock DE4 2AH. Alan & Alesia Clements, 01629 822813, www.derbyshiregarden.com. *5m SW of Matlock. From Cromford A6 T-lights turn towards Wirksworth. Turn R along Via Gellia, signed Buxton & Bonsall. After 1m turn R up hill towards Bonsall. Cascades on R at top of hill before village.* Cream teas. **Adm £4, chd free. For NGS: Sun 7 June, Sun 12 July (10-5). For other opening times and information, please phone or see garden website.** Fascinating 4 acre garden in spectacular natural surroundings with woodland, high cliffs, stream, ponds, a ruined corn mill and old lead mine. Secluded garden rooms provide peaceful views of the extensive collection of unusual plants, shrubs and trees. Featured on BBC East Midlands Today. Gravel paths, some steep slopes.

12 ◆ CHERRY HILL
The Nook, Eyam S32 5QP. June Elizabeth Skinner, 01433 631036, juneliza.s@btinternet.com, www.peakdistrictart.com. *6m NW of Chatsworth in Peak National Park. Off A623. In Eyam past church on R take 1st R up Hawkhill Rd. Car Park opp museum. 200yds up hill walk on to The Nook, entrance drive on R. Disabled parking at Cherry Hill up drive next to house.* Home-made teas. Delicious cakes baked by my husband. **Adm £3.50, chd free. Sun 21 June (1-5).** Visitors also welcome by arrangement May to June. One acre naturally planted artists' garden. The S facing aspect with beautiful country view. This garden has a delightful blend of herbaceous borders, secret areas, and a geranium carpeted orchard. Sculptures hidden amongst the foliage reflect the quirky and different style, which the present owner has brought to this garden. Artist's Studio open with a display of ceramics for sale. Garden sculptures made by the owner to be found around the garden. Special delight for children is a secret tree den. Featured in Sheffield Telegraph, Derbyshire Times and Peak Courier.

The Cottage

13▶ 10 CHESTNUT WAY
Repton DE65 6FQ. Robert &
Pauline Little, 01283 702267,
rlittleq@gmail.com,
www.littlegarden.org.uk. *6m S of
Derby. From A38, S of Derby, follow
signs to Willington, then Repton. In
Repton turn R at r'about. Chestnut
Way is ¼ m up hill, on L.* Home-made
teas. **Adm £3, chd free. Sun 19 Apr,
Mon 25 May, Sun 13 Sept (1.30-
5.30). Combined with Askew
Cottage and 22 Pinfold Close,
single garden adm £3, combined
adm £6 (Sun 13 Sep). Visitors also
welcome by arrangement Apr to
Sept for groups of 10+ (adm £6 incl
home-made teas and guided tour).**
Wander through an acre of sweeping
mixed borders, spring bulbs, mature
trees to a stunning butterfly bed, 10yr
old arboretum, established prairie and
annual meadow. Meet a pair of
passionate, practical, compost loving
gardeners who gently manage this
plantsman's garden. Designed and
maintained by the owners. Expect a
colourful display throughout the yr.
Plenty of seats, conservatory if wet.
Excellent plant stall. Special interest in
viticella clematis and organic
vegetables. Featured in Daily
Telegraph - Gardens to Visit. Level
garden, good solid paths to main
areas. Some grass/bark paths.

14▶ CHEVIN BRAE
Milford, Belper DE56 0QH. Dr
David Moreton, 01332 843553.
*1½ m S of Belper. Park in Mill House
PH car park. Cross A6 turn R & cont
up Chevin Rd immed on L. After 300
yds follow arrow to L up Morrells
Lane. After 300 yds Chevin Brae on L
with silver garage.* Home-made teas.
Many cakes and pies featuring fruit
and jam from the garden. **Adm
£2.50, chd free. Sun 29 Mar (1-5).
Visitors also welcome by
arrangement Feb to Oct. Please
leave message on answer phone if
no reply.**
A large garden, with swathes of
daffodils in the orchard a spring
feature. Extensive wild flower planting
along edge of wood features
aconites, snowdrops, wood
anemones, fritillaries and dog tooth
violets. Other parts of garden will
have hellebores and early camelias.
Tea and home made pastries to be
served from summer house in the
middle of the orchard.

15▶ 13 CHILTERN DRIVE
West Hallam, Ilkeston DE7 6PA.
Jacqueline & Keith Holness. *Approx
7m NE of Derby. From A609, 2m W
of Ilkeston, nr The Bottle Kiln, take St
Wilfreds Rd. Take 1st R onto*

*Derbyshire Av, Chiltern Drive is 3rd
turning on L.* Home-made teas.
Gluten free also available. **Adm
£2.50, chd free. Share to Teenage
Cancer Trust. Sun 31 May
(11-4.30).**
Pretty as a picture. A secret walled
suburban garden, every corner
brimming with plants, many rare and
unusual. Paris, podophyllum, beesia,
schefflera to name but a few and
more than 30 varieties of hosta and
lots of foxgloves. A pretty
summerhouse, two small ponds and
fernery, together with over 60 different
acers and some well hidden lizards!!
Garden is on two levels separated by
steps. Featured in The Derbyshire
magazine.

16▶ CLOVERMEAD
Commonpiece Lane, Findern
DE65 6AF. David & Rosemary
Noblet, 01283 702237,
daverose1221@btinternet.com. *4m
S of Derby. From Findern village
green, turn R at church into Lower
Green, R turn into Commonpiece
Lane, approx 500yds on R.* Home-
made teas. **Adm £3, chd free.
Sun 28 June (12.30-5.30).**
Cottage garden set in approx 1 acre.
Garden rooms packed full of
perennial flowers. Honeysuckle,
roses, jasmine and sweet peas scent

the air. Clematis ramble everywhere. Pergolas and archways give height to the garden. Fishponds and bandstand with seating. Greenhouses, large vegetable plot, wildlife orchard. New long rose walk. Pathway to village nature park and canal. Featured in Derbyshire Life Garden Weekly.

17 THE COTTAGE

25 Plant Lane, Old Sawley, Long Eaton NG10 3BJ. **Ernie & Averil Carver, 01158 491960, erniecarver@outlook.com.** *2m SW of Long Eaton. From town centre take B6540 to Old Sawley, R at Nags Head PH into Wilne Rd, 400yds take R turn Plant Lane at The Railway Inn. Garden 200yds on R.* Light refreshments. **Adm £3, chd free. Share to Canaan Trust. Sun 26 July, Sun 2, Sun 16 Aug (12.30-5.30); Sun 30, Mon 31 Aug (12-5.30). Visitors also welcome by arrangement July to Aug, adm £5.50 incl light refresments.**
Cottage garden full of colour steeped in herbaceous borders. Annual plants raised from the greenhouse. Number of surprising features. Summerhouse in a walled sheltered garden, providing a charming environment. After a short break for tea and home-made cakes why not step back in time to a bygone era and visit our Victorian nursery and the maid's room (extra cost) £2.50. Some gravelled areas.

18 COXBENCH HALL

Alfreton Road, Coxbench, Derby DE21 5BB. **Mr Brian Ballin.** *4m N of Derby close to A38. After passing through Little Eaton, turn L onto Alfreton Rd. After 1m Coxbench Hall is on L next to Fox & Hounds PH between Little Eaton & Holbrook.* Home-made teas incl diabetic and gluten free. **Adm £3, chd free. Sun 10 May, Sun 13 Sept (2.30-4.30).**
Formerly the ancestral home of the Meynell family, the gardens reflect the Georgian house standing in 4$^{1}/_{2}$ acres of grounds most of which is accessible and wheelchair friendly. The garden has 2 fishponds connected by a stream, a sensory garden for the sight impaired, a short woodland walk through shrubbery, vegetable plot and seasonal displays in the mainly lawned areas. As a Residential Home for the Elderly, our Gardens are developed to inspire our

residents from a number of sensory perspectives - different colours, textures and fragrances of plants, growing vegetables next to the C18 potting shed. There is also a veteran (500 - 800 yr old) Yew tree. Most of garden is lawned or block paved. Regret no wheelchair access to woodland area.

Pretty as a picture . . . a secret walled suburban garden, every corner brimming with plants . . .

19 CRAIGSIDE

Reservoir Road, Whaley Bridge SK23 7BW. **Jane & Gerard Lennox, 07939 012634, jane@lennoxonline.net, www.craigside.info.** *11m SE of Stockport. 11m NNW of Buxton. Turn off A6 onto A5004 to Whaley Bridge. Turn R at train station 1st L under railway bridge onto Reservoir Rd. Park on roadside or in village. Garden is $^{1}/_{2}$ m from village.* Home-made teas incl gluten free. **Adm £3.50, chd free. Fri 19 June (3-8); Sat 20, Sun 21 June (1-5). Visitors also welcome by arrangement May to Aug.**
1 acre garden rising steeply from the Reservoir giving magnificent views across Todbrook reservoir into Peak District. Gravel paths, stone steps with stopping places. Many mature trees incl 450yr old oak. Spring bulbs, summer fuchsias, herbaceous borders, alpine bed, steep mature rockery many heucheras and hydrangeas. Herbs, vegetables and fruit trees. Refreshments also available for 4 legged visitors with a selection of home-made dog biscuits! Featured in Amateur Gardening Weekly.

20 CUCKOOSTONE COTTAGE

Chesterfield Road, Matlock Moor, Matlock DE4 5LZ. **Barrie & Pauline Wild, 07960 708415, paulinewild246@btinternet.com.**

2$^{1}/_{2}$ m N of Matlock on A632. Past Matlock Golf Course look for Cuckoostone Lane on L. Turn here & follow for $^{1}/_{4}$ m. 1st cottage on bend. Light refreshments. **Adm £4, chd free. Visitors welcome by arrangement May to Sept. Groups welcome.**
Situated on a sloping, SW facing rural hillside at 850ft, this $^{1}/_{2}$ acre is a plantsman's garden. Colour themed borders, several ponds, bog garden and conservatory. Large collection of unusual trees, shrubs and perennials make this a yr-round garden but best from late May to late summer. In total over 1200 different species of plants, shrubs, trees.

21 8 CURZON LANE

Alvaston, Derby DE24 8QS. **John & Marian Gray, 01332 601596, maz@curzongarden.com, www.curzongarden.com.** *2m SE of Derby city centre. From city centre take A6 (London Rd) towards Alvaston. Curzon Lane on L, approx $^{1}/_{2}$ m before Alvaston shops.* Tea. **Adm £2.50, chd free. Sun 19, Sun 26 July (1-6). Visitors also welcome by arrangement July to Aug.**
Mature garden with lawns, borders packed full with perennials, shrubs and small trees, tropical planting. Ornamental and wildlife ponds, greenhouse, gravel area, large patio with container planting. Also recently added extra mixed borders and potager garden.

22 DAM STEAD

3 Crowhole, Barlow, Dronfield S18 7TJ. **Derek & Barbara Saveall, 01142 890802, barbarasaveall@hotmail.co.uk.** *Chesterfield B6051 to Barlow. Tickled Trout PH on L. Springfield Rd on L then R on unnamed rd. Last cottage on R.* Light refreshments. **Adm £2.50, chd free. Visitors welcome by arrangement Apr to Oct for 6+ visitors.**
Approx 1 acre with stream, weir, fragrant garden, rose tunnel, orchard garden and dam with an island. Long woodland path, alpine troughs, rockeries and mixed planting. A natural wildlife garden large summerhouse with seating inside and out. 3 village well dressings and carnival over one week mid August.

23 NEW 77 DEVONSHIRE ROAD

Dore, Sheffield S17 3NU. Ron & Pat Blake, 01142 360575, ron.blake@blake-uk.com. *Dore SW of Sheffield. Take A621 from city signed Bakewell approx 5m. Pass Millhouses Park & take 2nd R after Abbeydale Sports Club up Devonshire Rd for 1/2 m. Roadside parking.* Home-made teas. **Adm £3, chd free. Sat 23, Sun 24 May (2-6). Visitors also welcome by arrangement May to Aug for groups 10+.**
A mature garden with curved lawn, trees, conifers, numerous shrubs and plants. There are three island beds, two of which are linked with a waterfall stream leading to a pool. These are planted with a variety of shrubs and rockery plants. An interesting woodland area completes the setting. The front garden has a curved drive, lawn, shrubs, topiary and a rockery.

A garden
which needs
exploring to
discover its
secrets . . .

24 DOVE COTTAGE

off Watery Lane, Clifton, Ashbourne DE6 2JQ. Stephen & Anne Liverman, 01335 343545, astrantiamajor@hotmail.co.uk. *1 1/2 m SW of Ashbourne. Enter Clifton village. Turn R at Xrds by church. After 100yds turn L, Dove Cottage 1st house on L. Always well signed on open days.* Light refreshments. **Adm £4, chd free. Share to British Heart Foundation. Sun 29 Mar (12-4); Sat 23, Sun 24 May (11-4). Visitors also welcome by arrangement Mar to July.**
Much admired, long standing NGS 3/4 acre cottage garden by the R Dove, with collections of new and traditional hardy plants and shrubs, notably Astrantias, alchemillas, alliums, geraniums, hostas, variegated and silver foliage plants.

This plantsman's garden is noted for the number of separate areas, incl a ribbon border of purple flowering plants and foliage, woodland glade planted with daffodils and shade loving plants. Anne delivers a number of day courses for the Royal Horticultural Society in the garden, during the yr.

GROUP OPENING

25 ELMTON GARDENS

Elmton, Worksop S80 4LS. *2m from Creswell, 3m from Clowne, 5m from J30, M1. From M1 take A616 to Newark. Follow approx 4m. Turn R at Elmton signpost. At junction turn R.* Light refreshments. Cream teas also available in School Room next to church. **Combined adm £4, chd free. Sat 27, Sun 28 June (1-5).**

> **NEW ELM TREE COTTAGE**
> Dianne & Chris Illsley
>
> **NEW ELMWOOD HOUSE**
> Ian & Liz Chapman
>
> **PINFOLD**
> Nikki Kirsop
>
> **WILMOTS**
> Barbara Kirsop

Elmton is a lovely little village situated on a stretch of rare magnesian limestone in the middle of attractive farm land. There are about 40 houses, a PH, a church, art gallery and a village green. This weekend is our Well Dressing weekend. There are 3 boards to see in different locations around the village. At Spring Cottage there is a small art gallery that you would be welcome to visit and in the church there will be an exhibition of local history devised by the History Group. Food and drink is also available throughout the day at the Elm Tree PH.

26 FIR CROFT

Froggatt Road, Calver S32 3ZD. Dr S B Furness, www.alpineplantcentre.co.uk. *4m N of Bakewell. At junction of B6001 with A625 (formerly B6054), adjacent to Power Garage.* **Adm by donation. Sun 14 June (2-5).**
Massive scree with many varieties. Plantsman's garden; rockeries; water garden and nursery; extensive collection (over 3000 varieties) of

alpines; conifers; over 800 sempervivums, 500 saxifrages and 350 primulas. Tufa and scree beds. Special opening in conjunction with Alpine Garden Society summer show at Bakewell (all proceeds to NGS).

27 GAMESLEY FOLD COTTAGE

Gamesley Fold, Glossop SK13 6JJ. Mrs G Carr, 01457 867856, gcarr@gamesleyfold.co.uk, www.gamesleyfold.co.uk. *2m W of Glossop. Off A626 Glossop - Marple Rd nr Charlesworth. Turn down lane directly opp St. Margaret's School, white cottage at bottom. Parking in adjacent field. If very wet park at St. Margaret's School.* Home-made teas. **Adm £2.50, chd free. Sun 17, Sun 31 May (1-4). Visitors also welcome by arrangement May to June adm £5 incl teas.**
Old fashioned cottage garden. Spring garden with herbaceous borders, shrubs and rhododendrons, wild flowers and herbs in profusion to attract butterflies and wildlife. Good selection of herbs and cottage garden plants for sale. Featured in local press.

28 GREEN MEADOWS

Cross Lane, Monyash, Bakewell DE45 1JN. Mr & Mrs Mike Cullen, 01629 810234, culherbs@btinternet.com. *5m W of Bakewell. From centre Bakewell take B5055 to Monyash. At Xrds by village green go straight onto Tagg Lane. At 2nd bend turn R into Cross Lane.* Home-made teas. **Adm £4, chd free. Visitors welcome by arrangement May to Sept for max 16 visitors.**
Compact cottage garden surrounded by enclosures, in superb countryside with far reaching views of the Dales. Herbaceous borders, shrubs, wild flowers, lavender hedges and kit parterre in daily use filled with a profusion of herbs to attract butterflies and wildlife. Water features and limestone garden. Large greenhouse and raised beds. Featured in The Derbyshire magazine, Garden News, Amateur Gardening Weekly and Reflections Magazine.

29 HIGH ROOST

27 Storthmeadow Road, Simmondley, Glossop SK13 6UZ. Peter & Christina Harris, 01457 863888, peter-harris9@sky.com.

³/₄ m SW of Glossop. From Glossop A57 to M/CL at 2nd r'about, up Simmondley Ln nr top R turn. From Marple A626 to Glossop, in Chworth R up Town Ln past Hare & Hound PH 2nd L. Light refreshments. **Adm £2.50, chd free. Share to Manchester Dogs Home. Sun 28 June (12-4). Visitors also welcome by arrangement June to July.**
Garden on terraced slopes, views over fields and hills. Winding paths, archways and steps explore different garden rooms packed with plants, designed to attract wildlife. Alpine bed, vegetable garden, water features, statuary, troughs and planters. A garden which needs exploring to discover its secrets tucked away in hidden corners. Craft Stall, childrens garden quiz and lucky dip. Featured in Weekend Mail supplement.

30 37 HIGH STREET, REPTON
Repton DE65 6GD. David & Jan Roberts. *6m S of Derby. From A38, A50 junction S of Derby follow signs to Willington, then Repton. In Repton cont past island & shops. Garden on L.* Home-made teas. **Adm £3, chd free. Sun 29 Mar, Sun 28 June (2-5.30).**
Over 1 acre of gardens with bridge over Repton Brook which meanders through. Formal and wildlife ponds, mixed borders of herbaceous, shrubs and trees. Rhododendrons and woodland, grasses, ferns and bamboos. Vegetable garden and greenhouses, container planting for spring and summer colour and alpine troughs. A surprising garden for all seasons with interest for everyone. Partial wheelchairs access.

31 HIGHFIELD HOUSE
Wingfield Road, Oakerthorpe, Alfreton DE55 7AP. Paul & Ruth Peat and Janet & Brian Costall, 01773 521342, highfieldhouseopengardens@ hotmail.co.uk, www.highfieldhouse.weebly.com. *Rear of Alfreton Golf Club. A615 Alfreton-Matlock Rd.* Home-made teas. **Adm £6, chd free. Visitors welcome by arrangement Feb to June. Refreshments incl. Groups 15+.**
Lovely country garden of approx 1 acre, incorporating a shady garden, woodland, tree house, laburnum tunnel, orchard, parterre, herbaceous

borders and productive vegetable garden. No general openings in 2015 whilst we undertake some major work on our house and garden. Groups welcome by arrangement, we suggest February to see our Snowdrops, and come inside for refreshments. A lovely day out and you must try our AGA baked cakes and light lunches. Some steps, slopes and gravel areas.

NGS support helps to boost our profile

32 HILLSIDE
286 Handley Road, New Whittington, Chesterfield S43 2ET. Mr E J Lee, 01246 454960, eric.lee5@btinternet.com. *3m N of Chesterfield. Between B6056 & B0652 N of village. SatNav friendly.* Tea. **Adm £2.50, chd free. Visitors welcome by arrangement Feb to Nov. Groups or visitors welcome.**
¹/₃ acre sloping site. Herbaceous borders, rock garden, alpines, streams, pools, bog gardens, asiatic primula bed, and alpine house. Acers, bamboos, collection of approx 150 varieties of ferns, eucalypts, euphorbias, grasses, conifers, Himalayan bed. 1000+ plants permanently labelled. Yr-round interest.

33 NEW HOLLIES FARM PLANT CENTRE
Uppertown, Bonsall, Matlock DE4 2AW. Robert & Linda Wells, www.holliesfarmplantcentre.co.uk. *From Cromford turn R off A5012 up The Clatterway. Keep R past Fountain Tearoom to village cross, take L up High St, then 2nd L onto Abel Lane. Garden straight ahead.* Light refreshments. **Adm £3, chd free. Sat 20, Sun 21 June (10-5).**
The best selection in Derbyshire with advice and personal attention from

Robert and Linda Wells at their family run business. Enjoy a visit to remember in our beautiful display garden - set within glorious Peak District countryside. Huge variety of hardy perennials incl the rare and unusual. Vast selection of traditional garden favourites. Award winning hanging baskets. Ponds, herbaceous borders and glorious views.

34 ◆ LEA GARDENS
Lea, nr Matlock DE4 5GH. Mr & Mrs J Tye, 01629 534380, www.leagarden.co.uk. *5m SE of Matlock. Off A6 & A615.* **For opening times and information, please phone or see garden website.**
Rare collection of rhododendrons, azaleas, kalmias, alpines and conifers in delightful woodland setting. Gardens are sited on remains of medieval quarry and cover about 4 acres. Specialised plant nursery of rhododendrons and azaleas on site. Open daily 1 March to 31 July (9-5). Plant sales by arrangement out of season. Visitors welcome throughout the yr. Coffee shop noted for home-baked cakes and light refreshments. Gravel paths, steep slopes. Free access for wheelchair users.

35 THE LEYLANDS
Moorwood Lane, Owler Bar (Holmesfield), Nr Sheffield S17 3BS. Matthew Fenlon, 07956 255878, fenny657@hotmail.com. *2m W of Dronfield. Take B6054, (Sheffield ring rd/Owler Bar). Moorwood Lane is 1m from Owler Bar junction with A621 (Sheffield - Bakewell).* Light refreshments. **Adm £3, chd free. Sat 11 Apr (11.30-4). Visitors also welcome by arrangement Apr to Sept for groups 20+.**
Situated on the edge of the Peak District National Park. A 2 acre country garden on a sloping site. The garden has been developed over recent decades, as a means of accommodating the wide variety of plants, habitats and water systems. Paths winding through the plantings provide further interest. A wildlife and family friendly. Plantsman's garden. Children's play equipment. Hard drive with loose gravel surface. Most of garden viewed from grass; mostly wheelchair accessible inclines.

Enjoy a visit
to remember
in our beautiful
display garden . . .

36 THE LILIES

Griffe Grange Valley, Grangemill, Matlock DE4 4BW. Chris & Bridget Sheppard, www.thelilies.com. *4m N Cromford. On A5012 via Gellia Rd 4m N Cromford. 1st house on R after junction with B5023 to Middleton. From Grangemill 1st house on L after Stancliffe Quarry.* Home-made teas. **Adm £3, chd free. Sun 28 June, Sun 6 Sept (11.30-5).**
1 acre garden gradually restored over the past 8yrs situated at the top of a wooded valley, surrounded by wildflower meadow and ash woodland. Area adjacent to house with seasonal planting and containers, mixed shrubs and perennial borders many raised from seed. 3 ponds, vegetable plot, barn conversion with separate cottage style garden. Natural garden with stream developed from old mill pond. Walks in large wild flower meadow and ash woodland both SSSI's. Handspinning and natural dyeing display using materials from the garden and wool from sheep in the meadow. Spinning demonstration in September. Light Lunches served 11:30am to 2:00pm, home-made teas all day. Featured as Garden of the Week in Garden News Magazine. Partial wheelchair access. Steep slope from car park, limestone chippings at entrance, some boggy areas if wet.

37 LOCKO PARK

Spondon, Derby DE21 7BW. Mrs Lucy Palmer, www.lockopark.co.uk. *6m NE of Derby. From A52 Borrowash bypass, 2m N via B6001, turn to Spondon. More directions on www.lockopark.co.uk. NB. Satnav input via Locko Rd.* Home-made teas. **Adm £3, chd free. Sun 14 June (2-5).**
An original 1927 open garden for the NGS. Large garden; pleasure gardens; rose gardens designed by William Eames. House (not open) by Smith of Warwick with Victorian additions. Chapel (open) Charles II, with original ceiling. Partial wheelchair access, steps to main garden.

38 9 MAIN STREET

Horsley Woodhouse DE7 6AU. Ms Alison Napier, 01332 881629, ibhillib@btinternet.com. *3m SW of Heanor. 6m N of Derby. Turn off A608 Derby to Heanor rd at Smalley, towards Belper, (A609). Garden on A609, 1m from Smalley turning.* Cream teas. **Adm £3, chd free. Sat 1, Sun 2 Aug (1.30-4.30). Visitors also welcome by arrangement Apr to Sept.** Refreshments by prior arrangement.
$^{1}/_{3}$ acre hilltop garden overlooking lovely farmland view. Terracing, borders, lawns and pergola create space for an informal layout with planting for colour effect. Features incl large wildlife pond with water lilies, bog garden and small formal pool. Emphasis on carefully selected herbaceous perennials mixed with shrubs and old fashioned roses. Additions incl gravel garden for sun loving plants and scree garden, both developed from former drive. Plant stall has a wide collection of home grown plants and a selection of sempervivums for sale. Featured as Reader's Garden in Garden Answers. Wheelchair adapted WC.

39 2 MANVERS STREET

Ripley DE5 3EQ. Mrs D Wood & Mr D Hawkins, 01773 743962, d.s.Hawkins@btinternet.com. *Ripley Town centre to Derby rd turn L opp Leisure Centre onto Heath Rd. 1st turn R onto Meadow Rd, 1st L onto Manvers St.* Home-made teas. **Adm £2.50, chd free. Sat 11, Sun 12 July (2-5). Visitors also welcome by arrangement July to Aug.**
Summer garden with backdrop of neighbouring trees, 10 borders bursting with colour surrounded by immaculate shaped lawn. Perennials incl 26 clematis, annuals, baskets, tubs and pots. Ornamental fish pond. Water features, arbour and summerhouse. Plenty of seating areas to take in this awe inspiring oasis.

40 ◆ MELBOURNE HALL

GARDENS

Church Square, Melbourne, Derby DE73 8EN. The Melbourne Trust, 01332 862502, www.melbournehallgardens.com. *6m S of Derby. At Melbourne Market Place turn into Church St, go down to Church Sq. Garden entrance across visitor centre next to Melbourne Hall tea room.* Light refreshments. **Adm £4.50, chd free. For NGS: Sat 30, Sun 31 May (1.30-5.30). For other opening times and information, please phone or see garden website.**
A 17 acre historic garden with an abundance of rare trees and shrubs. Woodland and waterside planting with extensive herbaceous borders. Meconopsis, candelabra primulas, various Styrax and Cornus kousa. Other garden features incl Bakewells wrought iron arbour, a yew tunnel and fine C18 statuary and water features. Featured in Derbyshire Life and The Financial Times. Gravel paths, uneven surface in places, some steep slopes.

41 ◆ MEYNELL LANGLEY TRIALS GARDEN

Lodge Lane (off Flagshaw Lane), Nr Kirk Langley, Derby DE6 4NT. Robert & Karen Walker, 01332 824358, www.meynell-langley-gardens.co.uk. *4m W of Derby, nr Kedleston Hall. Head W out of Derby on A52. At Kirk Langley turn R onto Flagshaw Lane (signed to Kedleston Hall) then R onto Lodge Lane. Follow Meynell Langley Gdns.* Light refreshments at adjacent tea rooms. **Adm £3, chd free. For NGS: Suns 21 June, 19 July, 23 Aug, 20 Sept, 11 Oct (10.30-4). For other opening times and information, please phone or see garden website.**
Formal $^{3}/_{4}$ acre Victorian style garden established 20 yrs, displaying and trialling new and existing varieties of bedding plants, herbaceous perennials and vegetable plants grown at the adjacent nursery. Over 180 hanging baskets and floral displays. 85 varieties of apple, pear and other fruit. Summer fruit pruning demonstrations on July NGS day and apple tasting on October NGS day. Adjacent tea rooms serving light lunches and refreshments daily. Level ground and firm grass. Full disabled access to tea rooms.

Fir Croft

42 MOORFIELDS

257/261 Chesterfield Road, Temple Normanton, Chesterfield S42 5DE. Peter, Janet & Stephen Wright, 01246 852306, peterwright100@hotmail.com. *4m SE of Chesterfield. From Chesterfield take A617 for 2m, turn on to B6039 through Temple Normanton, taking R fork signed Tibshelf. Garden ¼ m on R. Limited parking.* Light refreshments. **Adm £3, chd free. Sun 3 May, Sun 28 June (1-5). Visitors also welcome by arrangement May to July for groups 10+.**
Two adjacent gardens, the larger with mature, mixed island beds and borders, a recently extended gravel garden to the front, a small wild flower area, large wildlife pond, orchard and soft fruit, and vegetable patch. Show of late flowering tulips. Smaller back and front gardens of No. 257 feature herbaceous borders. Views across to mid Derbyshire. Free range eggs for sale.

43 NEW MILLS SCHOOL

Church Lane, New Mills, High Peak SK22 4NR. Mr Craig Pickering, 07833 373593, www.newmillsschool.co.uk/ngs. html. *12m NNW of Buxton. From A6 take A6105 signed New Mills, Hayfield. At C of E Church turn L onto Church Lane. School on L. Parking on site.* Light refreshments in School Library. **Adm £3, chd free. Sat 11 July (10-5), Sun 12 July (1-5).**
Mixed herbaceous perennials/shrub borders, with mature trees and lawns and gravel border situated in the semi rural setting of the High Peak incl a Grade II listed building with 4 themed quads. Hot and cold Beverages and a selection of sandwiches, cream teas and home made cakes available. Ramps allow wheelchair access to most of outside, flower beds and into Grade II listed building and library.

44 9 NEWFIELD CRESCENT

Dore, Sheffield S17 3DE. Mike & Norma Jackson, 01142 366198, mandnjackson@googlemail.com. *Dore - SW Sheffield. Turn off Causeway Head Rd on Heather Lea Av. 2nd L into Newfield Crescent. Parking on roadside.* Light refreshments. **Adm £3, chd free. Sat 23, Sun 24 May (2-6). Visitors also welcome by arrangement.**
Mature, wildlife friendly garden

planted to provide all yr interest. Upper terrace with alpines in troughs and bowls. Lower terrace featuring pond with cascade and connecting stream to second pond. Bog garden, rock gardens, lawn alpine bed, wilder areas, mixed borders with trees, shrubs and perennials. Featuring azaleas, rhododendrons, primulas. Wheelchair access without steps to top terrace offering full view of garden.

45 ◆ OLD ENGLISH WALLED GARDEN, ELVASTON CASTLE COUNTRY PARK

Borrowash Road, Elvaston, Derby DE72 3EP. Derbyshire County Council, 01629 533870, www.derbyshire.gov.uk/elvaston. *4m E of Derby. Signed from A52 & A50. Car parking charge applies.* Delicious home-made cakes. **Adm £2.50, chd free. For NGS: Sat 18 Apr, Sat 15 Aug (12-4). For other opening times and information, please phone or see garden website.**
Come and discover the beauty of the Old English walled garden at Elvaston Castle.Take in the peaceful atmosphere and enjoy the scents and colours of all the varieties of trees, shrubs and plants. Spring bulbs, summer bedding, large herbaceous borders. After your visit to the walled garden take time to walk around the wider estate featuring romantic topiary gardens, lake, woodland and nature reserve. Estate gardeners on hand during the day.

46 THE PADDOCK

12 Manknell Road, Whittington Moor, Chesterfield S41 8LZ. Mel & Wendy Taylor, 01246 451001, debijt9276@gmail.com. *2m N of Chesterfield. Whittington Moor just off A61 between Sheffield & Chesterfield. Parking available at Lidl supermarket, garden signed from here.* Home-made teas. **Adm £3.50, chd free. Sun 17 May, Sun 9 Aug (11-5). Visitors also welcome by arrangement Apr to Sept.**
½ acre garden incorporating small formal garden, stream and koi filled pond. Stone path over bridge, up some steps, past small copse, across the stream at the top and back down again. Past herbaceous border towards a pergola where cream teas can be enjoyed.

Treat yourself to a plant from the plant stall ✿

Park Hall

47 **PARK HALL**
Walton Back Lane, Walton, Chesterfield S42 7LT. Kim & Margaret Staniforth, 01246 567412, kim.staniforth@btinternet.com. *2m SW of Chesterfield centre. From town on A 619 L into Somersall Lane. On A632 R into Acorn Ridge. Park on field side only of Walton Back Lane.* Light refreshments. **Adm £5, chd free. Visitors welcome by arrangement** Apr to July for groups 20+.
Romantic 2 acre plantsmans garden, in a stunningly beautiful setting surrounding C17 house (not open) 4 main rooms, terraced garden, parkland area with forest trees, croquet lawn, sunken garden with arbours, pergolas, pleached hedge, topiary, statuary, roses, rhododendrons, camellias, several water features. Newly planted driveside. Two steps down to gain access to garden.
🚾 🕷 ✿ 🚐 🍵

48 **22 PINFOLD CLOSE**
Repton DE65 6FR. Mr O Jowett, 01283 701964. *6m S of Derby. From A38, A50 J, S of Derby follow signs to Willington then Repton. Off Repton High St find Pinfold Lane, Pinfold*

Close 1st L. **Adm £3, chd free. Sun 13 Sept (1.30-5.30). Combined with 10 Chestnut Way and Askew Cottage, single garden adm £3, combined adm £6. Visitors** also welcome by arrangement.
Small garden with an interest in tropical plants. Palms, gingers, cannas, bananas. Mainly foliage plants.
🕷 ✿ 🍵

49 **RECTORY HOUSE**
Kedleston, Derby DE22 5JJ. Helene Viscountess Scarsdale. *5m NW Derby. A52 from Derby turn R Kedleston sign. Drive to village turn R. Brick house standing back from rd on sharp corner.* Home-made teas. **Adm £3.50, chd free. Sat 30 May (2-5).**
The garden is next to Kedleston Park and is of C18 origin. Many established rare trees and shrubs also rhododendrons, azaleas and unusual roses. Large natural pond with amusing frog fountain. Primulas, gunneras, darmeras and lots of moisture loving plants. The winding paths go through trees and past wild flowers and grasses. Partial wheelchair access. Uneven grass paths.
🚾 🕷 ✿ 🍵

50 ♦ **RENISHAW HALL & GARDENS**
Renishaw, nr Sheffield S21 3WB. Alexandra Hayward, 01246 432310, www.renishaw-hall.co.uk. *10m from Sheffield city centre. By car: Renishaw Hall only 3m from J30 on M1, well signed from junction r'about.* **Adm £6.50, chd £3. For NGS: Tue 5 May, Tue 7 July (10.30-4). For other opening times and information, please phone or see garden website.**
Renishaw Hall and Gardens boasts 7 acres of stunning gardens created by Sir George Sitwell in 1885. The Italianate gardens feature various rooms with extravagant herbaceous borders. Rose gardens, rare trees and shrubs, National Collection of Yuccas, sculptures, woodland walks and lakes create a magical and engaging garden experience. Wheelchair route around garden.
🚾 🕷 ✿ 🚐 **NCH** 🍵

51 **ROSEBANK**
303 Duffield Road, Allestree, Derby DE22 2DF. Patrick & Carol Smith, 01332 559161, padsmith@ntlworld.com. *2m N of Derby. Follow A6 from Derby towards Matlock. On crossing A38 island cont for 150 metres turning L into Gisborne Crescent then R into service rd.* Cream teas. **Adm £2.50, chd free. Sat 13 June (2-6). Visitors** also welcome by arrangement Apr to Sept for groups max 20 adults.
Interesting garden of variety on a gentle, upward sloping site. Access by steps and path incl colourful borders with imaginative planting and a water feature in a natural setting. Small orchard and soft fruit garden, lawns, incl a camomile lawn, rockery, shrubs, trees and greenhouse. Wildlife friendly. Children welcomed. Auricula Theatre housing a vivid display of Streptocarpus during the Summer. Running computer display in the summerhouse featuring the garden in different seasons plus photographs and wildlife information such as a checklist of birds observed in the garden. Wheelchair access to front and terrace in rear garden. Remainder of garden difficult.
🚾 🕷 ✿ 🍵

52 **THORNBRIDGE HALL**
Ashford in the Water DE45 1NZ. Jim & Emma Harrison, www.thornbridgehall.co.uk. *2m NW of Bakewell. From Bakewell take A6, signed Buxton. After 2m, R onto*

A6020. *¹/₂ m turn L, signed Thornbridge Hall. Light refreshments.* **Adm £5, chd free. Sun 16 Aug (10-4).**
A stunning C19, 10 acre garden, set in the heart of the Peak District overlooking rolling Derbyshire countryside. Designed to create a vision of 1000 shades of green, the garden has many distinct areas. These incl, koi lake and water garden, Italian garden with statuary, grottos and temples, 100ft herbaceous border, kitchen garden, scented terrace, hot border and refurbished glasshouses. Contains statuary from Clumber Park, Sydnope Hall and Chatsworth. Tea, coffee, sandwiches, cakes and award winning ice cream available. Mentioned in Garden News. Gravel paths, steep slopes, steps.

53 **TILFORD HOUSE**
Hognaston, Ashbourne DE6 1PW. Mr & Mrs P R Gardner, 01335 372001, peter.rgardner@mypostoffice.co.uk. *5m NE of Ashbourne. A517 Belper to Ashbourne. At Hulland Ward follow signs to Hognaston. Downhill (2m) to bridge. Roadside parking 100 metres.* Home-made teas. **Adm £3, chd free. Sun 10 May, Wed 17 June (2-5). Visitors also welcome by arrangement May to July.**
A 1¹/₂ acre streamside country garden. Woodland, wildlife areas and ponds lie alongside colourful borders. Collections of primulas, hostas, iris and clematis as well as many unusual plants and trees. Raised vegetable beds and fruit trees. Relax in a magical setting to listen to the sounds of the countryside. Featured in the Derbyshire Magazine, Derby Telegraph and Ashbourne Telegraph.

54 ◆ **TISSINGTON HALL**
nr Ashbourne DE6 1RA. Sir Richard & Lady FitzHerbert, 01335 352200, www.tissingtonhall.co.uk. *4m N of Ashbourne. E of A515 on Ashbourne to Buxton Rd in the centre of the beautiful Estate Village of Tissington.* Tea. **Adm £5, chd £2.50. For NGS: Mon 25 May, Mon 31 Aug (12-3). For other opening times and information, please phone or see garden website.**
Large garden celebrating over 75yrs in the NGS, with stunning Rose garden on West Terrace, herbaceous borders and 5 acres of grounds. Refreshments available at the award

winning Herberts Fine English Tearooms in village (Tel 01335 350501). Wheelchair access advice from ticket seller.

Marie Curie's hospice gardens provide tranquillity for patients

55 NEW **12 WATER LANE**
Middleton, Matlock DE4 4LY. Hildegard Wiesehofer, 01629 825543, wiesehofer@btinternet.com. *Approx 2¹/₂ m SW of Matlock. 1¹/₂ m NW of Wirksworth. A6 to Cromford, B5023 to Wirksworth, B5035 from Ashourne. Parking on main rd. Limited parking in Water Lane.* Home-made teas. **Adm £3.50, chd free. Sun 24, Mon 25 May, Sun 30, Mon 31 Aug (11.30-5.30). Visitors also welcome by arrangement Apr to Sept for groups 10+.**
Small, eclectic hillside garden on different levels, created as a series of rooms over the last 10 yrs. Incl woodland walk, ponds, eastern garden, and terrace with stunning panoramic views. Winner of Middleton in Bloom competition. Wheelchair access to front terrace and conservatory only, views over some of garden possible.

56 NEW **WELEDA HERB GARDEN**
The Field, off Hassock Lane North, Shipley, Heanor DE75 7JH. Weleda (UK) Ltd, claire.hattersley@weleda.co.uk. *Approx 1¹/₂ m N of Ilkeston off A6007. The Field is signed just before Shipley Garden Centre. Car parking at Michael House Steiner School DE75 7JH. Garden 5 mins walk away.* Home-made teas at Michael House Steiner School. **Adm £3, chd free.**

Sun 12 July (1-5). Visitors also welcome by arrangement May to July for groups 10+.
A 13 acre working herb garden which supplies fresh plant ingredients for Weleda Medicines. Registered Biodynamic for 30yrs, the garden provides many different habitats for plants and wildlife incl fixed beds, meadows, fields, ponds and woodland. Come and find out more about our medicinal plants and products, compost making, bee keeping and Biodynamics. Wheelchair access to part of the garden. Rest of site could be challenging.

57 **13 WESTFIELD ROAD**
Swadlincote DE11 0BG. Val & Dave Booth, 01283 221167, valerie.booth@sky.com. *5m E of Burton-on-Trent, off A511. Take A511 from Burton-on-Trent. Follow signs for Swadlincote. Turn R into Springfield Rd, take 3rd R into Westfield Rd.* Cream teas. **Adm £3, chd free. Sun 7 June, Sun 2 Aug (12-5). Visitors also welcome by arrangement June to Aug, adm £5 incl tea and cake.**
A garden on 2 levels of approx ¹/₂ acre. (7 steps with handrail). Packed herbaceous borders designed for colour. Roses and clematis scrambling over pergolas. A passion of ours is roses with over 40 varieties. Shrubs, baskets and tubs. Greenhouses, raised bed vegetable area, fruit trees and bushes. Free range chicken area. Plenty of seating.

58 **WESTGATE**
Combs Road, Combs, Chapel-en-le-Frith, High Peak SK23 9UP. Maurice & Chris Lomas, ca-lomas@sky.com. *N of Chapel-en-le-Frith off B5470. Turn L immed before Hanging Gate PH, signed Combs Village. ³/₄ m on L by railway bridge.* Tea. **Adm £3, chd free. Sun 31 May, Sun 28 June (1-5). Visitors also welcome by arrangement May to July for groups 10+.**
Large sloping garden in quiet village with beautiful views. Features incl mixed borders and beds containing many perenials, hosta and heuchera. Large rockery. Vegetable and fruit beds Natural pond and stream with bog area and two formal ponds. Wild flower area.

59 WHARFEDALE

34 Broadway, Duffield, Belper DE56 4BU. Roger & Sue Roberts, 01332 841905, rogerroberts34@outlook.com, www.garden34.co.uk. *4m N of Derby. Turn onto B5023 Wirksworth rd (Broadway) off A6 midway between Belper & Derby.* Home-made teas. **Adm £3, chd free. Sun 28 June (10-8.30); Sun 26 July, Sun 30 Aug (11-5). Visitors also welcome by arrangement June to Aug for 20+ visitors. Min fee applies.**

Plant enthusiasts' garden with over 500 varieties and rare specimens. 12 distinct areas incl Piet Oudolf inspired, tropical and single colour schemes. Italianate walled garden and woodland with pond and raised walkway. Japanese landscape garden with stream, moon gate and pavilion. Front cottage garden. Eclectic garden crammed with replicable planting styles. Every plant labelled. Completed in annual projects over 15yrs. Comfortable seating around the garden. Close to Kedleston Hall and Derwent Valley World Heritage Site. Featured in Derby Telegraph and Derbyshire magazine.

🌼 🚐 ☕

60 24 WHEELDON AVENUE

Derby DE22 1HN. Laura Burnett. *1m N Derby city centre. Off Kedleston Rd. Limited on street parking.* Home-made teas at 28 Wheeldon Avenue. **Combined adm £4, chd free. Sun 14 June (2-5). Combined with 26 Wheeldon Avenue.**

Small Victorian garden, with original walling supporting many shrubs and climbers with contrasting colour and texture. Circular lawn surrounded by herbaceous border with main colour scheme of blue, purple, black, yellow and orange tones. This leads to a small area at rear of garden given to more natural planting to suit shade and natural habitat. This is a garden produced on a low income budget, with varied tones and textures throughout the planting. Wheelchair access to side of property.

♿ 🌼 🌸 ☕

61 26 WHEELDON AVENUE

Derby DE22 1HN. Ian Griffiths, 01332 342204, idhgriffiths@gmail.com. *1m N of Derby. 1m from city centre & approached directly off the Kedleston Rd or from A6 Duffield Rd via West*

Bank Ave. Limited on-street parking. Home-made teas at 28 Wheeldon Avenue. **Combined adm £4, chd free. Sun 14 June (2-5). Combined with 24 Wheeldon Avenue. Visitors also welcome by arrangement May to July for groups 4+. Refreshments by arrangement.**

Tiny Victorian walled garden near to city centre. Lawn and herbaceous borders with newly expanded old rose collection, lupins, delphiniums and foxgloves. Small terrace with topiary, herb garden and lion fountain. Rose collection. Featured on BBC & ITV local news and in Period Living and Derbyshire Life magazines. Garden all on one level, lawn may be soft if wet conditions.

♿ 🌼 🌸 ☕

Come and find out more about our medicinal plants and products . . .

62 26 WINDMILL RISE

Belper DE56 1GQ. Kathy Fairweather. *From Belper Market Place take Chesterfield Rd towards Heage. Top of hill, 1st R Marsh Lane, 1st R Windmill Lane, 1st R Windmill Rise - limited parking only.* Light refreshments. Home baking and light lunches. **Adm £3, chd free. Sat 4, Sun 5 July (11.30-4.30).**

Behind a deceptively ordinary looking façade, step into an organic world of enchantment, wonder and surprises. Meander along extensive pathways lined with an interwoven tapestry of texture, colour, light and shade with a lush and restful atmosphere. A plant lovers' garden divided into sections: woodland, Japanese, secret garden, cottage, edible, ponds, small stream with some unusual specimen trees. One of only 3 Midland's finalists featured in Sky TV's new gardening programme. Featured in Belper News and the Belper 2015 calendar.

🌼 🚐 ☕

63 WINDWARD

62 Summer Lane, Wirksworth, Matlock DE4 4EB. Audrey & Andrew Winkler, 01629 822681, audrey.winkler@w3z.co.uk, www.grandmafrogsgarden.co.uk. *5m S of Matlock. From Wirksworth Market Place take B5023 towards Duffield. After 300yds turn R onto Summer Lane at mini r'about. Windward approx 500yds on R.* Home-made teas. **Adm £4, chd free. Share to Framework Knitters Museum. Sun 17 May (2-5). Visitors also welcome by arrangement Apr to Sept for groups 10+.**

A lush green garden of 1 acre, with pockets of colour throughout the yr. All wildlife is welcome, although the squirrels make sure we never get any walnuts. Winding paths make sure you don't miss anything, as something unexpected comes into view. The crinkle crankle Leyllandii hedge and a lolly holly add a surprising touch of formality. A garden for all seasons, with plenty of places to sit. Although on the edge of a small town, the garden is remarkably peaceful.

☕

64 WOODEND COTTAGE

134 Main Street, Repton DE65 6FB. Wendy & Stephen Longden, 01283 703259, wendylongden@btinternet.com. *6m S of Derby. From A38, S of Derby, follow signs to Willington, then Repton. In Repton straight on at r'about through village. Garden is 1m on R.* Home-made teas. **Adm £3, chd free. Sun 12 July, Sun 23 Aug (1.30-5.30). Visitors also welcome by arrangement June to Sept for groups 10+.**

Plant lover's garden with glorious views on a sloping 2½ acre site developed organically for yr-round interest. On lower levels herbaceous borders are arranged informally and connected via lawns, thyme bed, pond and pergolas. Mixed woodland and grassed labyrinth lead naturally into fruit, vegetable and herb potager with meadows beyond. Especially colourful in July and Aug. Easy and unusual perennials and grasses for sale. Why not visit St Wystans Church, Repton as part of your visit. Wheelchair access on lower levels only.

🌼 🚐 ☕

Thornbridge Hall

Share your day out on Facebook and Twitter

DEVON

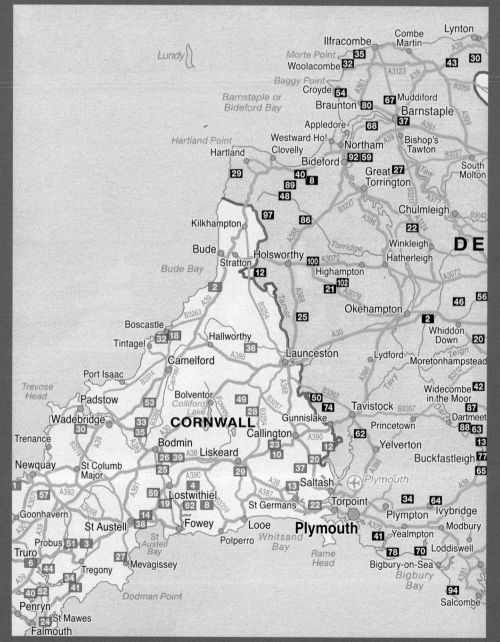

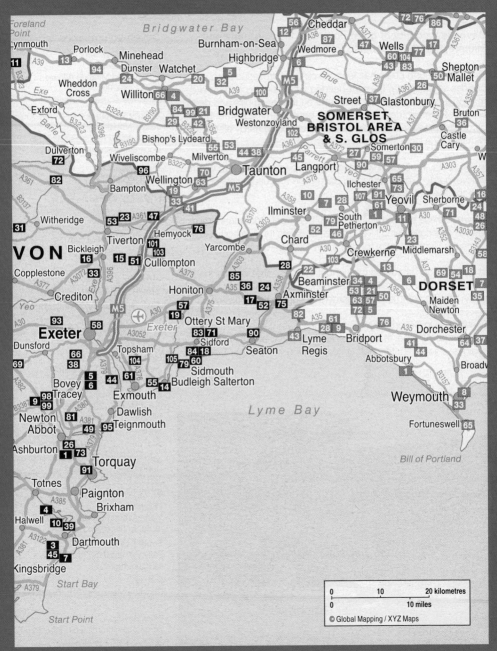

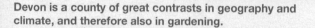

Devon

Devon is a county of great contrasts in geography and climate, and therefore also in gardening.

The rugged north coast has terraces clinging precariously to hillsides so steep that the faint-hearted would never contemplate making a garden there. But here, and on the rolling hills and deep valleys of Exmoor, despite a constant battle with the elements, NGS gardeners create remarkable results by choosing hardy plants that withstand the high winds and salty air.

In the south, in peaceful wooded estuaries and tucked into warm valleys, gardens grow bananas, palms and fruit usually associated with the Mediterranean.

Between these two terrains is a third: Dartmoor, 365 square miles of rugged moorland rising to 2000 feet, presents its own horticultural demands. Typically, here too are many NGS gardens.

In idyllic villages scattered throughout this very large county, in gardens large and small, in single manors and in village groups within thriving communities – gardeners pursue their passion.

Everywhere in Devon the NGS flourishes, with gardens on windswept cliff tops, in sub-tropical havens and on exposed hillsides; if you are interested in gardens you will find that Devon has it all!

Below: Sedgewell Coach House Gardens

Since our foundation we have donated more than £42.5 million to charity

Devon Volunteers

County Organiser & Central Devon
Edward and Miranda Allhusen
01647 440296
Miranda@allhusen.co.uk

County Treasurer
Julia Tremlett
01392 832671
jandjtremlett@hotmail.com

Publicity
Brian Mackness
01626 356004
brianmackness@clara.co.uk

Cath Pettyfer
01837 89024
cathpettyfer@gmail.com

Booklet Coordinator
Edward Allhusen
01647 440296
edward@allhusen.co.uk

Assistant County Organisers

East Devon
Peter Wadeley 01297 631210
wadeley@btinternet.com

Exeter
Jenny Phillips 01392 254076
jennypips25@hotmail.co.uk

Exmoor
Juliet Moss 01398 341604
julietm@onetel.com

North Devon
Jo Hynes 01805 804265
hynesjo@gmail.com

North East
Jill Hall 01884 38812
jill22hall@gmail.com

Plymouth
Maria Ashurst 01752 351396
maria.ashurst@sky.com

South Devon
Sally Vincent 01803 722227
salv@hotmail.co.uk

Torbay
Christine Mackness 01626 356004
christinemack@clara.co.uk

West Devon
Sara-Jane Cumming 01822 860281
sj@broadparkdesigns.co.uk

Opening Dates

All entries subject to change.
For latest information check www.ngs.org.uk

February

Sunday 1
22 Cherubeer Gardens

Saturday 7
58 Little Cumbre

Sunday 8
58 Little Cumbre

Saturday 14
58 Little Cumbre

Sunday 15
58 Little Cumbre

Friday 20
22 Cherubeer Gardens

March

Sunday 1
31 East Worlington House

Sunday 8
31 East Worlington House
78 Rowden House

Sunday 22
37 Gorwell House
93 Summers Place

Saturday 28
41 The Haven

Sunday 29
41 The Haven
42 Heathercombe

April

Friday 3
47 Holbrook Garden

Saturday 4
21 Chapel Farm House
38 Haldon Grange
47 Holbrook Garden

Sunday 5
21 Chapel Farm House
38 Haldon Grange
47 Holbrook Garden
51 Kia-Ora Farm & Gardens
105 Yonder Hill

Monday 6
38 Haldon Grange
47 Holbrook Garden
51 Kia-Ora Farm & Gardens
105 Yonder Hill

Saturday 11
38 Haldon Grange

Sunday 12
23 Chevithorne Barton
38 Haldon Grange
103 Wood Barton
105 Yonder Hill

Saturday 18
38 Haldon Grange
83 Sidbury Manor

Sunday 19
37 Gorwell House
38 Haldon Grange
51 Kia-Ora Farm & Gardens
80 St Merryn
82 Shapcott Barton Estate
83 Sidbury Manor
103 Wood Barton
105 Yonder Hill

Wednesday 22
38 Haldon Grange

Thursday 23
47 Holbrook Garden

Friday 24
47 Holbrook Garden

Saturday 25
25 NEW Cleave House
38 Haldon Grange
47 Holbrook Garden

Sunday 26
2 Andrew's Corner
25 NEW Cleave House
38 Haldon Grange
82 Shapcott Barton Estate
105 Yonder Hill

Wednesday 29
38 Haldon Grange

May

Saturday 2
28 Dicot
38 Haldon Grange
47 Holbrook Garden
70 Mothecombe House

Sunday 3
2 Andrew's Corner
28 Dicot
37 Gorwell House
38 Haldon Grange
45 Higher Ash Farm
47 Holbrook Garden
51 Kia-Ora Farm & Gardens
70 Mothecombe House
98 Whitstone Bluebells
100 Wick Farm Gardens
103 Wood Barton
105 Yonder Hill

Monday 4
2 Andrew's Corner
28 Dicot
33 Fursdon

Sunday 12
38 Haldon Grange
47 Holbrook Garden
51 Kia-Ora Farm & Gardens
100 Wick Farm Gardens
105 Yonder Hill

Wednesday 6
38 Haldon Grange

Saturday 9
11 Brendon Gardens
21 Chapel Farm House
34 Galen Way
38 Haldon Grange
81 Sedgewell Coach House Gardens
88 Spitchwick Manor

Sunday 10
2 Andrew's Corner
6 Bickham House
11 Brendon Gardens
20 Castle Drogo
21 Chapel Farm House
34 Galen Way
38 Haldon Grange
67 Marwood Hill
81 Sedgewell Coach House Gardens
87 Southcombe Gardens
88 Spitchwick Manor
100 Wick Farm Gardens
103 Wood Barton
105 Yonder Hill

Creative landscaping . . . quirky and eclectic . . .

Monday 11
53 Knightshayes Court Garden

Wednesday 13
38 Haldon Grange

Friday 15
69 Moretonhampstead Gardens

Saturday 16
30 Durcombe Water
38 Haldon Grange
54 Langtrees
56 Lewis Cottage
63 Lower Spitchwick Garden
69 Moretonhampstead Gardens

71 The Old Dairy
72 The Old Vicarage
97 NEW West Down House

Sunday 17
23 Chevithorne Barton
30 Durcombe Water
38 Haldon Grange
42 Heathercombe
45 Higher Ash Farm
51 Kia-Ora Farm & Gardens
54 Langtrees
56 Lewis Cottage
63 Lower Spitchwick Garden
69 Moretonhampstead Gardens
71 The Old Dairy
72 The Old Vicarage
77 Ridgehill
80 St Merryn
87 Southcombe Gardens
97 NEW West Down House
100 Wick Farm Gardens
105 Yonder Hill

Thursday 21
47 Holbrook Garden

Friday 22
47 Holbrook Garden

Saturday 23
8 Bocombe Mill Cottage
38 Haldon Grange
42 Heathercombe
47 Holbrook Garden
79 Runnymede

Sunday 24
2 Andrew's Corner
8 Bocombe Mill Cottage
30 Durcombe Water
38 Haldon Grange
42 Heathercombe
51 Kia-Ora Farm & Gardens
79 Runnymede
87 Southcombe Gardens
100 Wick Farm Gardens
105 Yonder Hill

Monday 25
2 Andrew's Corner
8 Bocombe Mill Cottage
19 Cadhay
30 Durcombe Water
38 Haldon Grange
51 Kia-Ora Farm & Gardens
79 Runnymede
87 Southcombe Gardens
100 Wick Farm Gardens
105 Yonder Hill

Saturday 30
1 Abbotskerswell Gardens
25 NEW Cleave House

Over 400 Volunteers help run the NGS – why not become one too?

38 Haldon Grange
89 Springfield

Sunday 31
1 Abbotskerswell Gardens
12 The Bridge Mill
15 NEW Burn Valley Butterleigh Gardens
25 NEW Cleave House
32 Foamlea
38 Haldon Grange
42 Heathercombe
57 Little Ash Bungalow
87 Southcombe Gardens
89 Springfield
100 Wick Farm Gardens
105 Yonder Hill

June

36 **Goren Farm (evenings)**
105 **Yonder Hill (every Sunday)**

Festival Weekend

Saturday 6
8 Bocombe Mill Cottage
36 Goren Farm
47 Holbrook Garden
56 Lewis Cottage
68 The Mill House

Sunday 7
8 Bocombe Mill Cottage
36 Goren Farm
42 Heathercombe
43 Heddon Hall
47 Holbrook Garden
50 Hotel Endsleigh
56 Lewis Cottage
68 The Mill House
74 Portington
87 Southcombe Gardens

Saturday 13
9 Bovey Tracey Gardens
10 Bramble Torre
18 Byes Reach
21 Chapel Farm House
36 Goren Farm
52 Kilmington (Shute Road) Gardens
65 NEW Luscombe Farm
80 St Merryn
88 Spitchwick Manor
96 Venn Cross Railway Gardens

Sunday 14
6 Bickham House
9 Bovey Tracey Gardens
10 Bramble Torre
15 NEW Burn Valley Butterleigh Gardens

18 Byes Reach
21 Chapel Farm House
29 Docton Mill
32 Foamlea
33 Fursdon
36 Goren Farm
51 Kia-Ora Farm & Gardens
52 Kilmington (Shute Road) Gardens
65 NEW Luscombe Farm
74 Portington
76 Regency House
78 Rowden House
80 St Merryn
87 Southcombe Gardens
88 Spitchwick Manor
96 Venn Cross Railway Gardens
102 Winsford Walled Garden

Monday 15
21 Chapel Farm House
102 Winsford Walled Garden

Tuesday 16
62 NEW Lower Grenofen

Wednesday 17
62 NEW Lower Grenofen

Friday 19
19 Cadhay
47 Holbrook Garden
66 NEW Marshall Farm

Saturday 20
25 NEW Cleave House
26 Collepardo
28 Dicot
47 Holbrook Garden
104 NEW Woodbury Gardens

Sunday 21
25 NEW Cleave House
26 Collepardo
27 The Croft
28 Dicot
32 Foamlea
42 Heathercombe
46 Higher Cullaford
66 NEW Marshall Farm
104 NEW Woodbury Gardens

Monday 22
26 Collepardo

Tuesday 23
26 Collepardo

Wednesday 24
26 Collepardo

Thursday 25
26 Collepardo

Friday 26
26 Collepardo
61 The Lookout

Saturday 27
25 NEW Cleave House
26 Collepardo
40 Harbour Lights
89 Springfield
92 Stone Farm
95 Teignmouth Gardens
101 Willand Old Village Gardens

Sunday 28
3 Ash Gardens
22 Cherubeer Gardens
24 Cleave Hill
26 Collepardo
32 Foamlea
40 Harbour Lights
42 Heathercombe
46 Higher Cullaford
51 Kia-Ora Farm & Gardens
61 The Lookout
89 Springfield
92 Stone Farm
95 Teignmouth Gardens
101 Willand Old Village Gardens

Delicious selection of home-made cakes and tray bakes . . .

July

36 **Goren Farm (evenings)**
105 **Yonder Hill (every Sunday)**

Wednesday 1
33 Fursdon

Thursday 2
44 High Garden

Friday 3
44 High Garden

Saturday 4
14 NEW Budleigh Salterton Gardens and Sea Gardens
21 Chapel Farm House
36 Goren Farm
44 High Garden
68 The Mill House
92 Stone Farm

Sunday 5
14 NEW Budleigh Salterton Gardens and Sea Gardens
21 Chapel Farm House
36 Goren Farm
68 The Mill House
92 Stone Farm

Friday 10
47 Holbrook Garden

Saturday 11
25 NEW Cleave House
36 Goren Farm
47 Holbrook Garden
75 Prospect House

Sunday 12
6 Bickham House
25 NEW Cleave House
36 Goren Farm
43 Heddon Hall
51 Kia-Ora Farm & Gardens
75 Prospect House
80 St Merryn
86 South Worden

Friday 17
19 Cadhay

Saturday 18
28 Dicot
48 Hole Farm
56 Lewis Cottage
89 Springfield
96 Venn Cross Railway Gardens

Sunday 19
27 The Croft
28 Dicot
48 Hole Farm
50 Hotel Endsleigh
56 Lewis Cottage
82 Shapcott Barton Estate
89 Springfield
96 Venn Cross Railway Gardens

Saturday 25
63 Lower Spitchwick Garden
90 NEW Springfield House

Sunday 26
51 Kia-Ora Farm & Gardens
60 Littlecourt Cottages
63 Lower Spitchwick Garden
82 Shapcott Barton Estate
90 NEW Springfield House
91 Squirrels

Monday 27
60 Littlecourt Cottages (Evening)

Take your Group to an NGS garden

August

Saturday 1
91 Squirrels

Sunday 2
91 Squirrels
93 Summers Place
99 Whitstone Farm
105 Yonder Hill

Saturday 8
72 The Old Vicarage

Sunday 9
6 Bickham House
51 Kia-Ora Farm & Gardens
72 The Old Vicarage
105 Yonder Hill

Saturday 15
11 Brendon Gardens
21 Chapel Farm House

Sunday 16
11 Brendon Gardens
21 Chapel Farm House
27 The Croft
57 Little Ash Bungalow
76 Regency House
86 South Worden
102 Winsford Walled Garden
105 Yonder Hill

Monday 17
21 Chapel Farm House
102 Winsford Walled Garden

Sunday 23
105 Yonder Hill

Friday 28
16 NEW Burnbridge Cottage
47 Holbrook Garden

Saturday 29
16 NEW Burnbridge Cottage
47 Holbrook Garden
56 Lewis Cottage
81 Sedgewell Coach House Gardens
84 Sidmouth Gardens

Sunday 30
16 NEW Burnbridge Cottage
47 Holbrook Garden
51 Kia-Ora Farm & Gardens
56 Lewis Cottage
81 Sedgewell Coach House Gardens
84 Sidmouth Gardens
105 Yonder Hill

Monday 31
19 Cadhay
51 Kia-Ora Farm & Gardens
84 Sidmouth Gardens

105 Yonder Hill

September

105 Yonder Hill (every Sunday)

Saturday 5
6 Bickham House
21 Chapel Farm House
69 Moretonhampstead Gardens
75 Prospect House

Sunday 6
6 Bickham House
21 Chapel Farm House
33 Fursdon
48 Hole Farm
69 Moretonhampstead Gardens
75 Prospect House
89 Springfield

Saturday 12
36 Goren Farm
96 Venn Cross Railway Gardens

Sunday 13
20 Castle Drogo
51 Kia-Ora Farm & Gardens
96 Venn Cross Railway Gardens

Saturday 19
13 NEW Brocton Cottage
85 South Wood Farm

Sunday 20
13 NEW Brocton Cottage
85 South Wood Farm

October

Sunday 4
45 Higher Ash Farm
93 Summers Place

Sunday 11
5 Bickham Cottage
76 Regency House

Sunday 18
2 Andrew's Corner
5 Bickham Cottage

Saturday 24
21 Chapel Farm House

Sunday 25
21 Chapel Farm House

February 2016

Saturday 6
58 Little Cumbre

Sunday 7
22 Cherubeer Gardens
58 Little Cumbre

Saturday 13
58 Little Cumbre

Sunday 14
58 Little Cumbre

Friday 19
22 Cherubeer Gardens

Gardens open to the public

7 Blackpool Gardens
17 Burrow Farm Gardens
19 Cadhay
20 Castle Drogo
29 Docton Mill
33 Fursdon
43 Heddon Hall
47 Holbrook Garden
50 Hotel Endsleigh
53 Knightshayes Court Garden
64 Lukesland
67 Marwood Hill
73 Plant World
82 Shapcott Barton Estate
102 Winsford Walled Garden

By arrangement only

4 Avenue Cottage
39 Hamblyn's Coombe
49 Hollycombe House
55 Lee Ford
59 Little Webbery
94 Tamarisks

Also open by arrangement

1 Abbotskerswell Gardens
1 Fairfield, Abbotskerswell Gardens
2 Andrew's Corner
3 Ash Tree Farm, Ash Gardens
8 Bocombe Mill Cottage
11 Brendon Gardens
12 The Bridge Mill
15 NEW Burn Valley Butterleigh Gardens
15 Shutelake, Burn Valley Butterleigh Gardens
18 Byes Reach
22 Cherubeer, Cherubeer Gardens
22 Cherubeer Gardens
22 Higher Cherubeer, Cherubeer Gardens
23 Chevithorne Barton
24 Cleave Hill
26 Collepardo
27 The Croft
32 Foamlea
34 Galen Way

36 Goren Farm
37 Gorwell House
38 Haldon Grange
40 Harbour Lights
41 The Haven
42 Heathercombe
44 High Garden
45 Higher Ash Farm
51 Kia-Ora Farm & Gardens
54 Langtrees
56 Lewis Cottage
57 Little Ash Bungalow
58 Little Cumbre
63 Lower Spitchwick Garden
68 The Mill House
69 Sutton Mead, Moretonhampstead Gardens
70 Mothecombe House
72 The Old Vicarage
74 Portington
75 Prospect House
76 Regency House
80 St Merryn
85 South Wood Farm
86 South Worden
87 Southcombe House, Southcombe Gardens
88 Spitchwick Manor
89 Springfield
91 Squirrels
93 Summers Place
96 The Engine House, Venn Cross Railway Gardens
96 Station House, Venn Cross Railway Gardens
99 Whitstone Farm
100 Wick Farm Gardens
103 Wood Barton
105 Yonder Hill

Flotsam and jetsam sit amongst naturalistic seaside planting . . .

Bring a bag for plants – help us give more to charity

The Gardens

GROUP OPENING

1 ABBOTSKERSWELL GARDENS

Abbotskerswell TQ12 5PN, 01626 356004, christinemack@clara.co.uk. *2m SW of Newton Abbot town centre. A 381 Newton Abbot/Totnes Road. Sharp L turn from NA, R from Totnes. Field parking at Fairfield. Maps available at all gardens, and at Church House.* Home-made teas at Church House. Teas available from 2 pm, but garden tickets and maps available from 1 pm. **Combined adm £5, chd free. Share to Friends of St Marys. Sat 30, Sun 31 May (1-5). Visitors also welcome by arrangement Apr to Aug, number of gardens available to be agreed.**

ABBOTSFORD
Mrs W Grierson

ABBOTSKERSWELL ALLOTMENTS
Margaret Crompton.
Access via the recreation ground

1 ABBOTSWELL COTTAGES
Ford Road. Jane Taylor

BRIAR COTTAGE
1 Monk's Orchard. Peggy & David Munden

FAIRFIELD
Christine & Brian Mackness
Visitors also welcome by arrangement Apr to Aug other gardens also by arrangement.
01626 356004
christinemack@clara.co.uk

NEW 37 WILTON WAY
Mrs Trish Turner

NEW 10 WILTON WAY
Mrs Margaret Crompton

In 2015 pretty and friendly Abbotskerswell adds 2 new gardens. 37 Wilton Way shows how to make the most of a steep site with shallow soil by creative landscaping, outdoor living areas and colourful pot planting. 10 Wilton Way is a quirky and eclectic mix! Japanese themes, ferns, hostas, grapevine, bamboo and grasses plus a few surprises. 4 other gardens have yet more new developments, and with the allotments, show a wide range of planting styles and innovative landscaping. Cottage gardens, terracing, wild flower areas, specialist plants, vegetable production methods. Many garden owners are winners in the annual Village Garden Show for produce or the garden itself. We offer inspirational ideas for large and small plots. Visitors are welcome to picnic in the field or arboretum at Fairfield. Children will enjoy the miniature Shetland ponies, plus finding their way through winding paths among high grasses. See You Tube

Abbotskerswell Gardens 2011 for a taster. Featured on Radio Devon The Potting Shed and in Newton Abbot and Mid Devon Advertiser and Herald Express. Disabled access to 3 gardens.

2 ANDREW'S CORNER
Belstone EX20 1RD. Robin & Edwina Hill, 01837 840332, edwinarobinhill@btinternet.com, www.belstonevillage.net. *3m E of Okehampton. Signed to Belstone. In village signed Skaigh. Parking restricted but cars may be left on nearby common.* Home-made teas. **Adm £4, chd free. Sun 26 Apr, Sun 3, Mon 4, Sun 10, Sun 24, Mon 25 May, Sun 18 Oct (2.30-5). Visitors also welcome by arrangement Feb to Nov.**
Well established, wildlife friendly, well labelled plantsman's garden in stunning high moorland setting. Variety of garden habitats incl woodland areas and pond; wide range of unusual trees, shrubs, herbaceous plants for yr-round effect with blue poppies, rhododendrons, bulbs and maples; spectacular autumn colour. Family friendly, with quiz sheet, fairy doors, playhouse, fruit, veg and chickens. Featured on BBC Radio Devon. Wheelchair access difficult when wet.

Wick Farm Gardens

GROUP OPENING

3 ASH GARDENS
Ash, Dartmouth TQ6 0LR. *2m SW of Dartmouth. Leave A3122 at Halwell for Dartmouth. R at Sportsman's Arms follow signs to Ash. 1¹/₂ m at 2nd Xrds, park at Ash Tree Farm.* Home-made teas. Combined adm £4.50, chd free. Sun 28 June (2-5).

ASH TREE FARM
Ash Cross, Dartmouth. Ms Stevie Rogers
Visitors also welcome by arrangement Mar to Oct, teas for groups.
01803 712437
stevie@ashtreefarm.com
www.ashtreefarm.com

BAY TREE COTTAGE
Jenny Goffe

HIGHER ASH FARM
Mr Michael Gribbin
(See separate entry)
3 delightful gardens of contrasting styles in the tiny hamlet of Ash. Ash Tree Farm with its rainbow garden planted for the benefit of wildlife. Full of original ideas. The beautiful intimate little garden at Bay Tree Cottage sits in a quiet secluded valley with wonderful sunlit views across open farmland. The perfect curved lawn leads the eye to small rooms filled with surprise and clever planting. Ornamental trees punctuate the boundary and a tiny vegetable garden of raised beds overflows with produce.

4 AVENUE COTTAGE
Ashprington, Totnes TQ9 7UT. Mr Richard Pitts and Mr David Sykes, 01803 732769,
richard.pitts@btinternet.com,
avenuecottage.com. *3m SW of Totnes. A 381 Totnes to Kingsbridge for 1m; L for Ashprington, into village then L by PH. Garden ¹/₄ m on R after Sharpham Estate sign.* Adm £4, chd free. Visitors welcome by arrangement Mar to Oct.
11 acres of mature and young trees and shrubs. Once part of an C18 landscape, the neglected garden has been cleared and replanted over the last 25 yrs. Good views of Sharpham House and R Dart. Azaleas and hydrangeas are a feature.

5 BICKHAM COTTAGE
Kenn. EX6 7XL. Steve Eyre. *6m S of Exeter. 1m off A38. Leave A38 at Kenn. 1st R in village, follow lane for ³/₄ m to end of no through rd.* Cream teas. Adm £3.50, chd free. Sun 11, Sun 18 Oct (2-5).
Small cottage garden divided into separate areas by old stone walls and hedge banks. Front garden with mainly South African bulbs and plants. Lawn surrounded by borders with agapanthus, eucomis, crocosmia, diorama etc. Stream garden with primulas. Pond with large Koi carp. Glasshouses with National Collection of Nerine sarniensis and cultivars, 3500 pots with in excess of 450 varieties.

NCH

6 BICKHAM HOUSE
Kenn. EX6 7XL. John & Julia Tremlett. *6m S of Exeter 1m off A38. Leave A38 at Kennford Services, follow signs to Kenn, 1st R in village, follow lane for ³/₄ m to end of no through rd.* Cream teas. Adm £5, chd free. Sun 10 May, Sun 14 June, Sun 12 July, Sun 9 Aug, Sat 5, Sun 6 Sept (2-5).
7 acre garden with much recent replanting. Colour co-ordinated borders, mature trees, croquet lawn. Fern garden and water garden. Formal parterre with lily pond. 1 acre walled garden with profusion of vegetables and flowers. Palm tree avenue leading to summerhouse. Spring garden with cowslips, bluebells, etc. Alpine house with over 100 immaculately displayed plants. Lakeside walk. Wide selection of well grown plants for sale. 5 Sept opening with Devon Open Studios for Kerry Tremlett's print maker's exhibition. Featured in Daily Telegraph, Western Morning News, Devon Country Gardener, Amateur Gardener, RHS Plantsman.

7 ◆ BLACKPOOL GARDENS
Dartmouth TQ6 0RG. Sir Geoffrey Newman, 01803 771801, www.blackpoolsands.co.uk. *3m SW of Dartmouth. From Dartmouth follow brown signs to Blackpool Sands on A379. Entrance to gardens via Blackpool Sands car park.* For opening times and information, please phone or see garden website.
Tenderly restored C19 subtropical plantsman's garden with collection of mature and newly planted tender and unusual trees, shrubs and carpet of spring flowers. Paths and steps lead gradually uphill and above the Captain's seat offering spectacular coastal views. Recent plantings follow the S hemisphere theme with callistemons, pittosporums, acacias and buddlejas. Open 1 Apr - Sept (10-4) weather permitting.

8 BOCOMBE MILL COTTAGE
Bocombe, Parkham, Bideford EX39 5PH. Mr Chris Butler & Mr David Burrows, 01237 451293, www.bocombe.co.uk. *6m E of Clovelly, 9m SW of Bideford. From A39 just outside Horns Cross village, turn to Foxdown. At Xrds follow signs for parking.* Home-made teas. Ploughmans lunch & traditional home-made cakes and cream teas. Adm £4, chd £1. Sat 23, Sun 24, Mon 25 May, Sat 6, Sun 7 June (12-5). Visitors also welcome by arrangement Mar to Sept for groups of 10+.
An undulating organic landscape of 5 acres punctuated with gardens and features. Flower gardens walk around house, plus relaxing circular walk around 1m, boots suggested. Streams, bog gardens, pools and 12 water features. White pergola. Hillside orchard and goats. Soft fruit and kitchen gardens. Garden kaleidoscope. Wild meadow, a wildlife haven. Garden plan incl 60+ specimen trees. Live hermits in new hermitage, with adjoining grotto. Goats on hillside.

GROUP OPENING

9 BOVEY TRACEY GARDENS
Bovey Tracey TQ13 9NA. *6m N of Newton Abbot. Gateway to Dartmoor. Take A382 to Bovey Tracey. Car parking at town car parks, on the road and at Parke.* Home-made teas at Pineholm. **Combined adm £4.50, chd free. Sat 13, Sun 14 June (2-6).**

> **NEW ASHWELL**
> East Street. Tony & Jeanette Pearce.
> *300m E of town centre. Landmark is large tree overhanging rd, shortly before Trough Lane. House set back from rd, on steep slope. Parking either in central Bovey, or in rd past church*

> **BOVEY COMMUNITY GARDEN**
> Parke, Home Farm. NT and Bovey Tracey Climate Action.
> *Follow signs to Parke, parking in visitors' car park*
> www.boveycommunitygarden.org.uk

> **5 BRIDGE COTTAGES**
> Pottery Rd. Cath Valentine.
> *Down lane at base of Pottery Rd, near r'about, opp Landrover dealership. R'about is approx 1m from Drumbridges junction of A38 (follow signs to Bovey Tracey/House of Marbles)*

> **NEW GREEN HEDGES**
> Moretonhampstead Road, Bovey Tracey. Alan and Linda Jackson.
> *Off A382 Bovey to Moretonhampstead Road. Turn R off A382, opp golf driving range. Green Hedges is 1st bungalow on L. Parking by 30mph sign before or in layby 100yds past property*

> **NEW PINEHOLM**
> High Close. Lynda Drake and Alan Pewsey.
> *B3344 from Chudleigh Knighton, directly on entering Bovey Tracey 1st R into Bradley Rd (or last L on Le Molay Littry way before exiting Bovey Tracey) then 1st R into High Close*

> **NEW 2 REDWOODS**
> Ashburton Road, Bovey Tracey. Mr & Mrs Tony Mooney.
> *Top of Pottery Rd turn R at Xrds into Ashburton Rd. 1st R into Redwoods Close. 2nd house on L*

Pretty cob and Dartmoor granite built town by R Bovey. 6 enormously varied gardens in or close to the town. Ashwell: steeply sloping Victorian stone walled garden with vineyard, colourful herbacaeous border, orchard with wild flowers and vegetables. 5 Bridge Cottages: productive, colourful and quirky cottage garden. Green Hedges: lovely views, well established with colourful borders, shrub, bulbs, perennials, annuals and vegetables. 2 Redwoods: woodland garden with moorland leat, extensive fern collection alongside large densely planted sunny gravel garden. Pineholm: terraced on steep slope, extensively planted with flowers, fruits and raised vegetable beds, also woodland, bogland and stream. The NT's Parke is a successful community garden, with productive fruit trees, and many vegetables (incl heritage varieties). Solar powered pump for irrigation. Limited wheelchair access at some gardens.

❀ ☕

6 enormously
varied gardens
in or close to
the town . . .

10 BRAMBLE TORRE
Dittisham, nr Dartmouth TQ6 0HZ. Paul & Sally Vincent, 01803 722227, salv@hotmail.co.uk, www.rainingsideways.com. *³/₄ m from Dittisham. Leave A3122 at Sportsman's Arms. Drop down into Village, at Red Lion turn L to Cornworthy. Continue ³/₄ m Bramble Torre straight ahead.* Cream teas. **Adm £4, chd free. Sat 13, Sun 14 June (2-6).**
Set in 20 acres of farmland, the 3-acre garden follows a rambling stream through a steep valley: lily pond, herbaceous borders, camellias, shrubs and roses dominated by huge embothrium glowing scarlet in late spring against a sometimes blue sky!

A formal herb and vegetable garden runs alongside the stream while chickens scratch in an orchard of Ditsum plums and cider apples. Well behaved dogs on leads welcome. Limited wheelchair access, parts of garden very steep and uneven. Tea area with wheelchair access and excellent garden view.

♿ 🐕 ☕

GROUP OPENING

11 BRENDON GARDENS
Brendon, Lynton EX35 6PU, 01598 741343, lalindevon@yahoo.co.uk. *1m S of A39 North Devon coast rd between Porlock and Lynton. Scenic 2m East Lyn River valley walk links 1 Deercombe Cottages, Doone Cottage and Hall Farm.* Light lunches and cream teas served at Higher Tippacott Farm. WC also available. Homemade cakes and drinks served at Hall Farm. **Combined adm £4.50, chd free. Sat 9, Sun 10 May, Sat 15, Sun 16 Aug (12-5). Visitors also welcome by arrangement May to Aug.**

> **HIGHER TIPPACOTT FARM**
> Tippacott Lane. Angela & Malcolm Percival.
> *From Xrds at Brendon village green follow signs to Tippacott, 1m to T-junction fronting moor. Turn R, proceed 200 yds. Parking on R*

> **1 DEERCOMBE COTTAGES**
> Valerie and Stephen Exley.
> *From village green in Brendon drive into village and park in Village hall car park. Garden 250yds on L. Set down possible close to garden*

> **NEW DOONE COTTAGE**
> Rockford. Carole & Jason Miller.
> *From Brendon village green drive to village hall, continue 1m to Rockford hamlet, garden on R. Limited parking in lane 100yds beyond*

> **HALL FARM**
> Mrs Janie Scott.
> *Not open for August dates. From village green in Brendon, over bridge turn R.100 yds on R. Limited parking in stable yard*

Stunningly beautiful part of Exmoor National Park. 3 gardens nestling in East Lyn river valley and one above, high up on heather moorland. Excellent walking incl dramatic

coastal path nearby. Cards, books and bric-a-brac for sale. Featured in Amateur Gardening (1 Deercombe Cottages) and Dorset County Gardener.

NGS donations have helped fund 358 Marie Curie Nurses

12 THE BRIDGE MILL

Mill Rd, Bridgerule, Holsworthy EX22 7EL. Rosie Beat, 01288 381341, rosie@thebridgemill.org.uk, www.thebridgemill.org.uk. *In Bridgerule village on R Tamar between Bude and Holsworthy. Between chapel by river bridge and church at top of hill towards Holsworthy. See above website for detailed directions.* Home-made teas. Refreshments in garden with ducks or in barn if wet! **Adm £3.50, chd free. Sun 31 May (10-5).** Visitors also welcome by arrangement May to July for groups of 15+.

1-acre organic gardens set around mill house and restored water mill. Small cottage garden; herb garden with medicinal and dye plants; very productive vegetable garden and woodland and water garden behind mill. The 16-acre smallholding will be open for lake, pond and riverside walks. Friendly sheep, pigs and poultry! The Bridge Mill is open for educational visits throughout the year to school groups. Details on website. Regular articles about the garden and smallholding in Country Smallholding magazine. Wheelchair access to part of garden. WC with access for wheelchairs.

13 NEW BROCTON COTTAGE

Pear Tree, Ashburton, Newton Abbot TQ13 7QZ. Mrs Naomi Hindley. *¹/₄ m from A38. From A38 take Ashburton Peartree junction. Turn R towards Princetown, then 1st*

L towards Buckfastleigh. Park on road or at Dartmoor Lodge Hotel (lunches available). Short walk to garden entrance.* Home-made teas. Lunches and refreshments also available at the Dartmoor Lodge Hotel. **Adm £3.50, chd free. Sat 19, Sun 20 Sept (2-5).**

1.3 acres recently recovered from neglect, combining established planting with newly developed areas. New orchard, woodland, ponds and productive area linked to established herbaceous borders and shrubberies. Developed as a single garden with views of Devon countryside. Dogs on leads only please.

GROUP OPENING

14 NEW BUDLEIGH SALTERTON GARDENS AND SEA GARDENS

Budleigh Salterton EX9 6JY. *Off B3178 Exmouth Rd through Budleigh Salterton. A map will be issued with your ticket which can be purchased from any of the gardens.* Home-made teas at 4 Cliff Terrace. **Combined adm £5, chd free. Sat 4, Sun 5 July (1-5).**

NEW 16 LITTLE KNOWLE

Mr & Mrs Frean.
No Parking in Little Knowle, please park in Public Car Parks or walk from other gardens

NEW THE SEA GARDENS 1,2,3,4,5A & 6 CLIFF TERRACE

Mrs Gilly Marshall-Lee.
Cliff Terrace is off Rolle Road on B3178 through Budleigh Salterton. Parking in Car Park opp Tourist Information is advised

NEW UPPER WESTCOTT

35, Northview Road. Mrs D Tremlett.
Parking locally in Northview Rd

NEW 4 WESTBOURNE TERRACE

Mr & Mrs Stewart.
Parking in public Car Parks or walk from other gardens

The Sea Gardens lie on cliff top along Jurassic Coastal Path above beach looking towards mouth of R Otter and on to Lyme Bay. The gardens are planted to tolerate strong winds and sea spray in winter and hot dry conditions in summer. The Sea Gardens are on opp side of road from the houses, creating a quillet (strips of

land together forming a larger plot). Upper Westcott, 35 Northview Rd is accessed from side of property off footpath leading to Jurassic Coastal Path. Situated behind 18th green of East Devon Golf Club this garden features many diverse herbaceous borders. 16 Little Knowle is accessed from rear of property across small bridge into tree lined secluded garden with herbaceous borders, fruit trees and weeping willow. 4 Westbourne Terrace is a very pretty well stocked enclosed garden with pond and curving path with a surprise around every corner. Limited wheelchair access.

GROUP OPENING

15 BURN VALLEY BUTTERLEIGH GARDENS

Butterleigh, Cullompton EX15 1PR, 01884 38812, jill22hall@gmail.com. *Follow signs for Silverton from Butterleigh village. Take L fork 100yds after entrance to Pound Farm. Car park sign on L after 150yds.* Home-made teas. Indoors if inclement. **Combined adm £5, chd free. Sun 31 May, Sun 14 June (2-6).** Visitors also welcome by arrangement Mar to Sept.

HIGHER BURNHAIES

Richard & Virginia Holmes

SHUTELAKE

Jill & Nigel Hall
Visitors also welcome by arrangement Mar to Oct cars/minibus only.
01884 38812
jill22hall@gmail.com

Higher Burnhaies is a 2¹/₂ acre site started in 1997. Situated in the beautiful Burn Valley, a plantsman's garden of herbaceous plantings with trees, shrubs, ponds and wildlife. Informal, country feel with Devon lane and wilderness walk. Vegetable garden. Live music. Cross a bridge over a babbling brook to Shutelake, a garden terraced into a hillside. Several levels blend a Mediterranean feel with natural local landscape. Borders, ponds, lake, sculptures, woodland walk. New rockery area. An oasis of calm. Uneven ground and steps in both gardens, not good for unsteady walkers.

16 NEW ► **BURNBRIDGE COTTAGE**
Cadeleigh, Tiverton EX16 8RY.
Kate Leevers and Martin
Callaghan. *From A3072 1½ m
from Bickleigh bridge, 6½ m from
Crediton, follow lane behind Blue
Cross centre for ¾ m. On R after
stone bridge. From Cadeleigh village
take lane opp PH. On L at bottom of
hill.* Home-made teas. Gluten free
cakes available. **Adm £3, chd free.
Fri 28, Sat 29, Sun 30 Aug (2-5).**
Mature trees and shrubs provide the
backdrop for this informal, secluded
1¼ acre garden. Reclaimed over last
6 years from long neglect and
developed for diversity of planting
and wildlife. Late summer flowerbeds
attract bees and butterflies. Other
moods and habitats created by
copse, pond, bog garden, hedges.
Streamside garden in development.
Also mini arboretum and hillside
wood. Sloping, mostly grass site -
main garden should be accessible by
wheelchairs if dry.

> Reclaimed over last
> 6 years from long
> neglect and
> developed for
> diversity of planting
> and wildlife . . .

17 ◆ **BURROW FARM
GARDENS**
Dalwood, Axminster EX13 7ET.
Mary & John Benger, 01404
831285,
www.burrowfarmgardens.co.uk.
*3½ m W of Axminster. From A35 turn
N at Taunton Xrds then follow brown
signs.* Light lunches, cream teas, tea,
coffees and cakes. **For opening
times and information, please
phone or see garden website.**
Beautiful 13 acre garden with unusual
trees, shrubs and herbaceous plants.
Traditional summerhouse looks
towards lake and ancient oak
woodland with rhododendrons and
azaleas. Early spring interest and
superb autumn colour. The more
formal Millennium garden features a
rill. Anniversary Garden featuring late

summer perennials and grasses. A
photographer's dream. Open 1 April -
31 Oct (10 - 7). Adm £7. Café and
gift shop. Various events incl plant fair
and open air Shakespeare held at
garden each year. Visit events page
on Burrow Farm Gardens website for
more details. Featured in Devon Life
magazine.

18 ► **BYES REACH**
26 Coulsdon Rd, Sidmouth
EX10 9JP. Lynette Talbot & Peter
Endersby, 01395 578081,
lfisher@talktalk.net. *Easterly on
A3052. R at Sidford X-lights. In ¾ m
turn L into Coulsdon Rd. On foot,
enter back gate via Livonia Field bike
path.* Gluten Free cakes available.
**Adm £2.50, chd free. Sat 13, Sun
14 June (2-5.30). Also open with
Sidmouth Gardens in Aug. Visitors
also welcome by arrangement
June to Sept for groups of 8+.**
3 yr old edible garden of approx ¼
acre. Potager style, raised beds,
espalier fruit trees on arched walkway.
Designed for those with mobility
problems. Colour themed
herbaceous borders, herbs, ferns,
hostas. Sitting areas, pond, rill,
rockery, greenhouse, studio. Backing
onto The Byes nature reserve and R
Sid; offering an opportunity for a short
walk from the garden gate. Long fruit
covered archway, use of recycled
materials and pond and rill.
Sculptured fountain. Views into
Livonia Field. Featured in Sidmouth
Herald, Express & Echo.

19 ◆ **CADHAY**
Ottery St Mary EX11 1QT. Rupert
Thistlethwayte, 01404 813511,
www.cadhay.org.uk. *1m NW of
Ottery St Mary. On B3176 between
Ottery St Mary and Fairmile. From E
exit A30 at Iron Bridge. From W exit
A30 at Patteson's Cross.* Home-
made teas. **Adm £3, chd £1. For
NGS: Mon 25 May, Fri 19 June, Fri
17 July, Mon 31 Aug (2-5). For
other opening times and
information, please phone or see
garden website.**
Tranquil 2-acre setting for Elizabethan
manor house. 2 medieval fish ponds
surrounded by rhododendrons,
gunnera, hostas and flag iris. Roses,
clematis, lilies and hellebores
surround walled water garden. 120ft
herbaceous border walk informally
planted with cottage garden
perennials and annuals. Walled

kitchen gardens have been turned
into allotments and old garden store
is now tearoom. Gravel paths.

20 ◆ **CASTLE DROGO**
Drewsteignton EX6 6PB. National
Trust, 01647 433306,
www.nationaltrust.org.uk. *12m W
of Exeter. 5m S of A30. Follow brown
signs SatNav EX6 6PB.* Home made
cakes & Devonshire cream teas. **Adm
£5.50, chd £3. For NGS: Sun 10
May, Sun 13 Sept (9.30-5.30). For
other opening times and
information, please phone or see
garden website.**
Medium-sized Grade II* listed garden
with formal structures designed by
Edwin Lutyens and George Dillistone
during the late 1920s. These consist
of formal rose beds, herbaceous
borders, shrubbery and circular
croquet lawn surrounded by mature
yew hedges. Garden tours available
with the head gardener. Partial
wheelchair access, purpose-built
access path to main terrace.

21 ► **CHAPEL FARM HOUSE**
Halwill Junction, Beaworthy
EX21 5UF. Robin & Toshie Hull.
*12m NW of Okehampton. On A3079.
At W end of village.* Home-made
teas. **Adm £3.50, chd £1. Sat 4,
Sun 5 Apr, Sat 9, Sun 10 May, Sat
13, Sun 14, Mon 15 June, Sat 4,
Sun 5 July, Sat 15, Sun 16, Mon 17
Aug, Sat 5, Sun 6 Sept, Sat 24,
Sun 25 Oct (11-5).**
Approx ½ acre garden started in
1992 by present owners, landscaped
with shrub borders, heathers,
rhododendrons and azaleas. Alpine
bed. Kitchen garden. 2 small
greenhouses for mixed use. Small
bonsai collection. 3 acres of mixed
young woodland with wildlife and
flowers. Japanese garden and stone
lantern. On May and Sept opening
dates a demonstration of Ikebana will
be given by Toshie Hull between
1 & 1.30 pm.

GROUP OPENING

22 ► **CHERUBEER GARDENS**
Dolton EX19 8PP, 01805 804265,
hynesjo@gmail.com,
www.sites.google.com/site/
cherubeergardens/the-gardens.
8m SE of Great Torrington. 2m E of

Dolton. From A3124 turn S towards Stafford Moor Fisheries, take 1st R, gardens 500m on L. Home-made teas at Higher Cherubeer. **Combined adm £4, chd free. Sun 1, Fri 20 Feb (2-5); Sun 28 June (2.30-5.30); Sun 7, Fri 19 Feb 2016 (2-5). Visitors also welcome by arrangement Feb to Oct groups of 10 +.**

CHERUBEER
Janet Brown
Visitors also welcome by arrangement Feb to July.

HIGHER CHERUBEER NCH
Jo & Tom Hynes
Visitors also welcome by arrangement Feb to Oct for groups of 10+.
01805 804265
hynesjo@gmail.com

The 2 Cherubeers, a family affair, form a small hamlet in rolling farmland at 500ft at top of SW facing valley. Despite the exposed location and stony acid clay soil, the gardens provide a wealth of colour right through the season. Cherubeer: cottage garden set around a C15 thatched house (not open). Ponds, paths, and steps filled with colourful perennials and herbs set off by mature shrubs and trees. Higher Cherubeer: 1-acre country garden with gravelled courtyard, raised beds and alpine house, large herbaceous border, shady woodland beds with over 200 varieties of snowdrops, colourful collection of basketry willows, vegetable garden and National Collection of hardy cyclamen. Featured in The English Garden and the Telegraph. Partial wheelchair access due to slopes and gravel. Very little wheelchair access at Cherubeer.

---

23 CHEVITHORNE BARTON
Tiverton EX16 7QB. Michael & Arabella Heathcoat Amory, pottinger985@gmail.com. *3m NE of Tiverton. Through Sampford Pev and Halberton to Tiverton, past Golf Club, turn R. R at next junction. Over bridge, L through Craze Lowman, carry on to T-junction, R then 1st L.* Home-made teas. Refreshments for church funds. **Adm £4, chd free. Sun 12 Apr, Sun 17 May (2-5). Visitors also welcome by arrangement Apr to Sept (state if booking via NGS yellow book).** Terraced walled garden, summer borders and romantic woodland of

rare trees and shrubs. In spring, garden features large collection of magnolias, camellias, rhododendrons and azaleas. Also incl one of only two NCCPG oak collections situated in 12 hectares of parkland and comprising over 200 different species. Featured in local press.

24 CLEAVE HILL
Membury, Axminster EX13 7AJ. Andy & Penny Pritchard, 01404 881437, penny@tonybengerlandscaping.co. uk. *4m NW of Axminster. From Membury Village, follow rd down valley. 1st R after Lea Hill B&B, last house on drive, approx 1m.* Light lunches, cream teas and cakes. **Adm £3.50, chd free. Sat 27, Sun 28 June (11-5). Visitors also welcome by arrangement, coach parking 1m.**
Artistic garden in pretty village situated on edge of Blackdown Hills. Cottage style garden, planted to provide all season structure, texture and colour. Designed around pretty thatched house and old stone barns. Wonderful views, attractive vegetable garden and orchard, wild flower meadow.

25 NEW CLEAVE HOUSE
Sticklepath EX20 2NL. Ann & Roger Bowden, https://www.bowdenhostas.com/pages/National-Hosta-Collection.html. *3½ m E of Okehampton. Follow brown tourist signs for Bowden Hostas. From Okehampton, Cleave House is on L, covered with Virginia Creeper.* Cream teas. Fantastic coffee and tea from the previous owners of The Best Tea House In The UK. **Adm £4, chd free. Share to NCCPG. Sats & Suns 25, 26 Apr, 30, 31 May, 20, 21 June, 11, 12 July (10-4).**
The National Collection of Hostas is housed in a beautifully mature garden of about ½ acre, alongside many interesting trees, shrubs and other plants. The new stumpery provides a focal point for ferns and tree ferns. Hostas, ferns, tree ferns and bamboos for sale with expert advice available. Garden audio guide. Treasure slug hunt and craft activities for children. General knowledge quiz. Featured on BBC TV Chelsea Flower Show, BBC1 with Benedict Cumberbatch and Wanda Ventham discussing our bamboos, Great British Garden Revival and in Devon Life. Partial wheelchair access.

Spitchwick Manor

26 ▶ COLLEPARDO
3 Keyberry Park, Newton Abbot
TQ12 1BZ. Betty & Don Frampton,
01626 354580,
collepardo@btinternet.com. *Take
A380 Newton Abbot. From Newton
Abbot (Penn Inn) r'about follow sign
for town centre. 1st L slip rd before T-
lights, then 1st R, 2nd L.* Home-made
teas. **Adm £3, chd free. Daily Sat
20 June to Sun 28 June (11-5).
Visitors also welcome by
arrangement May to June for
groups of 10+.**
⅓ acre garden laid out in series of
interlinked colour themed garden
rooms, explored via 400 metres of
meandering paths. Circular rockery of
30 metres enclosing new lawn.
Herbaceous and shrub borders,
pond, raised walkway and gazebo
allow the visitor every opportunity to
view 1500 varieties of hardy plants,
shrubs and trees.

27 ▶ THE CROFT
Yarnscombe, Barnstaple
EX31 3LW. Sam & Margaret Jewell,
01769 560535. *8m S of Barnstaple,
10m SE of Bideford, 12m W of South
Molton, 4m NE of Torrington. From
A377, turn W opp Chapelton railway
stn. Follow Yarnscombe signs, after
3m. From B3232, ¼ m N of
Huntshaw Cross TV mast, turn E and
follow Yarnscombe signs for 2m.
Parking in village hall car park.* Home-
made teas. **Adm £3.50, chd free.
Share to N Devon Animal
Ambulance. Sun 21 June, Sun 19
July, Sun 16 Aug (2-6). Visitors
also welcome by arrangement min
3 days noticed required.**
1-acre plantswoman's garden
featuring exotic Japanese garden
with tea house, koi carp pond and
cascading stream, tropical garden
with exotic shrubs and perennials,
herbaceous borders with unusual
plants and shrubs, bog garden with
collection of irises, astilbes and
moisture loving plants, duck pond.
Exotic borders, new beds around
duck pond and bog area, large
collection of rare and unusual plants.

28 ▶ DICOT
Chardstock EX13 7DF. Mr & Mrs F
Clarkson, www.dicot.co.uk. *5m N
of Axminster. Axminster to Chard
A358 at Tytherleigh to Chardstock. R
at George Inn, L fork to Hook, R to
Burridge, 2nd house on L.* Home-
made teas. **Adm £3.50, chd free.**

**Sat 2, Sun 3, Mon 4 May, Sat 20,
Sun 21 June, Sat 18, Sun 19 July
(2-5.30).**
Secret garden hidden in East Devon
valley. 3 acres of unusual and exotic
plants - some rare. Rhododendrons,
azaleas and camellias in profusion.
Meandering stream, fish pool,
Japanese style garden and interesting
vegetable garden with fruit cage,
tunnel and greenhouses. Surprises
round every corner. Featured on
Radio Devon and in local press.
Partial wheelchair access.

NGS support makes a vital difference to our patient care

29 ▶ ◆ DOCTON MILL
Lymebridge, Hartland EX39 6EA.
Lana & John Borrett, 01237
441369, www.doctonmill.co.uk. *8m
W of Clovelly. Follow brown tourist
signs on A39 nr Clovelly.* Cream teas
and light lunches available all day.
**Adm £4.50, chd free. For NGS: Sun
14 June (10-5). For other opening
times and information, please
phone or see garden website.**
Situated in stunning valley location.
Garden surrounds original mill pond
and the microclimate created within
the wooded valley enables tender
species to flourish. Recent planting of
herbaceous, stream and summer
garden give variety through the
season.

30 ▶ DURCOMBE WATER
Furzehill, Barbrook, Lynton
EX35 6LN. Pam & David
Sydenham, 01598 753658,
pam.sydenham@virgin.net. *3m S of
Lynton. From Lynton/Lynmouth head
for Barnstaple. At T-junction in
Barbrook (petrol station opp) turn L,
follow yellow signs. From Barnstaple*

*follow A39 (signed Lynton) to
Barbrook and follow signs.* Home-
made teas. **Adm £4, chd free. Sat
16, Sun 17, Sun 24, Mon 25 May
(11-5).**
Stunning views across Exmoor. A
silent relaxing 2½ acres, enlivened
with streams, ponds and waterfalls
falling 40ft through 8 tiered ponds.
Different types of garden - cottage,
landscaped terraces, oriental and art
gallery, each with colour, scents and
beauty. A feast of colour with
rhododendrons, azaleas, perennials
and shrubs. Lots of seats to enjoy the
peace, views and beauty. The garden
has been created single-handedly by
the owner over the last 13 years since
his retirement, and is maintained
solely by him. Superb views, water
features, peace and quiet.

31 ▶ EAST WORLINGTON HOUSE
East Worlington, Witheridge,
Crediton EX17 4TS. Mr & Mrs
Barnabas Hurst-Bannister. *In centre
of East Worlington, 2m W of
Witheridge. From Witheridge square
R to East Worlington. After 1½ m R at
T-junction in Drayford, over bridge
then L to Worlington. After ⅓ m L at
T-junction. Garden 200 yds on L.
Disabled parking at house. Parking
nearby.* Cream teas in thatched
parish hall next to house. **Adm £3.50,
chd free. Sun 1, Sun 8 Mar
(1.30-5).**
Thousands of crocuses. In 2 acre
garden, set in lovely position with
views down valley to Little Dart river,
these spectacular crocuses have
spread over many years through the
garden and into the neighbouring
churchyard. Cream teas in the parish
hall (in aid of its thatch fund) next
door. Dogs on leads please.

32 ▶ FOAMLEA
Chapel Hill, Mortehoe EX34 7DZ.
Beth Smith, 01271 871182,
bethmortepoint@fmail.co.uk. *¼ m
S of Mortehoe village. A361 N from
Barnstaple. L onto B3343 to
Mortehoe car park. No parking at or
near garden. On foot L past church,
down hill, then 200yds.* Home-made
teas. **Adm £3, chd free. Suns 31
May, 14, 21, 28 June (2-5). Visitors
also welcome by arrangement May
to Sept max 20.**
12 yr old collection of plants thriving
in open cliff top site with
uninterrupted view to Morte Point

Lemon drizzle cake, Victoria sponge … yummy!

(NT). The mild climate and a gradient providing natural drainage favour many temperate and semi-tropical species. Wide range of shrubs and perennials. Drystone walling, slate steps and shillet paths feature throughout. Colour-schemed areas, rockery and mixed plantings. National Collection of Phlomis. Featured on Coast and ITV with Alan Titchmarsh and in RHS The Garden, Devon Life, Amateur Gardening and SAGA magazines.

✿ **NCH** ☕

33 ◆ FURSDON
Cadbury, Thorverton, Exeter EX5 5JS. David & Catriona Fursdon, 01392 860860, www.fursdon.co.uk. *2m N of Thorverton. From Tiverton S on A396. Take A3072 at Bickleigh towards Crediton. L after 2¹/₂ m. From Exeter N on A396. L to Thorverton and R in centre.* Cream teas in Coach Hall. Light lunches served from 12 noon. **Adm £4, chd free. For NGS: Mon 4 May, Sun 14 June, Wed 1 July, Sun 6 Sept (12-5). For other opening times and information, please phone or see garden website.**
The garden surrounds Fursdon House, home of the same family for 7 centuries. Hillside setting with extensive views S over parkland and beyond. Sheltered by house, hedges and cob walls, there are terraces of roses, herbs and perennials in mixed traditional and contemporary planting. Woodland walk and pond in meadow garden. Fursdon House open for guided tours on NGS days. Some steep slopes, grass and gravel paths.

♿ 🐱 ⊨ ☕

34 GALEN WAY
Sparkwell, Plymouth PL7 5DF. Peter & Ann Tremain, 01752 837532, peteranntremain@talktalk.net. *Car parking Sparkwell Hall PL7 5DD. Follow signs approx 300yds. Limited disabled park at Galen Way.* Home-made teas. **Adm £4, chd free. Sat 9, Sun 10 May (1-5). Visitors also welcome by arrangement May to Sept.**
Quirky garden full of surprises, developed over last 40yrs. Incl fish ponds, floating Island, water wheel, cave and sunken greenhouse. Fully organic and compost system. Vegetable garden (no dig system). Flower borders with shrubs. Various seating areas and a 'follow the sun

house'! Complete walled garden. Mostly wheelchair access.

♿ 🐱 ✿ 🚂 ☕

35 THE GATE HOUSE
Lee EX34 8LR. Mrs H Booker. *3m W of Ilfracombe. Park in Lee village car park. Take lane alongside The Grampus PH. Garden approx 30 metres past inn buildings. Open most days but wise to check by tel 01271 862409 between 7pm & 9pm.* **Adm by donation. Daily Fri 1 May to Thur 1 Oct (10-4).**
Described by many visitors as a peaceful paradise, this streamside garden incl collection of over 100 rodgersia (at their best end of June), interesting herbaceous areas, patio gardens with semi-hardy exotics, many unusual mature trees and shrubs and large organic vegetable garden. Level gravel paths.

♿ 🐱 ☕

2 pretty gardens and gallery . . .

36 GOREN FARM
Broadhayes, Stockland, Honiton EX14 9EN. Julian Pady, 01404 881335, gorenfarm@hotmail.com, www.goren.co.uk. *6m E of Honiton, 6m W of Axminster. Old Taunton Rd from Shute on A35 or Otter Vale motors on A30. 100 metres N of Stockland television mast, signed at Ridge Cross.* Light refreshments. **Adm £3, chd free. Evening Openings Daily Mon 1 June to Fri 31 July (5-10). Sat 6, Sun 7, Sat 13, Sun 14 June, Sat 4, Sun 5, Sat 11, Sun 12 July (10-5); Sat 12 Sept (11-5). Visitors also welcome by arrangement June to Aug.**
Wander through 50 acres of natural species rich wild flower meadows. Dozens of varieties of wild flowers and grasses. Orchids early June, butterflies July. Stunning views of Blackdown Hills. Georgian house and gardens, guided walks 10.30 and

2.30 on open weekends, evenings, or by arrangement. Sept12: green apple day, tour around orchards, see apples pressed on 250yr press. BBQ lunches. Partial wheelchair access to meadows.

♿ 🐱 ✿ 🚂 ⊨ ☕

37 GORWELL HOUSE
Goodleigh Rd, Barnstaple EX32 7JP. Dr J A Marston, 01271 323202, artavianjohn@gmail.com, www.gorwellhousegarden.co.uk. *³/₄ m E of Barnstaple centre on Bratton Fleming road. Drive entrance between two lodges on L coming uphill.* Cream teas. **Adm £4, chd free. Sun 22 Mar, Sun 19 Apr, Sun 3 May (2-6). Visitors also welcome by arrangement, groups preferred.**
Created mostly since 1979, this 4-acre garden overlooking the Taw estuary has a benign microclimate which allows many rare and tender plants to grow and thrive, both in the open and in walled garden. Several strategically placed follies complement the enclosures and vistas within the garden. Opening in March especially for the magnolias. Featured in N Devon Journal, The English Garden and Devon Life magazines and on BBC Radio Devon. Recently on web-based SW1TV Summer Gardens. Mostly wheelchair access but some steep slopes.

♿ 🐱 ✿ ☕

38 HALDON GRANGE
Dunchideock, Exeter EX6 7YE. Ted Phythian, 01392 832349. *5m SW of Exeter. From A30 go through Ide Village to Dunchideock 5m. Turn L to Lord Haldon, Haldon Grange is next L. From A38 (S) turn L on top of Haldon Hill follow Dunchideock signs, R at village centre to Lord Haldon.* Home-made teas. **Adm £4, chd free. Sat 4, Sun 5, Mon 6, Sat 11, Sun 12, Sat 18, Sun 19, Wed 22, Sat 25, Sun 26, Wed 29 Apr, Sat 2, Sun 3, Mon 4, Wed 6, Sat 9, Sun 10, Wed 13, Sat 16, Sun 17, Sat 23, Sun 24, Mon 25, Sat 30, Sun 31 May (1-5). Visitors also welcome by arrangement Apr to June refreshments by arrangement.**
12 acre well established garden with camellias, magnolias, azaleas, various shrubs and rhododendrons; rare and mature trees; small lake and ponds with river and water cascades. 5 acre arboretum planted 2011 with wide range of trees and shrubs. Wheelchair access to main features.

♿ ✿ ☕

High Garden

39 HAMBLYN'S COOMBE

Dittisham, Dartmouth TQ6 0HE.
Bridget McCrum, 01803 722228,
mccrum.sculpt@waitrose.com. *3m
N of Dartmouth. From A3122 L to
Dittisham. In village R at Red Lion,
The Level, then Rectory Lane, past
River Farm to Hamblyn's Coombe.*
Adm £5, chd free. **Visitors
welcome by arrangement** Mar to
Nov, parking difficult for more than
20.
7-acre garden with stunning views
across the river to Greenway House
and sloping steeply to R Dart at
bottom of garden. Extensive planting
of trees and shrubs with unusual
design features accompanying
Bridget McCrum's stone carvings and
bronzes. Wild flower meadow and
woods. Good rhododendrons and
camellias, ferns and bamboos, acers
and hydrangeas. Exceptional autumn
colour.

40 HARBOUR LIGHTS

Horns Cross, Bideford EX39 5DW.
Brian & Faith Butler, 01237 451627,
brian.nfu@gmail.com. *7m W of
Bideford, 3m E of Clovelly. On main
A39 between Bideford and Clovelly,
halfway between Hoops Inn and
Bucks Cross.* Light lunches, home
made cakes and cream teas. Adm
£3.50, chd free. **Sat 27, Sun 28
June (11-6).** Also open Springfield

27/28 June. Visitors also welcome
by arrangement May to Aug for
groups of 10+.
½ acre colourful garden with Lundy
views. A garden of wit, humour,
unusual ideas and surprises. Water
features, shrubs, herbaceous, foliage
area, grasses in an unusual setting,
fernery, bonsai and polytunnel.
Interesting time saving ideas. You will
never have seen a garden like this!
Superb conservatory for cream teas.
Free leaflet. We like our visitors to
leave with a smile! Child friendly. A
'must visit' garden. Intriguing artwork
of various kinds. Featured in Amateur
Gardening and local press.

HARCOMBE HOUSE
See Dorset.

41 THE HAVEN

Wembury Road, Hollacombe,
Wembury, South Hams PL9 0DQ.
Mrs S Norton & Mr J Norton, 01752
862149,
suenorton1@hotmail.co.uk. *20
minutes from Plymouth city centre.
Use A379 Plymouth to Kingsbridge
rd. At Elburton r'about follow signs to
Wembury. Parking on roadside. Bus
stop outside, route 48 from
Plymouth.* Cream teas. Adm £3.50,
chd free. **Sat 28, Sun 29 Mar
(10-4.30).** Visitors also welcome by
arrangement Mar to Sept.

½ -acre sloping plantsman's garden
in the South Hams AONB. Tearoom
and seating areas. 2 ponds.
Substantial collection of large
flowering Asiatic and hybrid tree
magnolias. Large collection of
camellias including camellia reticulata.
Rare dwarf, weeping and slow
growing conifers. Daphnes, early
azaleas and rhododendrons, spring
bulbs, fritillaria and hellebores.
Michelias, manglietias. Wheelchair
access to top part of garden only.

42 HEATHERCOMBE

Manaton, nr Bovey Tracey
TQ13 9XE. Claude & Margaret Pike
Woodlands Trust, 01626 354404,
gardens@pike.me.uk,
www.heathercombe.com. *7m NW
of Bovey Tracey. From Bovey Tracey
take scenic B3387 to Haytor
/Widecombe. 1.7m past Haytor
Rocks (before Widecombe hill) turn R
to Hound Tor & Manaton. 1.4m past
Hound Tor turn L at Heatree Cross to
Heathercombe.* Cream teas in pretty
cottage garden or conservatory if
wet. Adm £4.50, chd free. Share to
Rowcroft Hospice. **Sun 29 Mar,
Sun 17, Sat 23, Sun 24, Sun 31
May, Sun 7, Sun 21, Sun 28 June
(1.30-5.30).** Visitors also welcome
by arrangement Apr to Oct home-
made teas.
Tranquil valley with tumbling streams

Look out for the NGS yellow arrows ...

and quiet ponds, setting for 30 acres of spring and summer interest - daffodils, extensive bluebells complementing large displays of rhododendrons, lovely cottage gardens, interesting herbaceous planting, woodland walks, many specimen trees, bog and fern gardens, orchard and wild flower meadow. Fine sculptures, seats and 2m mainly level sandy paths. Cottage gardens set around Heathercombe's traditional Dartmoor longhouses.

3 acres of exciting gardens with established pergola walk . . .

43 ◆ HEDDON HALL
Parracombe EX31 4QL. Mr & Mrs de Falbe, 07577 406238, Jdefalbe@gmail.com. *10m NE of Barnstaple. Follow A39 towards Lynton around Parracombe (avoiding village centre), then L. towards village; entrance 200 yds on L.* Home-made teas. **Adm £5, chd free. For NGS: Sun 7 June, Sun 12 July (11-4). For other opening times and information, please phone or email.** Stunning walled garden laid out by Penelope Hobhouse with clipped box and cordoned apple trees, herbaceous secret garden and natural rockery leading to a bog garden and 3 stew ponds. Very much a gardeners' garden, beautifully maintained, with many rare species, ferns, mature shrubs and trees all thriving in 4 acres of this sheltered Exmoor valley. Wheelchair access to walled garden only.

44 ▶ HIGH GARDEN
Chiverstone Lane, Kenton EX6 8NJ. Chris & Sharon Britton, 01626 899106, highgarden@highgarden.co.uk, highgardennurserykenton. wordpress.com. *5m S of Exeter on A379 Dawlish Rd. Leaving Kenton*

towards Exeter, L into Chiverstone Lane, 50yds along lane. Entrance clearly marked. Home-made teas. Evening openings with wine, nibbles and live music. **Adm £3.50, chd free. Thur 2, Fri 3 July (2-9); Sat 4 July (2-5.30). Visitors also welcome by arrangement Apr to July all size groups catered for.** Stunning garden of over 4 acres with huge range of interesting, rare and exciting plants. 70m double herbaceous border for high summer colour. Tropical border, large vegetable and fruit garden. Adjoining plantsman's nursery open on NGS days and all yr Tues to Fri. Slightly sloping site but the few steps can be avoided.

45 ▶ HIGHER ASH FARM
Ash, Dartmouth TQ6 0LR. Mr Michael Gribbin, 07595 507516, matthew.perkins18@yahoo.co.uk. *Leave A3122 at Halwell for Dartmouth. R at Sportsman's Arms to Ash. After 1½ m at 2nd Xrds turn R to Higher Ash Farm.* Home-made teas. **Adm £4.50, chd free. Sun 3, Sun 17 May, Sun 4 Oct (2-5). Also open 28 June with Ash Gardens. Visitors also welcome by arrangement Mar to Oct for 1-10.** Evolving garden, high up in South Devon countryside. Sitting in 2.5 acres there is a large kitchen garden terraced into the hillside adjoining orchard under planted with a variety of daffodils. A vibrant array of azaleas and rhododendrons surround the barns and courtyard. The farmhouse is surrounded by a mix of herbaceous borders, shrubs and lawns. Pond, stream, autumn interest.

46 ▶ HIGHER CULLAFORD
Spreyton, Crediton EX17 5AX. Dr and Mrs Kennerley. *Approx ¾ m from centre of Spreyton, 20m W of Exeter, 10 E of Okehampton. From A30 at Whiddon Down follow signs to Spreyton. Yellow signs from A3124, the centre of the village and Spreyton parish church.* Cream teas. **Adm £3.50, chd free. Sun 21, Sun 28 June (1.30-5.30).** Traditional cottage style garden developed over past 10yrs from steep field and farmyard on northern edge of Dartmoor National Park. Mixed borders of herbaceous plants, roses and shrubs. 30ft pergola covered with seagull rose and many varieties

of clematis, raised vegetable beds and wildlife pond. Additional vegetable garden with polytunnel and fruit trees. Wheelchair access limited but can drive in to garden on request.

47 ▶ ◆ HOLBROOK GARDEN
Sampford Shrubs, Sampford Peverell EX16 7EN. Martin Hughes-Jones & Susan Proud, 01884 821164, www.holbrookgarden.com. *1m NW from M5 J27. From M5 J27 follow signs to Tiverton Parkway. At top of slip rd off A361 follow brown sign to Holbrook Garden, 1m from J27.* **Adm £4, chd free. For NGS: Fri 3, Sat 4, Sun 5, Mon 6, Thur 23, Fri 24, Sat 25 Apr, Sat 2, Sun 3, Mon 4, Thur 21, Fri 22, Sat 23 May, Sat 6, Sun 7, Fri 19, Sat 20 June, Fri 10, Sat 11 July, Fri 28, Sat 29, Sun 30 Aug (10-5). For other opening times and information, please phone or see garden website.** 2 acre S-facing garden with plantings inspired by natural plant populations; the garden continually evolves - many experimental plantings - wet garden, stone garden. Perfumes, songbirds and nests everywhere in spring and early summer. Fritillaries, pulmonarias April; crocosmia, heleniums, Salvias, late perennials Aug/Sept. Productive vegetable garden and polytunnel. Coach parties by arrangement please phone or see holbrookgarden.com. Narrow paths restrict access for wheelchairs and child buggies.

48 ▶ HOLE FARM
Woolsery, Bideford EX39 5RF. Heather Alford. *11m SW of Bideford. Follow directions for Woolfardisworthy, signed from A39 at Bucks Cross. From village follow NGS signs from school for approx 2m.* Home-made teas in converted barn. **Adm £3.50, chd free. Sat 18, Sun 19 July, Sun 6 Sept (2-6). Also open Springfield.** 3 acres of exciting gardens with established pergola walk, waterfall, ponds, vegetable and bog garden. Terraces and features incl round house have all been created using natural stone from original farm quarry. Peaceful walks through Culm grassland and water meadows border R Torridge and host a range of wildlife. Home to a herd of pedigree native Devon cattle. Riverside walk not accessible with wheelchair.

49 HOLLYCOMBE HOUSE
Manor Rd, Bishopsteignton
TQ14 9SU. Jenny Charlton &
Graham Jelley, 01626 870838,
hollycombealpacas@live.co.uk,
www.hollycombealpacas.co.uk.
*Situated between Newton Abbot
& Teignmouth. From Newton
Abbot A381, L after Jack's Patch
GC, or from Teignmouth R at sign
Old Walls Vineyard - Church Rd -
R at PH, Radway Hill, L Manor Rd,
R at Rock.* **Adm £3.50, chd free.
Visitors welcome by
arrangement.**
Nearly 5 acres of stunning garden
with views over Teign Estuary. Some
say the best view in Devon. Stylish
borders, shrubs for every day of the
year. Organic vegetables in raised
beds - compost from alpacas!
Attractive large pond, water lilies, koi
carp, call ducks, alpacas with their
babies and free range chickens all
create an area of individuality: also we
have Harley the Harris Hawk! Limited
wheelchair access to view pond,
white silkie chickens, ducks, fish and
alpacas.

50 ◆ HOTEL ENDSLEIGH
Milton Abbot, Tavistock PL19 0PQ.
Olga Polizzi, 01822 870000,
www.hotelendsleigh.com/garden.
*7m NW of Tavistock, midway
between Tavistock and Launceston.
From Tavistock, take B3362 to
Launceston. 7m to Milton Abbot
then 1st L, opp school. From
Launceston & A30, B3362 to
Tavistock. At Milton Abbot turn R opp
school.* Tea in old stable yard opp
Hotel. Hotel also open to non
residents for lunch, teas and dinner.
**Adm £5, chd free. For NGS: Sun 7
June, Sun 19 July (11.30-4.30).** For
other opening times and
information, please phone or see
garden website.
200 year old Repton-designed
garden in 3 parts; formal gardens
around house, picturesque dell with
pleasure dairy and rockery and
arboretum. Gardens were laid out in
1814 and have been renovated over
last 10yrs. Bordering the R Tamar, it is
a hidden oasis of plants and views.
Hotel was built by Sir Jeffry Wyattville
for the Duchess of Bedford in the
romantic cottage Orne style. Nursery
adjoins hotel's 108 acres. Partial
wheelchair access.

51 KIA-ORA FARM & GARDENS
Knowle Lane, Cullompton
EX15 1PZ. Mrs M B Disney, 01884
32347, rosie@kia-orafarm.co.uk,
www.kia-orafarm.co.uk. *On W side
of Cullompton and 6m SE of Tiverton.
M5 J28, through town centre to
r'about, 3rd exit R, top of Swallow
Way turn L into Knowle Lane, garden
beside Cullompton Rugby Club.*
Home-made teas, undercover tea
barn for shelter or shade whatever
the British weather. **Adm £3, chd
free. Suns & Mons 5, 6, 19 Apr, 3,
4, 17, 24, 25 May, 14, 28 June, 12,
26 July, 9, 30, 31 Aug, 13 Sept
(2-5.30). Visitors also welcome by
arrangement**
Charming, peaceful 10 acre garden
with lawns, lakes and ponds. Water
features with swans, ducks and other
wildlife. Mature trees, shrubs,
rhododendrons, azaleas, heathers,
roses, herbaceous borders and
rockeries. Nursery avenue, novelty
crazy golf. Lots to see and enjoy, and
no afternoon would be complete
without sampling a home-made
Devon cream tea or a slice of one of
the many tempting cakes.

GROUP OPENING

52 KILMINGTON (SHUTE ROAD) GARDENS
Kilmington, Axminster EX13 7ST,
www.Kilmingtonvillage.com.
*1½ m W of Axminster. Signed off
A35.* Home-made teas at The Acorn.
**Combined adm £5, chd free.
Sat 13, Sun 14 June (1.30-5).**

NEW THE ACORN
Shute Road. Mike & Mary Tyler

BREACH
J A Chapman & B J Lewis.
Off Shute Rd

NEW LAMBLEY BROOK
Springhead Lane. David and
Stephanie.
nr Breach

SPINNEY TWO
Paul & Celia Dunsford

Set in rural E Devon in AONB yet
easily accessed from A35. 4 gardens
within ¼ m circle. Spinney Two: ½
acre on southerly slope with yr round
colour, foliage and texture. Spring
flowering bulbs, shrubs and trees
including acers and cornus, climbers
including clematis and roses. Mixed

borders and vegetable plot. Breach:
set in over 3 acres with majestic
woodland partially underplanted with
rhododendrons, also extensive areas
of grass, colourful beds, ponds,
orchard and vegetable garden.
Lambley Brook: Near Breach. ½ acre
tucked away location backing onto
fields and woodland. Bounded by 2
streams, incl bog garden, rockery and
numerous colour themed beds
containing many unusual plants and
shrubs. A surprise round every
corner! The Acorn: Enjoy teas with a
lovely view and in 1¼ acre informal
garden, with mature trees and shrubs
and wildlife ponds. Disabled Parking.

hospiceUK
The NGS funds vital
hospice care projects

53 ◆ KNIGHTSHAYES COURT GARDEN
Tiverton EX16 7RQ. National Trust,
01884 254665,
www.nationaltrust.org.uk. *2m N of
Tiverton. Via A396 Tiverton to
Bampton rd; turn E in Bolham, signed
Knightshayes; entrance ½ m on L.*
**Adm £9, chd £4.50. For NGS: Mon
11 May (11-4).** For other opening
times and information, please
phone or see garden website.
Large, beautiful 'Garden in the
Wood', 50 acres of landscaped
gardens with pleasant walks and
views over Exe valley. Choice
collections of unusual plants, incl
acers, birches, rhododendrons,
azaleas, camellias, magnolias, roses,
spring bulbs, alpines and herbaceous
borders; formal gardens; walled
kitchen garden.

54 LANGTREES
10 Cott Lane, Croyde, Braunton
EX33 1ND. Paul & Helena Petrides,
01271 890202,
angelrest@lineone.net,
www.langtrees.info. *10m W of
Barnstaple. From Braunton direction
Cott Lane on R as road narrows
towards village centre. No parking in
lane, parking in village car park
200yds L.* Home-made teas. **Adm**

£4, chd free. **Sat 16, Sun 17 May (1-5). Visitors also welcome by arrangement.**
1 acre plantsman's garden with eclectic selection of plants. Many S hemisphere shrubs and other tender species. Yr-round interest with landscaping and design features. Flowers all seasons from rhododendrons, viburnums and magnolias in spring to salvias, schizostylis and ginger lilies in autumn. Interesting selection of trees. Featured in Garden News.

55 LEE FORD
Knowle, Budleigh Salterton EX9 7AJ. Mr & Mrs N Lindsay-Fynn, 01395 445894, crescent@leeford.co.uk. *3¹/₂ m East of Exmouth in village of Knowle. For SatNav use postcode EX9 6AL.* Refreshments only available for pre booked groups of 10+. Morning coffee/coffee & cake/cream teas/afternoon tea & cake. **Adm £6, chd free. Visitors welcome by arrangement** Mar to Oct groups of 20+ discount, adm £5.
Extensive, formal and woodland garden, largely developed in 1950s, but recently much extended with mass displays of camellias, rhododendrons and azaleas, incl many rare varieties. Traditional walled garden filled with fruit and vegetables, herb garden, bog garden, rose garden, hydrangea collection, greenhouses. Ornamental conservatory with collection of pot plants. Lee Ford has direct access to the Pedestrian route and National Cycle Network route 2 which follows the old railway line that linked Exmouth to Budleigh Salterton. Garden is ideal destination for cycle clubs or rambling groups. Formal gardens are lawn with gravel paths. Moderately steep slope to woodland garden on tarmac with gravel paths in woodland.

56 LEWIS COTTAGE
Spreyton, nr Crediton EX17 5AA. Mr & Mrs M Pell and Mr R Orton, 07773 785939, rworton@mac.com, https://www.lewiscottageplants.co.uk. *5m NE or Spreyton, 8m W of Crediton. From Hillerton Cross, keep Stone Cross to your R. Drive approx 1¹/₂ m, Lewis Cottage on L, proceed across cattle grid.* Home-made teas. **Adm £4, chd free. Sats & Suns 16,** 17 May, 6, 7 June, 18, 19 July, 29, 30 Aug (11-5). **Visitors also welcome by arrangement** May to Aug for groups of 20 max.
Located on SW-facing slope in rural Mid Devon, the 4 acre garden at Lewis Cottage has evolved primarily over last two decades, harnessing and working with the natural landscape. Using informal planting and natural formal structures to create a garden that reflects the souls of those who garden in it, it is an incredibly personal space that is a joy to share. New rose garden and iris bed created for 2015. Featured in Devon Life and RHS The Garden and on Radio Devon.

57 LITTLE ASH BUNGALOW
Fenny Bridges, Honiton EX14 3BL. Helen & Brian Brown, 01404 850941, helenlittleash@hotmail.com, www.facebook.com/littleashgarden. *3m W of Honiton. Leave A30 at Iron Bridge from Honiton 1m, Patteson's Cross from Exeter ¹/₂ m and follow NGS signs.* Tea. **Adm £3.50, chd free. Sun 31 May, Sun 16 Aug (1.30-5.30). Visitors also welcome by arrangement** June to Sept for groups of 10+.
Plantswoman's 1¹/₂ acre garden packed with different and unusual herbaceous perennials, shrubs and bamboos. Designed for yr-round interest, wildlife and owners' pleasure. Inspirational, voluptuous colour coordinated mixed borders provide interest through late spring, summer and autumn. Natural stream, pond and damp woodland area, mini wildlife meadows and expanding gravel/alpine garden. Featured in Garden News, Devon Life, local press and on BBC Radio Devon. Grass paths.

58 LITTLE CUMBRE
145 Pennsylvania Rd, Exeter EX4 6DZ. Dr Margaret Lloyd, 01392 258315. *1m due N of city centre. From town centre take Longbrook St, continue N up hill approx 1m. Near top of hill. P bus within 75 yds of gate, every 20 mins, hourly on Suns.* **Adm £3.50, chd free. Sat & Sun 7, 8, 14, 15 Feb 2015, 6, 7, 13, 14 Feb 2016 (12-3.30). Visitors also welcome by arrangement** Feb to May for groups of 10+.
1 acre garden and woodland on S-facing slope with extensive views. Interesting areas of garden on different levels linked by grassy paths. Wonderful display of snowdrops, many varieties, and colourful hellebores. Scented winter shrubs and camellias, spring bulbs. Top garden managed to encourage wildlife. Partial wheelchair access.

59 LITTLE WEBBERY
Webbery, Bideford EX39 4PS. Mr & Mrs J A Yewdall, 01271 858206, jyewdall1@gmail.com. *2m E of Bideford. From Bideford (East the Water) along Alverdiscott Rd, or from Barnstaple to Torrington on B3232. Take road to Bideford at Alverdiscott, pass through Stoney Cross.* Home-made teas. **Adm £4, chd free. Visitors welcome by arrangement** Apr to Oct.
Approx 3 acres in valley setting with pond, lake, mature trees, 2 ha-has and large mature raised border. Large walled kitchen garden with yew and box hedging incl rose garden, lawns with shrubs and rose and clematis trellises. Vegetables and greenhouse and adj traditional cottage garden. Partial wheelchair access.

60 LITTLECOURT COTTAGES
Seafield Rd, Sidmouth EX10 8HF. Geoffrey Ward & Selwyn Kussman, www.littlecourtcottages.com. *500yds N of Sidmouth seafront off Station Rd. Take A3052 to Sidmouth. At Bowd PH take B3176 to Sidmouth. Continue towards seafront, turn R into Seafield Rd. Littlecourt is 75yds on R.* Home-made teas. **Adm £3.50, chd free. Sun 26 July (2-5). Evening Opening £3.50, chd free, wine, Mon 27 July (6-9).**
Oasis of calm in middle of Sidmouth. A series of rooms for the plantaholic. Courtyard gardens behind house; in front, main lawn and water feature. Rare and tender plants everywhere. Exceptional basket colour. New features in front garden. Recent redesign of rear garden with Victorian greenhouse.

1 acre plantsman's garden with eclectic selection of plants . . .

61 ▶ THE LOOKOUT

Sowden Lane, Lympstone EX8 5HE. Will & Jackie Michelmore, www.lympstone.org/businesses/lookout-landscapes/. *9m SE of Exeter, 2m N of Exmouth off A376. 12mins from M5. Follow signs off A376 to Exmouth after marine camp.* Cream teas. Coffees, cakes & soft drinks available. **Adm £4, chd free. Fri 26 June (2-5); Sun 28 June (2-6).**

2 wildlife-friendly acres on edge of Exe Estuary. Lovingly created from derelict site to harmonise with coastal location and maximise on far reaching views. Flotsam and jetsam sit amongst naturalistic seaside planting to give that washed up from the beach look. Circular walk through wild flower meadow to pond, through copse and along riverbank. Walled Mediterranean courtyard, small jungly area. Giant sandpit with buckets and spades for children. Photographic display showing how the site has evolved from 1920's to present day. Love-Local pop up shop featuring nautically inspired West Country craft and gifts. Featured in Country Homes & Interiors. Limited wheelchair access to lower garden, some gravel paths, steps and slopes. Drop off area at gate. Level access to stalls and refreshments.

& ⊗ ☕

62 NEW ▶ LOWER GRENOFEN

Grenofen, Tavistock PL19 9ES. Nicola Evans & Steven Nash, www.lowergrenofen.co.uk. *From A386 Tavistock to Plymouth road take lane opp Half Way House Inn at Grenofen, take 2nd L, signed 'narrow bridge', after 400yds we're last house on R immed before bridge.* Cream teas. Tea & coffee, cold drinks, biscuits. **Adm £4, chd free. Tue 16, Wed 17 June (11-5).**

46 acres in AONB (mainly SSSI) with woodland walks on banks of R Walkham. 2 acre cultivated secluded garden with lawns, wildlife ponds, rill with raised beds, bog and waterfall to terrace with glazed outdoor rooms. Perennial cottage plants and native wild flowers. Specimen acers. Mainly white and themed planting reflecting property's use as summer outdoor wedding venue. Gentle slopes. Some areas (eg raised orchard) would not be accessible to wheelchairs. Some shallow steps with alternative non step access.

& ☕

63 ▶ LOWER SPITCHWICK GARDEN

Poundsgate TQ13 7NU. Pauline Lee, 01364 631593, paulineleeceramics@hotmail.com. *4m NW of Ashburton. By Spitchwick Common, nr New Bridge, Dartmoor.* Home-made teas. **Adm £3.50, chd free. Sat 16, Sun 17 May, Sat 25, Sun 26 July (1.30-5). Visitors also welcome by arrangement May to Sept.**

Beautiful valley alongside R Dart. East Lower Lodge: atmospheric woodland garden with imaginative planting in natural setting. Contains jungle area with bamboo teahouse, meandering grass pathways, lawns, borders with stream, potager and vegetable garden. Ceramic sculpture inspired by plant forms. Artist's studio.

🏠 ⊗ ☕

> *It has a magical feel and great views across the dart valley . . .*

64 ◆ LUKESLAND

Harford, Ivybridge PL21 0JF. Mrs R Howell & Mr & Mrs J Howell, 01752 691749, www.lukesland.co.uk. *10m E of Plymouth. Turn off A38 at Ivybridge. 1¹/₂ m N on Harford rd, E side of Erme valley.* Home-made soups and home baking available at all openings. **For other information, please phone or see garden website.**

24 acres of flowering shrubs, wild flowers and rare trees with pinetum in Dartmoor National Park. Beautiful setting of small valley around Addicombe Brook with lakes, numerous waterfalls and pools. Extensive and impressive collections of camellias, rhododendrons, azaleas and acers; also champion magnolia campbellii and huge Davidia involucrata. Superb spring and autumn colour. Children's trail. Open Suns, Weds and BH (11-5) 29 Mar-14 June and 4 Oct-15 Nov. Adm £5, chd free. Champion magnolia and davidia featured in The Times, The Telegraph, The Daily Mail and

Western Morning News. Also on ITV West Country. Partial wheelchair access incl tearoom and WC.

🏠 ⊗ 🚐 ☕

65 NEW ▶ LUSCOMBE FARM

Colston Road, Buckfastleigh TQ11 0LP. Mr Julian David. *2¹/₂ m from A38 junction at Buckfastleigh. Follow yellow signs off A384.* **Adm £3.50, chd free. Sat 13, Sun 14 June (10.30-5).**

This walled garden was designed and created by Julian and Jasmin David in the 60's. A formal garden with fastigiate yews and box hedging and topiary, loosely planted with roses, shrubs, perennials, annuals and bi-annuals. It has a magical feel and great views across the dart valley.

& 🏠 ⊗

66 NEW ▶ MARSHALL FARM

Ide, nr Exeter EX2 9TN. Jenny Tuckett. *Between Ide and Dunchideock. Drive through Ide to top of village r'about, straight on for 1¹/₂ m. Turn R onto concrete drive, parking in farmyard at rear of property.* Home-made teas. Cream teas. **Adm £3, chd free. Fri 19, Sun 21 June (1-5).**

Garden approached along lane lined with home grown lime, oak and chestnut trees. A country garden created approx 1967. One acre featuring wild flower gardens, gravel beds, pond, parterre garden and a vegetable and cutting garden. Stunning views of Woodbury, Sidmouth gap and Haldon. Limited wheelchair access.

⊗ ☕

67 ◆ MARWOOD HILL

Marwood EX31 4EB. Dr J A Snowdon, 01271 342528, www.marwoodhillgarden.co.uk. *4m N of Barnstaple. Signed from A361 & B3230. Look out for brown signs. See website for map. New coach & car park.* Home-made teas. **Adm £6, chd free. For NGS: Sun 10 May (10-5). For other opening times and information, please phone or see garden website.**

Marwood Hill is a very special private garden covering an area of 20 acres with lakes and set in a valley tucked away in North Devon. From early spring snowdrops through to late autumn there is always a colourful surprise around every turn. National Collections of astilbe, iris ensata and tulbaghia, large collections of camellia, rhododendron and

Venn Cross Railway Gardens

magnolia. Winner of MacLaren Cup at rhododendron and camellia show RHS Rosemoor. Partial wheelchair access.

68 THE MILL HOUSE
Fremington, Barnstaple EX31 3DQ. Martin & Judy Ash, martin_s_ash@yahoo.co.uk. *3m W of Barnstaple. Off A39, take A3125 N. At 3rd r'about (Cedars) L on B3233. In Fremington L at top of Church Hill onto Higher Rd. All parking signed 100m away.* Home-made teas. **Adm £3.50, chd free. Sat 6, Sun 7 June, Sat 4, Sun 5 July (12-5). Visitors also welcome by arrangement May to Sept for groups of 10+ only.**
3/4 acre garden, surrounding thatched mill house and bordered by Fremington water; the topography is the first wow factor here. Stepped ups and downs, ins and outs, surprises around every corner. There is so much on a small scale; bridges, borders, ponds, walkways, rockery, terracing, lawns, bog garden, quarry garden, wild garden, a small art gallery, oh and a henge. Wandering minstrels!

GROUP OPENING

69 MORETONHAMPSTEAD GARDENS
Moretonhampstead TQ13 8PW. *12m W of Exeter & N of Newton Abbot. On E slopes of Dartmoor National Park. Parking at both gardens.* Cream teas. **Combined adm £5, chd free. Fri 15, Sat 16, Sun 17 May, Sat 5, Sun 6 Sept (2-6).**

MARDON
Graham & Mary Wilson.
From centre of village, head towards church, turn L into Lime St. Bottom of hill on R

SUTTON MEAD
Edward & Miranda Allhusen.
1/2 m N of village on A382. R at r'about
Visitors also welcome by arrangement, coach possible but 100yd walk from main road. 01647 440296 miranda@allhusen.co.uk

2 large gardens close to moorland town. One in a wooded valley, the other higher up with magnificent views of Dartmoor. Dogs on leads welcome. Plant sale, teas are a must. Both have mature orchards and year round vegetable gardens. Substantial rhododendron, azalea and tree planting, croquet lawns, summer colour and woodland walks through hydrangeas and acers. Something for all the family. Mardon: 4 acres based on its original Edwardian design. Long herbaceous border, rose garden and formal granite terraces supporting 2 borders of agapanthus. Fernery beside stream-fed pond with its thatched boathouse. New arboretum with 60 specimen trees. Sutton Mead: Paths wander through tranquil woodland, unusual planting. Lawns surrounding granite-lined pond with seat at water's edge. Elsewhere dahlias, grasses, bog garden, rill-fed round pond, secluded seating and an unusual concrete greenhouse. Sedum roofed summerhouse. A garden of variety. Limited wheelchair access.

70 MOTHECOMBE HOUSE
Holbeton, nr Plymouth PL8 1LB.
Mr & Mrs A Mildmay-White, 01752
830444, annemildmay@gmail.com,
www.flete.co.uk. *12m E of
Plymouth. From A379 between
Yealmpton and Modbury turn S for
Holbeton. Continue 2m to
Mothecombe.* Cream teas. **Adm £5,
chd free. Sat 2, Sun 3 May (2-5).
Visitors also welcome by
arrangement coach access limited
by 11¼ ft bridge.**
Queen Anne house (not open) with
Lutyens additions and terraces set in
private estate hamlet. Walled pleasure
gardens, borders and Lutyens
courtyard. Orchard with spring bulbs,
unusual shrubs and trees, camellia
walk. Autumn garden, streams, bog
garden and pond. Bluebell woods
leading to private beach. Yr-round
interest. New bumblebee garden.
Sandy beach at bottom of garden,
unusual shaped large liriodendron
tulipifera. New planting of bee friendly
walled garden, featured in Western
Morning News. Gravel paths, one
slight slope.
&♿ ⊗ ☕

71 THE OLD DAIRY
Sidbury, Sidmouth EX10 0QR.
Dame Alison Carnwath & Peter
Thomson. *½ m from Sidbury. Enter
village of Sidbury from either Honiton
or Sidford and turn into Church St
next to church.* Yellow signs visible at
church. Home-made teas. Variety of
home made cakes. Juices, teas and
coffees. Beautiful terrace to enjoy tea
or conservatory if wet. **Adm £5, chd
free. Sat 16, Sun 17 May (2-6).**
25 year old garden carved out of
woodland and meadows, built on
hillside. Rhododendrons and wisteria,
bluebells and roses. Some
herbaceous around the house. Small
pond and bog garden. Splendid
views over Sid Valley. The essence of
peaceful Devon countryside.
Continue from house along East
Devon way to extend your experience
of glorious East Devon. Limited areas
for wheelchair tours but magnificent
views of course!
♿ ⛩ ⊗ ☕

72 THE OLD VICARAGE
West Anstey, South Molton
EX36 3PE. Tuck & Juliet Moss,
01398 341604,
julietmoss@btinternet.com. *9m E of
South Molton. From S Molton go E
on B3227 to Jubilee Inn. Follow NGS
signs to house. From Tiverton r'about*

take A396 7m to B3227 (L) to Jubilee
Inn. Cream teas. **Adm £4, chd free.
Sat 16, Sun 17 May, Sat 8, Sun 9
Aug (12-5). Visitors also welcome
by arrangement May to Aug.**
Croquet lawn leads to multi-level
garden overlooking three large ponds
with winding paths, climbing roses
and overviews. Brook with waterfall
flows through garden past fascinating
summerhouse built by owner.
Benched deck overhangs first pond.
Features rhododendrons, azaleas and
primulas in spring and large collection
of Japanese iris in July and wonderful
hydrangeas in August.
⛩ 🚌 ⊗ ☕

**NGS funding
helps us support
more carers**

73 ♦ PLANT WORLD
St Marychurch Road, Newton
Abbot TQ12 4SE. Ray Brown,
01803 872939, www.plant-world-
gardens.co.uk. *2m SE of Newton
Abbot. 1½ m from Penn Inn r'about.
Follow brown tourist signs at end of
A380 dual carriageway from Exeter.*
**For opening times and information,
please phone or see garden
website.**
The 4 acres of landscape gardens
with fabulous views have been called
Devon's 'Little Outdoor Eden'.
Representing each of the five
continents, they offer an extensive
collection of rare and exotic plants
from around the world. Superb
mature cottage garden and
Mediterranean garden will delight the
visitor. Attractive new viewpoint café
and shop. Open 28 March - end Sept
(9.30-5.00). Wheelchair access to
café and nursery only.
⛩ ⊗ 🚌 ☕

74 PORTINGTON
nr Lamerton PL19 8QY. Mr & Mrs I
A Dingle, 01822 870364. *3m NW of
Tavistock. From Tavistock B3362 to
Launceston. Turn L at Carrs garage.*

1st R (signed Horse Bridge) then L
(signed Portington). From Launceston
turn R at Carrs garage then as above.
Home-made teas. **Adm £3, chd free.
Share to Plymouth Samaritans.
Sun 7, Sun 14 June (2-5.30).
Visitors also welcome by
arrangement June to July.**
Garden in peaceful rural setting with
fine views over surrounding
countryside. Mixed planting with
shrubs and borders. Walk to small
lake through woodland and fields,
which have been designated a county
wildlife site. Partial wheelchair access.
♿ ⛩ ⊗ ☕

75 PROSPECT HOUSE
Lyme Road, Axminster EX13 5BH.
Peter Wadeley, 01297 631210,
wadeley@btinternet.com. *½ m
uphill from centre of Axminster. Just
before service station.* Home-made
teas. **Adm £3.50, chd free. Sat 11,
Sun 12 July, Sat 5, Sun 6 Sept
(1.30-5). Visitors also welcome by
arrangement June to Sept groups
of 6+.**
1 acre plantsman's garden hidden
behind high stone walls with Axe
Valley views. Well stocked borders
with rare shrubs, many reckoned to
be borderline tender. 200 varieties of
salvia, and other late summer
perennials including rudbeckia,
helenium, echinacea, helianthus,
crocosmia and grasses creating
a riot of colour. A gem, not to be
missed.
⛩ ⊗ ☕

76 REGENCY HOUSE
Hemyock EX15 3RQ. Mrs Jenny
Parsons, 01823 680238,
jenny.parsons@btinternet.com,
www.regencyhousehemyock.
co.uk. *8m N of Honiton. M5 J26.
From Hemyock take Dunkeswell-
Honiton road. Entrance ½ m on R
from Catherine Wheel PH and
church.* Disabled parking (only) at
house. Home-made teas. **Adm
£4.50, chd free. Sun 14 June, Sun
16 Aug, Sun 11 Oct (2-5.30).
Visitors also welcome by
arrangement Apr to Oct no
coaches.**
5-acre plantsman's garden
approached across private ford.
Many interesting and unusual trees
and shrubs. Visitors can try their hand
at identifying plants with the plant list
or have a game of croquet. Plenty of
space to eat your own picnic. Walled
vegetable and fruit garden, lake,
ponds, bog plantings and sweeping

lawns. Horses, Dexter cattle and Jacob sheep. Scarecrow competition around the garden for June opening. Gently sloping gravel paths give wheelchair access to the walled garden, lawns, borders and terrace, where teas are served.

77 RIDGEHILL
5 Dart Bridge Road, Buckfastleigh TQ11 0DY. Paul & Pip Wadsworth, www.facebook.com/ ridgehillgarden.devon. *On Eastern edge of Buckfastleigh. A38, either direction. Dart Bridge exit Buckfastleigh/Buckfast/Totnes. Turn to B'leigh/B'fast. Over Dart L into Dart Bridge Rd. Ridgehill 400yds on R.* Home-made teas. Delicious selection of home made cakes and tray bakes. **Adm £4, chd free. Sun 17 May (2-5).**
Compact, $1/2$ acre, mature garden in Dart valley. Several distinct, heavily planted beds, many uncommon plants, alpine/rockery, wildlife pond, herbaceous and ferns, copse, grasses and bamboo, small orchard, fruit and veg, work area, shrubbery, roses. Several DIY projects using fencing poles, footer boards and old tools! Child's Find The Animal quiz and other surprises.

78 ROWDEN HOUSE
Stoke Road, Noss Mayo, Plymouth PL8 1JG. Mr & Mrs Andrew Kingsnorth. *1/2 m from village of Noss Mayo. From Plymouth or Modbury take A379 to Yealmpton. Opp The Volunteer take B3186 to Noss Mayo, after 3m take L to Bridgend & Noss Mayo, cross creek through village to church. L after 1/2 m, last house on R.* Home-made teas. **Adm £3.50, chd free. Sun 8 Mar, Sun 14 June (2-5).**
Beautiful 1 acre sloping S-facing garden in rural setting with views across adjacent fields. Landscaped with drystone walls, steps and grassy paths, mature trees and shrubs provide a framework for underplanted bulbs and perennial beds, giving yr-round interest. A pond and stream complete the bucolic picture.

79 RUNNYMEDE
2 Orchard Close, Manor Rd, Sidmouth EX10 8RS. Veronica Wood. *12m SE of Exeter. A3052 to Sidmouth. 1st R (Bowd) onto B3176 $1^{1}/_{2}$ m. R into Manor Rd at Manor Pavilion Theatre, 1/2 m to Manor Rd Car Park (advised as disabled parking only in Orchard Close).* Home-made teas. **Adm £3, chd free. Sat 23, Sun 24, Mon 25 May (2-5).**
On western edge of Sidmouth. Beautiful tranquil garden of approx 1/4 acre artistically landscaped with circles, pool and rill designed by Naila Green RHS Chelsea medallist. Abundance of colourful and unusual plants. Woodland and gravel areas. Microclimate, tender plants, plentiful seating, level paths. Raised vegetable beds and greeenhouse with vines. Pictures and articles in Sidmouth Herald.

80 ST MERRYN
Higher Park Road, Braunton EX33 2LG. Dr W & Mrs Ros Bradford, 01271 813805, ros@st-merryn.co.uk. *5m W of Barnstaple. On A361, R at 30mph sign, then R into Lower Park Road, then L into Seven Acre Lane, at top of lane R into Higher Park Rd. Pink house 200 yds on R.* Cream teas. **Adm £4, chd free. Sun 19 Apr, Sun 17 May, Sat 13, Sun 14 June, Sun 12 July (2-6). Visitors also welcome by arrangement Apr to July any small group.**
Very sheltered, peaceful, gently sloping, S-facing, artist's garden, emphasis on shape, colour, scent and yr-round interest. A garden for pleasure with thatched summerhouse leading down to herbaceous borders. Winding crazy paving paths, many seating areas. Shrubs, mature trees, fish ponds, grassy knoll, gravel areas, hens. Many environmental features. Open gallery (arts & crafts).

Haldon Grange

Southcombe Gardens

Support the NGS – eat more cake! ☕

81 SEDGEWELL COACH HOUSE GARDENS
Olchard TQ12 3GU. Heather Jansch, 01626 852777, heather@heatherjansch.com, www.heatherjansch.com. *4m N of Newton Abbot. 12m S of Exeter on A380, L for Olchard, straight ahead on private drive.* Tea. **Adm £4, chd free. Sat 9, Sun 10 May, Sat 29, Sun 30 Aug (11-5).**
Heather Jansch, world-famous sculptor, brings innovative use of recycled materials to gardening. 14 acres incl stunning driftwood sculpture, fabulous views from thrilling woodland bluebell trail down to timeless stream-bordered water meadow walk, pools, herbaceous border, medicinal herb garden. Plentiful seating, come and picnic.

82 ◆ SHAPCOTT BARTON ESTATE
(East Knowstone Manor), East Knowstone, South Molton EX36 4EE. Anita Allen, 01398 341664. *13m NW of Tiverton. J25 M5 take Tiverton exit. 6½ m to r'about take exit South Molton 10m on A361. Turn R signed Knowstone. Leave A361 travel ¼ m to Roachhill through hamlet turn L at Wiston Cross, entrance on L ¼ m.* Cream teas. **Adm £4, chd free. Share to Cats Protection. For NGS: Suns 19, 26 Apr, 19, 26 July (10.30-4.30). Openings by arrangement, groups welcome.**
Large, ever developing garden of 200 acre estate around ancient historic manor house. Wildlife garden. Restored old fish ponds, stream and woodland rich in bird life. Unusual fruit orchard. Scented bulbs in Apr. Flowering burst July/Aug of National Plant Collections *Leucanthemum superbum* (shasta daisies) and buddleja davidii. Many butterfly plants incl over 40 varieties of phlox. Kitchen garden and standard orchard. Featured in Western Morning News.
NCH

83 SIDBURY MANOR
Sidbury, Sidmouth EX10 0QE. Sir John & Lady Cave, www.sidburymanor.co.uk. *1m NW of Sidbury. Signed in Sidbury village off A375 between Honiton and Sidmouth.* Home-made teas. **Adm £4.50, chd free. Sat 18, Sun 19 Apr (2-5).**
Built in 1870s this Victorian manor house built by owner's family and set within East Devon AONB comes complete with 20 acres of garden incl substantial walled gardens, an extensive arboretum containing many fine trees and shrubs, a number of champion trees, and areas devoted to magnolias, rhododendrons and camellias. Partial wheelchair access.

Cottage garden divided by rose and clematis clad pergola . . .

GROUP OPENING

84 SIDMOUTH GARDENS
Sidmouth, EX10 9JP & EX10 9DX. *Road plan provided at each Garden.* Home-made teas. **Combined adm £4, chd free. Sat 29, Sun 30, Mon 31 Aug (2-5.30).**

BYES REACH
Lynette Talbot & Peter Endersby
(See separate entry)

ROWAN BANK
44 Woolbrook Park. Barbara & Alan Mence.
A3052. 10 m from Exeter turn R at bottom of hill beyond Bowd Inn into Woolbrook Rd. After ½ m turn R beside St Francis Church. Garden on L

Situated on Jurassic Coast World Heritage Site, Sidmouth has fine beaches, beautiful gardens and magnificent coastal views. 2 contrasting gardens about 1m apart. Byes Reach: edible garden of ⅛ acre. Potager style, raised beds, espalier fruit trees on arched walkway, designed for those with mobility problems. Herbaceous borders, colour themed flower beds combining perennials, herbs, ferns and hostas. Pond, rockery, greenhouse and studio. Backing onto The Byes nature reserve and R Sid, offering an opportunity for a short walk from the garden gate. Rowan Bank is approx ¼ acre on a NW facing slope, generously planted with trees, shrubs, perennials and bulbs for yr-round interest. Steps lead to wide zigzag path rising gently to woodland edge of birch and rowan, with shady bench under Mexican pine. Seats at every corner and summerhouse looking towards wooded hills. Wheelchair access at Byes Reach, regret none at Rowan Bank.

85 SOUTH WOOD FARM
Cotleigh, Honiton EX14 9HU. Dr Clive Potter, 07764 606037, c.potter@imperial.ac.uk. *3m NE of Honiton. From Honiton head N on A30, take 1st R past Otter Dairy layby. Follow for 1m. Go straight over Xrds and take first L. Entrance on R.* Home-made teas. **Adm £4, chd free. Sat 19, Sun 20 Sept (2-5). Visitors also welcome by arrangement Apr to Sept, guided tours of garden available.**
Large country garden surrounding a listed C17 Devon farmhouse set deep in the Blackdown Hills. Includes walled courtyard planted with late summer herbaceous and yew topiary, kitchen garden of raised beds with step over pears, fruit cages and trained fruit trees, sunken dry stream bed walk and reflecting pond, formal plum orchard, nuttery and traditional Devon cobbled yard with lean to glasshouse. Gravel pathways, cobbles and steps.

86 SOUTH WORDEN
West Putford, Holsworthy EX22 7LG. Colonel Michael French, 01409 261448, mike@southworden.co.uk, www.southworden.co.uk. *2m from main A388 at Venn Green Xrds Milton Damerel. Pick up NGS signs at Venn Green Xrds. Follow road signs to East/West Putford at Five lanes X, L to Bradworthy. After 800m 1st turning on R for South Worden.* Home-made teas. **Adm £3.50, chd free. Sun 12 July, Sun 16 Aug (2.30-5). Visitors also welcome by arrangement July to Sept no more than groups of 10.**
¾ acre peaceful garden in the beautiful Devon countryside. Cottage garden divided by rose and clematis clad pergola. Several large herbaceous beds incl white and hot beds, conifer bed, many roses, peonies and sweet peas. Separate ½ acre wild flower garden with large granite stone feature, cherry trees, statues and Japanese inspired garden with water features and seating. Lovely views. Mainly flat but some gravel and grass paths.

GROUP OPENING

SOUTHCOMBE GARDENS

Dartmoor, Widecombe-in-the-Moor TQ13 7TU. *6m W of Bovey Tracey. B3387 from Bovey Tracey after village church take rd SW for 400yds then sharp R signed Southcombe, after 200yds pass C17 farmhouse and park on L.* Home-made teas at Southcombe Barn. **Combined adm £5, chd free. Sun 10, Sun 17, Sun 24, Mon 25, Sun 31 May, Sun 7, Sun 14 June (2-5).**

SOUTHCOMBE BARN
Amanda Sabin & Stephen Hobson

SOUTHCOMBE HOUSE
Dr & Mrs J R Seale
Visitors also welcome by arrangement May to July.
01364 621365

Village famous for its Fair, Uncle Tom Cobley and its C14 church - the Cathedral of the Moor. Featured in RHS The Garden. Southcombe Barn: 4 acres, trees and drifts of flowers, abundantly wild and intensely colourful. Beautiful all year round and busy with wildlife but this is its zenith six weeks of breathtaking glory. You can spend hours in it. People do. Southcombe House: 5 acres, SE-facing garden, arboretum and orchid rich restored wild flower meadow with bulbs in spring and four orchid species (early purple, southern marsh, common spotted and greater butterfly). On steep slope at 900ft above sea level with fine views to nearby tors. The teas are legendary. People starting their own wildflower meadows have used Southcombe House seed-rich fresh-cut hay to seed their newly cleared ground. Yellow rattle is then usually abundant in the first year and orchids begin to appear in the fourth year.

88 SPITCHWICK MANOR

Poundsgate, Newton Abbot TQ13 7PB. Mr & Mrs P Simpson, 01364 631209, admin@bennah.co.uk. *4m NW of Ashburton. Princetown rd from Ashburton through Poundsgate, 1st R at Lodge. From Princetown L at Poundsgate sign. Past Lodge. Park after 300yds at Xrds.* Home-made teas. **Adm £5, chd free. Sat 9, Sun 10 May, Sat 13, Sun 14 June (11-4.30). Visitors also welcome by**

arrangement May & June.
6½ -acre garden with extensive beautiful views. Mature garden undergoing refreshment. A variety of different areas; lower walled garden with glass houses, formal rose garden with fountain, camellia walk with small leat and secret garden with Lady Ashburton's plunge pool built 1763. 2.6 acre vegetable garden sheltered by high granite walls housing 9 allotments and lily pond. Mostly wheelchair access.

89 SPRINGFIELD

Woolsery, Bideford EX39 5PZ. Ms Asta Munro, 01237 431162. *Ignore SatNav. 8m W of Bideford. 3m S of Clovelly. Turn off A39 at Buck's Cross. T-junction at school turn L past village hall. L signed Putford. 1m L.* Tea. **Adm £3.50, chd free. Sat 30, Sun 31 May, Sat 27, Sun 28 June, Sat 18, Sun 19 July, Sun 6 Sept (1-6). Also open 27/28 June Harbour Lights. Visitors also welcome by arrangement May to Sept.**
2 acre S sloping rural plot with views. Plantaholic's garden crammed with shrubs, perennials inc 100+ hardy geraniums. Paved suntrap with containers. Gravel area surrounded with herbs, aromatic, silver and pastel plants. Shade area. Small wildlife pond. Meadow with meandering paths. Kitchen garden fruit, vegetables, edible flowers. Wildlife haven including bats. Little old fashioned 'sweetie shop' nursery.

90 NEW SPRINGFIELD HOUSE

Seaton Road, Colyford EX24 6QW. Wendy Pountney. *Colyford. Starting on 3052 coast road, at Colyford PO take Seaton Rd. House 500m on R.* Ample parking in field. Home-made teas. **Adm £3.50, chd free. Sat 25, Sun 26 July (2-5).**
1 acre garden of mainly fairly new planting. Numerous beds, majority of plants from from cuttings and seed keeping cost to minimum. Full of colour with wonderful views over River Axe and bird sanctuary.

91 SQUIRRELS

98 Barton Road, Torquay TQ2 7NS. Graham & Carol Starkie, 01803 329241, calgra@talktalk.net. *5m S of Newton Abbot. From Newton Abbot take A380 to Torquay. After ASDA store on L, turn L at T-lights up*

Old Woods Hill. 1st L into Barton Rd. Bungalow 200yds on L. Also could turn by B&Q. Parking nearby. Home-made teas. **Adm £3.50, chd free. Sun 26 July, Sat 1, Sun 2 Aug (2-5). Visitors also welcome by arrangement**
Plantsman's small town environmental garden, landscaped with small ponds and 7ft waterfall. Interlinked through abutilons to Japanese, Italianate, tropical areas. Specialising in fruit incl peaches, figs, kiwi. Tender plants incl bananas, tree fern, brugmansia, lantanas, oleanders. Mandevilla. Collections of fuchsia, abutilons, bougainvilleas, topiary and more. Environmentally friendly water features and waterfall. 24 cleverly hidden rain water storage containers. Advice on free electric from solar pv panels and solar hot water heating. Fruit pruning advice. 3 Sculptures. Many topiary birds, animals and balls. Huge 18mtr Torbay palm. Featured on BBC Radio Devon & BBC Radio 4 and in local press & Devon Life Magazine. No wheelchair access. Mainly level paths. Parking nearby. Conservatory for shelter and seating.

Full of colour with wonderful views over River Axe and bird sanctuary . . .

92 STONE FARM

Alverdiscott Rd, Bideford EX39 4PN. Mr & Mrs Ray Auvray. *1½ m from Bideford towards Alverdiscott. From Bideford cross river using Old Bridge and turn L onto Barnstaple Rd. 2nd R onto Manteo Way and 1st L at mini r'about.* Home-made teas. **Adm £3.50, chd free. Sat 27, Sun 28 June, Sat 4, Sun 5 July (2-5).**
1-acre country garden with striking herbaceous borders, dry stone wall terracing, white garden, dahlia bed

wild meadow area and woodland area. We also have an extensive fully organic vegetable garden with raised beds, soft fruit cage and polytunnels, together with an orchard with traditional varieties of apples, pears and nuts. Some gravel paths but access to whole garden with some help.

& 🐾 ✿ ☕

93 SUMMERS PLACE
Little Bowlish, Whitestone EX4 2HS. Mr & Mrs Stafford Charles, 01647 61786. *6m NW of Exeter. From M5, A30 Okehampton. After 7m, R to Tedburn St Mary, immed R at r'about past golf course. 1st L after ¹/₂ m signed Whitestone, straight ahead at Xrds, follow signs. From Exeter on Whitestone rd 1m beyond Whitestone, follow signs from Heath Cross. From Crediton, follow Whitestone rd through Fordton.* Light refreshments. Soup & light snacks 12.30-1.45, home-made teas 2.30-4.30. **Adm £4.50, chd free. Sun 22 Mar, Sun 2 Aug, Sun 4 Oct (12-5). Visitors also welcome by arrangement Mar to Oct 24 hrs notice required. Refreshments by arrangement.**
Extensive woodland garden, interesting trees, shrubs, herbaceous and wildflowers, bulbs in spring, summer shrub roses, autumn fruit and colour. Paths, steps and walkways lead to follies, sculptures, ponds, streamside strolls, grass steps to dewpond with Dartmoor views. Conservation and planting equally emphasized. Intimate house garden, rare breed poultry. Children (prize trail) and dog friendly. William Robinson inspired garden. Featured in local press.

🐾 ✿ ☕

94 TAMARISKS
Inner Hope Cove, Kingsbridge TQ7 3HH. Barbara Anderson, 01548 561745, bba@talktalk.net. *6m SW of Kingsbridge. Follow signs through Hope Cove to Inner Hope Cove and the sea.* **Adm £3.50, chd free.** Share to Butterfly Conservation. **Visitors welcome by arrangement.**
Sloping ¹/₃ acre directly above the sea with magnificent views, rustic steps, extensive stonework, ponds, rockeries and wild terrace overlooking sea. Very colourful demonstration of seaside planting: hydrangeas, mallows, crocosmia, achillea, sea holly, convolvulus, lavender, sedum,

roses, grasses, ferns, conifers, fruit trees. A bird and butterfly haven.

🐾 ✿ ☕

GROUP OPENING

95 TEIGNMOUTH GARDENS
Cliff Road, Teignmouth TQ14 8TW. *1m from Teignmouth town centre. From Teignmouth take A379 towards Dawlish, at top of hill L into New Rd, park in New Rd, walk back to A379 and follow signs to gardens.* Home-made teas at High Tor. **Combined adm £4, chd free. Sat 27, Sun 28 June (1-5).**

BERRY COTTAGE
Cliff Road. Maureen Fayle

HIGH TOR
Cliff Road. Gill Treweek

LITTLE CLANAGE
Oak Hill Cross Rd. Gill and Paul Derbyshire.
No parking available in road

Three contrasting gardens within walking distance of one another. At Berry Cottage the artist owner has developed a lovely secluded wildlife haven and will have a display of her stunning artwork. The large garden at Little Clannage has a huge selection of interesting trees, shrubs and soft fruit with superb views of the sea. High Tor has abundant cottage garden style planting with a new pebble pond water feature. Plants have been chosen to encourage bees and butterflies including lavender, buddleja, catmint, hebes and wild flowers. Mostly wheelchair access, limited at Berry Cottage.

& ✿ ☕

Lovely secluded wildlife haven . . . display of stunning artwork . . .

GROUP OPENING

96 VENN CROSS RAILWAY GARDENS
Venn Cross, Waterrow, Taunton TA4 2BE, 01398 361392, venncross@btinternet.com. *Devon/Somerset border. 4m W of Wiveliscombe, 6m E of Bampton on B3227. Easy access. Ample tarmac parking.* Light refreshments. Selection of gluten-free cakes also available. **Combined adm £4, chd free. Sat 13, Sun 14 June, Sat 18, Sun 19 July, Sat 12, Sun 13 Sept (2-5.30).**

THE ENGINE HOUSE
Kevin & Samantha Anning
Visitors also welcome by arrangement May to Sept.
01398 361392
venncross@btinternet.com

STATION HOUSE
Pat & Bill Wilson
Visitors also welcome by arrangement June to Sept.
01398 361665
bill_wilson.daveneer@btinternet.com

Set in beautiful countryside straddling Devon/Somerset border between Bampton and Wiveliscombe. 2 large adjoining gardens covering site of former station and goods yard on GWR line between Taunton and Barnstaple. The Engine House: approx 4 acres with colour from trees, shrubs and bulbs in spring to the wildflower meadow, bog gardens and sweeping herbaceous borders as summer progresses. Streams, ponds (incl koi), vegetable plot, hornbeam walkway and woodland paths. Railway and sculptural features add interest throughout. Station House: 2-acre sheltered garden in deep cutting. Site of old station. Steep banks featuring hostas and other plants. Deep herbaceous beds packed with flowers. Vegetable beds. Tunnel (no entry permitted) at end forming part of dell garden. Access to top of tunnel with view of garden. Woodland walk. Historic railway interest (many photographs) and garden sculptures. Wheelchair access to main areas. Some gravel paths, gentle grass slopes.

& ✿ 🚐 ☕

97 NEW WEST DOWN HOUSE
Bradworthy, Holsworthy EX22 7RZ.
Dawn Brookes-Ensor, 01409
241400,
mail@westdownhouse.co.uk,
www.artofdrawingdevon.com. *1m
outside Bradworthy. From
Bradworthy Square, take Mill Rd,
past school and 1m following the
signs to West Down.* Adm £4, chd
free. Sat 16, Sun 17 May (10-4).
Our interesting and mature gardens
excite at every turn as they are not
only very beautiful, but filled with over
50 wonderful sculptures. The 5 acre
vista has many sections incl
woodland, copse, meadow and more
formally planted gardens. The
ephemeral ponds, huge Cedars and
Victorian tunnels make it a unique
place to visit. We look forward to
welcoming you soon. Beautiful
mature rhododendron, azalea,
hydrangea bushes and 300 yr old
trees. Featured in North Devon
Journal, Western Morning News,
Devon Home and Coast Magazine.
Whole garden is on level ground.

98 WHITSTONE BLUEBELLS
Bovey Tracey, Newton Abbot
TQ13 9NA, 01626 832258,
katie@whitstonefarm.co.uk.
*Whitstone Lane. From A382 turn
towards hospital (sign opp golf
range), after* 1/3 *m L at swinging sign
'Private road leading to Whitstone'.
Follow NGS signs.* Tea at Whitstone
Farm. Tea/coffee/cakes including
gluten free option. **Combined adm
£4, chd free. Sun 3 May (2-5).**
Stunning spring gardens each with its
own character and far reaching views
over Dartmoor. Whitstone House has
clouds of bluebells throughout
woodland walk area and at Whitstone
Farm: bluebells intermingle among
camellias, azaleas, rhododendrons
and magnolias. Plus a display of
architectural metal sculptures and
ornaments. Exhibition of work by
Matt Dingle, a talented Devon
Blacksmith, artist and forgemaster,
will also be on display at Whitstone
Farm.

99 WHITSTONE FARM
Whitstone Lane, Bovey Tracey
TQ13 9NA. Katie & Alan Bunn,
01626 832258,
katie@whitstonefarm.co.uk. 1/2 *m N
of Bovey Tracey. From A382 turn
towards hospital (sign opp golf*

range), after 1/3 m L at swinging sign
'Private road leading to Whitstone'.
Follow NGS signs. Tea. Home made
cakes and gluten free option. **Adm
£4, chd free. Sun 2 Aug (2-5).**
Visitors also welcome by
arrangement May to Aug for group
and society tours.
Nearly 4 acres of steep hillside
garden with stunning views of Haytor
and Dartmoor. Arboretum planted 40
yrs ago, over 200 trees from all over
the world incl magnolias, camellias,
acers, alders, betula, davidias and
sorbus. Major plantings of
rhododendron and cornus. Late
summer opening for flowering
eucryphias. National Collection of
Eucryphias. Beautiful yr-round
garden.

NCH

> The ephemeral
> ponds, huge
> Cedars and
> Victorian tunnels
> make it a unique
> place to visit . . .

100 WICK FARM GARDENS
Cookbury, Holsworthy EX22 6NU.
Martin & Jenny Sexton, 01409
253760. *3m E of Holsworthy. From
Holsworthy take Hatherleigh Rd for
2m, L at Anvil Corner,* 1/4 *m then R to
Cookbury, garden 1*1/2 *m on L.* Light
refreshments. Home-made teas.
Adm £4, chd free. Sun 3, Mon 4,
Sun 10, Sun 17, Sun 24, Mon 25,
Sun 31 May (11-6). Visitors also
welcome by arrangement May.
8 acre pleasure garden around
Victorian farmhouse arranged in
rooms with many attractive features.
Fernery, ornamental pond, borders,
sculptures, oriental garden with stone
bell, lake with carp. Plants in long
border to attract butterflies and bees.
Crocosmia, croquet lawn, tropical
oasis, stone henge with sacrificial

stone, arboretum with over 300 trees,
flowering cherries, rhodendrons and
azaleas. Woodland bluebell walk 1m.
Some gravel paths, motor wheelchair
friendly.

GROUP OPENING

**101 WILLAND OLD VILLAGE
GARDENS**
Willand Old Village, Cullompton
EX15 2RH. *From J27 or J28 of M5
follow signs B3181 to Willand. Turn at
PO sign, gardens approx 200 yds,
follow yellow signs. Parking in village.*
Home-made teas. **Combined adm
£4, chd free. Sat 27, Sun 28 June
(2-5.30).**

CHURCH LEA
Mrs D Anderson

THE FIRS
Silver Street. Mrs Sylvia
Statham

NEW HARPITT BUNGALOW
Jane & Phil Hoare

NEW THE NEW HOUSE
Celia & Bryan Holmes

**NONSUCH, DYE HOUSE
LANE**
E Whiteley

NEW OLD JAYCROFT FARM
D. Keating M. Hollings

THE VILLAGE ALLOTMENTS
Silver Street. c/o Mrs S.
Statham

Church Lea: ideas for limited space in
an evolving garden, pond, rockery
with alpines, many pots create a
garden within a garden, vegetables,
fruit and vistas. The Firs: a small
garden backing onto an old drovers'
road, laid out to attract wildlife.
Instructive competitions for children.
Harpitt Bungalow: cottage-style
garden surrounding three sides of
bungalow, planting to attract wildlife.
The New House: garden and large
pond at rear of house designed for
low maintenance by Chelsea Flower
Show designer. Nonsuch: imaginative
use of space in this tranquil garden
planted for all year interest, plus
inquisitive bantams. Old Jaycroft
Farm: surrounding the 300 year old
Grade II listed farmhouse, this
deceptively large garden is laid out to
form several individual areas, some
hidden, with imaginative use of
ornaments and mirrors, and a large
koi pond. The 56 allotment plots

demonstrate a wide range of skills and production methods. Fascinating composting scheme producing 10,000 bags. Gardens, village and church have good accessibility for wheelchair users with modest slopes and few changes of level. Allotments have partial access.

102 ◆ WINSFORD WALLED GARDEN

Halwill Junction EX21 5XT. Dugald and Adel Stark, 01409 221477, www.winsfordwalledgarden.org.uk. *10m NW of Okehampton. On A3079 follow brown tourism signs from centre of Halwill Junction (1m). Straight on through Anglers Paradise.* Home-made teas. **Adm £4, chd free. For NGS: Sun 14, Mon 15 June, Sun 16, Mon 17 Aug (10-5). For** other opening times and information, please phone or see garden website.

Under new ownership of the landscape painter, Dugald Stark. Historic walled gardens, redesigned and brimming with colourful and interesting planting. Large restored Victorian glasshouses and extensive mature bamboo grove. Studio open. Garden open May - Sept, Wed - Sun (10-5).

103 WOOD BARTON

Kentisbeare EX15 2AT. Mrs Rosemary Horton, 01884 266285. *8m SE of Tiverton, 3m E of Cullompton. 3m from M5 J28. A373 Cullompton to Honiton. 2m L to Bradfield/Willand, Horn Rd. After 1m at Xrds turn R. Farm drive 1/2 m on L. Bull on sign.* Home-made teas. **Adm £5, chd free. Suns 12, 19 Apr, 3, 10 May (2.30-5.30). Visitors also welcome by arrangement Mar to Oct refreshments only by arrangement.**

Established 2-acre arboretum with species trees on S-facing slope. Magnolias, 2 davidia, azaleas, camellias, rhododendrons, acers; several ponds and water feature. Autumn colour. New planting of woodland trees and bluebells opp house (this part not suitable for wheelchairs but dogs are welcome here). Sculptures and profiles in bronze resin.

Knightshayes Court Garden

© Val Corbett

GROUP OPENING

104 NEW WOODBURY GARDENS

Greenway, Woodbury, Exeter EX5 1LW. *E of Exeter on B3179 Clyst St George to Budleigh Salterton Rd.* Cream teas at Greenside, between the 2 open gardens. **Combined adm £3.50, chd free. Sat 20, Sun 21 June (1-5).**

NEW HAYDONS, BONFIRE LANE
Mr & Mrs M Jeans

NEW TIM ANDREWS GALLERY AND GARDEN
Cobb End. Mr Tim Andrews

2 pretty gardens in the centre of this attractive East Devon village. Tim Andrews Gallery & Garden is a compact, well stocked garden with emphasis on foliage planting, punctuated by sculptures from leading Artists. Pond/water feature and vegetable/fruit garden. Attached gallery with current international exhibition will also be open. Haydons is a cottage style corner garden landscaped into 3 different areas. S-facing front garden with greenhouse leading to lawned area with raised fishpond, then shallow steps under pergola to third enclosed garden. Mixed planting of trees, shrubs and herbaceous borders throughout.

105 YONDER HILL

Shepherds Lane, Colaton Raleigh, Sidmouth EX10 0LP. Judy McKay, Eddie Stevenson, Sharon Attrell, Bob Chambers, 07864 055532, judy@yonderhill.me.uk, www.yonderhill.org.uk. *4m N of Budleigh Salterton B3178 between Newton Poppleford and Colaton Raleigh. Take turning signed to Dotton and immed R into small lane, 1/4 m 1st R at top of hill opp public footpath.* Cream teas. Large choice of teas DIY just as you like it. **Adm £3, chd £1. Every Sun 5 Apr to 27 Sept (1.30-4.30). Mons 6 Apr, 4, 25 May, 31 Aug (1.30-4.30). Visitors also welcome by arrangement Apr to Sept.**

Enjoy a warm welcome to 3 1/2 acres planted with love. Blazing herbaceous borders buzzing with insects, cool woods alive with birdsong, rustling bamboos, delicious scents. Eucalyptus, grasses, conifer and fern collections. Rare plants, unusual planting, wildlife pond, wild flower meadow, woodland tunnels, lots of benches. This garden will awaken your senses and soothe your soul. Garden attracts great variety of birds and insects. Limited wheelchair access, some slopes. Wheelchair and large mobility scooter available, phone to book. WC.

DORSET

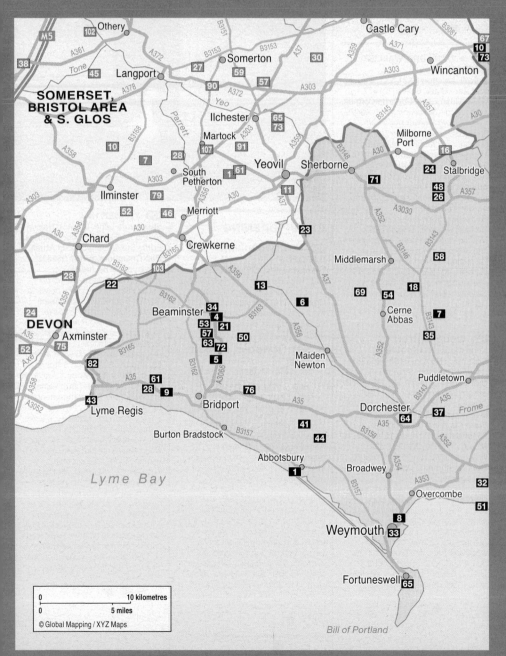

SOMERSET,
BRISTOL AREA
& S. GLOS

DEVON

Lyme Bay

Bill of Portland

0   10 kilometres
0   5 miles
© Global Mapping / XYZ Maps

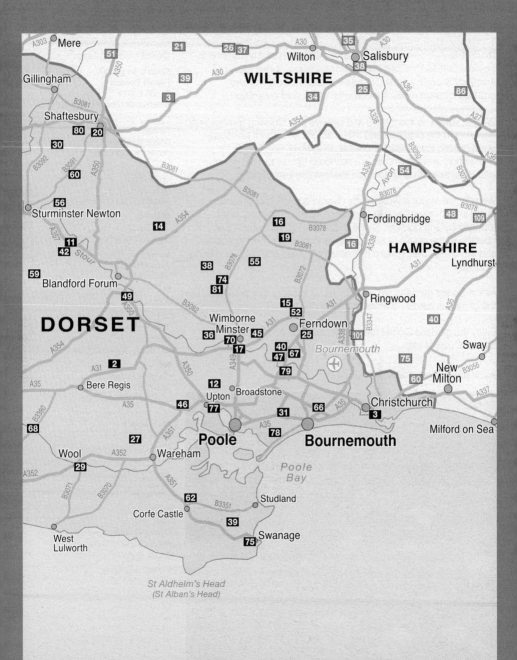

Dorset

Dorset is not on the way to anywhere. It has no motorway and no Cathedral, but what it does have is the glorious Jurassic Coast and thousands of acres of farmland, ancient monuments, heathland, cliffs and beaches.

Woods, valleys, ancient trees and byways give stunning glimpses and views down the coastline and inland across an ancient landscape. Small historic towns like Dorchester, Blandford, Sherborne, Shaftesbury and Weymouth are scattered throughout the county, with Bournemouth and Poole as the main centres of population.

We offer the visitor a wonderfully diverse collection of gardens found in both towns and in deep countryside. They vary in size, topography and content. Some of the loveliest gardens in England opening to the public to support us, and between the larger ones and the tiniest, they reward the visitor with their originality and bring much joy.

All the Dorset gardens are well planted and beautifully presented by the generous garden owners who open for the NGS.

Enjoy the gardens Dorset has to offer with the added bonus of a delicious cup of tea!

Below: Littlebredy Walled Gardens © Roger Lane

Currently the NGS donates around £2.5 million every year

Dorset Volunteers

County Organiser
Harriet Boileau
01935 83612
h.boileau@btinternet.com

County Treasurer
Richard Smedley
01202 528286
richard@carter-coley.co.uk

Publicity
Gillian Ford
01935 83645
gillianford33@btinternet.com

Di Reeds
01305 833500
digardengate@hotmail.co.uk

Booklet Editor
Judith Hussey
01258 474673
judithhussey@hotmail.com

Assistant County Organisers

Central East/Bournemouth
Trish Neale
01425 403565
trishneale1@yahoo.co.uk

North Central
Caroline Renner
01747 811140
croftfarm12@gmail.com

North East/Ferndown/Christchurch
Mary Angus
01202 872789
mary@gladestock.co.uk

North West & Central
Victoria Baxter
01935 815992
victoria@lborchard.co.uk

South Central
Helen Hardy
01929 471379
helliehardy@hotmail.co.uk

South West
Christine Corson
01308 868203
christinekcorson@gmail.com

West Central
Alison Wright
01935 83652
wright.alison68@yahoo.com

Opening Dates

All entries subject to change.
For latest information check www.ngs.org.uk

February

Sunday 22
42 Lawsbrook

Saturday 28
47 Manor Farm, Hampreston

March

Sunday 1
47 Manor Farm, Hampreston

Saturday 7
38 NEW Kitemoor Cottage

Sunday 8
38 NEW Kitemoor Cottage

Sunday 15
23 Frankham Farm
64 Q

Sunday 22
10 Chiffchaffs
29 Herons Mead

Saturday 28
26 Grange Cottage
35 Ivy House Garden
48 Manor Farm, Stourton Caundle
73 Snape Cottage Plantsman's Garden

Sunday 29
26 Grange Cottage
31 22 Holt Road
35 Ivy House Garden
48 Manor Farm, Stourton Caundle
60 The Old Vicarage
64 Q

April

Saturday 4
59 Old Smithy

Sunday 5
9 Chideock Manor
29 Herons Mead

Monday 6
9 Chideock Manor
19 Edmondsham House
35 Ivy House Garden

Wednesday 8
19 Edmondsham House

Saturday 11
8 24 Carlton Road North

Sunday 12
8 24 Carlton Road North
18 Domineys Yard
64 Q

Monday 13
8 24 Carlton Road North

Wednesday 15
19 Edmondsham House
57 The Old Rectory, Netherbury

Saturday 18
7 Butts Cottage
43 NEW Little Cliff
51 Marren

Sunday 19
6 Broomhill
7 Butts Cottage
31 22 Holt Road
51 Marren

Wednesday 22
16 Cranborne Manor Garden
19 Edmondsham House

Thursday 23
43 NEW Little Cliff

Friday 24
76 Uploders Place

Saturday 25
73 Snape Cottage Plantsman's Garden
76 Uploders Place

Sunday 26
12 Corfe Barn
23 Frankham Farm
25 The Glade
53 The Mill House
64 Q
78 Western Gardens

Wednesday 29
19 Edmondsham House
34 Horn Park

May

Sunday 3
29 Herons Mead
32 Holworth Farmhouse
35 Ivy House Garden
79 1692 Wimborne Road

Monday 4
32 Holworth Farmhouse
35 Ivy House Garden
58 The Old Rectory, Pulham

Saturday 9
69 The Secret Garden

Sunday 10
18 Domineys Yard
25 The Glade
53 The Mill House
59 Old Smithy
63 2 Pyes Plot
64 Q
69 The Secret Garden

79 1692 Wimborne Road

Tuesday 12
5 Braddocks

Wednesday 13
57 The Old Rectory, Netherbury

Thursday 14
74 NEW Staddlestones

Saturday 16
7 Butts Cottage
28 Harcombe House

Sunday 17
7 Butts Cottage
28 Harcombe House
31 22 Holt Road
58 The Old Rectory, Pulham
80 Wincombe Park
82 Wolverhollow

Monday 18
82 Wolverhollow

Tuesday 19
28 Harcombe House
82 Wolverhollow

Wednesday 20
80 Wincombe Park

Friday 22
39 Knitson Old Farmhouse

Saturday 23
39 Knitson Old Farmhouse
51 Marren

Sunday 24
11 Coombe Cottage
25 The Glade
39 Knitson Old Farmhouse
51 Marren
60 The Old Vicarage
72 Slape Manor

Monday 25
39 Knitson Old Farmhouse

Thursday 28
2 Anderson Manor

Saturday 30
73 Snape Cottage Plantsman's Garden

Sunday 31
3 Annalal's Gallery
12 Corfe Barn
47 Manor Farm, Hampreston

June

Wednesday 3
17 Deans Court

Festival Weekend

Saturday 6
7 Butts Cottage
14 Cottage Row (Evening)
20 Edwardstowe

Sunday 7
7 Butts Cottage
14 Cottage Row
20 Edwardstowe
23 Frankham Farm
24 Frith House
25 The Glade
55 Old Down House
62 Puddledock Cottage

Tuesday 9
5 Braddocks

Wednesday 10
55 Old Down House

Thursday 11
2 Anderson Manor

Saturday 13
8 24 Carlton Road North

Sunday 14
8 24 Carlton Road North
21 Farrs
31 22 Holt Road
56 The Old Rectory, Manston
64 Q

Tuesday 16
61 Pilsdon View

Wednesday 17
4 Beaminster Gardens
6 Broomhill
34 Horn Park
55 Old Down House
56 The Old Rectory, Manston
57 The Old Rectory, Netherbury
68 Sculpture by the Lakes

Thursday 18
43 NEW Little Cliff

Friday 19
29 Herons Mead (Evening)

Saturday 20
9 Chideock Manor
43 NEW Little Cliff
46 Lytchett Minster Gardens

Damselflies dance in the sunshine . . .

Visit a garden on National Gardens Festival Weekend 6 & 7 June

Sunday 21
- **4** Beaminster Gardens
- **9** Chideock Manor
- **10** Chiffchaffs
- **27** Greenacres
- **32** Holworth Farmhouse
- **46** Lytchett Minster Gardens
- **66** 25 Richmond Park Avenue
- **78** Western Gardens

Tuesday 23
- **44** Littlebredy Walled Gardens

Thursday 25
- **81** NEW Witchampton Gardens

Friday 26
- **81** NEW Witchampton Gardens

Saturday 27
- **36** Kingston Lacy
- **73** Snape Cottage Plantsman's Garden

Sunday 28
- **3** Annalal's Gallery
- **12** Corfe Barn
- **36** Kingston Lacy
- **61** Pilsdon View

Tuesday 30
- **44** Littlebredy Walled Gardens

July

Wednesday 1
- **17** Deans Court
- **75** Stone Rise

Saturday 4
- **45** 55 Lonnen Road

Sunday 5
- **6** Broomhill
- **13** Corscombe House
- **32** Holworth Farmhouse
- **45** 55 Lonnen Road
- **66** 25 Richmond Park Avenue
- **67** 357 Ringwood Road

Wednesday 8
- **68** Sculpture by the Lakes
- **75** Stone Rise

Thursday 9
- **43** NEW Little Cliff

Saturday 11
- **16** Cranborne Manor Garden

Sunday 12
- **30** Hilltop
- **48** Manor Farm, Stourton Caundle

Tuesday 14
- **5** Braddocks
- **61** Pilsdon View

Wednesday 15
- **75** Stone Rise

Thursday 16
- **66** 25 Richmond Park Avenue
- **74** NEW Staddlestones

Saturday 18
- **33** Holy Trinity Environmental Garden

Sunday 19
- **3** Annalal's Gallery
- **21** Farrs
- **30** Hilltop
- **31** 22 Holt Road
- **33** Holy Trinity Environmental Garden
- **52** Meadow Views

Wednesday 22
- **67** 357 Ringwood Road
- **75** Stone Rise

Thursday 23
- **70** The Secret Garden and Serles House

Sunday 26
- **15** Cottesmore Farm
- **27** Greenacres
- **30** Hilltop
- **58** The Old Rectory, Pulham
- **61** Pilsdon View
- **66** 25 Richmond Park Avenue
- **70** The Secret Garden and Serles House

Wednesday 29
- **53** The Mill House (Evening)
- **63** 2 Pyes Plot (Evening)
- **75** Stone Rise

Bees and butterflies abound . . .

August

Saturday 1
- **45** 55 Lonnen Road

Sunday 2
- **15** Cottesmore Farm
- **30** Hilltop
- **45** 55 Lonnen Road
- **47** Manor Farm, Hampreston
- **70** The Secret Garden and Serles House

Wednesday 5
- **47** Manor Farm, Hampreston
- **75** Stone Rise

Thursday 6
- **70** The Secret Garden and Serles House

Sunday 9
- **21** Farrs
- **30** Hilltop
- **32** Holworth Farmhouse
- **52** Meadow Views
- **62** Puddledock Cottage
- **65** Queen Ann House
- **70** The Secret Garden and Serles House

Wednesday 12
- **75** Stone Rise

Thursday 13
- **28** Harcombe House
- **74** NEW Staddlestones

Saturday 15
- **20** Edwardstowe
- **28** Harcombe House

Sunday 16
- **18** Domineys Yard
- **20** Edwardstowe
- **28** Harcombe House
- **30** Hilltop
- **31** 22 Holt Road
- **67** 357 Ringwood Road
- **82** Wolverhollow

Monday 17
- **82** Wolverhollow

Wednesday 19
- **75** Stone Rise

Sunday 23
- **6** Broomhill
- **15** Cottesmore Farm
- **70** The Secret Garden and Serles House
- **78** Western Gardens

Wednesday 26
- **75** Stone Rise

Sunday 30
- **11** Coombe Cottage
- **70** The Secret Garden and Serles House

Monday 31
- **70** The Secret Garden and Serles House

September

Thursday 3
- **70** The Secret Garden and Serles House

Saturday 5
- **70** The Secret Garden and Serles House

Sunday 6
- **49** The Manor House
- **70** The Secret Garden and Serles House

Wednesday 9
- **49** The Manor House

Thursday 10

74 NEW Staddlestones

Friday 11
- **39** Knitson Old Farmhouse

Saturday 12
- **39** Knitson Old Farmhouse

Sunday 13
- **21** Farrs
- **39** Knitson Old Farmhouse
- **70** The Secret Garden and Serles House

Sunday 20
- **10** Chiffchaffs
- **29** Herons Mead

October

Sunday 4
- **60** The Old Vicarage

Wednesday 7
- **19** Edmondsham House

Sunday 11
- **23** Frankham Farm

Wednesday 14
- **19** Edmondsham House

Saturday 17
- **36** Kingston Lacy

Sunday 18
- **36** Kingston Lacy

Wednesday 21
- **19** Edmondsham House

Wednesday 28
- **19** Edmondsham House

November

Sunday 1
- **42** Lawsbrook

Gardens open to the public

- **1** Abbotsbury Gardens
- **10** Chiffchaffs
- **16** Cranborne Manor Garden
- **19** Edmondsham House
- **22** Forde Abbey Gardens
- **30** Hilltop
- **36** Kingston Lacy
- **37** Kingston Maurward Gardens and Animal Park
- **40** Knoll Gardens
- **44** Littlebredy Walled Gardens
- **50** Mapperton Gardens
- **54** Minterne House
- **68** Sculpture by the Lakes
- **71** Sherborne Castle
- **73** Snape Cottage Plantsman's Garden

77 Upton Country Park	**7** Butts Cottage	**34** Horn Park	**58** The Old Rectory, Pulham
By arrangement only	**9** Chideock Manor	**35** Ivy House Garden	**59** Old Smithy
	11 Coombe Cottage	**38** NEW Kitemoor Cottage	**60** The Old Vicarage
41 Langebride House	**12** Corfe Barn		**61** Pilsdon View
	14 Cottage Row	**39** Knitson Old Farmhouse	**62** Puddledock Cottage
Also open by arrangement	**18** Domineys Yard		**64** Q
	23 Frankham Farm	**42** Lawsbrook	**66** 25 Richmond Park Avenue
2 Anderson Manor	**24** Frith House	**43** NEW Little Cliff	**67** 357 Ringwood Road
3 Annalal's Gallery	**25** The Glade	**45** 55 Lonnen Road	**72** Slape Manor
5 Braddocks	**26** Grange Cottage	**49** The Manor House	**78** Western Gardens
6 Broomhill	**28** Harcombe House	**51** Marren	**79** 1692 Wimborne Road
	29 Herons Mead	**53** The Mill House	**82** Wolverhollow
	31 22 Holt Road	**56** The Old Rectory, Manston	
	32 Holworth Farmhouse		

The Gardens

1 ◆ ABBOTSBURY GARDENS
nr Weymouth DT3 4LA. Ilchester Estates, 01305 871412, www.abbotsburygardens.co.uk. *8m W of Weymouth. From B3157 Weymouth-Bridport, 200yds W of Abbotsbury village.* **For opening times and information, please phone or see garden website.** 30 acres, started in 1760 and considerably extended in C19. Much recent replanting. The maritime micro-climate enables Mediterranean and southern hemisphere garden to grow rare and tender plants. National collection of Hoherias (flowering Aug in NZ garden). Woodland valley with ponds, stream and hillside walk to view the Jurassic Coast. Open all yr except Christmas week. Featured on Countrywise and Gardeners' World. Limited wheelchair access, some very steep paths and rolled gravel.

2 ANDERSON MANOR
Anderson, Blandford Forum DT11 9HD. Jeremy & Rosemary Isaac, 01929 471320, www.andersonmanor.co.uk. *3m E Bere Regis, 12m W Wimborne, 8m SW Blandford. Turn off A31 at Red Post Xrds to Anderson, follow rd around corner, entrance on R.* Homemade teas. **Adm £3.50, chd free. Thur 28 May, Thur 11 June (2-5). Visitors also welcome by arrangement May to Oct min 10.** Approx 3 acres of mature topiary, old roses and herbaceous borders surrounding Elizabethan/Jacobean manor house (Grade 1 listed, not open). Formal garden, gazebos, bowling green, walled garden, parterre and orchard. Yew and box hedges, pleached lime walk, old rose walk by R Winterborne and avenue of walnut trees. C12 church open next

to house. Separate car parking via Church Lane. All gardens accessible. No gravel, mainly grass.

3 ANNALAL'S GALLERY
25 Millhams Street, Christchurch BH23 1DN. Anna & Lal Sims, 01202 567585, anna.sims@ntlworld.com, www.annasims.co.uk. *Town centre. Park in Saxon Square PCP - exit to Millham St via alley at side of church.* **Adm £3, chd free. Sun 31 May, Sun 28 June, Sun 19 July (2-4). Visitors also welcome by arrangement May to Dec.** Enchanting 100 yr-old cottage, home of two Royal Academy artists. 32ft x 12½ ft garden on 3 patio levels. Pencil gate leads to colourful scented Victorian walled garden. Sculptures and paintings hide among the flowers and shrubs.

Old Smithy

© Heather Edwards

You are always welcome at an NGS garden!

GROUP OPENING

4 ▶ BEAMINSTER GARDENS
Shadrack Street, Beaminster DT8 3BE. *6m N of Bridport, 6m S of Crewkerne on B3162. All gardens within short walk of town square or main car park. In pairs, all well signed from town square. Lots of yellow arrows and balloons. Map issued with tickets.* Home-made teas in Beaminster Church, long gradual stairway to main church door and lift for wheelchairs etc. West door open for wheelchair access. **Combined adm £5, chd free.** Wed 17, Sun 21 June (2-5).

BARTON END
50 Fleet Street. Mr & Mrs Philip Crawford

NEW **63 EAST STREET**
Miss Jane Hooper.
Limited disabled parking

29 FLEET STREET
Mrs Jane Pinkster

NEW **HURFORD HOUSE**
East Street, Beaminster. Mr & Mrs Arnold Shipp.
Limited disabled parking in forecourt

SHADRACK HOUSE
Shadrack Street. Mr & Mrs Hugh Lindsay

SHORTS ORCHARD
Shorts Lane. Mrs Sally Mallinson

Five charming small town gardens, two by the river, and one a much larger town garden. All a total delight, masses of roses, unusual climbers, shrubs and swaithes of perennials. A first opening for the 2 East St gardens. Barton End won 1st in Large Gardens competition in 2014 Melplash show. Barton End, 29 Fleet St & Shorts Orchard are wheelchair friendly, Hurford House partially accessible.

5 ▶ BRADDOCKS
Oxbridge, Bridport DT6 3TZ. Dr & Mrs Roger Newton, 01308 488441, rogernewton329@btinternet.com, www.braddocksgarden.co.uk. *3m N of Bridport. From Bridport, A3066 to Beaminster 3m, just before Melplash, L into Camesworth Lane signed Oxbridge. Single track rd, down steep hill. Garden signed.* Home-made teas. **Adm £4, chd free.**

Tue 12 May, Tue 9 June, Tue 14 July (2-5). **Visitors also welcome by arrangement Apr to Oct.**
3 acres of plant-packed sloping gardens, conceived, planted and looked after by owner. 'A feast of a garden at all times of the year'. Wild flower meadows and water. Herbaceous, underplanted shrubs and roses of all types and hues. Shady woodland garden and fine mature specimen trees. Featured in Dorset Life. Steep slopes and gravel paths make the garden unsuitable for wheelchairs.

6 ▶ BROOMHILL
Rampisham DT2 0PU. Mr & Mrs D Parry, 01935 83266, carol.parry2@btopenworld.com. *11m NW of Dorchester. From Dorchester A37 Yeovil, 4m L A356 to Crewkerne, 6m R to Rampisham. From Yeovil A37 Dorchester, 7m R Evershot. From Crewkerne A356, 1½ m after Rampisham Garage L Rampisham. Follow Signs.* Home-made teas. **Adm £4, chd free.** Sun 19 Apr, Wed 17 June, Sun 5 July, Sun 23 Aug (2-5). **Visitors also welcome by arrangement May to Aug.**
Once a farmyard now a delightful, tranquil garden set in 1½ acres. Island beds and borders are planted with shrubs, roses, masses of unusual perennials and choice annuals to give vibrancy and colour from spring to autumn. Lawns and paths lead to a less formal area with a large wildlife pond, shaded areas, a bog garden and a late summer border. Featured in Roger Lane's Gardens of Dorset. Gravel entrance, the rest is grass, some gentle slopes.

7 ▶ BUTTS COTTAGE
Plush DT2 7RJ. John & Jane Preston, 01300 348545. *9m N Dorchester. At Piddletrenthide (on B3143) take turning E to Plush; after 1½ m follow No Through Rd sign then 1st R.* Teas. **Adm £3.50, chd free.** Sat 18, Sun 19 Apr, Sat 16, Sun 17 May, Sat 6, Sun 7 June (2-5). **Visitors also welcome by arrangement May & June for groups of 10+.**
Tranquil village garden of ¾ acre sheltered by mature beech trees around C18 cottage in fold of N Dorset Downs. Stream, pond, wild flowers and marsh orchids. Pleasant place to sit or wander amongst wide variety of flowers, vegetables, shrubs and trees. Partial wheelchair access.

8 ▶ 24 CARLTON ROAD NORTH
Weymouth DT4 7PY. Anne Mellars and Rob Tracey. *8m S of Dorchester. A354 from Dorchester, R into Carlton Rd N. On R after Alexandra Rd. From Town Centre follow esplanade towards A354 Dorchester and L into C Rd N.* Home-made teas. **Adm £3, chd free.** Sat 11, Sun 12, Mon 13 Apr, Sat 13, Sun 14 June (2-5).
Long garden on several levels. Steps and narrow sloping paths lead to beds and borders overflowing with trees, shrubs and herbaceous plants. Unusual plants incl exotics in interesting combinations merit a second look. A garden of discovery reflecting an interest in texture, shape, colour, wildlife and above all plants.

9 ▶ CHIDEOCK MANOR
Chideock, nr Bridport DT6 6LF. Mr & Mrs Howard Coates, 0788 555 1795, deidrecoates@btinternet.com. *2m W of Bridport on A35. In centre of village turn N at church. The Manor is ¼ m along this rd on R.* Home-made teas. **Adm £5, chd free.** Sun 5, Mon 6 Apr, Sat 20, Sun 21 June (2-5). **Visitors also welcome by arrangement Apr to Oct.**
6/7 acres of formal and informal gardens. Bog garden beside stream and series of ponds. Yew hedges and mature trees. Lime and crab apple walks, herbaceous borders, colourful rose and clematis arches, fernery and nuttery. Walled vegetable garden and orchard. Woodland and lakeside walks. Fine views. Partial wheelchair access.

> Diana (formally of Welcome Thatch) has created a new garden full of treasures . . .

10 ◆ CHIFFCHAFFS

Chaffeymoor, Bourton, Gillingham SP8 5BY. Mr K R Potts, 01747 840841. *3m E of Wincanton. W end of Bourton. N of A303 on border of Somerset and Wiltshire.* Adm £4.50, chd free. For NGS: Sun 22 Mar, Sun 21 June, Sun 20 Sept (2-5). For other opening times and information, please phone.

Well known mature garden for all seasons planted round stone cottage with many interesting plants, bulbs, shrubs, herbaceous border and shrub roses. Attractive walk to woodland garden with far reaching views across Blackmore Vale. New stream and waterfall feature.

11 COOMBE COTTAGE

Shillingstone DT11 0SF. Mike & Jennie Adams, 01258 860220, mikeadams611@gmail.com. *5m NW of Blandford. On main rd (A357) in middle of village between Gunn Lane and Old Ox PH. Parking advised in Gunn Lane.* Adm £3, chd free. Sun 24 May, Sun 30 Aug (2-6). Visitors also welcome by arrangement May to Sept.

0.4 acre profusely planted mixed garden with broad borders edged by walls, hedges, fences and arbours.

Cottage favourites jostle with more unusual herbaceous and bulbous perennials, shrubs, trees and climbers, and self-seeders rub shoulders with late flowering and bold leaved subtropicals. Large glasshouse and some non-botanical surprises. Licensed tearoom, The Willows, 3 mins walk away, is open when Coombe Cottage is open.

12 CORFE BARN

Corfe Lodge Road, Broadstone BH18 9NQ. Mr & Mrs John McDavid, 01202 694179. *1m W of Broadstone centre. From main r'about in Broadstone, W along Clarendon Rd ³/₄ m, N into Roman Rd, after 50yds W into Corfe Lodge Rd.* Home-made teas. Adm £2.50, chd free. Sun 26 Apr, Sun 31 May, Sun 28 June (2-5). Visitors also welcome by arrangement May to July.

Very varied garden in pleasant semi-rural environment extending to about ²/₃ acre. Mixture of usual and unusual trees, shrubs and flowers on three levels in and out of the barnyard. Wildlife friendly garden (so say Dorset Wildlife Trust).

13 CORSCOMBE HOUSE

Corscombe DT2 0NU. Jim Bartos. *3¹/₂ m N of Beaminster. On A356 take southern of two signed turnings E to Corscombe, then R signed Church; or on A37 turn W signed Corscombe, L signed Church.* Cream teas in village hall. Adm £4.50, chd free. Sun 5 July (2-5.30).

Strong architectural hedges define multiple rooms on different levels with yew columns, parterre and cool beds in lower garden. Reflecting pool and hot beds in upper garden. Wildflower meadow and orchard. Part walled vegetable garden and secret garden with Mediterranean planting and lemons in pots.

14 COTTAGE ROW

School Lane, Tarrant Gunville, nr Blandford Forum DT11 8JJ. Carolyn & Michael Pawson, 01258 830212, michaelpawson637@btinternet. com. *6m NE of Blandford Forum. From Blandford take A354 towards Salisbury, L at Tarrant Hinton. After 1¹/₂ m R in Tarrant Gunville into School Lane.* Cream teas. Adm £4, chd free. Evening Opening wine,

Sat 6 June (5-8). Sun 7 June (2-5.30). Visitors also welcome by arrangement May to Sept roses/clematis at best June/July, cyclamen Sept, min 6.

Maturing ¹/₂ acre partly walled garden. Formal and informal areas separated by yew hedges. Pergola, arbours, brick paths, tree house, kitchen garden and the sound of water; bees and butterflies abound in this tranquil spot. This sophisticated cottage garden reflects the owners' love of unusual plants, structure and an artist's eye for sympathetic colour also evident in new box plantings.

15 COTTESMORE FARM

Newmans Lane, West Moors, Ferndown BH22 0LW. Paul & Valerie Guppy. *Newmans Lane, 1m N of West Moors. Off B3072 Bournemouth to Verwood rd. Car parking in owner's field.* Home-made teas. Adm £4, chd free. Sun 26 July, Sun 2, Sun 23 Aug (2-5).

Gardens of over an acre, created from scratch over 17yrs. Wander through a plantsman's tropical paradise of giant gunneras, bananas, towering bamboos and over 100 palm trees, into a floral extravaganza. Large borders and sweeping island beds overflowing with phlox, heliopsis, helenium and much more combine to drown you in scent and colour. Featured in Gardens of Dorset and Dorset Life.

16 ◆ CRANBORNE MANOR GARDEN

Cranborne BH21 5PP. Viscount Cranborne, 01725 517289, www.cranborne.co.uk. *10m N of Wimborne on B3078. Enter garden via Cranborne Garden Centre, on L as you enter top of village of Cranborne.* Light refreshments. Adm £6, chd £1. For NGS: Wed 22 Apr, Sat 11 July (9-4). For other opening times and information, please phone or see garden website.

Beautiful and historic garden laid out in C17 by John Tradescant and enlarged in C20, featuring several gardens surrounded by walls and yew hedges: blue and white garden, cottage style and mount gardens, water and wild garden. Many interesting plants, with fine trees and avenues. Mostly wheelchair access.

The Old Rectory, Manston

17 DEANS COURT

Deans Court Lane, Wimborne Minster BH21 1EE. Sir William Hanham, 01202 849314, jonathan@deanscourt.org, www.deanscourt.org. *¼ m SE of Minster. Pedestrians: From Deans Court Lane, continuation of High St, over Xrds at Holmans shop (BH21 1EE). Cars: Entrance on Poole Rd, Wimborne (A349); heading S, 300m on R after Rodways r'about (BH21 1QF). Home-made teas. Our Squash Court Cafe will also be open.* **Adm £4, chd free. Share to Friends of Victoria Hospital. Wed 3 June, Wed 1 July (11-6).**
13 acres of peaceful, partly wild gardens in ancient setting with mature specimen trees, Saxon fish pond, herb garden and apiary beside R Allen close to town centre. Apple orchard with wild flowers. 1st Soil Association accredited kitchen garden within C18 serpentine walls. Lunches and teas served in garden and tearoom, using estate produce (also for sale). Tours of house by owner, pre-booking essential. Follow signs for parking closer to the gardens. Some paths have deeper gravel.

18 DOMINEYS YARD

Buckland Newton, Dorchester DT2 7BS. Mr & Mrs W Gueterbock, 01300 345295, cottages@domineys.com, www.domineys.com. *11m N of Dorchester, 11m S of Sherborne. 2m E A352 or take B3143. No thro' road between church & Gaggle of Geese. Enter 100yds on L. Home-made teas.* **Adm £4, chd free. Sun 12 Apr, Sun 10 May, Sun 16 Aug (2-6). Visitors also welcome by arrangement, refreshments by request.**
Welcome to 54 years of change. Attractive setting around our thatched and other cottages. Superb soil with good micro climate. Plant diversity to enjoy throughout the year. Naturalised arboretum. Rare and well known trees, shrubs, herbaceous, bulbs, annuals and pots, fruit and vegetables. Varied layout with something to see around every corner. A peaceful place to relate to and share with us. Wheelchair access excludes arboretum.

19 ◆ EDMONDSHAM HOUSE

Edmondsham, nr Cranborne, Wimborne BH21 5RE. Mrs Julia Smith, 01725 517207, Julia.edmondsham@yahoo.co.uk. *9m NE of Wimborne. 9m W of Ringwood. Between Cranborne & Verwood. Edmondsham off B3081. Wheelchair access West front. Tea, coffee and cake 3.30-4pm except Mon 6 April.* **Adm £2.50, chd £0.50. For NGS: Mon 6, Wed 8, Wed 15, Wed 22, Wed 29 Apr, Wed 7, Wed 14, Wed 21, Wed 28 Oct (2-5). For other opening times and information, please phone or see garden website.**
6 acres of mature gardens, grounds, views, trees and shaped hedges surrounding C16/C18 house, giving much to explore incl C12 church adjacent to garden. Large Victorian walled garden is productive and managed organically (since 1984) using 'no dig' vegetable beds. Wide herbaceous borders planted for seasonal colour. Traditional potting shed and working areas. House also open on NGS days.

20 EDWARDSTOWE

50-52 Bimport, Shaftesbury SP7 8BA. Mike & Louise Madgwick. *Park in town's main car park, garden 500m. Walk along Bimport (B3091) to end, Edwardstowe last house on L.* **Adm £3.50, chd free. Sat 6, Sun 7 June, Sat 15, Sun 16 Aug (11-5).**
An evolving cottage garden with yr-round interest, set behind oldest house in Shaftesbury. Enormous magnolia tree greets visitors exiting courtyard drive to long lawns, divided by 2 colourful borders and self sufficiency vegetable garden. Chickens and bees complete the scene. Seasonal plant and produce sales.

21 FARRS

Whitcombe Rd, Beaminster DT8 3NB. Mr & Mrs John Makepeace, 01308 862204, info@johnmakepeacefurniture.com, www.johnmakepeacefurniture.com. *Southern edge of Beaminster. On B3163. Car parking on site only for disabled. Enter through garden door in wall adjacent to Museum. Park in the Square or side streets. Light refreshments.* **Adm £5, chd free. Suns 14 June, 19 July, 9 Aug, 13 Sept (2-5).**
Enjoy several distinctive walled gardens, rolling lawns, sculpture and giant topiary around the house. John's inspirational grasses garden, Jennie's riotous potager with cleft oak fruit cage. Glasshouse, straw bale studio, geese in orchard. Remarkable trees, planked and seasoning in open sided barn. House also open on NGS days with selection of furniture by John Makepeace, and paintings, sculpture and applied arts by living artists. 2pm talks by John and Jennie Makepeace and Neil Lucas. Plants for sale. Reviews in Gardeners' World, Daily Mail, Telegraph and Hortus. Some gravel paths, alternative wheelchair route through orchard.

Treat yourself to a plant from the plant stall

22 ◆ **FORDE ABBEY GARDENS**
Chard TA20 4LU. Mr & Mrs Julian
Kennard, 01460 221290,
www.fordeabbey.co.uk. *4m SE of
Chard. Signed off A30 Chard-
Crewkerne and A358 Chard-
Axminster. Also from Broadwindsor
B3164.* **For opening times and
information, please phone or see
garden website.**
30 acres of fine shrubs, magnificent
specimen trees, ponds, herbaceous
borders, rockery, bog garden
containing superb collection of Asiatic
primulas, Ionic temple, working
walled kitchen garden supplying the
tearoom. Centenary fountain,
England's highest powered fountain.
Gardens open daily (10-6, last adm
4.30pm). Please ask at reception for
best wheelchair route. Wheelchairs
available to borrow/hire, advance
booking advised.

23 **FRANKHAM FARM**
Ryme Intrinseca, Sherborne
DT9 6JT. Susan Ross, 07594 427
365, neilandsusanross@gmail.com.
*3m S of Yeovil. A37 Yeovil-
Dorchester; turn E; ¹/₄ m; drive is on
L.* Home-made teas. **Adm £4, chd
free. Sun 15 Mar, Sun 26 Apr, Sun
7 June, Sun 11 Oct (2-5).** Visitors
also welcome by arrangement.
3¹/₂ acre garden, created since 1960
by the late Jo Earle for yr-round
interest. This large and lovely garden
is filled with a wide variety of well
grown plants, roses, unusual labelled
shrubs and trees from around the
world. Productive vegetable garden.
Climbers cover the walls. Spring
bulbs through to autumn colour,
particularly oaks. Sorry, no dogs.

24 **FRITH HOUSE**
Stalbridge DT10 2SD. Mr & Mrs
Patrick Sclater, 01963 250809,
rosalynsclater@btinternet.com.
*5m E of Sherborne. Between
Milborne Port and Stalbridge. From
A30 1m, follow sign to Stalbridge.
From Stalbridge 2m and turn W by
PO.* Home-made teas. **Adm £4,
chd free. Sun 7 June (2-5).**
Visitors also welcome by
arrangement May to July for
groups, Mon-Fri only.
Approached down long drive with
fine views. 4 acres of garden
around Edwardian house and self
contained hamlet. Range of mature
trees, lakes and flower borders.
House terrace edged by rose border

and featuring Lutyensesque wall
fountain and game larder. Well
stocked kitchen gardens.

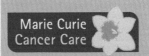

25 **THE GLADE**
Woodland Walk, Ferndown
BH22 9LP. Mary & Roger Angus,
01202 872789,
mary@gladestock.co.uk. *³/₄ m NE of
Ferndown, nr Tricketts Cross r'about.
N off Wimborne Rd East, Woodland
Walk is a single track lane with no
parking. Please leave cars on main
road and access on foot (5 mins/330
yds).* Home-made and cream teas.
**Adm £3.50, chd free. Sun 26 Apr,
Sun 10, Sun 24 May, Sun 7 June
(1-5).** Visitors also welcome by
arrangement Apr to June for
groups of 20+, refreshments by
arrangement.
The name captures the setting. Award
winning 1³/₄ acre spring garden.
Terraced lawns for lingering over tea.
Woodland walks through blossom
trees, wild anemones, primroses and
bluebells. Extensive shrubbery with
camellias, azaleas and rhododendrons. Stream and large wildlife pond
with primulas, marginals and
waterlilies. Bog garden, wet meadow,
spring bulbs and herbaceous and
mixed borders. Featured in Gardens of
Dorset, 15 min interview on Radio
Solent. Gravel, grass and slopes make
wheelchair access difficult, notably if
wet. Drop-off/pick-up for those with
restricted mobility, please phone
ahead.

26 **GRANGE COTTAGE**
Golden Hill, Stourton Caundle
DT10 2JP. Fleur Miles, 01963
364651, fleurmiles@ekit.com. *6m
SE of Sherborne. Park near The
Trooper Inn or close to Grange
Cottage.* **Adm £4, chd free. Sat 28,
Sun 29 Mar (2-5).** Also open Manor
Farm, Stourton Caundle, combined

adm £8. Visitors also welcome by
arrangement Mar to Sept for
groups of 10+, teas by
arrangement.
Come to our thatched cottage and
discover the peace and tranquillity of
a real cottage garden. Follow the
meandering paths and find many
flower borders, box and yew hedging,
two ponds, topiary creatures and
much more to delight you. Hellebores
and spring bulbs a particular feature.

27 **GREENACRES**
Bere Road, Coldharbour, Wareham
BH20 7PA. John & Pat Jacobs.
*2¹/₂ m NW of Wareham. From r'about
adjacent to stn take Wareham-Bere
Regis rd. House ¹/₂ m past Silent
Woman Inn on R.* Home-made teas.
**Adm £3.50, chd free. Sun 21 June,
Sun 26 July (2-5.30).**
Approx 1 acre plantswoman's garden
situated in Wareham Forest. Lawns
punctuated by colourful island beds
designed mainly for summer interest.
Unusual perennials, shrubs and
specimen trees, spectacular flowering
tulip tree. Themed areas and stone
water feature with 2 ponds. Stumpery
with collection of ferns and grasses.
Live music. Static display of radio
controlled aircraft. Plenty of off road
parking.

28 **HARCOMBE HOUSE**
Pitmans Lane, Morcombelake,
Bridport DT6 6EB. Jan & Martin
Dixon, 01297 489229,
Harcombe@hotmail.co.uk. *A35 4m
W of Bridport - ignore satnav. A35
from Bridport: R to Whitchurch just
past The Artwave Gallery. Immed R,
bear L into Pitmans Lane. Approx
800m, park in paddock on L.* Home-
made teas. All cakes are home-made
by Jan Dixon, all proceeds to NGS.
**Adm £4, chd free. Sat 16, Sun 17,
Tue 19 May, Thur 13, Sat 15, Sun
16 Aug (11-5).** Visitors also
welcome by arrangement May to
Sept groups are welcome but no
coaches.
Landscaped into the hillside with
wonderful views across Lyme Bay,
the garden is laid out as a series of
gravel paths and terraces connected
by steps. Featuring mature shrubs
and perennials, many of which are
unusual and visually stunning, the
garden offers something for every
season. The garden will present a
challenge to the less mobile visitor
and is unsuitable for wheelchairs and
buggies.

29 HERONS MEAD
East Burton Road, East Burton,
Wool BH20 6HF. Ron & Angela
Millington, 01929 463872,
ronamillington@btinternet.com. *6m
W of Wareham on A352.
Approaching Wool from Wareham,
turn R just before level crossing into
East Burton Rd. Herons Mead ³/₄ m
on L.* Home-made teas. Wine and
nibbles at evening opening in June.
Adm £3, chd free. Sun 22 Mar, Sun
5 Apr, Sun 3 May (2-5). Evening
Opening £4.50, chd free, wine, Fri
19 June (6-8). Sun 20 Sept (2-5).
**Visitors also welcome by
arrangement Mar to Sept for
groups of 10+.**
¹/₂ acre plantlover's garden full of
interest from spring (bulbs, many
hellebores, pulmonaria, fritillaries)
through abundant summer
perennials, old roses scrambling
through trees and late seasonal
exuberant plants amongst swathes of
tall grasses. Wildlife pond and plants
to attract bees, butterflies, etc. Tiny
woodland. Cacti. Local community
choir at June opening. Featured in WI
Life, Dorset Life & Amateur
Gardening.

Discover, by
degrees and at
every turn, its
element of
surprise . . .

30 ◆ HILLTOP
Woodville, Stour Provost,
Gillingham SP8 5LY. Josse & Brian
Emerson, 01747 838512,
www.hilltopgarden.co.uk. *7m N of
Sturminster Newton, 5m W of
Shaftesbury. On B3092 turn E at
Stour Provost Xrds, signed Woodville.
After 1¹/₄ m thatched cottage on R.
On A30, turn S opp Kings Arms.* Home-made teas.
Adm £3, chd free. For NGS: Suns
12, 19, 26 July, 2, 9, 16 Aug (2-6).
**For other opening times and
information, please phone or see
garden website.**

Summer at Hilltop is a gorgeous riot
of colour and scent, the old thatched
cottage barely visible amongst the
flowers. Unusual annuals and
perennials grow alongside the
traditional and familiar, boldly
combining to make a spectacular
display, which attracts an abundance
of wildlife. Always something new, the
unique, gothic garden loo a great
success. Nursery.

31 22 HOLT ROAD
Branksome, Poole BH12 1JQ. Alan
& Sylvia Lloyd, 01202 387509,
alan.lloyd22@ntlworld.com. *2.5m W
of Bournemouth Square 3m E of
Poole Civic Centre. From Alder Rd
turn into Winston Ave, 3rd R into
Guest Ave 2nd R into Holt Rd at end
of cul de sac. Park in Holt Rd or
alternatively in Guest Ave.* Home-made teas. Adm £3.50, chd free.
Suns 29 Mar, 19 Apr, 17 May, 14
June, 19 July, 16 Aug (2-5.30).
**Visitors also welcome by
arrangement Mar to Aug for groups
of 10+.**
³/₄ acre walled garden for all seasons.
Garden seating throughout the
diverse planting areas, comprising
Mediterranean courtyard garden,
wisteria pergola. Walk up slope
beside rill and bog garden to raised
bed vegetable garden. Return
through shrubbery and rockery back
to waterfall cascading into a pebble
beach. Partial wheelchair access.

32 HOLWORTH FARMHOUSE
Holworth, nr Dorchester DT2 8NH.
Anthony & Philippa Bush,
01305 852242,
bushinarcadia@yahoo.co.uk,
www.inarcadia-
gardendesign.co.uk. *7m E of
Dorchester. 1m S of A352. Follow
signs to Holworth. Through farmyard
with duckpond on R. 1st L after
200yds of rough track. Ignore no
access signs.* Home-made teas.
Adm £3.50, chd free. Sun 3, Mon 4
May, Sun 21 June, Sun 5 July, Sun
9 Aug (2-5). **Visitors also welcome
by arrangement May to Sept, we
can supply teas or wine.**
This unusual garden is tucked away
without being isolated and has an
atmosphere of extraordinary peace
and tranquility. At no point do visitors
perceive any idea of the whole, but
have to discover, by degrees and at
every turn, its element of surprise, its
variety of features and its appreciation

of space. At all times you are invited
to look back, to look round and to
look up. Birds and butterflies.
Beautiful unspoilt views. Limited
wheelchair access.

33 HOLY TRINITY
ENVIRONMENTAL GARDEN
Cross Rd, Weymouth DT4 9QX.
Holy Trinity C E Primary School &
Nursery,
holytrinityenvironmentalgarden.
blogspot.co.uk. *1m W of Weymouth
centre. Follow A354 from Weymouth
harbour junction by Asda. R at top of
hill into Wyke Rd. 3rd L into Cross
Rd. 200yds on R school car park.*
Home-made teas. Adm £4, chd free.
Sat 18, Sun 19 July (1-5).
Award winning wildlife garden, started
in 2008 with the donation of a
winning RHS Show garden. There are
also children's raised beds; large
wildlife pond; WWII garden with
genuine Anderson shelter; small
orchard and bird garden. Dorset's
largest living willow classroom which
seats 30 is now well established and
a recently installed composting toilet
complements the garden. Butterfly
hunt for children. Wheelchair access
to most of garden and WC.

34 HORN PARK
Tunnel Rd, Beaminster DT8 3HB.
Mr & Mrs David Ashcroft,
01308 862212,
angieashcroft@btinternet.com.
*1¹/₂ m N of Beaminster. On A3066
from Beaminster, L before tunnel (see
signs).* Home-made teas. Adm
£4.50, chd free. Wed 29 Apr, Wed
17 June (2.30-4.30). **Visitors also
welcome by arrangement Apr to
Oct on Tues to Thurs only.**
Large, plantsman's garden with
magnificent view to sea. Many rare
and mature plants and shrubs in
terraced, herbaceous, rock and water
gardens. Woodland garden and
walks in bluebell woods. Good
autumn colouring. Wild flower
meadow with 164 varieties incl
orchids.

35 IVY HOUSE GARDEN
Piddletrenthide DT2 7QF. Bridget
Bowen, 01300 348255,
bridgetpbowen@hotmail.com. *9m
N of Dorchester. On B3143. In middle
of Piddletrenthide village, opp
PO/village stores near Piddle Inn.*
Home-made teas. Adm £4, chd free.

Sat 28, Sun 29 Mar, Mon 6 Apr, Sun 3, Mon 4 May (2-5). **Visitors also welcome by arrangement Apr to May for groups of 10+.** Unusual and challenging ¹/₂ acre garden set on steep hillside with fine views. Wildlife friendly garden with mixed borders, ponds, propagating area, vegetable garden, fruit cage, greenhouses and polytunnel, chickens and bees, nearby allotment. Daffodils, tulips and hellebores in quantity for spring openings. Come prepared for steep terrain and a warm welcome! Run on organic lines with plants to attract bees and other insects. Insect-friendly plants usually for sale. Honey and hive products available and, weather permitting, observation hive of honey bees in courtyard. Beekeeper present to answer queries!

36 ◆ KINGSTON LACY
Wimborne Minster BH21 4EA. National Trust, 01202 883402, www.nationaltrust.org.uk. *1¹/₂ m W of Wimborne Minster. On Wimborne-Blandford rd B3082.* Full restaurant on site. **Adm £8, chd £4. For NGS: Sat 27, Sun 28 June, Sat 17, Sun 18 Oct (10.30-6). For other opening times and information, please phone or see garden website.**
35 acres of formal garden, incorporating parterre and sunk garden planted with Edwardian schemes during spring and summer. 5 acre kitchen garden and allotments, Victorian fernery containing over 35 varieties. Rose garden, mixed herbaceous borders, vast formal lawns and Japanese garden restored to Henrietta Bankes' creation of 1910. 2 National Collections: Convallaria and Anemone nemorosa. Deep gravel on some paths but lawns suitable for wheelchairs. Slope to visitor reception and S lawn.

37 ◆ KINGSTON MAURWARD GARDENS AND ANIMAL PARK
Kingston Maurward, Dorchester DT2 8PX. Kingston Maurward College, 01305 215003, www.morekmc.com. *1m E of Dorchester. Off A35. Follow brown Tourist Information signs.* **For opening times and information, please phone or see garden website.**
35 acres of gardens laid out in C18 and C20 with 5 acre lake. Generous terraces and gardens divided by hedges and stone balustrades. Stone features and interesting plants. Elizabethan walled garden laid out as demonstration. National Collections of penstemons and salvias. Open early Jan to mid Dec (10-5.30) or dusk if earlier. Partial wheelchair access, not all areas accessible. Gravel paths and steep slope to lake.

hospice UK

There's a hospice close to every NGS garden

38 NEW KITEMOOR COTTAGE
Manswood, Wimborne BH21 5BQ. Alan and Diana Guy, 01258 840894, diana.kitemoor@btinternet.com. *6m N of Wimborne. From B3078 turn to Witchampton, then from village centre follow signs to Manswood.* Tea. Homemade soup and roll at lunchtime, tea and cake in the afternoon. **Adm £3.50, chd free. Sat 7, Sun 8 Mar (11-4). Visitors also welcome by arrangement Mar to June for groups of 15 +.**
¹/₂ acre plantsperson's garden with glorious countryside views. Diana (formally of Welcome Thatch) has created a new garden full of treasures incl large collection of hellebores. Pond, mini meadow, naturalistic planting and cottage garden borders. Fruit and vegetable gardens. Exquisite holmlea hybrid hellebores for sale. Partial wheelchair access. Narrow pathways and different levels.

39 KNITSON OLD FARMHOUSE
Corfe Castle, Wareham BH20 5JB. Rachel Helfer, 01929 421681, rachel@knitson.co.uk. *1m NW of Swanage. 3m E of Corfe Castle. Signed L off A351 to Knitson. Very narrow rds for 1m. Ample parking in yard or in adjacent field.* Cream teas. Home-made cakes. **Adm £3, chd free. Fri 22, Sat 23, Sun 24, Mon 25 May, Fri 11, Sat 12, Sun 13 Sept**
(1-5). **Visitors also welcome by arrangement Mar to Dec, max 25.** Mature cottage garden with exceptional views nestled at base of chalk downland in dry coastal conditions. Herbaceous borders, rockeries, climbers and shrubs. Evolved and designed over 50yrs for yr-round colour and interest. Large wildlife friendly kitchen garden for self sufficiency. Rachel is delighted to welcome visitors and discuss gardening. Uneven, sloping paths.

40 ◆ KNOLL GARDENS
Hampreston, Wimborne BH21 7ND. Mr Neil Lucas, 01202 873931, www.knollgardens.co.uk. *2¹/₂ m W of Ferndown. ETB brown signs from A31. Large car park.* Close by The Old Thatch pub and restaurant serves coffee, snacks and meals, under a thatched roof, with a log fire and its own ghost! 01202 877192. **For opening times and information, please phone or see garden website.**
Originally a private botanic, an exciting collection of grasses and perennials now thrive within an informal setting of shrubs, mature and unusual trees. Owned by the UK's leading ornamental grass specialist, Neil Lucas, a recently extended Mediterranean-style gravel garden and new meadow planting complement his acclaimed naturalistic style. National Collection of Pennisetum and renowned nursery. Featured in The English Garden & Dorset magazine. Some slopes. Various surfaces incl gravel, paving, grass and bark.

41 LANGEBRIDE HOUSE
Long Bredy DT2 9HU. Mrs J Greener, 01308 482257. *8m W of Dorchester. S off A35, midway between Dorchester and Bridport. Well signed. 1st gateway on L in village.* **Adm £4.50, chd free. Visitors welcome by arrangement Jan to July.**
This old rectory garden has carpets of anemones spreading out under huge copper beech tree on lawn. A lovely place to visit in spring and early summer, with a large variety of daffodils and early spring bulbs amongst flowering shrubs, trees and herbaceous borders with kitchen garden. Some steep slopes.

42 LAWSBROOK
Brodham Way, Shillingstone, Dorset DT11 0TE. Clive, Faith & Gina Nelson, 01258 860148, cne70bl@aol.com, www.facebook.com/Lawsbrook. *5m NW of Blandford. Follow signs to Shillingstone on A357. Turn off at old PO, continue up Gunn Lane, 2nd junction on R, 1st house on R (200yds).* Home-made teas. **Adm £3, chd free. Sun 22 Feb, Sun 1 Nov (10-4).** Visitors also welcome by arrangement Feb to Nov, garden can accommodate large numbers. 6 acres. Over 200 trees incl the mature and unusual. Formal borders, wildflower and wildlife areas, vegetable garden. Relaxed and friendly, lovely opportunity for family walks in all areas incl wildlife, stream, meadow. Children and dogs welcome. Yr-round interest incl extensive snowdrops, hellebores and bulbs in early spring through full summer colour to intense autumn hues. Large and unusual labelled tree collection. Garden activities for all the family. More than an acre coverage of snowdrops in the early spring. Gravel path at entrance, grass paths over whole garden.

43 NEW LITTLE CLIFF
Sidmouth Road, Lyme Regis DT7 3EQ. Mrs Debbie Bell, 01297 444833. *Edge of Lyme Regis. Turn off A35 onto B3165 to Lyme Regis.Through Uplyme to mini r'about by Travis Perkins. 3rd exit on R, up to fork and L down Sidmouth Rd following NGS signs from mini r'about. Garden on R.* **Adm £3.50, chd free. Sat 18, Thur 23 Apr, Thur 18, Sat 20 June, Thur 9 July (2-5).** Visitors also welcome by arrangement Apr to June. South facing seaward, Little Cliff

looks out over spectacular views of Lyme Bay. Spacious garden sloping down hillside through series of garden rooms where visual treats unfold. Vibrant herbaceous borders, with hot garden, white garden, bog garden all intermingled with mature specimen trees, shrubs and wall climbers. Steep slopes.

44 ♦ LITTLEBREDY WALLED GARDENS
Littlebredy DT2 9HL. The Walled Garden Workshop, 01305 898055, www.littlebredy.com. *8m W of Dorchester. 10m E of Bridport. 1½ m S of A35. NGS days: park on village green then walk 300yd. For the less mobile (and on normal open days) use gardens car park.* Cream teas. **Adm £5, chd free. For NGS: Tue 23, Tue 30 June (2-7). For other opening times and information, please phone or see garden website.**
1 acre walled garden on S facing slopes of Bride River Valley. Herbaceous borders, riverside rose walk, lavender parterre and potager vegetable and cut flower gardens. Original Victorian glasshouses, one under renovation. Gardens also open 2-5pm on Wed & Sun (see website for other days) from Easter to end Sept, weather permitting. Featured in Country Living and several national and regional magazines. Partial wheelchair access, some steep grass slopes. For disabled parking please follow signs to main entrance.

45 55 LONNEN ROAD
Colehill, Wimborne BH21 7AT. Malcolm Case & Jenny Parr, 01202 883549. *1½ m N of Wimborne. From Canford Bottom r'about where A31 meets B3073, exit N marked Colehill for 1¼ m, R into Lonnen Rd.* Home-made teas. **Adm £3, chd free. Sat 4, Sun 5 July, Sat 1, Sun 2 Aug (2-5).** Visitors also welcome by arrangement July & Aug.
Perfectionist's garden on 3 levels. Colour co-ordinated planting using wide range of plants, with borrowed view over adjacent fields. Circular box parterre infilled with vegetables. Watering cans hang in a row behind tool shed, by bridge over little stream. New white border. Lots for the eye and senses to enjoy.

GROUP OPENING

46 LYTCHETT MINSTER GARDENS
Lytchett Minster BH16 6JF. *3m W of Wimborne. From A35 Bakers Arms PH r'about (junction with A351), follow signs to Lytchett MInster B3067. L opp St Peters Finger PH, follow parking signs. Garden guide/adm at car park.* Home-made teas at The Old Bakehouse, 55 Dorchester Rd. **Combined adm £5, chd free. Sat 20, Sun 21 June (2-5).**

15 ASHBROOK WALK
Sue & Terry Allison

NEW 57 DORCHESTER ROAD
Maureen & Stephen Kirkham. *Thatched house on corner of Dorchester Rd and New Rd*

NEW FRIARS GREEN
New Road. Jane & Robin SeQueira

HERON HOUSE
17 Ashbrook Walk. Phillip & Geraldine Stevens

OLD BUTTON COTTAGE
58 Dorchester Road. Thelma & Paul Johns

4 OLD FORGE CLOSE
Liz & Derek Allen

10 ORCHARD CLOSE
Daphne Turner

'The Gateway to the Purbecks', is W of Poole on the old Dorchester rd. Mixture of old and new houses, 2 churches, 2 PHs and an ancient pound. The 7 small to medium sized gardens offer variation in cottage style planting with many varieties of herbaceous perennials and hardy geraniums, some lush waterside planting, magnificent displays of climbing roses, small fruit and vegetable plots and many other interesting features. Flower festival in village. Dogs on leads in 3 gardens.

47 MANOR FARM, HAMPRESTON
Wimborne BH21 7LX. Guy & Anne Trehane. *2½ m E of Wimborne, 2½ m W of Ferndown. From Canford Bottom r'about on A31, take exit B3073 Ham Lane. ½ m turn R at Hampreston Xrds. House at bottom of village.* Home-made teas. **Adm**

Harcombe House

£3.50, chd free. **Sat 28 Feb, Sun 1 Mar (12-3); Sun 31 May, Sun 2 Aug (1-5); Wed 5 Aug (2-5).**
Traditional farmhouse garden designed and cared for by 3 generations of the Trehane family through over 100 years of farming and gardening at Hampreston. Garden is noted for its herbaceous borders and rose beds within box and yew hedges. Mature shrubbery, water and bog garden. Opening for hellebores in Feb. Dorset Hardy Plant Society sales at later openings.
&♿ ❀ ☕

48 MANOR FARM, STOURTON CAUNDLE
Stourton Caundle DT10 2JW. Mr & Mrs O S L Simon. *6m E of Sherborne, 4 m W of Sturminster Newton. From Sherborne take A3030. At Bishops Caundle, L signed Stourton Caundle. After 1½ m, L opp Trooper Inn in middle of village.* Home-made teas. **Adm £5, chd free. Sat 28, Sun 29 Mar, Sun 12 July (2-5). Also open Grange Cottage 28/29 March, combined adm £8.**
C17 farmhouse and barns with walled garden in middle of village. Mature trees, shrubberies, herbaceous borders, lakes and vegetable garden. Lovingly created over last 40 yrs by current owners. Wheelchair access to lower areas of garden, steps to top areas of garden.
♿ ❀ ☕

49 THE MANOR HOUSE
Church Lane, Lower Blandford St Mary, Blandford DT11 9ND. Mr & Mrs Jeremy Mains, 01258 451692. *¼ m E of Blandford. Signed off A350 to Poole from Blandford Forum Ring Road (Tesco r'about).* Cream teas. **Adm £4.50, chd free. Sun 6, Wed 9 Sept (2-5). Visitors also welcome by arrangement Apr to Sept.**
Traditional 3 acre walled garden surrounding Jacobean House (not open). Formal rose beds with mixed herbaceous borders. Working fruit and vegetable garden. Large and varied shrub borders with extensive collection of roses. Something of interest at all times of year.
♿ ❀ ☕

50 ◆ MAPPERTON GARDENS
nr Beaminster DT8 3NR. The Earl & Countess of Sandwich, 01308 862645, www.mapperton.com. *6m N of Bridport. Off A356/A3066. 2m SE of Beaminster off B3163.* Sawmill café open during garden opening hours. **For further information, please phone or see garden website.**
Terraced valley gardens surrounding Tudor/Jacobean manor house. On upper levels, walled croquet lawn, orangery and Italianate formal garden with fountains, topiary and grottos. Below, C17 summerhouse and fishponds. Lower garden with shrubs and rare trees, leading to woodland and spring gardens. Garden open

1 Mar to 31 Oct (except Sats) (11-5); café open 1 Apr to 30 Sept. Partial wheelchair access (lawn and upper levels).
♿ ❀ 🚐 ☕

51 MARREN
Holworth, Dorchester DT2 8NJ. Mr & Mrs Peter Cartwright, 01305 851503, wcartwright@tiscali.co.uk, www.wendycartwright.net. *SE of Dorchester. Don't use SatNav. Off A353 At Poxwell turn L to Ringstead. Straight on to NT Car Park at top of hill. Park before gate marked No Cars. Walk through gate, signed path, on R.* Home-made teas. **Adm £3.50, chd free. Sat 18, Sun 19 Apr, Sat 23, Sun 24 May (2-5). Visitors also welcome by arrangement Apr to June, refreshments by arrangement.**
4 acres. From National Trust car park down steep public footpath and 64 grass steps to woodland garden with tree sculptures.. Views of Weymouth Bay and Portland. More formal garden around house with wonderful arbour and Mediterranean feel. Strong structural planting. Italianate courtyard. Stout footwear and strong knees recommended. Fedge in willow. Hornbeam house. Italianate courtyard with fountain. Hornbeam arbour on terrace. Willow arbour at the bottom. Not suitable for wheelchairs. Disabled access to house for tea by prior arrangement.
❀ 🛏 Ⓓ ☕

52 MEADOW VIEWS

32 Riverside Road, West Moors, Ferndown BH22 0LQ. Sue & Norman Lynch. *2m from Ferndown towards Verwood, off B3072. From Station Rd through West Moors going N, turn L. Last house on R. Parking in rd, avoiding driveways.* Home-made teas. **Adm £2.50, chd free.** Sun 19 July, Sun 9 Aug (2-5).
Small, informal, wildlife friendly garden overlooking Manning Brook and open farmland. Island beds showing colourful herbaceous mixed planting with additional perennials for 2015. Newly enlarged and improved fernery. Damselflies dance in the sunshine over the water whilst butterflies and bees visit their chosen blooms. Some steps and gravel paths/driveway.

53 THE MILL HOUSE

Crook Hill, Netherbury DT6 5LX. Michael & Giustina Ryan, 01308 488267, themillhouse@dsl.pipex.com. *1m S of Beaminster. Turn R off A3066 Beaminster to Bridport rd at signpost to Netherbury. Car park at Xrds at bottom of hill.* Cream teas. Teas in aid of Friends of Netherbury Church. **Adm £5, chd free.** Sun 26 Apr, Sun 10 May (1-5). Evening Opening £5, chd free, wine, Wed 29 July (5.30-8.30). Combined with Pye's Plot, Netherbury 10th May & 29th July, 2 gardens £7. Visitors also welcome by arrangement Apr to Sept min 6, max 30.
6½ acres of garden around R Brit, mill stream and mill pond. Formal walled, terraced and vegetable gardens. Bog garden. Emphasis on spring bulbs, scented flowers, hardy geraniums, lilies, clematis and water irises. Wander through the wild garden planted with many rare and interesting trees including conifers, magnolias, fruit trees and oaks underplanted with bulbs. Partial wheelchair access.

54 ◆ MINTERNE HOUSE

Minterne Magna, Dorchester DT2 7AU. The Hon Henry & Mrs Digby, 01300 341370, www.minterne.co.uk. *2m N of Cerne Abbas. On A352 Dorchester-Sherborne rd.* For opening times and information, please phone or see garden website.
Voted one of the 10 Prettiest gardens in England in The Times. Famed for their display of rhododendrons, azaleas, Japanese cherries and magnolias in April/May. Small lakes, streams and cascades offer new vistas at each turn around the 1m horseshoe shaped gardens covering 23 acres. The season ends with spectacular autumn colour. Open mid February to 9 Nov (10-6). Featured on BBC2 Gardeners' World. Voted one of the 10 Prettiest Gardens in England by The Times, described by Simon Jenkins as 'A Corner of Paradise'. Regret unsuitable for wheelchairs.

> Series of garden rooms where visual treats unfold . . .

55 OLD DOWN HOUSE

Horton, Wimborne BH21 7HL. Dr & Mrs Colin Davidson, 07765 404248, pipdavidson59@gmail.com. *7½ m N of Wimborne. Horton Inn at junction of B3078 with Horton Rd, pick up yellow signs which take you up through North Farm. No garden access from Matterley Drove. 5min walk to garden down farm track.* Home-made teas. **Adm £3, chd free.** Sun 7, Wed 10, Wed 17 June (2-5).
Nestled down a farm track, this ¾ acre garden on chalk surrounds C18 farmhouse. Stunning views over Horton Tower and farmland. Cottage garden planting with formal elements, climbing roses clothe pergola and house walls along with stunning wisteria sinensis and banksia rose. Part walled potager. Not suitable for wheelchairs.

56 THE OLD RECTORY, MANSTON

Manston, Sturminster Newton DT10 1EX. Andrew & Judith Hussey, 01258 474673, judithhussey@hotmail.com. *6m S of Shaftesbury, 2½ m N of Sturminster Newton. From Shaftesbury, take B3091. On reaching Manston, past Plough Inn, L for Child Okeford on R-hand bend. Old Rectory last house* on L. Home-made teas. **Adm £4, chd free.** Sun 14, Wed 17 June (2-5). Visitors also welcome by arrangement May to Sept for groups of 4+.
Beautifully restored 5 acre garden. S-facing wall with 120ft herbaceous border edged by old brick path. Enclosed yew hedge flower garden. Wildflower meadow marked with mown paths and young plantation of mixed hardwoods. Well maintained walled Victorian kitchen garden. Knot garden introduced in 2011 now well established. New garden room surrounded by box and rose and yew introduced in 2013.

57 THE OLD RECTORY, NETHERBURY

nr Beaminster DT6 5NB. Simon & Amanda Mehigan, oldrectorynetherbury.tumblr.com. *2m SW of Beaminster. Please park considerately in the village, bearing in mind that large tractors and the school bus have to pass.* Home-made teas. Refreshments from 11 am. **Adm £5, chd free.** Wed 15 Apr, Wed 13 May, Wed 17 June (10-5).
5 acre garden surrounding C16 house. Formal areas with topiary near house, natural planting elsewhere. Extensive bog garden with pond and stream planted with drifts of irises, primulas and other moisture lovers. Woodland areas with magnolias, cornus, species peonies, wood anemones. Spring bulbs including many erythroniums. Hornbeam walk. Decorative vegetable garden. Featured in RHS The Garden.

58 THE OLD RECTORY, PULHAM

Dorchester DT2 7EA. Mr & Mrs N Elliott, 01258 817595. *13m N of Dorchester. 8m SE of Sherborne. On B3143 turn E at Xrds in Pulham. Signed Cannings Court.* Home-made teas. **Adm £5, chd free.** Mon 4, Sun 17 May, Sun 26 July (2-5). Groups also welcome by arrangement, weekdays May to Aug.
4 acres formal and informal gardens surround C18 rectory with splendid views. Yew hedges enclose circular herbaceous borders with late summer colour. Exuberantly planted terrace with purple and white beds. Box parterres, mature trees, pond, fernery, ha-ha, pleached hornbeam circle. 10 acres woodland walks. Flourishing and newly extended bog garden with

islands; awash with primulas and irises in May. Home-made teas and cakes, interesting plants for sale. Featured in Country Life, Home and Gardens, Country Homes and Interiors. Mostly wheelchair access.

59 OLD SMITHY
Ibberton DT11 0EN. Carol & Clive Carsley, 01258 817361, carolcarsley@btinternet.com. *9m NW of Blandford Forum. From Blandford A357 to Sturminster Newton. After 6.5m L to Okeford Fitzpaine. Follow signs to Ibberton, 3m, park by village hall, 5 min walk to garden.* Home-made teas in Village Hall. Adm £3.50, chd free. Sat 4 Apr, Sun 10 May (2-5). Visitors also welcome by arrangement Feb to Sept.
Worth driving twisty narrow lanes to reach rural 2½ acre streamside garden framing thatched cottage. Back of beyond setting which inspired international best seller Mr Rosenblum's List. Succession of ponds. Mown paths. Spring bulbs, aquilegia and hellebores. Sit beneath rustling trees. Views of Bulbarrow and church. Featured in Period Living & Dorset Life.

60 THE OLD VICARAGE
East Orchard, Shaftesbury SP7 0BA. Miss Tina Wright, 01747 811744, tina_lon@msn.com. *4½ m S of Shaftesbury, 3½ m N of Sturminster Newton. On B3091, on 90 degree bend, next to lay-by with phone box. Park in field opp. Walk along verge, cross at 2nd open gate carefully checking in mirror.* Home-made teas. Adm £4, chd free. Sun 29 Mar (1.30-4.30); Sun 24 May, Sun 4 Oct (2-5.30). Visitors also welcome by arrangement Feb to Dec.
1.7 acre, award winning wildlife friendly garden. Swathes of crocus, primula and unusual snowdrops in spring. A large number of different daffodils follow, then herbaceous borders and wild flowers. Sit by the bubbling stream or gaze at beautiful reflections in the swimming pond. Dogs welcome and children can pond dip. Swing and tree platform overlooking Duncliffe woods. Teas indoors and various shelters around the garden if wet. Featured in Independent and Mail on Sunday. Not suitable for wheelchairs if very wet.

61 PILSDON VIEW
Junction Butts Lane and Pitman's Lane, Ryall, Bridport DT6 6EH. D Lloyd, 01297 489377, davidlloyd001@hotmail.com. *5m W of Bridport, through Chideok. From E through Morecombelake A35. Take the Ryall turning opp Felicity's farm shop on A35. Garden ¾ m on L at junction Butts Lane/Pitmans Lane. High hedge with PO box in wall.* Light refreshments. Tea, coffee, cakes. Adm £3.50, chd free. Tue 16, Sun 28 June, Tue 14, Sun 26 July (12-4). Visitors also welcome by arrangement Apr to Aug no coaches.
Started over 25 yrs ago, the hard landscaping provides different levels with breathtaking views over the Marshwood Vale towards Pilson Pen. Mature copper beech and evolving garden gives all yr round interest. Water features with wildlife add to the essence of the garden. Bring your own picnic. Partial wheelchair access.

Small but perfectly formed front and back courtyard garden . . .

62 PUDDLEDOCK COTTAGE
Scotland Heath, Norden, nr Corfe Castle, Wareham BH20 5DY. Ray and Ann George, 07715 749147, malcolmorgee@yahoo.co.uk. *Scotland Heath, Norden. From Wareham to Corfe Castle turn L at Norden Park and Ride then L signed Slepe and Arne. Garden 500m on R.* Home-made teas. Adm £4, chd free. Sun 7 June, Sun 9 Aug (12-4). Visitors also welcome by arrangement Feb to Nov for any size groups.
Puddledock Cottage was originally a quarryman's cottage. Newly renovated, it now stands at the centre of a big lovingly created garden with

streams and ponds edged with nectar rich plants that attract a myriad of butterflies and bees. Shady walks snake though birch and willow, underplanted with rhododendrons and ferns. Views to Corfe Castle and Scotland Heath. Children's activities. Good wheelchair access.

63 2 PYES PLOT
St. James Road, Netherbury, Bridport DT6 5LP. Ms Sarah Porter. *2m SW of Beaminster. 2m SW of Beaminster. Turn off A3066. Go over R Brit into centre of village. L into St James Rd, signed to Waytown, R corner Hingsdon Lane.* Adm £3, chd free. Sun 10 May (2-5.30). Evening Opening £3, chd free, Light refreshments, Wed 29 July (5-7). Combined with The Mill House both days, 2 gardens £7, home-made teas at The Mill House.
Small but perfectly formed front and back courtyard garden, created from new in 2007. Cream walls and black paintwork make a striking framework for softer planting. Climbing plants, foliage and running water feature enhance the tranquil feel to this space, which uses every inch creatively. Featured in Dorset Life and Good Housekeeping.

64 Q
113 Bridport Road, Dorchester DT1 2NH. Heather & Chris Robinson, 01305 263088, hmrobinson45@gmail.com. *Approx 300m W of Dorset County Hospital. From Top o' Town r'about head W towards Dorset County Hospital, Q 300 metres further on.* Home-made teas. Adm £3, chd free. Suns 15, 29 Mar (2-4.30); 12, 26 Apr, 10 May, 14 June (2-5). Visitors also welcome by arrangement Feb to June for 40 max, 1wk notice preferred.
Q is essentially all things to all men, a modern cottage town garden with many facets, jam packed with bulbs, shrubs, trees, climbers and bedding plants. Gazebo, statues, water, bonsai and topiary. Planting reflects the owners many and varied interests including over 100 clematis, 1000+ spring bulbs purchased yearly. Mothering Sunday and Fathers Day celebrated for participants. Small number of paths available for wheelchair users.

© Roger Lane

Braddocks

65 ▶ QUEEN ANN HOUSE
Fortuneswell, Portland DT5 1LP.
Mrs Margaret Dunlop, 01305
820028,
margaretdunlop@tiscali.co.uk. *4m
S of Weymouth. Follow A354 to
Portland. Up hill into one way traffic.
When two way traffic 50 metres on L.
Free parking available on R and L just
before house. Street parking available
beyond house.* Cream teas. **Adm
£3.50, chd free. Sun 9 Aug (2-5).**
A hidden gem with sectioned
areas/gardens with different planting.
Fern garden, tropical garden, English
garden with rockery and two ponds.
Also a single cast ornate cast iron
horses drinking trough.

66 ▶ 25 RICHMOND PARK AVENUE
Bournemouth BH8 9DL. Barbara
Hutchinson and Mike Roberts,
01202 531072,
barbarahutchinson@tiscali.co.uk.
*2¹/₂ m NE Bournemouth Town Centre.
From T-lights at junction with Alma Rd
and Richmond Park Rd, head N on
B3063 Charminster Rd, 2nd turning
on R into Richmond Park Ave.* Home-
made teas. **Adm £3, chd free. Sun
21 June, Sun 5 July (11-5); Thur 16**

July (2-5); Sun 26 July (11-5). Also
open nearby 21 June Western
Gardens. **Visitors also welcome by
arrangement July groups of 10+.**
Beautifully designed town garden with
pergola leading to ivy canopy over
raised decking. Cascading waterfall
connects 2 wildlife ponds enhanced
with domed acers. Circular lawn with
colourful herbaceous border planted
to attract bees and butterflies.
Fragrant S-facing courtyard garden at
front, sparkling with vibrant colour
and Mediterranean planting incl Asian
lilies, brugmansias and lemon tree.
Featured in Dorset Country Gardener.
Partial wheelchair access.

67 ▶ 357 RINGWOOD ROAD
Ferndown BH22 9AE. Lyn &
Malcolm Ovens, 01202 896071,
lynandmalc@btinternet.com,
www.lynandmalc.co.uk. *³/₄ m S of
Ferndown. On A348 towards
Longham. Parking in Glenmoor Rd or
other side rds. Avoid parking on main
rd.* Home-made teas. **Adm £3, chd
free. Sun 5 July (11-5); Wed 22
July (2-5); Sun 16 Aug (11-5).
Visitors also welcome by
arrangement July & Aug.**
The original Dorset His and Hers

garden. Hers in cottage style with
clematis, phlox, lilies, roses, monarda,
encouraging butterflies and bees,
providing a riot of colour and perfume
into late summer. Walk through a
Moorish keyhole doorway into His
exotic garden with brugmansias,
canna, oleander, banana, dahlia and
bougainvillea. A good example of
what can be achieved in a small
plantaholics' garden. Ferndown
Common nearby.

68 ▶ ◆ SCULPTURE BY THE LAKES
Pallington Lakes, Pallington,
Dorchester DT2 8QU. Mrs Monique
Gudgeon, 07720 637808,
www.sculpturebythelakes.co.uk.
*6m E of Dorchester. ¹/₂ m E of
Tincleton, see beech hedge and
security gates. From other direction
0.8m from Xrds. Purbeck ice cream
available. No children under 14. No
dogs allowed.* **Adm £6. Wed 17
June, Wed 8 July (11-5). For
opening times and information,
please phone or see garden
website.**
Recently created modern garden with
inspiration taken from all over the
world. Described as a modern

arcadia it follows traditions of the landscape movement, but for C21. Where sculpture has been placed, the planting palette has been kept simple, but dramatic, so that the work remains the star. Home to Monique and her husband, renowned British sculptor Simon Gudgeon, the sculpture park features over 30 of his most iconic pieces including Isis, which is also in London's Hyde Park and a dedicated gallery where some of his smaller pieces can be seen and purchased. Disabled access limited though possible to go round paths on mobility scooter or electric wheelchair if care taken.

69 THE SECRET GARDEN
The Friary, Hilfield DT2 7BE. The Society of St Francis, 01300 341345, hilfieldssf@franciscans.org.uk, www.hilfieldfriary.org.uk. *10m N of Dorchester, on A352 between Sherborne & Dorchester. 1st L after Minterne Magna, 1st turning on R signed The Friary. From Yeovil turn off A37 signed Batcombe, 3rd turning on L.* Home-made teas. **Adm £4, chd free. Sat 9, Sun 10 May (2-5).** Ongoing reclamation of neglected woodland garden. Vegetables and courtyard garden. New plantings from modern day plant hunters. Mature trees, bamboo, rhododendrons, azaleas, magnolias, camellias, other choice shrubs with stream on all sides crossed by bridges, and in spring a growing collection of loderi hybrids with other choice shrubs. Stout shoes recommended for woodland garden. Friary grounds open where meadows, woods and livestock can be viewed. Friary Shop selling a variety of gifts. Featured in Guardian colour supplement.

70 THE SECRET GARDEN AND SERLES HOUSE
47 Victoria Road, Wimborne BH21 1EN. Ian Willis. *Centre of Wimborne. On B3082 W of town, very near hospital, Westfield car park 300yds. Off-road parking close by.* Home-made teas. **Adm £3, chd free. Share to Wimborne Civic Society and NADFAS. Thur 23, Sun 26 July, Sun 2, Thur 6, Sun 9, Sun 23, Sun 30, Mon 31 Aug, Thur 3, Sat 5, Sun 6, Sun 13 Sept (2-5).** Alan Titchmarsh described this amusingly creative garden as 'one of the best 10 private gardens in

Britain'. The ingenious use of unusual plants complements the imaginative treasure trove of garden objects d'art. The enchanting house is also open. A feeling of a by gone age accompanies your tour as you step into a world of whimsical fantasy that is theatrical and unique. New Oriental garden. Featured in Stour & Avon magazine and on Solent Radio. Wheelchair access to garden only. Narrow steps may prohibit wide wheelchairs.

> Plenty of areas just to sit and enjoy the wildlife. Wire bird sculptures by local artist . . .

71 ◆ SHERBORNE CASTLE
New Rd, Sherborne DT9 5NR. Mr J K Wingfield Digby, 01935 812072, www.sherbornecastle.com. *¹/₂ m E of Sherborne. On New Road B3145. Follow brown signs from A30 & A352.* **For opening times and information, please phone or see garden website.** 40+ acres. Grade I Capability Brown garden with magnificent vistas across surrounding landscape, incl lake and views to ruined castle. Herbaceous planting, notable trees, mixed ornamental planting and managed wilderness are linked together with lawn and pathways. Dry Grounds Walk. Partial wheelchair access, gravel paths, steep slopes, steps.

72 SLAPE MANOR
Netherbury DT6 5LH. Mr & Mrs Antony Hichens, 01308 488232, sczhichens@btinternet.com. *1m S of Beaminster. Turn W off A3066 to Netherbury. House ¹/₃ m S of Netherbury on back rd to Bridport signed Waytown.* Home-made teas. **Adm £4, chd free. Sun 24 May (2-5).** Visitors also welcome by arrangement May to Sept for groups of 10+.

River valley garden with spacious lawns and primula fringed streams down to lake. Walk over stream with magnificent hostas and gunneras, horizontal cryptomeria Japonica Elegans and around lake. Admire the mature wellingtonias, ancient wisterias, rhododendrons and planting around house. Mostly flat with some sloping paths and steps.

73 ◆ SNAPE COTTAGE PLANTSMAN'S GARDEN
Chaffeymoor, Bourton, nr Gillingham SP8 5BZ. Ian & Angela Whinfield, 01747 840330 (evenings), www.snapecottagegarden.co.uk. *5m NW of Gillingham. On border of Somerset & Wiltshire, at W end of Bourton, N of A303. Opp Chiffchaffs, 5 mins from Stourhead (NT).* Cream teas. Home-made cakes. **Adm £3.50, chd free. For NGS: Sat 28 Mar, Sat 25 Apr, Sat 30 May, Sat 27 June (2-5). For other opening times and information, please phone or see garden website.** Mature country garden containing exceptional collection of hardy plants and bulbs, artistically arranged in informal cottage garden style, organically managed and clearly labelled. Specialities incl snowdrops, hellebores, 'old' daffodils, pulmonarias, auriculas, herbs, irises and geraniums. Wildlife pond, beautiful views, tranquil atmosphere. Home of Snape Stakes Plant Supports and Obelisks. Featured in many publications worldwide.

74 NEW STADDLESTONES
14 Witchampton Mill, Witchampton, Wimborne BH21 5DE. Mrs Annette Lockwood. *5m N of Wimborne off B3078. Follow signs through the village and park in the sports field, 5 min walk to garden, limited disabled parking near garden.* Home-made teas. **Adm £3, chd free. Thur 14 May, Thur 16 July, Thur 13 Aug, Thur 10 Sept (2-5).** Cottage garden with colour themed borders, pleached limes and hidden gems, leading over chalk stream, to shady area which has some unusual plants, incl hardy orchids and arisaemas. Plenty of areas just to sit and enjoy the wildlife. Wire bird sculptures by local artist. Wheelchair access to first half of garden.

75 STONE RISE
25 Newton Road, Swanage
BH19 2EA. Mr & Mrs Suzanne
Nutbeem. *1/2 m S of Swanage town
centre. From town follow signs to
Durlston Country Park. At top of hill
turn R at red postbox into Bon
Accord Rd. 4th turn R into Newton
Rd.* Adm £3, chd free. Every Wed 1
July to 26 Aug (2-5.30).
Access down stone steps. Pause at
top of metal stairs then descend into
transformed stone quarry. Explore
densely planted beds in a relatively
confined space. Pieces of medieval
London Bridge lurk in the stonework.
'A beautiful and intriguing sunken
garden with exceptional richness
and arrangements of colour, textures
and form'. Featured in Amateur
Gardening.

A honey pot of
gardens spanning
1.2 miles . . .

76 UPLODERS PLACE
Uploders, Bridport DT6 4PF. Mrs
Venetia Ross Skinner. *3m E of
Bridport. From A35 to Bridport or
Dorchester take turning for Uploders
on S side of main rd. R and R again
under A35. At Crown Inn PH
(excellent food) R, 2 bends and
Private Parking notice.* Tea. Adm
£4.50, chd free. Fri 24, Sat 25 Apr
(2-5).
Old yews, cedar of Lebanon and a
tulip tree form the bones of this
newish garden created from
wilderness in 1993. Trees and shrubs
with unusual barks and flowers with
rhododendrons and camellias. A
quiet contemplative meander with the
R Asker flowing through. Spring
bulbs. Wheelchair access only to
terrace by request.
🏵 ✿ ☕

77 ◆ UPTON COUNTRY PARK
Upton, Poole BH17 7BJ. Borough
of Poole, 01202 262753,
www.uptoncountrypark.com.
*3m W of Poole town centre. On S
side of A35/A3049. Follow brown
signs.* For opening times and
information, please phone or see
garden website.
Over 100 acres of award winning
parkland incl formal gardens, walled
garden, woodland and shoreline.
Maritime micro-climate offers a
wonderful collection of unusual trees,
vintage camellias and stunning roses.
Home to Upton House, Grade II*
listed Georgian mansion. Regular
special events. Plant centre, art
gallery and tea rooms. Free car
parking and entry to park. Open 9am
- 6 pm (winter) and 9am - 8pm
(summer). www.facebook.com/
uptoncountrypark.
♿ 🏵 ✿ 🚐 ☕

WATERDALE HOUSE
See Wiltshire.

78 WESTERN GARDENS
(formerly 24A Western Ave), 24A
Western Ave, Branksome Park,
Poole BH13 7AN. Mr Peter
Jackson, 01202 708388,
peter@branpark.wanadoo.co.uk.
*3m W of Bournemouth. From S end
Wessex Way (A338) take The Avenue.
At T-lights turn R into Western Rd. At
church turn R into Western Ave.*
Home-made teas. Adm £4.50, chd
free. Sun 26 Apr, Sun 21 June, Sun
23 Aug (2-5.30). Also open nearby
21 June, 25 Richmond Park Ave
2-6. Visitors also welcome by
arrangement Apr to Sept,
refreshments by arrangement, min
12.
'This secluded and magical 1-acre
garden captures the spirit of warmer
climes and begs for repeated visits'
(Gardening Which?). Created over 40
yrs it offers enormous variety with
rose, herbaceous walk, courtyard and
woodland gardens and exuberant
foliage and flowers giving yr-round
colour and interest enhanced by
sculpture and topiary. 'A garden of
tremendous colour and interest which
in its use of lush foliage and
exuberant hues owes much to
Christopher Lloyd'. Featured in
Dorset Society. Wheelchair access
to 3/4 garden.
♿ 🚐 ☕

79 1692 WIMBORNE ROAD
Bear Cross BH11 9AL. Sue & Mike
Cleall, 01202 573440. *5m NW of
Bournemouth. On A341, 200yds E of
Bear Cross r'about.* Home-made
teas. Adm £3, chd free. Sun 3, Sun
10 May (2-5). Visitors also
welcome by arrangement Apr to
June for groups of 10+.
Suburban garden 120ft x 50ft.
Rhododendrons, acers and azaleas
are underplanted with woodland
plants for spring. Tulips add colour.
Man-made stream with waterfall and
water feature runs through lawned
area. Pond with statue. Fountain
attracts wildlife. Various seating areas
around garden and tea in
summerhouse is a pleasant
experience. Mostly flat areas.
♿ 🚐 ☕

80 WINCOMBE PARK
Shaftesbury SP7 9AB. John &
Phoebe Fortescue. *2m N of
Shaftesbury. A350 Shaftesbury to
Warminster, past Wincombe Business
Park, 1st R signed Wincombe &
Donhead St Mary. 3/4 m on R.* Cream
teas. Home-made cakes. Adm
£4.50, chd free. Sun 17, Wed 20
May (2-5).
Extensive mature garden with
sweeping panoramic views from lawn
over parkland to lake and enchanting
woods through which you can
wander amongst bluebells. Garden is
a riot of colour in spring with azaleas,
rhododendrons and camellias in
flower amongst shrubs and unusual
trees. Beautiful walled kitchen garden.
Partial wheelchair access, slopes and
gravel paths.
♿ 🏵 ✿ 🚐 ☕

GROUP OPENING

**81 NEW WITCHAMPTON
GARDENS**
Witchampton BH21 5AG. *Approx
3 1/2 m N of Wimborne. From B3078
take Witchampton turning. Follow
signs into village. Parking at 3 places.
Garden guide/admission at any of
gardens.* Home-made teas in village
shop/cafe. Combined adm £5, chd
free. Thur 25, Fri 26 June (2-5.30).

NEW **ABBEY COTTAGE**
Witchampton, Wimborne. Ms
Helen de Mattos

NEW **STADDLESTONES**
Mrs Annette Lockwood
(See separate entry)

Plant specialists: look for the Plant Heritage symbol **NCH**

NEW **SWISS COTTAGE**
Mr Simon Meyrick-Jones

NEW **WILLOW COTTAGE**
15 Witchampton Mill. Mark &
Chris Young

A honey pot of gardens spanning
1.2m with parking in 3 places or
enjoy picturesque walk in
conservation area passing Abbey
House, a grade II listed building,
village Church and lychgate and Ivy
house built 1580, now a club, village
shop and café. The 4 gardens incl
Abbey Cottage, 2 yr old garden with
herbaceous borders, trees, roses and
koi pond and views of the old abbey
ruins. Swiss Cottage: delightful,
densely planted, more mature formal
cottage garden borrowing elements
from larger and more formal garden.

Staddlestones and Willow cottage are
adjacent gardens built on former
paper mill with chalk stream
separating their back gardens.
Staddlestones is a plant lover's
garden with colour themed borders,
leading to shady area and lush
riverside plants. Willow Cottage has
central lawn leading down to river
with a mixture of sculptured borders
of perennial plants, evergreen shrubs,
trees and rose bed with an area of
ferns and grasses.

☸ ☕

82 **WOLVERHOLLOW**
Elsdons Lane, Monkton Wyld
DT6 6DA. Mr & Mrs D Wiscombe,
01297 560610. *4m N of Lyme Regis.
4m NW of Charmouth. Monkton Wyld
is signed from A35 approx 4m NW of
Charmouth off dual carriageway.
Wolverhollow is next to the church.*
Home-made teas. **Adm £3.50, chd
free. Sun 17, Mon 18, Tue 19 May,
Sun 16, Mon 17 Aug (11.30-4.30).
Visitors also welcome by
arrangement.**
Over 1 acre of informal garden on
different levels. Lawns lead past
borders and rockeries down to shady
lower garden. Numerous paths take
you past a variety of uncommon
shrubs and plants. Managed
meadow has an abundance of
primulas growing close to stream. A
garden not to be missed! There is
now a cabin in meadow area of
garden from which vintage, retro and
other lovely things can be purchased.
🐾 ☸ ☕

Snape Cottage Plantsman's Garden

© Heather Edwards

NGS supports nursing and caring charities

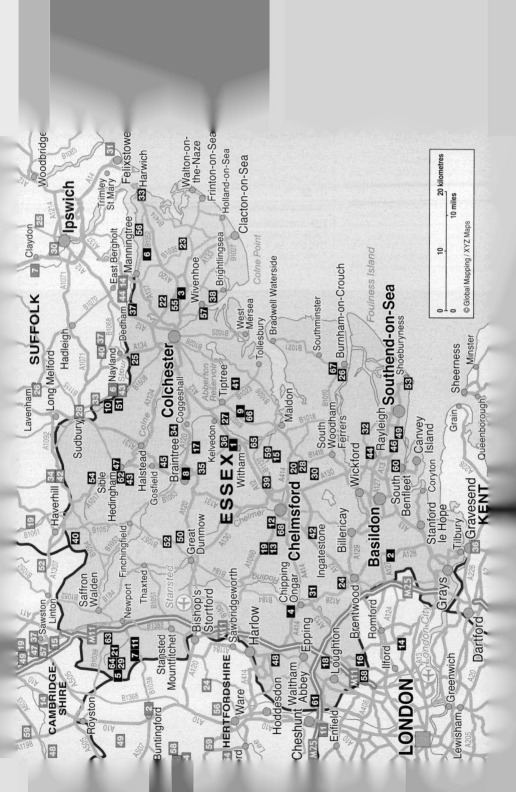

Essex

Close to London but with its own unique character, Essex is perhaps England's best kept secret – with a beautiful coastline, rolling countryside, exquisite villages and great pubs.

There are wide horizons, ancient woodlands and hamlets pierced by flint church spires. Essex is the home of 'Constable Country', and we have a range of attractive gardens in and around that delightful picturesque area including Strandlands in Wrabness, overlooking the River Stour.

In north-east Essex we have possibly the most famous garden in the UK at Beth Chatto Gardens, and near Maldon is the internationally renowned tulip garden at Ulting Wick.

Our biggest open garden is just south of Brentwood at Barnards Farm, with 60 sculptures to enjoy within 40 acres of garden and woodland.

For 2015 we have lots of exciting new groups of gardens to discover including the Rayleigh Gardens group which is opening no less than three times!

Why not take the time to visit our gardens, hidden away down narrow country lanes, in attractive towns and along the estuaries of the east coast? Visitors can be assured of a warm welcome at every open garden gate.

So forget the clichés – rediscover Essex!

Essex Volunteers

County Organiser
Susan Copeland
01799 550553
susan.copeland2@btinternet.com

County Treasurer
Richard Steers
01702 713221
steers123@aol.com

**Publicity &
Assistant County Organisers**
Doug Copeland
01799 550553
dougcopeland@btinternet.com

Linda Holdaway
01621 782137
lindaholdaway@btinternet.com

Ray Spencer
01702 713221
arjeyeski@courtview.demon.co.uk

Booklet Coordinator
Doug Copeland
(as above)

Groups and Talks
Linda Holdaway
(as above)

Assistant County Organisers
Neil Holdaway
01621 782137
mail@neilholdaway.com

Edwin Parsons
07540 798135
edwin@edwin.freeserve.co.uk

Ian Roxburgh
07540 798135
ianinessex@gmail.com

Left: Ulting Wick © Clive Nicholls

Join us on Facebook and spread the word

Opening Dates

All entries subject to change.
For latest information check www.ngs.org.uk

February

Saturday 21
39 The Old Rectory

Sunday 22
39 The Old Rectory
68 Writtle College

April

2 Barnards Farm (every Thursday from April 23)
17 Feeringbury Manor (every Thursday & Friday from April 2)

Sunday 5
57 Tudor Roost
66 Wood View

Monday 6
57 Tudor Roost
66 Wood View

Sunday 12
53 South Shoebury Hall

Friday 17
59 Ulting Wick

Sunday 19
42 Peacocks

Sunday 26
59 Ulting Wick

Wednesday 29
20 Furzelea

May

2 Barnards Farm (every Thursday)
17 Feeringbury Manor (every Thursday & Friday)

Friday 1
59 Ulting Wick

Sunday 3
40 Parsonage House
43 Peppers Farm
57 Tudor Roost
66 Wood View

Monday 4
5 NEW The Chestnuts
57 Tudor Roost
64 Wickets
66 Wood View

Sunday 10
66 Wood View

Wednesday 13
27 NEW Kelvedon Hall

Saturday 16
22 NEW Green Island

Sunday 17
15 Elwy Lodge
22 NEW Green Island
49 NEW 22 St Clements Drive

Saturday 23
56 NEW Strandlands

Sunday 24
29 NEW Langley Village Gardens
55 NEW Spring Cottage
56 NEW Strandlands
57 Tudor Roost

Monday 25
16 Fairwinds
55 NEW Spring Cottage
56 NEW Strandlands

Wednesday 27
36 Miraflores
47 Rookwoods

Thursday 28
36 Miraflores

Friday 29
12 8 Dene Court
30 The Limes (Evening)

Saturday 30
6 Chippins
30 The Limes

Sunday 31
10 NEW Daws Hall
38 Moverons
39 The Old Rectory
41 NEW Paternoster House
52 Snares Hill Cottage

June

2 Barnards Farm (every Thursday)
17 Feeringbury Manor (every Thursday & Friday)

Festival Weekend

Saturday 6
50 St Helens
55 NEW Spring Cottage

Sunday 7
46 Reprise
54 Spencers
55 NEW Spring Cottage
61 Waltham Abbey
63 Wendens Ambo Gardens
68 Writtle College

Tuesday 9
12 8 Dene Court

Wednesday 10
20 Furzelea

Thursday 11
15 Elwy Lodge
59 Ulting Wick

Friday 12
44 NEW Rayleigh Gardens

Saturday 13
21 Great Becketts
36 Miraflores

Sunday 14
7 Clavering Gardens
18 56 Forest Drive
36 Miraflores
42 Peacocks
45 NEW Rayne Hatch Farm
49 NEW 22 St Clements Drive
58 37 Turpins Lane

Tuesday 16
12 8 Dene Court
13 Dragons

Saturday 20
64 Wickets

Sunday 21
4 Blake Hall
26 Keeway
36 Miraflores
40 Parsonage House
62 Washlands

Wednesday 24
26 Keeway
62 Washlands (Evening)

Thursday 25
15 Elwy Lodge

Tranquil, peaceful place to linger and enjoy . . .

Saturday 27
2 Barnards Farm (Evening)
8 352 Coggeshall Road
32 262 Main Road

Sunday 28
2 Barnards Farm
8 352 Coggeshall Road
19 Fudlers Hall
58 37 Turpins Lane
60 NEW 37 Underhill Road
62 Washlands

July

2 Barnards Farm (every Thursday)
17 Feeringbury Manor (every Thursday & Friday)

Thursday 11
15 Elwy Lodge
59 Ulting Wick

Friday 12
44 NEW Rayleigh Gardens

Saturday 13
21 Great Becketts
36 Miraflores

Sunday 14
7 Clavering Gardens
18 56 Forest Drive
36 Miraflores
42 Peacocks
45 NEW Rayne Hatch Farm
49 NEW 22 St Clements Drive
58 37 Turpins Lane

Tuesday 16
12 8 Dene Court
13 Dragons

Saturday 20
64 Wickets

Sunday 21
4 Blake Hall
26 Keeway
36 Miraflores
40 Parsonage House
62 Washlands

Wednesday 24
26 Keeway
62 Washlands (Evening)

Thursday 25
15 Elwy Lodge

Saturday 4
12 8 Dene Court
57 Tudor Roost

Sunday 5
6 Chippins
31 Little Myles
46 Reprise
57 Tudor Roost

Wednesday 8
35 60 Mill Lane

Friday 10
15 Elwy Lodge

Saturday 11
1 Barnardiston House
15 Elwy Lodge
48 69 Rundells

Sunday 12
1 Barnardiston House
12 8 Dene Court
42 Peacocks
44 NEW Rayleigh Gardens

Friday 17
12 8 Dene Court
13 Dragons

Saturday 18
1 Barnardiston House
24 NEW 262 Hatch Road

Sunday 19
1 Barnardiston House
15 Elwy Lodge
19 Fudlers Hall
24 NEW 262 Hatch Road
28 Kingsteps
53 South Shoebury Hall

Sunday 26
18 56 Forest Drive
45 NEW Rayne Hatch Farm
58 37 Turpins Lane
60 NEW 37 Underhill Road

Tuesday 28
12 8 Dene Court

August

2 Barnards Farm (every Thursday)

Saturday 1
33 447 Main Road

Sunday 2
33 447 Main Road
46 Reprise

Tuesday 4
12 8 Dene Court
13 Dragons

Saturday 8
32 262 Main Road

Sunday 9
14 6 Elms Gardens
35 60 Mill Lane

Since our foundation we have donated more than £42.5 million to charity

Saturday 15
57 Tudor Roost
Sunday 16
44 NEW Rayleigh Gardens
57 Tudor Roost
Sunday 23
28 Kingsteps
60 NEW 37 Underhill Road
Sunday 30
11 Deers

September
17 Feeringbury Manor (every Thursday & Friday from Sep 3)
Thursday 3
2 Barnards Farm
Saturday 5
67 Woodpeckers
Sunday 6
2 Barnards Farm
20 Furzelea
60 NEW 37 Underhill Road
61 Waltham Abbey
Saturday 12
50 St Helens
67 Woodpeckers

Sunday 13
52 Snares Hill Cottage
54 Spencers
59 Ulting Wick
Friday 18
59 Ulting Wick
Saturday 19
67 Woodpeckers
Wednesday 23
13 Dragons
Saturday 26
67 Woodpeckers

October
Thursday 1
17 Feeringbury Manor
Friday 2
17 Feeringbury Manor
Sunday 18
68 Writtle College

November
Sunday 29
66 Wood View

February 2016
Sunday 21
68 Writtle College

Gardens open to the public
3 Beth Chatto Gardens
10 NEW Daws Hall
22 NEW Green Island
34 Marks Hall Gardens & Arboretum
54 Spencers

By arrangement only
9 60 Colchester Road
23 Hannams Hall
25 Horkesley Hall
37 Monks Cottage
51 Shrubs Farm
65 Wickham Place Farm

Also open by arrangement
1 Barnardiston House
2 Barnards Farm
6 Chippins
8 352 Coggeshall Road
12 8 Dene Court
13 Dragons
15 Elwy Lodge
16 Fairwinds
17 Feeringbury Manor
18 56 Forest Drive

20 Furzelea
24 NEW 262 Hatch Road
27 NEW Kelvedon Hall
32 262 Main Road
36 Miraflores
38 Moverons
39 The Old Rectory
41 NEW Paternoster House
42 Peacocks
43 Peppers Farm
44 NEW 1 Cherrydown, Rayleigh Gardens
44 NEW 36 London Road, Rayleigh Gardens
46 Reprise
47 Rookwoods
48 69 Rundells
50 St Helens
52 Snares Hill Cottage
53 South Shoebury Hall
56 NEW Strandlands
57 Tudor Roost
58 37 Turpins Lane
59 Ulting Wick
60 NEW 37 Underhill Road
62 Washlands
64 Wickets
66 Wood View
67 Woodpeckers

The Gardens

1 BARNARDISTON HOUSE
35 Chipping Hill, Witham CM8 2DE.
Ruth & Eric Teverson, 01376 502266,
ruthteverson@yahoo.co.uk. *10m NE of Chelmsford. A12 S-bound J22 & A12 N-bound J21 to town centre. Into Collingwood Rd at George PH. L at 2 mini r'abouts. Garden opp. White Horse PH. Use postcode CM8 2JU.* Home-made teas. **Adm £3, chd free. Sat 11, Sun 12, Sat 18, Sun 19 July (2-5). Visitors also welcome by arrangement July to Aug.**
A medium-sized town garden, designed and created over last 17yrs by the owners. A wide range of unusual and insect friendly plants, as well as fruit, heritage vegetables and succulents are grown, all of which must enjoy hot and dry conditions. Partial wheelchair access.
♿ ⊗ 🚌 ☕

2 BARNARDS FARM
Brentwood Road, West Horndon, Brentwood CM13 3LX. Bernard & Sylvia Holmes & The Christabella Charitable Trust, 01277 811262, sylvia@barnardsfarm.eu, www.barnardsfarm.eu. *5m S of Brentwood. On A128 1½ m S of A127 Halfway House flyover. From Junction continue on A128 under the railway bridge. Garden on R just past bridge.* Soup and filled rolls (Thurs), home-made cakes, teas (Suns). **Pre-booking essential for Musical Evening Sat 27 June adm £15, please contact Ray Spencer on arjeyeski@courtview.demon.co.uk or 01702 713221. Adm £6 (Thurs), £7.50 (Sun), chd £2.50.** Share to St Francis Church. **Every Thur 23 Apr to 3 Sept (11-4). Musical Evening Opening featuring 'Funky Voices' adm £15, chd free, incl wine, strawberries and cream, Sat 27 June (6-9). Sun 28 June, Sun 6 Sept (2-5.30). Visitors also welcome by arrangement Apr to Sept for groups of 20 min.**
A garden for all tastes and ages: 67 sculptures from the grand to the quirky carefully placed in the 17 hectares of garden and woodland bring surprise and delight. Daffodils by the stream, crab apple blossom; rose covered belvedere; summer flowers and climbers around the house; vegetable plot; Japanese garden; fountains, ponds, lake: frogs, dragonflies, butterflies and bees. Car museum (Suns only). Barnards Miniature Railway rides (BMR). Sunday extras: Bernard's Sculpture tour 3pm;. Veteran & vintage vehicle collection; 1920s Cycle shop Collect loyalty points on Thur visits and earn a free Sun or Thur visit. Aviators welcome (PPO), see website for details. Wheelchair accessible WC Golf buggy tour available.
♿ ⊗ NCH ☕

Daffodils by the stream, crab apple blossom and rose covered belvedere . . .

3 ◆ BETH CHATTO GARDENS

Elmstead Market, Colchester CO7 7DB. Mrs Beth Chatto, 01206 822007, www.bethchatto.co.uk. *1/4 m E of Elmstead Market. On A133 Colchester to Clacton Rd in village of Elmstead Market.* £6.95, chd under 14 free. For opening times and information, please phone or see garden website.

Internationally famous gardens, including dry, damp and woodland areas. The result of over fifty years of hard work and application of the huge body of plant knowledge possessed by Beth Chatto and her late husband Andrew. Visitors cannot fail to be affected by the peace and beauty of the garden. Large plant nursery and modern Tea Room. Disabled WC & parking.

4 BLAKE HALL

Bobbingworth CM5 0DG. Mr & Mrs H Capel Cure, www.blakehall.co.uk. *10m W of Chelmsford. Just off A414 between Four Wantz r'about in Ongar & Talbot r'about in North Weald. Signed on A414.* Home-made teas in C17 barn. Adm £4, chd free. Sun 21 June (11-4.30).

25 acres of mature gardens within the historic setting of Blake Hall (not open). Arboretum with broad variety of specimen trees. Spectacular rambling roses clamber up ancient trees. Traditional formal rose garden and herbaceous border. Sweeping lawns. Some gravel paths.

5 NEW THE CHESTNUTS

Langley Upper Green. CB11 4RY. Jane & David Knight. *7m W of Saffron Walden. 10m N of Bishops Stortford. At Newport take B1038 After 3m turn R at Clavering, signed Langley Upper Green is 3m further on. House is on cricket green. Parking at Village Hall 80yds away.* Light refreshments at village hall on green or in garden. Light lunches and home-made teas. Adm £3, chd free. Mon 4 May (11-5). Combined adm with Wickets £5.

Large, garden with many mature trees surrounding thatched cottage on village green. New planting beds, designed and installed by Tristen Knight, RHS Young Designer of the Year 2012. Featuring reclaimed sleeper jetty, yorkstone waterfall and herbaceous borders. Extensive grass meadow with mature oak trees and newly planted hornbeam avenue. A tranquil, peaceful place to linger and enjoy. Country walks to enjoy from rear of meadow. Disabled parking near to garden gate.

6 CHIPPINS

Heath Road, Bradfield CO11 2UZ. Kit & Ceri Leese, 01255 870730, ceriandkit1@btinternet.com. *3m E of Manningtree. On B1352, take main rd through village. Bungalow is directly opp primary school.* Home-made teas. Adm £3.50, chd free. Sat 30 May, Sun 5 July (11-4.30). Visitors also welcome by arrangement May to July groups very welcome.

Artist's garden and plantaholics paradise packed with interest. Springtime heralds irises, hostas and alliums. Stream and wildlife pond brimming with bog plants. Summer hosts an explosion of colour-abundance of tubs and hanging baskets. Wide borders feature hemerocallis with swathes of lilies, later dahlias and exotics (South African streptocarpus, aeonium and unusual agaves). Kit is a landscape artist, pictures always on display.

GROUP OPENING

7 CLAVERING GARDENS

Clavering CB11 4PX. *7m N of Bishop's Stortford. On B1038. Turn W off B1383 at Newport.* Home-made teas at Deers. Plants at April Cottage. Combined adm £6, chd free. Sun 14 June (2-5).

DEERS
Mr S H Cooke
(See separate entry)

NEW APRIL COTTAGE
Mr & Mrs Harris

Popular village with many C16/17 timber-framed dwellings. Beautiful C14 church, village green with thatched cricket pavilion and pitch. Deers (see separate entry) for 9 acres, judged by visitors to be a very romantic garden. April Cottage, charming and thatched with well established colourful garden packed with many unusual plants, old fashioned roses, clematis, wildlife and ornamental pond. Lined damp garden with primula candelabras and astilbes. Hosta collection. All to be discovered down winding paths.

Ideas for different situations. Plant list available. Jamie Oliver was brought up in Clavering where his parents still run The Cricketers PH. Dogs on leads please. Wheelchair access at Deers main lawn and flowerbeds plus vegetable garden. April cottage has some narrow paths.

8 352 COGGESHALL ROAD

Braintree CM7 9EH. Sau Lin Goss, 01376 329753, Richandsally.goss@yahoo.com. *15m W of Colchester, 10m N of Chelmsford. From M11 J8 take A120 Colchester. Follow A120 to Braintree r'about (McDonalds). 1st exit into Cressing rd follow to T-lights. R into Coggeshall rd.* Light refreshments. Adm £3, chd free. Sat 27, Sun 28 June (1.30-5.30). Visitors also welcome by arrangement May to July min 10, max 30.

Sau Lin arrived from Hong Kong to become enthralled with English gardening. 'My little heaven', she says of her garden which has themed areas, perennials, roses and many other plants. Japanese mixed border, fruit trees and shrubs. Seating and relaxing areas, fish pond with plants and wildlife. Mediterranean patio with water feature and wide array of pots. Partial wheelchair access, ramp from patio to main garden.

9 60 COLCHESTER ROAD

Great Totham, nr Maldon CM9 8DG. Mrs Sue Jackman, 01621 891155, susanjackman750@hotmail.com. *5m NE of Maldon. On B1022 Maldon to Colchester Rd at Totham North.* Adm £4, chd free. Visitors welcome by arrangement Apr to Sept groups of 15+. Refreshments by arrangement.

A 3/4 acre keen plantwoman's garden with large colour-themed borders, situated in both sun and shade. Borders are planted for a long season of interest with many unusual

species, particularly perennials. Rock garden full of spring and autumn bulbs and alpines. A rill leading to watersteps, and circular pool overlooked by a summerhouse. Small vegetable garden. Large Liriodendron Tulipfera (Tulip Tree) is a beautiful feature when in flower for approx six weeks in May/June. Featured in The East Anglian.

10 ▶ NEW ▶ ◆ DAWS HALL
Henny Road, Lamarsh, Bures CO8 5EX. Major & Mrs Iain Grahame, 01787 269213, www.dawshallnature.co.uk. *3m from Sudbury. 2m from Bures on Essex side of R. Stour.* Tea. **Adm £5, chd 10 & over £1. For NGS: Sun 31 May (1-5). For other opening times and information, please phone or see garden website.**
8 acres of scarce and unusual trees and shrubs. Over 100, mainly old fashioned, shrub roses. All labelled. 250 yr-old tulip tree, collection of waterfowl and observation beehive. 'Exotic shrubs plus a superb collection of trees and plants offer colour and interest throughout the year, creating a plantsman's paradise' - Philippa Pearson. Essex Life. Guided tours for groups in aid of The Daws Hall Trust. Featured in Essex Life.

11 ▶ DEERS
Clavering CB11 4PX. Mr S H Cooke. *7m N of Bishop's Stortford on B1038. Turn W off B1383 (old A11) at Newport & follow signs to Clavering then Langley & 1st L to Ford End (¼ m).* Home-made teas. **Adm £5. Share to Clavering Jubilee Field. Sun 30 Aug (2-5). Also open with Clavering Gardens 14 June.**
9 acres. Judged by visitors to be a romantic set of gardens. The river Stort runs through the gardens. Shrub and herbaceous borders, 3 ponds with water lilies, old roses in formal garden, pool garden, walled vegetable garden, moon gate, field and woodland walks. Plenty of seats to enjoy the tranquility of the gardens. A wildlife oasis in a farming desert. Dogs on leads please. Wheelchair access main lawn and flower beds plus vegetable garden only.

12 ▶ 8 DENE COURT
Chignall Road, Chelmsford CM1 2JQ. Mrs Sheila Chapman, 01245 266156. *W of Chelmsford*

Kelvedon Hall

© Nicola Stocken Tomkins

(Parkway). Take A1060 Roxwell Rd for 1m. Turn R at T-lights into Chignall Rd. Dene Court 3rd exit on R. Parking in Chignall Rd. **Adm £3, chd free. Fri 29 May, Tue 9, Tue 16 June, Sat 4, Sun 12, Fri 17, Tue 28 July, Tue 4 Aug (2-5). Also open Dragons 16 June, 17 July, 4 Aug. Visitors also welcome by arrangement June to Aug refreshments by arrangement.**
Beautifully maintained and designed compact garden (250sq yds). Owner is well-known RHS gold medal-winning exhibitor (now retired). Circular lawn, long pergola and walls festooned with roses and climbers. Large selection of unusual clematis. Densely-planted colour coordinated perennials add interest from May to Sept in this immaculate garden.

13 ▶ DRAGONS
Boyton Cross, Chelmsford CM1 4LS. Mrs Margot Grice, 01245 248651, mandmdragons@tiscali.co.uk. *3m W of Chelmsford. On A1060. ½ m W of The Hare PH or ½ m E of The Coriander.* Tea. **Adm £4, chd free. Tue 16 June, Fri 17 July, Tue 4 Aug, Wed 23 Sept (2-5). Also open 8 Dene Court, 16 June, 17 July, 4 Aug. Visitors also welcome by arrangement Jan to Oct**

refreshments on request.
A plantswoman's ¾ -acre garden, planted to encourage wildlife. Sumptuous colour-themed borders with striking plant combinations, featuring specimen plants, fernery, clematis, mature dwarf conifers and grasses. Meandering paths lead to ponds, patio, scree garden and small vegetable garden. Two summerhouses, one overlooking stream and farmland.

14 ▶ 6 ELMS GARDENS
Dagenham RM9 5TX. Peter & Kathy Railton. *1m from Becontree Heath. A124 Wood Ln towards Barking. Elms Gardens located off Five Elms Rd/Halbutt St.* Home-made teas. **Adm £3, chd free. Sun 9 Aug (1-5).**
Plant lovers garden (approx 80ft x 60ft) featuring wide range of herbaceous plants and shrubs with year round interest. Colourful begonias in baskets and containers. Large collection of Heucheras create foliage interest. Magnificent Magnolia grandifloras. Winding paths lead to quiet seating, Koi fishpond and small woodland shade area.

15 ELWY LODGE

West Bowers Rd, Woodham Walter CM9 6RZ. David & Laura Cox, 01245 222165, elwylodge@gmail.com. *Just outside Woodham Walter village. From Chelmsford, A414 to Danbury. L at 2nd mini r'about into Little Baddow Rd. From Colchester, A12 to Hatfield Peverel, L onto B1019. Follow NGS signs.* Light refreshments. **Adm £4, chd free. Sun 17 May (11-5); Thur 11, Thur 25 June, Fri 10, Sat 11, Sun 19 July (10.30-5.30). Also open Kingsteps 19 July. Visitors also welcome by arrangement May to Oct not open in Aug.**

Rural location offering peace, tranquility and lovely countryside views. Scented roses in front garden leading to flowing lawns, herbaceous/shrub borders, trees, wildlife pond and meadow area. The garden then slopes down to a secluded chamomile-scented lower garden with raised vegetable beds, soft fruits and fruit trees. This is an ever-changing garden being developed to blend with the rural setting. Sloping uneven lawn in parts. Please check wheelchair access with garden owner before visiting.

16 FAIRWINDS

Chapel Lane, Chigwell Row, Chigwell IG7 6JJ. Sue & David Coates, 07731 796467, scoates@forest.org.uk. *2m SE of Chigwell. Grange Hill Tube, turn R at exit, 10 mins walk uphill. Nr M25 J26 & N Circular, turn off Lambourne Rd signed Chigwell. Park in Lodge Close Car Park.* Home-made teas. Free refills of tea/coffee. **Adm £3.50, chd free. Mon 25 May (2-5). Visitors also welcome by arrangement Jan to Sept, refreshments only by arrangement. Groups preferred.**

A gravelled front garden and three differently styled back garden areas, Places for you to sit, relax and enjoy. A rich variety of planting influenced by Beth Chatto, Penelope Hobhouse and Christopher Lloyd. Start with themed flower borders. Hidden beyond is a woodland garden; home to shade loving plants and our hens. Finally, beyond the rustic fence, lies the wildlife pond and vegetable plot. Space for 2 disabled cars to park by the house. Wood chip paths in woodland area may require assistance.

17 FEERINGBURY MANOR

Coggeshall Road, Feering, Colchester CO5 9RB. Mr & Mrs Giles Coode-Adams, 01376 561946, seca@btinternet.com. *12m SW of Colchester. Between Feering & Coggeshall on Coggeshall Rd, 1m from Feering village.* **Adm £5, chd free. Share to Firstsite. Every Thur & Fri 2 Apr to 31 July (9-4). Every Thur & Fri 3 Sept to 2 Oct (9-4). Visitors also welcome by arrangement Apr to Oct.**

There is always plenty to see in this 10 acre garden with two ponds and river Blackwater. Jewelled lawn in early April then spectacular tulips and blossom lead on to a huge number of different and colourful plants, many unusual, culminating in a purple explosion of michaelmas daisies in Sept. Sculpture by Ben Coode-Adams. No wheelchair access to arboretum, steep slope.

> Secluded chamomile-scented lower garden with raised vegetable beds, soft fruits and fruit trees . . .

18 56 FOREST DRIVE

Theydon Bois CM16 7EZ. John & Barbara, 01992 814459, john.vale@live.co.uk. *2m S of Epping. J26 on M25 onto A121 to Wake Arms r'about 2nd exit B 172 into Theydon Bois. Turn L at The Bull PH 1st L into rd. Central line station 2nd on R.* Cream teas. Teas, coffee, available in the summerhouse. **Adm £3, chd free. Sun 14 June, Sun 26 July (12-5). Also open 37 Turpins Lane. Visitors also welcome by arrangement viewing after midday on weekdays due to parking.**

Elegant, tranquil garden set on a sloping site, developed by us since 1996, featuring specimen trees and plants. Shaded seating areas in this surprisingly secluded natural garden allow visitors to sit and watch the birds and admire Gladys in her reflective pool along with a collection of historic motorcycles.

19 FUDLERS HALL

Fox Road, Mashbury, Chelmsford CM1 4TJ. Mr & Mrs A J Meacock. *7m NW of Chelmsford. Chelmsford take A1060, R into Chignal Rd. 1/2 m L to Chignal St James approx 5m 2nd R into Fox Rd signed Gt. Waltham. From Gt Waltham take Barrack Lane.* Home-made teas. **Adm £4, chd free. Sun 28 June, Sun 19 July (2-6).**

An award winning, romantic 2 acre garden surrounding C17 farmhouse with lovely pastoral views. Old walls divide garden into many rooms, each having a different character, featuring long herbaceous borders, ropes and pergolas festooned with rambling old fashioned roses. Enjoy the vibrant hot border in late summer. Yew hedged kitchen garden. Ample seating.

20 FURZELEA

Bicknacre Road, Danbury CM3 4JR. Avril & Roger Cole-Jones, 01245 225726, randacj@gmail.com. *4m E of Chelmsford, 4m W of Maldon A414 to Danbury. At village centre turn S into Mayes Lane Take first R past Cricketers PH, L on to Bicknacre Rd see NT carpark on L garden 50m further on R.* Home-made teas. **Adm £4, chd free. Wed 29 Apr, Wed 10 June, Sun 6 Sept (11-5). Visitors also welcome by arrangement May to Sept groups 15+ (not August).**

A Victorian country house surrounded by a garden designed, created and maintained by the owners to provide maximum all year round interest. The colour coordinated borders and beds are enhanced with topiary, grasses, climbers and many unusual plants. Spring incl tulips and summer bursts into colour with roses and perennials continuing into autumn with vibrant showy dahlias and many other exotics. Opp Danbury Common (NT), short walk to Danbury Country Park and Lakes and short drive to RHS Hyde Hall. Featured in Gardens Illustrated. Partial wheelchair access, some steps and gravel paths.

21 GREAT BECKETTS

Duddenhoe End Road, Arkesden, Saffron Walden CB11 4HG. Mr & Mrs John Burnham. *5m W of Saffron Walden 10m N of Bishops Stortford. Approx 2/3m NW of Arkesden in the direction of Duddenhoe End, near Newland End. Access from S on B1038 via*

Arkesden village or from N on B1039. Home-made teas. served in old timber barn & courtyard. **Adm £5, chd free. Sat 13 June (1-5).**
In the middle of arable farm land, surrounding tudor house and outbuildings: a garden to explore. Perennials and climbers are the focus. Several perennial borders; courtyard; pergola; arbour; herb garden; two ponds; cutting garden; mini-orchard; paths through two established meadows. Newly planted trees and meadows on 5 additional acres across the road.

☕

22 NEW ◆ GREEN ISLAND
Park Road, Ardleigh CO7 7SP. Fiona Edmond, 01206 230455, www.greenislandgardens.co.uk. *3m NE of Colchester. From Ardleigh village centre, take B1029 towards Great Bromley. Park Rd is 2nd on R after level Xing. Garden is last on L.* Home-made teas at the Bluebell Bazaar and light lunches. **Adm £6, chd free. For NGS: Sat 16, Sun 17 May (10-4). For other opening times and information, please phone or see garden website.**
Bluebell Bazaar, a chance to see 19 acre garden in spring glory. Bluebell carpeted woods,scented Azaleas, Acers. Stalls selling garden wares, sculptures, jewellery, artwork, locally produced foods, sweets, preserves and fresh produce. Art, wildlife photography, garden design exhibitions plus children's entertainment.Unusual plants, woodland walks, gravel, seaside and Japanese garden. For more details of Bluebell Bazaar and to pre-purchase tickets at reduced price of £5, visit website [see above]. Recommended in Great Gardens to visit. Featured in Garden Answers, Garden Illustrated and front cover of Homes and Gardens.

♿ ❀ 🚌 ☕

23 HANNAMS HALL
Thorpe Road, Tendring CO16 9AR. Mr & Mrs W Gibbon, 01255 830292, w.gibbon331@btinternet.com. *10m E of Colchester. From A120 take B1035 at Horsley Cross, through Tendring Village (approx 3m) pass Cherry Tree PH on R, after 1/3m over small bridge 1st house L.* Light refreshments. **Adm £6, chd free. Visitors welcome by arrangement Mar to Nov max 30.**
C17 house (not open) set in 6 acres

of formal and informal gardens and grounds with extensive views over open countryside. Herbaceous borders and shrubberies, many interesting trees incl flowering paulownias. Lawns and mown walks through wild grass and flower meadows, woodland walks, ponds and stream. Walled vegetable potager and orchard. Lovely autumn colour. Some gravel paths.

♿ ❀ ☕

Plenty of seating to enjoy the views . . .

24 NEW 262 HATCH ROAD
Pilgrims Hatch, Brentwood CM15 9QR. Mike & Liz Thomas, 01277 220584. *2m N of Brentwood town centre. On A128 N toward Ongar turn R onto Doddinghurst Rd at mini-r'about (to Brentwood Centre) After the Centre turn next L into Hatch Rd.* Home-made teas. **Adm £4, chd free. Sat 18, Sun 19 July (1-5.30). Visitors also welcome by arrangement July to Aug.**
A formal frontage with lavender. An eclectic rear garden of around an acre divided into 'rooms' with themed borders, several ponds, three green houses, fruit and vegetable plots and oriental garden. There is also a secret white garden, spring and summer wild flower meadows, a folly and an exotic area. There is plenty of seating to enjoy the views and a cup of tea.

♿ ❀ ☕

25 HORKESLEY HALL
Little Horkesley, Colchester CO6 4DB. Mr & Mrs Johnny Eddis, 07808 599290, pollyeddis@hotmail.com. *6m N of Colchester City Centre. 2m W of A134. Drive through Little Horkesley Church car park & access is via low double black gates at the far end. 10 mins from A12, 20 from Sudbury & 1hr from Newmarket.* Light refreshments. We are happy to discuss your requirements with you - coffee, teas or light lunch available by arrangement. **Adm £5, chd free. Visitors welcome by arrangement Feb to Nov very flexible and warm welcome assured!**
8 acres of romantic garden surrounding classical house (not open) in mature parkland setting. Stream feeds 2 lakes. Wonderful and

enormous trees, some very rare. Largest ginkgo tree outside Kew. Many acers, several eucalyptus. Walled garden, pear avenue, acer walk. Blossom and spring bulbs. Formal terrace overlooking sweeping lawns to wild woodland. A timeless, family garden. Plants sometimes for sale. Wonderful natural setting, vast plane trees and stunning tree barks. Limited wheelchair access to some areas, gravel paths and slopes but quite easy access to tea area which has lovely views over lake and garden.

♿ 🚲 🚐 🛏 ☕

26 KEEWAY
Ferry Road, Creeksea, nr Burnham-On-Crouch CM0 8PL. John & Sue Ketteley. *2m W of Burnham-on-Crouch. B1010 to Burnham on Crouch. At town sign take 1st R into Ferry Rd signed Creeksea & Burnham Golf Club & follow NGS signs.* Home-made teas. **Adm £4, chd free. Sun 21, Wed 24 June (2-5).**
Large, mature country garden with stunning views over the R Crouch. Formal terraces surround the house with steps leading to sweeping lawns, mixed borders packed full of bulbs and early perennials, a formal rose and herb garden with interesting water feature. Further afield there are wilder areas, fields and paddocks. A productive greenhouse, vegetable and cutting gardens complete the picture.

♿ ❀ ☕

27 NEW KELVEDON HALL
Kelvedon, Colchester CO5 9BN. Mr & Mrs Jack Inglis, v_inglis@btinternet.com. *Take Maldon Rd from Kelvedon High St over A12. After bridge turn R onto Kelvedon Rd. Turn 1st L, single gravel road.* Light refreshments. **Adm £4, chd free. Wed 13 May (1.30-4). Visitors also welcome by arrangement May to June, private tour with gardeners.**
Varied 6 acre garden surrounding a pretty C18 Farmhouse. A blend of formal and informal spaces interspersed with modern sculpture. Pleached hornbeam and topiary provide structure. Courtyard Walled Garden juxtaposes a Modern Walled Pool Garden, both providing season long displays. Herbaceous borders offset an abundance of roses around the house. Lily covered ponds with a new wet garden.

❀ Ⓓ ☕

The Old Rectory

28 KINGSTEPS
Moor Hall Lane, Danbury
CM3 4ER. Mr David Greenwood.
*Bicknacre/Danbury. A414 from
Chelmsford Turn R at The Bell in
Danbury. L at T-junction approx
1¹/₂ m. R turn by post box into Moor
Hall Lane.* Home-made teas.
**Adm £3, chd free. Sun 19 July,
Sun 23 Aug (12-5). Also open Elwy
Lodge 19 July.**
Country garden in ¹/₂ acre plot.
Gardens front and rear with good
selection of herbaceous plants and
shrubs, roses, fuchsias, dahlias,
begonias, bedding plants, tubs and
hanging baskets. Fish pond with Koi
carp and others. Well kept lawns and
plenty of colour, especially late
summer. Large horse chestnut tree in
rear. Many seating areas.

GROUP OPENING

29 NEW LANGLEY VILLAGE GARDENS
Langley Upper Green, Saffron
Walden CB11 4RY. *7m W of Saffron
Walden 10m N of Bishops Stortford.
At Newport take B1038 After 3m turn
R at Clavering, signed Langley. Upper
Green is 3m further on. Sheepcote
Green will also be signed on day.*
Light refreshments at village hall on
Langley Village Green. Light lunches
& home-made teas. **Combined adm
£7, chd free. Sun 24 May (11-5).**

APRIL COTTAGE
Mr & Mrs Harris.

*At Sheepcote Green midway
between Clavering & Langley.
Also open with Clavering Gardens
14 June*

NEW THE CHESTNUTS
Jane & David Knight
(See separate entry)

NEW CHURCH COTTAGE
Langley Upper Green. Jago
Russell & Maeve Polkinhorn

NEW OLD BELL COTTAGE
Langley Upper Green. Richard
Vallance.
*On rd to and from Clavering, opp
the children's playground, house
is painted red*

WICKETS
Susan & Doug Copeland
(See separate entry)

April Cottage, at Sheepcote Green
just 2m from Langley is a charming
thatched cottage, with well
established and colourful garden
packed with unusual plants; roses,
clematis, wildlife and ornamental
ponds, lined damp garden, hosta
collection. The Chestnuts is a large
garden with many mature trees
surrounding thatched cottage on
village green, new planting beds,
extensive grass meadow. Church
Cottage is a ¹/₃ acre informal cottage
garden, countryside views. Interesting
planting, perennials, grasses, roses,
climbers and shrubs, Seating to relax
and enjoy garden. May highlights incl.
abundant roses, chocolate-scented
flowers of akebia quinata. Old Bell
Cottage incorporates part of former

field, many rather labour intensive
beds, well stocked cottage garden;
spring bulbs, alliums, lupins and
delphiniums; views across valley.
Greenhouse and patio area for
potting out, raised veg. beds, BBQ
area, natural pond. Wickets has wide,
mixed borders, landscaped
meadows, lily pond, parterre and
gravel garden. Langley is highest
Essex village set in rolling
countryside.

30 THE LIMES
The Tye, East Hanningfield
CM3 8AA. Stan & Gil Gordon. *6m
SE of Chelmsford. In centre of East
Hanningfield across village green opp
The Windmill PH.* Home-made teas.
**Adm £4, chd free. Evening
Opening, wine, Fri 29 May (6-9).
Sat 30 May (2-6).**
Plant lovers' 1-acre well-established
garden of many rooms, designed to
encourage you to explore this
peaceful place with its mature trees,
shrubs, perennials, roses, clematis
and grasses. Also orchard, soft fruit
and vegetable area, formal garden
and courtyard pots. Seek and Find
sheet for family fun. Lots to enjoy,
several seats and easy parking
nearby. Approx 1m from RHS Hyde
Hall. Gravel drive and grass paths.

31 LITTLE MYLES
Ongar Road, Stondon Massey,
Brentwood CM15 0LD. Judy &
Adrian Cowan,
Littlemyles@gmail.com. *1¹/₂ m SE of
Chipping Ongar. Off A128 at Stag
PH, Marden Ash, towards Stondon
Massey. Over bridge, 1st house on R
after S bend. 400yds Ongar side of
Stondon Church.* Home-made teas.
**Adm £3.50, chd £1. Sun 5 July
(11-4).**
Romantic garden full of hidden
features, set in 3 acres. Full borders,
tranquil benches, meandering paths
to Beach Garden, with seaside
planting. Asian garden with pots,
monkeys and bamboo. New exotic
planting around wire elephant. Slate
garden, hornbeam pergola,
ornamental vegetable patch and
pond. Herb garden that inspired Little
Myles handmade herbal cosmetics.
Crafts and handmade herbal
cosmetics for sale. Explorers sheet
and map for children. Gravel paths.

32 **262 MAIN ROAD**
Hawkwell, Hockley SS5 4NW.
Karen Mann, 07976 272999,
karenmann10@hotmail.com. *3m NE
of Rayleigh. From A127 at Rayleigh
Weir take B1013 towards Hockley.
Garden on L after White Hart PH &
village green.* Home-made teas. **Adm
£3.50, chd free. Sat 27 June, Sat 8
Aug (1-5.30). Visitors also welcome
by arrangement July to Aug.**
The garden comprises of 185 metres
of island beds and borders sited on
¹/₃ acre. Some of the borders are
elevated from the house resulting in
steep banks which provide a different
and interesting aspect. Salvia, dahlia,
hedychium, brugmansia peak in the
summer months.

33 **447 MAIN ROAD**
Harwich CO12 4HB. J Shrive & S
McGarry. *1m out of Dovercourt town
centre. Follow the signs along the
A120 to Harwich. Straight over 1st
r'about, carry on A120. Turn R, 4th
exit & up Parkeston Hill, turn R at mini
r'about. 300 yds on L. All signed.*
Home-made teas. **Adm £3, chd free.
Sat 1, Sun 2 Aug (11-4).**
Come and view something different.
Large town garden totally redesigned
in 2007 as a tropical oasis, with its
own Treasure island and treasure
chest and a new Tree fern walk,now
fully complete. Extensive herbaceous
border, brimming with colour, many of
the plants available to buy. A decking
area for teas and Sharon's Mums
delicious cakes!

34 **◆ MARKS HALL GARDENS
& ARBORETUM**
Coggeshall CO6 1TG. Marks Hall
Estate, 01376 563796,
www.markshall.org.uk. *1¹/₂ m N of
Coggeshall. Follow brown & white
tourism signs from A120 Coggeshall
bypass.* **Adm £5, chd over 5 £2,
family ticket £12. For opening
times and information, please
phone or see garden website.**
The walled garden is a unique blend
of traditional long borders within C17
walls and 5 contemporary gardens.
Inventive landscaping, grass
sculpture and stunningly colourful
mass plantings. On opp. lake bank is
millennium walk designed for winter
interest, scent and colour, surrounded
by over 100 acres of arboretum, incl.
species from all continents. New
bridge across the brook making
central area usable whatever the

weather, from snowdrops to autumn
colour. A partner garden to the RHS.
Hard paths now lead to all key areas
of interest.

35 **60 MILL LANE**
Tye Green, Cressing CM77 8HW.
Pauline & Arthur Childs. *2m S of
Braintree. 15m W of Colchester, 5m
N of Witham. From M11 J8 follow
A120 to Braintree r'about
McDonalds, take B1018 to Witham
approx ³/₄ m turn R into Mill Lane.*
Home-made teas. **Adm £2.50, chd
free. Wed 8 July, Sun 9 Aug (2-5).**
A hidden little gem. Plantaholic's
paradise packed with interesting
flowers and ferns. Very colourful
garden with hostas, penstemons,
fuchsias and clematis in profusion,
some rather unusual. 3 water features
add a sense of calm. Relax on patio
with delicious home-made cakes
while admiring our beautiful
containers, topiary and hanging
baskets. Please phone 01376
325904 if bad weather. Cressing
Temple Barns nearby.

36 **MIRAFLORES**
5 Rowan Way, Witham CM8 2LJ.
Yvonne & Danny Owen, 07976
603863, danny@dannyowen.co.uk.
*ACCESS via CM8 2PS. For SATNAV
house postcode is not to be used, as
access is from the rear of the garden
via Forest Rd & please follow yellow
signs.* Tea. Typical English Tea Event,
June 21, incl 40's and 50's
background music. £10 all incl. Must
be pre-booked, max of 20 people.
**Adm £3, £10 (Sun 21 June), chd
free. Wed 27, Thur 28 May, Sat 13,
Sun 14 June (1-5); Sun 21 June
(2-5). Visitors also welcome by
arrangement May to June, min 10.**
An award-winning, medium-sized

garden described by one visitor as a
'little bit of heaven'. A blaze of colour
with roses and clematis, pergola rose
arch, triple fountain with box hedging.
A blaze of colour with Roses and
poppy's galore. Come and see our
'Folly', our exuberant, and cascading
hanging baskets, as featured in
Garden Answers and Essex Life.
Tranquil seating areas and cakes to
die for.

37 **MONKS COTTAGE**
Monks Lane, Dedham nr
Colchester CO7 6DP. Nicola Baker,
01206 322210,
nicola_baker@tiscali.co.uk. *6m NE
of Colchester. Leave Dedham village
with the church on L. Take 2nd main
rd on R (Coles Oak Lane) Monks
Lane is first rd on L.* Home-made
teas. **Adm £3.50, chd free. Visitors
welcome by arrangement May to
Aug small groups.**
¹/₂ acre cottage garden on a sloping
site in the heart of Constable country.
Colour-themed borders filled with
bulbs, shrubs and perennials. Mature
trees and pond. Highlights include
roses, clematis and box-edged
parterre beds. Features incl boggy
area with strong foliage shapes and a
small woodland garden. Gin-and-
tonic balcony with views of the
garden.

38 **MOVERONS**
Brightlingsea CO7 0SB. Lesley &
Payne Gunfield, 01206 305498,
lesleyorrock@me.com,
www.moverons.co.uk. *7m SE of
Colchester. At old church turn R
signed Moverons Farm. Follow lane &
garden signs for approx 1m. Beware
some SatNavs take you the wrong
side of the river.* Home-made teas.
**Adm £5, chd free. Sun 31 May
(11-5). Visitors also welcome by
arrangement June to Sept for
groups of 10+.**
Beautiful tranquil 4 acre garden in
touch with its surroundings and
enjoying stunning estuary views. A
wide variety of planting in mixed
borders to suit different growing
conditions. Small courtyard, reflection
pool garden, large natural ponds,
plenty of seating, sculptures.
Magnificent trees some over 300yrs
old give this garden real presence.
New for 2015 deck and
summerhouse 'floating' over pond.

39 THE OLD RECTORY
Church Road, Boreham CM3 3EP.
Sir Jeffery & Lady Bowman,
01245 467233,
bowmansuzy@btinternet.com.
4m NE of Chelmsford. Take B1137 Boreham Village, turn into Church Rd at the Lion PH. 1/2 m along on R opp church. Home-made teas. In February we serve hot soup and hot sausages in rolls. **Adm £5, chd free. Sat 21, Sun 22 Feb (12-3); Sun 31 May (2-5). Visitors also welcome by arrangement Feb to June.**
2 1/2 -acre garden surrounding C15 house (not open). Ponds, stream, with bridges and primulas, small wild flower meadow and wood with interesting trees and shrubs, herbaceous borders with emphasis on complementary colours. Vegetable garden. February opening for crocus, snowdrops and cyclamen. Possibly largest gunnera in Essex. Lovely views over Chelmer/Blackwater canal. Featured in Country Homes and Interiors. Wheelchair access, gravel drive but large part of garden accessible.
  ♿ ❀ 🚐 ☕

40 PARSONAGE HOUSE
Wiggens Green, Helions Bumpstead, Haverhill CB9 7AD.
The Hon & Mrs Nigel Turner. *3m S of Haverhill. From the Xrds in the village centre go up past the Church for approx 1m. Parking on R through a five bar gate into the orchard.* Home-made teas. **Adm £4, chd free. Sun 3 May, Sun 21 June (2-5).**
C15 house (not open) surrounded by 3 acres of formal gardens with mixed borders, topiary, pond, potager and greenhouse. Further 3-acre wild flower meadow with orchids and rare trees and further 3 acre orchard of old East Anglian apple varieties. Featured in Country Life, The English Garden, Gardens Illustrated and Hortus. Gravel drive and small step into WC.
  ♿ ❀ ☕

41 NEW PATERNOSTER HOUSE
Barnhall Road, Tolleshunt Knights, Maldon CM9 8HA. Julia & Michael Bradley, juliaabradley@gmail.com. *From A12 J24 (Kelvedon) Take B1023 to Tiptree through Tiptree on B1023 bottom of Factory Hill turn L to Tolleshunt Knights on Brook Rd S bend onto Barnhall Rd. Continue to 30mph sign house on R.* Teas. **Adm £4, chd free. Sun 31 May (10-5). Visitors also welcome by**
arrangement Apr to Sept small groups, children supervised because of ponds.
Peaceful 5 acre garden rescued from a derelict state some 15yrs ago. It now has 2 meadows, orchards of apples, pears, stone fruit, mulberry trees and peaches. Ornamental kitchen garden and extensive lawns with large shrubberies. Some rare and unusual shrubs, incl collection of viburnums. Young and mature trees. 2 beautiful ponds. Enclosed flower garden. Some vintage tractors and machinery. Chickens, mandarin ducks, guinea fowl (The Freds), golden pheasants and semi-permanent mallards. Gravel drive. Rough grass in meadows (parking), otherwise reasonably level.
  ♿ ☕

42 PEACOCKS
Roman Road, Margaretting CM4 9HY. Phil Torr, 07802 472382, phil.torr@btinternet.com.
Margaretting Village Centre. From village Xrds go 75yds in the direction of Ingatestone, entrance gates will be found on L set back 50 feet from the road frontage. Light refreshments. **Adm £5, chd free. Share to St Francis Hospice. Sun 19 Apr (1-4); Sun 14 June, Sun 12 July (2-6). Visitors also welcome by arrangement Apr to July adm incl refreshments.**
5-acre garden surrounding Regency house with mature native and specimen trees. Restored horticultural buildings. Formal walled garden (2nd under construction), long herbaceous/mixed border. Vegetable garden. Temple and lake. Large areas for wildlife incl woodland walk and orchard/ wildflower meadow. Sunken dell. An exhibition of old Margaretting postcards.
  ♿ ❀ 🚐 ☕

43 PEPPERS FARM
Forry Green, Sible Hedingham CO9 3RP. Mrs Pam Turtle, 01787 460221, pam@peppersfarm.entadsl.com.
1m SW of Sible Hedingham. From S after Gosfield L for Southey Green. L for Forry Green. From N for Sible Hedingham R at Sugar Loaves, Rectory Rd. L at White Horse until Forry Green. Home-made teas. **Adm £3.50, chd free. Sun 3 May (2-5). Visitors also welcome by arrangement Feb to Oct.**
1/2 acre country garden set high on quiet rural green with farmland views.

Hedges divide informal borders featuring flowering shrubs, fruit and specimen trees, many grown from seed. Beautiful alpine scree and sinks overlook spring fed pond. Garden owner has been a 'seedaholic' since small enough to seek fairies in tulips. Free standing Wisteria, and set in Essex countryside. Featured in Garden News. Partial wheelchair access, large pond with steep sides. Some gravel.
  ♿ 🌺 ❀ ☕

A decking area for teas and Sharon's Mum's delicious cakes . . . !

18 PETTITS BOULEVARD, RM1 See London.

GROUP OPENING

44 NEW RAYLEIGH GARDENS
Rayleigh SS6 9ND. *All the group gardens are within 1m from Rayleigh station. From A127 take A1245 towards Chelmsford. At r'about turn towards Rayleigh on A129, London Rd. At Travellers Joy PH turn L (Downhall Rd) to access 3 gardens, the 4th is off A129 on R.* Home-made teas at all three gardens. **Combined adm £5, chd free. Fri 12 June, Sun 12 July, Sun 16 Aug (12-5).**

> #### NEW 1 CHERRYDOWN
> Richard & Gill Thrussell.
> *At Travellers Joy 3rd R into Gayleighs, then R into Cherrydown*
> **Visitors also welcome by arrangement June to Aug for groups of 6 plus.**
> 01268 781057
> richardthrussell@lineone.net

> #### NEW 35 LANGDON ROAD
> Mrs Louise Reed
> *From A129 turn R into Langdon Rd*

> #### NEW 36 LONDON ROAD
> Jenny & Ron Coutts.
> *L at Travellers Joy PH, L again to park in Cordelia Crescent. Entering the post code into SATNAV directs you there*
> **Visitors also welcome by arrangement June to July.**
> 01268 781329
> couttsier2@btinternet.com

NEW ▶ 2 LOWER LAMBRICKS
Linda & Alan Davison.
not open 16 Aug. At end of rd, at T- Junction, turn R onto Hambro Hill. Under railway bridge turn first R

Four diverse town gardens to delight and inspire the visitor. Cherrydown's 3 levels burst with over 350 perennial cultivars. Shade planting leads to a terrace with views over raised borders. Up steps to fruit trees, a greenhouse, parterre herb garden bordered with roses, agapanthus and annuals. London Rd boasts hot planting, succulents, Koi ponds to the front, with a lawn, pergolas groaning with climbers and baskets to the rear. Gingers, brugmansia, shrubs and perennials can be enjoyed from seating areas. Lower Lambricks sloping garden is imaginatively terraced with vertical planting, a trained fruit arbour and secluded seating, water features and containers. Perennials, grasses, greenhouse and productive area fill this great garden. Langden Rd is a delightful white garden boasting over 100 roses, unusual perennials and ferns, all crammed into a tiny plot. Shady fernery, arches, pond and a succession of bloom surround a handkerchief lawn providing interest all summer long. Wheelchair access to 36 London Rd and partial access to 2 Lower Lambricks.

♿ ❋ ☕

---

45 ▶ NEW ▶ RAYNE HATCH FARM
Rayne Hatch, Stisted, Braintree CM77 8BY. Dr Jill Chaloner. *1m NE Braintree. From Braintree bypass take A131 towards Sudbury passing through High Garrett & Three Counties Crematorium on L take R turn signed Stisted 2 then R at T-junction 4th house on R.* Light refreshments. **Adm £4, chd free. Sun 14 June, Sun 26 July (11-4).**
2½ acre garden surrounding grade II listed Elizabethan farmhouse lovingly created in past 14 yrs by plantaholic owner with 4 ponds providing a rich wildlife habitat. Enjoy waterside paths, ornamental bridge, well stocked herbaceous borders, woodland walk, orchard and walled garden. Fragrant arbours and ample seating throughout aid contemplation and tranquility.

❋ ☕

46 ▶ REPRISE
5 Mornington Crescent, Hadleigh, Benfleet SS7 2HW. David & Rosemary King, 01702 557632, david.rosie@talktalk.net. *5m W of Southend-on-Sea. A13 E through Hadleigh town, Woodfield Rd L. A13 W pass Hadleigh Boundary sign, Woodfield Rd R. Follow signs.* Home-made teas. **Adm £3, chd free. Sun 7 June, Sun 5 July, Sun 2 Aug (2-5). Visitors also welcome by arrangement June to July adm £7.50 incl cream tea.**
A 250 sq-metre garden, created over 5yrs. Patio, with flower-filled containers, gives garden views. The gravel path winds through colourful perennials to a raised seating area screened by apple tree and climbers. Beyond the lawn is a pond, backed by shrubs and trees. Vegetable plot and greenhouse tucked away completes the scene. Gold Medal for Best Small Garden, Castle Point in Bloom. Featured in Evening Echo.

❋ ☕

47 ▶ ROOKWOODS
Yeldham Road, Sible Hedingham CO9 3QG. Peter & Sandra Robinson, 07770 957111, sandy1989@btinternet.com. *8m NW of Halstead. Entering Sible Hedingham from the direction of Haverhill on A1017 take 1st R just after 30mph sign.* Cream teas. **Adm £3.50, chd free. Wed 27 May (1.30-5). Visitors also welcome by arrangement May to Sept, cream teas can be organised in advance.**
Rookwoods is a tranquil garden. You will find a mix of mature and young trees and shrubs. The herbaceous borders feature columns of tumbling roses. A few pleached hornbeam rooms lead to a young wild flower bed. All this surrounded by a Victorian red brick wall enhanced with clematis and vitis coignetiae. An ancient oak wood lies beyond a meadow of buttercups. Gravel drive.

♿ ❋ 🛏 🛌 ☕

48 ▶ 69 RUNDELLS
Harlow CM18 7HD. Mr & Mrs K Naunton, 01279 303471, k_naunton@hotmail.com. *Harlow. M11 J7 A414 exit T-lights take L exit Southern Way, mini r'about 1st exit Trotters Rd leading into Commonside Rd, take 2nd L into Rundells.* Home-made teas. **Adm £2.50, chd free. Sat 11 July (2-5). Visitors also welcome by arrangement Apr to Sept please give plenty of notice.**

As featured on Alan Titchmarsh's first 'Love Your Garden' series ('The Secret Garden') 69, Rundells is a very colourful, small town garden packed with a wide variety of shrubs, perennials, herbaceous and bedding plants in over 200 assorted containers. Hard landscaping on different levels incls summer house, various seating areas and water features. Steep steps. Access to adjacent allotment, open to view. Honey and other produce for sale (conditions permitting). Full size hot tub/jacuzzi.

❋ ☕

49 ▶ NEW ▶ 22 ST CLEMENTS DRIVE
Leigh-On-Sea SS9 3BJ. Lesley & Alan Kirkman. *3m W of Southend on Sea. From A127 take R filter at Progress Road towards Leigh on Sea & follow signs along the Fairway. From A13 follow signs from Kingswoods Chase.* Home-made teas. **Adm £3.50, chd free. Sun 17 May, Sun 14 June (11-4).**
Modern circular designed rear garden created for high impact and low maintenance. A rich mixture of planting incorporating semi exotics, a wide range of perennials and shrubs for all year round interest. 'Hot beds' full of colour and architectural planting. Designed to be an extension of the house for entertaining both friends and wildlife. Featured on television in Sky 1's 'Show me your Garden' gardening programme. Wheelchair access would be via the sideway to the main decked area.

♿ ☕

---

50 ST HELENS

High Street, Stebbing CM6 3SE. Stephen & Joan Bazlinton, 01371 856495, revbaz@care4free.net. *3m E of Great Dunmow. Leave Gt Dunmow on B1256. Take 1st L to Stebbing, at T-junction turn L into High St, garden 2nd on R.* Tea. **Adm £3.50, chd free. Share to Dentaid. Sat 6 June, Sat 12 Sept (1-5). Visitors also welcome by arrangement Apr to Aug.**

A garden of contrasts due to moist and dry conditions, laid out on a gentle Essex slope from a former willow plantation. These contours give rise to changing vistas and unanticipated areas of seclusion framed with hedging and generous planting. Walkways and paths alongside natural springs and still waters. Featured in Amateur Gardening. Partial wheelchair access.

51 SHRUBS FARM

Lamarsh, Bures CO8 5EA. Mr & Mrs Robert Erith, 01787 227520, bob@shrubsfarm.co.uk, www.shrubsfarm.co.uk. *1¼ m from Bures. On rd to Lamarsh, the drive is signed to Shrubs Farm.* Home-made teas in the barn. Refreshments to suit parties can be negotiated. **Adm £6, chd free. Visitors welcome by arrangement Apr to Oct groups of any size.**

2 acres with shrub borders, lawns, roses and trees. 50 acres parkland and meadow with wild flower paths and woodland trails. Over 70 species of oak. Superb 10m views over Stour valley. Ancient coppice and pollards incl largest goat (pussy) willow (*Salix caprea*) in England. Wollemi and Norfolk pines, and banana trees. Full size black rhinoceros. Display of Bronze age burial urns. Guided Tour to incl park and ancient woodland. Restored C18 Essex barn is available for refreshments. Some ground may be boggy in wet weather.

52 SNARES HILL COTTAGE

Duck End, Stebbing CM6 3RY. Pete & Liz Stabler, 01371 856565, lizstabler@hotmail.com. *Between Dunmow & Bardfield. On B1057 from Great Dunmow to Great Bardfield, ½ m after Bran End on L.* Home-made teas. **Adm £4, chd free. Sun 31 May, Sun 13 Sept (10.30-4). Visitors also welcome by arrangement Apr to Sept.**

A 'quintessential English Garden' - Gardeners World. Our quirky 1½ acre garden has surprises round every corner and many interesting sculptures. A natural swimming pool is bordered by romantic flower beds, herb garden and Victorian folly. A bog garden borders woods and leads to silver birch copse, beach garden and 'Roman' temple. Natural Swimming Pond.

53 SOUTH SHOEBURY HALL

Church Road, Shoeburyness SS3 9DN. Mr & Mrs M Dedman, 01702 299022, michael@shoeburyhall.co.uk. *4m E of Southend-on-Sea. Enter Southend on A127 to Eastern Ave A1159 signed Shoebury. R at r'about to join A13. Proceed S to Ness Rd. R into Church Rd. Garden on L 50 metres.* Home-made teas. **Adm £3.50, chd free. Sun 12 Apr, Sun 19 July (2-5). Visitors also welcome by arrangement Apr to July.**

Delightful, 1-acre established walled garden surrounding Grade II listed house (not open) and bee house. New agapanthus and hydrangea beds. April is ablaze with 3000 tulips and fritillaria. July shows 200+ varieties of agapanthus. Unusual trees, shrubs, rose borders, with 40yr old plus geraniums, Mediterranean and Southern Hemisphere planting in dry garden. St Andrews Church open to visitors. Garden close to sea. Featured on Mony Donn's Gardeners World and in Country Living, Amateur Gardening and Essex Life.

54 ◆ SPENCERS

Tilbury Road, Great Yeldham CO9 4JG. Mr & Mrs Colin Bogie, 01787 238175, www.spencersgarden.net. *Just N of Gt Yeldham on Tilbury Rd. In village centre, turn at 'Blasted Oak' (huge oak stump) onto Tilbury Rd. Spencers is clearly signed on L after approx ¼ m.* Home-made teas. **Adm £5, chd free. For NGS: Sun 7 June, Sun 13 Sept (2-5). For other opening times and information, please phone or see garden website.**

Romantic C18 walled garden laid out by Lady Anne Spencer, overflowing with blooms following Tom Stuart-Smith's renovation. Huge wisteria, armies of Lord Butler delphiniums ('Rab' lived at Spencers). Many varieties of roses, spectacular herbaceous borders, vibrant clover

---

lawn, oldest greenhouse in Essex. Parkland with many specimen trees. Victorian woodland garden. Open Thurs May to Sep 2-5, by arrangement for groups. Featured in The Guardian.

Designed to be an extension of the house for entertaining both friends and wildlife . . .

55 NEW SPRING COTTAGE

Chapel Lane, Elmstead Market, Colchester CO7 7AG. Mr & Mrs Roger & Sharon Sciachettano. *3m from Colchester. Overlooking village green N of A133 through Elmstead Market. Parking limited adjacent to cottage, village car park nearby on S side of A133.* Home-made teas. **Adm £3, chd free. Sun 24, Mon 25 May, Sat 6, Sun 7 June (1-5). Also open Strandlands 24, 25 May.**

From Acteas to Zauscherias and Aressima to Zebra grass we hope our large variety of plants will please. Our award winning garden features a range of styles and habitats e.g. Woodland dell, stumpery, Mediterranean area, perennial borders and pond. Our C17 thatched cottage and garden show cases a number of plants found at the world famous Beth Chatto gardens ½ m down the road.

56 NEW STRANDLANDS

off Rectory Road, Wrabness, Manningtree CO11 2TX. Jenny & David Edmunds, 01255 886260, strandlands@outlook.com. *1km along farm track from the corner of Rectory Rd. If using a SatNav, the post code will leave you at the corner of Rectory Road. Turn onto a farm track, signed to Woodcutters Cottage & Strandlands, & continue for 1km.* Sat & Sun light ploughman's lunches,

homemade teas. Mon wine, light canapés & tea/coffee. **Adm £3.50 (Sat & Sun), adm £4 (Mon), chd free. Sat 23, Sun 24 May (10-6); Mon 25 May (2.30-7.30). Also open Spring Cottage 24, 25 May. Visitors also welcome by arrangement Apr to Oct.**
Cottage surrounded by 4 acres of land bordering the beautiful and unspoilt Stour Estuary. One acre of decorative garden: formal courtyard with yew, box and lavender hedges, lily pond, summerhouse and greenhouse; 2 large island beds, secret 'moon garden', madly and vividly planted 'Madison' garden, 3 acres of wildlife meadows with groups of native trees, large wildlife pond, also riverside bird hide. View the Stour Estuary from our own bird hide. Grayson Perry's 'A House for Essex' can be seen just one field away from Strandlands. Featured in The English Garden. Mostly accessible and flat although parking area is gravelled.

♿ ❀ ☕

57 TUDOR ROOST

18 Frere Way, Fingringhoe, Colchester CO5 7BP. Chris & Linda Pegden, 01206 729831, pegdenc@gmail.com. *5m S of Colchester. In centre of village by Whalebone PH, follow sign to Ballast Quay, after ¹/₂ m turn R into Brook Hall Rd, then 1st L into Frere Way.* Home-made teas. **Adm £3.50, chd free. Sun 5, Mon 6 Apr, Sun 3, Mon 4, Sun 24 May, Sat 4, Sun 5 July, Sat 15, Sun 16 Aug (2-5). Visitors also welcome by arrangement Apr to Aug min 10 people, £6 per head incl tea & cake.**
An unexpected hidden colourful ¹/₄-acre garden. Well manicured grassy paths wind round island beds and ponds. Densely planted subtropical area with architectural and exotic plants - cannas, bananas, palms, agapanthus, agaves and tree ferns surround a colourful gazebo. Garden planted to provide yr-round colour and encourage wildlife. Many peaceful seating areas. Within 1m of Fingringhoe Wick Nature Reserve. Local PH that serves meal. PLEASE CONFIRM OPENING DATES ON NGS WEBSITE OR TELEPHONE. Featured in Essex Life Magazine, Garden News, Yours magazine. Also cover garden of the 2015 Essex Booklet.

🐇 ❀ 🚌 ☕

58 37 TURPINS LANE

Chigwell, Woodford Green IG8 8AZ. Fabrice Aru & Martin Thurston, 0208 5050 739, martin.thurston@talktalk.net. *Between Woodford & Epping. Tube: Chigwell, 2m from North Circular Rd at Woodford, follow the signs for Chigwell (A113) through Woodford Bridge into Manor Rd & turn L, Bus 275.* **Adm £3, chd free. Sun 14, Sun 28 June, Sun 26 July (11-6). Also open 56 Forest Drive, 14 June and 26 July. Visitors also welcome by arrangement May to Oct max 8.**
An unexpected hidden, magical, small part-walled garden showing how much can be achieved in a small space. An oasis of calm with densely planted rich, lush foliage, tree ferns, hostas, topiary and an abundance of well maintained shrubs complemented by a small pond and 3 water features designed for yr round interest. Awarded 2nd place by Gardening News for Best Small Garden.

☕

59 ULTING WICK

Crouchmans Farm Road, Maldon CM9 6QX. Mr & Mrs B Burrough, 01245 380216, philippa.burrough@btinternet.com, www.ultingwickgarden.co.uk. *3m*

Strandlands

NW of Maldon. Take turning to Ulting off B1019 as you exit Hatfield Peverel. Garden on R after 2m. Soup, filled rolls at lunch & teas 17 Apr, 13 Sept. Home-made teas 26 Apr. Cream teas 1 May, 11 June, 18 Sept. **Adm £5, chd free. Share to All Saints Ulting Church. Fri 17 Apr (2-5); Sun 26 Apr, Fri 1 May (11-5); Thur 11 June (2-5); Sun 13 Sept (11-5); Fri 18 Sept (2-5). Visitors also welcome by arrangement Mar to Oct groups of 15+. Other catering by arrangement.**
Listed black barns provide backdrop for colourful and exuberant planting in 8 acres. Thousands of tulips, flowing innovative spring planting, herbaceous borders, pond, mature weeping willows, kitchen garden, dramatic late summer beds with zingy, tender, exotic plant combinations. Drought tolerant wild flower meadow and front border. Woodland. New shrub and grass border. Many plants propagated in-house. Lots of unusual plants for sale. All Saints Church Ulting will be open in conjunction with the garden for talks on its history on Sun openings only. Featured in Essex Life, House and Garden, Period Homes and Interiors. Some gravel around the house but main areas of interest are accessible for wheelchairs.

♿ 🐇 ❀ 🚌 ☕

60 **NEW** **37 UNDERHILL ROAD**
Benfleet SS7 1EP. Mr Allan & Mrs Diane Downey, 01268 565291, allan.downey@yahoo.co.uk. *Approx 2m from Sadlers Farm r'about on A13. Towards Southend, take R turn at Tarpots Harvester continue to South Benfleet School turn L opp, in to Thundersley Park Rd, continue to Underhill Rd 500yds on R.* Home-made teas. **Adm £3.50, chd free. Suns 28 June, 26 July, 23 Aug, 6 Sept (1-6). Visitors also welcome by arrangement June to Sept weekdays only min 10.**
A ¼ acre garden offering a relaxing visit featuring topiary shrubs and climbers incl campsis, clematis, honeysuckle and jasmine. Over 40 heucheras in beds with sedums, rudbeckias and hydrangeas. Lovely views from all areas. Undercover Bonsai area, many colourful baskets and containers. Several cast iron and stone sculptures. Patio area to enjoy refreshments.

GROUP OPENING

61 **WALTHAM ABBEY**
Waltham Abbey EN9 1LG. *8m W of Epping Town. M25, J26 to Waltham Abbey. At T-lights by McD turn R to r'about. Take 2nd exit to next r'about. Take 3rd exit (A112) to T-lights. L to Monkswood Av.* Home-made teas at Silver Birches, Quendon Drive. **Combined adm £5, chd free. Sun 7 June, Sun 6 Sept (12-6).**

62 EASTBROOK ROAD
Caroline Cassell.
not open Sept. No Parking in Eastbrook Rd. Off Honey Lane, walking distance from Halfhides & The Glade Way approx 7mins

39 HALFHIDES
Chris Hamer

76 MONKSWOOD AVENUE
Cathy & Dan Gallagher

SILVER BIRCHES
Quendon Drive. Linda & Frank Jewson

Historic Waltham Abbey is near Epping Forest. The Abbey is purported to be last resting place of King Harold. Lee Valley Regional Park is nearby. Silver Birches boasts 3 lawns on 2 levels. This surprisingly secluded garden has many mixed borders packed with all year interest.

Mature shrubs and trees create a short woodland walk. Crystal clear water flows through a shady area of the garden. At 39 Halfhides the garden has evolved over 45yrs. It features mixed shrubs and perennial borders on 2 levels. Waterfall linking two ponds leads to shade garden. Alpines thrive on scree and in troughs. Beautiful autumn colour. 76 Monkswood Ave is a plantswoman's garden. Mixed borders filled with specimen trees, shrubs and perennials incl asters, dahlias and late-flowering anemones. Wildlife pond. 62 Eastbrook Rd is a small cottage garden, traditional perennial planting, topiary and circular themed hard landscaping. Reclaimed chimney pots for sale as planters. 62 Eastbrook Rd not suitable for wheelchairs.

> ¼ acre garden offering a relaxing visit featuring topiary shrubs and climbers . . .

62 **WASHLANDS**
Prayors Hill, Sible Hedingham CO9 3LE. Tony & Sarah Frost, 01787 460732, tony@washlands.co.uk. *¼ m NW of Sible Hedingham Church. At former Sugar Loaves PH on A1017 turn SW into Rectory Rd, R at former White Horse PH, pass St Peters Church on RH-side, ¼ m NW on Prayors Hill.* Home-made teas. **Adm £3.50, chd free. Sun 21 June (2-6). Evening Opening, wine, Wed 24 June (5.30-8.30). Sun 28 June (2-6). Visitors also welcome by arrangement June to Aug, groups of 10+.**
Informal, tranquil garden approx 1 acre with good views over rolling countryside. Features incl a horse pond. Wide herbaceous, shrub and woodland borders incl roses and peonies. Many young and mature

trees enhance the garden. A developing retirement project. Pond has steep banks. Woodland walk unsuitable for wheelchairs.

GROUP OPENING

63 **WENDENS AMBO GARDENS**
Saffron Walden CB11 4UJ. *Parking at village hall nr Church & Chinnel Barn signed on day.* Home-made teas at Crossways. **Combined adm £5, chd free. Sun 7 June (2-5).**

> **NEW** **2 CHURCH PATH**
> Mr Rupert Fulford

> **NEW** **3 CHURCH PATH**
> Ms Liz Hartley

> **COURTLANDS HOUSE**
> Dr & Mrs C Glazebrook

> **NEW** **CROSSWAYS**
> Rookery Lane. Mrs Andrea Reynolds.
> *Leave Newport on B1383 towards Cambridge over 1st r'about then immed L- 250 yds on R between main rd & level crossing*

> **NEW** **KATIE'S MILLENNIUM WOOD**
> Duck Street. Dr Katie Petty-Saphon.
> *Turn off B1039 into Duck St at phone box just E of The Bell PH. After 400yds Duck St bends sharp L but continue straight ahead. Wood is to L & R before tunnel under M11*

Wendens Ambo is a meandering historic village. 3 Church Path, quintessential cottage garden adjacent to historic church set behind a chocolate box thatched cottage. Terraced garden with mixed shrubs, perennials, beautiful clematis and roses. Hidden vegetable garden and fruit trees. 2 Church Path, sweeping lawn and orchard area complement cottage. Garden affords wonderful views of historic village. Courtlands House, low maintenance, minimalistic garden with interesting topiary, varieties of hostas, seasonal pots. Ferns and gunnera in shady areas. Crossways, 5 acre informal 'family' garden with mixed planting. Sweeping lawn and wild flowers. Wildlife areas and large pond, a haven for frogs! Specimen trees. Katie's Millenium Wood,10,000 trees planted as whips in 2000 - 2001,

mainly oak, ash, hazel, hawthorn, cherry, poplar and Scots pine. Great care taken to optimise the growing environment - remarkable height and volume achieved in 14yrs. Plants at Courtlands House. Village very close to Audley End House (English Heritage).

64 WICKETS

Langley Upper Green CB11 4RY. Susan & Doug Copeland, 01799 550553, susan.copeland2@btinternet.com. *7m W of Saffron Walden, 10m N of Bishops Stortford. At Newport take B1038 After 3m turn R at Clavering, signed Langley. Upper Green is 3m further on. At cricket green turn R. House 200m on R.* Home-made teas in village hall (opp) or in garden. Light Lunches & home-made teas on 4 May. **Adm £4, chd free. Mon 4 May (11-5); Sat 20 June (1-5). Combined adm with The Chestnuts, Sunday 4 May £5. Visitors also welcome by arrangement May to June min 15.** Peaceful country garden 'Far from the Madding Crowd'. Wide, informal mixed borders include camassia, shrub roses and alliums. Two landscaped meadows and shepherd's hut with fine pastoral views. Large lily pond sheltered by silver birch. New Griffin Glasshouse nearby. Curvilinear design links themed planting areas. Espalier apples enclose parterre with sweet peas, delphiniums, lavender. Secluded gravel garden. Featured in Country Homes and Interiors and Essex Life. Gravel drive.

65 WICKHAM PLACE FARM

Station Road, Wickham Bishops, Witham CM8 3JB. Mrs J Wilson, 01621 891282, info@wickhamplacefarm.co.uk, www.wickhamplacefarm.co.uk. *2¹/₂ m SE of Witham. On B1018 from Witham to Maldon. After going under A12 take 3rd L (Station Rd). 1st house on L.* **Adm £4.50, chd free. Share to Farleigh Hospice. Visitors welcome by arrangement for groups of 15+. Nursery by appt any day/time.** 14 acres for all seasons. 2 acre walled garden is home to climbers, shrubs, perennials & bulbs. Renowned for enormous wisterias in May (one over 250ft long) with further

flowering in July. Ponds, intricate box knot garden & lovely woodland walks with rabbit resistant plants. In September cyclamen carpet the woodland, replacing earlier bluebells. Adjacent to unique wooden trestle railway viaduct. Note, wisterias face all aspects, extending flowering time during May. Featured on Gardeners World, Great British Garden Revival & RHS The Garden.

3 acres of wildlife meadows with groups of native trees, large wildlife pond, also riverside bird hide . . .

66 WOOD VIEW

24 Chapel Road, Great Totham, nr Maldon CM9 8DA. Edwin Parsons & Ian Roxburgh, 07540 798135, edwin@edwin.freeserve.co.uk. *5m NE of Maldon. Situated in Great Totham North. Chapel Rd is off B1022 Maldon/Colchester Rd.* Light refreshments at URC Hall (opp). Home made soup using produce from our allotments will be available in season. November opening adm £7 to incl seasonal refreshments. **Adm £4, chd free. Sun 5, Mon 6 Apr, Sun 3, Mon 4, Sun 10 May (12-4); Sun 29 Nov (3-6). Visitors also welcome by arrangement pre booked groups adm £7 incl refreshments.** Expect the unexpected at this plantsmans garden for all seasons. Designed and maintained by the garden owners, there is interest at any time of year. Winter flowering shrubs, spring bulbs, roses, hostas and dahlias. Pergolas and terraces (also constructed by the garden owners) create seating areas in this haven for wildlife and visitors describe our garden as peaceful and tranquil. We also have 3 allotments nearby where home made teas, WC and car parking facilities are available. Some gravel paths.

67 WOODPECKERS

Mangapp Chase, Burnham-on-Crouch CM0 8QQ. Neil & Linda Holdaway, & Lilian Burton, 01621 782137, lindaholdaway@btinternet.com, www.essexgardens.co.uk. *1m N of Burnham-on-Crouch. B1010 to Burnham-on-Crouch. Just beyond town sign turn L into Green Lane. Turn L after ¹/₂ m. Garden 200yds on R.* Light refreshments. (Our ever popular home made soup, bread and sandwiches available at lunchtime and delicious cakes and bakes for tea). **Adm £4, chd free. Sats 5, 12, 19, 26 Sept (12-5). Visitors also welcome by arrangement Sept open for groups with home-made lunch or cream tea.** Hedges divide and add structure to the exuberant planting in this 1¹/₂ acre country garden. Although maintained for a long season of interest, the densely planted borders are probably at their best in late summer when asters, bulbs, grasses, sedums and dahlias, together with a wide variety of other nectar rich varieties of annuals and perennials, encourage foraging bees and clouds of butterflies. Photographs and articles in Essex Life, Landscape Magazine, Homes and Gardens (German edition), Gartnern Leicht Gemacht and Garden News.

68 WRITTLE COLLEGE

Writtle CM1 3RR. Writtle College, www.writtle.ac.uk. *4m W of Chelmsford. On A414, nr Writtle village, clearly signed.* Light refreshments in The Garden Room (main campus) & The Lordship tea room (Lordship campus). **Adm £4, chd free. Sun 22 Feb, Sun 7 June, Sun 18 Oct (10-3), 21 Feb 2016.** 15 acres; informal lawns with naturalised bulbs and wild flowers. Large tree collection, mixed shrubs, herbaceous borders. Landscaped gardens designed and built by students. Development of 13-acre parkland. Orchard meadow started. Landscaped glasshouses and wide range of seasonal bedding. Herbaceous perennial borders renovated during 2013. Extended naturalised bulb areas on front campus lawns. Rockery being renovated during 2014 for full open access by summer 2015. Some gravel, however majority of areas accessible to all.

GLOUCESTERSHIRE

(for South Gloucestershire see Somerset, Bristol Area & S Glos)

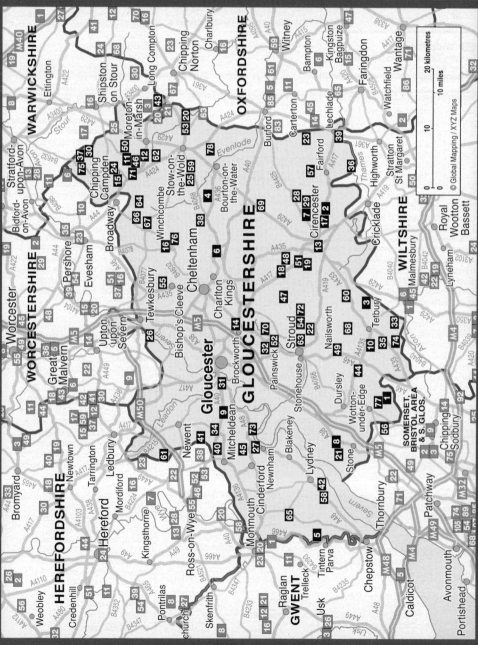

Investec Wealth & Investment supports the NGS

Gloucestershire

Gloucestershire is one of the most beautiful counties in England, spanning as it does a large part of the Cotswolds, as well as the Forest of Dean, and the Wye and Severn Valleys.

The Cotswolds is an expanse of gently sloping green hills, wooded valleys and ancient, picturesque towns and villages; it is designated as an Area of Outstanding Natural Beauty, and its quintessentially English charm attracts many visitors.

Like the county itself, many of the gardens which open for the NGS are quite outstanding. There are major public gardens such as Hidcote Manor Garden, as well as large private gardens such as Highnam Court and Stowell Park.

There are, however, many more modest gardens whose gates only open on an NGS open day, such as 25 Bowling Green Road with over 400 varieties of Hemerocallis. This tiny garden has opened for the NGS for over thirty years! The National Collection of Rambling Roses is held at Moor Wood, and that of Juglans and Pterocarya at Upton Wold.

Several Cotswold villages also open their gardens, and a wonderful day can be had strolling from cottage to house, marvelling at the gardens, only to pause for the obligatory tea and cake!

Gloucestershire Volunteers

County Organiser
Norman Jeffery
01793 762805
normjeffery28@btinternet.com

County Treasurer
Graham Baber
01285 650961
grayanjen@onetel.com

Publicity
Norman Jeffery
(as above)

Booklet Coordinator
Nick Kane
07768 478668
nick@kanes.org

Assistant County Organisers
Sue Hunt
01453 521263
suehunt2@btinternet.com

Trish Jeffery
01793 762805
trishjeffery@aol.com

Valerie Kent
01993 823294

Shirley & Gordon Sills
01242 820606
shirleysills@btinternet.com

Pat Willey
01285 762946
patwilley1@gmail.com

Gareth & Sarah Williams
01531 821654
dgwilliams84@hotmail.com

Left: Home Farm

Currently the NGS donates around £2.5 million every year

Opening Dates

All entries subject to change.
For latest information check www.ngs.org.uk

February

Sunday 1
34 Home Farm

Sunday 8
36 Kempsford Manor

Saturday 14
51 The Old Rectory, Duntisbourne Rous

Sunday 15
34 Home Farm
36 Kempsford Manor
70 Trench Hill

Wednesday 18
36 Kempsford Manor

Sunday 22
21 Dr Jenner's House & Garden
70 Trench Hill

March

Sunday 1
36 Kempsford Manor

Sunday 8
36 Kempsford Manor

Sunday 15
34 Home Farm
46 Mill Dene Garden

Sunday 29
55 Pear Tree Cottage

April

Sunday 5
10 Beverston Castle
31 Highnam Court
47 Misarden Park
70 Trench Hill

Monday 6
10 Beverston Castle
70 Trench Hill

Saturday 11
65 South Lodge

Sunday 12
34 Home Farm
36 Kempsford Manor
50 The Old Chequer

Monday 13
37 Kiftsgate Court

Tuesday 14
7 Barnsley House

Sunday 19
71 Upton Wold

Sunday 26
11 Blockley Gardens
34 Home Farm

May

Sunday 3
22 Eastcombe, Bussage and Brownshill Gardens
31 Highnam Court
58 Ramblers
65 South Lodge

Monday 4
22 Eastcombe, Bussage and Brownshill Gardens

Wednesday 6
42 Lydney Park Spring Garden

Sunday 10
17 The Coach House Garden
36 Kempsford Manor
67 Stanway Fountain & Water Garden
69 Stowell Park
70 Trench Hill

Monday 11
51 The Old Rectory, Duntisbourne Rous

Saturday 16
16 Charingworth Court

Sunday 17
16 Charingworth Court
36 Kempsford Manor
46 Mill Dene Garden
60 Rodmarton Manor

Saturday 23
35 Hookshouse Pottery

Sunday 24
35 Hookshouse Pottery
53 Pasture Farm

Monday 25
35 Hookshouse Pottery
41 Lower Farm House
53 Pasture Farm

Tuesday 26
35 Hookshouse Pottery

Wednesday 27
14 Brockworth Court
35 Hookshouse Pottery
41 Lower Farm House

Thursday 28
35 Hookshouse Pottery

Friday 29
35 Hookshouse Pottery

Saturday 30
18 Cotswold Farm
35 Hookshouse Pottery
40 Longhope Gardens
65 South Lodge

Sunday 31
4 NEW Aylworth Manor
6 Barn House, Sandywell Park
18 Cotswold Farm
28 Greenacres
33 Hodges Barn
35 Hookshouse Pottery
40 Longhope Gardens

June

Monday 1
33 Hodges Barn

Tuesday 2
28 Greenacres

Wednesday 3
70 Trench Hill

Festival Weekend

Saturday 6
63 Slad Valley House
75 NEW White House

Sunday 7
3 Ashley Grange and Dillycott
8 Berkeley Castle
36 Kempsford Manor
44 Matara Gardens of Wellbeing
63 Slad Valley House
68 18 Star Lane
75 NEW White House

Wednesday 10
15 Campden House
24 Ernest Wilson Memorial Garden
25 Eyford House
59 Rockcliffe House
70 Trench Hill
76 Woodlands Farm

Saturday 13
40 Longhope Gardens
61 Rose Cottage

Sunday 14
2 Ampney Brook House
11 Blockley Gardens
31 Highnam Court
36 Kempsford Manor
40 Longhope Gardens
58 Ramblers
61 Rose Cottage
66 Stanton Village Gardens
75 NEW White House
76 Woodlands Farm

Wednesday 17
15 Campden House
24 Ernest Wilson Memorial Garden
39 NEW Loders Gate
70 Trench Hill

76 Woodlands Farm

Saturday 20
9 Berrys Place Farm

Sunday 21
5 Barn House, Chepstow
9 Berrys Place Farm
27 The Gables
47 Misarden Park
49 NEW Nailsworth Gardens - off Chestnut Hill
54 Paulmead
57 Quenington Gardens
65 South Lodge
69 Stowell Park
72 Wells Cottage
76 Woodlands Farm

Rural Cotswold garden nestled in quiet hamlet . . .

Tuesday 23
77 NEW Wortley House

Wednesday 24
9 Berrys Place Farm
14 Brockworth Court
20 Daylesford House
25 Eyford House
59 Rockcliffe House
70 Trench Hill

Thursday 25
9 Berrys Place Farm

Friday 26
64 Snowshill Manor & Garden

Sunday 28
6 Barn House, Sandywell Park
10 Beverston Castle
29 Herbs for Healing
38 Littlefield Garden
48 Moor Wood
62 Sezincote

July

Saturday 4
30 Hidcote Manor Garden

Sunday 5
- **13** 25 Bowling Green Road
- **31** Highnam Court
- **36** Kempsford Manor
- **38** Littlefield Garden

Monday 6
- **13** 25 Bowling Green Road

Saturday 11
- **26** Forthampton Court

Sunday 12
- **6** Barn House, Sandywell Park
- **13** 25 Bowling Green Road

Monday 13
- **13** 25 Bowling Green Road

Saturday 18
- **43** NEW The Manor

Sunday 19
- **70** Trench Hill
- **74** Westonbirt School Gardens

August

Sunday 2
- **6** Barn House, Sandywell Park
- **31** Highnam Court

Sunday 9
- **36** Kempsford Manor

Monday 10
- **37** Kiftsgate Court

Sunday 16
- **12** Bourton House Garden
- **36** Kempsford Manor

Sunday 23
- **27** The Gables

Sunday 30
- **70** Trench Hill

Monday 31
- **32** Hilles House

September

Sunday 6
- **31** Highnam Court
- **67** Stanway Fountain & Water Garden
- **78** Wyck Rissington Gardens

Wednesday 9
- **14** Brockworth Court
- **15** Campden House
- **24** Ernest Wilson Memorial Garden

Saturday 12
- **61** Rose Cottage

Sunday 13
- **61** Rose Cottage
- **70** Trench Hill
- **73** Westbury Court Garden

Wednesday 16
- **39** NEW Loders Gate

January 2016

Sunday 31
- **34** Home Farm

February 2016

Saturday 13
- **64** Snowshill Manor & Garden

Sunday 14
- **34** Home Farm
- **36** Kempsford Manor
- **64** Snowshill Manor & Garden
- **70** Trench Hill

Sunday 21
- **70** Trench Hill

Sunday 28
- **36** Kempsford Manor

Gardens open to the public

- **12** Bourton House Garden

- **17** The Coach House Garden
- **21** Dr Jenner's House & Garden
- **29** Herbs for Healing
- **30** Hidcote Manor Garden
- **36** Kempsford Manor
- **37** Kiftsgate Court
- **42** Lydney Park Spring Garden
- **44** Matara Gardens of Wellbeing
- **46** Mill Dene Garden
- **47** Misarden Park
- **52** Painswick Rococo Garden
- **60** Rodmarton Manor
- **62** Sezincote
- **64** Snowshill Manor & Garden
- **67** Stanway Fountain & Water Garden
- **73** Westbury Court Garden
- **74** Westonbirt School Gardens

By arrangement only

- **1** Alderley Grange
- **19** Daglingworth House
- **23** Eastleach House
- **45** The Meeting House

- **56** Pemberley Lodge

Also open by arrangement

- **2** Ampney Brook House
- **3** Ashley Grange
- **4** NEW Aylworth Manor
- **5** Barn House, Chepstow
- **6** Barn House, Sandywell Park
- **13** 25 Bowling Green Road
- **14** Brockworth Court
- **16** Charingworth Court
- **18** Cotswold Farm
- **27** The Gables
- **33** Hodges Barn
- **34** Home Farm
- **40** Longhope Gardens
- **48** Moor Wood
- **50** The Old Chequer
- **51** The Old Rectory, Duntisbourne Rous
- **53** Pasture Farm
- **55** Pear Tree Cottage
- **65** South Lodge
- **70** Trench Hill
- **71** Upton Wold
- **76** Woodlands Farm

25 Bowling Green Road

© Mandy Bradshaw

Find a garden near you – download our free Android app

The Gardens

❶ ALDERLEY GRANGE

Alderley GL12 7QT. The Hon Mrs Acloque, 01453 842161, milly@acloque-alderley.co.uk. *2m S of Wotton-under-Edge. Turn NW off A46 Bath to Stroud rd at Dunkirk. L signed Hawkesbury Upton & Hillesley. In Hillesley follow sign to Alderley.* Adm £5, chd free. Visitors welcome by arrangement June for small or large groups max 40.
Walled garden with fine trees, old fashioned roses, herb garden and aromatic plants. A garden of character, charm and historical interest. Some gravel paths.
&

WE ARE
MACMILLAN.
CANCER SUPPORT

The NGS
has funded
147 different
Macmillan projects

❷ AMPNEY BROOK HOUSE

Ampney Crucis, Cirencester GL7 5RT. Allan and Louise Hirst, 01285 851098, allan.hirst@clmail.co.uk. *From Cirencester go E on A417 toward Fairford. After passing the Crown of Crucis take 1st L and follow yellow arrows.* Home-made teas. Additional refreshments for groups prior arrangement. Adm £5, chd free. Sun 14 June (11.30-4.30). Visitors also welcome by arrangement May to Sept, group arrangements encouraged.
Striking Grade II Cotswold country house on 4.3 acres fronting Ampney Brook. The gardens are 3yrs into a 5yr project to create a haven for wildlife with fun and stimulating spaces yr-round. Incl woodland, kitchen garden, herbaceous borders, meadows, lawns for picnicking (encouraged). No wheelchair access to kitchen garden and greenhouse.
& 🚧 ❀ ☕

GROUP OPENING

❸ ASHLEY GRANGE AND DILLYCOTT

Ashley, Tetbury GL8 8SX. *Between Tetbury and Cirencester off A433. Dillycot is at Culkerton. Ashley has no signage. Parking is available at both Ashley and Culkerton. See individual gardens for directions.* Home-made teas. Refreshments at Ashley Grange. Combined adm £5, chd free. Sun 7 June (2-5.30).

ASHLEY GRANGE
Mr & Mrs Richard Atkinson. *Ashley has no signage. Ashley Grange is opp entrance to C12 church (indicated)* Visitors also welcome by arrangement June. richard@richardatkinson.eu

DILLYCOT
Culkerton, nr Ashley. Mr & Mrs M Oates. *Signed from A433 Cirencester/Tetbury road. Entering hamlet Dillycot is on L just past parking area on R*

Ashley Grange: Original garden was designed by the late Miss Avice Pearson and opened in 1990s through NGS. Current owners have extended the garden and added new borders. Peonies and iris borders are a feature in June. Plants and cakes for sale. Dillycot: Pottager garden with flowers, fruit and vegetables. Exuberant planting grown on biodynamic principles. Wildlife friendly planting. Featured in Gardens Illustrated. WCs at refreshments venue. Dillycot not accessible by wheelchair. Mostly level access at Ashley.
& 🚧 ❀ ☕

❹ NEW AYLWORTH MANOR

Aylworth, Cheltenham GL54 3AH. Dr & Mrs John Ireland, 01451 850850, enquiries@aylworthmanor.co.uk. *Aylworth Manor lies between A436 and B4068, about 1m from village of Naunton.* Home-made teas in aid of Maggie's Cancer Charity. Adm £4, chd free. Sun 31 May (2-5.30). Visitors also welcome by arrangement May & June.
Rural Cotswold garden nestled in quiet hamlet, the garden has developed to splendid maturity over last 12yrs. Mixture of attractive herbaceous borders, shrubs, trees

and ponds, set in quiet valley directly on Windrush Way. Access to site of Medieval village, stunning walks and good disabled access. Most parts of garden are accessible for wheelchairs.
& 🛏 ☕

❺ BARN HOUSE, CHEPSTOW

Brockweir Common, Chepstow NP16 7PH. Mrs Kate Patel, 01291 680041, kate.patel@btinternet.com, thegardenbarnhouse.com. *10m S of Monmouth & N of Chepstow, under 1 hr from Hereford, Cheltenham & Cardiff. From Chepstow A466 to Monmouth. 2m past Tintern Abbey R across Brockweir Bridge then up Mill Hill 1/2 m, turn L at The Rock (cottage), signed to Cold Harbour. Narrow lane, no large coaches.* Home-made teas. Adm £3.50, chd free. Sun 21 June (2-5.30). Visitors also welcome by arrangement June to Sept.
Boldly and generously planted garden of an acre. Wealth of ornamental grasses plus long, late flowering perennials. Stunning mass plantings incl 70m miscanthus hedge. Imaginatively designed contrasting areas incl tranquil sunken terrace with lush Asian grasses, hot border of potted tender perennials, orchard and exuberantly planted vegetable garden screened by bamboos. Featured in The English Garden, Amateur Gardening & The Telegraph.
❀ ☕

❻ BARN HOUSE, SANDYWELL PARK

Whittington, Cheltenham GL54 4HF. Shirley & Gordon Sills, 01242 820606, shirleysills@btinternet.com. *4m E of Cheltenham on A40. 1m from Andoversford, 100 yds from turning to Whittington village on opp side of rd.* Home-made teas. Adm £4.50, chd free. Suns 31 May, 28 June, 12 July, 2 Aug (11-5). Visitors also welcome by arrangement June & July for groups of 10+.
2 1/2 -acre plantaholic's garden inside weathered walls of former Victorian kitchen garden. Designed, created and maintained by the owners as a series of exuberantly planted enclosures both formal and informal, sometimes quirky. Herbaceous, climbers, shrubs, trees, lawns, hedges, structures, vistas, water features. Featured in Glos Echo. Fairly level site although mostly grass paths.
& ❀ ☕

7 BARNSLEY HOUSE
Barnsley, Cirencester GL7 5EE.
Calcot Health & Leisure Ltd, 01285
740000,
reception@barnsleyhouse.com,
www.barnsleyhouse.com. *4m NE of
Cirencester. From Cirencester, take
B4425 to Barnsley. House entrance
on R as you enter village.* Tea. **Adm
£6, chd free. Tue 14 Apr (11-4).**
The beautiful garden at Barnsley
House, created by Rosemary Verey, is
one of England's finest and most
famous gardens incl knot garden,
potager garden and mixed borders in
Rosemary Verey's successional
planting style. The House also has an
extensive kitchen garden which will
be open with plants and vegetables
available for purchase. Narrow paths
mean restricted wheelchair access
but happy to provide assistance.

8 BERKELEY CASTLE
Berkeley GL13 9PJ. Mr & Mrs J R
G Berkeley, www.berkeley-
castle.com. *Half-way between
Bristol & Gloucester, 10mins from J14
of M5. Follow signs to Berkeley from
A38 & B4066. Visitors' entrance is on
L of Canonbury St, just before town
centre.* Light refreshments in a yurt,
next to ticket office/gift shop. **Adm
£5, chd free. Sun 7 June (11-4.30).**
Unique historic garden of a keen
plantsman, with far-reaching views
across R Severn. Gardens contain
many rare plants which thrive in the
warm micro-climate against stone
walls of mediaeval castle. Woodland,
historic trees and stunning terraced
borders. Butterfly house with free-
flying tropical butterflies. Lunches,
snacks and afternoon tea available in
Yurt Restaurant. Gift shop and plant
sales. Difficult for wheelchairs due to
terraced nature of gardens.

9 BERRYS PLACE FARM
Bulley Lane, Churcham, Gloucester
GL2 8AS. Anne Thomas, 07950
808022,
g.j.thomas@btconnect.com. *6m W
of Gloucester. A40 towards Ross.
Turning R into Bulley Lane at
Birdwood.* Home-made teas.
Ploughmans lunches, cream teas.
**Adm £3, chd free. Sat 20, Sun 21,
Wed 24, Thur 25 June (11-5).**
Country garden, approx 1 acre,
surrounded by farmland and old
orchards. Lawns and large sweeping
mixed herbaceous borders with over
100 roses. Formal kitchen garden

and beautiful rose arbour leading to
lake and summerhouse with a variety
of water lilies and carp. All shared
with peacocks and ducks.

10 BEVERSTON CASTLE
nr Tetbury GL8 8TU. Mrs A L Rook.
*2m W of Tetbury. On A4135 to
Dursley between Tetbury & Calcot
Xrds.* **Adm £4, chd free. Sun 5, Mon
6 Apr, Sun 28 June (2-5.30).**
Overlooked by romantic C12-C17
castle ruin (not open), copiously-
planted paved terrace leads from C18
house (not open) across moat to
sloping lawn with spring bulbs in
abundance, and full herbaceous and
shrub borders. Large walled kitchen
garden and greenhouses. Partial
wheelchair access.

BLICKS HILL HOUSE
See Wiltshire.

GROUP OPENING

11 BLOCKLEY GARDENS
Blockley GL56 9DB. *3m NW of
Moreton-in-Marsh. Just off the
Morton-in-Marsh to Evesham Rd
A44.* Home-made teas at Mill Dene &
St George's Hall (April)/at St George's
Hall and The Manor House (June).
**Combined adm £6, chd free. Sun
26 Apr, Sun 14 June (2-6).**

CHURCH GATES
High Street. Mrs Brenda
Salmon.
April 26 and June 14

COLEBROOK HOUSE
Richard & Melanie Slimmon.
April 26 only

LANDGATE
Draycott. Mrs Hilary Sutton.
June 14 only

MALVERN MILL
Mr & Mrs J Bourne.
April 26 only

THE MANOR HOUSE
George & Zoe Thompson.
April 26 and June 14

◆ MILL DENE GARDEN
Mr & Mrs B S Dare.
April 26 only
(See separate entry)

THE OLD CHEQUER
Mr & Mrs H Linley.
April 26 and June 14
(See separate entry)

PORCH HOUSE
Mr & Mrs Johnson.
April 26 only

SNUGBOROUGH MILL
Mr Rupert Williams-Ellis.
June 14 only
01386 701310
rupert.williams-
ellis@talk21.com

WOODRUFF
Mr Paul & Mrs Maggie Adams.
April 26 and June 14

This popular historic hillside village
has a great variety of high quality,
well-stocked gardens - large and
small, old and new. Blockley Brook,
an attractive stream which flows right
through the village, graces some of
the gardens; these incl gardens of
former water mills, with millponds
attached. From some gardens there
are wonderful rural views. Shuttle
coach service provided. Children
welcome but close supervision
required. Access to some gardens
quite steep and allowances should be
made.

The beautiful garden at Barnsley House . . .

12 ◆ BOURTON HOUSE
GARDEN
Bourton-on-the-Hill GL56 9AE. Mr
& Mrs R Quintus, 01386 700754,
info@bourtonhouse.com,
www.bourtonhouse.com. *2m W of
Moreton-in-Marsh. On A44.* Tea in
C16 Tithe Barn. **Adm £6, chd free.
For NGS: Sun 16 Aug (10-5).** For
other opening times and
information, please phone or see
garden website.
Award winning 3 acre garden
featuring imaginative topiary, wide
herbaceous borders with many rare,
unusual and exotic plants, water
features, unique shade house and
many creatively planted pots.
Fabulous at any time of year but
magnificent in summer months. New:
Walk in 7 acre pasture with free guide
to specimen tree planting available to
garden visitors. Featured in Garden
Answers and Country Life. 70%
access for wheelchairs.

Berrys Place Farm

13▶ 25 BOWLING GREEN ROAD
Cirencester GL7 2HD. Fr John &
Susan Beck, 01285 653778,
sjb@beck-hems.org.uk. *On NW
edge of Cirencester. Take A435 to
Spitalgate/Whiteway T-lights, turn into
The Whiteway [Chedworth turn], then
1st L into Bowling Green Rd.* **Adm
£3, chd free. Sun 5 July (2-5); Mon
6 July (11-4); Sun 12 July (2-5);
Mon 13 July (11-4). Visitors also
welcome by arrangement June &
July maximum group size 35-40.**
Wander at will along winding
walkways and billowing borders in a
mini jungle of heavenly hemerocallis,
gorgeous grasses, curvaceous
clematis, romantic roses and hopeful
hostas to glimpse friendly frogs and a
graceful giraffe, rated by visitors as a
wonderful hidden gem (and even as
'cool' by the young!).

🐸 ❀

BRETFORTON MANOR
See Worcestershire.

14▶ BROCKWORTH COURT
Court Road, Brockworth GL3 4QU.
Tim & Bridget Wiltshire, 01452
862938,
timwiltshire@hotmail.co.uk. *6m E of
Gloucester. 6m W of Cheltenham. Adj
St Georges Church on Court Rd.
From A46 turn into Mill Lane, turn R,
L, R at T junctions. From Ermin St,
turn into Ermin Park, then R at r'about
then L at next r'about.* Home-made
teas in tithe barn. Light refreshments
available for groups. **Adm £6, chd
free. Wed 27 May, Wed 24 June,
Wed 9 Sept (2-5.30). Visitors also
welcome by arrangement May to
Sept, house tour available for
groups of 10+.**
This intense yet informal tapestry style
garden beautifully complements the
period manor house which it
surrounds. Organic, with distinct
cottage-style planting areas that
seamlessly blend together. Natural
pond, which is home to moorhens,
with Monet bridge leading to small
island with thatched Fiji house.
Kitchen garden once cultivated by the

monks. Historic tithe barn. Views to
Crickley and Coopers Hill. Adjacent
Norman Church (open). Vintage
Tractors. Featured in Cotswold Life,
on Cotswold TV and in The Citizen
paper. Partial wheelchair access.

♿ ❀ ☕

15▶ CAMPDEN HOUSE
Chipping Campden GL55 6UP. The
Hon Philip & Mrs Smith. *Entrance
on Chipping Campden to Weston
Subedge Rd (Dyers Lane), approx ¼
m SW of Campden, 1¼ m drive. Do
not use SatNav.* Tea. **Combined adm
£5, chd free. Wed 10, Wed 17 June
(2-6); Wed 9 Sept (2-5). Combined
with The Ernest Wilson Memorial
Garden.**
2 acres featuring mixed borders of
plant and colour interest around
house and C17 tithe barn (neither
open). Set in fine parkland in hidden
valley with lakes and ponds.
Woodland walk, vegetable garden.
Gravel paths, steep slopes.

♿ 🐸 ☕

16 CHARINGWORTH COURT
Broadway Road, Winchcombe
GL54 5JN. Susan & Richard
Wakeford, 01242 603033,
susanwakeford@googlemail.com,
www.charingworthcourtcotswolds
garden.com/. *8m NE of Cheltenham.
400 metres N of Winchcombe town
centre car park in Bull Lane; walk
down Chandos St, L onto Broadway
Rd. Garden is on L or park along
Broadway Rd.* Home-made teas
from 2pm. **Adm £4, chd free.
Sat 16, Sun 17 May (11-6).** Visitors
also welcome by arrangement May
& June incl evenings.
Artistically and lovingly created 1½
acre gardens surrounding restored
Georgian/Tudor house (not open).
Relaxed country style with Japanese
influences, large pond and productive
walled vegetable garden. Mature
copper beech trees, cedar of
Lebanon and wellingtonia; and
younger trees replacing an earlier
excess of cupressus leylandii. Garden
will be backdrop for garden sculpture
selling exhibition.

**17 ◆ THE COACH HOUSE
GARDEN**
Ampney Crucis, Cirencester
GL7 5RY. Mr & Mrs Nicholas
Tanner, 01285 850256,
www.thecoachhousegarden.co.uk.
*3m E of Cirencester. Turn into village
from A417, immed before Crown of
Crucis Inn. Over hump-back bridge,
parking immed to R on cricket field
(weather permitting).* Home-made
teas. **Adm £5, chd free. For NGS:
Sun 10 May (2-5).** For other
opening times and information,
please phone or see garden
website.
Approx 1½ acres and full of structure
and design. Garden is divided into
rooms which incl rill garden, gravel
garden, rose garden, herbaceous
borders, green garden with pleached
lime allee and potager. Created over
last 25yrs by present owners. Rare
plant sales and garden lecture days
(www.thegenerousgardener.co.uk).
Limited wheelchair access. Ramp
available to enable access to main
body of garden but some other
areas are reached via short flights of
steps.

CONDERTON MANOR
See Worcestershire.

8 native orchids, hundreds of wild flowers and Roman snails . . .

18 COTSWOLD FARM
Duntisbourne Abbots, Cirencester
GL7 7JS. Mrs Mark Birchall, 01285
821857,
iona@cotswoldfarmgardens.org.uk,
www.cotswoldfarmgardens.org.uk.
*5m NW of Cirencester off old A417.
From Cirencester L sign
Duntisbourne Abbots Services, R and
R underpass. Drive ahead. From
Gloucester L signed Duntisbourne
Abbots Services. Pass Services.
Drive L.* Home-made Teas by WI.
**Adm £5, chd free. Share to A
Rocha. Sat 30, Sun 31 May (2-5).**
Visitors also welcome by
arrangement.
Arts and Crafts garden in lovely
position overlooking quiet valley on
descending levels with terrace
designed by Norman Jewson in
1930s. Snowdrops named and
naturalised, aconites in Feb. Winter
garden, bog garden best in May,
White border overflowing with texture
and scent. Shrubs, trees, shrub
roses. Allotments in old walled
garden, 8 native orchids, hundreds of
wild flowers and Roman snails. Family
day out. Croquet and toys on lawn.
Picnics welcome. Partial wheelchair
access.

19 DAGLINGWORTH HOUSE
Daglingworth, nr Cirencester
GL7 7AG. David & Henrietta
Howard, 01285 885626,
daglingworthhse@aol.com. *3m
from Cirencester off A417/419.
House beside church in
Daglingworth.* **Adm £6, chd free.
Visitors welcome by arrangement
Apr to Sept, groups welcome up to
25 persons.**
Walled garden, water features, temple
and grotto. Classical garden of

2 acres, views and vistas with
humorous contemporary twist.
Attractive planting, hedges, topiary
shapes, herbaceous borders.
Pergolas, woodland, pool, cascade
and mirror canal. Lovely Cotswold
village setting beside church.
Featured in Glos Echo and local
newspapers.

20 DAYLESFORD HOUSE
Daylesford GL56 0YG. Lord
Bamford & Lady Bamford, 01608
658888,
estate.office@daylesford.co.uk. *5m
W of Chipping Norton. Off A436.
Between Stow-on-the-Wold &
Chipping Norton.* Home-made teas.
**Adm £5, chd free. Wed 24 June
(1-5).**
Magnificent C18 landscape grounds
created 1790 for Warren Hastings,
greatly restored and enhanced by
present owners. Lakeside and
woodland walks within natural wild
flower meadows. Large walled
garden planted formally, centred
around orchid, peach and working
glasshouses. Trellised rose garden.
Collection of citrus within period
orangery. Secret garden with pavilion
and formal pools. Very large garden
with substantial distances to be
walked. General pathways allow
access however the terraine is not
always easy for pushing a wheelchair.

**21 ◆ DR JENNER'S HOUSE &
GARDEN**
Church Lane, Berkeley GL13 9BN.
The Jenner Trust, 01453 810631,
www.jennermuseum.com. *Mid-way
between Bristol & Gloucester just off
A38. Follow signs to Berkeley, then
brown tourist signs to Jenner
Museum.* Light refreshments. **Adm
£3.50, chd free. For NGS: Sun 22
Feb (11-4).** For other opening
times and information, please
phone or see garden website.
Informal woodland garden at former
home of Dr Edward Jenner.
Snowdrops and wild garlic guide you
around, past herb garden to Grade II*
listed Temple of Vaccinia, the 200yr
old plane tree and into vinery where
Jenner's Hampton Court Palace vine
grows. House not open for NGS.
Information sheets and children's
trails. Hot snack lunches and
afternoon teas. Full access statement
available at www.jennermuseum.
com/access.html.

Loders Gate
is a plant
lover's haven
of 1^1/$_2$ acres . . .

GROUP OPENING

22 EASTCOMBE, BUSSAGE AND BROWNSHILL GARDENS

Eastcombe GL6 7DS. *3m E of Stroud. 2m N of A419 Stroud to Cirencester rd on turning signed to Bisley & Eastcombe. Please park considerately in villages.* Teas at Eastcombe Village Hall. Cream teas/home-made cakes. **Combined adm £6, chd free.** Share to Acorns Children's Hospice; Breast Cancer Care; Hope for Tomorrow. **Sun 3, Mon 4 May (2-6).**

CADSONBURY
The Ridge, Bussage. Natalie & Glen Beswetherick

THE CHALFONT
St. Mary's Way, Brownshill. Mr & Mrs I Lambert

NEW HAWKLEY COTTAGE
Fidges Lane, Eastcombe. Mrs Helen Westendorp
www.essencegardens.co.uk

12 HIDCOTE CLOSE
Eastcombe. Mr & Mrs K Walker

HIGHLANDS
Dr Crouch's Road, Eastcombe. Helen & Bob Watkinson

1 THE LAURELS
Eastcombe. Andrew & Ruth Fraser

MIDDLEGARTH
Bussage Hill, Bussage. Peter Walker

REDWOOD
Bussage. Rita Collins

ROSE COTTAGE
The Street, Eastcombe. Mrs Juliet Shipman

VATCH RISE
Eastcombe, Stroud. Peggy Abbott

A group of gardens, medium and small, set in picturesque hilltop location. Some approachable only by foot. (Exhibitions may be on view in Eastcombe village hall). Glos Plant Heritage may have a sale of plants at Eastcombe Village Hall. There may also be other small plant sales in some gardens. Please visit the NGS website www.ngs.org.uk for further information.

23 EASTLEACH HOUSE

Eastleach Martin, Cirencester GL7 3NW. Mrs David Richards, garden@eastleachhouse.com, www.eastleachhouse.com. *5m NE of Fairford, 6m S of Burford. Entrance opp church gates in Eastleach Martin. Lodge at gate and driveway is quite steep up to house.* Refreshments at Victoria Inn, Eastleach, must book. **Visitors welcome by arrangement May to Sept for any size group.** Large traditional all-yr-round garden. Wooded hilltop position with long views S and W. New parkland, lime avenue and arboretum. Wild flower walk, wildlife pond, lawns, walled and rill gardens, with modern herbaceous borders, yew and box hedges, iris and paeony borders, lily ponds, formal herb garden and topiary. Rambling roses into trees. Featured in Country Life. Gravel paths and some steep slopes.

24 ERNEST WILSON MEMORIAL GARDEN

Leysbourne, Chipping Campden GL55 6DL. EWMG Trust. *High St. Chipping Campden, at Leysbourne below church.* **Combined adm £5, chd free. Wed 10, Wed 17 June, Wed 9 Sept (9-6).** Combined with Campden House.
The Ernest Wilson Memorial Garden was created in 1984 in memory of Ernest Wilson, the celebrated plant hunter who was born in Chipping Campden in 1876. This small tranquil walled garden in the centre of town features entirely plants, shrubs and trees introduced by Ernest Wilson.

25 EYFORD HOUSE

Upper Slaughter, Nr Cheltenham GL54 2JN. Mrs C Heber-Percy. *2^1/$_2$ m from Stow on the Wold on B4068 Stow to Andoversford Rd.* Cream teas. **Adm £4, chd free. Wed 10, Wed 24 June (12-6).** Also open Rockliffe House.
1^1/$_2$ -acre sloping N facing garden, ornamental shrubs and trees. Laid out originally by Graham Stuart Thomas, 1976. West garden and terrace, red border, walled kitchen garden, two lakes with pleasant walks and views, boots recommended! Holy well. Walled garden now open after reconstruction.

26 FORTHAMPTON COURT

Forthampton, Tewkesbury GL19 4RD. John Yorke. *W of Tewkesbury. From Tewkesbury A438 to Ledbury. After 2m turn L to Forthampton. At Xrds go L towards Chaceley. Go 1m turn L at Xrds.* Home-made teas. **Adm £4.50, chd free. Sat 11 July (12-4).**
Charming and varied garden surrounding North Gloucestershire Medieval manor house (not open) within sight of Tewkesbury Abbey. Incl borders, lawns, roses and magnificent Victorian vegetable garden.

27 THE GABLES

Riverside Lane, Broadoak, Newnham on Severn GL14 1JE. Bryan & Christine Bamber, bryanbamber@sky.com. *1m NE of Newnham on Severn. Park in White Hart PH unsurfaced car park, to R when facing river. Walk 250 metres along rd past PH to The Gables. Access through marked field gate.* Light refreshments. **Adm £3, chd free. Sun 21 June, Sun 23 Aug (11-5). Visitors also welcome by arrangement June to Aug for groups of 10+.**
Garden was started in 2006 from a blank canvas. Large flat garden with formal lawns, colourful herbaceous borders and shrubberies. Incl wild flower meadow incorporating soft fruits and fruit trees, an allotment-size productive vegetable plot, greenhouse and composting area. All areas of garden visible for wheelchair users but with limited access.

28 GREENACRES
Hay Lane, Bibury, Cirencester
GL7 5LZ. Alan & Liz Franklin,
www.greenacresgarden.uk. *¹/₂ m W
of Bibury. From Cirencester, take
B4425 to Bibury. Take L turn 50yds
before entering Bibury signed Fosse
Cross/Chedworth. House on R.*
Home-made teas. All proceeds from
sale of teas and plants to Alzheimer's
Society. **Adm £4, chd free. Sun 31
May (2-6); Tue 2 June (1-5).**
1 acre level garden developed by
present owners over 17yrs. Trees,
shrubs, perennials and bulbs to
create large informal borders
providing variety with yr-round
interest. Focus gardens incl
courtyard, pump, pipe (alpines),
gazebo, wild/orchard, heather, coach
house and vegetables/herbs with
raised beds, polytunnel and
greenhouses. Seating integrated in
garden design. 9 hole putting course.
Featured in Gloucestershire Echo
magazine and on BBC Radio
Gloucestershire.

29 ◆ HERBS FOR HEALING
Claptons Lane (behind Barnsley
House Hotel), Barnsley GL7 5EE.
Davina Wynne-Jones, 07773
687493, www.herbsforhealing.net.
*4m NE of Cirencester. Coming into
Barnsley from Cirencester - turn R
after Barnsley House Hotel and R
again at dairy barn. Follow signs.*
Home-made teas. Teas, herb teas
and home made cakes for donations.
**Adm £4, chd free. For NGS: Sun 28
June (2-5). For other opening times
and information, please phone or
see garden website.**
Not a typical NGS garden, rural and
naturalistic. Davina, the daughter of
Rosemary Verey, has created a
unique nursery, specialising in
medicinal herbs and a tranquil
organic garden in secluded field
where visitors can enjoy the beauty of
plants and learn more about
properties and uses of medicinal
herbs. Tours of garden explaining
current and historical uses of the
plants. Access to WC is difficult for
wheelchair users.

30 ◆ HIDCOTE MANOR GARDEN
Hidcote Bartrim, Chipping
Campden, nr Mickleton GL55 6LR.
National Trust, 01386 438333,
www.nationaltrust.org.uk/hidcote.
4m NE of Chipping Campden. Off
B4081. **Adm £10.45, chd £5.22. For
NGS: Sat 4 July (10-6). For other
opening times and information,
please phone or see garden
website.**
One of England's great gardens. 10¹/₂
acre Arts and Crafts masterpiece
created by Major Lawrence Johnston.
Series of outdoor rooms, each with a
different character, separated by walls
and hedges of many different
species. Rare trees, shrubs,
outstanding herbaceous borders, and
unusual plant species from all over
the world. Motorised buggies
available to borrow. One or two areas
not completely accessible to
wheelchairs.

31 HIGHNAM COURT
Highnam, Gloucester GL2 8DP. Mr
and Mrs R J Head,
www.HighnamCourt.co.uk. *2m W of
Gloucester. On A40/A48 from
Gloucester.* Light refreshments in
Orangery. **Adm £5, chd free. Suns 5
Apr, 3 May, 14 June, 5 July, 2 Aug,
6 Sept (11-5).**
40 acres of Victorian landscaped
gardens surrounding magnificent
Grade I house (not open), set out by
artist Thomas Gambier Parry. Lakes,
shrubberies and listed Pulhamite
water gardens with grottos and
fernery. Exciting ornamental lakes,
and woodland areas. Extensive 1
acre rose garden and many features,
incl numerous wood carvings. Some
gravel paths and steps to refreshment
area. Disabled WC.

32 HILLES HOUSE
Sevenleaze Lane, nr Painswick
GL6 6NN. Mr Matthew Reid
(Gardener), www.hilleshouse.co.uk.
*From Gloucester, take B4073
towards Painswick and turn R into
Sevenleaze Lane. From Stroud take
A4173 and turn R into Sevenleaze
Lane at Edge.* Home-made teas.
**Adm £3, chd free. Mon 31 Aug
(2-5).**
Small Arts and Crafts garden with
spectacular views towards the Black
Mountains, Malverns and Shropshire
Hills. Laid out exactly 100 yrs ago by
architect Detmar Blow, in a series of
elegant rectangles comprising yew
hedges, lawns and herbaceous
borders with planting inspired by
palette and patterns of Morris & Co.
House is currently home to his
grandson, also called Detmar Blow.
Teas served in main hall. Picnickers

welcome. Access via steep track and
steps within garden. Featured in
Country Life.

33 HODGES BARN
Shipton Moyne, Tetbury GL8 8PR.
Mr & Mrs N Hornby, 01666 880202,
hornby@cernocapital.com. *3m S of
Tetbury. On Malmesbury side of
village.* **Adm £10, chd free. Sun 31
May, Mon 1 June (2-6). Visitors
also welcome by arrangement Apr
to July for groups.**
Very unusual C15 dovecote
converted into family home. Cotswold
stone walls host climbing and
rambling roses, clematis, vines,
hydrangeas and together with yew,
rose and tapestry hedges create
formality around house. Mixed shrub
and herbaceous borders, shrub
roses, water garden, woodland
garden planted with cherries,
magnolia and spring bulbs. Some
gravel, mostly grass.

34 HOME FARM
Newent Lane, Huntley GL19 3HQ.
Mrs T Freeman, 01452 830210,
torill@ukgateway.net. *4m S of
Newent. On B4216 ¹/₂ m off A40 in
Huntley travelling towards Newent.*
**Adm £3, chd free. Suns 1, 15 Feb,
15 Mar, 12, 26 Apr (11-4) 2015;
Suns 31 Jan, 14 Feb 2016 (11-3).
Visitors also welcome by
arrangement Jan to Apr.**
Set in elevated position with
exceptional views. 1m walk through
woods and fields to show carpets of
spring flowers. Enclosed garden with
fern border, sundial and heather bed.
White and mixed shrub borders.
Stout footwear advisable in winter.

35 HOOKSHOUSE POTTERY

Hookshouse Lane, Tetbury GL8 8TZ. **Lise & Christopher White,** hookshousepottery.co.uk. *2½ m SW of Tetbury. Follow signs from A433 at Hare and Hounds Hotel, Westonbirt. Alternatively take A4135 out of Tetbury towards Dursley and follow signs after ½ m on L.* Home-made teas. **Adm £3.50, chd free. Sat 23, Sun 24, Mon 25, Tue 26, Wed 27, Thur 28, Fri 29, Sat 30, Sun 31 May (11-6).**
Garden offers a combination of dramatic open perspectives and intimate corners. Planting incl wide variety of perennials, with emphasis on colour interest throughout the seasons. Borders, shrubs, woodland glade, water garden containing treatment ponds (unfenced) and flowform cascades. Kitchen garden with raised beds, orchard. Sculptural features. Run on organic principles. Pottery showroom with hand thrown wood-fired pots incl frostproof garden pots. Art & Craft exhibition incl garden furniture and sculptures. Garden games and tree house. Apart from 1 small area, garden fully accessible to wheelchairs.

Dramatic open perspectives and intimate corners . . .

36 ◆ KEMPSFORD MANOR

High Street, Kempsford GL7 4EQ. **Mrs Z I Williamson,** 01285 810131, www.kempsfordmanor.com. *3m S of Fairford. Take A419 from Cirencester or Swindon. Kempsford is signed 10m (approx) from each. Manor is in centre of village.* Home-made teas. **Adm £4, chd free. For NGS: Sun 8, Sun 15, Wed 18 Feb, Suns 1, 8 Mar, 12 Apr, 10, 17 May, 7, 14 June, 5 July, 9, 16 Aug, 14, 28 Feb 2016 (2-5). For other opening times and information, please phone or see garden website.**
Early spring garden with variety of bulbs incl snowdrop walk along old canal followed by a lovely display of tulips and other spring bulbs. Roses and herbacious borders to follow.

Occasional musical events, art exhibitions, occasional talks on gardening. Canal path unsuitable for wheelchairs. Disabled parking at garden entrance. WC in house with 2 steps up.

37 ◆ KIFTSGATE COURT

Nr Chipping Campden GL55 6LN. **Mr & Mrs J G Chambers,** 01386 438777, www.kiftsgate.co.uk. *4m NE of Chipping Campden. Adj to Hidcote NT Garden. 3m NE of Chipping Campden.* Home-made teas. **Adm £8, chd £2.50. For NGS: Mon 13 Apr, Mon 10 Aug (2-6). For other opening times and information, please phone or see garden website.**
Magnificent situation and views, many unusual plants and shrubs, tree peonies, hydrangeas, abutilons, species and old-fashioned roses incl largest rose in England, Rosa filipes Kiftsgate. Featured in BBC Great British Garden Revival and BBC Gardens from the Air. Steep slopes and uneven surfaces.

38 LITTLEFIELD GARDEN

Hawling, Cheltenham GL54 5SZ. **Mr & Mrs George Wilk.** *From A40 Cheltenham to Oxford at Andoversford turn onto A436 towards Stow-On-The-Wold. Take 2nd signed rd to Hawling.* Home-made teas. **Adm £4, chd free. Sun 28 June, Sun 5 July (11-5).**
Surrounded by idyllic countryside with fine views over small valley, site of old medieval village of Hawling, Littlefield Garden was originally designed by Jane Fearnley-Whittingstall. More recently the planting in the yew walk was created by Sherborne Gardens. Rose garden, mixed borders, lily pond, wildflower meadow and lavender borders. Visitors can stroll 200yds across meadow to natural pond or have tea and relax under the pergola. Featured in Cotswold Life, Gloucestershire Echo and on BBC Radio Gloucestershire. Mostly wheelchair access. Gravel path and paved terraces.

39 NEW LODERS GATE

Fairford Road, Downington, Lechlade GL7 3DL. **Mr Jim Pymer.** *½ m from centre of Lechlade off A417 to Fairford. Turn R into gravel drive 100yds past West Alcott sign.* Light refreshments. **Adm £5. Wed 17**

June, Wed 16 Sept (1-4.30).
Loders Gate is a plant lover's haven of 1½ acres. Front garden with long deep borders of herbaceous plants, ornamental grasses and yew hedging, is repeated in walled garden to rear of house. Beyond is large garden with 2 wildlife ponds, small wooded area, greenhouse, lawns, mature trees, rose garden and long herbaceous and shrub borders.

GROUP OPENING

40 LONGHOPE GARDENS

Longhope GL17 0NA, 01452 830406, sally.j.gibson@btinternet.com. *10m W of Gloucester. 6m E of Ross on Wye. A40 take Longhope turn off to Church Rd. From A4136 follow Longhope signs and turn onto Church Rd. Parking available on Church Rd.* Home-made teas. **Combined adm £5, chd free. Sat 30 May (12-5); Sun 31 May (2-6); Sat 13 June (12-5); Sun 14 June (2-6). Visitors also welcome by arrangement May & June for groups of 5+.**

NEW CHESSGROVE COTTAGE
Chessgrove Lane, Longhope. **Mr Peter Evans.**
Access via very steep single track lane, parking available in orchard next to garden

3 CHURCH ROAD
Longhope. **Rev Clive & Mrs Linda Edmonds**

SPRINGFIELD HOUSE
Station Lane, Longhope. **Sally & Martin Gibson**

NEW WOODBINE COTTAGE
Church Road, Longhope. **Mrs Lucille Roughley.**
Opp recreation ground

Small village, sited in valley, with wonderful views and splendid C12 church. 4 well planted gardens, with different planting styles, 2 open for first time. Ample parking in village or if you're feeling energetic you can walk to all gardens. Refreshments and plant sales available at some gardens. 3 Church Road: long garden divided into rooms with large collection of hardy geraniums. Springfield House: large enclosed terraced garden with wide variety of shrubs and trees mingling with sweeping borders and a wildlife

pond. Woodbine Cottage: tranquil garden with traditional planting. Chessgrove Cottage: delightful garden with spectacular views and access to 12 acres of surrounding woodland.

41 LOWER FARM HOUSE
Cliffords Mesne, Newent GL18 1JT. Gareth & Sarah Williams. *2m S of Newent. From Newent, follow signs to Cliffords Mesne and Birds of Prey Centre (1¹/₂ m). Approx ¹/₂ m beyond Centre, turn L at Xrds (before church).* Home-made teas. **Adm £4, chd free. Mon 25, Wed 27 May (2-6).**
2 acre garden, incl woodland, stream and large natural lily pond with rockery and bog garden. Herbaceous borders, pergola walk, terrace with ornamental fishpond, kitchen and herb garden; Collections of irises, hostas and paeonies. Many interesting and unusual trees and shrubs incl. magnolias and cornus. Some gravel paths.

42 ♦ LYDNEY PARK SPRING GARDEN
Lydney GL15 6BU. The Viscount Bledisloe, 01594 842844/842922, www.lydneyparkestate.co.uk. *¹/₂ m SW of Lydney. On A48 Gloucester to Chepstow rd between Lydney & Aylburton. Drive is directly off A48.* Home-made teas. Light lunches. **Adm £5, chd £0.50. For NGS: Wed 6 May (10-5).** For other opening times and information, please phone or see garden website.
Spring garden in 8 acre woodland valley with lakes, profusion of rhododendrons, azaleas and other flowering shrubs. Formal garden; magnolias and daffodils (April). Picnics in deer park which has fine trees. Important Roman Temple site and museum.

43 NEW THE MANOR
Little Compton, Moreton-In-Marsh GL56 0RZ. Mr T Morgan. *Next to church in little Compton. 1m from A44 and then 2m from A3400 follow signs to Little Compton and then pick up yellow NGS signs.* Home-made teas. **Adm £5, chd free. Sat 18 July (2-5).**
C16 historic manor house (not open) and 4 acres of stunning gardens set in a beautiful location in village of

Little Compton. Enjoy the many garden rooms, the long herbaceous borders, deer walk, Japanese garden, flower garden, arboretum and specimen trees. Garden staff on site, croquet and tennis courts available to play.

44 ♦ MATARA GARDENS OF WELLBEING
Kingscote, Tetbury GL8 8YA. Herons Mead Ltd, 01453 861050, www.matarawellbeing.com. *5¹/₂ m NW of Tetbury. Approx 20mins from either J18 of M4 (12m) or J13 of M5 (8.5m).* Home-made teas. **Adm £5, chd free. For NGS: Sun 7 June (1-5).** For other opening times and information, please phone or see garden website.
Trees of life - enjoy the tranquil beauty of Matara's Gardens of Wellbeing and its dedication to the symbolic, spiritual and cultural role of trees. What makes us special are our Chinese scholar garden, Japanese tea garden, Shinto woodland, Celtic wishing tree, labyrinth, healing spiral, field of dreams and ornamental herb and flower gardens. Woodland walk, Chinese cloistered courtyard, barefoot trail, ponds, strolling walk,

walled garden and vegetable garden. Limited wheelchair access. Some steps around house area. Some grass paths.

45 THE MEETING HOUSE
New Road, Flaxley, Newnham GL14 1JS. Chris & Sally Parsons, 01452 760733. *Off A48, close to Westbury-on-Severn. S from Westbury-on-Severn, turn R signed Flaxley. Take 2nd L. 1st house on L. Park in field. Parking for coaches 500yds away (drop off at garden).* **Adm £5, chd free. Visitors welcome by arrangement** Apr to Sept, please leave clear message on answering machine.
Cottage with 2 acres developed by owners over last 20 yrs. Hedges, lawns, herbaceous borders, organic fruit trees, soft fruit and vegetables, greenhouse, orchard with wild flowers, reed bed sewage system and summerhouse. Also open: surrounding 17 acres of wild flower meadows, old and new orchards and ponds, managed for conservation. Featured in Gloucestershire Citizen - We're All Wild At Heart.

Painswick Rococo Garden
© Heather Edwards

4 acres of stunning gardens set in a beautiful location . . .

46 ♦ MILL DENE GARDEN

School Lane, Blockley, Moreton-in-Marsh GL56 9HU. Mr & Mrs B S Dare, 01386 700457, info@milldenegarden.co.uk, www.milldenegarden.co.uk. *3m NW of Moreton-in-Marsh. From A44 follow brown signs from Bourton-on-the-Hill to Blockley. Approx 1¹/₄ m down hill turn L behind village gates. Limited parking. Coaches by appt.* Tea. 15 March Mothering Sunday 2 - 5, book a special tea early: limited numbers. Entry incl tea £14. **Adm £7 excl tea, chd free. For NGS: Sun 15 Mar, Sun 17 May (2-5). For other opening times and information, please phone or see garden website.**

50 shades of green (!) at least in this 2¹/₂ acre garden hidden in the Cotswolds. Centrepiece is water mill dating from C10 (probably), with mill pond and stream. The owners have had fun creating a varied garden, from informal woodland full of bulbs, to rose walk, cricket lawn, then herb garden looking out over hills with church as backdrop. Garden trail for children. Booklet re development of garden available £2.50. Featured in Countryfile & Love your Garden. Half of garden wheelchair accessible. Please ring for reserved parking/ramps. Garden in a valley but sides have slope or step alternatives.

  ♿ 🚲 ☕

47 ♦ MISARDEN PARK

Miserden, Stroud GL6 7JA. Major M T N H Wills, 01285 821303, www.misardenpark.co.uk. *6m NW of Cirencester. Follow signs off A417 or B4070 from Stroud.* Home-made teas on terrace. **Adm £6, chd free. For NGS: Sun 5 Apr, Sun 21 June**

(2-5). For other opening times and information, please phone or see garden website.

This lovely, unspoilt garden, positioned high on the Wolds and commanding spectacular views was created in C17 and still retains a wonderful sense of timeless peace and tranquillity. Perhaps finest features in garden are double 92metre mixed border incl roses and clematis, in different colour sections. Much of original garden is found within ancient Cotswold stone walls. Partial access for wheelchairs.

♿ ❀ 🚲 ☕

48 MOOR WOOD

Woodmancote GL7 7EB. Mr & Mrs Henry Robinson, 01285 831692, susie@moorwoodhouse.co.uk. *3¹/₂ m NW of Cirencester. Turn L off A435 to Cheltenham at North Cerney, signed Woodmancote 1¹/₄ m; entrance in village on L beside lodge with white gates.* Home-made teas. **Adm £4, chd free. Sun 28 June (2-6). Visitors also welcome by arrangement June.**

2 acres of shrub, orchard and wild flower gardens in beautiful isolated valley setting. Holder of National Collection of Rambler Roses. Not recommended for wheelchairs.

 ☕

GROUP OPENING

49 NEW NAILSWORTH GARDENS - OFF CHESTNUT HILL

Nailsworth GL6 0RN. *4m S of Stroud. From A46 at mini r'about turn up Springhill then immed L onto Old Market, Park in Nailsworth, Chestnut Hill is further 200yds on R. Chestnut Close is up hill on L.* Light refreshments in Floris House. Tea, coffee, squash and cake. **Combined adm £4, chd free. Sun 21 June (1-6).**

> **NEW FLORIS HOUSE**
> Elly Austin

> **NEW SPRINGFIELDS**
> Mr Andrew Joyce

2 gardens on steep hill both offering completely different designs, features and planting. Featured in Gloucester Citizen. Both Gardens on steep hill so many steps.

☕

50 THE OLD CHEQUER

Draycott, Moreton in Marsh GL56 9LB. Mr & Mrs H Linley, 01386 700647, g.f.linley1@btinternet.com. *3m NW of Moreton-in-Marsh. Off the Moreton-in-Marsh to Evesham Rd A44. Through Blockley.Turn R by cemetery to Draycott.* Home-made teas. **Adm £3, chd free. Sun 12 Apr (2-5). Also open with Blockley Gardens on 26 April and 14 June. Visitors also welcome by arrangement Apr to July for groups of 10+.**

Cottage garden, created by owner, set in 2 acres of old orchard with original ridge and furrow. Emphasis on spring planting but still maintaining yr-round interest. Kitchen garden/soft fruit, herbaceous, shrubs, Croquet lawn, unusual plants, alpines and dry gravel borders.

♿ ❀ ☕

51 THE OLD RECTORY, DUNTISBOURNE ROUS

Cirencester GL7 7AP. Charles & Mary Keen, mary@keengardener.com. *4m NW of Cirencester. From Daglingworth take rd to Duntisbournes. Or from A417 from Gloucester take Duntisbourne Leer turning, follow signs for Daglingworth.* Tea in schoolroom DIY teas or coffee with a fire in winter. **Adm £5, chd free. Sat 14 Feb, Mon 11 May (12-4.30). Visitors also welcome by arrangement Feb to Sept for groups of 10+ and short talk from Mary Keen.**

Garden in an exceptional setting made by designer and writer Mary Keen. Subject of many articles and Telegraph column. Designed for atmosphere and all yr interest, but collections of galanthus, hellebores, auriculas and half hardies - especially dahlias - are all features in their season. Snowdrops and auriculas for sale. Difficult access for wheelchairs but a shortened version of garden is possible, find me for help.

❀ 🚲 ☕

OVERBURY COURT

See Worcestershire.

52 ♦ PAINSWICK ROCOCO GARDEN

Painswick GL6 6TH. Painswick Rococo Garden Trust, 01452 813204, www.rococogarden.org.uk. *¹/₂ m N of Painswick. ¹/₂ m outside village on*

B4073, follow brown tourism signs.
For opening times and information, please phone or see garden website.
Unique C18 garden from the brief Rococo period, combining contemporary buildings, vistas, ponds, kitchen garden and winding woodland walks. Anniversary maze, plant nursery. Snowdrop display late winter. Limited wheelchair access to garden due to it being set in a valley. Disabled access to WC and restaurant.

53 PASTURE FARM
Upper Oddington, Moreton-In-Marsh GL56 0XG. Mr & Mrs John LLoyd, 01451 830203, ljmlloyd@yahoo.com. *Mid-way between Upper and Lower Oddington. Oddington lies about 3m from Stow-on-the-Wold just off A436.* Home-made teas. **Adm £4, chd free. Sun 24, Mon 25 May (11-5.30).** **Visitors also welcome by arrangement Apr to Oct.**
Medium sized informal country garden that has evolved over 30yrs by current owners. It has all-yr interest with mixed borders, topiary, hedging both formal and informal, orchard and wealth of garden trees. In rural setting with very large spring fed pond inhabited by collection of ducks. Large plant stalls of herbaceous, shrubs and vegetables (proceeds to Kate's Home Nursing). Public footpath across 2 small fields arrives at C11 church, St. Nicholas, with doom paintings, set in ancient woodlands. Truly worth a visit. See Simon Jenkins' Book of Churches. Featured in Glos Echo. Coaches by appt only on open days.

54 PAULMEAD
Bisley GL6 7AG. Judy & Philip Howard. *5m E of Stroud. S edge of Bisley at head of Toadsmoor Valley on top of Cotswolds. Signed from Bisley village.* Disabled visitors can be dropped off at garden. Home-made teas. **Adm £6, chd free. Sun 21 June (2-6).** Combined with Wells Cottage, combined entry fee £6.00.
Approx 1 acre landscaped garden constructed in stages over last 25yrs. Terraced in 3 main levels: natural stream garden; formal herbaceous and shrub borders; yew and beech hedges; formal vegetable garden; lawns; summerhouse with exterior

wooden decking by pond and thatched roof over well head. Unusual tree house.

55 PEAR TREE COTTAGE
58 Malleson Road, Gotherington GL52 9EX. Mr & Mrs E Manders-Trett, 01242 674592, edandmary@talktalk.net. *4m N of Cheltenham. From A435, travelling N, turn R into Gotherington 1m after end of Bishop's Cleeve bypass at garage. Garden on L approx 100yds past Shutter Inn.* Light refreshments. **Adm £4, chd free. Sun 29 Mar (2-5).** **Visitors also welcome by arrangement Mar to June for 30 max.**
Mainly informal country garden of approx ½ acre with pond and gravel garden, grasses and herbaceous borders, trees and shrubs surrounding lawns. Wild garden and orchard lead to greenhouses, herb and vegetable gardens. Spring bulbs, early summer perennials and shrubs particularly colourful. Several small steps and some narrow paths.

56 PEMBERLEY LODGE
Churchend Lane, Old Charfield GL12 8LJ. Rob & Yvette Andrewartha, 01454 260885, www.gryfindor.info/ourgarden.html. *3m S of Wotton-under-Edge. From M5 take J14 towards Wotton-under-Edge. At r'about take 2nd exit on to Churchend Lane. Garden approx 600 metres on R.* Light refreshments. **Visitors welcome by arrangement Apr to Sept, prior notice required, for groups of 10+.**
Small private garden planted to delight all yr round. Garden wraps round house and has been densely planted for interest and low maintenance. It incorporates trees, shrubs, perennials, grasses, water, gravel, lawns and hard landscaping to give an informal and peaceful feel. Roof garden added in 2006. New garden area added in 2010/11. Roof garden not accessible.

GROUP OPENING

57 QUENINGTON GARDENS
nr Fairford GL7 5BW. *8m NE of Cirencester. Gardens well signed once in village.* Home-made teas at The Old Rectory. **Combined adm £5, chd free. Sun 21 June (2-5.30).**

THE OLD POST HOUSE
Mrs D Blackwood

THE OLD RECTORY, QUENINGTON
Church Rd. Mr & Mrs David Abel Smith
www.freshairsculpture.com

POOL HAY
Mrs E A Morris

YEW TREE COTTAGES
Mr J Lindon

A rarely visited Coln Valley village delighting its infrequent visitors with C12 Norman church and C17 stone cottages (not open). An opportunity to discover the horticultural treasures behind those Cotswold stone walls and visit 4 very different but charming gardens incorporating everything from the exotic and the organic to the simple cottage garden; a range of vistas from riverside to seclusion. Fresh Air 2015 sculpture show.

hospiceUK
Visit a garden and support hospice care

58 RAMBLERS
Lower Common, Aylburton, nr Lydney GL15 6DS. Jane & Leslie Hale. *1½ m W of Lydney. Off A48 Gloucester to Chepstow Rd. From Lydney through Aylburton, out of de-limit turn R signed Aylburton Common, ¾ m along lane.* Home-made teas. **Adm £3.50, chd free. Sun 3 May, Sun 14 June (1.30-5.30).**
Peaceful medium sized country garden with informal cottage planting, herbaceous borders and small pond looking through hedge windows onto wild flower meadow. Front woodland garden with shade loving plants and topiary. Large productive vegetable garden. Apple orchard. Winner of The English Garden magazine's competition Britain's Best Gardener's Garden for 2014.

Herbs for Healing

© P

RIVER BARN
See Wiltshire.

59 ▶ **ROCKCLIFFE HOUSE**
Upper Slaughter, Cheltenham
GL54 2JW. **Mr & Mrs Simon**
Keswick. *2m SW of Stow-on-the-*
Wold. 1¹/₂ m from Lower Swell on
B4068 towards Cheltenham. Leave
Stow on the Wold on B4068 through
Lower Swell. Continue on B4068 for
1¹/₂ m. Rockcliffe is well signed on L.
Teas £3.50. **Adm £5, chd free.**
Share to Kates Home Nursing.
Wed 10, Wed 24 June (12-6). Also
open Eyford House.
Large traditional English garden of 8
acres incl pink garden, white and blue
garden, herbaceous border, rose
terrace, large walled kitchen garden
and orchard. Greenhouses and
pathway of topiary birds leading up
through orchard to stone dovecot.
Dramatic pond surrounded by
6 large cornus contraversa
variegata. Featured in several
magazines. 2 wide stone steps
through gate, otherwise good
wheelchair access.

60 ◆ **RODMARTON MANOR**
Cirencester GL7 6PF. **Mr Simon**
Biddulph, 01285 841442,
www.rodmarton-manor.co.uk. *5m*
NE of Tetbury. Off A433. Between
Cirencester & Tetbury. Home-made
teas. **Adm £5, chd £1. For NGS:**
Sun 17 May (2-5). For other
opening times and information,
please phone or see garden
website.
The 8 acre garden of this fine Arts
and Crafts house (not open on NGS
day) is a series of outdoor rooms
each with its own distinctive
character. Leisure garden, winter
garden, troughery, topiary, hedges,
lawns, rockery, containers, wild
garden, kitchen garden, magnificent
herbaceous borders. Snowdrop
collection. Wheelchair access to most
of garden.

61 ▶ **ROSE COTTAGE**
Kempley, Nr Dymock GL18 2BN.
Naomi Cryer. *3m from Newent*
towards Dymock. From Newent on
B4221 take turning just after PH, on
R from Gloucester direction, signed
Kempley. Follow rd for approx 3m.

Home-made teas. **Adm £3.50, chd**
free. Sat 13, Sun 14 June, Sat 12,
Sun 13 Sept (11-5).
Open this year in June and in dahlias
time. About 1 acre of flat garden, put
mostly to herbaceous borders. Hot
bed and long border leading to
borrowed view, small parterre in
orchard area, grass bed and pond.
Small wild flower pasture, at its best
in June. Rose garden, iris bed,
hydrangea bed, over 200 dahlias,
vegetable plot, nursery bed and
cutting garden. Home made cakes
and plants for sale. Featured in
Gloucester Citizen. Although quite
flat, access mostly via lawn and grass
which may make wheelchair use
difficult.

SANDYWELL. BARN HOUSE
See Barn House, Sandywell

62 ◆ **SEZINCOTE**
nr Moreton-in-Marsh GL56 9AW.
Mr & Mrs D Peake, 01386 700444,
www.sezincote.co.uk. *3m SW of*
Moreton-in-Marsh. From Moreton-in-
Marsh turn W along A44 towards
Evesham; after 1¹/₂ m (just before

Bourton-on-the-Hill) turn L, by stone lodge with white gate. Home-made teas. **Adm £5, chd free. For NGS: Sun 28 June (2-6). For other opening times and information, please phone or see garden website.**
Exotic oriental water garden by Repton and Daniell with lake, pools and meandering stream, banked with massed perennials. Large semi-circular orangery, formal Indian garden, fountain, temple and unusual trees of vast size in lawn and wooded park setting. House in Indian manner designed by Samuel Pepys Cockerell. Garden on slope with gravel paths, so not all areas wheelchair accessible.

63 SLAD VALLEY HOUSE
203 Slad Road, Stroud GL5 1RJ. Mr & Mrs Michael Grey. *Situated in Slad Valley 1m W of Stroud on rd to Slad. Follow B4070 along valley towards Stroud. House is situated on R through gates up steep gravel drive. From Stroud drive 1m on B4070 towards Slad. Parking on Slad Road.* Home-made teas. **Adm £3.50, chd free. Sat 6, Sun 7 June (12-4).**
Delightful informal steep terraced garden and woodland area of approx 1 acre around C18 manor house (not open). Garden restoration work in progress in all areas. Numerous trees (incl 2 magnificent magnolia trees), shrubs, flowers and well stocked borders being developed. NB lots of steps and uneven paths, no handrails. The garden is a chosen site for local art exhibitions. Unsuitable for wheelchairs.

64 ◆ SNOWSHILL MANOR & GARDEN
Snowshill, nr Broadway WR12 7JU. National Trust, 01386 842810, www.nationaltrust.org.uk. *2¹/₂ m SW of Broadway. Off A44 bypass into Broadway village.* Light refreshments. **Adm £6.10, chd £3.10 June; £3.50, chd free Feb. For NGS: Fri 26 June (11-5); Sat 13, Sun 14 Feb 2016 (2-4). For other opening times and information, please phone or see garden website.**
Delightful hillside garden surrounding beautiful Cotswold manor, designed in Arts & Crafts style. Garden consists of a series of contrasting outdoor rooms. Simple, colourful plantings tumble and scramble down the terraces and around byres and

ponds. Enjoy produce from kitchen garden in restaurant. Garden produce and plants for sale (when available). In Feb see the snowdrops, cultivated by the garden team over many years. Enjoy warming refreshments in our tearoom. Not suitable for wheelchairs as garden is terraced with many steps.

65 SOUTH LODGE
Church Road, Clearwell, Coleford GL16 8LG. Andrew & Jane MacBean, 01594 837769, southlodgegarden@btinternet.com, www.southlodgegarden.co.uk. *2m S of Coleford. Off B4228. Follow signs to Clearwell. Garden on L of castle driveway. Please park on rd in front of church or in village.* Home-made teas. **Adm £3.50, chd free. Sat 11 Apr, Sun 3, Sat 30 May, Sun 21 June (1-5). Visitors also welcome by arrangement Apr to June for groups of 15+.**
Peaceful country garden in 2 acres with stunning views of surrounding countryside. High walls provide a backdrop for rambling roses, clematis, and honeysuckles. Organic garden with large variety of perennials, annuals, grasses, shrubs and specimen trees with yr-round colour. Vegetable garden, wildlife and formal ponds. Rustic pergola planted with English climbing roses and willow arbour amongst wild flowers. Gravel paths and steep slopes.

66 STANTON VILLAGE GARDENS
Stanton, nr Broadway WR12 7NE. Group Opening. *3m S of Broadway. Off B4632, between Broadway (3m) & Winchcombe (6m).* Home-made teas in Burland Hall in centre of village & in several open gardens. **Adm £6, chd free. Share to local charities. Sun 14 June (2-6).**
Over 20 gardens open in this picturesque Cotswold village. Many houses border the street with long gardens behind, hidden from general view. Gardens range from large houses with colourful herbaceous borders, established trees, shrubs and formal vegetable gardens, to tiny cottage gardens packed with interest. Some also have natural water features. Popular plant stall and legendary homemade teas. Regret not all gardens suitable for wheelchair users.

67 ◆ STANWAY FOUNTAIN & WATER GARDEN
nr Winchcombe GL54 5PQ. The Earl of Wemyss & March, 01386 584528, www.stanwayfountain.co.uk. *9m NE of Cheltenham. 1m E of B4632 Cheltenham to Broadway rd or B4077 Toddington to Stow-on-the-Wold rd.* Home-made teas. **Adm £7, chd free. For NGS: Sun 10 May, Sun 6 Sept (2-5). For other opening times and information, please phone or see garden website.**
20 acres of planted landscape in early C18 formal setting. The restored canal, upper pond and 165ft high fountain have re-created one of the most interesting Baroque water gardens in Britain. Striking C16 manor with gatehouse, tithe barn and church. Britain's highest fountain at 300ft, the world's highest gravity fountain which runs at 2.45 & 4.00pm for 30 mins each time. Limited wheelchair access in garden, some flat areas, able to view fountain and some of garden. House is not wheelchair suitable.

Rustic pergola planted with English climbing roses . . .

68 18 STAR LANE
Avening, Tetbury GL8 8NT. Anita Collins. *3m NW of Tetbury off B4014. SE on B4014 from Nailsworth. NW on B4014 from Tetbury 3m. A419 from Cirencester 6.5m. 1st exit at r'about. L at Ragged Cot. L at junction.* Home-made teas in cottage garden. **Adm £3, chd free. Sun 7 June (2-6).**
Hillside garden overflowing with cottage garden plants in calming pastel colours. Steps lead up garden from cosy seating area and winding paths and borders draw visitors to different areas incl rose circle, pond, hotbed and wooded area with lovely views across the valley. A romantic plant lover's paradise grown over time on a limited budget.

69 STOWELL PARK
Yanworth, Northleach, Cheltenham
GL54 3LE. The Lord & Lady Vestey,
www.stowellpark.co.uk. *8m NE of
Cirencester. Off Fosseway A429 2m
SW of Northleach.* Home-made teas.
Adm £6, chd free. Sun 10 May, Sun
21 June (2-5).
Magnificent lawned terraces with
stunning views over Coln Valley. Fine
collection of old-fashioned roses and
herbaceous plants, with pleached
lime approach to C14 house (not
open). Two large walled gardens
containing vegetables, fruit, cut
flowers and range of greenhouses.
Long rose pergola and wide, plant
filled borders divided into colour
sections. New water features and
hazel arch at bottom of garden. Open
continuously for 50yrs.

Peaceful sitting
areas . . . enjoy the
plants or simply
relax in
contemplation . . .

70 TRENCH HILL
Sheepscombe GL6 6TZ. Celia &
Dave Hargrave, 01452 814306,
celia.hargrave@btconnect.com.
*1¹⁄₂ m E of Painswick. From
Cheltenham A46 take 1st turn signed
Sheepscombe and follow lane
towards Sheepscombe for about
1¹⁄₄ m. Garden on L opp lane.* Home-
made teas. Adm £4, chd free. Sun
15, Sun 22 Feb (11-5); Sun 5, Mon
6 Apr, Sun 10 May (11-6); Weds 3,
10, 17, 24 June (2-6); Suns 19 July,
30 Aug, 13 Sept (11-6); Suns 14,
21 Feb 2016 (11-5). Visitors also
welcome by arrangement Feb to
Oct, not suitable for large coaches
max 42 seater.
Approx 3 acres set in small woodland
with panoramic views. Variety of
herbaceous and mixed borders, rose
garden, extensive vegetable plots,
wild flower areas, plantings of spring
bulbs with thousands of snowdrops
and hellebores, woodland walk, 2
small ponds, waterfall and larger

conservation pond. Interesting
wooden sculptures, many within the
garden. Run on organic principles.
Featured in Country Homes and
Interiors. Mostly wheelchair access
but some steps and slopes.

71 UPTON WOLD
Moreton-in-Marsh GL56 9TR. Mr &
Mrs I R S Bond, 01386 700667,
www.uptonwoldgarden.co.uk.
*4¹⁄₂ m W of Moreton-in-Marsh. On
A44 1m past A424 junction at
Troopers Lodge Garage, on R. Look
out for marker posts.* Home-made
teas. Adm £10, chd free. Sun 19
Apr (11-5). Visitors also welcome
by arrangement Apr to Sept.
Ever developing and changing
garden, architecturally and
imaginatively laid out around C17
house (not open) with commanding
views. Yew hedges, herbaceous
walk, some unusual plants and trees,
vegetables, pond and woodland
gardens, labyrinth. National
Collections of Juglans and
Pterocarya. 2 Star award from GGG.
NCH

72 WELLS COTTAGE
Wells Road, Bisley GL6 7AG. Mr &
Mrs Michael Flint, 01452 770289,
flint_bisley@talktalk.net. *5m N E of
Stroud. Gardens & car park well
signed in Bisley village. Gardens on S
edge of village at head of Toadsmoor
Valley, N of A419.* Adm £6, chd free.
Sun 21 June (2-6). Combined with
Paulmead, combined entry fee
£6.00.
Just under 1 acre. Terraced on
several levels with beautiful views
over valley. Much informal planting of
trees and shrubs to give colour and
texture. Lawns and herbaceous
borders. Collection of grasses.
Formal pond area. Rambling roses on
rope pergola. Vegetable garden with
raised beds. No access to upper
terraces for wheelchair users.

**73 ♦ WESTBURY COURT
GARDEN**
Westbury-on-Severn GL14 1PD.
National Trust, 01452 760461,
www.nationaltrust.org.uk. *11m SW
of Gloucester on A48. look for the
brown tourist signs as you enter the
village of Westbury on Severn.* Adm
£5.50, chd £2.70. For NGS: Sun 13
Sept (10-5). For other opening
times and information, please
phone or see garden website.

The finest example of a Dutch water
garden in the country. Wheelchair
access to most of garden.

**74 ♦ WESTONBIRT SCHOOL
GARDENS**
Tetbury GL8 8QG. Holfords of
Westonbirt Trust, 01666 880333,
jbaker@holfordtrust.com,
www.holfordtrust.com. *3m SW of
Tetbury. Opp Westonbirt Arboretum,
on A433. Enter via Holford wrought
iron gates to Westonbirt House.* Tea,
coffee & biscuits in Great Hall. Adm
£8, chd free. For NGS: Sun 19 July
(11-5). For other opening times and
information, please phone or see
garden website.
28 acres. Former private garden of
Robert Holford, founder of Westonbirt
Arboretum. Formal Victorian gardens
incl walled Italian garden now
restored with early herbaceous
borders and exotic border. Rustic
walks, lake, statuary and grotto. Rare,
exotic trees and shrubs. Beautiful
views of Westonbirt House open with
guided tours to see fascinating
Victorian interior on designated days
of the year. Tea, coffee and biscuits
available on NGS and Open House
and Garden Days. Afternoon tea with
sandwiches and scones available for
pre-booked private tours - groups of
10-60. Only some parts of garden
accessible to wheelchairs. Ramps
and lift allow access to house.

WHITCOMBE HOUSE
See Worcestershire.

75 NEW WHITE HOUSE
Chapel Lane, Mickleton, Chipping
Campden GL55 6SD. Mr & Mrs
James Bend. *2m NW of Chipping
Campden. Approaching Mickleton
heading N on B4632, turn L into
Chapel Lane by Three Ways House
Hotel. After 100yds White House can
be found on the L opp Butchers
Arms PH.* Tea. Adm £3.50, chd free.
Sat 6, Sun 7, Sun 14 June (11-4).
An Arts & Crafts inspired cottage
garden encircling the house and
arranged in a series of informal
rooms. Incl rose garden, holly-pop
walk, sunken terrace and collection of
topiary faces originally established by
artist Richard Sorrell. Garden has
been designed to offer peaceful
sitting areas from which to enjoy the
plants or simply relax in
contemplation.

76 **WOODLANDS FARM**
Rushley Lane, Winchcombe
GL54 5JE. Mrs Morag Dobbin,
01242 604261. *On N side of
Winchcombe, just off B4632. Rushley
Lane comes off B4632 through
Winchcombe, at Footbridge. Proceed
up Rushley Lane for 50yds, gate is
behind Stancombe Lane sign.
Parking available in field next to
garden.* **Adm £4, chd free. Wed 10,
Sun 14, Wed 17, Sun 21 June
(10-4). Visitors also welcome by
arrangement May to Sept min 6,
max 20.**
1½ acre garden with generously
sized garden rooms. The planting and
landscaping are both thoughtful and
tranquil. Generous borders
throughout with colourful and
harmonious planting schemes. Tall
hornbeam hedge creates dramatic
vista to stone monolith. Long
contemporary pond. New prairie style
border, roses, delphiniums, cottage
borders. Wheelchair assistance
needed with one steepish slope to
access garden.

77 **NEW** **WORTLEY HOUSE**
Wortley, Wotton-Under-Edge
GL12 7QP. Simon and Jessica
Dickinson. *1m from Wotton-under-
Edge. Full directions will be provided
with ticket. Pre booking essential by
phoning 01483 211535 or visit
www.ngs.org.uk. Tea.* **Adm £15, chd
free. Tue 23 June (2-5).**
This diverse garden of over 20 acres
has been created through the last 30
yrs by current owners and incl walled
garden, pleached lime avenues, nut
walk, potager, ponds, Italian garden,
shrubberies and wild flower
meadows. Follies urns and statues
have been strategically placed
throughout to enhance extraordinary
vistas, and the garden has been filled
with plants, arbours, roses through
trees and up walls and herbaceous
borders. The stunning surrounding
countryside is incorporated into the
garden with views up the steep valley
that are such a feature in this part of
Gloucestershire. Wheelchair access
to most areas of the garden, golf
buggy available as well.

GROUP OPENING

78 **WYCK RISSINGTON
GARDENS**
Cheltenham GL54 2PN. *Nr Stow-
on-the-Wold & Bourton-the-
Water. 1m from Fosse Way A429.*
Home-made teas in village hall.
**Combined adm £6, chd free. Share
to Friends of St Laurence. Sun 6
Sept (1-5).**

CHESTNUT COURT
Mrs Georgina Hampton.
*Walk up road on L of pond, turn L
between 2 houses, Chestnut
Court on R with silver post box*

GREENFIELDS FARM
Andrew & Elizabeth Ransom

LAURENCE HOUSE
Wyck Rissington. Mr & Mrs
Robert Montague.
*Off A429 between Bourton-on-
the-Water & Stow-on-the-Wold.
Last house in village behind high
bank on R*

MACES COTTAGE
Tim & Pippa Simon

An unspoilt Cotswold village set
round wide village green planted with
fine horse chestnuts. The gardens are
within easy reach of convenient
parking and of contrasting styles. You
will find inspiration for autumn
planting and can delight in the mellow
hues of September. A popular group
opening providing an enjoyable
afternoon in a perfect Cotswold
setting. Plant sale, garden produce,
and subject to the season, honey for
sale. Greenfields featured in Cotswold
Life. Wheelchair access available at
all gardens.

Laurence House, Wyck Rissington Gardens

© Val Corbett

Raising millions for charity since 1927

HAMPSHIRE

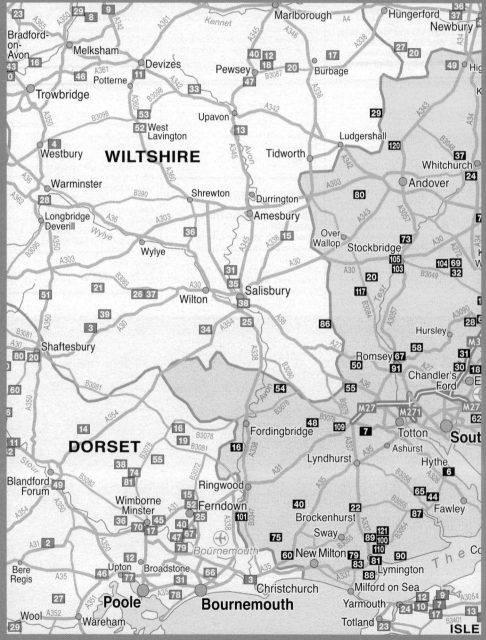

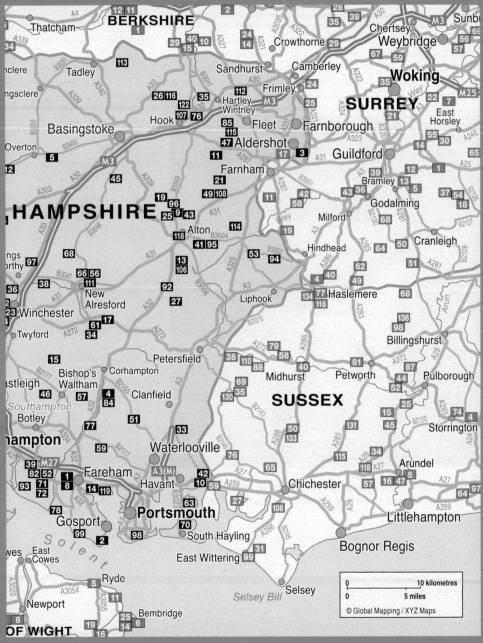

Hampshire

Hampshire is a large, diverse county. The landscape ranges from clay/gravel heath and woodland in the New Forest National Park in the south west, across famous trout rivers – the Test and Itchen – to chalk downland in the east, where you will find the South Downs National Park.

Our open gardens are spread right across the county, and offer a very diverse range of interest for both the keen gardener and the casual visitor.

We have a large number of gardens with rivers running through them, such as those in Longstock, Bere Mill, Dipley Mill and Weir House; gardens with large vegetable kitchen gardens such as Dean House and Bramdean House; and unique gardens such as Hanging Hosta Gardens which has over 1300 hosta cultivars.

You will be assured of a warm welcome by all our garden owners and we hope you enjoy your visits.

Since our foundation we have donated more than £42.5 million to charity

Hampshire Volunteers

County Organiser
Mark Porter 01962 791054
markstephenporter@gmail.com

County Treasurer
Fred Fratter 01962 776243
fred@tanglefoot-house.demon.co.uk

Publicity
Mark Porter
(as above)

Booklet Coordinator
Mark Porter
(as above)

Assistant County Organisers

Central East
Sue Alexander 01962 732043
suealex13@gmail.com

Central West
Patricia Elkington 01962 776365
elkslc@btinternet.com

East
Linda Smith 01329 833253
linda.ngs@btinternet.com

North
Cynthia Oldale 01420 520438
c.k.oldale@btinternet.com

North East
Mary Trigwell-Jones 01420 83389
mary.trigwell-jones@virgin.net

North West
Carol Pratt 01264 710 305
carolacap@yahoo.co.uk

South
Barbara Sykes 02380 254521
barandhugh@aol.com

South West
Elizabeth Walker 01590 677415
elizabethwalker13@gmail.com

West
Christopher Stanford 01425 652133
stanfordsnr@gmail.com

Above: Weir House © Ellen Rooney

Opening Dates

All entries subject to change.
For latest information check www.ngs.org.uk

January

79 The Mill at Gordleton (every Monday)

February

79 The Mill at Gordleton (every Monday)

Sunday 15
17 Bramdean House

Friday 20
69 Little Court

Sunday 22
38 The Down House
69 Little Court

Tuesday 24
69 Little Court

March

79 The Mill at Gordleton (every Monday)

Sunday 15
12 Bere Mill
46 Flintstones
69 Little Court

Wednesday 25
11 Beechenwood Farm

Thursday 26
23 12 Christchurch Road

Sunday 29
23 12 Christchurch Road
40 Durmast House

April

11 Beechenwood Farm (every Wednesday)
79 The Mill at Gordleton (every Monday excl Bank Hols)

Sunday 5
90 Pylewell Park

Monday 6
32 Crawley Gardens
100 Spinners Garden

Tuesday 7
32 Crawley Gardens

Saturday 18
67 The Island
95 'Selborne'

Sunday 19
17 Bramdean House
67 The Island
85 Old Thatch & The Millennium Barn
95 'Selborne'
99 Spindles

Saturday 25
6 Atheling Villas
81 Moore Blatch
108 Walbury

Sunday 26
6 Atheling Villas
81 Moore Blatch
107 Tylney Hall Hotel
108 Walbury

May

11 Beechenwood Farm (every Wednesday)
79 The Mill at Gordleton (every Monday excl Bank Hols)

Friday 1
9 NEW Bavins

Saturday 2
9 NEW Bavins
70 Littlewood

Sunday 3
30 The Cottage
70 Littlewood
92 Rotherfield Park

Monday 4
5 Ashe Park
30 The Cottage
94 Sandy Slopes

Thursday 7
69 Little Court
104 Tanglefoot

Saturday 9
19 Brick Kiln Cottage
61 Hinton Ampner

Sunday 10
19 Brick Kiln Cottage
30 The Cottage
65 The House in the Wood
69 Little Court
97 NEW Shroner Wood
104 Tanglefoot
105 Terstan
110 Walhampton

Monday 11
30 The Cottage
107 Tylney Hall Hotel

Saturday 16
22 21 Chestnut Road
71 NEW 99 Locks Heath Park Road
72 NEW 101 Locks Heath Park Road

93 NEW 2 Sampan Close
95 'Selborne'

Sunday 17
22 21 Chestnut Road
33 Crookley Pool
54 Heathermoor House
60 Hinton Admiral
71 NEW 99 Locks Heath Park Road
72 NEW 101 Locks Heath Park Road
93 NEW 2 Sampan Close
95 'Selborne'

Saturday 23
28 30 Compton Way
39 7 Downland Close
52 NEW Hambrooks Show Gardens (Evening)
62 NEW Hollybrook

Sunday 24
7 Aviemore
13 Berry Cottage
28 30 Compton Way
35 Dipley Mill
39 7 Downland Close
48 Fritham Lodge
62 NEW Hollybrook
80 Monxton & Amport Gardens
86 Ordnance House
90 Pylewell Park
91 Romsey Gardens
106 The Thatched Cottage
109 Waldrons
113 West Silchester Hall

Monday 25
39 7 Downland Close
80 Monxton & Amport Gardens
91 Romsey Gardens
94 Sandy Slopes
113 West Silchester Hall

Lots of ideas for the smaller garden . . .

Wednesday 27
28 30 Compton Way
34 Dean House

Saturday 30
2 Alverstoke Crescent Garden
62 NEW Hollybrook

Sunday 31
46 Flintstones
62 NEW Hollybrook
77 Meon Orchard
96 Shalden Park House

June

79 The Mill at Gordleton (every Monday)

Monday 1
46 Flintstones

Tuesday 2
112 NEW West Green House Gardens

Wednesday 3
76 1 & 2 Maple Cottage
11 Beechenwood Farm

Thursday 4
33 Crookley Pool
76 1 & 2 Maple Cottage

Festival Weekend

Saturday 6
6 Atheling Villas
12 Bere Mill
49 Froyle Gardens
61 Hinton Ampner
74 NEW Lower Norton Farmhouse

Sunday 7
6 Atheling Villas
12 Bere Mill
15 Blackdown House
49 Froyle Gardens
74 NEW Lower Norton Farmhouse
76 1 & 2 Maple Cottage
98 Southsea Gardens
107 Tylney Hall Hotel

Tuesday 9
47 Four Seasons Hotel

Wednesday 10
4 Appletree House
76 1 & 2 Maple Cottage

Thursday 11
32 Crawley Gardens
68 Lake House
76 1 & 2 Maple Cottage

Saturday 13
22 21 Chestnut Road
101 The Stable Family Home Trust Garden

Over 400 Volunteers help run the NGS – why not become one too?

Sunday 14
13 Berry Cottage
17 Bramdean House
22 21 Chestnut Road
24 NEW 2 Church Cottages
31 Cranbury Park
32 Crawley Gardens
35 Dipley Mill
36 The Dower House
37 NEW Down Farm House
68 Lake House
101 The Stable Family Home Trust Garden
106 The Thatched Cottage

Tuesday 16
3 23 Anglesey Road

Wednesday 17
24 NEW 2 Church Cottages
34 Dean House
37 NEW Down Farm House

Thursday 18
103 Stockbridge Gardens

Saturday 20
39 7 Downland Close
88 Pennington House
118 NEW 42 Whitedown
119 Wicor Primary School Community Garden

Sunday 21
8 19 Barnwood Road
39 7 Downland Close
42 Emsworth Gardens
45 Farleigh House
73 Longstock Park
88 Pennington House
99 Spindles
103 Stockbridge Gardens
105 Terstan
118 NEW 42 Whitedown

Tuesday 23
47 Four Seasons Hotel

Wednesday 24
4 Appletree House
13 Berry Cottage (Evening)
106 The Thatched Cottage (Evening)

Thursday 25
117 NEW The White House

Saturday 27
41 East Worldham Gardens
67 The Island
120 Wildhern Gardens

Sunday 28
27 Colemore House Gardens
29 Conholt Park
38 The Down House

40 Durmast House
41 East Worldham Gardens
67 The Island
117 NEW The White House
120 Wildhern Gardens

Monday 29
27 Colemore House Gardens

July

79 The Mill at Gordleton (every Monday)

Wednesday 1
5 Ashe Park
21 Bury Court
34 Dean House
38 The Down House

Thursday 2
32 Crawley Gardens
108 Walbury

Saturday 4
26 The Coach House
61 Hinton Ampner
98 Southsea Gardens (Evening)

Sunday 5
5 Ashe Park
16 Braemoor
25 Clover Farm
32 Crawley Gardens
35 Dipley Mill
105 Terstan
119 Wicor Primary School Community Garden

Monday 6
25 Clover Farm

Tuesday 7
47 Four Seasons Hotel

Sunday 12
10 7 Beacon Square
13 Berry Cottage
84 Old Droxford Station
106 The Thatched Cottage
113 West Silchester Hall
122 1 Wogsbarne Cottages

Monday 13
122 1 Wogsbarne Cottages

Tuesday 14
3 23 Anglesey Road

Wednesday 15
4 Appletree House

Saturday 18
22 21 Chestnut Road
82 NEW 4 Nightingale Mews
83 Oak Tree Cottage

Sunday 19
16 Braemoor
17 Bramdean House
22 21 Chestnut Road
34 Dean House
78 Michaelmas
82 NEW 4 Nightingale Mews
83 Oak Tree Cottage
85 Old Thatch & The Millennium Barn

Monday 20
78 Michaelmas

Tuesday 21
47 Four Seasons Hotel

Thursday 23
104 Tanglefoot

Saturday 25
14 8 Birdwood Grove
41 East Worldham Gardens
55 Hideaway

Sunday 26
29 Conholt Park
41 East Worldham Gardens
55 Hideaway
77 Meon Orchard
104 Tanglefoot
121 Willows

Tuesday 28
112 NEW West Green House Gardens (Evening)

Thursday 30
56 Hill House

Large collection of herbs and plants of botanical and historical interest . . .

August

79 The Mill at Gordleton (every Monday excl Bank Hols)

Saturday 1
20 The Buildings
44 Fairweather's Nursery
82 NEW 4 Nightingale Mews
95 'Selborne'

Sunday 2
16 Braemoor
20 The Buildings
34 Dean House
35 Dipley Mill
44 Fairweather's Nursery
56 Hill House
63 The Homestead
82 NEW 4 Nightingale Mews
95 'Selborne'

Monday 3
95 'Selborne'

Tuesday 4
47 Four Seasons Hotel
56 Hill House

Wednesday 5
43 Fairbank

Saturday 8
121 Willows

Sunday 9
17 Bramdean House
113 West Silchester Hall
121 Willows

Wednesday 12
43 Fairbank

Sunday 16
13 Berry Cottage

Tuesday 18
47 Four Seasons Hotel

Wednesday 19
34 Dean House

Saturday 29
66 The Hyde

Sunday 30
50 Gilberts Nursery
64 NEW The Hospital of St Cross
66 The Hyde
121 Willows

Monday 31
66 The Hyde
121 Willows

September

79 The Mill at Gordleton (every Monday)

Tuesday 1
47 Four Seasons Hotel

Saturday 5
20 The Buildings
61 Hinton Ampner

Sunday 6
17 Bramdean House
20 The Buildings
77 Meon Orchard
85 Old Thatch & The
Millennium Barn
102 **NEW** Stanford
House
105 Terstan

Saturday 12
71 **NEW** 99 Locks
Heath Park Road
72 **NEW** 101 Locks
Heath Park Road
114 Wheatley House

Sunday 13
12 Bere Mill
35 Dipley Mill
71 **NEW** 99 Locks
Heath Park Road
72 **NEW** 101 Locks
Heath Park Road
111 Weir House
114 Wheatley House

Tuesday 15
47 Four Seasons Hotel

Sunday 20
45 Farleigh House
57 Hill Top

Tuesday 22
3 23 Anglesey Road

Tuesday 29
47 Four Seasons Hotel

October
79 **The Mill at
Gordleton (every
Monday)**

Sunday 4
107 Tylney Hall Hotel

Saturday 17
52 **NEW** Hambrooks
Show Gardens
(Evening)

November
79 **The Mill at
Gordleton (every
Monday)**

Gardens open to the public
2 Alverstoke Crescent
Garden
58 Hillier Gardens
61 Hinton Ampner
64 **NEW** The Hospital of
St Cross
75 Macpennys Woodland
Garden & Nurseries
87 Patrick's Patch
100 Spinners Garden
112 **NEW** West Green
House Gardens

By arrangement only
1 80 Abbey Road
18 6 Breamore Close
51 Hambledon House
53 Hanging Hosta Garden
59 2 Hillside Cottages
89 Pilley Hill Cottage
115 Whispers

Also open by arrangement
3 23 Anglesey Road
4 Appletree House
6 Atheling Villas
7 Aviemore
8 19 Barnwood Road
11 Beechenwood Farm
12 Bere Mill
13 Berry Cottage
14 8 Birdwood Grove
15 Blackdown House
16 Braemoor
17 Bramdean House
19 Brick Kiln Cottage
20 The Buildings
21 Bury Court
22 21 Chestnut Road
23 12 Christchurch Road
29 Conholt Park
30 The Cottage
33 Crookley Pool

35 Dipley Mill
38 The Down House
39 7 Downland Close
40 Durmast House
43 Fairbank
46 Flintstones
47 Four Seasons Hotel
48 Fritham Lodge
54 Heathermoor House
55 Hideaway
56 Hill House
57 Hill Top
63 The Homestead
66 The Hyde
67 The Island
68 Lake House
69 Little Court
77 Meon Orchard
78 Michaelmas
83 Oak Tree Cottage
86 Ordnance House
91 4 Mill Lane, Romsey
Gardens
95 'Selborne'
97 **NEW** Shroner Wood
99 Spindles
104 Tanglefoot
105 Terstan
106 The Thatched Cottage
108 Walbury
111 Weir House
113 West Silchester Hall
114 Wheatley House
121 Willows

The Gardens

1 **80 ABBEY ROAD**
Fareham PO15 5HW. Brian &
Vivienne Garford, 01329 843939,
vgarford@aol.com. *1m W of
Fareham. From M27 J9 take A27 E to
Fareham for approx 2m. At top of hill,
turn L at lights into Highlands Rd.
Turn 4th R into Blackbrook Rd. Abbey
Rd is 4th L.* Light refreshments.
Visitors welcome by arrangement
Apr to Sept for groups of 30 max.
Unusual small garden with large
collection of herbs and plants of
botanical and historical interest, many
for sale. Box hedging provides
structure for relaxed planting.
Interesting use of containers and
ideas for small gardens. Two ponds
and tiny meadow for wildlife. A
garden trail for children. Living willow
seat, summerhouse, and trained
grapevine.

2 **♦ ALVERSTOKE CRESCENT
GARDEN**
Crescent Road, Gosport
PO12 2DH. Gosport Borough
Council, 01329 313359,
www.alverstokecrescentgarden.
co.uk. *1m S of Gosport. From A32 &
Gosport follow signs for Stokes Bay.
Continue alongside bay to small
r'about, turn L into Anglesey Rd.
Crescent Garden signed 50yds on R.*
Adm by donation. **For NGS: Sat 30
May (10-4).** For other opening
times and information, please
phone or see garden website.
Restored Regency ornamental
garden, designed to enhance fine
crescent (Thomas Ellis Owen 1828).
Trees, walks and flowers lovingly
maintained by community and council
partnership. Garden's considerable
local historic interest highlighted by
impressive restoration and creative
planting of adjacent St Mark's
churchyard. Worth seeing together.
Heritage, history and horticulture, a
fascinating package. Plant sale and
refreshments. Green Flag Award.

3 **23 ANGLESEY ROAD**
Aldershot GU12 4RF. Adrian &
Elizabeth Whiteley, 01252 677623.
*On E edge of Aldershot. Off A331
take A323 Aldershot. In quick
succession, R at 1st T-light North
Lane, 1st L Lower Newport Rd, L
bend, immed R Newport Rd, 1st R
Wilson Rd, L bend, 1st R Roberts Rd.
Anglesey Rd 1st L.* Home-made teas.
Adm £2.50, chd free. Tue 16 June,
Tue 14 July, Tue 22 Sept (2-5).
**Visitors also welcome by
arrangement** Apr to Oct for groups
of 15 max.
A garden so packed with intriguing
plants combining hardy with exotic,
rare with commonplace, bold with
petite, that the curious visitor hardly
notices its diminutive size. Ferns,
hollies, asters and large tender
perennials feature strongly. Leisurely
close inspection is richly rewarded, so
linger over tea and a chat, and maybe
be inspired to leave with something
unfamiliar to grow at home.

Bring a bag for plants – help us give more to charity

The Buildings

4 APPLETREE HOUSE

Station Road, Soberton SO32 3QU. Mrs J Dover, 01489 877333, jennie.dover@yahoo.co.uk. *10m N of Fareham. A32 to Droxford, at Xrds turn onto B2150. Turn R under bridge into Station Rd, garden 1m. Parking in lay-by 300yds or on the road.* Light refreshments. **Adm £3, chd free.** Wed 10, Wed 24 June, Wed 15 July (12-4). **Visitors also welcome by arrangement June to Aug with light lunches on request.**

Designed to look larger than its 40ftx90ft, this garden has both a shady woodland style area and also sunny areas allowing a variety of planting, which incl a large collection of Clematis viticella. Winding paths lead to different views across the garden and of the meadows beyond. Lots of ideas for the smaller garden.

5 ASHE PARK

nr Ashe, Overton RG25 3AF. Graham & Laura Hazell. *2m E of Overton. Entrance on B3400, approx 500yds W of Deane Gate Inn.* Home-made teas. **Adm £5, chd free.** Mon 4 May, Wed 1, Sun 5 July (2-6).

Extensive new gardens within the grounds of a Georgian Country House and Estate, with further development in progress. Parkland and specimen trees, woodland and bluebell walks, large contemporary potager, lime avenue and several newly planted areas. Featured in the Private View section of the English Garden magazine (June 2014), written by Deborah Curtis with photographs by Marianne Majerus.

6 ATHELING VILLAS

16 Atheling Road, Hythe, Southampton SO45 6BR. Mary & Peter York, 02380 849349, athelingvillas@gmail.com. *W side of Southampton Water. At M27 J2, take A326 for Hythe & Fawley. Cross all r'abouts until Dibden r'about. L to Hythe. After Shell garage take 2nd L & immed R.* Home-made teas in the Old Laundry. **Adm £3, chd free. Share to The Children's Society.** Sat 25, Sun 26 Apr, Sat 6, Sun 7 June (2-5). **Visitors also welcome by arrangement Apr to June for groups of 10+.**

Inspirational, imaginatively designed and comprehensively planted ⅓ acre Victorian villa garden, this yr celebrating its 10th yr of opening for the NGS. Explore meandering paths set amongst structural planting and delight in the flowering trees and shrubs (many rare), bulbs and herbaceous planting of this tranquil and welcoming garden. Several seating areas throughout garden. Features incl a self-guide leaflet, children's quiz, and a display of original art by owners in Garden Room Gallery. Featured in the Mail on Sunday gardening supplement, and an online Australian magazine 'A Magazine'.

7 AVIEMORE

Chinham Road, Bartley, Southampton SO40 2LF. Sandy & Alex Robinson, 02380 813651. *3m N of Lyndhurst, 7m W of Southampton. From M27 J1 go towards Lyndhurst on A337. After ¾ m turn L to Bartley & follow NGS signs.* Home-made teas. **Adm £3.50, chd free.** Sun 24 May (1.30-5). **Visitors also welcome by arrangement Apr to June with refreshments on request.**

Richly planted, small garden in north New Forest. Our aim is to please the plant connoisseur and introduce enthusiasts to new plants and ideas for smaller plots. Every plant must play its part within a seasonal symphony of shrubs, climbers, perennials and grasses. Oak bridges criss-cross a small stream. Old alpine troughs and quirky artifacts add texture, structure and colour to this yr-round garden. No wheelchair access to some gravel and stream areas.

8 19 BARNWOOD ROAD
Fareham PO15 5LA. Jill & Michael
Hill, 01329 842156,
Jillhillflowers@icloud.com. *1m W of
Fareham. M27 J9, A27 towards
Fareham. At top of Titchfield Hill, L at
T-lights, 4th R Blackbrook Rd, 4th R
Meadow Bank. Barnwood Rd is off
Meadow Bank. Please consider
neighbours when parking.* Home-
made teas. **Adm £3, chd free.**
Sun 21 June (11-4). Visitors also
welcome by arrangement May to
July for groups of 10-20.
Step through the gate to an
enchanting garden designed for
peace with an abundance of floral
colour and delightful features. Greek
style courtyard leads to natural pond
with bridge and bog garden,
complemented by a thatched
summerhouse and jetty, designed
and built by owners. Secret
pathways, hexagonal greenhouse
and new mosaic seating area.
Featured in Women's Weekly (May
2014).

9 NEW BAVINS
New Odiham Road, Shalden, Alton
GU34 5SX. Mrs Jennifer Ospici,
www.bavins.co.uk. *On the corner of
Stancombe Lane & the B3349 2½ m
N of Alton.* Light refreshments.
Adm £5, chd free. Fri 1, Sat 2 May
(11-4).
A unique 100 acre ancient bluebell
woodland. If you are a keen walker
you will have much to explore on the
long meandering paths and rides
dotted with secluded seats. Those
who enjoy a more leisurely pace will
experience the perfume of the carpet
of blue, listen to the birdsong and
watch the contrasting light through
the trees nearer to the entrance of
the woods. Refreshments will be served
in an original rustic wooden building
and incl soups using natural
woodland ingredients.

10 7 BEACON SQUARE
Emsworth PO10 7HU. Annette &
Michael Wood. *½ m W of Emsworth
village. From Emsworth village, take
A259 towards Havant. Take 3rd L
(Warblington Rd). After about 200yds,
turn L into Seafields, R at end of
road, garden around corner on L.*
Light refreshments. **Adm £3.50, chd
free.** Sun 12 July (10-1.30).
7 Beacon Square is an award-
winning, medium sized, sheltered
garden close to the sea. Exuberant,

densely planted, herbaceous beds
and borders in soft, pastel colours,
creating an ambiance of peace and
tranquillity. Tree ferns, fruit trees,
herbs, pond and small sculptures.
Seating areas designed for sun or
shade. Small raised beds with
vegetables, herbs and salad leaves.
Small greenhouse and a
summerhouse. Owner has designed
and built a garden at the Hampton
Court Palace Flower Show which
won a silver medal. Stained glass
work on display and for sale.

11 BEECHENWOOD FARM
Hillside, Odiham RG29 1JA. Mr &
Mrs M Heber-Percy, 01256 702300,
beechenwood@totalise.co.uk. *5m
SE of Hook. Turn S into King St from
Odiham High St. Turn L after cricket
ground for Hillside. Take 2nd R after
1½ m, modern house ½ m.* Home-
made teas. **Adm £4, chd free.**
Every Wed 25 Mar to 3 June (2-5).
Visitors also welcome by
arrangement Mar to June.
2 acre garden in many parts. Lawn
meandering through woodland with
drifts of spring bulbs. Rose pergola
with steps, pots with spring bulbs
and later aeoniums. Fritillary and
cowslip meadow. Walled herb garden
with pool and exuberant planting.
Orchard incl white garden and hot
border. Greenhouse and vegetable
garden. Rock garden extending to
grasses, ferns and bamboos. Shady
walk to belvedere. 8 acre copse of
native species with grassed rides.
Help available with gravel drive, and
some avoidable shallow steps.

12 BERE MILL
London Road, Whitchurch
RG28 7NH. Rupert & Elizabeth
Nabarro, 01256 892210,
rnabarro@aol.com. *9m E of
Andover, 12m N of Winchester. In
centre of Whitchurch, take London
Rd at r'about. Uphill 1m, turn R
50yds beyond The Gables on R.
Drop-off point for disabled at garden.*
Home-made teas. **Adm £5, chd free.**
Share to Smile Train. Sun 15 Mar,
Sat 6, Sun 7 June, Sun 13 Sept
(1.30-5). Visitors also welcome by
arrangement Feb to Oct for groups
of 10+.
Sits beside the fast flowing Upper
Test, surrounded by water meadows
and wooded valleys. Herbaceous
borders, bog and Mediterranean
plants as well as a replanted orchard

and two small arboretums; features
early bulbs, species tulips, Japanese
prunus, peonies, wisteria, irises and
roses. At heart it aims to complement
the natural beauty of the site, and to
incorporate elements of oriental
garden design and practice. The
working mill was where Portals first
made paper for the Bank of England
in 1716. Unfenced and unguarded
rivers and streams. Partial wheelchair
access if very wet.

Experience
the perfume
of the carpet
of blue, listen
to the
birdsong . . .

13 BERRY COTTAGE
Church Road, Upper Farringdon,
nr Alton GU34 3EG. Mrs P Watts,
01420 588318. *3m S of Alton off
A32. Turn L at Xrds, 1st L into Church
Rd. Follow road past Massey's Folly,
2nd house on R opp church.* Home-
made teas. **Adm £2.50, chd free.**
Sun 24 May, Sun 14 June (2-5.30).
Evening Opening, wine, Wed 24
June (6-8). Sun 12 July, Sun 16
Aug (2-5.30). Combined adm with
The Thatched Cottage (next door)
on 24 May, 14, 24 June, 12 July
£5.00, chd free. Visitors also
welcome by arrangement Apr to
Sept.
Small organic cottage garden with yr-
round interest. Spring bulbs, roses,
clematis and herbaceous borders.
Pond and bog garden. Shrubbery
and small kitchen garden. The owner
designed and maintained garden
surrounding C16 house (not open).
The borders are colour themed and
contain many unusual plants. Close
to Massey's Folly built by the Victorian
rector incl 80ft tower with unique
handmade floral bricks, C11 church
and some of the oldest yew trees in
the county.

14 8 BIRDWOOD GROVE

Downend, Fareham PO16 8AF.
Jayne & Eddie McBride,
01329 280838,
jayne.mcbride@ntlworld.com. *¹/₂ m
E of Fareham. M27 J11, L lane slip to
Delme r'about, L on A27 to
Portchester over 2 T-lights,
completely around small r'about,
Birdwood Grove 1st L.* Home-made
teas. **Adm £2.50, chd free.** Sat 25
July (1-5). **Visitors also welcome
by arrangement** July to Aug for
groups of 25 max.
The subtropics in Fareham! This small
garden is influenced by the flora of
Australia and New Zealand and incl
many indigenous species and plants
that are widely grown 'down under'.
The 4 climate zones; arid, temperate,
lush fertile and a shady fernery, are all
densely planted to make the most of
dramatic foliage, from huge bananas
to towering cordylines. Gold award
and category winner small
plantsman's back garden in Fareham
in Bloom. Featured garden in
Amateur Gardening (Sept 2014).
Short gravel path not suitable for
mobility scooters.

♿ 🐕 🌼 ☕

Well established
wild flower
meadow with
orchids and
butterflies . . .

15 BLACKDOWN HOUSE

Blackdown Lane, Upham
SO32 1HS. Mr & Mrs Tom Sweet-
Escott, 01962 777375,
rosamond@sweet-escott.co.uk. *5m
SE of Winchester, 5m N of Bishops
Waltham. 1m N of Upham, best
accessed off Morestead Rd Xrds with
Longwood Dean Lane from
Winchester or through the village of
Upham from Bishops Waltham.*
Cream teas. **Adm £4, chd free.**
Sun 7 June (2-6). **Visitors also
welcome by arrangement** Apr to
Oct for groups of 20+.
A 5 acre family garden. 100 metre
long colourful successional
herbaceous border set against a flint
wall. Well established wild flower
meadow with orchids and butterflies.
Part-walled working kitchen garden
with new summerhouse and orchard
with free range hens and sunny
terrace. Alpacas and Jacob sheep
roam the parkland. A constantly
evolving garden with new planting for
2015. Flautissimo (a flute quartet) will
be playing in the garden. Wheelchair
access with assistance, due to grass
slopes.

☕

16 BRAEMOOR

Bleak Hill, Harbridge, Ringwood
BH24 3PX. Tracy & John
Netherway & Judy Spratt,
01425 652983,
jnetherway@btinternet.com. *2¹/₂ m
S of Fordingbridge. Turn off A338 at
Ibsley. Go through Harbridge Village
to T-junction at top of hill, turn R for
¹/₄ m.* Home-made teas. **Adm £3.50,
chd free.** Sun 5, Sun 19 July, Sun 2
Aug (2-5.30). **Visitors also welcome
by arrangement** July to Aug.
³/₄ acre garden brimming with bold,
colourful planting and interest. One of
our moongates leads to a seaside
haven of painted beach huts and
driftwood gems. Another enters the
cottage garden with overflowing
herbaceous borders, stream and
pond. Greenhouses with cacti and
carnivorous plants. Vegetable area
with bantam chickens. Small adjacent
nursery. Some gravel paths.

♿ 🌼 🚐 ☕

17 BRAMDEAN HOUSE

Bramdean, Alresford SO24 0JU. Mr
& Mrs H Wakefield, 01962 771214,
victoria@bramdeanhouse.com. *4m
S of Alresford. In centre of village on
A272. Entrance opp sign to the
church.* Home-made teas. **Adm £5,
chd free.** Sun 15 Feb (2-4); Suns
19 Apr, 14 June, 19 July, 9 Aug,
6 Sept (2-4.30). **Visitors also
welcome by arrangement** Mar to
Oct.
Beautiful 5 acre garden famous for its
mirror image herbaceous borders.
Carpets of spring bulbs especially
snowdrops. A large and unusual
collection of plants and shrubs giving
yr-round interest. 1 acre walled
garden featuring prize-winning
vegetables, fruit and flowers. Small
arboretum. Trial of hardy Nerine
cultivars in association with RHS.
Features incl a wild flower meadow,
boxwood castle, a large collection of
old fashioned sweet peas. Home of
the nation's tallest sunflower 'Giraffe'.
Featured in Country Life, The English
Garden, The Times, Daily Mail, and
Southern TV.

♿ 🌼 ☕

18 6 BREAMORE CLOSE

Eastleigh SO50 4QB. Mr & Mrs R
Trenchard, 02380 611230,
dawndavina6@yahoo.co.uk. *1m N
of Eastleigh. M3 J12, follow signs to
Eastleigh. Turn R at r'about into
Woodside Ave, then 1st L into
Broadlands Ave (park here).
Breamore Close 3rd on L.* Home-
made teas. **Adm £3.50, chd free.**
Visitors welcome by arrangement
May to July for groups of 10+.
Delightful plant lover's garden with
coloured foliage and unusual plants,
giving a tapestry effect of texture and
colour. Many hostas displayed in pots.
The garden is laid out in
distinctive planting themes with
seating areas to sit and contemplate.
In May, magnificent wisteria over a
pergola with flowers 3ft-4ft long; in
June many clematis scramble
through roses followed by phlox in
July. Small gravel area.

♿ 🌼 🚐 ☕

19 BRICK KILN COTTAGE

The Avenue, Herriard, Nr Alton
RG25 2PR. Barbara Jeremiah,
01256 381301,
barbara@klca.co.uk. *4m NE of
Alton. A339 Basingstoke to Alton, L
along The Avenue, past Lasham
Gliding Club on R, then past Back
Lane on L & take next track on L.*
Home-made teas. **Adm £4, chd free.**
Sat 9, Sun 10 May (12-4). **Visitors
also welcome by arrangement** in
May.
Woodland garden filled with deep
blue English bluebells against the lime
green of sprouting trees. 2 acres incl
garden rooms of pebbles, rose and
vegetables, a treehouse, waterhole,
fernery, stumpery and a traditional
cottage garden filled with herbs.
Refurbished shepherd's hut with its
own garden is a new feature. Families
welcome to this wild garden in a
former brick works, with excellent
cream teas, home-made cakes,
sandwiches and pots of tea.

🐕 ☕

20 THE BUILDINGS

Broughton, Stockbridge
SO20 8BH. Dick & Gillian Pugh,
01794 301424,
richard260@btinternet.com. *3m W
of Stockbridge. NGS yellow signs 2m
W of Stockbridge off A30, or 6m N of*

Romsey off B3084. Home-made teas. **Adm £4, chd free. Share to Friends of St Mary's Broughton & St James' Bossington. Sat 1, Sun 2 Aug, Sat 5, Sun 6 Sept (2-5). Visitors also welcome by arrangement June to Sept for groups of 10+. Coaches need driver briefing.**
High on the Hampshire Downs, with wonderful views, our 1 acre offers modern planting in gravel, borders and an exuberant pergola all on thin chalk soil. At its best in late summer, it is often described as inspirational, the planting and layout widely admired. Many unusual plants and varieties especially in the Salvia, Clematis viticella, and Pelargonium families. Featured in The Garden RHS magazine (Aug 2014) and Radio Solent interview (7 Sept 2014).

21 BURY COURT
Bentley GU10 5LZ. John Coke, Jcoke46@gmail.com, www.burycourtbarn.com. *5m NE of Alton. 1m N of Bentley. Take Hole Lane, then follow signs towards Crondall.* Home-made teas. **Adm £6, chd free. Wed 1 July (2-6). Visitors also welcome by arrangement Apr to Oct.**
Designed in cooperation with Piet Oudolf, created from old farmyard, in the continental naturalistic style, making heavy use of grasses in association with perennials selected for an extended season of interest. Area designed by Christopher Bradley-Hole in minimalist style, featuring grid of gravel paths bisecting chequerboard of naturalistically planted raised squares edged in rusted steel.

22 21 CHESTNUT ROAD
Brockenhurst SO42 7RF. Iain & Mary Hayter, 01590 622009, maryiain.hayter@gmail.com, www.21-chestnut-rdgardens.co.uk. *New Forest, 4m S of Lyndhurst. At Brockenhurst turn R B3055 Grigg Lane. Limited parking, village car park nearby. Leave M27 J2, follow Heavy Lorry Route. Mainline station less than 10 mins walk.* Home-made teas. Gluten free catered for. **Adm £3.50, chd free. Sat 16 May (11-5); Sun 17 May (1-5); Sat 13 June (11-5); Sun 14 June (1-5); Sat 18 July (11-5); Sun 19 July (1-5). Visitors also welcome by arrangement May to Sept for groups of 10+.**

Welcome, in our 10th yr of opening, we have some surprises. Mature colourful borders and productive areas mingle with fantasia. Imaginative ideas for planting in different conditions, where the perennial is king. Fruit, vegetables, flowers and shrubs sympathetically blend with wildlife. There are formal and relaxed areas to enjoy home-made cakes and tea. Visit Brockenhurst Village and enjoy seeing the ponies, donkeys and cattle roam freely. Visit St Nicholas Church home to New Zealand War Graves. Some gravel areas, and no wheelchair access to raised deck or some parts of the garden when wet.

23 12 CHRISTCHURCH ROAD
Winchester SO23 9SR. Iain & Penny Patton, 01962 854272, pjspatton@yahoo.co.uk, For B&B info www.visitwinchester.com. *S side of city. Leave centre of Winchester by Southgate St, 1st R into St James Lane, 3rd L into Christchurch Rd.* Home-made teas. **Adm £3.50, chd free. Thur 26, Sun 29 Mar (2-5). Visitors also welcome by arrangement Mar to Apr for groups of 20 max.**
Small town garden with strong design enhanced by exuberant and vertical planting. All yr interest incl winter flowering shrubs, bulbs and hellebores. Two water features, incl slate edged rill and pergolas provide structure. Small front garden designed to be viewed from the house with bulbs, roses and herbaceous planting. Featured in The English Garden, Gardens Illustrated & Gardeners World. Partial wheelchair access due to small changes in levels.

24 NEW 2 CHURCH COTTAGES
Tufton, Whitchurch RG28 7RF. Jane & John Huxford. *N on A34, at Whitchurch exit, turn L off slip road, R at Xrds, house 2nd on R. From Whitchurch centre take Winchester Rd S. Before slip road bear R, turn R, turn R at Xrds, house 2nd on R.* Home-made teas. **Adm £3.50, chd free. Sun 14, Wed 17 June (1.30-5). Also open Down Farm House.**
A stone's throw from the R Test, formerly an estate cowman's cottage, the front and back is a traditional cottage garden. But there's more, through the gate in the hedge you'll

find a nursery, greenhouses, vegetables, cutting garden and small orchard. A stroll through the fields to see sheep, pigs and chickens leads to an area under development to form a walk with wild flowers in the summer.

2015 sees the NGS total to Macmillan pass £15 million

25 CLOVER FARM
Shalden Lane, Shalden, Alton GU34 4DU. Mrs Sarah Floyd. *Approx 3m N of Alton in the village of Shalden. Take A339 out of Alton. After approx 2m turn R up lane. At top turn sharp R next to church sign.* Tea. **Adm £4, chd free. Sun 5 July (1.30-5); Mon 6 July (2-4).**
3 acre garden with views to die for! Herbaceous borders and sloping lawns down to reflection pond, wild flower meadow, lime avenue, rose and kitchen garden.

26 THE COACH HOUSE
Reading Road, Sherfield on Loddon RG27 0EX. Jane & Peter Jordan. *5m N of Basingstoke. Follow A33 & signs to Sherfield on Loddon. Follow signs to free car parks. Some on-road parking. Drop off only at house.* Home-made teas. **Adm £3.50, chd free. Sat 4 July (2-5).**
A hidden gem, this 510 sq-metre walled garden has been replanted extensively over the past 7 yrs. Incl mature trees, a wide range of unusual plants and grasses chosen for texture and colour, herb garden, formal pond and sunken brick terrace. The style is relaxed, the content stimulating and the tea fresh, so come and enjoy! A couple of low steps in garden.

27 COLEMORE HOUSE GARDENS

Colemore, Alton GU34 3RX. Mr & Mrs Simon de Zoete. *4m S of Alton (off A32). Approach from N on A32, turn L (Shell Lane), ¼ m S of East Tisted. Go under bridge, keep L until you see Colemore Church. Park on verge of church.* Home-made teas. **Adm £4.50, chd free.** Sun 28, Mon 29 June (2-6).

4 acres in lovely unspoilt countryside, featuring rooms containing many unusual plants and different aspects. A spectacular arched rose walk, water rill, mirror pond, herbaceous and shrub borders and a new woodland walk. Many admire the lawns, new grass gardens and thatched pavilion (built by students from the Prince's Trust). A small arboretum is being planted. Change and development is ongoing, and increasing the diversity of interesting plants is a prime motivation. We propagate and sell plants, many of which can be found in the garden. Some are unusual and not readily available elswhere.

A stroll through the fields to see sheep, pigs and chickens . . .

28 30 COMPTON WAY

Winchester SO22 4HS. Susan Summers, www.summersgd.co.uk. *2m SW of Winchester. From M3 J11, follow A3090 Badger Farm Rd uphill. Turn L into Oliver's Battery Rd South. Take 2nd L into Compton Way. House on R before Austen Ave.* Home-made teas. **Adm £3, chd free.** Sat 23, Sun 24, Wed 27 May (2-5).

Contemporary garden owned by local garden designer on the outskirts of Winchester. Sunny hilltop ¼ acre plot. Themed borders of colourful mixed planting on chalky soil, incl alliums and aquilegias. Kitchen and herb gardens, and pond.

29 CONHOLT PARK

Hungerford Lane, Andover SP11 9HA. Conholt Park Estate, 07917 796826, conholt.garden@hotmail.com. *7m N of Andover. Turn N off A342 at Weyhill Church, 5m N through Clanville. L at T-junction, Conholt ½ m on R. A343 to Hurstbourne Tarrant, turn & go through Vernham Dean, L signed Conholt.* Home-made teas. **Adm £5, chd free.** Sun 28 June, Sun 26 July (11-5). **Visitors also welcome by arrangement May to July on weekends only.**

10 acres surrounding Regency house (not open), with mature cedars. Rose, sensory, winter and secret gardens, fern dell and poppy garden. Glasshouses, flower cartwheel, berry wall and orchard occupy the walled garden. New summer border and gravel garden. An Edwardian Ladies Walk. Large laurel maze with viewing platform. Visitors welcome to picnic.

30 THE COTTAGE

16 Lakewood Road, Chandler's Ford SO53 1ES. Hugh & Barbara Sykes, 02380 254521, barandhugh@aol.com. *2m NW of Eastleigh. Leave M3 J12, follow signs to Chandler's Ford. At King Rufus on Winchester Rd, turn R into Merdon Ave, then 3rd road on L.* Home-made teas. **Adm £3.50, chd free.** Sun 3, Mon 4, Sun 10, Mon 11 May (2-6). **Visitors also welcome by arrangement Apr to May.**

¾ acre. Azaleas, bog garden, camellias, dogwoods, erythroniums, free-range bantams, geraniums, hostas, irises, jasmines, kitchen garden, landscaping began in 1950, maintained by owners, new planting, osmunda, ponds, quiz for children, rhododendrons, sun and shade, trilliums, unusual plants, viburnums, wildlife areas, eXuberant foliage, yr-round interest, zantedeschia. 'A lovely tranquil garden', Anne Swithinbank. Hampshire Wildlife Trust Wildlife Garden Award. Honey from our garden hives for sale.

COTTAGE IN THE TREES

See Wiltshire.

31 CRANBURY PARK

Otterbourne, nr Winchester SO21 2HL. Mrs Chamberlayne-Macdonald. *3m NW of Eastleigh. Main entrance on old A33 at top of Otterbourne Hill. Entrances also in Hocombe Rd, Chandlers Ford & next to Otterbourne Church.* Home-made teas. **Adm £4.50, chd free.** Share to St Matthew's Church, Otterbourne. Sun 14 June (2-6).

Extensive pleasure grounds laid out in late C18 and early C19 by Papworth; fountains, rose garden, specimen trees and pinetum, lakeside walk and fern walk. Family carriages and collection of prams will be on view, also photos of King George VI, Eisenhower and Montgomery reviewing Canadian troops at Cranbury before D-Day. All dogs on leads please. Disabled WC.

GROUP OPENING

32 CRAWLEY GARDENS

Crawley, nr Winchester SO21 2PR, 01962 776243. *5m NW of Winchester. Between B3049 (Winchester - Stockbridge) & A272 (Winchester - Andover). Parking throughout village.* Home-made teas in the village hall. **Combined adm £6 (Apr & July) & £7.50 (June), chd free.** Mon 6, Tue 7 Apr (2-5.30); Thur 11, Sun 14 June, Thur 2, Sun 5 July (2-6).

BAY TREE HOUSE D
Julia & Charles Whiteaway.
Open June & July dates

GABLE COTTAGE
Patrick Hendra & Ken Jones.
Open April dates only

LITTLE COURT
Mrs A R Elkington.
Open April & June dates
(See separate entry)

PAIGE COTTAGE
Mr & Mrs T W Parker.
Open April, June & July dates

TANGLEFOOT
Mr & Mrs F J Fratter.
Open June & July dates
(See separate entry)

Crawley is an exceptionally pretty village nestling in chalk downland with thatched houses, C14 church and delightful village pond with ducks. A different combination of gardens opens each month providing seasonal interest with varied character, and with traditional and contemporary approaches to landscape and planting. Most of the gardens have beautiful country views and there are other excellent gardens to be seen from the road. The spring

gardens are Paige Cottage, Gable Cottage and the 3 acre traditional English country garden at Little Court with carpets of spring bulbs. In summer, other gardens open. At Bay Tree House there are pleached limes, a rill and contemporary borders; while at Tanglefoot there are colour themed borders, herb wheel, exceptional kitchen garden and a traditional Victorian boundary wall supporting trained fruit incl apricots. Also in the summer, Little Court has a mass of colourful herbaceous planting while Paige Cottage is a typical mixed cottage garden. This year, the June openings comprise the 4 large, varied and exciting gardens.

Old Swan House, Stockbridge Gardens

33 CROOKLEY POOL

Blendworth Lane, Horndean PO8 0AB. **Mr & Mrs Simon Privett,** 02392 592662, simon.privett123@btinternet.com. *5m S of Petersfield. 2m E of Waterlooville, off A3. From Horndean up Blendworth Lane between bakery & hairdresser. Entrance 200yds before church on L with white railings.* Home-made teas. **Adm £4.00, chd free.** Sun 17 May, Thur 4 June (2-5). **Visitors also welcome by arrangement Mar to Oct with teas on request.**
Here the plants decide where to grow. Californian tree poppies elbow valerian aside to crowd round the pool. Evening primroses obstruct the way to the door and the steps to wisteria shaded terraces. Hellebores bloom under the trees. Salvias, Pandorea jasminoides, Justicia, Pachystachys lutea and passion flowers riot quietly with tomatoes in the greenhouse. Not a garden for the neat or tidy minded, although this is a plantsman's garden full of unusual plants and a lot of tender perennials. Bantams stroll throughout. Watercolour paintings of flowers found in the garden will be on display.

34 DEAN HOUSE

Kilmeston Road, Kilmeston, Alresford SO24 0NL. **Mr P H R Gwyn,** www.deanhousegardens.co.uk. *5m S of Alresford. Via village of Cheriton or off A272 signed at Cheriton Xrds. Follow signs for Kilmeston, through village & turn L at Dean House sign.* Home-made teas in The Orangery. **Adm £6, chd free.**

Wed 27 May, Wed 17 June, Wed 1 July (10-4); Sun 19 July, Sun 2 Aug (12-4); Wed 19 Aug (10-4).
The 7 acres have been described as 'a well-kept secret hidden behind the elegant facade of its Georgian centrepiece'. Sweeping lawns, York stone paths, gravel pathways, many young and mature trees and hedges, mixed and herbaceous borders, symmetrical rose garden, pond garden, working walled garden, with 125 different varieties of vegetable, and glasshouses all help to create a diverse and compact sliver of Eden. Over 1700 individually documented plant species and cultivars in our collection. Gravel paths.

35 DIPLEY MILL

Dipley Road, Hartley Wintney, Hook RG27 8JP. **Miss Rose McMonigall,** rose@rosemcm.demon.co.uk, www.dipley-mill.co.uk. *2m NE of Hook. Turn E off B3349 at Mattingley (1½ m N of Hook) signed Hartley Wintney, West Green & Dipley. Dipley Mill ½ m on L just over bridge.* Cream teas. **Adm £5, chd free.** Suns 24 May, 14 June, 5 July, 2 Aug, 13 Sept (2-5.30). **Visitors also welcome by arrangement May to Sept for groups of 15+.**
A romantic adventure awaits as you wander by the meandering streams surrounding this Domesday Book

listed mill! Explore many magical areas, such as the Rust garden, the pill box grotto and the ornamental courtyard, or just escape into wild meadows. 'One of the most beautiful gardens in Hampshire' according to Alan Titchmarsh in his TV programme Love Your Garden. Animals. Local fruit stalls (depending on availability). Featured in Period Living magazine (May 2014).

36 THE DOWER HOUSE

Springvale Road, Headbourne Worthy, Winchester SO23 7LD. **Mrs Judith Lywood,** www.thedowerhousewinchester. co.uk. *2m N of Winchester. Entrance is directly opp watercress beds in Springvale Rd & near The Good Life Farm Shop. Parking at main entrance to house, following path to garden.* Home-made teas. **Adm £3.50, chd free.** Sun 14 June (2.30-5.30).
5½ acres with easy paths, numerous seats, good views, colourful perennials, shrubs and mature trees (incl large Indian bean tree and cercis Forest Pansy). Large geranium border overlooking grounds, bog garden, good pond with fish and water lilies, newly installed scented garden at entrance, small secret courtyard garden and container planting on The Dower House residents' patios.

37 NEW **DOWN FARM HOUSE**
Hurstbourne Priors, Whitchurch
RG28 7RT. Pat & Steve Jones.
1½ m from the centre of Whitchurch.
Please do not use SatNav. From the
centre of Whitchurch take the
Newbury road up the hill, then 1st L
after railway Xing. Approx 1m from
the railway bridge. Tea. **Adm £3.50,**
chd free. Sun 14, Wed 17 June
(2-5.30). **Also open 2 Church**
Cottages.
Step back in time in this 2 acre
garden, created from an old walled
farmyard and the surrounding land.
Many of the original features are used
as hard landscaping. Incl organic
vegetables, succulents, alpine bed
created from the old concrete capped
well, informal, naturalistic planting,
wooded area and orchard. The
garden has been created slowly over
the last 30 yrs. Wheelchair access by
gravel drive onto lawn.

Marie Curie
Cancer Care

Our nurses
work in
communities
covering 95%
of the UK

38 **THE DOWN HOUSE**
Itchen Abbas SO21 1AX. Jackie &
Mark Porter, 01962 791054,
markstephenporter@gmail.com,
www.thedownhouse.co.uk. *5m E of*
Winchester on B3047. 5th house on
R after the Itchen Abbas village sign if
coming on B3047 from Kings Worthy.
300yds on L after Plough PH if
coming on B3047 from Alresford.
Home-made teas. **Adm £4, chd free.**
Share to PCaSo, Prostate Cancer
Support. Sun 22 Feb (12-4); Sun 28
June, Wed 1 July (2-6). **Visitors**
also welcome by arrangement
June to July for groups of 20+.
3 acre garden developed by owners
since 2001, laid out in rooms
overlooking Itchen Valley, adjoining
the Pilgrim's Way, with walks through

a meadow to the river. Carpet of
snowdrops and crocus, plus borders
of coloured stems in winter. Roped
fountain garden, hot borders, wildlife
pond and shady places in summer.
Pleached hornbeams, yew lined
avenues, woodland nut and orchard
walk. Working vineyard and potager.
Live jazz on Sun 28 June. The garden
in winter was featured in Period
Homes & Interiors, Hampshire Life, &
Garden Answers magazines (Feb
2014).

39 **7 DOWNLAND CLOSE**
Locks Heath, nr Fareham
SO31 6WB. Roy Dorland, 07768
107779, roydorland@hotmail.co.uk.
3m W of Fareham. M27 J9 follow
A27 on Southampton Rd to Park
Gate. Past Kams Palace Restaurant,
L into Locks Rd, 3rd R into Meadow
Ave. 2nd L into Downland Close.
Please park in Locks Rd (only 2 mins
from garden). Home-made teas. **Adm**
£3, chd free. Sat 23, Sun 24, Mon
25 May, Sat 20, Sun 21 June (1-6).
Visitors also welcome by
arrangement May to July for
groups of 10-20.
Visit this prize-winning, beautiful,
restful and inspirational 50ft x 45ft
plantsman's garden, packed with
ideas for the modest sized plot. Many
varieties of hardy geraniums, hostas,
heucheras, shrubs, ferns and other
unusual perennials, weaving a
tapestry of harmonious colour.
Attractive water feature, plenty of
seating areas and charming
summerhouse. A garden to fall in love
with!

40 **DURMAST HOUSE**
Bennetts Lane, Burley BH24 4AT.
Mr & Mrs P E G Daubeney, 01425
402132, philip@daubeney.co.uk,
www.durmasthouse.co.uk. *5m SE*
of Ringwood. Off Burley to Lyndhurst
Rd, nr White Buck Hotel. Cream teas.
Adm £4, chd free. Share to Delhi
Commonwealth Women's Assn
Medical Clinic. Sun 29 Mar, Sun 28
June (2-5). **Visitors also welcome**
by arrangement Apr to July, incl
talk on the history and planting of
the garden for groups only.
Designed by Gertrude Jekyll,
Durmast has contrasting hot and cool
colour borders, formal rose garden
edged with lavender and a long
herbaceous border. Many old trees,
Victorian rockery and orchard with
beautiful spring bulbs. Rare azaleas:

Fama, Princeps and Gloria Mundi
from Ghent. Features incl new rose
bowers with rare French roses,
Eleanor Berkeley and Euphrosyne.
New Jekyll border with a blue, yellow
and white scheme. Many stone paths
and some gravel paths.

GROUP OPENING

41 **EAST WORLDHAM**
GARDENS
East Worldham, Alton GU34 3AE,
01420 83389, www.worldham.org.
2m SE of Alton on B3004. Gardens &
car parking off B3004 signed in
village. Tickets & maps available at
each garden. Home-made teas at
East Worldham Manor & 'Selborne'
(June). At 'Selborne' & Three
Horseshoes PH (July). **Combined**
adm £5, chd free. Sat 27, Sun
28 June, Sat 25, Sun 26 July
(2-5.30).

> **EAST WORLDHAM MANOR**
> Worldham Hill. Mrs H V Wood.
> *Open June dates only*
>
> **THE OLD HOP KILN**
> Blanket Street. John & Kate
> Denyer.
> *Open June dates only*
>
> **'SELBORNE'**
> Brian & Mary Jones.
> *Open June & July dates*
> **(See separate entry)**
>
> **SILVER BIRCHES**
> Old House Gardens. Jenny &
> Roger Bateman.
> *Open July dates only*
>
> **WYCK HOUSE**
> Wyck Lane. Chris & Penny
> Kehoe.
> *Open July dates only*

A honeypot of gardens. East
Worldham Gardens offers a different
combination of gardens with varied
characters and styles and far-
reaching views on each of the two
openings. East Worldham Manor is a
large walled Victorian garden with
restored greenhouses, vegetable area
and rose garden. Gravel paths wind
through the garden. The Old Hop
Kiln's terraced garden, with many
changes of level, has free-flowing
planting that complements the hard
landscaping. A series of cascades
links the upper and lower levels.
'Selborne' has an old orchard
providing dappled shade, metal and
stone sculptures and mixed borders,

densely planted with a range of hardy geraniums. The garden at Silver Birches, redesigned from an overgrown jungle, offers mixed borders of shrubs and herbaceous plants, small copse, fishpond, stream, rockery and rose garden. Wyck House's mature garden contains interesting shrubs and trees, roses, perennials, vegetables and fruit, shady area and features a large collection of clematis. Garden quizzes, sandpit and bookstall at 'Selborne'. C13 church with some modern stained glass windows and Medieval monument of a lady. Featured in Tindle Group of Newspapers. Access to Old Hop Kiln is by a steep gravel track that is unsuitable for some wheelchairs.

♿ ❇ ☕

GROUP OPENING

42 EMSWORTH GARDENS
Emsworth PO10 7PR. Lucy Watson & Mike Rogers. *7m W of Chichester, 2m E of Havant. Take A259 W of Chichester, follow signs to Emsworth r'about N of town centre. Park at recreation ground opp Talara Cottage if no space on roads.* Home-made teas at Talara Cottage. **Combined adm £5, chd free.** Sun 21 June (1-5.30).

23 NEW BRIGHTON ROAD
Lucy Watson & Mike Rogers. *From main Emsworth r'about head N. Underneath railway bridge & flyover. Garden immed on L up the slope*

NEW **TALARA COTTAGE, 42 HORNDEAN ROAD**
Mrs Angela Baldry. *A 5 min walk from 23 New Brighton Rd, up Horndean Rd*

Two contrasting gardens close to the centre of Emsworth; an historic fishing and sailing village on Chichester Harbour with numerous PH, small local museum, walks along the foreshore and around mill pond. With its eclectic mix of plants and ornaments, 23 New Brighton Road features a narrow 250ft long garden which ranges from full sun to full shade where informal planting maximises the available space. A large number of containers, ponds, greenhouse, summerhouse, shady reading area and mixed borders. Unusual plants and an unusual garden for the plantsperson. Display of old garden tools. Talara Cottage is

a secluded garden wrapping around an Edwardian villa. Vegetable gardens, Mediterranean garden, mixed herbaceous borders, glorious 1920's ornamental pond, and, if you are lucky, fairies behind the pavilion. Wheelchair access at Talara Cottage only.

♿ ❇ ☕

A unique
100 acre
ancient bluebell
woodland . . .

---

43 FAIRBANK
Old Odiham Road, Alton GU34 4BU. Jane & Robin Lees, 01420 86665, j.lees558@btinternet.com. *1½ m N of Alton. From S, past Sixth Form College, then 1½ m beyond road junction on R. From N, turn L at Golden Pot & then 50yds turn R. Garden 1m on L before road junction.* Home-made teas. **Adm £3, chd free.** Wed 5, Wed 12 Aug (2-5). Visitors also welcome by arrangement July to Sept for individuals or groups of 30 max.
A young garden, begun in 2006, planted for yr-round interest. Features incl roses, herbaceous borders, a wide variety of trees and shrubs, orchard and a large vegetable garden. Please be aware of uneven ground in some areas of the garden.

♿ 🚐 ☕

44 FAIRWEATHER'S NURSERY
Hilltop, Beaulieu, Brockenhurst SO42 7YR. Patrick & Aline Fairweather, www.fairweathers.co.uk. *1½ m NE of Beaulieu Village. Signed Beacon Gate on B3054 between Heath r'about (A326) & Beaulieu Village.* Cream teas. **Adm £2.50, chd free.**

Sat 1, Sun 2 Aug (10-4). Fairweather's holds a specialist collection of over 300 Agapanthus grown in pots and display beds, the collection should be looking at its best. Features incl; guided tours of the Nursery at 11.30am and 2.30pm, demonstrations of how to get the best from Agapanthus and companion planting, and Agapanthus and a range of other traditional and new perennials for sale. Aline Fairweather's garden (adjacent to the nursery) will also be open; it has mixed shrub and perennial borders containing many unusual plants.

♿ ♿ ❇ 🚐 **NCH** ☕

45 FARLEIGH HOUSE
Farleigh Wallop, nr Basingstoke RG25 2HT. Viscount Lymington. *3m SE of Basingstoke. Off B3046 Basingstoke to Preston Candover road.* Home-made teas. **Adm £5, chd free.** Sun 21 June, Sun 20 Sept (2-5).
Contemporary garden of great tranquillity designed by Georgia Langton, surrounded by wonderful views. 3 acre walled garden in 3 sections; ornamental potager, formal rose garden and wild rose garden. Greenhouse full of exotics, serpentine yew walk, contemplative pond garden and lake with planting for wildlife. The grounds cover approx 10 acres and will take about 1 hour to walk around.

♿ ♿ 🚐 ☕

46 FLINTSTONES
Sciviers Lane, Durley SO32 2AG. June & Bill Butler, 01489 860880, j.b.butler@hotmail.co.uk. *5m E of Eastleigh. M3 J11 towards Marwell Zoo. On B2177 turn R opp Woodman PH. M27 J7 follow signs for Fair Oak, then Durley, turn L at Robin Hood PH.* Teas (March), Home-made teas (May & June). **Adm £3.50, chd free.** Sun 15 Mar (2-5); Sun 31 May, Mon 1 June (2-6). Visitors also welcome by arrangement May to Sept for groups of 10+.
Garden of great tranquillity. Yr-round pleasing tapestry effect of contrasting and blending foliage and flowers. Plantswoman's garden developed from a field on fertile acid clay. Large perennial plant collections, especially hardy geraniums. Interesting island beds to wander round and explore. Plants for sale May and June only. Wheelchair access only when dry, please telephone prior to visit.

♿ ❇ ☕

Farleigh House

47 FOUR SEASONS HOTEL
Chalky Lane, Dogmersfield, Hook
RG27 8TD. Darren Moakes,
01252 853000,
reservations.ham@fourseasons.
com,
www.fourseasons.com/hampshire.
*3m from M3 J5. Follow A287 towards
Farnham for approx 3m. Follow signs
for the Four Seasons Hotel.* Adm £4,
chd free. Tues 9, 23 June, 7, 21
July, 4, 18 Aug, 1, 15, 29 Sept
(9.30-3.30). Visitors also welcome
by arrangement for groups of 10+.
Steeped in nearly 1000 yrs of history,
Dogmersfield Park was first
mentioned in the Domesday book of
1086. Let us welcome you to explore
the country estate where Henry VIII
met Catherine of Aragon. Walk
through the splendour of the walled
garden, rose walk and apple orchard
before relaxing with an afternoon tea
in the Grade I listed Manor House
(reservations required). Set in 500
acres of English heritage parkland,
see the oldest dovecote in Hampshire
built in 1570. Walk in the footsteps of
Earls, Lords and Kings through an
historic estate and enjoy the peace,
serenity, flowers and birdsong.

Guided tours 11am and 2pm.
Wheelchair access to the majority of
the gardens.

48 FRITHAM LODGE
Fritham SO43 7HH. Sir Chris &
Lady Powell, 02380 812650,
chris.powell@ddblondon.com. *6m
N of Lyndhurst. 3m NW of M27 J1
(Cadnam). Follow signs to Fritham.*
Cream teas. Adm £4, chd free. Sun
24 May (2-5). Visitors also
welcome by arrangement May to
July.
Set in the heart of the New Forest in
18 acres with 1 acre old walled
garden round Grade II listed C17
house (not open), originally one of
Charles II hunting lodges. Parterre of
old roses, potager with wide variety of
vegetables, pergola, wisterias,
herbaceous and blue and white
mixed borders, tulips, and ponds.
Features incl a walk across hay
meadows to woodland and stream,
with ponies, donkeys, sheep and rare
breed hens. Featued in The Daily
Telegraph (2014).

Look out for the NGS yellow arrows …

GROUP OPENING

49 FROYLE GARDENS
Walbury, Lower Froyle, Froyle
GU34 4LJ. Ernie & Brenda Milam.
*5m NE of Alton. Access to Lower
Froyle from A31 between Alton &
Farnham at Bentley. Follow signs
from Lower Froyle to Upper Froyle.
Maps given to all visitors.* Home-
made teas at Froyle Village Hall.
Combined adm £5, chd free.
Sat 6, Sun 7 June (2-6).

BRAMLINS
Mrs Anne Blunt

DAY COTTAGE
Mr Nick Whines & Ms Corinna
Furse
www.daycottage.co.uk

FORDS COTTAGE
Mr & Mrs M Carr

GLEBE COTTAGE
Barbara & Michael Starbuck

THE OLD SCHOOL
Nigel & Linda Bulpitt

WALBURY
Ernie & Brenda Milam
(See separate entry)

Visitors have been returning to Froyle
(The Village of Saints) for 15 yrs to
enjoy the wonderful variety of gardens
on offer, the warm welcome and the
excellent home-made teas. The
gardens harmonise gently with their
surroundings, many with lovely views
of beautiful countryside. Six gardens
will open their gates this year, not only
providing plant interest, colour and
scent, but animals frequently
associated with a true cottage
garden, as well as vegetables,
orchards, greenhouses and wild
flower meadows. Large display of
richly decorated C18 church
vestments in St Mary's Church Upper
Froyle (separate donation). No
wheelchair access to Glebe Cottage
and a gravel drive at Bramlins.

50 GILBERTS NURSERY
Dandysford Lane, Sherfield
English, nr Romsey SO51 6DT.
Nick & Helen Gilbert,
gilbertsdahlias.co.uk. *Midway
between Romsey & Whiteparish on
A27, in Sherfield English Village. From
Romsey 4th turn on L, just before
small petrol station on R, visible from
main road.* Light refreshments. Adm
£3, chd free. Sun 30 Aug (10-4).

This may not be a garden but do come and be amazed by the sight of over 300 varieties of dahlias in our dedicated 1½ acre field. The blooms are in all colours, shapes and sizes and can be closely inspected from wheelchair friendly hard grass paths. An inspiration for all gardeners. 2014 medals awarded: Gold in the New Forest Show and Taunton Flower Show; Large Gold and Best in Show in the Dorset County Show, Romsey Show and Newbury Show.

MANOR HOUSE
See Wiltshire.

51 HAMBLEDON HOUSE
Hambledon PO7 4RU. Capt & Mrs David Hart Dyke, 02392 632380, dianahartdyke@talktalk.net. *8m SW of Petersfield, 5m NW of Waterlooville. In village centre, driveway leading to house in East St. Do not go up Speltham Hill even if advised by SatNav.* **Adm £4, chd free. Visitors welcome by arrangement Apr to Sept with teas by prior request.**
3 acre partly walled plantsman's garden for all seasons. Large borders filled with a wide variety of unusual shrubs and perennials with imaginative plant combinations culminating in a profusion of colour in late summer. Hidden, secluded areas reveal surprise views of garden and village rooftops. Planting a large central area, started in 2011, has given the garden an exciting new dimension. Featured in Period Houses & Interiors and Hampshire Life. Partial wheelchair access as garden is on several levels.

52 NEW HAMBROOKS SHOW GARDENS
135 Southampton Road, Titchfield, Fareham PO14 4PR. Mr Mike Hodges. *On the old A27 opp B&Q.* **Evening Openings £3, chd free, Light refreshments, Sat 23 May, Sat 17 Oct (5-7.30).**
16 individually designed showcase gardens ranging from the traditional to the contemporary. Each has its own unique character, demonstrating versatile and visionary styles. The gardens contain different features that incl outdoor kitchens, fireplaces, stylish garden sofas, chandeliers, rusty crowned obelisks, babbling brooks, ponds and streams. Garden designers will be available to talk to

visitors, and at the Oct opening the gardens will be illuminated with garden lighting.

53 HANGING HOSTA GARDEN
Narra, Frensham Lane, Lindford, Bordon GU35 0QJ. June Colley & John Baker, 01420 489186, hanginghostas@btinternet.com. *Approx 1m E of Bordon. From the A325 at Bordon take the B3002, then B3004 to Lindford. Turn L into Frensham Lane, 3rd house on L.* **Adm £3.50, chd free. Visitors welcome by arrangement in July from Mon 6 to Fri 10 & Mon 13 to Fri 17 only.**
This garden is packed with almost 2000 plants. The collection of over 1500 hosta cultivars is one of the largest in England. Hostas are displayed at eye level to give a wonderful tapestry of foliage and colour. Islamic garden, waterfall and stream garden, cottage garden. Talks given to garden clubs. Featured in Daily Mail Supplement (2014).

 NCH

Working vineyard and potager . . .

54 HEATHERMOOR HOUSE
Hale Purlieu, Fordingbridge SP6 2NN. Andrew & Judy Pownall-Gray, 01725 513033, judypg@btinternet.com. *11m S of Salisbury, 5m NE of Fordingbridge. Yellow NGS signs at Downton & Breamore on A338 Salisbury & Fordingbridge, & at Cadnam M27 J1 B3078 to Downton.* Home-made teas. **Adm £4, chd free. Share to Wilton Group Riding for the Disabled (RDA). Sun 17 May (2-5). Visitors also welcome by arrangement May to Sept for groups of 10+.**
Our tranquil 4 acre garden leads directly onto the New Forest and abounds with azaleas, camellias,

rhododendrons, magnolias and acers, filling the garden with colour and fragrance. Large lawns, surrounded by herbaceous borders, are the perfect setting for tea and cake. The raised bed vegetable garden leads to the cabin in the woods, a joy for wildlife enthusiasts. No wheelchair access to cabin in woods.

55 HIDEAWAY
Hamdown Crescent, East Wellow, Romsey SO51 6BJ. Caroline & Colin Hart, 01794 322445, hart.caroline@yahoo.com. *3m W of Romsey. From M27 J2 take A36 NW towards Salisbury. After 2m, turn R by speed camera into Whinwhistle Rd. Hamdown Crescent is 3rd L.* Home-made teas. **Adm £3.50, chd free. Sat 25, Sun 26 July (2-5.30). Visitors also welcome by arrangement in July for groups of 20+.**
Stroll through our pretty ½ acre garden and be amazed at the colour and diversity of the plants. Wander down to the summerhouse passing beds of grasses, perennials and annuals then pause awhile. A small vegetable patch and fruit cage supply the kitchen. The natural world is not forgotten with bog gardens and a wildlife pond. Lovely all yr-round, particularly in midsummer and is full of inspiration. Many plants for sale and an art exhibition by a local group of artists. Featured in Garden News (23 Aug 2014).

56 HILL HOUSE
Old Alresford SO24 9DY. Mrs S Richardson, 01962 732720, hillhouseolda@yahoo.co.uk. *1m W of Alresford. From Alresford 1m along B3046 towards Basingstoke, then R by church.* Home-made teas. **Adm £3.50, chd free. Thur 30 July, Sun 2, Tue 4 Aug (1.30-5). Visitors also welcome by arrangement mid July to mid Aug.**
Traditional English 2 acre garden, established 1938, divided by yew hedge. Large croquet lawn framing the star of the garden, the huge multicoloured herbaceous border. Dahlia bed and butterfly attracting sunken garden in lavender shades. Prolific old fashioned kitchen garden with hens and bantams both fluffy and large. Small Dexter cows. Dried flowers.

57 HILL TOP

Damson Hill, Upper Swanmore SO32 2QR. David Green, 01489 892653, tricia1960@btinternet.com. *1m NE of Swanmore. Junction of Swanmore Rd & Church Rd, up Hampton Hill, sharp L bend. After 300yds junction with Damson Hill, house on L. Disabled parking by house. Home-made teas.* **Adm £4, chd free.** Sun 20 Sept (1-5). **Visitors also welcome by arrangement Apr to Oct.**

2 acres with extensive colourful borders and wide lawns, this garden has stunning views to the Isle of Wight. The glasshouses produce unusual fruit and vegetables from around the world. The outdoor vegetable plots bulge with well grown produce, much for sale on the day. Potted specimen plants and interesting annuals. Featured in Hampshire Life.

hospice UK

There's a hospice close to every NGS garden

58 ◆ HILLIER GARDENS

Jermyns Lane, Ampfield, Romsey SO51 0QA. Hampshire County Council, 01794 369317, www.hilliergardens.org.uk. *2m NE of Romsey. Follow brown tourist signs from A3090 Romsey to Winchester, or A3057 Romsey to Andover. Disabled parking available.* **For opening times and information, please phone or see garden website.**

Established by the plantsman Sir Harold Hillier, this 180 acre garden is landscaped with a unique collection of 12,000 different hardy plants from across the world. It incl the famous Winter Garden, Centenary Border, Himalayan Valley, Gurkha Memorial Garden, Magnolia Avenue, spring woodlands, fabulous autumn colour,

13 National Collections and over 400 champion trees. The Centenary Border is believed to be the longest double border in the country, a feast from early summer to autumn. Celebrated Winter Garden is one of the largest in Europe. Featured in Financial Times and RHS The Garden (Summer 2014). Electric scooters are available for hire (please pre-book). Disabled toilets. Guide and hearing dogs only.

59 2 HILLSIDE COTTAGES

Trampers Lane, North Boarhunt PO17 6DA. John & Lynsey Pink, 01329 832786, landjpink@tiscali.co.uk. *5m N of Fareham. 3m E of Wickham. From A32 at Wickham take B2177 E. Trampers Lane 2nd on L (approx 2m). Hillside Cottages approx 1/2 m on L.* **Adm £2.50, chd free.** Visitors welcome by arrangement **Feb to Nov.**

This 1 acre garden, on gently rising ground, contains so much of interest for plantspeople. Many rare and unusual specimens are shown off in sweeping borders in a tranquil setting. The National Collection of salvias is well displayed, all colours, sizes and growing habits. Something for everyone and an ideal venue for a group visit from spring through to autumn.

NCH

60 HINTON ADMIRAL

Christchurch BH23 7DY. Robin Mason, MEM Ltd. *4m NE of Christchurch. On N side of A35, 3/4 m E of Cat & Fiddle PH.* **Adm £6, chd free.** Share to Julia's House Childrens Hospice. Sun 17 May (1-4.30).

Magnificent 20 acre garden within a much larger estate, now being restored and developed. Mature plantings of deciduous azaleas and rhododendrons amidst a sea of bluebells. Wandering paths lead through rockeries and beside ponds and a stream with many cascades. Orchids appear in the large lawns. The 2 walled gardens are devoted to herbs and wild flowers and a very large greenhouse. The terrace and rock garden were designed by Harold Peto. No refreshments available, but picnics are welcome in the orchard. Some gravel paths.

61 ◆ HINTON AMPNER

Alresford SO24 0LA. National Trust, 01962 771305, www.nationaltrust.org.uk/hinton-ampner. *3 1/2 m S of Alresford. On A272 Petersfield to Winchester road, between Bramdean & Cheriton.* Light lunches & afternoon tea in the tea-room. **Adm £10.30, chd £5.15.** For NGS: Sats 9 May, 6 June, 4 July, 5 Sept (10-5). **For other opening times and information, please phone or see garden website.**

C20 garden created by Ralph Dutton covering 14 acres. Manicured lawns and topiary combine with unusual shrubs, climbers and herbaceous plants. Vibrant dahlias alternate in spring with tulips. Rose border incorporates over 45 old and new rose varieties. Dramatic foliage planting in the Dell; orchard with spring bulbs; magnolia and philadelphus walks; restored walled garden. Wheelchair access maps available from visitor reception.

62 NEW HOLLYBROOK

20a Chalk Hill, West End, Southampton SO18 3BZ. Michael Hook & Janet Galpin. *3m E of Southampton. Exit M27 J5 or J7, take A27, Chalk Hill at T-lights by Tesco. Park on hill & side roads. Small car parks, courtesy of Swan System Wardrobes & The Master Builder PH on A27, 2 mins from Chalk Hill. Home-made teas.* **Adm £2.50, chd free.** Sat 23, Sun 24, Sat 30, Sun 31 May (2-6).

Small 25x12 metre town garden started in 2008. Raised beds built using railway sleepers and imaginative use of other recycled and new materials to make interesting artistic garden pieces to complement small herbaceous border, pergola and two ponds, one with a variety of fish. Structural planting incl bamboos, grasses and hostas. Tiny vegetable patch. Friends' vegetable competition 2014 - heaviest parsnip.

63 THE HOMESTEAD

Northney Road, Hayling Island PO11 0NF. Stan & Mary Pike, 02392 464888, jhomestead@aol.com, www.homesteadhayling.co.uk. *3m S of Havant. From A27 Havant & Hayling Island r'about, travel S over Langstone Bridge & turn immed L into Northney Rd. Car park entrance*

on R after Langstone Hotel. Home-made teas. **Adm £3, chd free.** Sun 2 Aug (2-5.30). **Visitors also welcome by arrangement May to Sept for groups of 10+.**
1¼ acre garden surrounded by working farmland with views to Butser Hill and boats in Chichester Harbour. Trees, shrubs, colourful herbaceous borders and small walled garden with herbs, vegetables and trained fruit trees. A quiet and peaceful atmosphere with plenty of seats to enjoy the vistas within the garden and beyond. Some gravel paths.

64 NEW ◆ THE HOSPITAL OF ST CROSS
St Cross Road, Winchester SO23 9SD. The Hospital of St Cross & Almshouse of Noble Poverty, 01962 851375, www.hospitalofstcross.co.uk. *½ m S of Winchester. From city centre take B3335 (Southgate St & St Cross Rd) S. Turn L immed before The Bell PH. If on foot follow riverside path S from Cathedral & College, approx 20 mins.* Home-made teas in the Hundred Men's Hall in the Outer Quadrangle. **Adm £4, chd free.** For NGS: Sun 30 Aug (2-5). **For other opening times and information, please phone or see garden website.**
The Medieval Hospital of St Cross nestles in water meadows beside the R Itchen and is one of England's oldest almshouses. The tranquil, walled Master's Garden, created in the late C17 by Bishop Compton, now contains colourful herbaceous borders, old fashioned roses, interesting trees and a large fish pond. The Compton Garden has unusual plants of the type he imported when Bishop of London. There is wheelchair access but please be aware surfaces are uneven in places.

65 THE HOUSE IN THE WOOD
Beaulieu SO42 7YN. Victoria Roberts. *New Forest. 8m NE of Lymington. Leaving the entrance to Beaulieu Motor Museum on R (B3056) take next R signed Ipley Cross. Take 2nd gravel drive on RH-bend, approx ½ m.* Cream teas. **Adm £4.50, chd free.** Sun 10 May (2-6).
Peaceful 12 acre woodland garden with continuing progress and improvement. New areas and

streams have been developed and good acers planted among mature azaleas and rhododendrons. Used in the war to train the Special Operations Executive. A magical garden to get lost in and popular with birdwatchers.

66 THE HYDE
Old Alresford SO24 9DH. Sue Alexander, 01962 732043, suealex13@gmail.com. *1m W of Alresford. From Alresford 1m along B3046 towards Basingstoke. House in centre of village, opp flag pole on village green.* Home-made teas. **Adm £4, chd free.** Sat 29, Sun 30, Mon 31 Aug (1.30-5). **Visitors also welcome by arrangement in Sept for groups of 10+.**
Tucked behind an old field hedge, a delightful ¾ acre garden created by the owner to attract wildlife and reflect her flower arranging passion for colour and texture. Flowing borders contain an abundant mixture of perennials, half-hardies, annuals, grasses and shrubs. Wonderful ideas for late summer colour. National Collection of Patrinia. Short gravel drive at entrance.

67 THE ISLAND
Greatbridge, Romsey SO51 0HP. Mr & Mrs Christopher Saunders-Davies, 01794 512100, ssd@littleroundtop.co.uk. *1m N of Romsey on A3057. Entrance alongside Greatbridge (1st bridge Xing the R Test), flanked by row of cottages on roadside.* Home-made teas. **Adm £5, chd free.** Sat 18, Sun 19 Apr, Sat 27, Sun 28 June (2-5). **Visitors also welcome by arrangement Apr to Sept for groups of 15-20 (mornings only).**
6 acres either side of the R Test. Fine

display of daffodils and spring flowering trees. Main garden has herbaceous and annual borders, fruit trees, rose pergola, lavender walk and extensive lawns. An arboretum planted in the 1930s by Sir Harold Hillier contains trees and shrubs providing interest throughout the yr.

68 LAKE HOUSE
Northington SO24 9TG. Lord Ashburton, 07795 364539, lukeroeder@hotmail.com. *4m N of Alresford. Off B3046. Follow English Heritage signs to The Grange, then directions.* Home-made teas. **Adm £4.50, chd free.** Thur 11, Sun 14 June (12-5.30). **Visitors also welcome by arrangement June to Sept for groups of 10+.**
2 large lakes in Candover Valley set off by mature woodland with waterfalls, abundant birdlife, long landscaped vistas and folly. 1½ acre walled garden with rose parterre, mixed borders, long herbaceous border, rose pergola leading to moon gate. Flowering pots, conservatory and greenhouses. Picnicking by lakes. Grass paths and slopes to some areas of the garden.

69 LITTLE COURT
Crawley, nr Winchester SO21 2PU. Mrs A R Elkington, 01962 776365, elkslc@btinternet.com. *5m NW of Winchester. Between B3049 (Winchester - Stockbridge) & A272 (Winchester - Andover).* Home-made teas in the village hall. Teas in the garden for group visits. **Adm £3 (Feb & May), £4 (Mar), chd free.** Fri 20, Sun 22, Tue 24 Feb (2-5); Sun 15 Mar, Thur 7, Sun 10 May (2-5.30). **Also open on 7, 10 May Tanglefoot. Opening with Crawley Gardens on 6, 7 April, 11, 14 June. Visitors also welcome by arrangement Feb to July.**
In a small and pretty village, a traditional walled country garden which is spectacular in spring, with countless bulbs, hellebores and snowdrops, and cowslips in the labyrinth. 3 acres with large beds of perennials in harmonious colours and a good lawn. Fun for children; treehouse and swings. The garden is sheltered with many seats and fine views. Field with butterflies. Classic kitchen garden. Visitors say 'timeless', 'entrancing', 'paradise for children'.

70 LITTLEWOOD

West Lane, Hayling Island
PO11 0JW. Mr & Mrs Steven
Schrier. *3m S of Havant. From A27
Havant & Hayling Island junction,
travel S for 2m, turn R into West Lane
& continue 1m. House set back from
road in a wood.* Home-made teas.
**Adm £3, chd free. Sat 2, Sun 3
May (11-5).**
2½ acre bluebell wood and spring
flowering garden surrounded by fields
and near sea, protected from sea
winds by multi barrier hedge.
Rhododendrons, azaleas, camellias
and many other shrubs. Woodland
walk to full size treehouse. Features
incl pond, bog garden, house plants,
summerhouse, conservatory and
many places to sit outside and under
cover. Dogs on leads and picnickers
welcome. Close to Hayling Billy
Coastal Trail.

71 NEW 99 LOCKS HEATH PARK ROAD

Locks Heath, Southampton
SO31 6LY. Linda & David Goringe.
*2m W of Fareham. From M27
J9 take A27 to Southampton. At 2nd
r'about sharp L into Hunts Pond Rd.
R at 1st of 2 mini-r'abouts into
Church Rd. Then L into Locks Heath
Park Rd.* Home-made teas.
**Combined adm with 101 Locks
Heath Park Road £4, chd free.
Sat 16, Sun 17 May, Sat 12,
Sun 13 Sept (11-5).**
Delightful plant lover's 150ftx50ft
garden designed for yr-round interest,
replanted over the last 5 yrs with
emphasis on coloured foliage. Island
bed, varied ground cover perennials,
sun and shade loving plants.
Hellebores and bulbs in spring and
unusual shrubs in bloom or with
attractive fruit in autumn. Fish pond
with water lilies, 5 raised vegetable
beds, and 2 greenhouses. Wheelchair
access: one small step (12cm) from
patio to main garden area and gentle
slope around raised vegetable beds.

72 NEW 101 LOCKS HEATH PARK ROAD

Locks Heath SO31 6LY. Barbara &
Graham Peckham. *2m W of
Fareham. From M27 J9 take A27 to
Southampton. At 2nd r'about sharp
L into Hunts Pond Rd. R at 1st of
2 mini-r'abouts into Church Rd.
Then L into Locks Heath Park Rd.*
Home-made teas. **Combined adm
with 99 Locks Heath Park Road £4,**
chd free. **Sat 16, Sun 17 May, Sat
12, Sun 13 Sept (11-5).**
A garden 120ft x 40ft that has been
created over the yrs by Barbara &
Graham, who just enjoy gardening.
Busy borders with yr-round interest,
incl many plants that attract
butterflies and bees. Herb and pot
garden. Unusual and varied selection
of fruit trees and bushes incl Asian
pear, honey berry and blueberry.
Vegetable plot with greenhouse.

*A magical garden to
get lost in and
popular with
birdwatchers . . .*

73 LONGSTOCK PARK

Leckford, Stockbridge SO20 6EH.
Leckford Estate Ltd, part of John
Lewis Partnership,
www.longstockpark.co.uk. *4m S of
Andover. From A30 turn N onto
A3057 & follow signs to Longstock.*
Home-made teas at Longstock Park
Nursery. **Adm £6, chd £2. Sun 21
June (2-5).**
Famous water garden with extensive
collection of aquatic and bog plants
set in 7 acres of woodland with
rhododendrons and azaleas. A walk
through park leads to National
Collections of *Buddleja* and *Clematis
viticella*; arboretum, herbaceous
border. Assistance dogs only.
 NCH

74 NEW LOWER NORTON FARMHOUSE

Norton, Sutton Scotney,
Winchester SO21 3NE. Tom &
Alison Coleman. *10m N of
Winchester. From Sutton Scotney,
follow Bullington Lane signed towards
A303 & A34. After ¾ m turn R,
signed Norton. At top of lane turn L at
T-junction & follow lane for further 500
metres.* Home-made teas. **Adm £3,
chd free. Sat 6, Sun 7 June (2-6).**

1 acre family garden with herbaceous
borders and box providing structure
to relaxed cottage garden planting.
Wildlife pond with call ducks and
chickens. Large lawn area with wild
flowers, set off by water feature. New
borders with iris, grasses and
agapanthus. Vegetable garden. Short
walk to redundant watercress beds,
now a chalk lake haven for wildlife,
access by tractor and trailer ride.
Wheelchair access, please note
gravel drive.

75 ♦ MACPENNYS WOODLAND GARDEN & NURSERIES

Burley Road, Bransgore,
Christchurch BH23 8DB. Mr & Mrs
T M Lowndes, 01425 672348,
www.macpennys.co.uk. *6m S of
Ringwood, 5m NE of Christchurch.
From Crown PH Xrds in Bransgore
take Burley Rd, following sign for
Thorney Hill & Burley. Entrance ¼ m
on R.* **For opening times and
information, please phone or see
garden website.**
12 acres of nursery with 4 acre gravel
pit converted into woodland garden
planted with many unusual plants.
Offering interest yr-round, but
particularly in spring and autumn.
Large nursery displaying for sale a
wide selection of trees, shrubs,
conifers, perennials, hedging plants,
fruit trees and bushes. Tearoom
offering home-made cakes, Dorset
tea, New Forest ice cream, locally
produced honey, jams and chutneys;
using locally sourced foods wherever
possible. Partial wheelchair access.

76 1 & 2 MAPLE COTTAGE

Searles Lane, off London Road
(A30), Hook RG27 9EQ. John & Pat
Beagley. *A30 Hartley Wintney side of
Hook opp Hampshire Prestige Cars.
Use Hook House overflow car park,
immed on L. ¼ m up lane to entrance
& parking for those with walking
difficulties. Follow yellow ribbons.*
Home-made teas. Gluten free cake &
biscuits available. **Adm £3, chd free.
Wed 3, Thur 4, Sun 7, Wed 10,
Thur 11 June (2-5).**
1 acre offering two differing
established gardens with views
towards R Whitewater. Mature fruit
trees and shrubs, vegetable plots,
cottage style herbaceous borders,
courtyard garden, small wildlife pond,
and named hostas. Features incl a
tree cave for children, a good

Old Thatch, Old Thatch & The Millennium Barn

© Leigh Clapp

selection of birds and the chance to purchase handcrafted wood carvings for the garden and wood turning for the home. Some paved paths, mainly grassed areas.

& ⊕ ☕

77 MEON ORCHARD

Kingsmead, N of Wickham PO17 5AU. Doug & Linda Smith, 01329 833253, meonorchard@btinternet.com. *5m N of Fareham. From Wickham take A32 N for 1¹/₂ m. Turn L at Roebuck Inn. Continue ¹/₂ m. Park on verge or in field N of property.* Home-made teas. **Adm £4, chd free. Sun 31 May, Sun 26 July, Sun 6 Sept (2-6). Visitors also welcome by arrangement May to Sept for groups of 20+ or minimum charge.** 1¹/₂ acre garden designed and constructed by current owners. An exceptional range of rare, unusual and architectural plants incl National Collection of Eucalyptus. Dramatic foliage plants from around the world, both hardy and tender. Big bananas, huge taros, tree ferns, cannas, gingers and palms dominate in Sept, flowering shrubs in May/June and perennials in July. Streams and ponds plus an extensive range of planters

complete the display. See plants you have never seen before. Features for 2015 incl the recently acquired 20 acre meadow behind property, with ¹/₂ m of Meon River frontage. Visitors are welcome to explore this wonderful addition. Plant sale of the exotic and rare on Sun 6 Sept only. Garden fully accessible by wheelchair, reserved parking.

& 🐾 ⊕ 🚌 **NCH** ☕

78 MICHAELMAS

2 Old Street, Hill Head, Fareham PO14 3HU. Ros & Jack Wilson, 01329 662593, jazzjack00@gmail.com. *4¹/₂ m S of Fareham. From Fareham follow signs to Stubbington, then Hill Head. Turn R into Bells Lane. After 1m pass Osborne View PH on L, next R is Old St.* Home-made teas. **Adm £3, chd free. Sun 19, Mon 20 July (2-5). Visitors also welcome by arrangement June to Aug for groups of 10-20.** Very cheerful, colourful small garden with the wow factor. A variety of tall plants for a tall lady! Many are grown from seed or cuttings. Small vegetable garden, greenhouse, garden room, pot grown vegetables and flowers. Styled in the fashion of a

country garden with a wide range of plants with the emphasis on perennials. As pictured in preface of The Gardens of England book. 1 min walk from beach, 5 mins walk from Titchfield Haven Nature Reserve.

⊕ ☕

79 THE MILL AT GORDLETON

Silver Street, Sway, Lymington SO41 6DJ. Mrs Liz Cottingham, 01590 682219, info@themillatgordleton.co.uk, www.themillatgordleton.co.uk. *2m W of Lymington. From Lymington town centre head N on A337, in 500yds turn L after PH, for Sway & Hordle. Garden is 2m. Tickets available from Reception Desk.* Light refreshments. **Adm £3. Every Mon 5 Jan to 30 Nov (11-4) excl Bank Hols.** This old mill is now a small country hotel and restaurant. The meandering stream which bisects the garden has many areas of different character. The Mill Art Walk is a fascinating display of metal, glass and wooden sculptures created by local artists. Ducks, salmon and trout are abundant in the river. Plentiful outside seating.

& 🛏 ☕

Qni The Queen's Nursing Institute

NGS support makes a vital difference to our patient care

GROUP OPENING

80 MONXTON & AMPORT GARDENS

Amport SP11 8AY. *3m SW of Andover. Turn off A303 signed to East Cholderton from E or Thruxton Village from W. Follow signs to Amport. Parking in field next to village green.* Tea at Monxton & Amport Village Hall. **Combined adm £5, chd free.** Sun 24, Mon 25 May (1.30-6).

AMPORT PARK MEWS
Amport Park Mews Ltd

BRIDGE COTTAGE
Jenny Burroughs

FLEUR DE LYS
Ian & Jane Morrison

GAYCORREL
Mr & Mrs Perren

NEW SANDLEFORD HOUSE
Mr & Mrs Valerie & Michael Taylor

WHITE GABLES
Mr & Mrs D Eaglesham

Monxton and Amport are two pretty villages linked by Pill Hill Brook. Visitors have 6 gardens to enjoy. New for 2015, Sandleford House with its locally built iron pergola walkway along part of the western boundary. The garden is entirely walled in brick and flint. Bridge Cottage a 2 acre haven for wildlife, with the banks of the trout stream and lake planted informally with drifts of colour, a large vegetable garden, fruit cage, small mixed orchard and arboretum with specimen trees. Amport Park Mews has 11 borders arranged around a communal space surrounded by converted stable and carriage blocks

in historic mews. Fleur de Lys garden is a series of rooms with glorious herbaceous borders, leading to a large orchard. Gaycorrel the ½ acre working garden of a National Vegetable Society Judge and Fellow. Vegetables, dahlias and fruit are grown for exhibition. White Gables a cottage style garden with a collection of trees, incl a young giant redwood, along with old roses and herbaceous plants. No wheelchair access to White Gables.

 ♿ 🌱 ☕

81 MOORE BLATCH

48 High Street, Lymington SO41 9ZQ. *Top end of Lymington High St, on S side. Follow signs for Lymington town centre and use High St car parks.* Home-made teas. **Adm £3.50, chd free.** Sat 25 Apr (9.30-1); Sun 26 Apr (2-5).
Situated behind this elegant Georgian town house lies a surprising s-facing walled garden of 1 acre. From the raised terrace, enjoy the long vista across the croquet lawn to mature gardens beyond and then over to the Isle of Wight. Amusing and varied topiary interplanted with stunning tulips and forget-me-nots. Attractions close by incl the Lymington Saturday Market and the lively waterfront at the bottom of the High St.

🌱 ♿ ☕

82 NEW 4 NIGHTINGALE MEWS

Locks Heath, Southampton SO31 6GA. Mrs Kath Stratton. *3m W of Fareham. M27 J9 follow A27 Southampton, L into Hunts Pond Rd. R into Church Rd, 2nd L St Johns Rd, R Woodpecker Copse, Nightingale Mews on L. Please park in Woodpecker Copse.* Home-made teas. **Adm £3, chd free.** Sat 18, Sun 19 July, Sat 1, Sun 2 Aug (2-6).
Very colourful steeply sloping terraced garden 65ftx75ft established over 5 yrs and divided into varied sections incl a shady white garden with a water feature. A shelled gazebo at the top has stunning views of the striking planting, sculptures and planted roof garden. A lower patio, with hanging baskets and pots, has seats to see different perspectives of trees and shrubs in the tiered garden. Gold award for hanging and wall baskets in Fareham in Bloom. Wheelchair access to lower patio only.

♿ ☕

83 OAK TREE COTTAGE

Upper Common Road, Pennington, Lymington SO41 8LD. Sue Kent, 01590 677294, Sue.Kent9@btinternet.com. *2m NW of Lymington. From N off A337, turn into Sway Rd, 1½ m to Wheel Inn. Turn L into Ramley Rd & follow signs. Leave M27 J2 & follow Heavy Lorry Route to avoid traffic in Lyndhurst.* Home-made teas. **Adm £3, chd free.** Sat 18, Sun 19 July (2-5). Visitors also welcome by arrangement May to Aug for groups of 20+.
This 1 acre garden has a wealth of surprises, but with continuity. Using a limited palette of plants, with repetition of blue and silver, it flows from one secluded space to another. Designed with a gentle variation of levels and using many trees, contrasting foliage and flowers, one can become delightfully lost. Partial wheelchair access.

♿ ☕

84 OLD DROXFORD STATION

Station Road, Soberton, Southampton SO32 3QU. Jo & Tony Williams. *12m E of Winchester, 12m SW of Petersfield. A32 N through Droxford. After ½ m turn R (opp petrol station), under bridge, turn R (before Hurdles PH), property 1st on R, park in road. Please call 01489 878271 to arrange disability parking.* Tea. **Adm £3.50, chd free.** Sun 12 July (11-4).
A sympathetically restored railway station with wild flower garden in the former track. Established specimen trees, perennials, annuals and bulbs. Raised vegetable beds, greenhouse and a new orchard. Winston Churchill was based here before D Day.

♿ 🌱 ☕

GROUP OPENING

85 OLD THATCH & THE MILLENNIUM BARN

Sprats Hatch Lane, Winchfield, Hook RG27 8DD. *From A287 Odiham to Farnham turn N to Dogmersfield, L by Queens Head PH & L at Barley Mow. From Winchfield to Dogmersfield, R after 1⅓ m at Barley Mow.* Home-made teas. **Combined adm £4, chd free.** Sun 19 Apr, Sun 19 July, Sun 6 Sept (2-6).

THE MILLENNIUM BARN
Mr & Mrs S White

OLD THATCH
Jill Ede
www.old-thatch.co.uk

Two gardens in one! A small secluded haven sits under the old oak tree next to the pond, surrounded by yr-round colour and seasonal fragrance from roses and honeysuckle. You can listen to birdsong, wind chimes and the trickling of a small waterfall whilst enjoying views of Old Thatch and the cottage garden beyond. Who could resist visiting Old Thatch, a chocolate box thatched cottage, featured on film and TV, and evolving smallholding with a 5 acre garden and woodland alongside the Basingstoke Canal (unfenced). A succession of spring bulbs, a profusion of wild flowers, perennials and home grown annuals pollinated by our own bees and fertilised by the donkeys, who await your visit. Over 30 named clematis and rose cultivars. Lambs in April and donkey foals in summer. Children enjoy our quiz on Sundays and the tree lookout (supervised, please), Dads love the cakes and Mums enjoy the music and craft stalls. On 19 July, why not linger, enjoy the music and a glass of wine. Arrive by boat! Slipway opp Barley Mow PH. Basingstoke Canal Society may have boat trips to coincide with Sunday openings. Wheelchair access by grass slopes and paths. Limited disabled parking on-site (ask at car park entrance).

♿ 🐕 ❀ 🚐 ☕

---

86 ORDNANCE HOUSE
West Dean, Salisbury SP5 1JE. Terry & Vanessa Winters, 01794 341797, terry.winters@ordnancehouse.com, www.ordnancehouse.com. *7m W of Romsey. Park at West Dean Recreation Ground, 350yds away. Disability parking only at garden.* Home-made teas. **Adm £3.50, chd free. Sun 24 May (12-5). Visitors also welcome by arrangement June to July for groups of 10+.**
The garden changes through the seasons from its late spring and summer displays of purple and white alliums and foxgloves to the rich colour pallet of June to August. Lavender is a signature plant and used throughout the garden. Comprises many herbaceous beds, small orchard, compact soft fruit and vegetable gardens and formal parterre. Seating areas have views of garden and countryside beyond. Featured in The English Garden (Aug 2014), Amateur Gardening (19 July 2014) and in Germany, Garden Style (Summer 2014).

🐕 ❀ 🚐 ☕

87 ◆ PATRICK'S PATCH
Fairweather's Garden Centre, High Street, Beaulieu SO42 7YB. Mr P Fairweather, 01590 612307, www.fairweathers.co.uk. *SE of New Forest at head of Beaulieu River. Leave M27 at J2 & follow signs for Beaulieu Motor Museum. Go up High St & park in Fairweather's on LH-side.* **For opening times and information, please phone or see garden website.**
Model kitchen garden with a full range of vegetables, trained top and soft fruit and herbs. Salads in succession used as an educational project for all ages. Maintained by volunteers, primary school children and a part-time gardener. A very productive garden enclosed by walls built from New Forest heather bales and local softwood.

♿ 🐕 ❀ 🚐 ☕

88 PENNINGTON HOUSE
Ridgeway Lane, Lower Woodside, Lymington SO41 8AA. Sue Stowell & John Leach. Head Gardener Tom Maskell. *1½ m S of Lymington. A337 S of Lymington. L at r'about. R into Ridgeway Lane. At Chequers Inn, turn R onto the drive of Pennington House. Car parking available at the house.* Home-made teas. **Adm £4, chd free. Sat 20, Sun 21 June (2-4.30).**
7 acre garden created around 1910 by Frederick Grotian. Expansive lawns and clipped yew hedging surround the Italian sunken garden, rose garden, rejuvenated rockeries, ponds and stream. The large Victorian walled garden and glasshouse are in full use and all has been organic for 24 yrs. A rural, tranquil setting overlooking the Solent. Some gravel paths.

♿ ❀ ☕

89 PILLEY HILL COTTAGE
Pilley Hill, Pilley, Lymington SO41 5QF. Steph & Sandy Glen, 01590 677844, stephglen@hotmail.co.uk, www.pilleyhillcottage.com. *New Forest. 2m N of Lymington off A337. To avoid traffic delays in Lyndhurst leave M27 at J2.* Cream teas.

Visitors welcome by arrangement Mar to May for groups of 10+. Naturalistic, wildlife friendly garden of surprises around every corner. Enter through the rose covered lych gate, to a spectacle of colour. Wild flowers rub shoulders with perennials among quaint objects and oak structures. Meander through the wild old orchard through willow walks and oak archways, onto the shady pond garden. Take tea on the front lawn surrounded by herbaceous borders. Some visitors with wheelchairs have managed our garden, so please phone to discuss.

♿ 🐕 ❀ 🚐 ☕

> A small secluded haven sits under the old oak tree next to the pond, surrounded by year-round colour and seasonal fragrance from roses and honeysuckle . . .

90 PYLEWELL PARK
South Baddesley, Lymington SO41 5SJ. Lord Teynham. *Coast road 2m E of Lymington. From Lymington follow signs for Car Ferry to Isle of Wight, continue for 2m to South Baddesley.* Home-made teas. **Adm £3.50, chd free. Sun 5 Apr, Sun 24 May (2-5).**
A large parkland garden laid out in 1890. Enjoy a walk along the extensive grass paths, bordered by fine rhododendrons, magnolias, embothriums and cornus. Wild daffodils in bloom at Easter and bluebells in May. Large lakes are bordered by giant gunnera, onto magnificent views of the Solent. Lovely for families and dogs. Wear suitable footwear for muddy areas.

🐕 ☕

© Leigh Clapp

Michaelmas

GROUP OPENING

91 ROMSEY GARDENS

Mill Lane, Romsey SO51 8EU. *Town centre, all gardens within walking distance of Romsey Abbey, clearly signed. Car parking by King John's Garden*. Home-made teas at King John's House. **Combined adm £6, chd free. Sun 24, Mon 25 May** (11-5.30).

KING JOHN'S GARDEN
Friends of King John's Garden & Test Valley Borough

4 MILL LANE
Miss J Flindall
Visitors also welcome by arrangement Mar to Oct.
01794 513926

NEW THE NELSON COTTAGE
68 Cherville Street. Margaret Prosser

NEW THE OLD THATCHED COTTAGE
Mill Lane. Genevieve & Derek Langford

Romsey is a small, unspoilt, historic market town with the majestic C12 Norman Abbey as a backdrop to 4 Mill Lane, a garden described by Joe Swift as 'the best solution for a long thin garden with a view'. King John's Garden, with its fascinating listed C13 house, has all period plants that were

available before 1700; it also has an award-winning Victorian garden with a courtyard where tea is served (no dogs, please). The Nelson Cottage was formally a PH; its ½ acre garden has a variety of perennial plants and shrubs, with a wild grass meadow bringing the countryside into the town. The Old Thatched Cottage (C15) has a small garden undergoing further development by new owners; it features a variety of shrubs, lawn, vegetable patch, fruit cordons, rockery and water feature. No wheelchair access at 4 Mill Lane.

♿ ♿ ♿ ♿

92 ROTHERFIELD PARK
East Tisted, Alton GU34 3QE. Sir James & Lady Scott. *4m S of Alton on A32. Please do not use SatNav*. Home-made teas. **Adm £4, chd free.** Sun 3 May (2-5).
Take some ancient ingredients: ice house, ha-ha, lime avenue; add a walled garden, fruit and vegetables, trees and hedges; set this 12 acre plot in an early C19 park (picnic here from noon) with views to coin clichés about. Mix in a bluebell wood and Kim Wilkie's modern take on an amphitheatre by the stable block. Top growers selling plants, incl Marcus Dancer and Phoenix Perennial Plants. Good disabled access to walled garden.

♿ ♿ ♿

93 NEW 2 SAMPAN CLOSE
Warsash, Southampton SO31 9BU. Amanda & Robert Bailey. *4½ m W of Fareham. M27 J9 take A27 W, L at Park Gate into Brook Lane by Esso garage. Straight over 3 r'abouts, L at 4th r'about into Schooner Way. Sampan Close, 4th on R. Please park in Schooner Way*. Home-made teas. **Adm £2.50, chd free.** Sat 16, Sun 17 May (11.30-4).
Sited on former strawberry fields this compact garden 50ftx27ft was designed by the owner, an enthusiastic horticulturalist, to give yr-round interest. Inspirational design ideas for tiny plots with perennials, grasses, old roses, trough planting and raised vegetable beds. A small brick rill edges a circle of lawn. A blue, lean to glasshouse, against a brick garden wall is an attractive feature.

♿

94 SANDY SLOPES
Honeysuckle Lane, Headley Down, Bordon GU35 8EH. Mr & Mrs R Thornton. *6m S of Farnham. From A3 exit S-side of Hindhead tunnel, proceed to Grayshott, then Headley Down via B3002. From Farnham proceed S, A325 to Bordon turn L onto B3002 via Lindford & Headley to Headley Down*. Tea. **Adm £3, chd free.** Mon 4, Mon 25 May (2-5.30).
A plantsman's garden with a remarkable collection of mature plants from China and other parts of the world. Many of these are rare and exciting. Some are naturalised and many are woodland shade lovers such as trilliums, areseamas, primulas and rare blue meconopsis, growing beneath mature rhododendrons, magnolias and rare trees. Rising terraced ground with a stream and wildlife pond. Steep slopes and steps, unsuitable for pushchairs and visitors with walking difficulties.

♿ ♿

95 'SELBORNE'
Caker Lane, East Worldham GU34 3AE. Brian & Mary Jones, 01420 83389, mary.trigwelljones@virgin.net. *2m SE of Alton. On B3004 at Alton end of East Worldham opp The Three Horseshoes PH (please note, not in the village of Selborne). Parking signed*. Home-made teas. **Adm £3, chd free.** Share to East Worldham Church Fabric Fund (Apr) & Tafara Mission Zimbabwe (Aug).

Sat 18, Sun 19 Apr, Sat 16, Sun 17 May, Sat 1, Sun 2, Mon 3 Aug (2-5). Also open with East Worldham Gardens on 27, 28 June; 25, 26 July. Visitors also welcome by arrangement Apr to Aug for individuals and groups.

A garden of surprises! This ¹/₂ acre mature garden, with views across farmland, features an old established orchard of named varieties. Mixed, densely planted borders contain hardy geraniums and other herbaceous plants and shrubs. Containers, metal and stone sculpture enhance the borders. Relax and enjoy tea sitting in the dappled shade of the orchard. Summerhouses and conservatory provide shelter. Book stall, garden quizzes for children and a sandpit. Featured in the Tindle Newspaper Group. Wheelchair access, please note some gravel paths.

96 SHALDEN PARK HOUSE
The Avenue, Shalden, Alton GU34 4DS. Mr & Mrs Michael Campbell. 4¹/₂ m NW of Alton. B3349 from Alton or M3 J5 onto B3349. Turn W at Golden Pot PH marked Herriard, Lasham, Shalden. Entrance ¹/₄ m on L. Disabled parking on entry. Home-made teas. **Adm £4, chd free.** Sun 31 May (2-5).

Large 4 acre garden to stroll round with beautiful views. Herbaceous borders incl kitchen walk and rose garden, all with large scale planting and foliage interest. Pond, arboretum, perfect kitchen garden and garden statuary.

97 NEW SHRONER WOOD
Basingstoke Road, Martyr Worthy, Winchester SO21 1AG. John Anstruther-Gough-Calthorpe, 01962 882073. 5m N of Winchester. From S, take A33 N from Kings Worthy & after 1¹/₂ m, just before the dual carriageway begins, turn R. From N, take A33 S from M3 J7 & after 8m, at the end of the dual carriageway, turn L. Home-made teas. **Adm £5, chd free.** Sun 10 May (2-5). Visitors also welcome by arrangement Mar to May for groups of 30+.

A return to the NGS after 30 yrs, a 7 acre arboretum of great historical significance begun over 100 yrs ago by the Hillier family. Many fine and unusual trees and shrubs incl rhododendrons, azaleas and magnolias on a carpet of bluebells and wild flowers in late spring. Extensive restoration work in recent yrs has resulted in a garden to explore with a wonderful feeling of sanctuary.

Creative use of every available space . . .

GROUP OPENING

98 SOUTHSEA GARDENS
Southsea, Portsmouth PO4 0PR. St Ronan's Rd can be found off Albert Rd, Southsea. Follow signs from Albert Rd or Canoe Lake on seafront. Parking in Craneswater School. Home-made teas at 28 St Ronan's Avenue (June), wine (July). **Combined adm £5, chd free.** Sun 7 June (2-6). Evening Opening £6, chd free, Sat 4 July (5-8).

27 ST RONAN'S AVENUE
Mr & Mrs S C Johns

28 ST RONAN'S AVENUE
Ian Craig & Liz Jones
www.28stronansavenue.co.uk

85 ST RONAN'S ROAD
Mr Mike Hodges

87 ST RONAN'S ROAD
Miss Judy Walker

Four town gardens conveniently within 100 metres of each other. Each has a distinctive style, with different designs showing what can be achieved in an urban setting. 85 St Ronan's Road is a city garden with a classical twist, featuring a Neptune water feature in a pool of smoke. The inside-out garden at 87 St Ronan's Road captures busy urban living at its best, with an impressive dining area and sitting room with a permanent outside fireplace. Clever evergreen planting has been used to create privacy in a city setting. 85 and 87 have both won national landscape design awards and have been featured on TV. There is exceptional design at 27 St Ronan's Avenue where landscaping has been used to create a modern family concept with exuberant planting. 28 St Ronan's Avenue showcases the more traditional with a mixture of tender, exotic and dry loving plants incl king proteas, bananas, ferns, agaves, echeverias and echiums.

---

99 SPINDLES
24 Wootton Road, Lee-on-the-Solent, Portsmouth PO13 9HB. Peter & Angela Arnold, 02393 115181, elijahblew22@sky.com. 6m S of Fareham. Exit A27, turn L Gosport Rd A32. At r'about 2nd exit Newgate Lane B3385. Through 3 r'abouts, turn L Marine Parade B3333 onto Wootton Rd. Home-made soup (April). Home-made teas (June). **Adm £3, chd free.** Sun 19 Apr (10-2); Sun 21 June (2-6). Visitors also welcome by arrangement May to July for groups of 30 max.

An exciting and constantly changing garden, cottage style planting alongside exotic and tropicals. Creative use of every available space, fine display of roses and clematis, tiny pond and bog garden. Hostas, ferns, herbs, grasses, succulents, grapes, figs, olives, strawberries and blueberries.

100 ◆ SPINNERS GARDEN
School Lane, Boldre, Lymington SO41 5QE. Andrew & Vicky Roberts, 07545 432090, www.spinnersgarden.co.uk. 1¹/₂ m N of Lymington. Follow the brown signs off the A337 between Lymington & Brockenhurst. Also signed off the B3054 Beaulieu to Lymington road. Map available on website. Cream teas incl in adm. **Adm £5, chd free.** For NGS: Mon 6 Apr (11-4). For other opening times and information, please phone or see garden website.

Peaceful woodland garden with azaleas, rhododendrons, magnolias, acers and other rare shrubs underplanted with a wide variety of choice woodland and ground cover plants. The garden has been extended over the last 5 yrs and the views opened up over the Lymington valley. More recently, building work has been completed on a new house in the grounds designed to complement the garden. Partial wheelchair access.

101 **THE STABLE FAMILY HOME TRUST GARDEN**
The Stables, Bisterne, Ringwood BH24 3BN. Mrs Marion Davies. *3½ m S of Ringwood. Follow B3347 through Bisterne Village from Ringwood. Past Manor House, entrance on L.* Cream teas. **Adm £3.50, chd free. Share to SFHT.**
Sat 13, Sun 14 June (2-5.30).
3 walled gardens lovingly tended by our head gardener and some of the 100 adults with learning difficulties in our care. Gravel garden a riot of colour with flowers, shrubs and herbs and adorned with pottery objects made here. Kitchen garden with polytunnels, greenhouse and raised vegetable beds. The small rose garden is a place of peace, leading to main lawn with pond and dragon head fountain, also made in our pottery.

102 **NEW** **STANFORD HOUSE**
St James Lane, Winchester SO22 4NX. Mrs Ann Hauser. *S-side of city, leave centre of Winchester by Southgate St. 1st R into St James Lane. Parking 3rd L in Christchurch Rd or over railway bridge on RH-side of road.* Tea. **Adm £3.50, chd free.**
Sun 6 Sept (1-5).
Lovely ¾ acre garden with strong design. Redeveloped since 2003 by architect owners to complement Georgian house, lawned garden, shady woodland and hot garden, with interwoven paths throughout. Long views to the south and east. Koi carp pond, kitchen garden with cutting borders, large greenhouse and Mediterranean outside sitting room. Wide range of hydrangeas, perennials and annuals.

103 **STOCKBRIDGE GARDENS**
Stockbridge SO20 6EX. *9m W of Winchester. On A30, at junction of A3057 & B3049. Parking on High St. All gardens on High St & Winton Hill.* Tea on St Peter's Church Lawn. **Combined adm £6, chd free. Share to St Peter's Church.** Thur 18, Sun 21 June (2-5.30).

LITTLE WYKE
High Street. Mrs Mary Matthews

NEW **OLD SWAN HOUSE**
High Street. Mr Herry Lawford

SHEPHERDS HOUSE
Winton Hill. Kim & Frances Candler

TROUT COTTAGE
High Street. Mrs Sally Milligan

Stockbridge with its many listed houses, excellent shops and PH is on the famous R Test. Four gardens are open this yr offering a variety of styles and character. Tucked in behind the High St, Trout Cottage's small walled garden flowers for almost 10 mths of the yr. Little Wyke, also on the High St next to the Town Hall, has a long mature town garden with mixed borders and fruit trees. Old Swan House, at the east end of the High St, is a newly designed garden offering mature fishpond with waterlilies, long lawn under a 100 yr old hazel facing mirror herbaceous borders, an ancient brick and flint wall sheltering mixed planting and shrub roses, and a gravel grass garden bounded by brick paths and a partly mature orchard. Shepherds House, 50yds east of the White Hart r'about, is a s-facing, ¾ acre maturing garden on rising ground with informal shrubberies, colourful borders, lawns, ponds, woodland glade and small orchard.

104 **TANGLEFOOT**
Crawley, Winchester SO21 2QB. Mr & Mrs F J Fratter, 01962 776243, fred@tanglefoot-house. demon.co.uk. *5m NW of Winchester. Between B3049 (Winchester - Stockbridge) & A272 (Winchester - Andover). Lane beside Crawley Court (Arqiva). Drop-off at house; parking in field.* **Adm £3 (May) & £3.50 (July), chd free.** Thur 7, Sun 10 May, Thur 23, Sun 26 July (2-5.30).

Also open on 7, 10 May Little Court. Opening with Crawley Gardens on 11, 14 June, 2, 5 July. Visitors also welcome by arrangement May to July.
Designed and developed by owners since 1976, Tanglefoot's ½ acre garden is a blend of influences, from Monet-inspired rose arch and small wildlife pond to Victorian boundary wall with trained fruit trees. Highlights include a raised lily pond, small wildflower meadow, herbaceous bed (a riot of colour later in the summer), herb wheel, large productive kitchen garden and unusual flowering plants. A recently purchased 2 acre field is being converted into spring and summer wildflower meadows, with (mostly native) trees and shrubs; we hope our garden visitors will enjoy seeing it develop over the years. Watercolour flower paintings. Plants from the garden for sale. Featured in Hampshire Life (July 2014).

105 **TERSTAN**
Longstock, Stockbridge SO20 6DW. Alexander & Penny Burnfield, penny.burnfield@andover.co.uk, www.pennyburnfield.wordpress. com. *½ m N of Stockbridge. From Stockbridge (A30) turn N to Longstock at bridge. Garden ½ m on R.* Home-made teas. **Adm £4, chd free.** Suns 10 May, 21 June, 5 July, 6 Sept (2-6). Visitors also welcome by arrangement May to Sept with coach parking available.
1 acre, intensively planted, with an artist's flair for colour and design. Relax on one of the many seats with views across the R Test to the Hampshire Downs and listen to gentle jazz. An exuberance of rare and unusual plants. Live summer afternoon music. Featured in several magazines. Wheelchair access, but some gravel paths and steps.

106 **THE THATCHED COTTAGE**
Church Road, Upper Farringdon, Alton GU34 3EG. Mr & Mrs David & Cally Horton, 01420 587922, dwhorton@btinternet.com. *3m S of Alton off A32. At S end of Lower Farringdon take road to Upper Farringdon. At top of hill turn L into Church Rd, follow road to cottage on R, opp church.* Home-made teas at Berry Cottage (next door). **Adm £3.50, chd free.**

Sun 24 May, Sun 14 June (2-5.30). Evening Opening, wine, Wed 24 June (6-8). Sun 12 July (2-5.30). **Combined adm with Berry Cottage (next door) £5.00, chd free. Visitors also welcome by arrangement May to Aug for groups of 10+.**
A once neglected 1½ acre garden that has been lovingly restored over the last 3 yrs. Running south from a beautiful C16 thatched cottage the formal lawn and packed borders blend into more informal areas of perennial and shrub planting, to vegetables, fruit and wild flowers surrounding a gypsy caravan. Chickens, ducks and guinea fowl. Fully accessible by wheelchair after a short gravel drive.

107 TYLNEY HALL HOTEL
Ridge Lane, Rotherwick RG27 9AZ. Elite Hotels, 01256 764881, sales@tylneyhall.com, www.tylneyhall.co.uk. *3m NW of Hook. From M3 J5 via A287 & Newnham, M4 J11 via B3349 & Rotherwick.* Light refreshments in the Chestnut Suite from 12.00pm. **Adm £5, chd free. Sun 26 Apr, Mon 11 May, Sun 7 June, Sun 4 Oct (10-4).**
Large garden of 66 acres with extensive woodlands and fine vista being restored with new planting. Fine avenues of wellingtonias; rhododendrons and azaleas, Italian garden, lakes, large water and rock garden, dry stone walls originally designed with assistance of Gertrude Jekyll. Partial wheelchair access.

108 WALBURY
Lower Froyle, Alton GU34 4LJ. Ernie & Brenda Milam, 01420 22216, walbury@uwclub.net. *5m NE of Alton. Access to Lower Froyle from A31 between Alton & Farnham at Bentley. Parking available near Walbury,* at village hall. Home-made teas. **Adm £3, chd free. Sat 25, Sun 26 Apr, Thur 2 July (2-5). Visitors also welcome by arrangement Apr to July.**
⅓ acre garden divided into 3 sections. Each section has a cottage garden atmosphere with different styles, packed with plants in colour themed borders incl many unusual plants. There are water features, an alpine house and fern walk. Wheelchair access to 2 of the 3 sections of the garden.

109 WALDRONS
Brook, Bramshaw SO43 7HE. **Major & Mrs J Robinson.** *4m N of Lyndhurst. On B3079 1m W from M27 J1. 1st house L past Green Dragon PH & directly opp Bell PH.* Home-made teas. **Adm £3, chd free.** Sun 24 May (2-5).
Come and be suprised by our 1 acre garden hidden behind a high hedge on the edge of the New Forest. The garden contains a raised alpine garden, raised vegetable beds, fruit cage, a fern and hosta wooded area, a greenhouse and large herbaceous beds with shrubs and unusual plants giving yr-round colour.

110 WALHAMPTON
Beaulieu Road, Walhampton, Lymington SO41 5ZG. Walhampton School Trust Ltd. *1m E of Lymington. From Lymington follow signs to Beaulieu (B3054) for 1m & turn R into main entrance at 1st school sign 200yds after top of hill.* Tea. **Adm £4, chd free. Share to St John's Church, Boldre.** Sun 10 May (2-5.30).
Glorious walks through large C18 landscape garden surrounding magnificent mansion (not open). Visitors will discover 3 lakes, serpentine canal, climbable prospect mount, period former banana house and orangery, fascinating shell grotto, glade and terrace by Peto (c1907), drives and colonnade by Mawson (c1914). Seating, guided tours with garden history. Gravel paths, some slopes.

111 WEIR HOUSE
Abbotstone Road, Old Alresford SO24 9DG. Mr & Mrs G Hollingbery, 01962 735549, jhollingbery@me.com. *½ m N of Alresford. From Alresford down Broad St (B3046) past Globe PH. Take 1st L, signed Abbotstone. Park in signed field.* Home-made teas. **Adm £5, chd free. Sun 13 Sept (2-5). Visitors also welcome by arrangement May to Sept for groups of 10+.**
Spectacular riverside garden with sweeping lawn backed by old walls, yew buttresses and mixed perennial beds. Contemporary vegetable and cut flower garden at its height in Sept. Also incl newly designed garden around pool area, bog garden (at best in May) and

wilder walkways through wooded areas. Children can use the playground (at their own risk). Wheelchair access to most of garden.

112 NEW ◆ WEST GREEN HOUSE GARDENS
Thackhams Lane, Hartley Wintney RG27 8JB. Miss Marylyn Abbott, 01252 844611, www.westgreenhouse.co.uk. *3m NE of Hook. Turn N off A30 at Phoenix Green at Thackhams Lane, follow signs.* Tea in the Courtyard Tearooms. On Tue 28 July there will be a champagne bar and the opportunity to picnic by the lake. The gardens will be illuminated at 9pm. **Adm £8, chd £4. For NGS: Tue 2 June (11-4.30). Evening Opening £12, chd £4, wine, Tue 28 July (7.30-10). For other opening times and information, please phone or see garden website.**
Within its C18 walls the magnificent Walled Garden is a tapestry of exuberantly planted lavish herbaceous borders, elaborate potager and parterres. Outside the walls an informal lake field is studded with neoclassical follies, chinoiserie bridges and cascades. A grand water staircase and Italianate fountain provide a dramatic focal point. New this year is a Meadow Garden with a stunning pagoda. The Garden is always changing and always inspirational. Featured in The English Garden, Gardens Illustrated, Country Life, & Hampshire Life. BBC Gardeners World from The Chelsea Flower Show 2014 featured West Green House Gardens and Marylyn Abbotts Topiarist Garden. Wheelchair access, but some of the paths around the garden are gravel.

A grand water staircase and Italianate fountain provide a dramatic focal point . . .

113 WEST SILCHESTER HALL
Silchester RG7 2LX. Mrs Jenny
Jowett, 01189 700278,
www.jennyjowett.com. *9m N of
Basingstoke. 9m S of Reading, off
A340 (signed from centre of village).*
Home-made teas. **Adm £4, chd free.**
Sun 24, Mon 25 May, Sun 12 July,
Sun 9 Aug (2-6). Visitors also
welcome by arrangement May to
Aug for groups of 10+, coaches
welcome.
This much loved 2 acre garden has
fascinating colour combinations
inspired by the artist owners with
many spectacular herbaceous
borders filled with rare and unusual
plants flowering over a long period.
Many pots filled with half hardies, a
wild garden surrounding a natural
pond, banks of rhododendron, a self
supporting kitchen garden with lovely
views across a field of grazing cattle.
Large studio with exhibition of the
owners botanical, landscape and
portrait paintings, cards and prints.
Wheelchair access to most of the
garden, gravel drive.
&. 🎍 ❀ 🚐 ☕

114 WHEATLEY HOUSE
Wheatley Lane, between Binsted &
Kingsley, Bordon GU35 9PA. Mr &
Mrs Michael Adlington, 01420
23113, susannah@westcove.ie. *4m
E of Alton, 5m SW of Farnham. Take
A31 to Bentley, follow sign to Bordon.
After 2m, R at Jolly Farmer PH
towards Binsted, 1m L & follow signs
to Wheatley.* Home-made teas. **Adm
£4, chd free.** Sat 12, Sun 13 Sept
(1.30-5.30). Visitors also welcome
by arrangement Apr to Oct for
groups of 10+, with refreshments
on request.
Magnificent setting with panoramic
views over fields and forests.
Sweeping mixed borders,
shrubberies and grasses. $1^{1}/_{2}$ acres,
designed by artist owner. The colours
are spectacular. Striking white and
black border, now with deep red
accents. Local craft stalls, paintings,
and home-made teas in Old Barn.
Wheelchair access with care on
lawns, good views of garden and
beyond from terrace.
&. ❀ 🚐 ☕

115 WHISPERS
Chatter Alley, Dogmersfield
RG27 8SS. Mr & Mrs John Selfe,
01252 613568. *3m W of Fleet. Turn
N to Dogmersfield off A287 Odiham
to Farnham Rd. Turn L by Queen's
Head PH.* **Adm £5, chd free.**

Visitors welcome by arrangement
June to Aug for groups of 20+.
Come and discover new plants in this
2 acre garden of manicured lawns
surrounded by large borders of
colourful shrubs, trees and long
flowering perennials. Wild flower area,
water storage system, greenhouse,
kitchen garden and living sculptures.
Spectacular waterfall cascades over
large rock slabs and magically
disappears below the terrace. A
garden not to be missed. Gravel
entrance.
&. ❀

117 NEW THE WHITE HOUSE
Queenwood, Broughton,
Stockbridge SO20 8DF. Susan &
Nick Snook. *5m SW of Stockbridge.
From the A30, take the B3084 to
Broughton. After approx 2m (having
gone past Broughton) turn R towards
East & West Tytherley & Lockerley.
The White House is 1m on R.* Home-
made teas. **Adm £3.50, chd free.**
Thur 25, Sun 28 June (2-5).
Developing garden of 1 acre
surrounding Regency house (not
open). Scented rose terrace leading
to lawn surrounded by delphinium
filled herbaceous borders. Small
potager (or vegetable garden if slugs
have been kind), mixed borders and
mown paths through hay paddock.
Set in lovely rural spot on sloping
ground, some gravel and steps.
☕

The planting
has been
chosen to provide
nectar and habitat
for Wicor's rich
wildlife . . .

118 NEW 42 WHITEDOWN
Alton GU34 1LU. Ms Jo Carter. *In
Alton, leave The Butts Green on your
L, go past stone fountain & L into
Borovere Gardens. Go down to
T-junction then L into Whitedown,
follow road round. 42 is on R. Park on
road or at Butts Green.* Home-made
teas. **Adm £2.50, chd free.** Sat 20,
Sun 21 June (2-5.30).

A warm welcome awaits at this small
town garden, which is a feast for the
eyes and shows what can be done
within a limited space and lots of
creativity. Garden designer Jo and her
sculptor husband Richard, have
created from scratch an exuberant
and varied collection of shapes,
colours and textures, where
traditional and exotic plants mingle
with sculptures.
❀ ☕

**119 WICOR PRIMARY SCHOOL
COMMUNITY GARDEN**
Portchester, Fareham PO16 9DL.
Louise Bryant. *$^{1}/_{2}$ way between
Portsmouth & Fareham on A27. Turn
S at Seagull PH r'about into
Cornaway Lane, 1st R into Hatherley
Drive. Entrance to school is almost
opp.* Home-made teas. **Adm £3.50,
chd free.** Sat 20 June, Sun 5 July
(10-2).
Beautiful school gardens tended by
pupils, staff and community
gardeners. Wander along the
Darwin's path to see the Jurassic
garden, orchard, tropical bed, wildlife
areas and allotment, plus one of the
few Camera Obscuras in the south of
England. The gardens are situated in
historic Portchester with views of
Portsdown Hill. The planting has been
chosen to provide nectar and habitat
for Wicor's rich wildlife.
&. ❀ ☕

GROUP OPENING

120 WILDHERN GARDENS
Andover SP11 0JE. *From Andover
or Newbury A343. After Enham
Alamein or Hurstbourne turn at Xrd to
Penton Mewsey. Wildhern is $^{3}/_{4}$ m on
R. Parking at village hall.* Home-made
teas in village hall. **Combined adm
£5, chd free.** Sat 27, Sun 28 June
(2-5.30).

> **ELM TREE COTTAGE**
> Ian & Rosie Swayne
>
> **NEW LITTLE ORCHARD**
> Mrs Sue McGregor
>
> **OAKWOOD**
> Jean Pittfield
>
> **STARLINGS**
> Annie Bullen & Roy Wardale

All four gardens are within easy
walking distance of the village hall car
park. Oakwood with its mature
borders is planted for yr-round
interest and has a large pond framed

Little Court, Crawley Gardens

by unusual plants. Mixed woodland behind the garden frames the well kept shrubs and perennials. Two newly planted gardens at Elm Cottage and Little Orchard offer different planting styles, the former already a traditional cottage garden, although planted only 3 yrs ago, meticulously kept and designed to wrap colourfully around the old thatched cottage. The vibrant front garden of Little Orchard with close packed colour and fruit trees in mounded beds, set off by tall grasses, leads into an embryonic forest garden with uncommon edibles and vegetables in raised beds. The restoration of the ³/₄ acre garden at Starlings, begun 4 yrs ago, features a sunken gravel garden with nectar bearing plants and grasses, a small winter garden, a rose bearing pergola and enclosed vegetable beds shared by a tortoise. No wheelchair access to sunken gravel garden at Starlings, but can be viewed from decking.

121 WILLOWS

Pilley Hill, Boldre, Lymington SO41 5QF. Elizabeth & Martin Walker, 01590 677415, elizabethwalker13@gmail.com, www.willowsgarden.co.uk. *New Forest. 2m N Lymington off A337. To avoid traffic in Lyndhust, leave M27 at J2 & follow Heavy Lorry Route.* Cream teas. **Adm £3.50, chd free. Sun 26 July, Sat 8, Sun 9, Sun 30, Mon 31 Aug (2-5). Visitors also welcome by arrangement July to Sept for groups of 20+.**
Bold brilliant borders frame Willow's front lawn. Rich red crocosmias, cannas, dahlias and zinnias star in succession, with contrasting variegated grasses, bamboos, bananas and gingers. Giant hostas, gunneras and ferns lead up the jungle walk to the upper garden. Here dark leaved dahlias and billowing grasses thrive with a backdrop of cool hydrangeas. Plant Sale Sun 30 & Mon 31 Aug with 3 or 4 of the best local nurseries attending with Chelsea Gold medal winners Heucheraholics, Marcus Dancer Clematis & Kevin Hughes Plants. Featured as Garden Of the Week in Gardeners News (Sept 2014).

122 1 WOGSBARNE COTTAGES

Rotherwick RG27 9BL. Miss S & Mr R Whistler. *2¹/₂ m N of Hook. M3 J5, M4 J11, A30 or A33 via B3349.* Home-made teas. **Adm £3, chd free. Sun 12, Mon 13 July (2-5).**
Small traditional cottage garden with a roses around the door look, much photographed, seen on calendars, jigsaws and in magazines. Mixed flower beds and borders. Vegetables grown in abundance. Ornamental pond and alpine garden. Views over open countryside to be enjoyed whilst you take afternoon tea on the lawn. The garden has been open for the NGS for more than 30 yrs. Small vintage motorcycle display (weather permitting). Some gravel paths.

HEREFORDSHIRE

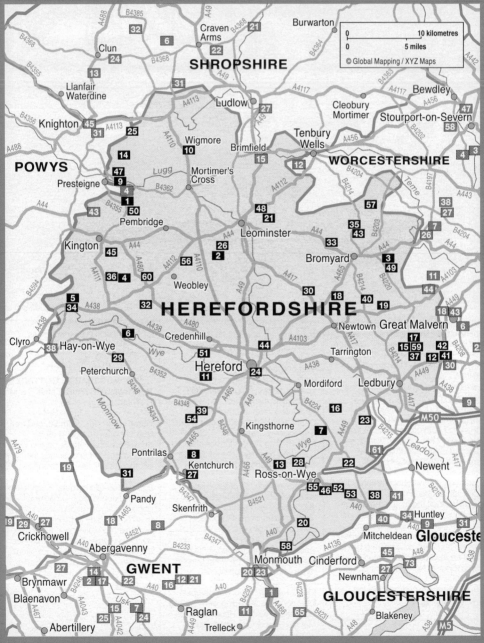

Herefordshire

Herefordshire is essentially an agricultural county, characterised by small market towns, black and white villages, fruit and hop orchards, meandering rivers, wonderful wildlife and spectacular, and often remote, countryside (a must for keen walkers).

As a major region in the Welsh Marches, Herefordshire has a long and diverse history, as indicated by the numerous prehistoric hill forts, medieval castles and ancient battle sites. Exploring the quiet country lanes can lead to many delightful surprises.

For garden enthusiasts there are many NGS gardens to visit, ranging from small town plots to informal cottage, wildlife, sculpture and grand formal gardens.

Widely contrasting in design and planting, they offer inspiration and innovative ideas to the garden visitor – and always a warm welcome. In addition, a range of excellent specialist nurseries propagate tempting collections of rare and unusual plants.

Herefordshire Volunteers

County Organiser
Rowena Gale
01568 615855
rowena.jimgale@btinternet.com

County Treasurer
Michael Robins
01531 632232
m.robins101@btinternet.com

Publicity
Sue Evans
01568 614501
s.evans.gp@btinternet.com

Booklet Coordinator
Chris Meakins
01544 370215
christine.meakins@btinternet.com

Booklet Distribution
Andrew Hallett
01981 570401
ar.hallett@gmail.com

Assistant County Organisers
David Hodgson
01531 640622
dhodgson363@btinternet.com

Sue Londesborough
01981 510148
slondesborough138@btinternet.com

Gill Mullin
01989 750593
gill@longorchard.plus.com

Penny Usher
01568 611688
pennyusher@btinternet.com

Left: Weston Hall

Currently the NGS donates around £2.5 million every year

Opening Dates

All entries subject to change.
For latest information check www.ngs.org.uk

February

Thursday 5
26 Ivy Croft

Thursday 12
26 Ivy Croft

Thursday 19
26 Ivy Croft

Wednesday 25
51 The Weir

Thursday 26
26 Ivy Croft

March

Sunday 1
32 Midland Farm

Saturday 14
15 Coddington Vineyard
59 Woofields Farm

Sunday 15
15 Coddington Vineyard
37 NEW Old Colwall House
38 The Old Corn Mill
59 Woofields Farm

Sunday 22
54 Whitfield

Saturday 28
43 NEW Ralph Court Gardens

Sunday 29
43 NEW Ralph Court Gardens

April

Wednesday 1
48 Stockton Bury Gardens

Sunday 5
10 Bury Court Farmhouse
38 The Old Corn Mill

Monday 6
38 The Old Corn Mill

Sunday 12
30 Lower Hope

Monday 13
35 Moors Meadow Gardens & Nursery

Wednesday 15
6 Brobury House Gardens

Sunday 19
2 Aulden Farm
26 Ivy Croft

Sunday 26
3 The Bannut
5 Brilley Court
54 Whitfield

May

13 Church Cottage (every Tuesday and Wednesday from May 19)
56 Windsor Cottage (every Tuesday and Thursday from May 26)

Friday 1
45 Rhodds Farm

Sunday 3
41 Perrycroft
58 Woodview

Sunday 10
6 Brobury House Gardens
32 Midland Farm

Monday 11
35 Moors Meadow Gardens & Nursery

Saturday 16
43 NEW Ralph Court Gardens

Sunday 17
4 Batch Cottage
43 NEW Ralph Court Gardens

Monday 18
9 Bryan's Ground
23 Hellens

Tuesday 19
23 Hellens

Sunday 24
2 Aulden Farm
10 Bury Court Farmhouse
11 The Carpenters
26 Ivy Croft
30 Lower Hope
38 The Old Corn Mill
47 Stapleton Castle Court Garden

Homemade ice cream and yummy cakes . . . !

Monday 25
2 Aulden Farm
26 Ivy Croft
38 The Old Corn Mill
47 Stapleton Castle Court Garden

Wednesday 27
3 The Bannut

Sunday 31
16 Croose Farm

June

13 Church Cottage (every Tuesday and Wednesday)
56 Windsor Cottage (every Tuesday and Thursday)

Monday 1
36 Newport House

Tuesday 2
36 Newport House

Wednesday 3
36 Newport House

Thursday 4
33 NEW Mistletoe Lodge
36 Newport House

Friday 5
33 NEW Mistletoe Lodge
36 Newport House
45 Rhodds Farm

Festival Weekend

Saturday 6
33 NEW Mistletoe Lodge
43 NEW Ralph Court Gardens
55 Wilton Castle on the Wye

Sunday 7
4 Batch Cottage
7 Brockhampton Cottage
12 Caves Folly Nurseries
16 Croose Farm
18 NEW Dovecote Barn
22 Grendon Court
33 NEW Mistletoe Lodge
37 NEW Old Colwall House
39 The Old Rectory
43 NEW Ralph Court Gardens
55 Wilton Castle on the Wye

Monday 8
35 Moors Meadow Gardens & Nursery

Saturday 13
17 The Cross
53 Weston Mews
57 Wolferlow House

Sunday 14
8 The Brooks
17 The Cross
18 NEW Dovecote Barn
27 Kentchurch Gardens
53 Weston Mews
60 Woonton & Almeley Gardens

Friday 19
20 NEW Goodrich Gardens
24 Hereford Cathedral Gardens

Sunday 21
11 The Carpenters

Sunday 28
1 Ashley Farm
3 The Bannut
14 Cloister Garden
41 Perrycroft

July

13 Church Cottage (every Tuesday and Wednesday)
56 Windsor Cottage (every Tuesday and Thursday)

Wednesday 1
6 Brobury House Gardens

Friday 3
45 Rhodds Farm

Monday 6
35 Moors Meadow Gardens & Nursery

Saturday 11
25 Hill House Farm

Sunday 12
11 The Carpenters
25 Hill House Farm
27 Kentchurch Gardens
30 Lower Hope
49 Stone House
58 Woodview

Saturday 18
49 Stone House

Sunday 19
58 Woodview

Wednesday 22
49 Stone House

Saturday 25
46 NEW Ross-on-Wye Community Garden

Sunday 26
46 NEW Ross-on-Wye Community Garden

August

13 Church Cottage (every Tuesday and Wednesday until Aug 12)

56 Windsor Cottage (every Tuesday and Thursday until Aug 27)

Saturday 1
42 The Picton Garden

Monday 3
35 Moors Meadow Gardens & Nursery

Friday 7
20 NEW Goodrich Gardens
45 Rhodds Farm

Sunday 9
42 The Picton Garden

Saturday 15
42 The Picton Garden
43 NEW Ralph Court Gardens

Sunday 16
43 NEW Ralph Court Gardens

Thursday 20
42 The Picton Garden

Monday 24
42 The Picton Garden

Friday 28
20 NEW Goodrich Gardens

Saturday 29
31 Middle Hunt House

Sunday 30
31 Middle Hunt House
39 The Old Rectory
42 The Picton Garden
47 Stapleton Castle Court Garden

Monday 31
47 Stapleton Castle Court Garden

September

Friday 4
45 Rhodds Farm

Saturday 5
42 The Picton Garden

Sunday 6
2 Aulden Farm
26 Ivy Croft

Friday 11
42 The Picton Garden

Sunday 13
8 The Brooks
10 Bury Court Farmhouse
34 Montpelier Cottage
37 NEW Old Colwall House

Thursday 24
51 The Weir

Friday 25
42 The Picton Garden

Sunday 27
30 Lower Hope

October

Friday 2
45 Rhodds Farm

Sunday 4
41 Perrycroft

Thursday 8
42 The Picton Garden

Sunday 11
36 Newport House

Sunday 18
42 The Picton Garden

February 2016

Thursday 4
26 Ivy Croft

Thursday 11
26 Ivy Croft

Thursday 18
26 Ivy Croft

Thursday 25
26 Ivy Croft

Gardens open to the public

3 The Bannut
6 Brobury House Gardens
9 Bryan's Ground
12 Caves Folly Nurseries
23 Hellens
24 Hereford Cathedral Gardens
31 Middle Hunt House
35 Moors Meadow Gardens & Nursery
42 The Picton Garden
48 Stockton Bury Gardens
51 The Weir

By arrangement only

19 NEW Evesbatch Court
21 Grantsfield
28 Lawless Hill
29 Little Llanavon
40 The Orchards
44 The Rambles
50 Upper Tan House
52 Weston Hall

Also open by arrangement

1 Ashley Farm
2 Aulden Farm
4 Batch Cottage
5 Brilley Court
10 Bury Court Farmhouse
13 Church Cottage
14 Cloister Garden
22 Grendon Court
25 Hill House Farm
26 Ivy Croft
30 Lower Hope
36 Newport House
38 The Old Corn Mill
39 The Old Rectory, Thruxton
41 Perrycroft
20 NEW Poole Cottage, Goodrich Gardens
47 Stapleton Castle Court Garden
53 Weston Mews
54 Whitfield
57 Wolferlow House
58 Woodview

The Gardens

1 ASHLEY FARM
Stansbatch HR6 9LN. Roger & Jackie Pietroni, 01544 267405, rogerpietroni@gmail.com, www.ashleyfarm.net. *2m S of Presteigne. 1m N of Titley. On B4355.* Home-made teas. Adm £5, chd free. Sun 28 June (2-5.30). Visitors also welcome by arrangement May to Sept.
5-acre garden started in 2005. A series of formal rooms surrounding the house becoming more informal further away. Many places to sit and contemplate. Wonderful views. Topiary, pleached limes, knot garden, colour-themed borders and orchards with wild flowers. Lots of roses and an autumn walk. There is a nuttery with species and wild roses too. Decorative and productive kitchen garden. Featured in The English Garden, House and Garden and Saturday Telegraph.
❀ ☕

2 AULDEN FARM
Aulden, Leominster HR6 0JT. Alun & Jill Whitehead, 01568 720129, web@auldenfarm.co.uk, www.auldenfarm.co.uk. *4m SW of Leominster. From Leominster take Ivington/Upper Hill rd, ³/₄ m after Ivington church turn R signed Aulden. From A4110 signed Ivington, take 2nd R signed Aulden.* Home-made teas. Homemade ice cream. Adm £3.50, chd free. Sun 19 Apr, Sun 24, Mon 25 May, Sun 6 Sept (2-5.30). Combined with Ivy Croft, adm £6. Visitors also welcome by arrangement Apr to Sept, individual or groups.
Informal country garden surrounding old farmhouse, 3 acres planted with wildlife in mind. Emphasis on structure and form, with a hint of quirkiness, a garden to explore with eclectic planting. Irises thrive around a natural pond, shady beds and open borders, seats abound, feels mature but ever evolving. Homemade ice cream and yummy cakes! National Collection of Siberian Iris and plant nursery.
❀ 🚐 NCH ☕

You are always welcome at an NGS garden!

3 ◆ **THE BANNUT**

Bringsty, Bromyard WR6 5TA.
Gareth & Tamla Bowdler,
thebannut@yahoo.com,
www.facebook.com/thebannut.
*2½ m E of Bromyard. On A44
Worcester Rd, ½ m E of entrance to
National Trust, Brockhampton.*
Home-made teas. **Adm £4.50, chd
free. For NGS: Sun 26 Apr, Wed 27
May, Sun 28 June (11-4). For other
opening times and information,
please email or see garden
website.**
This well-known and established 3-acre garden is starting a new chapter
with new owners for 2015. Traditional
garden with stunning Rhododendron
and Laburnum walks. Garden rooms
including a unique knot garden,
specimen trees and an extensive
heather garden. Some areas will be
undergoing transformation. Nature
trail and potting area for children. Tea
room serving homemade cakes and
refreshments. Some garden rooms
not accessible to wheelchairs.

THE BARTON
See Worcestershire.

4 **BATCH COTTAGE**

Almeley HR3 6PT. Jeremy &
Elizabeth Russell, 01544 327469.
*16m NW of Hereford. 2m off A438-
A4111 to Kington, turn R at Eardisley.*
Home-made teas. **Adm £4, chd free.
Sun 17 May, Sun 7 June (2-5.30).
Visitors also welcome by
arrangement Mar to Sept.**
Established unregimented,
conservation-oriented garden of
some 2½ acres with streams and
large pond, set in a natural valley,
surrounded by woodland and
orchard. Over 360 labelled trees and
shrubs, mixed borders, fern and bog
beds, wild flower bank, stumpery,
woodland walk. Fritillaries and
spotted orchids abound in season.
Partial wheelchair access- some
gravel paths and steep slopes.

BIRTSMORTON COURT
See Worcestershire.

BRIDGES STONE MILL
See Worcestershire.

5 **BRILLEY COURT**

Whitney-on-Wye HR3 6JF. Mr &
Mrs David Bulmer, 01497 831467,
rosebulmer@hotmail.com. *6m NE of
Hay-on-Wye. 5m SW of Kington.*

*1½ m off A438 Hereford to Brecon rd
signed to Brilley.* Home-made teas.
**Adm £4, chd free. Sun 26 Apr
(2-5.30). Visitors also welcome by
arrangement Apr to Sept
individuals and groups.**
3-acre garden, walled ornamental
kitchen garden. Spring tulip
collection, summer rose and
herbaceous borders. 7-acre
arboretum/wild stream garden, wild
flowers and rhododendron collection.
Partial wheelchair access.

Two hidden gems
of Goodrich:
contrasting in
terms of style
and size . . .

6 ◆ **BROBURY HOUSE
GARDENS**

Brobury by Bredwardine HR3 6BS.
Keith & Pru Cartwright, 01981
500229, www.broburyhouse.co.uk.
*10m W of Hereford. S off A438
signed Bredwardine & Brobury.
Garden 1m on L (before bridge).*
Home-made teas. **Adm £5, chd £2.
For NGS: Wed 15 Apr (2-5); Sun 10
May (11-5); Wed 1 July (2-5).
For other opening times and
information, please phone or see
garden website.**
9 acres of gardens, set on the banks
of an exquisitely beautiful section of
the R Wye, offer the visitor a delightful
combination of Victorian terraces with
mature specimen trees, inspiring
water features, architectural planting
and woodland areas. Redesign and
development is ongoing. Bring a
picnic, your paint brushes, binoculars
and linger awhile. Wheelchair users,
strong able-bodied assistant
advisable.

7 **BROCKHAMPTON
COTTAGE**

Brockhampton HR1 4TQ. Peter &
Ravida Clay. *8m SW of Hereford;.
5m N of Ross-on-Wye on B4224. In
Brockhampton take rd signed to*

church, cont up hill for ½ m, after set
of farm buildings, driveway on L, over
cattle grid. Car park 500yds from
garden. **Adm £5, chd free. Sun 7
June (10.30-2). Combined adm
with Grendon Court £8, (2-5).**
Created from scratch in 1999 by the
owners and Tom Stuart-Smith, this
beautiful hilltop garden looks S and W
over miles of unspoilt countryside. On
one side a woodland garden and wild
flower meadow, on the other side a
Perry pear orchard and in valley
below: lake, stream and arboretum.
Picnic parties welcome by lake until
2pm. Visit Grendon Court (2-5) after
your visit to us.

8 **THE BROOKS**

Pontrilas HR2 0BL. Marion & Clive
Stainton,
www.marionet.co.uk/the_brooks.
*12m SW of Hereford. From the A465
Hereford to Abergavenny rd, turn L at
Pontrilas onto B4347, take 2nd L
signed Orcop & Garway Hill. Garden
1¾ m on L.* Home-made teas. **Adm
£4, chd free. Sun 14 June, Sun 13
Sept (2-5.30).**
This 2½ -acre Golden Valley garden
incl part-walled enclosed vegetable
garden and greenhouse (wind/solar-powered), orchard, ornamental,
perennial, shade and shrub borders,
wildlife pond, evolving arboretum cum
coppice, and meadow with stunning
views. Surrounding a stone 1684
farmhouse (not open), the garden has
mature elements, but much has been
created since 2006, with future
development plans.

9 ◆ **BRYAN'S GROUND**

Letchmoor Lane, nr Stapleton,
Presteigne LD8 2LP. David Wheeler
& Simon Dorrell, 01544 260001,
www.bryansground.co.uk. *12m NW
of Leominster. Between Kinsham &
Stapleton. At Mortimer's Cross take
B4362 signed Presteigne. At Combe,
follow signs. SATNAV is misleading.
Coaches: please pre-book.* Home-made teas. **Adm £6, chd £2. For
NGS: Mon 18 May (2-5). For other
opening times and information,
please phone or see garden
website.**
8-acre internationally renowned
contemporary reinterpretation of an
Arts and Crafts garden dating from
1912, conceived as series of rooms
with yew and box topiary, parterres,
colour-themed flower and shrub
borders, reflecting pools, potager,

Edwardian greenhouse, heritage apple orchard, follies. Arboretum of 400 specimen trees and shrubs with wildlife pool beside R Lugg. Home of Hortus, garden journal. The majority of the garden is accessible by wheelchair, though there are some steps adjoining the terrace.

 ♿ ☢ 🚐 ☕

10 ▶ BURY COURT FARMHOUSE

Ford Street, Wigmore, Leominster HR6 9UP. Margaret & Les Barclay, 01568 770618, **l.barclay2@virgin.net.** *10m from Leominster, 10m from Knighton. On A4110 from Leominster, at Wigmore turn R just after shop & garage. Follow signs to parking and garden.* Home-made teas. **Adm £3.50, chd free. Sun 5 Apr, Sun 24 May, Sun 13 Sept (2-5). Visitors also welcome by arrangement Mar to Sept visitors and groups up to 20.** ³/₄ acre garden, 'rescued' since 1997, surrounds the 1840's stone farmhouse (not open). The courtyard contains a pond, mixed borders, fruit trees and shrubs, with steps up to a terrace which leads to lawn and vegetable plot. The main garden (semi-walled) is on two levels with mixed borders, greenhouse, pond, mini-orchard with daffodils in spring, and wildlife areas. Year-round colour.

♿ ☕

11 ▶ THE CARPENTERS

Eaton Bishop, Hereford HR2 9QD. Christine & Alan Morris. *4m SW Hereford. A465 towards Abergavenny. After 2¹/₂ m turn R on B4349, after Clehonger turn R to Eaton Bishop. Park at village hall, continue on foot about 100yds.* Home-made teas. **Adm £3.50, chd free. Sun 24 May, Sun 21 June, Sun 12 July (2-6).** 2 acre garden with 25 planted areas incl herbaceous and mixed borders, ditch border, shrubberies, wild life areas, many trees and pond. Amateur gardener never satisfied, always changing and developing new and existing areas. Mainly flat with no significant slopes but all paths grass. Suitable for disability scooters but not wheelchairs.

🚗 ♿ ☕

12 ◆ CAVES FOLLY NURSERIES

Evendine Lane, Colwall WR13 6DX. Wil Leaper & Bridget Evans, 01684 540631, www.cavesfolly.com.

The Carpenters

1¹/₄ m NE of Ledbury. B4218. Between Malvern & Ledbury. Evendine Lane, off Colwall Green. Home-made teas. **Adm £3, chd free. For NGS: Sun 7 June (2-5). For other opening times and information, please phone or see garden website.** Organic nursery and display gardens. Specialist growers of Cottage garden plants and Alpines. All plants are grown in peat free organic compost. This is not a manicured garden! It is full of drifts of colour and wild flowers and a haven for wildlife.

♿ 🚗 ♿ 🚐 🛌 ☕

13 ▶ CHURCH COTTAGE

Hentland, Ross-on-Wye HR9 6LP. Sue Emms & Pete Weller, 01989 730222, sue.emms@mac.com. *6m from Ross-on-Wye. A49 from Ross. R turn to Hentland/Kynaston. At bottom of hill sharp R to St Dubricius Church. Narrow lane - please take care. Unsuitable for motor homes/caravans.* Tea. **Adm £3, chd free. Every Tue & Wed 19 May to 12 Aug (2-5). Visitors also welcome by arrangement May to Aug groups welcome.** Garden designer and plantswoman's ¹/₂ -acre evolving garden packed with plants, many unusual varieties mixed with old favourites, providing interest over a long period. Wildlife pond, rose garden, potager, mixed borders,

white terrace, gravel garden. Interesting plant combinations and design ideas to inspire.

♿ ☕

14 ▶ CLOISTER GARDEN

Pant Hall, Willey, Presteigne LD8 2LY. Malcolm Temple & Karen Roberts, 01544 260066, karmal@live.co.uk, www.karenontheborders. wordpress.com. *3m N of Presteigne. Exactly 3m from Lugg Bridge at St Andrews Church in Presteigne. Follow rd from bridge, signed to Willey. Pass Stapleton Castle on R. Pant Hall on L on 3rd hill - blue house.* Home-made teas. **Adm £4, chd free. Sun 28 June (2-5). Visitors also welcome by arrangement May to Sept groups or individuals - please ring.** In total 6 acres. The ¹/₂ -acre ornamental garden incorporates terraced lawns, flower beds and shrubberies leading down to a small pond and bog area. Bordering one side is a stream over which a bridge leads to a steep bank cut through with paths rising to a recently terraced orchard field and a half acre wild field with large pond. Beyond is a 3 acre recently planted woodland with avenues and meadow. Artist designed garden.

♿ 🛌 ☕

15 CODDINGTON VINEYARD
Coddington HR8 1JJ. Sharon & Peter Maiden. *4m NE of Ledbury. From Ledbury to Malvern A449, follow brown signs to Coddington Vineyard.* Cream teas. Light lunches pre booked only. **Adm £3.50, chd free.** Sat 14, Sun 15 Mar (12-4.30). Combined with Woofields, adm £6. 5 acres incl 2-acre vineyard, listed farmhouse, threshing barn and cider mill. Garden with terraces, wild flower meadow, woodland with masses spring bulbs, pond and stream. Unusual perennials, trees and shrubs.

16 CROOSE FARM
Woolhope HR1 4RD. Mrs C Malim. *5m N of Ross-on-Wye. Woolhope signed off the B4224 Ross to Hereford rd. From Woolhope take rd opp the Church signed Sollars Hope & The Hyde. Follow garden signs.* Home-made teas. **Adm £5, chd free.** Sun 31 May, Sun 7 June (1-5). 3-acre country garden, set in middle of lovely Woolhope dome, created from original farmyard in 1987. Now well established it has as its theme a number of separate small gardens. These incl a 'hot bed', rose garden, white garden, courtyards, knot garden, water garden and wild flower meadow. The garden is stocked with a great variety of shrubs, trees and herbaceous plants.

17 THE CROSS
Coddington, Ledbury HR8 1JL. Brian & Megan Taylor. *4m N of Ledbury. From Colwall take Mill Lane to Coddington (3m), then follow NGS signs. From Bosbury, take B4220, turn R at sign to Coddington and Colwall. After 2m follow NGS signs.* Home-made teas. **Adm £3, chd free.** Sat 13, Sun 14 June (2-5). 1-acre informal country garden. Generous mixed borders lavishly planted with shrubs, roses, perennials and bulbs. Wildlife pond and native flower patch. Gravel garden and vegetables. Pleasant walk through paddock leads to a tranquil path through 5 acres of mature woodland. Lovely views of the Malvern Hills. Display of willow and wire sculpture by Chelsea exhibitor Victoria Westaway. All paths are gravel.

18 NEW DOVECOTE BARN
Stoke Lacy, Bromyard HR7 4HJ. Gill Pinkerton & Adrian Yeeles. *4m S of Bromyard on A465. Turn into lane running alongside Stoke Lacy Church. Parking in 50 metres.* Home-made teas at Stoke Lacy Church adjacent to Dovecote Barn. **Adm £4, chd free.** Sun 7, Sun 14 June (2-5). Nestling in the unspoilt Lodon Valley, a 2-acre, organic, wildlife-friendly garden designed in 2008. Featuring ornamental vegetable and fruit gardens, peaceful and romantic pond area, copse with specimen trees for spring and autumn colour, winter walk, wildflower meadow and dry garden. The C17 barn, framed by cottage garden planting, looks out over the garden to the Malvern Hills beyond. Gravel paths.

19 NEW EVESBATCH COURT
Bishops Frome, Worcester WR6 5BD. Mr & Mrs J Blackwell, 07722 377590, phil.telos@gmail.com. *10m W of Worcester. 1m from A4103, next to the church in Evesbatch.* Tea. **Adm £5, chd free. Visitors welcome by arrangement** Apr to Sept for groups of 6 - 30. A new garden, mostly created since 2008. It features mixed borders, formal lawns, a kitchen, fountain temple gardens. The planting is traditional, with a good variety of old shrub roses. Much of the garden is wheelchair accessible via gravel paths and gently sloping lawns.

GROUP OPENING

20 NEW GOODRICH GARDENS
Goodrich, Ross on Wye HR9 6HX. *5m from Ross on Wye 7m from Monmouth. Close to Goodrich Castle in Wye Valley AONB. Goodrich signed from A40 or take B4234 from Ross on Wye. Park in village & follow signs to gardens. Very limited parking close to Poole Cottage - please walk from village if possible - 10mins uphill.* Home-made teas. **Combined adm £5, chd free.** Fri 19 June, Fri 7, Fri 28 Aug (11-5).

NEW MULBERRY HOUSE
Knapp Close. Tina & Adrian Barber

NEW POOLE COTTAGE D
Jo Ward-Ellison & Roy Smith
Visitors also welcome by arrangement June to Sept individuals & groups. 01600 890148 jo@ward-ellison.com

Two hidden gems of Goodrich: contrasting in terms of style and size but each making the most of their very different settings. One in village centre, the other a 10 min walk up Coppett Hill overlooking the R Wye. Mulberry House: a delightful rear garden with views out to beautiful listed village buildings. Imaginatively planted and nurtured by a plant lover with an artistic eye. Themed herbaceous borders and areas of shrub planting provide a long season of colour and interest. Roses, peonies and alliums enhance the predominately cottage garden feel. Poole Cottage: created from scratch over the past 4yrs, this 2 acre hillside garden has a predominately naturalistic style with many grasses and later flowering perennials. Home to designer Jo Ward-Ellison, the garden continues to evolve with new plantings to extend the seasons. Some steep slopes, steps and uneven paths. Features incl a pond loved by wildlife, small orchard and kitchen garden with fabulous views.

21 GRANTSFIELD
nr Kimbolton, Leominster HR6 0ET. Colonel & Mrs J G T Polley, 01568 613338. *3m NE of Leominster. A49 N from Leominster, at A4112 turn R, then immed R (signed Hamnish), 1st L, then R at Xds. Garden on R after*

$^1/_2$ m. Tea. **Adm £3.50, chd free.**
Visitors welcome by arrangement
Apr to Sept visitors and groups welcome.
Contrasting styles in gardens of old stone farmhouse; wide variety of unusual plants, trees and shrubs, old roses, climbers, herbaceous borders, superb views. 1$^1/_2$ -acre orchard and kitchen garden with flowering and specimen trees and shrubs. Spring bulbs. Comma butterfly saved from extinction here by Emma Hutchinson in 1890s.

22 GRENDON COURT
Upton Bishop, Ross on Wye, Herefordshire HR9 7QP. Mark & Kate Edwards, 079713 39126, kate@grendoncourt.co.uk. *3m NE of Ross-on-Wye. M50, J3. Hereford B4224 Moody Cow PH, 1m open gate on R. From Ross. A40, B449, Xrds R Upton Bishop. 100yds on R by cream cottage.* Home-made teas in the recently renovated barn. **Adm £4, chd free. Sun 7 June (2-5).**
Combined adm with Brockhampton Cottage £8 (morning opening 10.30 - 2). Visitors also welcome by arrangement June to Sept. Can provide lunch 50 max.
A contemporary garden designed by Tom Stuart-Smith. Planted on 2 levels, a clever collection of mass-planted perennials and grasses of different heights, textures and colour give all-yr round interest. The upper walled garden with a sea of flowering grasses makes a highlight. Views of pond and valley walk. Visit Brockhampton Cottage (10.30-2) before you visit us (picnic in parking field).

23 ◆ HELLENS
Much Marcle, Ledbury HR8 2LY. PMMCT, 01531 660504, www.hellensmanor.com. *6m from Ross-on-Wye. 4m SW of Ledbury, off A449. L at Xrds in front of The Walwyn PH. Continue past school on R & Memorial Hall on L. Drive on L 300yds past the Memorial Hall.* Home-made teas. **Adm £2.50, chd free. For NGS: Mon 18, Tue 19 May (9-5). For other opening times and information, please phone or see garden website.**
In the grounds of Hellens manor house, the gardens are being gently redeveloped to reflect the C17 ambience of the house. Incl a rare

octagonal dovecote, knot garden, physic garden and yew labyrinth, lawns, herb and kitchen gardens, short woodland and pond walk. Longer walk to Hall Wood, SSSI. Gardens are fairly level but pathways are gravel.

Small but charmingly, secluded garden, centred around a natural pond with lush planting . . .

24 ◆ HEREFORD CATHEDRAL GARDENS
Hereford HR1 2NG. Dean of Hereford Cathedral, 01432 374202, www.herefordcathedral.org. *Centre of Hereford. Approach rds to the Cathedral are signed. Tours leave from information desk in the cathedral building.* Tea in Cathedral's Cloister Café. **Adm £5, chd free. Share to Homeless Charity. For NGS: Fri 19 June (11-4). For other opening times and information, please phone or see garden website.**
Guided tours of historic gardens which won 2 top awards in 'It's Your Neighbourhood 2012'. The tour incl: a courtyard garden; an atmospheric cloisters garden enclosed by C15 buildings; the Vicar's Choral garden; the Dean's own garden; and 2 acre Bishop's garden with fine trees, vegetable and cutting garden, outdoor chapel for meditation in a floral setting, all sloping to the Wye. Collection of plants with ecclesiastical connections in College Garden. Partial wheelchair access.

HIGH VIEW
See Worcestershire.

HIGHFIELD COTTAGE
See Worcestershire.

25 HILL HOUSE FARM
Knighton LD7 1NA. Simon & Caroline Gourlay, 01547 528542, simongourlay@btinternet.com. *4m SE of Knighton. S of A4113 via Knighton (Llanshay Lane, 3m) or Bucknell (Reeves Lane, 3m).* Cream teas. **Adm £4, chd free. Sat 11, Sun 12 July (2-5.30). Visitors also welcome by arrangement May to Sept.**
5-acre south facing hillside garden developed over past 40 years with magnificent views over unspoilt countryside. Some herbaceous around the house with extensive lawns and mown paths surrounded by roses, shrubs and specimen trees leading to the half acre Oak Pool 200ft below house. Transport available from bottom of garden if required.

26 IVY CROFT
Ivington Green, Leominster HR6 0JN. Sue & Roger Norman, 01568 720344, ivycroft@homecall.co.uk, www.ivycroftgarden.co.uk. *3m SW of Leominster. From Leominster take Ryelands Rd to Ivington. Turn R at church, garden $^3/_4$ m on R. From A4110 signed Ivington, garden 1$^3/_4$ m on L.* Tea. **Adm £3.50, chd free. Thurs 5, 12, 19, 26 Feb (9-4); Sun 19 Apr, Sun 24, Mon 25 May, Sun 6 Sept (2-5.30); Thurs 4, 11, 18, 25 Feb 2016. Combined adm with Aulden Farm £6 (not Feb). Visitors also welcome by arrangement all year.**
A maturing rural garden with areas of meadow, wood and orchard, blending with countryside and providing habitat for wildlife. The cottage is surrounded by borders, raised beds, trained pears and containers giving all year interest. Paths lead to the wider garden including herbaceous borders, vegetable garden framed with espalier apples and seasonal pond with willows, ferns and grasses. Snowdrops. Partial wheelchair access.

The Picton Garden

GROUP OPENING

27 KENTCHURCH GARDENS
Pontrilas HR2 0DB. *12m SW of Hereford. From Hereford A465 to Abergavenny, at Pontrilas turn L signed Kentchurch. After 2m fork L, after Bridge Inn. Drive opp church.* Home-made teas. **Combined adm £5, chd free.** Sun 14 June, Sun 12 July (11-5).

KENTCHURCH COURT 🛏
Mrs Jan Lucas-Scudamore
01981 240228
jan@kentchurchcourt.co.uk
www.kentchurchcourt.co.uk

UPPER LODGE
Jo Gregory

Kentchurch Court is sited close to the Welsh border. The large stately home dates to C11 and has been in the Scudamore family for over 1000yrs The deer-park surrounding the house dates back to the Knights Hospitallers of Dinmore and lies at the heart of an estate of over 5000 acres. Historical characters associated with the house incl Welsh hero Owain Glendower, whose daughter married Sir John Scudamore. The house was modernised by John Nash in 1795. First opened for NGS in 1927. Formal rose garden, traditional vegetable garden redesigned with colour, scent and easy access. Walled garden and herbaceous borders, rhododendrons and wild flower walk. Deer-park and ancient woodland. Extensive collection of mature trees and shrubs. Stream with habitat for spawning trout. Upper Lodge is a tranquil and well-established walled cottage garden situated at the centre of the main garden. Incl a wide variety of herbaceous plants, bulbs and shrubs ranging from traditional favourites to the rare and unusual. Most of the garden can be accessed by wheelchairs.

♿ ✿ 🚐 ☕

28 LAWLESS HILL
Sellack, Ross-on-Wye HR9 6QP. Keith Meehan & Katalin Andras, 07595 678837, katalin_andras@yahoo.co.uk. *4m NW of Ross-on-Wye. Western end of M50. On A49 to Hereford, take 2nd R, signed Sellack. After 2m, turn R by white house, to Sellack church. At next church sign, turn L. Garden halfway down lane, before church.* **Adm £3, chd free. Visitors welcome by arrangement** Mar to Oct individuals and small groups welcome.
Modernist Japanese-influenced garden with dramatic views over R Wye. Collection of 'rooms' sculpted from the steep hillside using network of natural stone walls and huge rocks. Among exotic and unusual plantings, natural ponds are held within the terracing, forming waterfalls between them. Due to steep steps and stepping stones open by water, the garden is unsuitable for the less mobile and young children. Tea and cake in the round house and magical views overlooking waterfall and the river valley.

🛏 ☕

29 LITTLE LLANAVON
Dorstone, Hereford HR3 6AT. Jenny Chippindale, 01981 550984, jennychip@hotmail.co.uk, www.goldenvalleybandb.co.uk. *2m W of Peterchurch. In the Golden Valley, 15m W of Hereford on B4348, ¹/₂ m towards Peterchurch from Dorstone.* **Adm £3, chd free. Visitors welcome by arrangement** May to Sept.
¹/₂ -acre S-facing cottage-style walled garden in lovely rural location. Meandering paths among shrubs in shady spring garden. Hot gravel area and herbaceous borders closely planted with select perennials and grasses, many unusual. Good late colour.

✿ 🚐 🛏 ☕

LITTLE MALVERN COURT
See Worcestershire.

30 ► LOWER HOPE
Lower Hope Farm, Ullingswick,
Hereford HR1 3JF. Mr & Mrs Clive
Richards, 01432 820557,
cliverichards@crco.co.uk. *5m S of
Bromyard. A465 N from Hereford,
after 6m turn L at Burley Gate onto
A417 towards Leominster. After
approx 2m turn R to Lower Hope.
After 1/2 m garden on L.* Tea. **Adm £5,
chd £1. Suns 12 Apr, 24 May, 12
July, 27 Sept (2-5).** Visitors also
welcome by arrangement visits
within 5 days after each open day.
5-acre garden facing S and W.
Herbaceous borders, rose walks and
gardens, laburnum tunnel,
Mediterranean garden, new Italian
garden, bog gardens. Lime tree walk,
lake landscaped with wild flowers,
streams, ponds. Conservatories and
large glasshouse with exotic species
incl orchids, colourful butterflies,
bougainvilleas. Prizewinning herd of
pedigree Hereford cattle, flock of
pedigree Suffolk sheep.

👤 ❀ 🚐 ☕

31 ► ◆ MIDDLE HUNT HOUSE
Walterstone, Hereford HR2 0DY.
Trustees of Monnow Valley Arts &
Rupert & Antoinetta Otten,
01873 860529,
www.monnowvalleyarts.org. *4m W
of Pandy, 17m S of Hereford, 10m N
of Abergavenny. A465 to Pandy, L
towards Longtown, turn R at Clodock
Church, 1m on R.* Disabled parking
available. Tea. **Adm £5, chd free.
For NGS: Sat 29, Sun 30 Aug (2-5).**
For other opening times and
information, please phone or see
garden website.
A modern garden using swathes of
herbaceous plants and grasses,
surrounding stone built farmhouse
and barns with stunning views of the
Black Mountains. Special features:
rose borders, hornbeam alley, formal
parterre with sensory plants, fountain
court with Wlliam Pye water feature,
architecturally designed greenhouse
complex, vegetable gardens. Carved
lettering and sculpture throughout,
garden covering about 4 acres.
Exhibitions take place during NGS
openings in the studio and gallery, for
2015 see website. Partial wheelchair
access.

👤 🏛 ☕

32 ► MIDLAND FARM
Pig Street, Norton Wood HR4 7BP.
Sarah & Charles Smith, 01544
318575, sarah@midlandfarm.co.uk.
*10m NW of Hereford. From Hereford
take the A480 towards Kington. 1/2 m
after Norton Canon turn L towards
Calver Hill. At bottom of the hill turn R
into Pig St, garden 1/4 m on L.* Home-
made teas. **Adm £4, chd free. Sun 1
Mar, Sun 10 May (11-3).**
A new 1.2 acre cottage garden
begun in 2008 and ongoing.
Designed as a series of rooms incl
flower, spring and kitchen gardens;
Perennials, roses and helebores a
speciality.

❀ ⟶ ☕

33 ► NEW ► MISTLETOE LODGE
Bredenbury, Wacton Lane,
Bromyard HR7 4TF. Jewels
Williams Peplow and Mark Peplow,
1885488029,
Jewelswilliams@hotmail.co.uk. *A44
between Bromyard & Leominster. At
Bredenbury turn onto Wacton Lane
between Three Pines Garage &
Barnaby Arms. Garden is 50yds on L.
Drop off for disabled, parking at
Barnaby Arms.* Home-made teas.
**Adm £2.50, chd free. Thur 4, Fri 5,
Sat 6, Sun 7 June (11-5).**
Small but charmingly, secluded
garden, centred around a natural
pond with lush planting. 'A tranquil
hidden gem.' Complimented by a
mixed media art exhibition, 'Coast
and Garden.' Homemade cakes, teas
and coffee to enjoy in the garden.

☕

34 ► MONTPELIER COTTAGE
Brilley, Whitney-on-Wye, Hereford
HR3 6HF. Dr Noel Kingsbury & Ms
Jo Eliot, noel.k57@virgin.net,
www.noelkingsbury.com. *Between
Hay-on-Wye & Kington. From A438
1/2 m E of Rhydspence Inn, take rd
signed Brilley, then 0.9m. From
Kington, follow rd to Brilley, then 0.6m
from Brilley Church.* Home-made
teas. **Adm £5, chd free. Sun 13
Sept (2-5).**
Exuberant wild-style garden created
by well-known garden writer. Approx
1 acre of garden and trial beds where
English cottage style meets German
parks and American prairie. Wide
range of perennials, plus ponds,
vegetable garden and fruit. A further
3 acres incl hay meadow habitat and
unusual wild flower-rich wet meadow.
Children's playground. Featured in
Gardens Illustrated, Country Life.

🏛 ❀ 🚐 ⟶ ☕

**35 ► ◆ MOORS MEADOW
GARDENS & NURSERY**
Collington, Bromyard HR7 4LZ.
Ros Bissell, 01885 410318,
www.moorsmeadow.co.uk. *4m N of
Bromyard, on B4214. 1/2 m up lane
follow yellow arrows.* **Adm £6, chd
£1. For NGS: Mons 13 Apr, 11
May, 8 June, 6 July, 3 Aug (11-5).**
For other opening times and
information, please phone or see
garden website.
Gaining international recognition for
its phenomenal range of wildlife and
rarely seen plant species, this
inspirational 7-acre organic hillside
garden is a 'must see'. Full of peace,
secret corners and intriguing features
and sculptures with fernery, grass
garden, extensive shrubberies,
herbaceous beds, meadow, dingle,
pools and kitchen garden. Resident
Artist Blacksmith. Featured in Country
Living magazine.

❀

36 ► NEWPORT HOUSE
Almeley HR3 6LL. David & Jenny
Watt, 07754 234903,
david.gray510@btinternet.com.
*5m S of Kington. 1m from Almeley
Church, on rd to Kington. From
Kington take A4111 to Hereford. After
4m turn L to Almeley, continue 2m,
garden on L.* Home-made teas. **Adm
£5, chd free. Mon 1, Tue 2, Wed 3,
Thur 4, Fri 5 June (11-7); Sun 11
Oct (11-5).** Visitors also welcome
by arrangement May to Oct.
20 acres of garden, woods and lake
(with walks). Formal garden set on 3
terraces with large mixed borders
framed by formal hedges, in front of
Georgian House (not open). 2 1/2 -acre
walled organic garden in restoration
since 2009.

👤 🏛 ☕

37 NEW OLD COLWALL HOUSE

Old Colwall, Malvern WR13 6HF. Mr & Mrs Roland Trafford-Roberts. *3m NE of Ledbury. From Ledbury, turn L off A449 to Malvern towards Coddington. Signed from 2½ m along lane. Signed from Colwall.* Tea. Adm by donation. **Sun 15 Mar, Sun 7 June, Sun 13 Sept (12-4).** Early C18 garden on a site owned by the Church till Henry VIII. Walled lawns and terraces on various levels. The heart is the yew walk, a rare survival from the 1700s: 100 yds long, 30ft high, cloud clipped, and with a transept-like quality inside. Later centuries have brought a summer house, water garden, and rock gardens. Fine trees, incl enormous veteran yew; fine views. Steep in places.

38 THE OLD CORN MILL

Aston Crews, Ross-on-Wye HR9 7LW. Mrs Jill Hunter, 01989 750059. *5m E of Ross-on-Wye. A40 Ross to Gloucester. Turn L at T-lights at Lea Xrds onto B4222 signed Newent, Garden ½ m on L. Parking for disabled down drive. DO NOT USE THE ABOVE POSTCODE IN YOUR SATNAV - try HR9 7LA.* Home-made teas. Teas and coffees with cake. Adm £3, chd free. **Sun 15 Mar, Sun 5, Mon 6 Apr, Sun 24, Mon 25 May (11-5).** Visitors also welcome by arrangement Jan to Oct max 50+.
Forget the stresses of life and experience the calm of this relaxed country garden. Birdsong and a babbling brook, numerous places to sit and dream. Interest all year with spectacular tulips and common spotted orchids in spring. A place of peace and tranquility. Children's trail and quirky garden sculptures.

39 THE OLD RECTORY, THRUXTON

Thruxton HR2 9AX. Mr & Mrs Andrew Hallett, 01981 570401, ar.hallett@gmail.com, www.thruxtonrectory.co.uk. *6m SW of Hereford. A465 to Allensmore. At Locks (Shell) garage take B4348 towards Hay-on-Wye. After 1½ m turn L towards Abbey Dore & Cockyard. Car park 150yds on L.* Home-made teas. Adm £4, chd free. **Sun 7 June, Sun 30 Aug (1-5).** Visitors also welcome by arrangement May to Sept.

Plantsman's garden created since 2007. Two acre formal garden: long borders stocked with shrubs, unusual perennials, roses, gazebo, woodland borders, glasshouse and vegetable parterre. Most of our plants are labelled. Two acre paddock with ornamental trees and shrubs, heritage fruit trees, wildlife pond and chickens. Plenty of places to sit and enjoy the garden and views of Herefordshire countryside. Some gravel paths.

> The heart is the yew walk, a rare survival from the 1700s: 100 yds long, 30ft high, cloud clipped, and with a transept-like quality inside . . .

40 THE ORCHARDS

Golden Valley, Bishops Frome, nr Bromyard WR6 5BN. Mr & Mrs Robert Humphries, 01885 490273, theorchards.humphries@btinternet.com. *14m E of Hereford. A4103 turn L at bottom of Fromes Hill, through Bishops Frome on B4214. Turn R immed after de-regulation signs. Follow NGS signs to car park, garden 250yds along track.* Home-made teas. Ploughman's Lunches. Adm £3, chd free. **Visitors welcome by arrangement Apr to Sept.**
Mature 1-acre garden, with many species of trees and shrubs. The garden is laid out on various levels and intensely planted, incorporating collections of roses, clematis, fuchsias and dahlias. There are 15 water features. Many herbaceous borders, the garden overflows with annuals in pots and baskets during the summer months. Several seating areas around the garden.

PEAR TREE COTTAGE

See Worcestershire.

41 PERRYCROFT

Jubilee Drive, Upper Colwall, Malvern WR13 6DN. Gillian & Mark Archer, 07858 393767, gillianarcher@live.co.uk. *Between Malvern & Ledbury. On B4232 between British Camp & Wyche cutting. Park in Gardiners Quarry pay & display car park opp, short walk to garden. No parking at house except for disabled by prior arrangement.* Home-made teas. Adm £5, chd free. **Sun 3 May, Sun 28 June, Sun 4 Oct (2-5).** Visitors also welcome by arrangement groups and individuals all year. Teas by prior arrangement for groups 10+.
10-acre garden and woodland on upper slopes of Malvern Hills with magnificent views. Arts and Crafts house (not open), garden partly designed by CFA Voysey. Walled garden with mixed and herbaceous borders, yew and box hedges and topiary, dry garden, natural wild flower meadows, ponds (unfenced), bog garden, woodland walks. Some steep and uneven paths. Featured in House and Garden, Gardens Illustrated and Country Life.

42 ◆ THE PICTON GARDEN

Old Court Nurseries, Walwyn Road, Colwall WR13 6QE. Mr & Mrs Paul Picton, 01684 540416, www.autumnasters.co.uk. *3m W of Malvern. On B4218 (Walwyn Rd) N of Colwall Stone. Turn off A449 from Ledbury or Malvern onto the B4218 for Colwall.* Adm £3.50, chd free. **For NGS: Sat 1, Sun 9, Sat 15, Thur 20, Mon 24, Sun 30 Aug, Sat 5, Fri 11, Fri 25 Sept, Thur 8, Sun 18 Oct (11-5).** For other opening times and information, please phone or see garden website.
1½ acres W of Malvern Hills. Interesting perennials and shrubs in Aug. In late Sept and early Oct colourful borders display the National Plant Collection of Michaelmas daisies, backed by autumn colouring trees and shrubs. Many unusual plants to be seen, incl bamboos, ferns and acers. Features raised beds and silver garden. National Plant Collection of autumn-flowering asters and an extensive nursery that has been growing them since 1906. Featured on Gardeners World, Great British Garden Revival and Countrylife.

NCH

Treat yourself to a plant from the plant stall

43 NEW RALPH COURT GARDENS
Edwyn Ralph, Bromyard HR7 4LU.
Mr & Mrs Morgan,
www.ralphcourtgardens.co.uk.
From Bromyard follow the Tenbury rd for approx 1m. On entering the village of Edwyn Ralph take 1st turning on R towards the church. Light refreshments. 80 seater Tea Room offering breakfast, light lunches and afternoon tea. **Adm £7.50, chd £4. Sats & Suns 28, 29 Mar, 16, 17 May, 6, 7 June, 15, 16 Aug (9-5).**
12 amazing gardens set in the grounds of a gothic rectory. A plants man's garden with a twist, incorporating an Italian Piazza, an African Jungle, Dragon Pool, Alice in Wonderland and the elves in their conifer forest. These are just a few of the themes within this stunning garden. Tea room overlooks Malvern Hills.

44 THE RAMBLES
Shelwick, Hereford HR1 3AL.
Shirley & Joe Fleming, 01432 357056, joe.eff@live.co.uk. *2m E of Hereford. A465/ A4103 r'about take the Sutton St Nicholas Rd, turn L signed Shelwick, under railway bridge, The Rambles is behind 1st house on L. Car parking on drive by house.* Tea. **Adm £3, chd free. Visitors welcome by arrangement June to Aug.**
Colourful plantaholics ⅓ acre garden packed with a wide range of interesting plants, colour-themed borders, and water feature. Many pots with tender plants. Good late colour.

45 RHODDS FARM
Lyonshall HR5 3LW. Richard & Cary Goode, 01544 340120, cary.goode@russianaeros.com, www.rhoddsfarm.co.uk. *1m E of Kington. From A44 take small turning S just E of Penrhos Farm, 1m E of Kington. Continue 1m garden straight ahead.* **Adm £5, chd free. Fris 1 May, 5 June, 3 July, 7 Aug, 4 Sept, 2 Oct (11-5).**
The garden began in 2005 and is still a work in progress. The site is challenging with steep banks rising to overhanging woodland but has wonderful views. Formal garden leads to new dovecote, mixed borders have interest throughout the year with the double herbaceous borders of hot colours being particularly good in

Wilton Castle on the Wye

© Val Corbett

summer. Woodland walks with wonderful bluebells in spring. See garden website for detailed description. Featured in English Garden and House and Garden.

46 NEW ROSS-ON-WYE COMMUNITY GARDEN
Old Gloucester Rd, Ross-On-Wye HR9 5AE. Haygrove Ltd. *The garden is situated half way along Old Gloucester Rd and opp the former Walter Scott School.* Tea. **Adm £3, chd free. Sat 25, Sun 26 July (10-4).**
The Community Garden is a three and a half acre site in the centre of Ross which is run by Haygrove Ltd to grow fruit and vegetables - see our Facebook page. The project works mainly with adults with learning disabilities, mental health illnesses and those who are long term unemployed. Produce and plants are for sale as well as garden tours, demonstrations and activities for children. Half of the site is accessible for those using wheelchairs.

SHUTTIFIELD COTTAGE
See Worcestershire.

47 STAPLETON CASTLE COURT GARDEN
Stapleton, Presteigne LD8 2LS.
Margaret & Trefor Griffiths, 01544 267327. *2m N of Presteigne. From Presteigne cross Lugg Bridge at bottom of Broad St & continue to Stapleton. Do not turn towards Stapleton but follow signs to garden on R.* Home-made teas. **Adm £4, chd free. Sun 24, Mon 25 May, Sun 30, Mon 31 Aug (2-5.30). Visitors also welcome by arrangement May to Aug, min group adm £25.**
Situated on a gentle slope overlooked by the remains of Stapleton Castle. The garden developed over the past 7 yrs by an enthusiastic plantswoman and benefits from considered and colour-themed borders. Guided tour of the castle remains: 2.30 and 3.30 each day. Display of site history incl house ruins, mill pond, mill pit and disused turbine, etc. Wheelchairs not suitable for castle tour.

48 ◆ STOCKTON BURY GARDENS

Kimbolton HR6 0HA. Raymond G Treasure, 07880 712649, www.stocktonbury.co.uk. *2m NE of Leominster. From Leominster to Ludlow on A49 turn R onto A4112. Gardens 300yds on R.* Light refreshments. Adm £6, chd £3. **For NGS: Wed 1 Apr (12-5). For other opening times and information, please phone or see garden website.**
Superb, sheltered 4-acre garden with colour and interest all yr. Extensive collection of plants, many rare and unusual set amongst medieval buildings. Features pigeon house, tithe barn, grotto, cider press, pools, ruined chapel and rill, all surrounded by unspoilt countryside. All plants sold are grown on site. Stockton Bury has a garden school which features courses from high profile speakers such as Chris Beardshaw. Our restaurant offers a varied and very tasty menu. We pride ourselves in offering great plant and gardening advice to our visitors. Featured monthly in The English Garden magazine. Partial wheelchair access.

49 STONE HOUSE

Linley Green, Whitbourne, Worcester WR6 5RG. Bill & Jill Cartlidge. *12m W of Worcester. A44 W from Worcester.After approx 12m turn L into B4220 Malvern Road, after 1m fork L to Linley Green, cottage on R after ¹/₂ m.* Light refreshments. Adm £4, chd free. Share to The Firefighters Charity. **Sun 12, Sat 18, Wed 22 July (2-5.30).**
The garden mixes the traditional features of the timeless cottage garden with innovative contemporary elements. Alongside glorious floral planting, orchard and potager stand a wall mosaic, living willow boat, iridescent sofa and crossword. Many plants grown from seed with lilies and sweet peas a speciality. Generally level garden. Beware molehills and tunnels in grass areas. One set of steps with alternative grass ramp access.

50 UPPER TAN HOUSE

Stansbatch, Leominster HR6 9LJ. James & Caroline Weymouth, 01544 260574, caroline.weymouth@btopenworld.com, www.uppertanhouse.com. *4m W of Pembridge. From A44 in Pembridge take turn signed Shobdon & Presteigne. After exactly 4m & at Stansbatch Nursery turn L down hill. Garden on L 100yds after chapel.* Adm £4, chd free. **Visitors welcome by arrangement** May to Sept, groups welcome. Coffee & biscuits £1, tea & cake £2.
S-facing garden sloping down to Stansbatch brook in idyllic spot. Deep herbaceous borders with informal and unusual planting, pond and bog garden, formal vegetable garden framed by yew hedges and espaliered pears. Reed beds, wild flower meadow with orchids in June. Good late summer colour and diverse wildlife.

51 ◆ THE WEIR

Swainshill, Hereford HR4 7QF. National Trust, 01981 590509, www.nationaltrust.org.uk/weir. *5m W of Hereford. On A438, signed The Weir Garden.* Adm £5, chd free. **For NGS: Wed 25 Feb, Thur 24 Sept (10.30-4.30). For other opening times and information, please phone or see garden website.**
Stunning riverside gardens with sweeping views along the R Wye and Herefordshire countryside. Drifts of snowdrops and spring bulbs give way to summer wild flowers in the woodland garden and in autumn the walled garden is full of fruit and vegetables. Spring bulbs in full bloom during February - May, productive walled garden including Foster and Pearson glasshouse. Riverside setting. Very limited wheelchair access.

52 WESTON HALL

Weston-under-Penyard, Ross-on-Wye HR9 7NS. Mr P & Miss L Aldrich-Blake, 01989 562597, aldrichblake@btinternet.com. *1m E of Ross-on-Wye. On A40 towards Gloucester.* Light refreshments by arrangement, at modest extra cost. Adm £4, chd free. **Visitors welcome by arrangement** Apr to July groups of 10+.
6 acres surrounding Elizabethan house (not open). Large walled garden with herbaceous borders, vegetables and fruit, overlooked by Millennium folly. Lawns with both mature and recently planted trees, shrubs with many unusual varieties. Ornamental ponds and lake. 4 generations in the family, but still evolving year on year.

53 WESTON MEWS

Weston-under-Penyard HR9 7NZ. Ann Rothwell & John Hercock, 01989 563823. *2m E of Ross-on-Wye. Going towards Gloucester on A40, continue approx 100yds past the Weston Cross PH & turn R into grey brick-paved courtyard.* Light refreshments. Adm £3, chd free. **Sat 13, Sun 14 June (11-5).** Visitors also welcome by arrangement May to Sept wine.
Walled ex-kitchen garden divided by yew and box hedges. Traditional in style and planting with large herbaceous beds and borders at different levels. Broad range of plants incl roses. Enclosed garden with sundial. Large vine house. Partial wheelchair access.

Italian Piazza, an African Jungle, Dragon Pool, Alice in Wonderland and the elves in their conifer forest . . .

54 WHITFIELD

Wormbridge HR2 9BA. Mr & Mrs Edward Clive, 01981 570202, tclive@whitfield-hereford.com, www.whitfield-hereford.com. *8m SW of Hereford. The entrance gates are off the A465 Hereford to Abergavenny rd, ¹/₂ m N of Wormbridge.* Home-made teas. Adm £4, chd free. **Sun 22 Mar, Sun 26 Apr (2-5.30).** Visitors also welcome by arrangement Mar to Oct tour & refreshments available for 15+ groups.
Parkland, wild flowers, ponds, walled garden, many flowering magnolias (species and hybrids), 1780 ginkgo tree, 1¹/₂ m woodland walk with 1851 redwood grove. Picnic parties welcome. Partial access to wheelchair users, some gravel paths and steep slopes.

55 ▶ WILTON CASTLE ON THE WYE

Wilton, Ross-on-Wye HR9 6AD. Alan & Suzie Parslow, www.wiltoncastle.co.uk. *½ m NW of Ross on R Wye. Sgnd at Wilton r'about on M50/A40/A449 trunk rd. Imm turn L opp garage. Castle entrance behind Castle Lodge Hotel. DO NOT cross bridge into Ross.* Light refreshments. **Adm £5, chd free. Sat 6, Sun 7 June (1-6).**
The romantic ruins of a restored C12 castle and C16 manor house (ruin) form the perfect backdrop for herbaceous borders, roses entwined around mullioned windows, an abundance of sweetly scented old-fashioned roses, gravel gardens and shrubberies. The 2-acre gardens are surrounded by a dry moat which leads down to the R Wye with swans, ducks, kingfishers etc. Featured in Country Life. No disabled access into dry moat area, or inside towers; disabled WC.

  🚻 🎵 🚐 ☕

56 ▶ WINDSOR COTTAGE

Dilwyn, Hereford HR4 8HJ. Jim & Brenda Collins. *6m W of Leominster off A4112. Turn L off A4112 into Dilwyn. From centre of village, with PH on L, turn L. After 100y turn R. Cottage 400yds on L.* Limited parking. Home-made teas. Home made cakes, ground coffee and choice of teas, gluten free available. **Adm £3, chd free.** Every Tue & Thur 26 May to 27 Aug (2-5.30). *½* -acre wildlife friendly garden redesigned over the last 4yrs by present owners. Herbaceous borders, shrub bed, wildlife ponds, fruit and vegetables in raised beds. Extensive use of gravel beds. Wide selection of plants for all year interest including peonies, irises, hostas and clematis. Exhibition of watercolour and oil paintings. Wildlife friendly garden. Plants chosen to encourage bees, birds, and butterflies. Gravelled drive giving access to level, lawned garden.

  🚻 🎵 ❀ ☕

57 ▶ WOLFERLOW HOUSE

Wolferlow, nr Upper Sapey HR7 4QA. Stuart & Jill Smith, 01886 853311, hillheadfm@aol.com, www.holidaylettings.co.uk/rentals/ worcester/210892. *5m N of Bromyard. Off B4203 or B4214 between Upper Sapey & Stoke Bliss. Disabled parking at the house.*

Home-made teas. **Adm £3.50, chd free.** Sat 13 June (10-5). **Visitors also welcome by arrangement May to Aug groups up to 20 or so.**
Surrounded by farmland this former Victorian rectory is set within formal and informal gardens with planting to attract wildlife. Walks through the old orchard and ponds to sit by, space to relax and reflect taking in the views of borrowed landscape. Fruit, vegetable and cutting garden and wild-flower meadow. Featured in The Independent - Tales from the Woods. Gravel paths.

  🚻 ❀ 🛏 ☕

Parkinson's UK are proud to be the NGS guest charity

58 ▶ WOODVIEW

Great Doward, Whitchurch, Ross-on-Wye HR9 6DZ. Janet & Clive Townsend, 01600 890477, clive.townsend5@homecall.co.uk. *6m SW of Ross-on-Wye, 4m NE of Monmouth. A40 Ross/Mon At Whitchurch follow signs to Symonds Yat west, then to Doward Park campsite. Take forestry rd 1st L garden 2nd L - follow NGS signs.* Light refreshments. **Adm £4, chd free.** Sun 3 May, Sun 12, Sun 19 July (1-6). **Visitors also welcome by arrangement June to Sept please phone for details.**
Formal and informal gardens approx 4 acres in woodland setting. Herbaceous borders, hosta collection, mature trees, shrubs and seasonal bedding. Gently sloping lawns. Statuary and found sculpture, local limestone, rockwork and pools. Woodland garden, wild flower meadow and indigenous orchids. Collection of vintage tools and memorabilia, garden games. Croquet, clock golf and garden games.

  🚻 🎵 ❀ ☕

59 ▶ WOOFIELDS FARM

Coddington, Ledbury HR8 1JJ. Mrs Rosemary Simcock. *3m N of Ledbury. From Ledbury to Malvern rd A449, follow brown signs to Coddington Vineyard.* **Adm £3.50, chd free.** Sat 14, Sun 15 Mar (12-4.30). **Combined with Coddington Vineyard, adm £6.**
2-acre garden on working farm: an eclectic mixture of planting, colour all yr round. Variety in shape and texture. Spring bulbs and shrubs. Borders planted with roses, clematis, wide range of herbaceous plants, many alstromeria, gravel garden, ornamental pond. Natural pond recently re-landscaped and planted by Peter Dowle.

  ❀

GROUP OPENING

60 ▶ WOONTON & ALMELEY GARDENS

Woonton, Hereford HR3 6QN. *12m W of Leominster. From Leominster follow A44 & then A4112, turn R after 10 metres onto A480 at Sarnesfield to Woonton & Almeley by following yellow signs.* Home-made teas at The Old Villa. **Combined adm £5, chd free. Sun 14 June (2-5.30).**

OAK HALL
Woonton. Tessa & Jeremy Plummer

THE OLD VILLA
Almeley. Mrs Caryl Mead

2 small but very different gardens. Oak Hall is an enchanting *¾* -acre walled cottage garden surrounding a C15 open-hall house (not open); herbaceous borders, herb garden, romantic rose garden with fountain, soft fruit and vegetables and lovely views over the countryside.
The Old Villa is a small garden of informal design with gravel paths and some steps. Borders are packed with plants, some old favourites like roses, iris and aster, some unusual like arisaema, climbing codonopsis and veratrum. Small raised pond, vegetable and fruit area, greenhouse, small collection of ferns and views to Hay Bluff. Homemade tea and cakes, plants for sale. Both gardens are accessible to wheelchairs users, although some areas of each would be restricted.

  ❀ ☕

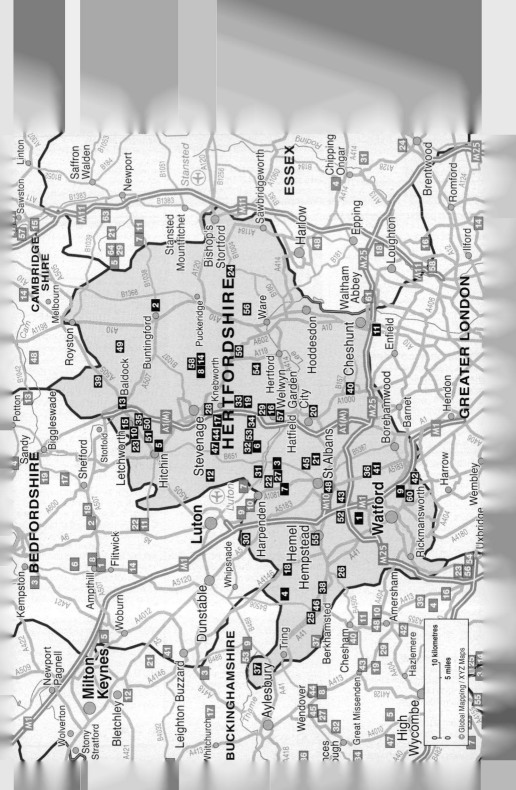

Hertfordshire

With its proximity to London, Hertfordshire became a breath of country air and a retreat for wealthy families wishing to escape the grime of the city – hence the county is peppered with large and small country estates, some of which open their garden gates for the NGS.

Hertfordshire was home for a long time to a flourishing fruit, vegetable and cut-flower trade, with produce sent up from nurseries and gardens to the London markets. There is a profusion of inviting rural areas with flower-filled country lanes and some of the best ancient woodlands carpeted with bluebells in late spring. Pretty villages sit in these rural pockets, with farmhouse and cottage gardens to visit.

Our towns, such as St Albans with its abbey, Baldock and Berkhamsted with their markets, and the garden cities of Welwyn and Letchworth, all have interesting town gardens, both modern and traditional in their approach. We have many gardens open 'By Arrangement', and we are happy to arrange tours for large groups.

So next time you are heading through our county, don't just drive on – stop and visit one of our gardens to enjoy the warm welcome Hertfordshire has to offer.

Hertfordshire Volunteers

County Organiser
Julie Wise
01438 821509
juliewise@f2s.com

County Treasurer
Peter Barrett
01442 393508
tterrabjp@ntlworld.com

Publicity
Julie Knight
01727 752375
jknight21@gmail.com

Chris Roper
07793 739732
chris.roper79@gmail.com

Booklet Coordinators
Edwina Robarts
01279 842422
edwina.robarts@gmail.com

Julie Ryan
01707 874957
julieannryan@tiscali.co.uk

Group Tours
Sarah Marsh
07813 083126
sarahkmarsh@hotmail.co.uk

Assistant County Organisers
Marion Jay
01707 334274
marion@garden84.net

Julie Loughlin
01438 871488
jloughlin11@gmail.com

Christopher Melluish
01920 462500
c.melluish@btopenworld.com

Karen Smith
01462 673133
hertsgardeningangel@googlemail.com

Left: St Michael's Croft

Since our foundation we have donated more than £42.5 million to charity

Opening Dates

All entries subject to change.
For latest information check www.ngs.org.uk

February

Saturday 7
58 Walkern Hall
Sunday 8
58 Walkern Hall
Saturday 14
37 NEW Old Church Cottage
Sunday 15
37 NEW Old Church Cottage

March

Saturday 7
11 Capel Manor Gardens
Saturday 28
20 Hatfield House West Garden

April

Sunday 19
2 Alswick Hall
3 Amwell Cottage
Wednesday 22
34 The Mill House
Friday 24
27 8 Kingcroft Road (Evening)
Saturday 25
34 The Mill House
Sunday 26
26 Huntsmoor
27 8 Kingcroft Road
34 The Mill House
35 324 Norton Way South
47 St Paul's Walden Bury

May

Saturday 2
44 Rustling End Cottage (Evening)
Sunday 3
38 Patchwork
57 84 Valley Road
Monday 4
4 Ashridge House
Friday 8
13 42 Church Street (Evening)
Sunday 10
13 42 Church Street

Friday 15
15 10 Cross Street (Evening)
Saturday 16
15 10 Cross Street
21 122 Hazelwood Drive
Sunday 17
15 10 Cross Street
32 The Manor House, Ayot St Lawrence
33 43 Mardley Hill
47 St Paul's Walden Bury
Saturday 23
44 Rustling End Cottage (Evening)
Sunday 24
40 Queenswood School
Friday 29
31 Mackerye End House (Evening)
Sunday 31
18 15 Gade Valley Cottages

June

Festival Weekend

Saturday 6
6 NEW Ayot Gardens
Sunday 7
6 NEW Ayot Gardens
39 Pembroke Farm
47 St Paul's Walden Bury
53 Shaw's Corner
56 Thundridge Hill House
Friday 12
17 NEW Field End House (Evening)
Saturday 13
30 The Lodge
49 Sandon Bury
Sunday 14
8 Benington Lordship
17 NEW Field End House
22 3 Highfield Avenue
30 The Lodge
49 Sandon Bury
Thursday 18
26 Huntsmoor (Evening)
Friday 19
3 Amwell Cottage (Evening)
Sunday 21
46 St Michael's Croft
52 Serge Hill Gardens
59 Woodhall Park
Wednesday 24

23 Hitchin Lavender (Evening)
Friday 26
29 NEW 322 Knightsfield (Evening)
51 Serendi (Evening)
Sunday 28
29 NEW 322 Knightsfield
48 St Stephens Avenue Gardens
51 Serendi

July

Friday 3
19 Greenwood House (Evening)
57 84 Valley Road (Evening)
Saturday 4
54 South Wing
Sunday 5
19 Greenwood House
31 Mackerye End House
41 Radlett Allotments
50 Scudamore
Friday 10
57 84 Valley Road (Evening)
Sunday 12
12 NEW 8 Chapel Road
18 15 Gade Valley Cottages
Wednesday 15
12 NEW 8 Chapel Road
Friday 17
43 The Royal National Rose Society (Evening)
Sunday 19
36 Oakridge Avenue Gardens
55 9 Tannsfield Drive
Friday 24
23 Hitchin Lavender (Evening)
Saturday 25
60 42 Falconer Road
Sunday 26
7 Beesonend Gardens
16 35 Digswell Road
60 42 Falconer Road
Friday 31
5 22a The Avenue (Evening)
10 44 Broadwater Avenue (Evening)

August

Saturday 1
44 Rustling End Cottage (Evening)
60 42 Falconer Road

Sunday 2
10 44 Broadwater Avenue
60 42 Falconer Road
Sunday 9
42 Reveley Lodge
55 9 Tannsfield Drive
Sunday 16
38 Patchwork
57 84 Valley Road
Monday 24
23 Hitchin Lavender (Evening)
Monday 31
14 Croft Cottage

September

Sunday 6
25 Hospice of St Francis Garden
48 St Stephens Avenue Gardens
Sunday 13
44 Rustling End Cottage
Sunday 20
26 Huntsmoor
Friday 25
45 3 St Marys Walk (Evening)
Sunday 27
45 3 St Marys Walk

October

Sunday 18
16 35 Digswell Road
Saturday 24
11 Capel Manor Gardens

November

60 42 Falconer Road (Evening)

Gardens open to the public

4 Ashridge House
8 Benington Lordship
11 Capel Manor Gardens
20 Hatfield House West Garden
23 Hitchin Lavender
24 Hopleys
28 Knebworth House Gardens
39 Pembroke Farm
43 The Royal National Rose Society
47 St Paul's Walden Bury
53 Shaw's Corner

Over 400 Volunteers help run the NGS – why not become one too?

Alswick Hall

The Gardens

1 THE ABBOTS HOUSE

10 High Street, Abbots Langley WD5 0AR. Peter & Sue Tomson, 01923 264946, peter.tomson@btinternet.com. *5m NW of Watford. M25, J20, take A4251 signed Kings Langley. R at r'about, R at T-junction, under railway bridge & follow yellow signs. Park in free village car park.* **Adm £4.50, chd free. Share to Friends of St Lawrence Church. Visitors welcome by arrangement Mar to Aug groups of 10 - 30.**
1³/₄ -acre garden with unusual trees, shrubs, mixed borders with interesting colour combinations, scented garden, sunken garden, pond, conservatory and a bed with many Himalayan plants. A garden of 'rooms' with different styles and moods. Many half-hardy plants. Oast House. Pea shingle path.

2 ALSWICK HALL

Hare Street Road, Buntingford SG9 0AA. Mike & Annie Johnson, www.alswickhall.co.uk. *1m from Buntingford on B1038. From the S take A10 to Buntingford, drive into town & take B1038 E towards Hare Street Village. Alswick Hall is 1m on R.* **Hog roast. Adm £5, chd free. Sun 19 Apr (12-4).**
Listed Tudor House with 5 acres of landscaped gardens set in unspoiled farmland. Two well established natural ponds with rockeries. Herbaceous borders, shrubs, woodland walk and wild flower meadow with a fantastic selection of daffodils, tulips, camassias and crown imperial. Spring blossom, formal beds, orchard and glasshouses. There will be a Hog Roast, and some interesting trade stands. Good access for disabled with lawns and wood chip paths. Slight undulations.

3 AMWELL COTTAGE

Amwell Lane, Wheathampstead AL4 8EA. Colin & Kate Birss. *¹/₂ m S of Wheathampstead. From St Helen's Church, Wheathampstead turn up Brewhouse Hill. At top L fork (Amwell Lane), 300yds down lane, park in field opp.* **Home-made teas. Adm £3.50, chd free. Sun 19 Apr (2-5). Evening Opening wine, Fri 19 June (6-9).**
Informal garden of approx 2¹/₂ acres around C17 cottage (not open). Large orchard of mature apples, plums and pear laid out with paths. Extensive lawns with borders, framed by tall yew hedges and old brick walls. A large variety of roses, stone seats with views, woodland pond, greenhouse and recently designed fire-pit area. Gravel drive.

4 ◆ ASHRIDGE HOUSE

Berkhamsted HP4 1NS. Ashridge (Bonar Law Memorial) Trust, 01442 843491, www.ashridge.org.uk. *3m N of Berkhamsted. A4251, 1m S of Little Gaddesden.* Light refreshments. **Adm £4.50, chd free. For NGS: Mon 4 May (2-6). For other opening times and information, please phone or see garden website.**
The gardens cover 190-acres forming part of the Grade II Registered Landscape of Ashridge Park. Based on designs by Humphry Repton in 1813 modified by Jeffry Wyatville. Small secluded gardens, as well as a large lawn area leading to avenues of trees. 2013 marked the 200th anniversary of Repton presenting Ashridge with the Red Book, detailing his designs for the estate.

5 22A THE AVENUE

Hitchin SG4 9RL. Martin Woods, www.mwgardendesign.co.uk. *¹/₂ m E of town centre. Opp St Mary's Church take Windmill Hill, continue to top, crossing Highbury Rd into Wymondley Rd The Avenue is 1st turning on L.* **Evening Opening £4, chd free, wine, Fri 31 July (6-9).**
A stylish town garden with a contemporary feel, combining elegant design with knowledgeable plantsmanship. A patio area is bordered by a formal raised pond. Steps up to the garden are lined with pots of unusual and interesting succulents, alpines, species pelargoniums and other tender plants.

GROUP OPENING

6 NEW AYOT GARDENS
Ayot St. Lawrence, Welwyn
AL6 9BT. *4m W of Welwyn, 20 mins J4 A1M. A1(M) J6 follow signs to Welwyn, Codicote (B656) then Ayot St Lawrence (Shaws Corner NT). Parking in field short walk to gardens.*. Home-made teas in nearby Palladian church also housing Art Exhibition. **Combined adm £5, chd free. Sat 6 June (11-5); Sun 7 June (2-5).**

2 RUINS COTTAGE
Joe & Heather Warwick

NEW WEST HOUSE
Alban & Susie Warwick

Two gardens in the centre of quaint, picturesque, tiny village.

GROUP OPENING

7 BEESONEND GARDENS
Harpenden AL5 2AN. *1m S of Harpenden. Take A1081 S from Harpenden, after 1m turn R into Beesonend Lane, bear R into Burywick to T-junction. Follow signs to Barlings Road & The Deerings.* Home-made teas at 17 The Deerings. **Combined adm £5, chd free. Sun 26 July (2-5.30).**

2 BARLINGS ROAD
Liz & Jim Machin

17 THE DEERINGS
Mr & Mrs Phillip Thompson

Set in a mature development these two gardens reflect their owners individual interests and needs. 2 Barlings Road is packed with unusual plants, shrubs and climbers to provide yr-round structure. The colourful courtyard garden with water feature and secluded shade garden add extra interest. 17 The Deerings

offers specimen trees, architectural plants, ornamental grasses, herbaceous borders as well as a compact kitchen garden and herb bed.

8 ◆ BENINGTON LORDSHIP
nr Stevenage SG2 7BS. Mr & Mrs R R A Bott, 01438 869668, www.beningtonlordship.co.uk. *4m E of Stevenage. In Benington Village, next to church. Signs off A602.* Home-made teas in Parish Hall. **Adm £5, chd free. For NGS: Sun 14 June (12-5). For other opening times and information, please phone or see garden website.**
7-acre garden incl historic buildings, kitchen garden, lakes, roses. Spectacular herbaceous borders, unspoilt panoramic views.

9 47 BOURNEHALL AVENUE
Bushey WD23 3AU. Caroline & Jim Fox, 0208 950 0727, carolinefox@f2s.com. *1m S of Watford. Bushey Village A411, Falconer Rd, Herkomer Rd, 2nd on L is Bournehall Ave. Map on www.jamespfox.co.uk.* Light refreshments. **Adm £4, chd free. Visitors welcome by arrangement Mar to Apr.**
Medium sized village garden on 3 levels, designed by owners. Garlanded planters overlook sunken garden with acers and pond. Wisteria and vine covered pergola leads to fruited potager. Step up to sculpted lawn edged with small trees, shrubs and sumptuous perennials.

10 44 BROADWATER AVENUE
Letchworth Garden City SG6 3HJ. Karen & Ian Smith. *½ m SW Letchworth town centre. A1(M) J9 signed Letchworth. Straight on at 1st three r'abouts, 4th r'about take 4th exit then R into Broadwater Ave.* Home-made teas. **Adm £4, chd free. Evening Opening wine, Fri 31 July (6-9). Sun 2 Aug (12-5).**
Town garden in the Letchworth Garden City conservation area that successfully combines a family garden with a plantswoman's garden. Out of the ordinary, unusual herbaceous plants and shrubs. Attractive front garden designed for yr-round interest.

11 ◆ CAPEL MANOR GARDENS
Bullsmoor Lane, Enfield EN1 4RQ. Capel Manor College, 08456 122 122, www.capelmanorgardens.co.uk. *2m from Cheshunt. 3 mins from J25 of M25/A10. Nearest train station is Turkey Street, then 20 mins walk.* Light refreshments. **Adm £5.50, chd £2.50. For NGS: Sat 7 Mar, Sat 24 Oct (10-5). For other opening times and information, please phone or see garden website.**
A beautiful 30-acre estate providing a colourful and scented oasis surrounding a Georgian Manor House and Victorian Stables. Be inspired by prize winning themed, model and historical gardens incl the latest additions the Old Manor House Garden and the Australian Garden (Chelsea Gold Medal winner). Jungle Gym Garden for under 5's Amazing holly maze to explore. Meercats, Shetland Ponies, Alpacas and reptile house. Wheelchair loan available and free with advanced booking.

12 NEW 8 CHAPEL ROAD
Breachwood Green, Hitchin SG4 8NU. Mr & Mrs Melvin Gore. *Midway between Hitchin Harpenden & Luton, Breachwood Green is well signed. We are just 2 doors from Red Lion PH.* Home-made teas. **Adm £3, chd free. Sun 12, Wed 15 July (12-5).**
Standing in the heart of the village surrounding a C17 cottage is an informal garden having no lawns or straight level pathways with a good selection of perennials, shrubs and alpines. With one of the largest collections of vintage garden tools and machinery on display.

13 42 CHURCH STREET
Baldock SG7 5AF. Leila Shafarenko. *Baldock town centre. 3m N of A1M J9 in the center of Baldock. 2m S of A1M J10. At the end of High St turn R at r'about, soon L into Sun St, continue Church St.* Home-made teas. **Adm £3, chd free. Evening Opening wine, Fri 8 May (6-8.30). Sun 10 May (2-5).**
Secluded walled garden hidden behind a C16 house in the heart of Baldock's conservation area. Mature trees, incl a magnificent magnolia, wisteria-clad walls, wide herbaceous borders. Cottage-style planting featuring species peonies, and many varieties of thornless roses.

14 CROFT COTTAGE

9 Church Green, Benington SG2 7LH. Richard Arnold-Roberts & Julie Haire. *4m E of Stevenage. A1 J7 onto A602 to Hertford. Onto single carridgeway. Next r'about L down hill to mini r'about. Up hill through Aston. 1¹/₂ m to Xrd. Then 1¹/₂ m. Park on road opp cottage. Tea in village hall.* **Adm £3.50, chd free. Mon 31 Aug (1-5).**
C16 cottage with small, extensively planted garden divided into several areas. Many variegated and colourful-leafed shrubs and perennials. Mixed border in pastel shades. Euphorbia and hosta collection. Pool with fish, waterspout and seat. Rose and clematis shaded arbour with view over fields. Japanese maple garden with pool overlooking C13 church. Featured in Garden News Garden of the Week. Gravel paths.

15 10 CROSS STREET

Letchworth Garden City SG6 4UD. Renata & Colin Hume, www.cyclamengardens.com. *nr town centre. From A1(M) J9 signed Letchworth, across 2 r'abouts, R at 3rd, across next 3 r'abouts L into Nevells Rd, 1st R into Cross St. Tea. Friday evening - wine.* **Adm £3.50, chd free. Evening Opening wine, Fri 15 May (5-8). Sat 16 May (11-2); Sun 17 May (2-5).**
A cottage garden fronts a Letchworth Garden City exhibition cottage of 1905. The back garden contains informal planting dictated by the gently sloping plot and three formal circular lawns. Trees, shrubs, grasses and herbaceous perennials combine to create interest in the different areas. The garden also contains a lily pond, a small pond for wildlife, a well-stocked greenhouse and an apple walk with a selection of old varieties.

16 35 DIGSWELL ROAD

Welwyn Garden City AL8 7PB. Adrian & Clare de Baat, 01707 324074, adrian.debaat@ntlworld.com, www.adriansgarden.org. *¹/₂ m N of Welwyn Garden City centre. From the Campus r'about in city centre take N exit just past the Public Library into Digswell Rd. Over the White Bridge, 300yds on L.* Home-made teas. **Adm £4, chd free. Sun 26 July (2-5.30); Sun 18 Oct (1.30-4.30). Visitors also welcome by arrangement June to Oct groups of up to 20,**

adm £7 incl tea & cake.
Town garden of around a third of an acre with naturalistic planting inspired by the Dutch garden designer, Piet Oudolf. The garden has perennial borders plus a small meadow packed with herbaceous plants and grasses. The contemporary planting gives way to the exotic, incl a succulent bed and under mature trees, a lush jungle garden incl bamboos, bananas, palms and tree ferns. Featured in Hertfordshire Life and Garden Answers magazines. Grass paths and gentle slopes to all areas of the garden.

60 142 FALCONER ROAD

Bushey, Watford WD23 3AD. Mrs Suzette Fuller 077142 94170 suzettesdesign@btconnect.com *M1 J 5 follow signs for Bushey From London A40 via Stanmore towards Watford. From Watford via Bushey Arches, through to Bushey High St turn L into Falconer Rd, opp St James church.* **Light refreshments. Adm £3, chd free. Sat 25, Sun 26 July, Sat 1, Sun 2 Aug (12-6). Evening Opening wine, Sat 7 Nov (4-8). Visitors also welcome by arrangement July.**
Enchanting magical unusual Victorian style space. Children so very welcome. Winter viewing for fairylight lighting, for all ages, bring a torch. Bird cages and chimneys a feature, plus a walk through conservatory with orchids.

17 NEW FIELD END HOUSE

The Green, Park Lane, Old Knebworth SG3 6QN. Paul & Sue Wood. *From J6 A1(M) Welwyn take B656 signed Codicote then follow NGS signs From J7 A1(M) Stevenage S exit take A602 to Knebworth. Follow NGS signs. Park in field short walk to garden.* Home-made teas. **Adm £3.50, chd free. Evening Opening wine, Fri 12 June (6-9). Sun 14 June (2-5.30).**
¹/₃ acre garden with views over countryside. Early summer planting in the prairie style has been incl to withstand windy conditions. A curved grass meadow under mature lime trees looks out on to arable farmland with distant views. A sheltered corner with exotic planting affords an enticing place to sit. Wheelchair access good in most areas of the garden.

18 15 GADE VALLEY COTTAGES

Dagnall Road, Great Gaddesden, Hemel Hempstead HP1 3BW. Bryan Trueman. *3m N of Hemel Hempstead. Follow A4146 N from Hemel Hempstead. Past Water End. Go past turning for Great Gaddesden. Gade Valley Cottages on R. Park in village hall car park.* Home-made teas. **Adm £3, chd free. Sun 31 May, Sun 12 July (1.30-5).**
165ft x 30ft sloping rural garden. Patio, lawn, borders and pond. Paths lead through a woodland area emerging by wildlife pond and sunny border. A choice of seating offers sunny rural views or quiet shady contemplation with sounds of rustling bamboos and bubbling water. Featured in Garden News.

A sheltered corner with exotic planting affords an enticing place to sit . . .

19 GREENWOOD HOUSE

2a Lanercost Close, Welwyn AL6 0RW. David & Cheryl Chalk. *1¹/₂ m E of Welwyn village, close to J6 on A1(M). Off B197 in Oaklands. Opp North Star PH turn into Lower Mardley Hill. Park here as limited at house (5min walk). Take Oaklands Rise to top of the hill & take L fork.* Home-made teas. **Adm £4, chd free. Evening Opening wine, Fri 3 July (6-9). Sun 5 July (1-5).**
Secluded garden of ¹/₃ acre surrounds our contemporary home and backs on to a beautiful ancient woodland. Garden has been transformed in last 6 years, with mature trees providing a natural backdrop to the many shrubs and perennials which provide interest and colour throughout the seasons. Access to rear garden across pebble paths and some steps.

© Rosalind Simon

Rustling End Cottage

20 ◆ HATFIELD HOUSE WEST GARDEN

Hatfield AL9 5NQ. The Marquess of Salisbury, 01707 287010, www.hatfield-house.co.uk. *Opp Hatfield Stn, 21m N of London, M25 J23. 7m A1(M) J4 signed off A414 & A1000. Free parking.* Light refreshments. **Adm £6, chd free. For NGS: Sat 28 Mar (11-5). For other opening times and information, please phone or see garden website.**

Visitors can enjoy the spring bulbs in the lime walk, sundial garden and view the famous Old Palace garden, childhood home of Queen Elizabeth I. The adjoining woodland garden is at its best in spring with masses of naturalised daffodils and bluebells. Restaurant open. Shopping in Stable Yard.

21 122 HAZELWOOD DRIVE

St. Albans AL4 0UZ. Phil & Becky Leach. *³/₄ m NE of St Albans city centre. From city centre take A1057 (Hatfield Rd). After ³/₄ m turn L into Beechwood Ave. Take 2nd R into Central Drive, then 2nd L into Hazelwood Drive.* Home-made teas. **Adm £3, chd free. Sat 16 May (2-5).**

A densely and informally planted small town garden divided into sections, with an emphasis on foliage and structure. Large-leaved plants incl foxglove tree (paulownia), giant rhubarb (gunnera) and rice-paper plant (tetrapanax). Structural plants incl onopordum, acanthus, cynara and eryngium. Many plants grown from seed; echinops, echium, teasel and melianthus. Featured on Radio Verulam and in St Albans Review. Access is via small section of gravel drive.

22 3 HIGHFIELD AVENUE

Harpenden AL5 5UB. Sue Gudgin. *²/₃ m from Harpenden Railway Stn. Station Rd, R into Milton Rd, over r'about, L into Fairmead Ave then Highfield Ave. No 3 on L.* Home-made teas. **Adm £3, chd free. Sun 14 June (2-5.30).**

Romantic, peaceful, garden (80' x 30', N-facing), designed over 10yrs for all-year colour. Informal garden rooms interlinked by winding grass paths and wide traditional borders creating seating areas with different atmospheres. Arches with wisteria, rose and lonicera. Trees incl silver birch, ash, rowan and acers. Small

raised herb patch, sedum roof on garden shed. **1 Highfield Avenue**, the garden of Brian & Sue Smith, will also be open with Plants for Sale.

23 ◆ HITCHIN LAVENDER

Cadwell Farm, Ickleford, Hitchin SG5 3UA. Mr Tim Hunter, 01462 434343, www.hitchinlavender.com. *2m N of Hitchin. From Hitchin take A600 N. At r'about R into Turnpike Lane. Continue into Arley Rd, garden on R after railway Xing.* **For NGS: Evening Openings £4, chd free, Wed 24 June, Fri 24 July, Mon 24 Aug (5-9). For other opening times and information, please phone or see garden website.**

Visitors are encouraged to walk through the miles of lavender rows at Hitchin Lavender. As well as taking home some great photos you can also pick a bunch of lavender. The fields are a great spot for photographers, artists or those just wanting to take life a little slower. Entrance incl pick your own bunch of lavender - please bring your own scissors! Partial wheelchair access.

Find a garden near you – download our free iPhone app

24 ◆ **HOPLEYS**
High Street, Much Hadham
SG10 6BU. Aubrey & Jan Barker,
01279 842509, www.hopleys.co.uk.
*5m W of Bishop's Stortford. On
B1004. M11 (J8) 7m or A10
(Puckeridge) 5m via A120. 50yds N of
Bull PH in centre of Much Hadham.*
**For opening times and information,
please phone or see garden
website.**
4 acres laid out in informal style with
island beds. The garden has become
a useful collection of stock plants and
trial ground for many new plants
collected over the years, and features
a wide selection of trees, shrubs,
perennials and grasses. The nursery
production area is hidden by an
avenue of fastigiate hornbeams.

25 **HOSPICE OF ST FRANCIS
GARDEN**
Spring Garden Lane, Berkhamsted
HP4 3GW. Hospice of St Francis.
*1¹⁄₂ m W of Berkhamsted town
centre. Leave A41 at A416 Chesham
exit. Follow signs for Berkhamsted,
When rd bends R go straight on into
Shootersway, signed Northchurch, for
1¹⁄₄ m.* Tea. **Adm £4, chd free. Sun 6
Sept (2-5.30).**
The hospice was built in 2006 on
seven acres of previously damaged
land and designed to resemble a
farmhouse, barns and outbuildings.
The garden has native woodland at
the boundaries and pergolas, paved
terraces, lawns, ponds, and flower
and shrub beds visible and
accessible from patients' bedrooms;
a peaceful oriental healing garden;
and a sensory garden with views
across to Ashridge. Most of the
woodland is not suitable for
wheelchairs.

26 **HUNTSMOOR**
Stoney Lane, Bovingdon, Hemel
Hempstead HP3 0DP. Mr Brian
Bradnock & Ms Jane Meir,
01442 832014,
b.bradnock@btinternet.com.
*Between Bovingdon & Hemel
Hempstead. Do not follow SatNav
directions along Stoney Lane. Huge
pot holes and ruts in lane. Approach
from Bushfield Rd.* Home-made teas.
Gluten free provided. **Adm £5, chd
free. Sun 26 Apr (2-5). Evening
Opening wine, Thur 18 June (7-9).
Sun 20 Sept (2-5). Visitors also
welcome by arrangement Apr to
Sept for groups of 10+.**

Rose garden, rhododendron border,
arboretum, Koi pond, nature pond,
shrub and herbaceous borders. Also
has a 'cave', and lots of places to sit.
Full access to garden including easy
access to WC.

27 **8 KINGCROFT ROAD**
Southdown, Harpenden AL5 1EJ.
Zia Allaway, 07770 780 231,
zia.allaway@ntlworld.com,
www.ziaallaway.com. *1¹⁄₂ m S of
Harpenden town centre. From
Harpenden take the St Albans Rd
A1081 S. At 1st r'about turn L onto
Southdown Rd. Continue straight
over 3 r'abouts to Grove Rd.* Home-
made teas. **Adm £3.50, chd free.
Evening Opening wine, Fri 24 Apr
(5.30-8.30). Sun 26 Apr (2-6).
Visitors also welcome by
arrangement Apr to Sept for small
groups.**
Beautiful mature town garden
designed by garden writer and
designer in a contemporary informal
style, with small pond and pebbled
beach area, gravel garden, a wide
range of tulips and spring bulbs,
herbaceous perennials and shrubs,
mature trees, shady borders,
greenhouse, and inspirational
container displays. A small courtyard
features flower-filled window boxes
and vegetables in raised beds.

28 ◆ **KNEBWORTH HOUSE
GARDENS**
Knebworth SG1 2AX. The Hon
Henry Lytton Cobbold, 01438
812661,
www.knebworthhouse.com. *28m N
of London. Direct access from A1(M)
J7 at Stevenage. Stn, Stevenage 3m.*
Open year round for corporate
hospitality and social functions. See
website for details. **For opening
times and information, please
phone or see garden website.**
Knebworth's magnificent gardens
were laid out by Lutyens in 1910.
Lutyens' pollarded lime avenues,
Gertrude Jekyll's herb garden, the
restored maze, yew hedges, roses
and herbaceous borders are key
features of the formal gardens with
peaceful woodland walks beyond.
Gold garden, green garden, brick
garden and walled kitchen garden.
Delicious afternoon teas served in the
Garden Terrace Tea Room. Featured
in Hertfordshire Life.

29 NEW ▶ **322 KNIGHTSFIELD**
Welwyn Garden City AL8 7NQ. Mrs
Judy Tucker. *Leave A1M at J6
signed WGC. At r'about turn R &
follow NGS signs. From town centre
leave by Digswell Rd & follow NGS
signs from 2nd r'about. Park at
school opp.* Home-made teas. **Adm
£3, chd free. Evening Opening
wine, Fri 26 June (5-8). Sun 28
June (2-5.30).**
Mature medium sized cottage style
town garden, with all year round
interest, Surrounded by beech
hedges and mature woodland trees.
The garden contains a variety of
trees, shrubs and perennials all
bordering a lawn and patio. Features
incl pond, ha ha, summerhouse,
small courtyard and secluded seating
area.

Features incl
pond, ha ha,
summerhouse,
small courtyard
and secluded
seating area . . .

30 ▶ **THE LODGE**
Luton Road, Markyate, St Albans
AL3 8QA. Jan & John Paul. *2m N of
M1 J9. Turn off A5 to Luton on
B4540. The garden is between the
villages of Markyate & Slip End.* Light
refreshments. Tea coffee or squash
and homemade cakes. **Adm £4, chd
free. Sat 13 June (11-5); Sun 14
June (11-4).**
The garden, of nearly 3 acres, has
evolved over 47yrs, partly through our
own efforts and partly through nature
growing plants wherever it chooses.
The garden, mainly informal with a
series of rooms, with small wooded
area, a wild flower meadow and
remains of an orchard full of common
spotted orchids and other lovely wild
flowers all of which arrived by
themselves. Come and see for
yourself. Main entrance gravel.
Garden mostly flat.

31 ▶ MACKERYE END HOUSE

Mackerye End, Harpenden
AL5 5DR. Mr & Mrs G Penn. *3m E
of Harpenden. A1 J4 follow signs
Wheathampstead. then turn R
Marshalls Heath Lane. M1 J10 follow
Lower Luton Road B653. Turn L
Marshalls Heath Lane. Follow signs.*
Home-made teas. **Adm £5, chd free.
Evening Opening wine, Fri 29 May
(6-9). Sun 5 July (12-5).**
C16 (Grade 1 listed) Manor House
(not open) set in 15 acres of formal
gardens, parkland and woodland,
front garden set in framework of
formal yew hedges. Victorian walled
garden with extensive box hedging
and box maze, cutting garden,
kitchen garden and lily pond.
Courtyard garden with extensive yew
and box borders. West garden
enclosed by pergola walk of old
English roses. Walled garden access
by gravel paths.

♿ ✿ ☕

32 ▶ THE MANOR HOUSE, AYOT ST LAWRENCE

Welwyn AL6 9BP. Rob & Sara
Lucas. *4m W of Welwyn. 20 mins J4
A1M. Take B653 Wheathampstead.
Turn into Codicote Rd follow signs to
Shaws Corner. Parking in field short
walk to garden.* Home-made teas.
**Adm £5, chd free. Sun 17 May
(11-5).**
A 6-acre garden set in mature
landscape around Elizabethan Manor
House (not open). 1-acre walled
garden incl glasshouses, fruit and
vegetables, double herbaceous
borders, rose and herb beds.
Herbaceous perennial island beds,
topiary specimens. Parterre and
temple pond garden surround the
house. Gates and water features by
Arc Angel. Garden designed by Julie
Toll.

Ⓓ ☕

33 ▶ 43 MARDLEY HILL

Welwyn AL6 0TT. Kerrie & Pete. *5m
N of Welwyn Garden City. On B197
between Welwyn & Woolmer Green,
on crest of Mardley Hill by bus stop
for Arriva 300/301.* Home-made teas.
**Adm £3, chd free. Sun 17 May
(1-5).**
Only one opening in 2015 for you to
see an unexpected garden
transformed by plantaholics since
2009 and packed with unusual plants
and inspiring combinations. Seating
areas give different perspectives on
the garden design and planting
composition, and from a small bridge

you can watch the man-made stream
cascade down into the pond. For sale
will be cakes, teas and a large
selection of plants.

✿ ☕

34 ▶ THE MILL HOUSE

31 Mill Lane, Welwyn AL6 9EU.
Sarah & Ian. *Old Welwyn. J6 A1M
approx ³/₄ m to garden, follow yellow
arrows to Welwyn Village.* Home-
made teas. **Adm £4, chd free. Wed
22, Sat 25, Sun 26 Apr (2-5).**
Listed millhouse (not open) with semi-
walled garden bordered by a bridged
millstream and mill race. This
romantic spring garden has ancient
apple trees underplanted with an
abundant display of tulips and white
narcissi. These set off a garden full of
perennial promise, within which
nestles a stylish summerhouse, a
hidden parterre and productive
potager. Featured in The Telegraph
and Countryside magazine.

♿ ✿ ☕

Garden around a 400 year old thatched cottage adjoining a disused churchyard with ancient yews . . .

35 ▶ 324 NORTON WAY SOUTH

Letchworth Garden City SG6 1TA.
Roger & Jill Thomson. *Just off the
A505, E of town centre. From the
A1M leave at J 9 (A505) to
Letchworth. At 2nd r'about turn L. to
Hitchin, still on A505. At T-lights turn
R into Norton Way South.* Tea. **Adm
£3.50, chd free. Sun 26 Apr (2-5).**
¹/₅ acre organic garden of a
sympathetically extended Garden City
house (1906). Features incl an
informal knot garden, a bespoke
David Harber armillary sphere as focal
point of a lawn surrounded by a
rockery, scree garden, borders,
summerhouse and pond. Mature
trees, shrubs and seasonal planting in
beds and containers, alpine troughs,
sculptures, greenhouse and kitchen
garden. Wheelchair access to most
areas of the garden.

♿ ✿ ☕

36 ▶ OAKRIDGE AVENUE GARDENS

Radlett WD7 8EW. *Radlett. 1m N of
Radlett off A5183, Watling St. From
S, through Radlett Village last turning
on L.* Cream teas. Pimms at No 47.
**Combined adm £4, chd free. Sun
19 July (2-5.30).**

45 OAKRIDGE AVENUE

Mr & Mrs Vaughan.
Follow yellow arrows
Visitors also welcome by
arrangement Apr to Sept.
01923 854650
ekvaughan@btinternet.com

47 OAKRIDGE AVENUE

Scott Vincent

Two varied interconnecting gardens in
attractive village near St Albans. Both
on the edge of a working farm. The
main features of no. 45 are the plants
carefully chosen to combine the use
of colour throughout the year. The
garden is in two halves approx 150ft
x 60ft on 3 levels of terracing, looping
around to a garden of vegetables and
soft fruit. Beds divided by sleepers.
Plants for sale are propagated from
the garden. No. 47 is a spacious and
mature garden, approx 1 acre with a
large pond, an impressive Victorian
wall and small orchard. A local brook
runs alongside.

✿ ☕

37 ▶ NEW ▶ OLD CHURCH COTTAGE

Chapel Lane, Long Marston, Tring
HP23 4QT. Dr John & Margaret
Noakes. *A41 to Aylesbury leave at
Tring exit. On outskirts of Tring take
B488 towards Ivinghoe. At first
r'about straight over to Long
Marston. Park at village hall, disabled
parking & drop off only at house.*
Light refreshments. Mulled wine and
muffins incl in the adm. **Adm £5, chd
free. Sat 14, Sun 15 Feb (11-3).**
Small garden around a 400yr old
thatched cottage adjoining a disused
churchyard with ancient yews and
Norman tower being the remnant of a
Chapel of Ease. Many species and
varieties of snowdrops together with
cyclamen, crocuses and other early
spring bulbs. Ancient listed buildings
in a conservation zone. Garden laid
out with raised beds with many
unusual snowdrops.

☕

Serendi

Join us on Facebook and spread the word

38 PATCHWORK

22 Hall Park Gate, Berkhamsted HP4 2NJ. Jean & Peter Block, 01442 864731. *3m W of Hemel Hempstead. Entering E side of Berkhamsted on A4251, turn L 200yds after 40mph sign.* Light refreshments. **Adm £3, chd free. Sun 3 May, Sun 16 Aug (2-5). Visitors also welcome by arrangement Mar to Oct groups of 10 to 50.**

¼-acre garden with lots of yr-round colour, interest and perfume, particularly on opening days. Sloping site with background of colourful trees, rockeries, two small ponds, patios, shrubs and trees, spring bulbs, herbaceous border, roses, bedding, fuchsias, dahlias, patio pots and tubs galore, and hanging baskets. Seating and cover from the elements. Not suitable for wheelchairs, as side entrance is narrow, and there are many steps and levels.

39 ◆ PEMBROKE FARM

Slip End, nr Ashwell, Baldock SG7 6SQ. Krysia Selwyn-Gotha, 01462 743100, pembrokefarmgarden.co.uk. *¼ m S of Ashwell. Turn off A505 (The Ashwell turn opp the Wallington & Rushden junction.) Go Under a railway bridge & past a cottage on R, after 200 yards enter the white farm gates on R.* Home-made teas in the courtyard. **Adm £3.50, chd free. For NGS: Sun 7 June (12-5). For other opening times and information, please phone or see garden website.**

A country house garden with a wildlife walk and formal surprises. You are invited to meander through changing spaces creating a palimpsest of nature and structure. Car park close to garden entry.

40 QUEENSWOOD SCHOOL

Shepherds Way, Brookmans Park, Hatfield AL9 6NS. Queenswood School. *3m N of Potters Bar. M25 J24 signed Potters Bar at T-lights turn R onto A1000 signed Hatfield. 2m turn R onto B157. School ½ m on R. From N A1000 from Hatfield turn L B157.* **Adm £4, chd free. Sun 24 May (11-5).**

120 acres of informal gardens and woodlands. Rhododendrons, fine specimen trees, shrubs and herbaceous borders. Glasshouses.

Fine views to Chiltern Hills. Picnic area. Full Sunday Roast served alongside Scampi and Chips, also a vegetarian option. Muffins, strawberries and cream teas. Some gravel areas.

> Behind lumpy hedges explore a simple box parterre, topiary, reflecting pool and abundant planting . . .

ALLOTMENTS

41 RADLETT ALLOTMENTS

Gills Hill, Radlett WD7 8DA. Aldenham Parish Council, None. *½ m W of Radlett centre - walk across recreation ground. Follow signs up Station Rd & Gills Hill. Park in Recreation Ground CP or surrounding streets. Disabled parking on site - entrance opp St Johns Church in Gills Hill Lane WD7 8DF.* Home-made teas. **Adm £3, chd free. Sun 5 July (2-5).**

84 well established allotments cultivated in a variety of styles in a peaceful environment. Wide selection of fruit, vegetable and flowers incl exhibition standard sweet peas. Some plots divided into mini allotments which will have been judged the day before. Many plot holders will be present. Fresh vegetables and plants for sale. Home made teas. Exhibition standard, cordon grown, sweet peas. Partial wheelchair access, main paths are accessible but paths between allotments are too narrow. Access to teas will be difficult.

42 REVELEY LODGE

88 Elstree Road, Bushey Heath WD23 4GL. Bushey Museum Property Trust, www.reveleylodge.org. *3½ m E of Watford & 1½ m E of Bushey Village. From A41 take A411 signed Bushey & Harrow. At mini-r'about 2nd exit into Elstree Rd. Garden ½ m on L. Disabled parking only onsite.* Home-

made teas. **Adm £4, chd free. Sun 9 Aug (2-6).**

2½-acre garden surrounding a Victorian house bequeathed to Bushey Museum in 2003 and in process of re-planting and renovation. Featuring colourful annual, tender perennial and medicinal planting in beds surrounding a mulberry tree. Conservatory, lean-to greenhouse, vegetable garden and beehive. Analemmatic (human) sundial constructed in stone believed unique to Hertfordshire. Partial wheelchair access.

43 ◆ THE ROYAL NATIONAL ROSE SOCIETY

Chiswell Green Lane, St Albans AL2 3NR. The Secretary, 0845 833 4344, www.rnrs.org.uk. *M25 J21a M1 J6. Follow brown signs, Gardens of the Rose off A405 Noke Lane 1st R Miriam Lane as you enter Butterfly World Ltd. For Satnav use postcode AL2 3NY.* **For NGS: Evening Opening £5, chd free, Tea, Fri 17 July (6-8). For other opening times and information, please phone or see garden website.**

The gardens were completely rebuilt to a design by Michael Balston & Co in 2007, in the winter of 2009 the garden design was further enhanced by the introduction of additional grass paths enabling visitors more access to the roses. Also at this time a decision was also taken to support general gardening trends by the introduction of many more companion plants. The garden showcases over 15,000 roses old and new, fragrant and colourful, displaying the stunning heritage of our favorite flower in a beautiful setting.

44 RUSTLING END COTTAGE

Rustling End, nr Codicote SG4 8TD. Julie & Tim Wise, www.rustlingend.com. *1m N of Codicote. From B656 turn L into '3 Houses Lane' then R to Rustling End. House 2nd on L.* Home-made teas. **Adm £4.50, chd free. Evening Openings wine, Sat 2, Sat 23 May, Sat 1 Aug (4-8). Sun 13 Sept (2-5.30).**

Meander through our wild flower meadow to a cottage garden with contemporary planting. Behind lumpy hedges explore a simple box parterre, topiary, reflecting pool and abundant planting. Late flowering borders

Lemon drizzle cake, Victoria sponge … yummy!

feature blue Camassia in late spring. Naturalistic planting incl the use of wild flowers with perennials and grasses. Our terrace hosts drought tolerant planting. Hens in residence.

45 3 ST MARYS WALK
St. Albans AL4 9PD. Mrs Rosemary Coldstream, 01727 860092, rose@rosemarycoldstream.com, www.rosemarycoldstream.com. *Marshalswick, North St Albans. Located off Pondfield Crescent or via walkway from The Ridgeway, follow yellow NGS signs.* Home-made teas. **Adm £3.50, chd free. Evening Opening wine, Fri 25 Sept (5.30-7.30). Sun 27 Sept (2-5.30). Visitors also welcome by arrangement Apr to Oct.**
This contemporary and late-summer garden features an unusual collection of antipodean and English plants. A garden designer's own family garden, pathways lead off in all directions from a central oval-shaped lawn. The borders are packed with grasses, perennials, ferns, tree ferns, exotic trees and shrubs and some quirky topiary. The garden also houses Rosemary's design studio. Featured in House Beautiful September and a Gardening book by Frances Tophill published April 2015.

46 ST MICHAEL'S CROFT
Woodcock Hill, Durrants Lane, Berkhamsted HP4 3TR. Sue & Alan O'Neill, www.stmichaelscroft.co.uk. *1¼ m W of Berkhamsted town centre. Leave A41 signed A416 Chesham. Follow sign to Berkhamsted, after 500 metres straight on to Shootersway. 1m on turn R into Durrants Lane. Garden 1st on L.* Home-made teas. **Adm £4, chd free. Sun 21 June (2-6).**
1-acre S-facing garden with variety of densely planted borders surrounded by mature trees. Rhododendrons, azaleas, hostas, ferns, alliums, palms and bananas. Water features and waterfall from lock gate. Pergolas with clematis and climbers, vegetable beds, 2 greenhouses. Working beehives. Seating and cover. Home produced honey and plants for sale. Featured in Garden News (Garden of the Week). Easy access for wheelchairs.

47 ◆ ST PAUL'S WALDEN BURY
Whitwell, Hitchin SG4 8BP. Simon & Caroline Bowes Lyon, 01438 871218, www.stpaulswaldenbury.co.uk. *5m S of Hitchin. On B651; ½ m N of Whitwell village. From London leave A1(M) J6 for Welwyn (not Welwyn Garden City). Pick up signs to Codicote, then Whitwell.* Home-made teas. **Adm £5, chd £1. For NGS: Sun 26 Apr, Sun 17 May, Sun 7 June (2-7). For other opening times and information, please phone or see garden website.**
Spectacular formal woodland garden, Grade 1 listed, laid out 1720. Long rides lined with clipped beech hedges lead to temples, statues, lake and a terraced theatre. Seasonal displays of snowdrops, daffodils, cowslips, irises, magnolias, rhododendrons, lilies. Wild flowers are encouraged. This was the childhood home of the late Queen Mother. Children welcome. Open Garden combined with Open Farm Sunday 7 June. Performances of Shakespeare's 'Merry Wives of Windsor' 25-27 July. Partial wheelchair access in part of the garden. Steep grass slopes in places.

GROUP OPENING

48 ST STEPHENS AVENUE GARDENS
St Albans AL3 4AD. *1m S of St Albans City Centre. From A414 take A5183 Watling St. At double mini-r'bout by St Stephens Church/King Harry PH take B4630 Watford Rd. St Stephens Ave is 1st R.* **Combined adm £5, chd free. Sun 28 June, Sun 6 Sept (2-6).**

20 ST STEPHENS AVENUE
Heather & Peter Osborne
Visitors also welcome by arrangement Apr to Oct for groups of 10+. 01727 856354 heather.osborne20@btinternet.com

30 ST STEPHENS AVENUE
Carol & Roger Harlow

Visit our gardens at a different time of year! As well as our late June date, this year for the first time we're also opening in September, when the pastel tones of high summer give way to shimmering grasses and a more exotic palette. The plantswoman's garden at number 20 has been developed to provide a range of

habitats from cool shade, hot and dry, to lush pondside displays. Successional planting ensures waves of colour from April to October. Serpentine paths weave through the carefully maintained borders. New areas are developed each year, recent additions include a bed of late season perennials and ornamental grasses. Number 30 has a southwest facing gravelled front garden that has a Mediterranean feel. Herbaceous plants, such as sea hollies and achilleas, thrive in the poor, dry soil. Clipped box, beech and hornbeam in the back garden provide a cool backdrop for the strong colours of the herbaceous planting. A gate beneath a beech arch frames the view to the park beyond. Plants for sale at June opening only.

49 SANDON BURY
Sandon, Buntingford SG9 0QY. Teddy & Louise Faure Walker. *5m N of Buntingford. A10 N of Buntingford. L at Buckland. Follow signs to Sandon. A1 N of Stevenage, A505 towards Royston. R after 2½ m to Sandon.* Tea at Sandon Village Hall. **Adm £5, chd free. Sat 13, Sun 14 June (2-5).**
1640 Manor House in 2 acre garden. The highest point in Hertfordshire with views over countryside. Large herbaceous borders, walled vegetable garden, parterre, dovehouse, mature trees. ART EXHIBITION in recently restored 1250 Saxon Barn one of the oldest in Europe. C13 church, village hall Teas WC, easy parking. Wheelchair access to garden, barn up sloping gravel path. Art Exhibition in recently restored C13 barn. Disabled Parking WC at Village Hall Church and Garden easy access. Access to barn up rough gravel drive not suitable for all wheelchairs.

50 SCUDAMORE

1 Baldock Road, Letchworth
Garden City SG6 3LB. Michael &
Sheryl Hann. *Opp Spring Rd,
between Muddy Lane & Letchworth
Lane. J9 A1. Follow directions to
Letchworth. Turn L to Hitchin A505.
After 1m House on L opp corner
shop. Parking in Muddy Lane &
Spring Rd.* Home-made teas. **Adm
£4, chd free. Share to Garden
House Hospice. Sun 5 July (11-5).**
1/2 acre garden surrounding early C17
cottages that were converted and
extended in 1920s to form current
house (not open). Family garden of
mature trees, mixed herbaceous
borders with shrubs, pond and
stream, wet bed, wild garden and
orchard/vegetable area. Many
sculptures add interest to the garden.
& 🐾 🕸 ☕ •

51 SERENDI

22 Hitchin Road, Letchworth
Garden City SG6 3LT. Valerie & Ian
Aitken. *1m from city centre. A1 M J9
signed Letchworth on A505. At 2nd
r'about turn L to Hitchin on A505.
Straight over T-lights. Garden 1m on
R.* Home-made teas. **Adm £4, chd
free. Evening Opening wine, Fri 26
June (6-9). Sun 28 June (1-5.30).**

1/3 acre plot comprising several
different areas. Front garden -
wisteria, an 'S' loop of lavender, blue
and pink bed, hot coloured narrow
border - dahlias, shrubs. A 'back
yard' of hostas and acers, memento
wall, formal planting and exuberant
cottage style planting with roses and
magnolias in larger beds.
Greenhouse, contemporary knot
garden, topiary and aeoniums. Gravel
entrance driveway.
& 🐾 🕸 ☕ •

GROUP OPENING

52 SERGE HILL GARDENS

Serge Hill Lane, Bedmond, Watford
WD5 0RT. *1/2 m E of Bedmond. Go to
Bedmond & take Serge Hill Lane,
where you will be directed past the
lodge & down the drive.* Home-made
teas at Serge Hill. **Combined adm
£7, chd free. Sun 21 June (2-5).**

THE BARN D
Sue & Tom Stuart-Smith

SERGE HILL
Kate Stuart-Smith

Two very diverse gardens. At its
entrance the Barn has an enclosed

courtyard, with tanks of water,
herbaceous perennials and shrubs
tolerant of generally dry conditions. To
the N there are views over the 5-acre
wild flower meadow, and the West
Garden is a series of different gardens
overflowing with bulbs, herbaceous
perennials and shrubs. Serge Hill is
originally a Queen Anne House (not
open), beautifully remodelled by
Busby (architect of Brighton and
Hove) in 1811. It has wonderful views
over the ha-ha to the park; a walled
vegetable garden with a large
greenhouse, roses, shrubs and
perennials leading to a long mixed
border. At the front of the house there
is an outside stage used for family
plays, and a ship. Featured in House
and Garden and Hertfordshire Life.
🕸 ☕

53 ◆ SHAW'S CORNER

Ayot St Lawrence, nr Welwyn
AL6 9BX. National Trust,
01438 820307,
www.nationaltrust.org.uk/
shawscorner. *2m NE of
Wheathampstead. At SW end of
village, approx 2m from B653 (A1 J4,
M1 J10). Signed from B653 (Shaw's
Corner/The Ayots).* Light

8 Kingcroft Road

Look out for the NGS yellow arrows ...

refreshments. **Adm £7.25, chd free. For NGS: Sun 7 June (12-5.30). For other opening times and information, please phone or see garden website.**
Approx 3½ acres with richly planted borders, orchard, small meadow, wooded areas and views over the Hertfordshire countryside. Historical garden, belonging to George Bernard Shaw from 1906 until his death in 1950. Hidden among the trees is the revolving writing hut where Shaw retreated to write his plays. Ionian Singers will perform in the garden on NGS open day. No wheelchair accessible WC.

54 SOUTH WING
Bramfield House, Bramfield, Hertford SG14 2QT. Mr Keith Henderson. *3m NE of Hertford. From Hertford take A119 towards Watton-at-Stone. Turn L to Bramfield. In Bramfield turn R into Well Green.* Home-made teas. **Adm £5, chd free. Sat 4 July (12-6).**
Just under 5 acres, and situated to the S of a wing of a Victorian villa. Perennial herbaceous beds follow the view to the lake. Summer beds planted fully and to succeed from spring to late autumn. Prairie-style beds near the lake, and more large perennial beds lead to a large meadow. Only in its 5th year since planting, the garden is one of long vistas with large flowering beds.

55 9 TANNSFIELD DRIVE
Hemel Hempstead HP2 5LG. Peter & Gaynor Barrett, 01442 393508, tterrabjp@ntlworld.com, www.peteslittlepatch.co.uk. *Approx 1m NE of Hemel Hempstead town centre & 2m W of J8 on M1. From J8 cross r'dabout to A414 Hemel Hempstead. Under ftbridge, cross r'dabout then 1st R across dual c'way to Leverstock Green Rd. Straight on to High St Green. L into Ellingham Rd then follow signs.* Home-made teas. **Adm £3, chd free. Sun 19 July, Sun 9 Aug (1.30-5). Visitors also welcome by arrangement June to Sept groups of up to 10 welcome.**
This small, town garden is decorated with over 400 plants creating a welcoming oasis of calm. The owners love to experiment with the garden planting scheme which ensures the look of the garden alters from year to year. Narrow paths divide, leading the

visitor on a discovery of the garden's many features. The sound of water is ever-present. Water features, metal sculptures, wall art and mirrors run throughout the garden. As a time and cost saving experiment all hanging baskets are planted with hardy perennials most of which are normally used for ground cover.

56 THUNDRIDGE HILL HOUSE
Cold Christmas Lane, Ware SG12 0UE. Christopher & Susie Melluish, 01920 462500, c.melluish@btopenworld.com. *2m NE of Ware. ³/₄ m from The Sow & Pigs PH off the A10 down Cold Christmas Lane, crossing new bypass.* Home-made teas. **Adm £4.50, chd free. Sun 7 June (2-5.30). Visitors also welcome by arrangement Apr to Aug.**
Well-established garden of approx 2½ acres; good variety of plants, shrubs and roses, attractive hedges. We are at present creating an unusual yellow-only bed. Several delightful places to sit. Wonderful views in and out of the garden especially down to the Rib Valley. 'A most popular garden to visit'.

57 84 VALLEY ROAD
Welwyn Garden City AL8 7DP. Marion Jay. *W side of Welwyn Garden City. Turn R off Great North Rd at Lemsford r'about, go under the bridge then 2nd turning next r'about. 200 yds on L.* Home-made & cream teas, home-made cake. **Adm £3.50, chd free. Sun 3 May (2-5.30). Evening Openings wine, Fri 3, Fri 10 July (7-9). Sun 16 Aug (2-5.30).**
This will be the final year of opening so do not miss the chance to visit this lovely garden. A dramatic garden rising steeply from the back of the house, using an 'amphitheatre' of stone wall terracing to accommodate

the slope. Planting is largely in the modern perennial style, mixing drifts of drought-tolerant herbaceous plants with a variety of grasses. Three ponds and new front garden prairie planting. Plants for sale. Featured in The English Garden and Garden Answers magazine. Difficult for those walking with sticks.

58 WALKERN HALL
Walkern, Stevenage SG2 7JA. Mrs Kate de Boinville, 079735 58838, katedeboinville@btconnect.com. *4m E of Stevenage. Turn L at War Memorial as you leave Walkern, heading for Benington (immed after small bridge). Garden 1m up hill on R.* Home-made teas. Warming homemade soup. **Adm £3.50, chd free. Sat 7, Sun 8 Feb (12-4.30).**
Walkern Hall is essentially a winter woodland garden. Set in 8 acres, the carpet of snowdrops and aconites is a constant source of wonder in Jan/Feb. This medieval hunting park is known more for its established trees such as the tulip trees and a magnificent London plane tree which dominates the garden. There is wheelchair access but no WC.

59 WOODHALL PARK
Watton-at-Stone, Hertford SG14 3NF. Mr & Mrs Ralph Abel Smith, www.woodhallestate.co.uk. *4m N of Hertford. 6m S of Stevenage, 4m NW of Ware, Main lodge entrance to Woodhall Park on A119.* Home-made teas. **Adm £5, chd free. Sun 21 June (12-5).**
Mature 4-acre garden created out of surrounding park in 1957 when C18 stable block was converted into a dwelling house (not open). Special features: courtyard, rose borders, rose arbours, herbaceous and mixed borders, swimming pool garden, kitchen garden and areas to sit with unspoilt views. Grassland park full of mature and ancient trees traversed by the R Beane and lake. Homemade teas served from Pavilion in the swimming pool garden. After seeing the gardens visitors are welcome to walk in C18 park. Long and short routes clearly marked. Featured in Hertfordshire Mercury.

60 142 FALCONER ROAD
see page 269

ISLE OF WIGHT

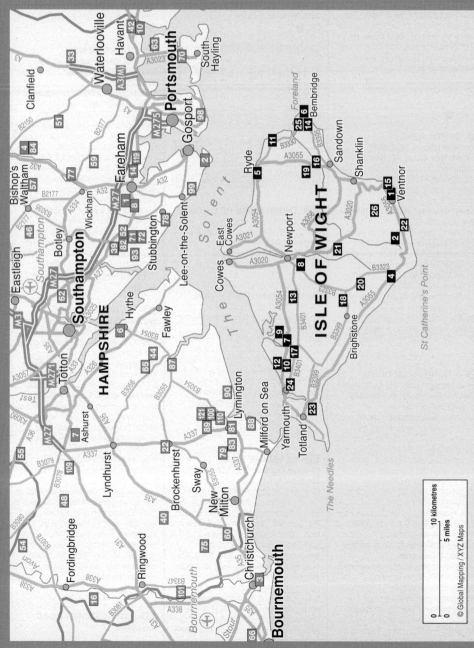

Isle of Wight

The island is a very special place to those who live and work here and to those who visit and keep returning. We have a range of natural features, from a dramatic coastline of cliffs and tiny coves to long sandy beaches.

Inland, the grasslands and rolling chalk downlands contrast with the shady forests and woodlands. Amongst all of this beauty nestle the picturesque villages and hamlets, many with gardens open for the NGS. Most of our towns are on the coast and many of the gardens have wonderful sea views.

The one thing that makes our gardens so special is our climate. The moderating influence of the sea keeps hard frosts at bay, and the range of plants that can be grown is therefore greatly extended. Conservatory plants are planted outdoors and flourish. Pictures taken of many island gardens fool people into thinking that they are holiday snaps of the Mediterranean and the Canaries.

Our gardens are very varied and our small enthusiastic group of garden owners are proud of their gardens, whether they are small town gardens or large manor gardens, and they love to share them for the NGS.

Below: Crab Cottage © Carole Drake

Isle of Wight Volunteers

County Organiser
Jennie Fradgley
01983 730805
jenniemf805@yahoo.co.uk

County Treasurer
Jennie Fradgley
(as above)

Publicity
Jennie Fradgley
(as above)

Booklet Coordinator
Jennie Fradgley
(as above)

Assistant County Organisers
Mike Eastwood
01983 721060
mike@aristia.co.uk

Louise Ness
01983 551701
louiseness@gmail.com

Sally Parker
01983 612495
sallyparkeriow@btinternet.com

Currently the NGS donates around £2.5 million every year

Opening Dates

All entries subject to change.
For latest information check www.ngs.org.uk

April

Saturday 25
23 Sunny Patch

May

Saturday 2
4 NEW The Beeches

Sunday 10
18 Northcourt Manor Gardens

Sunday 17
3 Badminton
16 NEW Morton Manor

Sunday 24
13 Meadowsweet

Wednesday 27
10 Funakoshi

Sunday 31
6 Blue Haze
14 Mill Farm
25 1 White Cottages

June

Festival Weekend

Saturday 6
5 Blenheim House
21 Rookley Manor

Sunday 7
5 Blenheim House
21 Rookley Manor

Sunday 14
7 NEW Bridge House
24 Thorley Manor

Saturday 20
1 Ashcliff

Sunday 21
1 Ashcliff
20 The Old Rectory

Saturday 27
6 Blue Haze
25 1 White Cottages

Sunday 28
17 NEW Ningwood Manor

July

Saturday 4
2 Ashknowle House

Sunday 5
2 Ashknowle House

Sunday 12
11 High Vista
19 Nunwell House

Saturday 25
23 Sunny Patch

August

Saturday 1
26 NEW Wroxall Village Gardens

Sunday 2
9 Crab Cottage
26 NEW Wroxall Village Gardens

Saturday 8
22 The Shute

Saturday 15
4 NEW The Beeches

Sunday 16
15 NEW Miramar Lodge

Sunday 30
16 NEW Morton Manor

Gardens open to the public

19 Nunwell House

By arrangement only

8 Clatterford House
12 Highwood

Also open by arrangement

5 Blenheim House
9 Crab Cottage
17 NEW Ningwood Manor
18 Northcourt Manor Gardens

The Gardens

1 ASHCLIFF

The Pitts, Bonchurch, nr Ventnor PO38 1NT. Judi & Sid Lines. *From A3055 follow directions for Bonchurch. Follow signs for Bonchurch pond & park in village or continue, following signs for parking in Bonchurch Shute.* Home-made teas. Adm £3.50, chd free. Sat 20, Sun 21 June (11-4).
The garden was started from a blank canvas 9 yrs ago and now contains many diverse areas of interest incl areas of sun and shade. Plantings are of interesting and unusual perennials, shrubs and trees over approx 1 acre blending into the natural landscape, part of which is a cliff.
🐕 ❀ ☕

2 ASHKNOWLE HOUSE

Ashknowle Lane, Whitwell, Ventnor PO38 2PP. Mr & Mrs K Fradgley. *4m W of Ventnor. Take the Whitwell Rd from Ventnor or Godshill. Turn into unmade lane next to Old Rectory. Field parking & disabled parking at house.* Home-made teas. Adm £4, chd free. Sat 4, Sun 5 July (11.30-4.30).
A variety of features to explore in the grounds of this Victorian house. Informative woodland walks, borders, wildlife pond and other water features. Ongoing development of ornamental areas. The well maintained kitchen garden is highly productive and boasts a wide range of fruit and vegetables grown in cages, tunnels, glasshouses and raised beds. New orchard incl protected cropping. Display and DVD of red squirrel antics.
🐕 ❀ ☕

3 BADMINTON

Clatterford Shute, Carisbrooke, Newport PO30 1PD. Mr & Mrs G S Montrose, 01983 526143. *1½ m SW of Newport. Free parking in Carisbrooke Castle car park. Garden signed approx 200yds. Parking for disabled can be arranged, please phone prior to opening.* Home-made teas. Adm £3.50, chd free. Sun 17 May (2-5).
1 acre garden on sheltered south and west facing site with good vistas. Planted for yr-round interest with many different shrubs, trees and perennials to give variety, structure and colour. Natural stream with bridges and waterfall. Pond being developed alongside kitchen garden.
🐕 ❀ ☕

4 NEW THE BEECHES

Chale Street, Chale, Ventnor PO38 2HE. Mr & Mrs Andrew & Anne Davidson, 01983 551876. *Turn off A3055 at Chale onto B3399. Entrance between Old Rectory & bus stop, in gap in stone wall. On entry turn up the gravel drive towards our house which is two storey, tile hung.* Tea. Adm £3, chd free. Sat 2 May, Sat 15 Aug (10-5).
A large garden laid out mainly to shrubs and border plants designed for colour and texture. A haven of peace with extensive 270 degree views of the countryside incl the south west coast of the island down to The Needles and Dorset beyond. Features incl a grassland meadow and pond for fish and wildlife (children to be supervised because of deep water). The garden is not easy for

© Carole Drake

wheelchairs due to gravel driveway and some steps, however can be accommodated with prior arrangement.

 🚰 ☕

5 ▶ BLENHEIM HOUSE

9 Spencer Road (use Market St entrance), Ryde PO33 2NY. **David Rosewarne & Magie Gray, 01983 614675.** *Market St entrance behind Ryde Town Hall/Theatre.* Tea. **Adm £3, chd free. Sat 6, Sun 7 June (2-5.30). Visitors also welcome by arrangement May to Sept.**
A garden developed over 9 yrs, exploring the decorative qualities and long term effects of pattern making, colour and texture. This terraced 116ft x 30ft sloping site is centred on a twisting red brick path that both reveals and hides interesting and contrasting areas of planting, creating intimate and secluded spaces that belie it's town centre location.

❀ ☕

6 ▶ BLUE HAZE

24 Beachfield Road, Bembridge PO35 5TN. Gerry Price, www.thecoastalgardener.co.uk. *Take B3395 for Bembridge. At Windmill Inn turn into Lane End, 2nd R into Egerton Rd, L into Howgate Rd, then 1st R onto unmade road.* Home-made teas. **Combined adm with 1 White Cottages £3, chd free. Sun 31 May, Sat 27 June (11-4).**
A passion for plants, art and the coast inspired the creation of this small coastal garden which wraps around Blue Haze. Native coastal plants thrive alongside more cultivated species whilst sculptures made from objects washed ashore augment the theme. Fruit, vegetables and a small nursery are integrated into the garden making it productive as well as attractive. Flat gravel garden, wheelchair access to some areas may be difficult.

🚰 ❀ 🚐 ☕

7 ▶ NEW ▶ BRIDGE HOUSE

Church Lane, Shalfleet, Newport PO30 4NF. Pam & Bruce. *On banks of R Calbourne. One-way lane off Newport/Yarmouth road & opp New Inn. House on L & parking in village hall grounds up lane on R.* Home-made teas at Shalfleet Village Hall. **Adm £3, chd free. Sun 14 June (2-4).**
A foliage garden on the banks of the little river Cal Bourne with its own waterfall and pool where eels and catfish come to feed each afternoon. Lots of lovely views, and planting for wildlife. Many different ferns and a good range of plants incl hostas, bulbs and trees. Features incl feeding the eels at 3pm and look out for the riverside treehouse. Partial wheelchair access.

🚰 🐕 ❀ ☕

Find a garden near you – download our free Android app

The Old Rectory

8 ▶ CLATTERFORD HOUSE
Clatterford Shute, Carisbrooke
PO30 1PD. Sylvia Clare & David
Hughes, 01983 537338,
sylvia.clare@btinternet.com,
www.mindfullyalive.org. *1¹/₂ m SW
of Newport. On-site parking available
for small groups of up to 10 cars.*
Adm £3.50, chd free. Visitors
welcome by arrangement Mar to
Apr on Sats & Suns from 21 Mar to
11 Apr only. Refreshments on
request.
Developing garden, reclaimed in the
year 2000 from derelict and overgrown
property. Fantastic views enhance the
naturalistic planting, managed for
wildlife conservation using organic
principles. Spring bulbs and early
summer plantings worth seeing.
Regular articles on the Hardy Plant
Society website. Partial wheelchair
access, please phone for details. Not
suitable for motorised chairs.

9 ▶ CRAB COTTAGE
Mill Road, Shalfleet PO30 4NE.
Mr & Mrs Peter Scott,
mencia@btinternet.com. *4¹/₂ m E of
Yarmouth. Turn past New Inn into Mill
Rd. Please park before going through
NT gates. Entrance 1st on L, less
than 5 mins walk.* Home-made teas.
Adm £3.50, chd free. Sun 2 Aug
(11.30-5). Visitors also welcome by
arrangement May to Aug.
1¹/₄ acres on gravelly soil. Part
glorious views across croquet lawn
over Newtown Creek and Solent
leading to wild flower meadow,
woodland walk and hidden waterlily

pond. Part walled garden protected
from westerlies, with mixed borders,
leading to terraced sunken garden
with ornamental pool and pavilion;
planted with exotics, tender shrubs
and herbaceous perennials. Gravel
path, uneven grass paths.

10 ▶ FUNAKOSHI
Cranmore Avenue, Yarmouth
PO41 0XR. Mrs Helen Mount,
01983 761321. *2m E of Yarmouth.
Just off the main Yarmouth/Newport
road. There is a bus shelter opp the
entrance to Cranmore Ave from the
main road.* Home-made teas. Adm
£3, chd free. Wed 27 May
(11-4.30).
Approx 1 acre of mixed planting
designed for yr-round interest on
heavy clay. Garden developed over
last 6 yrs after being retrieved from
yrs of neglect. Particular interest in
growing South African plants and
cultivated plants that are good for
pollinating insects. Owner grows
some less common or hard to find
perennial plants blended with annuals
and coordinates Hardy Plant Society
National Conservation Scheme.
Partial wheelchair access.

11 ▶ HIGH VISTA
Seaview Lane, Seaview PO34 5DJ.
Mrs Linda Bush. *Location is at the
top of Seaview Lane, just outside
Nettlestone. Please park on main &
side roads only.* Home-made teas.
Adm £3, chd free. Sun 12 July
(10.30-5).

A small new garden by a new
gardener which defies its size with
immense variety and riot of colour. Sit
under a vine covered pergola and
enjoy the feeling of the
Mediterranean. Lots of climbers, pots
and planters with a kaleidoscope of
colour. Small area given over to
vegetables and a glasshouse. Sloping
driveway from main road.

12 ▶ HIGHWOOD
Cranmore Avenue, Cranmore
PO41 0XS. Mr & Mrs Cooper,
01983 760550,
ross.cooper1934@talktalk.net. *2m
E of Yarmouth on Yarmouth to
Newport road. Bus shelter opp
entrance to Cranmore Ave.* Tea.
Visitors welcome by arrangement.
A garden for all seasons. In spring,
snowdrops, hepaticas and
hellebores. In summer, perennials,
grasses, ferns, wild flowers, and
orchids particularly. In autumn, asters,
berries and much colour. A wonderful
contrast of sunny borders and shady
woodland garden. S-facing slope
leads to an oak copse. Clay soil, so
good footwear needed if inclement
weather. Features incl galanthus, wild
orchids, and unusual perennials.

13 ▶ MEADOWSWEET
5 Great Park Cottages, off Betty-
Haunt Lane, Carisbrooke
PO30 4HR. Gunda Cross. *4m SW of
Newport. From A3054 Newport/
Yarmouth road, turn L at Xrd
Porchfield/Calbourne, over bridge*

into 1st lane on R. Parking along one side, on grass verge past house. Home-made teas. **Adm £3.50, chd free.** Sun 24 May (11.30-4.30). From windswept barren 2 acre cattle field to developing tranquil country garden. Natural, mainly native, planting and wild flowers. Cottagey front garden, herb garden, orchard, fruit cage and large pond. The good life and a haven for wildlife! Flat level garden with grass paths.

14 MILL FARM
Mill Road, Bembridge PO35 5PD. Peter, Alice & Kirsty Summerhayes. *Follow brown signs to Bembridge Windmill, come through NT gate, past windmill to the R. Limited parking on roadside.* Home-made teas. **Adm £3, chd free.** Sun 31 May (2-5.30). Delightful informal cottage garden surrounding C17 farmhouse (not open) in windswept location with wonderful views. The garden is set out in a number of areas incl a gravel garden, vegetable patch and orchard. Gravel drive.

15 NEW MIRAMAR LODGE
Bonchurch Shute, Ventnor PO38 1NX. Mrs Jane Buitenhuis. *Off A3055 just E of Ventnor town. Entrance to small private country lane, which leads to Miramar Lodge, is adjacent to the V66 landslip & coastal path of landslip area. Road is also highlighted as East & West Miramar.* Home-made teas. **Adm £3, chd free.** Sun 16 Aug (11-4.30). Miramar Lodge sits on the famous Bonchurch landslip. Newly landscaped in 2014. Interesting hard scape products, which work with the various garden levels. Plants range from tropical, country garden and raised vegetable beds, with a careful choice of planting, colours and textures. Chris Barnes resident islander designed areas of Miramar. Miramar was once stables to the larger estate.

16 NEW MORTON MANOR
Morton Manor Road, Brading, Sandown PO36 0EP. Mr & Mrs G Godliman. *Off A3055 5m S of Ryde just out of Brading. At Yar Bridge T-lights turn into lower Adgestone Rd. Take next L into Morton Manor Rd.* Home-made teas. **Adm £4, chd £1.** Sun 17 May, Sun 30 Aug (11-4).

A colourful garden of great plant variety. Mature trees incl many acers with a wide variety of leaf colour. Early in the season a display of rhododendrons, azaleas and camellias. Ponds, sweeping lawns, roses set on a sunny terrace and much more to see in this extensive garden surrounding a picturesque C16 Manor House (not open).

17 NEW NINGWOOD MANOR
Station Road, Ningwood, Nr Newport PO30 4NJ. Nicholas & Claire Oulton, 01983 761352, claireoulton@gmail.com. *Nr Shalfleet. From Newport, turn L opp the Horse & Groom PH. Ningwood Manor is 300-400yds on the L. Please use 2nd set of gates.* Tea. **Adm £4, chd free.** Sun 28 June (12-4.30). Visitors also welcome by arrangement June to July. A 3 acre, landscape designed country garden with a walled courtyard garden, croquet lawn garden, white garden and kitchen garden. Much new planting has taken place over the last few yrs. The owners have several new garden projects underway, so the garden is a work in progress. Features incl a vegetable garden with raised beds and a small summerhouse, part of which is alleged to be Georgian.

18 NORTHCOURT MANOR GARDENS
Main Road, Shorwell PO30 3JG. Mr & Mrs J Harrison, 01983 740415, john@northcourt.info, www.northcourt.info. *4m SW of Newport. On entering Shorwell from Newport, entrance at bottom of hill on R. If entering from other directions head through village in direction of Newport. Garden on the L, on bend after passing the PO.* Tea. **Adm £4.50, chd free.** Sun 10 May (12-7). Visitors also welcome by arrangement May to Oct with tea or light lunch for groups available. 15 acre garden surrounding large C17 Manor House (not open), incl walled kitchen garden, chalk stream, terraces, magnolias and camellias. Subtropical planting. Boardwalk along jungle garden. A large variety of plants enjoying the different microclimates. There are roses, primulas by the stream and hardy geraniums in profusion. Picturesque wooded valley around the stone manor house. Bathhouse and snail

mount leading to terraces. 1 acre walled garden being restored. The house celebrates its 400th year anniversary in 2015. Wheelchair access on main paths only.

19 ◆ NUNWELL HOUSE
West Lane, Brading PO36 0JQ. Mr & Mrs S Bonsey, 01983 407240, www.nunwellhouse.co.uk. *3m S of Ryde. Signed off A3055 into Coach Lane.* Home-made teas. **Adm £4, chd £1.** For NGS: Sun 12 July (1-5). For other opening times and information, please phone or see garden website. 5 acres of beautifully set formal and shrub gardens and old fashioned shrub roses prominent. Exceptional Solent views from the terraces. Small arboretum and walled garden with herbaceous borders. House (not open) developed over 5 centuries and full of architectural interest.

20 THE OLD RECTORY
Kingston Road, Kingston PO38 2JZ. Derek & Louise Ness, www.theoldrectorykingston.co.uk. *8m S of Newport. Entering Shorwell from Carisbrooke, take L turn at mini r'about towards Chale (B3399). Follow road until Kingston sign, house 2nd on L after this. Park in adjacent field.* Home-made teas. **Adm £3.50, chd free.** Sun 21 June (2-5). Constantly evolving romantic country garden. Areas of interest incl the walled kitchen garden, orchard, formal and wildlife ponds and a wonderfully scented collection of old and English roses.

21 ROOKLEY MANOR

Niton Road, Rookley PO38 3NR.
Mr M Eastwood & Mr M von
Brasch. *Enter Niton Rd from Rookley
Village. Manor is 8th house on R.*
Home-made teas. **Adm £3.50, chd
free. Sat 6, Sun 7 June (11-4).**
A private, romantic 1 acre garden
developed over a decade by an artist
and a writer respecting the older trees
and Georgian house built in 1782 (not
open). Within the framework of the
garden is a continuous exploration of
the possibilities of new planting ideas
that take into account shade, light
and space. There will also be an art
exhibition of six artists work as well as
live harp music with Anna Sacchini.

❀ ☕

22 THE SHUTE

Seven Sisters Road, St. Lawrence,
Ventnor PO38 1UZ. Mr & Mrs C
Russell. *½ way along Seven Sisters
Rd, opp bottom of St Lawrence
Shute. Parking in Fishers or Twining
Rd (2 mins walk) or in Undercliff Drive
(10 min uphill walk). Sorry, no parking
in our shared drive.* Home-made
teas. **Adm £3, chd free. Sat 8 Aug
(11-5).**
Approx ¾ acre, formerly part of a
large Victorian garden. Views from the
terrace across the lawn and white
border to the sea. In the lower area
we mix herbaceous planting with fruit
and vegetables. Phlox perfumes the
shaded pink border whilst annuals
complement the dahlias and
perennials in the hot border for a
show of late summer colour.

❀ ☕

23 SUNNY PATCH

Victoria Road, Freshwater
PO40 9PP. Mrs Eileen Pryer. *½ way
between Freshwater Village &
Freshwater Bay. Down Afton Rd, L at
garage up Stroud Rd. Keep L just up
from Parish Hall on same side.
Parking in road outside house.*
Home-made teas. **Adm £3, chd free.
Sat 25 Apr, Sat 25 July (10-4.30).**
A garden of an eccentric plantaholic
and ornament collector. A light
hearted garden of rooms which incl
acers, magnolias and many
herbaceous plants and shrubs, 2
ponds, a fairy wood, and a folly. Each
season brings another treasure to the
fore and the borders continue to
grow. There are no paths and
numerous yrs of moles has made the
ground very uneven.

☕

24 THORLEY MANOR

Thorley, Yarmouth PO41 0SJ. Mr &
Mrs Anthony Blest. *1m E of
Yarmouth. From Bouldnor take
Wilmingham Lane. House ½ m on L.*
Home-made teas. **Adm £3.50, chd
free. Sun 14 June (2-5).**
Delightful informal gardens of over 3
acres surrounding Manor House (not
open). Garden set out in a number of
walled rooms incl herb garden,
colourful perennial and self seeding
borders, sweeping lawn and shrub
borders, plus unusual island croquet
lawn. Venue renowned for excellent
home-made teas and the eccentric
head gardener.

❀ ☕

*A passion for
plants, art and the
coast inspired the
creation of this
small coastal
garden . . .*

25 1 WHITE COTTAGES

109 High Street, Bembridge
PO35 5SF. Mr Nick Inigo Peirce,
whitecottagedaylilies.com. *B3395
for Bembridge. The Old High St is
straight on through village or past the
NT Windmill if coming from Sandown
or Brading.* Home-made teas.
**Combined adm with Blue Haze £3,
chd free. Sun 31 May, Sat 27 June
(11-4).**
A dry gravel garden, mainly used to
grow and breed daylilies
(Hemerocallis). They are in full bloom
at the end of June and at the
beginning of July. The garden is
predominantly herbaceous mixed
with grasses and thus the garden
changes dramatically over the yr.
Spring flowers provide interest before
the daylilies and grasses, and the late
perennials. The garden is long and
narrow with narrow winding paths.
100 registered daylilie varieties and
seedlings in garden setting with
seedling borders.

❀ ☕

GROUP OPENING

26 NEW WROXALL VILLAGE GARDENS

Wroxall Community Centre, Station
Road, Wroxall PO38 3DP. *2m N of
Ventnor on B3327. Enter village from
N & take Station Rd, R after church.
Entering from S take Station Rd, R
before church. Free car park opp
community centre where tickets &
map will be available.* Cream teas in
Wroxall Community Centre.
**Combined adm £4.50, chd free.
Sat 1, Sun 2 Aug (11-4).**

NEW **BOX COTTAGE,
BEACHFIELD ROAD**
Mr & Mrs Vic & Yvette Hickin

NEW **22 COOMBE PARK**
Mr Graham Dix

NEW **HEBRON, COOMBE
PARK**
Eric Wilkinson & Julie Cole

NEW **LITTLE FOXES,
COOMBE PARK**
Mr & Mrs Mike & Pat Botell

NEW **MEADOW VIEW,
COOMBE PARK**
Mr & Mrs Wilfred & Patricia Gill

NEW **54 MOUNTFIELD
ROAD**
Mr & Mrs Alf & Rose Gallop

NEW **32 WEST STREET**
Mr & Mrs Peter & Joyce
Bayford

NEW **3 WORSLEY DRIVE**
Mr & Mrs Richard & Lynn
Dasham

NEW **47 YARBOROUGH
ROAD**
Stephanie Smith

Nestled in the heart of the small
village of Wroxall you will find a
collection of gardens in different
styles, incl traditional cottage,
productive and modern style planting.
Some have been created from a
blank canvas, while others have been
cared for over many yrs. One garden
features a natural spring that flows
through many of the gardens that are
open. All are within comfortable
walking distance. The community
centre will host a variety of stalls incl
plants, house and garden signs,
decorative painted stones, fruit and
vegetables, clothes, and cream teas.

🐕 ❀ ☕

Blue Haze

Spread the word about the NGS: tell your family and friends

KENT

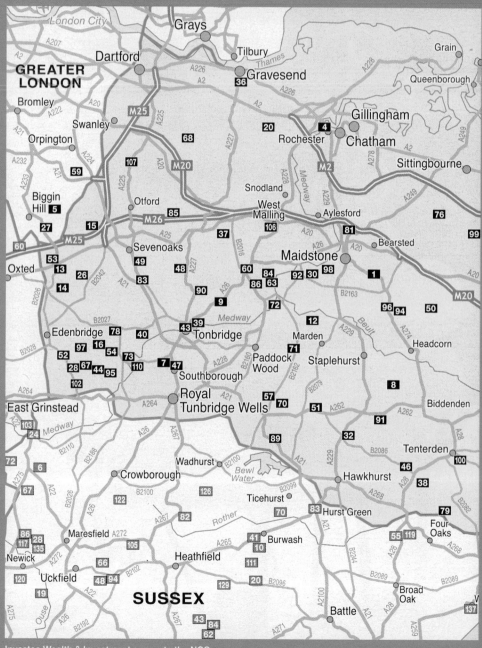

London City

Grays

Tilbury

Grain

Dartford

Thames

GREATER
LONDON

A226

Gravesend

36

Queenborough

Bromley

A226

Gillingham

A20

M25

Swanley

20

Rochester

4

Chatham

Sittingbourne

Orpington

68

107

M20

Snodland

West
Malling

85

M26

Otford

Aylesford

81

76

Biggin
Hill **5**

106

Bearsted

99

27

15

M25

Sevenoaks

37

Maidstone

60

53

49

48

60

84

92 **30** **98**

1

Oxted

13

26

83

86 **63**

M20

14

90

9

72

96 **94**

50

Medway

12

Edenbridge **78**

40

43 **39**

Tonbridge

Marden

71

Headcorn

97 **16**

54

73

Paddock
Wood

Staplehurst

52

28 **67** **44** **95**

110

7 **47**

Southborough

8

102

Royal
Tunbridge Wells

57 **70**

Biddenden

East Grinstead

103

Medway

51

91

24

89

32

Tenterden

72

6

Wadhurst

Bewl
Water

Hawkhurst

46

100

67

Crowborough

126

38

122

Ticehurst

70

83 Hurst Green

79

Maresfield

82

Rother

Four
Oaks

86

28

105

41

Burwash

55 **119**

117 **135**

10

Newick

111

120

66

Heathfield

129

20

Broad
Oak

19

Uckfield

48 **94**

SUSSEX

137

43 **84**

Battle

62

Investec Wealth & Investment supports the NGS

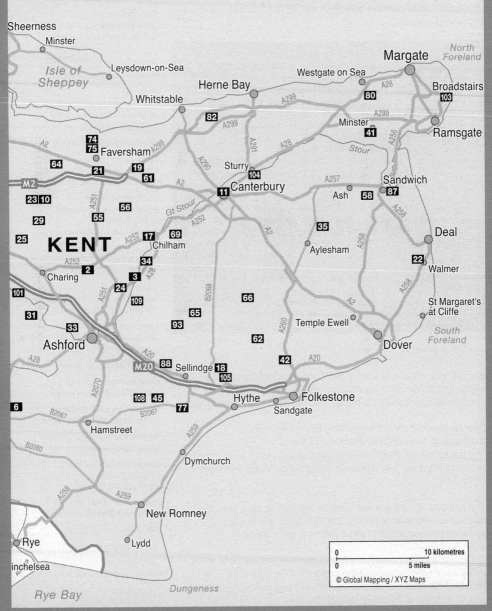

KENT

Sheerness
Minster
Isle of Sheppey
Leysdown-on-Sea
Whitstable
Herne Bay
Westgate on Sea
Margate
North Foreland
Broadstairs
103
80
A28
A299
A299
Minster
41
A256
Ramsgate
82
A299
A291
A28
Stour
74
75 Faversham
A299
A2
A290
Sturry
104
A257
Sandwich
64
21
19
61
A2
11 Canterbury
Ash **58** **87**
M2
23 **10**
56
Gt Stour
A251
A252
A35
A258
Deal
29
55
A2
25
KENT
17 **69**
Chilham
A252
35
A256
22
A252 **2**
34
Aylesham
Walmer
Charing
3 A28
B2068
A258
101
24
66
St Margaret's at Cliffe
31
109
65
A260
Temple Ewell
South Foreland
33
93
A2
Ashford
62
Dover
A28
A20
M20
88 Sellindge **18**
42 A20
105
6
108 **45**
77
Hythe
Folkestone
B2067
B2067
Sandgate
Hamstreet
A259
B2080
Dymchurch
A259
A259
New Romney
Rye
Lydd
inchelsea
Rye Bay
Dungeness

0   10 kilometres
0   5 miles
© Global Mapping / XYZ Maps

Kent

Famously known as 'The Garden of England', Kent is a county full of natural beauty, special landscapes and historical interest.

Above: Watergate House

Being England's oldest county, Kent unsurprisingly boasts an impressive collection of castles and historic sites, notably the spectacular Canterbury Cathedral, and the medieval Ightham Mote.

Twenty eight per cent of the county forms two Areas of Outstanding Natural Beauty: the Kent Downs and the High Weald. The landscapes of Kent are varied and breathtaking, and include haunting marshes, rolling downs, ancient woodlands and iconic white cliffs.

The gardens of Kent are well worth a visit too, ranging from the landscaped grounds of historic stately homes and castles, to romantic cottage gardens and interesting back gardens.

Never has a county been so close to London and yet feels so far away, so why not escape to the peace of a Kent garden? The variety of the gardens and the warmth of the garden owners will ensure a memorable and enjoyable day out.

Since our foundation we have donated more than £42.5 million to charity

Kent Volunteers

County Organiser
Jane Streatfeild 01342 850362
jane@hoath-house.freeserve.co.uk

County Treasurer (Acting)
Nicholas Ward 01732 810525
hookwood1@yahoo.co.uk

Publicity
Victoria Henderson 01892 870625
victoria_henderson@hotmail.com

Publicity (Radio)
Jane Streatfeild (as above)

Booklet Advertising
Marylyn Bacon 01797 270300
ngsbacon@ramsdenfarm.co.uk

Booklet Coordinator
Ingrid Morgan Hitchcock
01892 528341
ingrid@morganhitchcock.co.uk

Booklet Distribution
Diana Morrish 01892 723905
diana.morrish@hotmail.co.uk

Group Tours
Sue Robinson 01622 729568
suerobinson.timbers@gmail.com

Assistant County Organisers
Jacqueline Anthony 01892 518879
jacquelineanthony7@gmail.com

Marylyn Bacon (as above)

Clare Barham 01580 241386
clarebarham@holepark.com

Bridget Langstaff 01634 842721
bridget.langstaff@btinternet.com

Virginia Latham 01303 862881
lathamvj@gmail.com

Caroline Loder-Symonds
01227 831203
caroline@dennehill.co.uk

Susan Moir 01892 722223
moirconsult@btinternet.com

Diana Morrish (as above)

Sue Robinson (as above)

Julia Stanton 01227 700421
familystanton@hotmail.com

Felicity Ward 01732 810525
hookwood1@yahoo.co.uk

Opening Dates

All entries subject to change.
For latest information check www.ngs.org.uk

February

Tuesday 3
8 1 Brickwall Cottages

Saturday 7
94 Spring Platt

Sunday 8
50 Knowle Hill Farm
94 Spring Platt

Tuesday 10
8 1 Brickwall Cottages

Sunday 15
21 Copton Ash

Tuesday 17
8 1 Brickwall Cottages

Thursday 19
9 Broadview Gardens

Sunday 22
50 Knowle Hill Farm
60 Mere House
110 Yew Tree Cottage

Tuesday 24
8 1 Brickwall Cottages

Wednesday 25
44 Hoath House
110 Yew Tree Cottage

March

Sunday 1
60 Mere House

Sunday 8
110 Yew Tree Cottage

Wednesday 11
110 Yew Tree Cottage

Sunday 15
21 Copton Ash
33 Godinton House & Gardens
61 Mount Ephraim

Wednesday 18
87 The Secret Gardens of Sandwich at The Salutation

Sunday 22
16 Chiddingstone Castle
33 Godinton House & Gardens
46 Hole Park
95 Stonewall Park
110 Yew Tree Cottage

Wednesday 25
110 Yew Tree Cottage

Sunday 29
34 Godmersham Park
37 Great Comp Garden
56 Luton House

Exceptionally pretty and colourful summer garden . . .

April

38 **Great Maytham Hall (every Wednesday)**

Sunday 5
21 Copton Ash

Monday 6
20 Cobham Hall
21 Copton Ash
40 Hall Place
60 Mere House
72 Parsonage Oasts

Wednesday 8
110 Yew Tree Cottage

Sunday 12
3 Bilting House
22 34 Cross Road
35 Goodnestone Park Gardens
55 Lords
70 Orchard End
110 Yew Tree Cottage

Wednesday 15
46 Hole Park

Sunday 19
72 Parsonage Oasts
79 Potmans Heath House
81 11 Raymer Road

Tuesday 21
49 Knole

Wednesday 22
110 Yew Tree Cottage

Thursday 23
65 NEW Oak Cottage
83 Riverhill Himalayan Gardens

Saturday 25
65 NEW Oak Cottage
67 Old Buckhurst
104 Watergate House

Sunday 26
6 Boldshaves

8 1 Brickwall Cottages
21 Copton Ash
67 Old Buckhurst
86 St Michael's Gardens
91 Sissinghurst Castle
110 Yew Tree Cottage

Monday 27
8 1 Brickwall Cottages

Wednesday 29
67 Old Buckhurst

May

38 **Great Maytham Hall (every Wednesday)**

Sunday 3
8 1 Brickwall Cottages
10 NEW Calico House
30 Gallants Manor
67 Old Buckhurst
88 Sandown
95 Stonewall Park

Monday 4
8 1 Brickwall Cottages
21 Copton Ash
30 Gallants Manor
88 Sandown

Saturday 9
67 Old Buckhurst

Sunday 10
13 Charts Edge
25 Eagleswood
51 Ladham House
56 Luton House
59 12 The Meadows
67 Old Buckhurst
75 Pheasant Farm
99 Torry Hill
110 Yew Tree Cottage

Tuesday 12
83 Riverhill Himalayan Gardens

Wednesday 13
23 Doddington Place
89 Scotney Castle
110 Yew Tree Cottage

Thursday 14
57 Marle Place

Sunday 17
3 Bilting House
40 Hall Place
78 NEW 3 Post Office Cottages

Wednesday 20
14 Chartwell
46 Hole Park

Saturday 23
67 Old Buckhurst

Sunday 24
2 Beech Court Gardens
21 Copton Ash
40 Hall Place
88 Sandown

110 Yew Tree Cottage

Monday 25
21 Copton Ash
25 Eagleswood
88 Sandown

Wednesday 27
110 Yew Tree Cottage

Saturday 30
11 Canterbury Cathedral Gardens
18 Churchfield
67 Old Buckhurst
105 West Court Lodge

Sunday 31
8 1 Brickwall Cottages
11 Canterbury Cathedral Gardens
18 Churchfield
66 Old Bladbean Stud
92 Smiths Hall
105 West Court Lodge
106 West Malling Early Summer Gardens

June

38 **Great Maytham Hall (every Wednesday)**

Monday 1
8 1 Brickwall Cottages

Wednesday 3
67 Old Buckhurst

Festival Weekend

Saturday 6
35 Goodnestone Park Gardens
45 NEW Hogben House
62 Mounts Court Farmhouse
67 Old Buckhurst
74 Pheasant Barn
75 Pheasant Farm
108 Wyckhurst

Sunday 7
45 NEW Hogben House
62 Mounts Court Farmhouse
63 Nettlestead Place
74 Pheasant Barn
75 Pheasant Farm
79 Potmans Heath House
86 St Michael's Gardens
108 Wyckhurst

Monday 8
64 Norton Court

Tuesday 9
64 Norton Court

Wednesday 10
84 Rock Farm
110 Yew Tree Cottage

Thursday 11
- **57** Marle Place
- **61** Mount Ephraim

Saturday 13
- **4** Bishopscourt
- **45** NEW Hogben House
- **70** Orchard End
- **78** NEW 3 Post Office Cottages
- **84** Rock Farm
- **90** Shipbourne Gardens
- **104** Watergate House
- **108** Wyckhurst

Sunday 14
- **4** Bishopscourt
- **12** 3 Chainhurst Cottages
- **21** Copton Ash
- **22** 34 Cross Road
- **28** Falconhurst
- **34** Godmersham Park
- **45** NEW Hogben House
- **66** Old Bladbean Stud
- **69** The Orangery
- **70** Orchard End
- **85** St Clere
- **90** Shipbourne Gardens
- **99** Torry Hill
- **100** Townland
- **101** Tram Hatch
- **107** The World Garden at Lullingstone Castle
- **108** Wyckhurst
- **110** Yew Tree Cottage

Wednesday 17
- **12** 3 Chainhurst Cottages (Evening)
- **26** Emmetts Garden
- **46** Hole Park
- **102** Upper Pryors

Saturday 20
- **53** Little Gables

Sunday 21
- **6** Boldshaves
- **10** NEW Calico House
- **15** Chevening
- **23** Doddington Place
- **41** Haven
- **43** NEW 37 The Haydens
- **53** Little Gables
- **80** NEW Quex Gardens
- **109** Wye Gardens

Wednesday 24
- **91** Sissinghurst Castle (Evening)
- **110** Yew Tree Cottage

Thursday 25
- **87** The Secret Gardens of Sandwich at The Salutation

Friday 26
- **33** Godinton House & Gardens

Saturday 27
- **19** The Coach House
- **31** Garden House
- **88** Sandown
- **97** NEW Thatched Cottage

Sunday 28
- **2** Beech Court Gardens
- **19** The Coach House
- **31** Garden House
- **55** Lords
- **66** Old Bladbean Stud
- **88** Sandown
- **97** NEW Thatched Cottage
- **110** Yew Tree Cottage

Monday 29
- **20** Cobham Hall

Something to see whatever the season . . .

July

- **38** Great Maytham Hall (every Wednesday)

Wednesday 1
- **96** Sutton Valence School

Saturday 4
- **50** Knowle Hill Farm (Evening)
- **62** Mounts Court Farmhouse
- **74** Pheasant Barn

Sunday 5
- **42** Hawkinge Allotments
- **59** 12 The Meadows
- **62** Mounts Court Farmhouse
- **81** 11 Raymer Road
- **92** Smiths Hall

Wednesday 8
- **67** Old Buckhurst
- **110** Yew Tree Cottage

Thursday 9
- **48** Ightham Mote

Saturday 11
- **71** Orchard House, Spenny Lane

Sunday 12
- **66** Old Bladbean Stud
- **71** Orchard House, Spenny Lane
- **82** 43 The Ridings
- **101** Tram Hatch
- **110** Yew Tree Cottage

Wednesday 15
- **67** Old Buckhurst

Saturday 18
- **36** Gravesend Gardens Group
- **70** Orchard End

Sunday 19
- **21** Copton Ash
- **36** Gravesend Gardens Group
- **70** Orchard End
- **99** Torry Hill
- **100** Townland

Wednesday 22
- **23** Doddington Place
- **110** Yew Tree Cottage

Saturday 25
- **27** Eureka
- **88** Sandown

Sunday 26
- **27** Eureka
- **32** Goddards Green
- **66** Old Bladbean Stud
- **69** The Orangery
- **88** Sandown
- **110** Yew Tree Cottage

Monday 27
- **5** NEW The Blacksmiths Arms

August

- **38** Great Maytham Hall (every Wednesday)

Saturday 1
- **27** Eureka
- **103** The Watch House

Sunday 2
- **27** Eureka
- **50** Knowle Hill Farm
- **52** Leydens
- **67** Old Buckhurst
- **88** Sandown
- **103** The Watch House

Monday 3
- **88** Sandown

Thursday 6
- **5** NEW The Blacksmiths Arms

Saturday 8
- **27** Eureka

Sunday 9
- **27** Eureka
- **110** Yew Tree Cottage

Wednesday 12
- **110** Yew Tree Cottage

Thursday 13
- **65** NEW Oak Cottage

Saturday 15
- **65** NEW Oak Cottage

Sunday 16
- **101** Tram Hatch

Wednesday 15
- **67** Old Buckhurst

Saturday 22
- **5** NEW The Blacksmiths Arms

Sunday 23
- **43** NEW 37 The Haydens
- **110** Yew Tree Cottage

Wednesday 26
- **110** Yew Tree Cottage

Friday 28
- **17** Chilham Castle (Evening)

Saturday 29
- **17** Chilham Castle
- **54** NEW Long Meadow
- **70** Orchard End
- **78** NEW 3 Post Office Cottages

Sunday 30
- **39** 115 Hadlow Road
- **54** NEW Long Meadow
- **66** Old Bladbean Stud
- **70** Orchard End
- **88** Sandown

Monday 31
- **88** Sandown

September

Saturday 5
- **4** Bishopscourt
- **67** Old Buckhurst
- **88** Sandown

Sunday 6
- **4** Bishopscourt
- **27** Eureka
- **88** Sandown

Monday 7
- **27** Eureka

Tuesday 8
- **49** Knole

Wednesday 9
- **67** Old Buckhurst
- **110** Yew Tree Cottage

Thursday 10
- **73** Penshurst Place & Gardens

Saturday 12
- **67** Old Buckhurst

Sunday 13
- **66** Old Bladbean Stud
- **67** Old Buckhurst
- **110** Yew Tree Cottage

Sunday 20
- **23** Doddington Place

Friday 25
- **33** Godinton House & Gardens

Saturday 26
- **77** Port Lympne, The Aspinall Foundation

Take your Group to an NGS garden

Sunday 27
61 Mount Ephraim
66 Old Bladbean Stud

October

Sunday 4
35 Goodnestone Park Gardens
63 Nettlestead Place

Monday 5
87 The Secret Gardens of Sandwich at The Salutation

Sunday 11
46 Hole Park

Sunday 18
37 Great Comp Garden

Sunday 25
37 Great Comp Garden
60 Mere House

February 2016

Sunday 7
50 Knowle Hill Farm

Sunday 14
21 Copton Ash

Sunday 21
50 Knowle Hill Farm
60 Mere House

Wednesday 24
110 Yew Tree Cottage

Sunday 28
60 Mere House
110 Yew Tree Cottage

Gardens open to the public

2 Beech Court Gardens
9 Broadview Gardens
13 Charts Edge
14 Chartwell
16 Chiddingstone Castle
17 Chilham Castle
20 Cobham Hall
23 Doddington Place
26 Emmetts Garden
33 Godinton House & Gardens
35 Goodnestone Park Gardens
37 Great Comp Garden
46 Hole Park
48 Ightham Mote
49 Knole
57 Marle Place
61 Mount Ephraim
73 Penshurst Place & Gardens
80 NEW Quex Gardens
83 Riverhill Himalayan Gardens
87 The Secret Gardens of Sandwich at The Salutation

89 Scotney Castle
91 Sissinghurst Castle
107 The World Garden at Lullingstone Castle

By arrangement only

1 Ashley
7 Boundes End
24 Downs Court
29 Frith Old Farmhouse
47 Honnington Farm Gardens
58 Marshborough Farmhouse
68 NEW The Old Rectory
76 Placketts Hole
93 South Hill Farm
98 Timbers

Also open by arrangement

3 Bilting House
5 NEW The Blacksmiths Arms
6 Boldshaves
8 1 Brickwall Cottages
18 Churchfield
19 The Coach House
21 Copton Ash
25 Eagleswood

27 Eureka
32 Goddards Green
34 Godmersham Park
39 115 Hadlow Road
41 Haven
44 Hoath House
50 Knowle Hill Farm
55 Lords
56 Luton House
62 Mounts Court Farmhouse
64 Norton Court
67 Old Buckhurst
69 The Orangery
70 Orchard End
72 Parsonage Oasts
74 Pheasant Barn
75 Pheasant Farm
77 Port Lympne, The Aspinall Foundation
79 Potmans Heath House
82 43 The Ridings
84 Rock Farm
94 Spring Platt
99 Torry Hill
100 Townland
105 West Court Lodge
108 Wyckhurst
109 Mistral, Wye Gardens

The Gardens

1 **ASHLEY**
White Horse Lane, Otham, Maidstone ME15 8RQ. Susan & Roger Chartier, 01622 861333, susanchartier@hotmail.com. *4m SE of Maidstone. From A20 or A274 follow signs for Otham or Stoneacre, garden located between White Horse PH & Simmonds Lane.* Light refreshments. **Adm £2.50, chd free.** Share to Kent Autistic Trust.
Visitors welcome by arrangement Apr to Sept. Groups 25 max.
Front garden developed into a parterre, leading to surprisingly large rear garden with many unusual perennials. Pond with bridge, kitchen garden, dry garden and scented leaf pelargonium collection. Two beehives, one handmade in an original design following the principles of natural beekeeping. G Scale garden railway layout with working model trains. Partial wheelchair access.
♿ 🌳 ❇ ☕ 💧

Orchard House, Spenny Lane

Bring a bag for plants – help us give more to charity

© Leigh Clapp

Godinton House & Gardens

2 ♦ BEECH COURT GARDENS
Canterbury Road, Challock, nr Ashford TN25 4DJ. Mr & Mrs Vyvyan Harmsworth, 01233 740735, www.beechcourtgardens.co.uk. *5m N of Ashford, Faversham 6m, Canterbury 9m. W of Xrds A251/A252, off the Lees.* Cream teas. **Adm £4.50, chd free. For NGS: Sun 24 May, Sun 28 June (10.30-5). For other opening times and information, please phone or see garden website.**
Informal woodland garden surrounding medieval farmhouse (not open). Spring bulbs, rhododendrons, azaleas and viburnums give superb spring colour; climbing roses, summer borders and hydrangeas follow; fine collection of trees incl acers give autumn colour. Extensive lawns, meandering paths and surprising vistas. Picnic area. Tree lists, pet animals, children's trail. Artists welcome. Good wheelchair access except when wet.

3 BILTING HOUSE
nr Ashford TN25 4HA. Mr John Erle-Drax, 07764 580011, jdrax@marlboroughfineart.com. *5m NE of Ashford. A28, 9m S from Canterbury. Wye 1½ m.*

Home-made teas. **Adm £5, chd free. Sun 12 Apr, Sun 17 May (2-6). Visitors also welcome by arrangement Apr to June for groups 10+.**
6 acre garden with ha-ha set in beautiful part of Stour Valley. Wide variety of rhododendrons, azaleas and ornamental shrubs. Woodland walk with spring bulbs. Mature arboretum with recent planting of specimen trees. Rose garden and herbaceous borders. Conservatory.
🚴 ⚘ 🚌 ☕

4 BISHOPSCOURT
24 St Margaret's Street, Rochester ME1 1TS. Mrs Bridget Langstaff. *Central Rochester, nr castle & cathedral. On St Margaret's St at junction with Vines Lane. Rochester train station 10 mins walk. Disabled parking only at garden but many car parks within 5-7 mins walk.* Delicious home-made teas served in tea tent. **Adm £3, chd free. Sat 13, Sun 14 June, Sat 5, Sun 6 Sept (1-5).**
The residence of the Bishop of Rochester, this 1 acre historic walled garden is a peaceful oasis in the heart of Rochester with views of the castle from a raised lookout. Mature trees, lawns, yew hedges, rose garden, gravel garden, sculptures, fountain, wild flowers and mixed borders with perennials. Greenhouse and small

vegetable garden. Featured in Amateur Gardener magazine. Child friendly. Most of garden is accessible by wheelchair. WC incl disabled.
🚴 ⚘ ⚘ ☕

5 NEW THE BLACKSMITHS ARMS
Cudham Lane South, Cudham, Sevenoaks TN14 7QB. Joyce Cole, 01959 572678, mail@theblacksmithsarms.co.uk. *Leave M25 at J4. At Hewitts r'about take 3rd exit onto A21. At Pratts Bottom r'about take 2nd exit onto A21. At r'about take 1st exit onto Cudham Lane North & follow for 4m.* Cream teas. **Adm £3.50, chd free. Mon 27 July, Thur 6, Sat 22 Aug (1-5). Visitors also welcome by arrangement June to Sept.**
Exceptionally pretty and colourful summer garden set in the grounds of a C17 inn. Unusual varieties of summer bedding plants and annuals, mostly grown and cared for by the landlady. Decking and seating areas surrounded by spectacular hanging baskets and patio displays. Open lawn area with deep colour coordinated beds. We also are proud of our small natural area to attract and sustain wildlife. Partial wheelchair access inside PH.
🚴 ⚘ 🚌 ☕

6 BOLDSHAVES
Woodchurch, nr Ashford TN26 3RA. Mr & Mrs Peregrine Massey, 01233 860302, masseypd@hotmail.co.uk, www.boldshaves.co.uk. *Between Woodchurch & High Halden off Redbrook St. From A28 towards Ashford turn R in High Halden at village green; 2nd R on to Redbrook St, then R down unmarked lane after ½ m to brick entrance to Boldshaves at bottom of hill.* Home-made teas in C18 Barn. **Adm £5, chd free. Share to Kent Minds. Sun 26 Apr, Sun 21 June (2-6). Visitors also welcome by arrangement for groups 8+. No large coaches.**
7 acre garden, partly terraced, S facing, with ornamental trees and shrubs, walled garden, Italian Garden, Diamond Jubilee Garden, Camellia Dell, herbaceous borders (incl flame bed and red borders), bluebell walks in April, woodland and ponds. For other opening times please see website. Featured in 25 Gorgeous Gardens - Kent Life. Grass paths.
🚴 ⚘ 🛏 ☕

7 BOUNDES END

2 St Lawrence Avenue, Bidborough, Tunbridge Wells TN4 0XB. Carole & Mike Marks, 01892 542233, carole.marks@btinternet.com, www.boundesendgarden.co.uk. *Between Tonbridge & Tunbridge Wells off A26. Take B2176 Bidborough Ridge signed to Penshurst. Take 1st L into Darnley Drive, then 1st R into St Lawrence Ave.* Home-made teas. **Adm £3, chd free. Share to Hospice in the Weald.** Visitors welcome by arrangement July to Aug. Groups 20 max.

Garden, designed by owners, on an unusually shaped ¹/₃ acre plot formed from 2 triangles of land. Front garden features raised beds, and the main garden divided into a formal area with terrace, pebble bed and 2 pergolas, an informal area in woodland setting with interesting features and specimen trees. Plenty of places to sit and enjoy the garden. Some uneven ground in lower garden.

&♿ 🐕 ✿ ☕

8 1 BRICKWALL COTTAGES

Frittenden, Cranbrook TN17 2DH. Mrs Sue Martin, 01580 852425, sue.martin@talktalk.net, www.geumcollection.co.uk. *6m NW of Tenterden. E of A229 between Cranbrook & Staplehurst & W of A274 between Biddenden & Headcorn. Park in village & walk along footpath opp school.* Home-made teas. **Adm £3.50, chd free.** Tues 3, 10, 17, 24 Feb, Suns & Mons 26, 27 Apr, 3, 4, 31 May, 1 June (2-5). Visitors also welcome by arrangement Apr to June for max 20 visitors.

Although less than ¹/₄ acre, the garden gives the impression of being much larger as it is made up of several rooms all intensively planted with a wide range of hardy perennials, bulbs and shrubs, with over 100 geums which comprise the National Collection planted throughout the garden. Pergolas provide supports for climbing plants and there is a small formal pond. Featured in Kent Life. Some paths are narrow and wheelchairs may not be able to reach far end of garden.

&♿ 🐕 ✿ 🚐 NCH ☕

9 ◆ BROADVIEW GARDENS

Hadlow TN11 0AL. Hadlow College, 01732 853211, www.broadviewgardens.co.uk. *On A26, 2¹/₂ m NE of Tonbridge on L, 200 metres before village of Hadlow, through main Hadlow College entrance.* Light refreshments. **Adm £3, chd free. For NGS: Thur 19 Feb (11-5).** For other opening times and information, please phone or see garden website.

10 acres of ornamental planting in attractive landscape setting; 100m double mixed border, island beds with mixed plantings, lakes and water gardens; series of demonstration gardens incl Italian, Oriental and Hampton Court show gardens. National Collections of Anemone japonica and Helleborus. Wheelchair access difficult when wet due to grass paths.

&♿ ✿ 🚐 NCH ☕

10 NEW CALICO HOUSE

The Street, Newnham, Sittingbourne ME9 0LN. Graham Lloyd-Brunt. *Centre of village. From A2 at Stone Chapel (W of Faversham) follow rd on valley floor signed Newnham & Doddington. 1st village is Newnham. Calico House is on R of Main St & has terracotta scraffito sign dated 1710 on gable end. From A20 at Lenham follow rd uphill signed Doddington & Newnham. Drive through 1st village, Doddington & into 2nd village, Newnham. Calico House is on L.* Cream teas. **Adm £4, chd free.** Sun 3 May, Sun 21 June (2-5).

The contemporary garden created at Calico House between 2008 and 2013 is set within a traditional English garden framework of topiary yew hedges and terraced lawns dating from the 1920s. Themed flower borders are at their best May to August set against the garden's strong structural backdrop.

☕

GROUP OPENING

11 CANTERBURY CATHEDRAL GARDENS

Canterbury CT1 2EP, 01227 865350, enquiriesisc@canterbury-cathedral.org, www.canterbury-cathedral.org. *Canterbury Cathedral Precincts.* **Enter precincts via main Christchurch gate**. No access for cars, use park & ride or public car parks. Home-made teas on Green Court. Sat 30 May (11-5) **Normal precinct charges apply plus £5 adm to Open Gardens Event per adult, chd free;** Sun 31 May (2-5) No precinct charges apply today, £5 adm to Open Gardens Event per adult, chd free.

ARCHDEACONRY
The Archdeacon, Sheila Watson

THE DEANERY
The Dean

15 THE PRECINCTS
Canon Papadapulos

19 THE PRECINCTS
Canon Irvine

22 THE PRECINCTS
Canon Clare Edwards

A wonderful opportunity to visit and enjoy five Canonical gardens within the historic precincts of Canterbury Cathedral: The Deanery Garden with wonderful roses, wildflower planting and orchard, unusual medlar tree, vegetable garden and wild fowl enclosure; the Archdeaconry incl the ancient mulberry tree, contrasting traditional and modern planting and a Japanese influence; the three further precinct gardens, varied in style, offer sweeping herbaceous banks, delightful enclosed spaces, and areas planted to attract and support birds, insects and wildlife. All the gardens now incl vegetable plots personal to each house. Step back in time and see the herb garden, which show the use of herbs for medicinal purposes in the Middle Ages. The walled Memorial Garden has wonderful wisteria, formal roses, mixed borders and the stone war memorial at its centre, and hidden Bastion Chapel in the city wall. Gardeners' plant stall and home-made refreshments. Dover Beekeepers Association, up close and personal opportunity with Birds of Prey and unique access to Bastion Chapel. Classic cars on Green Court. Wheelchair access to all gardens. Archdeaconry has separate entrance for wheelchairs.

&♿ ✿ 🛏 ☕

Extensive lawns, meandering paths and surprising vistas . . .

Every garden visit makes a difference

12 CHAINHURST COTTAGES
Chainhurst, Marden TN12 9SU.
Heather & Richard Scott. *6m S
of Maidstone, 3m N of Marden. From
Marden follow Pattenden Lane; at
T-junction turn L, to Chainhurst. In
Chainhurst take 2nd turning on L.
From Maidstone take A229; at Stile
Bridge Inn fork R, then 1st R then
follow NGS signs.* Home-made teas.
Adm £4, chd free. Sun 14 June
(2-5). Evening Opening £5, chd
free, Wine, Wed 17 June (6-8).
The garden surrounding this Kent peg
tiled cottage is formally designed with
relaxed cottage style planting in
shades of soft purple, pink and
burgundy. Low box hedging, brick
paths, hornbeam and beech hedging
divide the garden into small areas
making the whole feel larger than it is.
Raised vegetable beds contain
cutting flowers as well as vegetables
and step over apples. An informal
gravelled area surrounded by a brick
wall marks the end of the garden. You
are welcome to linger here with
homemade cake and tea served all
afternoon.

13 ◆ CHARTS EDGE
Westerham TN16 1PL. Mr & Mrs J
Bigwood, 07906 408848 (Liz
Seaton),
www.chartsedgegardens.co.uk.
*¹/₂ m S of Westerham, 4m N of
Edenbridge. On B2026 towards
Chartwell.* Home-made teas. Adm
£5, chd free. For NGS: Sun 10 May
(2-5). For other opening times and
information, please phone or see
garden website.
8 acre hillside garden being updated
by present owners. Large collection
of rhododendrons, azaleas and
magnolias; among specimen trees, 2
copper beech recorded as the tallest
in UK. Majority of plants labelled, rock
garden, water gardens, rainbow
borders and rill. Beds showing the
origin of plants from around the
world. Fine views over N Downs.
Featured in Kent Life magazine -
Garden of the Month. Partial access
for wheelchair users.

14 ◆ CHARTWELL
Mapleton Road, nr Westerham
TN16 1PS. National Trust, 01732
868381, www.nationaltrust.org.uk.
*4m N of Edenbridge, 2m S of
Westerham. Fork L off B2026 after
1¹/₂ m.* Adm £6.50, chd £3.25. For
NGS: Wed 20 May (10-5). For other

opening times and information,
please phone or see garden
website.
Informal gardens on hillside with
glorious views over Weald of Kent.
Water garden and lakes together with
red brick wall built by Sir Winston
Churchill, former owner of Chartwell.
Lady Churchill's rose garden. Avenue
of golden roses runs down the centre
of a must see productive kitchen
garden. Hard paths to Lady
Churchill's rose garden and the
terrace. Some steep slopes and
steps.

15 CHEVENING
Nr Sevenoaks TN14 6HG. The
Board of Trustees of the Chevening
Estate, www.cheveninghouse.com.
*4m NW of Sevenoaks. Turn N off A25
at Sundridge T-lights on to B2211; at
Chevening Xrds 1¹/₂ m turn L.* Home-
made teas. Adm £5, chd £2. Sun 21
June (2-5).
27 acres with lawns, woodland, lake,
maze and parterre. Gentle slopes,
gravel paths throughout.

You are
welcome
to linger here
with homemade
cake and
tea . . .

**16 ◆ CHIDDINGSTONE
CASTLE**
Hill Hoath Road, Chiddingstone,
Edenbridge TN8 7AD. Trustees of
the Denys Eyre Bower Bequest,
01892 870347,
www.chiddingstonecastle.org.uk.
*From B2027 in village of Bough
Beech follow signs to Castle via Mill
Lane. Entrance is on Hill Hoath Road.*
Cream teas. Adm £4.50, chd free.
For NGS: Sun 22 Mar (11-4). For
other opening times and
information, please phone or see
website.

Chiddingstone Castle, a historic
garden, is surrounded by 35 acres of
unspoilt informal gardens incl a large
fishing lake, waterfall and woodland.
During spring, the East Meadow is a
riot of golden daffodils and cherry
trees blossom in the Japanese
Earthquake Memorial Orchard.
Beautiful views from the North Lawn,
and the South Lawn leads to the
restored Grade II* Victorian Orangery.
Chiddingstone Castle's history can be
traced to C16. It now houses the
remarkable collections of the late
antiquarian, Denys Eyre Bower -
featuring Japanese Samurai armour
and lacquerware, antiquities from
Ancient Egypt and rare paintings and
memorabilia of the Stuarts and
Jacobites. Tea rooms serving cream
teas and gift shop also open. The
path to village across lake suitable for
wheelchairs, although steep in
places. All other paths are either
grass or gravel.

17 ◆ CHILHAM CASTLE
Canterbury CT4 8DB. Mr & Mrs
Wheeler, 01227 733100,
www.chilham-castle.co.uk. *6m SW
of Canterbury, 7m NE of Ashford,
centre of Chilham Village. Follow NGS
signs for garden open day from A28
or A252 up to Chilham village square
& through main gates of Chilham
Castle.* Light refreshments (Fri),
home-made teas (Sat). Adm £5, chd
free. For NGS: Evening Opening,
Fri 28 Aug (5-8). Sat 29 Aug (2-5).
For other opening times and
information, please phone or see
garden website.
The garden surrounds Jacobean
house 1616 (not open). C17 terraces
with herbaceous borders. Topiary
frames the magnificent views with
lake walk below. Extensive kitchen
and cutting garden beyond spring
bulb filled Quiet Garden. Established
trees and ha-ha lead onto park.
Partial wheelchair access only.

18 CHURCHFIELD
Pilgrims Way, Postling, Hythe
CT21 4EY. Mr & Mrs C Clark, 01303
863558, coulclark@hotmail.com.
*2m NW of Hythe. From M20 J11 turn
S onto A20. 1st L after ¹/₂ m on bend
take rd signed Lyminge. 1st L into
Postling.* Home-made teas in Village
hall. Combined adm £5, single
garden £3, chd free. Sat 30, Sun 31
May (1-5). Combined with West
Court Lodge. Visitors also

welcome by arrangement May to Sept for max 20 people.

At the base of the Downs, springs rising in this garden form the source of the East Stour. Two large areas are home to wildfowl and fish and the banks have been planted with drifts of primula and large leaved herbaceous. The rest of the 5 acre garden is a Kent cobnut platt and vegetable garden, large grass areas and naturally planted borders with an area under development as a prairie garden. Postling Church open for visitors. Areas around water may be slippery. Children must be carefully supervised.

19 THE COACH HOUSE
Kemsdale Road, Hernhill, Faversham ME13 9JP. Alison & Philip West, 07801 824867, alison.west@kemsdale.plus.com. *3m E of Faversham. At J7 of M2 take A299, signed Margate. After 600 metres take 1st exit signed Hernhill, take 1st L over dual carriageway to T-junction, turn R & follow yellow NGS signs.* Cream teas. **Adm £3.50, chd free. Sat 27, Sun 28 June (1-6).** Also open Lords (Sun 28 June). Visitors also welcome by arrangement Apr to Sept.

The ½ acre garden has views over surrounding fruit producing farmland. Sloping terraced site, and island beds with yr round interest, a pond room, herbaceous borders containing bulbs, shrubs, and perennials, and a developing tropical bed.The different areas are connected by flowing curved paths. Unusual planting on light sandy soil where wildlife is encouraged. Most of garden accessible to wheelchairs. Seating available in all areas.

20 ◆ COBHAM HALL
Cobham DA12 3BL. Mr D Standen (Bursar), 01474 823371, www.cobhamhall.com. *3m W of Rochester, 8m E of M25 J2. Ignore SatNav directions to Lodge Lane. Entrance drive is off Brewers Rd, 50 metres E from Cobham/Shorne A2 junction.* Tea in Gilt Hall. **Adm £2.50, chd free. For NGS: Mon 6 Apr, Mon 29 June (2-5). For other opening times and information, please phone or see website.**

1584 brick mansion (open for tours) and parkland of historical importance, now a boarding and day school for girls. Some herbaceous borders,

formal parterres, drifts of daffodils, C17 garden walls, yew hedges and lime avenue. Humphry Repton designed 50 hectares of park, most garden follies restored in 2009. Combined with tours to the Darnley Mausoleum (see NT book for details). Film location for BBC's Bleak House series and films by MGM and Universal. Gravel and slab paths through gardens. Land uneven, many slopes. Stairs and steps in Main Hall. Please call in advance to ensure assistance.

21 COPTON ASH
105 Ashford Road, Faversham ME13 8XW. Drs Tim & Gillian Ingram, 01795 535919, coptonash@yahoo.co.uk, www.coptonash.plus.com. *½ m S of Faversham. On A251 Faversham to Ashford rd. Opp E bound J6 with M2.* Home-made teas. **Adm £3.50, chd free. Sun 15 Feb (12-4); Sun 15 Mar, Sun 5, Mon 6, Sun 26 Apr, Mon 4, Sun 24, Mon 25 May, Sun 14 June, Sun 19 July (2-5.30); Sun 14 Feb 2016 (12-4).** Visitors also welcome by arrangement Mar to Oct.

Garden grown out of a love and fascination with plants from an early age. Contains very wide collection incl many rarities and newly introduced species raised from wild seed. Special interest in woodland flowers, snowdrops and hellebores with flowering trees and shrubs of spring. Wide range of drought tolerant plants. Raised beds with choice alpines and bulbs. Small alpine nursery. Gravel drive and some narrow grass paths.

22 34 CROSS ROAD
Walmer CT14 9LB. Mr Peter Jacob & Mrs Margaret Wilson. *A258 Dover to Deal. In Upper Walmer turn L into Station Rd. Under railway bridge, Cross Rd is 2nd R. N.B. Do not approach from Ringwould as SatNav suggests.* **Adm £3.50, chd free. Sun 12 Apr, Sun 14 June (11-5).**

An exciting and lovely garden combining great artistic sensibility with an extensive and fascinating variety of plants. Collection of Daphnes, hardy Geraniums, herbaceous beds, unusual trees, shrubs and alpines.

23 ◆ DODDINGTON PLACE
Church Lane, Doddington, nr Sittingbourne ME9 0BB. Mr & Mrs Richard Oldfield, 01795 886101, www.doddingtonplacegardens.co. uk. *6m SE of Sittingbourne. From A20 turn N opp Lenham or from A2 turn S at Teynham or Ospringe (Faversham), all 4m.* Cream teas. **Adm £6, chd £2. For NGS: Wed 13 May, Sun 21 June, Wed 22 July, Sun 20 Sept (11-5). For other opening times and information, please phone or see garden website.**

10 acre garden, landscaped with wide views; trees and cloud clipped yew hedges; woodland garden with azaleas and rhododendrons; Edwardian rock garden recently renovated (not wheelchair accessible); formal garden with mixed borders. Gothic folly. Wheelchair access possible to majority of gardens.

24 DOWNS COURT
Church Lane, Boughton Aluph, Ashford TN25 4EU. Mr & Mrs Bay Green, 07984 558945, bay@baygee.com. *4m NE of Ashford. From A28 Ashford or Canterbury, after Wye Xrds take next turn NW to Boughton Aluph Church. Fork R at pillar box, garden only drive on R.* Light refreshments. **Adm £5, chd free. Visitors welcome by arrangement May to July.**

Three acre downland garden on alkaline soil with fine trees, mature yew and box hedges, mixed borders with many unusual plants. Shrub roses and rose arch pathway, small parterre. Sweeping lawns and lovely views over surrounding countryside.

25 EAGLESWOOD

Slade Road, Warren Street, Lenham ME17 2EG. Mike & Edith Darvill, 01622 858702, mike.darvill@btinternet.com. *Going E on A20 nr Lenham, L into Hubbards Hill for approx 1m then 2nd L into Slade Rd. Garden 150yds on R. Coaches permitted.* Tea. **Adm £3.50, chd free. Share to Demelza House Hospice. Sun 10, Mon 25 May (11-5).** Visitors also welcome by arrangement May to Oct.

2 acre plantsman's garden situated high on N Downs, developed over the past 27yrs. Wide range of trees and shrubs (many unusual), herbaceous material and woodland plants grown to give yr-round interest, particularly in spring and for autumn colour. Some gravel areas. Grass paths may be slippery when wet.

26 ◆ EMMETTS GARDEN

Ide Hill, Sevenoaks TN14 6BA. National Trust, 01732 750367, www.nationaltrust.org.uk. *5m SW of Sevenoaks. 1¹/₂ m S of A25 on Sundridge-Ide Hill Rd. 1¹/₂ m N of Ide Hill off B2042.* **Adm £7.50, chd £3.75. For NGS: Wed 17 June (10-4).** For other opening times and information, please phone or see garden website.

5 acre hillside garden, with the highest tree top in Kent, noted for its fine collection of rare trees and flowering shrubs. The garden is particularly fine in spring, while a rose garden, rock garden and extensive planting of acers for autumn colour extend the interest throughout the season. Hard paths to the Old Stables for light refreshments and WC. Some steep slopes. Volunteer driven buggy available for lifts up steepest hill.

27 EUREKA

Buckhurst Road, Westerham Hill TN16 2HR. Mr & Mrs Gordon & Suzanne Wright, 01959 570848, sb.wright@btinternet.com. *1¹/₂ m N of Westerham, 1m S from centre of Biggin Hill. 5m from J5 & J6 of M25, parking at Westerham Heights Garden Centre on A233. Limited disabled parking at house.* Home-made teas. **Adm £4, chd free. Sat 25, Sun 26 July, Sat 1, Sun 2, Sat 8, Sun 9 Aug, Sun 6, Mon 7 Sept (1.30-5).** Visitors also welcome by arrangement June to Sept for groups 30+.

A blaze of colourful displays in perennial borders and the cartwheel centre beds, 50 hanging baskets, 150 tubs and troughs, plenty of garden art. Many surprises, chickens, lots of seating, and a viewing platform. Garden art incl a 12ft red dragon, a horse's head carved out of a 200yr old yew tree stump and 12ft dragon fly on a reed. Viewing platform to see garden from above. Featured in Amateur Gardening magazine.

> A riot of plants growing together as if in the wild . . .

28 FALCONHURST

Cowden Pound Road, Markbeech, Edenbridge TN8 5NR. Mr & Mrs Charles Talbot, www.falconhurst.co.uk. *3m SE of Edenbridge. B2026 at Queens Arms PH turn E to Markbeech. 2nd drive on R before Markbeech village. Parking 1st L in paddock if dry.* Home-made teas. **Adm £4.50, chd free. Sun 14 June (1-5).**

4 acre garden with fabulous views devised and cared for by the same family for 160yrs. Deep mixed borders with old roses, peonies, shrubs and a wide variety of herbaceous and annual plants; ruin garden; walled garden; interesting mature trees and shrubs; kitchen garden; wild flower meadows with woodland and pond walks. Woodland pigs; orchard chickens; lambs in the paddocks.

29 FRITH OLD FARMHOUSE

Frith Road, Otterden, Faversham ME13 0DD. Drs Gillian & Peter Regan, 01795 890556, peter.regan@cantab.net. *¹/₂ m off Lenham to Faversham rd. From A20 E of Lenham turn up Hubbards Hill, follow signs to Eastling. After 4m turn L signed Newnham, Doddington. From A2 in Faversham, turn S towards Brogdale & cont through Painters Forstal & Eastling. Turn R 1¹/₂ m beyond Eastling.* Tea. **Adm £4, chd free. Visitors welcome by arrangement Apr to Sept. Groups 50 max; please book in advance.**

A riot of plants growing together as if in the wild, developed over 30yrs. No neat edges or formal beds, but a very wide range of unusual and interesting plants, together with trees and shrubs chosen for yr-round appeal. Special interest in bulbs and woodland plants. Visitor comments - 'a plethora of plants', 'inspirational', 'a hidden gem'. Featured in Kent Life and RHS The Garden.

30 GALLANTS MANOR

Gallants Lane, East Farleigh, Maidstone ME15 0LF. Michael & Barbara Bartlett. *From E Farleigh Church cont in direction of W Farleigh/Yalding. Take 1st turning on L into Gallants Lane. Entrance & parking about 400m on L.* Home-made teas. **Adm £5, chd free. Share to Heart of Kent Hospice & East Farleigh Church. Sun 3, Mon 4 May (11-4).**

A 10 acre country garden surrounding C14 house (not open) designed for ease of maintenance. Formal rose garden, pond with stream leading into small lake. Spring bulbs. Azaleas, rhododendrons, japanese maples, herbaceous and shrub borders. Lawns, paved courtyard. Views of North Downs. Wheelchair access on grass.

31 GARDEN HOUSE

off Swan Lane, Surrenden, Pluckley TN27 0PR. Michael & Gillian Bushell. *7m W of Ashford. A20, Take turn to Pluckley at Charing Xrds. Proceed 3m & immed after sign for Pluckley & 30mph, L into Swan Lane. ¹/₂ m down hill, 1st entrance through high wall on R. SatNav unreliable.* Home-made teas. **Adm £4.50, chd free. Sat 27, Sun 28 June (1-6).**

Originally the kitchen garden to the Surrenden Dering Estate containing a 2 acre walled garden. Collection of magnolia, unusual specimen trees, yew topiary and parterre leading onto a cobnut walk underplanted with spring bulbs. Deep herbaceous beds and productive potager. A few changes to the garden since its last opening in 2013. Plenty of seating to enjoy the tranquillity of this garden. Wheelchair access through blue iron gate on left of drive.

Charts Edge

© Leigh Clapp

32 GODDARDS GREEN

Angley Road, Cranbrook
TN17 3LR. John & Linde Wotton,
01580 715507,
jpwotton@gmail.com,
http://goddardsgreen.btck.co.uk.
*1/2 m SW of Cranbrook. On W of
Angley Rd. (A229) at junction with
High St, opp War Memorial*. Home-
made teas. **Adm £5, chd free.** Sun
26 July (12.30-4.30). **Visitors also
welcome by arrangement May to
Sept, coaches welcome, but no
parking on site.**
Garden of about 2 acres, surrounding
beautiful 500yr old clothier's hall (not
open), laid out in 1920s and
redesigned over past 22yrs to
combine traditional and modern
planting schemes. Fountain, rill and
water garden, borders with bulbs,
herbaceous plants, flowering shrubs,
trees and exotics, birch grove, grass
border, pond, kitchen garden and
mature mixed orchard.

33 ◆ GODINTON HOUSE & GARDENS

Godinton Lane, Ashford TN23 3BP.
Godinton House Preservation
Trust, 01233 643854,
info@godintonhouse.co.uk,
www.godintonhouse.co.uk.
*1 1/2 m W of Ashford. M20 J9 to
Ashford. Take A20 towards
Charing & Lenham, then follow
brown tourist signs*. Home-made
teas. **Adm £5, chd free.** For NGS:
Sun 15, Sun 22 Mar, Fri 26 June

(1-6); Fri 25 Sept (10.30-12.30).
**For other opening times and
information, please phone or see
garden website.**
12 acres complement the
magnificent Jacobean house.
Terraced lawns lead through
herbaceous borders, rose garden
and formal lily pond to intimate
Italian garden and large walled
garden with delphiniums, potager,
cut flowers and iris border.
March/April the wild garden is a mass
of daffodils, fritillaries, other spring
flowers. Large collection of Bearded
Iris flowering late May. Delphinium
Festival (21-28 June). Garden
sculpture show (25 July-16 Aug).
Macmillan Coffee Morning (25 Sept).
Garden workshop and courses
throughout the yr, see website for
details. Partial wheelchair access to
ground floor of house and most of
gardens.

34 GODMERSHAM PARK

Godmersham CT4 7DT. Mrs Fiona
Sunley, 01227 730293. *5m NE of
Ashford. Off A28, midway between
Canterbury & Ashford*. Home-made
teas. **Adm £5, chd free. Share to
Godmersham Church.** Sun 29 Mar,
Sun 14 June (1-5). **Visitors also
welcome by arrangement Mar to
Sept min group 6.**
24 acres restored wilderness and
formal gardens set around C18
mansion (not open). Topiary, rose
garden, herbaceous borders, walled

kitchen garden and recently restored
Italian garden. Superb daffodils in
spring and roses in June. Historical
association with Jane Austen. Also
visit the Heritage Centre. Deep gravel
paths.

35 ◆ GOODNESTONE PARK GARDENS

Wingham, Canterbury CT3 1PL.
Margaret, Lady FitzWalter,
01304 840107,
www.goodnestoneparkgardens.
co.uk. *6m SE of Canterbury. Village
lies S of B2046 from A2 to Wingham.
Brown tourist signs off B2046.*
Delicious home-made cakes, cream
teas and light lunches. **Adm £6, chd
£2. For NGS: Sun 12 Apr, Sat 6
June, Sun 4 Oct (12-5). For other
opening times and information,
please phone or see garden
website.**
One of Kent's outstanding gardens
and the favourite of many visitors. 14
acres around C18 house (not open)
and with views over cricket ground
and parkland. Something special yr-
round from snowdrops and spring
bulbs to the famous walled garden
with old fashioned roses and kitchen
garden. Outstanding trees and
woodland garden with cornus
collection and hydrangeas later. 2
arboretums, contemporary gravel
garden. Picnics welcome. Featured in
The Lady magazine.

GROUP OPENING

GRAVESEND GARDENS GROUP

Gravesend DA12 1JZ. *Approx ½ m from Gravesend town centre. From A2 take A227 towards Gravesend. At T-lights with Cross Lane turn R then L at next T-lights following yellow NGS signs. Park in Sandy Bank Rd.* Cream teas. **Combined adm £3.50, chd free.** Sat 18, Sun 19 July (12-5).

58A PARROCK ROAD
Mr Barry Bowen

68 SOUTH HILL ROAD
Judith Hathrill

Enjoy two lovely gardens, very different in character, close to Windmill Hill which has extensive views over the Thames estuary. 58A Parrock Road is a beautiful, well established town garden, approx 120ft x 40ft, nurtured by owner for 50yrs. There is a stream running down to a pond, luscious planting along the rocky banks, fascinating water features, mature trees and shrubs, magnificent display of hostas and succulents. 68 South Hill Road is an award winning wildlife garden, showing that wildlife friendly gardens need not be wild. Colourful herbaceous borders, flowers, herbs and salads in the potager, raised vegetable and herb beds, ferns, grasses and colourful containers. Mediterranean vegetables thrive in the greenhouse, two ponds planted with native species. Jazz Trio at 58A Parrock Road.

◆ GREAT COMP GARDEN

Comp Lane, Platt, nr Borough Green, Sevenoaks TN15 8QS. Great Comp Charitable Trust, 01732 885094, www.greatcompgarden.co.uk. *7m E of Sevenoaks. 2m from Borough Green Station. Accessible from M20 & M26 motorways. A20 at Wrotham Heath, take Seven Mile Lane, B2016; at 1st Xrds turn R; garden on L ½ m.* Light refreshments at The Old Dairy Tearooms. **Adm £6.50, chd free.** For NGS: Sun 29 Mar, Sun 18, Sun 25 Oct (11-5). For other opening times and information, please phone or see garden website.
Skilfully designed 7 acre garden of exceptional beauty. Spacious setting of well maintained lawns and paths lead visitors through plantsman's

collection of trees, shrubs, heathers and herbaceous plants. Good autumn colour. Early C17 house (not open). Magnolias, hellebores and snowflakes (leucojum), hamamellis and winter flowering heathers are a great feature in the spring. A great variety of perennials in summer incl salvias, dahlias and crocosmias. Tearoom open daily for morning coffee, homemade lunches and afternoon teas. Featured on BBC Gardeners' World. Most of garden accessible to wheelchair users. Disabled WC.

NGS donations have helped fund 358 Marie Curie Nurses

GREAT MAYTHAM HALL

Maytham Road, Rolvenden, Tenterden TN17 4NE. The Sunley Group. *3m from Tenterden. Maytham Rd off A28 at Rolvenden Church, ½ m from village on R. No access down drive for double decker buses. Designated parking for visitors.* **Adm £5, chd free.** Every Wed 1 Apr to 26 Aug (1-4.30). Also open, Hole Park (Weds 15 April, 20 May, 17 June).
Lutyens designed gardens famous for having inspired Frances Hodgson Burnett to write The Secret Garden (pre Lutyens). Parkland, woodland with bluebells. Walled garden with herbaceous beds and rose pergola. Pond garden with mixed shrubbery and herbaceous borders. Interesting specimen trees. Large lawned area, rose terrace with far reaching views.

115 HADLOW ROAD

Tonbridge TN9 1QE. Mr & Mrs Richard Esdale, 01732 353738. *1½ m N of Tonbridge stn. Take A26 from N end of High St signed Maidstone, house 1m on L in service rd.* **Adm £3.50, chd free.** Sun 30 Aug (2-5). Visitors also welcome by

arrangement June to Aug. Refreshments by request.
Almost ½ acre unusual terraced garden with large collection of modern roses, island herbaceous border, many clematis, hardy fuchsias, heathers, grasses, hostas, phormiums, and ferns, shrub borders, alpines, annuals, kitchen garden and pond; well labelled.

HALL PLACE

Leigh TN11 8HH. Robin Hope-Morley. *4m W of Tonbridge. From A21 Sevenoaks to Tonbridge, B245 to Hildenborough, then R onto B2027 through Leigh & on R.* Tea. **Adm £7, chd £3.50.** Mon 6 Apr, Sun 17, Sun 24 May (2-6).
Large outstanding garden with 11 acre lake, lakeside walk crossing over picturesque bridges. Many rare and interesting trees and shrubs.

HAVEN

22 Station Road, Minster, Ramsgate CT12 4BZ. Robin Roose-Beresford, 01843 822594, robin.roose@hotmail.co.uk. *Off A299 Ramsgate Rd, take Minster exit from Manston r'bout, straight rd, R fork at church is Station Rd.* **Adm £3, chd free.** Sun 21 June (10-5). Also opening Quex Park Gardens. Visitors also welcome by arrangement Feb to Nov.
A smallish (300ft x 30ft) garden, designed with wildlife in mind, devised and maintained by the owner, densely planted in a natural style with meandering stepping stone paths. Two ponds (one for wildlife), gravel garden, rock garden, bog areas, fernery, Japanese garden, hostas and carnivorous plant beds, many exotic and unusual trees, shrubs and plants, colourful in leaf and flower.

HAWKINGE ALLOTMENTS

Stombers Lane, Hawkinge, Folkestone CT18 7AP. Mr Nick Lord, www.hawkingeallotments.org.uk. *E side of Hawkinge village. From village centre, turn off Canterbury Rd along The Street, follow to end & take next L into Stombers Lane, parking immed on L, entrance 200m on L.* Home-made teas. **Adm £3, chd free.** Sun 5 July (1-5). Also open Mounts Court Farmhouse, Acrise.
An allotment site with over 60 families having plots of varying sizes, incl

Lemon drizzle cake, Victoria sponge … yummy!

raised beds for those less able. A diverse range of vegetables and flowers are grown and the site is self managed by plot holders. The site which includes a compostable toilet and its own club house has only existed for 6yrs and has already won many awards. No specific disabled parking area, please make marshals aware if you need assistance on arrival, area is mostly flat rough or grass terrain.

43 NEW 37 THE HAYDENS
Tonbridge TN9 1NS. Angie Boakes.
N Tonbridge, off Yardley Park Rd (between Shipbourne Rd & Hadlow Rd). Please park on Yardley Park Rd by green & follow signs. Limited disabled parking on rd. Home-made teas. **Adm £3, chd £2.50. Sun 21 June, Sun 23 Aug (11.30-5).**
A small modern garden redesigned by the current owner in 2014 after trying to grow a peony on a N facing wall! Split into sections which mirror the house, the borders (separated by a slate path) feature roses, Cornus, birches, Salvia, perennials and grasses plus a small area of planting from a Chelsea Show Garden. Hopefully it will give visitors ideas for typical modern house sized gardens. Note - slate paths.

44 HOATH HOUSE
Chiddingstone Hoath, Edenbridge TN8 7DB. Mr & Mrs Richard Streatfeild, 01342 850362, jane@hoath-house.freeserve.co.uk. *4m SE of Edenbridge via B2026. At Queens Arms PH turn E to Markbeech. Approx 1m E of Markbeech.* Home-made teas. **Adm £5, chd free. Wed 25 Feb (11-4). Visitors also welcome by arrangement Feb to Dec.**
Mediaeval/Tudor family house (not open) surrounded by both mature and unusual young trees, gravel garden in former stable yard, knot garden, shaded garden, herbaceous borders, yew hedges. Sea of single snowdrops with doubles from great grandmother's garden, growing collection of more special snowdrops. Home-made teas/soup in this enchanting garden with stunning views over rural Kent. Wheelchair access to many snowdrop views via rough gravel drive.

45 NEW HOGBEN HOUSE
Church Lane, Aldington, Ashford TN25 7EG. Margaret & Rod Gibbs.
From A20 heading towards Sellindge, past sign for Aldington, take next turning on R immed after KOS business centre, Church Lane. Hogben House is 6th property on R. Home-made teas. **Adm £4, chd free. Sat 6, Sun 7, Sat 13, Sun 14 June (11-4.30).**
Pretty period cottage (not open) situated in the old part of Aldington, with typical cottage garden plantings, herbaceous borders of roses, perennials, shrubs and ornamental trees to the front garden and vegetable garden and orchard to the side and rear. Small water feature and hand crafted gypsy type caravan in orchard. Partial wheelchair access to front cottage garden.

Lavender ribbons are magnets for bees . . .

46 ◆ HOLE PARK
Benenden Road, Rolvenden, Cranbrook TN17 4JB. Mr & Mrs E G Barham, 01580 241344, www.holepark.com. *4m SW of Tenterden. Midway between Rolvenden & Benenden on B2086. Follow brown tourist signs from Rolvenden.* Light lunches and home-made teas. **Adm £7, chd £1. For NGS: Sun 22 Mar, Wed 15 Apr, Wed 20 May, Wed 17 June, Sun 11 Oct (11-6). For other opening times and information, please phone or see garden website.**
Hole Park is proud to stand amongst the group of gardens which first opened in 1927 soon after it was laid out by my great grandfather. Our 15 acre garden is surrounded by parkland with beautiful views and contains fine yew hedges, large lawns with specimen trees, walled gardens, pools and mixed borders combined with bulbs, rhododendrons and azaleas. Massed bluebells in woodland walk, standard wisterias, orchids in flower meadow and glorious autumn colours make this a garden for all seasons. The Sundial Garden was redesigned and planted in 2013. Good wheelchair access

throughout but beware of steep inclines. Wheelchairs are available for free hire and may be reserved.

47 HONNINGTON FARM GARDENS
Vauxhall Lane, Southborough, Tunbridge Wells TN4 0XD. Mrs Ann Tyler, 01892 536990, ann.honnington@btinternet.com, www.honningtonfarmgardens. co.uk. *Between Tonbridge & Tunbridge Wells. A21 to A26. Large coaches must only access Vauxhall Lane from A26 & use Equestrian Centre car park. Ring for additional directions.* Light refreshments. **Adm £5, chd free. Visitors welcome by arrangement Mar to Oct. Min group 20. Coach 60 seater max.**
6 acre garden, with natural pool in wild flower meadow and extensive gravel garden. Rose walkways, rockery, lakes and water features. Heavy clay soil enriched yearly producing a wide range of habitats, incl water and bog gardens, primrose and bluebell walks. Wildlife promotion a priority. Wonderful views and herbaceous beds. Glass houses and large vegetable garden. Newly renovated Kent Barn which holds 60 for teas/lunches by prior arrangement. Steep slopes and gravel drives. WC incl disabled.

48 ◆ IGHTHAM MOTE
Ivy Hatch, Sevenoaks TN15 0NT. National Trust, 01732 810378, www.nationaltrust.org.uk. *6m E of Sevenoaks. Off A25, 2½ m S of Ightham. Buses from train stns Sevenoaks or Borough Green to Ivy Hatch & Ightham Mote on weekdays.* Light refreshments in The Mote Café. **Adm £12, chd £6. For NGS: Thur 9 July (10.30-5). For other opening times and information, please phone or see garden website.**
14 acre garden and moated medieval manor c1320, first opened for NGS in 1927. North lake and pleasure gardens, ornamental pond and cascade created in early C18. Orchard, enclosed formal vegetable and cutting gardens all contribute to the sense of tranquillity. Free guided tours of garden (donations to NGS welcome). Garden team on hand for tips and advice. Hot food served 12.00-2.30, cream teas and sandwiches all day. Wheelchairs available from visitor reception and shop. Ask for a wheeled access guide at visitor reception.

© Leigh Clapp

Upper Pryors

49 ◆ KNOLE

Knole, Sevenoaks TN15 0RP. Lord Sackville, 01732 462100, www.nationaltrust.org.uk. 1½ m SE of Sevenoaks. Leave M25 J5 (A21). Park entrance S of Sevenoaks town centre off A225 Tonbridge Road (opp St Nicholas church). For SatNav use TN13 1HU. Tea at the Bookshop Cafe. **Adm £12, chd £6.** For NGS: **Tue 21 Apr, Tue 8 Sept (11-4).** For other opening times and information, please phone or see garden website.

Lord Sackville's 26 acre private walled garden incl features which transport you back centuries to horticultural fashions long forgotten. Enjoy bluebells in spring and return in late summer to lose yourself in the C16 Wilderness garden and enjoy little seen views of the house. Last entry at 3.30pm. Knole's garden is accessed via the beautiful Orangery space off Green Court. Refreshments are available in the new Bookshop Café or from the Outdoor Café in the park. Wheelchair access possible but difficult in poor weather.

&. ☕

50 ▶ KNOWLE HILL FARM

Ulcombe, Maidstone ME17 1ES. The Hon Andrew & Mrs Cairns, 01622 850240, elizabeth.cairns@btinternet.com, www.knowlehillfarmgarden.co.uk. 7m SE of Maidstone. From M20 J8 follow A20 towards Lenham for 2m. Turn R to Ulcombe. After 1½ m, L at Xrds, after ½ m 2nd R into Windmill Hill. Past Pepper Box PH, ½ m 1st L to Knowle Hill. Light refreshments. Adm £5. **Sun 8, Sun 22 Feb (11-3). Evening Opening, wine, Sat 4 July (5-8). Sun 2 Aug (2-6); Sun 7, Sun 21 Feb 2016.** Visitors also welcome by arrangement May to Sept. Access for 25-30 seater coaches.

2 acre garden, created over 30yrs, on S facing slope of N Downs with spectacular views. Snowdrops: Mediterranean and tender plants, roses, agapanthus, verbenas, salvias and grasses, flourish on the light soil. Many unusual plants. Evolving topiary. Lavender ribbons are magnets for bees. Pool and rill enclosed in small walled garden planted mainly with white flowers. New green garden is being developed. Some steep slopes.

&. 🐕 ✿ 🚐 ☕

51 ▶ LADHAM HOUSE

Goudhurst TN17 1DB. Mr Guy Johnson. 8m E of Tunbridge Wells. On NE of village, off A262. Through village towards Cranbrook, turn L at The Goudhurst Inn. 2nd R into Ladham Rd, main gates approx 500yds on L. Tea. **Adm £4, chd £1. Sun 10 May (2-5).**

Large garden and parkland with rhododendrons, camellias, azaleas and magnolias. Spectacular twin borders, a rose garden and an arboretum containing some fine specimens. Also, an Edwardian sunken rockery, woodland walk, ha-ha and vegetable garden.

✿ ☕

52 ▶ LEYDENS

Hartfield Road, Edenbridge TN8 5NH. Roger Platts, www.rogerplatts.com. 1m S.of Edenbridge. On B2026 towards Hartfield (use Nursery entrance & car park). Tea. **Adm £4, chd free. Sun 2 Aug (12-5). Also open Old Buckhurst.**

Small private garden of garden designer, nursery owner and author who created NGS Garden at Chelsea in 2002, winning Gold and Best in Show, and in 2010 Gold and People's Choice for the M&G Garden. Constant development with wide range of shrubs and perennials incl late summer flowering perennial border adjoining wild flower hay meadow. Kitchen garden. Plants clearly labelled and fact sheet available.

&. ✿ 🚐 ☕

53 ▶ LITTLE GABLES

Holcombe Close, Westerham TN16 1HA. Peter & Elizabeth James. Centre of Westerham. Off E side of London Rd A233, 200yds from The Green. Please park in public car park. No parking available at house. Home-made teas. **Adm £3.50, chd free. Sat 20, Sun 21 June (2-5).**

¾ acre plant lover's garden extensively planted with a wide range of trees, shrubs, perennials etc, incl many rare ones. Collection of climbing and bush roses. Large pond with fish, water lilies and bog garden. Fruit and vegetable garden. Large greenhouse. Featured in Kent Life.

☕

Look out for the NGS yellow arrows …

54 NEW LONG MEADOW

1 Bourne Row, Wellers Town Road, Chiddingstone TN8 7BQ. Ian & Jo Peel. *5m SE of Edenbridge via B2027. 1m S of Chiddingstone Village. Garden on L, parking on R after Wellers Town sign.* Adm £3, chd free. Sat 29, Sun 30 Aug (11-4).

A contemporary cottage garden of 1/3 of an acre that wraps around the house with a pond and wonderful countryside views. A gorgeous mix of traditional and modern varieties of late summer perennials and grasses. The colour palette is kept simple but the planting is dense and many plants are designed to peak at the end of summer with shades of pink, purple, copper and bronze. Featured in Country Homes & Interiors magazine.

55 LORDS

Sheldwich, Faversham ME13 0NJ. John Sell, 01795 536900, john@sellwade.co.uk. *4m S of Faversham. From A2 or M2 take A251 towards Ashford. 1/2 m S of Sheldwich church find entrance lane on R adjacent to wood. (3 1/2 m N of Challock Xrds).* Lemon Barley water & shortbread biscuits available (sorry, no hot drinks). Adm £5, chd free. Sun 12 Apr, Sun 28 June (2-5). Visitors also welcome by arrangement Apr to July adm £6 incl refreshments.

C18 canted walled garden and greenhouse. A herb terrace overlooks a citrus standing. A flowery mead beneath medlar and quince trees. Across a grass tennis court is a cherry orchard grazed by Jacob sheep. A shady fernery, lawns, ponds and wild area. Old specimen trees include redwoods, planes, copper beech, yew hedges and 120ft tulip tree. Daffodils, primroses, cowslips, fritillaries in spring. Some gravel paths.

56 LUTON HOUSE

Selling ME13 9RQ. Sir John & Lady Swire, 01227 752234, moiraswire@aol.com. *4m SE of Faversham. From A2 (M2) or A251 make for White Lion, entrance 30yds E on same side of rd.* Adm £4, chd free. Sun 29 Mar, Sun 10 May (2-5). Visitors also welcome by arrangement Mar to Oct. Please apply in writing, or by email.

6 acres; C19 landscaped garden; ornamental ponds; trees underplanted with azaleas, camellias,

woodland plants, hellebores, spring bulbs, magnolias, cherries, daphnes, halesias, maples, Judas trees and cyclamen. Depending on the weather, those interested in camellias, early trees and bulbs may like to visit in late Mar/early April. Partial wheelchair access.

Discover this beautiful cottage garden in the heart of the countryside . . .

57 ◆ MARLE PLACE

Marle Place Road, Brenchley TN12 7HS. Mr & Mrs Gerald Williams, 01892 722304, www.marleplace.co.uk. *8m SE of Tonbridge. At Forstal Farm r'about N of Lamberhurst bypass on A21 take B2162 Horsmonden direction approx 3m. From Brenchley follow brown & white tourism signs 1 1/2 m.* Adm £6.50, chd £4. For NGS: Thur 14 May, Thur 11 June (11-5). For other opening times and information, please phone or see garden website.

Victorian gazebo, plantsman's shrub borders, walled scented garden, Edwardian rockery, herbaceous borders, bog and kitchen gardens. Woodland walks, mosaic terrace, artists' studios and gallery with contemporary art. Autumn colour. Restored Victorian 40ft greenhouse with orchids. C17 listed house (not open). Collection of interesting chickens. Nature trail, Art exhibition. Guided tour at 2 pm. Tea room with homemade cakes. Ramps in place for stepped areas. Access incl some sloping lawns and gravel paths. Wheelchair users enter free of charge.

58 MARSHBOROUGH FARMHOUSE

Farm Lane, Marshborough, Sandwich CT13 0PJ. David & Sarah Ash, 01304 813679. *1 1/2 m W of Sandwich, 1/2 m S of Ash. From Ash take R fork to Woodnesborough. After 1m Marshborough sign. L into Farm Lane at white thatched cottage,*

garden 100yds on L. Coaches must phone for access information. Home-made teas. Adm £4, chd free. Visitors welcome by arrangement 21 May to 21 Jun and 17 Aug to 31 Aug.

Fascinating 2 1/2 acre plantsman's garden, developed enthusiastically over 17yrs. Original lawns are rapidly shrinking, giving way to meandering paths around informal island beds with many unusual shrubs, trees and perennials creating yr-round colour and interest. Herbaceous borders, pond, rockery, raised dry garden, succulents and tender pot plants.

59 12 THE MEADOWS

Chelsfield, Orpington BR6 6HS. Mr & Mrs Roger & Jean Pemberton. *3m from J4 on M25. Exit M25 at J4. At r'about 1st exit for A224, next r'about 3rd exit - A224, 1/2 m, take 2nd L, Warren Rd. Bear L into Windsor Drive. 1st L The Meadway, follow signs to garden.* Home-made teas. Adm £4, chd free. Sun 10 May, Sun 5 July (1-5.30).

Front garden Mediterranean style gravel with sun loving plants. Rear 3/4 acre garden in 2 parts. Semi formal area with two ponds, one Koi and one natural (lots of Spring interest). Mature bamboos, acers, grasses etc and semi wooded area, children's path with 13ft high giraffe and lots of points of interest. Designated children's area. Only children allowed access! Wheelchair access to all parts except small stepped area at very bottom of garden.

60 MERE HOUSE

Mereworth ME18 5NB. Mr & Mrs Andrew Wells, www.mere-house.co.uk. *7m E of Tonbridge. From A26 turn N on to B2016 & then into Mereworth village. 3 1/2 m S of M20/M26 junction, take A20, then B2016 to Mereworth.* Home-made teas. Adm £4, chd free. Sun 22 Feb, Sun 1 Mar, Mon 6 Apr, Sun 25 Oct (2-5); Sun 21, Sun 28 Feb 2016 (2-5).

6 acre garden with C18 lake. Snowdrops, daffodils, lawns, herbaceous borders, ornamental shrubs and trees with foliage contrast and striking autumn colour. C19 woodland walk and major tree planting and landscaping last 20yrs. Park and lake walks.

There's a hospice close to every NGS garden

61 ◆ MOUNT EPHRAIM
Hernhill, Faversham ME13 9TX. Mr & Mrs E S Dawes & Mr W Dawes, 01227 751496, www.mountephraimgardens.co.uk. *3m E of Faversham. From end of M2, then A299 take slip rd 1st L to Hernhill, signed to gardens.* Adm £6, chd £2.50. For NGS: Sun 15 Mar (11-4); Thur 11 June, Sun 27 Sept (11-5). For other opening times and information, please phone or see garden website.
Herbaceous border, topiary, daffodils and rhododendrons, rose terraces leading to small lake. Rock garden with pools, water garden, young arboretum. Rose garden with arches and pergola planted to celebrate the Millennium. Magnificent trees. Grass maze. Superb views over fruit farms to Swale estuary. Village craft centre. Teas and lunches available. Partial wheelchair access due to being on a slope. Disabled WC. Full access to tea room.

62 MOUNTS COURT FARMHOUSE
Acrise, nr Folkestone CT18 8LQ. Graham & Geraldine Fish, 01303 840598, geraldine_fish@btinternet.com. *6m NW of Folkestone. From A260 Folkestone to Canterbury rd, turn L at Densole opp Black Horse Inn, 1½ m towards Elham & Lyminge, on N side.* Home-made teas. Adm £5, chd free. Sat 6, Sun 7 June, Sat 4, Sun 5 July (1-5). Also open Hawkinge Allotment Society (Sun 5 July). Visitors also welcome by arrangement May to Sept.
Developed from a 1½ acre horse paddock over 30yrs in surroundings designated as an Area of Outstanding Natural Beauty at a height of 150 metres. Variety of trees, shrubs and grasses and herbaceous plants. Wide winding paths flow through deep, densely planted mixed borders varying from cottage to woodland in character, with an eye to foliage

pattern and changing colour mixes. Pond and bog garden. Featured in Gardens Illustrated magazine.

63 NETTLESTEAD PLACE
Nettlestead ME18 5HA. Mr & Mrs Roy Tucker, www.nettlesteadplace.co.uk. *6m W/SW of Maidstone. Turn S off A26 onto B2015 then 1m on L, next to Nettlestead Church.* Tea. Adm £5, chd free. Sun 7 June, Sun 4 Oct (2-5).
C13 manor house in 10 acre plantsman's garden. Large formal rose garden. Large herbaceous garden of island beds with rose and clematis walkway leading to garden of China roses. Fine collection of trees and shrubs; sunken pond garden, terraces, bamboos, glen garden, acer lawn. Young pinetum adjacent to garden. Sculptures. Wonderful open country views. Gravel paths, partial access: sunken pond garden. New large steep bank and lower area in development.

64 NORTON COURT
Teynham, Sittingbourne ME9 9JU. Tim & Sophia Steel, 01795 522941, sophia@nortoncourt.net. *Off A2 between Teynham & Faversham. L off A2 at Texaco garage into Norton Lane; next L into Provender Lane; L signed Church for car park.* Tea. Adm £5, chd free. Mon 8, Tue 9 June (2-5). Visitors also welcome by arrangement May to June.
10 acre garden within parkland setting. Mature trees, topiary, wide lawns and clipped yew hedges. Orchard with mown paths through wild flowers. Walled garden with mixed borders and climbing roses. Pine tree walk. Formal box and lavender parterre. Tree house in the Sequoia. Church open, adjacent to garden. Gravel paths.

65 NEW OAK COTTAGE
Elmsted, Ashford TN25 5JT. Martin & Rachael Castle. *6m NW of Hythe. From Stone St (B2068) turn W opp the Stelling Minnis turning. Follow signs to Elmsted. Turn L at Elmsted village sign. Limited parking at house. Further parking at Church (7mins walk).* Home-made teas. Adm £3.50, chd free. Thur 23, Sat 25 Apr, Thur 13, Sat 15 Aug (11-4).
Get off the beaten track and discover

this beautiful ½ acre cottage garden in the heart of the Kent countryside. This plantsman's garden is filled with unusual and interesting perennials, incl a wide range of salvias. There is a small specialist nursery packed with herbaceous perennials. For our April opening a large auricula collection will be show cased in a range of traditional theatres.

66 OLD BLADBEAN STUD
Bladbean, Canterbury CT4 6NA. Carol Bruce, www.oldbladbeanstud.co.uk. *6m S of Canterbury. From B2068, follow signs into Stelling Minnis, turn R onto Bossingham Rd, then follow yellow NGS signs through single track lanes.* Cream teas. Adm £5.50, chd free. Suns 31 May, 14, 28 June, 12, 26 July, 30 Aug, 13, 27 Sept (2-6).
Five interlinked gardens all designed and created from scratch by the garden owner on 3 acres of rough grassland between 2003 and 2011. Romantic walled rose garden with over 90 labelled old fashioned rose varieties, tranquil yellow and white garden, square garden with blended pastel borders and Victorian style greenhouse, 300ft long colour schemed symmetrical double borders. An experimental self sufficiency project comprises a wind turbine, rain water collection, solar panels and a ground source heat pump, an organic fruit and vegetable garden. The gardens are maintained entirely by the owner and were designed to be managed as an ornamental ecosystem with a large number of perennial species encouraged to set seed, and with staking, irrigation, mulching and chemical use kept an absolute minimum. Each garden has a different season of interest - please see the garden website for more information. Featured in Kent Life, Country Life, The English Garden, Period Living plus many other publications.

67 OLD BUCKHURST
Markbeech, nr Edenbridge TN8 5PH. Mr & Mrs J Gladstone, 01342 850825, www.oldbuckhurst.co.uk. *4m SE of Edenbridge. B2026, at Queens Arms PH turn E to Markbeech. In approx 1½ m, 1st house on R after leaving Markbeech. Parking in paddock if dry.* Adm £4, chd free. Sat 25, Sun 26, Wed 29 Apr, Sun 3, Sat 9, Sun 10,

Sat 23, Sat 30 May, Wed 3, Sat 6 June, Wed 8, Wed 15 July, Sun 2 Aug, Sat 5, Wed 9, Sat 12, Sun 13 Sept (11-5). Also open Stonewall Park (Sun 3 May) & Leydens (Sun 2 Aug). Visitors also welcome by arrangement Apr to Sept. Tours by arrangement. No coaches.
1 acre partly walled cottage garden around C15 Grade II listed farmhouse with catslip roof (not open). Comments from Visitors' Book: 'perfect harmony of vistas, contrasts and proportions. Everything that makes an English garden the envy of the world'. 'The design and planting is sublime, a garden I doubt anyone could forget'. Stefan Buczacki in Garden News said – 'My favourite cottage garden is Old Buckhurst in Kent'. Mixed borders with roses, clematis, wisteria, poppies, iris, peonies, lavender, July/Aug a wide range of day lilies.

68 **NEW** **THE OLD RECTORY**
Valley Road, Fawkham, Longfield DA3 8LX. Karin & Christopher Proudfoot, 01474 707513, keproudfoot@firenet.uk.net. *1m S of Longfield. Midway between A2 & A20, on Valley Rd 1¹/₂ m N of Fawkham Green, 0.3m S of Fawkham church, opp sign for Gay Dawn Farm/Corinthian Sports Club. Parking on drive only. Not suitable for coaches.* Home-made teas. **Adm £4, chd free. Visitors welcome by arrangement in Feb for individuals and groups 20 max.**
1¹/₂ acres with impressive display of long established naturalised snowdrops and winter aconites; over 70 named snowdrops added recently. Garden developed around the snowdrops over 30yrs, incl hellebores, pulmonarias and other early bulbs and flowers, with foliage perennials, shrubs and trees, also natural woodland. Gentle slope, gravel drive, some narrow paths.

69 **THE ORANGERY**
Mystole, Chartham, Canterbury CT4 7DB. Rex Stickland & Anne Prasse, 01227 738348, rex@mystole.fsnet.co.uk. *5m SW of Canterbury. Turn off A28 through Shalmsford Street. In 1¹/₂ m at Xrds turn R downhill. Cont, ignoring rds on L & R. Ignore drive on L - Mystole House only. At sharp bend in 600yds turn L into private drive.* Home-made teas. **Adm £4, chd free.** Sun 14

June, Sun 26 July (1-6). **Visitors also welcome by arrangement Apr to Sept. Coaches welcome, contact owner for parking information.**
1¹/₂ acre gardens around C18 orangery, now a house (not open). Front gardens, established well stocked herbaceous border and large walled garden with a wide variety of shrubs and mixed borders. Splendid views from terraces over ha-ha and paddocks to the lovely Chartham Downs. Water features and very interesting collection of modern sculptures set in natural surroundings. Ramps to garden.

70 **ORCHARD END**
Cock Lane, Spelmonden Road, Horsmonden TN12 8EQ. Mr Hugh Nye, 01892 723118, hughnye@aol.com. *8m E of Tunbridge Wells. From A21 going S turn L at r'bout onto B2162 to Horsmonden. After 2m turn R onto Spelmonden Rd. Atfter ¹/₂ m turn R into Cock Lane. Garden on R.* Home-made teas. **Adm £4, chd free. Share to The Amyloidosis Foundation.** Sun 12 Apr, Sats & Suns 13, 14 June, 18, 19 July, 29, 30 Aug (11-5). **Visitors also welcome by arrangement. Max group 40.**
Contemporary classical garden within a 4 acre site. Made over 15yrs by resident landscape designer. Divided into rooms with linking vistas. Incl hot borders, white garden, exotics, oak and glass summerhouse amongst magnolias. Dramatic changes in level. Formal pool with damp garden, ornamental vegetable potager. Wildlife orchards and woodland walks.

71 **ORCHARD HOUSE, SPENNY LANE**
Claygate, Marden, Tonbridge TN12 9PJ. Mr & Mrs Lerwill. *Just off B2162 between Collier St & Horsmonden. Spenny Lane is adjacent to the White Hart PH. Orchard House is 1st house on R about 400m from PH.* Home-made teas. **Adm £3.50, chd free.** Sat 11, Sun 12 July (11-4).
A relatively new garden created within the last 9yrs. Gravel garden with potted tender perennials, cottage garden and herbaceous borders. Potager with vegetables, fruit and flowers for cutting. Bee friendly borders. Hornbeam avenue underplanted with camassia. Small nursery on site

specialising in herbaceous perennials and ornamental grasses. Access for wheelchairs but some pathways are gravel, grassed areas uneven in places.

The 70 year old garden is now looked after by the grandchildren of the original owner . . .

72 **PARSONAGE OASTS**
Hampstead Lane, Yalding ME18 6HG. Edward & Jennifer Raikes, 01622 814272, jmraikes@parsonageoasts.plus. com. *6m SW of Maidstone. On B2162 between Yalding village & stn, turn off at Anchor PH over canal bridge, cont 150yds up lane. House & car park on L.* Cream teas. **Adm £3. Mon 6, Sun 19 Apr (2-5.30). Visitors also welcome by arrangement Mar to Sept.**
Our garden has a lovely position on the bank of the R Medway. Typical Oast House (not open) often featured on calendars and picture books of Kent. 70yr old garden now looked after by grandchildren of its creator. ³/₄ acre garden with walls, daffodils, crown imperials, shrubs, clipped box and a spectacular magnolia. Small woodland on river bank. Featured in The English Garden Magazine. Unfenced river bank. Gravel paths.

73 **◆ PENSHURST PLACE & GARDENS**
Penshurst TN11 8DG. Lord & Lady De L'Isle, 01892 870307, www.penshurstplace.com. *6m NW of Tunbridge Wells. SW of Tonbridge on B2176, signed from A26 N of Tunbridge Wells.* Cream teas. **Adm £8.50, chd £6. For NGS: Thur 10 Sept (10.30-6). For other opening times and information, please phone or see garden website.**
11 acres of garden dating back to C14; garden divided into series of rooms by over a mile of yew hedge; profusion of spring bulbs; formal rose garden; famous peony border. Woodland trail and arboretum. Yr-round interest. Toy museum. Garden is wheelchair accessible.

74 PHEASANT BARN

Church Road, Oare ME13 0QB. Paul & Su Vaight, 01795 591654, paul.vaight@mac.com. *2m NW of Faversham. Entering Oare from Faversham, turn R at Three Mariners PH towards Harty Ferry. Garden 400yds on R, before church. Parking on roadside.* Home-made teas at Pheasant Farm (Sun 7 June) and Pheasant Barn (Sat 6 June). **Adm £4, chd free.** Sat 6, Sun 7 June, Sat 4 July (1-5). **Combined with Pheasant Farm Sat 6 & Sun 7 June, combined adm £7, chd free. Visitors also welcome by arrangement Apr to July, refreshments by request.**

Series of smallish gardens around award winning converted farm buildings in beautiful situation overlooking Oare Creek. Main area is nectar rich planting in formal design with a contemporary twist inspired by local landscape. Also vegetable garden, parterre, water features, wild flower meadow and labyrinth. July optimum for wild flowers. Spring blossom. Kent Wildlife Trust Oare Marshes Bird Reserve within 1m. Two village inns serving lunches/dinners.

75 PHEASANT FARM

Church Road, Oare, Faversham ME13 0QB. Jonathan & Lucie Neame, 01795 535366, lucie@neame.eclipse.co.uk. *2m NW of Faversham. Enter Oare from Faversham. R at 3 Mariners PH towards Harty Ferry. Garden 450yds on R, beyond Pheasant Barn, before church. Parking on roadside.* Home-made teas at Pheasant Barn (Sat 6 June) and Pheasant Farm (Sun 7 June). **Adm £3.50, chd free.** Sun 10 May, Sat 6, Sun 7 June (1-5). **Combined with Pheasant Barn Sat 6 & Sun 7 June. Combined adm £7, chd free. Visitors also welcome by arrangement May to June, refreshments incl in price. Groups 20 max.**

Redesigned in 2008, a walled garden surrounding C17 farmhouse with outstanding views over Oare marshes and creek. Main garden with shrubs and herbaceous plants. Infinity lawn overlooking creek, orchard and circular walk through adjoining churchyard. Two local Public Houses serving lunches. Wheelchair access in main garden only.

&♿ ☕

76 PLACKETTS HOLE

Bicknor, nr Sittingbourne ME9 8BA. Allison & David Wainman, 01622 884258, aj@aj-wainman.demon.co.uk. *5m S of Sittingbourne. W of B2163. Bicknor is signed from Hollingbourne Hill & from A249 at Stockbury Valley. Placketts Hole is midway between Bicknor & Deans Hill.* Light refreshments. **Adm £5, chd free. Visitors welcome by arrangement** May to Oct for 1 to 30 max.

Mature 3 acre garden in Kent Downland valley incl herbaceous borders, rose and formal herb garden, small, walled kitchen garden and informal pond intersected by walls, hedges and paths. Many unusual plants, trees and shrubs and small wildflower calcareous meadow. Most of garden accessible by wheelchair.

♿ ❀ ☕

> The design and planting is sublime, a garden I doubt anyone could forget . . .

77 PORT LYMPNE, THE ASPINALL FOUNDATION

Aldington Road, Lympne, Hythe CT21 4PD. The Aspinall Foundation, 08448 424647, info@aspinallfoundation.org. *Follow signs from M20, J11, to Port Lympne Reserve. Park in the Main customer car park.* Cream teas at the Mansion hotel. **Adm £6, chd £3.** Howletts/Port Lympne passport holders half-price. Sat 26 Sept (10-3). **Visitors also welcome by arrangement Sept.**

Port Lympne Mansion Hotel. 15 acres of beautiful landscaped grounds cut out of the old sea cliffs overlooking Romney Marsh and out to the English Channel. Features incl formal ponds, chessboard and striped gardens with an outdoor staircase - Italian inspired. Partial wheelchair access. Historical site with steps and terraces.

♿ ❀ 🚐 🛏 ☕

78 NEW 3 POST OFFICE COTTAGES

Chiddingstone Causeway, Tonbridge TN11 8JP. Julie & Graham Jones-Ellis. *Approx 6m W of Tonbridge & approx 6m E of Edenbridge. On B2027 Clinton Lane into Chiddingstone Causeway same side as PO, garden is end of terrace cottage with hedge & small gravel driveway.* Home-made teas. **Adm £3.50, chd free.** Sun 17 May, Sat 13 June, Sat 29 Aug (12-6).

Small but charming cottage garden, with large selection of clematis and over 30 varieties of roses. Herbaceous borders filled with colour in May and June. Several seating areas and small water features.

79 POTMANS HEATH HOUSE

Wittersham TN30 7PU. Dr Alan & Dr Wilma Lloyd Smith, 01797 270221, potmansheath@hotmail.com. *1½ m W of Wittersham. Between Wittersham & Rolvenden, 1m from junction with B2082. 200yds E of bridge over Potmans Heath Channel. Nearest WC at Wittersham Church.* Home-made teas. **Adm £5, chd free.** Sun 19 Apr, Sun 7 June (2-6). **Visitors also welcome by arrangement groups welcome.**

Large compartmentalised country garden. Our specialities are widespread naturalised bulbs and spectacular blossom in spring, followed by a variety of climbing roses and mixed borders in summer. Part walled vegetable garden, greenhouses. Specimen trees, some unusual. Orchards. Adjoining parkland with duck ponds. Rich variety of garden birds. Recent article with photographs in Country Living and Kent Life. Wheelchair users welcome. Some awkward slopes but generally good.

80 NEW ♦ QUEX GARDENS

Quex Park, Birchington CT7 0BH. Powell-Cotton Museum, 01843 842168, http://www.quexpark.co.uk/museum/quex-gardens/. *3m W of Margate. Follow signs for Quex Park on approach from A299 then A28 towards Margate, turn R into B2048 Park Lane. Quex Park is on L.* **Adm £4, chd £3.** For NGS: Sun 21 June (10-5). **For other opening times and information, please phone or see garden website.**

10 acres of woodland and gardens with fine specimen trees unusual on Thanet, spring bulbs, wisteria, shrub borders, old figs and mulberries, herbaceous borders. Victorian walled garden with cucumber house, long glasshouses, cactus house, fruiting trees. Peacocks, dovecote, woodland walk, wildlife pond, children's maze, croquet lawn, picnic grove, lawns and fountains. Head Gardener will be available on NGS open days to give tours and answer questions. Mama Feelgoods Boutique Café serving morning coffee, lunch or afternoon tea. Quex Barn farmers market selling local produce and serving breakfasts to evening meals. Picnic sites available. Garden almost entirely flat with tarmac paths. Sunken garden has sloping lawns to the central pond.

81 ▶ 11 RAYMER ROAD

Penenden Heath, Maidstone ME14 2JQ. Mrs Barbara Badham. *1m from J6 M20. At M20, J6 at Running Horse r'about take Penenden Heath exit along Sandling Lane towards Bearsted. At T-lights turn into Downsview Rd & follow yellow NGS signs*. Home-made teas. **Adm £3, chd free.** Sun 19 Apr, Sun 5 July (11-4).

Inspirational small garden with lovely views of the Downs, divided into different areas and intensely planted for yr-round interest. Cottage garden border, oriental themed pond, secret woodland garden plus a selection of ferns and hostas arranged under the canopy of a strawberry tree. Organic fruit and vegetables in raised beds and containers, minarette fruit trees underplanted with wild flowers.

82 ▶ 43 THE RIDINGS

Chestfield, Whitstable CT5 3QE. David & Sylvie Sayers, 01227 500775, sylviebuat-menard@hotmail.com. *Nr Whitstable. From M2 heading E cont onto A299. In 3m take A2990. From r'about on A2990 at Chestfield, turn onto Chestfield Rd, 5th turning on L onto Polo Way which leads into The Ridings*. Home-made teas. **Adm £3.50, chd free.** Sun 12 July (11-4). Visitors also welcome by arrangement Apr to Sept for groups +8.

Delightful small garden brimming with interesting plants both in the front and behind the house. Many different areas. Dry gravel garden in front, raised beds with Alpines and bulbs and borders with many unusual perennials and shrubs.

83 ▶ ◆ RIVERHILL HIMALAYAN GARDENS

Riverhill, Sevenoaks TN15 0RR. The Rogers Family, 01732 459777, www.riverhillgardens.co.uk. *2m S of Sevenoaks on A225. Leave A21 at A225 & follow signs for Riverhill Himalayan Gardens*. Light refreshments. **Adm £7.75, chd £5.75.** For NGS: Thur 23 Apr, Tue 12 May (10.30-5). **For other opening times and information, please phone or see garden website.**

Beautiful hillside garden, privately owned by the Rogers family since 1840. Extensive views across the Weald of Kent. Spectacular rhododendrons, azaleas and fine specimen trees. Bluebell and natural woodland walks. Walled Garden has extensive new planting, terracing and water feature. Children's adventure playground, den building trail, hedge maze and Yeti Spotting. Cafe serving freshly ground coffee, speciality teas, light lunches, homemade cream teas, cakes, gluten free cakes and soya milk. Wheelchair access to Walled Garden only. Good access to café, shop and tea terrace.

Scotney Castle

Recycle – bring a bag for your plant purchases

84 ROCK FARM

Gibbs Hill, Nettlestead ME18 5HT. Mrs S E Corfe, 01622 812244. *6m SW of Maidstone. Turn S off A26 onto B2015, then 1m S of Wateringbury turn R up Gibbs Hill.* **Adm £4, chd free. Share to Nettlestead Church.** Wed 10, Sat 13 June (11-6). **Visitors also welcome by arrangement May to Sept.**

2 acre garden set around old Kentish farmhouse (not open) in beautiful setting; created with emphasis on yr-round interest and ease of maintenance. Plantsman's collection of shrubs, trees and perennials for alkaline soil; extensive herbaceous border, vegetable area, bog garden and plantings around two large natural ponds. Steep paths.

85 ST CLERE

Kemsing, Sevenoaks TN15 6NL. Mr & Mrs Simon & Eliza Ecclestone, www.stclere.com. *6m NE of Sevenoaks. 1m E of Seal on A25, turn L signed Heaverham. In Heaverham turn R signed Wrotham. In 75yds straight ahead marked private rd; 1st L to house.* **Home-made teas in Garden Room. Adm £5, chd free.** Sun 14 June (2-5).

4 acre garden, full of interest. Formal terraces surrounding C17 mansion (not open), with beautiful views of the Kent countryside. Herbaceous and shrub borders, productive kitchen and herb gardens, lawns and rare trees. Garden tours with Head Gardener at 2.30pm & 3.45pm (£1 per head). Some gravel paths and small steps.

☕

GROUP OPENING

86 ST MICHAEL'S GARDENS

Roydon Hall Road, East Peckham TN12 5NH. *5m NE of Tonbridge, 5m SW of Maidstone. Turn off A228 between Mereworth & Paddock Wood into Roydon Hall Rd. Gardens ½ m up hill on L.* **Home-made teas. Combined adm £5, chd free. Share to Friends of St Michael's Church, Roydon.** Sun 26 Apr, Sun 7 June (2-4.30).

ST MICHAEL'S COTTAGE
Mr Peter & Mrs Pauline Fox

ST MICHAEL'S HOUSE
The Magan family

A Victorian house and cottage garden come together to provide colour, scent and inspiration in April and June in this rural village. The year unfolds at the grey stone old vicarage with a lovely display of tulips in spring, followed by irises, then a mass of roses from red hot to old soft colours, all complemented by yew topiary hedges and wonderful views from the meadow. The traditional cottage garden, with a wildlife area, was designed so it cannot be seen all at once. Explore and enjoy the collection of lavenders, hostas, clematis, ferns, heathers and heucheras. Southdown sheep and lambs, chickens. Carp lake. Partial wheelchair access to St Michael's Cottage.

87 ◆ THE SECRET GARDENS OF SANDWICH AT THE SALUTATION

Knightrider Street, Sandwich CT13 9EW. Mr & Mrs Dominic Parker, 01304 619919, www.the-secretgardens.co.uk. *In the heart of Sandwich. Turn L at Bell Hotel & into Quayside car park. Entrance in far R corner of car park.* **Light refreshments. Adm £12, chd £6.** For NGS: Wed 18 Mar (10-4.30); Thur 25 June (10-5.30); Mon 5 Oct (10-4.30). **For other opening times and information, please phone or see garden website.**

3½ acres of ornamental and formal gardens designed by Sir Edwin Lutyens and Gertrude Jekyll in 1911 surrounding Grade I listed house. Designated historic park and garden, lake. White, yellow, spring, woodland, rose, kitchen, vegetable and herbaceous gardens. Designed to provide yr-round changing colour. Unusual plants for sale. Tea Rooms open offering cream teas and light lunches. Gardens, tearoom and shop are wheelchair friendly.

88 SANDOWN

Plain Road, Smeeth, nr Ashford TN25 6QX. Malcolm & Pamela Woodcock. *4m SE of Ashford. Exit J10 onto A20, take 2nd L signposted Smeeth, at Woolpack PH turn R, past garage on L, past next L, garden on L. From A20 in Sellindge at Church, turn R carry on 1m. Park in layby on hill.* **Cream teas. Adm £3.50.** Suns & Mons 3, 4, 24, 25 May, Sats & Suns 27, 28 June, 25, 26 July, Suns & Mons 2, 3, 30, 31 Aug, Sat 5, Sun 6 Sept (1-5).

Our small compact Japanese style garden and Koi pond has visitor book comments such as: inspirational, just like Japan, stunning a hidden gem. There is a Japanese arbour, tea house/veranda, waterfall and stream. Acers, bamboos, ilex crenata (Cloud Trees), ginkgo, fatsia japonica, akebia quinata, clerodendrum trichotomum, pinus mugos, wisterias, hostas and mind your own business for ground cover. WC available. Regret no children owing to deep pond. Featured in local Parish magazines and mentioned on Radio Kent.

89 ◆ SCOTNEY CASTLE

Lamberhurst TN3 8JN. National Trust, 01892 893820, www.nationaltrust.org.uk. *6m SE of Tunbridge Wells. On A21 London - Hastings, brown tourist signs. Bus: (Mon to Sat) Tunbridge Wells - Wadhurst, alight Lamberhurst Green.* **Light refreshments. Adm £13, chd £6.50.** For NGS: Wed 13 May (10-5). **For other opening times and information, please phone or see garden website.**

Scotney Castle's garden has seen many changes since the 1920s when it first opened as part of the NGS open days. You could say it has been a true survivor - from bombs in WW2 to the great storm of 1987 which brought down over 90 substantial trees. Its doors however are still proudly open and the full glory of this romantic setting still encapsulates the original picturesque inspiration. March is all about atmosphere, with low mists across the moat and the first signs of spring to come. With over 20 acres of garden to explore it is a great time to get back out into the garden after the winter. Wheelchairs available for loan.

♿ ❀ 🚐 ☕

GROUP OPENING

90 SHIPBOURNE GARDENS
Shipbourne TN11 9RJ. Off A227 between Tonbridge & Borough Green. Gardens & car parking signed from Chaser PH. Combined group ticket & map available at each garden. Home-made teas in Village Hall. **Combined adm £6, chd free. Sat 13, Sun 14 June (11-5).**

NEW GREAT BUDDS HOUSE
Sarah & Martin Miles

HOOKWOOD HOUSE
Mr & Mrs Nicholas Ward

PLANTATION HOUSE
Viv Packer

Contrasting gardens around the parish will incl Hookwood House, with herbaceous borders, herb garden, topiary, nut plat, vegetable garden; Plantation House, an informal garden with roses, perennials, organic vegetable garden, sculptures; Great Budds House, a 4 acre garden around an old farmhouse, mature oaks, specimen trees, shrubs and roses, dew ponds and lawns. Teas in our pretty village hall on the village green which in June is a mass of wild flowers. Partial wheelchair access to all gardens if wet.

91 ◆ SISSINGHURST CASTLE
Sissinghurst TN17 2AB. National Trust, 01580 710700, www.nationaltrust.org.uk. *On A262 1m E of Sissinghurst. Bus: Arriva Maidstone-Hastings, alight Sissinghurst 1¼ m. Approx 30 mins walk from village.* **Adm £12.90, chd £6.25. For NGS: Sun 26 Apr (11-5.30). Special evening opening, pre-booking essential (see contact details below), £20, chd £10, wine, Wed 24 June (7-9). For other opening times and information, please phone or see garden website.**
Garden created by Vita Sackville-West and Sir Harold Nicolson. Spring garden, herb garden, cottage garden, white garden, rose garden. Tudor building and tower, partly open to public. Moat. Vegetable garden and estate walks. Pre-book tickets for an exclusive evening with Troy Scott-Smith, head gardener, and the garden team. Wed 24 June (7-9). Book tickets at www.nationaltrust.org.uk/sissinghurst

-castle or 0844 249 1895. Free welcome talks and estate walks leaflets. Cafe, restaurant and shop open from 10am-5.30pm daily, closed Christmas Eve and Christmas Day. Some areas unsuitable for wheelchair access due to narrow paths and steps.

Lose yourself in numerous themed rooms . . .

92 SMITHS HALL
Lower Road, West Farleigh ME15 0PE. Mr S Norman, www.smithshall.com. *3m W of Maidstone. A26 towards Tonbridge, turn L into Teston Lane B2163. At T-junction turn R onto Lower Rd B2010. Opp Tickled Trout PH.* Home-made teas. **Adm £5, chd free. Share to Free Me. Sun 31 May, Sun 5 July (11-5).**
Delightful 3 acre gardens surrounding a beautiful 1719 Queen Anne House (not open). Lose yourself in numerous themed rooms: sunken water garden, iris beds, scented old fashioned rose walk, formal rose garden, intense wild flowers, peonies, deep herbaceous borders and specimen trees. Walk 9 acres of park and woodland with great variety of young native and American trees and fine views of the Medway valley. Cakes, quiche, jams and preserves available. Gravel paths.

93 SOUTH HILL FARM
Tamley Lane, Hastingleigh, Ashford TN25 5HL. Sir Charles Jessel, 01233 750325, sircjj@btinternet.com. *4½ m E of Ashford. Turn off A28 to Wye, through village & ascend Wye Downs. 2m turn R at Xrds, Brabourne &*

South Hill, then 1st L. From Stone St (B2068) turn W opp Stelling Minnis, follow signs to Hastingleigh. Cont towards Wye, turn L at Xrds marked Brabourne & South Hill, then 1st L. Tea, coffee and homemade biscuits. **Adm £4.50, chd free. Visitors welcome by arrangement in June, adm incl guided tour and tea.**
2 acres high up on N Downs, C17/18 house (not open). Old walls, ha-ha, formal water garden; old and new roses, unusual shrubs, perennials and coloured foliage plants. A few paths not accessible to wheelchairs.

94 SPRING PLATT
Boyton Court Road, Sutton Valence, Maidstone ME17 3BY. Mr & Mrs John Millen, 01622 843383, carolyn.millen@virginmedia.com, www.kentsnowdrops.com. *5m SE of Maidstone. From A274 nr Sutton Valence follow yellow NGS signs.* Limited parking. Light refreshments. incl home made soup, bread and cakes. **Adm £4, chd free. Sat 7, Sun 8 Feb (11-3). Visitors also welcome by arrangement Feb to Mar. Limited parking but large groups by coach welcome.**
1 acre garden under continual development with panoramic views of the Weald. Over 500 varieties of snowdrop grown in tiered display beds with spring flowers in borders. An extensive collection of alpine plants in a large greenhouse. Vegetable garden and water feature under construction. Garden on a steep slope and many steps.

95 STONEWALL PARK
Chiddingstone Hoath, nr Edenbridge TN8 7DG. The Fleming Family. *4m SE of Edenbridge. via B2026. Halfway between Markbeech & Penshurst.* Home-made teas. **Adm £5, chd free. Share to Sarah Matheson Trust & St Mary's Church, Chiddingstone. Sun 22 Mar, Sun 3 May (1.30-5). Also open Chiddingstone Castle (Sun 22 Mar) and Old Buckhurst (Sun 3 May).**
Romantic woodland garden in historic setting featuring species rhododendrons, magnolias, azaleas, bluebells, a range of interesting trees and shrubs, sandstone outcrops, wandering paths and lakes. Historic parkland with cricket ground, sea of wild daffodils in March.

© Leigh Clapp

Thatched Cottage

96 SUTTON VALENCE SCHOOL

North Street, Sutton Valence, Maidstone ME17 3HL. Sutton Valence School, www.svs.org.uk. *Approx 6m S of Maidstone on A274. M20, J8. Turn L A20, Lenham. 2nd r'about, B2163, Sutton Valence. Xrds A274, Sutton Valence. School on L after 1m.* Home-made teas. **Adm £5 (incl teas), chd free. Wed 1 July (11-3).**
Sutton Valence School garden surrounds the main buildings with a mixture of formal and more naturalistic planting. The borders reflect the style of the older buildings, with the newer areas having a gravel garden and a Mediterranean border. There are steps and gradients to contend with as the gardens are built around a sloping site with several changes of level. A shorter tour can be taken comprising some of the highlights.

97 NEW THATCHED COTTAGE

Hever Road, Hever, Edenbridge TN8 7NH. Ivor & Wendy Macklin, 07970 156681. *200m from Hever Castle. 100m down hill from Henry VIII PH & St Peters Church.* Home-made teas. **Adm £4, chd free. Sat 27, Sun 28 June (1-5).**
Charming cottage garden with many roses, herbaceous and shrub borders. Herb garden, Tudor Well, natural pond with bridge and vegetable plot with small poly tunnel. Orchard leading onto meadow with wild flowers. Stunning views in AONB. Most of garden wheelchair accessible but some uneven surfaces.

98 TIMBERS

Dean Street, East Farleigh, nr Maidstone ME15 0HS. Mrs Sue Robinson, 01622 729568, suerobinson.timbers@gmail.com, www.timbersgardenkent.co.uk. *2m S of Maidstone. From Maidstone take B2010 to East Farleigh. After Tesco's on R follow Dean St for ¹⁄₂ m. Timbers on L behind 8ft beech hedge. Parking through gates. Access for 54 seater coaches.* Light refreshments. **Adm £5, chd free. Visitors welcome by arrangement Apr to July; day and evening openings.**
5 acre garden stocked with unusual hardy plants, annuals and shrubs, designed with flower arranger's eye.

Formal areas (parterre, pergola) herbaceous, vegetables, lawns and mature specimen trees surrounded by 100yr old Kentish cobnut platt, wild flower meadows and woodland. Rock pool with waterfalls. Valley views. Plant list. Newly designed walled garden in progress. Kent Wildlife Trust Gold Award. Featured in Kent Life. Most of garden is flat, some steep slopes to rear.

A water feature and unusual artifacts compliment this exciting courtyard garden . . .

99 TORRY HILL

Frinsted/Milstead, Sittingbourne ME9 0SP. Lady Kingsdown, 01795 830258, lady.kingsdown@btinternet.com. *5m S of Sittingbourne. From M20 J8 take A20 (Lenham). At r'about by Mercure Hotel turn L Hollingbourne (B2163). Turn R at X'rds at top of hill (Ringlestone Rd). Thereafter Frinsted-Doddington (not suitable for coaches), then Torry Hill/NGS signs. From M2 J5 take A249 towards Maidstone, then 1st L (Bredgar), L again (follow Bredgar signs), R at War Memorial, 1st L (Milstead), Torry Hill/NGS signs from Milstead. Please use entrance marked D (on red background) for disabled parking.* Home-made teas. **Adm £4, chd free. Share to St Dunstan's Church (May/June), MS Society (July). Sun 10 May, Sun 14 June, Sun 19 July (2-5). Visitors also welcome by arrangement May to July weekdays only. Tea/coffee and biscuits available.**
8 acres; large lawns, specimen trees, flowering cherries, rhododendrons, azaleas and naturalised daffodils; walled gardens with lawns, shrubs, herbaceous borders, rose garden incl shrub roses, wild flower areas and

vegetables. Extensive views to Medway and Thames estuaries. Some shallow steps. No wheelchair access to rose garden but can be viewed from pathway.

100 TOWNLAND

Sixfields, Tenterden TN30 6EX. Alan & Lindy Bates, 01580 764505, alanandlindybates@yahoo.co.uk. *From centre of Tenterden High St, turn into Jackson's Lane next to Webbs Ironmongers. Follow lane to end (400m). Townland is on the R.* Home-made teas. **Adm £4, chd free. Share to Pilgrims Hospice and ShelterBox. Sun 14 June, Sun 19 July (2-5.30). Visitors also welcome by arrangement June to July for groups 10+. Adm £5 incl tea and biscuits.**
A 1 acre family garden in a unique position. Mixed borders, with a wide range of shrubs and flowers providing a riot of colour throughout the yr, flow into the more naturalistic planting which is adjacent to meadow areas and fruit trees. A gravel garden, rose arbour and intensive fruit and vegetable areas complete the experience. Small area redesigned this yr due to encroaching development. Also wild flowers grown specially to attract bees. Featured in Kent Life.

101 TRAM HATCH

Charing Heath, Ashford TN27 0BN. Mrs P Scrivens, www.tramhatchgardens.co.uk. *10m NW of Ashford. A20 turn towards Charing Railway Stn on Pluckley Rd, over motorway then 1st R signed Barnfield to end, turn L carry on past Barnfield, Tram Hatch ahead.* Home-made teas. **Adm £5, chd free. Sun 14 June, Sun 12 July, Sun 16 Aug (1-5.30).**
Meander your way off the beaten track to a mature, extensive garden changing through the seasons. You will enjoy a garden laid out in rooms - what surprises are round the corner? Large selection of trees, vegetable, rose and gravel gardens, colourful containers. The R Stour and the Angel of the South enhance your visit. Please come and enjoy, then relax in our new garden room for tea. The garden is totally flat, apart from a very small area which can be viewed from the lane.

102 UPPER PRYORS
Butterwell Hill, Cowden TN8 7HB. Mr & Mrs S G Smith. *4¹/₂ m SE of Edenbridge. From B2026 Edenbridge-Hartfield, turn R at Cowden Xrds & take 1st drive on R.* Home-made teas. **Adm £5, chd free. Wed 17 June (12-6).**
Ten acres of English country garden surrounding C16 house - a garden of many parts; colourful profusion, interesting planting arrangements, immaculate lawns, mature woodland, water and a terrace on which to appreciate the view, and tea!

Please come and enjoy, then relax in our new garden room for tea . . .

103 THE WATCH HOUSE
7 Thanet Road, Broadstairs CT10 1LF. Dan Cooper & Alex Dawson, www.frustratedgardener.com. *Off Broadstairs High St on narrow side rd. At Broadstairs station, cont along High St (A255) towards sea front. Turn L between Lloyds Bank & Estate Agent then immed turn R.* Light refreshments. **Adm £3, chd free. Sat 1, Sun 2 Aug (12-4).**
Adjoining an historic fishermen's cottage in the town centre, this tiny garden measures just 20ft x 30ft. Sheltered, and enjoying a unique microclimate, the garden is home to an array of exotic and unusual plants and trees. A constantly changing display of tender plants in containers demonstrates how yr-round interest can be achieved in the smallest of spaces. Within a few mins walk of Viking Bay, The Dickens Museum and Bleak House.

104 WATERGATE HOUSE
King Street, Fordwich, Canterbury CT2 0DB. Fiona Cadwallader, www.cadwallader.co.uk. *2m E of Canterbury. From Canterbury A257 direction, Sandwich, 1m L to Fordwich. 1m L on Moat Lane, direct to Watergate House bottom of High St. Follow parking instructions.* Home-made teas. **Adm £4, chd free. Sat 25 Apr, Sat 13 June (2-6).**
Magical walled garden by the R Stour: defined areas of formal, spring, woodland, vegetable and secret garden reveal themselves in a naturally harmonious flow, each with its own colour combinations. Ancient walls provide the garden's basic structure, while a green oak pergola echoes a monastic cloister. Featured in Country Homes and Interiors and The English Garden magazines (see our website for links). The garden is mainly on one level with one raised walkway under pergola.

105 WEST COURT LODGE
Postling Court, The Street, Postling, nr Hythe CT21 4EX. Mr & Mrs John Pattrick, 01303 863285, malliet@hotmail.co.uk. *2m NW of Hythe. From M20 J11 turn S onto A20. Immed 1st L. After ¹/₂ m on bend take rd signed Lyminge. 1st L into Postling.* Tea in village hall. **Combined adm £5, single garden £3, chd free. Sat 30, Sun 31 May (1-5). Combined with Churchfield.** Visitors also welcome by arrangement May to Aug for max 20 people.
S facing 1 acre walled garden at the foot of the N Downs, designed in 2 parts: main lawn with large sunny borders and a romantic woodland glade planted with shadow loving plants and spring bulbs. Lovely C11 church will be open next to the gardens.

GROUP OPENING

106 WEST MALLING EARLY SUMMER GARDENS
West Malling ME19 6LW. *On A20, nr J4 of M20. Park in West Malling for Little Went & Went House where maps, directions & combined tickets available for other gardens.* Tea at Went House & 2 New Barns Oast. **Combined adm £6, chd free. Share to St Mary's Church. Sun 31 May (12-5).**

BROME HOUSE
John Pfeil & Shirley Briggs

LITTLE WENT
Anne Baring

2 NEW BARNS OAST
Nick Robinson & Becky Robinson Hugill

TOWN HILL COTTAGE
Mr & Mrs P Cosier

WENT HOUSE
Alan & Mary Gibbins

West Malling is an attractive small market town with some fine buildings. Enjoy five lovely gardens that are entirely different from each other and cannot be seen from the road. In the middle of the town, Little Went's long narrow secret garden has fish ponds, an aviary, conservatory, gravel garden, parterre and statues. Brome House has colour themed herbaceous borders, specimen trees and an ornamental vegetable garden. Went House is a Queen Anne house surrounded by a secret garden with a stream, specimen trees, old roses, mixed borders, attractive large kitchen garden, fountain and parterre. Approx ³/₄ m S of the town, 2 New Barns Oast is a child friendly garden with interesting hard landscaping features and raised vegetable garden. Town Hill Cottage is a part walled garden with mature and interesting planting. Little Went has no disabled parking, Town Hill Cottage garden is difficult to access but remaining gardens have wheelchair access.

107 ◆ THE WORLD GARDEN AT LULLINGSTONE CASTLE
Eynsford DA4 0JA. Guy Hart Dyke, 01322 862114, www.lullingstonecastle.co.uk. *1m from Eynsford. Over Ford Bridge in Eynsford Village. Follow signs to Roman Villa. Keep Roman Villa immed on R then follow Private Rd to Gatehouse.* Light refreshments. **Adm £7, chd free. For NGS: Sun 14 June (12-5). For other opening times and information, please phone or see garden website.** Interactive world map of plants laid out as a map of the world within a walled garden. The oceans are your pathways as you navigate the world in 1 acre. You can see Ayers Rock and walk alongside the Andes whilst reading tales of intrepid plant hunters. Discover the origins of some 6,000 different plants - you'll be amazed

where they come from! Plant Hunters Nursery and Lullingstone World Garden seeds for sale. Wheelchairs available upon request.

 ♿ ⊛ 🚐 **NCH** ☕

108 ▸ WYCKHURST

Mill Road, Aldington, Ashford, Kent TN25 7AJ. **Mr & Mrs Chris Older,** 01233 720395, cdo@rmfarms.co.uk. *4m SE of Ashford. From M20 J10 take A20 2m E to Aldington turning; turn R at Xrds & proceed 1¹/₂ m to Aldington Village Hall. Turn R & immed L by Walnut Tree Inn down Forge Hill. After ¹/₄ m turn R into Mill Rd.* Home-made teas, soup and rolls. **Adm £4.50, chd free.** Sat 6, Sun 7, Sat 13, Sun 14 June (11-6). **Visitors also welcome by arrangement June.**

C16 Kent Cottage (not open) nestles in romantic seclusion at the end of a drive. This enchanting garden is a mixture of small mixed herbaceous borders, roses and unusual topiary incl a wild flower meadow. There is plenty of seating round the lawns to enjoy the garden, teas and the extensive views across Romney Marsh towards the sea. Shepherds Hut, small water feature and meadow to stroll in. Recently featured on ART TV in France and Germany. Some gentle slopes which limit wheelchair access to some small areas.

 ♿ ⊛ ☕

GROUP OPENING

109 ▸ WYE GARDENS

Wye TN25 5BJ. *3m NE of Ashford. From A28 take turning signed Wye. Bus: Ashford to Canterbury via Wye. Train: Wye. Collect map of gardens at Church.* Home-made teas at Wye Church. **Combined adm £5, chd free.** Sun 21 June (2-6).

3 BRAMBLE CLOSE
Dr M Copland

CUMBERLAND COURT Ⓓ
Mr & Mrs F Huntington

MISTRAL
Dr & Mrs G Chapman
Visitors also welcome by arrangement.
01233 813011

SPRING GROVE FARM HOUSE
Heather Van den Bergh

YEW TREES
Ian & Elizabeth Coulson

Start at the centre of an historic village to visit 5 unusual gardens. 3 Bramble Close is a unique experience, a very wild garden with meadow, pond and ditches, mown paths, hedges and research carried out on the effects of wildlife. A water feature and unusual artefacts complement an exciting courtyard garden at Cumberland Court, once an asphalt car park now densely planted with a wide range of unusual plants, pots and secret garden. Mature shrub pruning of particular interest. 250 species of botanical interest (labelled) flourish at Mistral, once part of a tennis court, incl white and alpine gardens and centre stage, a mini outdoor theatre! Spring Grove Farm House a country garden full of colour and interest with stream, lily pond and gravel garden. Yew Trees is a traditional garden divided into 3 distinct, secluded areas with lawns, naturalised wildlife area, pond, mature trees, wide borders planted with shrubs, grasses and herbaceous perennials and enclosed potager. Wye Gardens opening coincides with Stour Music Festival and Wye Food Festival.

 ♿ ☕

110 ▸ YEW TREE COTTAGE

Penshurst TN11 8AD. **Mrs Pam Tuppen.** *4m SW of Tonbridge. From A26 Tonbridge to Tunbridge Wells, join B2176 Bidborough to Penshurst rd. 2m W of Bidborough, 1m before Penshurst. Please phone for further directions. Unsuitable for coaches.* Light refreshments. **Adm £2.50, chd free.** Sun 22, Wed 25 Feb, Sun 8, Wed 11, Sun 22, Wed 25 Mar, Wed 8, Sun 12, Wed 22, Sun 26 Apr, Sun 10, Wed 13, Sun 24, Wed 27 May, Wed 10, Sun 14, Wed 24, Sun 28 June, Wed 8, Sun 12, Wed 22, Sun 26 July, Sun 9, Wed 12, Sun 23, Wed 26 Aug, Wed 9, Sun 13 Sept (12-5), Wed 24, Sun 28 Feb 2016 (12-5).

Small, romantic, cottage garden with steep hillside entrance. Lots of seats and secret corners, many unusual plants - hellebores, spring bulbs, old roses, many special perennials. Small pond; something to see in all seasons. Created and maintained by owner, a natural garden full of plants.

 ⊛ ☕

Chiddingstone Castle

© Leigh Clapp

312

LANCASHIRE

Merseyside, Greater Manchester and Isle of Man

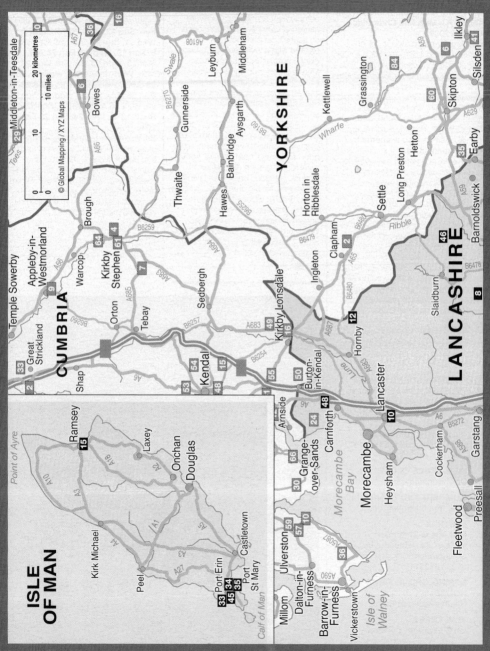

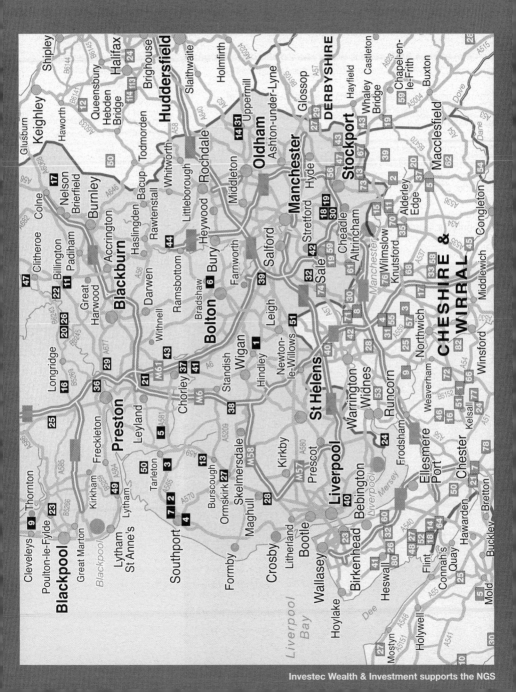

Lancashire, Merseyside, Greater Manchester & Isle of Man

You can always be sure of a really warm red-rose welcome when you visit any of Lancashire's beautiful gardens.

From the tiniest of cottage gardens to spectacular views of Pendle Hill – there is something to delight every taste in all parts of the county.

From Chorley Cakes to Eccles Cakes, from Lemon Drizzle to Victoria Sponge, we have delicacies to tempt every palate. Add a few choice plants to the mix and you can have a fantastic day out for under £10.

Where else can you get such value for money and at the same time support your favourite charities?

Over 400 Volunteers help run the NGS – why not become one too?

Lancashire, Merseyside, Greater Manchester & Isle of Man Volunteers

County Organiser
Margaret Fletcher
01704 567742
geoffwfletcher@hotmail.co.uk

County Treasurer
Geoff Fletcher
01704 567742
geoffwfletcher@hotmail.co.uk

Publicity
Lynn Kelly
01704 563740
lynn-kelly@hotmail.co.uk

Christine Ruth
01517 274877
caruthchris@aol.com

Booklet Coordinator
Brenda Doldon
01704 834253
doldon@btinternet.com

Assistant County Organisers
Anne Britt
01614 458100
annebritt@btinternet.com

Peter & Sandra Curl
01704 893713
peter.curl@btinternet.com

Ray & Brenda Doldon
(as above)

Sharon & Eric Rawcliffe
01253 883275
ericrawk@talktalk.net

Isle of Man
Caroline Couch
01624 832266
carolinecouch@manx.net

Left: Becconsall

Opening Dates

All entries subject to change.
For latest information check www.ngs.org.uk

February

Sunday 8
51 Weeping Ash Garden
Sunday 15
51 Weeping Ash Garden
Sunday 22
51 Weeping Ash Garden

March

Sunday 1
51 Weeping Ash Garden

April

Sunday 5
39 The Secret Valley
Saturday 18
16 Dale House Gardens
Sunday 19
16 Dale House Gardens
51 Weeping Ash Garden

May

49 Warton Hall (every day May 9 to May 17)
Sunday 3
4 Birkdale Village Gardens

---

6 Bridge House
39 The Secret Valley
Monday 4
6 Bridge House
37 The Ridges
Sunday 10
19 3 The Drive
30 Moor Cottage
Sunday 17
13 79 Crabtree Lane
Sunday 24
5 Bretherton Gardens
12 Clearbeck House
47 Waddow Lodge Garden
Monday 25
12 Clearbeck House
Saturday 30
29 Mill Barn
38 NEW Roby Mill Gardens
Sunday 31
21 NEW 17 Glenmore
29 Mill Barn
38 NEW Roby Mill Gardens

June

Festival Weekend

Saturday 6
14 NEW 5 Crib Lane
31 NEW Moordale Paddock
39 The Secret Valley

Sunday 7
3 Becconsall
4 Birkdale Village Gardens
14 NEW 5 Crib Lane
18 Didsbury Village Gardens
31 NEW Moordale Paddock
39 The Secret Valley
Saturday 13
17 Dent Hall
28 Maghull Gardens
Sunday 14
5 Bretherton Gardens
11 Casa Lago
13 79 Crabtree Lane
17 Dent Hall
28 Maghull Gardens
Saturday 20
29 Mill Barn
48 NEW Warton Gardens
Sunday 21
9 NEW The Calder Gardens
12 Clearbeck House
27 NEW 72 Ludlow Drive
29 Mill Barn
48 NEW Warton Gardens
Saturday 27
10 Carr House Farm
16 Dale House Gardens
20 Dutton Hall
22 Great Mitton Hall
24 NEW Hale Village Gardens

Sunday 28
1 40 Acreswood Avenue
10 Carr House Farm
12 Clearbeck House
16 Dale House Gardens
20 Dutton Hall
22 Great Mitton Hall
23 Green Farm Cottage
24 NEW Hale Village Gardens

July

Saturday 4
25 Hallidays Farm
Sunday 5
3 Becconsall
4 Birkdale Village Gardens
8 NEW Browsholme Hall
25 Hallidays Farm
39 The Secret Valley
40 Sefton Park Gardens
Saturday 11
42 Southlands
Sunday 12
5 Bretherton Gardens
13 79 Crabtree Lane
42 Southlands
44 The Stubbins Gardens
Saturday 18
2 NEW 8 Bankfield Lane
7 4 Brocklebank Road
43 The Stones & Roses Garden
Sunday 19
2 NEW 8 Bankfield Lane

14 Saxon Road, Birkdale Village Gardens

© Julia Stanley

7 4 Brocklebank Road
32 NEW Mossfield Allotments
43 The Stones & Roses Garden
47 Waddow Lodge Garden

Saturday 25
41 Silver Birches

Sunday 26
41 Silver Birches

August

Saturday 1
6 Bridge House

Sunday 2
6 Bridge House
36 NEW Ribbleton Library
39 The Secret Valley

Saturday 8
26 Lower Dutton Farm

Sunday 9
26 Lower Dutton Farm

Monday 31
37 The Ridges

September

Sunday 6
5 Bretherton Gardens
39 The Secret Valley

Isle of Man Gardens

March

Friday 20
33 NEW Port Erin Group

April

Friday 17
33 NEW Port Erin Group

May

Friday 15
33 NEW Port Erin Group

June

Friday 19
33 NEW Port Erin Group

Sunday 21
35 NEW Red Roofs
45 Thie-ny-Chibbyr

July

Saturday 4
34 Primrose Lodge

Sunday 12
15 NEW Cummal Beg

Friday 17
33 NEW Port Erin Group

Sunday 19
35 NEW Red Roofs

August

Friday 21
33 NEW Port Erin Group

September

Sunday 6
35 NEW Red Roofs

February 2016

Sunday 14
51 Weeping Ash Garden

Sunday 21
51 Weeping Ash Garden

Sunday 28
51 Weeping Ash Garden

Gardens open to the public

8 NEW Browsholme Hall
12 Clearbeck House
37 The Ridges

By arrangement only

46 Varley Farm
50 Wedgwood

Also open by arrangement

3 Becconsall
4 71 Dunbar Crescent, Birkdale Village Gardens
4 14 Saxon Road, Birkdale Village Gardens
5 Hazel Cottage, Bretherton Gardens
5 Owl Barn, Bretherton Gardens
7 4 Brocklebank Road
10 Carr House Farm
11 Casa Lago
13 79 Crabtree Lane
15 NEW Cummal Beg
16 Dale House Gardens
18 38 Willoughby Avenue, Didsbury Village Gardens
19 3 The Drive
29 Mill Barn
33 NEW Port Erin Group
34 Primrose Lodge
35 NEW Red Roofs
39 The Secret Valley
40 Sefton Villa, Sefton Park Gardens
41 Silver Birches
42 Southlands
43 The Stones & Roses Garden

The Gardens

1 **40 ACRESWOOD AVENUE**
Hindley Green, Wigan WN2 4NJ.
Angie Barker,
www.angiebarker.co.uk. *4m E of Wigan. Take A577 from Wigan to Manchester, L at Victoria Hotel, at T-junction L for parking on Dray King car park. Walk back to T-junction & take 1st L.* Tea. **Adm £3.50, chd free. Sun 28 June (11-4).**
This small garden in the middle of a modern housing estate, has been created from scratch over the last 8 years. It uses planting to bring privacy to an overlooked space and has a mix of contemporary and cottage garden styles. It features a formal decked pond area and a small wildlife pond and manages to squeeze in a small vegetable plot.

2 NEW **8 BANKFIELD LANE**
Churchtown, Southport PR9 7NJ.
Mr & Mrs A Swift. *2½ m N of Southport. Turn R at T-lights on A565*

in Churchtown 1st L at r'about past Hesketh Arms PH & Botanic Gardens main entrance on L. Garden is 200yds on R. Home-made teas. **Combined adm with 4 Brocklebank Road £4, chd free. Share to Southport Spinal Unit. Sat 18, Sun 19 July (11-5).**
Open aspect to rear of garden, double herbaceous borders, small vegetable garden, greenhouse, chickens coup, two raised patio areas. Front garden has trees, shrubs and roses. Restricted parking on Bankfield Lane. Parking available at rear of Botanic Gardens on Veralum Road. A short walk from Botanic Gardens to Bankfield Lane via main or side gate. Wheelchair access to most areas.

3 **BECCONSALL**
Hunters Lane, Tarleton Moss, Preston PR4 6JL. John & Elizabeth Caunce, 01772 814788, johnelizabeth.caunce@yahoo. co.uk. *11m S of Preston. From Preston, take A59 then A565 towards*

Southport. *After 2m rd goes down to one lane turn R, & back on other side of rd. Hunters Lane ½ m on L. Parking in nearby field.* Home-made teas. **Adm £3, chd free. Sun 7 June, Sun 5 July (11-5). Visitors also welcome by arrangement June to July.**
1 acre sympathetically combining different areas lawn, rill, arboretum, herbaceous border, wild flower area and raised vegetable beds. Music in the afternoon. Wheelchair access to most of the garden.

Situated close to historic Marsh Mill and less than 2m from the sea . . .

Green Farm Cottage

GROUP OPENING

BIRKDALE VILLAGE GARDENS

Birkdale, Southport PR8 2AX. *1m S of Southport. Off A565 Southport to Liverpool rd. 4th on L after r'about, opp St James Church. Maps available at each location.* Home-made teas at Saxon Rd,. **Combined adm £4.50, chd free. Share to Southport Inshore Lifeboat.**
Sun 3 May, Sun 7 June, Sun 5 July (11-5).

23 ASHTON ROAD
PR8 4QE. John & Jennifer Mawdsley.
Open 3 May. ³/₄ m S from village along Liverpool Rd, turn R into Sandon Rd (church on corner) 2nd L Ashton Rd

71 DUNBAR CRESCENT
PR8 3AA. Mrs Kimberley Gittins.
Open all 3 dates. S along A565 from town centre, over railway bridge at Hillside. Dunbar Crescent is 3rd rd on L
Visitors also welcome by arrangement May to July, refreshments may be incl for group bookings.
01704 579325
kgo611@ymail.com

10 MEADOW AVENUE
PR8 5HF. John & Jenny Smith.
Open 3 May 5 July. S on A5267 through Birkdale Village, L at T-lights, continue past 1 zebra Xing, just before next turn R into Warwick St, then 2nd L

14 SAXON ROAD
Margaret & Geoff Fletcher.
Open all 3 dates
Visitors also welcome by arrangement May to July for groups of 10+.
01704 567742
geoffwfletcher@hotmail.co.uk

66 SHAWS ROAD
PR8 4LR. Brian & Vivienne Rimmer.
Open all 3 dates. From Birkdale village head S through T-lights at Crescent Rd. Shaws Rd is 6th rd on L

An established group of gardens encircling the attractive, bustling Victorian village of Birkdale, some within easy walking distance, others reached by a short car journey. Some gardens opening on all 3 dates, others less. Gardens feature new this year a plantswoman's garden in cottage garden style, a quirky large family garden full of reclaimed materials and surprises, a walled garden with an array of tender plants amongst informal island beds and a developing family garden with pond, mini orchard, reclaimed materials and lots of good ideas. Finally a garden of different rooms with inspirational fruit and vegetable plot. Wheelchair access to some gardens.
&♿ ❀ ☕

GROUP OPENING

BRETHERTON GARDENS

Flag Lane, Bretherton, nr Leyland PR26 9AD. *8m SW of Preston. Between Southport & Preston, from A59, take B5247 towards Chorley for 1m. Gardens off North Rd (B5248) & South Rd (B5247).* Home-made teas at Bretherton Congregational Church. Light lunches (July only). **Combined adm £5, £4 (Sept), chd free. Share to St Catherine's Hospice.**
Suns 24 May, 14 June, 12 July, 6 Sept (12-5).

GLYNWOOD HOUSE
Eyes Lane, PR26 9AS. Terry & Sue Riding

HAZEL COTTAGE
PR26 9AN. John & Kris Jolley
Visitors also welcome by arrangement.
01772 600896
jolley@johnjolley.plus.com

◆ HAZELWOOD
North Road, PR26 9AY.
Jacqueline Iddon & Thompson Dagnall.
01772 601433
Not open on 6 September
For other opening times and information, please see garden website.
www.jacquelineiddon.co.uk

OWL BARN
PR26 9AD. Richard & Barbara Farbon.
From Croston train stn, follow Bretherton Rd. This goes over the R Lostock & becomes Flag Lane. Stay on main rd until you see a bungalow on R. Owl Barn is 20yds further on R
Visitors also welcome by arrangement May to Aug small groups only (less than 10).
01772 600750
farbons@btinternet.com

PEAR TREE COTTAGE
Eyes Lane, PR26 9AS. John & Gwenifer Jackson.
In Bretherton turn into Eyes Lane at the War Memorial

Five contrasting gardens spaced across 3m in an attractive village with conservation area. Glynwood House has ³/₄-acre mixed borders, pond with drystone-wall water feature, woodland walk, patio garden with pergola and raised beds, all in a peaceful location with spectacular open aspects. Pear Tree Cottage garden blends seamlessly into its rural setting with informal displays of ornamental and edible crops, water and mature trees, against a backdrop of open views to the West Pennine Moors. Owl Barn has a working kitchen garden and mixed borders with exuberant planting to complement an historic C18 listed building (not open). Hazelwood Garden, Nursery and Sculpture Gallery cover 1¹/₂ acres of mature orchard, with a wide range of habitats, showing the finest plants for every situation, from moist shade to well-drained sun. Hazel Cottage garden has evolved from a Victorian subsistence plot to encompass a series of themed spaces packed with plants to engage the senses and the mind. Sculpture demonstration 2pm at Hazelwood, live music at Hazelwood and Glynwood. Home-made preserves for sale at Pear Tree Cottage.
&♿ ❀ 🚐 ☕

Reclaimed materials and lots of good ideas . . .

◆ BRIDGE HOUSE
Bolton Road, Bradshaw, Bolton BL2 3EU. Glenda & Graham Ostick.
2m NE of Bolton. On A676 to Ramsbottom, 2m from centre of Bolton. In Bradshaw half way between 'Erico's Restaurant & 'The Crofter's'. Enter Bolton Rd for Satnav. Cream teas. **Adm £2.50, chd free. Share to The Prostatic Cancer Endowment Fund. Sun 3, Mon 4 May, Sat 1, Sun 2 Aug (1-5).**

An impressive and beautiful garden of more than 1 acre created by 2 dedicated gardeners over many years. Spring interest in bulbs, azaleas and some unusual shrubs and trees, 2 ponds. Summer, herbaceous borders, challenging 'wild area'. Views across meadow and brook, extensive lawns, prolific vegetable garden and beautiful wall mosaic. Garden for all seasons, not to be missed. Wheelchair access to main garden only 'wild part unsuitable'.

 4 BROCKLEBANK ROAD
Southport PR9 9LP. Alan & Heather Sidebotham, 01704 543389, alansidebotham@yahoo.co.uk. *1¼ m N of Southport. Off A565 Southport to Preston Rd, opp North entrance to Hesketh Park.* Home-made teas. **Combined adm with 8 Bankfield Lane £4, chd free. Sat 18, Sun 19 July (11-5). Visitors also welcome by arrangement May to Aug groups of 8+.**
A walled garden incorporating a church folly. Landscaped with reclaimed materials from historic sites in the Southport area. There are several water features, an extensive herbaceous border and various areas of differing planting, thus creating a garden with much interest. Featured in Lancashire Life.

8 NEW ◆ **BROWSHOLME HALL**
Clitheroe Road, Cow Ark, Clitheroe BB7 3DE. Mr & Mrs R Parker, cturner@browsholme.com, www.browsholme.com. *5m NW of Clitheroe. From Clitheroe, leave on B6243 via Eidisford Bridge, R to Bashall Eaves. From Whalley turn L to Great Mitton, then to Bashall Eaves. From Longridge follow signs to Trough of Bowland.* Light refreshments in the Tithe Barn (licensed). **Adm £3.50, chd free. For NGS: Sun 5 July (11-4). For other opening times and information, please email or see garden website.**
Historic garden and parkland in the setting of a 500 year old grade 1 listed Hall (open). Evidence remains of the C17 garden with magnificent yew walk and 'wilderness' undergoing restoration. The parkland setting is in the style of Capability Brown with C18 origins of lakes, woodland views and a ha-ha; while the immediate

garden area reflects the later Edwardian period. Guided tours (separate charge). Gravel paths and lawns. Car park 300 yds.

GROUP OPENING

9 NEW **THE CALDER GARDENS**
Thornton-Cleveleys FY5 2TR. *Approx 7m N of Blackpool. From M6 then M55 until J3. Follow A585 towards Fleetwood. At Morrisons store r'bout, last exit E towards Thornton. 1st L Meadows Ave, 1st L Calder Ave.* Home-made teas. **Combined adm £4, chd free. Sun 21 June (11-5).**

> **NEW** **4 CALDER AVE**
> Sue & Emmett Hughes

> **NEW** **6 CALDER AVE**
> Jackie and Pete Newey

> **NEW** **8 CALDER AVE**
> Marjorie & Alan Brogden

> **NEW** **10 CALDER AVE**
> Roy Powney

Situated close to historic Marsh Mill and less than 2m from the sea, these 4 neighbouring gardens show completely different styles. No. 4 garden with the length of one side as ornamental rockery and stream leading to large Koi pool. The rest is laid to lawn and low maintenance borders with various shrubs and trees. No. 6 is closely planted to attract insects and birds with a variety of perennials, evergreens, shrubs and trees. There is a small wildlife pond and a native hedgerow. No. 8 is laid to lawn with specimen trees. It is bordered by close planted flowers, shrubs and trees with the aim of low maintenance. There is a vegetable plot, a small greenhouse and

ornamental pond with water feature. No.10 is laid to lawn near the house The established borders contain specimen trees, shrubs, perennials, roses, climbers and fruit trees. There are 2 small greenhouses with begonias, geranium, succulents and streptocarpus. All gardens are on one level.

 CARR HOUSE FARM
Carr House Lane, Lancaster LA1 1SW. Robin & Helen Loxam, 01524 60646. *SW of Lancaster City. From A6 Lancaster city centre turn at hospital, past B&Q & 1st R, straight under railway bridge into farm.* Home-made teas. **Adm £4, chd free. Share to Fairfield Flora & Fauna Association. Sat 27, Sun 28 June (10-5). Visitors also welcome by arrangement May to Aug.**
A hidden gem in historic City of Lancaster. Farmhouse gardens incl Mediterranean, rustic and cottage flowers and trees intertwined beautifully with 2 ponds fed naturally by 'Lucy Brook' attracting all manner of wildlife. Apple, pear, plum, lemon and orange trees mix well within the scene. See rare breed cattle and enjoy nature walk in adjoining fields. Featured in Lancashire & Lancashire Life. Slope towards pond.

11 CASA LAGO
1 Woodlands Park, Whalley BB7 9UG. Carole Ann & Stephen Powers, 01254 824903, powers@carolepowers6. orangehome.co.uk. *2½ m S of Clitheroe. From M6 J31, take A59 to Clitheroe. 9m take 2nd exit at r'about for Whalley. After 2m reach village & follow yellow signs. Parking in village car parks or nearby.* Light refreshments. **Adm £3, chd free. Sun 14 June (1-5). Visitors also welcome by arrangement June to Sept.**
Casa Lago has koi ponds, acers, bamboos, hosta collection, grasses, bananas and a succulent garden. Black limestone wall, oak pergolas, and a secluded haven encased in glass. A raised decked area surrounded by a pebbled beach with box insets, alpine display and a beautiful green, white and lemon prairie meadow. Visitor comments include 'stupendous' 'Inspiring and magical'.

© Julia Stanley

Bridge House

12 ◆ CLEARBECK HOUSE

Mewith Lane, Higher Tatham via Lancaster LA2 8PJ. Peter & Bronwen Osborne, 01524 261029, www.clearbeckgarden.org.uk. *13m NE of Lancaster. Signed from Wray (M6 J34, A683, B6480) & Low Bentham.* Light refreshments. **Adm £4, chd free. For NGS: Sun 24, Mon 25 May, Sun 21, Sun 28 June (11-5). For other opening times and information, please phone or see garden website.**

'A surprise round every corner' is the most common response as visitors encounter fountains, streams, ponds, sculptures, boathouses and follies: Rapunzel's tower, temple, turf maze, giant fish made of CDs, walk-through pyramid. 2-acre wildlife lake attracts many species of insects and birds. Planting incl herbaceous borders, grasses, bog plants and many roses. Vegetable and fruit garden. Painting studio open. Children- friendly incl quiz. Artists and photographers welcome by arrangement. Featured in Lancashire Magazine & on BBC2 programme 'Alan's Garden Secrets'. Many grass paths, some sloped.

13 79 CRABTREE LANE

Burscough L40 0RW. Sandra & Peter Curl, 01704 893713, peter.curl@btinternet.com. *3m NE of Ormskirk. A59 Preston - Liverpool Rd. From N before bridge R into Redcat Lane signed for Martin Mere. From S over 2nd bridge L into Redcat Lane after ³/₄ m L into Crabtree Lane.* Home-made teas. **Adm £3.50, chd free. Sun 17 May, Sun 14 June, Sun 12 July (11-4). Visitors also welcome by arrangement May to July.**

³/₄ acre garden that over recent yrs has been changed and replanted but still has many established and contrasting hidden areas. Patio surrounded by shrubs and alpine bed. Colour themed herbaceous and island beds with shrubs. Rose garden, fish pond surrounded by a large rockery and a koi pond with waterfall, recently rebuilt and shallow area for wildlife. Spring and woodland garden, gravel garden with tender Mediterranean planting and late summer hot bed. Hosta and fern walk. A derelict, dry stone bothy and stone potting shed. Featured in Lancashire Life. Flat grass paths.

14 NEW 5 CRIB LANE

Dobcross, Oldham OL3 5AF. Helen Campbell. *5m E of Oldham. From Dobcross village-head towards Delph on Platt Lane. Crib Lane is opp Dobcross Band Club - go straight up the lane, there is limited parking across from a double green garage door.* Light refreshments. **Combined adm with Moordale Paddock £3.50, chd free. Sat 6, Sun 7 June (1-4).**

A well loved and well used family garden which is challenging as on a high stony hillside and encompasses hens, a site for annual bonfires, some small wildlife ponds, vegetable garden, a poly tunnel and areas that are always being re thought and dug up and changed depending on time and aged bodies aches and pains!

15 NEW CUMMAL BEG

Jurby Road, Ramsey, Isle Of Man IM8 3PF. June Nicholls, 01624 815745, gardenmad@hotmail.com. *On A13 ¹/₂ m N of Ramsey town centre. From Ramsey Town Hall head N along Bowring Road. Turn L into Jurby Road (opp St Olaves Church) bungalow is approx. 200 yds on L, just before Mount Auldyn.* **Adm £3, chd free. Sun 12 July (12-5). Visitors also welcome by arrangement June to July.**

An interesting garden on ¹/₃ acre, which is continually evolving. Lots of colourful perennials, shrubs etc. Some colour themed flower beds. Small raised fish pond with adjoining flower bed. Separate sections with roses and clematis on trellises, 2 arbours, fruit trees, large well stocked fruit cage, vegetable beds, 2 greenhouses, 2 polytunnels. Winner of Ramsey in Bloom Best Large garden.

16 DALE HOUSE GARDENS

off Church Lane, Goosnargh, Preston PR3 2BE. Caroline & Tom Luke, 01772 862464, tomlukebudgerigars@hotmail.com. *2¹/₂ m E of Broughton. M6 J32 signed Garstang Broughton, T-lights R at Whittingham Lane, 2¹/₂ m to Whittingham at r'about turn L at Church Lane garden between nos 17 & 19.* **Adm £3.50, chd free. Share to Goosnargh Scout Group. Sat 18, Sun 19 Apr, Sat 27, Sun 28 June (10-4). Visitors also welcome by arrangement Apr to Sept.**

¹/₂ -acre tastefully landscaped gardens comprising of limestone

rockeries, well stocked herbaceous borders, raised alpine beds, well stocked koi pond, lawn areas, greenhouse and polytunnel, patio areas, specialising in alpines rare shrubs and trees, large collection unusual bulbs. All year round interest. Large indoor budgerigar aviary. 300+ budgies to view. Gravel path, lawn areas.

♿ ❀ 🚐 ☕

A fabulous wisteria, pond, terraced dining area and a quirky collection of frogs . . .

17▶ DENT HALL
Colne Road, Trawden, Colne BB8 8NX. Mr Chris Whitaker-Webb. *Turn L at end of M65. Follow A6068 for 2m; after 3rd r'about turn R down B6250. After 1½ m, in front of church, turn R, signed Carry Bridge. Parking 200yds in village 5 mins walk on public footpaths.* Home-made teas. **Adm £3.50, chd free. Share to Pendleside Hospice. Sat 13, Sun 14 June (12-5).** Country garden surrounding 400 year old grade II listed hall (not open). Garden reflects nature of house and surrounding countryside. Parterre, lawns, herbaceous borders, shrubbery, wildlife pond with bridge to seating area, hidden summerhouse in woodland area. Plentiful seating. Some uneven paths and gradients.

❀ ☕ ♿

GROUP OPENING

18▶ DIDSBURY VILLAGE GARDENS
South Manchester M20 3GZ. *5m S of Manchester. From M60 J5 follow signs to Northenden. Turn R at T-lights onto Barlow Moor Rd to Didsbury. From M56 follow A34 to Didsbury.* Home-made teas at Moor Cottage & 68 Brooklawn Drive. **Combined adm £6, chd free. Sun 7 June (12-5).**

68 BROOKLAWN DRIVE
M20 3GZ. Anne & Jim Britt. *Off Wilmslow Rd then last R on Westhome Rd*

3 THE DRIVE
Peter & Sarah Clare
(See separate entry)

GROVE COTTAGE, 8 GRENFELL ROAD
M20 6TQ. Mrs Susan Kaberry. *From the centre of village at T-lights Xrds go down Barlow Moor Rd. Grenfell Rd is 3rd on L*

30 LIDGATE GROVE
M20 2TS. Mary Powell. *From Didsbury village take rd by Oxfam into Grove Lane, which then becomes Lidgate Grove. Follow NGS sign into garden*

MOOR COTTAGE
William Godfrey
(See separate entry)

2 PARKFIELD ROAD SOUTH
M20 6DA. Conrad & Kate Jacobson

38 WILLOUGHBY AVENUE
Mr Simon Hickey. *Garden at closed end of cul-de-sac; some may prefer to park further up & walk a short distance* Visitors also welcome by arrangement. 016147 85589

Didsbury is an attractive South Manchester suburb which retains its village atmosphere. There are interesting shops, cafes and restaurants, well worth a visit in themselves! This year we have seven gardens, one of which is new. The gardens demonstrate a variety of beautiful spaces- one is a large family garden divided into several enchanting areas incl pretty courtyard and Jewel garden, another is an expertly planted shade garden with many rarities, whilst another reflects the charm of the cottage garden ethos with rose covered pergola, old fashioned perennials and tranquil raised pool. Our smaller gardens show beautifully how suburban plots, with limited space, can be packed full of interesting features and a range of planting styles. Dogs allowed at some gardens. Wheelchair access to some gardens.

♿ 🐶 ❀ ☕

19▶ 3 THE DRIVE
M20 6HZ. Peter & Sarah Clare, 07710 321913, peter_clare@ntlworld.com. *From M60 J5 follow signs to Northenden. Turn R at T-lights onto Barlow Moor Rd to Didsbury. From M56. A tiny*

road off Fog Lane with an old gatehouse on the corner. No 3 is the first gap in the hedge immed on L. **Adm £5, chd free. Sun 10 May (12-5). Also open with Moor Cottage.** Visitors also welcome by arrangement Mar to Sept. Secluded woodland garden with winding paths wandering romantically from ponds and waterfalls to pergolas and ferneries. Stone steps lead to different levels and hidden views emerge from old seats tucked into leafy corners. There is a mix of formality and informality with subtle use of colour and a wide range of shade planting and foliage for spring,summer and autumn. Partial wheelchair access, gravel paths and drive.

♿

20▶ DUTTON HALL
Gallows Lane, Ribchester PR3 3XX. Mr & Mrs A H Penny, www.duttonhall.co.uk. *2m NE of Ribchester. Signed from B6243 & B6245 also directions on website.* Home-made teas. **Adm £5, chd free. Sat 27, Sun 28 June (1-5).** Formal garden at front with backdrop of C17 house (not open). 2 acres at rear which incl large collection of old fashioned roses, water feature, wild orchid meadow and viewing platforms with extensive views over the Ribble Valley. Visitors requested to keep to mown paths in meadow areas. Also Orangery and collection of Pemberton roses. Analemmatic sundial. Featured in English Garden Magazine.

❀ ☕

21▶ NEW▶ 17 GLENMORE
Clayton-le-Woods, Chorley PR6 7TA. Mr & Mrs P Hothersall. *1m E of J28 M6 Leyland, take B5256 towards Chorley, turn R into Glenmore at crest of hill, after thatched cottage on R.* Light refreshments. **Adm £3, chd free. Sun 31 May (11-4.30).** This ⅓ acre corner on the fringe of Cuerden Valley Park is home to a constantly evolving garden incorporating lawns, shrubs, colourful borders and peaceful seating areas for sun and shade, amidst a borrowed backdrop of surrounding trees. Features incl a fabulous wisteria, pond, terraced family dining area and a quirky collection of frogs. Most of garden accessible to wheelchair users.

♿ ❀ ☕

22 GREAT MITTON HALL
Mitton Road, Mitton, nr Clitheroe BB7 9PQ. Jean & Ken Kay. *2m W of Whalley. Take Mitton Rd out of Whalley pass Mitton Hall on L, Aspinall Arms on R over bridge. Hall is on R next to Hillcrest tearooms.* Home-made teas. **Adm £3.50, chd free. Share to Help for Heroes. Sat 27, Sun 28 June (1-5).** Overlooked by C12 Allhallows Church, with stunning views to the river and Pendle Hill the terraced gardens with herbaceous borders, lawn, topiary and raised lily pond, sympathetically surround the medieval hall (not open). Chickens, fruit and vegetables, summer house and seating add to the overall experience. Stalls on village green at side of Hall.

23 GREEN FARM COTTAGE
42 Lower Green, Poulton-le-Fylde FY6 7EJ. Eric & Sharon Rawcliffe. *500yds from Poulton-le-Fylde Village. M55 J3 follow A585 Fleetwood. T-lights turn L. Next lights bear L A586. Poulton 2nd set of lights turn R Lower Green. Cottage on L.* Light refreshments. **Adm £3, chd free. Sun 28 June (10-5).** 1/2 acre well established formal cottage gardens. Feature koi pond, paths leading to different areas. Lots of climbers and rose beds. Packed with plants of all kinds. Many shrubs and trees. Themed colour borders. Well laid out lawns. Said by visitors to be 'a real hidden jewel'.

GROUP OPENING

24 NEW HALE VILLAGE GARDENS
Liverpool L24 4BA. *6m S of M62 J6. Take A5300, A562 towards Liverpool, then A561, L for Hale opp the RSPCA. The 82a bus route passes through the village. Additional parking is available by the church and in the village.* **Combined adm £4, chd free. Sat 27, Sun 28 June (2-5).**

> #### NEW 37 CHURCH ROAD
> Hale Village, Liverpool. Betty Henson.
> *Enter through gate right of property*

> #### NEW 56 CHURCH ROAD
> Geraldine & John Trevaskis

> #### NEW 66 CHURCH ROAD
> Liz Kelly-Hines & David Hines

A cluster of very different neighbouring gardens in the delightful village of Hale, set in rural S Merseyside between Widnes and Liverpool Airport. Church Road is also home to the cottage, sculpture and grave of the famous Childe of Hale.

PERENNIAL
GARDENERS' ROYAL BENEVOLENT SOCIETY
Helping Horticulturists In Need Since 1839

Perennial; supporting horticulturists since 1839

25 HALLIDAYS FARM
Moss Lane, Bilsborrow, Preston PR3 0RU. Lisa Walling. *4m S of Garstang. Leave M6 at J32. Follow signs for Garstang 4m, turn L onto St Michaels Rd, take your 1st L onto Moss Lane, 1st Farm on R.* Light refreshments. **Adm £3.50, chd free. Sat 4, Sun 5 July (10-4).** A relatively new garden, with lots to see including a wildlife pond with waterfall and a log water feature on the patio with a settee to sit on and relax and listen to the sound of trickling water. The garden is planted with lots of colour and planting combinations with shrubs perennials, bulbs climbers and roses. Raised bed vegetable patch.

26 LOWER DUTTON FARM
Gallows Lane, Ribchester PR3 3XX. Mr R Robinson. *1 1/2 m NE of Ribchester. Leave M6 J31. Take A59 towards Clitheroe, turn L at T-lights towards Ribchester. Signed from B6243 & B6245. Ample car parking.* Home-made teas. Wine. **Adm £3.50, chd free. Sat 8, Sun 9 Aug (1-5).** Traditional long Lancashire farmhouse and barn (not open), with 1 1/2 acre garden. Formal gardens nr house with mixed herbaceous beds, wild flower beds and shrubs, sweeping lawns leading to wildlife area and established large pond and small woodland with mix of trees and plants. Ample parking on adjacent field. Lawns may be difficult in very wet weather.

27 NEW 72 LUDLOW DRIVE
Ormskirk L39 1LF. Mr & Mrs Jones. *1/2 m W of Ormskirk. Take Southport Rd (A570) turn R onto Heskin Lane then 1st R onto Ludlow Drive.* Home-made teas. **Adm £3, chd free. Sun 21 June (11-4).** Plantswoman's small corner house garden with well stocked colourful herbaceous and shrub borders. The garden also features a gravel garden with sun loving plants, raised beds with some unusual shade loving plants, modern and old roses and many clematis. There are also alpine troughs and a raised fish pond. The owners are beekeepers and will have observation hive on show. Wheelchair access to front garden but limited access to rear garden.

GROUP OPENING

28 MAGHULL GARDENS
Maghull, Liverpool L31 7DR. *7m N of Liverpool. End of M57/M58/A59 take A59 towards O/skirk after 1 1/2 m take next slip rd on L, L at bridge onto Liverpool Rd Sth, L Balmoral Rd, R Buckingham Rd.* Home-made teas. **Combined adm £2.50, chd free. Sat 13, Sun 14 June (12-5).**

> #### 136 BUCKINGHAM ROAD
> L31 7DR. Debbie & Mark Jackson

> #### MAGHULL STATION
> Station Road, Maghull, L31 7DE. Merseyrail.
> *Turn R at Town Hall over canal bridge. Follow signs to Maghull Station*

One garden and an award winning station. 136 Buckingham Road: small suburban garden owned by a plantaholic. The garden is brimming with cottage garden plants, containers and hanging baskets full of colour and small pond stocked with fish.The garden is planted to attract wildlife, plenty of seating and exceedingly good homemade cakes available. Maghull Station: Named The Best Small Station of the year 2013. Filled with herbaceous plants, shrubs, rockery, hanging baskets, troughs and large planters tumbling with a wide variety of bedding plants - a wonderful sight for commuters arriving in Maghull.

29 MILL BARN
Goosefoot Close, Samlesbury, Preston PR5 0SS. Chris Mortimer, 01254 853300, chris@millbarn.net. *6m E of Preston. From M6 J31 2½ m on A59/A677 B/burn. Turn S. Nabs Head Lane, then Goosefoot Lane.* Cream teas. **Adm £4, chd free. Sat 30, Sun 31 May, Sat 20, Sun 21 June (1-5).** Visitors also welcome by arrangement May to July, min group donation £40.
Tranquil terraced garden along the banks of R Darwen. A garden on many levels, both physical and psychological. A sense of fun and mystique is present and an adventurous spirit may be needed to negotiate the various parts. Flowers, follies and sculptures engage the senses, moving up from the semi formal to the semi wild where nature is only just under control. A grotto dedicated to alchemy, a suspension bridge over the R Darwen 20 metres wide at this point, and a tower on the far bank above the 'Lorelei' rocks where a princess might wait for her lover. Partial wheelchair access, visitors have not been disappointed in the past.
⟨accessibility symbols⟩

30 MOOR COTTAGE
Grange Lane. M20 6RW. William Godfrey. *From M60 J5 follow signs to Northenden. Turn R at T-lights onto Barlow Moor Rd to Didsbury. From M56. Off Wilmslow Rd.* Home-made teas. **Adm £5, chd free. Sun 10 May (12-5).** Also open with 3 The Drive.
Moor Cottage is a delightful walled garden hidden from the street. It opens up into a series of flower-filled rooms packed with choice planting combinations. Lawn and yew hedging create firm structure and design. Kitchen garden.
⟨accessibility symbols⟩

31 NEW MOORDALE PADDOCK
Huddersfield Road, Diggle, Oldham OL3 5NT. Mrs H Barnes. *5m E of Oldham. The garden is located up the driveway beside 109 Huddersfield Rd, Diggle. Garden is on R as you go up the drive. NB Parking is available on Huddersfield Rd only.* Home-made teas. **Combined adm with 5 Crib Lane £3.50, chd free. Sat 6, Sun 7 June (1-4).**
The mature gardens are to the front and rear of the large stone built house and consist of deep beds containing a range of herbaceous perennials,

roses and shrubs and a shade bed at the rear planted with hostas, There are ponds front and rear and a vegetable plot at the top of the garden with greenhouse.
⟨symbol⟩

ALLOTMENTS

32 NEW MOSSFIELD ALLOTMENTS
Flixton Road, Urmston, Manchester M41 5DR. *1m town centre. M60 J10 for Urmston, across 2 r'abouts to T-lights, turn R onto Moorside Rd. Next r'about 2nd exit, park Bowfell Rd OR straight across T-lights past Sainsburys R onto Flixton Rd. 1m gates on R.* Home-made teas. on site, under a large gazebo on a pleasant grassed area. **Combined adm £3, chd free. Sun 19 July (1-4.30).**
We are an attractive allotment site voted by Trafford Council Best in Urmston 2014. We have 81 plots with a mixed group of tenants from young families to retired people, with varying methods of growing a wide variety of crops. The allotments are laid out either side and between green walkways providing a lovely circular walk along beautiful coloured flower borders. Our site is wheelchair friendly throughout with accessible WC. A limited amount of parking is reserved for blue badge holders.
⟨accessibility symbols⟩

GROUP OPENING

33 NEW PORT ERIN GROUP
Thornhill Close, Maine Road & Grammah Avenue, Port Erin, Isle of Man IM9 6NF. Group Co-ordinator Sylvia Constantine, 01624 830607, thieshey@wm.im. *Gardens are between 200 - 600 metres inland of the lighthouse on Port Erin beach. From Castletown A5, R to Port Erin. Straight across r'about. 4th R Ballafesson Rd, 2nd L Bay View Rd. Park on Bay View Rd near Ballakneale Ave (2nd R). Short walk to Thie Shey.* Home-made teas. Refreshments offered in the garden and conservatory of Thie Shey. **Combined adm £3, chd free. Fri 20 Mar, 17 Apr, 15 May, 19 June, 17 July, 21 Aug (10-4).** Visitors also welcome by arrangement Mar to Aug for groups of 4+.

NEW 9 GRAMMAH AVENUE
Peter Hudson.
open 17 July & 21 Aug

NEW MOVILLE
Maine Road. John Moore.
open 20 March, 17 April, 19 June & 17 July

NEW THIE SHEY ⟨symbol⟩
6 Thornhill Close. Sylvia Constantine.
open all dates with extended opening until 7 in May, June & July. From Bay View Rd turn onto Ballakneale Ave (near bus shelter) and first L onto Thornhill Close
01624 830607
thieshey@wm.im

NEW 1 THORNHILL CLOSE
Ann Stevens.
open 20 March & 15 May

With a climate warmed by the Gulf Stream and similar average hours of sunshine to southern England, the Isle of Man is a paradise for gardeners. Port Erin is in the south of the island with a beautiful sheltered bay. Winter storms can cause havoc with salt-sensitive plants, but Manx palms, agapanthus, fuchsias and a wide variety of herbaceous plants thrive in these conditions. Gardening is a passion shared by many in the island and with typical generosity most gardeners will invite you to have a 'skeet' (Manx Gaelic for 'have a nosy').This group typifies the variety of plants, stunning colours and delicious garden produce grown throughout the island. Please obtain tickets from Thie Shey. Parking is very limited outside gardens. All gardens are within 400 metres of one another via footpaths between the roads.
⟨symbols⟩

Church Road
is also home
to the cottage,
sculpture and
grave of the
famous Childe
of Hale . . .

34 PRIMROSE LODGE
Athol Park, Port Erin, Isle Of Man
IM9 6ES. Caroline Couch, 01624
832266, carolinecouch@manx.net.
*Centre of Port Erin village. From
Castletown A5, R to Port Erin village.
L into Droghadfayle Rd, cross railway
lines then R into Athol Park. On L on
junction with Sunnydale Ave.* Light
refreshments. **Adm £3, chd free. Sat
4 July (11-4). Visitors also welcome
by arrangement May to Sept.**
A delightful cottage style garden
gradually evolving after being
replanted from scratch in 2008.
Packed with shrubs and perennials
designed to give interest and colour
all year round. In addition to the lawns
and flower beds there are espalier
fruit trees, a greenhouse and
vegetable and fruit garden.

35 NEW RED ROOFS
Fistard, Port St. Mary, Isle Of Man
IM9 5PG. Maggie Wright, 01624
833050, maggiewright@manx.net.
*¹/₄ m from the centre of Port St Mary.
Drive through PSM & then follow 1
way system into Park Rd. Continue
up the hill on Fistard Rd, until it
narrows & bears L. Garden on R.*
Light refreshments. **Adm £3, chd
free. Share to Women's Aid IOM.
Sun 21 June, Sun 19 July, Sun 6
Sept (11-5). Visitors also welcome
by arrangement Apr to Aug.**
Three distinctly different gardens on 3
sides of the property, each with their
own planting style and colour palette.
Mature shrubs and perennials;
containers and vegetable plot. Some
semi-wild areas. Winner of Port St
Mary in Bloom.

**36 NEW RIBBLETON
LIBRARY**
Ribbleton Hall Drive, Ribbleton,
Preston PR2 6EE. Friends of
Ribbleton Library Gardening Club.
*E of Preston. M6 J31 Tickled Trout,
follow A59 to Preston,R at 1st r'about
Hesketh Arms along Blackpool Rd
A5085, R at 2nd set of T- lights -
Ribbleton Ave. Ribbleton Hall Dr is on
R.* Light refreshments. **Adm £3.50,
chd free. Sun 2 Aug (12-5).**
This is a community garden created
and maintained by a group of
volunteers - the Friends of Ribbleton
Library Gardening Club. We have a
pleasant area with lots of flowers,
annuals and perennials with benches
for sitting and enjoying the colours
and fragrances. Library users and

people who work nearby often use
the garden to read or to eat their
lunch. The garden is all on a flat level.
The library building can be accessed
via a ramp.

37 ◆ THE RIDGES
Weavers Brow (cont. of Cowling
Rd), Limbrick, Chorley PR6 9EB.
Mr & Mrs J M Barlow, 01257
279981, www.bedbreakfast-
gardenvisits.com. *2m SE of Chorley
town centre. From M6 J27, M61 J8.
Follow signs for Chorley A6 then
signs for Cowling & Rivington.
Passing Morrison's up Brooke St,
mini r'about 2nd exit.* Home-made
teas. **Adm £4, chd free. For NGS:
Mon 4 May, Mon 31 Aug (11-5).
For other opening times and
information, please phone or see
garden website.**
3 acres, incl old walled orchard
garden, cottage-style herbaceous
borders, and perfumed rambling
roses through the trees Arch leads to
formal lawn, surrounded by natural
woodland, shrub borders and trees
with contrasting foliage. Woodland
walks and dell. Natural looking
stream, wildlife ponds. Walled water
feature with Italian influence, and
walled herb garden. Classical music
played. Home made cakes, baked
and served by ladies of St James
Church, Chorley. Some gravel paths
and woodland walks not accessible.

GROUP OPENING

**38 NEW ROBY MILL
GARDENS**
Roby Mill, Upholland,
Skelmersdale WN8 0SY,
www.robymillgardens.shutterfly.
com. *Approx 3m from Parbold - 6m
from Wigan. J27 M6 - follow Parbold
A5209. In approx 1¹/₄ m turn L into
Appley Lane North. Continue for 2m
until sharp L bend. Turn R for Lees
Lane, bear L for Bank Brow.* Home-
made teas at Appledene. **Combined
adm £5, chd free. Sat 30, Sun 31
May (12-5).**

NEW APPLEDENE
Bank Brow. Keith & Mavis Till

**NEW DOUGLAS BANK
FARM**
Lees Lane. Mr & Mrs S Gilmore

NEW HALLIWELL FARM
Lees Lane. David & Val
Edwards

Roby Mill Gardens are three
neighbouring gardens of very diverse
styles:- Appledene cottage garden,
on different levels. Rear garden is a
series of terraces with a wide variety
of plants. Side garden is mainly given
over to fruit and vegetables.
Alongside is a fish pond and mini
waterfall. Front garden is stocked with
a wide variety of herbaceous plants.
Douglas Bank Farm country garden
with a laburnum walk leading to a
walled garden planted with
vegetables, fruit trees and
herbaceous borders. Beyond are an
orchard, shrubbery, nuttery and
hornbeam circle up to a formal area.
Untamed areas beyond.
Halliwell Farm 7 acres of garden
surrounding a C17 farmhouse.
Peacocks wander around and with a
wildlife pond and a fish pond looked
over by a bronze of Peter Pan with
Tinkerbell a lovely place to rest.
Home-made jams and chutneys for
sale also Plant sale [pay and collect
by car later] WC available here.

Fish pond
looked over
by a bronze of
Peter Pan with
Tinkerbell a lovely
place to rest . . .

39 THE SECRET VALLEY
The Reach, off Hopefold Drive,
Worsley, Manchester M28 3PN.
Sally Berry, 7999422731,
sallyuk@gmail.com,
www.thesecretvalley.com. *7¹/₂ m
from central Manchester. 1¹/₂ m from
J13 M60. Straight over r'about onto
Walkden Rd, at 1st T-lights turn R
onto A580, Take 1st L onto Old
Clough Lane, turn L at T-junction onto
A6. Park on A6 please. No parking on
The Reach.* Light refreshments. **Adm
£5, chd free. Sun 5 Apr, Sun 3 May,
Sat 6, Sun 7 June, Sun 5 July, Sun
2 Aug, Sun 6 Sept (11-5). Visitors
also welcome by arrangement Mar
to Sept.**

Dutton Hall

This reclaimed space was once an inaccessible swamp filled with rubbish and noxious weeds (including invasive species such as Himalayan Bolsom and Japanese Knotweed). The space has now been transformed into a water garden with ponds, streams, waterfalls, islands and a lake. It is a haven for waterfowl and local wildlife (including swans, geese, coots, moorhens, grebes) The space is an ongoing family project to create and protect habitats for local wildlife. We are in the 4th year of a 6 year plan of action to transform this area and this is the first time visitors can come and visit.

GROUP OPENING

40 ▶ SEFTON PARK GARDENS
Sefton Drive, Sefton Park, Liverpool L8 3SD. *1m S of Liverpool city centre. From end of M62 take A5058 Queens Drive ring rd S through Allerton to Sefton Park. Parking roadside in Sefton Park.* Home-made teas. **Combined adm £5, chd free. Sun 5 July (12-5).**

NEW ▶ BUCKINGHAM HOUSE
Croxteth Drive. Val Covey

NEW ▶ THE COMMUNITY ORCHARD AND WILDLIFE GARDEN
Arundel Avenue. The Society of Friends.
From end of M 62, take A5058 Queens Dr ring rd S across Allerton Rd to Sefton Park. Parking roadside in Sefton Park www.tann.org.uk

NEW ▶ FERN GROVE COMMUNITY GARDEN
Liverpool City Council

PARKMOUNT
38 Ullet Road. Jeremy Nicholls.
L17 3BP

SEFTON PARK ALLOTMENTS
Greenbank Drive. Sefton Park Allotments Society.
L17 1AS Next door to Sefton Park cricket club

SEFTON VILLA
Patricia Williams.
L8 3SD
Visitors also welcome by arrangement Mar to Sept.
0151 281 3687
seftonvilla@live.co.uk

YORK HOUSE GARDENS
Croxteth Drive. Jean Niblock & Your Housing

A varied group showing a range of city gardening, from the long colour themed herbaceous borders at Park Mount to the 6 acres of vegetables and flowers of the allotments. A Community Garden featuring raised beds, and a Community Orchard with young fruit trees in the former Quaker Burial ground join the scheme this year. A second inspirational garden surrounding a tower block also joins in with roses, herbaceous borders and colourful containers. Surprises and rare and unusual plants at Park Mount as well as Paddy Christian's special plants for sale and refreshments. The small walled garden at Sefton Villa is secluded and tranquil, with rare plants for sale and an enclosed Japanese garden. Beekeeping demonstration at Fern Grove Community Garden at 2pm. Children's activities also at Fern Grove. Wheelchair access at York House, Buckingham House and wheelchair access WC at Sefton Park allotments.

41 SILVER BIRCHES
Rawlinson Lane, Heath Charnock, Chorley PR7 4DE. Margaret & John Hobbiss, 01257 480411. *2¹/₂ m S of Chorley. From the A6 turn into Wigan Lane (A5106). After 0.4m turn L into Rawlinson Lane. Silver Birches is 0.2m on L. Disabled parking only next to the house.* Home-made teas. **Adm £3, chd free.** Share to St George's Church, Chorley. **Sat 25, Sun 26 July (1-5).** Visitors also welcome by arrangement July to Aug.
The garden has evolved from a family garden into one with a variety of features. There are herbaceous borders, sunken shaded dell, an African hut, lawns, 2 ponds, polytunnel, vegetable plot and orchard. The embankment of a disused railway has been turned into rockeries with a wood of native trees. There are paths for exploring which lead to the nearby Leeds-Liverpool canal. Wheelchair access is possible to many areas of the garden.

 ♿ ❀ ☕

42 SOUTHLANDS
12 Sandy Lane, Stretford M32 9DA. Maureen Sawyer & Duncan Watmough, 0161 283 9425, moe@southlands12.com, www.southlands12.com. *3m S of Manchester. Sandy Lane (B5213) is situated off A5181 (A56) ¹/₄ m from M60 J7.* Home-made teas. Cake-away service (take a slice of your favourite cake home). **Adm £3.50, chd free. Sat 11, Sun 12 July (1-6).** Visitors also welcome by arrangement June to Aug guided tours for groups over 10.
Artist's multi-award winning, inspirational s facing garden unfolding into a series of beautiful garden 'rooms' each with its own theme incl courtyard, Mediterranean, ornamental and woodland garden. Organic kitchen garden with large glasshouse containing vines and tomatoes. Extensive herbaceous borders, stunning containers of exotics, succulents and annuals, 2 ponds and water feature. Featured in Garden News magazine, Lancashire Life magazine and Rustica magazine.

 ❀ ☕

43 THE STONES & ROSES GARDEN
White Coppice Farm, White Coppice, Chorley PR6 9DF. Raymond & Linda Smith, 01257 277633, stonesandroses@btinternet.com,

www.stonesandroses.org. *3m NE of Chorley. J8 M61 (next to the Mormon Temple & Botany Bay) take A674 to Blackburn, 3rd R to Heapey & White Coppice. Parking up hill next to the garden.* Home-made teas. **Adm £3.50, chd free. Sat 18, Sun 19 July (10.30-4.30).** Visitors also welcome by arrangement July individuals may be added to groups 7 - 24 July.
The garden where the cows used to live set in the beautiful hamlet of White Coppice with wonderful views. Sunken rose garden, fountains, waterfalls, herbaceous borders, all with colour themed planting and formal kitchen garden. Fruit tree walk down to the Gentleman's Lodge with wild flower planting. Wonderful walking area with beautiful cricket field. Featured in Lancashire Life. Gravel paths ³/₄ of garden accessible by wheelchair and entrance into the house.

 ♿ ❀ ❀ 🚌 ☕

GROUP OPENING

44 THE STUBBINS GARDENS
Ramsbottom, Bury BL0 0SD. *4m N of Bury. Exit at J1 M66 turn R onto A56 signed Ramsbottom, continue straight until yellow NGS signs.* Home-made teas at 1 School Court. **Combined adm £3.50, chd free. Sun 12 July (12-5).**

 AREVINTI 🛌
 1 School Court. Lavinia Tod
 01706 822474
 vinnie.tod@hotmail.com

 NEW 155 BOLTON ROAD NORTH
 David Ireland.
 As you climb the hill garden on R, behind houses just before Stubbins Primary School

 NUTWOOD
 3 School Court. Sheila Sherris.
 2¹/₂ m on main rd, past The Duckworth Arms on R, L over bridge, L at r'about

 NEW 4 SCHOOL COURT
 Barbara Morris

A fine opportunity to see 4 different examples of how to make small gardens into attractive areas. Water features, mixed planting, unusual ornamentation, mirror, statuary and much more besides. Nutwood a traditional garden with lawn, clematis, sweet peas, delphiniums, lupins. Variety of hanging baskets, troughs

and containers. Arevinti has 3 gardens rooms- court yard garden with topiary, curvicular garden with lawns raised pond interesting planting leading to church yard garden with herbaceous borders. Tea and cakes served here in our flower filled garden room shaded with vine and thornless blackberry. 4 School Court,a walled garden with colour coordinated planting described as artist meets cottage garden. 155 Bolton Rd North a well designed shaded garden on an usual plot with collection of hostas. An area rich in history in a rural setting, wood, hills, waterfalls and steam trains also in Ramsbottom. Across the rd is the hamlet of Chatterton site of the 1826 riots. The church is open when we open. Partial wheelchair access in 3 gardens.

 ♿ ❀ ☕

> The garden where the cows used to live set in the beautiful hamlet of White Coppice with wonderful views . . .

45 THIE-NY-CHIBBYR
Surby Road, Surby, Port Erin, Isle Of Man IM9 6TA. Mike & Wendy Ingram. *1m from Port Erin. From Douglas, take A7 through Colby to Ballachurry. Take 1st R then R again, (B47 to Fleshwick). At top of hill fork L, 2nd house on L.* Home-made teas. **Adm £3, chd free. Sun 21 June (12-5).**
Hillside cottage garden which has evolved from three long, narrow gardens. Small lawns, a variety of mixed colourful borders, patios and interesting nooks and crannies. Small pond, stone troughs and containers. Shrubs maintained to enjoy the superb views over the south of the Island. Gravel drive.

 ♿ ❀ ☕

46 ▶ VARLEY FARM

Anna Lane, Forest Becks, Bolton-by-Bowland, Clitheroe BB7 4NZ. Mr & Mrs B Farmer, 078876 38436, varleyforestbecks@btinternet.com. *7m N of Clitheroe. A59 off at Sawley follow Settle 2nd L after Copy Nook onto Settle Rd turn L at rd sign on L. Follow lane 1m to a sharp R hand bend garden on L.* Home-made teas. **Visitors welcome by arrangement July to Aug for groups of 10+. Adm £6 incl tea, coffee and a slice of cake.**

1½ -acre garden that's been developing from 2004. Varley Farm is 700ft above sea level with views across the Forest of Bowland and Pendle. Herbaceous lawned cottage garden, flagged herb garden and walled gravel garden, steps to orchard and organic kitchen garden. Stream and pond area planted in 2009 still maturing with a grassed walk through natural meadow and wild flower meadow.

47 ▶ WADDOW LODGE GARDEN

Clitheroe Road, Waddington, Clitheroe BB7 3HQ. Liz & Peter Foley, www.gardentalks.co.uk. *1½ m N of Clitheroe. From M6 J31 take A59 (Preston-Skipton). A671 to Clitheroe then B6478. 1st house on L in village. Parking available on rd before entering village; blue badges in drive parking area on gravel.* Home-made teas. **Adm £3.50, chd free. Sun 24 May, Sun 19 July (1-5).** Inspirational 2-acre organic garden for all seasons surrounding Georgian house (not open) with views to Pendle and Bowland. An enthusiast's collection of many unusual plants with herbaceous borders, large island beds, shrubs, heathers, rhododendrons, small mature wooded area, old fashioned and hybrid roses. Extensive kitchen garden of vegetables and soft fruit, interesting heritage apple orchard, herbs, alpines and greenhouse plus developing wildlife meadow. Colourful containers. Some gravel/bark paths, otherwise level surfaces.

&♿ ✿ ☕

GROUP OPENING

48 ▶ NEW WARTON GARDENS

Warton LA5 9PJ. *1½ m N of Carnforth. From M6 J35 take A601M NW for 1m, then N on A6 for 0.7m turn L signed Warton Old Rectory.*

Warton Village 1m down Borwick Lane. From Carnforth pass train stn and follow signs Warton & Silverdale. Home-made teas at 111 Main Street. **Combined adm £3.50, chd free. Sat 20, Sun 21 June (11-4.30).**

NEW ▶ 2 CHURCH HILL AVENUE

Mr & Mrs J Street. *S end of village opp The Malt Shovel PH*

NEW ▶ 111 MAIN STREET

Mr & Mrs J Spendlove. *In the centre of village opp Ashleigh Interiors*

NEW ▶ TUDOR HOUSE

137 Main Street. Mr & Mrs T Singleton. *N end of village on corner of Main St & Croftlands*

The 3 gardens are spread across the village and offer a wide variety of planting and design ideas incl cottage charm, unusual herbaceous and more formal approaches.

✿ ☕

49 ▶ NEW WARTON HALL

Lodge Lane, Lytham, Lytham St. Annes FY8 5RP. Nicola Thompson, www.total-art.co.uk. *Lytham 10mins J3 exit M55. L for Kirkham, follow signs for Wrea Green, L towards Warton to the BAE T-lights, R, Lodge Lane on R after The Golf Academy & 2m before Lytham town centre.* Home-made teas. Light refreshments in the week. **Adm £3, chd free. Daily Sat 9 May to Sun 17 May (11-4).** A small Georgian Manor house rebuilt in 1871, with woodland bluebell walk and garden sculpture trail in 4 acres of natural gardens with vegetable patch and bog garden. Impressive 400 year old Weeping Hornbeam tree in the centre of the lawn. Story Telling, in the tepee each day and Children's Trail. Please check NGS website for times of Story Telling and Music. The main driveway is gravel and may be difficult to push a wheelchair on but the woodland paths are compacted and should be fine.

&♿ ☕

50 ▶ WEDGWOOD

Shore Road, Hesketh Bank, Preston PR4 6XP. Denis & Susan Watson, 01772 816509, heskethbank@aol.com, www.wedgwoodgarden.com. *10m SW of Preston & 8m E of Southport. From Preston: A59. Turn R at Coe Lane, Tarleton T-lights. Turn R onto Hesketh Lane for 2½ m onto Shore Rd. Garden 1.3m on L. Park on rd. Yellow NGS sign in hedge.* Tea. **Adm £5, chd free. Visitors welcome by arrangement** June to July adm incl tea and biscuits.

1-acre country garden containing gravel garden with pots, formal pond, 2 lawns surrounded by extensive herbaceous borders in sun or shade, with mature trees, 50ft square glasshouse, 50ft x 30ft sheltered patio, leading to 90ft parterre with colour themed beds, archways, pergolas and rose covered gazebo, wild flower meadow, fruit trees. Wood chip paths in parterre.

&♿ ✿ 🚐 ☕

WE ARE MACMILLAN. CANCER SUPPORT

2015 sees the NGS total to Macmillan pass £15 million

51 ▶ WEEPING ASH GARDEN

Bents Garden & Home, Warrington Road, Glazebury WA3 5NS. John Bent, www.bents.co.uk. *15m W of Manchester. Located next to Bents Garden & Home, just off the East Lancs Rd A580 at Greyhound r'about near Leigh. Follow brown 'Garden Centre' signs.* **Adm £3, chd free. Suns 8, 15, 22 Feb, 1 Mar, 19 Apr (12-4); Suns 14, 21, 28 Feb 2016.** Created by retired nurseryman and photographer John Bent, Weeping Ash is a garden of all-yr interest with beautiful display of early snowdrops. Broad sweeps of colour lend elegance to this beautiful garden. Weeping Ash Garden is located immed adjacent to Bents Garden & Home with its award winning Fresh Approach Restaurant and children's adventure play area. Partial wheelchair access and weather dependent.

✿ 🚐 ☕

LEICESTERSHIRE & RUTLAND

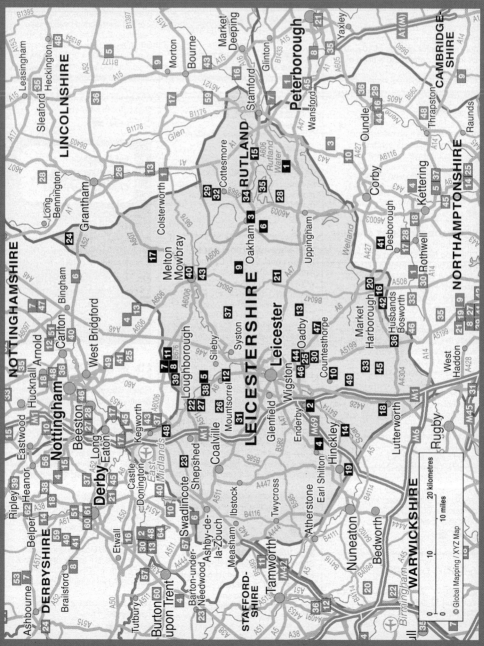

Leicestershire & Rutland

Leicestershire is very much in the centre of England, and has a diverse landscape and wide range of settlements.

Our open gardens are of corresponding variety. From compact Victorian terraces with inspirational planting, large country houses with broad vistas, an arboretum with four national 'champion' trees, to an allotment with over 100 plots. Most gardens welcome groups, sell plants and offer tea and cake.

Confident in the knowledge that your donation goes to wonderful causes, you can look for inspiration for your own garden or plot, or simply take pleasure looking at beautiful gardens.

'Much in Little' is Rutland's motto. They say small is beautiful and never were truer words said.

Rutland is rural England at its best. Honey-coloured stone cottages make up pretty villages nestling amongst rolling hills; the passion for horticulture is everywhere you look, from stunning gardens to the hanging baskets and patio boxes showing off seasonal blooms in our two attractive market towns of Oakham and Uppingham.

There's so much to see in and around Rutland whatever the time of year, including many wonderful NGS gardens.

Left: University Botanic Garden

Leicestershire & Rutland Volunteers

Leicestershire

County Organiser
Colin Olle
01858 575791
colin.olle@tiscali.co.uk

County Treasurer
Martin Shave
01455 556633
martinshave@kilworthaccountancy.co.uk

Publicity
Janet Currie
01509 212191
janet.currie@me.com

Assistant County Organisers
Mary Hayward
01162 884018
maryehayward@googlemail.com

Verena Olle
01858 575791
colin.olle@tiscali.co.uk

David & Beryl Wyrko
01664 840385

Rutland

County Organiser
Rose Dejardin
01572 737557
rosedejardin@btopenworld.com

County Treasurer
David Wood
01572 737465
rdavidwood@easynet.co.uk

Publicity
Jane Alexander-Orr
01572 737368
janealexanderorr@hotmail.com

Leicestershire & Rutland

Booklet Coordinator
Mary Hayward
01162 884018
maryehayward@googlemail.com

Bring a bag for plants – help us give more to charity

Opening Dates

All entries subject to change.
For latest information check www.ngs.org.uk

February

Sunday 22
19 7 Hall Road

March

Sunday 1
24 The Homestead
47 Westview
Sunday 22
20 Hammond Arboretum

April

26 Long Close (every Wednesday to Sunday)
Sunday 12
37 Parkside

May

26 Long Close (every Wednesday to Sunday)
Sunday 3
3 Barleythorpe Gardens
21 Hedgehog Hall
43 Tresillian House
Monday 4
21 Hedgehog Hall
Sunday 17
28 Manton Gardens
47 Westview
Sunday 24
10 NEW Countesthorpe Gardens

17 Goadby Marwood Hall
30 Mill House
34 The Old Vicarage, Burley
Sunday 31
2 12 Alexander Avenue
9 Burrough Gardens
38 Quorn Orchard Gardens

June

26 Long Close (every Wednesday to Sunday)
Wednesday 3
41 Stoke Albany House
42 Thorpe Lubenham Hall

Festival Weekend

Sunday 7
10 NEW Countesthorpe Gardens
45 Walton Gardens
Wednesday 10
41 Stoke Albany House
45 Walton Gardens
Saturday 13
27 Loughborough Gardens
Sunday 14
7 88 Brook Street
8 109 Brook Street
11 Cradock Cottage
27 Loughborough Gardens
32 The Old Hall
33 The Old Stables
Wednesday 17
41 Stoke Albany House
Thursday 18
22 134 Herrick Road (Evening)

Saturday 20
29 NEW Market Overton Gardens
Sunday 21
6 Braunston Gardens
16 2 Fairway
Wednesday 24
41 Stoke Albany House
Thursday 25
34 The Old Vicarage, Burley (Evening)
Sunday 28
15 Empingham Gardens
16 2 Fairway
21 Hedgehog Hall
48 Whatton Gardens

July

26 Long Close (every Wednesday to Sunday to July 12)
Wednesday 1
41 Stoke Albany House
Sunday 5
23 Hill Park Farm
31 Mountain Ash
35 Orchard House
43 Tresillian House
Wednesday 8
41 Stoke Albany House
Sunday 12
1 Acre End
5 Beveridge Street Gardens
18 Green Wicket Farm
30 Mill House
31 Mountain Ash
Wednesday 15
18 Green Wicket Farm
Saturday 18
13 Cupplesfield
Sunday 19
13 Cupplesfield
40 119 Scalford Road
49 Willoughby Gardens
Sunday 26
36 Orchard House

August

Sunday 2
25 NEW Knighton Sensory
Sunday 9
44 University Botanic Garden
Sunday 30
43 Tresillian House
Monday 31
47 Westview

September

26 Long Close (every Wednesday to Sunday)
Sunday 6
46 Washbrook Allotments

October

26 Long Close open every Wednesday to Sunday to Oct 11)
Sunday 11
20 Hammond Arboretum
Sunday 18
43 Tresillian House

Gardens open to the public

48 Whatton Gardens

By arrangement only

4 Barracca
12 7 The Crescent
14 Dairy Cottage
39 Ridgewold Farm

Also open by arrangement

1 Acre End
5 Apricot Cottage, Beveridge Street Gardens
7 88 Brook Street
8 109 Brook Street
10 NEW 2 Elliots Yard, Countesthorpe Gardens
17 Goadby Marwood Hall
18 Green Wicket Farm
21 Hedgehog Hall
22 134 Herrick Road
24 The Homestead
25 NEW Knighton Sensory
26 Long Close
30 Mill House
31 Mountain Ash
32 The Old Hall
33 The Old Stables
34 The Old Vicarage, Burley
36 Orchard House
37 Parkside
40 119 Scalford Road
43 Tresillian House
47 Westview
49 Farmway, Willoughby Gardens

143 Herrick Road, Loughborough Gardens

Since our foundation we have donated more than £42.5 million to charity

The Gardens

1 ACRE END

The Jetties, North Luffenham
LE15 8JX. Jim & Mima Bolton,
01780 720906, mmkb@mac.com.
*7m SE of Oakham. Via Manton &
Edith Weston, 7m SW of Stamford via
Ketton. 2m off A47 through Morcott
village.* Light refreshments at North
Luffenham Community Centre. **Adm
£5, chd free. Sun 12 July (11-5).**
Visitors also welcome by
arrangement June to Aug.
1 acre garden, imaginatively
designed, intensively planted, incl
knot garden, oriental courtyard
garden, mixed borders, circular lawn
with island beds, herb and scented
garden. Working fruit and vegetable
garden, long herbaceous borders,
woodland garden. Many unusual
trees, shrubs, herbaceous perennials,
tender exotics in containers. All
organically managed to encourage
wildlife. Paintings, cards, crafts.
Wildlife wood carvings display.
Featured in GGG. Mainly grass paths
and lawns, some gravel.

  ♿ ✿ ☕

2 12 ALEXANDER AVENUE

Enderby, Leicester LE19 4NA. Mr &
Mrs J Beeson. *4m S of Leicester.
From M1 J21 take A5460 to Fosse
Park, turn R on B4114. Turn R to
Enderby at next r'about, straight on
to church then follow yellow NGS
signs.* Home-made teas. **Adm £2,
chd free. Sun 31 May (11-5).**
Our small town garden has been
carefully designed to make full use of
the space available and to provide
interest all yr-round. We have
dispensed with the lawn giving us
space to create different areas in the
garden, incl a pond, and to
accommodate a wide variety of
plants chosen for colour and to
attract wildlife. Our garden is an
extension of the house, a place to
potter, relax and enjoy. Some gravel
areas.

  ♿ ✿ ☕

GROUP OPENING

3 BARLEYTHORPE GARDENS

Barleythorpe, nr Oakham
LE15 7EQ. *1m from Oakham on
A6006 towards Melton Mowbray. Car
park in Pasture Lane 1st L in
Barleythorpe by post box. Please
park in field on L not on lane.* Home-

The Old Stables

made teas at Dairy Cottage.
Combined adm £5, chd free. Share
to East Midlands Immediate Care
Scheme. **Sun 3 May (2-5).**

BARLEYTHORPE HOUSE
Richard Turner

DAIRY COTTAGE
Mr & Mrs W Smith

THE LODGE
Dr & Mrs T J Gray

Visit 3 beautiful gardens in this
Rutland village. Dairy Cottage (opp
car park), is a cottage style garden at
rear with interesting and unusual
shrubs and spring bulbs.
Paved/walled garden to front (with
pond) and lime hedge. Orchard with
spring bulbs and unusual shrubs and
trees. The Lodge (next door), with
mixed flowers within walled garden,
½ lawn and part walled kitchen
garden with small stretch of gravel
path between lawned area and
vegetable garden. Follow path
alongside Dairy Cottage, turn left into
Barleythorpe House, 8 Manor Lane -
offering both water and woodland.
Flowering shrubs, large weeping
trees, small lake and woodland walk.

  ♿ 🏵 ✿ ☕

4 BARRACCA

Ivydene Close, Earl Shilton
LE9 7NR. Mr & Mrs John & Sue
Osborn, 01455 842609,
susan.osborn1@btinternet.com,
www.barraccagardens.co.uk. *10m
W of Leicester. From A47 after
entering Earl Shilton, Ivydene Close is
4th on L from Leicester side of A47.*
**Adm £6, chd free. Visitors
welcome by arrangement** May to
July for groups 10+. Adm incl
tea/coffee and cake.
1 acre garden with lots of different
areas, silver birch walk, wildlife pond
with seating, apple tree garden,
Mediterranean planted area and
lawns surrounded with herbaceous
plants and shrubs. Patio area with
climbing roses and wisteria. There is
also a utility garden with greenhouse,
vegetables in beds, herbs and
perennial flower beds, lawn and fruit
cage. Part of the old gardens owned
by the Cotton family who used to
open approx 9 acres to the public in
the 1920's. Partial wheelchair access.

  ♿ ☕

GROUP OPENING

5 BEVERIDGE STREET GARDENS

Barrow upon Soar LE12 8PL. *2m S of Loughborough. Follow NGS signs & turn opp church.* Combined adm £3, chd free. Sun 12 July (11.30-5).

APRICOT COTTAGE
Jane Atkinson
Visitors also welcome by arrangement Mar to Sept.
01509 414528
atkinsonjane@me.com

THE OLD WALLED GARDEN
Roger & Jo Chappell

An old Leicestershire village with pleasant walks along banks of the R Soar. The two gardens are very different. Apricot Cottage is small and very modern. The Old Walled Garden is much larger and as the name suggests, enclosed by a wall which creates its own microclimate.

GROUP OPENING

6 BRAUNSTON GARDENS

Braunston, nr.Oakham LE15 8QS. *Braunston & Braunston Rd in Oakham direction. Quaintree Hall is located in Braunston, 2m S of Oakham. Hill Top Farm is ¹/₂ m out of Oakham in the direction of Braunston.* Home-made teas at Hill Top Farm. Combined adm £5, chd free. Sun 21 June (2-6).

HILL TOP FARM 🏠
Jane & William Cross
01572 755744
janecross49@yahoo.co.uk
www.cross-in-rutland.co.uk

QUAINTREE HALL
Mrs Caroline Lomas

Two large gardens belonging to keen gardening friends with different styles. Hill Top Farm - Fabulous views of the surrounding countryside from this aptly named property. The terrace surrounding the house is host to containers and beds packed with sun loving plants. Paths invite the visitor to stroll amongst borders of interesting shrubs and perennials. A woodland area with hazel walk has recently been extended with plantings of oak and fir and a new wildlife pond. Quaintree Hall in Braunston - An established garden surrounding the medieval hall house (not open) incl a formal box parterre to the front of the

house, a woodland walk, formal walled garden with yew hedges, a small picking garden and a terraced courtyard garden with conservatory. A wide selection of interesting plants can be enjoyed here, each carefully selected for its specific site by the knowledgeable garden owner. Some gravel and steps.

♿ 🐕 ⊗ ☕

WE ARE MACMILLAN. CANCER SUPPORT

The NGS is Macmillan's largest single donor

7 88 BROOK STREET

Wymeswold LE12 6TU. Adrian & Ita Cooke, 01509 880155, itacooke@btinternet.com. *4m NE of Loughborough. From A6006 Wymeswold turn S by church onto Stockwell, then E along Brook St. Roadside parking on Brook St.* Combined adm £4, chd free. Sun 14 June (11-5). Combined with Craddock Cottage and 109 Brook Street. Visitors also welcome by arrangement May to June.

The ¹/₂ acre garden is set on a hillside, which provides lovely views across the village, and comprises 3 distinct areas: firstly, a cottage style garden; then a water garden with a stream and champagne pond; and finally at the top there is a vegetable plot, small orchard and wild flower meadow. The ponds are a breeding ground for great crested and common newts, frogs and toads.

🐕 ⊗

8 109 BROOK STREET

Wymeswold LE12 6TT. Maggie & Steve Johnson, 01509 880866, sameuk@tiscali.co.uk. *4m NE of Loughborough. From A6006 Wymeswold turn S onto Stockwell, then E along Brook St. Roadside parking along Brook St. Steep drive with limited disabled parking at house.* Home-made teas. Combined adm £4, chd free. Sun 14 June

(11-5). Combined with 88 Brook Street and Cradock Cottage. Visitors also welcome by arrangement May to June for groups 10+. Min 2 wks notice please.

S facing ³/₄ acre gently sloping garden with views to open country. Mature garden much improved. Patio with roses and clematis, wildlife and fish ponds, mixed borders, vegetable garden, orchard, hot garden and woodland garden. Something for everyone. Demonstration of rain water harvesting on limited budget. Some gravel paths.

♿ 🐕 ⊗ ☕

GROUP OPENING

9 BURROUGH GARDENS

Burrough on the Hill, Nr Melton Mowbray LE14 2QZ. *In the village of Burrough on the Hill. Close to B6047. 10 mins from A606. 20 mins from Melton Mowbray.* Home-made teas at Burrough Hall. Combined adm £5, chd free. Sun 31 May (2-5).

BURROUGH HALL
Richard & Alice Cunningham

BURROUGH HOUSE
Roger & Sam Weatherby

2 Large gardens, both with magnificent views over High Leicestershire. Burrough House, in the middle of the village, has an extensive garden surrounding a former stone farmhouse with stunning views over the surrounding countryside. The current owners are adding to the former established garden to create a series of vistas and spaces and maximise the views in and out of the garden with the use of clipped hedges and avenues. Burrough Hall, outside the village between Somerby and Burrough, was built in 1867 as a classic Leicestershire hunting lodge. The garden, framed by mature trees and shrubs, was extensively redesigned by garden designer George Carter in 2007. This family garden, which continues to develop for the enjoyment of all generations, consists of extensive lawns, mixed borders, a vegetable garden and woodland walks. There will be a small collection of vintage and classic cars on display at Burrough Hall.

♿ ⊗ ☕

GROUP OPENING

🔟 NEW COUNTESTHORPE GARDENS

Countesthorpe, Leicester LE8 5RG. *5m S Leicester. From r'bout in centre of village follow yellow NGS arrows.* Home-made teas. **Combined adm £3, chd free. Sun 24 May, Sun 7 June (11-5).**

NEW 2 ELLIOTS YARD

Sue Hobson
Visitors also welcome by arrangement May to June, max 15 visitors.
01162 788070
martinandsuehobson@btinternet.com

NEW 4 PACKMAN GREEN

Roger Whitmore

Both gardens are close to the village centre, but about 400yds apart. Elliots yard is a small sheltered garden planted with an emphasis on variegated and contrasting foliage, interspersed with some seasonal flowers. A water feature and small pond add additional interest. 4 Packman Green is a small town house garden, which is packed with hardy perennials and surrounded by climbing roses, clematis, honeysuckle and jasmine, making it an enclosed peaceful haven filled with colour and scent.

🔟🔟 CRADOCK COTTAGE

74 Brook St, Wymeswold LE12 6TU. Mike & Carol Robinson. *4m NE of Loughborough. From A6006 Wymeswold turn S by church onto Stockwell, then E along Brook St. Roadside parking on Brook St.* Home-made teas at 109 Brook Street. **Combined adm £4, chd free. Sun 14 June (11-5).** Combined with 109 and 88 Brook Street.
³/₄ acre S facing country garden developed over the last 14yrs. Paddock beyond with attractive views of the village and countryside. Colour themed borders with formal mature hedging. Enclosed vegetable garden.

🔟🔟 7 THE CRESCENT

Rothley LE7 7RW. Mrs Fiona Dunkley, 01162 376301, fiona.dunkley@btinternet.com. *Off Montsorrel Lane, Rothley. Parking on Montsorrel Lane.* Home-made teas.

Adm £2, chd free. Visitors welcome by arrangement May to Aug for groups 10 - 30 max.
Small, well designed garden with interesting and unusual plants. Good display of alliums in spring. Many diverse grasses and bamboos combined with verbena bonariensis create a very special effect in late summer and autumn.

Small in size but big on ideas . . .

🔟🔟 CUPPLESFIELD

2 Stoughton Road, Gaulby LE7 9BB. Roger & Ruth Harris. *6m E of Leicester. Follow NGS yellow arrows.* **Sat 18, Sun 19 July (2-5.30).** One acre garden packed full of surprises! Themes range from a contemporary Japanese style area to a long informal herbaceous border and Piet Oudolf inspired prairie beds. Interesting borders incl a hidden jungle, a small wild life pond and low walled potager. The garden is alive with sculptures and hedge art which add that extra interest. Such a lot in so little. Featured in Garden News. Most parts accessible by wheelchair in dry conditions but reduced when wet.

🔟🔟 DAIRY COTTAGE

15 Sharnford Road, Sapcote LE9 4JN. Mrs Norah Robinson-Smith, 01455 272398, nrobinsons@yahoo.co.uk. *9m SW of Leicester. Sharnford Rd joins Leicester Rd in Sapcote to B4114 Coventry Rd. Follow NGS signs at both ends.* Home-made teas. **Adm £3, chd free. Visitors welcome by arrangement** May to Aug.
From a walled garden with colourful mixed borders to a potager approached along a woodland path, this mature cottage garden combines extensive perennial planting with

many unusual shrubs and specimen trees. More than 90 clematis and climbing roses are trained up pergolas, arches and into trees 50ft high - so don't forget to look up!

GROUP OPENING

🔟🔟 EMPINGHAM GARDENS

Empingham LE15 8PS. *Empingham Village. 5m E of Oakham, 5m W of Stamford on A606.* Home-made teas at Prebendal House. **Combined adm £5, chd free. Sun 28 June (2-5.30).**

LAVANDER COTTAGE

Virginia Todd

PREBENDAL HOUSE

Mr J Partridge

2 gardens the absolute opposite in scale in a lovely Rutland village. Park and start your visit at Prebendal House, next door to the Church and explore the 4 acres surrounding the house (not open), built in 1688 as a summer palace for the Bishop of Lincoln. Incl are extensive herbaceous borders, topiary and a water garden. In complete contrast is the tiny garden of Lavander Cottage in Nook Lane, opp the White Horse Inn. Developed over 10yrs into a series of rooms linked by rose and honeysuckle arches and packed with climbing, shrub and standard roses, richly underplanted with lavender, alliums and clematis and full of colour, scent and the occasional surprise. Wheelchair access at Prebendal House only.

🔟🔟 2 FAIRWAY

Market Harborough LE16 9QL. Mr & Mrs J Coombs. *³/₄ m N of Harborough, L off Leicester Rd. Follow yellow NGS arrows.* Light refreshments. **Adm £2, chd free. Sun 21, Sun 28 June (10.30-4.30).** A small plantwomans garden started 3yrs ago, planting had to be rare, unusual, a touch of normal but only plants we really love. Come and see just what can be done in a short time. There are lots of plants and grasses, some trees, some exotics, a real mix of old and new ideas and some very interesting climbers. Small in size but planted with big ideas. Cream teas, coffee and cake, lunchtime savouries all on offer.

88 Brook Street

17 GOADBY MARWOOD HALL

Goadby Marwood LE14 4LN. Mr & Mrs Westropp, 01664 464202. *4m NW of Melton Mowbray. Between Waltham on the Wolds & Eastwell.* Tea in Village Hall. **Adm £5, chd free. Sun 24 May (11-4). Visitors also welcome by arrangement.**
Redesigned in 2000 by the owner based on C18 plans. A chain of 5 lakes (covering 10 acres) and several ironstone walled gardens all interconnected. Lakeside woodland walk. Planting for yr-round interest. Landscaper trained under plantswoman Rosemary Verey at Barnsley House. Beautiful C13 church open. Featured on Castles in the Country on BBC. Gravel paths and lawns.

18 GREEN WICKET FARM

Ullesthorpe Road, Bitteswell, Lutterworth LE17 4LR. Mrs Anna Smith, 01455 552646, greenfarmbitt@hotmail.com. *2m NW of Lutterworth J20 M1. From Lutterworth follow signs through Bitteswell towards Ullesthorpe. Green Wicket Farm is situated behind*
Bitteswell Cricket Club. Field parking available. Home-made teas. **Adm £3, chd free. Sun 12, Wed 15 July (2-5). Visitors also welcome by arrangement June to Aug. Groups 10+.**
A developing garden created in 2008 on a working farm. Clay soil and very exposed but beginning to look established. Many unusual hardy plants along with a lot of old favourites have been used to provide a long season of colour and interest. Formal pond and water features. Some gravel paths.

19 7 HALL ROAD

Burbage, Hinckley LE10 2LU. Don & Mary Baker. *Sketchley Manor Est. From M69 J1, take B4109 signed Hinckley. At 2nd r'about follow NGS yellow arrows.* Light refreshments. **Adm £2.50, chd free. Sun 22 Feb (11-5).**
Medium sized garden with a good mix of shrubs, snowdrops, spring bulbs and hellebores. Partial wheelchair access.

20 HAMMOND ARBORETUM

Burnmill Road, Market Harborough LE16 7JG. The Robert Smyth Academy. *15m S of Leicester on A6. From High St, follow signs to The Robert Smyth Academy via Bowden Lane to Burnmill Rd. Park in 1st entrance on L.* Home-made teas. **Adm £3, chd free. Sun 22 Mar, Sun 11 Oct (2-5).**
A site of just under 2½ acres containing an unusual collection of trees and shrubs, many from Francis Hammond's original planting dating from 1913 to 1936 whilst headmaster of the school. Species from America, China and Japan with malus and philadelphus walks and a moat. Proud owners of 4 champion trees identified by national specialist. Guided walks and walk plans available. Some steep slopes.

21 HEDGEHOG HALL

Loddington Road, Tilton on the Hill LE7 9DE. Janet & Andrew Rowe, 01162 597339, janetnandrew@btinternet.com. *8m W of Oakham. 2m N of A47 on B6047 between Melton & Market Harborough.* Follow yellow NGS signs in Tilton towards Loddington. Cream teas. **Adm £3, chd free. Sun 3, Mon 4 May, Sun 28 June (11-5). Visitors also welcome by arrangement May to June for groups 10+.**
½ acre organically managed plant lover's garden. Steps leading to three stone walled terraced borders filled with shrubs, perennials and bulbs. Lavender walk, herb border, beautiful spring garden, colour themed herbaceous borders. Sheltered courtyard with hostas, and acers, Hot terraced border. New this yr - patio built at the top of the terraces overlooking the valley. Cakes for sale. Featured in Garden News. Regret, no wheelchair access to terraced borders.

22 134 HERRICK ROAD

LE11 2BU. Janet Currie, 01509 212191, janet.currie@me.com, www.thesecateur.com. *1m SW of Loughborough. From M1 J23 take A512 Ashby Rd to Loughborgh. At r'about R onto A6004 Epinal Way. At Beacon Rd r'about L, Herrick Rd 1st on R.* Evening Opening **£2, chd 50p, Thur 18 June (4-7). Combined with Loughborough Gardens Sat 13, Sun 14 June (12-5), combined adm £3, chd free. Visitors also**

welcome by arrangement June to Sept.

A small garden brimming with texture, colour and creative flair. Trees, shrubs and climbers give structure. A sitting area surrounded by lilies, raised staging for herbs and alpines. A lawn flanked with deeply curving and gracefully planted beds of perennials growing through handmade willow structures. A shaded area under the Bramley apple tree, raised vegetable beds and potting area. The excellent Secret Craft Fair held during the Loughborough Gardens Group open gardens weekend 13 and 14 June provides additional delight and surprises for visitors who can find specially selected high quality contemporary crafts, many with garden themes, on sale and displayed amongst the plants.

❀ ☕

23 HILL PARK FARM
Dodgeford Lane, Belton LE12 9TE. John & Jean Adkin. *6m W of Loughborough. Dodgeford Lane off B5324 between Belton & Osgathorpe.* Home-made teas. **Adm £3, chd free. Sun 5 July (2-6).**
Beautiful medium sized garden to a working farm. Shrubs, fruit trees and vegetable garden. Rock garden and herbaceous borders brimming with colour. Pergola with clematis and roses, water features, and many planted stone troughs and window boxes.

🏠 ❀ ☕

24 THE HOMESTEAD
Normanton-by-Bottesford NG13 0EP. John & Shirley Palmer, 01949 842745. *8m W of Grantham. From A52, turn N in Bottesford, signed Normanton; last house on R. From A1, 1st house on L.* Tea. **Adm £2.50, chd free. Sun 1 Mar (2-5). Visitors also welcome by arrangement Feb to May.**
³/₄ acre informal plant lover's garden. Vegetable garden, small orchard, woodland area, many hellebores, growing collection (over 100) of snowdrops and some single peonies and salvias. Collections of hostas and sempervivums. National Collection of heliotropes. A garden where plants (incl vegetables) come first to produce a peaceful and relaxed overall effect.

🏠 ❀ ☕

25 NEW KNIGHTON SENSORY
Knighton Park, Leicester LE2 3YQ. Mike Chalk, kpgc@hotmail.co.uk, www.knightonparkgardeningclub.com. *Off A563 (Outer Ring Rd) S of Leicester. From Palmerston Blvd, turn into South Kingsmead Rd then 1st L into Woodbank Rd. Park entrance at end of rd. Enter park, follow path to R, garden then on R.* Light refreshments. **Adm by donation. Sun 2 Aug (1-5). Visitors also welcome by arrangement May to Aug. Groups 12 max.**
This ¹/₄ acre community garden stands in a secluded corner of Knighton Park away from the bustle of the city, It is a feast for all the senses. It incl shrubs, some traditional bedding, herbaceous borders, bog garden with bridge, dry riverbed with wild flowers and wildlife area, Separate area contains raised beds for edibles. Twice awarded outstanding by the It's Your Neighbourhood Scheme.

♿ 🏠 ❀ ☕

A small garden brimming with texture, colour and creative flair . . .

26 LONG CLOSE
Main St, Woodhouse Eaves LE12 8RZ. John Oakland, 01509 890376, longclosegardens@btinternet.com, www.longclose.org.uk. *4m S of Loughborough. Nr M1 J23. From A6, W in Quorn.* **Adm £4, chd 50p. Every Wed, Thur, Fri, Sat & Sun 1 Apr to 12 July and 2 Sept to 11 Oct (10.30-4.30). Also open Bank Holiday Mons. Visitors also welcome by arrangement Apr to July and Sep to Oct. Groups min 15. Tea/coffee and biscuits by request.**
5 acres spring bulbs, rhododendrons, azaleas, camellias, magnolias, many rare shrubs, mature trees, lily ponds; terraced lawns, herbaceous borders,

potager in walled kitchen garden, wild flower meadow walk. Winter, spring, summer and autumn colour, a garden for all seasons.

🏠 ❀ 🚌 ☕

GROUP OPENING

27 LOUGHBOROUGH GARDENS
Herrick Road & Parklands Drive, Loughborough LE11 2BU, www.thesecateur.com. *1m SW Loughborough. From M1 J23 take A512 Ashby Rd to Loughborough. At r'about R onto A6004 Epinal Way. At Beacon Rd r'about L, Herrick Rd 1st on R.* Tea at 134 and 94 Herrick Road, and 47 Parklands Drive. **Combined adm £3, chd free. Sat 13, Sun 14 June (12-5).**

80 HERRICK ROAD
Sarah Fazakerley

NEW 94 HERRICK ROAD
Marion Smith

134 HERRICK ROAD
Janet Currie
(See separate entry)

NEW 47 PARKLANDS DRIVE
Lynda & Alan Burton

This side of Loughborough is a quiet leafy area with a mix of Victorian and mid century homes. The four gardens in this group contain plenty of horticultural and creative interest. 134 Herrick Road is a garden designed for tranquility, wildlife and produce brimming with texture, colour and creative flair. The excellent Secret Craft Fair held during the open gardens weekend provides additional delight and surprises for visitors. 80 Herrick Road is an intriguing garden in several sections linked by a winding path, the owner's collection of dwarf conifers and eight elderly tortoises are of particular interest. 94 Herrick Road is a traditional old fashioned English garden with mainly perennial planting, an interest in hardy geraniums and Heucheras, and home to two active and productive beehives. 47 Parklands Drive has mixed borders with a wide variety of shrubs, herbaceous perennials and bulbs, planted to attract and support wildlife as well as creating an attractive place to sit and relax. Herrick Road Honey will also be on sale.

❀ ☕

Home-made cakes for sale . . . !

GROUP OPENING

28 MANTON GARDENS

Oakham LE15 8SR. *3m N of Uppingham. 3m S of Oakham. Manton is on S shore of Rutland Water ¼ m off A6003. Please park carefully in village.* Ploughman's lunches and home-made teas in Village Hall. **Combined adm £5, chd free. Sun 17 May (12.30-5).**

NEW 22 LYNDON ROAD
Chris & Val Carroll

MANTON GRANGE
Anne & Mark Taylor

MANTON LODGE FARM
Caroline Burnaby-Atkins
www.mantonlodge.co.uk

NEW 3 ST MARY'S ROAD
Ruth Blinch

SHAPINSAY
Mr & Mrs Tony & Jane Bews

5 gardens in small village on S shore of Rutland Water. Manton Grange - 2½ acre garden with interesting trees, shrubs and herbaceous borders. Incl a rose garden, water features, a lime tree walk and clematis pergola. Shapinsay - ⅔ acre garden with mature trees framing views over the Chater Valley, incl a woodland walk, perennial borders, island shrub borders and a stream linking numerous ponds constructed in November 2011 by a local RHS gold medal garden designer. 22 Lyndon Rd - a beautiful combination of cottage garden and unusual plants in overflowing borders, hanging baskets and decorative pots. 3 St Mary's Road - a tiny garden where the use of every available space is maximised to create a series of areas within which to sit and enjoy beds, and numerous pots, packed with plants. Manton Lodge Farm - Stone country house (not open) nestled into hillside, with wonderful views from the steeply sloping gardens. Paths lead through borders of shrubs, roses and perennials. Wheelchair access to Manton Grange and Shapinsay only.

  ♿ ❀ ☕

GROUP OPENING

29 NEW MARKET OVERTON GARDENS

Market Overton, Oakham
LE15 7PP. *7m NE of Oakham. Turn R off Ashwell/Wymondham rd at Teigh.* Home-made teas at the Cricket Pavilion. **Combined adm £5, chd free. Sat 20 June (1.30-5).**

NEW 7 MAIN STREET
Ann Tibbert

NEW 35 THISTLETON ROAD

NEW 37 THISTLETON ROAD
Nick Buff
Richard Carruthers

NEW 45 THISTLETON ROAD
Jean Hutton

NEW 47 THISTLETON ROAD
Jane Smeetem

NEW 49 THISTLETON ROAD
Alan Hubbard

59 THISTLETON ROAD
Wg Cdr Andrew Stewart JP

A Rutland village group visit incl, on Thistleton Rd, 5 tiny, very individual gardens behind a row of pretty red brick terraced house all overlooking the village Cricket Green, and a 1.8 acre garden converted over the last 11yrs into a restful haven for wildlife with large pond, shrubbery, orchard and large colourful perennial beds. At the other end of the village, at 7 Main Street, is an illustration of how to develop a square patch of grass over 4yrs into an interesting garden divided into a series of areas richly planted to provide yr round interest and featuring specimen trees and unusual shrubs and colourful planted pots and containers. Wheelchair access at 59 Thistleton Road and 7 Main Street only.

  ♿ ❀ ☕

30 MILL HOUSE

118 Welford Road, Wigston
LE18 3SN. Mr & Mrs P Measures,
01162 885409,
petemeasures@hotmail.co.uk. *4m S of Leicester. From Leicester to Wigston Magna follow A5199 Welford Rd S towards Kilby, up hill past Mercers Newsagents, 100yds on L.* Home-made teas. **Adm £2.50, chd free. Sun 24 May, Sun 12 July (12-5).** Visitors also welcome by arrangement May to July. Flexible times for groups, max 30.
Walled town garden with an extensive plant variety, many rare and unusual. A plant lovers garden, with interesting designs incorporated in the borders, rockery and scree. It is full of surprises with memorabilia and bygones a reminder of our past. Good variety of reasonably priced plants for sale.

  ❀ ☕

31 MOUNTAIN ASH

140 Ulverscroft Lane, Newtown Linford LE6 0AJ. Mike & Liz Newcombe, 01530 242178, mjnew12@gmail.com. *7m SW of Loughborough, 7m NW of Leicester, 1m NW of Newtown Linford. Head ½ m N along Main St towards Sharpley Hill, fork L into Ulverscroft Lane.* Light refreshments. **Adm £3.50, chd free. Sun 5, Sun 12 July (11-5).** Visitors also welcome by arrangement May to Oct for groups 10+ (afternoon or evening).
2 acre SW facing garden with stunning views across Charnwood countryside. Near the house are patios, lawns, water features, flower and shrub beds, fruit trees, greenhouses and vegetable plots. Lawns then slope down to a gravel garden, a large wildlife pond with waterfall and three areas of woodland, with pleasant walks though many species of trees. Several places to sit and relax around the garden.

  🐕 ❀ ☕

32 THE OLD HALL

Main Street, Market Overton
LE15 7PL. Mr & Mrs Timothy Hart, 01572 767145, stefa@hambleton.co.uk. *6m N of Oakham. Beyond Cottesmore; 5m from A1 via Thistleton. 10m E from Melton Mowbray via Wymondham.* Home-made teas. **Adm £4.50, chd free. Sun 14 June (2-6).** Visitors also welcome by arrangement Apr to Sept weekdays only. Light lunches or teas served with produce of Hambleton Bakery. Price on request with pre-payment required.
Set on a southerly ridge overlooking Catmose Vale, the garden is now on 4 levels. Stone walls and yew hedges

divide the garden into enclosed areas with herbaceous borders, shrubs, and young and mature trees. In 2006 the lower part of garden was planted with new shrubs to create a walk with mown paths. Terrace and lawn give a great sense of space, enhancing the view. Neil Hewertson has been involved in the gardens design since 1990s.

33 THE OLD STABLES
Bruntingthorpe LE17 5QL. Gordon & Hilary Roberts, 01162 478713, gordon.hilary.1943@btinternet.com. *10m S of Leicester. Leicester A5199, R at Arnesby to Bruntingthorpe; R towards Peatling Parva. M1, J20 for Lutterworth; R in front of police station to Bruntingthorpe.* Home-made teas. **Adm £3, chd free. Sun 14 June (11-5). Visitors also welcome by arrangement June to July for groups 15 - 35 max.** Plant lovers' delightful 1 acre country garden. Plant compositions in interconnecting areas give a feeling of spaciousness and tranquillity. Wide grass walks set off the large herbaceous borders packed with a collection of interesting perennials, shrubs and climbers. Many mature trees, wild life area with pond; striking views to Leicester. Rockery and raised alpine beds, tender plants in containers. Featured in Leicester Mercury's Magazine.

34 THE OLD VICARAGE, BURLEY
Church Road, Burley, Nr Oakham LE15 7SU. Jonathan & Sandra Blaza, 01572 770588, sandra.blaza@btinternet.com, www.theoldvicarageburley.com. *1m NE of Oakham. In Burley just off B668 between Oakham & Cottesmore. Church Rd is opp the village green, the Old Vicarage 1st L off Church Rd.* Home-made teas. **Adm £4, chd free. Share to Eden Valley Hospice. Sun 24 May (1.30-5). Evening Opening £4, chd free, Light refreshments, Thur 25 June (6-9). Visitors also welcome by arrangement May to June for groups.**
Country garden, planted for yr round interest, incl a walled garden (with vine house) producing fruit, herbs, vegetables and cut flowers. Formal lawns and borders, lime walk, rose gardens and a rill through an avenue of standard wisteria. Wildlife garden

with pond, 2 orchards and mixed woodland. Some gravel and steps between terraces.

35 ORCHARD HOUSE
Lyndon Road, Hambleton, Nr Oakham LE15 8TJ. Richard & Celia Foulkes. *Next to Rutland Water, 400 yds from centre of Hambleton. Enter village, turn R at church, down hill, only house at bottom on R.* Home-made teas. **Adm £3.50, chd free. Sun 5 July (2-5).**
Beautifully situated partly bordering Rutland Water. Series of garden rooms incl formal, Japanese and vegetable gardens; newly planted orchard; and large informal garden with rose pergola and copses.

NGS donations have helped fund 358 Marie Curie Nurses

36 ORCHARD HOUSE
14 Mowsley Rd, Husbands Bosworth, Lutterworth LE17 6LR. David & Ros Dunmore, d.dunmore@yahoo.com. *6m W of Market Harborough. A4304 from Market Harborough enter village. Mowsley Rd is 3rd R. A4304 from Lutterworth/ M1, enter village. Mowsley Rd is 3rd L.* Home-made teas. **Adm £3, chd free. Share to Rainbows children's hospice. Sun 26 July (11-5). Visitors also welcome by arrangement June to Aug, groups 10 - 20.**
A hidden gem. Small enclosed cottage garden with elements of surprise around each corner. Five garden rooms shaded by mature trees and linked by Victorian gravel paths. Patio area with summer planting, small pond and other water features. Alpine bed and varied use of container planting. Wheelchair access to main features of the garden. Some gravel paths.

37 PARKSIDE
6 Park Hill, Gaddesby LE7 4WH. Mr & Mrs D Wyrko, 01664 840385. *8m NE of Leicester. From A607 Rearsby bypass turn off for Gaddesby. L at Cheney Arms. Garden 400yds on R.* Tea. **Adm £4, chd free. Sun 12 Apr (11-5). Visitors also welcome by arrangement Mar to July adm £6 incl tea and cake, groups max 30.**
Woodland garden of approx 1¼ acres containing many spring flowers and bulbs. Vegetable garden with cordon fruit trees and soft fruit. Greenhouse, cold frame and pond with bog garden and other features. Informal mixed borders planted to encourage wildlife and to provide a family friendly environment.

GROUP OPENING

38 QUORN ORCHARD GARDENS
Barrow Road, Quorn LE12 8DH. *2m S of Loughborough. From A6 follow signs towards Great Central Railway then straight on to Quorn village centre. Extra parking available to the end of Barrow Rd.* Home-made teas at 45 Barrow Road. **Combined adm £2.50, chd free. Sun 31 May (11-5).**

> **35 BARROW ROAD**
> Sally Ash

> **37 BARROW ROAD**
> Jacqui Fowler & Pat Manning

> **45 BARROW ROAD**
> Mr & Mrs D Cox

> **NEW** **56 BARROW ROAD**
> Mr & Mrs R Jones

These neighbours and friends with a common interest in creating a beautiful green space in their own individual style, would like to invite you to share their passion for an afternoon. Three gardens are typical of 1930s urban properties with generous proportions, created upon an old orchard. The fourth garden, hidden behind an Victorian terraced cottage, is a wonderful surprise. Leicestershire Master Composters demonstration. Some small steps and narrow paths, but generally wheelchair friendly.

39 RIDGEWOLD FARM

Burton Lane, Wymeswold
LE12 6UN. Robert & Ann Waterfall,
01509 881689,
robert.waterfall@yahoo.co.uk. *5m
SE of Loughborough. Off Burton
Lane between A6006 & B676. Ample
car & coach parking.* **Adm £3.50,
chd free. Visitors welcome by
arrangement June to July for
groups 10 - 50 max. Home-made
teas and pre-booked lunches
available.**
2½ acre rural garden in the Leics
Wolds. Conducted tours of garden
and working farm, start at the
sweeping drive of specimen trees.
Beech, Laurel and Saxon hedges
divide different areas. Lawn, rill, water
feature, summer house, shrubs, rose
fence, clematis arch, wisteria, ivy
tunnel, rose garden, herbaceous,
orchard, vegetable patch. Birch
avenue gives view of the village.
Woodland walk. Wild life pond.

40 119 SCALFORD ROAD

Melton Mowbray LE13 1JZ.
Richard & Hilary Lawrence, 01664
562821, randh1954@me.com. *½ m
N of Melton Mowbray. Take Scalford
Rd from town centre past Cattle
Market. Garden 100yds after 1st
turning on L (The Crescent).* Home-
made teas. **Adm £2.50, chd free.
Sun 19 July (11-5). Visitors also
welcome by arrangement June to
Aug for groups 10 - 25 max.**
Larger than average town garden
which has evolved over the last
25yrs. Mixed borders with traditional
and exotic plants, enhanced by
container planting particularly
begonias. Vegetable parterre and
greenhouse. Various seating areas for
viewing different aspects of the
garden. Water features incl ponds.
Partial wheelchair access. Gravelled
drive, ramp provided up to lawn but
paths not accessible.

41 STOKE ALBANY HOUSE

Desborough Road, Stoke Albany
LE16 8PT. Mr & Mrs A M Vinton,
www.stokealbanyhouse.co.uk. *4m
E of Market Harborough. Via A427 to
Corby, turn to Stoke Albany, R at the
White Horse (B669) garden ½ m on
L.* **Adm £3.50, chd free. Share to
Marie Curie Cancer Care. Weds 3,
10, 17, 24 June, 1, 8 July (2-4.30).**
4 acre country house garden; fine
trees and shrubs with wide
herbaceous borders and sweeping

striped lawn. Good display of bulbs in
spring, roses June and July. Walled
grey garden; nepeta walk arched with
roses, parterre with box and roses.
Mediterranean garden. Heated
greenhouse, potager with topiary,
water feature garden and sculptures.

SULBY GARDENS

See Northamptonshire.

> Contrasting sizes
> and styles that,
> together, they make
> the perfect visit . . .

42 THORPE LUBENHAM HALL

Farndon Road, Lubenham
LE16 9TR. Sir Bruce & Lady
MacPhail. *2m W of Market
Harborough. From Market
Harborough take 3rd L off main rd,
down Rushes Lane, past church on
L, under old railway bridge & straight
on up private drive.* Cream teas. **Adm
£3.50, chd free. Wed 3 June (10-4).**
15 acres of formal and informal
garden surrounded by parkland and
arable. Many mature trees. Traditional
herbaceous borders and various
water features. Walled pool garden
with raised beds. Ancient moat area
along driveway. Gravel paths, some
steep slopes and steps.

43 TRESILLIAN HOUSE

67 Dalby Road, Melton Mowbray
LE13 0BQ. Mrs Alison Blythe,
01664 481 997,
studentsint@aol.com,
www.studentsint.com. *S of Melton
Mowbray. Follow signs B6047 (Dalby
Rd) S. Parking on site.* Cream teas
and ploughman's lunches. Soup
(Oct only). **Adm £2.50, chd free.
Suns 3 May, 5 July, 30 Aug, 18 Oct
(11-4.30). Visitors also welcome by
arrangement May to Oct. Max 30
visitors.**
¾ acre garden re-established by new
owner between 2009 and 2012.
Beautiful blue cedar trees, excellent
specimen tulip tree. Parts of garden
original, others reinstated with variety
of plants and bushes. Original bog
garden and natural pond. Vegetable
plot. Parts left uncultivated with wild

cowslips and grasses. Quiet oasis.
Slate paths, steep in places.

44 UNIVERSITY BOTANIC GARDEN

'The Knoll' entrance, Glebe Road,
Oadby LE2 2LD. University of
Leicester,
www.le.ac.uk/botanicgarden. *2m
SE of Leicester off A6. On outskirts of
city opp race course.* Light
refreshments. **Adm by donation.
Sun 9 Aug (10-4).**
16 acre garden, whose formal
planting centres around a restored
Edwardian garden. Plantings originate
from around the world and incl an
arboretum, a herb garden, woodland
and herbaceous borders, rock
gardens, a water garden, special
collections of skimmia, aubretia and
hardy fuchsia, and a series of
glasshouses displaying temperate
and tropical plants, alpines and
succulents. Open daily. Please phone
or see garden website.

GROUP OPENING

45 WALTON GARDENS

Walton LE17 5RG. *4m NE of
Lutterworth. M1 J20, via Lutterworth
follow signs for Kimcote & Walton, or
from Leicester take A5199. After
Shearsby turn R signed
Bruntingthorpe. Follow signs.* Cream
teas at The Dog and Gun (proceeds
to NGS). **Combined adm £4, chd
free. Sun 7, Wed 10 June (11-5).**

ORCHARDS
Mr & Mrs G Cousins
www.grahamsgreens.com

RYLANDS FARMHOUSE
Mark & Sonya Raybould

SANDYLAND
Martin & Linda Goddard

TOAD HALL
Sue Beardmore

Small village set in beautiful south
Leicestershire countryside. The four
gardens at Walton are in such
contrasting sizes and styles that,
together, they make the perfect
garden visit. There is a plantsman's
garden filled with gorgeous rare
plants; a Modernist garden where all
the leaves are green (no variegated,
gold or purple foliage) featuring the
extensive use of grasses and a lovely
view across the surrounding

Lemon drizzle cake, Victoria sponge ... yummy!

landscape; a traditional garden featuring serpentine hedging and another which is walled and has a unique water feature; last but not least, a really delightful enclosed cottage garden. Orchards was a winning garden when featured in the new programme on Sky TV - Welcome to my Garden. Some wood chip and cobbled paths that can be accessed by wheelchairs but may prove difficult.

46 WASHBROOK ALLOTMENTS

Welford Road, Leicester LE2 6FP. Sharon Maher. *Approx 2¹/₂ m S of Leicester, 1¹/₂ m N of Wigston. Regret no onsite parking. Welford Rd is difficult to park on. Please use nearby side rds & Pendlebury Drive (LE2 6GY).* Tea. **Adm £3, chd free. Sun 6 Sept (11-3).**
Our allotment gardens have been described as a hidden oasis off the main Welford Road. There are over 100 whole and half plots growing a wide variety of fruit and vegetables. We have a fledgling wildflower meadow, a composting toilet and a shop. Keep a look out for the remains of Anderson Shelters, and see how woodchip is put to good use. Circular route around the site is uneven in places but is suitable for wheelchairs.

47 WESTVIEW

1 St Thomas' s Road, Great Glen, Leicester LE8 9EH. Gill & John Hadland, 01162 592170, gill@hadland.wanadoo.co.uk. *7m S of Leicester. Take either r'about from A6 into village. At centre (War Memorial) follow NGS signs.* Home-made teas. **Adm £2, chd free. Sun 1 Mar (12-4); Sun 17 May, Mon 31 Aug (12-5). Visitors also welcome by arrangement Mar to Sept for groups 20 max.**
Organically managed small walled cottage style garden with yr-round interest. Interesting and unusual plants, many grown from seed. Formal box parterre herb garden, courtyard, herbaceous borders, small wildlife pond, greenhouse, beehives, vegetable and fruit area. Auricula display. Handmade sculptures and artefacts made from recycled materials on display. Collection of Galanthus (snowdrops).

Green Wicket Farm

48 ◆ WHATTON GARDENS

nr Kegworth LE12 5BG. Lord & Lady Crawshaw, 01509 842225, www.whattonhouseandgardens.co.uk. *4m NE of Loughborough. On A6 between Hathern & Kegworth; 2¹/₂ m SE of M1J24.* Home-made teas. **Adm £4, chd free. For NGS: Sun 28 June (11-6). For other opening times and information, please phone or see garden website.**
A wonderful extensive 15 acre C19 country house garden. Arboretum with many fine trees, large herbaceous borders, traditional rose garden, ornamental ponds, flowering shrubs and many spring bulbs. Nooks and crannies to explore. A hidden treasure and a truly relaxing experience for all the family. Open daily (not Sat) March to Oct. Available for group bookings. Gravel paths.

GROUP OPENING

49 WILLOUGHBY GARDENS

Willoughby Waterleys LE8 6UD. *9m S of Leicester. Follow yellow NGS rd arrows.* Tea in Village Hall. **Combined adm £4, chd free. Sun 19 July (11-5).**

> NEW **1 CHURCH FARM LANE**
> Kathleen & Peter Bowers

> NEW **2 CHURCH FARM LANE**
> Valerie & Peter Connelly

> **FARMWAY**
> Eileen Spencer

Visitors also welcome by arrangement June to Aug, max 25 visitors. 01162 478321 eileenfarmway9@msn.com

> NEW **HIGH MEADOW**
> Phil & Eva Day

> **JOHN'S WOOD**
> John & Jill Harris

> NEW **KAPALUA**
> Richard & Linda Love

> NEW **3 ORCHARD ROAD**
> Diane & Roger Brearley

Willoughby Waterleys lies in the South Leicestershire countryside. The Norman Church will be open, hosting a film of the local bird population filmed by a local resident. 7 gardens are open, 5 for the first time. John's Wood is a 1¹/₂ acre nature reserve planted to encourage wildlife. 1, Church Farm Lane is a well stocked garden with lawn, trees and shrubs, roses,and climbers. 2, Church Farm Lane has been professionally designed with many interesting features. Farmway is a plant lovers garden with many unusual plants in colour themed borders. High Meadow has been evolving over 5yrs. Incl mixed planting and ornamental vegetable garden. Kapalua has interesting planting design incorporating open views of countryside. 3, Orchard Road is a small garden packed with interest. Lawncare advice clinic 2-4pm. Willoughby embroidery on display in village hall.

LINCOLNSHIRE

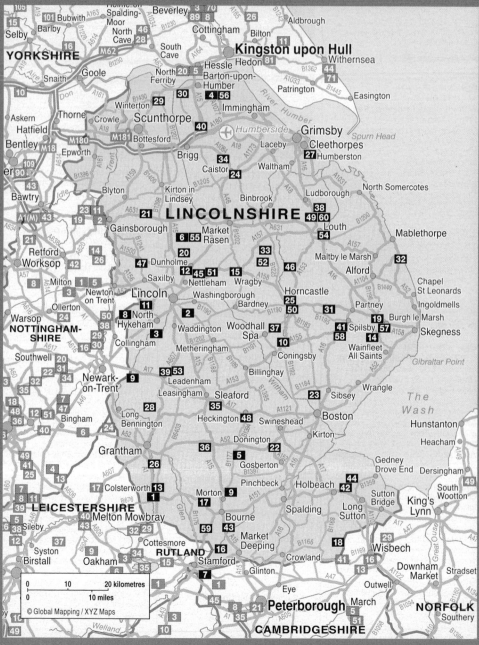

Lincolnshire

Lincolnshire is a county shaped by a rich tapestry of fascinating heritage, passionate people and intriguing traditions; a mix of city, coast and countryside.

The city of Lincoln is dominated by the iconic towers of Lincoln Cathedral. The eastern seaboard contains windswept golden sands and lonely nature reserves. The Lincolnshire Wolds is a nationally important landscape of rolling chalk hills and areas of sandstone and clay, which underlie this attractive landscape.

To the south is the historic, religious and architectural heritage of The Vales, with river walks, the fine Georgian buildings of Stamford and historic Burghley House. In the east the unique Fens landscape thrives on an endless network of waterways inhabited by an abundance of wildlife.

Beautiful gardens of all types, sizes and designs are cared for and shared by their welcoming owners. Often located in delightful villages, a visit to them will entail driving through quiet roads often bordered by verges of wild flowers.

Lincolnshire is rural England at its very best. Local heritage, beautiful countryside walks, aviation history and it is the home of the Red Arrows.

Lincolnshire Volunteers

County Organiser
Sally Grant
01205 750486
sallygrant50@btinternet.com

County Treasurer
Helen Boothman
01652 628424
boothmanhelen@gmail.com

Publicity
Margaret Mann
01476 585905
marg_mann2000@yahoo.com

Erica McGarrigle
01476 585909
ericamcg@hotmail.co.uk

Assistant County Organisers
Lynne Barnes
01529 497462
lynnebarnes14@googlemail.com

Helen Boothman
(as above)

Susie Dean
01476 565456
susie@dean0.plus.com

Tricia Elliot
01427 788517
triciaelliot921@btinternet.com

Stephanie Lee
01507 442151
marigoldlee@btinternet.com

Sylvia Ravenhall
01507 526014
sylvan@btinternet.com

Left: 2 Mill Cottage

Currently the NGS donates around £2.5 million every year

Opening Dates

All entries subject to change.
For latest information check www.ngs.org.uk

February

Saturday 14
26 Little Ponton Hall
Sunday 15
26 Little Ponton Hall
Saturday 21
9 21 Chapel Street
Sunday 22
9 21 Chapel Street

March

Sunday 8
11 Doddington Hall Gardens
Sunday 29
6 Brightwater Gardens
9 21 Chapel Street

April

Friday 3
13 Easton Walled Gardens
Saturday 4
57 Willow Cottage
Sunday 5
60 Woodlands
Monday 6
57 Willow Cottage
Saturday 11
7 Burghley House Private South Gardens
Sunday 12
7 Burghley House Private South Gardens
14 NEW Firsby Manor
17 Grimsthorpe Castle
Sunday 19
15 Goltho House
Sunday 26
41 The Old Rectory

May

Saturday 2
16 Greatford Mill
32 Marigold Cottage
57 Willow Cottage
Sunday 3
2 Ashfield House
32 Marigold Cottage
49 Shepherds Hey
60 Woodlands

Monday 4
57 Willow Cottage
Sunday 10
12 Dunholme Lodge
Sunday 17
42 The Old Vicarage
44 Old White House
46 Pear Tree Cottage
Saturday 23
32 Marigold Cottage
57 Willow Cottage
Sunday 24
14 NEW Firsby Manor
31 Manor House
32 Marigold Cottage
Monday 25
57 Willow Cottage
Sunday 31
23 Holly House
41 The Old Rectory

June

Festival Weekend

Sunday 7
4 NEW The Barn
18 Guanock House
20 Hackthorn Hall
52 The Walled Garden
56 NEW 3 Westcote Farm House
60 Woodlands
Wednesday 10
17 Grimsthorpe Castle
Saturday 13
43 NEW The Old Vicarage, Thurlby
57 Willow Cottage
Sunday 14
5 NEW 10 Brewery Lane
25 Horncastle Gardens
30 Manor Farm
57 Willow Cottage
Sunday 21
8 NEW 45 Chapel Lane
22 The Hawthorns
29 19 Low Street
36 The Moat
37 Nova Lodge
48 NEW Shangrila
58 NEW Windrush
59 Witham Hall School
Saturday 27
45 Overbeck
51 NEW Thornham
Sunday 28
32 Marigold Cottage
35 11 Millfield Terrace

July

Saturday 4
21 Hall Farm
28 The Long House
33 2 Mill Cottage
Sunday 5
21 Hall Farm
38 Nut Tree Farm
60 Woodlands
Sunday 12
1 NEW Ashcroft House
3 Aubourn Hall
10 Courtlands
12 Dunholme Lodge
47 73 Saxilby Road
50 Sir Joseph Banks Tribute Garden
Wednesday 15
54 68 Watts Lane
Sunday 19
46 Pear Tree Cottage

August

Sunday 2
6 Brightwater Gardens
19 Gunby Hall & Gardens
32 Marigold Cottage
39 The Old House
53 Walnut Tree Cottage
54 68 Watts Lane
55 West Barn
60 Woodlands
Sunday 9
50 Sir Joseph Banks Tribute Garden
54 68 Watts Lane
Sunday 16
40 Old Quarry Lodge
54 68 Watts Lane
Sunday 23
54 68 Watts Lane
Saturday 29
32 Marigold Cottage
Sunday 30
31 Manor House
32 Marigold Cottage
54 68 Watts Lane

September

Sunday 6
21 Hall Farm
38 Nut Tree Farm
49 Shepherds Hey
60 Woodlands
Wednesday 23
11 Doddington Hall Gardens
Sunday 27
15 Goltho House

October

Sunday 25
2 Ashfield House

February 2016

Saturday 13
26 Little Ponton Hall
Sunday 14
26 Little Ponton Hall
Saturday 27
9 21 Chapel Street
Sunday 28
9 21 Chapel Street

Gardens open to the public

6 Brightwater Gardens
7 Burghley House Private South Gardens
11 Doddington Hall Gardens
13 Easton Walled Gardens
15 Goltho House
19 Grimsthorpe Castle
19 Gunby Hall & Gardens
21 Hall Farm

By arrangement only

24 Hope House
27 1 Lomond Grove
34 Mill Farm

Also open by arrangement

2 Ashfield House
9 21 Chapel Street
10 Courtlands
20 Hackthorn Hall
23 Holly House
25 15 Elmhirst Road, Horncastle Gardens
28 The Long House
31 Manor House
32 Marigold Cottage
36 The Moat
37 Nova Lodge
38 Nut Tree Farm
40 Old Quarry Lodge
41 The Old Rectory
42 The Old Vicarage
45 Overbeck
46 Pear Tree Cottage
54 68 Watts Lane
57 Willow Cottage
60 Woodlands

The Gardens

Hope House

1 NEW ASHCROFT HOUSE

45 Newton Way, Woolsthorpe By Colsterworth, Grantham NG33 5NP. **Lucienne Bennett.** *7m from Grantham, 400 metres from Woolsthorpe Manor (NT). No parking in Newton Way. Plenty of parking along Woolsthorpe Rd or at Woolsthorpe Manor (if visiting property).* Home-made teas. **Adm £3, chd free. Sun 12 July (12-5).** Back garden created in 2012 from part of a pony paddock on a filled in ironstone quarry. Sloping ground necessitated terracing and having natural springs running down one side, and boggy ground in deep shade at the bottom of the plot meant that this small garden needed careful planning.

2 ASHFIELD HOUSE

Lincoln Road, Branston, Lincoln LN4 1NS. John & Judy Tinsley, 07977 505682, jmt@ashtreedevelopments.co.uk. *3m S of Lincoln. From Branston off B1188 Lincoln Rd on L; 1m from Branston Hall Hotel signed Ashfield Farms.* Home-made teas. **Adm £3.50, chd free. Sun 3 May (11-4.30); Sun 25 Oct (11-4). Visitors also welcome by arrangement Feb to Oct.** 10 acre garden constructed around a planting of trees and shrubs. The main feature in the spring is the collection of some 110 flowering cherries of 40 different varieties. Sweeping lawns with massed plantings of spring flowering bulbs around a large pond. In the autumn the colours can be amazing. A recently planted magnolia collection in a newly constructed woodland garden. Early spring is a great time to visit by arrangement to see the masses of bulbs. Fairly level garden. Grass paths.

3 AUBOURN HALL

Harmston Road, Aubourn, nr Lincoln LN5 9DZ. Mr & Mrs Christopher Nevile, www.aubournhall.co.uk. *7m SW of Lincoln. Signed off A607 at Harmston & off A46 at Thorpe on the Hill.* Home-made teas. **Adm £4.50, chd free. Sun 12 July (2-5).** Approx 8 acres. Lawns, mature trees, shrubs, roses, mixed borders, new rose garden, new large prairie and topiary garden, spring bulbs and ponds. C11 church adjoining. Access to garden is fairly flat and smooth. Depending on weather some areas may be inaccessible to wheelchairs. Parking in field not on tarmac.

4 NEW THE BARN

6 Westcote Farm, Wold Road, Barrow-Upon-Humber DN19 7DY. **Lesley & Ian Pepperdine.** *Outskirts of Barrow upon Humber, 3m S of Humber Bridge. From A15 follow B1206 towards Barrow upon Humber. Indicate L turn at 30 mph sign on entering village, lane down to Westcote Farm is on immed L.* Light refreshments. **Combined adm £3, chd free. Sun 7 June (11-5). Combined with Westcote Farmhouse.** A new and evolving garden set in approx 1 acre of land with orchard, formal yew hedging, mature trees, topiary, herbaceous border, shrubbery and vegetable area. Garden Room to shelter if weather is inclement. Wheelchair and scooter access over lawn and most hard surfaces.

5 NEW 10 BREWERY LANE

Billingborough, Sleaford NG34 0LN. Jim & Maureen Cowley. *On entering village from N take last turning on L at top of High St. From S take 1st turning on R into Brewery Lane.* Home-made teas. **Adm £3, chd free. Sun 14 June (11-5).** Created over the last 6 yrs this small garden has been designed for easy management with as much interest as possible. A stone ruin and pergola with wisteria add height. Unusual plants and many hostas create contrast in the borders. There is also a collection of Streptocarpus.

6 ◆ BRIGHTWATER GARDENS

The Garden House, Saxby, Market Rasen, Lincoln LN8 2DQ. Chris Neave & Jonathan Cartwright, 01673 878820, www.brightwatergardens.co.uk. *8m N of Lincoln; 2¼ m E of A15. Turn off A15 signed Saxby.* Home-made teas. **Combined adm £4.50, chd free. For NGS: Sun 29 Mar, Sun 2 Aug (11-4). For other opening times and information, please phone or see garden website.** 8 acre landscaped garden packed with interest. Yew hedging and walls enclose magical garden rooms full of roses and herbaceous plants. Solar garden, long terrace, Dutch, pergola and obelisk gardens, lavender walk. Large natural damp garden. Dry garden, specimen trees overlooking a large reflective pond. Native woodland areas, prairie and wild flower meadow planted with massed bulbs. Wonderful views. Adjacent to C18 classical church. Gravel paths, steep slopes.

7 ◆ BURGHLEY HOUSE PRIVATE SOUTH GARDENS

Stamford PE9 3JY. Burghley House Preservation Trust, 01780 752451, www.burghley.co.uk. *1m E of Stamford. From Stamford follow signs to Burghley via B1443.* **Adm £3.50, chd £2. For NGS: Sat 11, Sun 12 Apr (11-4). For other opening times and information, please phone or see garden website.**

On 11 and 12 April the Private South Gardens at Burghley House will open for the NGS with spectacular spring bulbs in park like setting with magnificent trees and the opportunity to enjoy Capability Brown's famous lake and summerhouse. Entry to the Private South Gardens via orangery. The Garden of Surprises, Sculpture Garden and house are open as normal. (Regular adm prices apply). Light refreshments. Gravel paths.

8 NEW 45 CHAPEL LANE

North Scarle, Lincoln LN6 9EX. Michael & Anna Peacock. *12m SW of Lincoln; 9m NW Newark. From A46 follow signs to Whisby & Eagle. On entering Eagle take 1st R, cont for approx 1m take 1st L. Cont to Xrds in centre of N Scarle. Turn R into Chapel Lane. Garden last on L.* Home-made teas. **Adm £2.50, chd free. Sun 21 June (1-5).**

This is a good example of a garden designed by the owners to provide a cottage style feel to a relatively modern village property. The ³/₄ acre garden was started from a blank canvas in 2011. Three offset circular lawns are edged with bee friendly hardy perennials, lavenders, roses, shrubs and fruit trees. Gravel area with low rockery. Small orchard to front. Pretty gazebo. Some features made from recycled materials. Archways too narrow for wheelchairs. One cobble path may prove difficult.

9 21 CHAPEL STREET

Hacconby, Bourne PE10 0UL. Cliff & Joan Curtis, 01778 570314, cliffordcurtis@btinternet.com. *3m N of Bourne. A15, turn E at Xrds into Hacconby, L at village green.* Hot soup (Feb) and light refreshments. **Adm £3, chd free. Sun 21, Sun 22 Feb, Sun 29 Mar (11-4); Sat 27 Feb (11-4), Sun 28 Feb 2016 (11-6). Visitors also welcome by arrangement.**

A cottage garden behind a 300yr old cottage. Snowdrops, primroses, hellebores and many different spring flowering bulbs. Colour with bulbs and herbaceous plants through the yr, autumn with asters, dahlias, salvias and many of the autumn flowering yellow daises. Part gravel and part grass paths.

NGS support makes a vital difference to our patient care

10 COURTLANDS

Tattershall Road, Kirkby-on-Bain, Woodhall Spa LN10 6YN. Peter & Jill Hilton, 01526 353115, peter@courtlandshilton.co.uk. *Kirkby on Bain. Garden located on S edge of village, on rd leading to Recycling Centre, gravel pits & Coningsby.* Home-made teas. **Adm £3, chd free. Sun 12 July (2-5). Visitors also welcome by arrangement May to Sept for groups 10+.**

Enjoy the peace and quiet of this lovely 3¹/₂ acre garden and paddock. A flat established garden with large trees (60 mature Scots Pines), open lawn, herbaceous borders, island beds, folly area, water feature, newly developed Japanese garden, tree house, and a large vegetable garden with raised beds. Full wheelchair access to garden but regret no accessible WC.

11 ◆ DODDINGTON HALL GARDENS

Doddington, Lincoln LN6 4RU. Claire & James Birch, 01522 812510, www.doddingtonhall.com. *5m W of Lincoln. Signed clearly from A46 Lincoln bypass & A57, 3m.* **Adm £6, chd £3. For NGS: Sun 8 Mar, Wed 23 Sept (11-5). For other opening times and information, please phone or see garden website.**

5 acres of romantic walled and wild gardens. Naturalised spring bulbs and scented shrubs from Feb to May. Spectacular iris display late May/early June in box edged parterres of West Garden. Sumptuous herbaceous borders throughout summer; ancient chestnut trees; turf maze; Temple of the Winds. Fully productive, walled kitchen garden. Wheelchair access possible via gravel paths. Ramps also in use. Access map available from Gatehouse Shop.

12 DUNHOLME LODGE

Dunholme, Lincoln LN2 3QA. Hugh & Lesley Wykes. *4m NE of Lincoln. Turn off A46 towards Welton at Hand Car Wash garage. After ¹/₂ m turn L up long concrete rd. Garden at top.* Cream teas. **Adm £2.50, chd free. Sun 10 May, Sun 12 July (11-5).**

3 acre garden. Spring bulb area, shrub borders, fern garden, topiary, large natural pond, wild flower area, orchard and vegetable garden. RAF Dunholme Lodge Museum and War Memorial in the grounds. Most areas wheelchair accessible but some loose stone and gravel.

13 ◆ EASTON WALLED GARDENS

Easton NG33 5AP. Sir Fred & Lady Cholmeley, 01476 530063, www.eastonwalledgardens.co.uk. *7m S of Grantham. 1m off A1. Follow village signposts via B6403.* Light refreshments. **Adm £6.95, chd £2.75. For NGS: Fri 3 Apr (11-4). For other opening times and information, please phone or see garden website.**

12 acres of 400yr old forgotten gardens undergoing extensive renovation. Set in parkland with dramatic views. C16 garden with Victorian embellishments. Italianate terraces; yew tunnel; snowdrops and cut flower garden. David Austin roses, meadows and sweet pea collections. Cottage and vegetable gardens. Please wear sensible shoes suitable for country walking. Childrens' Trail. Regret no wheelchair access to lower gardens but tearoom, shop and upper gardens all accessible.

14 **NEW** **FIRSBY MANOR**
Firsby, Spilsby PE23 5QJ. David &
Gill Boldy. *5m E of Spilsby. From
Spilsby take B1195 to Wainfleet all
Saints. In Firsby, turn R into Fendyke
Rd. Firsby Manor is 0.8m along lane
on L.* Home-made teas. **Adm £2.50,
chd free. Sun 12 Apr, Sun 24 May
(1-5).**
Firsby Manor is a garden of 3 acres
surrounding a Georgian farmhouse. It
has been developed by the current
owners over two decades and has
been designed to provide interest
throughout the year, although it is at
its most lovely in late spring and early
summer. Most of garden accessible
by wheelchair, but no disabled WC.

15 ◆ **GOLTHO HOUSE**
Lincoln Road, Goltho, Nr Wragby,
Market Rasen LN8 5NF. Mr & Mrs S
Hollingworth, 01673 857768,
www.golthogardens.com. *10m E of
Lincoln. On A158, 1m before Wragby.
Garden on L (not in Goltho Village).*
**Adm £5, chd free. For NGS: Sun 19
Apr, Sun 27 Sept (10-4). For other
opening times and information,
please phone or see garden
website.**
4¹/₂ acre garden started in 1998 but
looking established with long grass
walk flanked by abundantly planted
herbaceous borders forming a focal
point. Paths and walkway span out to
other features incl nut walk, prairie
border, wild flower meadow, rose
garden and large pond area.
Snowdrops, hellebores and shrubs
for winter interest.

16 **GREATFORD MILL**
Greatford PE9 4QA. Mr & Mrs D
Lygo. *4m E of Stamford. At T-
junction in village nr Hare & Hounds
PH, take route to Carlby &
Braceborough. Garden is 2nd on L.*
Home-made teas. **Adm £4, chd free.
Sat 2 May (2-4.30).**
Lovely ¹/₂ acre village garden with
special spring interest overlooking St
Thomas' church. Situated on the R
Glen, original water wheel and open,
unfenced mill pond. Informal planting
of shrubs, Japanese Maples,
herbaceous borders around lawn and
formal parterre garden of
fruit/vegetables. Large decking with
seating area and prairie planting.
Duck race. Some gravel paths.

17 ◆ **GRIMSTHORPE CASTLE**
Grimsthorpe, Bourne PE10 0LZ.
Grimsthorpe & Drummond Castle
Trust, 01778 591205,
www.grimsthorpe.co.uk. *3m NW of
Bourne. 8m E of A1 on A151 from
Colsterworth junction. Main entrance
indicated by brown tourist sign.* Light
refreshments. **Adm £5.50, chd £2.
For NGS: Sun 12 Apr, Wed 10 June
(11-5). For other opening times and
information, please phone or see
garden website.**
15 acres of formal and woodland
gardens incl bulbs and wildflowers.
Formal gardens encompass fine
topiary, roses, herbaceous borders
and unusual ornamental kitchen
garden. Gift shop, cycle hire and
adventure playground. Gravel paths.

Enjoy tea
and cake in
the garden . . .

18 **GUANOCK HOUSE**
Guanock Gate, Sutton St Edmund
PE12 0LW. Mr & Mrs Michael
Coleman. *16m SE of Spalding. From
village church turn R, cross rd, then L
Guanock Gate. Garden at end of rd
on R.* Home-made teas. **Adm £3,
chd free. Sun 7 June (1.30-5).**
Garden designed by Arne Maynard.
5 acres. Herbaceous border, knot
garden, rose garden and lime walk.
Orchard, walled kitchen garden,
Italian garden. Guanock House is a
C16 manor house built in the flat fens
of S Lincolnshire. Plant stall. Partial
wheelchair access. Garden on
different levels.

19 ◆ **GUNBY HALL &
GARDENS**
Spilsby PE23 5SS. National Trust,
01754 890102,
www.nationaltrust.org.uk. *2¹/₂ m
NW of Burgh-le-Marsh. 7m W of
Skegness. On A158. Signed off
Gunby r'about.* Home-made teas in
Gunby tea-room. **Adm £5, chd

£2.50. For NGS: Sun 2 Aug (11-5).
For other opening times and
information, please phone or see
garden website.**
8 acres of formal and walled gardens;
old roses, herbaceous borders; herb
garden; kitchen garden with fruit trees
and vegetables. Greenhouses, carp
pond and sweeping lawns.
Tennyson's Haunt of Ancient Peace.
House built by Sir William
Massingham in 1700. Wheelchair
access in gardens but not hall.

20 **HACKTHORN HALL**
Hackthorn, Lincoln LN2 3PQ. Mr &
Mrs William Cracroft-Eley, 01673
860423, office@hackthorn.com,
www.hackthorn.com. *6m N of
Lincoln. Follow signs to Hackthorn.
Approx 1m off A15 N of Lincoln.*
Home-made teas at Hackthorn Hall
Gardens. **Adm £3.50, chd free. Sun
7 June (1-5). Visitors also welcome
by arrangement for groups 20+.**
Formal and woodland garden,
productive and ornamental walled
gardens surrounding Hackthorn Hall
and church extending to approx 15
acres. Parts of the formal gardens
designed by Bunny Guinness. The
walled garden boasts a magnificent
Black Hamburg vine, believed to be
second in size to the vine at Hampton
Court. Partial wheelchair access,
gravel paths, grass drives.

21 ◆ **HALL FARM**
Harpswell, Gainsborough
DN21 5UU. Pam & Mark Tatam,
01427 668412, www.hall-
farm.co.uk. *7m E of Gainsborough.
On A631, 1¹/₂ m W of Caenby
Corner.* Light refreshments. **Adm
£3.50, chd free. For NGS: Sat 4,
Sun 5 July, Sun 6 Sept (10-5).
For other opening times and
information, please phone or see
garden website.**
The garden is now about 3 acres,
encompassing mature area, formal
and informal areas, a parterre filled
with salad crops, herbs and annuals.
There is also a sunken garden,
courtyard with rill, a walled
Mediterranean garden, double
herbaceous borders for late summer,
lawns, pond, giant chess set, and a
flower and grass meadow. A short
walk to a medieval moat. Free seed
collecting on Sun 6 Sept. Most of
garden suitable for wheelchairs.

Visit a garden in your own time – look for by arrangement gardens

Guanock House

© Rosalind Simon

22 THE HAWTHORNS
Bicker Road, Donington PE11 4XP.
Colin & Janet Johnson, 01775
822808, colinj04@hotmail.com,
www.thehawthornsrarebreeds.
co.uk. ½ m NW of Donington. Bicker
Rd is directly off A52 opp Church Rd.
Parking available in Church Rd or
village centre car park. Home-made
teas. **Adm £3.50, chd free.**
Sun 21 June (11-4).
Traditional garden with extensive
herbaceous borders, pond, large old
English rose garden, vegetable and
fruit areas with feature greenhouse.
Cider orchard and area housing rare
breed animals incl pigs, sheep and
chickens.

♿ ⦿ ☕

23 HOLLY HOUSE
Fishtoft Drove, Frithville, Boston
PE22 7ES. Sally & David Grant,
01205 750486,
sallygrant50@btinternet.com. 3m N
of Boston. 1m S of Frithville.
Unclassified rd. On W side of West
Fen Drain. Marked on good maps.
Home-made teas. **Adm £3.50, chd
free.** Sun 31 May (12-5). Visitors
also welcome by arrangement May
to June for groups 10+.
Approx 1 acre informal mixed
borders, steps leading down to pond
with cascade and stream. Small
woodland area. Quiet garden with
water feature. Extra 2½ acres
devoted to wildlife, especially bumble
bees and butterflies. Partial
wheelchair access with some steep
slopes and steps.

♿ ☠ ⦿ 🚐 ☕

24 HOPE HOUSE
15 Horsemarket, Caistor LN7 6UP.
Sue Neave, 01472 852307,
hopehousegardens@aol.com,
www.hopehousegardens.co.uk. Off
A46 Between Lincoln & Grimsby.
Centre of town. Home-made teas at
Hope House and Caistor Arts &
Heritage Centre. **Visitors welcome
by arrangement** May to Aug.
A country garden in an attractive
historic town in the heart of the
Lincolnshire Wolds. Small walled
garden attached to an interesting
Georgian house. Roses, perennials,
shrubs, trees, fruit and a small
raised vegetable area. Wildlife
pond and formal water trough in the
dining area. Yr-round colour and
interest in a tranquil space created
by its garden designer owner.
Caistor Arts and Heritage Centre is
opposite who organise walks
around the historic town and local
areas of interest. Featured in Garden
News, Lincolnshire life, Garden
Design Journal and many local
publications.

☠ ⦿ 🛋 ☕

GROUP OPENING

25 HORNCASTLE GARDENS
Horncastle LN9 5AS, 01507
526014, sylvan@btinternet.com.
Take A158 from Lincoln. Just inside
40mph turn L into Accommodation
Rd. Gardens signed from here.
Roadside parking only. Please park
sensibly. Home-made teas at 15
Elmhirst Road. Gluten free cake, hot
and cold drinks. **Combined
adm £4, chd free.** Sun 14 June
(11-4.30).

40 ACCOMMODATION ROAD
Eddie & Marie Aldridge

NEW 30 ELMHIRST ROAD
Andy & Yvonne Mathieson

15 ELMHIRST ROAD
Sylvia Ravenhall
Visitors also welcome by
arrangement June to July
daytime or evening visits.
01507 526014
sylvan@btinternet.com

The market town of Horncastle some
20m to the east of Lincoln on the
A158 is often called The Gateway to
the Wolds. It is well known for its
Antique and bric-a-brac shops.
These three very different gardens are
within easy walking distance of each
other, maps provided. 40
Accommodation Road is packed with
herbaceous perennials and climbers
in a garden which wraps around three
sides of a bungalow. The rear garden
has suffered from flooding in the past,
hence the raised beds. 15 Elmhirst
Road is a long and narrow town
garden, two thirds walled, winding
gravel paths and shallow steps take
you around secret corners. It is
planted with mixed perennials,
shrubs, climbers, small trees and
lawn. Many hostas are grown in pots
and in the ground. There are plenty of
seats. 30 Elmhirst Road is a new
garden for 2015 (but a previous NGS
opener). It contains colourful planting,
raised vegetable beds, small
greenhouse and fruit. The quirky
handmade features raise a smile on
most faces.

⦿ 🚐 ☕

26 LITTLE PONTON HALL
Grantham NG33 5BS.
Mrs A McCorquodale,
www.littlepontonhallgardens.org.uk.
2m S of Grantham. ½ m E of A1 at
S end of Grantham bypass. Disabled
parking. Light refreshments. **Adm £5,
chd free.** Sat 14, Sun 15 Feb
(11-4), Sat 13, Sun 14 Feb 2016.
3 to 4 acre garden. Massed
snowdrops and aconites in Feb.
Stream, spring blossom and
hellebores, bulbs and river walk.
Spacious lawns with cedar tree over
200yrs old. Formal walled kitchen
garden and listed dovecote, with
recently developed herb garden.
Victorian greenhouses with many

plants from exotic locations. Wheelchair access on hard surfaces, unsuitable on grass. Disabled WC.

27 1 LOMOND GROVE
Humberston, Grimsby DN36 4BD. Mike & Josie Ireland, 01472 319579, m.ireland1@ntlworld.com, www.alpinegarden.co.uk. *1m S of Cleethorpes. From A16 Peaks Parkway turn onto A1098 Hewitts Ave. Turn R at r'about onto A1031, 3rd R into Derwent Drive. 2nd R into Lomond Grove.* **Adm £2.50, chd free. Visitors welcome by arrangement Feb to Oct for groups 20 max. Refreshments by arrangement.**
Small S facing garden for alpines, bulbs, dwarf conifers and other interesting genera which grow alongside alpines. Acers grown from seed provide shade. Trillium, corydalis, primula, pulsatilla, crocus, fritillaria, anemone and sanguinaria are just some of the species grown. Raised tufa bed in alpine house and new tufa wall in the garden.

28 THE LONG HOUSE
Gelston NG32 2AE. Dr Lisanne Radice, lisanne@radice.plus.com. *5m N of Grantham. 16m S of Lincoln. Between Hough-on-the-Hill & Marston.* Home-made teas. **Adm £3.50, chd free. Sat 4 July (2-5). Visitors also welcome by arrangement May to July.**
2 acre garden with extensive views over the Vale of Belvoir. Roses in abundance, knot garden, informal arrangement of borders and a large pond to encourage wildlife. Work in progress incl an extended grass bed together with a new shade garden to incorporate the existing phormium and bamboo border.

29 19 LOW STREET
Winterton DN15 9RT. Jane & Allan Scorer, www.hoehoegrow.blogspot.com. *Winterton, North Lincs. Winterton is on A1077 4m N of Scunthorpe and 7m S of the Humber Bridge. Garden is signed from A1077. Parking on Low Street & nearby Market place (2 mins walk from Low Street).* Light refreshments. **Adm £3, chd free. Sun 21 June (11-5).**
Informal, varied ½ acre garden of several clearly defined spaces and styles, including herbaceous borders,

dovecote, ornamental pond, Subtropical garden. Vegetable garden with wildlife pond beyond. Packed with interesting plants and many places to sit.

30 MANOR FARM
Horkstow Road, South Ferriby, Barton-upon-Humber DN18 6HS. Geoff & Angela Wells. *3m from Barton-upon-Humber on A1077, turn L onto B1204, opp Village Hall.* Home-made teas. **Adm £3, chd free. Sun 14 June (11-5).**
A traditional farmhouse set within approx 1 acre with mature shrubberies, herbaceous borders, gravel garden and pergola walk. Many old trees with preservation orders. New rose garden planted 2013. Wildlife pond set within a paddock.

31 MANOR HOUSE
Manor Road, Hagworthingham, Spilsby PE23 4LN. Gill Maxim & David O'Connor, 01507 588530, vcagillmaxim@aol.com. *5m E of Horncastle. S of A158 in Hagworthingham, turn into Bond Hayes Lane downhill, becomes Manor Rd. Please follow signs down gravel track to parking area.* Home-made teas. **Adm £3, chd free. Sun 24 May, Sun 30 Aug (2-5). Visitors also welcome by arrangement May to Oct.**
2 acre garden on S facing slope, partly terraced and well protected by established trees and shrubs. Redeveloped over 10yrs with natural and formal ponds. Shrub roses, laburnum walk, hosta border, gravel bed and other areas mainly planted with hardy perennials, trees and shrubs.

32 MARIGOLD COTTAGE
Hotchin Road, Sutton-on-Sea LN12 2NP. Stephanie Lee & John Raby, 01507 442151, marigoldlee@btinternet.com, www.marigoldcottage.webs.com. *16m N of Skegness on A52. 7m E of Alford on A1111. 3m S of Mablethorpe on A52. Turn off A52 on High St at Cornerhouse Cafe. Follow rd past playing field on R. Rd turns away from the dunes. House 2nd on L.* Home-made teas. **Adm £3, chd free. Sat 2, Sun 3, Sat 23, Sun 24 May, Sun 28 June, Sun 2, Sat 29, Sun 30 Aug (2-5). Visitors also**

welcome by arrangement Apr to Sept for groups. Home-made teas available.
Slide open the Japanese gate to find secret paths, lanterns, a circular window in a curved wall, water lilies in pots and a gravel garden, vegetable garden and propagation area. Take the long drive to see the sea. Back in the garden, find a seat, enjoy the birds and bees. We face the challenges of heavy clay and salt ladened winds but look for unusual plants not the humdrum for these conditions. Most of garden accessible to wheelchairs along flat, paved paths.

> Exciting mixture of the flamboyant and the quintessentially English garden . . .

33 2 MILL COTTAGE
Barkwith Road, South Willingham, Market Rasen LN8 6NN. Mrs Jo Rouston, 01673 858656, jo@rouston-gardens.co.uk. *5m E of Wragby. On A157 turn R at PH in East Barkwith then immed L to South Willingham. Cottage 1m on L. Please email or phone for more directions.* Home-made teas. **Adm £3, chd free. Sat 4 July (12-5).**
A garden of several defined spaces, packed with interesting features, unusual plants and well placed seating areas, created by garden designer Jo Rouston. Original engine shed, a working well, raised beds using local rock with small pond. Clipped box, alpines, roses, summerhouses and water feature. Box and lavender hedge to greenhouse and herb garden. Late season bed. Woven metal and turf tree seat. Featured in Garden News. Partial wheelchair access. Gravel at far end of garden. Steps down to main greenhouse.

34 MILL FARM

Brigg Road, Grasby, Caistor DN38 6AQ. Mike & Helen Boothman, 01652 628424, boothmanhelen@gmail.com, www.millfarmgarden.co.uk. *3m NW of Caistor on A1084. Between Brigg & Caistor. From Cross Keys PH towards Caistor for approx 200yds.* Home-made teas. **Visitors welcome by arrangement** Apr to Sept.

Over 3 acres of garden with many diverse areas. The frontage is formal with shrubs and trees. The rear a plantsman haven. There is a peony and rose garden, wildlife ponds, specimen trees, vegetable area, an old windmill adapted into a fernery, alpine house and a shade house with a variety of shade loving plants. There are a number of herbaceous beds with many different grasses and hardy perennials. Small nursery on site with home grown plants available.

35 11 MILLFIELD TERRACE

Sleaford NG34 7AD. Mrs Weston. *Opp Northgate Sports Hall & Carres Grammar School where parking is available.* Adm £3, chd free. **Sun 28 June (12-5).**

11 Millfield Terrace is a charming small town garden. On entry there is an intimate courtyard garden, with an abundance of ferns, hostas and various perennials. Venturing through an ivy arch you enter the main gravel garden which features a large variety of clematis, heucheras and grasses. Also an imaginative planting of pots and finally on to a thoughtfully planted allotment. The garden also backs on to an allotment full of fruit trees, vegetables and flowers.

36 THE MOAT

Newton NG34 0ED. Mr & Mrs Mike Barnes, 01529 497462, lynnebarnes14@googlemail.com. *Off A52 halfway between Grantham & Sleaford. In Newton village, opp church. Please park sensibly in village.* Home-made teas. **Adm £4, chd free. Sun 21 June (11-5). Visitors also welcome by arrangement May to Sept.**

Delightful 2½ acre country garden established 12yrs. Created to blend with its country surroundings and featuring island beds planted with a variety of unusual perennials, large natural pond and ha-ha, again imaginatively planted. Topiary,

courtyard and orchard. Small vegetable garden. Garden on slope but accessible to wheelchair users.

37 NOVA LODGE

150 Horncastle Road, Roughton Moor, Woodhall Spa LN10 6UX. Leo Boshier, 01526 354940, moxons555@btinternet.com. *On B1191. Approx 2m E of centre of Woodhall Spa on Horncastle Rd. Roadside parking.* Home-made teas. **Adm £3, chd free. Sun 21 June (12-5). Visitors also welcome by arrangement May to July for groups 10+.**

²/₃ acre traditional garden set within mature trees started 2009. Herbaceous borders and beds, rare and unusual perennials. Shrub beds with grasses and ferns, large collection of hostas and heucheras, area for vegetables, fruit and herbs. Summerhouse, greenhouses, lawns and ponds. Central arbour with climbing roses and clematis. Featured in Lincolnshire Today.

> Home produced honey for sale . . . yummy . . . !

38 NUT TREE FARM

Peppin Lane, Fotherby, Louth LN11 0UP. Tim & Judith Hunter, 01507 602208, nuttreefarm@hotmail.com. *2m N of Louth. At end of Peppin Lane cont on farm track for approx ¹/₂ m. Transport available for those with mobility problems from Woodlands.* **Sun 5 July, Sun 6 Sept (11-5). Combined with Woodlands on Sun 5 July, adm £3.50, chd free and with Shepherds Hey and Woodlands Sun 6 Sept, adm £4, chd free. Visitors also welcome by arrangement Apr to Sept.**

A garden of over an acre recently established with stunning views of the Lincolnshire Wolds. There is a sweeping herbaceous border framing the lawn. A double wall planted with pelargoniums surround the house

with a rill running from the raised terrace to the large pond. There is also an attractive brick potager. Pedigree flock of prize winning Hampshire Down sheep in fields surrounding part of garden. Honey for sale. Some gravel paths.

39 THE OLD HOUSE

1 The Green, Welbourn, Lincoln LN5 0NJ. Mr & Mrs David Close. *Turn off A607 to S end of village, on village green opp red phone box.* Home-made teas at Welbourn Village Hall, ice creams at The Old House. **Combined adm £3, chd free. Sun 2 Aug (2-6). Combined with Walnut Tree Cottage.**

The formal front garden of this listed Georgian house was redesigned by Guy Petheram. Gravel, paving and pebble mosaics provide hard landscaping around beds with box hedging, clipped Portuguese laurel, lavender and roses. Herbaceous border, white hydrangea bed, and small enclosed paved garden. Welbourn Blacksmiths shop and forge dating from 1864 and still in full working order open with Friends of Forge on hand to answer questions. Plant stall, artisan honey and products, metal sculpture, will have stands within the gardens. Some gravel.

40 OLD QUARRY LODGE

15 Barnetby Lane, Elsham, nr Brigg DN20 0RB. Mel & Tina Welton, 01652 680309, melwelton60@hotmail.com. *6m S of Humber Bridge. Leave M180 at J5. Take 1st exit L passing petrol station into Elsham village. Old Quarry Lodge is 1st house on R on entering village.* Cream teas at Village Hall. **Adm £3.50, chd free. Sun 16 Aug (10.30-5). Visitors also welcome by arrangement Apr to Sept.**

Approx ¹/₂ acre sloping garden with formal and informal features. Abundant borders and island beds with architectural focal points, Mediterranean influence in parts. Highly imaginative garden with exciting mixture of the flamboyant and the quintessentially English. Garden is always packed with yr round interest. Featured in Amateur Gardening Magazine, Lincolnshire Today magazine and Lincolnshire Journal. Gravel drive, sloping site.

41 THE OLD RECTORY
East Keal, Spilsby PE23 4AT. Mrs Ruth Ward, 01790 752477, rfjward@btinternet.com. *2m SW of Spilsby. Off A16. Turn into Church Lane by PO.* Home-made teas. **Adm £3, chd free. Sun 26 Apr, Sun 31 May (2-5). Visitors also welcome by arrangement Feb to Oct. Refreshments on request.**
Beautifully situated, with fine views, rambling cottage garden on different levels falling naturally into separate areas, with changing effects and atmosphere. Steps, paths and vistas to lead you on, with seats well placed for appreciating special views or relaxing and enjoying the peace. Dry border, vegetable garden, orchard, woodland walk, wild flower meadow.

42 THE OLD VICARAGE
Low Road, Holbeach Hurn PE12 8JN. Mrs Liz Dixon-Spain, 01406 424148, lizdixonspain@gmail.com. *2m NE of Holbeach. Turn off A17 N to Holbeach Hurn, past post box in middle of village, 1st R into Low Rd. Old Vicarage on R approx 400yds.* Home-made teas at Old White House. **Combined adm £5, chd free. Sun 17 May (1-5). Combined with Old White House. Visitors also welcome by arrangement Mar to Sept.**
2 acres of garden with 150yr old tulip, plane and beech trees: borders of shrubs, roses, herbaceous plants. Shrub roses and herb garden in old paddock area, surrounded by informal areas with pond and bog garden, wild flowers, grasses and bulbs. Small fruit and vegetable gardens. Kids love exploring winding paths through the wilder areas. Garden is managed environmentally. Lots of areas for kids to explore.

43 NEW THE OLD VICARAGE, THURLBY
Church Street, Thurlby, Bourne PE10 0EH. Roy Grundy. *2m S of Bourne. From A15 turn east at Horseshoe PH in Thurlby. The Old Vicarage is 200yds on R.* Tea and cake served in the Parish Hall. **Adm £4, chd free. Sat 13 June (11-5).**
This wonderful ²/₃ acre garden was created by its current owner and his talented late wife Sue. It is a mix of formal and informal areas all defined by clever use of yew hedges comprising, wild flower area, wildlife

pond, formal pond, herbaceous beds, woodland area, and a beautifully planted courtyard/herb garden.

44 OLD WHITE HOUSE
Holbeach Hurn PE12 8JP. Mr & Mrs A Worth. *2m N of Holbeach. Turn off A17 N to Holbeach Hurn, follow signs to village, cont through, turn R after Rose & Crown PH at Baileys Lane.* Home-made teas. **Combined adm £5, chd free. Sun 17 May (1-5). Combined with The Old Vicarage.**
1¹/₂ acres of mature garden, featuring herbaceous borders, roses, patterned garden, herb garden and walled kitchen garden. Large catalpa, tulip tree that flowers, ginko and other specimen trees. Flat surfaces, some steps but wheelchair access to all areas without using steps.

45 OVERBECK
46 Main Street, Scothern LN2 2UW. John & Joyce Good, 01673 862200, jandjgood@btinternet.com. *4m E of Lincoln. Scothern signed from A46 at Dunholme & A158 at Sudbrooke. Overbeck is at E end of Main St.* Light refreshments. **Combined adm £4, chd free. Sat 27 June (11-5). Combined with Thornham. Visitors also welcome by arrangement May to Aug, daytime and evenings.**
Approx ¹/₂ acre garden in quiet village. Long herbaceous borders and colour themed island beds with some unusual perennials. Hosta border, gravel bed with grasses, fernery, trees, numerous shrubs and climbers and large prolific vegetable and fruit area.

46 PEAR TREE COTTAGE
Butt Lane, Goulceby, Louth LN11 9UP. Jill Mowbray & Miranda Manning Press, 01507 343201, chirpy@theraggedrobin.co.uk,

www.theraggedrobin.co.uk. *6m N of Horncastle & 8m SW of Louth. 2m off A153 between Louth & Horncastle. 2m off Caistor High St (B1225).* Home-made teas. **Adm £3, chd free. Sun 17 May, Sun 19 July (11-4). Visitors also welcome by arrangement Apr to Aug for groups 10+.**
Situated in the heart of the Wolds, the garden which surrounds the house on three sides, is an oasis of bright colour within the delightful village of Goulceby. The balance of perennials and annuals ensure a vibrant display throughout the seasons. Productive fruit and vegetable plots and greenhouses lie alongside the borders which only serves to add to the verdant atmosphere within the garden. Visit The Three Horseshoes PH, Shoe Lane, for refreshments (www.the3horseshoes.com) and Workshop in the Wolds displaying home and garden wooden furniture (www.workshopinthewolds.co.uk). Featured on Radio Lincolnshire, in Lincolnshire Today Magazine and Horncastle News. Wheelchair access via front gate with access on grass paths only.

47 73 SAXILBY ROAD
Sturton by Stow LN1 2AA. Charles & Tricia Elliott. *9m NW of Lincoln. On B1241. Halfway between Lincoln & Gainsborough.* Home-made teas. **Adm £2.50, chd free. Sun 12 July (11-4.30).**
Heleniums, phlox, monarda, daylilies, grasses and wide range of usual and unusual summer and autumn flowering plants in this extensively planted smallish garden, much beloved by wildlife. Open to the elements, good views. Approx 170 tender fuchsias on display.

48 NEW SHANGRILA
Little Hale Road, Great Hale, Sleaford NG34 9LH. Marilyn Cooke & John Knight. *On B1394 between Heckington & Helpringham.* Home-made teas. **Adm £3.50, chd free. Sun 21 June (11-5).**
Approx 3 acre garden with sweeping lawns long herbaceous borders, colour themed island beds, hosta collection, lavender bed with seating area, topiary, acers, small raised vegetable area, 3 ponds and new exotic borders. Wheelchair access to all areas.

Support the NGS – eat more cake!

49 SHEPHERDS HEY

Peppin Lane, Fotherby, Louth LN11 0UW. Barbara Chester. *2m N of Louth. Leave A16 to Fotherby. Peppin Lane is no-through rd running E from village centre. Please park on R verge opp allotments.* Home-made teas at Woodlands. **Adm £3.50 £4, chd free. Sun 3 May, Sun 6 Sept (11-5).** Combined with Woodlands, Sun 3 May, adm £3.50, chd free and with Nut Tree Farm and Woodlands, Sun 6 Sept, adm £4, chd free.

Small garden packed with unusual and interesting perennials. Open frontage gives visitors a warm welcome, with a small pond, terraced border and steep bank side to a small stream. Rear garden takes advantage of the panoramic views over open countryside, with colour themed borders. Featured in Lincolnshire Life. Wheelchair access to rear garden possible with care. Front garden can be viewed from road.

50 SIR JOSEPH BANKS TRIBUTE GARDEN

Bridge Street, Horncastle LN9 5HZ. Sir Joseph Banks Society. *From Horncastle Market Square 100yds along Bridge St. Garden on L, entrance through shop.* Home-made teas. **Adm £2.50, chd free. Sun 12 July, Sun 9 Aug (1.30-4).**

Sir Joseph Banks (1743-1820) Tribute Garden is a courtyard providing an attractive oasis in a busy market town. It features 60 different species of plants, many collected on his voyage with Capt Cook on HMS Endeavour. Interpretation material is available. Gift shop selling amongst other things art and crafts from talented local artisans. New Garden Cafe serving tea, coffee and delicious cakes in vintage style. Level gravel path.

51 NEW THORNHAM

Northing Lane, Scothern, Lincoln LN2 2WL. Janis Mason. *4m E of Lincoln. Scothern is signed from A46 at Dunholme & A158 at Sudbrooke. Thornham is a 150 metre walk up Northing Lane, which is opp Overbeck at E end of Main St.* Light refreshments at Overbeck. **Combined adm £4, chd free. Sat 27 June (11-5).** Combined with Overbeck.

Medium sized, densely planted, naturalistic, perennial garden. Many hardy plants, some unusual. Plantaholic gardener aims to have something in flower yr round. Gravel pathways lead through the flower beds as there is no lawn.

Children, find where the frogs are hiding! Many butterflies and bees but how many different types . . . ?

52 THE WALLED GARDEN

Benniworth Road, Panton, Market Rasen LN8 5LQ. David & Jenny Eckford. *5m NE of Wragby. Turn off A157 at E Barkwith. From E turn off B1225 to Benniworth. Garden on Benniworth to Panton Rd.* Home-made teas. **Adm £3, chd free. Sun 7 June (11-5).**

Atmospheric 2 acre C18 walled garden in woodland setting. Rescued from dereliction and carefully restored by present owners. Informal planting within a formal framework. Long herbaceous borders with gravel paths. Many unusual plants and trees. Panoramic view from the roof terrace. Craft and Plant Stalls. Partial wheelchair access due to varying levels of gravel and step leading to garden.

53 WALNUT TREE COTTAGE

6 Hall Lane, Welbourn, Lincoln LN5 0NN. Malcolm & Nina McBeath. *On A607 from Lincoln take R turn into Hall Lane by W. Nursing Home. From Leadenham take L turn. Garden is 3rd gate on L.* Home-made teas at Welbourn Village Hall, Beck Street. LN5 0LZ. Ice Cream available at The Old House. **Combined adm £3, chd free. Sun 2 Aug (2-6).** Combined with The Old House.

A peaceful 1/2 acre garden full of interesting perennials planted in long, curved and colour themed borders. Winding paths surrounded by shrubs and climbing roses provide varied vistas and secluded seating areas. Many old varieties of roses feature throughout. Local honey and bee products for sale, and a local metal sculptor will exhibit and sell in this garden. Nearby, Welbourn Blacksmith's shop and forge, dating from 1864 and still in full working order, will be open, with Friends of the Forge on hand to answer questions. Gravel drive to front, some steps, some narrow paths at rear.

54 68 WATTS LANE

Louth LN11 9DG. Jenny & Rodger Grasham, 07977 318145, sallysing@hotmail.co.uk, www.facebook.com/thesecretgardenoflouth. *1/2 m S of Louth town centre. Watts Lane off Newmarket (on B1200). Turn by pedestrian lights & Co-op.* Home-made teas. **Adm £2.50, chd free. Wed 15 July, Suns 2, 9, 16, 23, 30 Aug (11-4).** Visitors also welcome by arrangement July to Aug incl teas.

Blank canvas of 1/5 acre in early 90s. Developed into lush, colourful, exotic plant packed haven. A whole new world on entering from street. Exotic borders, raised island, long hot border, ponds, stumpery, developing prairie style border. Conservatory, grapevine. Intimate seating areas along garden's journey. Facebook page - The Secret Garden of Louth. Children, find where the frogs are hiding! Many butterflies and bees but how many different types? Feed the fish. Grass pathways, main garden area accessible by wheelchair.

55 WEST BARN

Saxby, Market Rasen LN8 2DQ. Mrs E Neave. *8m N of Lincoln. 2 1/4 m E of A15. Turn of A15 signed Saxby.* Home-made teas. **Combined adm £4.50, chd free. Sun 2 Aug (11-4).** Combined with Brightwater Gardens.

Formal walled courtyard garden with loggia, box hedging, shrub roses, climbers and herbaceous planting. Water feature and pots with seasonal planting. Gravel paths, some steps.

56 NEW 3 WESTCOTE FARM HOUSE

Wold Road, Barrow-upon-Humber DN19 7DY. Gary & Ali Baugh. *On outskirts of Barrow-upon-Humber, 3m from Humber Bridge. From A15 follow B1206 towards Barrow-upon-*

Humber, indicate L turn at 30 mph sign then L down lane signed *Westcote Farm*. Light refreshments. **Combined adm £3, chd free. Sun 7 June (11-5). Combined with The Barn, 6 Westcote Farm.** The garden has been designed to offer a place to relax and enjoy the surrounding countryside. Yew hedges are used to give a formal but contemporary feel throughout the garden giving unity and seclusion to each individual area. Large drifts of herbaceous plants add a new dimension during the summer months. Trees and shrubs form the backbone of the garden. Wheelchair and scooter access over lawn and most hard surfaces.

57 WILLOW COTTAGE
Gravel Pit Lane, Burgh-le-Marsh PE24 5DW. Bob & Karen Ward, 01754 811450, robertward055@aol.com, www.willowcottagecl.webs.com. *6m W of Skegness. S of Gunby r'about on A158, take 1st R signed Bratoft & Burgh-le-Marsh. 1st R again onto Bratoft Lane. L at T-junction, parking on R 25yds.* Home-made teas. **Adm £3, chd free. Sat 4, Mon 6 Apr, Sat 2, Mon 4, Sat 23, Mon 25 May, Sat 13, Sun 14 June (2-5). Visitors also welcome by arrangement Apr to Sept with garden tours.** Surround yourself with the natural world of a delightful hidden English cottage garden, where wildlife abounds, enjoy the many tranquil spots to take a moment or two to appreciate the joy of plants flowers and shrubs created for your delight! A wonderful place to enjoy afternoon tea on the terrace with a few friends. Woodland walk and Victorian glasshouse. Partial wheelchair access. For assistance please phone ahead of visit.

58 NEW WINDRUSH
Main Road, East Keal, Spilsby PE23 4BB. Mr & Mrs Ian & Suzie MacDonald. *On A16, 4m S of Spilsby, opp A155 turning signed West Keal.* Tea. **Adm £3.50, chd free. Sun 21 June (11-4).** Country garden of approx 4 acres with herbaceous borders, shrub and climbing roses, clematis and grasses. Woodland walks and ponds, and vegetable garden. Meadow planted in

Burghley House Private South Gardens

2013 with orchard of Lincolnshire apples. Shallow steps and some uneven ground.

59 WITHAM HALL SCHOOL
Witham-on-the-Hill, Bourne PE10 0JJ. Mr & Mrs C Banks, www.withamhall.com. *7m NNE of Stamford. 4m SW of Bourne. From Stamford take A6121 to Bourne. After approx 7m turn L at Xrds, signed Witham-on-the-Hill. Entrance to Witham Hall after 1m on L.* **Adm £3, chd free. Sun 21 June (2-4).** One of the first gardens that opened in 1927, and now home of Witham Hall School. Formal garden with ornamental pond and paved rosewalk, and mature cedar parkland, pupils' wilderness area, herbaceous borders surrounded by acres of quality sports grounds. Wheelchair access to garden only, gravel driveway.

60 WOODLANDS
Peppin Lane, Fotherby, Louth LN11 0UW. Ann & Bob Armstrong, 01507 603586, annbobarmstrong@btinternet.com, www.woodlandsplants.co.uk. *2m N of Louth on A16 signed Fotherby.*

Please park on R verge opp allotments & walk approx 350 yds to garden. No parking at garden. Please do not drive beyond designated area. Home-made teas. **Adm £2.50, chd free. Suns 5 Apr, 3 May, 7 June, 5 July, 2 Aug, 6 Sept (11-5). Combined with Shepherds Hey Sun 3 May, Nut Tree Farm Sun 5 July, adm £3.50, chd free and Shepherds Hey and Nut Tree Farm Sun 6 Sept, adm £4, chd free. Visitors also welcome by arrangement Mar to Oct.** A lovely mature woodland garden with many unusual plants set against a backdrop of an ever changing tapestry of greenery. A peaceful garden where wildlife is given a chance to thrive. The front garden has been developed into a crevice area for alpine plants. The nursery, featured in RHS Plantfinder, gives visitors the opportunity to purchase plants seen in the garden. Award winning professional artist's studio/gallery open to visitors. Specialist collection of Codonopsis for which Plant Heritage status has been granted. New National Plant collection featured in Daily Mail, The Garden, The Plantsman, Garden News and Garden Answers.

LONDON

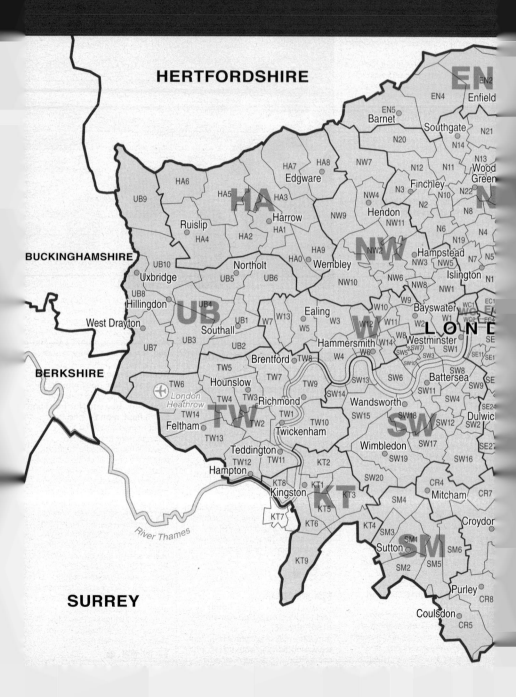

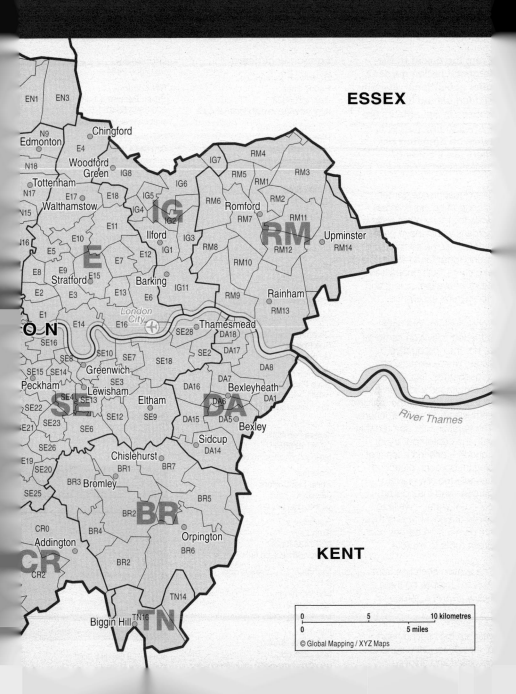

London

From the tiniest to the largest, London gardens offer exceptional diversity. Hidden behind historic houses in Spitalfields are exquisite tiny gardens, while on Kingston Hill there are 9 acres of landscaped gardens.

The oldest private garden in London boasts 5 acres, while the many other historic gardens within these pages are smaller – some so tiny there is only room for a few visitors at a time – but nonetheless full of innovation, colour and horticultural excellence.

London allotments have attracted television cameras to film their productive acres, where exotic Cape gooseberries, figs, prize-winning roses and even bees all thrive thanks to the skill and enthusiasm of city gardeners. The traditional sit comfortably with the contemporary in London – offering a feast of elegant borders, pleached hedges, topiary, gravel gardens and the cooling sound of water – while to excite the adventurous there are gardens on barges and green roofs to explore.

The season stretches from April to October, so there is nearly always a garden to visit somewhere in London. Our gardens opening this year are the beating heart of the capital just waiting to be visited and enjoyed.

Since our foundation we have donated more than £42.5 million to charity

London Volunteers

County Organiser
Penny Snell
01932 864532
pennysnellflowers@btinternet.com

County Treasurer
Richard Raworth
07831 476 088
raworthrichard@gmail.com

Publicity
Penny Snell
(as above)

Booklet Coordinator
Sue Phipps
07771 767196
sue@suephipps.com

Booklet Distributor
Joey Clover
020 8870 8740
joeyclover@dsl.pipex.com

Assistant County Organisers

Clapham & surrounding area
Sue Phipps
(as above)

Dulwich & surrounding area
Clive Pankhurst
07941 536934
alternative.ramblings@gmail.com

E London
Teresa Farnham
07761 476651
farnhamz@yahoo.co.uk

Hackney
Philip Lightowlers
020 8533 0052
plighto@gmail.com

Hampstead
Ruth Levy
020 7435 4124
ruthlevy@tiscali.co.uk

Highgate, St John's Wood & Holland Park
Sue Whittington
020 8348 2785
suewhittington@hotmail.co.uk

Islington
Nell Darby Brown
020 7226 6880
pendarbybrown@blueyonder.co.uk

Gill Evansky
020 7359 2484

NW London
Susan Bennett & Earl Hyde
020 8883 8540
suebearlh@yahoo.co.uk

Caroline Broome
020 8444 2329
carosgarden@virginmedia.com

Outer NW London
James Duncan Mattoon
020 8830 7410

SE London
Janine Wookey
07711 279636
j.wookey@btinternet.com

SW London
Joey Clover
(as above)

Outer S London
Mhairi Clutson
020 8402 3978
mhairi@grozone.co.uk

W London, Barnes & Chiswick
Jenny Raworth
020 8892 3713
jraworth@gmail.com

Outer W London
Julia Hickman
020 8339 0931
julia.hickman@virgin.net

Above: 7 St George's Road
© Marianne Majerus

London gardens listed by postcode

Inner London postcodes

E & EC London

Spitalfields Gardens Group E1
17 Greenstone Mews E11
16 St Margarets Road E12
87 St Johns Road E17
46 Cheyne Avenue E18
5 Brodie Road E4
Homerton Gardens E5
Lower Clapton Gardens E5
42 Latimer Road E7
London Fields Gardens E8
17a Navarino Road E8
12 Bushberry Road E9
The Charterhouse EC1
Amwell Gardens Group EC1R
The Inner Temple Garden EC4

N & NW London

37 Alwyne Road N1
Arlington Square Gardens N1
4 Canonbury Place N1
23 Canonbury Place N1
11 Cloudesley Street N1
De Beauvoir Gardens N1
Islington Gardens N1
King Henry's Walk Garden N1
5 Northampton Park N1
20 St Mary's Grove N1
5 Cecil Road N10
60 Church Crescent N10
19 Hillfield Park N10
66 Muswell Avenue N10
Princes Avenue Gardens N10
5 St Regis Close N10
14 Tetherdown N10
27 Wood Vale N10
33 Wood Vale N10
21 Woodland Rise N10
94 Brownlow Road N11
Golf Course Allotments N11
The Rose Garden at Golf Course Allotments N11
5 Russell Road N13
Handsworth Road Gardens N17
Harmony Garden at Broadwater Farm N17
159 Higham Road N17

94 Marsh Lane Allotments N17
30 Mercers Road N19
79 Church Lane N2
58 Summerlee Avenue N2
91 Vicar's Moor Lane N21
Alexandra Park Road Gardens N22
23 Imperial Road N22
Railway Cottages N22
31 Church Crescent N3
Gordon Road Allotments N3
18 Park Crescent N3
160a Stapleton Hall Road N4
Olden Garden Community Project N5
7 The Grove N6
2 Millfield Place N6
3 The Park N6
Southwood Lodge N6
9 Furlong Road N7
1a Hungerford Road N7
62 Hungerford Road N7
11 Park Avenue North N8
12 Warner Road N8
70 Gloucester Crescent NW1
The Holme NW1
4 Park Village East (Tower Lodge Gardens) NW1
Royal College of Physicians Medicinal Garden NW1
4 Asmuns Hill NW11
48 Erskine Hill NW11
74 Willifield Way NW11
86 Willifield Way NW11
121 Anson Road NW2
20 Exeter Road NW2
27 Menelik Road NW2
93 Tanfield Avenue NW2
58A Teignmouth Road NW2
208 Walm Lane, The Garden Flat NW2
17 Belsize Lane, NW3 NW3
Fenton House NW3
88 Frognal NW3
Frognal Gardens NW3
Little House A NW3
27 Nassington Road NW3
21 Thurlow Road NW3
Copthall Group NW7
Highwood Ash NW7
116 Hamilton Terrace NW8
2 Hillside Close NW8

S, SE & SW London

Garden Barge Square at Downings Roads Moorings SE1
The Garden Museum SE1
Lambeth Palace SE1
Roots and Shoots SE11
41 Southbrook Road SE12

Choumert Square SE15
Lyndhurst Square Group SE15
Walworth Garden Farm SE17
Penge Gardens SE20
Court Lane Garden Group SE21
Dulwich Village Two Gardens SE21
6 Frank Dixon Way SE21
4 Cornflower Terrace SE22
9 The Gardens SE22
174 Peckham Rye SE22
86 Underhill Road SE22
45 Underhill Road SE22
Tewkesbury Lodge : Over the Hill SE23
Tewkesbury Lodge: Top of the Hill SE23
5 Burbage Road SE24
2 Shardcroft Avenue SE24
South London Botanical Institute SE24
Stoney Hill House SE26
St Gothard Mews SE27
35 Camberwell Grove SE5
81 Camberwell Grove SE5
24 Grove Park SE5
Cadogan Place South Garden SW1
Eccleston Square SW1
6 Cornford Grove SW12
81 Tantallon Road SW12
61 Arthur Road SW19
97 Arthur Road SW19
9a Calonne Road SW19
123 South Park Road SW19
Paddock Allotments & Leisure Gardens SW20
Chelsea Physic Garden SW3
51 The Chase SW4
Clapham Manor Street Gardens SW4
4 Macaulay Road SW4
Trinity Hospice SW4
35 Turret Grove SW4
286 Earl's Court Road SW5
The Hurlingham Club SW6
Bina Gardens East SW7
Natural History Museum Wildlife Garden SW7

W London

57 St Quintin Avenue W10
29 Addison Avenue W11
Arundel & Ladbroke Gardens W11
12 Lansdowne Road W11
49 Loftus Road W12
Cleveland Square W2
Capel Manor College, Gunnersbury Park Campus W3

65 Mill Hill Road W3
41 Mill Hill Road W3
Zen Garden W3
Chiswick Mall Gardens W4
The Orchard W4
All Seasons W5
60 Ranelagh Road W5
27 St Peters Square W6
1 York Close W7
Edwardes Square W8
7 Upper Phillimore Gardens W8

Outer London postcodes

22 Kelsey Way BR3
White Cottage BR5
2 Springhurst Close CR0
Elm Tree Cottage CR2
55 Warham Road CR2
Whitgift School CR2
33a Brookhill Road and 33B Brookhill Road EN4
207 East Barnet Road EN4
Elm Court Gardens EN4
West Lodge Park EN4
190 Barnet Road EN5
7 Byng Road EN5
45 Great North Road EN5
13 Greenhill Park EN5
53 Brook Drive HA1
Treetops HA6
4 Stradbroke Grove IG9
7 Woodbines Avenue KT1
Warren House KT2
The Watergardens KT2
Little Lodge KT7
Speer Road Gardens KT7
Hampton Court Palace KT8
6 Manor Road KT8
61 Wolsey Road KT8
239a Hook Road KT9
18 Pettits Boulevard RM1
7 St George's Road TW1
Ormeley Lodge TW10
Petersham House TW10
St Michael's Convent TW10
Stokes House TW10
Hampton Hill Gardens TW12
63 Rosecroft Gardens TW2
20 Beechwood Avenue TW9
Kew Green Gardens TW9
Old Palace Lane Allotments TW9
Trumpeters House & Sarah's Garden TW9
31 West Park Road TW9

Delicious home-made cakes . . .

Opening Dates

All entries subject to change.
For latest information check www.ngs.org.uk

March

Sunday 29
7 The Grove, N6

April

Wednesday 1
Chelsea Physic Garden, SW3
Saturday 11
4 Canonbury Place, N1
23 Canonbury Place, N1
Natural History Museum Wildlife Garden, SW7
20 St Mary's Grove, N1
Trinity Hospice, SW4
Sunday 12
Trinity Hospice, SW4
Sunday 19
Edwardes Square, W8
NEW 6 Frank Dixon Way, SE21
17a Navarino Road, E8
South London Botanical Institute, SE24
Wednesday 22
51 The Chase, SW4 (Evening)
Sunday 26
53 Brook Drive, HA1
51 The Chase, SW4
NEW Cleveland Square, W2
6 Cornford Grove, SW12
Southwood Lodge, N6
7 Upper Phillimore Gardens, W8
NEW 21 Woodland Rise, N10
Monday 27
6 Cornford Grove, SW12 (Evening)
Wednesday 29
NEW Cleveland Square, W2

May

Sunday 3
2 Millfield Place, N6
5 St Regis Close, N10
Wednesday 6
The Inner Temple Garden, EC4

Thursday 7
Hampton Court Palace, KT8 (Evening)
27 Wood Vale, N10 (Evening)
Sunday 10
Arundel & Ladbroke Gardens, W11
Cadogan Place South Garden, SW1
9a Calonne Road, SW19
Eccleston Square, SW1
Elm Tree Cottage, CR2
Olden Garden Community Project, N5
The Orchard, W4
NEW 27 St Peters Square, W6
86 Underhill Road, SE22
Warren House, KT2
The Watergardens, KT2
Saturday 16
The Hurlingham Club, SW6
Walworth Garden Farm, SE17
33 Wood Vale, N10
Sunday 17
94 Brownlow Road, N11
5 Burbage Road, SE24
Princes Avenue Gardens, N10
Stoney Hill House, SE26
91 Vicar's Moor Lane, N21
Walworth Garden Farm, SE17
West Lodge Park, EN4
33 Wood Vale, N10
Wednesday 20
12 Lansdowne Road, W11
4 Park Village East (Tower Lodge Gardens), NW1 (Evening)
Thursday 21
Lambeth Palace, SE1 (Evening)
Saturday 23
NEW 1 York Close, W7 (Evening)
Sunday 24
13 Greenhill Park, EN5
Kew Green Gardens, TW9
Penge Gardens, SE20
NEW 1 York Close, W7
Thursday 28
NEW 4 Macaulay Road, SW4 (Evening)
Saturday 30
NEW 20 Beechwood Avenue, TW9 (Evening)
The Garden Museum, SE1
31 West Park Road, TW9 (Evening)
Sunday 31
37 Alwyne Road, N1

190 Barnet Road, EN5
Chiswick Mall Gardens, W4
Garden Barge Square at Downings Roads Moorings, SE1
Islington Gardens, N1
Little Lodge, KT7
3 The Park, N6
58 Summerlee Avenue, N2
Tewkesbury Lodge : Over the Hill, SE23
208 Walm Lane, The Garden Flat, NW2

June

Tuesday 2
The Charterhouse, EC1 (Evening)
Thursday 4
Hampton Court Palace, KT8 (Evening)

Festival Weekend

Saturday 6
Hampton Hill Gardens, TW12
7 St George's Road, TW1 (Evening)
Sunday 7
Arlington Square Gardens, N1
35 Camberwell Grove, SE5
Choumert Square, SE15
4 Cornflower Terrace, SE22
De Beauvoir Gardens, N1
Elm Tree Cottage, CR2
48 Erskine Hill, NW11
9 Furlong Road, N7
7 The Grove, N6
Hampton Hill Gardens, TW12
NEW Homerton Gardens, E5
1a Hungerford Road, N7
62 Hungerford Road, N7
Lower Clapton Gardens, E5
30 Mercers Road, N19
27 Nassington Road, NW3
11 Park Avenue North, N8
174 Peckham Rye, SE22
Petersham House, TW10
NEW 63 Rosecroft Gardens, TW2
123 South Park Road, SW19
Southwood Lodge, N6
Speer Road Gardens, KT7
160a Stapleton Hall Road, N4
Stokes House, TW10
12 Warner Road, N8
NEW Whitgift School, CR2

Wednesday 10
239a Hook Road, KT9 (Evening)
Saturday 13
NEW Capel Manor College, Gunnersbury Park Campus
18 Pettits Boulevard, RM1
41 Southbrook Road, SE12
Spitalfields Gardens Group, E1
Zen Garden , W3
Sunday 14
61 Arthur Road, SW19
97 Arthur Road, SW19
17 Belsize Lane, NW3
81 Camberwell Grove, SE5
79 Church Lane, N2
NEW Copthall Group, NW7
Court Lane Garden Group, SE21
88 Frognal, NW3
Handsworth Road Gardens, N17
22 Kelsey Way, BR3
London Fields Gardens, E8
NEW 6 Manor Road, KT8
17a Navarino Road, E8
18 Pettits Boulevard, RM1
St Michael's Convent, TW10
41 Southbrook Road, SE12
NEW 2 Springhurst Close, CR0
4 Stradbroke Grove, IG9
Trumpeters House & Sarah's Garden, TW9
74 Willifield Way, NW11
61 Wolsey Road, KT8
Zen Garden , W3
Tuesday 16
49 Loftus Road, W12 (Evening)
Wednesday 17
2 Millfield Place, N6 (Evening)

Lawn and lots of hidden corners give space to sit and enjoy . . .

61 Wolsey Road, KT8
(Evening)
Thursday 18
Lambeth Palace, SE1
(Evening)
Friday 19
Roots and Shoots, SE11
Saturday 20
Tewkesbury Lodge: Top of
the Hill, SE23 (Evening)
Sunday 21
29 Addison Avenue, W11
Amwell Gardens Group,
EC1R
33a Brookhill Road and
33B Brookhill Road, EN4
60 Church Crescent, N10
Clapham Manor Street
Gardens, SW4
Dulwich Village Two
Gardens, SE21
Frognal Gardens, NW3
116 Hamilton Terrace, NW8
(Evening)
Little House A, NW3
Lyndhurst Square Group,
SE15
Ormeley Lodge, TW10
18 Park Crescent, N3
7 St George's Road, TW1
(Evening)
5 St Regis Close, N10
Tewkesbury Lodge: Top of
the Hill, SE23
Tuesday 23
Fenton House, NW3
(Evening)
Saturday 27
The Holme, NW1
Paddock Allotments &
Leisure Gardens, SW20
Sunday 28
12 Bushberry Road, E9
NEW▶ 11 Cloudesley
Street, N1
116 Hamilton Terrace, NW8
(Evening)
Highwood Ash, NW7
The Holme, NW1
The Rose Garden at Golf
Course Allotments, N11
208 Walm Lane, The
Garden Flat, NW2
White Cottage, BR5
Monday 29
Royal College of Physicians
Medicinal Garden, NW1

July

Saturday 4
All Seasons, W5
5 Northampton Park, N1
(Evening)
Zen Garden , W3

Sunday 5
All Seasons, W5
121 Anson Road, NW2
7 Byng Road, EN5
5 Cecil Road, N10
NEW▶ 20 Exeter Road
NEW▶ 159 Higham Road
NEW▶ 2 Hillside Close,
NW8
27 Menelik Road, NW2
66 Muswell Avenue, N10
Railway Cottages, N22
81 Tantallon Road, SW12
58A Teignmouth Road,
NW2
NEW▶ 14 Tetherdown, N10
NEW▶ 21 Thurlow Road,
NW3
Zen Garden , W3

Wednesday 8
King Henry's Walk Garden,
N1 (Evening)

Thursday 9
NEW▶ 286 Earl's Court
Road, SW5 (Evening)
27 Wood Vale, N10
(Evening)

Friday 10
41 Mill Hill Road, W3
(Evening)

Saturday 11
NEW▶ 20 Beechwood
Avenue, TW9 (Evening)

Sunday 12
70 Gloucester Crescent, NW1
4 Park Village East (Tower
Lodge Gardens), NW1
Royal College of Physicians
Medicinal Garden, NW1
NEW▶ St Gothard Mews,
SE27
57 St Quintin Avenue, W10
2 Shardcroft Avenue, SE24
Treetops, HA6
NEW▶ 45 Underhill Road,
SE22
86 Underhill Road, SE22

Saturday 18
42 Latimer Road, E7

Sunday 19
4 Asmuns Hill, NW11
190 Barnet Road, EN5
Elm Court Gardens, EN4
NEW▶ 9 The Gardens,
SE22 (Evening)
19 Hillfield Park, N10
42 Latimer Road, E7
94 Marsh Lane Allotments,
N17
5 St Regis Close, N10
35 Turret Grove, SW4
86 Willifield Way, NW11

Saturday 25
18 Pettits Boulevard, RM1

Sunday 26
29 Addison Avenue, W11
45 Great North Road, EN5

18 Park Crescent, N3
18 Pettits Boulevard, RM1
57 St Quintin Avenue, W10
55 Warham Road, CR2

Thursday 30
Hampton Court Palace,
KT8 (Evening)

August

Saturday 1
The Holme, NW1
Trinity Hospice, SW4

Sunday 2
Alexandra Park Road
Gardens, N22
NEW▶ 31 Church
Crescent, N3
NEW▶ Harmony Garden at
Broadwater Farm, N17
The Holme, NW1
93 Tanfield Avenue, NW2
Trinity Hospice, SW4

Sunday 9
Elm Tree Cottage, CR2
70 Gloucester Crescent,
NW1
65 Mill Hill Road, W3
41 Mill Hill Road, W3
Old Palace Lane
Allotments, TW9
NEW▶ 60 Ranelagh Road,
W5
16 St Margarets Road, E12

The Garden Museum

Bring a bag for plants – help us give more to charity

70 Gloucester Crescent

Saturday 15
5 Brodie Road, E4

Sunday 16
5 Brodie Road, E4
46 Cheyne Avenue, E18
17 Greenstone Mews, E11
87 St Johns Road, E17
33 Wood Vale, N10
7 Woodbines Avenue, KT1

Sunday 23
87 St Johns Road, E17

Thursday 27
Hampton Court Palace, KT8
(Evening)

September

Friday 4
65 Mill Hill Road, W3 (Evening)

Sunday 6
NEW 20 Beechwood Avenue, TW9
(Evening)
94 Brownlow Road, N11
Golf Course Allotments, N11
Gordon Road Allotments, N3
24 Grove Park, SE5
Petersham House, TW10
5 Russell Road, N13

Wednesday 9
The Inner Temple Garden, EC4

Sunday 20
Bina Gardens East, SW7

October

Sunday 4
23 Imperial Road, N22

Sunday 11
Warren House, KT2
The Watergardens, KT2

Sunday 25
West Lodge Park, EN4

Gardens open to the public

Chelsea Physic Garden, SW3
Fenton House, NW3
The Garden Museum, SE1
Hampton Court Palace, KT8
Natural History Museum Wildlife
 Garden, SW7
Roots and Shoots, SE11

By arrangement only

207 East Barnet Road, EN4

Also open by arrangement

Arundel & Ladbroke Gardens, W11
4 Asmuns Hill, NW11
190 Barnet Road, EN5

NEW 20 Beechwood Avenue, TW9
17 Belsize Lane, NW3
33a Brookhill Road and 33B Brookhill
 Road, EN4
5 Burbage Road, SE24
7 Byng Road, EN5
Cadogan Place South Garden, SW1
35 Camberwell Grove, SE5
51 The Chase, SW4
Field House, Chiswick Mall Gardens,
 W4
21 Northchurch Terrace, De Beauvoir
 Gardens, N1
3 Elm Court, Elm Court Gardens,
 EN4
48 Erskine Hill, NW11
NEW 20 Exeter Road
70 Gloucester Crescent, NW1
45 Great North Road, EN5
17 Greenstone Mews, E11
7 The Grove, N6
116 Hamilton Terrace, NW8
Highwood Ash, NW7
NEW 2 Hillside Close, NW8
1a Hungerford Road, N7
23 Imperial Road, N22
1 Battlebridge Court, Islington
 Gardens, N1
Little Lodge, KT7
53 Mapledene Road, London Fields
 Gardens, E8
8 Almack Road, Lower Clapton
 Gardens, E5
94 Marsh Lane Allotments, N17
27 Menelik Road, NW2
65 Mill Hill Road, W3
41 Mill Hill Road, W3
2 Millfield Place, N6
66 Muswell Avenue, N10
17a Navarino Road, E8
3 The Park, N6
4 Park Village East (Tower Lodge
 Gardens), NW1
26 Kenilworth Road, Penge Gardens,
 SE20
Penge Gardens, SE20
Royal College of Physicians Medicinal
 Garden, NW1
7 St George's Road, TW1
87 St Johns Road, E17
57 St Quintin Avenue, W10
5 St Regis Close, N10
41 Southbrook Road, SE12
Southwood Lodge, N6
Stokes House, TW10
93 Tanfield Avenue, NW2
58A Teignmouth Road, NW2
27 Horniman Drive, Tewkesbury
 Lodge: Top of the Hill, SE23
White Cottage, BR5
86 Willifield Way, NW11
33 Wood Vale, N10

The Gardens

29 ADDISON AVENUE, W11

London W11 4QS. Shirley Nicholson. *No entry for cars from Holland Park Ave, approach via Queensdale Rd. Tube: Holland Park or Shepherds Bush. Buses: 31, 94, 148, 228, 295, 316.* **Adm £3, chd free. Sun 21 June, Sun 26 July (2-6). Also open 57 St Quintin Ave (Sun 26 July).**

The small lawn is dominated by an ancient pear tree and surrounded by shrubs and hardy geraniums. The colour scheme is of soft blues and pinks; no yellow allowed! In June roses and clematis (a speciality here) cover the walls, while in late July phlox, salvia and monarda make a bright splash in the centre beds. Plenty of ideas for those who think their gardens are finished by the end of June.

🎪 ❀

GROUP OPENING

ALEXANDRA PARK ROAD GARDENS, N22

Nos 270, 272, 279, 289 & 300, Alexandra Park Road, London N22 7BG. *Tube: Bounds Green or Wood Green, then bus 10 mins. Train: Alexandra Park. Buses: 184, W3. Alight at junction of Alexandra Park Rd & Palace Gates Rd.* Home-made teas at No 272. **Combined adm £4.50, chd free. Sun 2 Aug (2-6).**

270 ALEXANDRA PARK ROAD
Dan McGiff.

272 ALEXANDRA PARK ROAD
Clive Boutle & Kate Tattersall

279 ALEXANDRA PARK ROAD
Gail & Wilf Downing

289 ALEXANDRA PARK ROAD
Julie Littlejohn

300 ALEXANDRA PARK ROAD
Paul Cox & Bee Peak

On the site of the original Alexandra Park estate are five front gardens and a back garden to enjoy: the surprisingly long rear garden of a 1920s house backing onto deer enclosure, and five exuberant contrasting front gardens. The back garden retains many pre war features incl an Anderson Shelter, rock garden, crazy paving and venerable trees as well as a tree house, greenhouse and wildlife friendly eclectic planting. The front gardens all provide colour and interest for the community and are inspiring examples of how much can be achieved in a very small space. There is a profusion of colour in pots, while tall plants hide a secret hidden from the street. One steeply sloping front garden has a semi tropical theme, with a rill running through a riverbed rockery, disappearing under the path and dropping into a pool surrounded by beautiful stones, another is a modern re-creation of a cottage country garden, another concentrates on scent and screening to hide its roadside location. Winner - London Green Corners Award.

❀ ☕

Wildlife friendly eclectic planting . . .

ALL SEASONS, W5

97 Grange Road, Ealing W5 3PH. Dr Benjamin & Mrs Maria Royappa. *Tube: Ealing Broadway/South Ealing/Ealing Common: 10-15 mins walk.* Home-made teas. **Adm £3, chd free. Sat 4 July (1-6); Sun 5 July (12.30-6).**

Garden designed, built and planted by owners, with new interesting planting, features incl ponds, pergolas, Japanese gardens, tropical house for orchids, exotics and aviaries. Several recycled features, composting and rain water harvesting, orchard, kiwi, grape vines, architectural and unusual plants incl ferns, bamboos, conifers and cacti. Partial wheelchair access.

♿ ❀ ☕

37 ALWYNE ROAD, N1

London N1 2HW. Mr & Mrs J Lambert. *Buses: 38, 56, 73, 341 on Essex Rd; 4, 19, 30, 43 on Upper St, alight at Town Hall; 271 on Canonbury Rd, A1. Tube: Highbury & Islington.* Home-made teas. **Adm £4, chd free. Share to The Friends of the Rose Bowl. Sun 31 May (2-6).**

The New River curves around the garden, freeing it from the restraints of the London rectangle and allowing degrees of formality. Roses along the river, topiary, an urban meadow next to the conservatory, a secluded spot where the life of the river is part of the charm. The garden continues to develop, visitors return to see what's new and enjoy the spectacular array of extremely good homemade cakes. Shelter available if wet. Wheelchair access with own assistant only for 3 entrance steps.

♿ ❀ ☕

GROUP OPENING

AMWELL GARDENS GROUP, EC1R

South Islington, London EC1R 1YE. *Tube: Angel, 5 mins walk. Buses: 19, 38 to Rosebery Ave; 30, 73 to Pentonville Rd.* Home-made teas at 11 Chadwell St. **Combined adm £6, chd free. Sun 21 June (2-5.30).**

11 CHADWELL STREET
Mary Aylmer & Andrew Post. *off Myddelton Sq*

LLOYD SQUARE
Lloyd Square Garden Committee. *off Amwell Street*

27 MYDDELTON SQUARE
Sally & Rob Hull

NEW RIVER HEAD
NRH Residents. *Myddelton Passage, off Myddelton Sq*

49 WHARTON STREET
London. David Sulkin & Geoffrey Milton. *off Lloyd Sq*

The Amwell Gardens Group is in a secluded corner of Georgian Clerkenwell. Contrasting gardens include Lloyd Square, a mature space with drifting borders in the centre of the Lloyd Baker Estate, and the nearby gardens surrounding the historic New River Head, where a stylish fountain and pergola have replaced the outer pond, which distributed fresh water to London. In Myddelton Square two courtyard gardens with contrasting styles complement this elegant terraced setting. New for 2013, a small garden in Wharton Street features a bandstand and musician.

☕

121 ANSON ROAD, NW2
London NW2 4AH. Helen Marcus. *Cricklewood. Tube: Willesden Grn or Kilburn, Thameslink: Cricklewood, Buses: 226, (Dawson Rd stop) 16, 32, 189, 245, 260, 266, 316 to Cricklewood Bdy.* **Adm £2.50, chd free. Sun 5 July (2-5.30). Also opening 27 Menelik Rd and 58A Teignmouth Rd, combined adm (3 gardens), £8, chld free.**
Lush country style garden brimming with colour and yr-round interest, surrounded by mature trees and shrubs creating a secluded haven. Lawned area with deep flower borders densely planted for sun and shade; wide variety of cottage garden and unusual plants, shrubs, perennials, clematis, roses. Trellises, urns and statues used to create unexpected vistas and focal points. Charming produce garden combining formal features with wild flower area, vegetables and fruit.
&

GROUP OPENING

ARLINGTON SQUARE GARDENS, N1
London N1 7DP, www.arlingtonassociation.org.uk. *South Islington. Off New North Rd via Arlington Ave or Linton St. Buses: 21, 76, 141, 271. Home-made teas at The Vicarage, 1A Arlington Square.* **Combined adm £6, chd free. Sun 7 June (1.30-5.30).**

> **26 ARLINGTON AVENUE**
> Mr Thomas Blaikie

> **21 ARLINGTON SQUARE**
> Ms Alison Rice

> **25 ARLINGTON SQUARE**
> Mr Michael Foley

> NEW ▶ **27 ARLINGTON SQUARE**
> Mr Geoffrey Wheat & Rev. Justin Gau

> NEW ▶ **28 ARLINGTON SQUARE**
> Mr & Mrs H Li

> **5 REES STREET**
> Gordon McArthur & Paul Thompson

> **ST JAMES' VICARAGE**
> John & Maria Burniston

Behind the early Victorian facades of Arlington Square are 7 town gardens that cover the full spectrum of gardening styles, from modern contemporary design to the traditional cottage garden. It is interesting to see how each garden has used the limited area available to create an inspiring and relaxing space. 2 new gardens have joined the group, both designed by local garden designer Paul Thompson-McArthur, whose own garden is part of the group. One is sleek and modern, utilising cutting edge hard landscaping to create an outside room very much in keeping with the house interior. The other is a classic cottage garden designed as a haven from the modern world. Adjacent to each other, it is intriguing how a similar palette of plants can be used to achieve very different results. The other gardens in the group are mature and reflect the diverse tastes and interests of each garden owner. It is hard to believe you are moments from the bustle of the City of London. Featured in The English Garden.
☕

Small but beautifully formed... a pure joy to see . . .

61 ARTHUR ROAD, SW19
Wimbledon, London SW19 7DN. Daniela McBride. *Tube: Wimbledon Park, then 8 mins walk. Mainline: Wimbledon, 18 mins walk.* Tea. **Adm £4, chd free. Sun 14 June (2-6). Also open 97 Arthur Rd.**
In spring, the main features of this steeply sloping garden are the woodland walks, filled with bulbs, flowering shrubs and ferns. In early summer the focus moves to the many roses grown around the garden, then later the autumn colour is provided by trees and shrubs. Partial wheelchair access to top lawn and terrace only, steep slopes elsewhere.
& ☕

97 ARTHUR ROAD, SW19
Wimbledon, London SW19 7DP. Tony & Bella Covill. *Wimbledon Park tube, then 200yds up hill on R.* Light refreshments. **Adm £3, chd free. Sun 14 June (2-6). Also open 61 Arthur Road.**
¹/₃ acre garden of an Edwardian house. Garden established for more than 20yrs and constantly evolving with a large variety of plants and shrubs. It has grown up around several lawns with pond and fountains. Abundance of wildlife and a bird haven. A beautiful place with much colour, foliage and texture.
& 🏵 ☕

ARUNDEL & LADBROKE GARDENS, W11
Kensington Park Road, Notting Hill W11 2LW. Arundel & Ladbroke Gardens Committee, 07957 640816, susan.lynn1@ntlworld.com, www.arundelladbrokegardens.co.uk. *Entrance on Kensington Park Rd, between Ladbroke & Arundel Gardens. Tube: Notting Hill Gate, Buses: 23, 52, 452.* Home-made teas. **Adm £4, chd free. Sun 10 May (2-6). Visitors also welcome by arrangement Mar to Nov for max 10 visitors.**
A private square, of mid Victorian design, planted as a woodland garden: massed rhododendrons, camellias, some crinodendron and flowering dogwoods, a glade of spring bulbs among birch, dogwood, cercis and amelanchier; Australasian plants, such as prostanthera, corokia, dianella and dicksonias, as well as acers, clerodendron and a Stachyurus chinensis for foliage interest. Wheelchair access possible but 2 steps and gravel paths to negotiate.
& 🏵 ☕

4 ASMUNS HILL, NW11
Hampstead Garden Suburb NW11 6ET. Peter & Yvonne Oliver, 020 8455 8741, yvonne.oliver@virgin.net. *Close to Finchley Rd & N Circular. Tube: Golders Green, then buses 82, 102 or 460 to Temple Fortune, then 2 mins walk along Hampstead Way, Asmuns Hill 2nd on L.* **Adm £3.50, chd free. Sun 19 July (1-6). Also open 86 Willifield Way. Visitors also welcome by arrangement May to Aug.**
Arts and Crafts cottage garden in the Artisan's Quarter of Hampstead

Garden Suburb. Many Clematis in front and back gardens. Heleniums. Crocosmias, Salvias and other bee friendly plants. Pond, patio, herbaceous bed, shade area. Succulents and Acers. Sculptures and objets trouvés. Garden visited by HRH Prince Edward in 2013. Featured in Hampstead & Highgate Express and winner of London Gardens Society Silver Gilt Medal and Cup.

  ♿ ❀

190 BARNET ROAD, EN5
Arkley, Barnet EN5 3LF. Hilde & Lionel Wainstein, 020 8441 4041, hildewainstein@hotmail.co.uk. *1m S of A1, 2m N of High Barnet tube. Garden is located on corner of A411, Barnet Rd & Meadowbanks cul-de-sac. Nearest tube: High Barnet, then 107 bus, Glebe Lane stop. Plenty of on rd unrestricted parking.* Selection of home-made cakes worthy of Mary Berry! **Adm £3.50, chd free. Sun 31 May, Sun 19 July (2-6). Visitors also welcome by arrangement Apr to Sept.**
Garden designer's walled garden, approx 90ft x 36ft. Modern, asymmetric design thickly planted in flowing, natural drifts around trees, shrubs and central pond; a changing array of interesting containers and found objects. Handmade beaten copper trellis divides the space into contrasting areas. The garden continues to evolve as new planted areas are expanded. This yr the lawn has to go! National Collection of akebias. Wide range of interesting plants for sale, incl akebia, all propagated from the garden. Single steps within garden.

  ♿ ❀ **NCH** ☕

NEW ▶ **20 BEECHWOOD AVENUE, TW9**
Kew, Richmond TW9 4DE. Dr Laura de Beden, lauradebeden@hotmail.com. *Within walking distance of Kew Gardens Tube Station.* **Evening Openings £5, chd free, wine, Sat 30 May, Sat 11 July, Sun 6 Sept (6-8). Also open 31 West Park Road (Sat 30 May). Visitors also welcome by arrangement May to Sept for groups 10 - 20 max.**
Delightful small town garden, minutes away from Royal Botanic Gardens and Kew Retail Pk. 'Follow your Bliss', Joseph Campbell's tenet words guided the creation of this garden. A decidedly minimal design

layout offsets exquisite favourite planting. Writing shed holds pride of place as the main idea-production centre. Topiary, pots, sculpture, surprises, good humour and Autumn colour all on offer. Wheelchair access to main patio only.

  ♿ ❀ ☕

The NGS has funded 147 different Macmillan projects

17 BELSIZE LANE, NW3
Hampstead NW3 5AD. Maureen Michaelson, 020 7435 0510, mm@maureenmichaelson.com, www.maureenmichaelson.com. *Trains: Belsize Park 5 mins; Hampstead Heath, Finchley Rd, Swiss Cottage 12 mins. Closest to Haverstock Hill buses & Belsize Park tube. From Swiss Cottage/Finchley Rd go past village shops on Belsize Lane & turn L to stay on Belsize Lane after Village Close. Opp School.* **Adm £3.50, chd free. Sun 14 June (2-6). Visitors also welcome by arrangement May to Sept.**
Professional garden art gallerist's own lushly planted garden. Backdrop of screening trees and focus on evergreens. Flashes of colour from perennials and flowering shrubs. Irregular shaped plot reveals different aspects. Pergolas with many climbers, small pond, deck with large planted pots. Works by contemporary artists incl sculptures and installations in ceramic, glass, copper; slate tables and chairs. Unusual plants for sale, all propagated from garden. Also open in association with Chelsea Fringe. See www.chelseafringe.com for details. Features in Ham & High and Fabric magazine. Access for wheelchair 69cm.

  ♿ ❀

BINA GARDENS EAST, SW7
Dove Mews, London SW7 4NH. Alice Ulm. *Pedestrian access through Dove Mews off Old Brompton Rd, or Rosary Gardens, Kensington. Tube: Gloucester Rd - 5 mins away.* Tea. **Adm £3, chd free. Sun 20 Sept (12-5).**
A private secret garden of ⅓ of an acre, hidden behind buildings. The original formal layout of 1880 is softened by generous and mature planting. Predominantly in shade there is enough light and warmth to grow unusual and exotic plants. As a winner of many London garden competitions, both plants and sculptures reflect a personal touch. Wonderful in September. Plant list available. Garden team attending opening.

  ☎ ❀ ☕

5 BRODIE ROAD, E4
Chingford, London E4 7HF. Mr & Mrs N Booth. *From Chingford train station, any bus to Chingford Green (Co-op), turn L at Prezzo, 2nd R (Scholars Rd), then 1st L.* Light refreshments. **Adm £3, chd free. Sat 15, Sun 16 Aug (2-5).**
A constantly evolving garden with new plantings annually obtained from specialist nurseries. The gardener's love of butterflies has moulded the planting style over the years, with two wide herbaceous borders packed with stunning colour from heleniums, rudbeckia, hydrangeas and dahlias. The borders are intersected by a narrow path leading to clematis and rose covered arches.

  ☕

53 BROOK DRIVE, HA1
Harrow HA1 4RT. Mr Brian Porter. *1m W of Harrow & Wealdstone stn & H9 bus to Pinner View, or 1m N of Harrow on the Hill stn & H14 bus Hatch End to Headstone Gdns/Drive.* Light refreshments at 51 Brook Drive. **Adm £3, chd free. Sun 26 Apr (2-5).**
Lots of lush colour, especially in spring with a selection of vegetables amongst a variety of perennials, bulbs, shrubs and trees incl two magnificent magnolias in a small suburban garden. Wheelchair access via side passage.

  ♿ ☕

33A BROOKHILL ROAD AND 33B BROOKHILL ROAD, EN4

Barnet EN4 8SE. Barbara Perry, 020 8400 0319. *Between E Barnet Rd & Cat Hill. Tube: Cockfosters on Piccadilly line then 384 bus to Brookhill Rd, High Barnet Northern line then 384 bus to Brookhill Rd.* Home-made teas. **Adm £3, chd free. Sun 21 June (2-5). Visitors also welcome by arrangement July to Sept for groups 6 to 12 max. Price on application.**
Award winning small secluded courtyard garden. An oasis of tranquillity packed with harmonising shrubs, perennials, trees and over 50 clematis. Easily maintained. New for 2015 the owner is developing the neighbouring garden as a dry garden, utilising gravel and reclaimed materials. A garden on a shoestring budget, this is work in progress and will evolve in time.

94 BROWNLOW ROAD, N11

Bounds Green, London N11 2BS. Spencer Viner, www.northeleven.co.uk. *Close to N Circular. Tube: Bounds Green then 5 mins walk, direction N Circular. Corner of Elvendon Rd & Brownlow Rd.* Light refreshments. **Adm £2.50, chd free. Sun 17 May, Sun 6 Sept (2-6). Also open Princess Av (Sun 17 May); 5 Russell Rd and Golf Course Allotments (Sun 6 Sept).**
A small courtyard for meditation. The conception of this garden by a designer has the ability to transport the visitor to a different, foreign place of imagination and tranquillity, far away from the suburbs. Features incl reclaimed materials, trees, water, pergola, pleached limes, seating and a strong theme of pared back simplicity. Design and horticultural advice.

5 BURBAGE ROAD, SE24

Herne Hill SE24 9HJ. Crawford & Rosemary Lindsay, 020 7274 5610, rl@rosemarylindsay.com, www.rosemarylindsay.com. *Nr junction with Half Moon Lane. Herne Hill & N Dulwich mainline stns, 5 mins walk. Buses: 3, 37, 40, 68, 196, 468.* Home-made teas. **Adm £3.50, chd free. Sun 17 May (2-5). Also open Stoney Hill House. Visitors also welcome by arrangement Mar to July.**
The garden of a member of The Society of Botanical Artists. 150ft x

40ft with large and varied range of plants. Herb garden, herbaceous borders for sun and shade, climbing plants, pots, terraces, lawns. Gravel areas to reduce watering. See our website for what the papers say. Very popular plant sale and home-made teas. Featured in The English Garden and Garden Answers.

12 BUSHBERRY ROAD, E9

Hackney E9 5SX. Molly St Hilaire. *Overground stn: Homerton, then 5 mins walk. Buses: 26, 30, 388, alight last stop in Cassland Rd.* Tea. **Adm £3, chd free. Sun 28 June (2-6).**
Petite courtyard garden with water feature. Rambling roses, jasmine, vine and clematis cover the overarching pergola. Small but beautifully formed... a pure joy to see.

7 BYNG ROAD, EN5

High Barnet EN5 4NW. Mr & Mrs Julian Bishop, 020 8440 2042. *Opp Foulds School - 10 mins walk from tube. Tube: High Barnet. Stn: Hadley Wood or New Barnet. Buses: 107, 263, 384 alight Ravenscroft Park or The Spires.* Home-made teas. **Adm £3, chd free. Sun 5 July (1-5). Visitors also welcome by arrangement Apr to Sept.**
Six different borders all in one London garden. One filled with tropical plants, another hot border, two with cooler coloured perennials. Lots of rare and unusual varieties with a modern design twist. Owner a Chelsea Flower Show TV producer for 10 yrs. Emphasis on salvias, day lilies, digitalis and unusual half hardy plants. Also vegetable/cutting garden, series of raised beds and colourful pots.

CADOGAN PLACE SOUTH GARDEN, SW1

Sloane Street, London SW1X 9PE. The Cadogan Estate, 07890 452992, Ric.Glenn@cadogan.co.uk. *Entrance to garden opp 97 Sloane St.* **Adm £3.50, chd free. Sun 10 May (10-4). Visitors also welcome by arrangement Mar to Nov with head gardener tours by request.**
Many surprises and unusual trees and shrubs are hidden behind the railings of this large London square. The first square to be developed by architect Henry Holland for Lord Cadogan at the end of C18, it was then called the London Botanic Garden. Mulberry trees planted for

silk production at end of C17. Cherry trees, magnolias and bulbs are outstanding in spring, when the fern garden is unfurling. Award winning Hans Sloane Garden exhibited at the Chelsea Flower Show. Pond. Spring walk on East side of garden. Feel free to bring a picnic to enjoy in the garden.

> Lots of lush colour, especially in spring . . .

9A CALONNE ROAD, SW19

London SW19 5HH. Mr & Mrs Neville & Marissa Quie. *Wimbledon. Tube & Mainline: Wimbledon 15-20 mins walk. Bus: 93 on Parkside.* Tea. **Adm £3, chd free. Sun 10 May (12-3).**
Japanese inspired garden with many acers, bamboo, sunken rock pool and Balinese summerhouse. Colourful display of rhododendrons and bulbs. Bird boxes to encourage wildlife. Interesting new planting still in progress.

81 CAMBERWELL GROVE, SE5

London SE5 8JE. Jane & Alex Maitland Hudson. *5 mins from Denmark Hill mainline & Overground stn. Buses: 12, 36, 68, 148, 171, 185, 436. Entrance at rear please follow yellow NGS signs.* Home-made teas. **Adm £3, chd free. Sun 14 June (2-6).**
A large Japanese maple and a tall trachycarpus palm shade York stone paving and borders filled with herbaceous perennials, roses, clematis and shade loving ground cover. There is a pond and bog garden. Pots are a feature of the garden bringing colour and diversity. A west facing garden room filled with scented leaf geraniums catches the afternoon sun, and small greenhouse allows propagation. We also pride ourselves on our home made cakes.

4 Stradbroke Grove

© Harpur GL

35 CAMBERWELL GROVE, SE5
London SE5 8JA. Lynette
Hemmant & Juri Gabriel, 020 7703
6186, juri@jurigabriel.com. *Backing
onto St Giles Church, Camberwell
Church St. From Camberwell Green
go down Camberwell Church St. Turn
R into Camberwell Grove.* Fruit juice
and biscuits available. **Adm £3.50,
chd free. Share to St Giles Church.
Sun 7 June (12-6). Also open 174
Peckham Rye and 4 Cornflower
Terrace. Visitors also welcome by
arrangement June to July.**
Plant packed 120ft x 20ft garden with
charming backdrop of St Giles
Church. Evolved over 30yrs into a
romantic country style garden
brimming with colour and overflowing
with pots. In June, spectacular roses
stretch the full length of the garden,
both on the artist's studio and
festooning an old iron staircase.
Artist's studio open. Lynette (who has
earned her living by pen and brush
throughout her life) has painted the
garden obsessively for the past 20yrs;
see her (lynettehemmant.com) and
NGS websites. Extensive press and
some tv coverage over the yrs.

4 CANONBURY PLACE, N1
London N1 2NQ. Mr & Mrs Jeffrey
Tobias. *Tube & Overground:
Highbury & Islington. Buses: 271 to
Canonbury Square. Located in the
old part of Canonbury Place, off*

Alwyne Villas in a cul de sac. Home-
made teas. **Adm £3.50, chd free.
Sat 11 Apr (2-5).**
A paved, 100ft garden behind a 1780
house. Spectacular mature trees
enclosed in a walled garden. Mostly
pots and also interesting shrubs and
climbers. Daffodils, tulips and
bluebells abound for this springtime
opening.

23 CANONBURY PLACE, N1
London N1 2NY. *Canonbury,
Islington. Highbury & Islington:
Overground & Tube. Buses: 271 to
Canonbury Sq 4, 19, 30 to St Paul's
Rd.* **Adm £2.50, chd free. Share to
Stand By Me. Sat 11 Apr (2-5).**
Award winning front and back
gardens featuring wisteria, spring
flowers, fruit trees and a small, wildlife
pond.

NEW ▶ **CAPEL MANOR
COLLEGE, GUNNERSBURY
PARK CAMPUS, W3**
The Walled Garden, Popes Lane
W3 8LQ. Sarah Neophytou,
www.capel.ac.uk/gunnersbury-
park-centre.html. *From Chiswick
r'about going N on A406, turn L into
Popes Lane at BP Garage. Entrance
to free car park on L just past
pedestrian Xing. Nearest tube; Acton
Town, 10 mins walk. Bus; E3 stops at*

entrance to car park. **Adm £4, chd
free. Sat 13 June (1-5).**
Sited within the Walled Garden in
Gunnersbury Park, formerly owned
by the Rothschild family, is one of the
Capel Manor College campuses,
specialising in teaching landbased
industries such as Horticulture,
Animal Care and Floristry. Usually
closed to the public, this garden is
maintained entirely by Horticulture
students, one member of staff and a
handful of student volunteers. There
are a range of loosely themed
borders, tropical, Mediterranean, and
herbaceous, together with raised
beds for vegetable growing. At the
top of the student practice area is a
new Stumpery garden, built by
students during 2013/2014. Tree
ferns, a range of deciduous trees,
woodland planting, incl drifts of
digitalis, give a magical feel.
Imaginative use of dead wood and
stumps contrast eerily with the
planting. Incl a dead hedge structure,
log seating and wildlife friendly areas.
Café in Gunnersbury Park (nr
museum) for refreshments. Paths
through Stumpery not suitable for
wheelchair users but area can be
viewed. Borders and vegetable areas
have good access.

CAPEL MANOR GARDENS
See Hertfordshire.

5 CECIL ROAD, N10
Muswell Hill N10 2BU. Ben Loftus.
*Off Alexandra Park Rd. Buses: 102,
299 from E Finchley or Bounds
Green, alight St Andrew's Church.*
**Adm £2.50, chd free. Sun 5 July
(2-5). Also open 66 Muswell Av and
14 Tetherdown.**
Garden designer's sloping garden
featured in several magazines.
Spectacular, well planted large pots
(irrigated), interesting small raised
pond, unusual South American trees,
shrubs and perennials with much
emphasis on foliage and shape.
Stylish garden office with green roof
of bulbs, thymes etc. Lush garden
with all soil and boundaries hidden by
plants.

**Marie Curie
Cancer Care**

Marie Curie's
hospice
gardens provide
tranquillity
for
patients

THE CHARTERHOUSE, EC1
Charterhouse Square, London
EC1M 6AN. The Governors of
Sutton's Hospital.
www.thecharterhouse.org. *Buses:
4, 55. Tube: Barbican. Turn L out of
stn, L into Carthusian St & into
square. Entrance through car park.*
**Evening Opening £5, chd free,
wine, Tue 2 June (6-9).**
Enclosed courtyard gardens within
the grounds of historic Charterhouse,
which dates back to 1347. English
country garden style featuring roses,
herbaceous borders, ancient
mulberry trees and small pond.
Various garden herbs found here are
still used in the kitchen today. In
addition, two other areas are being
opened for the NGS. Pensioners
Court, which is partly maintained by

the private tenants and Master's
Garden, the old burial ground
which now consists of lawns,
borders and wildlife garden planted
to camouflage a war time air raid
shelter. A private garden for the
Brothers of Charterhouse, not usually
open to the public. (Buildings not
open).
♿

51 THE CHASE, SW4
London SW4 0NP. Mr Charles
Rutherfoord & Mr Rupert Tyler,
020 7627 0182,
mail@charlesrutherfoord.net,
www.charlesrutherfoord.net. *Off
Clapham Common Northside. Tube:
Clapham Common. Buses: 137, 452.*
Light refreshments. **Adm £4, chd
free. Evening Opening £4, chd
free, Light refreshments, Wed 22
Apr (6-8). Sun 26 Apr (12-6).
Visitors also welcome by
arrangement Apr to Oct.**
Member of the Society of Garden
Designers, Charles has created the
garden over 30yrs. 2015 will see a
remodelling of the main garden.
Spectacular in spring, when 2000
tulips bloom among irises and tree
peonies. Scented front garden.
Rupert's geodetic dome shelters
seedlings, succulents and
subtropicals.
🄿 🍵

**♦ CHELSEA PHYSIC GARDEN,
SW3**
66 Royal Hospital Road, London
SW3 4HS. Chelsea Physic Garden
Company, 020 7352 5646,
www.chelseaphysicgarden.co.uk.
*Tube: Sloane Square (10 mins). Bus:
170. Parking: Battersea Park
(charged). Entrance in Swan Walk
(except wheelchairs).* **Adm £9.90,
chd £6.60. For NGS: Wed 1 Apr
(11-6). For other opening times and
information, please phone or see
garden website.**
Come and explore London's oldest
botanic garden situated in the heart
of Chelsea. With a unique living
collection of around 5000 plants this
walled Garden is a celebration of the
importance of plants and their beauty.
Highlights of the Garden incl Europe's
oldest pond rockery, the Garden of
Edible and Useful plants and the
Garden of Medicinal Plants which
opened in 2014. Tours also available.
Wheelchair access is via 66 Royal
Hospital Rd.
♿ ✿ 🚌 🍵

46 CHEYNE AVENUE, E18
South Woodford, London E18 2DR.
Helen Auty. *Nearest tube S
Woodford. Short walk. From station
take Clarendon Rd. Cross High Rd
into Broadwalk, 3rd on L Bushey Ave.
1st R Cheyne Ave.* Light
refreshments. **Adm £3.50, chd free.
Sun 16 Aug (12-4).**
On site of Lord Cheyne's original
market garden, typical suburban
garden with lawn and borders of
shrubs, climbers and perennials -
greenhouse and productive fruit and
vegetable garden.
✿ 🍵

GROUP OPENING

CHISWICK MALL GARDENS, W4
Chiswick W6 9TN. *Car: Towards
Hogarth r'about, A4 (W) turn Eyot
Grds S. Tube: Stamford Brook or
Turnham Green. Buses: 27, 190, 267
& 391 to Young's Corner. From
Chiswick High Rd or Kings St S under
A4 to river.* Tea at 16 Eyot Gardens.
**Combined adm £6, chd free.
Sun 31 May (2-6).**

16 EYOT GARDENS
Ms Dianne Farris

FIELD HOUSE
Rupert King
**Visitors also welcome by
arrangement Apr to Oct.**
kingrupert@hotmail.com
www.fieldhousegarden.co.uk

SWAN HOUSE
Mr & Mrs George Nissen

This peaceful riverside setting offers
three very different gardens. An
informal walled garden with
herbaceous borders, fruit trees and
small vegetable garden. An Eastern
inspired water garden with exotic and
unusual planting. And lastly an end of
terrace inner city garden with wisteria,
Canary Bird Rosa, and two lovingly
maintained lawns.
🌿

CHOUMERT SQUARE, SE15
London SE15 4RE. The Residents.
*Off Choumert Grove. Trains from
London Bridge, Clapham Junction to
Peckham Rye; buses (12, 36, 37, 63,
78, 171, 312, 345). Car park 2 mins.*
Home-made teas. **Adm £4, chd free.
Share to St Christopher's Hospice.
Sun 7 June (1-6). Also open 174
Peckham Rye and 4 Cornflower
Terrace.**

Lemon drizzle cake, Victoria sponge … yummy!

About 46 mini gardens with maxi planting in Shangri-la situation that the media has described as a Floral Canyon, which leads to small communal secret garden. The popular open gardens will combine this yr with our own take on a village fete with home produce stalls, arts, crafts and music. Regular national and local press coverage since first opening in 1999.

NEW 31 CHURCH CRESCENT, N3
Finchley Church End, London N3 1BE. Gerald & Margaret Levin. *7 min walk from Finchley Central Underground (Northern Line, High Barnet branch). Buses nearby incl 82, 460, 125, 326, 143 and 382. No parking restrictions on Sun.* Home-made teas. **Adm £3.50, chd free. Sun 2 Aug (2-6).**
120ft x 30ft E facing garden designed and built by us with no straight lines, three season interest and a wildlife pond as the focal point. A sunny terrace with tubs, three beds around the pond with interesting shrubs and perennials, and a more challenging shadier area with trees, shrubs and ferns. Recent removal of a large birch has given us many new planting opportunities. Partial wheelchair access. Two shallow steps from public footpath into garden, one within garden. Level access to refreshments in conservatory.

60 CHURCH CRESCENT, N10
Muswell Hill, London N10 3NE. Liz Gill. *Tube: Highgate, then 12 mins walk. Buses: 43, 134 along Muswell Hill Rd then 1 min walk.* Home-made teas. **Adm £3.50, chd free. Sun 21 June (2-6). Also open 5 St Regis Close.**
Panoramic views over parkland walk and beyond set off writer's garden constructed over 4 levels. Raised deck with herb filled tubs, patio with colourful containers and mini alpine garden. Horseshoe lawn surrounded by lushly planted borders, rose covered arch leads to romantic secluded gravel area with wildlife pond.

79 CHURCH LANE, N2
London N2 0TH. Caro & David Broome. *Tube: E Finchley, then East End Rd for ³/₄ m, R into Church Ln. Buses: 143 to Five Bells PH, 3 min walk; 263 to E Finchley Library, 5 min walk.* Home-made teas. Mouth watering selection incl gluten free. **Adm £3.50, chd free. Sun 14 June (2-6).**
Constantly evolving, a garden writer's garden with a twist. Enter through catatorium, a plant filled open air conservatory, into the patio garden beyond, packed full of shrubs, roses and unusual perennials to create a colour coordinated palette, with curved rill, hidden water features and quirky ornamentals! Rustic archway leads to secluded ferny glen, home to a secret hideaway. Locally propagated perennials ideal for London clay soils. Ever popular raffle and always something new to see in the planting schemes. Columnist for Garden News - Over The Fence. Featured in Amateur Gardener and on The One Show and Love Your Garden. Thompson and Morgan plant triallists and bloggers. Highly Commended by The London Gardens' Society.

GROUP OPENING

CLAPHAM MANOR STREET GARDENS, SW4
Clapham Old Town, London SW4 6DZ. *Tube: Clapham Common. Off Clapham High St.* Home-made teas. **Combined adm £6, chd free. Sun 21 June (2-5).**

40 CLAPHAM MANOR STREET
Mrs Nina Murdoch

44 CLAPHAM MANOR STREET
Mrs Annette Marchini

Two creatively inspired secret, romantic walled gardens. No.40 is a large garden divided by trained arches of apple trees. It contains a cobbled courtyard, a stream, ferns and ivy garden, 2 ponds and many climbers. No.44 has the emphasis on lush green planting with white flowers, creating a soft, organic counterpoint to the contemporary extension. Perfect habitats for breeding birds, especially sparrows.

NEW CLEVELAND SQUARE, W2
London W2 6DD. The Residents, www.clevelandsquare.org. *Entrance on W side. 5 mins from Paddington, Queensway, Lancaster Gate, Royal Oak & Bayswater tube. 5 mins from many bus routes, eg 23, 27, 36, 94, 148. Metered parking on & nr Square.* **Adm £4, chd free. Sun 26, Wed 29 Apr (2-5).**
This garden will have special appeal to horticulturists with its emphasis on design and sequential colour and form. Planting is for a sequence of colour design, biodiversity, and flowers for insect and bird life twelve months of the yr. The garden is in the London square tradition of renewal, but incl horticultural elements from domestic country gardens with fruit and herbs for cutting. The garden has gravel paths but these are usable by wheelchairs.

> Constantly evolving, a garden writer's garden with a twist . . .

NEW 11 CLOUDESLEY STREET, N1
London N1 0HU. Mr & Mrs David & Gilvrie Lock. *Barnsbury, N1. 5mins from Angel Underground & buses, parallel to Liverpool Rd.* Light refreshments. **Adm £3.50, chd free. Sun 28 June (2-6).**
An intriguing garden on two levels, designed by Barbara Hunt, MSGD, for low maintenance, some privacy and to work when viewed from above. The lower patio has shrubs and herbs in pots, and climbers. The upper area has a stainless steel pergola, water feature and dry section with bamboos, an olive tree, clematis, climbing roses, akebia quinata, underplanted with ajuga, epimedium, stachys.

© Sarah Lee

12 Bushberry Road

GROUP OPENING

NEW COPTHALL GROUP, NW7
Mill Hill, London NW7 2NB. *Short bus ride (221) from Edgware tube or Mill Hill East. Free parking vouchers available if restrictions are in force.* Home-made teas at 2 Copthall Drive. **Combined adm £4.50, chd free. Sun 14 June (2-5.30).**

> NEW **2 COPTHALL DRIVE**
> Mrs. Janet Jomain

> NEW **13 COPTHALL GARDENS**
> Mrs Lise Marshfield

Two small town gardens enthusiastically gardened by their plantaholic owners. 13 Copthall Gardens is a mature leafy garden in a quiet cul-de-sac. Emphasis on form and texture. Clipped shrubs, topiary, perennials and roses. Small pond, portal to third dimension. Traditional Finnish swing seat. 2 Copthall Drive is a small east facing town garden with more than 40 roses and many clematis, alliums, hydrangeas and a wildlife pond. A small but productive fruit and vegetable patch incl nectarines and kiwi fruit, and in the greenhouse there may be a pineapple nearly ready to pick.

4 CORNFLOWER TERRACE, SE22
East Dulwich SE22 0HH. Clare Dryhurst. *5 mins walk from 63 bus stop at bottom of Forest Hill Rd. Turn into Dunstans Rd, then 2nd on L. Mainline: Peckham Rye or Honor Oak Park.* Light refreshments. **Adm £3.50, chd free. Sun 7 June (2-5.30). Also open 174 Peckham Rye.**
Still defying size limits, now featuring wrought iron trellises to use every available inch. A pretty, secluded and tiny courtyard cottage garden, only 50ft x 9ft in a quiet street in the heart of artistic East Dulwich. Around a sunken patio with a bench and solar fountain are clustered climbers, roses, ferns, annuals and herbs in raised beds and pots backed by a charming painted garden shed.

6 CORNFORD GROVE, SW12
London SW12 9JF. Susan Venner & Richard Glassborow, 020 8675 8574, sv@vennerlucas.co.uk. *Tube & mainline Balham, then 8 mins walk.* Home-made teas. **Adm £3.50, chd free. Sun 26 Apr (2-6). Evening Opening £3.50, chd free, wine, Mon 27 Apr (6-8).**
This medium sized garden is an integral extension of sustainable low carbon living. The guiding principles within the garden combine aesthetic values with productivity, biodiversity and low maintenance. Technically an orchard, 20 fruiting trees and forest berries merge with herbaceous planting and two working bee hives.

GROUP OPENING

COURT LANE GARDEN GROUP, SE21
Dulwich, London SE21 7EA. *Court Lane, Dulwich, London SE21 7EA. Buses P4, 12, 40, 176, 185 (to Dulwich Library), 37, 176. Mainline: N Dulwich then 20 mins walk. Ample free parking.* Home-made teas at 125, Court Lane. **Combined adm £7, chd free. Share to St Christopher's Hospice. Sun 14 June (2-5.30).**

> NEW **22 COURT LANE**
> Liz & Chris Campbell-Warner

> **122 COURT LANE**
> Jean & Charles Cary-Elwes

> **125 COURT LANE**
> Stephen Henden & Neil Ellis

> **142 COURT LANE**
> Dulwich, London. Jeremy & Jackie Prescott.

Court Lane Garden Group aka South London Urban Gardeners (SLUGS) bring you four gardens with very different planting styles which make for a very interesting visit. Partial wheelchair access.

Look out for the NGS yellow arrows …

High fences are covered with clematis, honeysuckle and passion flowers . . .

GROUP OPENING

DE BEAUVOIR GARDENS, N1
London N1 4HU. *Highbury & Islington tube then 30 or 277 bus; Angel tube then 38, 56 or 73 bus; Bank then 21, 76 or 141 bus. 10 min walk from Dalston Overground stations. Street parking available.* Home-made teas at 158 Culford Road. **Combined adm £6, chd free. Sun 7 June (11-3).**

132 CULFORD ROAD
Mr & Mrs J Ward

158 CULFORD ROAD
Gillian Blachford

NEW **102 DOWNHAM ROAD**
Mr Paul Beard

21 NORTHCHURCH TERRACE
Nancy Korman
Visitors also welcome by arrangement June to July. 0207 249 4919 nancylkorman@hotmail.co.uk

Four gardens to explore in De Beauvoir, a leafy enclave of Victorian villas near to Islington and Dalston. The area boasts some of Hackney's keenest gardeners and a thriving gardening club. New this yr is 102 Downham Road, a formally laid out town house garden with ornamental features, two patios and curved borders with a good mix of flowering shrubs and herbaceous perennials. Returning to the Group this yr, 132 Culford Road has been designed for low maintenance with a sunken garden at house level, a large paved area with a vine and hop covered pergola divided by an island bed from a high rear bed planted with shrubs. 158 Culford Road is a long narrow garden with a romantic feel and a path winding through full borders with shrubs, small trees, perennials and many unusual plants. The walled garden at 21 Northchurch Terrace has a more formal feel, with deep herbaceous borders, pond, fruit trees, pergola, patio pots and herb beds.

GROUP OPENING

DULWICH VILLAGE TWO GARDENS, SE21
London SE21 7BJ. *Rail: N Dulwich or W Dulwich then 10 -15 mins walk. Tube: Brixton then P4 bus passes the gardens, alight Dulwich Picture Gallery stop. Street parking.* Home-made teas at No 103. **Combined adm £5, chd free. Share to Macmillan. Sun 21 June (2-5).** Also open Tewkesbury Lodge: Top of the Hill and Lyndhurst Square Group.

103 DULWICH VILLAGE
Mr & Mrs N Annesley

105 DULWICH VILLAGE
Mr & Mrs A Rutherford

2 Georgian houses with large gardens, 3 mins walk from Dulwich Picture Gallery and Dulwich Park. 103 Dulwich Village is a country garden in London with a long herbaceous border, lawn, pond, roses and fruit and vegetable gardens. 105 Dulwich Village is a very pretty garden with many unusual plants, lots of old fashioned roses, fish pond and water garden. A destination opening! Amazing collection of plants for sale. Wind band provided by Dulwich Symphony Orchestra will be playing in the garden of No.103.

NEW **286 EARL'S COURT ROAD, SW5**
SW5 9AS. Ms Camilla Shivarg, www.gallery286.com. *By Earl's Court Sq, opp Branham Gardens.* **Evening Opening adm £20 incl talk by owner, wine and canapés, Thur 9 July (6-8).** Pre-booked tickets from www.ngs.org.uk or ring 01483 211535.

70ft garden behind the busy Earl's Court Rd comes as a surprise to everyone who sees it for the first time. Started from scratch in 1997, Camilla has created imaginative plant associations and collected many rare tender plant specimens. Garden has a pond, sculpture, and raised beds with circular lawn and two paved areas. Art gallery. Advance booking essential. Featured in many gardening magazines and in Secret Gardens of London book.

207 EAST BARNET ROAD, EN4
New Barnet, London EN4 8QS. Margaret Chadwick, 020 8440 0377, magg1ee@hotmail.com. *M25 J24 then A111 to Cockfosters. Tube: Northern line to High Barnet or Piccadilly line to Cockfosters. Buses: 184, 307 & 326.* Tea. **Adm £3, chd free. Visitors welcome by arrangement Apr to Sept.** Delightful example of a minute courtyard garden 25ft x 30ft. High fences are covered with clematis, honeysuckle and passion flowers; roses and vines scramble over an arch above a seat. Small pond sustains frogs and tadpoles and water plants. An old barrel is home to the Goldfish. Many interesting and unusual plants, mainly in pots. Clever use of mirrors lends added dimensions to this pretty garden. Good use of space, packed full of plants and designed not to reveal itself all at once.

ECCLESTON SQUARE, SW1
London SW1V 1NP. Roger Phillips & the Residents, roger.phillips@rogersroses.com, www.rogerstreesandshrubs.com. *Off Belgrave Rd nr Victoria Stn, parking allowed on Suns.* Home-made teas. **Adm £4, chd free. Sun 10 May (2-5).** Planned by Cubitt in 1828, the 3 acre square is subdivided into mini gardens with camellias, iris, ferns and containers. Dramatic collection of tender climbing roses and 20 different forms of tree peonies. National Collection of ceanothus incl more than 70 species and cultivars. Notable important additions of tender plants being grown and tested. World collection of Ceanothus, Tea Roses and Tree Peonies. Featured on BBC coverage of the Chelsea Flower Show.

EDWARDES SQUARE, W8
South Edwardes Square, Kensington W8 6HL. Edwardes Square Garden Committee. *Tube: Kensington High St & Earls Court. Buses: 9, 10, 27, 28, 31, 49 & 74 to Odeon Cinema. Entrance in South Edwardes Square. Light refreshments.* **Adm £4, chd free. Sun 19 Apr (11.30-5).**
One of London's prettiest secluded garden squares. 3½ acres laid out differently from other squares, with serpentine paths by Agostino Agliothe, Italian artist and decorator who lived at no.15 from 1814-1820, and a beautiful Grecian temple which is traditionally the home of the head gardener. Romantic rose tunnel winds through the middle of the garden. Good displays of bulbs and blossom. Very easy wheelchair access.

  ♿ ☕

GROUP OPENING

ELM COURT GARDENS, EN4
Oakhurst Avenue, East Barnet EN4 8HA. *200 yds from Oakleigh Pk Stn on rail line to Welwyn Garden City. M25 J24, then A111 to Cockfosters & A110 down Cat Hill to East Barnet Village.* Home-made teas. **Combined adm £4.50, chd free. Sun 19 July (2-6).**

> **3 ELM COURT**
> Mike & Alyne Lidgley
> Visitors also welcome by arrangement July to Aug no min, max 20.
> 020 8361 2642

> **4 ELM COURT**
> Simon Moor & Jayne Evans

Two, larger than average, contrasting gardens. Front gardens - one a formal parterre, one natural, with gravel, grasses, conifers and reclaimed materials. Back gardens: No 3 with hot planting, full size and miniature topiary, annuals, perennials, shrubs, baskets, interesting containers, water feature, themed pink, blue, spiky and heuchera beds, a ball bed, greenhouse, sheds that bear close scrutiny, 2 rockeries, alpine display and home grown bonsai. No 4 is long and shady, with curving lawns, a gravel area with containers full of colour, a white bed, a rockery and the whole emphasis is on attracting pollinators - blue, pink, purple and yellow shrubs and perennials. Jayne is a successful artist and has her studio in the garden. A developing garden, still evolving, and gradually triumphing over poor soil, overhanging trees and lack of water. A new stumpery, full of ferns, is loving the shade, and many more perennials are now in place. Plant crÈche: plants purchased delivered locally; raffle prizes are high quality; great cakes, jolly helpers and gazebos for sun or rain make this worth the journey. Both gardens featured in Garden News.

  ❀ ☕

hospiceUK

Visit a garden and support hospice care

ELM TREE COTTAGE, CR2
85 Croham Road, South Croydon CR2 7HJ. Wendy Witherick & Michael Wilkinson, 020 8681 8622, elmtreecottage@sky.com. *2m S of Croydon. Off B275 from Croydon, off A2022 from Selsdon, bus 64. Station: East or South Croydon.* **Adm £3.50. Sun 10 May, Sun 7 June, Sun 9 Aug (1-4). Also open Whitgift School (Sun 7 June).**
Picture this! Come through the gate of our c1855 flint cottage and welcome to the Mediterranean! Meander up the sloping brick path to the sound of running water, see lemon trees, olives, palms and other drought-tolerant plants. Look inside the glasshouse and you will find wonderful agaves! Take a seat before you carry on your journey, past lavender, rosemary and much much more! Featured in Garden Answers. Steep garden, unsuitable for those unsteady on their feet. Regret no dogs or children.

48 ERSKINE HILL, NW11
Hampstead Garden Suburb, London NW11 6HG. Marjorie & David Harris, 020 8455 6507, marjorieharris@btinternet.com. *1m N of Golders Green. Nr A406 & A1. Tube: Golders Green. H2 Hail & Ride bus from Golders Green to garden, or 82, 460, 102 buses to Temple Fortune (10 mins walk).* Home-made teas. **Adm £3.50, chd free. Sun 7 June (2-6). Visitors also welcome** by arrangement May to Sept no min, max 20.
Bird friendly organic garden, wrapped around Arts and Crafts artisan's cottage, featuring perennials, shrubs, roses, clematis, old apple tree and flowering cherry. Terrace with well planted containers. Intriguing brick paved area with four raised beds. Greenhouse. Visited by LGS patron, HRH Prince Edward. Nest boxes, miniature long grass areas, organic and pesticide free. Find the hidden creatures quiz for under 10s. London Gardens Society - Highly Recommended Back Garden. Featured in Ham & High; British General Peoples Gardens by Keiko Igata, pp106-111 (Mr.Partner Publishing Ltd). Some single steps and narrow paths. Rail to lawn.

  ♿ ❀ 🚐 ☕

NEW ▶ 20 EXETER ROAD, NW2
London NW2 4SP. Theo & Renee Laub, 020 8208 0004, reneelaub2@gmail.com. *Nearest tube Kilburn few mins walk.* Home-made teas. **Adm £3.50, chd free. Sun 5 July (2-6).** Also open 121 Anson Rd, 27 Menelik Rd and 58a Teignmouth Rd. **Visitors also welcome by arrangement for groups of 10 max.**
Garden designer's very new garden started from scratch 2½ yrs ago. Small but with interesting features: sculpture and pots. No lawn, good collection of interesting plants - many perennials grown from seed. Water feature and living wall behind it.

  ❀ ☕

♦ FENTON HOUSE, NW3
Hampstead Grove, Hampstead NW3 6SP. National Trust, www.nationaltrust.org.uk. *300yds from Hampstead tube. Entrances: Top of Holly Hill & Hampstead Grove.* **For NGS: Evening Opening, wine, Tue 23 June (6.30-8). Pre booking essential for Special Evening tour, £10 with wine and light refreshments. For tickets please visit www.ngs.org.uk or phone 01483 211535. For other opening times and information, please phone or see garden website.**
Join the Gardener in Charge for a special evening tour. Andrew Darragh who brings over 10 yrs experience from Kew to Fenton House will explore this timeless 1½ acre walled garden. Laid out over 3 levels, and featuring formal walks and areas, a small sunken rose garden, a 300yr

old orchard and a kitchen garden, Andrew will present the garden and his plans for its future development. Special conducted tour by Head Gardener.

NEW▶ 6 FRANK DIXON WAY, SE21
Dulwich, London SE21 7BB. Margaret Hogarth. *Rail: West Dulwich 10 mins walk or North Dulwich 20mins walk. Tube: Brixton then P4 bus to Dulwich College stop. Frank Dixon Way is off College Rd. Street parking.* Home-made teas. **Adm £3.50, chd free. Sun 19 Apr (2-6). Also open South Botanical Institute.**
A serene and tranquil garden in the heart of Dulwich which feels as though you could be in the countryside. In Spring it is filled with a lovely collection of bulbs and early herbaceous plants. The garden is walled on two sides with a mature yew hedge on the other and features a beautiful mirror detail. There is a small vegetable patch and apple, pear, fig and mulberry trees. Wheelchair access to garden via garage.
&♿ ☕

88 FROGNAL, NW3
Frognal, London NW3 6XB. Mr & Mrs M. Linell. *Tube: Hampstead then 7 mins walk. Buses: 46, 268, 13, 113, 82. Garden entrance at 12B Church Row, nr corner with Frognal.* Home-made teas. **Adm £4, chd free. Sun 14 June (2-5.30).**
½ acre garden hidden from view by historic high walls, designed on 2 levels with a terrace and large C19 conservatory near the house leading to lawns all surrounded by herbaceous borders and ornamental trees, shrubs and climbers, many rare, planted and underplanted for yr round effect. Home propagated plants for sale. Bark chip sloping path gives wheelchair access to main lawn from entrance. Steps elsewhere in garden.
♿ ⊛ ☕

GROUP OPENING

FROGNAL GARDENS, NW3
Hampstead NW3 6UY. *Tube: Hampstead. Buses: 46, 268 to Hampstead High St. Frognal Gdns 2nd R off Church Row from Heath St.*

Home-made teas. **Combined adm £5, chd free. Sun 21 June (2-5.30).**

5 FROGNAL GARDENS
Ruth & Brian Levy

5A FROGNAL GARDENS
Ian & Barbara Jackson

Two neighbouring gardens divided by path lined with trellises of cascading roses and clematis, underplanted with carpets of flowers. At No.5, the long narrow structured garden is romantically planted with soft colours and a profusion of unusual climbers and cottage perennials. The small, beautifully landscaped garden at 5A is a garden to enjoy and relax in with lawn, colourful flower beds and containers. 4" step from patio doors for wheelchair users to negotiate.
♿ ⊛ ☕

A serene and tranquil garden in the heart of Dulwich . . .

9 FURLONG ROAD, N7
Islington, London N7 8LS. Nigel Watts & Tanuja Pandit. *Tube & Overground: Highbury & Islington, 3 mins walk along Holloway Rd, 2nd L. Furlong Rd joins Holloway Rd & Liverpool Rd. Buses: 43, 271, 393.* Home-made teas. **Adm £2, chd free. Sun 7 June (2-6).**
Award winning small garden designed by Karen Fitzsimon which makes clever use of an awkwardly shaped plot. Curved lines are used to complement a modern extension. Raised beds contain a mix of tender and hardy plants to give an exotic feel and incl loquat, banana, palm, cycad and tree fern. Contrasting traditional front garden. Featured in Small Family Gardens and Modern Family Gardens by Caroline Tilston.
⊛ ☕

GARDEN BARGE SQUARE AT DOWNINGS ROADS MOORINGS, SE1
31 Mill Street, London SE1 2AX. Mr Nick Lacey. *Close to Tower Bridge & Design Museum. Mill St off Jamaica*

Rd, between London Bridge & Bermondsey stns, Tower Hill also nearby. Buses: 47, 188, 381, RV1. Tea. **Adm £3.50, chd free. Share to RNLI. Sun 31 May (2-5.30).**
Series of 7 floating barge gardens connected by walkways and bridges. Gardens have an eclectic range of plants for yr round seasonal interest. Marine environment: suitable shoes and care needed. Small children must be closely supervised.
☕

◆ THE GARDEN MUSEUM, SE1
Lambeth Palace Road, London SE1 7LB. The Garden Museum, 020 7401 8865, www.gardenmuseum.org.uk. *E side of Lambeth Bridge. Tube: Lambeth North, Vauxhall, Waterloo. Buses: 507 Red Arrow from Victoria or Waterloo mainline & tube stns, also 3, 77, 344.* **Adm £7.50, chd free. Share to Garden Museum. For NGS: Sat 30 May (10.30-4). For other opening times and information, please phone or see garden website.**
Reproduction C17 knot garden with period plants, topiary and box hedging. Wild garden in front of graveyard area; front border designed by Dan Pearson. Temporary exhibitions focusing on leading garden designers or garden related themes, permanent display of tools, paintings and ephemera, shop and café housed in former church of St Mary at Lambeth. Cafe offering delicious home baked menu. The Museum is accessible for wheelchair users via ramps and access lift.
♿ ⊛ ☕

NEW▶ 9 THE GARDENS, SE22
East Dulwich, London SE22 9QD. Nigel Watts. *Off Peckham Rye, Dulwich side. Stations: Peckham Rye & Honor Oak, both on Overground. Buses: 12, 37, 63,197, 363. Free parking in square.* **Evening Opening £5, chd free, wine, Sun 19 July (5-8).**
A riot of salvias in the front garden gives no hint of what lies behind this Victorian house. A collection of camellias and shade loving perennials leads to a jewel coloured palette of massed plantings many unusual, as well as dramatic exotics packed into a formal box framework with two towering yews. All within 40ft x 20ft! Local honey, Kentish fruit juice, art cards and paintings.
⊛ ☕

70 GLOUCESTER CRESCENT, NW1

London NW1 7EG. Lucy Gent, gent.lucy@gmail.com. *Tube: Camden Town 2 mins, Mornington Crescent 10 mins. Metered parking in Oval Rd.* **Adm £3.50, chd free. Sun 12 July, Sun 9 Aug (2-5.30).** Also open 4 Park Village East and Royal College of Physicians (Sun 12 July). Visitors also welcome by arrangement Mar to Oct.

One of three beautiful and unusual gardens in NW1 opening on the same day in July. Here is an oasis in Camden's urban density, where resourceful planting outflanks challenges of space and shade. An August opening (solo) features pomegranates and shows how wonderful the month can be in a town garden.

A riot of salvias in the front garden gives no hint of what lies behind . . .

ALLOTMENTS

GOLF COURSE ALLOTMENTS, N11

Winton Avenue, London N11 2AR. GCAA/Haringey, www.golfcourseallotments.co.uk. *Tube: Bounds Green. Buses: 102 184 299 to Sunshine Garden Centre, Durnsford Rd. Through park to Bidwell Gdns. Straight on up Winton Ave. No cars on site.* Light refreshments. **Adm £3.50, chd free. Share to GCAA. Sun 6 Sept (1-4.30).** Also open 94 Brownlow Rd and 5 Russell Rd.

Large, long established allotment with over 200 plots, some organic. Maintained by culturally diverse community growing wide variety of fruit, vegetables and flowers. Picturesque corners and quirky sheds - a visit feels like being in the countryside. Autumn Show on Sun 6 Sept features prize winning horticultural and domestic exhibits. Tours of best plots. Fresh allotment produce, chutneys, jams, cakes and light lunches for sale. Wheelchair access to main paths only. Gravel and some uneven surfaces. WC incl disabled.

 ♿ 🐕 ❀ ☕

ALLOTMENTS

GORDON ROAD ALLOTMENTS, N3

Gordon Road, London N3 1EL. Judy Woollett, www.finchleyhorticulturalsociety.org.uk. *Finchley Central. 10 mins walk from Finchley Central tube. 326 bus. Parking in Gordon Rd & adjacent st. No parking on site.* Home-made teas. **Adm £3.50, chd free. Sun 6 Sept (1.30-5.30).**

Founded in 1940 to promote the interests of gardeners throughout Finchley with over 70 plots. Allotments comprise a mixture of traditional plots and raised beds for those with physical disabilities and for children from local schools. Also a wildlife area with slow worms and an area set aside for bee hives. Tours of best plots. Seasonal vegetables on sale incl perennial flowers. Wheelchair access on main paths only. Disabled WC.

 ♿ ❀ ☕

45 GREAT NORTH ROAD, EN5

Barnet EN5 1EJ. Ron & Miriam Raymond, 020 8449 4453, ron.raymond91@yahoo.co.uk. *1m S of Barnet High St, 1m N of Whetstone. Tube: Midway between High Barnet & Totteridge & Whetstone stns. 20 mins walk. Buses 34 234 263 326 alight junc Great N Rd & Lyonsdown Rd.* Tea. **Adm £3, chd free. Sun 26 July (2-5.30). Visitors also welcome by arrangement May to Sept.**

45 Great North Road is designed to give a riot of colour during August. The 90ft x 90ft cottage style front garden is packed with interesting perennials. Tiered stands line the side entrance with over 64 pots displaying a variety of flowering and foliage plants. Rear garden incl over 100 tubs and hanging baskets. Small pond surrounded by tiered beds. Named begonias a speciality. Children's fun trail (for 3-6yr olds), prizes. Adult's garden quiz, also with prizes. Partial wheelchair access.

 ♿ ❀ ☕

13 GREENHILL PARK, EN5

Barnet EN5 1HQ. Sally & Andy Fry. *1m S of High Barnet. ¹/₂ m S of High Barnet tube stn. Take 1st L after Odeon Cinema, Weaver PH on corner. Buses: 34, 84, 234, 263, 326.* Home-made teas. **Adm £3, chd free. Sun 24 May (2-5.30).**

An oasis in suburbia. Approx ¹/₄ acre. Colourful herbaceous borders, wildlife pond, summerhouse in which to relax, Victorian plant house and shady fern garden. Series of rustic arches link main garden to path through wildlife friendly secret garden, incorporating tree fern collection, stumpery and Shepherd's hut. Japanese themed area and hidden courtyard vegetable garden with rare breed chickens.

 ❀ ☕

17 GREENSTONE MEWS, E11

Wanstead, London E11 2RS. Mr & Mrs S Farnham, 07761 476651, farnhamz@yahoo.co.uk. *Wanstead. Tube: Snaresbrook or Wanstead, 5 mins walk. Bus: 101, 308, W12, W14 to Wanstead High St.* Light refreshments. **Adm £5. Sun 16 Aug (2-5). Visitors also welcome by arrangement June to Aug min 6, max 8 visitors.**

Slate paved garden (20ft x 17ft). Height provided by a mature strawberry tree. A buried bath used as a fishpond is surrounded by climbers clothing fences underplanted with herbs, vegetables, shrubs and perennials grown from cuttings. Plants for sale grown from cuttings. Ideas aplenty for small space gardening. Entry incl cup of tea. Homemade cakes for sale. Book and plant sale. Wheelchair access through garage. Limited turning space.

 ♿ ❀ ☕

7 THE GROVE, N6

Highgate Village, London N6 6JU. Mr Thomas Lyttelton, 07713 638161. *The Grove is between Highgate West Hill & Hampstead Lane. Tube: Archway or Highgate. Buses: 143, 210, 214 and 271.* Home-made teas. **Adm £3.50, chd free. Share to The Harington Scheme. Sun 29 Mar, Sun 7 June (2-5.30).** Also open Southwood Lodge (Sun 7 June). Visitors also welcome by arrangement Mar to

Sept. Refreshments by arrangement.

½ acre designed for all year interest making a tapestry of greens and yellows. A wild garden with mature trees giving a woodland feel. Brilliant for hide and seek and young explorers. Water garden, vistas, 19 paths, some leading to sunny clearings. Exceptional camellias and magnolia in late March. Wheelchair access to main lawn only; many very narrow paths.

24 GROVE PARK, SE5

Camberwell SE5 8LH. Clive Pankhurst, www.alternative-planting.blogspot.com. *Chadwick Rd end of Grove Park. Stns: Peckham Rye or Denmark Hill, both 10 mins walk. Easy bus from Oval (185) or Elephant and Castle (176, 40). Good street parking.* Lots of home-made cakes. **Adm £3.50, chd free. Sun 6 Sept (2-5.30).**
An exotic garden full of the exuberance of late summer inspired by travel in Southeast Asia. A jungle of big leafed plants, bold colours and shapes incl bananas, dahlias and towering Paulownias. Huge hidden garden gives unexpected size with ponds, bee hives, sunken terrace, productive area. Lawn and lots of hidden corners give spaces to sit and enjoy. Renowned for delicious cake and no Styrofoam cups to be seen! Featured on BBC Gardeners World and in the Independant.

116 HAMILTON TERRACE, NW8

London NW8 9UT. Mr & Mrs I B Kathuria, 020 7625 6909, gkathuria@hotmail.co.uk. *Tube: Maida Vale (5 mins) or St.Johns Wood (10 mins) Buses: 16, 98 to Maida Vale, 139, 189 to Abbey Rd. Free parking on Sundays.* **Share to St. Mark's Church. Evening Openings £5, chd free, wine, Sun 21, Sun 28 June (5-9).** Visitors also welcome by arrangement Apr to Aug for groups 10 +.
Lush front garden full of dramatic foliage with a water feature and tree ferns. Large back garden of different levels with Yorkshire stone paving, many large terracotta pots and containers, water feature and lawn. Wide variety of perennials and flowering shrubs, many unusual and subtropical plants, succulents, acers, ferns, climbers, roses, fuchsias and prizewinning hostas. A great example

23 Imperial Road

© Jacqui Hurst

of container gardening and varied foliage.

◆ HAMPTON COURT PALACE, KT8

East Molesey KT8 9AU. Historic Royal Palaces, 0844 482 7777, hamptoncourt@hrp.org.uk, www.hrp.org.uk. *Follow brown tourist signs on all major routes. Junction of A308 with A309 at foot of Hampton Court Bridge.* **For NGS: Evening Openings £12, chd free, wine, Thur 7 May, Thur 4 June, Thur 30 July, Thur 27 Aug (6.30-8). Special evening tours with specialist talks.** Please visit www.ngs.org.uk for information and bookings, or phone 01483 211535. For other opening times and information, please phone or see garden website.

Take the opportunity to join 4 very special NGS private tours, after these wonderful historic gardens have closed to the public. 7th May - The heart of all - a behind the scenes tour of the garden's nursery. 4th June - HCP 500 - celebrate 500yrs of Hampton Court Palace hear about the monarchs and people associated with the gardens. 30th July - Summertime in the Tiltyard Gardens - tour this changing area of the gardens. 27th August - Time for trees - discover how trees shape the landscape. With specialist talks, and the chance to go behind the scenes, come and learn about the 500 year history of these royal gardens and find out what goes into creating and maintaining them. Some un-bound gravel paths.

 NCH

GROUP OPENING

HAMPTON HILL GARDENS, TW12
Hampton Hill TW12 1DW. *3m from Twickenham. 4m from Kingston-upon-Thames. Between A312 (Uxbridge Rd & A313 (Park Rd). Bus: 285 from Kingston stops on Uxbridge Rd. Stn: Fulwell 15 mins walk.* Home-made teas at 99 Uxbridge Rd and 30 St James's Rd. **Combined adm £5, chd free. Sat 6, Sun 7 June (2-5).**

18 CRANMER ROAD
Bernard Wigginton

30 ST JAMES'S ROAD
Jean Burman

99 UXBRIDGE ROAD
Anne & Bob Wagner

3 gardens of diverse interest in an attractive West London suburb. With the backdrop of St James's Church spire, 18 Cranmer Rd is a colourful garden with herbaceous and exotic borders and a WW2 air raid shelter transformed as rockery and water garden with azaleas, helianthemums and foliage plants. The SE facing garden at 30 St James's Rd is subdivided into 5 rooms. Decking with seating leads to ponds surrounded by grasses and shrubs and an African themed thatched exterior sitting room. 99 Uxbridge Rd is a wildlife friendly, urban cottage garden. Secluded and peaceful, many pots and containers, lawn, shrubs, flowers, fruit trees, ponds and an organic kitchen garden. Lots of places to sit and relax. Partial wheelchair access at Cranmer Rd and Uxbridge Rd.
♿ 🏡 ⊗ ☕

The Queen's Nursing Institute
Qni

NGS support makes a vital difference to our patient care

GROUP OPENING

HANDSWORTH ROAD GARDENS, N17
Handsworth Road, London N17 6DB. *Tube: Seven Sisters (15 min walk). Buses: 341, 230 or W4 (alight Broadwater Lodge). Driving: one way rd, entry Philip Lane.* Home-made teas at No 47. **Combined adm £3.50, chd free. Sun 14 June (2-6).**

47A HANDSWORTH ROAD, N17
Hazel Griffiths & Andy D'Cruz

77 HANDSWORTH ROAD, N17
Serge Charles

In a quiet Tottenham street sit these two contrasting gardens, united by their owners' love of plants and creative use of space. First time June opening and new features. At 47A a gravel path leads beneath a vine covered pergola to emerge into a sunny, Mediterranean inspired garden. A geometric pattern of paths and trellis provides a framework for the informal planting. Many unusual plants, some propagated for sale. A mature quince tree, rill pool with waterfall, raised herb bed, sculpture (by resident artist) and terracotta pots contribute to the atmosphere. Adjoining tea garden with covered seating. At 77 a long, narrow front garden is home to bamboos, roses and clematis which screen a secret knot garden of box. Container planted trees incl olive and mimosa. A shady path, planted with a wide range of ferns and shade tolerant plants, leads to a small back garden where the bamboos reach 25ft underplanted with tree ferns.
⊗ ☕

NEW **HARMONY GARDEN AT BROADWATER FARM, N17**
Adams Road, Tottenham, London N17 6HE. Dornelle St Cyr, www.back2earth.org.uk. *Tube to Seven Sisters/Wood Green or Turnpike Lane or train to Bruce Grove. Buses 123/243 to Lordship Lane, park gates, enter park & keep L or W4 bus to Higham Rd. Cross park, garden on R behind community centre (yellow brick).* Light refreshments at Broadwater Farm Community Cafe and Harmony Garden outdoor BBQ. **Adm £3.50, chd free. Sun 2 Aug (1-6).**
Regeneration at its most inspiring. In

2010 Back2Earth charity raised funds to create a community garden at Tottenham's Broadwater Farm. Gabions walls using recycled materials surround vegetable plots, flowers and pond. Arches support apples, pears and climbing roses. A poly tunnel houses exotic tropical plants from Jamaica provided by Head Gardener Robert Samuda. Exotic plant garden and recycled materials for planters. Featured in The Guardian, The Gleaner, on The Voice and Inside Out London BBC TV. Partial wheelchair access.
🏡 ⊗ ☕

NEW **159 HIGHAM ROAD, N17**
Downhills Park, London N17 6NX. Jess Kitley & Sally Gray. *Tube: Turnpike Lane then 15 mins walk/W4 alight Higham Rd or Seven Sisters then 41 bus alight Philip Lane, walk up through Downhills Park. Buses 341, 230,41,W4. Free parking on Higham Rd.* Tea. **Adm £3.50, chd free. Sun 5 July (2-6).**
Designers developing their 80ft x 30ft garden incorporating sculptural elements, unity of design and materials. Densely planted with shrubs, perennials and grasses. Areas to sit, contemplate and enjoy as birds, bees and butterflies abound. A natural wildlife pond dug into clay harnesses natural springs, mitigating constant flooding. Backing on to woodland, big skies...and this is Tottenham!
☕

HIGHWOOD ASH, NW7
Highwood Hill, Mill Hill NW7 4EX. Mr & Mrs R Gluckstein, 020 8959 1183. *Totteridge & Whetstone on Northern line, then bus 251 stops outside - Rising Sun/Mill Hill stop. By car: House on A5109 from Apex Corner to Whetstone. Garden located opp The Rising Sun PH.* **Adm £4.50, chd free. Sun 28 June (2-5.30). Visitors also welcome by arrangement May to July for groups of 2 to 20.**
3¼ acre incl new gravel garden, shrub and herbaceous borders, rhododendrons, azaleas, lake with waterfall, terrace with raised herb garden, a mixture of formal and informal. About half of the garden is accessible for wheelchairs but the lowest parts are too steep.
♿ 🏡

19 HILLFIELD PARK, N10
London N10 3QT. Zaki & Ruth Elia. *Off Muswell Hill Broadway, corner HSBC Bank. Buses: W7, 43, 102, 144, 134, 234. Tube: Highgate, E Finchley, Finsbury Park.* Tea at 5 St Regis Close. **Adm £3, chd free. Sun 19 July (2-6). Also open 5 St Regis Close.**
An orientalist garden in Edwardian Muswell Hill. Created by owner/designer, inspired by the original British Raj features within the house. Three tiled terraces with ceramic containers unfold around a traditional fountain. A bespoke Eastern style shed crowns the top terrace, while dramatic planting by Declan Buckley cocoons visitors in lush seclusion. Featured on ITV's Love Your Garden.

Take a seat before you carry on your journey past lavender, rosemary and much more . . . !

NEW 2 HILLSIDE CLOSE, NW8
Off Carlton Hill, St. John's Wood, London NW8 0EF. Kris & Barry Musikant, 020 7624 3836, krismusi@aol.com. *Nr to Maida Vale end of Carlton Hill, look for large black entrance gates. Parking in Carlton Hill. Tube: Maida Vale (8mins); St. John's Wood (15mins). Buses: 16, 98, 139, 189.* Home-made teas. **Adm £4, chd free. Sun 5 July (11-5). Visitors also welcome by arrangement Apr to Aug. Min group 6.**
Set in a secluded cul de sac with attractively planted flowerbeds, the house has four gardens. To the front is a small parterre. To the rear a walled courtyard with fruit trees and raised vegetable beds. From here, water flows from a trough along a 52ft rill and drops into a wild life pond which is situated in a country style lawned garden with herbaceous beds, shrubs and wild flowers.

THE HOLME, NW1
Inner Circle, Regents Park NW1 4NT. Lessee of The Crown Commission. *In centre of Regents Park on The Inner Circle. Within 10 mins walk from Great Portland St or Baker St Underground Stations, opp Regents Park Garden Cafe.* **Adm £4.50, chd free. Sat 27, Sun 28 June, Sat 1, Sun 2 Aug (2.30-5.30).**
4 acre garden filled with interesting and unusual plants. Sweeping lakeside lawns intersected by islands of herbaceous beds. Extensive rock garden with waterfall, stream and pool. Formal flower garden with unusual annual and half hardy plants, sunken lawn, fountain pool and arbour. Gravel paths and some steps which gardeners will help wheelchair users to negotiate.

GROUP OPENING

NEW HOMERTON GARDENS, E5
London E5 0DS. *Gardens close to Homerton High St. Nearest station Homerton Overground. Nearest buses 236, 488, 276 or W15.* Home-made teas at 79 Glyn Rd. **Combined adm £4, chd free. Sun 7 June (2-6.30).**

NEW 79 GLYN RD
Ms Pat Hornsby

NEW 80 RODING ROAD
Ms Joan Wadge

These are small family gardens used to relax and enjoy. Both combine mixed established borders with seating areas. Roding Road has a paved area surrounded by borders. The aim is to combine texture with colour and smell depending on the mood of the owner. Glyn Road has a lawn and makes the most of its fencing for climbers.

239A HOOK ROAD, KT9
Chessington KT9 1EQ. Mr & Mrs D St Romaine, www.gardenphotolibrary.com. *4m S of Kingston. A3 from London, turn L at Hook underpass onto A243. Gdn. 300yds on L. Parking opp in Park or on rd, no restrictions at night. Buses K4, 71, 465 from Kingston & Surbiton to North Star PH.* **Evening Opening £5, chd free, wine, Wed 10 June (8.30-10.30).**

Garden photographer's garden. Contemporary flower garden with entertaining area, gravel garden, colour themed herbaceous borders, fernery, pond and rose tunnel. Traditional potager with 20 varieties of fruit and 50+ varieties of vegetables and herbs. Late night opening to show how over 500 candles and lighting, used in imaginative ways with containers and architectural foliage, can effectively transform areas of a garden at night. Images by Derek St Romaine.

1A HUNGERFORD ROAD, N7
London N7 9LA. David Matzdorf, davidmatzdorf@blueyonder.co.uk, www.growingontheedge.net. *Between Camden Town & Holloway. Tube: Caledonian Rd tube. Buses: 17, 29, 91, 253, 259 & 393.* **Adm £2, chd free. Share to Terrence Higgins Trust. Sun 7 June (12-6). Also open 62 Hungerford Rd.** Visitors also welcome by arrangement Apr to Oct.
Unique eco house with walled, lush front garden planted in modern exotic style. Front garden densely planted with palms, acacia, ginger lilies, brugmansias, bananas, ferns, yuccas, abutilons and bamboo. Floriferous and ambitious green roof resembling scree slope planted with agaves, aloes, yuccas, dasylirions, euphorbias, alpines, sedums, bulbs, grasses, Mediterranean shrubs and aromatic herbs. Sole access to roof is via built in ladder. Garden and roof each 50ft x 18ft. Featured in Small Green Roofs (Timber Press) and on BBC Great British Garden Revival.

62 HUNGERFORD ROAD, N7
London N7 9LP. John Gilbert & Lynne Berry. *Between Camden Town & Holloway. Tube: Caledonian Rd, 6 mins walk. Buses: 29 & 253 to Hillmarton Rd stop in Camden Rd. Also 17, 91, 259, 393 to Hillmarton Rd. 10 to York Way.* **Adm £2.50, chd free. Sun 7 June (2-6). Also open 1A Hungerford Road.**
Densely planted mature town garden at rear of Victorian terrace house which has been designed to maximise space for planting and create several different sitting areas, views and moods. NW facing with considerable shade, it is arranged in a series of paved rooms with a good range of perennials, shrubs and trees. Professional garden designer's own garden.

190 Barnet Road

THE HURLINGHAM CLUB, SW6
Ranelagh Gardens, London
SW6 3PR. The Members of the
Hurlingham Club,
www.hurlinghamclub.org.uk. *Main
gate at E end of Ranelagh Gardens.
Tube: Putney Bridge (110yds). Please
note there is no parking onsite. Meter
parking on local streets & restricted
parking on Sats (9-5).* Light
refreshments in the Napier Servery.
Adm £5, chd £2. Sat 16 May (12-4).
Rare opportunity to visit this 42 acre
jewel with many mature trees, 2 acre
lake with water fowl, expansive lawns
and a river walk. Capability Brown
and Humphry Repton were involved
with landscaping. The gardens are
renowned for their roses, herbaceous
and lakeside borders, shrubberies
and stunning bedding displays. The
riverbank is a haven for wildlife with
native trees, shrubs and wild flowers.
Garden Tour at 2pm.

23 IMPERIAL ROAD, N22
London N22 8DE. Kate Gadsby,
07958 901679,
kate@kategadsby.co.uk. *Off
Bounds Green Rd between Bounds
Green Tube & Wood Green Tube. 5
mins from Alexandra Palace mainline.*
Home-made teas. **Adm £2.50, chd
free. Sun 4 Oct (12.30-4.30).**
Visitors also welcome by
arrangement Apr to Oct.
Tiny back garden overflowing with
interesting and unusual plants where
an inventive and inspiring approach to

planting, has created a surprising
number of perspectives. An early
October opening to show how many
varieties of aster can be fitted into a
very small space. Semi covered deck
allows enjoyment in sun and rain.

**THE INNER TEMPLE GARDEN,
EC4**
Crown Office Row, Inner Temple,
London EC4Y 7HL. **The
Honourable Society of the Inner
Temple, www.innertemple.org.uk.**
*Entrance: Main Garden Gate on
Crown Office Row, access via Tudor
Street gate or Middle Temple Lane
gate. For map visit www.ngs.org.uk.*
**Wed 6 May, Wed 9 Sept (11-2.30),
adm £40 to incl conducted tour of
the garden by the Head Gardener
and lunch in the Inner Temple
Luncheon room. Advance booking
only. Please visit www.ngs.org.uk
or phone 01483 211535.**
A 3 acre garden between the Thames
and Fleet St with sweeping lawns,
unusual trees, and charming
woodland areas. The well known
herbaceous borders show off
inspiring plant combinations from
early spring through till autumn, filled
with colour and texture. Featured in
Country Life, Which? Gardening,
Evening Standard and Sunday Times.
Wheelchair access gate along Crown
Office Row.

GROUP OPENING

ISLINGTON GARDENS, N1
London N1 1BE. *Barnsbury N1.
Tube: Kings Cross, Caledonian Rd or
Angel. Buses: 17, 91, 259 to
Caledonian Rd.* Home-made teas at
36 Thornhill Square. **Combined adm
£8, chd free. Sun 31 May (2-6).**

BARNSBURY WOOD
London Borough of Islington

1 BATTLEBRIDGE COURT
Visitors also welcome by
arrangement Mar to Sept.
horticulturist@blueyonder.co.uk
www.gardeningforbeginners.
org.uk

44 HEMINGFORD ROAD
Peter Willis & Haremi Kudo

36 THORNHILL SQUARE
Anna & Christopher McKane

Walk through Islington's historic
Georgian squares and terraces to
view these four contrasting gardens,
all within walking distance of the new
vibrant development at King's Cross.
Barnsbury Wood is Islington's hidden
secret, a tranquil oasis of wild flowers
and massive trees, a wildlife haven
just minutes from Caledonian Road.
The three gardens in the group have
extensive collections of unusual
plants; specimen trees, shrubs and
perennials and a pond at 44
Hemingford Road; old and new roses
and many herbaceous perennials at

Support the NGS – eat more cake!

36 Thornhill Square, a 120ft long garden with a country atmosphere. There is also a bonsai collection. 1 Battlebridge Court is a small plantsman's garden making optimum use of sun and shade with the additional attraction of being beside the canal basin. All the gardens have evolved over many yrs, to incl plants to suit their particular growing conditions, and show what can be achieved while surmounting the difficulties of dry walls and shade.

22 KELSEY WAY, BR3
Beckenham BR3 3LL. *Janet & Steve Wright. From Beckenham town centre, take Kelsey Park Rd, R into Manor Way. Kelsey Way is turning off this. Bus: 367 Sunday service to Village Way stop.* Home-made teas. **Adm £3, chd free. Sun 14 June (2-5).**
Multiple award winning garden. Colourful herbaceous borders with many tropical plants incl bananas, colocasias, alocasias, cannas and several different varieties of brugmansias. Displays of potted plants and a conservatory with a magnificent bougainvillea. Extensive and varied vegetable garden with a large fruit cage.

GROUP OPENING

KEW GREEN GARDENS, TW9
Kew TW9 3AH. *Kew Green. NW side of Kew Green. Tube: Kew Gardens. Mainline stn: Kew Bridge. Buses: 65, 391. Entrance via riverside.* Home-made teas at 67 Kew Green. **Combined adm £6, chd free. Sun 24 May (2-6).**

65 KEW GREEN
Giles & Angela Dixon

67 KEW GREEN
Lynne & Patrick Lynch

69 KEW GREEN
John & Virginia Godfrey

71 KEW GREEN
Mr & Mrs Jan Pethick

73 KEW GREEN
Sir Donald & Lady Elizabeth Insall

Five long gardens behind a row of C18 houses on the Green, close to the Royal Botanic Gardens. These gardens feature the profusely planted and traditional borders of a mature English country garden, and contrast formal gardens, terraces and lawns, laid out around tall old trees, with wilder areas and woodland and wild flower planting. One has an unusual architect designed summerhouse, while another offers the surprise of a modern planting of espaliered miniature fruit trees.

Unexpected havens from the city's hustle and bustle . . .

KING HENRY'S WALK GARDEN, N1
11c King Henry's Walk, London N1 4NX. *Friends of King Henry's Walk Garden, www.khwgarden.org.uk. Buses incl: 21, 30, 38, 56, 141, 277. Behind adventure playground on KHW, off Balls Pond Rd.* Light refreshments. **Share to Friends of KHW Garden. Evening Opening £5.50, chd free, wine, Wed 8 July (6-9).**
Vibrant ornamental planting welcomes the visitor to this hidden oasis and leads you into a verdant community garden with secluded woodland area, beehives, wildlife pond, wall-trained fruit trees, and plots used by local residents to grow their own fruit and vegetables. Live music. Art exhibition. Disabled WC.

LAMBETH PALACE, SE1
Lambeth Palace Rd, London SE1 7JU. *The Church Commissioners, www.archbishopofcanterbury.org. Entrance via Main Gatehouse facing Lambeth Bridge. Station: Waterloo Tube: Westminster, Lambeth North & Vauxhall all 10 mins walk. Buses: 3, C10, 76, 77, 77a, 344, 507.* **Evening Openings £6, chd free, wine, Thur 21 May, Thur 18 June (5.30-8).**
Lambeth Palace garden is one of the oldest and largest private gardens in London. Site occupied by Archbishops of Canterbury since end C12. Formal Courtyards with historic White Marseilles fig planted in 1556. Parkland style garden with mature trees, woodland and native planting, orchard and pond. Also formal terrace, summer gravel border, scented chapel garden and beehives. Ramped path to rose terrace, disabled WC.

12 LANSDOWNE ROAD, W11
London W11 3LW. *The Lady Amabel Lindsay. Tube: Holland Park. Buses: 12, 88, GL 711, 715 to Holland Park, 4 mins walk up Lansdowne Rd.* **Adm £3.50, chd free. Wed 20 May (2-6).**
A country garden in the heart of London. An old mulberry tree, billowing borders, rambling Rosa banksiae, a greenhouse of climbing geraniums and a terrace filled with tender perennials. Partial wheelchair access.

42 LATIMER ROAD, E7
Forest Gate, London E7 0LQ. *Janet Daniels. 8 mins walk from Forest Gate or Wanstead Park stn. From Forest Gate cross to Sebert Rd, then 3rd rd on L.* Home-made teas. **Adm £3.50, chd free. Sat 18, Sun 19 July (11-4).**
Passionate plant collector's garden 90ft x 15ft. An abundance of baskets, climbers, shrubs and fruit trees. Raised koi carp pond. Step down to large secret garden containing exuberant borders, wildlife pond with gunnera, small green oasis lawn with arbour. Unusual and exotic plants, herb ladders and other quirky features. Wildlife friendly. Summerhouse full of collectables, dinky toys and collection of old wooden tools.

LITTLE HOUSE A, NW3
16A Maresfield Gardens, Hampstead NW3 5SU. *Linda & Stephen Williams. 5 mins walk Swiss Cottage or Finchley Rd tube. Off Fitzjohn's Ave & 2 doors from Freud Museum (signed).* Home-made teas. **Adm £3.50, chd free. Sun 21 June (2-6).**
1920's Arts and Craft house (not open) built by Danish Artist Baron Arild Rosenkrantz. Award winning front and rear garden created in 2002 and set out formally with water features, stream and sculpture. Wide collection of unusual and rare shrubs and perennials.

LITTLE LODGE, KT7

Watts Road, Thames Ditton KT7 0BX. Mr & Mrs P Hickman, 020 8339 0931, julia.hickman@virgin.net. *2m SW of Kingston. Mainline Stn Thames Ditton 5 min walk. House opp Thames Ditton Library after Giggs Hill Green, Parking in Library Car Park.* Home-made teas. **Adm £4, chd free. Sun 31 May (11.30-5.30).** Visitors also welcome by arrangement May to June for groups 10+.
Partly walled ½ acre informal cottage garden filled with usual and unusual shrubs, perennials, native plants and topiary. Lots of stone sinks, troughs and terracotta pots, plus a Victorian style glasshouse. Productive hidden parterre vegetable garden edged with espalier apple trees. Garden designed and maintained by owners. Plants for sale, also propagated and grown by owners.

49 LOFTUS ROAD, W12

London W12 7EH. Emma Plunket, www.plunketgardens.com. *Shepherds Bush or Shepherds Bush Market tube or train or bus to Uxbridge Rd. Free street parking.* **Evening Opening £4, chd free, wine, Tue 16 June (5.30-8).** Professional garden designer, Emma Plunket, opens her acclaimed walled garden. Richly planted, it is the ultimate hard working city garden with all yr structure and colour; fruit, vegetables and herbs. Set against a backdrop of trees, it is unexpectedly open and peaceful. Garden plan, plant list and advice.

D ☕

GROUP OPENING

FIELDS GARDENS, E8

London E8 3LS. *On W side of London Fields park. Short walk from Haggerston stn, London Overground; or London Fields stn (from Liverpool St) or tube to Bethnal Green or Angel then bus towards Hackney.* Home-made teas at 61 Lansdowne Drive and 84 Lavender Grove. **Combined adm £6, chd free. Sun 14 June (2-6).**

> **61 LANSDOWNE DRIVE**
> Chris Thow & Graham Hart

> **84 LAVENDER GROVE**
> Anne Pauleau

> **36 MALVERN ROAD**
> Kath Harris

53 MAPLEDENE ROAD

Tigger Cullinan
Visitors also welcome by arrangement May to July max 10 visitors.
020 7249 3754
tiggerine8@blueyonder.co.uk

A diverse group of 4 gardens in London Fields, an area which takes its name from fields on the London side of the old village of Hackney. They are unexpected havens from the city's hustle and bustle, with an exciting range and variety of colours, scents and design. This yr we have a fascinating plantsman's garden, lush tropical plantings, a scented cottage garden and a serene designer garden filled with the sound of running water. Expect everything from courtyards to areas of banana, from showers of roses to clusters of clematis, ponds with water lilies and giant gunnera.

GROUP OPENING

LOWER CLAPTON GARDENS, E5

Hackney, London E5 0RL. *10 mins walk from Hackney Central or Hackney Downs stns. Buses 38, 55, 106, 253, 254 or 425, alight Lower Clapton Rd.* Home-made teas at 16 & 99 Powerscroft Rd. **Combined adm £6, chd free. Sun 7 June (2-6).** Also open Homerton Gardens.

> **8 ALMACK ROAD**
> Philip Lightowlers
> Visitors also welcome by arrangement May to July.
> 07910 850276
> plighto@gmail.com

16 POWERSCROFT ROAD
Elizabeth Welch

NEW **68B POWERSCROFT ROAD**
Molly & Paul Jason

NEW **70 POWERSCROFT ROAD**
Mr David Lake

99 POWERSCROFT ROAD
Rose Greenwood

Lower Clapton is an area of mid Victorian terraces sloping down to the R Lea. This group of gardens reflect their owner's tastes and interests. New this yr we have 68b and 70 Powerscroft Rd which are revamped south facing gardens featuring a gravel garden, raised beds and mixed borders. No.16 has sun and space for meditation, while No. 99 has a high level patio looking out across the garden to a thatched gazebo. No. 8 Almack Rd is a long thin garden with two different rooms, one incl a classic blue agave named Audrey.

☸ ☕

GROUP OPENING

LYNDHURST SQUARE GROUP, SE15

Lyndhurst Square, London SE15 5AR, 07969 641955, martin.lawlor@sky.com. *London. Rail & London Overground orbital network - Clapham Junction to Highbury & Islington; Peckham Rye (check timetables), then 5 mins walk NW. Buses:36 from Oval tube, 171 from Waterloo, 63 from Kings Cross, 12 from oxford Circus. Free parking in Lyndhurst Square.* Home-made teas at No 4. **Combined adm £7, chd free. Share to MIND. Sun 21 June (1.30-5).** Also open Tewkesbury Lodge: Top of the Hill and 103 & 105 Dulwich Village Two Gardens.

> **1 LYNDHURST SQUARE**
> Josephine Pickett-Baker

> **3 LYNDHURST SQUARE**
> Stephen Haines

> **4 LYNDHURST SQUARE**
> Amelia Thorpe & Adam Russell

> **5 LYNDHURST SQUARE**
> Martin Lawlor & Paul Ward

> **6 LYNDHURST SQUARE**
> Iain Henderson & Amanda Grygelis

7 LYNDHURST SQUARE
Pernille Ahlström & Barry Joseph

Six very attractive gardens open in this small, elegant square of 1840s listed villas. Each approx 90ft x 50ft has its own shape and style as the Square curves in a U shape. No. 1, Eclectic and comfortable walled garden reflecting the creative background of the gardener. Mostly evergreen foliages of varying colours and textures with surprising details. No. 3 is a pretty, classic English garden with shrubs, fruit trees and sculpted topiary. A delightful greenhouse enhances the impression of peace. No. 4 is for a family, with a generous lawn, vegetables and herbs, and mature fruit trees adding lushness. At No. 5, the design combines Italianate and Gothic themes with roses, lavender, olives, euphorbia and ferns within yew and box parterres. Plants for sale here. No. 6 is an up to date family garden given drama with architectural plants. A wisteria pergola frames the vegetables bordered by espaliered apples. Check out the treehouse! Simplicity, Swedish style, is key at No. 7, with roses and raised beds, framed by yew hedges. Home-made teas, hot and cold drinks and other treats available.

🎞 ✿ ☕

NEW▶ 4 MACAULAY ROAD, SW4
Clapham SW4 0QX. Mrs Diana Ross. *Clapham Common Tube. Buses 88, 87, 77, 77A, 137, 137A, 37, 35, 345, 452 from tube cross Common towards large church ahead on R. Macaulay Rd opp. Free parking on The Chase.* **Evening Opening adm £20 incl talk by owner, wine and canapes, Thur 28 May (6.30-8.30). Pre-booked tickets from www.ngs.org.uk or ring 01483 211535.**
A garden writer's inspirational prize winning garden. Extensive planting incl many rare plants. Jungle, grotto and fountain. Many pots and containers and an eclectic mix of mature shrubs, trees and herbaceous plants. Expertly designed by the owner to make use of every inch (85' x 50'). Before and after photographs, taken over the yrs, on display. Advance booking essential. Featured in House & Garden.

☕

NEW▶ 6 MANOR ROAD, KT8
East Molesey KT8 9JX. Ann & Peter Pope. *10 min walk from Hampton Court station.* Light refreshments. **Combined adm £5, single garden adm £3, chd free. Sun 14 June (2-6). Combined with 61 Wolsey Road.**
A charming country garden with softly planted borders of roses, lavenders and sages. Perennial and annual flowers provide a nectar rich mix for bees throughout most of the yr. Rambling rose and sweet pea arches intermingle with clematis. Hand tame robins visit this wildlife friendly garden daily. Under glass is an 80yr old grapevine originally a cutting from the Great Vine at Hampton Court.

✿ ☕

ALLOTMENTS

94 MARSH LANE ALLOTMENTS, N17
Marsh Lane, Tottenham N17 OHY. Chris Achilleos, 07903 211715, a_c_h1964@yahoo.co.uk. *Opp Northumberland Park stn, on the corner of Marsh Lane & Marigold Rd. Buses: W3, 318, 341, 476.* **Adm £4, chd free. Sun 19 July (2-6). Visitors also welcome by arrangement July to Aug. Groups welcomed before 6pm.**
An oasis in the city, a unique allotment exuding peace and tranquillity. An exuberant collection of decorative, edible and exotic plants. Gravel plants lined with potted tender specimens. Established herbaceous border, mini orchard of Mediterranean and native fruit trees. Central gazebo, wildlife pond, sculptures - something for everyone. Artwork and mosaics. Featured in The City Planter - a plot with a twist, and My Cool Allotment by Lia Leendertz. Also feature in Ham & High and on Gardeners World.

✿ ☕

12 THE MEADOWS
See Kent.

27 MENELIK ROAD, NW2
London NW2 3RJ. C Klemera, cklemera@hotmail.com. *West Hampstead, E of Shoot up Hill. From Kilburn tube, buses 16, 32,189, 316, 332 to Mill Lane on Shoot up Hill, then Minster Rd/Menelik Rd at end. From W Hampstead tube, C11 bus to Menelik Rd.* **Adm £4, chd free. Sun 5 July (2-5.30). Also opening 58a**

Teignmouth Rd and 121 Anson Rd, combined adm (3 gardens) £8, chd free. Visitors also welcome by arrangement Apr to Sept for groups 10+.
A garden full of surprises and humour. A 30yr old Trachycarpus overlooks many exotic plants of strong shape, texture and colour. Discover a cloud pruned tree in the oriental corner from your seat in the tea house. Topiary pops up in the lush colourful borders and the piazza is secluded by bay trees and a banana, often in flower. Paths will lead you on a magical journey through plants from around the world. Plants for sale will be from cuttings of many of my favourites from this garden.

✿ ☕

A unique allotment exuding peace and tranquillity . . .

30 MERCERS ROAD, N19
London N19 4PJ. Ms Joanne Bernstein, www.joannebernstein-gardendesign.com. *Tufnell Park. Tube: Tufnell Park then 10 mins walk. Holloway Rd, then 5 min Bus 43, 271 to Manor Gardens stop.* Teas. **Adm £4, chd free. Sun 7 June (2-6).**
Created by the garden designer owner, strong geometry complements the contemporary architecture of the house extension, softened by billowing Prairie style planting in the sunny area and shade tolerant shrubs and perennials in the woodland. There is openness and seclusion, light and shade, created by generous planting and simple hard landscaping. Featured in BBC Gardeners' World.

Ⓓ ☕

65 MILL HILL ROAD, W3
London W3 8JF. Anna Dargavel,
020 8992 1723,
Annadargavel@mac.com. *Tube:
Acton Town, turn R, Mill Hill Rd on R
off Gunnersbury Lane.* **Adm £5, chd
free. Sun 9 Aug (2-6). Evening
Opening £5, chd free, wine, Fri 4
Sept (6-8).** Also open 41 Mill Hill
Road (Sun 9 Aug). Visitors also
welcome by arrangement June to
Sept max 12 visitors.
Garden designer's own garden. A
secluded and tranquil space, paved,
with changes of level and borders.
Sunny and shady areas, topiary, fruit
trees and interesting planting
combine to provide a wildlife haven.
Ponds and organic principles are
used to promote a green environment
and give a stylish walk to a studio at
the end.

41 MILL HILL ROAD, W3
London W3 8JE. Marcia Hurst, 020
8992 2632/07989 581940,
marcia.hurst@sudbury-
house.co.uk. *Acton, W London.
Piccadilly Line to Acton Town, turn R,
Mill Hill Rd 3rd on R off Gunnersbury
Lane.* Tea. **Adm £4, chd free.
Evening Opening £5, chd free,
wine, Fri 10 July (6-8). Sun 9 Aug
(2-6).** Also open 65 Mill Hill Road
(Sun 9 Aug). Visitors also welcome
by arrangement May to Oct no
min, max 20 visitors.
120ft x 40ft garden. A surprisingly
large and sunny garden, with
lavender and hornbeam hedges,
herbaceous planting and climbers,
incl unusual plants as the owner is a
compulsive plantaholic. Lots of space
to sit and enjoy the garden. Some of
the plants growing in the garden are
for sale in pots. Articles in the Daily
Mail weekend features.

2 MILLFIELD PLACE, N6
Highgate, London N6 6JP. c/o
Peter Lloyd, 020 8348 6487,
daisydogone@aol.com. *Off
Highgate West Hill, E side of
Hampstead Heath. Buses: C2, C11
or 214 to Parliament Hill Fields.North
London Line to Gospel Oak.* Home-
made teas. **Adm £4.50, chd free.
Sun 3 May (2-6). Evening Opening
£5, chd free, wine, Wed 17 June
(5.30-9).** Visitors also welcome by
arrangement May to Sept.
1½ acre spring and summer garden
with camellias, rhododendrons, many
flowering shrubs and unusual plants.

Spring bulbs, herbaceous borders,
spacious lawns, small pond and
extensive views over Hampstead
Heath. Partial wheelchair access with
separate entrance, assistance
available, please ask at gate.

Imaginatively planted lawn area leads through pergola to a little bit of Cornwall in London . . .

66 MUSWELL AVENUE, N10
London N10 2EL. Kay Thomson &
Nick Wood-Glover, 020 8883 6697,
kaythomson378@gmail.com. *1st L
into Muswell Ave from Alexandra Park
Rd. Tube: Bounds Green or E
Finchley then bus 102 or 299, alight
Colney Hatch stop.* Home-made
teas. **Adm £3.50, chd free. Sun 5
July (2-6).** Visitors also welcome
by arrangement May to Oct.
Coastal echoes in suburbia. Four
contrasting atmospheres and
environments. Tiny courtyard opens
onto terrace of mainly containerized
Mediterranean planting incl oleander,
jasmine, grapevine and herbs.
Imaginatively planted lawn area leads
through pergola to a little bit of
Cornwall in London incl boat, pebble
beaches and pond. Dry stone wall
behind the patio with unexpected
delights. Fish feeding - 4.00 pm.
Garden photographed by one of the
world's finest garden photographers:
Marianne Majerus. Featured in Daily
Mail's Visit this... column; Ham & High
article, A Garden of Delights; Article
by author Abigail Willis, A Garden
Written in the Stars.

27 NASSINGTON ROAD, NW3
Hampstead, London NW3 2TX.
Lucy Scott-Moncrieff. *From
Hampstead Heath rail stn & bus
stops at South End Green, go up*

*South Hill Park, then Parliament Hill, R
into Nassington Rd.* Home-made
cakes and light refreshments. **Adm
£4, chd free. Sun 7 June (2-5.30).**
Double width town garden planted for
colour and to support wildlife.
Spectacular ancient wisteria, herbs,
fruit and vegetables in with the
flowers. The main feature is a large
eco pond, designed for swimming,
with colourful planting in and out of
the water.

◆ **NATURAL HISTORY MUSEUM
WILDLIFE GARDEN, SW7**
Cromwell Road, London SW7 5BD.
Natural History Museum, 020 7942
5011, www.nhm.ac.uk/wildlife-
garden. *Natural History Museum.
Tube: South Kensington, 5 mins walk.*
Tea. **Adm by donation. For NGS:
Sat 11 Apr (12-5).** For other
opening times and information,
please phone or see garden
website.
Celebrate Spring in the Wildlife
Garden. Set in the Museum grounds
the Wildlife Garden has provided a
lush and tranquil habitat in the heart
of London since 1995. It reveals a
range of lowland habitats incl
deciduous woodland, heathland,
meadow and ponds. With over 2500
plant and animal species it
demonstrates the potential for wildlife
conservation in the inner city. Spring
inspired workshops, nature live talks
12.30 and 2.30 and garden tours.
Discover how to attract butterflies
and bees to your garden. Learn
about amphibians and pond life.
Wildlife inspired crafts and learn how
to identify seeds and fruits using a
microscope. Wild flower plants for
sale. Received Brighter Kensington
and Chelsea Scheme Wildlife Garden
Award.

17A NAVARINO ROAD, E8
London E8 1AD. Ben Nel & Darren
Henderson, 07734 773990,
darren.henderson@hotmail.co.uk.
*Buses 30, 38, 242 or 277 alight
Graham Rd. Short walk from Hackney
Central or London Fields stns on
Overground line.* Teas with cakes
made specially by local company.
**Adm £3, chd free. Sun 19 Apr, Sun
14 June (2-5).** Visitors also
welcome by arrangement Apr to
July. Tour groups welcome.
Established Italian and Japanese
water garden. Features a square
pond with Corinthian fountain, topiary

yew border, lilies and Mediterranean trees. Leading to Japanese garden with pond, bridge and stream cutting the Soleirolia soleirolii landscape, with acer, cypress, ferns and bamboo, overlooked by a beautiful Japanese Tea House. Featured in The Sunday Times, The New London Garden by George Carter and Marianne Majerus and The London Garden Book by Abigail Willis.

272 Alexandra Park Road, Alexandra Park Road Gardens

5 NORTHAMPTON PARK, N1
Islington N1 2PP. Andrew Bernhardt & Anne Brogan. *5 mins walk from Canonbury stn, 10 mins from Highbury & Islington Tube (Victoria Line) Bus: 30, 277, 341, 476.* **Evening Opening £4, chd free, wine, Sat 4 July (4-7.30).**
Early Victorian S facing walled garden, (1840's) saved from neglect and developed over the last 22yrs. Arches, palms, box and yew hedging frame the cool North European blues, whites and greys moving to splashes of red/orange Mediterranean influence. The contrast of the cool garden shielded by a small park creates a sense of seclusion from its inner London setting.

ALLOTMENTS

OLD PALACE LANE ALLOTMENTS, TW9
Old Palace Lane, Richmond TW9 1PG. Old Palace Lane Allotment Group. *Next to White Swan PH, through gate in wall. Mainline & tube: Richmond. Parking on meters in lane or round Richmond Green, or in Old Deer Park car park, entrance on A316 Twickenham Rd.* Home-made teas. **Adm £3, chd free. Sun 9 Aug (2-5).**
Hidden behind a door in an ancient wall, the Old Palace Lane Allotments in Richmond are like a secret garden. Each of the 33 plots has its own identity; some resemble cottage gardens with patchwork sheds where sun flowers and fennel mingle haphazardly with squash and zucchini, while others sport raised beds, regimented rows of runner beans and gleaming greenhouses. Allotment featured in the Evening Standard and Amateur Gardening.

OLDEN GARDEN COMMUNITY PROJECT, N5
Islington N5 1NH. London Borough of Islington. *Opp 22 Whistler Street & Drayton Park Train Station.* Home-made teas. **Adm £3.50, chd free. Sun 10 May (2-5).**
Olden Garden Community Project is a 2 acre oasis of beauty and retreat from the busy streets surrounding it. A top terrace of beautiful herbaceous borders, lawn and patio and a stunning Rambling Rector rose. On the lower slopes there is an orchard, a meadow, vegetable beds and a greenhouse. In springtime, there is blossom and golden daffodils. Islington in Bloom - Overall Winner Community Garden with Gold and Silver Awards. Wheelchair access to all areas of top terrace. Disabled WC.

THE ORCHARD, W4
40A Hazledene Road, Chiswick, London W4 3JB. Vivien Cantor. *10 mins walk from Chiswick mainline & Gunnersbury tube. Off Fauconberg Rd. Close to junction of A4 & Sutton Court Rd,.* Home-made teas. **Adm £4, chd free. Sun 10 May (2-5.30).**
Informal, romantic ¼ acre garden with mature flowering trees, shrubs and imaginative planting in flowing herbaceous borders. Climbers, fern planting and water features with ponds, a bridge and waterfall in this ever evolving garden.

ORMELEY LODGE, TW10
Ham Gate Avenue, Richmond, Surrey TW10 5HB. Lady Annabel Goldsmith. *From Richmond Pk exit at Ham Gate into Ham Gate Ave, 1st house on R. From Richmond A307, after 1½ m, past New Inn on R at T-lights turn L into Ham Gate Ave.* Tea. **Adm £4, chd free. Sun 21 June (3-6).**
Large walled garden in delightful rural setting on Ham Common. Wide herbaceous borders and box hedges. Walk through to orchard with wild flowers. Vegetable garden, knot garden, aviary and chickens. Trellised tennis court with roses and climbers. A number of historic stone family dog memorials.

ALLOTMENTS

PADDOCK ALLOTMENTS & LEISURE GARDENS, SW20
51 Heath Drive, Raynes Park SW20 9BE. Paddock Horticultural Society. *Bus:57, 131, 200 to Raynes Pk station then 10 min walk or bus 163. 152 to Bushley Rd 7 min walk; 413, 5 min walk from Cannon Hill Lane. Street parking.* Home-made teas. **Adm £3, chd free. Sat 27 June (12-5).**
An allotment site not to be missed, over 150 plots set in 5½ acres. Our tenants come from diverse communities growing a wide range of flowers, fruits and vegetables, some plots are purely organic. Plants, jams and produce for sale. Display of arts and crafts by members of the Paddock Hobby Club. Winners of London in Bloom Best Allotment. Paved and grass paths, mainly level.

3 THE PARK, N6
off Southwood Lane, London N6 4EU. Mr & Mrs G Schrager, 020 8348 3314, buntyschrager@gmail.com. *3 mins from Highgate tube, up Southwood Lane. The Park is 1st on R. Buses: 43, 134, 143, 263.* Home-made teas. **Adm £3.50, chd free. Sun 31 May (2.30-5.30). Visitors also welcome by arrangement Mar to July.**
Established large garden with informal planting for colour, scent and bees. Pond with fish, frogs and tadpoles. Tree peonies, Crinodendron hookerianum and a new Heptacodium. Plants, tea and home-made jam for sale. Children particularly welcome - a treasure hunt with prizes!

11 PARK AVENUE NORTH, N8
Crouch End, London N8 7RU. Mr Steven Buckley & Ms Liz Roberts. *Tube: Finsbury Park & Turnpike Lane, nearest bus stop W3.* Home-made teas. **Adm £3.50, chd free. Sun 7 June (11-5.30). Also open 160A Stapleton Hall Rd and 12 Warwick Rd.**
An exotic 250ft T-shaped garden, threaded through an old orchard and rose garden. Dramatic, mainly spiky, foliage dominates, with the focus on palms, agaves, dasylirions, aeoniums, bananas, tree ferns, nolinas, cycads, bamboos, yuccas, cacti and many species of succulents. Flowering aloes are a highlight. Rocks and terracotta pots lend a Mediterranean accent.

Parkinson's UK are proud to be the NGS guest charity

18 PARK CRESCENT, N3
Finchley N3 2NJ. Rosie Daniels. *Tube: Finchley Central. Buses: 82 to Essex Park, also 125, 460, 626, 683.* Home-made teas. **Adm £3.50, chd free. Sun 21 June, Sun 26 July (2-6).**
Constantly evolving, charming small garden designed and densely planted by owner. Roses and clematis with interesting plants through the summer. New small pond, tub water feature and bird haven. Stepped terrace with lots of pots. Glass installations and sculptures by owner. Hidden seating with view through garden. Secluded, peaceful, restorative. Children's treasure hunt.

4 PARK VILLAGE EAST (TOWER LODGE GARDENS), NW1
Regents Park, London NW1 7PX. Eveline Carn, 020 7388 1113, evelinecbcarn@icloud.com. *Tube: Camden Town or Mornington Crescent 7 mins. Bus: C2 or 274 3 mins. Opp The York & Albany, just off junction of Parkway/Prince Albert Rd.* Home-made teas. **Adm £4, chd free. Evening Opening £5, chd free, wine, Wed 20 May (6-8.30). Sun 12 July (2.30-6). Also open 70 Gloucester Crescent and The Royal College of Physicians Sun 12 July. Visitors also welcome by arrangement May to Aug.**
One of three beautiful and unusual gardens in NW1 opening on the same day in July. Here is an unexpectedly large garden tucked behind a John Nash house, screened by trees and descending over three terraces to what used to be the Regents Canal. A garden of shapes, textures and many shades of green, where box and yew combine with good landscape architecture to provide structure for looser planting. Featured in Country Life.

174 PECKHAM RYE, SE22
London SE22 9QA. Mr & Mrs Ian Bland. *Stn: Peckham Rye. Buses: 12, 37, 63, 197, 363. Overlooks Peckham Rye Common from Dulwich side.* Home-made teas. **Adm £3.50, chd free. Share to St Christopher's Hospice. Sun 7 June (2.30-5.30). Also open 4 Cornflower Terrace and 35 Camberwell Grove.**
Visitors call our garden an oasis of calm in Peckham. Every yr the garden changes and matures. It is densely planted with a wide variety of contrasting foliage. Unusual plants are combined with old favourites. It remains easy care and child friendly. Garden originally designed by Jude Sharpe. Our ever popular plant sale and famed cakes will be available again. Easy access via side alley into a flat garden.

GROUP OPENING

PENGE GARDENS, SE20
London SE20 7QG, 020 8402 3978, mhairi@grozone.co.uk. *Nr junction A213 & A234, off Beckenham Rd nr Kenthouse Station.* Home-made teas. **Combined adm £6, chd free. Sun 24 May (2-5). Visitors also welcome by arrangement May to Sept.**

43 CLEVEDON ROAD
Elizabeth Parker

26 KENILWORTH ROAD D
Mhairi & Simon Clutson Visitors also welcome by arrangement to Sept. Refreshments available for groups 10+. 020 8402 3978 mhairi@grozone.co.uk

Two contrasting gardens: One is a contemporary garden with clever juxtaposition of hard landscaped areas complemented by dynamic planting, and the other is a cottage garden. 43 Clevedon Rd is 50ft x 22ft, with unusual trees and shrubs incl snake bark maple, sorbus cashmiriana and itea ilicifolia.

Abundant rambler roses, incl Félicité Perpétue, colourful mixed borders, and pots on terrace. Several interesting and unusual water features. 26 Kenilworth Rd is a garden designers' inspirational garden providing maximum impact in a small space. An inventive layout extends the living space and planted areas to create a flexible low maintenance garden. Creative use of drought tolerant flowering Mediterranean shrubs ensure that the garden looks green even in the Winter. Contrasting foliage textures and colours are complemented with interesting perennials and bold planters filled with Agapanthus.

❀ ☕

A Wendy house and hidden wooden castle provide delight for children . . .

PETERSHAM HOUSE, TW10
Petersham Road, Petersham, Richmond TW10 7AA. Francesco & Gael Boglione, www.petershamnurseries.com. *Stn: Richmond, then 65 bus to Dysart PH. Entry to garden off Petersham Rd, through nursery. Parking very limited on Church Lane.* **Adm £4, chd free. Sun 7 June, Sun 6 Sept (11-4).**
Broad lawn with large topiary, generously planted double borders. Productive vegetable garden with chickens. Adjoins Petersham Nurseries with extensive plant sales, shop and cafe.

♿ 🚲 ❀ ☕

18 PETTITS BOULEVARD, RM1
Rise Park, Romford RM1 4PL. Mr & Mrs Nutley. *From M25 take A12 towards London, at Pettits Lane junction turn R then R again into Pettits Boulevard.* Tea. **Adm £3, chd free. Sat 13, Sun 14 June, Sat 25, Sun 26 July (1-6).**
Small garden on 3 levels with trees,

shrubs and perennials, many in pots. There is an ornamental pond, woodland themed area and interesting agricultural implements and garden ornaments. There are seating areas situated throughout the garden. Agricultural implements on show. Partial wheelchair access.

♿ 🚲 ☕

GROUP OPENING

PRINCES AVENUE GARDENS, N10
Muswell Hill N10 3LS. *Buses: 43 & 134 from Highgate tube; also W7, 102, 144, 234, 299. Princes Ave opp M&S in Muswell Hill Broadway, or John Baird PH in Fortis Green.* Home-made teas at No 15 & No 28. **Combined adm £4, chd free. Sun 17 May (2-6). Also open 94 Brownlow Rd.**

15 PRINCES AVENUE
Eliot & Emma Glover

28 PRINCES AVENUE
Ian & Viv Roberts

In a beautiful Edwardian avenue in the heart of Muswell Hill Conservation Area, two very different gardens reflect the diverse life styles of their owners. The large S facing family garden at No. 15 has been designed for entertaining and yr-round interest. White, blue and blush pink themed beds with alliums and a wide variety of perennials and shrubs frame an exceptional lawn. A Wendy house and hidden wooden castle provide delight for children of all ages. The charming annexe garden at No.17, where tea can be enjoyed, has a superb Hosta display. No. 28 is a well-established traditional garden reflecting the charm typical of the era. Mature trees, shrubs, mixed borders and woodland garden creating an oasis of calm just off the bustling Broadway.

♿ 🚲 ❀ ☕

GROUP OPENING

RAILWAY COTTAGES, N22
Dorset Road, Alexandra Palace N22 7SL. *Tube: Wood Green, 10 mins walk. Overground: Alexandra Palace, 3 mins. Buses W3, 184. 3 mins. Free parking in local streets on Sundays.* Home-made teas at 2 Dorset Rd. **Combined adm £4, chd free. Sun 5 July (2-5.30).**

2 DORSET ROAD
Jane Stevens

4 DORSET ROAD
Mark Longworth

14 DORSET ROAD
Cathy Brogan

22 DORSET ROAD
Mike & Noreen Ainger

24A DORSET ROAD
Eddie & Jane Wessman

A row of historical railway cottages, tucked away from the bustle of Wood Green nr Alexandra Palace, takes the visitor back in time. No. 4 Is a pretty secluded woodland garden, (accessed through the rear of No. 2) sets off sculptor owner's figurative and abstract work among acers, sambucus nigra, species shrubs and old fruit trees. Within the pretty surroundings sits the owner's working studio. Three front gardens at Nos. 14, 22 and 24a, one nurtured by the grandson of the original railway worker occupant, show a variety of planting, incl aromatic shrubs, herbs, jasmine, flax, fig, fuchsia and vines. A modern raised bed vegetable garden is a new addition this yr. The tranquil country style garden at No. 2 Dorset Rd flanks 3 sides of the house. Hawthorn topiary (by the original owner) and clipped box hedges contrast with climbing roses, clematis, honeysuckle, abutilon and cottage plants. Trees incl mulberry, quince, fig, apple and a mature willow creating an opportunity for an interesting shady corner. There is an emphasis on scented flowers that attract bees and butterflies and the traditional medicinal plants found in cottage gardens.

❀ ☕

NEW ▶ **60 RANELAGH ROAD, W5**
Ealing, London W5 5RP. Mr Antony Watkins & Mr Christopher Hutchings. *Ealing. South Ealing Tube - 10 mins; Ealing Broadway tube - 20 mins. Off Ealing Common - Uxbridge Rd. Entry to garden via Baillies Walk.* Tea. **Adm £4, chd free. Sun 9 Aug (2-6).**
Palms, bamboos and sub tropical planting throughout a 50ft south facing garden with a flow of bright flowers, such as salvias, tithonias, cleome, abutilons to name some. Walk around the sunken path and stop off in the seating areas.

❀ ☕

30 St James's Road, Hampton Hill Gardens

◆ ROOTS AND SHOOTS, SE11
Walnut Tree Walk, Kennington
SE11 6DN. Trustees of Roots and
Shoots,
www.rootsandshoots.org.uk. *Tube:
Lambeth North. Buses: 3, 59, 159,
360. Just S of Waterloo Stn, off
Kennington Rd, 5 mins from Imperial
War Museum. No car parking on site.*
Cream teas. **Adm £2, chd free. For
NGS: Fri 19 June (2-7).** For other
opening times and information,
please phone or see garden
website.
1/2 acre wildlife garden run by
innovative charity providing training
and garden advice. Summer
meadow, observation beehives, 2
large ponds, hot borders,
Mediterranean mound, old roses and
echiums. Learning centre with
photovoltaic roof, solar heating,
rainwater catchment, three planted
roofs, one brown roof. Wildlife garden
study centre exhibition with photo,
video and other wildlife interpretation
materials.
&♿ ✿ ☕

ALLOTMENTS

**THE ROSE GARDEN AT GOLF
COURSE ALLOTMENTS, N11**
Winton Avenue, London N11 2AR.
GCAA Mr George Dunnion,
www.gcaa.pwp.blueyonder.co.uk.
*Tube: Bounds Green, 1km Buses:
102,184 299 to Sunshine Garden
Centre Durnsford Rd*. Home-made
teas in main allotment chalet. **Adm
£3.50, chd free. Sun 28 June
(1-5.30).**
Large allotment plot displaying over
120 different roses comprising much
of the history of the rose; there are
Gallicas, Damasks, Albas, Portlands
etc, as well as around 40 Austin
roses and many others. The roses are
interplanted with a wide range of
perennials as well as vegetables.
Colourful chards and red cabbages,
grasses, clematis and rare exotic
plants. Owners will share their
extensive knowledge with visitors.
Featured in Gardeners World and
local press. Awarded Best Allotment
in Haringey in Bloom competition.
♿ ✿ ☕

**NEW ▸ 63 ROSECROFT
GARDENS, TW2**
Twickenham TW2 7PU. Valerie
Hedley. *Off A316 W towards M3.
Pass Harlequins Rugby Grd on L.
After 150yds turn into Rosebine Ave.
At T-junction turn R then L into
Rosecroft Gdns. Garden at bottom of
rd. SW trains to Whitton stn 15mins
walk.* **Adm £3.50, chd free. Sun 7
June (2-5).**
Informal plantsman's garden for wild
life and birds on an Art Deco

bungalow estate in Twickenham.
Mixed borders, interesting shrubs,
perennials, climbers and ground
cover. Woodland area. Sunny terrace
with terracotta pots.
&♿ ✿

**ROYAL COLLEGE OF
PHYSICIANS MEDICINAL
GARDEN, NW1**
11 St Andrews Place, London
NW1 4LE. Royal College of
Physicians of London, 0207 034
4901,
henry.oakeley@rcplondon.ac.uk,
www.rcplondon.ac.uk/museum-
and-garden/garden. *Tubes: Great
Portland St & Regent's Park. Garden
is one block N of station exits, on
Outer Circle opp SE corner of
Regent's Park.* **Adm £4, chd free.
Mon 29 June, Sun 12 July (10-4).**
Also open 4 Park Village East and
70 Gloucester Crescent (Sun 12
July). Visitors also welcome by
arrangement.
One of three beautiful and unusual
gardens in NW1 opening on the same
day in July. 1100 different plants used
in conventional and herbal medicines
around the world during the past
3000 yrs; plants named after
physicians and plants with medical
implications. The plants are labelled,
and arranged by continent except for
the plants from the College's
Pharmacopoeia of 1618. Guided

tours all day, explaining the uses of the plants, their histories and stories about them. Books about the plants in the medicinal garden will be on sale. Wheelchair ramps at steps.

5 RUSSELL ROAD, N13
Bowes Park, London N13 4RS. **Angela Kreeger.** *Close to N Circular Rd & Green Lanes. Tube: Bounds Green, 10 mins walk. Mainline: Bowes Park, 3 mins walk. Numerous bus routes. Off Whittington Rd.* Home-made teas. **Adm £3, chd free. Sun 6 Sept (2-6).**
A poem for the eyes. Billowing, overflowing, balanced by flat lawn. Airy, dreamy planting in small woodland, a pebble garden marks the border. Not manicured. Simple, unfussy with a contemporary feel, calm, quiet and peaceful. Autumn is rusty, loose and soft. Golden in sunlight. Small bespoke greenhouse reminiscent of Dungeness and Hastings. Front garden vegetable bed. The garden is being extensively revised in 2015. Featured in Gardens Illustrated.

Creative and witty placing of bits and bobs . . .

7 ST GEORGE'S ROAD, TW1
St Margarets, Twickenham TW1 1QS. **Richard & Jenny Raworth, 020 8892 3713,** jraworth@gmail.com, www.raworthgarden.com. *1½ m SW of Richmond. Off A316 between Twickenham Bridge & St Margarets r'about.* **Evening Openings £6, chd free, wine, Sat 6, Sun 21 June (6-8). Visitors also welcome by arrangement May to July for groups 10+.**
Exuberant displays of Old English roses and vigorous climbers with unusual herbaceous perennials. Massed scented crambe cordifolia. Pond with bridge converted into child-safe lush bog garden and waterfall.Large N facing luxuriant conservatory with rare plants and

climbers. Pelargoniums a speciality. Sunken garden and knot garden. Pergola covered with climbing roses and clematis. New water feature and fernery. Filmed for Gardener's World with MontyDon.

NEW ST GOTHARD MEWS, SE27
17 St Louis Road, London SE27 9QW. **Linda & Philip Newcombe.** *Bus 322 to St Gothard Rd (hail & ride section). From Gipsy Hill stn, 322 towards Clapham. Or bus 3 Gipsy Hill stop, walk along Gipsy Rd, turn R at St Gothard Rd, R into St Louis. Garden on R.* Tea. **Adm £3, chd free. Sun 12 July (2-5). Also opening 2 Shardcroft Ave, 45 & 86 Underhill Rd.**
Small private mews. A hidden gem; quirky and unexpected communal courtyard with interesting nooks and crannies. Lush exotic and Mediterranean planting in temporary, raised and makeshift beds, unusual plant combinations in pots, wall planters and containers. Tiny toad garden. Creative and witty placing of bits and bobs. Delightful sub courtyard adds theatre and surprise. Wheelchair access to main courtyard only.

87 ST JOHNS ROAD, E17
London E17 4JH. **Andrew Bliss, 07790 230053,** blisshand@yahoo.co.uk. *15 mins walk from W'stow tube/overground or 212/275 bus. Ring bell at petrol station. 10 mins walk from Wood St overground. Very close to N Circular.* Home-made teas. **Adm £3, chd free. Sun 16, Sun 23 Aug (1-5). Visitors also welcome by arrangement.**
My garden epitomises what can be achieved with imagination, design and colour consideration in a small typical terraced outdoor area. The reoccurring circular theme, whether horizontal or vertical maintains continuity and together with overplanting creates a most beautiful and relaxing space. Seeing is believing, come and enjoy it!!!! Variety of stalls selling arts and crafts.

16 ST MARGARETS ROAD, E12
London E12 5DP. **Julie & Brian Linden.** *Nearest tube Wanstead or mainline Manor Park. Bus 101. Alight at Empress Avenue.* Tea. **Adm £3.50, chd free. Sun 9 Aug (2-6).**

Stylish modern suburban garden 100ft x 25ft. Well established trees inc. Indian bean, robinia, olive, white lilac and bananas. Formal lawn, box hedging, dazzling beds of dahlias, cannas and other exotics. Secret second garden at the end to discover. Emphasis on lots of colour and low maintenance. Featured in Amateur Gardening.

20 ST MARY'S GROVE, N1
London N1 2NT. **Mrs B Capel.** *Canonbury, Islington. Tube & Overground: Highbury & Islington. Buses: 4, 19, 30, 277 to St Paul's Rd. 271 to Canonbury Square.* **Adm £2.50, chd free. Sat 11 Apr (2-5).**
Come and discover this delightful, small paved garden with sweet smelling spring flowers and shrubs - coronilla, tree peony, sarcococca, camellias, lilac. Don't miss the auricula theatre with a variety of little potted favourites.

ST MICHAEL'S CONVENT, TW10
56 Ham Common, Ham, Richmond TW10 7JH. **Community of the Sisters of the Church.** *2m S of Richmond. On Ham Common nr A307 between Richmond & Kingston or 65 bus, alight at Ham Gate Av.* Tea. **Adm £3, chd free. Sun 14 June (2-4.30).**
4 acre organic garden comprises walled vegetable garden, orchards, vine house, ancient mulberry tree, extensive borders, meditation and Bible gardens. Some gravel paths.

NEW 27 ST PETERS SQUARE, W6
London W6 9NW. **Oliver Leigh Wood.** *Tube to Stamford Brook exit station & turn S down Goldhawk Rd. At T-lights cont ahead into British Grove. Entrance to garden is at 50 British Grove 100 yds on the L.* **Adm £4, chd free. Sun 10 May (2-6).**
This long, secret space, is a plantsman's eclectic semi tamed wilderness. Created over the last 8yrs it contains lots of camellias, magnolias and fruit trees. Much of the hard landscaping is from skips and the whole garden is full of other people's unconsidered trifles of fancy incl a folly and summer house.

57 ST QUINTIN AVENUE, W10

London W10 6NZ. Mr H Groffman, 020 8969 8292. *1m from Ladbroke Grove or White City tube. Buses: 7, 70, 220 all to North Pole Rd. Free parking on Sundays.* Home-made teas. **Adm £3, chd free. Sun 12, Sun 26 July (2-6). Also open 29 Addison Ave (Sun 26 July). Visitors also welcome by arrangement July to Aug. Refreshments available if ordered in advance.**
30ft x 40ft walled garden; wide selection of plant material incl evergreen and deciduous shrubs for foliage effects. Patio area mainly furnished with bedding material, colour themed. Focal points throughout. Refurbished with new plantings and special features. Theme for the garden this yr is the 70th anniversary of the end of World War II (VE and VJ days). All London Championship 1st Prize winner.

5 ST REGIS CLOSE, N10

Alexandra Park Road, London N10 2DE. Ms S Bennett & Mr E Hyde, 020 8883 8540, suebearlh@yahoo.co.uk. *Muswell Hill. Tube: Bounds Green then 102 or 299 bus, or E. Finchley take 102. Alight St Andrew Church. 134 or 43 bus stop at end of Alexandra Pk Rd, follow arrows.* Home-made teas. **Adm £3.50, chd free. Sun 3 May, Sun 21 June, Sun 19 July (2-6.30). Visitors also welcome by arrangement Apr to Oct for groups 10+. Home-made teas/light lunches.**
A cornucopia of sensual delights! Artists' garden renowned for unique architectural features and delicious cakes. Baroque temple, pagodas, oriental raku tiled mirrored wall conceals plant nursery. American Gothic shed overlooks newly built

Liberace Terrace. Maureen Lipman's favourite garden, combining colour, humour and trompe l'oeil with wildlife friendly ponds, waterfalls, weeping willow and lawns. Imaginative container planting and abundant borders, creating an inspirational and re-energising experience. Open studio with ceramics and prints home grown plants. Featured in House Beautiful and on ITV's Britains Best Gardens. Wheelchair access to all parts of garden unless waterlogged.

2 SHARDCROFT AVENUE, SE24

Herne Hill, London SE24 0DT. Catriona Andrews. *Short walk from Herne Hill rail station & bus stops. Buses: 3, 68, 196, 201, 468 to Herne Hill. Parking in local streets.* Home-made teas. **Adm £3, chd free. Sun 12 July (2-6). Also open 45 & 86 Underhill Rd.**
A designer's garden with loose, naturalistic planting. Geometric terracing accommodates a natural slope, framing vistas from the house. Drought tolerant beds with cascading perennials and grasses, scented courtyard, formal wildlife pond, woodland glade with fire pit and green roofed shed provide wildlife habitats and a feast for the senses. Planted ecologically to benefit wildlife, pond, nesting boxes and log piles, green roofed shed, seating circle with fire pit.

SOUTH LONDON BOTANICAL INSTITUTE, SE24

323 Norwood Road, London SE24 9AQ. South London Botanical Institute, www.slbi.org.uk. *Mainline stn: Tulse Hill. Buses: 68, 196, 322 & 468 stop at junction of Norwood & Romola Rds.* Home-made teas. **Adm £3, chd free. Share to South London Botanical Institute. Sun 19 Apr (2-5). Also open 6 Frank Dixon Way.**
London's smallest botanical garden, densely planted with 500 labeled species grown in a formal layout of themed borders. Wildflowers flourish beside medicinal herbs. Carnivorous, scented, native and woodland plants are featured, growing among rare trees and shrubs. Unusually this yr we are opening in spring to highlight our newly created moss trail. The fascinating SLBI building is also open. Unusual plants for sale.

123 SOUTH PARK ROAD, SW19

Wimbledon, London SW19 8RX. Susan Adcock. *Mainline & tube: Wimbledon, 10 mins; S Wimbledon tube 5 mins. Buses: 57, 93, 131, 219 along High St. Entrance in Bridges Rd (next to church hall) off South Park Rd.* Home-made teas. **Adm £3, chd free. Sun 7 June (2-6).**
This small L shaped garden has a high deck amongst trees overlooking a woodland area, patio with pots, several small water containers, a fish pond, and a secluded courtyard with raised beds for flowers and herbs, as well as a discreet hot tub. Lots of ideas for giving a small space atmosphere and interest.

41 SOUTHBROOK ROAD, SE12

Lee, London SE12 8LJ. Barbara & Marek Polanski, 020 8333 2176, polanski101@yahoo.co.uk. *United Kingdom. Situated at Southbrook Rd, off S Circular, off Burnt Ash Rd. Train: Lee & Hither Green, both 10 mins walk. Bus: P273,202.* Home-made teas. **Adm £3.50, chd free. Sat 13, Sun 14 June (2-5.30). Also open 2 Springhurst Close. Visitors also welcome by arrangement May to July (2-5.30).**
Developed over 14yrs, this large garden has a formal layout, with wide mixed herbaceous borders full of colour and interest, surrounded by mature trees, framing sunny lawns, a central box parterre and an Indian pergola. Ancient pear trees festooned in June with clouds of white Kiftsgate and Rambling Rector roses. Discover fishes and damselflies in 2 lily ponds. Many places to sit and relax. Enjoy refreshments in a small classical garden building with interior wall paintings. Appeared as Garden of the Week in Garden News magazine also featured in Bises, a Japanese publication for English country garden enthusiasts. Side access available for standard wheelchairs.

SOUTHWOOD LODGE, N6

33 Kingsley Place, Highgate N6 5EA. Mr & Mrs C Whittington, 020 8348 2785, suewhittington@hotmail.co.uk. *Tube: Highgate then 6 mins walk up Southwood Ln. 4 min walk from Highgate Village along Southwood Ln. Buses: 143, 210, 214, 271.* Home-made teas. **Adm £4, chd free. Sun 26 Apr, Sun 7 June (2-5.30).**

Also open 7 The Grove (Sun 7 June). Visitors also welcome by arrangement Apr to July. Refreshments available if ordered in advance.

Unusual garden hidden behind C18 house (not open), laid out last century on steeply sloping site, now densely planted. Ponds, waterfall, frogs and newts. Lots of different topiary shapes formed from self sown yew trees. Beautiful working greenhouse, also good for tea on rainy days! Many unusual plants grown and propagated for sale - rare pelargoniums a speciality at June opening. Toffee hunt for children. Featured in Englische Garten Ikonen by Heidi Howcroft and Marianne Majerus.

❀ 🚐 ☕

GROUP OPENING

SPEER ROAD GARDENS, KT7
Thames Ditton KT7 0PJ. *2m SW of Kingston. Thames Ditton stn 5mins walk.* Home-made teas at 37 Speer Road. **Combined adm £5, chd free. Sun 7 June (2-5.30).**

37 SPEER ROAD
Diana Brown & Dave Matten

53 SPEER ROAD
Mrs Jayne Thomas

2 contrasting gardens within 4 mins walking distance of each other. 53 Speer Rd is a garden designer's family garden, transformed to provide areas of interest with large mixed shrub and herbaceous borders, planted to give a long season of interest incl a late season display of colour. Ornamental trees and silver birches create a calm woodland setting with a wild meadow. Many plants from designer's gardens at Hampton Court. 37 Speer Rd is an 1920s landscaped garden, maintained by present owners to the original design with emphasis on imaginative and carefully clipped topiary. The boundary is edged by 7 small fish pools, which also mark an ancient public right of way for villagers to drive their sheep to pastures beyond. The garden is an evocative reminder of the '20s. Croquet on the lawn at 37 Speer Rd (Underwood).

❀ ☕

Beautiful working greenhouse, also good for tea on rainy days . . . !

GROUP OPENING

SPITALFIELDS GARDENS GROUP, E1
London E1 6QH. Not for publication. *10 mins walk from Aldgate E Tube & 5 mins walk from Liverpool St stn. Overground: Shoreditch High St - 3 mins walk.* Home-made teas at Town House, 5 Fournier St. **Combined adm £12, chd free. Sat 13 June (10-4).**

NEW▶ 7 ELDER STREET 🅳

7 FOURNIER STREET
John Nicolson

20 FOURNIER STREET
Ms Charlie de Wet

NEW▶ 29 FOURNIER STREET
Juliette Larthe

31 FOURNIER STREET
Rodney Archer

21 WILKES STREET
Rupert Wheeler

Six hidden treasures behind some of the finest merchants and weavers houses in Spitalfields. Two gardens opening for the first time: 7 Elder St: a small garden featuring cloud hedging, a chequerboard brick and chamomile lawn, a row of pleached evergreen oaks, and climbers. Across Commercial St. - 29 Fournier St: a country house feel in a recently created garden - wisteria, fig, jasmine and blue and white borders. Next door: 31 Fournier St: an idyllic green courtyard with vine covered arch - a rill, a pond, a silver birch and a surprise await the visitor! Opp: 20 Fournier St: a S-facing retreat

---

where fig, mulberry, cherry and vines flourish. 7 Fournier St, opp Christ Church: a magical shady garden with a single ash tree. Imaginative planting for shade complemented by salvaged artefacts and water. Around the corner, 21 Wilkes Street - a contemporary garden on three levels within a redundant factory. Moat, bridge, light wells, rock pool and raised beds. Roses, jasmines and vines. Featured in Country Life.

☕

NEW▶ 2 SPRINGHURST CLOSE, CR0
Shirley Church Road, Croydon CR0 5AT. Ben & Peckham Carroll. *2m S of Croydon. Off A2022 from Selsdon. Off A232 from Croydon. Tram line 3 to Addington Village. East Croydon Station.* Home-made teas. **Adm £3.50, chd free. Sun 14 June (2-6). Also opening 41 Southbrook Road.**

A new country courtyard garden of grasses, topiary and specimen perennials in a woodland setting. Water feature and planting in a soft colour palette of blues, purples and pinks designed to attract bees and wildlife. Vegetable garden in raised beds, fernery, large collection of hostas and hydrangea walk add interest and variety to ¹/₂ acre woodland garden. Mainly level with grass paths but a few steps.

♿ ❀ ☕

160A STAPLETON HALL ROAD, N4
Stroud Green, London N4 4QJ. Peter Beardsley. *Nr to Parkland Walk; www.parkland-walk.org.uk. Local Buses: W3, W5. Nearest trains: Crouch Hill, Harringay Rail.* Home-made teas. **Adm £3.50, chd free. Sun 7 June (1-5). Also open 11 Park Av North and 12 Warren Rd.**

Designer's hillside garden. A long London patch maximised; a descent that frays into a wild blossom wood. S facing. Mature trees and hedges compartmentalise a sequence of loosely planted perennial gardens. A meander of woodland tracks and narrow steps connect a series of sitting glades. Richly planted and floral. Vegetable patch. Greenhouse. Vintage horticultural ware. Full plant list. Cake! Featured in Gardens Illustrated.

❀ ☕

STOKES HOUSE, TW10
Ham Street, Ham, Richmond
TW10 7HR. Peter & Rachel
Lipscomb, 020 8940 2403,
rlipscomb@virginmedia.com. *2m S
of Richmond off A307. ¼ m from
A307. Trains & tube to Richmond &
train to Kingston which link with 65
bus to Ham Common.* Home-made
teas. **Adm £3, chd free. Sun 7 June
(2-5).** Visitors also welcome by
arrangement Apr to Sept. Garden
groups welcome.
Originally an orchard, this ½ acre
walled country garden is abundant
with roses, clematis and perennials.
There are mature trees incl ancient
mulberries and wisteria. The yew
hedging, pergola and box hedges
allow for different planting schemes
throughout the yr. Supervised children
are welcome to play on the slide and
swing. Georgian house, herbaceous
borders, brick garden, wild garden,
large compost area and interesting
trees. Many plants for sale.
Wheelchair access via double doors
from street with 2 wide steps.

Professional plantsman's petite hillside paradise . . . !

STONEY HILL HOUSE, SE26
Rock Hill, London SE26 6SW.
Cinzia & Adam Greaves. *Off
Sydenham Hill. Train: Sydenham,
Gipsy Hill or Sydenham Hill (closest)
stations. Buses: To Crystal Palace,
202 or 363 along Sydenham Hill,
House at end of cul-de-sac on L
coming from Sydenham Hill.* Delicious
home-made cakes! Generous mugs
of tea (with free refills) also available.
**Adm £4, chd free. Sun 17 May
(2-6). Also open 5 Burbage Road.**
Garden and woodland of approx 1
acre providing a secluded secret
green oasis in the city. Paths
meander through mature
rhododendron, oak, yew and holly
trees, offset by pieces of

contemporary sculpture. The garden
is on a slope and a number of
viewpoints set at different heights
provide varied perspectives. The
planting in the top part of the garden
is fluid and flows seamlessly into the
woodland. We hope to have a living
sculpture carved into an oak tree
damaged in high winds. Shallow,
wide steps at entrance to garden with
grass slope alongside. Wheelchair
access possible if these can be
negotiated.

4 STRADBROKE GROVE, IG9
Buckhurst Hill IG9 5PD. Mr & Mrs
Brighten. *Between Epping &
Woodford, 5m from M25 J26. Tube:
Buckhurst Hill, turn R cross rd to
Stradbroke Grove.* Home-made teas.
**Adm £3, chd free. Sun 14 June
(2-5.30).**
Secluded garden, designed to
enhance its strong sloping aspect.
Central gravelled bed. Rose screened
vegetable and fruit garden. Large
lawn with good herbaceous borders
and pergola to disguise conifer
hedge.

58 SUMMERLEE AVENUE, N2
London N2 9QH. Edwina & Nigel
Roberts. *Tube to E Finchley, cross
main rd, Summerlee Ave located off
Southern Rd. Walking distance from
Muswell Hill. Entry via alley at back of
house.* Home-made teas. **Adm
£3.50, chd free. Sun 31 May (2-6).**
Beautiful acer, densely planted
borders with mixture of shrubs and
herbaceous perennials and spring
and summer bulbs. Fences clothed
with climbing roses, wisteria, clematis
and honeysuckle. Woodland planting
under acer. Small wildlife pond and
planting is chosen to attract birds and
insects and for fragrance. Several
seating areas arranged to allow
different views of garden. Gravel
garden. Featured in Ham & High.

93 TANFIELD AVENUE, NW2
Dudden Hill, London NW2 7SB. Mr
James Duncan Mattoon, 020 8830
7410. *Dudden Hill - Neasden.
Nearest station: Neasden - Jubilee
line then 10 mins walk; or various bus
routes to Neasden Parade or Tanfield
Av.* Home-made teas. **Adm £4, chd
free. Sun 2 Aug (2-6).** Visitors also
welcome by arrangement May to
Sept for groups 20 max.
Professional plantsman's petite

hillside paradise! Arid/tropical deck
with panoramic views of Wembley
and Harrow, descends through
Mediterranean screes and warm
sunny slopes, to sub-tropical oasis
packed with many rare and exotic
plants e.g. Hedychium, Plumbago,
Punica, Tetrapanax. To rear, jungle
shade terrace and secret summer
house offer cool respite on sunny
days. Stunning panoramic views.
Previous garden was Tropical Kensal
Rise (Doyle Gardens) featured on
BBC2 Open Gardens and Sunday
Telegraph. Jim Carter and Imelda
Staunton say 'A beautiful and
surprising garden; an absolute delight
that will inspire any gardener!'.

81 TANTALLON ROAD, SW12
Balham, London SW12 8DQ. Mr
Jonathan McKee. *5 mins from
Balham or Wandsworth Common
stations. No parking restrictions.*
Refreshments. **Adm £3.50, chd free.
Sun 5 July (1-5).**
Very small, but stunning garden, in a
Victorian terrace, a blaze of colour
throughout with structural and annual
planting. Espalier apple trees reach
into a carefully managed plot and
gardeners will notice that maturing
specimens provide interest as the
planting scheme evolves over time in
a garden that is thoughtfully
constructed to optimise space in
early summer.

58A TEIGNMOUTH ROAD, NW2
Cricklewood NW2 4DX. Drs Elayne
& Jim Coakes, 020 8208 0082,
elayne.coakes@btinternet.com,
www.facebook.com/
gardening4bees. *Cricklewood. Tube:
Willesden Green or Kilburn 10 mins
walk. Buses: 16, 32, 189, 226, 260,
266, 316, 332, 460. Teignmouth Rd
just off Walm Ln.* Home-made teas.
**Adm £3.50, chd free. Sun 5 July (3-
6.30).** Also opening 121 Anson Rd
and 27 Menelik Rd, combined
admission (3 gardens) £8 chld free.
Visitors also welcome by
arrangement Apr to Sept. 15 max.
Plenty of notice required please.
Front and back gardens with eclectic
planting schemes incl restrained
palate coordinated beds, pergola with
wisteria, climbing roses and 40+
clematis, 2 ponds, water features,
acers, hardy, and unusual plants.
Rainwater harvesting with integral
watering system, native plants and
organic treatment means a home for

frogs, newts and bees. Under the terrace is a 3¹/₂ ton tank for the water harvesting system that feeds water to taps around the garden; Clematis and other climbing plants clothe the pergola and woodland walk as well as the fences. Featured in Japanese Lifestyle magazine Mr Partner, British Clematis Society's journal and The Great British Garden Revival. Some areas accessible only by stepping stones. Deep pond.

NEW **14 TETHERDOWN, N10**
London N10 1NB. Laura Wahburn Hutton & Ian Pollock. *Opp the entrance to Fortismere Secondary school.* Home-made teas. **Adm £3.50, chd free. Sun 5 July (2-6).** Also open 5 Cecil Rd and 66 Muswell Av.
The theme is based on circles using a variety of materials. Ornamental plants accompany espaliered fruit trees, soft fruit, step overs and masses of herbs. One of the owners is a cookery writer, so the edible aspect of the garden is important. The scheme is meant to attract bees and butterflies, be scented and have movement. An example of what can be done in a small space with eastern exposure.

GROUP OPENING

TEWKESBURY LODGE : OVER THE HILL, SE23
Forest Hill, London SE23 3DE. *Off S Circular (A205) behind Horniman Museum & Gardens. Stn: Forest Hill, 10 mins walk. Buses: 176, 185, 312, P4. Tickets available from any garden.* Home-made teas (incl gluten free) available. **Combined adm £7, chd free. Sun 31 May (1-6).**

7 CANONBIE ROAD
Mrs June Wismayer

THE COACH HOUSE
Pat Rae

25 WESTWOOD PARK
Beth & Steph Falkingham-Blackwell

Three gardens all within 5 mins walk of each other with art, sculpture, delicious home-made teas and many plants for sale. An exuberantly planted city sanctuary garden built on 3 levels has rose and jasmine draped arches, woodland planting in both dry and damp shade, jewel garden and

65 Mill Hill Road

topiary and incl many new grasses and plants. A sculptor's courtyard garden crammed with unusual plants and sculptures and ceramics for sale has been beautifully redesigned and now incl a seating area and a fruit cage. An organic garden overlooking the Horniman Park has been completely redesigned to incl more bee friendly plants and warm colours, grasses, a unique slate water feature, seating areas and large fruit cage.

GROUP OPENING

TEWKESBURY LODGE: TOP OF THE HILL, SE23
London SE23 3DE. *Off S Circular (A205) behind Horniman Museum & Gardens. Station: Forest Hill, 10 mins walk. Buses: 176, 185, 312, P4.* Home-made teas at 53 Ringmore Rise (Sun). **Combined adm £7, chd free. Share to St Christopher's Hospice and Marsha Phoenix Trust. Evening Opening, wine, Sat 20 June (5-8). Sun 21 June (2-6). Combined with The Coach House. Also open 103 & 105 Dulwich Village (Sun 21 June).**

HILLTOP, 28 HORNIMAN DRIVE
Frankie Locke

27 HORNIMAN DRIVE
Rose Agnew
Visitors also welcome by arrangement Apr to Oct groups welcome.
020 8699 7710
roseandgraham@talktalk.net

53 RINGMORE RISE
Valerie Ward

Three very different hillside gardens within a short walk of each other, with spectacular views over London and the North Downs. A small SE facing garden has richly coloured borders within formal outlines to complement a modern extension plus mini meadow and a tranquil vegetable garden with seating, greenhouse and compost area. The front garden of another, inspired by Beth Chatto's dry garden, has stunning borders in soft mauves, yellows and white, with a rear garden on three levels, with themed beds, some shady, others sunny. A country style garden has informal flower borders, raised vegetable beds, a fruit cage, greenhouse, chickens, and wildlife areas. Story Hunt for children. New for 2015 - alpine garden. Great views. Plants for sale at 27 Horniman Drive.

Over 400 Volunteers help run the NGS – why not become one too?

NEW ▶ 21 THURLOW ROAD, NW3
The Garden Flat, Hampstead, London NW3 5PP. Jenny & Howard Ross. *tube: Hampstead, buses 268, 46. Thurlow Rd 5 mins walk from Hampstead tube down Rosslyn Hill on R. Also nearby Belsize Park tube, Hampstead Heath Silverlink, 168 bus.* Home-made teas incl gluten free cakes. **Adm £3.50, chd free. Sun 5 July (2-5.30).**
Hidden beyond iron gates is a charming walled garden just 5yrs old, with a sunken area bordered by densely planted flowerbeds. The garden consists of herbaceous beds and plants incl lavenders, agapanthus, delphiniums, exceptional hydrangeas propagated from a Dorset garden and C19 roses, all in subtle muted tones.

The NGS is Macmillan's largest single donor

TREETOPS, HA6
Sandy Lane, Northwood HA6 3ES. Mrs Carole Kitchner. *Opp Northwood HQ. Tube: Northwood, 10 mins walk. Bus 8 stops at bottom of lane. Parking in Lane.* Tea. **Adm £4, chd free. Sun 12 July (2-6).**
Nestling in quiet lane in Northwood conservation area, sloping garden with long terrace and large pots. Rose covered pergola, water feature, small lawn, wide variety unusual shrubs incl magnolia grandiflora, paulownias, trochodendron. Peaking in high summer, heleniums, agapanthus, lobelias, eryngiums, crocosmias present a vibrant vision - well worth a visit! Mentioned in an article by Robin Lane Fox in the Financial Times.

TRINITY HOSPICE, SW4
30 Clapham Common North Side, London SW4 0RN. Trinity Hospice, www.trinityhospice.org.uk. *Tube: Clapham Common. Buses: 35, 37, 345,137 stop outside.* Tea, coffee and biscuits. **Adm £2.50, chd free.**

Sat 11, Sun 12 Apr, Sat 1, Sun 2 Aug (10-4).
Trinity's beautiful, award winning gardens play an important therapeutic role in the life and function of Trinity Hospice. Over the years, many thousands of people have enjoyed our gardens and today they continue to be enjoyed by patients, families and visitors alike. Set over nearly two acres, they offer space for quiet contemplation, family fun and make a great backdrop for events. Ramps and pathways.
 ♿ 🐕 ☕

TRUMPETERS HOUSE & SARAH'S GARDEN, TW9
Richmond TW9 1PD. Baron & Baroness Van Dedem. *Richmond riverside. 5 mins walk from Richmond Station via Richmond Green in Trumpeter's Yard. Parking on Richmond Green & Old Deer Park car park only.* Home-made teas. **Adm £5, chd free. Sun 14 June (2-5).**
The 2 acre garden is on the original site of Richmond Palace. Long lawns stretch from the house to banks of the River Thames. There are clipped yews, a box parterre and many unusual shrubs and trees, a rose garden and oval pond with carp. The ancient Tudor walls are covered with roses and climbers. Discover Sarah's secret garden behind the high walls. Wheelchair access on grass and gravel.
☕

35 TURRET GROVE, SW4
Clapham Old Town SW4 0ES. Wayne Amiel, www.turretgrove.com. *Off Rectory Grove. 10 mins walk from Clapham Common Tube & Wandsworth Rd Mainline. Buses: 87, 137.* Home-made teas. **Adm £4, chd free. Sun 19 July (10-5).**
This garden shows what can be achieved in a small space (8m x 25m). The owners, who make no secret of disregarding the rule book, describe this visual feast of intoxicating colours as Clapham meets Jamaica. This is gardening at its most exuberant, where bananas, bamboos, gingers, tree ferns and fire bright plants flourish beside the traditional.

NEW ▶ 45 UNDERHILL ROAD, SE22
London SE22 0QZ. Nicola Bees. *Approx 200 metres from Lordship Lane. Train: Forest Hill 20 mins walk.*

Bus: Routes P13, P4, 63, 176, 185, 197, 363. Car: Off A205 nr junction with Lordship Lane. Free parking. Home-made teas. **Adm £3.50, chd free. Sun 12 July (2-5.30). Also open 86 Underhill Road.**
An intermittently loved and neglected Victorian garden being brought back to its former glory. A majestic cedar tree stands sentry over the garden. The eclectic and informal planting includes some unusual and interesting plants and the wildlife pond is a haven for frogs and newts. A corner summer house provides a tranquil retreat at the bottom of the garden.

86 UNDERHILL ROAD, SE22
East Dulwich, London SE22 0QU. Claire & Rob Goldie. *Between Langton Rise & Melford Rd. Stn: Forest Hill. Buses: P13, 363, 63, 176, 185 & P4.* Home-made teas. **Adm £3.50, chd free. Sun 10 May, Sun 12 July (2-6). Also open 45 Underhill Rd, Shardcroft Rd and St Gothard Mews (Sun 12 July).**
A generous family space bursting with colour. Mixed beds of medicinal, fragrant and edible planting. Secluded seating set among water barrels and bamboo. See if you can spot our friendly newts and enjoy tea and cake in the spacious garden room built on tyres.

7 UPPER PHILLIMORE GARDENS, W8
Kensington, London W8 7HF. Mr & Mrs B Ritchie. *From Kensington High St turn into Phillimore Gdns or Campden Hill Rd; entrance at rear in Duchess of Bedford Walk.* Light refreshments. **Adm £3, chd free. Sun 26 Apr (2-6).**
Well planned mature garden on different levels creating areas of varied character and mood. Pergola with Italian fountain and fishpond, lawn with border plants leading to the sunken garden with rockery. Also groundcover, mature trees (making a secluded haven in central London), flowering shrubs and a fine display of spring bulbs.
🐕 ☕

91 VICAR'S MOOR LANE, N21
Winchmore Hill N21 1BL. Mr David & Dr Malkanthie Anthonisz. *Tube: Southgate then W9 to Winchmore Hill Green then short walk. Train: Winchmore Hill then short walk via*

Wades Hill. Light refreshments. **Adm £3.50, chd free. Sun 17 May (2-6).** Established characterful garden. Paths wind through species acers, clematis, climbers shrubs, perennials planted for colour and form. Waterfall and stream flows under raised pergola, viewing platform to home bred koi carp pond. Exotic elements, and art abound in this much loved evolving paradise. Summerhouse, terraces, sunken garden provide tranquil, comfortable places to sit and contemplate. Featured in Gardeners Weekly and on Sky TV.

☕

Exotic elements, and art abound in this much loved evolving paradise . . .

208 WALM LANE, THE GARDEN FLAT, NW2

London NW2 3BP. Miranda & Chris Mason, www.thegardennw2.co.uk. *Tube: Kilburn. Garden at junction of Exeter Rd & Walm Lane. Buses: 16, 32, 189, 226, 245, 260, 266, 316 to Cricklewood Broadway, then consult A-Z. Home-made teas.* **Adm £3.50, chd free. Sun 31 May, Sun 28 June (2-6).** Tranquil oasis of green. Meandering lawn with island beds, curved and deeply planted borders of perennials, scented roses and flowering shrubs. An ornamental fishpond with fountain. Shaded mini woodland area of tall trees underplanted with rhododendrons, ferns, hostas and lily of the valley with winding path from oriental inspired summerhouse to secluded circular seating area. Live music, plant sale and raffle prizes.

♿ ⛲ ✿ ☕

WALWORTH GARDEN FARM, SE17

206 Manor Place, corner Braganza Street/Manor Place, Kennington SE17 3BN. Trustees of Walworth

Garden Farm, www.walworthgardenfarm.org.uk. *Kennington. Tube: Kennington, 500yds down Braganza St, corner of Manor Place. From Walworth Rd down Manor Place to the corner with Braganza St.* **Adm £2, chd free. Sat 16, Sun 17 May (10-4.30).** Walworth Garden Farm is an oasis in Southwark. From a derelict site this charity has created a productive garden full of organically grown fruit and vegetables surrounded by colourful flowerbeds. It is a working garden with greenhouses, bee hives, pond and wildlife areas and a vital part of the local community providing free training and development in horticulture. Majority of garden accessible by wheelchair users.

♿ ⛲ ✿ 🚐

55 WARHAM ROAD, CR2

South Croydon CR2 6LH. Shanthee Siva. *Off A23, S of central Croydon. Train: South or East Croydon, then buses 119, 405, 455. Free parking.* Tea. **Adm £3.50, chd free. Sun 26 July (2-5.30).** Large suburban garden with broad, immaculate lawn edged by sweeping flower packed borders with a variety of exotic perennials, punctuated by fruit trees and interesting shrubs, peaking at this time. Dahlias as big as plates! All framed by exotic trees. Wide choice of plants for sale, many taken from garden cuttings. Teas with a fusion of English and Sri Lankan snacks.

✿ ☕

12 WARNER ROAD, N8

London N8 7HD. Linnette Ralph. *Nr Alexandra Palace, between Crouch End & Muswell Hill. Turning off Priory Rd. Tube to Finsbury Park then take W3 bus to Hornsey Fire Station. Buses W7 & 144. Home-made teas.* **Adm £3.50, chd free. Sun 7 June (2-6). Also open 11 Park Av North and 160A Stapleton Hall Rd.** A secluded courtyard area leads to a formal garden with borders surrounding a circular lawn. Established climbers clothe the tall fences maintaining the feeling of seclusion and peace. A curved path leads into the kitchen garden where raised beds are divided by gravel paths. The planting is mixed with grasses, ferns, bulbs and perennials planted between box balls and shrubs.

✿ ☕

WARREN HOUSE, KT2

Warren Road, Kingston Hill, Kingston-upon-Thames KT2 7HY. Andrew Fuller, Head Gardener, www.warrenhouse.com. *16m from M25, J10. From the A3 Robin Hood junction take A308 for 1m. Turn L at Zebra crossing into Warren Rd.* Tea. **Adm £3.50, chd free. Sun 10 May, Sun 11 Oct (2-5). Also open The Watergardens.** A 4 acre garden with Grade II listed features and yr-round interest. Italianate terrace, grotto, sunken garden and wild flower meadow. Rose garden and many spring flowers. Terrace area for dining and teas. Most of the site is accessible by wheelchair. Some pathways are loose gravel or grass. All main areas have paving. Disabled parking available.

♿ ☕

THE WATERGARDENS, KT2

Warren Road, Kingston-upon-Thames KT2 7LF. The Residents' Association. *1m E of Kingston. From Kingston take A308 (Kingston Hill) towards London; after approx ½ m turn R into Warren Rd.* **Adm £4.50, chd free. Sun 10 May, Sun 11 Oct (2-4.30). Also open Warren House.** Japanese landscaped garden originally part of Coombe Wood Nursery, planted by the Veitch family in the 1860s. Approx 9 acres with ponds, streams and waterfalls. Many rare trees which, in spring and autumn, provide stunning colour. For the tree lover this is a must see garden. Gardens attractive to wildlife.

WEST LODGE PARK, EN4

Cockfosters Road, Hadley Wood EN4 0PY. Beales Hotels, 020 8216 3904, headoffice@bealeshotels.co.uk. *2m S of Potters Bar. On A111. J24 from M25 signed Cockfosters. Cream teas in hotel, booking advisable.* **Adm £5, chd free. Sun 17 May (2-5); Sun 25 Oct (1-4).** Open for the NGS for over 25yrs, the 35 acre Beale Arboretum consists of over 800 varieties of trees and shrubs, incl National Collection of Hornbeam cultivars (Carpinus betulus) and 2 planned collections (Taxodium and Catalpa). Network of paths through good selection of conifers, oaks, maples and mountain ash - all specimens labelled. Beehives and 2 ponds. Stunning collection within the M25. Guided tours available.

♿ 🛏 ☕

33 Wood Vale

31 WEST PARK ROAD, TW9
Kew, Richmond TW9 4DA. Anna
Anderson. *Within Walking distance of
Kew Gardens station.* **Evening
Opening £3, chd free, Sat 30 May
(5-8). Also open 20 Beechwood
Avenue.**
Modern botanical garden with an
oriental twist. Emphasis on foliage
and an eclectic mix of plants,
reflecting pool and rotating willow
screens which provide varying views
or privacy. Dry bed, shady beds,
mature trees and a private paved
dining area with dappled light and
shade.

WHITE COTTAGE, BR5
Crockenhill Road, Kevington
BR5 4ER. John Fuller & Alida
Burdett, 01689 875134,
alidaburdett@aol.com. *3m NE of
Orpington. Crockenhill Rd is B258.
Garden at junction with Waldens Rd.*
Home-made teas. **Adm £4, chd free.
Sun 28 June (1-5). Visitors also
welcome by arrangement June to
Sept.**
Traditional box, clipped hedging and
reclaimed materials give structure to
this informal garden surrounding a
Victorian gardener's cottage. Colour
themed beds contain grasses,
perennials, shrubs and fruit trees.
There is a small but productive
vegetable garden, a pond, rare

chickens and bees. Wildlife
promotion is a priority. Plenty of
places to sit and enjoy the garden.
Produce for sale. Majority of garden
accessible by wheelchair.
♿ 🏠 ❀ ☕

NEW ▸ WHITGIFT SCHOOL, CR2
Haling Road, South Croydon
CR2 6YT. Sophie Tatzkow,
www.whitgift.co.uk. *Train: South
Croydon then 5min walk. Buses:
119,197, 312, 466. School entrance
on Nottingham Rd.* Tea, coffee,
home-made (and professionally
made) cakes. **Adm £3.50, chd free.
Sun 7 June (1-5). Also open Elm
Tree Cottage.**
Whitgift Gardens are a series of
fascinating well maintained gardens in
a number of original styles within the
extensive grounds of Whitgift, all of
which help to provide a stimulating
environment for students. Head
gardener Sophie Tatzkow is on a
mission to make sure there isn't
another school garden as excellent as
this, to be found in the UK. Wildlife
and Birds (wallabies, flamingos,
peacocks in an enclosed area) area,
a feature of the school grounds. Most
garden areas accessible by
wheelchair. The Andrew Quadrangle
can be accessed, but non accessible
steps within garden.
♿ ❀ 🚌 ☕

74 WILLIFIELD WAY, NW11
London NW11 6YJ. David
Weinberg. *From Golders Green
Tube, H2 bus or 82,102,460 to
Temple Fortune. Walk up Hampstead
Way, turn L at The Orchard, walk
through to Willifield Way.* Cream teas.
**Adm £3.50, chd free. Sun 14 June
(2-6).**
A very peaceful English country
garden packed with herbaceous
borders and perfumed rose beds with
wonderful containers to the patio area
with a beautiful handmade lead
fountain. A haven of tranquillity to be
enjoyed. A large variety of herbacious
plants together with highly perfumed
roses to the side and back flower
beds together with a central white
rose flower bed edged with box
hedging. Wheelchair access to patio
area only.
♿ ☕

86 WILLIFIELD WAY, NW11
Hampstead Garden Suburb
NW11 6YJ. Diane Berger, 020 8455
0455, dianeberger@hotmail.co.uk.
*1m N of Golders Green. Tube:
Golders Green, then H2 bus to
Willifield Way. Buses 82, 102, 460 to
Temple Fortune, walk along
Hampstead Way, turn L at The
Orchard.* Home-made teas. **Adm
£3.50, chd free. Sun 19 July (1-6).
Also open 4 Asmuns Hill. Visitors**

also welcome by arrangement June to Sept for groups 6+.
Beautiful, constantly evolving cottage garden with yr round interest set behind listed Arts and Crafts cottage. Wildlife pond, gazebo, pergola, private decked area, spectacular colour themed herbaceous borders all encased by host of mature trees, shrubs and perennials. A plant enthusiasts delight. Visited by HRH Prince Edward Earl of Wessex. Received the London Garden Society, Guild Hall Award for Best Back Garden in London and Winner of (HGS) suburb in bloom. Wheelchair access on front lawn. Back garden has very narrow and uneven pathways.

An unexpected adventure unfolds through herbaceous borders, winding paths with water features . . .

61 WOLSEY ROAD, KT8
East Molesey KT8 9EW. Jan & Ken Heath. *A short walk from Hampton Court station.* Home-made teas. **Sun 14 June (2-6). Evening Opening £5, chd free, wine, Wed 17 June (8.30-10.30).** Combined with 6 Manor Road, single garden adm £3, combined adm £5, chd free (Sun 14 June).
Romantic, secluded and peaceful garden of two halves designed and maintained by the owners. Part is shaded by two large copper beech trees with woodland planting. The second reached through a beech arch has cottage garden planting, pond and wooden obelisks covered with roses and sweet peas. Beautiful octagonal gazebo overlooks pond plus a new oak framed summerhouse designed and built by the owners. Most of garden wheelchair accessible.

♿ ✿ ☕

27 WOOD VALE, N10
London N10 3DJ. Mr & Mrs A W Dallman. *Muswell Hill 1m. A1 to Woodman PH; signed Muswell Hill. From Highgate tube, take Muswell Hill Rd, sharp R into Wood Lane leading to Wood Vale.* Wine, soft drinks and snacks. **Evening Openings £5, chd free, wine, Thur 7 May, Thur 9 July (6-9).**
One of London's most popular gardens. Winner of London Gardens Society best large garden. An unexpected adventure unfolds through herbaceous borders, winding paths with water features, to lawn with orchard, vegetable garden and greenhouses. This yr, we are opening on two evenings, as above, so come along and join us for a glass of wine or soft drink in our ³/₄ acre garden.

✿ ☕

33 WOOD VALE, N10
Highgate, London N10 3DJ. Mona Abboud, 0208 883 4955, monaabboud@hotmail.com, www.monasgarden.co.uk. *Tube: Highgate, 10 mins walk. Buses: W3, W7 to top of Park Rd.* **Adm £2.50, chd free. Sat 16, Sun 17 May (2-6); Sun 16 Aug (2-5.30).** Visitors also welcome by arrangement Apr to Sept.
The garden opens with a view of a Sedum roof atop a greenhouse. Emphasis is on texture, shapes, contrasting foliage, colour of unusual Mediterranean type plants and exotics. Formal planting surrounds a centrepiece fountain followed by a meandering path flanked by shrubs, trees and two 30m mixed borders of perennials and grasses. The garden widens onto raised beds, small rockery, bog area and willow hedge. Featured in Ham & High.

7 WOODBINES AVENUE, KT1
Kingston-upon-Thames KT1 2AZ. Mr Tony Sharples & Mr Paul Cuthbert. *Kingston-upon-Thames. Take K2, K3,71 or 281 bus. From Surbiton, bus stop outside Waitrose & exit bus Kingston University Stop. From Kingston, walk or get the bus from Eden Street (opposite Heals).* Home-made teas. **Adm £4, chd free. Sun 16 Aug (12-5).**
We have created a winding path through our 70ft garden with trees, evergreen structure, perennial flowers and grasses. We have used deep borders to create depth, variety, texture and interest around the garden. We like to create a garden

party so feel welcome to stay as long as you like. Wide herbaceous borders, an ancient grapevine, a box hedge topiary garden, and a hot summer terrace providing a contrast.

☕

NEW▶ **21 WOODLAND RISE, N10**
London N10 3UP. Ian Potts & Jill Pack. *Close to Highgate Wood. Tube: Highgate, 10-15 mins walk. Bus 43 or 134 to Cranley Gardens stop. Off Muswell Hill Road.* Tea. **Adm £3.50, chd free. Sun 26 Apr (2-6).**
N facing terraced garden; the garden is particularly spectacular in spring with a mature tree peony, wisteria brachybotrys Shiro kapitan, ceanothus and paeonia mlokosewitschii, as well as the blossom of a malus transitoria tree.

✿ ☕

NEW▶ **1 YORK CLOSE, W7**
London W7 3JB. Tony Hulme & Eddy Fergusson. *By rd only, entrance to York Close is via Church Rd. Nearest station Hanwell mainline. Buses E3, 195, 207.* **Adm £3, chd free. Evening Opening £4.50, chd free, wine, Sat 23 May (6-8). Sun 24 May (2-5).**
Tiny quirky garden extensively planted with eclectic mix incl hosta collection, many unusual and tropical plants. Plantaholics paradise. Many surprises in this unique and very personal garden.

☕

ZEN GARDEN, W3
55 Carbery Avenue, Acton, London W3 9AB. Three Wheels Shin Buddhist Temple, www.threewheels.co.uk. *Tube: Acton Town 5 mins walk, 200yds off A406.* **Adm £3, chd free. Sat 13, Sun 14 June, Sat 4, Sun 5 July (2-5.30).**
Pure Japanese Zen garden (so no flowers) with 12 large and small rocks of various colours and textures set in islands of moss and surrounded by a sea of grey granite gravel raked in a stylised wave pattern. Garden surrounded by trees and bushes outside a cob wall. Oak framed wattle and daub shelter with Norfolk reed thatched roof. Japanese tea ceremony demonstration and talks by designer/creator of the garden. Buddha Room open to visitors. Featured in Daily Mail article Things to do this Week.

☕

NORFOLK

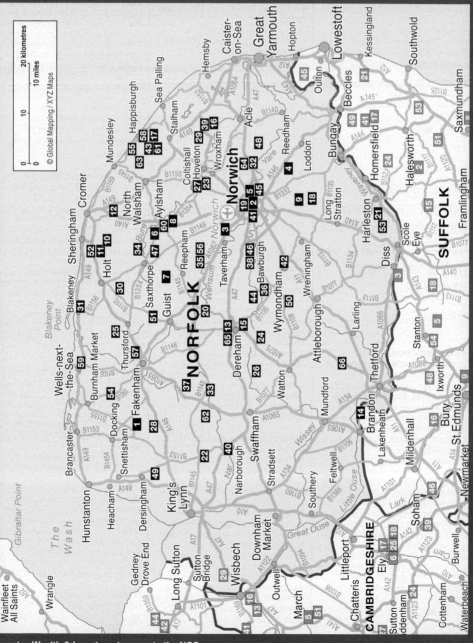

Norfolk

Norfolk is a large low-lying county, predominantly agricultural with a relatively small population. Visitors come because they are attracted to the tranquillity of the countryside, the medieval churches, the coastal area, and the large network of rivers and waterways of the Norfolk Broads.

Gardens vary in size from large historic parks and smaller manor houses, to cottages and courtyards, and are situated throughout the county. Some are old and traditional, whilst others are modern or naturalistic.

Norfolk NGS is honoured to have the support of Her Majesty the Queen at Sandringham, and is grateful to our many garden owners who include not only the descendants of our first Prime Minister, Robert Walpole at Houghton Hall and Mannington Hall, but also the Bishop of Norwich. We are also fortunate to have the beautiful gardens at East Ruston Old Vicarage, home to NGS Ambassador Alan Gray.

'Oh! Rare and beautiful Norfolk,' said the landscape painter John Sell Cotman. We think so too and feel sure you will also enjoy Norfolk's beautiful gardens.

Norfolk Volunteers

County Organisers
Fiona Black
01692 650247
ridlingtonoldrectory@gmail.com

Julia Stafford Allen
01760 755334
jstaffordallen@btinternet.com

County Treasurer
Neil Foster
01328 701288
neilfoster@lexhamestate.co.uk

Publicity
Graham Watts
01362 690065
grahamwatts@dsl.pipex.com

Booklet Coordinator
Julia Stafford Allen
(as above)

Assistant County Organisers
Isabel Cator
01603 270748
isabel@markcator.co.uk

Jennifer Dyer
01263 761811
jandrdyer@btinternet.com

Sue Guest
01362 858317
guest63@btinternet.com

Stephanie Powell
01328 730113
stephaniepowell@creake.com

Below: Houghton Hall Walled Garden
© Val Corbett

Currently the NGS donates around £2.5 million every year

Opening Dates

All entries subject to change.
For latest information check www.ngs.org.uk

February

Saturday 21
27 Horstead House
Sunday 22
1 Bagthorpe Hall
Thursday 26
11 Chestnut Farm

March

Sunday 1
11 Chestnut Farm
Sunday 29
22 Gayton Hall
25 Hindringham Hall

April

Sunday 5
14 Desert World Gardens
66 Wretham Lodge
Monday 6
14 Desert World Gardens
66 Wretham Lodge
Saturday 11
17 East Ruston Old Vicarage
53 Shorelands Wildlife Gardens
Sunday 12
64 16 Witton Lane
Sunday 19
34 Mannington Hall
Sunday 26
11 Chestnut Farm

May

Sunday 3
12 Daisy Cottage
32 Lake House
48 Plovers Hill
Monday 4
32 Lake House
48 Plovers Hill
63 Witton Hall
Sunday 10
11 Chestnut Farm
26 Holme Hale Hall
54 Sly's Farm
Sunday 17
29 How Hill Farm
33 Lexham Hall
36 Manor Farm, Coston

Thursday 21
52 Sheringham Park
Sunday 24
18 NEW Elm House
44 The Old Rectory, Brandon Parva
Sunday 31
8 Bolwick Hall
43 The Old Rectory, Ridlington
47 Oulton Hall
61 West View

June

Thursday 4
52 Sheringham Park

Festival Weekend

Saturday 6
42 167 Norwich Road
53 Shorelands Wildlife Gardens
Sunday 7
35 Manor Farm House, Swannington
42 167 Norwich Road
56 Swannington Manor
59 Wells-Next-The-Sea Gardens
65 Wood Hill
Saturday 13
20 Elsing Hall Gardens
Sunday 14
24 High House Gardens
57 NEW Thorpland Hall
Tuesday 16
10 Chaucer Barn
Wednesday 17
24 High House Gardens
40 Narborough Hall

Mature trees in wooded area with stream running the length of the garden . . .

Sunday 21
3 NEW 9 Bellomonte Crescent
7 Blickling Lodge
37 Manor House Farm, Wellingham
Tuesday 23
38 4 Mill Road
46 NEW The Old Smithy
Thursday 25
34 Mannington Hall (Evening)
Saturday 27
2 The Bear Shop
Sunday 28
2 The Bear Shop
19 68 Elm Grove Lane
23 Heggatt Hall

July

Saturday 4
58 Walcott House
Sunday 5
4 Bergh Apton Manor
14 Desert World Gardens
26 Holme Hale Hall
Sunday 12
5 Bishop's House
62 The Wicken
Saturday 18
6 Blickling Estate
Sunday 19
31 Kettle Hill
60 West Lodge
Sunday 26
9 NEW Brick Kiln House
13 Dale Farm
19 68 Elm Grove Lane

August

Sunday 2
15 Dunbheagan
41 North Lodge
9 NEW The Old Rectory, Kirby Bedon
Sunday 9
41 North Lodge
51 Severals Grange
Sunday 16
50 Sea Mere
Sunday 23
39 The Mowle
Saturday 29
55 Suil Na Mara
Sunday 30
55 Suil Na Mara
Monday 31
55 Suil Na Mara

September

Sunday 6
12 Daisy Cottage
30 Hunworth Hall Garden
Sunday 13
24 High House Gardens
Wednesday 16
24 High House Gardens
Sunday 20
53 Shorelands Wildlife Gardens

October

Saturday 10
6 Blickling Estate
17 East Ruston Old Vicarage

Gardens open to the public

6 Blickling Estate
17 East Ruston Old Vicarage
25 Hindringham Hall
28 Houghton Hall Walled Garden
34 Mannington Hall
34 Mannington Hall
40 Narborough Hall
49 Sandringham Gardens
51 Severals Grange
52 Sheringham Park

By arrangement only

16 The Dutch House
21 Furze House

Also open by arrangement

7 Blickling Lodge
11 Chestnut Farm
12 Daisy Cottage
13 Dale Farm
14 Desert World Gardens
15 Dunbheagan
20 Elsing Hall Gardens
22 Gayton Hall
26 Holme Hale Hall
32 Lake House
39 The Mowle
42 167 Norwich Road
45 The Old Rectory, Kirby Bedon
48 Plovers Hill
50 Sea Mere
55 Suil Na Mara
60 West Lodge

The Gardens

1 ▶ BAGTHORPE HALL
Bagthorpe, nr Bircham PE31 6QY.
Mr & Mrs D Morton, 01485 578528,
dgmorton@hotmail.com. *3¹/₂ m N of
East Rudham, off A148. At King's
Lynn take A148 to Fakenham. At East
Rudham (approx 12m) turn L opp
The Crown, 3¹/₂ m into hamlet of
Bagthorpe. Farm buildings on L,
wood on R, white gates set back
from rd, at top of drive.* Light
refreshments. Homemade soups
made with vegetables from the farm,
homemade cakes and teas. **Adm £4,
chd free. Sun 22 Feb (11-4).**
Snowdrops carpeting woodland walk,
walled garden and main garden.
Some access for wheelchairs in the
garden, but not the woodland walk.

🎭 ⊛ 🚐 🛏 ☕

2 ▶ THE BEAR SHOP
Elm Hill, Norwich NR3 1HN. Robert
Stone. *Norwich City Centre. From St
Andrews, L to Princes St, then L to
Elm Hill. Garden at side of shop
through large wooden gate & along
alleyway.* Teas. **Adm £3, chd free.
Sat 27, Sun 28 June (11-4.30).**
Considered to be based on a design
by Gertrude Jekyll, a small terraced
garden behind a C15 house in the
historic Cathedral Quarter of Norwich.
Enjoy the tranquillity of the riverside.

🎭 ⊛ ☕

**3 ▶ NEW ▶ 9 BELLOMONTE
CRESCENT**
Drayton, Norwich NR8 6EJ. Wendy
& Chris Fitch. *5m N of Nowich. Take
A1067. In Drayton,R turn past Red
Lion PH. Access either through gate
at back of Drayton churchyard or
continue 1st exit r'about to School
Rd, 1st L turn to Bellomonte Cres.*
Home-made teas. **Adm £3, chd free.
Sun 21 June (11-4.30).**
¹/₅ acre garden with deep mixed
borders of traditional shrubs,
perennials and exotic mediterranean
plants. A large deck overlooks main
lawn with planted pergolas. Borrowed
landscape with views of Drayton
church give interest and privacy.
Terraced upper garden with fruit and
vegetables and secluded courtyard.
No wheelchair access to upper levels.

⊛ ☕

4 ▶ BERGH APTON MANOR
Threadneedle Street, Bergh Apton
NR15 1BL. Kip & Alison Bertram.
8m SW of Norwich. Take A146

68 Elm Grove Lane

*(Beccles Rd) from Norwich. Exactly
5m from Southern bypass see
signpost pointing down Mill Rd to
Bergh Apton. Take this turning, ¹/₂ m
on Xrds turn L. Garden ¹/₂ m on L.*
Light refreshments. **Adm £5, chd
free. Sun 5 July (11-4.30).**
Established walled garden as part of
Georgian Manor House (not open).
This beautiful garden is planted for
colour throughout the yr with formal
edged borders and beds, pond,
summerhouse, and terrace with
vistas across 60 acres of wooded
parkland which can be walked. It has
arguably the best lawns in Norfolk.
No disabled WC.

♿ 🎭 ☕

5 ▶ BISHOP'S HOUSE
Bishopgate, Norwich NR3 1SB.
The Bishop of Norwich,
www.dioceseofnorwich.org/about/
bishops/norwich/bishops-
gardens/. *City centre. Located in the
city centre near the Law Courts &
Adam & Eve PH.* Home-made teas.
**Adm £3, chd free. Sun 12 July
(1-5).**
4-acre walled garden dating back to
C12. Extensive lawns with specimen
trees. Borders with many rare and
unusual shrubs. Spectacular
herbaceous borders flanked by yew

hedges. Rose beds, meadow
labyrinth, kitchen garden, woodland
walk and long border with hostas and
bamboo walk. Popular plant sales.
Gravel paths, slopes.

♿ ⊛ ☕

6 ▶ ♦ BLICKLING ESTATE
Aylsham, Norwich NR11 6NF.
National Trust, 01263 738030,
www.nationaltrust.org.uk/blickling.
*14m N of Norwich just off the A140.
1¹/₂ m NW of Aylsham on N side of
B1354.* Light refreshments. **Adm
£8.95, chd £4.95. For NGS: Sat 18
July, Sat 10 Oct (10.30-5.30). For
other opening times and
information, please phone or see
garden website.**
Four centuries of good husbandry
have made this 55 acre garden one
of the greatest in England. Norah
Lindsay, the society gardener, created
the garden you see today, which
includes an C18 Orangery, Temple,
secret garden, beautiful double
borders and parterre, lake and
ancient yew hedges. The new rose
garden is taking shape. Sorry, no
dogs. Garden open every day of the
year except Christmas. Wheelchairs
and powered mobility vehicles
available to borrow. WC, gravel paths.

♿ ⊛ 🚐 ☕

7 BLICKLING LODGE

Blickling, Norwich NR11 6PS. Michael & Henrietta Lindsell, 078819 56646, henrietta@lindsell.co.uk. *¹/₂ m N of Aylsham. Leave Aylsham on old Cromer rd towards Ingworth. Over hump back bridge & house is immed on R.* Home-made teas. **Adm £4.50, chd free. Sun 21 June (2-5.30). Visitors also welcome by arrangement Apr to Sept min 10, max 20.**
Georgian house (not open) set in 17 acres of parkland incl cricket pitch, mixed border, walled kitchen garden, yew garden, new woodland/water garden and river walk. Some variation of levels.

&♿ ✿ 🚐 ☕

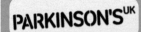

Thank you
to the
NGS for
supporting
Parkinson's
nurses

8 BOLWICK HALL

Marsham NR10 5PU. Mr & Mrs G C Fisher. *8m N of Norwich off A140. Heading N towards Aylsham, at Marsham take 1st R after Plough PH, signed 'By Road' then next R onto private rd to front of Hall.* Home-made teas. **Adm £5, chd free. Sun 31 May (1-5).**
Landscaped gardens and park surrounding a late Georgian hall. The original garden design is attributed to Humphry Repton. The current owners have rejuvenated the borders, planted gravel and formal gardens and clad the walls of the house in old roses. Enjoy a woodland walk around the lake as well as as stroll through the working vegetable and fruit garden with its double herbaceous border. Please ask at gate for wheelchair directions.

&♿ ✿ ☕

9 NEW BRICK KILN HOUSE

Priory Lane, Shotesham St Mary, Norwich NR15 1UJ. Jim & Jenny Clarke. *9/10m S of Norwich. Take A 146 to Poringland, then Shotesham Rd after church. Priory Lane is 200 metres from Shotesham All Saints Church on rd to Saxlingham Nethergate.* Home-made teas. **Adm £5, chd free. Sun 26 July (11-5).**
1³/₄ acre garden with a mixture of different types of planting. A large terrace, lawns and herbaceous borders near the house. A pergola with wisteria and clematis through a rose garden surrounded by a 'topiaried 'yew hedge. Mature trees in wooded area with stream running the length of the garden. Parking in field but easy access to brick path.

&♿ 🐕 ☕

10 CHAUCER BARN

Holt Road, Gresham NR11 8RL. James Mermagen, www.chaucerbarn.com. *3m S of Sheringham. Turn off A149 nr junction of A149 & A1082 signed Gresham/East Beckham. Turn L at T-junction. 1st building in Gresham, gravel drive on L.* Home-made teas. **Adm £3.50, chd free. Tue 16 June (2-6.30).**
5-acre garden created by owner over 20 years in ruins of farmyard. Uphill drive flanked by topiary leads to award winning barn conversion. Knot/herb garden leads to lawn flanked by walled herbaceous borders and pergola leading through contemporary topiary garden to stunning views over rolling hills to woodland. Woodland path leads downhill to wild flower meadow and young arboretum.

&♿ 🛏 ☕

11 CHESTNUT FARM

Church Road, West Beckham NR25 6NX. Mr & Mrs John McNeil Wilson, 01263 822241, john@mcneil-wilson.freeserve.co.uk. *2¹/₂ m S of Sheringham. On A148 opp Sheringham Park entrance. Take the rd signed BY WAY TO WEST BECKHAM, about ³/₄ m to the village sign & you have arrived.* Light refreshments. Light lunches and teas available at all openings. **Adm £4.50, chd free. Thur 26 Feb, Sun 1 Mar (11-4); Sun 26 Apr, Sun 10 May (11-5). Visitors also welcome by arrangement Feb to July refreshments by arrangement.**
Mature 3 acre garden for all seasons

with recent additions, created over 50yrs by enthusiastic plant lovers. Lawns, formal areas, herbaceous borders, vegetables and fruit. Woodland garden and small arboretum. Handkerchief tree, Tulip tree, Ginko etc. In Spring see 90 varieties of snowdrops with crocus, hellebores and daphnes planted in natural surroundings. There is always something new to see. Blacksmith Toby Winterbourn will exhibit a collection of his Garden Sculpture on Sun 1 March. Plant sales and visiting nurseries at all openings. Refreshments at all events. Featured in Garden Answers, Norfolk Magazine, and on Radio Norfolk. Wheelchair access weather dependent.

&♿ 🐕 ✿ 🚐 ☕

12 DAISY COTTAGE

Chapel Road, Roughton, Norwich NR11 8AF. Miss Geraldine Maelzer & Miss Anne Callow, 01263 768322, anne.callow@sky.com. *3¹/₂ m S of Cromer. A140 from Norwich, in Roughton Village take B1436, signed Felbrigg Hall NT. Daisy Cottage is 150yds on L.* Light refreshments. **Adm £4.50, chd free. Sun 3 May, Sun 6 Sept (11-5). Visitors also welcome by arrangement May to Sept for groups of 10+. Refreshments by arrangement.**
2 acre garden not to be missed with areas dedicated for wildlife, incl stream, pond, and more formally a Japanese style garden. Among its features are mixed borders for autumn colour, vegetable garden and apiary, chickens and ducks. For the early opening a huge planting of late spring bulbs will delight, The garden has an individual charm whatever the season. Produce and plants for sale. Bees and bugs in the garden demo. Featured in 'Let's Talk' magazine. Partial wheelchair access to pathed areas only.

&♿ ✿ ☕

13 DALE FARM

Sandy Lane, Dereham NR19 2EA. Graham & Sally Watts, 01362 690065, grahamwatts@dsl.pipex.com. *16m W of Norwich. 12m E of Swaffham. From A47 take B1146 signed to Fakenham, turn R at T-junction, ¹/₄ m turn L into Sandy Lane (before pelican crossing).* Home-made teas. **Adm £4, chd free. Sun 26 July (11-5). Visitors also welcome by**

arrangement **June to July** groups of 10+.
2 acre plant lover's garden with a large spring fed pond. Over 800 plant varieties featured in exuberantly planted borders and waterside gardens.These incl a collection of 70 species and varieties of hydrangea. Kitchen garden, orchard, naturalistic planting areas, gravel garden and sculptures. Gravel drive and some grass paths. Wide range of plants for sale incl rare hydrangeas. Rutland Wind Ensemble playing. Finalist in Britain's Best Gardeners Garden competition.

14 **DESERT WORLD GARDENS**
Thetford Road (B1107), Santon Downham IP27 0TU. **Mr & Mrs Barry Gayton, 01842 765861.** *4m N of Thetford. On B1107 Brandon 2m.* Light refreshments. **Adm £3.50, chd free. Sun 5, Mon 6 Apr, Sun 5 July (10-5). Visitors also welcome by arrangement Apr to Sept.**
1¼ acres plantsman's garden, specialising in tropical and arid plants. Hardy succulents - sempervivums and plectranthus. Bamboos, herbaceous, ferns, spring/summer bulbs, primula theatre, over 70 varieties of magnolias. View from roof garden. New area of primula auriculas. National Gardeners Question Time. Radio Cambridge gardener. Glasshouses cacti/succulents 12500, viewing by appt. Large primula area incl theatre, large collection of hardy Ferns. Featured on BBC Radio Cambridgeshire.

15 **DUNBHEAGAN**
Dereham Road, Westfield NR19 1QF. **Jean & John Walton, 01362 696163,** jandjwalton@btinternet.com. *2m S of Dereham. From Dereham take A1075 towards Shipdham. L into Westfield Rd at Vauxhall Gge. At Xrds ahead into lane, becomes Dereham Rd. Parking at Anema's Farm.* Home-made teas. **Adm £4, chd free. Sun 2 Aug (12.30-5). Visitors also welcome by arrangement June to July.**
Relax and enjoy walking among the borders and island beds, a riot of colour well into late Summer with plants of all descriptions. Extensive collection of rare and unusual plants plus the more recognisable in this ever changing plantsman's garden.

Reepham Ensemble playing 2-4. Featured in Garden News, Daily Telegraph and local press. Gravel driveway.

16 **THE DUTCH HOUSE**
Ludham NR29 5NS. **Mrs Peter Seymour, 01692 678225,** janes.seymour@gmail.com. *5m W of Wroxham. B1062 Wroxham to Ludham 7m. Turn R by Ludham village church into Staithe Rd. Garden ¼ m from village.* Home-made teas. **Adm £6, chd free. Visitors welcome by arrangement June to July.**
Romantic 2½ acre garden originally designed and planted by painter Edward Seago. Informal borders lead to wild areas of old fashioned roses and shrubs. Steep bridge and uneven paths through Marsh and Wood lead one to Womack water (limited access). Partial wheelchair access to main part of garden.

17 ◆ **EAST RUSTON OLD VICARAGE**
East Ruston, Norwich NR12 9HN. **Alan Gray & Graham Robeson, 01692 650432,** www.eastrustonoldvicarage.co.uk. *3m N of Stalham. Turn off A149 onto B1159 signed Bacton, Happisburgh. After 2m turn R 200yds N of East Ruston Church (ignore sign to East Ruston).* Tea. **Adm £8, chd £1. For NGS: Sat 11 Apr, Sat 10 Oct (1-5.30). For other opening times and information, please phone or see garden website.**
20-acre exotic coastal garden incl traditional borders, exotic garden, desert wash, sunk garden, topiary, water features, walled and Mediterranean gardens. Many rare and unusual plants, stunning plant combinations, wild flower meadows, old-fashioned cornfield, vegetable and cutting gardens.

18 **NEW** **ELM HOUSE**
The Green, Saxlingham Nethergate, Norwich NR15 1TH. **Linda Woodwark.** *9m S of Norwich. Travel S on A140 turn L onto B1527 to Hempnall, turn L at Kilbourne Garage, through the village & turn R signed Shotesham / Brooke. Elm House is last on L.* Home-made teas. **Adm £4, chd free. Sun 24 May (11-5).**
2 acre country garden filled with

extensive planting in mixed island beds, and late summer herbaceous borders. Pergola with climbing roses. clematis and honeysuckle underplanted with nepeta. A large natural pond is home to ducks and moorhens and a haven for wildlife. Pygmy goats, chickens and grandchildren all share the paddock area. Wheelchair access to parts of the garden.

Ducks and moorhens and a haven for wildlife. Pygmy goats, chickens and grandchildren all share the paddock area . . .

19 **68 ELM GROVE LANE**
Norwich NR3 3LF. **Selwyn Taylor.** *1¾ m N of Norwich city centre. Proceed from Norwich city centre to Magdalen St, to Magdalen Rd, bear L to St. Clements Hill turn L into Elmgrove Lane. No.68 is at bottom on R.* Home-made teas. **Adm £3, chd free. Sun 28 June, Sun 26 July (11-4).**
This extended living/working space is the owner's endeavour to redefine a suburban garden and to provide inspiration when viewed from his studio window. Aesthetic values, initially took precedent over gardening know-how, but over 30yrs a more balanced approach has resulted in an eclectic array of informal planting, rich in colour and form and full of surprises. Feature Garden of the Week in Garden News.

Dale Farm

and shrubs have been planted over the years with a magnificent display of rambling roses in June. An abundance of spring bulbs and also autumn colour. Wheelchair access to most areas, paths are gravel and grass.

23 HEGGATT HALL

Horstead NR12 7AY. Mr & Mrs Richard Gurney. *6m N of Norwich. Take B1150 North Walsham rd out of Norwich go for N 6m. R at small Xrds signed Heggatt Hall. Turn L at T-junction house 400yds on L.* Light refreshments. **Adm £4, chd free. Sun 28 June (12-5).**
Elizabethan house (not open) set in large gardens surrounded by parkland with ancient chestnut trees. Herbaceous border, sunken garden. Walled knot/rose garden leading into kitchen garden with wisteria walk and further flower beds. Some Gravel paths and steps.

24 HIGH HOUSE GARDENS
Blackmoor Row, Shipdham, Thetford IP25 7PU. Mr & Mrs F Nickerson. *6m SW of Dereham. Take the airfield or Cranworth Rd off A1075 in Shipdham. Blackmoor Row is signed.* Home-made teas. **Adm £4, chd free. Sun 14, Wed 17 June, Sun 13, Wed 16 Sept (2-5.30).**
Plantsman's garden with colour-themed herbaceous borders with extensive range of perennials. Box-edged rose and shrub borders. Woodland garden, pond and bog area. Newly planted orchard and vegetable garden. Wildlife area. Glasshouses. Gravel paths.

20 ELSING HALL GARDENS
Elsing Hall, Hall Road, Elsing, Dereham NR20 3DX. Patrick Lines & Han Yang Yap, 01362 637866, Patrick.lines@gmail.com, www.elsinghall.com. *6km NW of Dereham. From A47 take the N Tuddenham exit. From A1067 take the turning to Elsing opp the Bawdeswell Garden Centre. Follow NGS signs to the garden.* Home-made teas. **Adm £4, chd free. Sat 13 June (11-5). Visitors also welcome by arrangement May to July group size 20+.**
C15 fortified manor house (not open) with working moat. 10 acre gardens and 10 acre park surrounding the house. Significant collection of old roses, walled garden, formal garden, marginal planting, Gingko avenue, viewing mound, moongate, interesting pinetum and terraced garden.

21 FURZE HOUSE
Harleston Road, Rushall, Diss IP21 4RT. Philip & Christine Greenacre, 01379 852375 or 07967 966698, philipgreenacre@hotmail.co.uk. *2m W of Harleston. From A140 Scole r'about to Dickleburgh Village, turn R*

at church, after 3m garden on L. Home-made teas. **Adm £3.50, chd free. Visitors welcome by arrangement May to Sept.**
A 6yr old 2-acre plantaholics' country garden with many unusual perennials, trees, shrubs and some seldom seen varieties. Informal island beds intensely planted create a long season of colour throughout. Interesting stone and wood feature in the borders, rockery, scree and wildlife pond. Some sheltered tender and rare specimens.

22 GAYTON HALL
Gayton, Kings Lynn PE32 1PL. Viscount & Viscountess Marsham, 01485 528432, ciciromney@icloud.com. *6m E of King's Lynn. On B1145; R on B1153. R down Back St 1st entrance on L.* Home-made teas. **Adm £5, chd free. Sun 29 Mar (1-5). Visitors also welcome by arrangement Mar to Oct.**
This rambling 20-acre water garden, with over 2 miles of paths, contains lawns, lakes, streams, bridges and woodland. In the traditional and waterside borders are primulas, astilbes, hostas, lysichiton and gunneras. A variety of unusual trees

25 ◆ HINDRINGHAM HALL
Blacksmiths Lane, Hindringham NR21 0QA. Mr & Mrs Charles Tucker, 01328 878226, www.hindringhamhall.org. *7m from Holt/Fakenham/Wells. Turn off A148 between Holt & Fakenham at Crawfish PH. Drive into Hindringham (2m). Turn L into Blacksmiths Lane.* **Adm £6, chd free. For NGS: Sun 29 Mar (10-4).** For other opening times and information, please phone or see garden website.
Tudor Manor House surrounded by complete C13 moat. Victorian nut walk, formal beds and wild garden. Surrounding the moat are thousands of narcissi (32 varieties), a working walled vegetable garden and stream

garden ablaze with hellebore and primula in the spring. The garden has something of interest throughout the year continuing well into autumn. Wheelchair access at visitors discretion.

26 ▶ HOLME HALE HALL

Holme Hale, Thetford IP25 7ED. Mr & Mrs Simon Broke, 01760 440328, simon.broke@hotmail.co.uk. *6m E of Swaffham, 8m W of Dereham, 5m N of Watton. 2m S of Necton off A47 main rd.* Light refreshments on NGS days all through the day. **Adm £5, chd free. Sun 10 May, Sun 5 July (12-4). Visitors also welcome by arrangement May to Sept coach parties very welcome.**
Noted for its spring display of tulips and aliums, historic wisteria plus mid and late summer flowering. Walled kitchen garden and front garden designed and planted in 2000 by Chelsea winner Arne Maynard. The garden incorporates herbaceous borders, trained fruit, vegetables and traditional greenhouse. We have created a terrace and nuttery and restored the Victorian Ice House. Featured in Country Life, with Front Cover photograph. Wheelchair access available to the Front Garden, Kitchen Garden and tearoom.

27 ▶ HORSTEAD HOUSE

Mill Road, Horstead, Norwich NR12 7AU. Mr & Mrs Matthew Fleming. *6m NE of Norwich on North Walsham rd, B1150. Down Mill Rd opp the Recruiting Sargeant PH.* Home-made teas. **Adm £4, chd free. Sat 21 Feb (11-4).**
Millions of beautiful snowdrops carpet the woodland setting with winter flowering shrubs. A stunning feature are the dogwoods growing on a small island in R Bure, which flows through the garden. Small walled garden. Wheelchair access to main snowdrop area.

28 ◆ HOUGHTON HALL WALLED GARDEN

New Houghton, King's Lynn PE31 6UE. The Cholmondeley Gardens Trust, 01485 528569, www.houghtonhall.com. *11m W of Fakenham. 13m E of King's Lynn. Signed from A148.* **For opening times and information, please phone or see garden website.**
Superbly laid out award-winning 5

acre walled garden designed by the Bannermans. Divided by clipped yew hedges into 'garden rooms' which incl a kitchen garden with large fruit cage, walks, fountains, pergolas, magnificent double herbaceous borders, glasshouse, statues, rustic temple, croquet lawn and rose parterre containing 120 varieties. Contemporary sculptures in surrounding parkland. Plants on sale. Gravel and grass paths. Electric buggies available for use in the walled garden.

29 ▶ HOW HILL FARM

Ludham NR29 5PG. Mr P D S Boardman. *2m W of Ludham. On A1062; then follow signs to How Hill. Farm garden S of How Hill.* Home-made teas. **Adm £4, chd free. Sun 17 May (1-5).**
Broadland garden. 2 very different gardens around the house. 3rd garden started 1968 on green field site with 3 acre broad dug 1978 with views of Turf Fen Mill, R Ant and Reedham Marshes. Approx 12 acres incl Broad, 4 ponds, site of old Broad with 100yr old Tussock sedges 5ft tall, approx 1 acre of indigenous ferns under oak and alder. Paths through rare conifers, rhododendrons, azaleas, ornamental trees, shrubs and herbaceous plants. Collection of holly species and varieties. Various very old stone carvings used for seats, excellent vistas.

30 ▶ HUNWORTH HALL GARDEN

Hunworth, Melton Constable NR24 2EQ. Henry & Charlotte Crawley. *2m S of Holt. Follow by rd to Thornage from Hunworth Green, adjacent to church.* Home-made teas. **Adm £5, chd free. Sun 6 Sept (2-5).**
1 hectare of walled formal gardens incl topiary, canals, pavilions and kitchen garden. Re-created in the Anglo-Dutch fashion over the last 20yrs, it reflects the style and period of the house, and is set in the peaceful wooded upper Glaven Valley. Partial wheelchair access.

31 ◀ KETTLE HILL

The Downs, Langham Road, Blakeney NR25 7PN. Mrs Winch. *Turning to garden is off Langham Rd.* Home-made teas. **Adm £4, chd free. Sun 19 July (11-4).**
Kettle Hill has been quietly simmering

but is now back on the boil! With a new fruit garden designed by Tamara Bridge, as well as re designed and re planted coastal and walled gardens. A newly re designed and re planted coastal and walled garden. A formal parterre, long herbaceous borders, wild flower meadow and a secret garden. Stunning rose garden and grass paths through woods, a real treat for any garden lover. Excellent views across Morston to the sea, framed by lavender, roses and sky. Gravel drive way and lawns but hard paving near the house. Ramps are situated around the garden making all except the wood accessible for wheelchairs.

> # A children's trail, plenty of seats to sit, relax and enjoy the view . . .

32 ▶ LAKE HOUSE

Postwick Lane, Brundall NR13 5LU. Mrs Janet Muter, 01603 712933, janetmuter28@talktalk.net. *5m E of Norwich. On A47; take Brundall turn at r'about. Turn R into Postwick Lane at T-junction.* Home-made teas at Plovers Hill, Strumpshaw. **Adm £4, chd free. Sun 3, Mon 4 May (11-5). Combined adm with Plovers Hill £6. Visitors also welcome by arrangement refreshments by arrangement.**
In the centre of Brundall Gardens, a series of ponds descends through a wooded valley to the shore of a lake. Steep paths wind through a variety of shrubs and flowers in season, which attract many kinds of rare birds, dragonflies and mammals. This is an historic water garden. Spectacular woodland in spring and autumn. Collection of geraniums and shrubs. Partial wheelcahir access only to viewing platform.

33 LEXHAM HALL

nr Litcham PE32 2QJ. Mr & Mrs Neil Foster, *www.lexhamestate.co.uk. 2m W of Litcham. 6m N of Swaffham off B1145.* Home-made teas. **Adm £5, chd free. Sun 17 May (11-5).**
Fine C17/C18 Hall (not open). Parkland with lake and river walks. Formal garden with terraces, yew hedges, roses and mixed borders. Traditional kitchen garden with crinkle crankle wall. A garden of all year round interest, acid loving shrubs are the highlight in May. Rhododendrons, azaleas, camellias and magnolias dominate the 3 acre woodland garden. Fine trees. Bulbs with emerging perennials and shrubs in the many walled garden borders.

34 ◆ MANNINGTON HALL

nr Saxthorpe/Corpusty NR11 7BB. The Lord & Lady Walpole, 01263 584175, *www.manningtongardens.co.uk. 18m NW of Norwich. 2m N of Saxthorpe via B1149 towards Holt. At Saxthorpe/Corpusty follow sign posts to Mannington.* Home-made teas. **Adm £6, chd free. For NGS: Sun 19 Apr (12-5). Evening Opening, Light refreshments, Thur 25 June (5-9). For other opening times and information, please phone or see garden website.**
20 acres feature shrubs, lake, trees and roses. Heritage rose and period gardens. Borders. Sensory garden. Extensive countryside walks and trails. Moated manor house and Saxon church with C19 follies. Wild flowers and birds. Gravel paths, one steep slope.

35 MANOR FARM HOUSE, SWANNINGTON

Swannington NR9 5NR. Mr & Mrs John Powles. *7m NW of Norwich. Almost ¹/₂ way between A1067 (to Fakenham) & B1149 (to Holt). In village parking in Romantic Garden Nursery.* Home-made teas. **Combined adm with Swannington Manor £5, chd free. Sun 7 June (11-5).**
Small garden including knot garden with central fountain, rose garden enclosed by hornbeam hedging, and terrace with large pots of lavender and agapanthus. Access to the Romantic Garden Nursery, which ajoins the garden.

36 MANOR FARM, COSTON

Coston Lane, Coston, nr Barnham Broom NR9 4DT. Mr & Mrs J O Hambro. *10m W of Norwich. Off B1108 Norwich - Watton Rd. Take B1135 to Dereham at Kimberley. After approx 300yds sharp L bend, go straight over down Coston Lane, house and garden on L.* Home-made teas. **Adm £4, chd free. Sun 17 May (11-5).**
Approx 3 acre country garden, several small garden rooms with both formal and informal planting. Walled kitchen garden, white, grass and late summer gardens, roses, herbaceous and shrub borders. Wild flower areas with new Pictorial Meadows borders. Many interesting plants. Dogs and picnics most welcome. Plant sale. Featured in Country Life. Some gravel paths and steps.

Unusual 'Taj' garden with old-fashioned roses, tree peonies, lilies and pond . . .

37 MANOR HOUSE FARM, WELLINGHAM

nr Fakenham, Kings Lynn PE32 2TH. Robin & Elisabeth Ellis, *www.manor-house-farm.co.uk. 7m from Fakenham. 8m from Swaffham. ¹/₂ m off A1065 N of Weasenham. Garden is beside the church.* Home-made teas. **Adm £5, chd free. Sun 21 June (11-5).**
Charming 4-acre garden surrounds an attractive farmhouse, with many interesting features: Formal quadrants with obelisks, 'Hot Spot' with grasses and gravel, small arboretum with specimen trees, pleached lime walk, vegetable parterre and rose tunnel. Unusual 'Taj' garden with old-fashioned roses, tree peonies, lilies and pond. Small herd of Formosan Sika deer. Some gravel and a few steps negotiable with assistance.

38 4 MILL ROAD

Marlingford NR9 5HL. Mrs Jean Austen. *6m W of Norwich. A47 to B1108 Watton Rd junction, 3rd on R. Bear R past mill & garden on R after village hall, (parking) before The Bell. From Easton, signed opp Des Amis.* Home-made teas. **Combined adm with The Old Smithy £5, chd free. Tue 23 June (10.30-4.30).**
Take home ideas from this small garden packed with unusual features. Designed as a collection of garden rooms divided by hedges, paths, arches and pleached limes. Colour-themed borders, Japanese garden, pond, vegetables and fruit. Wind sculpture. Views to the water meadows beyond. A children's trail, plenty of seats to sit, relax and enjoy the view New colour scheme for 2015. Two small steps, ramps available.

39 THE MOWLE

Staithe Road, Ludham NR29 5NP. Mrs N N Green, 01692 678213, nivea.green@icloud.com. *5m E of Wroxham. A1062 Wroxham to Ludham 7m. Turn R by Ludham village church into Staithe Rd. Garden ¹/₄ m from village.* Home-made teas. **Adm £4.50, chd free. Sun 23 Aug (1.30-5.30). Visitors also welcome by arrangement Mar to Oct any number from 2 to 100.**
Approx 2¹/₂ acres running down to marshes. The garden incl several varieties of catalpa. Japanese garden and enlarged wildlife pond with bog garden. A special border for gunnera as in Aug 2008 we were given full National Collection status. Boardwalk into wild area. 85% of the garden is acessable to wheelchairs.

40 ◆ NARBOROUGH HALL

Narborough Hall Gardens, Main Road, Narborough PE32 1TE. Dr Joanne Merrison, 01760 338827, *www.narboroughhallgardens.com. 2m W of Swaffham off A47. Narborough located off A47 between Swaffham & King's Lynn.* Light refreshments. **Adm £5, chd free. For NGS: Wed 17 June (11-5). For other opening times and information, please phone or see garden website.**
Gently evolving, romantic English garden. Herbs, wild flowers and fruit are planted through out, with yew hedging and sumptuous herbaceous borders. Lake, river and woodland

walks, ancient parkland, willow sculpture. Subtle and unusual colour schemes, lots of planting for wildlife, particularly in the gravel paths and the 'wild at heart' garden. Partial wheelchair access but with some gravel paths. Home-made teas.

41 NORTH LODGE
51 Bowthorpe Road, Norwich NR2 3TN. Bruce Bentley & Peter Wilson. *1½ m W of Norwich City Centre. Turn into Bowthorpe Rd off Dereham Rd, garden 150 metres on L. By bus,5,19,20,21,22,23,24 from city.* Home-made teas. **Adm £3, chd free. Sun 2, Sun 9 Aug (11-5).**
Town garden of almost ⅕ acre on difficult triangular plot surrounding Victorian Gothic Cemetery Lodge (not open). Strong structure and attention to internal vista with Gothic conservatory, formal ponds and water features, pergola, classical-style summerhouse and 80ft deep well! Predominantly herbaceous planting. Self guided walk around associated historic parkland cemetery also available. House extension won architectural award. Slide show of house and garden history. Featured on BBC Radio Norfolk 'Garden Party'.

42 167 NORWICH ROAD
Wymondham NR18 0SJ. Rachel & Richard Dylong, 07884 120685, richarddylong@hotmail.co.uk. *¾ m N of Wymondham centre. A11 to Wymondham. Take exit, straight to Waitrose and turn L at r'about. Garden on R after ¼ m.* Home-made teas. **Adm £3, chd free. Sat 6, Sun 7 June (10-5). Visitors also welcome by arrangement Apr to July.**
In our ¼ -acre town garden, created from a blank canvas 12 years ago, meandering pathways round a circular lawn to a secluded tropical haven, on to a sunken pergola, greenhouse with cacti collection and fruit and vegetable plot. We love to recycle and experiment.

43 THE OLD RECTORY, RIDLINGTON
Ridlington, nr North Walsham NR28 9NZ. Peter & Fiona Black, 01692 650247, ridlingtonoldrectory@gmail.com, www.oldrectorynorthnorfolk.co.uk. *4m E of North Walsham 4m N of Stalham. Take B1159 Stalham to Bacton Rd, turn L at By Way to*

Foxhill sign, ½ m to Xrds turn R, ½ m to garden. Home-made teas. Barbecue 12-2. **Combined adm with West View £5, chd free. Sun 31 May (12-5).**
A tranquil 2 acre garden around a former rectory. Established trees and topiary. Mixed borders of shrubs, perennials, roses and bulbs, raised vegetable beds. Enjoy a cup of tea in the garden and listen to Stalham Brass Band 2-4pm. Children's treasure hunt. Gravel drive and some paths might be difficult if wet.

44 THE OLD RECTORY, BRANDON PARVA
Stone Lane, Brandon Parva NR9 4DL. Mr & Mrs S Guest. *9m W of Norwich. Leave Norwich on B1108 towards Watton, turn R at sign for Barnham Broom. L at T-junction, stay on rd approx 3m until L next turn to Yaxham. L at Xrds.* Home-made teas. **Adm £4, chd free. Sun 24 May (11-5).**
4-acre, mature garden with large collection (70) specimen trees, huge variety of shrubs and herbaceous plants combined to make beautiful mixed borders. The garden comprises several formal lawns and borders, woodland garden incl rhododendrons, pond garden, a walled garden and pergolas covered in wisteria, roses and clematis which create long shady walkways. Croquet lawn open for visitors to play.

45 NEW THE OLD RECTORY, KIRBY BEDON
Kirby Bedon, Norwich NR14 7DX. Mr & Mrs Peter de Bunsen, 01508 492382, adebunsen@hotmail.com. *3m SE of Norwich. From bypass take A146 exit. Filter L at T-lights signed Kirby Bedon. 2m turn L to Woods End, entrance 50yds on L. Parking in church car park.* Teas. **Adm £4, chd free. Sun 2 Aug (2-5). Visitors also welcome by arrangement May to Sept.**
Early C18 house (not open) situated in a 1½ acre garden has formal lawns, paving, box balls, yew and hornbeam hedges. There are two lawns one oval, and the main lawn having a fine view to the west and an architectural summerhouse. A hedge-enclosed sunken rose garden has a small pond and unusual fountain. An area of rough grass with mown paths is planted with a collection of birches.

46 NEW THE OLD SMITHY
Mill Road, Marlingford, Norwich NR9 5HL. Kirsty Reader & David Eagles. *6m W of Norwich. A47 to B1108 Watton Road, take 3rd R down past mill, garden on R after village hall. Parking before the Bell. From Easton signed opp Des Amis.* Home-made teas at 4 Mill Road. also light refreshments. **Combined adm with 4 Mill Road £5, chd free. Tue 23 June (10.30-4.30).**
A garden for the family designed by a plantsman, with unusual cottage garden perennials and shrubs. Large marsh facing border filled with colour for all seasons. Woodland planting, specimen trees, stumpery, vegetables and hens.

47 OULTON HALL
Oulton, Aylsham NR11 6NU. Bolton Agnew. *4m W of Aylsham. From Aylsham take B1354. After 4m turn L for Oulton Chapel, Hall ½ m on R. From B1149 (Norwich/Holt rd) take B1354, next R, Hall ½ m on R.* **Adm £5, chd free. Sun 31 May (1-5).**
C18 manor house (not open) and clocktower set in 6-acre garden with lake and woodland walks. Chelsea designer's own garden - herbaceous, Italian, bog, water, wild, verdant, sunken and parterre gardens all flowing from one tempting vista to another. Developed over 16yrs with emphasis on structure, height and texture, with a lot of recent replanting in the contemporary manner.

48 PLOVERS HILL
Buckenham Road, Strumpshaw
NR13 4NL. Jan Saunt, 01603
714587, jan@saunt.vispa.com. *9m
E of Norwich. Off A47 at Brundall
continuing through to Strumpshaw
village. Turn R 300yds past The
Huntsman, then take 1st R., at T
junction R, Plovers Hill is 1st on R up
the hill.* Home-made teas. **Adm £4,
chd free. Sun 3, Mon 4 May (11-5).
Combined adm with Lake House
£6. Visitors also welcome by
arrangement May to Sept.**
1-acre garden of contrasts, small C18
house (not open) with RIBA award
winning orangery. Formal lawn
hedged with yew and lesser species,
huge mulberry, gingko, liquidambar
and Japanese bitter orange,
herbaceous borders with a range of
varied plants and spring bulbs.
Kitchen garden with orchard and soft
fruits. Garden sculptures. Water
feature. Cast aluminium silver birches.
Wheelchair access to main part of
garden, some gentle steps to teas.

49 ◆ SANDRINGHAM GARDENS
Sandringham PE35 6EH. Her
Majesty The Queen, 01485 545408,
www.sandringhamestate.co.uk. *6m
NW of King's Lynn. By gracious
permission, the House, Museum &
Gardens at Sandringham will be
open.* **Adm £9, chd £4.40 (5-15).
For opening times and information,
please phone or see garden
website.**
60 acres of glorious gardens,
woodland and lakes, with rare plants
and trees. Colour and interest
throughout the year with sheets of
spring-flowering bulbs, avenues of
rhododendrons and azaleas, beds of
lavender and roses, and dazzling
autumn colour. Donations are given
from the Estate to various charities.
Gravel paths (not deep), long
distances - please tel or visit website
for our Accessibility Guide. Open
4 Apr to 18 Oct, Closed 29 July.

50 SEA MERE
Seamere Road, Hingham,
Norwich NR9 4LP. Judy Watson,
01953 850217,
judywatson@seamere.com,
www.seamere.com. *Off the B1108,
1m E of Hingham. From Norwich
B1108, 2m after Kimberley railway
crossing, turn L into Seamere Rd.
Sea Mere drive is 2nd on L.* Home-

made teas in Sea Mere Study Centre,
adjacent to house. Tea or coffee and
home made cakes. **Adm £5, chd
free. Sun 16 Aug (11-5).** Visitors
also welcome by arrangement Apr
to Aug groups of 10+, guided tour
with the garden owner.
The gardens border a 20 acre circular
mere with spectacular views to the
water over terraced lawns, gunnera
and a new wetland garden. Mature
trees, shrubs and perennials frame
the view. The 5 acre garden incl an
ornamental potager, formal oval
garden with herbaceous borders,
woodland garden, shrub roses in the
orchard and a bamboo glade. The
higher levels, near the house are
wheelchair accessible. WC suitable
for disabled use.

Large marsh facing
border filled with
colour for all
seasons . . .

51 ◆ SEVERALS GRANGE
Holt Road, Wood Norton
NR20 5BL. Jane Lister, 01362
684206, www.hoecroft.co.uk. *8m S
of Holt, 6m E of Fakenham. 2m N of
Guist on L of B1110. Guist is situated
5m SE of Fakenham on A1067
Norwich rd.* Home-made teas. **Adm
£3, chd free. For NGS: Sun 9 Aug
(1-5). For other opening times and
information, please phone or see
garden website.**
The gardens surrounding Severals
Grange and the adjoining nursery
Hoecroft Plants are a perfect example
of how colour, shape and form can
be created by the use of foliage
plants, from large shrubs to small
alpines. Movement and lightness is
achieved by interspersing these
plants with a wide range of
ornamental grasses, which are at
their best in late summer. Extensive
range of ornamental grasses,
herbaceous plants and shrubs in
various garden settings. Groups for
guided tours by appt July - Sept.

52 ◆ SHERINGHAM PARK
Wood Farm Visitors Centre, Upper
Sheringham NR26 8TL. National
Trust, 01263 820550,
www.nationaltrust.org.uk/
sheringham. *2m SW of Sheringham.
Access for cars off A148 Cromer to
Holt Rd, 5m W of Cromer, 6m E of
Holt, signs in Sheringham town.* Light
refreshments in Courtyard Cafe. **Adm
£5 per car, chd free. For NGS: Thur
21 May, Thur 4 June (10-5). For
other opening times and
information, please phone or see
garden website.**
80 acres of species rhododendron,
azalea and magnolia. Also numerous
specimen trees incl handkerchief tree.
Viewing towers, waymarked walks,
sea and parkland views. No adm
charge to Sheringham Park, car park
charge payable, £5 for non NT
members. Special walkway and WCs
for disabled. 1½ m route is
accessible for wheelchairs, mobility
scooters available to hire.

53 SHORELANDS WILDLIFE GARDENS
Langmere Road, Langmere, Diss
IP21 4QA. Ben & Sarah Potterton,
www.shorelands.org.uk. *1½ m from
A140, follow Brown Tourist signs from
Dickleburgh Village.* Light
refreshments. **Adm £4, chd £3. Sat
11 Apr, Sat 6 June, Sun 20 Sept
(10-5).**
Shorelands offers something for
visitors of all ages, borders
overflowing with unusual perennials,
gravel beds with grasses and bulbs,
shrubberies containing rare and
unusual trees and a new edible
garden situated next to our collection
of rare breed poultry. The garden is
predominantly known for its free
roaming animals that incl flocks of
cranes on the lawns and marmoset
monkeys in the trees. Largest crane
(Birds) breeder in the country, birds
can bee seen on all lawns. Free
Range Monkeys! 4 groups of
Marmosets and Tamarins free in the
garden. Visitors with wheelchairs can
be dropped directly at the entrance
ramp to the main gardens, all paths in
the main garden are on grass.

54 SLY'S FARM
North Creake, Fakenham
NR21 9JQ. Mr & Mrs J Finch.
*Between N & S Creake. From
Fakenham take B1355 (off the A148)
towards Burnham Market. After S*

Creake, pass the L turn signed
Walsingham. Sly's Farm is next house
on L. Home-made teas. **Adm £4,
chd free. Sun 10 May (12-5).**
To the rear of the house is a walled 1-
acre mature garden with hidden
rooms and pathways revealing a wide
variety of texture, colour and diversity
of plants. At its best in spring. In front
of the house there are mature trees
and stream with a small pond. Partial
wheelchair access.

55 SUIL NA MARA
North Walsham Road, Bacton,
Norwich NR12 0LG. Bill Kerr & Bev
Cole, 01692 652386,
billkerr1@btinternet.com. *19m N of
Norwich on N Norfolk coast. Take
B1152 from North Walsham to
Bacton. When you reach the
Coastguard Station in Pollard St we
are the 3rd bungalow on L past it.*
Light refreshments. **Adm £3.50, chd
free. Sat 29, Sun 30, Mon 31 Aug
(11-5.30). Visitors also welcome by
arrangement May to Sept no min
number.**
This 1/4 acre exotic garden
incorporates more than 200 plant
varieties in an unusual mix of lush
semi tropical planting meets Norfolk
Coast meets Industrial and rural
decay. Set in a series of garden
rooms the striking architectural plants
mixed with beachcombed wood,
rusty metal and unusual water
features all provides plenty to look at
and enjoy. Often described as a
'Tardis' of a garden! Small
photographic and Art Studio also on
site with photos and artwork featuring
the beautiful North Norfolk Coast.
Featured in Amateur Gardening. Sorry
all paths are gravelled and are difficult
for wheelchair/mobility access.

56 SWANNINGTON MANOR
Norwich NR9 5NR. David Prior.
*7m NW of Norwich. Almost 1/2 way
between A1067 (to Fakenham) &
B1149 (to Holt). In village parking in
Romantic Garden Nursery.* Light
refreshments. **Combined adm with
Manor Farm House £5, chd free.
Sun 7 June (11-5).**
The C17 manor house (not open)
creates a stunning backdrop to this
romantic garden which is framed by
extensive 300yr old hedges, thought
to be unique in this country. Mixed
shrub and herbaceous borders, water
garden, sunken rose and knot
gardens, specimen trees and sloping

167 Norwich Road

lawns combine to make this garden
both delightful and unusual.Once
again this year the gardens will
provide a stunning backdrop to
wonderful outdoor works by local
artists from NOVA - North Norfolk
Organisation for Visual Artists.

57 NEW THORPLAND HALL
Thorpland, Fakenham NR21 0HD.
Mr & Mrs N R Savory. *1m N of
Fakenham bypass A148. Turn off
r'about by Morrisons superstore,
signed Thorpland Rd. Additional
parking for wheelchair users only.*
Home-made teas. **Adm £5, chd free.
Sun 14 June (2-5.30).**
Mature English garden in a superb
setting, containing ruins of an old
chapel, and surrounding a fine Tudor
house (not open). The 6 acres of
garden, with some recent re-planting,
incl peony beds, herbaceous borders
and a rose garden. The walled garden
is in full working order and kept to a
high standard. A small lake, and
nearby restored shepherd's hut, are

surrounded by interesting trees and
shrubs. Gravel paths, paved areas
and lawns. Some grass paths maybe
a little uneven.

58 WALCOTT HOUSE
Walcott Green, Walcott, Norwich
NR12 0NU. Mr Nick Collier. *3m N of
Stalham. Off the Stalham to Walcott
rd (B1159).* Light refreshments. **Adm
£3.50, chd free. Sat 4 July (1.30-5).**
A garden in the making with
emphasis on formal structure around
the house and a traditional set of
Norfolk farm buildings. These provide
a series of connecting gardens which,
through a south facing garden wall,
lead to further gardens of clipped
box, pleached hornbeam, fruit trees
and roses. All set within recently
planted woodland providing avenues
and vistas. Small single steps to
negotiate when moving between
gardens in the yards.

Share your passion: open your garden

Wood Hill

GROUP OPENING

59 WELLS-NEXT-THE-SEA GARDENS

Wells-Next-The-Sea NR23 1DP.
*10m N of Fakenham. B1105 from
Fakenham. Also off A149 (King's Lynn
- Cromer rd). Wells is served by
Norfolk Green Coast Hopper bus
X29. Car park at Stearman's Yard
behind the Captain's Table PH, The
Buttlands or Market Lane (close to
gardens on Burnt St). Advisable to
tour gardens on foot.* Home-made
teas at Bishop Ingle House.
Combined adm £5, chd free.
Sun 7 June (11-5).

BISHOP INGLE HOUSE
Clubbs Lane. Gilly & Peter
Cook

CAPRICE
Clubbs Lane. David & Joolz
Saunders.
*Coasthopper/Norfolk Green Bus
to 'The Buttlands' follow NGS
signs 1 min from stop*

7 MARKET LANE
Hazel Ashley.
Off Burnt St

NORFOLK HOUSE
Burnt St. Katrina & Alan
Jackson.
Next to Poacher Cottage

POACHER COTTAGE
Burnt St. Roger & Barbara
Oliver.
*Next door to Norfolk House.
Coasthopper + X29 buses pass
the house*

Support the NGS – eat more cake!

Wells-next-the-Sea is a small friendly coastal town on the glorious North Norfolk Coast: popular with families, walkers and bird watchers. The harbour has shops, cafes, fish and chips, while a mile along The Run lies Wells Beach, served by a narrow gauge railway. Of the five in the group four are smaller town gardens and one is somewhat larger: all demonstrate a variety of design and planting approaches incorporating herbaceous borders, 'cottage', shrub and fruit, with two of the gardens providing different 'rooms'. The route around the five gardens takes in the Parish Church of St Nicholas, the High Street with its beautiful once-shop windows and the tree lined Georgian green square, The Buttlands. Wheelchair access at all gardens.

60 WEST LODGE
Aylsham NR11 6HB. Mr & Mrs Jonathan Hirst, jonathan.hirst@btinternet.com. *1/4 m NW of Aylsham. Off B1354 Blickling Rd out of Aylsham, turn R down Rawlinsons Lane, garden on L.* Home-made teas. **Adm £5, chd free. Sun 19 July (12-5). Visitors also welcome by arrangement Feb to Aug please email.**
9-acre garden with lawns, splendid mature trees, rose garden, well-stocked herbaceous borders, ornamental pond, magnificent 2 1/2 acre C19 walled kitchen garden (maintained as such). Georgian house (not open) and outbuildings incl a well-stocked tool shed (open) and greenhouses. Most of the garden is easliy accessible to wheelchair users. Some recently repaired gravel areas a bit more difficult.

61 WEST VIEW
Youngmans Lane, East Ruston, nr Stalham NR12 9JN. Chris & Bev Hewitt. *3m N of Stalham. Take B1159 Stalham to Bacton Rd turn L after East Ruston Church, continue 3/4 m turn L by Butchers Arms PH.* **Combined adm with The Old Rectory, Ridlington £5, chd free. Sun 31 May (12-5).**
1 acre plantsmans garden incl borders with trees and shrubs underplanted with carpets of hellebores and bulbs, pergolas with roses and clematis, greenhouse with many interesting plants, a summer

border with mixed perennials, vegetable parterre, tropical border, orchard and pond. Featured in Amateur Gardening Magazine and EDP Norfolk Magazine. Gravel Paths.

62 THE WICKEN
Castle Acre, King's Lynn PE32 2BP. Mr & Mrs Alastair Keith. *2m N of Castle Acre. Castle Acre is off A1065 just N of Swaffham. The Wicken is to the N of the village on the Great Massingham Rd, (Peddars Way) at Xrds signed to the R.* Home-made teas. **Adm £5, chd free. Sun 12 July (11-4.30).**
6 acres of garden incl three walled gardens, formal and informal in planting and design, a woodland garden with stumpery which hosts many unusual Hosta and Fern varieties planted amongst Mecanopsis and Dactoloryza., and a working kitchen garden. Beautifully maintained lawns, flanked by mixed perennial and shrub borders, open to stunning views of the surrounding landscape beyond the ha-ha. Wheelchair access to most areas.

63 WITTON HALL
nr North Walsham NR28 9UF. Sally Owles. *3 1/2 m from North Walsham. From North Walsham take Happisburgh Rd or Byway to Edingthorpe Rd off North Walsham bypass.* Light refreshments. **Adm £3, chd free. Mon 4 May (12-4).**
A natural woodland garden. Walk past the handkerchief tree and wander through carpets of English bluebells, rhododendrons and azaleas. Walk from the garden down the field to the church. Stunning views over farmland to the sea. Wheelchair access difficult if wet.

64 16 WITTON LANE
Little Plumstead NR13 5DL. Sally Ward & Richard Hobbs. *5m E of Norwich. Take A47 to Yarmouth, 1st exit after Postwick, turn L to Witton Green & Gt Plumstead, then 1st R into Witton Lane for 1 1/2 m. Garden on L.* Home-made teas. **Adm £3, chd free. Sun 12 Apr (11-4).**
An 'Aladdin's Cave' for the alpine and woodland plant enthusiast. Tiny garden with wide range of rare and unusual plants will be of great interest with its species tulips, daffodils, Scillas, dog's tooth violets, other bulbous plants and many Trilliums

and wood anemones. A garden for the plant specialist. National Collection of Muscari.

65 WOOD HILL
Hill Farm, Gressenhall, East Dereham NR19 2NR. Mr & Mrs John Bullard. *1m W of East Dereham. 1/2 m W of Dereham off A47 N on Draytonhall Lane, B1146, R at T junction, 1st L Rushmeadow Rd, 1m over small bridge, entrance on R.* Home-made teas. **Adm £4, chd free. Sun 7 June (12-5.30).**
3 acres, the garden is set in mature parkland, incl water features, statues/stones, lily pond, varied rose gardens, yew hedging, vegetable garden, lawns with floodlighting for mature hardwood trees. One of East Anglia's oldest Tulip trees, beautiful Oaks and copper Beech.

66 WRETHAM LODGE
East Wretham IP24 1RL. Mr Gordon Alexander. *6m NE of Thetford. A11 E from Thetford, L up A1075, L by village sign, R at Xrds then bear L.* Tea in Church. **Adm £4, chd free. Sun 5, Mon 6 Apr (11-5).**
In spring masses of species tulips, hellebores, fritillaries, daffodils and narcissi; bluebell walk. Walled garden, with fruit and interesting vegetable plots. Mixed borders and fine old trees. Double herbaceous borders. Wild flower meadows.

NORTH EAST

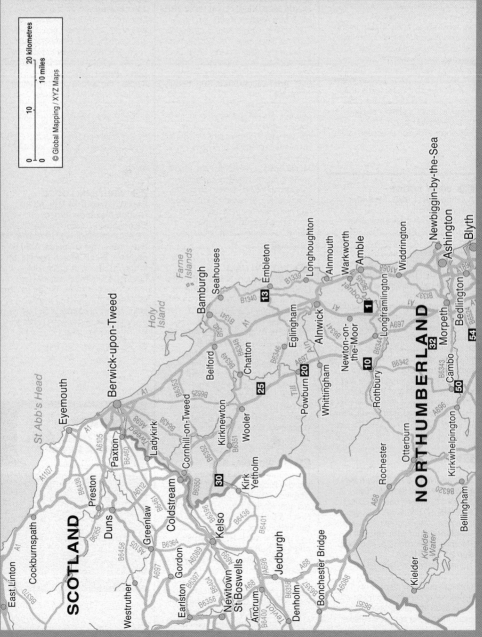

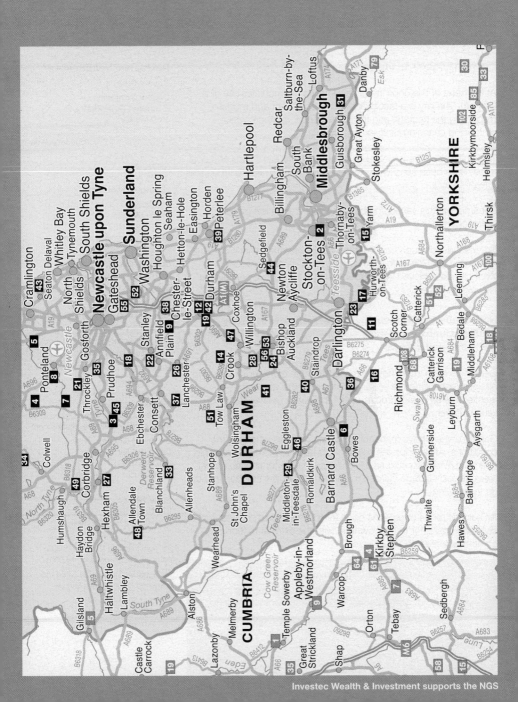

North East

County Durham: an unsung county.

At the heart of this once industrial land lies the medieval city of Durham. The city is a fascinating blend of ancient and modern, respecting the heritage and traditions of its forefathers whilst embracing changing lifestyles and culture.

This epitomises the county as a whole; old, industrial sites and coal mines have been sensitively cleared to restore the land to its original 'green' beauty.

Set amongst this varied and beautiful countryside are gardens which open their gates for the NGS.

So, meander through our delightfully quirky former miner's cottage garden in Low Row with its knowledgeable gardener, or see what can be achieved in a garden at 1000 feet above sea level at Newbiggin House.

Northumberland is a county rich in history with sturdy castles, stunning coastline and a wild landscape threaded with sheltered valleys.

Gardeners have learnt how to make the most of the land; terracing hillsides, enhancing the soil and often using the wonderful architecture as a backdrop, such as at Seaton Delaval Hall and Lilburn Tower.

Garden owners have managed to create gardens whatever the conditions. At Blagdon the solution has been to plant within an old quarry, at Wallington to use a long narrow valley for shelter, and at Newonstead Cottage Garden to choose perennials that can stand up to the wind.

An eclectic range of gardens open for the NGS. Each reflects the style and character of their owners, with the extra attraction of home-made teas and plant sales.

North East Volunteers

County Durham

**County Organiser
& Booklet Coordinator**
Jean Morley
01609 748066
morley@the-willows.wanadoo.co.uk

County Treasurer
Gill Naisby
01325 381324
gillnaisby@gmail.com

Publicity
Alison Morgan
01913 843842
morganalisonm@gmail.com

Assistant County Organisers
Sue Douglas 01325 332289
pasm.d@btinternet.com

Alison Morgan
(as above)

Mary Smith 01388 832727
mary@maryruth.plus.com

Sue Walker 01325 481881
walker.sdl@gmail.com

Northumberland & Tyne and Wear

**County Organiser
& Booklet Coordinator**
Maureen Kesteven
01914 135937
maureen@patrickkesteven.plus.com

County Treasurer
David Oakley
01434 618994
david@susie-white.co.uk

Publicity
Susie White
07941 077595
susie@susie-white.co.uk

Assistant County Organisers
Patricia Fleming 01668 217009
patriciaflemingwoop@gmail.com

Natasha McEwen 07917 754155
natashamcewengd@aol.co.uk

Liz Reid 01914 165981
lizreid52@ntlworld.com

Left: Mindrum

Since our foundation we have donated more than £42.5 million to charity

Opening Dates

All entries subject to change.
For latest information check www.ngs.org.uk

February

Sunday 15
9 **NEW** Congburn Arboretum

March

Wednesday 18
12 Crook Hall & Gardens

April

Sunday 5
9 **NEW** Congburn Arboretum
Sunday 12
36 The Old Vicarage
53 West House

May

Sunday 3
22 **NEW** Harperley Hall Farm
Sunday 10
50 Wallington
Sunday 17
5 Blagdon
Sunday 24
2 Barnard Avenue Gardens
Sunday 31
15 **NEW** Forest Lane Gardens
25 Lilburn Tower
46 **NEW** Stobgreen House
48 Thornley House

June

Festival Weekend

Saturday 6
17 Gardens On The Green
43 Seaton Delaval Hall
Sunday 7
11 Croft Hall
37 Oliver Ford Garden
52 Washington Old Hall
Saturday 13
29 Middleton-in-Teesdale

Sunday 14
3 The Beacon
41 Ravensford Farm
Sunday 21
16 The Forge
30 Mindrum
32 **NEW** Netherwitton Village and surrounds
Saturday 27
13 Fallodon Hall
51 **NEW** Warrenfell,
55 Woodlands
Sunday 28
6 Browside
23 Hidden Gardens of Croft Road
51 **NEW** Warrenfell,
54 Whalton Manor Gardens

July

Saturday 4
7 Cheeseburn (Evening)
33 Newbiggin House
Sunday 5
4 **NEW** Bitchfield Tower
24 Hillside Cottages
27 Loughbrow House
44 Sedgefield Gardens
Saturday 11
10 Cragside
Sunday 12
14 The Fold
39 **NEW** Peterlee Gardens Safari
42 St Margaret's Allotments

49 **NEW** Wall Village Gardens
50 Wallington
Sunday 19
31 **NEW** Moorsholm Village
56 Woodside House
Sunday 26
35 No. 2 Ferndene

August

Sunday 2
47 4 Stockley Grove
Sunday 9
20 **NEW** Greenfields

September

Sunday 6
18 Gibside
Sunday 13
21 Halls of Heddon
Sunday 27
26 **NEW** Lizards Farm

October

Sunday 11
26 **NEW** Lizards Farm

Gardens open to the public

10 Cragside
12 Crook Hall & Gardens
18 Gibside
21 Halls of Heddon
30 Mindrum

40 Raby Castle
43 Seaton Delaval Hall
50 Wallington
52 Washington Old Hall
54 Whalton Manor Gardens

By arrangement only

1 Acton House
8 Coldcotes Moor Farm
19 14 Grays Terrace
28 10 Low Row
34 Newonstead Cottage Garden
38 25 Park Road South
45 Skara Brae

Also open by arrangement

3 The Beacon
14 The Fold
16 The Forge
22 **NEW** Harperley Hall Farm
24 2 Hillside Cottage, Hillside Cottages
27 Loughbrow House
35 No. 2 Ferndene
46 **NEW** Stobgreen House
47 4 Stockley Grove
48 Thornley House
55 Woodlands
56 Woodside House

Forest Lane Gardens

Over 400 Volunteers help run the NGS – why not become one too?

The Gardens

1 ACTON HOUSE
Felton, Morpeth NE65 9NU.
Mr Alan & Mrs Eileen Ferguson,
Contact Head Gardener 077798
60217. *N of Morpeth. On old A1 N of
Felton, take turning to Acton, follow
rd for 1/2 m until fork and follow sign to
Acton House.* **Adm £4, chd free.**
Visitors welcome by arrangement
May to Aug for groups of 10+.
This stunning walled garden has
structure, colour and variety of
planting, with abundant herbaceous
perennials and different grasses.
Planted in the spring of 2011, it has
sections devoted to fruit and
vegetables, David Austin rose
borders, standard trees and climbers
spreading over the brick walls. There
are additional mixed borders, a ha-
ha, and developing woodland
planting, in total extending over 5
acres. Herbaceous perennial
plantings include species and
varieties favoured by butterflies and
bees (info available).

&

GROUP OPENING

2 BARNARD AVENUE GARDENS
Stockton-On-Tees TS19 7AB. *10m
E of Darlington off A66. Heading E or
W from or towards Middlesbrough
take slip rd marked Hartburn &
Stockton W. L into Greens Lane,
follow yellow signs. Off Gainford Rd &
Oxbridge Rd W side of Stockton.
Park in Gainford Rd.* Home-made
teas at Briarcroft (no 27). **Combined
adm £3.50, chd free.** Sun 24 May
(1-5).

10 BARNARD AVENUE
Dennis & Jennifer Hodgson

22 BARNARD AVENUE
Laura & Peter Davison

BRIARCROFT
27 Barnard Avenue. Mr Glenn
Sunman

Enjoy a visit to three, small urban
gardens. No. 10 is a mature secluded
garden with several seating areas.
Recently landscaped, it is divided into
'rooms' and backed by mature trees.
There are two small ponds, a water
feature, a Judas tree which is
magnificent when in flower in spring
and, apart from hanging baskets, no
annuals. No. 22 is a quiet and
relaxing suburban garden divided into

three areas: a secluded sunny seating
area, a larger lawned area with mixed
borders and a shady section under a
mature ash tree. No 27 has a wisteria
covered pergola, wild flower area,
willow tunnel and arbour, aerial
hedge, kitchen garden and
herbaceous borders. Gravel paths in
some areas.

& ⊗ ☕

WE ARE MACMILLAN. CANCER SUPPORT

2015 sees the NGS
total to Macmillan
pass £15 million

3 THE BEACON
10 Crabtree Road, Stocksfield
NE43 7NX. Derek & Patricia
Hodgson, 01661 842518,
patandderek@btinternet.com. *12m
W of Newcastle upon Tyne. From
A69 follow signs into village. Station &
cricket ground on L. Turn R into
Cadehill Rd then 1st R into Crabtree
Rd (cul de sac) Park on Cadehill.*
Home-made teas. **Adm £4, chd free.**
Sun 14 June (2-6). Visitors also
welcome by arrangement May to
July groups of 10+.
This garden illustrates how to make a
cottage garden with loads of interest
at different levels. Planted with acers,
roses and a variety of cottage garden
and formal plants. Water runs gently
through it and there are tranquil
places to sit and talk or just reflect.
Steep, so not wheelchair friendly but
wheelchair users have negotiated the
drive and enjoyed the view of the
main garden.

⊗ 🚌 ☕

4 NEW BITCHFIELD TOWER
Belsay, Newcastle Upon Tyne
NE20 0JP. Lesley & Stewart
Manners, 075114 39606,
lesleymanners@gmail.com. *Private
rd off B6309, 4m N of Stamfordham
and SW of Belsay village.* Home-
made teas in the gingang house.
cream teas, scones, cake and cold
beverages. **Adm £4, chd free.**
Sun 5 July (1-4).
A 6 acre garden, currently being
rejuvenated, set around a Medieval

Pele Tower with an impressive stone
water feature, large lake, mature
woodland, cottage gardens, meadow
and 2 walled gardens. Good views of
the surrounding countryside.There
are large herbaceous borders around
the garden with extensive lawns.
Vegetable garden with raised beds
and cutting garden. Historic building,
tennis court, woodland walk, lake.

⊗ 🛏 ☕

5 BLAGDON
Seaton Burn NE13 6DE. Viscount
Ridley, www.blagdonestate.co.uk.
*5m S of Morpeth on A1. 8m N of
Newcastle on A1, N on B1318, L at
r'about (Holiday Inn) & follow signs to
Blagdon. Entrance to parking area
signed.* Home-made teas. **Adm £4,
chd free.** Sun 17 May (1-4.30).
Unique 27 acre garden
encompassing formal garden with
Lutyens designed 'canal', Lutyens
structures and walled kitchen garden.
Valley with stream and various follies,
quarry garden and woodland walks.
Large numbers of ornamental trees
and shrubs planted over many
generations. National Collections of
Acer, Alnus and Sorbus. Trailer rides
around the estate (small additional
charge) and stalls selling local
produce. Partial wheelchair access.

& 🏵 ⊗ **NCH** ☕

6 BROWSIDE
Boldron, Barnard Castle
DL12 9RQ. Mr & Mrs R D Kearton.
*3m S of Barnard Castle. A66 W of
Greta Bridge, turn R to Boldron, then
proceed 1/2 m. Entrance opp junction.
From Barnard Castle take A67 to
Bowes, after 2m turn L to Boldron.*
Home-made teas. **Adm £2.50, chd
free.** Sun 28 June (1-5.30).
1 1/4 acres with unusual water features
and large collection of conifers,
topiary and acers, with a wide range
of plants and imaginative stone
objects. Wonderfully tranquil seating
areas. Off road wheelchair access to
most of garden but over grass and
slight raised lawn areas to bottom of
garden.

& 🏵 ⊗ ☕

7 CHEESEBURN
Cheeseburn Grange Hall,
Stamfordham, Newcastle upon
Tyne NE18 0PT. Mr & Mrs S Riddell,
www.cheeseburn.com. *8m W of
Newcastle upon Tyne. From
Newcastle, take B6324
(Stamfordham Rd) heading west.
Cheeseburn is exactly 1.8m beyond*

Plough Inn on R. **Evening Opening £5, chd £2, wine, Sat 4 July (5-8).** 11 acres of gardens surround the beautiful Dobson designed house (not open) and church of St Francis Xavier (open). Cheeseburn provides a showcase for contemporary sculpture, design and art. A classic English country garden with formal lawns, rose borders, parterre, herbaceous borders, woodland walks and mature trees. Contemporary sculpture in the garden. Partial wheelchair access.

8 COLDCOTES MOOR FARM
Ponteland, Newcastle Upon Tyne NE20 0DF. Ron & Louise Bowey, 01661 822579, ron@theboweys.co.uk. *Off A696 N of Ponteland. From S, leave Ponteland on A696 towards Jedburgh, after 1m take L turn marked 'Milbourne 2m'. After 400yds turn L into drive.* Home-made teas. **Adm £5, chd free. Visitors welcome by arrangement** July to Aug for groups of 10+.
The garden, landscaped grounds and woods cover around 15 acres. The wooded approach opens out to lawned areas surrounded by new ornamental and woodland shrubs and trees. A courtyard garden leads to an ornamental walled garden, beyond which is an orchard, vegetable garden and rose arbour. To the south the garden looks out over a lake and field walks, with woodland walk to the west. Small children's play area. Most areas can be accessed though sometimes by circuitous routes or an occasional step. WC access involves three steps.

9 NEW CONGBURN ARBORETUM
Edmondsley, Durham DH7 6DY. Mr Alan Herbert, www.congburnnurseries.co.uk. *From B6532 at Edmondsley, follow yellow NGS signs.* Light refreshments in café / gift shop on site where live music will be playing between 2- 3. Café open 10 'til 4 serving lunches and teas. **Adm £3, chd free. Sun 15 Feb, Sun 5 Apr (10-4).**
Come and enjoy a woodland walk: snowdrops in February followed in April by daffodils and narcissi. On the Easter Sunday opening there is a 'Hunt The Easter Egg' trail for the children. The arboretum is in the process of development and you will

therefore see plenty of new planting amongst the already established trees. The site is on a hillside so please wear sturdy footwear.

Garden, currently being rejuvenated, set around a Medieval Pele Tower with a stone water feature . . .

10 ◆ CRAGSIDE
Rothbury NE65 7PX. National Trust, 01669 620333, www.nationaltrust.org.uk/cragside/things-to-see-and-do/garden/. *13m SW of Alnwick. (B6341); 15m NW of Morpeth (A697).* Light refreshments. **Adm £10.70, chd £5.40. For NGS: Sat 11 July (10-7). For other opening times and information, please phone or see garden website.**
The Formal Garden is in the 'High Victorian' style created by the 1st Lord and Lady Armstrong. Incl orchard house, carpet bedding, ferneries and Italian terrace. New rose garden for 2014. The largest sandstone Rock Garden in Europe with its tumbling cascades. Extensive grounds of over 1000 acres famous for rhododendrons in June, large lakes and magnificent conifer landscape. The House, mainly the design of Norman Shaw, with its very fine arts and crafts interiors is worth a separate visit. Featured in The Daily Telegraph, The Times and local publications. Partial access to the Formal Garden.

11 CROFT HALL
Croft-on-Tees DL2 2TB. Mr & Mrs Trevor Chaytor Norris. *3m S of Darlington. On A167 to Northallerton, 6m from Scotch Corner. Croft Hall is 1st house on R as you enter village from Scotch Corner.* Home-made teas. **Adm £4, chd free. Sun 7 June (2-5).**
A lovely lavender walk leads to a Queen Anne-fronted house (not open) surrounded by a 5-acre garden, comprising a stunning herbaceous border, large fruit and vegetable plot,

two ponds and wonderful topiary arched wall. Pretty rose garden and mature box Italianate parterre are beautifully set in this garden offering peaceful, tranquil views of open countryside. Some gravel paths.

12 ◆ CROOK HALL & GARDENS
Sidegate, Durham City DH1 5SZ. Maggie Bell, 0191 384 8028, www.crookhallgardens.co.uk. *Centre of Durham City. Crook Hall is short walk from Durham's Market Place. Follow the tourist info signs. Parking available at entrance.* **Adm £7, chd £5. For NGS: Wed 18 Mar (10-3). For other opening times and information, please phone or see garden website.**
Described in Country Life as having 'history, romance and beauty'. Intriguing medieval manor house surrounded by 4 acres of fine gardens. Visitors can enjoy magnificent cathedral views from the 2 walled gardens. Other garden 'rooms' incl the silver and white garden. An orchard, moat pool, maze and Sleeping Giant give added interest! Featured on Radio 4 with John McCarthy, and Clare Balding, on Radio 4 Gardeners Question Time and in Independent and the ' I ' as number 9 in the top ten places to visit in Britain.

13 FALLODON HALL
Alnwick NE66 3HF. Mr & Mrs Mark Bridgeman, 01665 576252, www.bruntoncottages.co.uk. *5m N of Alnwick, 2m off A1. From the A1 turn R on B6347 signed Christon Bank & Seahouses, & turn into Fallodon gates after exactly 2m, at the Xrds. Follow drive for 1m.* Home-made teas in stable yard. **Adm £4, chd free. Sat 27 June (2-5).**
Extensive, well established garden, including a 30 metre border, finishing beside a hot greenhouse and bog garden. The late C17 walls of the kitchen garden surround cutting and vegetable borders and the fruit greenhouse. The sunken garden from 1898 has been replanted by Natasha McEwen. Woodlands, pond and arboretum extend over 10 acres to explore. Renowned home-made teas in stable yard, and plant sale, predominantly of Fallodon plants. Featured on BBC Look North. Partial wheelchair access.

Lilburn Tower

© Susie White

small wildlife ponds with two natural stone features. There is a variety of trees, shrubs and mixed borders leading to a meadow. Featured in the Teesdale Mercury and Northern Echo. Wheelchair access across gravel path.

GROUP OPENING

17 GARDENS ON THE GREEN
Hurworth-on-Tees, Darlington DL2 2JA. *2m SE of Darlington. Follow main Rd through Hurworth Place. Off A66- follow signs to Hurworth.* Home-made teas at 50 The Green. **Combined adm £5, chd free.** Sat 6 June (1-5).
A variety of village gardens of different sizes and aspects on the north and south sides of the village green, incl two new gardens this year. Three of the gardens have spectacular views over the R Tees. There is a courtyard garden, formal and cottage gardens with vegetable areas. One of the gardens is a previous winner in the Darlington in Bloom competition.

14 THE FOLD
High Wooley, Stanley Crook DL15 9AP. Mr & Mrs G Young, 01388 768412, g898young@btinternet.com. *3m N of Crook. Turn R at Xrds in Brancepeth, opp turn to the Castle, drive 3m along the single track rd until you reach the junction on bend with the main rd.* Cream teas. **Adm £3.50, chd free.** Sun 12 July (1.30-5). **Visitors also welcome by arrangement May to Sept for groups of 10+.**
Garden, approx ½ acre at 700ft and with splendid views over countryside. Herbaceous borders and island beds. Ponds and numerous mature trees. Small roof garden, wide range of plants, many grown from seed and cuttings. Emphasis on colour, harmony and texture. Different styles of planting to create variety. Featured in Northern Echo. No disabled access due to steep slopes and gravel paths.

GROUP OPENING

15 NEW FOREST LANE GARDENS
52 (The Hollies) & 48 Forest Lane, Kirklevington, Yarm TS15 9ND. Fiona & Terry Dunn, Marian & David McDonald. *200yds after village hall on R. Travelling N on A19 exit A67 to Yarm (or take Crathorne exit when heading S). At the Crown Hotel Kirklevington turn into Forest Lane & the gardens are 500yds on R.* Home-made teas. Hot & cold drinks & cakes. **Combined adm £4, chd free.** Sun 31 May (1-5).
The Hollies, informal 1 acre gardens, large island beds plus borders with shrubs and perennials with rhododendrons, wisteria, alliums, clematis and 70+ trees incl wooded wild flower area, and kitchen garden. 48 Forest Lane, superbly manicured lawns and expertly planted beds with wide variety of flowering shrubs, camellias, perennials, climbers and fruit trees. Double tiered pond, water features and lilies. Featured in Darlington and Stockton Times. The Hollies: gravel drive and paths plus shallow slopes in the garden should be OK for wheelchairs. No.48 has narrow side access only.

16 THE FORGE
Ravensworth, Richmond DL11 7EU. Mr & Mrs Peter & Enid Wilson, 01325 718242, enid.wilson@btconnect.com. *7m N of Richmond. Travel 5½ m W on A66 from Scotch Corner. Turn L to Ravensworth & follow NGS signs.* Cream teas. **Adm £2.50, chd free.** Sun 21 June (1-5). **Visitors also welcome by arrangement June to Oct.**
The Blacksmith's Secret Garden - the garden is hidden from view behind The Forge House, Cottage and the working Blacksmith's Forge. It has

18 ◆ GIBSIDE
Rowlands Gill NE16 6BG. National Trust, 01207 541820, www.nationaltrust.org.uk/gibside. *6m SW of Gateshead. Follow brown signs from the A1 & take the A694 towards Rowlands Gill.* Light refreshments in Potting Shed Cafe. Locally-sourced produce with fruit & vegetables from walled garden. **Adm £7.90, chd £4.05. For NGS:** Sun 6 Sept (10-6). **For other opening times and information, please phone or see garden website.**
C18 landscape park designed by Stephen Switzer for one of the richest men in Georgian England, George Bowes, and his celebrated daughter Mary Eleanor. Inner pleasure grounds with tree-lined avenue and productive walled garden, plus miles of woodland and riverside walks in the Derwent Valley. Ongoing restoration of the gardens and woodland, one of the National Trust's most ambitious such projects. Behind the scenes guided talks by the head gardener; see the walled garden come back to life as we restore it. If you have special access needs, please call us on 01207 541820 in advance of your visit.

19 **14 GRAYS TERRACE**
Redhills, Durham DH1 4AU.
Mr Paul Beard, 0191 5972849,
pauljofraeard@yahoo.co.uk. *Just off
A167 on W side of Durham. ¹/₂ m S of
A167 / A691 r'about, turn L into
Redhills Lane. When road turns R
with no entry sign, Grays Terrace is
ahead. No.14 is at the very end.* **Adm
by donation. Visitors welcome by
arrangement Apr to Aug.**
A steeply sloping garden of about
²/₃ acre with a superb view over
Durham Cathedral, Castle and
surroundings. Very informal garden;
no bedding and a significant wild
area. Planting is mixed with
interest throughout the yr. Many
unusual and rare plants. Particularly
knowledgeable owner who is
happy to escort groups round the
garden.

20 **NEW** **GREENFIELDS**
Powburn, Alnwick NE66 4HR. Mr &
Mrs A Samuels. *N of Rothbury. Off
A697, take L to Glanton upon
entering Powburn. House ¹/₂ m on R.
Park on roadside.* **Light refreshments.
Special event for limited number
so pre-booking essential please
contact NGS 01483 211535
www.ngs.org.uk. Adm £20, incl
refreshments 2.30pm talk by
garden designr, Mark Robson.
Sun 9 Aug (2-4.30).**
A southern hemisphere inspired
garden in rural Northumberland! A
special opportunity to see a recently
created, but still developing, unique
garden surrounding Grade II listed
historic manse, Greenfield. Designed
by landscape architect, Mark Robson
of Bide-a-wee Cottage, to give the
feel of the African landscape in which
the owners had lived for many years.
It contains a formal garden with box-
edged beds full of blocks of swaying
grasses and colourful perennials,
providing spectacular late summer
colour that flows into the
Northumbrian landscape. In addition,
there is a potager, an orchard, and a
greenhouse with tender and unusual
plants. Large numbers of bulbs have
been planted for spring colour,
including a fabulous display from
10,000 fritillarias. Featured in Homes
and Gardens and has also been
extensively photographed by
international landscape and garden
photographer, Andrea Jones.

21 **◆ HALLS OF HEDDON**
West Heddon Nursery, Heddon-on-
the-Wall, Newcastle Upon Tyne
NE15 0JS. Mr David Hall, 01661
852445, www.hallsofheddon.co.uk.
*Approx 5m W of Newcastle upon
Tyne. Approx 1m NW of Heddon on
the Wall signed off B6318 (Military
Rd) at the bridge crossing the A69.*
Home-made teas. Teas, coffees and
home made cakes % sales to NGS.
**Adm by donation. For NGS: Sun 13
Sept (10.30-4).** For other opening
times and information, please
phone or see garden website.
Halls is a world renowned family
owned nursery, full of plants set
against the backdrop of an orginal
heated wall garden. September sees
a spectacular display of colour and
foliage in its dahlia and
chrysanthemum trial fields. Row upon
row of brilliant hues of plants
arranged to show type, colour and
height. It lifts the spirits as winter
approaches and makes a
dahlia/chrysanthemum lover of every
gardener. Introductory talks with a
question and answer session will be
provided throughout the day by David
Hall.

> Come and
> enjoy a woodland
> walk: snowdrops
> in February
> followed in April by
> daffodils and
> narcissi . . .

22 **NEW** **HARPERLEY HALL
FARM**
Harperley, Stanley DH9 9UB. Gary
McDermott, 01207 233318,
enquiries@
harperleyhallfarmnurseries.co.uk,
www.harperleyhallfarmnurseries.
co.uk. *A1 leave J63 at r'about take
2nd exit A693, continue for 5m. After
T-turn R Shieldrow Lane, then R Kyo
Lane at end turn R Harperley Lane,
garden 500yds on L.* Home-made
teas. **Adm £3, chd free. Sun 3 May
(10-5).** Visitors also welcome by

arrangement Mar to Oct. Group
visits welcome daytime or
evenings.
An evolving garden, attached to an
award winning specialist plant
nursery. The garden is set within 5
acres of countryside and we grow a
wide range of bog and woodland
plants around a series of ponds. The
garden is heavily planted with Primula
'Inverewe' and blue Himalayan
poppies as well as the very rare
Meconopsis punicea 'Sichuan Silk'
For nursery opening times see our
website. The garden is in a tranquil
setting and a flock of Rainbow and
other Lorikeet fly at liberty around the
garden. Several features, written by
owner, for Living North Magazine and
its website. The majority of the
garden and nursery can be accessed
by wheelchair users.

GROUP OPENING

23 **HIDDEN GARDENS OF
CROFT ROAD**
Darlington DL2 2SD. *2m S of
Darlington on A167. ³/₄ m S from
A167/A66 r'about between
Darlington & Croft.* Home-made teas
at Oxney Cottage & Orchard
Gardens. **Combined adm £5, chd
free. Share to Great North Air
Ambulance. Sun 28 June (1-5).**
4 very different and interesting
gardens, well named as 'Hidden
Gardens'. All are behind tall hedges.
Oxney Cottage is a very pretty
cottage garden with lawns,
herbaceous borders and roses,
colourful and varied unusual plants.
Nags Head Farm has a wonderful rill
running alongside a sloping garden
with a variety of plants leading to a
quiet, peaceful courtyard. There is a
large vegetable garden in which
stands a magnifcent glass-house with
prolific vines and chilli plants. A
woodland walk enhances the
tranquility of this garden. Orchard
Gardens is a large interesting garden
of mixed planting, stump sculptures,
colourful themed beds, fruit trees and
different imaginative ornaments.
Oxney Flatts has well-stocked
herbaceous borders, a newly
developed fruit garden and a wild life
pond planned for 2015. Partial
wheelchair access.

Every garden visit makes a difference

GROUP OPENING

24 HILLSIDE COTTAGES
Low Etherley, Bishop Auckland **DL14 0EZ**. *Off the B6282 in Low Etherley, Near Bishop Auckland. To reach the gardens walk down the track opp number 63 Low Etherley. Parking will be available at Green Croft Farm on S side of the rd.* Home-made teas. **Combined adm £4, chd free.** Sun 5 July (1.30-5).

2 HILLSIDE COTTAGE
Mrs M Smith
Visitors also welcome by arrangement Apr to Oct.
01388 832727
mary@maryruth.plus.com

1 HILLSIDE COTTAGES
Eric & Delia Ayres

The gardens of these two C19 cottages offer contrasting styles. At Number 1, grass paths lead you through a layout of trees and shrubs including many interesting specimens. Number 2 is based on island beds and has a cottage garden feel with a variety of perennials among the trees and shrubs and also incl a wild area, vegetables and fruit. Both gardens have ponds and water features. 2 Hillside Cottages was featured in Garden News. There are steps in both gardens.

25 LILBURN TOWER
Alnwick NE66 4PQ. Mr & Mrs D Davidson. *3m S of Wooler. On A697.* Home-made teas. **Adm £4, chd free.** Sun 31 May (2-6).
10 acres of magnificent walled and formal gardens set above river; rose parterre, topiary, scented garden, Victorian conservatory, wild flower meadow. Extensive fruit and vegetable garden, large glasshouse with vines. 30 acres of woodland with walks. Giant lilies, meconopsis around pond garden. Rhododendrons and azaleas. Also ruins of Pele Tower, and C12 church. Partial wheelchair access.

26 NEW LIZARDS FARM
Kitswell Road, Lanchester, Durham **DH7 0RE**. Mr Peter Robinson, 07713 627329, treetransplanters@tiscali.co.uk, www.northerntreetransplanters. com. *Drive full length of Kitswell Rd*

(signed as no through rd) & then continue straight ahead down single track to parking area. Light refreshments in the cosy farmhouse. Warming soup & bread roll, teas & cakes available all day. **Adm £4, chd free.** Sun 27 Sept, Sun 11 Oct (10-4).
Lizards Farm: a plantation and nursery for trees. Extensive range, with unusual species inc. many maples. Glorious autumn colour. Saplings to full size trees on sale. Very knowledgeable owner available to answer queries. Tree spade demonstration can be arranged - just ask. The site has lakes, extended walks and an area dedicated to a fascinating range of chicken breeds. Wear sturdy footwear.

27 LOUGHBROW HOUSE
Hexham NE46 1RS. Mrs K A Clark, 01434 603351, patriciaclark351@btinternet.com. *1m S of Hexham. 1m S of Hexham on B6306. Dipton Mill Rd. Rd signed Blanchland, ¹/₄ m take R fork; then ¹/₄ m at fork, lodge gates & driveway at intersection.* Home-made teas. **Adm £4, chd free.** Sun 5 July (2-5).
Visitors also welcome by arrangement Mar to Oct.
Country house garden with sweeping, colour themed herbaceous borders set around large lawns. Unique Lutyens inspired rill with grass topped bridges. Part walled kitchen garden and paved courtyard. Bog garden with pond. Developing new border and rose bed. Wild flower meadow with specimen trees. Woodland quarry garden with rhododendrons, azaleas, hostas and rare trees. Home made jams and chutneys.

28 10 LOW ROW
North Bitchburn, Crook DL15 8AJ. Mrs Ann Pickering, 01388 766345, keightleyann@yahoo.co.uk. *3m NW of Bishop Auckland. From Bishop*

Auckland take A689 (N) to Howden-le-Wear. R up Bank before petrol stn, 1st R in village at 30mph sign. Park in the village. **Adm £2, chd free.**
Visitors welcome by arrangement for individuals and groups of 20 max.
Quirky, original and truly organic, rambling garden: 90% grown from seeds and cuttings. Created without commercially bought plants or expense. Environmentally friendly. A haven for wildlife! Sloping garden with a myriad of paths and extensive views over the Wear valley. Colour yr-round from snowdrops to autumn leaves. Knowledgeable garden owner who will make your visit one to remember. Open all yr except Tuesdays. Book by phone or e-mail. Refreshments offered in adjacent PH.

GROUP OPENING

29 MIDDLETON-IN-TEESDALE
Market Place, Middleton-In-Teesdale, Barnard Castle **DL12 0ST**. Joanna & Brian Tait-Lovatt. *Gardens are all located in & near the village. Tickets & map with directions to each garden available from the Tourist Information Centre, in the centre of the village.* Home-made teas in Tourist Information Centre. Gluten free scones available. **Combined adm £4, chd free.** Sat 13 June (2-4.30).
Middleton in Teesdale sits amongst the outstanding scenery of Upper Teesdale. It welcomes Pennine Way walkers, and is just 4 miles to the W of the famous High Force Waterfall. 6 + gardens will be open in this delightfully picturesque village, covering a variety of sizes, designs and planting. The gardens, in and near the village, range in elevation from 1,200ft - 750ft above sea level, and present both alpine and cottage planting. Plants available for sale. Teas offered in the Tourist Information Centre. Wheelchair access to most gardens.

30 ◆ MINDRUM
Mindrum, nr Cornhill on Tweed & Yetholm TD12 4QN. Mr & Mrs T Fairfax, 01890 850228, www.mindrumestate.com. *6m SW of Coldstream, 9m NW of Wooler. Off B6352, 4m N of Yetholm. 5m from Cornhill on Tweed.* Home-made teas.

Adm £4, chd free. **For NGS: Sun 21 June (2-5). For other opening times and information, please phone or see garden website.**
3 acres of romantic planting with old fashioned roses, violas, hardy perennials, lilies, herbs, scented shrubs, and intimate garden areas. Glasshouses with vines, jasmine. Large hillside limestone rock garden with water leading to a pond, delightful stream, woodland and wonderful views across Bowmont valley with further river walks. Large plant sale, mostly home grown. Featured in English Garden Magazine. Partial wheelchair access due to landscape. Blue badge parking close to house. Wheelchair accessible WC available.

GROUP GARDEN

31 NEW MOORSHOLM VILLAGE
Moorsholm, Saltburn-By-The-Sea TS12 3JF. Mrs Valerie Rudd. *Moorsholm is 6m E of Guisborough on A171. Turn L at signed for Moorsholm. Village 1m from A171. Visitors proceed to Church Hall next to St Mary's Church High Street.Guides & maps available.* Home-made teas in the Church Hall. Cakes and scones, tea and coffee. **Combined adm £4, chd free.**
Sun 19 July (10.30-4).
At least 4 cottage gardens and up to 16 allotments in a moorland village, farming and former ironstone setting, 5m from the North Sea. 3 times winner of Northumbria in Bloom best village; finalist in Britain in Bloom. The village boasts a range of heritage features and cultivated public areas, notably the 'Long Border' and wild flower areas. An interesting heritage walk takes in village allotment gardens, green lanes with wildlife habitats and conservation schemes. Victorian Churchyard, Church Hall and Quiet Garden won 'Best Grounds of a Religious Establishment' Northumbria in Bloom. Printed map and interpretation boards ensure visitors enjoy local features and natural history. Warm welcome from Moorsholm in Bloom volunteers. Gold winners Britain in Bloom. Depending on weather some of the green lanes could be unsuitable for wheelchairs.

GROUP GARDEN

32 NEW NETHERWITTON VILLAGE AND SURROUNDS
Netherwitton, Morpeth NE61 4NN. Mr Nick Myerscough. *5m W of Morpeth. The gardens are spread throughout this small village & surrounding farms. Parking in the village at Netherwitton Hall.* Home-made teas in Netherwitton Village Hall on the village green. **Combined adm £5, chd free. Share to The RDA Pegasus Centre, Morpeth & St Giles Church, Netherwitton.** Sun 21 June (12-5).
Netherwitton is a hidden gem nestling in the Font Valley west of Morpeth. The gardens of this picturesque village are very private and very rarely open to the public.There are a wide variety of gardens ranging from small shady courtyards, to colourful cottage gardens, to large rural gardens, and the C17 Netherwitton Hall. Most gardens are within the village, but some larger gardens are on outlying farms within a mile of the village. Not all the gardens are accessible for wheelchairs. Netherwitton Open Gardens is a real community event, raising money for the NGS and the RDA Pegasus Centre in Morpeth. Most of the gardens are accessible for wheelchairs but some have steps.

Netherwitton is a hidden gem nestling in the Font Valley . . . a picturesque village . . .

---

33 NEWBIGGIN HOUSE
Blanchland DH8 9UD. Mrs A Scott-Harden. *12m S of Hexham. From Blanchland village take Stanhope Rd. 1/2 m along narrow rd follow yellow signs up tarmac drive into car park.* Home-made teas. **Adm £4, chd free.**
Sat 4 July (2-5).
5-acre landscaped garden at 1000ft, started in 1996 and maturing beautifully. Enjoy old-fashioned herbaceous borders, peonies, shrubs, roses, bog and wild gardens

---

incl a wild rose walk. Magnificent collection of unusual trees and shrubs. The garden is still being developed and there are new plants and features to enjoy. Partial wheelchair access.

34 NEWONSTEAD COTTAGE GARDEN
Great Bavington, Newcastle Upon Tyne NE19 2BJ. Philippa Hodkinson, 01830 540409, philippahodkinson@yahoo.co.uk. *NW of Newcastle upon Tyne. From A696 turn onto B6342 past Kirkharle Courtyard, then R to Great Bavington. From A68 turn onto B6342 approx half way to A696, take L turn to Great Bavington. Follow yellow signs.* **Adm £4, chd free. Visitors welcome by arrangement June to Aug for groups of 10 or more.**
Developing cottage garden on 1/2 -acre site set in wild landscape. Dramatic backdrop of outcrop of whin sill. Stunning late season colour from hardy annuals and unusual perennials. Chickens wander amongst young trees set in the lawn. This is an artist's garden, which is run on green gardening principles. Grass paths may be difficult after heavy rain.

35 NO. 2 FERNDENE
2 Holburn Lane Court, Holburn Lane, Ryton NE40 3PN. Maureen Kesteven, 0191 413 5937, maureen@patrickkesteven.plus. com. *8m W of Gateshead, off B6317, on Holburn Lane in Old Ryton Village. Park in Co-op carpark on High St, cross rd and walk through Ferndene Park.* Home-made teas. pizzas from wood fired oven. **Adm £4, chd free.** Sun 26 July (1-4.30). **Visitors also welcome by arrangement Apr to May groups of 10+.**
A garden, approx. 3/4 acre, developed over the last 5yrs, surrounded by mature trees. Informal areas of herbaceous perennials, more formal box bordered area, vegetable patch, sedum roof, wildlife pond, bog and fern gardens. Early interest - hellebores, snowdrops, daffodils, bluebells and tulips, as well as later summer flowering perennials. 1 1/2 acre mixed broadleaf wood being restored. Pizzas cooked in wood fired oven. Featured in Amateur Gardening and The Northumbrian.

36 THE OLD VICARAGE

Hutton Magna, nr Richmond, N Yorkshire DL11 7HJ. Mr & Mrs D M Raw. *8m SE of Barnard Castle. 6m W of Scotch Corner on A66. Turn R, signed Hutton Magna. Continue to, and through, village. Garden 200yds past village on L, on corner of T-junction.* Home-made teas. **Adm £3, chd free.** Sun 12 Apr (2-5). S-facing garden, elevation 450ft. Plantings, since 1978, now maturing within original design contemporary to 1887 house (not open). Cut and topiary hedging, old orchard, rose and herbaceous borders featuring hellebores in profusion, with tulips and primulas. Large and interesting plant sale. Recent introduction of a loggery to encourage wildlife.

37 OLIVER FORD GARDEN

Longedge Lane, Rowley, Consett DH8 9HG. Bob & Bev Tridgett, www.gardensanctuaries.co.uk. *5m NW of Lanchester. Signed from A68 in Rowley. From Lanchester take rd towards Sately. Garden will be signed as you pass Woodlea Manor.* Light refreshments. **Adm £3, chd free.** Sun 7 June (1-5). Spectacular 1½ -acre woodland garden developed and planted by 2007 BBC gardener of the year. Mini arboretum specialising in bark that includes rare acers, stewartia, betula and prunus. Stream, wildlife pond and bog garden. Semi-shaded Japanese maple and dwarf rhododendron garden. 80 sq metre rock garden. Large insect nectar garden. Orchard and 1½ -acre upland meadow. Annual wild flower area. Featured as a double page spread in the Northern Echo.

38 25 PARK ROAD SOUTH

Chester le Street DH3 3LS. Mrs A Middleton, 0191 388 3225. *4m N of Durham. Located at S end of A167 Chester-le-St bypass rd. Precise directions provided when booking visit.* Tea. **Adm £2.50, chd free.** Visitors welcome by arrangement May to July. Plantswoman's garden with all-yr round interest, colour, texture and foliage. Unusual perennials, grasses, shrubs and container planting. Cool courtyard garden using foliage only. Small front gravel garden. Lots of unusual plants for sale!

An interesting heritage walk takes in village allotment gardens, green lanes with wildlife habitats and conservation schemes . . .

GROUP OPENING

39 NEW PETERLEE GARDENS SAFARI

Shotton Hall Banqueting Suites, Old Shotton, Peterlee SR8 2PH. Peterlee Town Council. *From S-bound carriageway of A19, turn L onto slip rd signed Peterlee. At mini r'about turn L & then take the 1st turn on R into the grounds of Shotton Hall Banqueting Suites.* Light refreshments at Shotton Hall Banqueting Suites. hot and cold refreshments, snacks and afternoon teas available. **Combined adm £3, chd free.** Sun 12 July (10-5). Peterlee is opening about 12 of its prettiest gardens together with its well-managed allotments and the colourful grounds of Shotton Hall. While some of the gardens are of medium size, many are small, bijou spaces full of colour and interest. All have been ingeniously planted by imaginative owners. Because of the size of the town, visiting all the venues will take the form of a circular safari for which a vehicle will be needed. So, purchase a ticket and collect a map from Shotton Hall and start your journey wherever you wish on the well-signed route. Refreshments will be available throughout the day at Shotton Hall. Wheelchair access to most but not all gardens.

40 ◆ RABY CASTLE

Staindrop, Darlington DL2 3AH. Lord Barnard, 01833 660202, www.rabycastle.com. *12m NW of Darlington, 1m N of Staindrop. On A688, 8m NE of Barnard Castle.* **For opening times and information, please phone or see garden website.** C18 walled gardens set within the grounds of Raby Castle. Designers

---

such as Thomas White and James Paine have worked to establish the gardens, which now extend to 5 acres, displaying herbaceous borders, old yew hedges, formal rose gardens and informal heather and conifer gardens. Assistance will be needed for wheelchairs.

41 RAVENSFORD FARM

Hamsterley DL13 3NH. Jonathan & Caroline Peacock, 01388 488305, caroline@ravensfordfarm.co.uk. *7m W of Bishop Auckland. From A68 at Witton-le-Wear turn off W to Hamsterley. Go through village & turn L just before tennis courts at far end.* Home-made teas. **Adm £4, chd free.** Sun 14 June (2-5). Was it the garden, the plants for sale, the home-baked cakes, the background music, the new ornamental features or the sunny weather that brought us our biggest ever number of visitors in 2014? All the same elements will be on offer again (incl the weather, we hope!) but in a much earlier season. The plants in flower will be very different - the welcome just as warm. Live music in the background. Featured in the Northern Echo, with a photograph in the paper and several other photos on the website. We also had an entry on the 'letters page' in the Teesdale Mercury. Some gravel, so assistance will be needed for wheelchairs.

ALLOTMENTS

42 ST MARGARET'S ALLOTMENTS

Margery Lane, Durham DH1 4QG, 0191 386 1049, pauline@dhent.fsnet.co.uk. *From A1 take A690 to City Centre/Crook. Straight ahead at T-lights after passing 4 r'abouts.* **Combined adm £4, chd free.** Sun 12 July (2-5). 5 acres of 82 allotments against the spectacular backdrop of Durham Cathedral. This site has been cultivated since the Middle Ages, and was saved from development 20yrs ago, allowing a number of enthusiastic gardeners to develop plots which display a great variety of fruit, vegetables and flowers. Display about successful campaign to save the allotments from development. Guided Tours. Art in the Allotments.

43 ◆ SEATON DELAVAL HALL

The Avenue, Seaton Sluice, nr Whitley Bay NE26 4QR. National Trust, www.nationaltrust.org.uk/seatondelaval-hall. *2m N of Whitley Bay. N of Newcastle, between Seaton Delaval & Seaton Sluice, A190 linking to A193 coastal rd & A19. 5m from A1. Follow brown signs.* Light refreshments in Stables Cafe. **Adm £6, chd £3. Plant sale for NGS. For NGS: Sat 6 June (11-4). For other opening times and information, please phone or see garden website.**

Formal gardens designed by James Russell in 1950 with topiary parterre, pond and fountain, rose garden and striking sculptures. Greatly improved in recent years, with colourful borders and new bee garden, to complement the magnificent C18 baroque hall, designed by Sir John Vanbrugh, said to be the finest house in North East England. (Normal entry charge applies to area beyond NGS plant stalls). Super Plant Sale.

 ♿ 🐕 ❀ 🚐 ☕

GROUP OPENING

44 SEDGEFIELD GARDENS

Sedgefield TS21 2AE. The Council Offices. *Village green. Sedgefield is E of the A1(M), ajacent to the r'about junctions of the A177 & A689.* Home-made teas at Ceddesfeld Hall, ajacent to village green. **Combined adm £3.50, chd free. Sun 5 July (1-5).**

Selection of 8-10 gardens in a beautiful town, featuring water gardens, cottage planting and oriental display. Northumbria in Bloom Gold award winners. Sedgefield boasts the magnificent C13 St Edmund's church set on traditional village green. Percy Boydell award for best overall entry and gardens in the whole of Northumberland Britain in Bloom and Northumbria in Bloom Gold award winners. As well as open gardens visitors can enjoy the numerous Sedgefield in Bloom winning projects around the village -check out the website. Partial wheelchair access.

 ♿ ❀ ☕

---

45 SKARA BRAE

20 Tynedale Gardens, Stocksfield NE43 7EZ. Ann Mates, 01661 843175, ann.mates@yahoo.com. *14m W of Newcastle upon Tyne. 9m E of Hexham. A1/A69 then B6309 to Stocksfield. From W, past station & cricket ground. At Quaker meeting house turn into New Ridley Rd. 2nd R is Tynedale Gardens.* Tea. **Adm £3, chd free. Visitors welcome by arrangement May to Aug minibuses acceptable.**

A charming, developing cottage-style garden, with established shrubs and herbaceous planting in wide borders, that is continuously being improved, on SW-facing site 150ft x 40ft. Added interest of statuary and water features, including small stream at bottom of the garden, and seating areas to sit and relax. Featured in Tynedale Life magazine.

🐕 ☕

---

46 NEW STOBGREEN HOUSE

Town Head, Eggleston, Barnard Castle DL12 0DB. Anna-Marie Gossage, 01833 650578, info@stobgreenhouse.co.uk. *Heading from Barnard Castle towards Eggleston take 1st turning to the village (on the junction with the Garage) The garden is set back from the road & will be signed from here.* Home-made teas. **Adm £2.50, chd free. Sun 31 May (1-4.30). Visitors also welcome by arrangement May to July.**

The gardens are arranged over an area of approx 3 acres. The largest area is a semi mature wooded area with a spring fed beck running through it, this is mostly naturalised, attracting lots of wildlife. The formal gardens are around the house. Established in 2011 after extensive build works there are terraces, a walled garden and sunken patio mainly with herbaceous planting.

❀ 🛏 ☕

---

47 4 STOCKLEY GROVE

Brancepeth DH7 8DU. Mr & Mrs Bainbridge, 079445 23551, fabb63@sky.com. *5m W of Durham City. Situated on the A690 between Durham & Crook. From Durham direction turn L at the end of village & from Crook turn 1st R on entering.* Home-made teas. **Adm £4, chd free. Sun 2 Aug (1-5).** Visitors also welcome by arrangement May to Sept.

A stunning ½ -acre garden with inspirational planting to provide yr-round colour and interest. Landscaped with hidden grassy paths with many unusual trees, shrubs and plants incl wildlife pond, rockery area and water features.

❀ ☕

Acton House
© Susie White

48 THORNLEY HOUSE
Thornley Gate, Allendale,
NE47 9NH. Ms Eileen Finn,
01434 683255,
enquiries@thornleyhouse.co.uk,
www.thornleyhouse.co.uk. *1km W
of Allendale. Take rd downhill from the
Allendale Inn for 1km to the 5 road
junction. Thornley House is just opp
on R.* Home-made teas. Tea, coffee.
fruit squash and homemade cakes.
**Adm £4, chd free. Share to Brooke
Charity for Working Animals.**
Sun 31 May (2-5). Visitors also
welcome by arrangement May to
Aug.
1-acre country garden with
perennials, wild flowers, shrubs,
conifers, stream and pond.
Vegetables and fruit, rose avenue and
peaceful woodland reached across
field. A feline theme is evident
throughout this child-friendly garden.
Seek and find quiz is available for
family fun. Maine Coon cats and
ornamental animals enhance this
garden. Tombola and live music.

GROUP OPENING

49 NEW WALL VILLAGE GARDENS
Hexham NE46 4DU. *4m NW of
Hexham. A69 towards Hexham. Turn
at B6079 signed Acomb/Chollerford,
2½ m through Acomb to Wall. Park
on village green. All gardens within a
few minutes walk.* Light refreshments
and home-made teas in village hall.
Combined adm £4, chd free.
Sun 12 July (12-4).

NEW BIBURY
Mr & Mrs Bob & Ros Elliott.
*From S on L after Hadrian PH in
Wall village*

NEW MIDDLE CHARE
Mr & Mrs W Soulsby.
*Turn R opp Hadrian Hotel on to
narrow lane, then immed L 2nd
bungalow on L*

NEW 1 WARDEN VIEW
Judith Longlands.
At southern edge of Wall Village

Three delightful gardens in Wall a
small picturesque village near
Hadrian's Wall and Chesters Roman
Fort. Bibury a 2 acre terraced garden,
set around three sides of a stone
house, on the edge of Wall Village,
with mature copper beech and lime
trees, pond, orchard, and borders of
colourful herbaceous perennials.

Extensive views over North Tyne
Valley. Middle Chare is a cottage
garden with herbaceous borders with
clematis, some topiary, bed of
grasses and fern and hosta border
with tree fern and small stumpery.
Good display of David Austin Roses.
Gravel paths in some areas. 1
Warden View this is a keen plants
woman's garden, with cottage garden
style planting on differing levels.
Mainly perennials, and many are
unusual plants chosen for their foliage
as much as for the flowers, to give
harmonious appeal. The garden is
packed with plants.

NGS support
makes a vital
difference to our
patient care

50 ◆ WALLINGTON
Cambo NE61 4AR. National Trust,
01670 774389,
www.nationaltrust.org.uk/
wallington. *12m W of Morpeth 20m
NW Newcastle. From N B6343; from
S via A696 from Newcastle, 6m W of
Belsay, B6342 to Cambo.* Light
refreshments in Clock Tower Cafe
and Garden Kiosk. **Adm £11.50, chd
£5.75.** For NGS: Sun 10 May, Sun
12 July (10-5). For other opening
times and information, please
phone or see garden website.
Walled, terraced garden with fine
herbaceous and mixed borders;
Edwardian conservatory; 100 acres
woodland and lakes. House dates
from 1688 but altered, interior greatly
changed c1740; exceptional rococo
plasterwork by Francini brothers. Peat
free plant sales. Head Gardener's
Question Time 12-4 both days 10
May & 12 July. Wheelchair access
limited to top terrace in Walled
Garden but elsewhere possible with
care and support.

51 NEW WARRENFELL,
2 Filter Cottages, Tunstall
Reservoir, Wolsingham, Bishop
Auckland DL13 3LX. Fran Toulson.
*W on A689 through Wolsingham
Village centre. On edge of village take
R turn by Wolsingham School, signed
to Tunstall Resrvoir. No through Road.
Garden 2m on R below dam wall.*
Home-made teas. **Adm £3, chd free.**
Sat 27, Sun 28 June (10.30-4.30).
A young garden, approx ¼ acre,
started in 2012 and still in
development. Sited in the stunning
Waskerley valley below Tunstall
Reservoir. Why not combine a garden
visit with a walk at the reservoir.
Borders with shrubs, perennials,
roses and peonies. Kitchen garden
with raised beds and espaliered
apples and pears. Also a formal lawn,
small wild flower area, lavender
hedging and small greenhouse.

52 ◆ WASHINGTON OLD HALL
The Avenue, Washington Village
NE38 7LE. National Trust, 0191 416
6879, www.nationaltrust.org.uk. *7m
SE of Newcastle upon Tyne. From
A19 onto A1231 From A1 exit J64
onto A195 In both cases stay on road
until you pick up brown signs to
Washington Old Hall.* Home-made
teas in Friends' tearoom. Delicious
home made cakes and pies. For
NGS: Sun 7 June (11-4). For other
opening times and information,
please phone or see garden
website.
The picturesque stone manor house
and its gardens provide a tranquil
oasis in an historic setting. It contains
a formal Jacobean garden with box
hedging borders around evergreens
and perennials, vegetable garden,
wild flower nut orchard with bee
hives. Places to sit out and enjoy a
picnic or afternoon tea. Refreshments
supplied by Friends of Washington
Old Hall. NGS Bargain Garden Plant
Sale 11 to 4. Garden lift which
wheelchair users full access to the
whole area.

53 WEST HOUSE
5 Etherley Lane, Bishop Auckland
DL14 7QR. Dr & Mrs R McManners.
*Park in Bondgate car park, Bishop
Auckland. 250 metre walk to house;
route clearly signed.* Home-made
teas. **Adm £3.50, chd free.** Sun 12
Apr (2-5).
A domestic, semi-rustic town garden
surrounding 3 sides of this mid C19

Lemon drizzle cake, Victoria sponge ... yummy!

town house (not open). Probably originally laid out in 1856, there is now a more recent terraced garden on the site of the original orchard. To the rear of the house is a small, walled 'Dutch Yard Garden', complete with fountain which may well have been enjoyed by Sir Edward Elgar during his many visits to West House. Wheelchair access to viewing point.

54 ◆ WHALTON MANOR GARDENS
Whalton NE61 3UT. Mr & Mrs T R P S Norton, 01670 775205, www.whaltonmanor.co.uk. *5m W of Morpeth. On the B6524, the house is at E end of the village & will be signed.* Tea. **Adm £4, chd free. For NGS: Sun 28 June (2-5). For other opening times and information, please phone or see garden website.**
The historic Whalton Manor, altered by Sir Edwin Lutyens in 1908, is surrounded by 3 acres of magnificent walled gardens, designed by Lutyens with the help of Gertrude Jekyll. The gardens have been developed by the

Norton family since the 1920s and incl extensive herbaceous borders, 30yd peony border, rose garden, listed summerhouses, pergolas and walls, festooned with rambling roses and clematis. Open by appt. See website. Featured in The English Garden magazine. Partial wheelchair access, some stone steps.

55 ▶ WOODLANDS
Peareth Hall Road, Gateshead NE9 7NT. Liz Reid, 077198 75750, lizreid52@ntlworld.com. *3¹/₂ m N Washington Galleries. 4m S Gateshead town centre. OnB1288 turn opp Guide Post PH (NE9 7RR) onto Peareth Hall Rd. Continue for ¹/₂ m passing 2 bus stops on L. Third drive on L past Highbury Ave.* Home-made teas. **Adm £4, chd free.**
Sat 27 June (1-4.30). Visitors also welcome by arrangement June to Aug groups of 10+.
Mature garden on a site of approx ¹/₇ acres- quirky, with tropical themed planting and Caribbean inspired bar. A fun garden with lots of deep mid-late summer colour, interesting plants, informal beds and borders, pond area

and decks. Featured in Amateur Gardening, Shields Gazette, The Journal and Sunderland Echo.

56 ▶ WOODSIDE HOUSE
Witton Park, Bishop Auckland DL14 0DU. Charles & Jean Crompton, 01388 609973, j.crompton@talktalk.net. *2m N of Bishop Auckland. from Bishop Auckland take A68 to Witton Park. In village DO NOT follow SatNav. Go down track next to St Pauls Church.* Home-made teas. **Adm £4, chd free.**
Sun 19 July (2-5). Visitors also welcome by arrangement Apr to Sept.
Stunning 3-acre, mature, undulating garden full of interesting trees, shrubs and plants. Superbly landscaped with island beds, flowing herbaceous borders, an old walled garden, rhododendron beds, fernery, 3 ponds and vegetable garden. Delightful garden full of interesting and unusual features: much to fire the imagination. Winner of Bishop Auckland in bloom. Partial wheelchair access.

Woodlands

© Susie White

NORTHAMPTONSHIRE

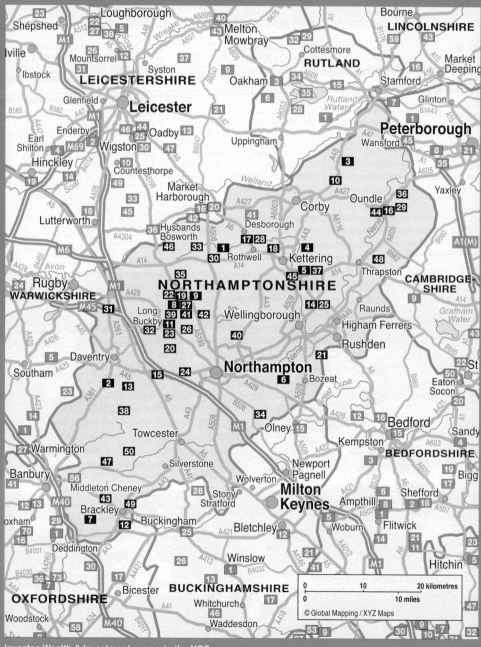

Northamptonshire

Northamptonshire, known as the County of Spires and Squires, and also as the Rose of the Counties, lies in the East Midlands area of the country and is bordered by eight counties.

Take a gentle stroll around charming villages with thatch and stone cottages and welcoming inns. Wander around stately homes, discovering art treasures and glorious gardens, many open for the NGS (Kelmarsh Hall, Castle Ashby, Cottesbrooke Hall and Boughton House). Explore historic market towns such as Oundle and Brackley in search of fine footwear, antiques and curiosities. Or visit wildlife sanctuaries such as Sulby Gardens with 12 acres of interesting flora and fauna.

The serenity of our waterways will delight, and our winding country lanes and footpaths will guide you around a rural oasis, far from the pressures of modern living, where you can walk knee-deep in bluebells and snowdrops in spring at gardens such as Greywalls and Rosemount.

Our NGS year starts in February and has openings nearly every month until November, giving a glimpse of gardens through the seasons.

Below: Mulberry Cottage, Spratton Gardens

Northamptonshire Volunteers

County Organisers
David Abbott
01933 680363
d_j_abbott@btinternet.com

Gay Webster
01604 740203
gay.webster6@gmail.com

County Treasurer
Michael Heaton
01604 846032
ngs@mimomul.co.uk

Publicity
Michael Heaton
(as above)

Booklet Coordinators
David Abbott
(as above)

Michael Heaton
(as above)

Assistant County Organisers
Philippa Heumann
01327 860142
pmheumann@gmail.com

Geoff Sage
01788 510334
geoffsage256@btinternet.com

Currently the NGS donates around £2.5 million every year

Opening Dates

All entries subject to change.
For latest information check www.ngs.org.uk

February

Sunday 22
29 Jericho
41 Rosemount

March

Sunday 1
4 Boughton House
21 Greywalls

Sunday 8
25 67-69 High Street

April

Saturday 4
33 The Maltings

Sunday 5
33 The Maltings

Monday 6
33 The Maltings

Sunday 12
15 Flore Gardens

Sunday 19
5 Briarwood
9 Cottesbrooke Hall Gardens

Thursday 23
46 Sulby Gardens

Sunday 26
35 NEW Naseby Lodge

May

Saturday 2
12 Evenley Wood Garden

Sunday 3
20 Great Brington Gardens

Saturday 9
22 Guilsborough Gardens

Sunday 10
22 Guilsborough Gardens

Sunday 17
10 Deene Park
29 Jericho
48 Titchmarsh House

Wednesday 20
30 Kelmarsh Hall

Sunday 24
7 Charlton Gardens
42 Spratton Gardens
50 Weedon Lois & Weston Gardens

Sunday 31
47 Sulgrave Gardens

June

Thursday 4
25 67-69 High Street (Evening)

Festival Weekend

Sunday 7
14 Finedon Gardens
24 Harpole Gardens
38 Preston Capes and Little Preston Gardens

Thursday 11
25 67-69 High Street (Evening)

Friday 12
13 NEW Everdon Hall (Evening)

Saturday 13
48 Titchmarsh House

Sunday 14
2 Badby and Newnham Gardens
31 Kilsby Gardens
36 NEW The Old Black Horse
37 34 Poplars Farm Road

Thursday 18
25 67-69 High Street (Evening)

Saturday 20
15 Flore Gardens

Sunday 21
15 Flore Gardens
16 Foxtail Lilly

Thursday 25
25 67-69 High Street (Evening)
46 Sulby Gardens

Saturday 27
34 The Menagerie (Evening)

Sunday 28
1 Arthingworth Open Gardens
14 Finedon Gardens
49 Turweston Gardens

July

Saturday 4
11 NEW East Haddon Hall
23 Haddonstone Show Gardens

Sunday 5
6 Castle Ashby Gardens
11 NEW East Haddon Hall

23 Haddonstone Show Gardens
32 Long Buckby Gardens

Sunday 12
39 Ravensthorpe Gardens

Sunday 19
40 Rosearie-de-la-Nymph
43 Steane Park

Sunday 26
3 NEW Blatherwycke Estate
17 Froggery Cottage
28 Hostellarie
40 Rosearie-de-la-Nymph

August

Sunday 2
26 Holdenby House Gardens
44 NEW Stoke Doyle Gardens

Sunday 9
27 Hollowell Gardens
45 67 Stratfield Way

Thursday 20
46 Sulby Gardens

September

Sunday 13
8 Coton Manor Garden
34 The Menagerie

October

Thursday 8
46 Sulby Gardens

Sunday 25
4 Boughton House

November

Thursday 12
46 Sulby Gardens

We aim to give visitors an afternoon of discovery . . .

February 2016

Sunday 28
29 Jericho

Gardens open to the public

4 Boughton House
6 Castle Ashby Gardens
8 Coton Manor Garden
9 Cottesbrooke Hall Gardens
10 Deene Park
12 Evenley Wood Garden
23 Haddonstone Show Gardens
26 Holdenby House Gardens
30 Kelmarsh Hall
43 Steane Park

By arrangement only

18 Glendon Hall
19 Gower House

Also open by arrangement

1 Bosworth House, Arthingworth Open Gardens
2 The Banks, Badby and Newnham Gardens
5 Briarwood
15 The Old Bakery, Flore Gardens
16 Foxtail Lilly
21 Greywalls
22 Dripwell House, Guilsborough Gardens
22 Four Acres, Guilsborough Gardens
24 The Close, Harpole Gardens
24 19 Manor Close, Harpole Gardens
25 67-69 High Street
29 Jericho
31 Pytchley House, Kilsby Gardens
32 Mill House, Long Lane, Long Buckby Gardens
33 The Maltings
36 NEW The Old Black Horse
37 34 Poplars Farm Road
39 Mill House, Ravensthorpe Gardens
39 Ravensthorpe Nursery, Ravensthorpe Gardens
46 Sulby Gardens
48 Titchmarsh House

Visit a garden on National Gardens Festival Weekend 6 & 7 June

The Gardens

GROUP OPENING

1 ARTHINGWORTH OPEN GARDENS

Arthingworth, nr Market Harborough LE16 8LA. *6m S of Market Harborough. From Market Harborough via A508, after 4m take L to Arthingworth. From Northampton, A508 turn R just after Kelmarsh.* Home-made teas at Bosworth House & village hall. **Combined adm £5, chd free.** Sun 28 June (2-6).

BOSWORTH HOUSE
Mr & Mrs C E Irving-Swift.
From the phone box, when in Oxendon Rd, take the little lane with no name, second to the R Visitors also welcome by arrangement Mar to July for groups of 15+.
01858 525202
irvingswift@btinternet.com

5 CHURCH FARM WAY
Mr & Mrs Leigh & Carol Brewin

CHURCH VIEW
Oxendon Road. Mr Greg Ellis

GLEBE FARM COTTAGE
Kelmarsh Road. Noel & Hannah Walsh.
Opp PH

THE HAWTHORNS
Kelmarsh Road. A Knott.
Entry through Bulls Head PH car park

ORCHARD HOUSE
Mr & Mrs Mike Osgood

NEW 7 OXENDON ROAD
John Parton

1 SUNNYBANK
Tim & Jane French

NEW 2 THE TITHE BARN
Mr & Mrs A Roe

Arthingworth welcomes you with 9 gardens to visit, from the good life to the manor born or nearly. Come and enjoy the diversity, we aim to give visitors an afternoon of discovery. Our gardens have been chosen because they are all different in spirit, and tended by young and weathered gardeners. We have gardens with stunning views, traditional with herbaceous borders and vegetables, walled, and artisan. The village is looking forward to welcoming you. Wheelchair access available to some gardens.

Titchmarsh House

© Leigh Clapp

GROUP OPENING

2 BADBY AND NEWNHAM GARDENS

Daventry NN11 3AR. *3m S of Daventry. E-side of A361. Maps provided for visitors.* Home-made teas at Badby & Newnham Churches. **Combined adm £4, chd free.** Sun 14 June (2-6).

THE BANKS
Newnham. Sue & Geoff Chester
Visitors also welcome by arrangement May to June.
07548 670020
sueandgeoffchester@btinternet.com
www.suestyles.co.uk

HILLTOP
Newnham. David & Mercy Messenger

SHAKESPEARES COTTAGE
Church Hill, Badby. Sarah & Jocelyn Hartland-Swann

SOUTHVIEW COTTAGE
Badby. Alan & Karen Brown

TRIFIDIA
Badby. Colin & Shirley Cripps

5 gardens within 2 beautiful villages with attractive old houses of golden coloured Hornton stone set around their village greens. In Badby, there are 3 gardens of differing styles; a wisteria clad thatched cottage with modern sculptures; a newly developed elevated garden with views over the village; and a garden with pond, conservatory, glasshouses and vegetables, also featuring unusual plants that aim for yr-round interest. In Newnham there are 2 gardens, a 3 acre organic garden around a picturesque C17 thatched cottage (not open) with lawns, densely planted borders, vegetable and cutting garden, and paddocks with feature trees. Then there is a garden designer's recently remodelled garden with pools, herbaceous borders, vegetables and herbs developed as rooms among mature trees, a garden to wander through. NB Both villages are hilly.

© Val Corbett

Deene Park

3 NEW ▶ BLATHERWYCKE ESTATE

Blatherwycke, Peterborough PE8 6YW. Mr George. *Blatherwycke is signed off the A43 between Stamford & Corby. Follow road through village & the gardens entrance is immed next to the large river bridge.* Home-made teas. **Adm £3, chd free.** Sun 26 July (11-4). Blatherwycke Hall demolished in the 1940's, its grounds and gardens lost until now! In April 2011 we started the renovation of the derelict 4 acre walled gardens. So far a large kitchen garden, wall trained fruit trees, extensive herbaceous borders, seasonal beds, parterre, pleaching orchard and wild flower meadows have been built, planted and sown. Also a very large arboretum is being planted. Grass and gravel paths, some slopes and steps with ramps.

&♿ 🐕 ✿ 🚌 ☕

4 ◆ BOUGHTON HOUSE

Geddington, Kettering NN14 1BJ. Duke of Buccleuch & Queensberry, KBE, 01536 515731, www.boughtonhouse.org.uk. *3m NE of Kettering. From A14, 2m along A43 Kettering to Stamford, turn R into Geddington, house entrance 1½ m on R.* Light refreshments in C18 Stable Block. **Adm £5, chd £2.**

For NGS: Sun 1 Mar, Sun 25 Oct (11-3). **For other opening times and information, please phone or see garden website.**
The Northamptonshire home of the Duke and Duchess of Buccleuch. The garden opening incl opportunities to see the historic walled kitchen garden and herbaceous border incl the newly created sensory and wildlife gardens. The wilderness woodland will open for visitors to view the spring flowers or the autumn colours. As a special treat the garden originally created by Sir David Scott (cousin of the Duke of Buccleuch) will also be open.

✿ 🚌 ☕

5 ◆ BRIARWOOD

4 Poplars Farm Road, Barton Seagrave, Kettering NN15 5AF. Elaine Christian & William Portch, 01536 522169, briarwood.garden@yahoo.co.uk, www.elainechristian-gardendesign.co.uk. *1½ m SE of Kettering Town Centre. J10 off A14 turn onto Barton Rd (A6) towards Wicksteed Park. R into Warkton Lane, after 200 metres R into Poplars Farm Rd.* Light refreshments. **Adm £3, chd free.** Sun 19 Apr (10-4). **Visitors also welcome by arrangement Apr to July.**
A garden in 2 parts with quirky

original sculptures and many faces. Firstly a s-facing lawn and colourful borders with spring bulbs, blossom trees, summer colour, hedging, palms, climbers, lily pond, and sunny terrace. Secondly, a secret garden with summerhouse, small orchard, raised bed potager and water feature. Crafts for sale and children's quiz.

&♿ ✿ ☕

6 ◆ CASTLE ASHBY GARDENS

Castle Ashby, Northampton NN7 1LQ. Earl Compton, 07771 871766, www.castleashbygardens.co.uk. *6m E of Northampton. 1½ m N of A428, turn off between Denton & Yardley Hastings. Follow brown tourist signs (SatNav will take you to the village, look for brown signs).* **Adm £5.50, chd free.** For NGS: Sun 5 July (10-5.30). **For other opening times and information, please phone or see garden website.**
35 acres within a 10,000 acre estate of both formal and informal gardens, incl Italian gardens with orangery and arboretum with lakes, all dating back to the 1860s as well as a farmyard with various animals. Rare breed farmyard, tearooms and gift shop. Gravel paths within gardens.

&♿ 🐕 ✿ 🚌 ☕

GROUP OPENING

7 **CHARLTON GARDENS**
Banbury OX17 3DR. *7m SE of Banbury, 5m W of Brackley. From B4100 turn off N at Aynho, or from A422 turn off S at Farthinghoe. Parking at village hall.* Home-made teas at Walnut House. **Combined adm £5, chd free.** Sun 24 May (2-5.30).

8 CARTWRIGHT ROAD
Miss Valerie Trinder

CHARLTON LODGE
Mr & Mrs Andrew Woods

HOME FARM HOUSE
Mrs N Grove-White

WALNUT HOUSE
Sir Paul & Lady Hayter

Pretty stone village with a selection of gardens large and small, incl a cottage garden with colourful planting, interesting corners and lovely views; a walled garden with roses and clematis; a large garden behind C17 farmhouse (not open) with colour themed borders, separate small gardens and a hot gravel garden created in 2011; and a large terraced garden with a 140ft long herbaceous border and raised bed vegetable patch, overlooking a lake.

8 **◆ COTON MANOR GARDEN**
Nr Guilsborough, Northampton NN6 8RQ. Mr & Mrs Ian Pasley-Tyler, 01604 740219, www.cotonmanor.co.uk. *10m N of Northampton, 11m SE of Rugby. From A428 & A5199 follow tourist signs.* Light refreshments at Stableyard Cafe. **Adm £7, chd £2.50. For NGS: Sun 13 Sept (12-5.30).** For other opening times and information, please phone or see garden website.
10 acre garden set in peaceful countryside with old yew and holly hedges and extensive herbaceous borders containing many unusual plants. Other areas incl rose, water, herb and woodland gardens, our famous bluebell wood, and wild flower meadow. Adjacent specialist nursery with over 1000 plant varieties propagated from the garden. Partial wheelchair access as some paths are narrow and the site is on a slope.

9 **◆ COTTESBROOKE HALL GARDENS**
Cottesbrooke NN6 8PF. Mr & Mrs A R Macdonald-Buchanan, 01604 505808, www.cottesbrooke.co.uk. *10m N of Northampton. Signed from J1 on A14. Off A5199 at Creaton, A508 at Brixworth.* Tea. **Adm £5.50, chd £3. For NGS: Sun 19 Apr (2-5.30).** For other opening times and information, please phone or see garden website.
Award winning gardens by Geoffrey Jellicoe, Dame Sylvia Crowe, James Alexander Sinclair and more recently Arne Maynard. Formal gardens and terraces surround Queen Anne house with extensive vistas onto the lake and C18 parkland containing many mature trees. Wild and woodland gardens, which are exceptional in spring, a short distance from the formal areas. Partial wheelchair access as paths are grass, stone and gravel. Access map identifies best route.

Varied mix of gardens, developed by friendly and enthusiastic owners . . .

10 **◆ DEENE PARK**
Nr Corby, Deene NN17 3EW. The Trustees, 01780 450278, www.deenepark.com. *6m N of Corby. Off A43 between Stamford & Corby.* Light refreshments in Old Kitchen tearoom. **Adm £6, chd £3. For NGS: Sun 17 May (2-5).** For other opening times and information, please phone or see garden website.
Interesting garden set in beautiful parkland. Large parterre with topiary designed by David Hicks echoing the C16 decoration on the porch stonework, long mixed borders, old fashioned roses, Tudor courtyard and white garden. Lake and waterside walks with rare mature trees in natural garden. Wheelchair access available to main features of garden.

11 NEW **EAST HADDON HALL**
Main Street, East Haddon, Northampton NN6 8BU. Mr & Mrs John Beynon. *Located in the centre of the village near the church.* **Combined adm with Haddonstone Show Gardens £4, chd free.** Sat 4, Sun 5 July (11-5).
First opened for the NGS in 1928 and now restored by the present owners. 8 acres of parkland surrounding a Grade I listed Georgian house (not open) with extensive lawns, mature specimen trees and lovely views. More formal planting surrounds the house with many exuberantly planted containers.

12 **◆ EVENLEY WOOD GARDEN**
Evenley, Brackley NN13 5SH. Timothy Whiteley, 07776 307849, www.evenleywoodgarden.co.uk. *³/₄ m S of Brackley. Turn off at Evenley r'about on A43 & continue through village towards Mixbury before taking 1st L.* Light refreshments. **Adm £5, chd £1. For NGS: Sat 2 May (11-5).** For other opening times and information, please phone or see garden website.
This 60 acre woodland is a plantsman's garden with a huge variety of plants all of which are labelled. Mainly trees, shrubs, bulbs and lilies. Many magnolias, azaleas, rhododendrons and camellias. All paths are grass.

13 NEW **EVERDON HALL**
Little Everdon, Daventry NN11 3BG. Mrs Charles Coaker. *Leave M1 at J16 & take A45 toward Daventry. In Dodford turn L & after 1¹/₂ m turn R. Go uphill & before double bend turn R to Little Everdon. Everdon Hall at end of road.* **Evening Opening £15, Fri 12 June (5.30-8).** Enjoy a summer's evening with a glass of wine. Pre-booking essential. For tickets please phone 01483 211535 or visit www.ngs.org.uk.
Everdon Hall sits in a wonderful setting with surrounding parkland. It incl a walled garden filled with roses and a lavender parterre. Terraces, and formal borders, with rugosa roses and rhododendrons behind.

GROUP OPENING

14 FINEDON GARDENS
Finedon NN9 5JN. *2m NE of Wellingborough. 6m SE Kettering. All gardens individually signed from A6 & A510 junction.* Cream teas at 67-69 High Street. **Combined adm £3.50, chd free. Sun 7, Sun 28 June (2-6).**

67-69 HIGH STREET
Mary & Stuart Hendry
(See separate entry)

11 THRAPSTON ROAD
John & Gillian Ellson

NEW THE VICARAGE
Church Hill. Revds Richard and David Coles

All 3 gardens are very different with everything from vegetables to flowers on show. 67-69 High Street is an ever evolving ⅓ acre garden of a C17 cottage (not open) with mixed borders, many obelisks and containers. Planting for varied interest spring to autumn. 11 Thrapston Road is a ⅓ acre cottage garden with lawns and mixed borders, gravel and paved seating areas with planters and water features. Pergola, rose arches, summerhouse and treehouse. Mixed vegetable plot, and soft fruit and apple trees. Built in the 90's, The Vicarage garden has many shrubs, raised beds, sculpture and ornaments and delightful summerhouse. Large selection of home raised plants for sale at some locations (all proceeds to the NGS). Wheelchair accesss, although some gravel paths and grassed areas.

♿ 🐕 ☕

GROUP OPENING

15 FLORE GARDENS
Flore, Northampton NN7 4LQ. *7m W of Northampton on A45. 2m W of M1 J16.* Home-made teas in chapel school room (Apr), chapel school room & church, with light lunches in the chapel school room (June). **Combined adm £5, chd free. Share to All Saints Church & United Reform Church, Flore. Sun 12 Apr (2-6); Sat 20, Sun 21 June (11-6).**

24 BLISS LANE
John & Sally Miller

THE CROFT
John & Dorothy Boast

THE GARDEN HOUSE
Edward & Penny Aubrey-Fletcher.
Open June dates only

THE OLD BAKERY
John Amos & Karl Jones
Visitors also welcome by arrangement Apr to Aug for groups of 20-50.
01327 349080
yeolbakery@aol.com
www.johnnieamos.co.uk

PRIVATE GARDEN OF BLISS LANE NURSERY
Christine & Geoffrey Littlewood

ROCK SPRINGS
Tom Higginson & David Foster

RUSSELL HOUSE
Peter Pickering & Stephen George

Flore gardens have been open for many yrs as part of the Flore Flower Festival, and the partnership with the NGS started in 1992. Flore is an attractive village with views over the upper Nene valley. There is a C12 church and Victorian chapel which are also open in June with floral displays. We have a varied mix of gardens, developed by friendly and enthusiastic owners. Our gardens provide interest throughout the yr. There is a varied selection of garden structures, incl greenhouses, gazebos and summerhouses with seating providing opportunities to rest while enjoying the gardens. In spring there are early flowering perennials, interesting trees, shrubs, and bulbs in pots and border drifts. There is planting for all situations from shade to full sun. The June gardens incl formal and informal designs with lots of roses, clematis and many varieties of trees, shrubs, perennials, herbs, fruit and some vegetables. June gardens open in association with Flore Flower Festival. Partial wheelchair access to most gardens, some assistance may be required.

♿ 🐕 � ☕

16 FOXTAIL LILLY
41 South Road, Oundle PE8 4BP. Tracey Mathieson, 01832 274593, tracey@foxtail-lilly.co.uk, www.foxtail-lilly.co.uk. *1m town centre. From A605 at Barnwell Xrds take Barnwell Rd, 1st R to South Rd.* Home-made teas. **Adm £3.50, chd free. Sun 21 June (10.30-5.30).** Visitors also welcome by arrangement May to July for groups of 40 max.

A cottage garden where perennials and grasses are grouped creatively together amongst gravel paths, complementing one another to create a natural look. Some unusual plants and quirky oddities create a different and colourful informal garden. Lots of flowers for cutting, and a shop in the barn. New meadow pasture turned into new cutting garden.

🐕 🐕 🚗 ☕

17 FROGGERY COTTAGE
85 Breakleys Road, Desborough NN14 2PT. Mr John Lee. *6m N of Kettering. 5m S of Market Harborough. Signed off A6 & A14.* Light refreshments. **Combined adm with Hostellarie £3, chd free. Sun 26 July (11.30-5).** 1 acre plantsman's garden full of rare and unusual plants. NCCPG Collection of 435 varieties of penstemons incl dwarfs and species. Mediterranean and water gardens with large herbaceous borders. Artifacts on display incl old ploughs and garden implements. Workshops throughout the day.

♿ 🐕 🐕 🚗 NCH ☕

18 GLENDON HALL
Kettering NN14 1QE. Rosie Bose, 01536 711732, rosiebose@googlemail.com. *1½ m E of Rothwell. A6003 to Corby (A14 J7) W of Kettering, turn L onto Glendon Rd signed Rothwell, Desborough, Rushton. Entrance 1½ m on L past turn for Rushton.* **Adm £3, chd free.** Visitors welcome by arrangement Apr to Sept for groups of 25 max.
Mature specimen trees, topiary, box hedges, and herbaceous borders stocked with many unusual plants. Large walled kitchen gardens with

glasshouse, and a shaded area well stocked with ferns. Some gravel and slopes, but wheelchair access via longer route.

 ♿ ✿ 🚐 ☕

19 ▶ GOWER HOUSE
Guilsborough, Northampton NN6 8PY. Ann Moss, 01604 740755, cattimoss@aol.com. *Off High St by The Witch & Sow PH, through PH car park.* Visitors welcome by arrangement Apr to July for combined visit with Dripwell House only.
Although Gower House garden is small it is closely planted with specimen trees, shrubs, perennials, orchids, thyme lawn, wild flowers and alpines, some rare or unusual, with foliage colour being important. Several seating areas designed for elderly relatives incorporating recycled materials. Soft fruit and vegetable garden, shared with Dripwell, is an important part of our gardening. Very steep site unsuitable for those with mobility difficulties.
☕

GROUP OPENING

20 ▶ GREAT BRINGTON GARDENS
Nr Northampton NN7 4JJ. *7m NW of Northampton. Off A428 Rugby Rd. From Northampton, 1st L turn past main gates of Althorp. Free parking. Programmes & maps available at car park.* Tea at parish church with morning coffee & lunches in the reading room. Combined adm £3.50, chd free. Sun 3 May (11-5).

7 BEDFORD COTTAGES
Mrs Felicity Bellamy

FOLLY HOUSE
Sarah & Joe Sacarello

ROSE COTTAGE
David Green & Elaine MacKenzie

SUNDERLAND HOUSE
Mrs Margaret Rubython

Great Brington, named Best Small Village in Northamptonshire 2013/2014, is renowned for its warm welcome with dozens of parish volunteers helping on the day; manning the free car park and plant stall, serving lunches and teas, stewarding and providing information about the village and its gardens. A particularly picturesque, predominately stone and thatch village, Great Brington is well worth a visit in its own right. The C12 church, rated as one of Simon Jenkins' 1000 Best, has connections with the Spencers of Althorp and George Washington. Our open gardens provide immense variety; many of the gardens continue to evolve each yr, several have unique water features, and most are planned and maintained by their owners. Features incl a local history exhibition.

✿ ☕

21 ▶ GREYWALLS
Farndish NN29 7HJ. Mrs P M Anderson, 01933 353495, greywalls@dbshoes.co.uk. *2½ m SE of Wellingborough. A609 from Wellingborough, B570 to Irchester, turn to Farndish by cenotaph. House adjacent to church.* Light refreshments. Adm £3, chd free. Sun 1 Mar (12-4). Visitors also welcome by arrangement, coaches welcome.
2 acre mature garden surrounding old vicarage (not open). Over 100 varieties of snowdrops, drifts of hardy cyclamen and hellebores. Alpine house and raised alpine beds. Water features and natural ponds with views over open countryside. Rare breed hens.

♿ ✿ 🚐 ☕

GROUP OPENING

22 ▶ GUILSBOROUGH GARDENS
Guilsborough NN6 8PT. *10m NW of Northampton. 10m E of Rugby. Between A5199 & A428. J1 off A14. Car parking in field on Hollowell Rd out of Guilsborough. Information & maps from village hall, next to primary school.* Home-made teas in the village hall. Combined adm £5, chd free. Sat 9, Sun 10 May (2-6).

DRIPWELL HOUSE
Mr J W Langfield & Dr C Moss
Visitors also welcome by arrangement Apr to July for combined visit with Gower House.
01604 740140
cattimoss@aol.com

FOUR ACRES
Mark & Gay Webster
Visitors also welcome by arrangement Apr to Aug for groups of 10+.
01604 740203
gay.webster6@gmail.com

THE GATE HOUSE
Mike & Sarah Edwards

GUILSBOROUGH HOUSE
Mr & Mrs John McCall

NEW **LINDEN HOUSE**
Mr & Mrs Dave Wooldridge

OAK DENE
Mr & Mrs R A Darker

THE OLD HOUSE
Richard & Libby Seaton Evans

THE OLD VICARAGE
John & Christine Benbow

Eight varied village gardens in an attractive rural setting. Three small cottage style gardens, one belonging to a keen flower arranger, one a secret walled garden crammed with fruit, flowers and vegetables and the other surrounding a recently built house. The remaining gardens are larger, ranging from a magical woodland garden on a very steep site to formal gardens with sweeping lawns, mature trees and beautiful views. There is plenty of room to sit and relax. Walled kitchen gardens and a potager are an important part of our gardening. Plants for sale incl both the rare and unusual from our plantsmen's gardens, a true highlight here. Dripwell House, has opened for the NGS since 1986, originally an individual garden. There is thus a lot to see and visitors find that they need the whole afternoon. Wheelchair access at Four Acres, Guilsborough House, Oak Dene, The Old House & The Old Vicarage only. Dogs not permitted at every garden.

♿ ✿ ☕

Conservation planting and efforts to improve wildlife habitats . . .

23 ◆ HADDONSTONE SHOW GARDENS
The Forge House, Church Lane, East Haddon, Northampton NN6 8DB. Haddonstone Ltd, 01604 770711, www.haddonstone.com. *7m NW of Northampton. Brown tourism signs from A428. Located in centre of village near church, opp school*. Home-made teas. **Combined adm with East Haddon Hall £4, chd free. For NGS: Sat 4, Sun 5 July (11-5). For other opening times and information, please phone or see garden website.**
See Haddonstone's classic garden ornaments in the beautiful setting of the walled Manor gardens incl planters, fountains, statues, bird baths, sundials, balustrades and follies. Garden is on different levels with roses, clematis, climbers, herbaceous borders, ornamental flowers, topiary, specimen shrubs and trees. Latest additions incl a new reception, contemporary garden and statue walk. The gardens incorporate plantings used at the company's acclaimed Chelsea Flower Show exhibits. Wheelchair access to all areas of main garden from new reception area.

GROUP OPENING

24 HARPOLE GARDENS
Harpole NN7 4BX. *On A45 4m W of Northampton towards Weedon. Turn R at The Turnpike Hotel into Harpole. Village maps given to all visitors.* Home-made teas at The Close. **Combined adm £5.00, chd free. Sun 7 June (1-6).**

BRYTTEN-COLLIER HOUSE
James & Lucy Strickland

THE CLOSE
Michael Orton-Jones
Visitors also welcome by arrangement.
01604 830332
michael@orton-jones.com

19 MANOR CLOSE
Caroline & Andy Kemshed
Visitors also welcome by arrangement in June.
01604 830512
carolinekemshed@live.co.uk

THE MANOR HOUSE
Mrs Katy Smith

THE OLD DAIRY
David & Di Ballard

Attractive Northamptonshire village well known for its annual scarecrow festival (2nd weekend in Sept). Enjoy a lovely farmhouse garden with an acre of lawn, mixed borders, mature trees, views overlooking the farm and strawberry field. Visit a partly walled s-facing garden with wonderful herbaceous borders, many climbing roses and clematis and a beautiful treehouse. See a sheltered cottage garden with clematis, roses and luxuriant planting. View a smaller garden (40x10yd) belonging to a more recently constructed house. This is a flower arranger's garden of interesting design with water features and mixed borders. Come and see a former walled vegetable garden enhanced into a family garden in the last 6 yrs. Take tea in an old fashioned country garden with large lawn, herbaceous borders and mature trees. An interesting and varied afternoon is guaranteed with a warm welcome to all. Wheelchair access at Brytten-Collier House, The Close & The Old Dairy only.

Water features and natural ponds with views over open countryside . . .

25 67-69 HIGH STREET
Finedon. NN9 5JN. Mary & Stuart Hendry, 01933 680414, stuart.hendryarcht@gmail.com. *6m SE Kettering. Garden signed from A6 & A510 junction.* Adm incl soup & a roll (Mar), wine & nibbles (June). **Adm £3.50, chd free. Sun 8 Mar (11-3). Evening Openings Thur 4, Thur 11, Thur 18, Thur 25 June (5-8.30). Visitors also welcome by arrangement Feb to Sept.**
Constantly evolving ⅓ acre rear garden of C17 cottage (not open). Mixed borders, many obelisks and containers, kitchen garden and herb bed, and rope border. Spring garden with snowdrops and hellebores, summer and autumn borders all giving varied interest from Feb through to Oct. Features incl plant

surgery by local expert (June only), bring along your plants or questions. Home raised plants for sale. Featured in The Daily Telegraph Saturday Gardening supplement (March 2014). Most areas accessible via hard paved paths, with some gravel paths and grass.

26 ◆ HOLDENBY HOUSE GARDENS
Northampton NN6 8DJ. Mr & Mrs James Lowther, 01604 770074, www.holdenby.com. *6m NW of Northampton. From A5199 or A428 between East Haddon & Spratton. Follow brown tourist signs.* Tea. **Adm £5, chd £3.50. For NGS: Sun 2 Aug (1-5). For other opening times and information, please phone or see garden website.**
The 20 acre Grade I listed garden set in stately lawns and hedges and has several special features. Away from the formal gardens lie the terraces of the Elizabethan rose garden, one of the best preserved examples of their kind. There is also a delightful walled kitchen garden with the original Victorian greenhouse. The estate incl gravel paths.

GROUP OPENING

27 HOLLOWELL GARDENS
Hollowell NN6 8RR. *8m N of Northampton. ½ m off A5199, turn off at Creaton. Roads are narrow & twisting, so please use car park, which is clearly signed.* Light refreshments at village hall. **Combined adm £4, chd free. Sun 9 Aug (11-6).**

HILLVIEW
Jan & Crawford Craig

IVY COTTAGE
Rev John & Mrs Wendy Evans

ROSEMOUNT
Mr & Mrs J Leatherland
(See separate entry)

Three contrasting gardens with plenty of interest. Rosemount is a plantsman's garden, developed over 50 yrs. The owners propagate their favourite plants, many of which are for sale. Ivy Cottage is a haven for wildlife with relaxed planting, a stream, orchard and vegetable area. Hillview is a traditional country garden on three levels, dating from the 1930s, with colourful, informal

planting. No wheelchair access at Hillview, partial access at remaining two gardens. Steep hills.

♿ ⚘ ♨

28 HOSTELLARIE

78 Breakleys Road, Desborough NN14 2PT. Stella & Stan Freeman. *6m N of Kettering. 5m S of Market Harborough. From church & war memorial turn R into Dunkirk Ave, then 3rd R. From cemetery L into Dunkirk Ave then 4th L.* Light refreshments at Froggery Cottage. **Combined adm with Froggery Cottage £3, chd free. Sun 26 July (11.30-5).**
Over 180ft long town garden. Divided into rooms of different character; courtyard garden with a sculptural clematis providing shade, colour themed flower beds, ponds and water features, cottage gardens and gravel borders, clematis and roses, all linked by lawns and gravel paths. The growing collection of hostas, with over 50 plants, are taking up more space each yr, and are the pride of the garden.

⚘ ♨

29 JERICHO

42 Market Place, Oundle PE8 4AJ. Stephen & Pepita Aris, 01832 275416, stephenaris@btinternet.com. *East Jericho. From the Jericho cul-de-sac at the E end of the market place, go through red door to the R of the shop, through passage, down yard to garden.* Tea. **Adm £3, chd free. Sun 22 Feb (12-4); Sun 17 May (12-5); Sun 28 Feb 2016 (12-4). Visitors also welcome by arrangement May to July for individuals and groups.**
Inspired by Vita Sackville-West 60 yrs ago, the 100 metre, s-facing, walled garden is divided into a series of secret spaces. The house is clothed in wisteria, clematis and roses. A plant led garden with massive hornbeam hedge, clipped box and lavender. Over 50 labelled species roses, a chamomile lawn, plus a hot border. Snowdrops, crocus and hellebore in early spring. Full-page feature in Peterborough Evening Telegraph.

⚘ ♨

30 ♦ KELMARSH HALL

Main Road, Kelmarsh, Northampton NN6 9LY. The Kelmarsh Trust, 01604 686543, www.kelmarsh.com. *From A14, exit at J2 & head N towards Market Harborough. Kelmarsh Hall is at Xrds. From A508 the hall is 5m S of Market Harborough & 11m N of Northampton.* Tea. **Adm £5.50, chd £3.50. For NGS: Wed 20 May (11-5). For other opening times and information, please phone or see garden website.**
Kelmarsh Hall is an C18 country house, set in gardens inspired by society decorator Nancy Lancaster and surrounded by woodland and an estate of rolling Northamptonshire countryside. Hidden gems incl a newly renovated orangery, double border, sunken garden, a 30 metre long border, rose garden and at the heart of it all an historic walled kitchen garden. Highlights incl our fritillaries, tulips, rare peonies, roses, cottage garden perennials and sweet peas. Visit late summer to see our rare dahlia collection. Disabled parking is available close to the Visitor Centre entrance. Blue badges must be displayed and please advise staff on arrival.

♿ 💮 ⚘ 🚌 ♨

GROUP OPENING

31 KILSBY GARDENS

Kilsby Village CV23 8XP. *5m SE of Rugby. 6m N of Daventry on A361. The road through village is the* B4038. Home-made teas at Kilsby Village Hall. **Combined adm £4, chd free. Sun 14 June (1-5).**

NEW BOLBERRY HOUSE
Mr & Mrs Richard Linnell

NEW PYTCHLEY GARDENS
Kathy Jenkins & Neighbours

PYTCHLEY HOUSE
Mr & Mrs T F Clay
Visitors also welcome by arrangement May to July.
01788 822373
the.clays@tiscali.co.uk

RAINBOW'S END
Mr & Mrs J Madigan

12 RUGBY ROAD
Mr & Mrs T Hindle

NEW THE THATCHED HOUSE
Mr & Mrs Tony Ward

Kilsby is a stone and brick village with historic interest, home of St Faith's Church dating from the C12. The village was the site of one of the first skirmishes of the Civil War in 1642 and also gave its name to Stephenson's nearby lengthy rail tunnel built in the 1830s. Six attractive gardens will be open this yr, all within easy walking distance. Do please come and see us.

♿ ⚘ ♨

Versions Farm, Turweston Gardens

The owners
propagate
their favourite
plants, many
of which
are for sale . . .

GROUP OPENING

32 LONG BUCKBY GARDENS
Northampton NN6 7RE. *8m NW of
Northampton, midway between A428
& A5. Maps will be available at each
garden. Mill House at junction of
A428 & Long Lane is 1m away with
plenty of parking. WC & parking
available in the village square.* Home-
made teas in community centre.
Combined adm £5, chd free.
Sun 5 July (1.30-5.30).

ASHMORE HOUSE
Mike Greaves & Sally Sokoloff

NEW 3 COTTON END
Mr & Mrs Roland & Georgina
Wells

NEW LIBRARY GARDEN

MILL HOUSE, LONG LANE
Ken & Gill Pawson
Visitors also welcome by
arrangement June to Aug for
groups of 40 max.
gillandken@pawsons.co.uk

NEW 4 SKINYARD LANE
Susie & William Mitchell

NEW 15 SYERS GREEN
CLOSE
Shona Mcnamee

NEW 16 SYERS GREEN
CLOSE
Bobbie & Christine Lamb

TORESTIN
June Ford

Eight village gardens, with a variety of
layout and planting. Selection of
water features, pergolas and other
garden structures. Variety of planting,
incl annuals, herbaceous and shrubs.
One large garden in the countryside,
with large fruit and vegetable plot,
wildlife areas, orchard, borders,
wooded area, wild flower plot and
pond, with foundations of East
Haddon windmill; owner is a Heritage
Seed Guardian.

33 THE MALTINGS
10 The Green, Clipston, Market
Harborough LE16 9RS. Mrs
Hamish Connell & Mr William
Connell, 01858 525336. *4m S of
Market Harborough, 9m W of
Kettering, 10m N of Northampton.
From A14 take J2, A508 N. After 2m
turn L for Clipston.* Home-made teas.
Adm £3, chd free. Sat 4 Apr
(2-5.30); Sun 5, Mon 6 Apr
(11-5.30). Visitors also welcome by
arrangement Apr to May for groups
of 10+.
We have raised £22,700 for the NGS
charities over the 9 yrs we have been
open. We are now moving house, so
this will be your last chance to visit
our ³/₄ acre sloping plantsman's
garden. Many unusual plants, shrubs,
old and new trees. Over 60 different
clematis, wild garden walk, spring
bulb area, over 30 different species
roses, and 2 ponds connected by a
stream. Features incl home-made
cake stall, and a swing and slide for
children. Partial wheelchair access
due to gravel drive, some narrow
paths, and some steps.

34 THE MENAGERIE
Newport Pagnell Road, Horton
NN7 2BX. Hugues Decobert. *6m S
of Northampton. 1m S of Horton. On
B526, turn E at lay-by, across field.*
Tea. Adm £6, chd free. Sun 13 Sept
(2-5.30). Enjoy an exclusive
evening visit with a glass of wine
on Sat 27 June (5.30-8). Adm £20.
Pre-booking essential. For tickets
please phone 01483 211535 or visit
www.ngs.org.uk.
Stunning garden set around C18 folly,
with 2 delightful thatched arbours.
Large formal walled garden with
fountain, used for vegetables, fruit
and cutting flowers. Recently
extended exotic bog garden and
native wetland area. Also rose
garden, shrubberies, herbaceous
borders and wild flower areas.

35 NEW NASEBY LODGE
Naseby, Northampton NN6 6BX.
Mr David Dollar. *Take Thornby Rd in
Thornby by Red Lion PH, garden 1m
on RH-side; or from Naseby take
Thornby Rd, then ¹/₂ m on LH-side.
SatNav Thornby. TomTom works
using postcode.* Tea. Adm £4, chd
free. Sun 26 Apr (2.30-5.30).
Easy going over lots of lawn with ha-
ha and magnificent views over short,
medium and long distances.
Established 6 yrs ago, when the old
house was demolished and current
house was built. Many young trees, a
pretty pond and lake. Good for both
the energetic and less energetic
visitor. No dogs, please.

36 NEW THE OLD BLACK HORSE
Main Street, Tansor, Peterborough
PE8 5HS. Mrs Pamela Metcalf,
01832 226302,
pamelametcalf@sky.com. *2m N of
Oundle off A605 towards
Peterborough, take L turn signed
Glapthorn & Cotterstock. Follow signs
to Tansor, turn R at Xrds signed Main
St. Parking on roadside.* Home-made
teas at Tansor Village Hall. Adm
£3.50, chd free. Sun 14 June (1-5).
Visitors also welcome by
arrangement Mar to Aug for groups
of 10+.
A cottage garden with mature trees,
lawns and mixed borders. Both full
sun and shady areas planted to give
a natural look. Spring bulbs, flowering
shrubs with colour going through the
summer season. Roses climb and
ramble over house, barn, arches,
trees and arbours. Productive
vegetable potager with greenhouse.
New wild meadow with views across
fields to Oundle.

37 34 POPLARS FARM ROAD
Barton Seagrave, Kettering
NN15 5AG. Revd Dr & Mrs J Smith,
01536 513786. *1¹/₂ m SE of
Kettering. J10 off A14 onto Barton Rd
(A6) towards Wicksteed Park &
Kettering. Turn R onto Warkton Lane,
then R into Poplars Farm Rd.* Tea.
Adm £3, chd free. Sun 14 June
(2-5). Visitors also welcome by
arrangement May to July.
A 1 acre garden divided by archways,
numerous mixed borders and beds
created from a large lawn 15 yrs ago.
A parterre planted with shrubs, herbs,
hostas and perennials leads to an
arch of roses and apple trees. There

is a profusion of anthemis, helenium, hostas, agapanthus and silver birch. A long hazel arch leads to a small meadow planted with specimen trees overlooking open countryside. The garden contains some gravel pathways.

♿ 🚻 ☕

Visit a garden and support hospice care

GROUP OPENING

38 PRESTON CAPES AND LITTLE PRESTON GARDENS

Little Preston, Daventry NN11 3TF. *6m SW of Daventry. 13m NE of Banbury. 3m N of Canons Ashby. Parking for Little Preston at Old West Farm, follow signs. For Preston Capes parking off High St. Very limited disabled parking at The Manor House & by church, blue badge holders only.* Home-made teas at Old West Farm. Lunch served from 12-2. **Combined adm £5, chd free.** Sun 7 June (12-5).

CITY COTTAGE
Mrs Gavin Cowen.
Off High St, Church Way. Garden behind letter box

LADYCROFT
Mervyn & Sophia Maddison

NEW THE MANOR
High Street. Mr Graham Stanton

NORTH FARM
Mr & Mrs Tim Coleridge.
³/₄ m E of Preston Capes

THE OLD RECTORY
Church Way. Luke & Victoria Bridgeman

OLD WEST FARM
Mr & Mrs Gerard Hoare.
³/₄ m E of Preston Capes on road to Maidford

VILLAGE FARM
High Street. Trevor & Julia Clarke

A selection of differing gardens in the beautiful unspoilt south Northamptonshire ironstone villages, most with a backdrop of fantastic views of the surrounding countryside. Gardens range from small contemporary, through to classical country style with old fashioned roses and borders, to large gardens with woodland walks and ponds. Features incl local sandstone houses and cottages, Norman church and wonderful views. Partial wheelchair access to some parts of the gardens.

♿ ❀ ☕

GROUP OPENING

39 RAVENSTHORPE GARDENS

Ravensthorpe NN6 8ES. *7m NW of Northampton. Signed from A428. Mill House immed R as you turn off A428 down Long Lane. 1m from village.* Home-made teas at village hall. **Combined adm £5, chd free.** Sun 12 July (1.30-5.30).

5 CHURCH GARDENS
Mr & Mrs Glynn Lewis.
Off the village green, L past the churchyard & next to the footpath to the allotments

MILL HOUSE
Ken & Gill Pawson
Visitors also welcome by arrangement June to Aug for groups of 40 max.
01604 770103
gillandken@pawsons.co.uk

2 THE ORCHARDS
Chris & Tricia Freeman.
A small close off Guilsborough Rd

RAVENSTHORPE NURSERY
Mr & Mrs Richard Wiseman
Visitors also welcome by arrangement.
01604 770548
ravensthorpenursery@hotmail.com

NEW WIGLEY COTTAGE
Mr & Mrs Dennis Patrick.
At the end of Bettycroft Close

Attractive village in Northamptonshire uplands near to Ravensthorpe reservoir and Top Ardles Wood Woodland Trust which have bird watching and picnic opportunities. Five established and developing gardens set in beautiful countryside displaying a wide range of plants, many of which are available from the Nursery. Offering inspirational planting, quiet contemplation, beautiful views, water features,

gardens encouraging wildlife, fruit and vegetable garden owned by a Heritage Seed Library Guardian, and flower arranger's garden. Two of the gardens have beehives and it is hoped that a representative from Northamptonshire Beekeepers' Association will be on hand to give information on beekeeping to visitors. Access to one of the gardens is via the village allotments, which incl a small vineyard. Partial wheelchair access to 2 The Orchards & Wigley Cottage.

♿ 🚻 ❀ ☕

40 ROSEARIE-DE-LA-NYMPH

55 The Grove, Moulton, Northampton NN3 7UE. Peter Hughes, Mary Morris, Irene Kay & Jeremy Stanton. *N of Northampton town. Turn off A43 at small r'about to Overstone Rd. Follow NGS signs in village. The garden is on the Holcot Rd out of Moulton.* **Adm £4, chd free.** Sun 19, Sun 26 July (11-5). We have been developing this garden for about 10 yrs and now have over 1000 roses, incl English, French and Italian varieties. Many unusual water features and specimen trees. Roses, scramblers and ramblers, climb into trees, over arbours and arches. We have tried to time our open days to cover the peak flowering period. Collection of Japanese maples. Mostly flat, but there are two standard width doorways to negotiate.

♿ 🚻 🚐

41 ROSEMOUNT

18 Church Hill, Hollowell NN6 8RR. Mr & Mrs J Leatherland, 01604 740354. *10m NW of Northampton, 5m S J1 A14. Between A5199 & A428. Parking at village hall.* Light refreshments at village hall. **Adm £3, chd free.** Sun 22 Feb (11-3). The Leatherlands have been developing this ¹/₂ acre garden for over 50 yrs. Both are keen and knowledgeable plantspeople, who love collecting and propagating favourite plants, many of which are for sale. February opening features their collection of over 200 different snowdrops, hellebores and unusual spring bulbs. In August the garden is full of colour and interest with unusual shrubs, herbaceous and clematis. Partial wheelchair access.

♿ ❀ ☕

1000 roses,
including English,
French and Italian
varieties . . .

GROUP OPENING

42 SPRATTON GARDENS
Spratton NN6 8HL. *6½ m NNW of
Northampton. From A5199 turn W at
Holdenby Rd for Spratton Grange
Farm. Others turn E at Brixworth Rd.
Car park in village with close access
to 1st garden.* Light refreshments at
St Andrew's Church. **Combined adm
£5, chd free. Sun 24 May (11-5).**

    DALE HOUSE 🔗
    Fiona & Chris Cox
    01604 846458
    fionacox19@aol.com

    11 HIGH STREET
    Philip & Frances Roseblade

    MULBERRY COTTAGE
    Michael & Morley Heaton

    SPRATTON GRANGE FARM
    Dennis & Christine Yardy

    THE STABLES
    Pam & Tony Woods

    WALTHAM COTTAGE
    Norma & Allan Simons

The last chance to enjoy this popular
event, as several of the garden
owners wish to retire after many yrs
of opening for the NGS. The old part
of this picturesque village has many
late C17 stone built houses and turn
of the C19/20 brick built ones. These
line the route between the five inner
village gardens, which are of a very
varied nature. One has a natural
stream and pond, one has a 300 yr
old Holm (evergreen) oak. Three
gardens are cottage style. Many
interesting shrubs with good use of
foliage colour. Three gardens show
how much can be made of a small
area. Several gardens have fine views
over rolling agricultural countryside.
The garden outside the village centre
was created from a farm and at 2
acres is the largest. Natural pond,
bog garden and beautiful courtyard

where once cows stood. One of the
gardens will be hosting a large plant
sale at bargain prices. Attractive
village with C12 Grade I Norman
church which is a very fine example
with many interior features, which can
be admired whilst enjoying some light
refreshments.

  ♿ 🔗 ⊕ ☕

43 ◆ STEANE PARK

Brackley NN13 6DP. Lady Connell,
01280 705899,
www.steanepark.co.uk. *2m from
Brackley towards Banbury. On A422,
6m E of Banbury.* Cream teas. **Adm
£4.50, chd free. For NGS: Sun 19
July (11-5). For other opening
times and information, please
phone or see garden website.**
The garden was in an extremely
dilapidated and overgrown state; over
the past 24 yrs we have tried to
recapture its original glory. There are
beautiful trees in 80 acres of
parkland, old waterway and
fishponds, 1620 church in grounds.
The gardens are constantly being
updated in sympathy with old stone
house and church. Amongst many
features and attractions there is the
The Monet Bridge, built by a
craftsman from Suffolk. It was
delivered in several pieces and
constructed on-site with the aid of a
lot of ropes, getting wet and crossed
fingers, but the end result looks
magnificent! Partial wheelchair
access.

  ♿ ⊕ ☕

GROUP OPENING

**44 NEW STOKE DOYLE
GARDENS**
Stoke Road, Stoke Doyle, Oundle
PE8 5TN. *In village of Stoke Doyle
2m SW of Oundle, nr Peterborough.
It can be reached from the N via
A605 from A1 & Peterborough, or
from the S from Thrapston via A605
turning off towards Lilford & Pilton.*
Home-made teas in St Rumbald
Church. **Combined adm £4, chd
free. Sun 2 Aug (12-5).**

    NEW THE FORGE
    Mrs Jenny Carter

    NEW OUNDLE LODGE
    Mrs Dawn Gent.
    *On Stoke Doyle Rd, take 2nd R
    after cemetery signed Oundle
    Lodge. Garden is at top of track
    on RH-side*

    **NEW ST RUMBALD
    CHURCH**
    Church Lane. Mrs Liz Doherty

    NEW SEVEN WELLS FARM
    Mrs Sally Knight

4 very different gardens and a
conservation churchyard in a village
setting. Oundle Lodge, has a series of
garden rooms, each with a different
feel, incorporating the super views
into the design and full of lovely plants
to enjoy. The larger garden at Seven
Wells Farm is a relatively recent
project and incl a vegetable plot.
Interesting planting schemes and
large agricultural trough containers.
The Forge, a smaller garden is more
mature and shows what can be
done with relatively little space!
Churchyard has won many awards
over the yrs for its conservation
planting and efforts to improve wildlife
habitats.

  ♿ ☕

45 67 STRATFIELD WAY

Kettering NN15 6GS. Mrs Paula
Mantle. *5 mins off A14 (J9) Kettering.
Leave J9 & turn off r'about at Park
Hotel & continue along the road, next
L, straight over r'about, next R, follow
signs.* Light refreshments. **Adm £3,
chd free. Sun 9 Aug (2-6).**
After an accident in 2010 that left me
injured, my garden became my
soulmate. This is a pretty garden with
structure and softness, work has
been done at a recovering pace with
bursts of energy and colour alongside
gentler combinations of delicate
willowy flowers. From a 3 metre fatsia
to dainty alpines, climbing hydrangea,
wisteria, bold dahlias, geraniums,
crocosmia, fuscia, alliums, hosta, and
maples. Featured in Amateur
Gardening magazine (Oct 2014).

  ♿ ☕

46 SULBY GARDENS

Sulby, Northampton NN6 6EZ.
Mrs Alison Lowe, 01858 880573,
ecolowe@btinternet.com. *16m NW
of Northampton, 2m NE of Welford
off A5199. Past Wharf House Hotel
take 1st R, signed Sulby. After R & L
bends, turn R at sign for Sulby Hall
Farm. Turn R at junction, garden is
1st L. Parking limited, no vans or
buses please.* Home-made teas.
**Adm £4, chd free. Thurs 23 Apr, 25
June, 20 Aug (2-5.30); 8 Oct (2-5);
12 Nov (1-4). Visitors also welcome
by arrangement for groups of 10-
30.**

Unusual property covering 12 acres comprising working Victorian kitchen garden, orchard, and C19 icehouse, plus nature reserve incl woodland, ponds, stream and wild flower meadows. Features incl April: snakeshead fritillaries, cowslips, and bluebells. June: wild flower meadows in full bloom. Aug: butterflies, dragonflies, aquatic plants. Oct: Apple Day, examples of apple varieties with information and new season's apple juice for sale. Nov: autumn colour and tree architecture. NB: Children welcome but under strict supervision because of deep water.

☕

GROUP OPENING

47 SULGRAVE GARDENS
Banbury OX17 2RP. *8m NE of Banbury. Just off B4525 Banbury to Northampton road, 7m from J11 off M40. Car parking at Church Hall.* Home-made teas at Church Cottage, Church St. **Combined adm £5, chd free. Sun 31 May (2-6).**

> **NEW THE COTTAGE**
> George & Jo Ann Jenkins

> **NEW EAGLE HOUSE**
> Sue & Andrew Dixon.
> *On corner of Little St & Helmdon Rd*

> **FERNS**
> George & Julia Metcalfe

> **THE HERB SOCIETY GARDEN AT SULGRAVE MANOR**
> The Herb Society

> **RECTORY FARM**
> Charles & Joanna Smyth-Osbourne

> **◆ SULGRAVE MANOR**
> The Sulgrave Manor Trust

> **THREEWAYS**
> Alison & Digby Lewis

Sulgrave is a small historic village having recently celebrated its strong American connections in 2014 as part of the 150 yrs of the signing of the Treaty of Ghent. An award winning community owned and run village shop which will be open. Seven gardens opening, two are new; Eagle House, a walled garden, which has been recently extensively replanted and The Cottage, a compact garden on two levels with strong architectural features. Ferns is

a plantsman's garden, Threeways, a small walled cottage garden with some vegetables grown in containers. Rectory Farm has lovely views, a rill and well, and planted arbours. The well established Manor garden planted by Sir Reginald Blomfield in the 1920s and the adjoining National Herb Garden featuring the herbs that could have been taken to America with the Washington family and others that have been introduced from America.

❀ ☕

---

48 TITCHMARSH HOUSE
Chapel Street, Titchmarsh NN14 3DA. Sir Ewan & Lady Harper, 01832 732439, jennifer.harper3@virginmedia.com. *2m N of Thrapston. 6m S of Oundle. Exit A14 at junction signed A605, Titchmarsh signed as turning to E.* Tea at community shop (May) & village fete (June). **Adm £3, chd free. Sun 17 May (2-6); Sat 13 June (12-5). Visitors also welcome by arrangement Apr to June.**
4½ acres extended and laid out since 1972. Cherries, magnolias, herbaceous, irises, shrub roses, range of unusual shrubs, walled borders and ornamental vegetable garden. Most of the garden can be visited without using steps.

♿ ☕

GROUP OPENING

49 TURWESTON GARDENS
Brackley NN13 5JY. *2m E of Brackley. A43 from M40 J10. On Brackley bypass turn R on A422 towards Buckingham, ½ m turn L signed Turweston.* Tea at Versions Farm. **Combined adm £4, chd free. Sun 28 June (2-5.30).**

> **TURWESTON MILL**
> Mr Harry Leventis

> **VERSIONS FARM**
> Mrs E T Smyth-Osbourne

Charming unspoilt stone built village in a conservation area. 2 quite large beautiful gardens. The Mill with bridges over the millstream and a spectacular waterfall, wildlife pond and newly designed kitchen garden. A 3 acre plantsman's garden with old stonewalls, terraces, pond and small water garden.

♿ ❀ ☕

GROUP OPENING

50 WEEDON LOIS & WESTON GARDENS
Weedon Lois, Towcester NN12 8PJ. Sir John & Lady Greenaway. *7m W of Towcester. 7m N of Brackley. Old Barn & Hillside are on High St, Weedon Lois. Home Close, Kettle End is just off High St & Ridgeway Cottage is on Weston High St.* Cream teas at Weston Community Centre. **Combined adm £5, chd free. Sun 24 May (2-5.30).**

> **HILLSIDE**
> Mrs Karen Wilcox

> **HOME CLOSE**
> Clyde Burbidge

> **LOIS WEEDON HOUSE**
> Sir John & Lady Greenaway

> **OLD BARN**
> Mr & Mrs John Gregory

> **RIDGEWAY COTTAGE**
> Jonathan & Elizabeth Carpenter

Two adjacent villages in south Northamptonshire with a handsome Medieval church in Weedon Lois. The extension churchyard contains the graves of the poets Dame Edith Sitwell and her brother Sir Sacheverel Sitwell who lived in Weston Hall. There are five gardens in Weedon Lois comprising a large garden with terracing, large borders and outstanding views, a plantsman's garden, an award-winning garden and a garden with lovely stone terracing. In Weston there is a charming cottage garden and teas being provided in the community centre.

♿ 🚐 ☕

Nottinghamshire

Nottinghamshire is best known as Robin Hood country. His legend persists and his haunt of Sherwood Forest, now a nature reserve, contains some of the oldest oaks in Europe. The Major Oak, thought to be 800 years old, still produces acorns.

Civil War battles raged throughout Nottinghamshire, and Newark's historic castle bears the scars. King Charles I surrendered to the Scots in nearby Southwell, after a night at The Saracen's Head, which is still an inn today.

The Dukeries in the north of the county provide an unmatched landscape of lakes, parks and woods, so called because four dukes lived there, and their estates were contiguous. The dukes are gone, but their estates at Clumber, Thoresby and Welbeck continue to offer a pre-industrial haven in a thickly populated county.

Oaks in Sherwood, apples in Southwell (where the original Bramley tree still stands) and 100 kinds of rhubarb in the ducal kitchen garden at Clumber Park – they await your visit.

Nottinghamshire Volunteers

County Organiser
Georgina Denison
01636 821385
campden27@aol.com

County Treasurers
Rowan & Janet McFerran
01636 636921
rowan.mcferran@gmail.com
janet.mcferran@gmail.com

Publicity
Richard & Ronnie Ogier
01159 116786
ronnie.ogier@ntlworld.com
ned.ogier@ntlworld.com

Booklet Coordinator
Dave Darwent
01142 665881
dave@poptasticdave.co.uk

Assistant County Organisers
Joan Arnold
01159 653789
trebleclef.arnold@btinternet.com

Judy Geldart
01636 823832
judygeldart@gmail.com

Beverley Perks
01636 812181
perks.family@talk21.com

Mary Thomas
01509 672056
admet123@btinternet.com

Left: Capability Barn

Currently the NGS donates around £2.5 million every year

Opening Dates

All entries subject to change.
For latest information check www.ngs.org.uk

February

Sunday 15
3 The Beeches

Wednesday 18
3 The Beeches

March

Sunday 22
3 The Beeches

April

Sunday 12
7 Capability Barn

Sunday 19
15 Felley Priory

Sunday 26
3 The Beeches
7 Capability Barn
44 Sycamores House

May

Sunday 3
32 Oxton Village Gardens

Monday 4
10 7 Collygate

Sunday 10
11 Cross Lodge
12 Dumbleside
16 Floral Media
27 NEW 6 Moor Lane
28 NEW 10 Moor Lane

Sunday 17
19 Gringley Gardens
30 Norwell Nurseries
35 NEW Patchings Art Centre
51 Woodpeckers

Sunday 24
33 Papplewick Hall
35 NEW Patchings Art Centre

Monday 25
22 Holbeck Lodge
23 Holmes Villa
31 The Old Vicarage

Sunday 31
25 Home Farm House, 17 Main Street
41 NEW Rose Cottage
47 West Farm and Church House Gardens

June

Festival Weekend

Sunday 7
20 NEW Halam Gardens and Wildflower Meadow

Sunday 14
4 Bishops Cottage
27 NEW 6 Moor Lane
28 NEW 10 Moor Lane
38 The Poplars
50 Woodbine Farmhouse

Sunday 21
1 Askham Gardens
2 NEW Beckingham Gardens
10 7 Collygate
18 The Glade
48 6 Weston Close

Sunday 28
29 Norwell Gardens

July

Wednesday 1
29 Norwell Gardens (Evening)

Sunday 5
9 NEW The Coach House

31 The Old Vicarage
36 48 Penarth Gardens

Wednesday 8
39 NEW Rhubarb Farm

Saturday 11
8 Clumber Park Walled Kitchen Garden

Sunday 12
45 Thrumpton Hall
48 6 Weston Close

Sunday 19
34 Park Farm
49 White House

Wednesday 22
36 48 Penarth Gardens (Evening)

Sunday 26
14 The Elms
37 Piecemeal

August

Sunday 2
37 Piecemeal

Sunday 9
17 The Forge
42 Squirrel Lodge

Sunday 16
5 Broadlea
24 The Holocaust Centre
46 University of Nottingham Gardens

Sunday 23
24 The Holocaust Centre
31 The Old Vicarage

Sunday 30
6 5 Burton Lane

September

Sunday 6
26 Lodge Mount

Sunday 20
40 Riseholme, 125 Shelford Road

October

Sunday 11
30 Norwell Nurseries

Gardens open to the public

8 Clumber Park Walled Kitchen Garden
15 Felley Priory
21 Hodsock Priory Gardens
30 Norwell Nurseries

Thrumpton Hall

Visit a garden on National Gardens Festival Weekend 6 & 7 June

A peaceful backwater in an urban setting . . .

The Gardens

GROUP OPENING

1 ASKHAM GARDENS

Markham Moor NG22 0RP. *6m S of Retford. On A638, in Rockley village turn E to Askham.* Home-made teas at Stone Lea. **Combined adm £3, chd free. Sun 21 June (2-6).**

DOVECOTE COTTAGE
Mrs C Slack

FERN LEA
Mr G Thompson & Miss N Loy

NURSERY HOUSE
Mr & Mrs D Bird
Visitors also welcome by arrangement May to Sept.
01777 838768
David@davidbird.eu

STONE LEA
Mr & Mrs J Kelly

Variety of pleasant English village gardens, with a flower festival in the church. Nursery House is a plantsman's garden, secluded and very private, with every plant meticulously labelled; waterfall and well stocked pond. Fern Lea is a small, ornamental garden with lawns and borders at different levels. Stone Lea has an interesting sequence of gardens surrounding the house. Dovecote Cottage is an enchanting cottage and garden with roses on the walls and attractive raised fish pond.
🎭 ❁ ☕

GROUP OPENING

2 NEW BECKINGHAM GARDENS

Doncaster DN10 4PS. *At junction of A620 & A631 r'about enter Beckingham Village on Low Street.*

Thistle Farm located on R at junction with The Green. Home-made teas in The Recreation Room. **Combined adm £3, chd free. Sun 21 June (1-5).**

PRIMROSE COTTAGE
Terry & Brenda Wilson

THISTLE FARM
Jayne & Russell Hanson

Two very different but complementary gardens within a short walking distance in the village of Beckingham. Primrose Cottage is an old fashioned cottage garden. Walled herbaceous border, well stocked shrubbery. Many old roses, feature pergola, kitchen garden, summerhouse. New for 2015 - greenhouse and secret garden. Thistle Farm is a garden gem entered via a small shrubbery and day garden with summerhouse. Rambling roses and old wisteria lead into French style parterre with clipped box, roses, culinary and medicinal herbs.
♿ ❁ ☕

3 THE BEECHES

The Avenue, Milton, Newark NG22 0PW. Margaret & Jim Swindin, 01777 870828. *1m S A1 Markham Moor. Exit A1 at Markham Moor, take Walesby sign into village (1m). From Main St, L up The Avenue.* Home-made teas. **Adm £3, chd free. Sun 15, Wed 18 Feb, Sun 22 Mar, Sun 26 Apr (11-4). Visitors also welcome by arrangement Feb to May.**
1 acre garden full of colour and interest to plant enthusiasts looking for unusual and rare plants. Spring gives some 250 named snowdrops together with hellebores and early daffodils. The lawn is awash with crocus, fritillarias, anemones, narcissi and cyclamen. Large vegetable garden on raised beds. Lovely views over open countryside. Newcastle Mausoleum (adjacent) open. Featured

in Daily Telegraph, English Gardens Diary, Daily Mail and various local publications. Some slopes and gravel areas.
♿ 🎭 ❁ 🚐 ☕

4 BISHOPS COTTAGE

89 Main Street, Kinoulton, Nottingham NG12 3EL. Ann Hammond, s.ahammond@btinternet.com. *8m SE of West Bridgford. Kinoulton is off A46, just N of intersection with A606. Into village, pass school & village hall. Garden on R after bend on Main St.* **Adm £3, chd free. Sun 14 June (1-5). Visitors also welcome by arrangement June to July, groups min 10, max 20.**
This is a large, mature cottage garden with mixed herbaceous borders, old fruit trees, two ponds - one formal with fish, one natural. Old varieties of roses with the emphasis on scent and colour coordination. Vegetable patch to the rear of the property. Open views across the countryside. Gravel drive.
♿ ❁

5 BROADLEA

North Green, East Drayton, Retford DN22 0LF. David & Jean Stone. *From A1 take A57 towards Lincoln, East Drayton is signed off A57. North Green runs N from church. Garden last gate on R.* Home-made teas. **Adm £3, chd free. Sun 16 Aug (2-5).**
Our aim in this 1 acre garden is to have interest throughout the yr and attract wildlife. There is plenty to see, woodland walk, many perennials, shrubs and spring bulbs. Large pond is a haven for wildlife and a kitchen garden together with wild bank and dyke add attraction to the formal vistas. Works of art by owner on show. Partial wheelchair access.
♿ ❁ ☕

6 5 BURTON LANE

Whatton in the Vale NG13 9EQ. Ms Faulconbridge, 01949 850942, jpfaulconbridge@hotmail.co.uk. *3m E of Bingham. Follow signs to Whatton from A52 between Bingham & Elton. Garden nr Church in old part of village. Follow yellow NGS signs.* Home-made teas. **Adm £3, chd free. Sun 30 Aug (1.30-5).** Visitors also welcome by arrangement May to Sept.

Modern cottage garden which is both productive and highly decorative. We garden organically and for wildlife. The garden is full of colour and scent from Spring to Autumn. Several distinct areas, incl fruit and vegetables. Large beds are filled with great variety of plants with paths through so you can wander and get close. Also features seating, gravel garden, pond, shade planting. Historic church, attractive village with walks. Featured in Bingham Advertiser, Nottingham Evening Post.

The NGS is Macmillan's largest single donor

7 CAPABILITY BARN

Gonalston Lane, Hoveringham NG14 7JH. Malcolm & Wendy Fisher, 01159 664322, wendy.fisher111@btinternet.com, www.capabilitybarn.co.uk. *8m NE of Nottingham. A612 from Nottingham through Lowdham. Take 1st R into Gonalston Lane. 1m on L.* Home-made teas. **Adm £3.50, chd free. Sun 12, Sun 26 Apr (1-4.30).** Visitors also welcome by arrangement Apr to June, adm **£5.00 incl refreshments.**

In early April see brilliant displays of daffodils, tulips and hyacinths. Fritillarias star in the wildflower meadow. Late April invites rhododendrons, azaleas and wisteria flowers and orchard apple blossom.

Herbaceous borders are filled with Spring beauties - erythroniums, anemones, primulas and pulmonarias. Roses, delphiniums, lupins, hostas, vegetables/fruit will greet by arrangement visitors later. Extensive collection of dhalias and flowering begonias.

8 ◆ CLUMBER PARK WALLED KITCHEN GARDEN

Clumber Park, Worksop S80 3AZ. National Trust, 01909 476592, www.nationaltrust.org.uk. *4m S of Worksop. From main car park or main entrance follow directions to the Walled Kitchen Garden.* Light refreshments. **Adm £4.10, chd free. For NGS: Sat 11 July (10-5). For other opening times and information, please phone or see garden website.**

Beautiful 4 acre walled kitchen garden, growing unusual and old varieties of vegetables and fruits. Herbs and flower beds, incl the magnificent 400ft double herbaceous borders. 450ft glasshouse with grapevines. Museum of gardening tools. Soft fruit garden, rose garden, collections of regional apples and culinary rhubarbs. Garden has been awarded National Collection status for its collection of culinary rhubarbs (over 130 varieties) and regional (Nottinghamshire, Derbyshire, Lincolnshire, Leicestershire, Yorkshire) apples (72 varieties). Featured in Grow Your Own and Kitchen Garden Magazine and on regional TV. Gravel paths and slopes.

9 NEW THE COACH HOUSE

Fosse Road, Farndon, Newark NG24 2SF. Sir Graeme Davies. *On old A46 W of Farndon approx 450yrds on R past new overbridge turn off to Hawton. Entrance driveway marked Private Road.* Home-made teas. **Adm £3.50, chd free. Sun 5 July (1-5).**

The Coach House has two major garden areas set in approx 0.9 acres. Both have several distinct sections and the planting throughout is designed to give colour and interest throug the seasons. There is a wide range of mainly perennial plants, shrubs, grasses and trees with many rare and unusual species. The planting in each areas of the garden is fully detailed for visitors.

10 7 COLLYGATE

Swingate, Kimberley NG16 2PJ. Doreen Fahey, 01159 192690, dfahey456@hotmail.com. *6m W of Nottingham. From M1 J26 take A610 towards Nottingham. L at next island (B600 to Kimberley) L at Sainsbury's mini island. L at top. Park here. Garden 500yds on R.* Light refreshments. **Adm £3, chd free. Mon 4 May, Sun 21 June (1-5).** Visitors also welcome by arrangement May to Aug. Refreshments on request.

Delightful garden created by serious plant enthusiast and tucked away at the end of a short narrow lane in Swingate. It greets you with an impact of unexpected colour and delights you with the variety and sensitivity of the planting. A peaceful backwater in an urban setting. Greenhouse and vegetable plot in cottage garden. Wheelchair access to parts but some gravel paths.

11 CROSS LODGE

Beckingham Road, Walkeringham DN10 4HZ. John & Betty Roberts. *A620 from Retford, A631 from Bawtry/Gainsborough, A161 to Walkeringham. Garden on A161. Parking at Village Hall approx 150 metres N of garden. For SatNav use DN10 4JF.* Home-made teas in Walkeringham Village Hall. **Adm £2.50, chd free. Sun 10 May (1-5).**

Ever changing 1¼ acre garden with successive displays of spring and summer flowers. Rhododendron walk in which there are over 50 varieties is at its best in May. Shrubs and perennial borders, rockeries, roses, conifers, old orchard and small woodland with large pond. Wheelchair access to all main features, except pond side paths.

12 DUMBLESIDE

17 Bridle Road, Burton Joyce NG14 5FT. Mr P Bates, 01159 313725. *5m NE of Nottingham. Very narrow lane to walk up 100 yds - please park on Lambley Lane & walk if possible. Drop off if necessary for less mobile.* Home-made teas. **Adm £3, chd free. Sun 10 May (2-6).** Visitors also welcome by arrangement, refreshments on request (not incl in adm).

2 acre garden of varied habitat. Raised gravel beds for small sun lovers. Natural springs planted with

primulas, fritillaries; the stream runs beside woodland paths, bordered by shade loving tree ferns, arisaemas and trilliums. 50yd mixed border. Stepping stones to meadow/orchard, with bulbs and extensive wild flowers in grass - recent tree deaths have led to changes and perhaps added interest!. Steep slopes towards stream.

13 ELM HOUSE
Main Street, Hickling, Melton Mowbray LE14 3AJ. David & Deborah Chambers, 01664 822928, davidgeorgechambers@gmail.com. *12m E of Nottingham. 7m W of Melton Mowbray. From Nottingham take A606 E. After crossing A46 turn L at Bridgegate Lane signed Hickling. In village turn R at T-junction. Elm House is last on R.* Home-made teas. **Adm £3, chd free. Visitors welcome by arrangement Apr to July for groups 10+.**
Large, interesting garden of over an acre with many different areas. Lovely in spring with more than 25 varieties of magnolia and many spring bulbs. Herbaceous in June/July. Other features incl a railway garden, seaside garden, small walled garden, and pond with fish. Newly formed stumpery best viewed mid April/early May or mid June /early July. Level garden with some gravel paths.

14 THE ELMS
Main Street, North Leverton DN22 0AR. Tim & Tracy Ward, 01427 881164, tracy@wardt2.fsnet.co.uk. *5m E of Retford, 6m SW of Gainsborough. From Retford take rd to Leverton for 5m, into North Leverton with Habblesthorpe.* Home-made teas. **Adm £3, chd free. Sun 26 July (2-5). Visitors also welcome by arrangement June to Sept.**
This garden is very different, creating an extension to the living space. Inspiration comes from Mediterranean countries, giving a holiday feel. Palms, bamboos and bananas, along with other exotics, create drama and yet make a statement true to many gardens, that of peace and calm. North Leverton Windmill may be open for visitors. The garden is fully viewable however wheelchair access onto decked and tiled areas is restricted.

University of Nottingham Gardens

15 ◆ FELLEY PRIORY
Underwood NG16 5FJ. Ms Michelle Upchurch for the Brudenell Family, 01773 810230, www.felleypriory.co.uk. *8m SW of Mansfield. Off A608 ½ m W M1 J27.* Light refreshments. **Adm £5, chd free. For NGS: Sun 19 Apr (10-4). For other opening times and information, please phone or see garden website.**
Garden for all seasons with yew hedges and topiary, snowdrops, hellebores, herbaceous borders and rose garden. There are pergolas, a white garden, small arboretum and borders filled with unusual trees, shrubs, plants and bulbs. The grass edged pond is planted with primulas, bamboo, iris, roses and eucomis. Bluebell woodland walk. Orchard with extremely rare daffodils. Featured in Garden Answers.

16 FLORAL MEDIA
Norwell Road, Caunton, Newark NG23 6AQ. Mr & Mrs Steve Routledge, www.floralmedia.co.uk. *Take Norwell Rd from Caunton. Approx ½ m from Caunton on L.* Home-made teas. **Adm £3, chd free. Sun 10 May (10-4).**
A beautifully well maintained country

garden. Beds overflowing with a variety of roses, shrubs and flowers. A gravel/oriental garden, wildlife pond, vegetable, herb and fruit garden. New for 2015 a contemporary purple/white garden. This garden has many different rooms for you to indulge in!. Full wheelchair access incl disabled WC.

17 THE FORGE
Barton in Fabis, Nottingham NG11 0AE. Angela Plowright & Paul Kaczmarczuk. *6m SW of Nottingham. A453 from Clifton 3rd exit Mill Hill r'about, 1st R Barton, house on R down hill by red phone box. From M1 J24 leave A453 at W Leake r'bout 2nd sign to Barton on L.* Home-made teas at Church or Village Hall if wet. **Adm £3, chd free. Sun 9 Aug (1-5.30).**
Step back in time in this romantic cottage garden divided into several intimate rooms, each overflowing with perennials and herbs chosen to attract butterflies and bees. Original buildings incl old farmyard with wildflowers, pond and agricultural bygones. Shepherd's Hut. Featured in Garden News and filmed for Britain's Best Gardens.

18 THE GLADE
2a Woodthorpe Avenue,
Woodthorpe, Nottingham
NG5 4FD. Tony Hoffman,
07836 207196,
a.hoffman@insideoutgroup.co.uk.
*3m N of Nottingham. A60 Mansfield
Rd from Nottingham. After Sherwood
shops turn R at T-lights by
Woodthorpe Park into Woodthorpe
Drive. 2nd L into Woodthorpe Av.*
Home-made teas at 6 Weston Close.
Combined adm £4, chd free.
**Sun 21 June (1-5). Combined with
6 Weston Close. Visitors also
welcome by arrangement June to
Sept.**
Exquisite medium sized garden
developed over 8yrs on the site of a
former Great Western Railway track
with very free draining soil which
allows Mediterranean plants to thrive.
Feature plants incl tree ferns, 30ft
high bamboos, fan palms, acers and
other shrubs rarely seen. The railway
arch, enclosed in trellis work,
provides shade for a variety of ferns
and hostas.

GROUP OPENING

19 GRINGLEY GARDENS
Gringley-on-the-Hill, Doncaster
DN10 4QT. *5m E of Bawtry. Gringley
is midway between Bawtry &
Gainsborough on A631. Follow yellow
NGS signs off by pass into village,
individual gardens will be signposted.*
Home-made teas at Ellicar Gardens.
Combined adm £5, chd free.
Sun 17 May (1-5).

ELLICAR GARDENS
Will & Sarah Murch
Visitors also welcome by
arrangement Mar to Oct for
groups 10+ during term time.
01777 817218
sarah@ellicargardens.co.uk
www.ellicargardens.co.uk

HONEYSUCKLE COTTAGE
Miss J Towler

THE SUMMER HOUSE
Helena Bishop
01777 217248
jbt@waitrose.com

Three diverse gardens in different
settings: The Summer House, a
charming English garden, lovingly
planted with outstanding views
framed by overflowing borders.
Highlights incl a romantic rose
garden, wildflower meadow and

water garden with stream.
Honeysuckle Cottage, a traditional
terraced cottage garden with
interesting use of bricks and boulders
for hard landscaping. Mixed borders
have relaxed planting. An old Bramley
Apple tree creates a focal point on
the top terrace alongside formal
elements of clipped box which create
a tranquil atmosphere. A productive
garden has vegetables in raised beds,
a soft fruit section and small
greenhouse. Ellicar Gardens, vibrant,
naturalistic, diverse, this 5 acre family
garden is a haven for garden lovers,
wildlife enthusiasts and
families.Gravel garden, old roses,
wildflower and perennial meadows,
orchard, potager winter garden, and
beautiful natural swimming pool.
Children love exploring the school
garden, willow maze and tree house.
Friendly rare breed pets. Wheelchair
access at Ellicar Gardens and The
Summer House only - grass and
some gravel paths.

> Step back in
> time in this
> romantic cottage
> garden . . .

GROUP OPENING

20 NEW HALAM GARDENS
AND WILDFLOWER MEADOW
Nr Southwell NG22 8AX. *Village
gardens within walking distance. Hill's
Farm wildflower meadow is a short
drive of ¹/₂ m towards Edingley village.*
Home-made teas at Hill's Farm.
Combined adm £5, chd free.
Sun 7 June (1-5).

NEW HILL'S FARM
John & Margaret Hill

HOLBECK LODGE
Paul & Jane Oakley
(See separate entry)

THE OLD VICARAGE
Mrs Beverley Perks
(See separate entry)

Unusual mixture of two long standing
NGS village gardens and a new 6
acre wildflower meadow - part of an
organic farm where the cattle are fed
the herb rich pasture which is cut in
July - visitors can be assured of an
inspiring discussion with a farmer;
passionate about the benefits of this
method of farming for the
environment, his Shorthorn cattle and
the meat produced.

---

21 ◆ HODSOCK PRIORY
GARDENS
Blyth, Worksop S81 0TY. Sir
Andrew & Lady Buchanan, 01909
591204, www.snowdrops.co.uk.
*4m N of Worksop off B6045. Blyth-
Worksop rd approx 2m from A1M.
Well signed locally.* **For opening
times and information, please
phone or see garden website.**
Enjoy exploring our estate and nearby
attractions. Visitors to the snowdrops
can enjoy a leisurely walk through the
gardens and woods. See our website
for special offers, opening times and
full details of our snowdrop events,
talk and tours. Some paths difficult
for wheelchairs when wet.

---

22 HOLBECK LODGE
Manor Fields, Halam, Newark
NG22 8DU. Paul & Jane Oakley.
*1¹/₂ m W of Southwell. From B6386 in
Halam village 350yds past church, R
into Manor Fields. Parking on Radley
Rd.* Home-made teas at The Old
Vicarage. **Combined adm £4.50,
chd free. Mon 25 May (1-5).
Combined with The Old Vicarage,
Halam.**
Starting with a blank canvas in 2001
when Holbeck Lodge was built, this
¹/₂ acre garden was designed and
planted to flow from semi formal to
more natural planting bordering open
countryside. A vegetable garden with
raised beds is contained by a rose
trellis, leading through herbaceous
beds, hostas, roses, betula, sorbus
and several spectacular Cornus
Kousa. Bordering beck. Some
sloping areas which may not be
suitable for wheelchairs.

---

23 HOLMES VILLA
Holmes Lane, Walkeringham, nr
Gainsborough DN10 4JP. Peter &
Sheila Clark, 01427 890233,
clarkshaulage@aol.com. *4m NW of
Gainsborough. A620 from Retford or*

A631 from Bawtry/Gainsborough and A161 to Walkeringham then towards Misterton. Follow yellow NGS signs for 1m. Reserved disabled parking. Home-made teas. **Adm £2.50, chd free. Mon 25 May (1-5). Visitors also welcome by arrangement Apr to July.**

1³/₄ acre plantsman's interesting and inspirational garden; surprises around every corner with places to sit and ponder, gazebos, arbours, ponds, hosta garden. Unusual perennials and shrubs for flower arranging. Lots of ideas to copy. Old tools, wildlife pond and scarecrows. A flower arranger's artistic garden. Specialist plant sale. Driftwood stall bric-a-brac. Featured in Lincolnshire Today, Lincolnshire Pride and local publications.

© Richard Bloom
Felley Priory

24 THE HOLOCAUST CENTRE

Laxton, Newark NG22 0PA. Janet Mills, www.holocaustcentre.net. *Take A614 from Nottingham. At Ollerton r'about take 4th exit A6075 signed Tuxford. On leaving Boughton turn sharp R signed Laxton.* Light refreshments. **Adm £3, chd free. Sun 16, Sun 23 Aug (10.30-4).**
Since 1995, over 1000 highly scented Margaret Merrill roses have been planted in this poignant memorial garden. Each individual plaque reminds us that those who were murdered during the Holocaust were people with names and families not just statistics. Explore also the delightful Koi pond and see other sculptures and memorials. Visitors are welcome to view museum exhibitions (seperate charge). Disabled parking and WC facilities.

25 HOME FARM HOUSE, 17 MAIN STREET

Keyworth, Nottingham NG12 5AA. Graham & Pippa Tinsley, 01159 377122, Graham_Tinsley@yahoo.co.uk. *7m S of Nottingham. Follow signs for Keyworth from A60 or A606 & head for church. Garden about 50yds down Main St. Car parks at village hall or on Bunny Lane.* Home-made teas. **Combined adm £4, chd free. Sun 31 May (1-5). Combined with Rose Cottage, 81 Nottingham Road. Visitors also welcome by arrangement June to July, groups max 30.**
A large garden hidden behind old farmhouse in the village centre with views over open fields. Many trees incl cedars, limes, oaks and chestnuts which, with high beech and yew hedges, create hidden places to be explored. Old orchard, ponds, turf mound, rose garden, winter garden and old garden with herbaceous borders. Pergolas with wisteria, ornamental vine and roses. Paintings and prints by members of Newark Art Club for sale. Interesting and unusual perennials for sale by Piecemeal Plants (www.piecemealplants.co.uk). Wheelchair access via gravel yard.

26 LODGE MOUNT

Town Street, South Leverton, Retford DN22 0BT. Mr A Wootton-Jones, 07427 400848, a.wj@live.co.uk. *4m E of Retford. Opp Bradley's Garage on Town Street.* Light refreshments. **Adm £3, chd free. Sun 6 Sept (12-6). Visitors also welcome by arrangement June to Oct.**
Originally a field, much of the ¹/₂ acre garden, although planned on paper for yrs, was landscaped within a few months during 2012 in order to fulfill an ambition following Helen Wootton-Jones' terminal cancer diagnosis. Following organic principles, an orchard and large vegetable and fruit plots are complemented by an area of unusual perennial edibles, and helpful plants, with a view to self sufficiency. Numerous clematis, roses, and climbers provide fragrance and a feeling of enclosure. Helen's aunt also had cancer and the garden was specifically designed to open for the NGS to raise money for cancer charities.

27 NEW 6 MOOR LANE

Bramcote, Nottingham NG9 3FH. Carol Ward. *4m W of Nottingham. From Nottingham take A52 W. At 3rd r'about signed A6007 Ilkeston, take 5th exit onto A52 E. After Bramcote Leisure Centre, 1st L into Moor Lane.* Roadside parking. Home-made teas. **Combined adm £4, chd free. Sun 10 May, Sun 14 June (1-5). Combined with 10 Moor Lane.**
A beautifully designed, modern garden with sinuous curves, creative hard landscaping and stunning structural planting from statuesque bamboos and grasses to unusual shrubs and perennials. A container planted pebbled area and water features add to the delights.

28 NEW 10 MOOR LANE

Bramcote, Nottingham NG9 3FH. Liz Ratcliffe. *4m W of Nottingham. From Nottingham take A52 W. At 3rd r'about signed A6007 Ilkeston, take 5th exit onto A52 E. After Bramcote Leisure Centre, 1st L into Moor Lane.* Roadside parking. Cream teas. **Combined adm £4, chd free. Sun 10 May, Sun 14 June (1-5). Combined with 6 Moor Lane.**
A traditional, established, quintessentially romantic English garden with yr-round colour and interest from camellias and rhododendrons to rose covered rope swags. The large ornamental trees and established shrubs provide a structural backdrop to perennial planting, chosen to attract bees and butterflies. There is a raised bed vegetable plot, soft fruit area and herb bed.

Treat yourself to a plant from the plant stall

GROUP OPENING

29 ▶ NORWELL GARDENS
Nr Newark NG23 6JX. *6m N of Newark. halfway between Newark & Southwell. Off A1 at Cromwell turning, take Norwell Rd at bus shelter. Or off A616 take Caunton turn.* Home-made teas in Village Hall (June) & Norwell Nurseries (July). **Combined adm £4, chd free. Sun 28 June (1-5). Evening Opening Wed 1 July (6.30-9).**

ARTISAN'S COTTAGE
Mr & Mrs B Shaw

NEW ▶ ASH HOUSE
Mrs Fiona Mountford

HOPBINE FARMHOUSE, OSSINGTON
Mr & Mrs Geldart

NORWELL ALLOTMENT PARISH GARDENS
Norwell Parish Council

◆ NORWELL NURSERIES
Andrew & Helen Ward
(See separate entry)

THE OLD FORGE
Adam & Hilary Ward

Range of different, very appealing gardens all making superb use of the beautiful backdrop of a quintessentially English countryside village. The beautiful medieval church and its peaceful churchyard with grass labyrinth will be the setting for - Humour in World War II - cartoons, poetry, songs and flowers will show how soldiers used humour to cope with the horrors of war.

30 ◆ NORWELL NURSERIES
Woodhouse Road, Norwell NG23 6JX. Andrew & Helen Ward, 01636 636337, www.norwellnurseries.co.uk. *6m N of Norwell halfway between Newark & Southwell. Off A1 at Cromwell turning, take rd to Norwell at bus stop. Or from A616 take Caunton turn.* Home-made teas. **Adm £2.50, chd free. For NGS: Sun 17 May, Sun 11 Oct (2-5). For other opening times and information, please phone or see garden website.**
Jewel box of over 2,500 different, beautiful and unusual plants sumptuously set out in a one acre plantsman's garden incl shady garden with orchids, woodland gems,

cottage garden borders, alpine and scree areas. Pond with opulently planted margins. Extensive herbaceous borders and effervescent colour themed beds. Innovative Grassoretum (like an arboretum but for grasses). New borders every yr. Nationally renowned nursery with over 1,000 different rare plants for sale also open. Autumn opening features UK's largest collection of hardy chrysanthemums. Featured in the highly prestigious - Best Gardens to Visit and in Country Living magazine. Grass paths, no wheelchair access to woodland paths.

Wildflower meadow with glorious views - soak up the peace and quiet . . .

31 ▶ THE OLD VICARAGE
Halam Hill, Halam NG22 8AX. Mrs Beverley Perks, 01636 812181, perks.family@talk21.com. *1m W of Southwell.* Please park diagonally into beech hedge on verge with speed interactive sign or in village - a busy road so no parking on roadside. Home-made teas in conservatory if wet. Home-made teas in conservatory if wet. **Mon 25 May (1-5), combined with Holbeck Lodge, adm £4.50, chd free. Sun 7 June (1-5), combined with Halam Gardens and Wildflower Meadow, adm £5, chd free. Sun 5 July, Sun 23 Aug (1-5), adm £3.50, chd free. Visitors also welcome by arrangement June to Aug for groups 20+.**
This beautifully planted, organic, relaxing garden on S facing hillside, offers history, wonder and design. Bounteous borders of unusual herbaceous plants, clematis, roses, shrubs and trees. Lots of hidden nooks and crannies, varied wildlife ponds, swimming pool planting, productive kitchen garden, wildflower meadow with glorious views - soak up the peace and quiet, slightly disturbed by our friendly chickens. Beautiful C12 Church open only short

walk into the village or across field through attractively planted churchyard - rare C14 stained glass window.

GROUP OPENING

32 ▶ OXTON VILLAGE GARDENS
Forest Road, Oxton NG25 0SZ. Oxton Village Gardens. *5m W of Southwell. From B6386 turn into village (Blind Lane). Gardens R up Windmill Hill & Chapel Lane, R at T-junction up Forest Rd & down Main St to New Rd & Water Lane.* Home-made teas. **Combined adm £5, chd free. Sun 3 May (12-6).**

CROWS NEST COTTAGE
Joan Arnold & Tom Heinersdorff
Visitors also welcome by arrangement Apr to Aug for groups 10+.
01159 653789
trebleclef.arnold@btinternet.com

LILAC COTTAGE
Matthew Bramble & Anita Garfield

WESLEY GRANGE
Judith & Phil Meats

THE WHITE BUNGALOW
Sue & Robin Aldridge

Enjoy several very different gardens in this lovely, rural village incl Wesley Grange's gravelled courtyard garden, set around a converted barn with a sunny Mediterranean feel; the White Bungalow, fronted by the Dover Beck stream and incorporating a vegetable plot in a child friendly garden; Lilac Cottage boasting spring bulbs, spectacular delphiniums and perennial borders and Crow's Nest Cottage, a larger, bird friendly garden with ponds, running water, a wealth of tulips and lovley clematis. Crows Nest Cottage featured as Garden of the Week in Garden News. Wheelchair access in some gardens will require assistance.

33 ▶ PAPPLEWICK HALL
Blidworth Waye, Papplewick, Nottinghamshire NG15 8FE. J R Godwin-Austen Esq, www.papplewickhall.co.uk. *7m N of Nottingham. 300 yards out of N end of Papplewick village, on B683 (follow*

yellow signs to Papplewick from A60 and B6011). Free parking at Hall. **Adm £3.50, chd free. Share to St James' Church. Sun 24 May (2-5).** This historic, mature, 8 acre garden, mostly shaded woodland, abounds with rhododendrons, hostas, ferns, and spring bulbs. Suitable for wheelchair users, but sections of the paths are gravel.

&

34 PARK FARM
Crink Lane, Southwell NG25 0TJ. Dr & Mrs Ian Johnston, 01636 812195, v.johnston100@gmail.com. *1m SE of Southwell. A612 from Southwell towards Newark, take Fiskerton Rd & 200yds up hill turn R into Crink Lane. Park Farm is on 2nd bend.* Home-made teas. **Adm £3.50, chd free. Sun 19 July (2-5). Visitors also welcome by arrangement May to July, guided tour 50p per person. Regret, no refreshments.** 3 acre garden remarkable for its extensive variety of trees, shrubs and perennials, many rare or unusual. All within long borders, pathways enclosed by shrubs and trees, woodland and alpine/scree gardens, and a large pond. Spectacular views of the Minster across a wildflower meadow and ha-ha.

&

35 NEW PATCHINGS ART CENTRE
Oxton Road, Calverton, Nottingham NG14 6NU. Chas & Pat Wood, 01159 653479, Chas@patchingsartcentre.co.uk, www.patchingsartcentre.co.uk. *N of Nottingham city take A614 towards Ollerton. Turn R on to B6386 towards Oxton. Patchings is on L nr turning to Calverton.* Light refreshments at Patchings Cafe. **Adm £3, chd free. Sun 17, Sun 24 May (10.30-4.30).** Something very different, a woodland walk linked to art history and dressed to celebrate colour and textiles. Spring wild flowers dominate the grass path walk, with a stunning display of Ox Eye Daisies in the rolling landscape of Patchings. To add further interest, the walk is divided into centuries from C14 to C21 with illustrations acknowledging some of giants of the art world. Grass paths, with some undulations and up hill sections accessible to wheelchairs with help. Please enquire for assistance.

36 48 PENARTH GARDENS
Sherwood Vale, Nottingham NG5 4EG. Josie & Geoff Goodlud, 01159 609067. *Approx 2½ m N of Nottingham. Take B684 (Woodborough Rd) from Nottingham. Turn L after Aldi superstore into Woodthorpe Rd, L again into Penarth Rise, then L into Penarth Gdns.* **Adm £3, chd free. Sun 5 July (1-5). Evening Opening £5, chd free, wine, Wed 22 July (6-9).** One of Nottingham city's hidden gems is to be found in the unlikely setting of the old Nottingham Brickwork Quarry. The landscape has been transformed with pathways, steps and a summer house. Clever planting with trees, fences, bamboos, palms and specimen shrubs, lead to flowing herbaceous borders which provide colour and interest with many unusual plants.

37 PIECEMEAL
123 Main Street, Sutton Bonington, Loughborough LE12 5PE. Mary Thomas, 01509 672056, admet123@btinternet.com. *2m SE of Kegworth (M1 J24). 6m NW of Loughborough. Almost opp St Michael's Church & Sutton Bonington Hall.* **Adm £2.50, chd free. Sun 26 July, Sun 2 Aug (1-5). Visitors also welcome by arrangement June to Aug for groups min 4, max 10. For 10+ please contact to discuss. Regret no refreshments available.** Pots of pots! Tiny, sheltered walled garden housing large collection of shrubs as well as various climbers, perennials and even a few trees, in around 400 containers as well as in small borders. Many unusual and not fully hardy. Focus on distinctive form, foliage shape and colour combination to provide interest from spring to autumn. Both garden and conservatory a jungle by mid summer!. Featured in BBC Gardeners' World Magazine.

38 THE POPLARS
60 High Street, Sutton-on-Trent, Newark NG23 6QA. Sue & Graham Goodwin-King. *7m N of Newark. Leave A1 at Sutton/Carlton/ Normanton-on-Trent junction. In Carlton turn L onto B1164. Turn R into Hemplands Lane then R into High Street. 1st house on R. Limited parking, more at Woodbine Farmhouse.* **Combined adm £3.50, chd free. Sun 14 June (11-6). Combined with Woodbine**

Farmhouse.
Mature ½ acre garden on the site of a Victorian flower nursery, now a series of well planted areas each with its own character: Kitchen terrace with potted exotics. Iron balcony overlooking pond and oriental style gravel garden. Jungle with castaway's shack and lookout. Black and white garden. Woodland area. Walled potager. Fernery and hidden courtyard, Lawns, borders and charming sitting places. Some gravel paths and shallow steps, but most areas accessible.

Visit a garden and support hospice care

39 NEW RHUBARB FARM
Hardwick Street, Langwith, Mansfield NG20 9DR. Community Interest Company, www.rhubarbfarm.co.uk. *On NW border of Nottinghamshire in village of Nether Langwith. From A632 in Langwith, by bridge (single file traffic) turn up steep Devonshire Drive. N.B. Turn off SatNav. Take 2nd L into Hardwick St. Rhubarb Farm at end. Parking to R of gates.* Home-made teas. **Adm £3, chd free. Wed 8 July (10.30-2.30).** 52 varieties of fruit and vegetables organically grown not only for sale but for therapeutic benefit. This 2 acre social enterprise provides training and volunteering opportunities to 50 ex offenders, drug and alcohol misusers, and people with mental and physical ill health and disability. Timed tours at 10.30am, 12.30pm and 2.30pm. Two 65ft polytunnels, willow domes and willow arches, 80 hens, sensory garden, water cress bed, outdoor pizza ovens, comfrey bed and comfrey fertiliser factory, composting toilet. Chance to meet and chat with volunteers who come to gain skills, confidence and training. Featured in The Daily Mirror (http://www.mirror.co.uk/news/uk-news/gardening-good-you-growing-veg-4071751), Derbyshire Times and on Radio Sheffield. Main path down site is suitable for wheelchairs but is a little bumpy.

Norwell Nurseries, Norwell Gardens

40▶ RISEHOLME, 125 SHELFORD ROAD
Radcliffe on Trent NG12 1AZ. John & Elaine Walker, 01159 119867. *4m E of Nottingham. From A52 follow signs to Radcliffe. In village centre take turning for Shelford (by Co-op). Approx ¾ m on L.* Home-made teas. **Adm £3, chd free. Sun 20 Sept (1-5). Visitors also welcome by arrangement July to Sept for groups 10+.**
Just under ½ acre, intensely planted plant lovers garden. Many varieties of perennials, grasses, shrubs and trees provide colour and interest all yr. Colour themed beds, jungle area with tropical style planting, tender perennials, particularly salvias, in pots. Unique garden mirrors and other interesting objects complement planting. New areas planned for 2015.

41 NEW ▶ ROSE COTTAGE
81 Nottingham Road, Keyworth, Nottingham NG12 5GS. Richard & Julie Fowkes. *7m S of Nottingham. Follow signs for Keyworth from A606, garden (white cottage) on R 100yrds*

after Sainsburys. From A60 follow Keyworth signs & turn L at church, garden is 400yrds on L. Light refreshments. **Combined adm £4, chd free. Sun 31 May (1-5). Combined with Home Farm House, 17 Main Street.**
Small cottage garden with informal planting and a private enclosed feel. A pebble mosaic, water feature with a Victorian pump, and original brick well all add unique interest. There is a decked seating area and summerhouse. A wildlife stream, installed in 2013 meanders down to a pond and bog garden. A new woodland area leads to a potage with herbs, fruit bushes and hens. Art studio will be open. Paintings and art cards designed by Julie will be on sale.
☕

42▶ SQUIRREL LODGE
2 Goosemoor Lane, Retford DN22 7JA. Peter & Joan Whitehead. *1m S of Retford on A638. Take A683 out of Retford towards A1. Turn R before railway bridge on outskirts of Retford.* Home-made teas. **Adm £3, chd free. Sun 9 Aug (1-5).**
Enjoy mature trees, well kept lawns, small ponds, walled vegetable garden, quirky features and wide variety of plants. Garden room, gazebo, veranda and summerhouse provide views of this skilfully crafted garden. A country feel within walking distance of town. Children's quiz. Partial wheelchair access.
& 🚐 ⊗ ☕

43▶ SUTTON BONINGTON ARBORETUM AND GARDENS
University Campus, College Road, Sutton Bonington LE12 5RD. Desmond O'Grady, 01159 513649, desmond.ogrady@nottingham.ac.uk, www.nottingham.ac.uk. *2m SE of Kegworth, 6m NW of Loughborough. Yellow NGS signs visible at junction of Melton Rd & College Rd. & top of Marlpit Hill, Sutton Bonington. Parking charges apply 8am - 4.15pm weekdays, £3 for 2hrs.* **Adm £3, chd free. Visitors welcome by arrangement June to Aug, midweek afternoons/evenings, groups 10 - 40 max.**
Sutton Bonington Arboretum is a little known resource that began life during the Plant a Tree in '73 campaign. The Arboretum has an interesting collection of over 300 evergreen and deciduous trees. Notable specimens

incl big cone pine, Corsican pine, cedar, eucalyptus, American chestnut, maple and Persian ironwood. The campus gardens are extensive and feature a lake and a historic lime avenue. Picnic area. Guided tours.
🚐 🚐 ☕

44▶ SYCAMORES HOUSE
Salmon Lane, Annesley Woodhouse, Nottingham NG17 9HB. Lynne & Barrie Jackson, 01623 750466, landbjackson@gmail.com, www.sycamoreshouse.weebly.com. *From M1 J27 follow Mansfield signs to Badger Box T-lights. Turn L. Gate on L just past No footway for 600 yds sign.* Home-made teas. **Adm £3, chd free. Sun 26 Apr (2-6). Visitors also welcome by arrangement Apr to May for groups 10+. Adults only from mid April.**
A grassy field in 2005, this 1⅓ acre plantsman's garden now comprises a range of growing environments incl a large, productive, organic vegetable garden, polytunnel and orchard. Visitors will discover the secret pathways and quirky ideas along with the glass garden art. All plants are named to interest experienced gardeners with good ideas for the novice. Children's trail for under 5s. Garden suitable for wheelchair users. Couple of short steep slopes. Gravel paths near house, grass further down. Ramp available for entrance steps.
& 🚐 ⊗ ☕

45▶ THRUMPTON HALL
Thrumpton NG11 0AX. Miranda Seymour, www.thrumptonhall.com. *7m S of Nottingham. M1 J24 take A453 towards Nottingham. Turn L to Thrumpton village & cont to Thrumpton Hall.* Tea. **Adm £3, chd free. Sun 12 July (2-5).**
2 acres incl lawns, rare trees, lakeside walks, flower borders, rose garden and box bordered sunken herb garden, all enclosed by C18 ha-ha and encircling a Jacobean house. Garden is surrounded by C18 landscaped park and is bordered by a river. Rare opportunity to visit Thrumpton Hall (separate ticket). Jacobean mansion, unique carved staircase, Great Saloon, State Bedroom, Priest's Hole.
& 🚐 ⊗ ☕

46 UNIVERSITY OF NOTTINGHAM GARDENS
Nottingham NG7 2RD. University of Nottingham,
www.nottingham.ac.uk/estates/grounds/home.aspx. *Approx 4m SW of Nottingham city centre. Tickets on sale in Millennium Garden in centre of University campus, signed from N & W entrances to University & within the internal rd network.* Light refreshments. **Adm £3, chd free. Sun 16 Aug (1.30-5).**
University Park has many beauitful gardens incl the award winning Millennium Garden with its dazzling flower garden, timed fountains and turf maze. Also the huge Lenton Firs rock garden, the dry garden and the Jekyll garden. During summer, the Walled Garden will be alive with exotic plantings. In total, 300 acres of landscape and gardens. Picnic area, cafe, walking tours, accessible minibus to feature gardens within campus. Some gravel paths and steep slopes.

GROUP OPENING

47 WEST FARM AND CHURCH HOUSE GARDENS
Hoveringham NG14 7JH. *Centre of Hoveringham village. 6m NE of Nottingham. Signed from A612 Nottingham to Southwell rd, on Southwell side of Lowdham.* Light refreshments at West Farm House. **Combined adm £4, chd free. Sun 31 May (1-5).**

  CHURCH HOUSE
  Alex & Sue Allan
  Visitors also welcome by arrangement Apr to June. Groups 30 max.
  07976 966795
  suziewoo109@hotmail.com

  WEST FARM HOUSE
  Richard & Carolyn Torr
  Visitors also welcome by arrangement May to June. Groups 30 max.
  01159 664771
  richard-torr1@tiscali.co.uk

2 contrasting gardens in the centre of Hoveringham village near St Michael's Church. West Farm House is a large cottage style garden and Church House is a small, but perfectly formed, walled garden. Both gardens host a wide range of features and plants, with specialist collections in each. Cacti and succulent collection at West Farm House. Auricula theatre and Japanese area at Church House. Gravel at both gardens. Narrow, uneven access at Church House, very difficult for wheelchairs.

48 6 WESTON CLOSE
Woodthorpe, Nottingham NG5 4FS. Diane & Steve Harrington, 01159 857506, mrsdiharrington@gmail.com. *3m N of Nottingham. A60 Mansfield Rd. Turn R at T-lights into Woodthorpe Drive. 2nd L Grange Road. R into The Crescent. R into Weston Close. Park in The Crescent.* Home-made teas. **Adm £3, chd free. Sun 21 June, Sun 12 July (1-5). Combined with The Glade Sun 21 June, combined adm £4, chd free. Visitors also welcome by arrangement June to Aug for groups 6+.**
Set on a substantial slope with 3 separate areas, dense planting creates a full, varied yet relaxed display incl many scented roses, clematis and a collection over 50 named mature hostas in the impressive colourful rear garden. Large plant sale packed with good value home propagated plants. Occasional craft stalls. Featured as Readers Garden in Garden Answers.

Spring wild flowers dominate the grass path walk . . .

49 WHITE HOUSE
39 Melton Road, Tollerton, Nottingham NG12 4EL. Joan Dean, 01159 375031, joandean4el@btinternet.com. *5m S of Nottingham. From A52 Wheatcroft island, take A606 towards Melton Mowbray. Garden is approx 1½ m on L. Parking in front of Post Office (45 Melton Rd).* Home-made teas. **Adm £3, chd free. Sun 19 July (1-5). Visitors also welcome by arrangement May to Aug, groups min 10, max 30.**
An interesting garden full of herbaceous plants, shrubs and trees. Wisteria and honeysuckle covered arches and pergola. Mirrors and ornaments enhance the garden. Hidden seating area with lots of interesting and unusual rooms. Secluded wild life pond, an orient inspired area along with seaside corner and a touch of the jungle. Well worth a visit.

50 WOODBINE FARMHOUSE
Ingram Lane, Sutton-on-Trent, Newark NG23 6RT. Peter & Jennie Searle, www.jenniesearle.co.uk. *7m N of Newark. Leave A1 at Sutton/Carlton/Normanton junction. Turn L onto B1164. Garage on L, take next R along Main St. Follow rd till school on L & church on R; bear R along Ingram Lane. Woodbine Farmhouse on L.* Home-made teas. **Combined adm £3.50, chd free. Sun 14 June (11-6). Combined with The Poplars.**
An artist's colourful garden surrounding C18 farmhouse with quirky sculptures and interesting planting. Follow the path through the woodland walk. Walled courtyard garden with water feature. Rediscovered well with self seeded ferns. Lawns, herbaceous borders and plenty of places to sit. Wild flower areas. Small pond and fruit trees. Fruit and vegetables. Jennie's Studio Gallery will be open. Mostly wheelchair accessible but some narrow paths and gravel.

51 WOODPECKERS
35 Lambley Lane, Burton Joyce, Nottingham NG14 5BG. Lynn & Mark Carr, 01159 313237, info@woodpeckersdining.co.uk. *6m N of Nottingham. In Burton Joyce, turn off A612 (Nottingham to Southwell rd) into Lambley Lane, turn L onto private drive to access gardens. Ample parking.* Home-made teas. **Adm £3.50, chd free. Sun 17 May (12-5). Visitors also welcome by arrangement.**
4 acres of mature woodland and formal gardens with spectacular views over the Trent Valley. 500 rhododendrons and azaleas. New scented rose tunnel leading from the main lawn to the wisteria arbour. Balustrade terrace for teas. Glade with 200 yr-old cedars overlooking ponds, waterfalls and croquet lawn. Bog garden and sunken area below ha-ha, then onwards towards ancient well. New areas opening. Gravel and grass paths, steep slopes.

OXFORDSHIRE

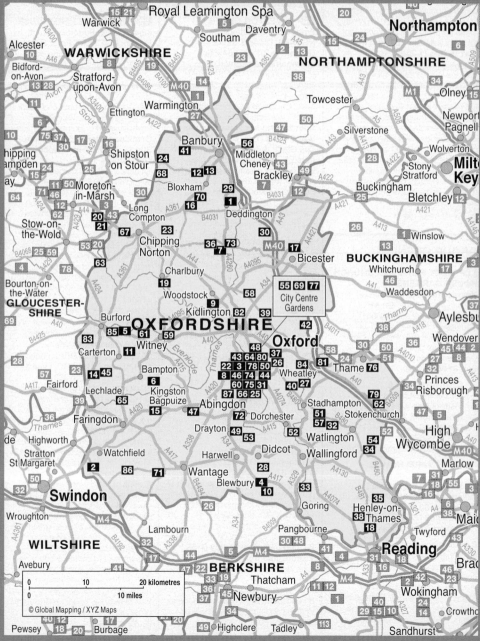

Oxfordshire

In Oxfordshire we tend to think of ourselves as one of the most landlocked counties, right in the centre of England and furthest from the sea.

We are surrounded by Warwickshire, Northamptonshire, Buckinghamshire, Berkshire, Wiltshire and Gloucestershire, and, like these counties, we benefit from that perfect British climate which helps us create some of the most beautiful and famous gardens in the world.

Many gardens opened last year for Oxfordshire NGS between spring and late-autumn. Amongst these were the perfectly groomed college gardens of Oxford University, and the grounds of stately homes and palaces designed by a variety of the famous garden designers such as William Kent, Capability Brown and Harold Peto, Rosemary Verey, Tom Stuart-Smith and the Bannermans of more recent fame.

But we are also a popular tourist destination for our honey-coloured mellow Cotswold stone villages, and for the Thames which has its spring near Lechlade. More villages open as 'groups' for the NGS in Oxfordshire than in any other county, and offer tea, hospitality, advice and delight with their infinite variety of gardens.

All this enjoyment benefits the excellent causes that the NGS supports.

Left: Gothic House, Charlbury Gardens
© Andrew Lawson

Currently the NGS donates around £2.5 million every year

Oxfordshire Volunteers

County Organisers
Marina Hamilton-Baillie
01367 710486
marina_hamilton_baillie@hotmail.com

David White
01295 812679
david.white@doctors.org.uk

County Treasurer
David White
(as above)

Publicity
Priscilla Frost
01608 810578
info@oxconf.co.uk

Booklet Coordinator
Catherine Pinney
01491 612638

Assistant County Organisers
Lynn Baldwin
01608 642754
elynnbaldwin@gmail.com

Graham & Rosemarie Lenton
01993 899033
grahamlenton@btopenworld.com

John & Joan Pumfrey
01189 722848
joanpumfrey@lineone.net

Charles & Lyn Sanders
01865 739486
sandersc4@hotmail.com

Opening Dates

All entries subject to change.
For latest information check www.ngs.org.uk

February

Sunday 15
39 Hollyhocks

Sunday 22
22 14 Chawley Lane

March

Sunday 15
58 Monks Head

Sunday 29
15 Buckland Lakes
77 Trinity College

April

41 Home Farm (every Monday & Tuesday)

Sunday 5
4 Ashbrook House

Monday 6
24 Church Farm Field
45 Kencot Gardens

Saturday 11
2 Allsorts

Sunday 12
39 Hollyhocks
49 Lime Close
50 Magdalen College
58 Monks Head
80 Wadham College

Sunday 19
81 Waterperry Gardens

Sunday 26
13 Broughton Grange
60 Old Boars Hill Gardens

May

41 Home Farm (every Monday & Tuesday)

Sunday 3
14 Broughton Poggs & Filkins Gardens
27 NEW Denton House

Monday 4
71 Sparsholt Manor

Sunday 10
39 Hollyhocks
58 Monks Head

Saturday 16
64 50 Plantation Road

Sunday 17
8 36 Bertie Road
22 14 Chawley Lane
31 Foxcombe Hall
36 The Grove
37 Headington Gardens
42 Horton cum Studley Gardens
48 Lady Margaret Hall
64 50 Plantation Road

Saturday 23
16 NEW Bush House
70 South Newington House

Sunday 24
7 Barton Abbey
16 NEW Bush House
67 Salford Gardens
70 South Newington House

Monday 25
54 Meadow Cottage

Wednesday 27
79 Upper Chalford Farm (Evening)

Friday 29
61 NEW Old Swan & Minster Mill

Sunday 31
24 Church Farm Field
49 Lime Close
82 Wayside
85 Whitehill Farm

June

41 Home Farm (every Monday & Tuesday)

Festival Weekend

Saturday 6
2 Allsorts
9 Blenheim Palace
53 The Manor House, Sutton Courtenay

Sunday 7
26 103 Dene Road
44 Iffley Gardens
46 Kennett Road Gardens
73 Steeple Aston Gardens
74 Tall Trees
75 NEW Tanglewood

Wednesday 10
87 NEW Wootton Gardens

Saturday 13
59 32 New Yatt Road

Sunday 14
5 Asthall Manor
11 Brize Norton Gardens

13 Broughton Grange
17 NEW Caversfield House
28 East Hagbourne Gardens
56 Middleton Cheney Gardens
59 32 New Yatt Road

Tuesday 16
34 Greenfield Farm (Evening)
35 Greys Court

Thursday 18
52 Manor House (Evening)

Saturday 20
52 Manor House

Sunday 21
10 Blewbury Gardens
51 The Manor
57 Mill Barn
63 The Old Vicarage, Bledington
68 Sibford Gower Gardens

Thursday 25
30 NEW Field Cottage
79 Upper Chalford Farm (Evening)

Friday 26
30 NEW Field Cottage
61 NEW Old Swan & Minster Mill

Sunday 28
1 Adderbury Gardens
69 Somerville College Gardens
84 Wheatley Gardens

July

41 Home Farm (every Monday & Tuesday)

Sunday 5
18 Chalkhouse Green Farm
25 NEW Copse Side
32 The Grange
66 NEW Ridgeway
76 Thame Gardens
83 Westwell Manor

Thursday 9
79 Upper Chalford Farm (Evening)

Sunday 12
33 Green and Gorgeous, The Cutting Garden
80 Wadham College

Sunday 19
20 Chastleton Glebe

Saturday 25
59 32 New Yatt Road

Sunday 26
12 Broughton Castle
13 Broughton Grange
55 Merton College Oxford Fellows' Garden
59 32 New Yatt Road
77 Trinity College

August

41 Home Farm (every Monday & Tuesday)

Sunday 9
3 Appleton Dene
43 NEW 86 Hurst Rise

Sunday 16
52 Manor House

Saturday 22
2 Allsorts

Sunday 23
65 Radcot House

Sunday 30
6 NEW Aston Pottery

September

41 Home Farm (every Monday & Tuesday)

Sunday 6
4 Ashbrook House
13 Broughton Grange
19 Charlbury Gardens
21 Chastleton House and Garden
47 Kingston Bagpuize House

Sunday 13
24 Church Farm Field
60 Old Boars Hill Gardens
86 Woolstone Mill House

Tuesday 15
78 University of Oxford Botanic Garden

Sunday 20
81 Waterperry Gardens

There are gardens where you can just sit, relax and enjoy the day . . .

October

41 Home Farm (every Monday & Tuesday)

Visit a garden on National Gardens Festival Weekend 6 & 7 June

Sunday 4
65 Radcot House

November

41 Home Farm (every Monday & Tuesday)

December

41 Home Farm (every Monday & Tuesday)

February 2016

Sunday 14
22 14 Chawley Lane
Sunday 21
39 Hollyhocks

Gardens open to the public

9 Blenheim Palace
12 Broughton Castle
21 Chastleton House and Garden
35 Greys Court
47 Kingston Bagpuize House
78 University of Oxford Botanic Garden
81 Waterperry Gardens

By arrangement only

23 Chivel Farm
29 Fairfield
38 Hearns House
40 Home Close
62 The Old Vicarage

72 64 Spring Road

Also open by arrangement

2 Allsorts
3 Appleton Dene
16 NEW Bush House
24 Church Farm Field
27 NEW Denton House
32 The Grange
33 Green and Gorgeous, The Cutting Garden
34 Greenfield Farm
37 40 Osler Road, Headington Gardens
39 Hollyhocks
41 Home Farm
42 Upper Green, Horton cum Studley Gardens
46 10 Kennett Road, Kennett Road Gardens
49 Lime Close

52 Manor House
58 Monks Head
59 32 New Yatt Road
60 Uplands, Old Boars Hill Gardens
63 The Old Vicarage, Bledington
66 NEW Ridgeway
67 Old Rectory, Salford Gardens
67 Willow Tree Cottage, Salford Gardens
70 South Newington House
73 Primrose Gardens, Steeple Aston Gardens
79 Upper Chalford Farm
82 Wayside
84 Wheatley Gardens
85 Whitehill Farm

The Gardens

GROUP OPENING

1 ADDERBURY GARDENS

Adderbury OX17 3LS. *3m S of Banbury. Adderbury is on A4260. At The Green turn into village.* Home-made teas at Church House (Library), High St. **Combined adm £5, chd free. Share to Katharine House Hospice.** Sun 28 June (2-6).

CANALIA NCH
Mr Jeffrey Moore

THE OLD VICARAGE
Christine & Peter Job

PLACKETTS
High Street. Dr D White.
Enter village after 300yds garden on L. From Bloxham garden straight ahead as you pass Tithe Barn in village

Attractive Ironstone village, with gardens ranging from quite small to very large. The Old Vicarage walled front garden, large rear garden stretching from ha-ha to small lake and flood meadows. Unusual plants and trees. Japanese maple plantation. Placketts 1/5 acre walled garden with sheltered gravel courtyard, main garden exposed, with views. Plethora of colourful plants throughout the yr with late summer colour. Canalia notable for remarkable collection of Mints. Restricted access at Placketts. Dogs allowed at The Old Vicarage.
♿ ⚘ ☕ ♨

Broughton Castle

© Andrew Lawson

Find a garden near you – download our free Android app

2 **ALLSORTS**
Cleycourt Road, Shrivenham
SN6 8BN. Mr & Mrs Jane-anne &
Andrew Morrison, 07521 448422.
*5m from Swindon. See signs from
each way of the B4000 & A420
Swindon-Oxon road.* Light
refreshments. **Adm £3, chd free.**
**Sat 11 Apr, Sat 6 June, Sat 22 Aug
(10.30-4.30).** **Visitors also welcome
by arrangement Apr to Sept for
groups of 8 max.**
A cottage garden with surprises.
Offering varied planting areas with
shrubs, climbers, herbaceous and
alpine plants, along with fun topiary
and a bank of wild flowers. The
entrance takes you under a wisteria
where we enjoy yr-round colour;
some of the plants with scent, and
some unusual ones. We enjoy
varieties of geranium, salvia and
lysimachia. Our pond holds fish and
wildlife. We enjoy a far reaching
view over our garden fence.
Assistant dogs only please. No WC
available.

3 **APPLETON DENE**
Yarnells Hill, Botley, Oxford
OX2 9BG. Mr & Mrs A Dawson,
07701 000977, annrobe@aol.com.
*3m W of Oxford. Take W road out of
Oxford, through Botley Rd, pass
under A34, turn L into Westminster
Way, Yarnells Hill 2nd on R, park at
top of hill. Walk 200 metres.* Home-
made teas. **Combined adm with 86
Hurst Rise £4, chd free.** Sun 9 Aug
(11-5). **Visitors also welcome by
arrangement May to Oct, please
phone in advance.**
Beautiful secluded garden set in a
hidden valley bordered by woods and
a field. The ¼ acre garden on a
steeply sloping site surrounds a
mature tulip tree. There is a skillfully
incorporated level lawn area
overlooked by deep borders incl a
wide variety of plants for long
seasonal interest. There will also be
some outdoor floral displays.
Featured in Garden News magazine.

4 **ASHBROOK HOUSE**
Blewbury OX11 9QA. Mr & Mrs S A
Barrett. *4m SE of Didcot. Turn off
A417 in Blewbury into Westbrook St.
1st house on R. Follow yellow signs
for parking in Boham's Rd.* Tea. **Adm
£4, chd free.** **Sun 5 Apr (2-5.30);
Sun 6 Sept (2.30-5.30).**
The garden where Kenneth Grahame
read Wind in the Willows to local

children and where he took
inspiration for his description of the
oak doors to Badger's House. Come
and see, you may catch a glimpse of
Toad and friends in this 3½ acre
chalk and water garden in a beautiful
spring line village. In spring the banks
are a mass of daffodils and in late
summer the borders are full of
unusual plants.

5 **ASTHALL MANOR**
Asthall, Nr Burford OX18 4HW.
Rosanna Pearson,
www.asthallmanor.com. *3m E of
Burford. Going from Witney to
Burford on A40, turn R at r'about.
Coming from Chipping Norton, come
through Shipton-under-Wychwood &
Swinbrook.* Tea in the village. **Adm
£6, chd free.** **Sun 14 June (2-6).**
6 acres of garden surround this C17
manor house (not open), once home
to the Mitford family and overlooking
the Windrush Valley. The gardens,
designed by I & J Bannerman in
1998, offer 'a beguiling mix of
traditional and contemporary' as
described by the Good Gardens
Guide. Exuberant scented borders,
sloping box parterres, wild flowers,
gypsy waggon, turf sculpture and
hidden lake are all part of the mix.
Featured in Telegraph Magazine
(2014). Partial wheelchair access.

6 **NEW** **ASTON POTTERY**
Aston, Bampton OX18 2BT.
Mr Stephen Baughan,
www.astonpottery.co.uk. *On
the B4449 between Bampton &
Standlake. 4m S of Witney.* Cream
teas. **Adm by donation.**
Sun 30 Aug (12-5).
4 stunning borders flowering
throughout the summer and into
autumn. Set around our pottery, gift
shop and cafe are a dense,
multilayered, traditional perennial
border. Large 72 metre double
bordered hornbeam walk with
summerhouse. 50 metre hot bank,
phlox, kniphofia and canna lilies
running 5 metre deep. New for
this yr, our seasons garden with
August offering a delight of 600
dahlias and agapanthus. Featured
in The English Garden (Sept 2014)
and The Saturday Telegraph (Sept
2014).

7 **BARTON ABBEY**
Steeple Barton OX25 4QS. Mr &
Mrs P Fleming. *8m E of Chipping
Norton. On B4030, ½ m from
junction of A4260 & B4030.* Home-
made teas. **Adm £5, chd free.**
Sun 24 May (2-5).
15 acre garden with views from
house (not open) across sweeping
lawns and picturesque lake. Walled
garden with colourful herbaceous
borders, separated by established
yew hedges and espalier fruit,
contrasts with more informal
woodland garden paths with vistas of
specimen trees and meadows.
Working glasshouses and fine display
of fruit and vegetables.

**WE ARE
MACMILLAN.**
CANCER SUPPORT

**2015 sees the
NGS total to
Macmillan pass
£15 million**

8 **36 BERTIE ROAD**
Cumnor, Oxford OX2 9PS. Esther &
Neil Whiting. *3½ m W of Oxford.
Take W road out of Oxford, through
Botley & continue uphill. At car
showrooms turn R. Park in Bertie &
Norreys Rd.* Home-made teas at 14
Chawley Lane. **Combined adm with
14 Chawley Lane £4, chd free.**
Sun 17 May (2-5).
Small, professionally designed garden
in a leafy suburban setting.
Rectangular plot with a structured
layout of three rooms incl a pergola
and raised vegetable bed. The
planting is relaxed with clumps of
hemerocallis, iris, bronze fennel and
ornamental grasses. Small area of
gravel path.

9 **◆ BLENHEIM PALACE**
Woodstock OX20 1PX. His Grace
the Duke of Marlborough,
www.blenheimpalace.com. *8m N of
Oxford. Bus: S3 Oxford-Chipping
Norton, alight Woodstock.* **Adm £4,
chd £2.** **For NGS: Sat 6 June (9-6).**

For other opening times and information, please see garden website.

Blenheim Gardens, originally laid out by Henry Wise, incl the formal Water Terraces and Italian Garden by Achille Duchêne, Rose Garden, Arboretum, and Cascade. The Secret Garden offers a stunning garden paradise in all seasons. Blenheim Lake, created by Capability Brown and spanned by Vanburgh's Grand Bridge, is the focal point of over 2,000 acres of landscaped parkland. The Pleasure Gardens complex incl the Herb and Lavender Garden and Butterfly House. Other activities incl the Marlborough Maze, adventure play area, giant chess and draughts. Some gravel paths, terrain can be uneven in places. Dogs allowed in park only.

GROUP OPENING

10 BLEWBURY GARDENS
Blewbury OX11 9QB. *4m SE of Didcot. On A417. Follow yellow signs for car parks.* Home-made teas at The Manor, all proceeds to the NGS. **Combined adm £5, chd free.** Sun 21 June (2-6).

BLEWBURY MANOR
Mr & Mrs M R Blythe

BROOKS END
Jean & David Richards

GREEN BUSHES
Phil Rogers

HALL BARN
Malcolm & Deirdre Cochrane

STOCKS
Norma & Richard Bird

As celebrated by Rachel de Thame in Gardener's World. Five gardens in charming downland village. Blewbury Manor a manor house with moat set in a garden of about 10 acres. Features incl a parterre; flower garden, herbaceous and mixed borders; pergola; vegetable and herb garden; stream planting and woodland area; lake and sunken gravel gardens. Large traditional courtyard with late season flowering borders. Brooks End 1960's bungalow, newly designed garden with colour themed beds, damp border, hidden garden, small orchard, new shady border area added, greenhouse and vegetable garden. Green Bushes created by plant lover

Rhon (dec'd 2007) around C15 cottage. Colour themed borders, ponds and poolside planting, alpine troughs, ferns, pleached limes and roses. Hall Barn extends over 4 acres with traditional herbaceous borders, kitchen garden and a croquet lawn. C16 dovecote, thatched cob wall and clear chalk streams. Stocks an early cruck-constructed thatched cottage, surrounded by densely planted lime tolerant herbaceous perennials offering tiers of colour yr-round. Plant stall in the car park by Special Plants Nursery. Wheelchair access to some gardens.

A series of ponds, and water gardens linked by a hidden boardwalk . . .

GROUP OPENING

11 BRIZE NORTON GARDENS
Brize Norton OX18 3LY. *3m SW of Witney. Brize Norton Village, S of A40, between Witney & Burford. Parking at various locations in village. Coaches welcome with plenty of parking nearby.* Home-made teas at Elderbank Hall. **Combined adm £4, chd free.** Sun 14 June (2-6).

BARNSTABLE HOUSE
Mr & Mrs P Butcher

CHURCH FARM HOUSE
Philip & Mary Holmes

CLUMBER
Mr & Mrs S Hawkins

16 DAUBIGNY MEAD
Bob & Margaret Watts

95 STATION ROAD
Mr & Mrs P A Timms

STONE COTTAGE
Mr & Mrs K Humphris

Pretty village on the edge of the Cotswold's offering a number of gardens open for your enjoyment. You can see a wide variety of planting incl ornamental trees, herbaceous borders, ornamental grasses and traditional fruit and vegetable gardens. Features incl a Mediterranean style patio, courtyard garden, water features, plus gardens where you can just sit, relax and enjoy the day. Plants will be available for sale at individual gardens. A Flower Festival will take place in the Brize Norton St Britius Church. Partial wheelchair access to some gardens.

12 ♦ BROUGHTON CASTLE
Nr Banbury OX15 5EB. Lord Saye & Sele, 01295 276070, www.broughtoncastle.com. *2¹/₂ m SW of Banbury. On Shipston-on-Stour road (B4035).* Home-made teas. **Adm £5, chd free. For NGS:** Sun 26 July (2-5). For other opening times and information, please phone or see garden website.

1 acre; shrubs, herbaceous borders, walled garden, roses, climbers seen against background of C14-C16 castle surrounded by moat in open parkland. House also open (additional charge).

13 BROUGHTON GRANGE
Wykham Lane, Broughton OX15 5DS, www.broughtongrange.com. *¹/₄ m out of village. From Banbury take B4035 to Broughton. Turn L at Saye & Sele Arms PH up Wykham Lane (one way). Follow road out of village for ¹/₄ m. Entrance on R.* Light refreshments. **Adm £7, chd free.** Suns 26 Apr, 14 June, 26 July, 6 Sept (10-5).

An impressive 25 acres of gardens and light woodland in an attractive Oxfordshire setting. The centrepiece is a large terraced walled garden created by Tom Stuart-Smith in 2001. Vision has been used to blend the gardens into the countryside. Good early displays of bulbs followed by outstanding herbaceous planting in summer. Formal and informal areas combine to make this a special site incl newly laid arboretum with many ongoing projects.

© Andrew Lawson

Gowers Close, Sibford Gower Gardens

GROUP OPENING

14▶ BROUGHTON POGGS & FILKINS GARDENS
Nr Lechlade GL7 3JH,
www.filkins.org.uk. *3m N of Lechlade. 5m S of Burford. Just off A361 between Burford & Lechlade on the B4477. Map of the gardens available.* Home-made teas in Filkins Village Hall. **Combined adm £5, chd free. Sun 3 May (2-6).**

> **BROUGHTON HALL**
> Karen & Ian Jobling
>
> **BROUGHTON POGGS MILL**
> Charlie & Avril Payne
>
> **NEW▶ THE CORN BARN**
> Ms Alexis Thompson
>
> **FIELD COTTAGE**
> Peter & Sheila Gray
>
> **FILKINS HALL**
> Filkins Hall Residents
>
> **LITTLE PEACOCKS**
> Colvin & Moggridge
>
> **MILLER'S COTTAGE**
> Mr Luke Bailey

PIGEON COTTAGE
Lynne Savege

PIP COTTAGE
G B Woodin

ST PETER'S HOUSE
John Cambridge

THE TALLOT
Mr & Mrs Don Stowell

TAYLOR COTTAGE
Mr & Mrs Ian & Ronnie Bailey

WILLOW COTTAGE
Emma Sparks

13 gardens in these beautiful and vibrant Cotswold stone twin villages. Scale and character vary from the grand landscape setting of Filkins Hall and the equally extensive but more intimate Broughton Hall, to the small but action packed Pigeon Cottage and The Tallot. Broughton Poggs Mill has a rushing mill stream with an exciting bridge, Pip Cottage combines topiary, box hedges and a fine rural view. In these and the other equally exciting gardens horticultural interest abounds. Features incl plant stall by professional local nursery,

Swinford Museum of Cotswolds tools and artefacts, and Cotswold Woollen Weavers. Many gardens have gravel driveways but most are suitable for wheelchair access. Most gardens welcome dogs on leads.

15▶ BUCKLAND LAKES
Nr Faringdon SN7 8QW. **The Wellesley Family.** *3m NE of Faringdon. Buckland is midway between Oxford (14m) & Swindon (15m), just off the A420. Faringdon 3m, Witney 8m. Follow the yellow NGS signs which will lead you to driveway & car park by St Mary's church.* Home-made teas at Memorial Hall. **Adm £4, chd free. Share to RWMT (community bus). Sun 29 Mar (2-5).**
Descend down wooded path to two large secluded lakes with views over undulating historic parkland, designed by Georgian landscape architect Richard Woods. Picturesque mid C18 rustic icehouse, cascade with iron footbridge, thatched boathouse and round house, and renovated exedra. Many fine mature trees, drifts of spring bulbs and daffodils amongst shrubs. Norman church adjoins. Cotswold village. Children must be supervised due to large expanse of open water which is unfenced.

16▶ NEW▶ BUSH HOUSE
Wigginton Road, South Newington, Banbury OX15 4JR. **Mr & Mrs John & Roberta Ainley, 01295 721207, rojoainley@btinternet.com.** *A361 from Banbury to Chipping Norton in South Newington, take 1st R to Wigginton, 1st house on the L in Wigginton Rd.* Home-made teas at South Newington House. **Adm £4.50, chd free. Sat 23, Sun 24 May (2-5). Also open South Newington House. Visitors also welcome by arrangement Mar to Sept for individuals or groups of 40 max.**
Set in 8 acres over 4 yrs, a 2 acre garden has emerged. Herbaceous borders partner dual level ponds and stream. The terrace leads to a walled parterre framed by roses and wisteria. The orchard is screened by rose and vine covered wrought iron trellis. Kitchen gardens, greenhouse and fruit cage provide organically grown produce. Stream and interconnecting ponds. Walled parterre and knot

garden. 1000 native broadleaved trees planted 2006, 2011 and 2014. Gravel drive, a few small steps with a ramp, and two gentle grass slopes on either side of the garden.

17 NEW CAVERSFIELD HOUSE
Caversfield, Bicester OX27 8TQ. Judith & Daniel Kleinman. *Off the B4100 between Bicester & Aynho.* Home-made teas. **Adm £5, chd free. Sun 14 June (1-6).**
A large garden, approx 30 acres managed organically. Comprising a variety of areas incl mixed borders, wild flower and wildlife areas, lake and wetland. We inherited some wonderful old trees and the beautiful lake, which we believe was made in Victorian times, and an old mixed border. We have added new borders, topiary and planted hundreds of new trees. There are some steps, gravelled areas and woodland paths.

18 CHALKHOUSE GREEN FARM
Nr Kidmore End RG4 9AL. Mr & Mrs J Hall, www.chgfarm.com. *2m N of Reading, 5m SW of Henley-on-Thames. Situated between A4074 & B481. From Kidmore End take Chalkhouse Green Rd. Follow yellow signs.* Home-made teas. **Adm £3, chd free. Sun 5 July (2-6).**
1 acre garden and open traditional farmstead. Herbaceous borders, herb garden, shrubs, old fashioned roses, trees incl medlar, quince and mulberries, walled ornamental kitchen garden. New cherry orchard. Rare breed farm animals incl an ancient breed of British White cattle, Suffolk Punch horses, donkeys, Berkshire pigs, piglets, chickens, ducks and turkeys. Plant and jam stall, donkey rides, swimming in covered pool, trailer rides, farm trail, horse logging demonstration, bee display. Partial wheelchair access.

GROUP OPENING

19 CHARLBURY GARDENS
Charlbury OX7 3PP. *6m SE of Chipping Norton. Large Cotswold village on B4022 Witney-Enstone Rd.* Tea in St Mary's Church, Charlbury. **Combined adm £4, chd free. Sun 6 Sept (2-5).**

GOTHIC HOUSE
Mr & Mrs Andrew Lawson.
In the centre of Charlbury, between church & The Bell Hotel

THE PRIORY GARDEN
Dr D El Kabir & Colleagues

2 varied gardens in the centre of this large Cotswold village, in the context of traditional stone houses. Gothic House with 1/3 acre walled garden designed with sculpture and colour in mind. New area of planted squares replaces lawn. False perspective, pleached lime walk, trellis, terracotta containers. The Priory Garden has 1 acre of formal terraced topiary gardens with Italianate features. Foliage colour schemes, shrubs, parterres with fragrant plants, old roses, water features, sculpture and inscriptions aim to produce a poetic, wistful atmosphere. Arboretum of over 3 acres borders the R Evenlode and incl wildlife garden and pond.

The windows in the wall taken in the 19th century from Brasenose College Chapel and Library . . .

20 CHASTLETON GLEBE
Moreton-in-Marsh GL56 0SZ. Prue Leith. *Chastleton. 3m SE of Moreton-in-Marsh off A44, 4m NW of Chipping Norton.* Cream teas & cold drinks. **Adm £4, chd free. Sun 19 July (2-6).**
5 acre garden with well watered lawns, rose tunnel, mature trees, borders (one devoted to hostas) and shrubberies, a small wild wood with a hellebore hill, and alpine terraces round the house. The Red Garden is a blaze of vulgar colour with hanging baskets and Victorian bird cages over the vine covered stone pergola, hybrid tea roses, fuchsias and red perennials. Backstage will interest the keen gardener with greenhouse, frames, 10 compost bays, and stableyard. The lake has a small island with Chinese bridge and

pagoda, and a boat you can row at your own risk! Lakeside planting, mostly by Mother Nature but with interventions of now mature trees, gunnera, bamboos, and several lysimachias. Wheelchair access dependent on weather as some gravel paths and grass areas.

21 ◆ CHASTLETON HOUSE AND GARDEN
Chastleton, Moreton-in-Marsh GL56 0SU. National Trust, 01608 674981, www.nationaltrust.org.uk. *Follow brown signs for Chastleton House from A44 between Moreton-in-Marsh & Chipping Norton.* Tea in Chastleton Brewhouse. **Adm £3.50, chd £1.80. For NGS: Sun 6 Sept (12.30-5). For other opening times and information, please phone or see garden website.**
Chastleton is a historic garden that represents the decline of one family from 1607-1991. Made up of various rooms, it still shows how certain areas were accessed depending on your status in the Jacobean household. The garden has a variety of topiaries, shrubs, fruit, vegetables, trees and herbaceous planting with an ancient feel. It has 2 croquet lawns and is home of croquet. Features incl garden tours, meet garden volunteers and the gardener. Plant and produce stall, honey from the garden for sale, meet the beekeeper, and garden fruit advice. Gravel, some slopes and steps.

22 14 CHAWLEY LANE
Cumnor, Oxford OX2 9PX. Alice & Paul Munsey. *3m W of Oxford. From W Oxford, at top of Cumnor Hill, turn R opp Maserati garage into Chawley Lane. Garden 50 metres on R. Parking in Norreys & Bertie Rd.* Home-made teas. **Adm £4, chd free. Sun 22 Feb (1.30-4); Sun 17 May (2-5); Sun 14 Feb 2016 (1.30-4). Combined adm with 36 Bertie Road on Sun 17 May only £4, chd free.**
Plantsman's 1/2 acre garden with wide and interesting range of plants, many unusual. Owner has a particular interest in alpines and woodland plants. Lovely views over valley and Wytham Woods. Area of developing meadow. Well laid out vegetable garden. Extensive range of snowdrops. One slight slope. Small step to WC.

23 CHIVEL FARM

Heythrop OX7 5TR. Mr & Mrs J D
Sword, 01608 683227,
rosalind.sword@btinternet.com.
*4m E of Chipping Norton. Off A361 or
A44.* Visitors welcome by
arrangement, adm dependent on
group size.
Beautifully designed country garden,
with extensive views, designed for
continuous interest, that is
continuously evolving. Colour
schemed borders with many unusual
trees, shrubs and herbaceous plants.
Small formal white garden and a
conservatory.

24 CHURCH FARM FIELD

Church Lane, Epwell, Banbury
OX15 6LD. Mrs D V D Castle,
01295 788473. *7¹/₂ m W of Banbury
on N side of Epwell Village. 7¹/₂ m W
of Banbury on N side of Epwell
Village.* Tea. Adm £2, chd free.
Mon 6 Apr, Sun 31 May, Sun 13
Sept (2-6). Visitors also welcome
by arrangement Mar to Oct.
Woods, arboretum with wild flowers
(planting started 1992), over 90
different trees and shrubs in 4¹/₂
acres. Paths cut through trees for
access to various parts.

25 NEW COPSE SIDE

Lincombe Lane, Boars Hill, Oxford
OX1 5DY. Rosemary & Colin
Maund. *3m S of Oxford. From S ring
road towards A34 at r'about follow
signs to Wootton & Boars Hill. Up
Hinksey Hill take R fork. Follow road
for just over 1m & take L into
Lincombe Lane.* Combined adm
with Ridgeway £5, chd free.
Sun 5 July (2-6).
A recently designed and landscaped
2¹/₂ acre garden slopes down to a
series of ponds, and water gardens
linked by a hidden boardwalk and
small woodland. Developing borders
and fruit and vegetable garden add to
the magic. Garden is situated on a
downward slope with woodland
terrain.

26 103 DENE ROAD

Headington, Oxford OX3 7EQ.
Mr & Mrs Steve & Mary Woolliams.
*S Headington nr Nuffield. Dene Rd
accessed from The Slade from the N,
or from Hollow Way from the S. Both
access roads are B4495. Garden on
sharp bend.* Home-made teas.

Combined adm with Kennett Road
Gardens £4, chd free. Sun 7 June
(2-5.30).
A surprising eco-friendly garden with
borrowed view over the Lye Valley
Nature Reserve. Lawns, a wild flower
meadow, pond and large kitchen
garden are incl in a suburban (60ft x
120ft) sloping garden. Fruit trees, soft
fruit and mixed borders of shrubs,
hardy perennials, grasses and bulbs,
designed for seasonal colour. This
garden has been noted for its wealth
of wildlife incl a variety of birds and
butterflies, incl the rare Brown
Hairstreak butterfly.

27 NEW DENTON HOUSE

Denton, Oxford OX44 9JF. Mr &
Mrs Luke, 01865 874440,
waveney@jandwluke.com. *In a
valley between Garsington &
Cuddesdon.* Home-made teas.
Adm £5, chd free. Sun 3 May
(2-5.30). Visitors also welcome by
arrangement Apr to Sept.
Large walled garden surrounds a
Georgian mansion (not open), with
shaded areas, walks, topiary and
many interesting mature trees. Large
lawns and herbaceous borders and
rose beds. The windows in the wall
were taken in the C19 from
Brasenose College Chapel and
Library. Wild garden and a further
walled fruit garden.

GROUP OPENING

28 EAST HAGBOURNE GARDENS

East Hagbourne OX11 9LN. *¹/₂ m
S of Didcot. Enter village via B4016
or, from A417 through W Hagbourne
& Coscote. Cycle path 44.* Home-
made teas available in the village.
Combined adm £5, chd free.
Sun 14 June (2-6).

NEW BOTTOM BARN

Manor Farm Lane. Mr Colin &
Dr Jean Millar.
*At village hall car park, turn R
along the main road. Manor Farm
Lane is on the L. Turn L after the
1st barn & Bottom Barn is
straight-ahead*

BUCKELS

12 Main Road. Felicity Topping.
*Garden access via Bakers Lane
off Main Rd opp Willowbrae
Barns*

NEW CHRISTMAS COTTAGE

9 Blewbury Road. Caroline
Hunt & Simon Stevenson

NEW 6 CHURCH CLOSE

Mrs Charlotte Warrington

5 HIGGS CLOSE

Mrs Jenny Smith

NEW KINGFISHER HOUSE

Fieldside. Mr & Mrs Nicola &
Robert Ainger

NEW LIME TREE COTTAGE

9 Main Road. Jane & Robin Bell

NEW LIME TREE FARM

Main Road. Mrs Erica Bevan

TUDOR HOUSE & TUDOR HOUSE ALLOTMENTS

Penny Kisby & Craig Barfoot

Pretty Domesday village, timber frame
and local clunch stone houses. Open
every 3 yrs. Follow main road or
explore pretty alleyways to visit 9
gardens; Bottom Barn, in the shadow
of the C12 church, with topiary and
perennial planting; Tudor House, a
garden surrounded by barns and
walls; Tudor House Allotments,
seasonal fruit and vegetables and fine
hemerocallis, roses and dahlias;
Buckels a sculptured walled garden
with cypresses, box and herbs; 5
Higgs Close a colourful garden with
herbaceous borders, small pond and
vegetable patch. New for 2014; 6
Church Close a C17 farm worker's
cottage garden with herbaceous
perennials and vegetables; Lime Tree
Farm a picturesque village garden
and orchard, separated by Hakkas
Brook; Lime Tree Cottage with water
plants, mature trees, and secret
garden; Kingfisher House a family
garden with mixed herbaceous
planting. Christmas Cottage a family
and wildlife friendly garden, pond and
flowing mixed borders. Features incl
access to wildflower meadow, plant
sales and home-made teas available
in the village.

A tapestry of
beautiful plants
and a patchwork
of colour . . .

29 ▶ FAIRFIELD
Cross Hill Road, Adderbury, Banbury OX17 3EQ. Mr Mike & Mrs Val Adams, 01295 810109. *From A4260 follow road via Adderbury Village. House 900yds on L.* **Adm £3, chd free.** Visitors welcome by arrangement June to Aug with Placketts (High Street, Adderbury). This exquisite, tiny, paved garden is a tapestry of beautiful plants and a patchwork of colour, interwoven with a large variety of clematis together with other interesting climbers.

30 ▶ NEW FIELD COTTAGE
Fritwell Road, Fewcott, Bicester OX27 7NZ. Mrs Wendy Farha. *Follow public footpath sign turning up drive past The Old Schoolhouse. Field Cottage is at the top of this drive & through the far R gate.* Light refreshments in wooden lodge on-site. **Adm £3.50, chd free.** Thur 25, Fri 26 June (10.30-3).
1 acre organic garden with perennial borders and specimen bushes and trees. Eco-friendly techniques employed to encourage a variety of wildlife and birds. Green roof primarily of sedum to counter balance the emissions from the main house heating system. Wildlife pond and wild flower bund to compliment the eco-friendly ethos. A series of woodchip and garden paths surround the garden with large lawn area for viewing borders.

31 ▶ FOXCOMBE HALL
Boars Hill, Oxford OX1 5HR. The Open University in the South. *3m S of Oxford. From Oxford ring road S, follow signs for Wootton & Boars Hill. At Berkeley Rd turn R. At 1st L bend look for car park on L.* Light refreshments, home-made cakes and local produce. **Adm £3, chd free.** Sun 17 May (1-5).
Come and explore 15 acres of beautiful garden at Foxcombe Hall, home to The Open University in the South and formerly owned by Lord Randall Berkeley. The grounds are mostly natural woodland and incl an artificial lake, Italian garden with terrace and rockery, rhododendrons and magnolias. The grounds are not usually open to the public. Indoor displays and presentations on cacti and succulents and on carnivorous plants by Open University experts. Tours of the building will also be available on the day. Partial

wheelchair access, some paths very slippery when wet.

32 ▶ THE GRANGE
Berrick Road, Chalgrove, Oxford OX44 7RQ. Mrs Vicky Farren, 01865 400883, vickyfarren@mac.com. *12m E of Oxford & 4m from Watlington off B480.* **Adm £4, chd free.** Sun 5 July (2-6). Visitors also welcome by arrangement May to Sept.
10 acre plot with an evolving garden incl herbaceous borders and a prairie with many grasses inspired by the Dutch style. Lake with bridges and an island, a brook running through the garden, wild flower meadow, a further pond, arboretum, old orchard and vegetable garden. There is deep water and bridges may be slippery when wet. Grass paths.

33 ▶ GREEN AND GORGEOUS, THE CUTTING GARDEN
Little Stoke, Wallingford OX10 6AX. Rachel Siegfried, 07977 445041, www.greenandgorgeousflowers.co.uk. *3m S of Wallingford. Off B4009 between N & S Stoke, follow single track road down to farm.* Home-made teas. **Adm £3.50, chd free.** Sun 12 July (12-5). Visitors also welcome by arrangement June to Aug.
6 acre working flower farm next to R Thames. Cut flowers (many unusual varieties) in large plots and polytunnels, planted with combination of annuals, bulbs, perennials, roses and shrubs, plus some herbs, vegetables and fruit to feed the workers! Flowers selected for scent, novelty, nostalgia and naturalistic style. Floristry demonstrations. Short grass paths, large concrete areas.

34 ▶ GREENFIELD FARM
Christmas Common, Nr Watlington OX49 5HG. Andrew & Jane Ingram, 01491 612434, andrew@andrewbingram.com. *4m from J5 of M40, 7m from Henley. J5 M40, A40 towards Oxford for ¹/₂ m, turn L signed Christmas Common. ³/₄ m past Fox & Hounds PH, turn L at Tree Barn sign.* Evening Opening £4, chd free, Tue 16 June (6-8). Visitors also welcome by arrangement May to Sept for groups of 8+.
10 acre wild flower meadow, surrounded by woodland, established

18 yrs ago under the Countryside Stewardship Scheme. Traditional Chiltern chalkmeadow in beautiful peaceful setting with 100 species of perennial wild flowers, grasses and 5 species of orchids. ¹/₂ m walk from parking area to meadow. Opportunity to return via typical Chiltern beechwood. A guided tour at 6.00pm. The tour will last approx 2hrs and is 1¹/₂ m long.

35 ▶ ◆ GREYS COURT
Rotherfield Greys, Henley-on-Thames RG9 4PG. National Trust, 01491 628529, www.nationaltrust.org.uk/greys-court. *2m W of Henley-on-Thames. From Nettlebed mini-r'about on A4130 take B481 & property is signed to the L after approx 3m.* **Adm £4, chd £2. For NGS: Tue 16 June (10-5).** For other opening times and information, please phone or see garden website.
The tranquil gardens cover 9 acres and surround a Tudor house with many alterations, as well as a Donkey Wheel and Tower. They incl lawns, a maze and small arboretum. The highlights are the series of enchanting walled gardens, a colourful patchwork of interest set amid Medieval walls. Meet the gardeners and volunteers who look after the gardens. Tea, coffee, lunches and afternoon teas served in The Cowshed. Partial wheelchair access. Loose gravel paths, slopes and some cobbles in garden.

36 ▶ THE GROVE

North Street, Middle Barton, Chipping Norton OX7 7BZ. Ivor & Barbara Hill. *7m E Chipping Norton. On B4030, 2m from junction A4260 & B4030, opp Carpenters Arms PH. Parking in street.* Home-made teas. **Adm £3, chd free.** Sun 17 May (1.30-5).
Mature informal plantsman's garden. ⅓ acre planted for yr-round interest around C19 Cotswold Stone cottage (not open). Numerous borders with wide variety of unusual shrubs, trees and hardy plants; several species weigela syringa viburnum and philadelphus. Pond area, well stocked greenhouse. Plant list available. Home-made preserves for sale. Wheelchair access to most of garden.
♿ ✿ ☕

GROUP OPENING

37 ▶ HEADINGTON GARDENS

Old Headington OX3 9BT. *2m E from centre of Oxford. After T-lights in the centre of Headington heading towards Oxford take the 2nd turn on R into Osler Rd. Gardens at end of road in Old Headington.* Tea in Crinkle Crankle Cafe at Ruskin College. **Combined adm £5, chd free.** Share to Ruskin College. Sun 17 May (2-6).

THE COACH HOUSE
The Croft. Bryony & David Rowe

40 OSLER ROAD
Nicholas & Pam Coote Visitors also welcome by arrangement May to Aug. 07804 932748 pamjcoote@gmail.com

RUSKIN COLLEGE ♿
Crinkle Crankle Wall and Walled Garden, Dunstan Road. Ruskin College http://www.headington.org.uk/crinklecrankle/history/index.html

NEW ▶ 9 STOKE PLACE
Clive & Veronica Hurst

WHITE LODGE
Osler Road. Denis & Catharine Macksmith & Roger & Frances Little

Situated above Oxford, Headington is centred round an old village that is remarkable for its mature trees, high stone walls, narrow lanes and Norman church. The 5 gardens in Old Headington provide a rare glimpse behind the walls. 40 Osler Road is a well established garden with an Italian theme brimming with exotic planting. White Lodge provides a large park like setting for a Regency property. The Coach House combines a formal setting with hedges, lawn and flowers and a sunny courtyard on 2 levels. The newly restored walled vegetable garden in the grounds of Ruskin College incorporates a Grade II listed Crinkle Crankle Wall designed to maximise the sunshine available to trained fruit trees, and teas will be available at the nearby Crinkle Crankle Cafe. New this yr is 9 Stoke Place, with a traditional lawn and mixed border on one side of the house, and a newly created formal garden on the other. Some gravel paths in one garden.
♿ 🐾 ✿ ☕

---

38 ▶ HEARNS HOUSE

Gallowstree Common RG4 9DE. John & Joan Pumfrey, 01189 722848, joanpumfrey@lineone.net. *5m N of Reading, 5m W of Henley. From A4074 turn E at Cane End.* Home-made teas. **Visitors welcome by arrangement** May to Sept with introductory talk by the owner.
2 acre garden provides yr-round interest with pergolas, crinkle-crankle walls, sculpture, ponds. Inspirational variety of indigenous and exotic planting. Some self-sown plants are allowed to flourish where they enhance the original design. The nursery is full of wonderful plants propagated from the garden. Optional tours of the National Collections of brunnera and omphalodes available in May.
♿ 🐾 ✿ **NCH** ☕

---

39 ▶ HOLLYHOCKS

North Street, Islip, nr Kidlington OX5 2SQ. Avril Hughes, 01865 377104, ahollyhocks@btinternet.com. *3m NE of Kidlington. From A34, exit Bletchingdon & Islip. B4027 direction Islip, turn L into North St.* Home-made teas. **Adm £3.50, chd free.** Sun 15 Feb (1.30-4.30); Sun 12 Apr, Sun 10 May (2-6); Sun 21 Feb 2016 (1.30-4). Combined adm with Monks Head on Sun 12 Apr & Sun 10 May only £5.00, chd free. Visitors also welcome by arrangement Feb to Sept.
Plantswoman's small Edwardian garden brimming with yr-round interest. Divided into areas with bulbs, herbaceous borders, roses, clematis, shade and woodland planting with a particular interest in woodland planting especially Trillium, Podophyllum and Arisaema. There are several alpine troughs as well as lots of pots around the house.
✿ ☕

---

40 ▶ HOME CLOSE

Southend, Garsington OX44 9DH. Ms M Waud & Dr P Giangrande, 01865 361394. *3m SE of Oxford. N of B480, opp Garsington Manor.* **Adm £4, chd free. Visitors welcome by arrangement** Apr to Sept with refreshments on request.
2 acre garden with listed house (not open) and listed granary. Unusual trees and shrubs planted for yr-round effect. Terraces, walls and hedges divide the garden and the planting reflects a Mediterranean interest. Vegetable garden and orchard. 1 acre mixed tree plantation with fine views.

---

100 varieties of tall bearded irises . . .

---

41 ▶ HOME FARM

Middle Lane, Balscote, Banbury OX15 6JP. Mr Godfrey Royle, 01295 738194. *½m off A422. Light refreshments.* **Adm by donation.** Every Mon & Tue 1 Apr to 31 Dec (10-5). Visitors also welcome by arrangement May to Dec, advanced notice required so help can be arranged.
Formerly a plant lover's peaceful garden, but now redesigned as low maintenance with flowering shrubs, mature trees and poetry! A unique Balscote-sur-Mer theme adds a touch of humour, with lovely views of surrounding countryside from various viewpoints in the garden. Two undulating lawns give a feeling of spaciousness and contrast beautifully with slate and gravel, continuing the beach theme. Poetry in the garden by artist and writer Zizi Lagadec.
♿ 🚐 ☕

GROUP OPENING

42 HORTON CUM STUDLEY GARDENS

Brill Road, Horton Cum Studley OX33 1BU. *6m NE of Oxford. From Headington & Green Rd r'about on Oxford ring road, take Bayswater Rd. After 1m, turn R & immed L at staggered Xrds. Continue to village.* Home-made teas at Studley Barn. **Combined adm £4, chd free.** Sun 17 May (2-5).

HILL TOP COTTAGE
Mrs Sarah Rogers.
Enter village. R up Horton Hill. Hill Top Cottage halfway up. 2 disabled spaces, other parking at bottom of hill

HORSESHOE COTTAGE
Jilly Heather

UPPER GREEN
Susan & Peter Burge.
Enter village, turn R up Horton Hill. At T-junction turn L into Brill Rd. Upper Green 250yds on R, 2 gates before pillar box. Roadside parking
Visitors also welcome by arrangement Feb to Oct.
01865 351310
sue.burge@ndm.ox.ac.uk

Explore three contrasting gardens in this Otmoor village with almshouses (1636) and church designed by William Butterfield (1867). Hilltop Cottage is a plantaholic's large cottage garden, with productive vegetable plot, soft fruit and ornamentals. Beds incl herbaceous, shrubbery and prairie look. Small trees incl Acer griseum, Sorbus spp, and silver leaved shrubs. Bursts of colour enrich the garden in May with shrubs and perennials incl irises, herbaceous clematis, peonies and roses. Horseshoe Cottage a garden full of interest with traditional cottage planting in front. The back split into rooms separated by mature shrubs and trees, incl a Japanese area and vegetable garden. Upper Green is a mature ½ acre garden with views to the Chilterns, with a gravel garden, alpine trough, informal mixed borders, potager, rock area, bog area and pond. Old apple trees support climbing roses and yr-round interest provided by wide range of perennials, bulbs, ferns, grasses and shrubs. Partial wheelchair access; gravel drive and path with shallow steps.

♿ ☕

Broughton Grange

© Suzanne Shacklock

43 NEW 86 HURST RISE

86 Hurst Rise Road, Cumnor Hill, Oxford OX2 9HH. Ms P Guy & Mr L Harris. *W side of Oxford. Take Botley interchange off A34 from N or S. Follow signs for Oxford & then turn R at Botley T-lights opp MacDonalds, & follow NGS yellow signs.* **Adm £3, chd free.** Sun 9 Aug (11-5).
Combined adm with Appleton Dene £4.00, chd free.
A small town garden designed and planted by the owners in 2013. Good use of a 40ft x 40ft space brimming with herbaceous perennial plants, roses, clematis, shrubs and small trees. Seasonal use of containers and hanging baskets incl tender succulents. An unusual stone water feature, two raised beds packed with interesting plants, an arch and pergola all add to a plantaholic's garden. Partial wheelchair access as path is partly pebble.

GROUP OPENING

44 IFFLEY GARDENS

Iffley, Oxford OX4 4EJ. *2m S of Oxford. Within Oxford's ring road, off A4158 Iffley road from Magdalen Bridge to Littlemore r'about to Iffley Village. Map provided at each garden.* Home-made teas in the village hall. **Combined adm £5, chd free.** Sun 7 June (2-6).

15 ABBERBURY ROAD
Allen & Boglarka Hill

NEW 17 ABBERBURY ROAD
Mrs Julie Steele

86 CHURCH WAY
Helen Beinart & Alex Coren

122 CHURCH WAY
Sir John & Lady Elliott

6 FITZHERBERT CLOSE
Tom & Eunice Martin

THE MALT HOUSE
Helen Potts

THE THATCHED COTTAGE
Martin & Helen Foreman

Secluded old village with renowned Norman church, featured on cover of Pevsner's Oxon Guide. Visit 7 gardens ranging in variety and style from an English cottage garden with Californian plants to a small professionally designed Japanese style garden, with maples and miniature pines. Varied planting throughout the gardens incl herbaceous borders and shade loving plants, roses, fine specimen trees and plants in terracing. Features incl water features, formal gardens, small lake and riverbank. Plant Sale at The Malt House.

♿ ⊛ ☕

14 Chawley Lane

© Mandy Bradshaw

GROUP OPENING

45 KENCOT GARDENS
Kencot, Nr Lechlade GL7 3QT. *5m NE of Lechlade. E of A361 between Burford & Lechlade. Village maps available.* Home-made teas in village hall. **Combined adm £4, chd free.** Mon 6 Apr (2-6).

THE ALLOTMENTS
Amelia Carter Trust

NEW **BELHAM HAYES**
Mr Joseph Jones

NEW **THE GARDENS**
Ms Maggie Sutton

HILLVIEW HOUSE
John & Andrea Moss

IVY NOOK
Gill & Wally Cox

KENCOT HOUSE
Tim & Kate Gardner

THE MALT HOUSE
Hilary & Chris Bradshaw

NEW **THE MALTINGS**
Mr Ray and Jay Mathews

NEW **4 PINNOCKS PIECE**
David & Stella Chapman

WELL HOUSE
Gill & Ian Morrison

Opening for the last 10 yrs, The Allotments have a range of vegetables, flowers and fruit. Hillview House a 2 acre garden, lime tree drive, shrubs, borders and spring flowers. Ivy Nook has flowers, shrubs, borders, rockery, small pond and waterfall, magnolia and fruit trees. Kencot House, 2 acres with gingko tree, shrubs, and a haven for wildlife. Clockhouse, summerhouse and carved C13 archway. The Malt House with roses, herbaceous borders, water features, fruit trees and vine framing late Medieval stone buildings. The Maltings a small cottage garden, herb wheel, pots, and mature trees. Stone steps provide background for climbing plants and pots of herbs and flowering plants. The Gardens, lovingly tended for over 30 yrs by previous owner. In spring something new appears which enhances the garden. 4 Pinnocks Piece developed over 40 yrs, three lawns, two patios with shrubs, containers and spring flowers. Belham Hayes with lawns, mature fruit trees and shrubs, borders with spring bulbs. Plant sale in the car park. No wheelchair access to The Allotments.

♿ 🐾 ✿ � ☕

GROUP OPENING

46 KENNETT ROAD GARDENS
Kennett Road, Headington, Oxford OX3 7BJ. *2m E of Oxford in central Headington. S of London Rd between New High St with the shark to the W & Windmill Rd to E. Residents' parking only.* **Combined adm £4, chd free.** Sun 7 June (2-5.30). Combined with 103 Dene Road.

10 KENNETT ROAD
Linda & David Clover
Visitors also welcome by arrangement for groups of 10 max.
01865 765881
lindaclover@yahoo.co.uk

29 KENNETT ROAD
Joyce & Brendan McCullagh

39 KENNETT ROAD
Stephanie Jenkins
www.headington.org.uk/private/garden

Three very different town gardens incl an award winning Oxford in Bloom Best Kept Rear Garden. Number 10 is a small, densely planted suburban oasis of mixed planting which incl a secluded fernery, small wildlife pond, greenhouse and an unparalleled view of Untitled 1986 Headington's world-famous rooftop sculpture. Number 29, a wider than average town garden, has areas of sun, shade and lawns, densely planted with a wide selection of unusual shrubs, trees, ferns and herbaceous plants, small vegetable plot and pond. Number 39 is a traditional long laundress garden that leads you on an adventure of discovery through mature shrubs, perennials and much more, brought to life by decorative hens that will keep the children amused.

✿ ☕

47 ◆ KINGSTON BAGPUIZE HOUSE
Kingston Bagpuize, Nr Abingdon OX13 5AX. Mrs Francis Grant, 01865 820259, www.kingstonbagpuizehouse.com. *5m W of Abingdon. In Kingston Bagpuize just off A415, ¼ m S of A415 & A420, accessed from Rectory Lane.* Home-made teas. **Adm £5, chd free.** For NGS: Sun 6 Sept (2-5). For other opening times and information, please phone or see garden website.

Support the NGS – eat more cake! ☕

Notable collection of unusual trees, incl magnolias, shrubs, perennials, snowdrops and other bulbs, providing yr-round interest and colour. Large mixed borders, interesting summer flowering trees and shrubs. Restoration of copses and new planting in garden and parkland continues. House open (additional adm £2.50). Guide Dogs only beyond carpark. Gravel and grass paths. Disabled WC.

48 LADY MARGARET HALL
Norham Gardens, Oxford OX2 6QA. Principal & Fellows of Lady Margaret Hall. *1m N of Carfax. From Banbury Rd, R at T-lights into Norham Gardens.* Cream teas. **Adm £3, chd free.** Sun 17 May (2-5.30). Beautiful college garden, full of interesting plants, wonderful buildings and riverside walk. One of the best college gardens, great trees, plenty of seats, the perfect retreat, grasses a speciality, 10 acres to wander at your leisure.

49 LIME CLOSE
35 Henleys Lane, Drayton, Abingdon OX14 4HU. M C de Laubarede, 07831 861463, mail@mclgardendesign.com. *2m S of Abingdon. Henleys Lane is off main road through Drayton.* Home-made teas. **Adm £4.50, chd free. Share to CLIC Sargent Care for Children.** Sun 12 Apr, Sun 31 May (2-5.30). **Visitors also welcome by arrangement Feb to June for groups of 10+.**
3 acre mature plantsman's garden with rare trees, shrubs, perennials and bulbs. Mixed borders, raised beds, pergola, unusual topiary and shade borders. Herb garden designed by Rosemary Verey. Listed C16 house (not open). Cottage garden designed by MCL Garden Design, focusing on colour combinations and an iris garden with over 100 varieties of tall bearded irises. Many winter bulbs, hellebores and shrubs.

50 MAGDALEN COLLEGE
Oxford OX1 4AU. Magdalen College, www.magd.ox.ac.uk. *Entrance in High St.* Light refreshments in the Old Kitchen. **Adm £5, chd £4.** Sun 12 Apr (1-6). 60 acres incl deer park, college lawns, numerous trees 150-200 yrs

old; notable herbaceous and shrub plantings. Magdalen meadow, where purple and white snake's head fritillaries can be found, is surrounded by Addison's Walk, a tree lined circuit by the R Cherwell developed since the late C18. Ancient herd of 60 deer. Press bell at the lodge for porter to provide wheelchair access.

51 THE MANOR
Mill Lane, Chalgrove, Oxford OX44 7SL. Paul & Rachel Jacques. *Chalgrove is 12m E of Oxford & 4m from Watlington off B480. The Manor is W of Chalgrove, 300yds S of Lamb PH.* Home-made teas. **Combined adm with Mill Barn £5, chd free.** Sun 21 June (2-5.30).
The Manor garden has a lake and wildlife areas. Mixed shrub and herbaceous beds surround the C15, Grade I listed Manor house. The kitchen garden incl hotbeds and companion planting. Parking on mown grass. Gavel paths, and shallow steps in the garden.

52 MANOR HOUSE
Manor Farm Road, Dorchester-on-Thames OX10 7HZ. Mr & Mrs S H Broadbent, 01865 340101, mab2@o2.co.uk. *8m SSE of Oxford. Off A4074, signs from village centre. Parking at Bridge Meadow 400 metres. Disabled parking at house.* Tea in Dorchester Abbey Guesthouse (90 metres). **Adm £4, chd free.** Evening Opening £7, chd free, wine, Thur 18 June (5.30-8). Sat 20 June, Sun 16 Aug (2-5.30). **Visitors also welcome by arrangement May to Sept for groups of 10+.**
2 acre garden in beautiful setting around Georgian house (not open)

and Medieval abbey. Spacious lawn leading to riverside copse of towering poplars, fine views of Dorchester Abbey. Terrace with rose and vine covered pergola around lily pond. Colourful herbaceous borders, small orchard and vegetable garden. Gravel paths.

53 THE MANOR HOUSE, SUTTON COURTENAY
Church Street, Sutton Courtenay OX14 4AD. Mr & Mrs Anthony Warne. *4m S of Abingdon. Out of Abingdon on the A415. Turn off to Culham-Sutton Courtenay. From A34 going N come into Milton Village take last road on R to Sutton Courtenay.* Home-made teas in listed barn overlooking the Thames. **Adm £6, chd free.** Sat 6 June (2-6).
Grade II listed gardens greatly influenced by two famous lady gardeners, Norah Lindsey who lived at the Manor House 1895-1940 and Brenda Colvin who remodelled the gardens which are regarded as her finest formal and wild divided gardens. Formal and kitchen gardens, river walks and woodlands. Please note: There are streams and a river in the garden, care required. Featured in Norah Lindsey, The Life and Art of a Garden Designer by Allyson Hayward, Brenda Colvin; A Career in Landscape by Trish Gibson and The Gardens of England: Treasures of the National Gardens Scheme by George Plumptre.

54 MEADOW COTTAGE
Christmas Common, Watlington OX49 5HR. Mrs Zelda Kent-Lemon. *1m from Watlington. Coming from Oxford M40 to J6. Turn R & go to Watlington. Turn L up Hill Rd to top. Turn L, then R. Down gravel track.* Home-made teas. **Adm £5, chd free.** Mon 25 May (12-5).
1³/₄ acre garden adjoining ancient bluebell woods created by the owner from 1995 onwards, with many areas to explore. A professionally designed vegetable garden, large composting areas, wild flower garden and pond, old and new fruit trees, many shrubs, much varied hedging and large areas of lawn. Shrubs, indigenous trees, copious hedges, C17 barn. Tennis court and swimming pool. During the month of May, bluebell woodland. Partial wheelchair access as gravel driveway and lawns.

55 MERTON COLLEGE OXFORD FELLOWS' GARDEN
Merton Street, Oxford OX1 4JD.
Merton College. *Merton St runs parallel to High St.* **Adm £4.50, chd free.** *Sun 26 July (2-5).*
Ancient mulberry, said to have associations with James I. Specimen trees, long mixed border, recently established herbaceous bed. View of Christ Church meadow.
&

GROUP OPENING

56 MIDDLETON CHENEY GARDENS
Cheney Gardens, Middleton Cheney OX17 2ST. *3m E of Banbury. From M40 J11 follow A422, signed Middleton Cheney. Map available at all gardens.* Home-made teas at Peartree House. **Combined adm £5, chd free.** *Sun 14 June (1-6).*

19 GLOVERS LANE
Michael Donohoe & Jane Rixon

21 GLOVERS LANE
Mr & Mrs Richard Walmsley

NEW **17 HORTON CLOSE**
Steve & Hannah Thompson

38 MIDWAY
Margaret & David Finch

PEARTREE HOUSE
Roger & Barbara Charlesworth

14 QUEEN STREET
Brian & Kathy Goodey

1 THE MOORS DRIVE
Charles & Anne Woolland

19 Glovers Lane has a strong modern design with flowing curves that create an elegant, serene feeling echoed in a cool, restrained water feature. Planted for foliage, texture and colour. 21 Glovers Lane incorporates formal elements of oak pergola, water feature and pleached trees contrasting with colourful beds and borders. 17 Horton Close transports you to an exotic haven with bamboos, bananas, tree ferns and cannas. At 38 Midway mature small front and back gardens planted in great profusion create a powerful sensation of a private, intimate haven incl pond and waterfall. Peartree House is a mature garden with an air of mystery and romance full of hidden corners and surprises, with the ever-changing sight and sound of water. 14 Queen Street is a densely planted

cottage garden where room can always be found for another plant. 1 The Moors Drive has colourful herbaceous borders round a central lawn leading to a bed of mature trees giving an overall sense of seclusion.
& ✿ ☕

57 MILL BARN
25 Mill Lane, Chalgrove OX44 7SL.
Pat Hougham. *12m E of Oxford. Chalgrove is 4m from Watlington off B480. Mill Barn is in Mill Lane on the W of Chalgrove, 300yds S of Lamb PH. Parking in field behind the Manor.* Home-made teas at The Manor (opposite). **Combined adm with Manor House £5, chd free.** *Sun 21 June (2-5.30).*
Mill Barn has an informal cottage garden with a variety of flowers, shrubs and fruit trees incl medlar, mulberry and quince in sunny and shaded beds. Wheelchair friendly brick paths with rose arches and a pergola leading to a vegetable plot surrounded by cordon of fruit trees all set in a mill stream landscape.
& ✿ ☕

58 MONKS HEAD
Weston Road, Bletchingdon OX5 3DH. Sue Bedwell, 01869 350155. *Approx 4m N of Kidlington. From A34 take B4027 to Bletchingdon, turn R at Xrds into Weston Rd.* Home-made teas. **Adm £3, chd free.** *Sun 15 Mar (2-5); Sun 12 Apr, Sun 10 May (2-6).*
Combined adm with Hollyhocks on Sun 12 Apr & Sun 10 May only £5.00, chd free. Visitors also welcome by arrangement.
Plantaholics' garden for all year interest. Bulb frame and alpine area, greenhouse.
✿ 🚐 ☕

59 32 NEW YATT ROAD
Witney OX28 1NZ. Montserrat & Nigel Holmes, 01993 704195, nigel-holmes@ntlworld.com. *¹/₂ m NE of Witney town centre. Turn off A4095 towards Wood Green. Follow New Yatt Rd in NE direction. Garden is close to District Council offices (Elmfield).* **Adm £3, chd free.** *Sat 13, Sun 14 June, Sat 25, Sun 26 July (2-6). Visitors also welcome by arrangement June to Aug for groups of 10+.*
An exuberant, plantswoman's suburban oasis, brimming with traditional and unusual plants in a small, but long, rear garden to an

Edwardian house. Features a 70 metre mixed herbaceous border with over 60 old fashioned roses. Also contains island beds, small shrubbery, vegetable patch plus a patio crammed with exotic and tender container plants. Short but flat shingle driveway to access garden.
& 🐕 ✿ 🚐 ☕

An exotic haven with bamboos, bananas, tree ferns and cannas . . .

GROUP OPENING

60 OLD BOARS HILL GARDENS
Jarn Way, Boars Hill, Oxford OX1 5JF. Charles & Lyn Sanders. *3m S of Oxford. From S ring road towards A34 at r'about follow signs to Wootton & Boars Hill. Up Hinksey Hill take R fork. 1m R into Berkley Rd to Old Boars Hill.* Home-made teas at Tall Trees & Uplands. **Combined adm £4 (Apr) & £5 (Sept), chd free.** *Sun 26 Apr, Sun 13 Sept (2-5.30).*

NEW **BLACKTHORN**
Louise Edwards.
Sept opening only

HEDDERLY HOUSE
Mrs Julia Bennett.
April opening only. Close to Jarn Mound

TALL TREES
Suzanne & David Clark
(See separate entry)

UPLANDS
Charles & Lyn Sanders
Visitors also welcome by arrangement Mar to Sept.
01865 739486
sandersc4@hotmail.com

WHITSUN MEADOWS
Berkeley Road. Jane & Nigel Jones.
Sept opening only

YEW COTTAGE
John Hewitt.
Sept opening only. House on L, descending Old Boars Hill, opp Orchard Lane

Six delightful gardens in a semi rural conservation area with views over Oxford. Each garden has a different setting. Hedderly House a terraced hillside garden with wooded walks and ponds with extensive views over the Vale of the White Horse. Yew Cottage, a thatched cottage nestled into it's new redesigned plot as well as the treat of seeing the owner's vintage cars. Whitsun Meadows an extensive perambulating garden incl mature trees, many herbaceous borders and other delights and surprises. Blackthorn an 8 acre parkland garden with woodland walks, floral herbaceous borders and ponds. Uplands a southerly facing garden full of colour and an extensive range of plants for all seasons and Tall Trees a cottage garden full of scents, roses and other floral treats.

61 NEW OLD SWAN & MINSTER MILL
Old Minster Lovell, Minster Lovell, Witney OX29 0RN. Patrick Jones, 01993 774441, enquiries@oldswanandminstermill.com, www.oldswanandminstermill.com. *5 min drive from Witney. Approx 14m after Oxford take the sliproad signed Carterton, Minster Lovell. Turn R at the junction & travel through Minster Lovell.* Light refreshments. **Adm £3, chd free. Fri 29 May, Fri 26 June (2-5).**
The hotel is set in 65 acres of picturesque gardens, located beside the majestic R Windrush, the grounds comprise of formal gardens, a kitchen garden that supplies the inn, and 40 acres of wild flower meadows which were created in 2011. The apiary sits amongst the wild flowers supplying the hotels honey. There are a few steps along garden paths and gravelled areas where help may be required.

62 THE OLD VICARAGE
Aston Rowant, Watlington OX49 5ST. Julian & Rona Knight, 01844 351315, jknight652@aol.com. *Between Chinnor & Watlington, off B4009. From M40 J6, take B4009 towards Chinnor & Princes Risborough. After 1m, turn L signed Aston Rowant Village only.* Tea & home-made cake, or wine & snacks. **Adm £4, chd free.**
Visitors welcome by arrangement June to Oct for groups of 10-30.
Romantic, 1³/₄ acre vicarage garden lovingly rejuvenated and enjoyed by the present family. Centered around a croquet lawn surrounded by beds brimming with shrubs and herbaceous plants, hot bed and roses. Lushly planted pond leading through a pergola overflowing with roses and clematis to a tranquil green garden. Small vegetable and cutting garden.

> The best gardens must offer drama, surprise and contrast and you can find all three here . . .

63 THE OLD VICARAGE, BLEDINGTON
Main Road, Bledington, Chipping Norton OX7 6UX. Sue & Tony Windsor, 01608 658525, tony.windsor@tiscali.co.uk. *6m SW of Chipping Norton. 4m SE of Stow-on-the-Wold. On the main street B4450, through Bledington. Not next to church.* Home-made teas. **Adm £4, chd free. Sun 21 June (2-6).**
Visitors also welcome by arrangement May to July with refreshments by prior request.
1¹/₂ acre garden around a late Georgian vicarage (1843) not open. Borders and beds filled with hardy perennials, shrubs and trees. Informal rose garden with 350 David Austin roses. Small pond and vegetable patch. Paddock with trees, shrubs and herbaceous border. Planted for yr-round interest. Gravel driveway and gentle sloped garden can be hard work.

64 50 PLANTATION ROAD
Oxford OX2 6JE. Philippa Scoones. *Central Oxford. N on Woodstock Rd take 2nd L. Coming into Oxford on Woodstock Rd turn R after Leckford Rd. No disabled parking nr house.* **Adm £3.50, chd free. Sat 16, Sun 17 May (2-6).**
Surprisingly spacious small city garden. North facing front garden, side alley filled with shade loving climbers, mature and unusual plants incl Mount Etna Broom, conservatory, terraced area and secluded water garden with rill, woodland plants and alpines.

65 RADCOT HOUSE
Radcot OX18 2SX. Robin & Jeanne Stainer, www.radcothouse.com. *1¹/₄ m S of Clanfield. On A4095 between Witney & Faringdon, 300yds N of Radcot bridge.* Cream teas. **Adm £5, chd free. Sun 23 Aug, Sun 4 Oct (2-6).**
Approx 3 acres of dramatic yet harmonious planting in light and shade, formal pond, fruit and vegetable cages. Convenient seating at key points enables relaxed observation and reflection. Extensive use of grasses and unusual perennials and interesting sculptural surprises. Spectacular autumn display. Featured in FT Weekend 'An exuberant new garden'; Cotswold Life (Sept) 'Radcot House ends the season in a blaze of glory'; Oxford Times: 'The best gardens must offer drama, surprise and contrast and you can find all three here. Radcot House is a gem'.

66 NEW RIDGEWAY
Lincombe Lane, Boars Hill, Oxford OX1 5DZ. John & Viccy Fleming, garden@octon.eu. *Between Oxford & Abingdon. Off Foxcombe Rd & Fox Lane between A34 Hinksey Hill r'about & B4017 Wootton to Abingdon road. Nearly opp Fox PH.* Home-made teas. **Combined adm with Copse Side £5, chd free. Sun 5 July (2-6). Visitors also welcome by arrangement Apr to Oct for groups of 10-20.**
Exceptional ³/₄ acre garden on sandy soil with some rare shrubs and plants. Developed over the last 10 yrs to provide yr-round interest. The intricate design incl 2 alpine beds, a fruit garden, a vegetable garden and multiple borders with varied planting.

GROUP OPENING

67 SALFORD GARDENS
Salford OX7 5YN. *2m W of Chipping Norton. Off A44 Oxford-Worcester road.* Tea in Salford Village Hall. **Combined adm £4, chd free. Sun 24 May (2-6).**

GREYSANDS HOUSE
Cooks Lane. DJ & LJ Stevens

OLD RECTORY
Mr & Mrs N M Chambers
Visitors also welcome by arrangement.
01608 643969

WILLOW TREE COTTAGE
Mr & Mrs J Shapley
Visitors also welcome by arrangement Apr to Sept.
01608 642478
john.shapley@virgin.net

Willow Tree Cottage with small walled twin gardens with shrub and herbaceous borders, many clematis; one garden created from old farmyard with large alpine garden. Small grass beds. Plantsman's garden with many interesting plants. Greysands House has been completely re-landscaped, only 7 yrs old. Walls, pond, raised beds, fantastic views, interesting corners. The Old Rectory a large garden surrounding Old Rectory (not open). Herbaceous borders, orchard and vegetable garden. Partial wheelchair access to Greysands as there are steep steps.

🔸 ✾ ☕

GROUP OPENING

68 SIBFORD GOWER GARDENS
Sibford Gower OX15 5RX, 01295 780348. *7m W of Banbury. Nr the Warwickshire border, S of B4035, in centre of village nr Wykham Arms PH.* Home-made teas at The Manor House. **Combined adm £5, chd free. Sun 21 June (2-6).**

BUTTSLADE HOUSE 🛏
Mrs Diana Thompson
01295 788818
diana@buttsladehouse.co.uk
www.buttsladehouse.co.uk

CARTER'S YARD
Sue & Malcolm Bannister

GOWERS CLOSE 🛏
Judith Hitching & John Marshall
01295 780348
j.hitching@virgin.net

GREEN ACRES
Paul & Margaret Hobson

THE MANOR HOUSE
Michael Donovan & Alison Jenkins

Charming small village off the beaten track, with thatched stone cottages. Five gardens open, all different, all very interesting. The cottage gardens complement the ancient houses they surround. Masses of roses, wisteria and clematis clamber over walls and pergolas. Box parterres, clipped yew hedges, herb gardens, bosky borders in pinks and purples plus productive kitchen gardens. Some new and innovative planting with unusual plants, plus a woodland walk with mown paths, rare trees and wild flowers.

✾ ☕

Delicious home-made teas and plant stall of donated plants . . .

69 SOMERVILLE COLLEGE GARDENS
Woodstock Road, Oxford OX2 6HD. Somerville College. *½ m E of Carfax Tower. Enter from Woodstock Rd, S of Radcliffe Infirmary.* Tea. **Adm £2.50, chd free. Share to Friends of Oxford Botanic Garden. Sun 28 June (1-6).**
Approx 2 acres, robust college garden planted for yr-round interest. Formal bedding, colour themed and extensive vibrant old fashioned mixed herbaceous borders.

🔸 ☕

70 SOUTH NEWINGTON HOUSE
South Newington OX15 4JW. Mr & Mrs David Swan, 01295 721866, claire_ainley@hotmail.com. *6m SW of Banbury. South Newington is between Banbury & Chipping Norton. Take Barford Rd off A361, 1st L after*

100yds in between oak bollards. For SatNav use OX15 4JL. Tea. **Adm £4.50, chd free. Sat 23, Sun 24 May (2-5).** Visitors also welcome by arrangement Feb to Oct for groups.
Meandering tree lined drive leads to 2 acre garden. Herbaceous borders designed for yr-round colour. Organic garden with established beds and rotation planting scheme. Orchard full of fruit trees with pond encouraging wildlife. Walled parterre planted for seasonal colour. A family garden with a small menagerie, all beautifully designed to blend seamlessly into the environment; a haven for all. Some gravel paths, otherwise full access for wheelchair users.

🔸 ✾ 🚐 🛏 ☕

71 SPARSHOLT MANOR
Nr Wantage OX12 9PT. Sir Adrian & Lady Judith Swire. *3½ m W of Wantage. Off B4507 Ashbury Rd.* Tea in the village hall. **Adm £3, chd free. Mon 4 May (2-6).**
Lakes and wildfowl; ancient boxwood, wilderness with walkways, and summer borders. Wheelchair access in most of the garden.

🔸 🐾 ☕

72 64 SPRING ROAD
Abingdon OX14 1AN. Mrs Janet Boulton, 01235 524514, j.boulton89@btinternet.com, www.janetboulton.co.uk. *S Abingdon from A34 take L turn after police station into Spring Rd. Minute's drive to number 64 on L.* **Adm £5. Visitors welcome by arrangement June to Oct for limited numbers only.**
An artists garden (4½ x 30½ metres) behind a Victorian terrace house, narrow with steps. Predominantly green it contains numerous sculptures with inscriptions relating to art, history and the human spirit. Featured in Homes & Gardens (2014).

☕

GROUP OPENING

73 STEEPLE ASTON GARDENS
Steeple Aston OX25 4SP. *14m N of Oxford, 9m S of Banbury. ½ m E of A4260.* Home-made teas in village hall. **Combined adm £5, chd free. Sun 7 June (1-5.30).**

ACACIA COTTAGE
Jane & David Stewart

COMBE PYNE
Water Lane. Chris & Sally
Cooper

 NEW **GRANGE COTTAGE**
South Side. Caroline &
Christopher Compston.
*On the same side as the Red Lion
PH & midway between the Red
Lion PH & the village shop*

KRALINGEN
Mr & Mrs Roderick Nicholson

THE LONGBYRE
Mr Vaughan Billings

PRIMROSE GARDENS
Richard & Daphne Preston.
*Approx 200yds W of the church
opp 2 thatched cottages*
Visitors also welcome by
arrangement May to July.
01869 340512
richard.preston5@btopenworld.
com

TOUCHWOOD
Gary Norris

Steeple Aston, often considered the
most easterly of the Cotswold
villages, is a beautiful stone built
village with gardens that provide a
huge range of interest. A stream
meanders down the hill as the
landscape changes from sand to clay.
The 7 open gardens incl; small
floriferous cottage gardens, large
landscaped gardens, natural
woodland areas, ponds and bog
gardens, themed borders. No
wheelchair access at Primrose
Gardens or Touchwood.
&ⓈⓇ☕

74 **TALL TREES**
Jarn Way, Boars Hill, Oxford
OX1 5JF. Suzanne & David Clark.
*At junction up Hinksey Hill turn R.
After 1m turn R into Berkley Rd &
next L into Jarn Way.* Home-made
teas. **Combined adm with
Tanglewood £5, chd free.** Sun 7
June (2-6).
A plantswoman's mature ¹/₂ acre
cottage garden adjoining Sir Arthur
Evans wild garden. Camellias,
clematis, rhododendrons, climbing
and shrub roses, flowering cherry and
crab apple trees, shrubs, spring bulbs
and perennials. Auricula theatre at
spring opening. All year interest with
colour coordination. Level access.
Delicious home-made teas and plant
stall of donated plants.
&Ⓢ🚐☕

75 **NEW** **TANGLEWOOD**
Jarn Way, Boars Hill, Oxford
OX1 5JF. Wendy Becker. *Hinksey
r'about, uphill. Turn R to Wootton &
Boars Hill, after 1m turn R into
Berkley Rd & next L into Jarn Way.
Property on L framed by a drystone
wall.* **Combined adm with Tall Trees
£5, chd free.** Sun 7 June (2-6).
Splendid 2 acre garden with a wide
variety of flowering plants in borders
and beds, especially roses. Features
incl a croquet lawn, an avenue of
Robinia, a sculptural area made from
fallen trees and drystone walling, a
small stumpery area, a multilevel
pond feature, a large vegetable
garden and greenhouse. Wide
entrances available but some gravel
drives, pathways and steps.
&

carers trust
action · help · advice

Carers Trust
improves support,
services and
recognition for
carers

GROUP OPENING

76 **THAME GARDENS**
Thame OX9 3TE. *From M40 J7/8
follow signs to Thame midway
between Oxford & Aylesbury on
A418.* Home-made teas. **Combined
adm £4, chd free.** Sun 5 July (2-
5.30).

19 CHINNOR ROAD
Thame. Dr Wendie Norris

10 HAMILTON ROAD
Lesley Winward & Wendy Reid

33 LUDSDEN GROVE
Sandra & Graham Matthews

**4 AND 6 PARLIAMENT
ROAD**
Shirley Denny & Peter
Lawrence

Four gardens set in the historic
market town of Thame. A small

cottage style garden filled with pots,
pools and perennials; a colourful
corner plot of beds, borders and
containers full of almost every plant
imaginable; a walled garden with
raised beds, fruit trees, climbers and
perennials; and neighbours
combining two gardens with water
features, tropical plants, sculptures
and spa.
&ⓈⓇ☕

77 **TRINITY COLLEGE**
Broad Street, Oxford OX1 3BH.
Paul Lawrence, Head Gardener,
www.trinity.ox.ac.uk. *Central
Oxford. Entrance in Broad St.* Home-
made teas in dining hall. **Adm £2.50,
chd free.** Sun 29 Mar, Sun 26 July
(1-5).
Historic main College Gardens with
specimen trees incl aged forked
catalpa, spring bulbs, fine long
herbaceous border and handsome
garden quad originally designed by
Wren. President's Garden surrounded
by high old stone walls, mixed
borders of herbaceous, shrubs and
statuary. Fellows' Garden: small
walled terrace, herbaceous borders;
water feature formed by Jacobean
stone heraldic beasts. Award-winning
lavender garden and walk-through
rose arbour.
&Ⓢ☕

78 ♦ **UNIVERSITY OF OXFORD
BOTANIC GARDEN**
Rose Lane, Oxford OX1 4AZ.
University of Oxford, 01865
286690, www.botanic-garden.
ox.ac.uk. *1m E of Oxford city centre.
Bottom of High St in central Oxford,
on banks of the R Cherwell by
Magdalen Bridge & opp Magdalen
College Tower.* **Adm £4.50, chd free.**
For NGS: Tue 15 Sept (9-5). **For
other opening times and
information, please phone or see
garden website.**
The Botanic Garden contains more
species of plants per acre than
anywhere else on earth. These plants
are grown in 7 glasshouses, water
and rock gardens, large herbaceous
border, walled garden and every
available space. In total there are
around 5,000 different plants to see.
Features incl glasshouses, systematic
beds, National Collection of
Euphorbia, herbaceous border,
Merton borders, fruit and vegetable
collection. Gravel paths.
&Ⓢ **NCH**

Plant specialists: look for the Plant Heritage symbol **NCH**

79 UPPER CHALFORD FARM
between Sydenham & Postcombe,
Chinnor OX39 4NH. Mr & Mrs Paul
Rooksby, 01844 351320,
paulrooksby@talktalk.net. *4¹/₂ m SE
of Thame. M40 exit J6. A40 to
Postcombe turn R to Chalford (L if on
A40 from Oxford). After 1m L at 1st
telegraph pole (between Sydenham &
Postcombe).* Wine or Pimms.
**Evening Openings £4, chd free,
Wed 27 May, Thur 25 June, Thur 9
July (5-8). Visitors also welcome
by arrangement Feb to Sept for
groups of up to 45. Refreshments
on request.**
Jacobean farmhouse garden, old
roses, shrubs and perennials.
Unusual trees and an ancient black
pine. Hidden gardens with different
plantings and peaceful places to sit.
Spring fed pond and stream with
damp planted banks leading to
reclaimed woodland with treehouse.
Newly established bog garden and
landscaping. Features incl a good
collection of unusual trees, topiary,
wildlife ponds, conservatory and
sundials. Short gravel drive from car
park. A closer drop-off point is
possible.

> A wildlife friendly
> garden packed with
> cottage garden
> favourites . . .

80 WADHAM COLLEGE
Parks Road, Oxford OX1 3PN. The
Warden & Fellows. *Central Oxford.
Wadham College gardens are
accessed through the main entrance
of the College on Parks Rd.* Adm £2,
chd free. Sun 12 Apr (2-5); Sun 12
July (2-5.30).
5 acres, best known for trees, spring
bulbs and mixed borders. In Fellows'
main garden, fine ginkgo and
Magnolia acuminata; bamboo
plantation; in Back Quadrangle very
large *Tilia tomentosa* 'Petiolaris'; in
Mallam Court white scented garden
est 1994; in Warden's garden an
ancient tulip tree; in Fellows' private
garden, Civil War embankment with

period fruit tree cultivars, recently
established shrubbery with unusual
trees and ground cover amongst
older plantings.

81 ◆ WATERPERRY GARDENS
Waterperry, nr Wheatley OX33 1JZ.
School of Economic Science,
01844 339226,
www.waterperrygardens.co.uk. *9m
E of Oxford. For SatNavs please use
OX33 1LA.* Adm £6.80, chd free.
For NGS: Sun 19 Apr, Sun 20 Sept
(10-5.30). **For other opening times
and information, please phone or
see garden website.**
Waterperry Gardens are an
inspiration. 8 acres of landscaped
gardens incl rose and formal knot
garden, water lily canal, riverside walk
and one of the country's finest purely
herbaceous borders. There is also a
plant centre, garden shop, teashop,
art gallery, museum and Saxon
church. National Collection of
Kabschia and Silver Saxifrages.
Fritillaries looking fantastic for April
opening. Michaelmas weekend
coincides with Sept opening.
Riverside Walk may be inaccessible
to wheelchair users if very wet.

82 WAYSIDE
82 Banbury Road, Kidlington
OX5 2BX. Margaret & Alistair
Urquhart, 01865 460180,
alistairurquhart@ntlworld.com. *5m
N of Oxford. On R of A4260 travelling
N through Kidlington.* Tea. Adm £3,
chd free. Sun 31 May (2-6). **Visitors
also welcome by arrangement May
to June.**
¹/₄ acre garden shaded by mature
trees. Mixed border with some rare
and unusual plants and shrubs. A
climber clothed pergola leads past a
dry gravel garden to the woodland
garden with an extensive collection of
hardy ferns. Conservatory, and large
fern house with a collection of
unusual species of tree ferns and
tender exotics.

83 WESTWELL MANOR
Westwell, Nr Burford OX18 4JT.
Mr Thomas Gibson. *2m SW of
Burford. From A40 Burford-
Cheltenham, turn L ¹/₂ m after Burford
r'about signed Westwell. After 1¹/₂ m
at T-junction, turn R & Manor is 2nd
house on L.* Adm £5, chd free.
Share to St Marys Church,
Westwell. Sun 5 July (2.30-6).

6 acres surrounding old Cotswold
manor house (not open), knot garden,
potager, shrub roses, herbaceous
borders, topiary, earth works,
moonlight garden, auricula ladder, rills
and water garden.

GROUP OPENING

84 WHEATLEY GARDENS
High Street, Wheatley OX33 1XX,
01865 875022,
echess@hotmail.co.uk. *5m E of
Oxford. Leave A40 at Wheatley, turn
into High St. Gardens at W end of
High St, S-side.* Cream teas at The
Manor House. **Combined adm £4,
chd free. Sun 28 June (2-6).
Visitors also welcome by
arrangement with refreshments
available.**

> **BREACH HOUSE GARDEN**
> Liz Parry
>
> **THE MANOR HOUSE**
> Mrs Edward Hess
>
> **THE STUDIO**
> S & A Buckingham.
> *At the rear of the Wheatley Manor
> garden*

Three adjoining gardens in the historic
coaching village of Wheatley. Breach
House Garden has an established
main area with extensive shrubs and
perennials, also a more contemporary
reflective space with a wild pond. The
Manor House is a 1¹/₂ acre garden
surrounding an Elizabethan manor
house (not open). Formal box walk,
herb garden, cottage garden with
rose arches and a shrubbery with old
roses. A romantic oasis in this busy
village. The Studio is a cottage style
walled garden developed from what
was once a farmyard. Herbaceous
borders, climbing roses and clematis,
shrubs, vegetable plot and fruit trees.
All in all a lovely little collection of
gardens set in the busy village of
Wheatley. Various musical events.
Wheelchair accessible with
assistance, although there are gravel
paths, 2 shallow steps and grass.

85 WHITEHILL FARM
Widford, Nr Burford OX18 4DT.
Mr & Mrs Paul Youngson, 01993
823218, a.youngson@virgin.net,
www.whitehillfarmnursery.co.uk.
*1m E of Burford. From A40 take turn
signed Widford. Follow signs to*

Radcot House

Whitehill Farm Nursery. Home-made teas. **Adm £3.50, chd free. Sun 31 May (2-6). Visitors also welcome by arrangement May to Sept with teas for groups of 10+ only.**
2 acres of hillside gardens and woodland with spectacular views overlooking Burford and Windrush valley. Informal plantsman's garden being continuously developed in various areas. Herbaceous and shrub borders, ponds and bog area, old fashioned roses, ground cover, ornamental grasses, bamboos and hardy geraniums.

86 ▶ **WOOLSTONE MILL HOUSE**
Woolstone, Nr Faringdon SN7 7QL. **Mr & Mrs Justin Spink.** *7m W of Wantage. 7m S of Faringdon. Woolstone is a small village off B4507 below Uffington White Horse Hill.* Home-made teas. **Adm £5, chd free. Sun 13 Sept (2-5.30).**
2 acre garden in pretty hidden village. Stream runs through garden. Large mixed herbaceous and shrub circular border bounded by yew hedges. Small gravel, cutting, kitchen and bog gardens. Topiary, medlars and old fashioned roses. Treehouse with spectacular views to Uffington White Horse and White Horse Hill. C18

millhouse and barn (not open). Partial wheelchair access.

GROUP OPENING

87 ▶ **NEW** ▶ **WOOTTON GARDENS**
Wootton OX13 6DP. *Wootton is 3m SW of Oxford. From the Oxford ring road S, take the turning signed Wootton.* Tea. **Combined adm £5, chd free. Wed 10 June (12-6).**

> **NEW** ▶ **60 BESSELSLEIGH ROAD**
> Mrs Freda East

> **NEW** ▶ **142 CUMNOR ROAD**
> Boars Hill, Oxford. **Mr & Mrs Ersin & Kate Aydin.**
> *From Bystander PH, turn L into Cumnor Rd, walk 10 mins towards Cumnor (over mini-r'about), 142 is on the R*

> **NEW** ▶ **8 MANOR ROAD**
> Mr & Mrs Dave & Gill Richards

> **NEW** ▶ **22 SANDLEIGH ROAD**
> Mr & Mrs Peter & Jennie Debenham

> **NEW** ▶ **35 SANDLEIGH ROAD**
> Hilal Baylav Inkersole

5 inspirational small gardens, all with

very different ways of providing a personal joy. 35 Sandleigh Road is a mature garden, laid to lawn on two levels. Grown mostly from cuttings the garden is brimming with vibrant flowers, pondside planting and mature shrubs. 22 Sandleigh Road is a wildlife friendly garden packed with cottage garden favourites beside brick paths. A kitchen garden is complete with chickens and a beach hut! 60 Besselsleigh Road has The Deadwood Stage, many semi-camouflaged garden creatures to find in the secret garden based on circles and plants! 8 Manor Road is an impeccable garden with brilliantly colourful planting as well as an area of shade loving plants. 142 Cumnor Road's sustainable garden was created in 2012, from an area previously full of leylandii and brambles. A membrane and tonnes of topsoil have allowed the planting of espaliered fruit as well as raised beds with organic flowers and vegetables. The garden incl a small wildlife pond. Partial wheelchair access.

466

SHROPSHIRE

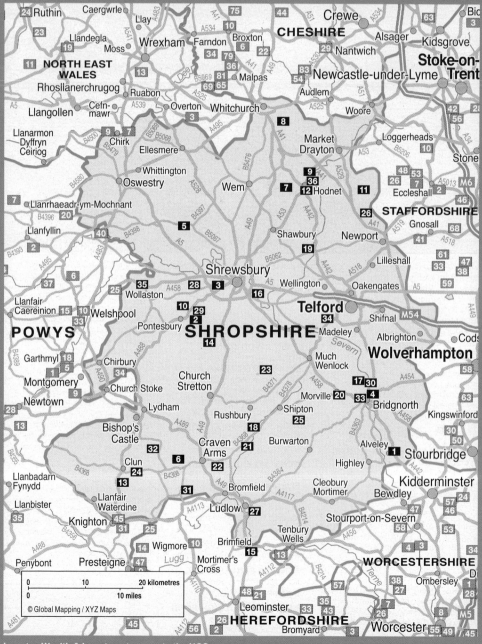

© Global Mapping / XYZ Maps

Investec Wealth & Investment supports the NGS

Shropshire

One of England's best kept secrets and one of the least populated areas in the country, Shropshire has a lot to offer visitors.

Our county has stunning gardens, majestic estates, interesting towns, history both modern and new (Shropshire was home to the ancient tribes of Mercia and also the birthplace of modern industry at Ironbridge), wonderful natural beauties such as the 'Blue Remembered Hills' that the poet A. E. Housman epitomised, and Shropshire is the self-proclaimed 'foodie' capital of Britain.

Above all, Shropshire's gardens are a must for the visitor; in 2015, generous garden owners and volunteers across the county have many open gardens, ranging from large estates – such as Walcot Hall, in the depths of the beautiful south Shropshire countryside, home to Clive of India and one of the original openers for the NGS when the charity started in 1927 – to small, beautifully designed town gardens, such as the exquisite Japanese-inspired garden at 8 Westgate Villas in Bridgnorth in the east of the county.

We want 2015 to be an outstanding year, so come to lovely Shropshire and enjoy our beautiful gardens, and raise money for the very important charities that the NGS supports.

Below: Goldstone Hall Gardens

Shropshire Volunteers

County Organiser
Chris Neil
01743 821651
bill@billfneil.fsnet.co.uk

County Treasurer
Suzanne Stevens
01588 660314
harrystevens@btconnect.com

Publicity
Allison Walter
01588 620055
allison.walter2@btinternet.com

Booklet Coordinator
Fiona Chancellor
01952 507675
fionachancellor@btinternet.com

Assistant County Organisers
Bill Neil
01743 821651
bill@billfneil.fsnet.co.uk

Penny Tryhorn
01746 783931
pennypottingshed@hotmail.co.uk

Since our foundation we have donated more than £42.5 million to charity

Opening Dates

All entries subject to change.
For latest information check www.ngs.org.uk

February

Sunday 15
18 Millichope Park
Sunday 22
18 Millichope Park

March

Sunday 29
19 Moortown

April

Tuesday 7
24 Radnor Cottage
Thursday 16
2 Avocet
Friday 17
33 8 Westgate Villas (Evening)
Sunday 19
33 8 Westgate Villas
Tuesday 28
5 Brownhill House

May

15 The Croft (every Tuesday)
Sunday 3
14 Holly Grove
16 Longner Hall
18 Millichope Park
Sunday 10
17 Lyndale House
Thursday 14
2 Avocet
Friday 15
36 Wollerton Old Hall

Sunday 17
1 Ancoireán
7 The Citadel
Saturday 23
31 NEW Upper Shelderton House
Sunday 24
31 NEW Upper Shelderton House
32 Walcot Hall
Monday 25
31 NEW Upper Shelderton House
32 Walcot Hall
Tuesday 26
5 Brownhill House
24 Radnor Cottage
Wednesday 27
35 NEW Wollaston Lodge
Sunday 31
11 Goldstone Hall Gardens
30 Stanley Hall

June

15 The Croft (every Tuesday)
Tuesday 2
21 Mynd Hardy Plants
Wednesday 3
10 Edge Villa

Festival Weekend

Sunday 7
20 Morville Hall Gardens
Saturday 13
25 Ruthall Manor
Sunday 14
12 Hodnet Hall Gardens
25 Ruthall Manor
34 Windy Ridge
Monday 15
25 Ruthall Manor

Thursday 18
2 Avocet
Saturday 20
27 Secret Garden
Sunday 21
28 Shoothill House
Tuesday 23
5 Brownhill House
Sunday 28
9 NEW Drayton Fields
11 Goldstone Hall Gardens
15 Holmcroft
18 Millichope Park

July

15 The Croft (every Tuesday)
Sunday 5
4 48 Bramble Ridge
Sunday 12
1 Ancoireán
21 Mynd Hardy Plants
26 Sambrook Manor
34 Windy Ridge
Wednesday 15
11 Goldstone Hall Gardens
Thursday 16
2 Avocet
Sunday 19
3 Bowbrook Allotment Community
Wednesday 22
11 Goldstone Hall Gardens
Sunday 26
13 NEW The Hollies
15 Holmcroft
Wednesday 29
11 Goldstone Hall Gardens

August

15 The Croft (every Tuesday)
Sunday 9
34 Windy Ridge
Wednesday 12
11 Goldstone Hall Gardens
Thursday 13
2 Avocet
Sunday 16
26 Sambrook Manor
Wednesday 19
11 Goldstone Hall Gardens
Wednesday 26
11 Goldstone Hall Gardens

Saturday 29
31 NEW Upper Shelderton House
Sunday 30
11 Goldstone Hall Gardens
31 NEW Upper Shelderton House
Monday 31
22 NEW Norton Farm
31 NEW Upper Shelderton House

September

Sunday 6
21 Mynd Hardy Plants
34 Windy Ridge
Sunday 13
10 Edge Villa
Sunday 20
18 Millichope Park

October

Sunday 4
21 Mynd Hardy Plants
Sunday 11
18 Millichope Park

Gardens open to the public

36 Wollerton Old Hall

By arrangement only

6 Caudibrook House
23 Preen Manor
29 Sibberscote Manor

Also open by arrangement

1 Ancoireán
2 Avocet
3 Bowbrook Allotment Community
5 Brownhill House
8 The Croft
10 Edge Villa
11 Goldstone Hall Gardens
14 Holly Grove
22 NEW Norton Farm
24 Radnor Cottage
25 Ruthall Manor
27 Secret Garden
28 Shoothill House
34 Windy Ridge

Windy Ridge

Over 400 Volunteers help run the NGS – why not become one too?

The Gardens

ANCOIREÁN
24 Romsley View, Alveley
WV15 6PJ. Judy & Peter Creed,
01746 780504, pdjc@me.com. *6m
S Bridgnorth off A442 Bridgnorth to
Kidderminster rd. N from
Kidderminster turn L just after Royal
Oak PH. S from Bridgnorth turn R
after Squirrel PH. Take 3rd turning on
R & follow NGS signs.* Home-made
teas. **Adm £3.50, chd free. Sun 17
May, Sun 12 July (1-5).** Visitors
also welcome by arrangement May
to July 20+.
Natural garden layout on several
levels, developed over 30yrs, with a
large variety of herbaceous plants
and shrubs, water features, wooded
area with bog garden containing
numerous varieties of ferns and
hostas, and colourful alpine scree.
Features incl chickens in wooded
area, stumpery, ornamental grass
border and Spring Bulb
collection,Clematis collection,
acer and azalea beds. Selection of
plants and bird and insect boxes
for sale. Close to Severn Valley
Railway and Country Park and
Dudmaston Hall NT. Featured in
Shropshire Star and other local
newspapers.

❷ AVOCET
3 Main Road, Plealey, Shrewsbury
SY5 0UZ. Malc & Jude Mollart,
01743 791743,
malcandjude@btinternet.com. *6m
SW of Shrewsbury. From A5 take
A488 signed Bishops Castle, approx
1/2 m past Lea Cross Tavern turn L
signed Plealey. In 3/4 m turn L, garden
on R.* Tea. **Adm £3, chd free. Thurs
16 Apr, 14 May, 18 June, 16 July,
13 Aug (2-5).** Visitors also welcome
by arrangement Apr to Aug groups
of 10+.
Cottage style garden with modern
twists owned by plantaholics and
shared with wildlife. Designed
around a series of garden
compartments and for year round

interest. Features incl a wildlife pool,
mixed borders, seaside garden,
gravel garden, trained fruit trees,
chickens and sculpture. Children are
welcome. Countryside views and
walks from the garden. Featured in
'Shropshire Magazine'.

❀ ☕

ALLOTMENTS

❸ BOWBROOK ALLOTMENT COMMUNITY
Mytton Oak Road, Shrewsbury
SY3 5BT, 01743 791743,
malcandjude@btinternet.com,
www.bowbrookallotments.co.uk.
*1/2 m from Royal Shrewsbury
Hospital. From A5 Shrewsbury
bypass take B4386 following signs for
hospital. Allotments situated 1/2 m
along B4386. (Mytton Oak Rd) on R.*
Tea. **Combined adm £3.50, chd
free. Sun 19 July (2-6).** Visitors also
welcome by arrangement July to
Aug groups of 10+.
Recipient of RHS National Certificate
of Distinction, this 5 acre site, recently
extended to 93 plots, has featured in a
variety of magazines and on local radio
stations and displays wide ranging
cultivation methods. Members
cultivate organically with nature in
mind using companion planting and
attracting natural predators. Green
spaces flourish throughout and include
Gardens of the 4 Seasons, orchards,
and many wildlife features including
wild flower meadows. The gardens
provide a peaceful haven for members
and visitors. Children are encouraged
to be part of the community and have
their own special places such as a
story telling willow dome, willow
tunnel, sensory garden and turf spiral
with textured totem pole. See how the
Contemplation Garden and the Prairie
Garden have developed. A large
wildlife pond is under development.
Visitors can participate in voting for
Favourite Plot and follow the interest
trail. Children are particularly welcome
and can enjoy their own quizzes.
Wheelchair access, flat wide grass
paths allow access to the main
features of the site and to the interest
trail.

♿ ❀ ☕

❹ 48 BRAMBLE RIDGE
Bridgnorth WV16 4SQ. Chris &
Heather. *From Bridgnorth N on
B4373 signed Broseley. 1st on R
Stanley Lane, 1st R Bramble Ridge.
From Broseley S on B4373, nr*

Bridgnorth turn L into Stanley Lane,
1st R Bramble Ridge. Home-made
teas. **Adm £4, chd free. Sun 5 July
(1-5).**
Steep garden with many steps, part
wild, part cultivated, terraced in
places and overlooking the Severn
valley with views to High Rock and
Queens Parlour. Described by some
as fascinating and full of interest; the
garden incl shrubs, perennials, small
vegetable plot, herbs, wildlife pond
and summerhouse. Full of interesting
plants.

❀ ☕

BROOK FARM
See Worcestershire.

❺ BROWNHILL HOUSE
Ruyton XI Towns, Shrewsbury
SY4 1LR. Roger & Yoland Brown,
01939 261121,
brownhill@eleventowns.co.uk,
www.eleventowns.co.uk. *10m NW
of Shrewsbury on B4397. On the
B4397 in the village of Ruyton XI
Towns.* Home-made teas. **Adm
£3.50, chd free. Tue 28 Apr, Tue 26
May, Tue 23 June (1.30-5).** Visitors
also welcome by arrangement Apr
to July individuals or groups.
Has to be seen to be believed. A
unique hillside garden (over 700
steps) bordering R Perry. Wide variety
of styles and plants from formal
terraces to woodland paths, plus
large kitchen garden. Kit cars on
show. Featured in GGG.

❀ 🛏 ☕

❻ CAUDIBROOK HOUSE
Hopesay, Craven Arms SY7 8HD.
Chris & Carol Clarke, 01588
660753, cc@caudibrook.plus.com.
*4m Craven Arms, 7m Bishops Castle,
11m Ludlow. From A49 take B4368
to Aston on Clun, R over bridge
signed Hopesay & Edgeton. After 1m
enter Hopesay, 1st R signed Round
Oak. Park as directed.* Home-made
teas. **Adm £3, chd free.** Visitors
welcome by arrangement May to
Sept.
Conceived as a 'no lawn' garden this
20yr old, 3/4 acre garden is set out in
mixed borders of ornamental shrubs
and hardy perennials accessed by
gravel paths. It leads through to a
stream and views of fields and
Hopesay Hill. There is an alpine
garden, large vegetable plot, fruit
cage and inner courtyard. Roses and
peonies predominate in June with a
thyme lawn giving a purple hue.

❀ ☕

7 THE CITADEL
Weston-under-Redcastle SY4 5JY.
Mr Beverley & Mrs Sylvia Griffiths,
01630 685204,
griffiths@thecitadelweston.co.uk,
www.thecitadelweston.co.uk. *12m
N of Shrewsbury on A49. At Xrds turn
for Hawkstone Park, through village of
Weston-under-Redcastle, 1/4 m on R
beyond village.* Home-made teas.
Adm £4, chd free. Sun 17 May
(2-5.30).
Imposing castellated house (not
open) stands in 4 acres. Mature
garden, with fine trees,
rhododendrons, azaleas, acers and
camellias. Herbaceous borders;
walled potager and Victorian thatched
summerhouse provide added
interest. Paths meander around and
over sandstone outcrop at centre.

8 THE CROFT
Ash Magna, Whitchurch SY13 4DR.
Peter & Shiela Martinson,
01948 663248,
smartinson@ashbounty.co.uk. *2m
S of Whitchurch. From Whitchurch
bypass take A525 Newcastle (A530
Nantwich). 'Ash' signposted at
r'about. Village centre 2m. Follow
signs to garden.* Home-made teas.
Adm £3, chd free. Every Tue 5 May
to 25 Aug (1-5). Visitors also
welcome by arrangement May to
Aug groups of 10+.
Just how much food can be
produced on about an acre, whilst
still indulging a love of colour and the
natural world? A wonderful place for
children to run, play and discover,
shared with contented animals,
flowers, fruit and vegetables with a
'green man' hiding in the woodland.
Bottle feeding lambs in the Spring,
free-ranging chickens, pond dipping.

9 NEW DRAYTON FIELDS
Wollerton, Market Drayton
TF9 3LU. Mr & Mrs Roberts.
*Northern edge of Wollerton Village,
Drayton Rd. Garden is set back with
white railings.* Home-made teas. Adm
£4, chd free. Sun 28 June (1-5).
3 1/2 acres of interesting trees, incl
Wellingtonias, herbaceous borders,
lawns, box hedging, lavender
parterre, rose garden. Vegetable
garden and greenhouse, small pond,
flowers abound and combining into
partly organised floral, scented
chaos.

10 EDGE VILLA
Edge, nr Yockleton SY5 9PY.
Mr & Mrs W F Neil, 01743 821651,
bill@billfneil.fsnet.co.uk. *6m SW of
Shrewsbury. From A5 take either
A488 signed to Bishops Castle or
B4386 to Montgomery for approx 6m
then follow NGS signs.* Home-made
teas. Adm £4, chd free. Wed 3
June (9.30-1); Sun 13 Sept (2-5).
Visitors also welcome by
arrangement Apr to Sept
group 10+.
Two acres nestling in South
Shropshire hills. Self-sufficient
vegetable plot. Chickens in orchard,
foxes permitting. Large herbaceous
borders. Dewpond surrounded by
purple elder, irises, candelabra
primulas and dieramas. Large
selection of fragrant roses. Teas in
sheltered courtyard. Wed 3 June is an
am opening with plant sale. Wendy
House and Teepee for children. See
website for spring opening. Some
gravel paths.

11 GOLDSTONE HALL GARDENS
Goldstone, Market Drayton
TF9 2NA. Miss Victoria Cushing,
01630 661202,
enquiries@goldstonehall.com,
www.goldstonehall.com. *5m N of
Newport on A41. Follow brown signs
from Hinstock. From Shrewsbury
A53, R for A41 Hinstock & follow
brown signs.* Home-made teas.
Adm £4.50, chd free. Sun 31 May,
Sun 28 June, Weds 15, 22, 29 July,
12, 19, 26, Sun 30 Aug (2-5).
Visitors also welcome by
arrangement May to Sept for
groups of 10+.
Mature setting of Goldstone Hall
Hotel and Restaurant with large well
ordered kitchen garden with raised
beds and herbal walkway cover over
a third of an acre; double tiered
herbaceous border; award winning
oak framed pavilion perfect for
afternoon tea; Unusual combination
of roses maturing into fine borders, all
in 5 acres. Majority of garden can be
accessed on gravel and lawns.

12 HODNET HALL GARDENS
Hodnet, Market Drayton TF9 3NN.
Sir Algernon & The Hon Lady
Heber-Percy,
www.hodnethallgardens.org.
*5 1/2 m SW of Market Drayton. 12m
NE Shrewsbury. At junction of A53 &
A442.* Light refreshments. Adm

£6.50, chd £3. Sun 14 June (12-5).
60-acre landscaped garden with
series of lakes and pools; magnificent
forest trees, great variety of flowers,
shrubs providing colour throughout
season. Unique collection of big-
game trophies in C17 tearooms.
Kitchen garden. For details please
see website. Maps are available to
show access for our less mobile
visitors.
NCH

> Flowers abound
> and combining
> into partly
> organised
> floral, scented
> chaos . . .

13 NEW THE HOLLIES
Clun, Craven Arms SY7 8LR. Pat &
Terry Badham. *10m W of Craven
Arms. 8m S of Bishops Castle. From
A49 Craven Arms take B4368 to
Clun. Turn L onto A488 continue for
1 1/2 m. Bear R signed Treverward &
follow signs.* Home-made teas. Adm
£3, chd free. Sun 26 July (2-6).
A still developing young garden of
approx 2 acres at 1000ft. Features
incl a kitchen garden, large island
beds and borders with perennials,
shrubs and grasses, specimen trees.
Wildlife dingle with stream and a large
badger set. There are plans for further
development in the pipeline.

14 HOLLY GROVE
Church Pulverbatch SY5 8DD.
Peter & Angela Unsworth, 01743
718221,
angela.unsworth@btinternet.com.
*6m S of Shrewsbury. Midway
between Stapleton & Church
Pulverbatch. From A49 follow signs
to Stapleton & Pulverbatch.* Home-
made teas. Adm £4, chd free. Sun 3
May (2-5). Visitors also welcome

by arrangement for 10+. Also in winter for snowdrops.

3-acre garden set in S Shropshire countryside. Yew and beech hedges enclosing 'rooms', box parterres, pleached limes, vegetable garden, rose and herbaceous borders containing many rare plants. Arboretum, lake and wild flower meadows. Opportunity to see rare White Park cattle and Soay sheep New summer house for 2015. Wheelchair access to most areas.

15 HOLMCROFT

Wyson Lane, Brimfield, nr Ludlow SY8 4NW. Mr & Mrs Michael Dowding. *4m S of Ludlow & 6m N of Leominster. From Ludlow or Leominster leave the A49 at the Salway Arms PH, turn into lane signed Wyson only. From Tenbury Wells cross the A49 into Wyson Lane.* Cream teas. **Adm £4, chd free. Sun 28 June, Sun 26 July (2-5.30).**

C17 thatched cottage set in terraced gardens of ¾ acre, which due to sudden illness did not open last year but will open twice in 2015 to take advantage of extended planting. Quintessential cottage garden planting. Roses, herbaceous borders, kitchen, gravel and woodland gardens all with spectacular views of surrounding countryside. Only the woodland walk is inaccessible for wheelchairs.

16 LONGNER HALL

Atcham, Shrewsbury SY4 4TG. Mr & Mrs R L Burton. *4m SE of Shrewsbury. From M54 follow A5 to Shrewsbury, then B4380 to Atcham. From Atcham take Uffington rd, entrance ¼ m on L.* Home-made teas. **Adm £4, chd free. Sun 3 May (2-5).**

A long drive approach through parkland designed by Humphry Repton. Walks lined with golden yew through extensive lawns, with views over Severn Valley. Borders containing roses, herbaceous and shrubs, also ancient yew wood. Enclosed walled garden containing mixed planting, garden buildings, tower and game larder. Short woodland walk around old moat pond. 1-acre walled garden currently being restored now open to visitors. Woodland walk not suitable for wheelchairs.

Bowbrook Allotment Community

© Julia Stanley

17 LYNDALE HOUSE

Astley Abbots, Bridgnorth WV16 4SW. Bob & Mary Saunders. *2m out of Bridnorth off B4373. From High Town Bridgnorth take B4373 Broseley Rd for 1½ m, then take lane signed Astley Abbotts & Colemore Green.* Tea. **Adm £3.50, chd free. Sun 10 May (2-5).**

Large 1½ acre garden which has evolved over 20yrs. Terrace with roses, alliums and iris surrounded by box hedging. Specimen trees planted in large lawn. Hundreds of tulips for spring colour. Clematis and allium walk to pool and waterfall. Vegetable garden and working greenhouses. Densely planted borders. Wealth of peonies, viburnums and acers. Stumpery with late spring bulbs. New scree bed in progress. Courtyard garden with topiary, pool with waterfall and 'pebble beach'. Masses of blossom in spring. Birds in abundance. Named the prettiest garden in the county. Please ask owner about wheelchair friendly access.

18 MILLICHOPE PARK

Munslow, Craven Arms, Munslow SY7 9HA. Mr & Mrs Frank Bury, www.boutsviolas.co.uk. *8m NE of Craven Arms. From Ludlow (11m) turn L off B4368, just ½ m outside village of Munslow.* Home-made teas. **Adm £5, chd free. Suns 15, 22 Feb (2-5); Suns 3 May, 28 June, 20 Sept (2-6); Sun 11 Oct (2-5).**

Historic landscape gardens covering 14 acres with lakes, cascades dating from C18, woodland walks and wildflowers. Snowdrops in February, Bluebells in May, Roses and wild flower meadows in June and Autumn colour in September and Octobe. Also open the Walled Garden at Millichope, an exciting restoration project bringing the walled gardens and C19 glasshouses back to life. Rare opportunity to see the Bouts Viola collection. UK's largest collection of hardy, perennial, scented violas. Many varieties for sale during the May opening. Partial wheelchair access, incl WC.

Morville Hall Gardens

19 MOORTOWN

nr Wellington TF6 6JE. Mr David Bromley. *8m N of Telford. 5m N of Wellington. Take B5062 signed Moortown 1m between High Ercall & Crudgington.* Home-made teas. **Adm £4, chd free.** Sun 29 Mar (2-5). Approx 1-acre plantsman's garden. Here may be found the old-fashioned, the unusual and even the oddities of plant life, in mixed borders of 'controlled' confusion.

GROUP OPENING

20 MORVILLE HALL GARDENS

Bridgnorth WV16 5NB. *3m W of Bridgnorth. On A458 at junction with B4368.* Home-made teas in Morville Church. **Combined adm £5, chd free. Share to Morville Church.** Sun 7 June (2-5).

THE COTTAGE
Mrs J Bolton

THE DOWER HOUSE
Dr Katherine Swift

1 THE GATE HOUSE
Mr & Mrs Rowe

2 THE GATE HOUSE
Mrs G Medland

MORVILLE HALL
Mr & Mrs M Irving

SOUTH PAVILION
Mr & Mrs B Jenkinson

An interesting group of gardens that surround a beautiful Grade I listed mansion (not open). The Cottage has a pretty walled cottage garden with plenty of colour. The Dower House is a horticultural history lesson about Morville Hall which incl a turf maze, cloister garden, Elizabethan knot garden, C18 canal garden, Edwardian kitchen garden and more. It is the setting of Katherine Swift's bestselling book 'The Morville Hours', and the sequel 'The Morville Year'. 1 & 2 The Gate House are cottage-style gardens with colourful borders, formal areas, lawns and wooded glades. The 4-acre Morville Hall (NT) garden has a parterre, medieval stew pond, shrub borders and large lawns, all offering glorious views across the Mor Valley. South Pavilion features new thoughts and new designs in a small courtyard garden. Mostly all level but areas of gravel and lawned areas in some gardens.

21 MYND HARDY PLANTS

Delbury Hall Estate, Mill Lane, Diddlebury, Craven Arms SY7 9DH. Mr & Mrs Rallings, www.myndhardyplants.co.uk. *8m W of Craven Arms. 1m off B4368, Craven Arms to Bridgnorth, through village of Diddlebury, turn R at Mynd Hardy Plants sign.* Home-made teas. **Adm £4.** Tue 2 June, Sun 12 July, Sun 6 Sept, Sun 4 Oct (10-5). Commercial nursery within old walled garden, offering and selling more than 800 varieties of herbaceous perennials. Speciality is hemerocallis with more than 150 day lilies, most unavailable elsewhere in the UK. There is also a large penstemon collection and a growing range of late summer flowering plants. Gravel and grass paths.

22 NEW **NORTON FARM**
Norton, Craven Arms SY7 9LT.
Holiday Property Bond, 01588
674050, nhmanager@hpb.co.uk,
www.hpb-uppernorton.co.uk.
*8m N of Ludlow. From A49 turn
L on B4368 signed Much Wenlock &
Bridgenorth 1½ m turn R for Norton,
Burley & Bache. From Bridgenorth
take A458 W. At Morville L B4368
signed Craven Arms, L for Bache &
Norton.* Tea. Squash drinks for
children. **Adm £4, chd free.**
Mon 31 Aug (12-4). Visitors also
welcome by arrangement May to
Aug.
Holiday cottages tastefully developed
from old farm and buildings
overlooking Clee Hills. Mediterranean
style planting covering old walls and
maturing herbaceous borders.
Emphasis on seasonal changes,
scent and bee friendly plants. Reed
bed, eco filtration system. New
heritage orchard and herb garden,
Ornamental pond with water lilies.

23 **PREEN MANOR**
Church Preen SY6 7LQ. Mrs Ann
Trevor-Jones, 01694 771207. *6m W
of Much Wenlock. Signed from
B4371.* Home-made teas. Tea and
biscuits £1. **Adm £6, chd free.**
Visitors welcome by arrangement.
May to Sept for groups of 10+.
Not August.
6-acre garden on site of Cluniac
monastery and Norman Shaw
mansion. Kitchen, chess, water and
wild gardens. Fine trees in park;
woodland walks. Developed for over
30yrs with changes always in
progress.

24 **RADNOR COTTAGE**
Clun SY7 0JA. Pam & David
Pittwood, 01588 640451. *7m W of
Craven Arms. 1m E of Clun on
B4368.* Home-made teas. **Adm £3,
chd free.** Share to Clun Methodist
Church. Tue 7 Apr, Tue 26 May
(2-6). Visitors also welcome by
arrangement Apr to June.
2 acres on S-facing slope,
overlooking Clun Valley. Wide variety
of garden habitats all densely planted.
Incl sunny terracing with paving and
dry-stone walling; alpine troughs;
cottage garden borders; damp shade
for white flowers and gold foliage;
pond, stream and bog garden;
orchard; rough grass with naturalised
bulbs and wild flowers. Lots of plants
for sale - shrubs, perennials, alpines;

from £1 - nearly all raised by us in the
garden, so you can see the parent
plants growing.

25 **RUTHALL MANOR**
Ditton Priors, Bridgnorth
WV16 6TN. Mr & Mrs G T Clarke,
01746 712608,
clrk608@btinternet.com. *7m SW of
Bridgnorth. Ruthall Rd signed nr
garage in Ditton Priors. See yellow
arrows.* Home-made teas. **Adm £4,
chd free.** Sat 13, Sun 14, Mon 15
June (12.30-6). Visitors also
welcome by arrangement May to
Aug refreshments by arrangement.
1-acre garden with ha-ha and old
horse pond planted with candelabra
primulas, iris and bog plants. Rare
specimen trees. Designed for easy
maintenance with lots of ground
cover and unusual plants. Gravel art
garden and other areas for low
maintenance incl stumpery. New
features being added year by year.
Jigsaws for sale.

26 **SAMBROOK MANOR**
Sambrook, Newport TF10 8AL. Mrs
E Mitchell, 01952 550256,
sambrookmanor@btconnect.com.
*Between Newport & Ternhill. 1m off
A41 in the village of Sambrook.*
Home-made teas. **Adm £4, chd free.**
Sun 12 July, Sun 16 Aug (12.30-5).
The garden surrounds the early C18
manor house (not open) and contains
a wide selection of herbaceous plants
and roses. Features incl a waterfall
down to a pond and various acers. A
new development leading to the river
along the edge of the garden is filled
with a variety of shrubs and trees.

27 **SECRET GARDEN**
21 Steventon Terrace, Steventon
New Road, Ludlow SY8 1JZ. Mr &
Mrs Wood, 01584 876037,
carolynwood2152@yahoo.co.uk.
*Park & Ride if needed, stops outside
garden.* Home-made teas. **Adm
£3.50, chd free.** Sat 20 June (12-5).
Visitors also welcome by
arrangement open throughout the
year.
½ -acre of very secret S-facing
garden, divided into different
sections, roses, herbaceous borders,
lawn and summer house. Developed
over 30yrs by present owners.
Terraced vegetable garden and
greenhouses. ¼ -acre project incl
poly tunnel, vegetable plot, chickens,

completed in 2011. Mediterranean
style terrace garden. 1st Ludlow in
Bloom.

28 **SHOOTHILL HOUSE**
Ford, Shrewsbury SY5 9NR. Colin
& Jane Lloyd, 01743 850795,
jane@lloydmasters.com. *5m W of
Shrewsbury. From A458 turn L
towards Shoothill (signed).* Home-
made teas. **Adm £4.50, chd free.**
Sun 21 June (2-5). Visitors also
welcome by arrangement May to
Sept groups 10+.
6-acre garden, incl small wood with
swamp garden, wild flower meadows,
tree house and several lawned areas
surrounded by mixed borders. Large
well maintained Victorian greenhouse
in renovated walled kitchen garden.
New areas of garden created in 2012.
Mature wildlife pond surrounded by
species trees and shrubs with
extensive views over Welsh hills.
Victorian manor house vintage tea
stall.

*A multitude of
colourful beds and
tranquil seating
areas from which
to enjoy
a moment in our
garden . . .*

29 **SIBBERSCOTE MANOR**
Lea Cross, Shrewsbury SY5 8JF.
Lady Kingsland, 01743 860985. *5m
S of Shrewsbury. Take A488 S off
Shrewsbury bypass, 4m take L turn in
Lea Cross to Arscott.* Home-made
teas. **Adm £5, chd free.** Visitors
welcome by arrangement June to
July min 20.
Garden created to complement C16
timbered farmhouse (not open).
Lovely views over 4-acre lake and S
Shropshire hills. Artistically planted
with roses, herbaceous and shrub
borders, interesting topiary and
showing a collection of sculpture.
Teas in renovated farm buildings.
Partial access on gravel and grass.

30 STANLEY HALL

Bridgnorth WV16 4SP. Mr & Mrs M J Thompson. ¹/₂ m N of Bridgnorth. *Leave Bridgnorth by N gate; B4373; turn R at Stanley Lane. Pass Golf Course Club House on L & turn L at Lodge.* Home-made teas. **Adm £4, chd free. Sun 31 May (2-6).**
Drive ¹/₂ m with rhododendrons, azaleas, fine trees and chain of pools. Restored ice-house. Woodland walks with steps, slopes and pools. Also open **The Granary** (Mr & Mrs Jack Major) Charming small trellis garden. Profusion of flowers in hanging baskets and herbaceous borders and also **Dower House** Mr & Mrs Colin Wells.

Plenty of places to sit and take in the views . . .

31 NEW UPPER SHELDERTON HOUSE

Shelderton, Clungunford, Craven Arms SY7 0PE. Andrew Benton & Trica McHaffie, 01547 540525. *Between Ludlow & Craven Arms. Heading from Shrewsbury to Ludlow on A49, take 1st R after Onibury railway crossing. Take 3rd R signed Shelderton. After approx 1m the house is last property on L. Garden will be signed.* Home-made teas. **Adm £4, chd free. Sat 23, Sun 24, Mon 25 May, Sat 29, Sun 30, Mon 31 Aug (2-5).**
Set in a stunning tranquil position, our naturalistic and evolving 6¹/₂ acre garden was originally landscaped in 1962. Most of the trees, azaleas and rhododendrons were planted then. There is a wonderful new kitchen garden designed and planted by Jayne and Norman Grove. Ponds and woodland walk encourage wildlife. A large sweeping lawn leads in various directions revealing a multitude of colourful beds and tranquil seating areas from which to enjoy a moment in our garden.

32 WALCOT HALL

Lydbury North SY7 8AZ. Mr & Mrs C R W Parish, 01588 680570, maria@walcothall.com, www.walcothall.com. *4m SE of Bishop's Castle. B4385 Craven Arms to Bishop's Castle, turn L by Powis Arms, in Lydbury North.* Home-made teas. **Adm £3.50, chd free. Sun 24, Mon 25 May (1.30-5.30).**
Arboretum planted by Lord Clive of India's son, Edward. Cascades of rhododendrons, azaleas amongst specimen trees and pools. Fine views of Sir William Chambers' Clock Towers, with lake and hills beyond. Walled kitchen garden; dovecote; meat safe; ice house and mile-long lakes. Outstanding ballroom where excellent teas are served. Russian wooden church, grotto and fountain now complete and working; tin chapel. Beautifully relaxed borders with some rare shrubs. Lakeside replanted, and water garden at western end re-established. The garden adjacent to the ballroom is accessible via a sloping bank, as is the walled garden and arboretum.

33 8 WESTGATE VILLAS

Salop Street, Bridgnorth WV16 4QX. Bill & Marilyn Hammerton. *From A458 Bridgnorth bypass, at Ludlow Rd r'about take rd into Bridgnorth signed town centre. At T-junction (free parking at council offices here) turn R, garden is 100yds on L past Victoria Road.* 17 April wine & canapés, 19 April tea & cake. **Adm £4, chd free. Evening Opening £5, chd free, Fri 17 Apr (7-9.30). Sun 19 Apr (2-5.30).**
Town garden having formal Victorian front garden with box hedging and water feature to complement house. Back garden has a shade border, lawn, small knot garden and orchard, together with a strong oriental influence incl Japanese style teahouse and zen garden and path in Chinese style. Wine, canapes, music and garden lighting incl at evening opening. Shakkei, Featured in The journal of the Japanese Garden Society. Partial wheelchair access.

34 WINDY RIDGE

Church Lane, Little Wenlock, Telford TF6 5BB. George & Fiona Chancellor, 01952 507675, fionachancellor@btinternet.com. *2m S of Wellington. Follow signs for Little Wenlock from N (J7, M54) or E*
(off A5223 at Horsehay). Parking signed. Do not rely on SatNav. Home-made teas. **Adm £5, chd free. Suns 14 June, 12 July, 9 Aug, 6 Sept (12-5).** Visitors also welcome by arrangement May to Sept suitable for coaches.
'Stunning' and 'inspirational' are how visitors frequently describe this multi-award-winning ²/₃ acre village garden. The strong design and exuberant colour-themed planting (over 1000 species, mostly labelled) offer a picture around every corner. The grass and perennial gravel garden has created a lot of interest and versions are now appearing in gardens all over the country! Some gravel paths but help available.

35 NEW WOLLASTON LODGE

Wollaston, Halfway House, Shrewsbury SY5 9DN. Sandy & Grant Williams, 01743 884831, enjoylife@wollastonlodge.co.uk, www.wollastonlodge.co.uk. *From A458, Shrewsbury - Welshpool Rd. 8m from Shrewsbury ringroad, 8m from Welshpool. Signed Wollaston.* Light refreshments. **Adm £4, chd free. Wed 27 May (12-5).**
Classic Italianate style gardens borrowing the views. Formal terraces, ornamental pool. Compact, plenty of places to sit and take in the views. Gardens surround award winning B&B.

36 ◆ WOLLERTON OLD HALL

Wollerton, Market Drayton TF9 3NA. Lesley & John Jenkins, 01630 685760, www.wollertonoldhallgarden.com. *4m SW of Market Drayton. On A53 between Hodnet & A53-A41 junction. Follow brown signs.* **Adm £6.50, chd free. For NGS: Fri 15 May (12-5). For other opening times and information, please phone or see garden website.**
4-acre garden created around C16 house (not open). Formal structure creates variety of gardens each with own colour theme and character. Planting is mainly of perennials, the large range of which results in significant collections of salvias, clematis, crocosmias and roses. Ongoing lectures by Gardening Celebrities including Chris Beardshaw, Jules Hudson and Sir Roy Strong. Partial wheelchair access.

Wollerton Old Hall

© Clive Nicholls

From tiny back plots to country estates ...

SOMERSET, BRISTOL AREA &
SOUTH GLOUCESTERSHIRE incl Bath

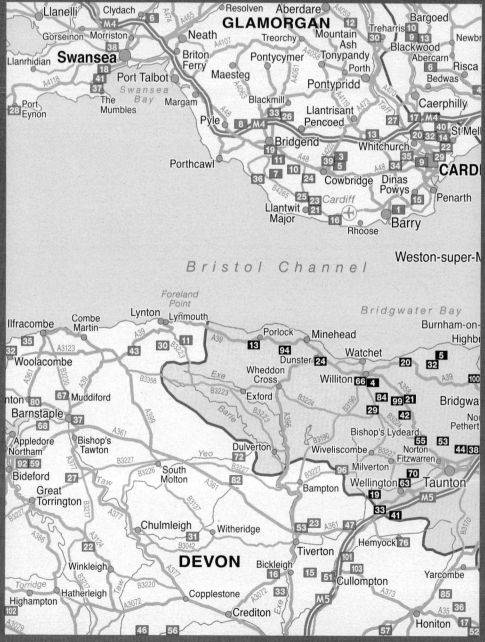

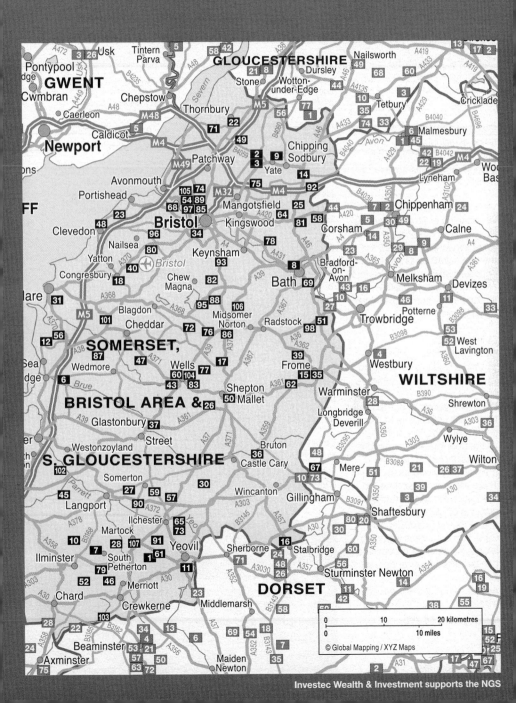

Somerset, Bristol Area & South Gloucestershire

Somerset is open for business with snowdrops and bulbs above the flood line.

Come and explore the fascinating range of mainly privately owned gardens in the county, usually offering delicious teas, and which benefit charity too.

View the Capability Brown landscaping of Ston Easton Park, the plantsman's garden for all seasons at Little Garth, the tree collection of rare and unusual cultivars at Little Yarford and much more - possibly finding a rarity from a plant stall along the way.

Bristol, South Gloucestershire, and Bath are also looking forward to another successful year.

We offer a variety of gardens from small urban plots to country estates. We have village openings and community projects, including gardens maintained by volunteers. There are tranquil gardens for meditation forming part of the grounds of St Peter's Hospice, and at Penny Brohn Cancer Care. Some gardens including allotments cater for groups and can be visited by arrangement.

Almost all our gardens will offer a delicious home-made tea to accompany your visit.

Somerset Volunteers

County Organiser
Lucy Hetherington 01934 713159
lucyhetherington@btinternet.com

County Treasurer
David Bull 01934 712609
d.bull08@btinternet.com

Publicity
Roger Peacock 01275 341584
barum@blueyonder.co.uk

Photographer
John Wyatt 07775 866224
jhg.wyatt@btopenworld.com

Booklet Distributor
Chris & Dianne McKinley
01278 421675
chrismckinley80@hotmail.com

Beneficiaries
Sarah Wilcox 01823 451402
wilcoxsarah@hotmail.co.uk

Presentations
Dave & Pru Moon 01373 473381
davidmoon202@btinternet.com

Assistant County Organisers
Patricia Davies-Gilbert
01823 412187
pdaviesgilbert@btinternet.com

Alison Highnam 01747 838133
allies1@btinternet.com

Laura Howard 01460 282911
laurafivehead@btinternet.com

Judith Stanford 01761 233045
judithstanford.ngs@hotmail.co.uk

Bristol Area Volunteers

County Organiser
Su Mills 01454 615438
susanlmills@gmail.com

County Treasurer
Ken Payne 01275 333146
kg.payne@yahoo.co.uk

Publicity
Jean Damey 01179 775587
jeandamey@gmail.com

Pat Davie 01275 790919
pattidavie@hotmail.com

County Booklet Advertising
Jean Damey (as above)

Booklet Coordinator
Jean Damey (as above)

Booklet Distributor
Graham Guest 01275 472393
gandsguest@btinternet.com

Assistant County Organisers
Angela Conibere 01454 413828
aeconibere@hotmail.com

Pat Davie (as above)

Christine Healey 01454 612795
christine.healey@uwclub.net

Margaret Jones 01225 891229
ian@weircott.plus.com

Jeanette Parker 01454 299699
jeanette_parker@hotmail.co.uk

Jane Perkins 01454 414570
janekperkins@gmail.com

Irene Randow 01275 857208
irene.randow@sky.com

Right: Ston Easton Park

Currently the NGS donates around £2.5 million every year

Opening Dates

All entries subject to change.
For latest information check www.ngs.org.uk

February

Sunday 1
71 Rock House
Sunday 8
28 East Lambrook Manor Gardens
71 Rock House
Sunday 15
76 Sherborne Garden
Monday 16
76 Sherborne Garden

March

Tuesday 17
44 Hestercombe Gardens
Sunday 29
32 Fairfield
82 Stanton Court Nursing Home

April

Thursday 2
29 Elworthy Cottage
Monday 6
29 Elworthy Cottage
Sunday 12
21 Crowcombe Court
42 Hartwood House
Wednesday 15
50 Kilver Court Secret Gardens
Thursday 16
29 Elworthy Cottage
Saturday 18
7 Barrington Court
Sunday 19
2 Algars Manor
3 Algars Mill
41 Hangeridge Farmhouse
72 Rose Cottage
Thursday 23
8 Bath Priory Hotel
Sunday 26
101 Watcombe
103 Wayford Manor

May

Saturday 2
11 1 Braggchurch
52 Little Garth

Sunday 3
11 1 Braggchurch
87 Stone Allerton Gardens
Monday 4
87 Stone Allerton Gardens
Friday 8
53 Little Yarford Farmhouse
Saturday 9
45 NEW Hillcrest
53 Little Yarford Farmhouse
Sunday 10
20 Court House
28 East Lambrook Manor Gardens
42 Hartwood House
45 NEW Hillcrest
53 Little Yarford Farmhouse
54 Lucombe House
59 Midney Gardens
69 Prior Park Landscape Garden
Monday 11
53 Little Yarford Farmhouse
Thursday 14
29 Elworthy Cottage
Sunday 17
4 Aller Farmhouse
41 Hangeridge Farmhouse
60 Milton Lodge
63 Nynehead Court
101 Watcombe
Thursday 21
29 Elworthy Cottage
86 Ston Easton Park
Saturday 23
58 Marshfield Gardens
Sunday 24
29 Elworthy Cottage
58 Marshfield Gardens
70 NEW Rendy Farm
Monday 25
70 NEW Rendy Farm
Tuesday 26
104 Wellfield Barn
Thursday 28
29 Elworthy Cottage
50 Kilver Court Secret Gardens
Saturday 30
6 Babbs Farm
30 Esotera
38 Glebe Court
106 Woodlea Bottom
Sunday 31
6 Babbs Farm
17 Church Farm House

30 Esotera
34 1 Frobisher Road
38 Glebe Court
49 Jekka's Herbetum
83 Stoberry Garden
106 Woodlea Bottom

June

Wednesday 3
17 Church Farm House
Thursday 4
29 Elworthy Cottage

Festival Weekend

Saturday 6
28 East Lambrook Manor Gardens
52 Little Garth
65 The Old Rectory, Limington
99 Vellacott
Sunday 7
18 Congresbury Gardens
54 Lucombe House
60 Milton Lodge
61 Montacute House
65 The Old Rectory, Limington
89 1 Sunnyside
91 Tintinhull
93 Tranby House
97 University of Bristol Botanic Garden
99 Vellacott
Tuesday 9
44 Hestercombe Gardens
Wednesday 10
15 9 Catherston Close
40 Goblin Combe House
Thursday 11
29 Elworthy Cottage
48 Jasmine Cottage
57 Lytes Cary Manor
101 Watcombe
Saturday 13
64 The Old Rectory, Doynton
74 St Peter's Hospice
102 NEW Waverley
Sunday 14
10 NEW Bradon Farm
35 Frome Gardens
42 Hartwood House
62 Nunney Gardens
63 Nynehead Court
74 St Peter's Hospice
80 Southfield Farm
85 NEW Stoke Bishop Gardens
102 NEW Waverley
105 West Bristol Gardens

Monday 15
79 South Meade
Tuesday 16
79 South Meade
Wednesday 17
15 9 Catherston Close
40 Goblin Combe House
79 South Meade
Thursday 18
79 South Meade
81 Special Plants
Friday 19
79 South Meade
Saturday 20
30 Esotera
56 Lympsham Gardens

Pair of interesting gardens adjacent to the Downs . . .

Sunday 21
23 NEW The Dairy
30 Esotera
55 Lydeard House
56 Lympsham Gardens
66 Orchard Wyndham
68 Penny Brohn Cancer Care
84 Stogumber Gardens
88 Stowey Gardens
Wednesday 24
40 Goblin Combe House
Thursday 25
48 Jasmine Cottage
Friday 26
25 Dyrham Park
Saturday 27
25 Dyrham Park
102 NEW Waverley
Sunday 28
17 Church Farm House
33 Fernhill
41 Hangeridge Farmhouse
102 NEW Waverley
107 Yews Farm
Monday 29
107 Yews Farm

July

Wednesday 1
17 Church Farm House

Visit a garden on National Gardens Festival Weekend 6 & 7 June

Friday 3
13 NEW Broomclose

Saturday 4
13 NEW Broomclose
52 Little Garth
58 Marshfield Gardens
95 Truffles

Sunday 5
13 NEW Broomclose
24 Dunster Castle Gardens
36 Gants Mill & Garden
37 Glastonbury Secret Gardens
41 Hangeridge Farmhouse
60 Milton Lodge
95 Truffles

Wednesday 8
15 9 Catherston Close

Thursday 9
48 Jasmine Cottage

Sunday 12
46 Hinton St George Gardens
49 Jekka's Herbetum

Monday 13
46 Hinton St George Gardens

Wednesday 15
41 Hangeridge Farmhouse
86 Ston Easton Park

Thursday 16
81 Special Plants

Saturday 18
7 Barrington Court
39 NEW Glebe Farmhouse

Sunday 19
12 Brent Knoll Gardens
20 Court House
31 22 Exeter Road
41 Hangeridge Farmhouse
47 Honeyhurst Farm
73 Rugg Farm
76 Sherborne Garden
77 Sole Retreat
90 Sutton Hosey Manor
93 Tranby House
96 Tyntesfield

Thursday 23
48 Jasmine Cottage

Saturday 25
51 NEW Linden
98 NEW 8 Upper Farm Close

Sunday 26
14 Camers
17 Church Farm House
19 Cothay Manor & Gardens

21 Crowcombe Court
31 22 Exeter Road
33 Fernhill
51 NEW Linden
98 NEW 8 Upper Farm Close

Wednesday 29
17 Church Farm House

August

Saturday 1
52 Little Garth

Sunday 2
23 NEW The Dairy

Sunday 9
49 Jekka's Herbetum

Sunday 16
34 1 Frobisher Road
41 Hangeridge Farmhouse
93 Tranby House

Thursday 20
81 Special Plants

Sunday 23
33 Fernhill

Thursday 27
29 Elworthy Cottage

Sunday 30
6 Babbs Farm
77 Sole Retreat

Monday 31
6 Babbs Farm
29 Elworthy Cottage
79 South Meade
83 Stoberry Garden

September

Tuesday 1
79 South Meade

Wednesday 2
79 South Meade
86 Ston Easton Park

Thursday 3
29 Elworthy Cottage
79 South Meade

Friday 4
79 South Meade

Saturday 5
52 Little Garth
67 Pen Mill Farm

Sunday 6
67 Pen Mill Farm
93 Tranby House

Monday 7
41 Hangeridge Farmhouse

Thursday 10
8 Bath Priory Hotel

Sunday 13
9 Beechwell House
21 Crowcombe Court

82 Stanton Court Nursing Home

Monday 14
50 Kilver Court Secret Gardens

Thursday 17
81 Special Plants

Friday 18
59 Midney Gardens

Saturday 26
100 The Walled Gardens of Cannington

Sunday 27
100 The Walled Gardens of Cannington

October

Thursday 15
81 Special Plants

February 2016

Sunday 7
28 East Lambrook Manor Gardens
71 Rock House

Sunday 14
71 Rock House
76 Sherborne Garden

Monday 15
76 Sherborne Garden

Gardens open to the public

7 Barrington Court
19 Cothay Manor & Gardens
20 Court House
24 Dunster Castle Gardens
25 Dyrham Park
28 East Lambrook Manor Gardens
29 Elworthy Cottage
44 Hestercombe Gardens
49 Jekka's Herbetum
50 Kilver Court Secret Gardens
57 Lytes Cary Manor
59 Midney Gardens
60 Milton Lodge
61 Montacute House
69 Prior Park Landscape Garden
76 Sherborne Garden
81 Special Plants
86 Ston Easton Park
91 Tintinhull
96 Tyntesfield
97 University of Bristol Botanic Garden
100 The Walled Gardens of Cannington

By arrangement only

1 Abbey Farm
5 Ash Cottage
16 Cherry Bolberry Farm
22 Daggs Allotments
26 East Burford House
27 East End Farm
43 Henley Mill
75 Serridge House
78 NEW South Kelding
92 Tormarton Court
94 NEW Troytes Farmstead

Also open by arrangement

4 Aller Farmhouse
6 Babbs Farm
12 Ball Copse Hall, Brent Knoll Gardens
13 NEW Broomclose
14 Camers
17 Church Farm House
33 Fernhill
40 Goblin Combe House
41 Hangeridge Farmhouse
42 Hartwood House
46 Hooper's Holding, Hinton St George Gardens
47 Honeyhurst Farm
48 Jasmine Cottage
52 Little Garth
53 Little Yarford Farmhouse
54 Lucombe House
63 Nynehead Court
65 The Old Rectory, Limington
67 Pen Mill Farm
71 Rock House
72 Rose Cottage
73 Rugg Farm
77 Sole Retreat
84 Knoll Cottage, Stogumber Gardens
87 Badgers Acre, Stone Allerton Gardens
90 Sutton Hosey Manor
95 Truffles
99 Vellacott
101 Watcombe
104 Wellfield Barn
105 4 Haytor Park, West Bristol Gardens
105 West Bristol Gardens
105 159 Westbury Lane, West Bristol Gardens
106 Woodlea Bottom
107 Yews Farm

The Gardens

1 ABBEY FARM
Montacute TA15 6UA. Alisdair & Elizabeth McFarlane, 01935 823556, ct.fm@btopenworld.com. *4m from Yeovil. Follow A3088, take slip rd to Montacute, turn L at T-junction into village. Turn R between Church & King's Arms (no through rd).* Refreshments by arrangement. **Adm £5, chd free. Visitors welcome by arrangement June to July.**
2½ acres of mainly walled gardens on sloping site provide the setting for Cluniac Medieval Priory gatehouse. Interesting plants incl roses, shrubs, grasses, clematis. Herbaceous borders, white garden, gravel garden. Small arboretum. Pond for wildlife - frogs, newts, dragonflies. Fine mulberry, walnut and monkey puzzle trees. Seats for resting. Gravel area and one steep slope.

2 ALGARS MANOR
Station Rd, Iron Acton BS37 9TB. Mrs B Naish. *9m N of Bristol, 3m W of Yate/Chipping Sodbury. Turn S off Iron Acton bypass B4059, past village green, 200yds, then over level Xing (Station Rd).* Tea. **Combined adm £5, chd free. Sun 19 Apr (2-5). Combined with Algars Mill.**
2 acres of woodland garden beside R Frome, mill stream, native plants mixed with collections of 60 magnolias and 70 camellias, rhododendrons, azaleas, eucalyptus and other unusual trees and shrubs. Partial wheelchair access, gravel paths, some steep slopes.

3 ALGARS MILL
Frampton End Rd, Iron Acton, Bristol BS37 9TD. Mr & Mrs John Wright. *9m N of Bristol, 3m W of Yate/Chipping Sodbury. (For directions see Algars Manor).* **Combined adm £5, chd free. Sun 19 Apr (2-5). Combined with Algars Manor.**
2-acre woodland garden bisected by R Frome; spring bulbs, shrubs; very early spring feature (Feb-Mar) of wild Newent daffodils. 300-400yr-old mill house (not open) through which millrace still runs.

Wayford Manor

© Val Corbett

4 ALLER FARMHOUSE
Williton, nr Taunton TA4 4LY. Mr & Mrs Richard Chandler, 01984 633702, sylvana.chandler@gmail.com. *7m E of Minehead, 1m S of Williton. From A358 Taunton turn L into Sampford Brett. Follow signs to Capton. Follow lane downhill to Aller Farm. Car park in field beyond house.* **Adm £4, chd free. Sun 17 May (2-5.30). Visitors also welcome by arrangement Apr to Oct for groups of 10+.**
2-3 acres. Hot, dry, sunny, S-facing, surrounded by pink stone walls and sub-divided into 5 separate compartments by same. Cliff Garden is old 3-sided quarry. Old magnolias, figs, Judas, etc; newer acacias; many unusual and/or tender plants incl eremurus, beschorneria, dendromecon, echiums in variety and buddleia colvilei. Partial wheelchair access.

5 ASH COTTAGE
Shurton, Stogursey, Bridgwater TA5 1QF. Barbara & Peter Oates, 01278 732258, oatespeter@gmail.com. *8m W of Bridgwater. From A39 nr Holford, follow signs to Stogursey then to Shurton. From A39 at Cannington follow signs to Hinkley Point then Shurton. Map supplied when arrangement is made.* Light refreshments. Details by prior arrangement. **Adm £4, chd free. Groups of 10+ welcome by arrangement May to June.**
Tranquil cottage garden in rural area, approx ⅔ acre, wrapping around 3 sides of early C16 cottage (not open). Colour-themed borders and flowerbeds incl island bed, with raised 40ft border reached by steps from either end. Admire our amazing S-facing wall! Natural stream with planted banks runs through garden. Children must be supervised at all times. Some gravel paths and shallow steps.

6 BABBS FARM
Westhill Lane, Bason Bridge, Highbridge TA9 4RF. Sue & Richard O'Brien, 01278 793244. *1½ m E of Highbridge, 1½ m SSE of M5 exit 22. Turn into Westhill Lane off B3141 (Church Rd), 100yds S of where it joins B3139 (Wells-Highbridge rd).* Tea. **Adm £3.50, chd free. Sat 30, Sun 31 May, Sun 30, Mon 31 Aug (2-5). Visitors also welcome by arrangement May to Sept.**
¾ acre plantsman's garden in Somerset Levels, gradually created out of fields surrounding old farmhouse over last 20 yrs and still being developed. Trees, shrubs and herbaceous perennials planted with an eye for form and shape in big flowing borders. Various ponds (formal and informal) box garden, patio area and conservatory. Featured in Somerset Country Gardener.

Barrington Court

7 ◆ BARRINGTON COURT

Barrington, Ilminster TA19 0NQ.
National Trust, 01460 241938,
www.nationaltrust.org.uk. *5m NE of
Ilminster. In Barrington village on
B3168. Follow brown NT signs.* **Adm
£12, chd £6. For NGS: Sat 18 Apr,
Sat 18 July (10.30-5).** For other
opening times and information,
please phone or see garden
website.
Well known garden constructed in
1920 by Col Arthur Lyle from derelict
farmland (the C19 cattle stalls still
exist). Gertrude Jekyll suggested
planting schemes for the layout.
Paved paths with walled rose and iris,
white and lily gardens, large kitchen
garden. The kitchen garden has been
in continuous production for over
90yrs. Some paths a little uneven.

&. ⊗ 🚐 ☕

8 BATH PRIORY HOTEL

Weston Rd, Bath BA1 2XT. Jane
Moore, Head Gardener,
www.thebathpriory.co.uk. *Close to
centre of Bath. From Bath centre take
Upper Bristol Rd, turn R at end of
Victoria Park and L into Weston Rd.
Please note no parking. Drop off and
parking for disabled only. Meter
parking available in Victoria Park.*
Home-made teas. **Adm £3, chd free.
Thur 23 Apr, Thur 10 Sept (2-5).**
Discover 3 acres of mature walled
gardens. Quintessentially English, the
garden has billowing borders, croquet
lawn, wild flower meadow and
ancient specimen trees. Spring is

bright with tulips and flowering
cherries; autumn alive with colour.
Perennials and tender plants provide
summer highlights while the kitchen
garden supplies herbs, fruit and
vegetables to the restaurant. Gravel
paths and some steps.

&. ⊗ **NCH** ☕

9 BEECHWELL HOUSE

51 Goose Green, Yate BS37 5BL.
Tim Wilmot, www.beechwell.com.
*10m NE of Bristol. From Yate centre,
go N onto Church Ln. After ¹/₂ m turn
L onto Greenways Rd then R onto
Church Ln. After 300yds take R fork,
garden 100yds on L.* Home-made
teas. **Adm £3.50, chd free. Sun 13
Sept (1-5).**
Enclosed, level, subtropical garden
created over last 26 yrs and filled with
exotic planting, incl palms (over 6
varieties), tree ferns, yuccas, agaves
and succulent bed, rare shrubs,
bamboos, bananas, aroids and other
architectural planting. Wildlife pond
and koi pond. C16 40ft deep well.
Rare plant raffle every hour. Featured
on BBC Gardeners World, ITV and in
Daily Mail, Daily Express, Daily
Telegraph. Some narrow pathways.

&. ☕

10 NEW BRADON FARM

Isle Abbotts, Taunton TA3 6RX. Mr
& Mrs Thomas Jones. *Take turning
to Ilton off A358. Bradon Farm is
1¹/₂ m out of this village on Bradon
Lane.* Home-made teas. **Adm £5,**

chd free. **Sun 14 June (2-5.30).**
A classic formal garden created in
recent years, demonstrating the
effective use of structure. There is
much to see incl parterre, knot
garden, pleached lime walk, formal
pond, herbaceous borders, orchard
and wildflower planting. Featured in
Somerset County Gazette and
Western Gazette.

&. ⊗ 🚐 ☕

11 1 BRAGGCHURCH

93 Hendford Hill, Yeovil BA20 2RE.
Veronica Sartin. *Walking distance of
Yeovil centre. Approaching Yeovil on
A30 from Quicksilver Mail PH r'about,
garden 1st driveway on R down
Hendford Hill, parking at Southwoods
(next R down hill). Car park at bottom
of Hendford Hill.* Home-made teas.
**Adm £4, chd free. Sat 2, Sun 3
May (2-6).**
Old garden of undulating lawns and
mature trees evolving since May 2002
to semi-wild, nature-friendly,
woodland garden with a few
surprises within the new planting -
refurbished tree house, dancing
figures, Anderson shelter, pond,
willow weaving, retreat with poetry,
medlar tree enclosure, rhododendron
hideaway and courtyard
curios/mosaics. Tree house for
children. Partial wheelchair access -
on main drive through garden to
refreshment area. Small paths leading
off not suitable.

&. 🐕 ⊗ ☕

Original stone terraces, Mediterranean garden, long borders . . .

GROUP OPENING

12 BRENT KNOLL GARDENS
nr Highbridge TA9 4DF. *2m N of Highbridge. Off A38 & M5 J22. From M5 take A38 N (Cheddar etc) first L into Brent Knoll.* Cream teas at Ball Copse Hall. Light refreshments. **Combined adm £7, chd free.** Sun 19 July (11-5).

BALL COPSE HALL
Mrs S Boss & Mr A J Hill.
From A38 follow signs to Woodlands Hotel then L into car park
Visitors also welcome by arrangement Feb to Oct.
01278 760301
susan.boss@gmail.com

PEN ORCHARD
Brent Street, Highbridge.
John & Wiet Harper.
From A38 into Brent Street, 100 yards on R after PO

ROSE COTTAGE
8 Brent St. Malcolm & Sheila Holness.
Off A38 at Fox & Goose L into village. White Cottage on R

NEW WOODBINE FARM
Brent Street. Matt & Sam Jackson.
Soon after Red Cow Inn on R

The distinctive hill of Brent Knoll, an iron age hill fort, is well worth climbing 449ft for the 360 degree view of surrounding hills incl Glastonbury Tor and the Somerset Levels. Lovely C13 church renowned for its bench ends. Ball Copse Hall: S-facing Edwardian house (not open) on lower slopes of Knoll. Front garden maturing well with curving slopes and paths. Ha-ha, wild

area and kitchen garden. Views to Quantock and Polden Hills. Kitchen garden enclosed by crinkle crankle wall. Pen Orchard is a lovely garden with several developements since last open. A busy person's garden to relax in. Rose Cottage is a level ³/₄ acre garden, started in 2000, redesigned under present ownership in 2002. Many roses, lilies and mature herbaceous beds. Small orchard, contemplation circle and wild area with pond. Woodbine Farm is a quintessential English garden with 3 areas. Cottage garden, main house garden and field with pond under huge willow tree. Flock of Soay sheep. Working beehive on show with honey for sale. Wheelchair access in all gardens, some restricted.

13 NEW BROOMCLOSE
Porlock, Somerset, Minehead TA24 8NU. David and Nicky Ramsay, 01643 862078, davidjamesramsay@gmail.com. *Off A39 on Porlock Weir Rd, between Porlock and West Porlock. Limited parking at property or park in Porlock (10 min walk). In Porlock, thro High St to Porlock Weir Rd, leaving houses behind, pass 3 fields, garden entrance on L.* Home-made teas. **Adm £3.50, chd free.** Fri 3, Sat 4, Sun 5 July (12-6). **Visitors also welcome by arrangement Mar to Oct.**
Large varied garden set around turn of century Arts and Crafts house overlooking the sea. Original stone terraces, Mediterranean garden, long borders, copse, camellia walk, wild flower meadow and vegetable garden. Maritime climate favours unusual sub-tropical trees, shrubs and herbaceous plants.

14 CAMERS
Old Sodbury BS37 6RG. Mr & Mrs A G Denman, 01454 322430, dorothydenman@camers.org, www.camers.org. *2m E of Chipping Sodbury. Entrance in Chapel Lane off A432 at Dog Inn.* Home-made teas. **Adm £5, chd free.** Sun 26 July (2-5). **Visitors also welcome by arrangement Feb to Sept for groups of 20+.**
Elizabethan farmhouse (not open) set in 4 acres of constantly developing garden and woodland with spectacular views over Severn Vale.

Garden full of surprises, formal and informal areas planted with very wide range of species to provide yr-round interest. Parterre, topiary, Japanese garden, bog and prairie areas, waterfalls, white and hot gardens, woodland walks. Some steep slopes.

15 9 CATHERSTON CLOSE
Frome. BA11 4HR. Dave & Prue Moon. *15m S of Bath. Town centre W towards Shepton Mallet (A361). R at Sainsbury's r'about, follow lane for ¹/₂ m. L into Critchill Rd. Over Xrds, 1st L Catherston Close.* **Adm £3.50, chd free.** Wed 10, Wed 17 June, Wed 8 July (12-5). **Also open with The Bastion Garden 14 June (Frome Gardens).**
A town garden which has grown over the years to ¹/₃ acre! Colour-themed shrub and herbaceous borders, pond, patios, pergolas and wild meadow areas lead to wonderful far reaching views. Productive vegetable and fruit garden with greenhouse. Exhibition of garden photography from near and far by the garden owner is displayed in the summerhouse. A surprise in waiting. Featured in Fosseway and Country Gardener magazines, regional press with Radio Bristol, Somerset and Glastonbury fm. Several shallow steps, gravel paths.

16 CHERRY BOLBERRY FARM
Furge Lane, Henstridge BA8 0RN. Mrs Jenny Raymond, 01963 362177, cherrybolberryfarm@tiscali.co.uk. *6m E of Sherborne. In centre of Henstridge, R at small Xrds signed Furge Lane. Continue straight up lane, over 2 cattle grids, garden at top of lane on R.* Home-made teas. **Adm £5, chd free.** Groups of 10+ welcome by arrangement June.
40 yr-old award winning, owner designed and maintained 1 acre garden planted for yr round interest with wildlife in mind. Colour themed island beds, shrub and herbaceous borders, unusual perennials and shrubs, old roses and an area of specimen trees. Vegetable and flower cutting garden, greenhouses, nature ponds. Wonderful extensive views. Garden surrounded by our dairy farm which has been in the family for nearly 100 years. You will see Jersey cows, sheep, horses and hens!

17 CHURCH FARM HOUSE

Turners Court Lane, Binegar, nr Wells BA3 4UA. Susan & Tony Griffin, 01749 841628, smgriffin@beanacrebarn.co.uk, www.beanacrebarn.co.uk. *5m NE of Wells. From Wells B3139 NE for 4½ m, turn R signed Binegar, yellow NGS sign at Xrds. From A37 in Gurney Slade, follow sign to Binegar, past church, at Xrds NGS sign turn R into Turners Ct Lane.* **Adm £3.50, chd free. Sun 31 May, Wed 3, Sun 28 June, Wed 1, Sun 26, Wed 29 July (11-4.30). Visitors also welcome by arrangement June to Aug.**

Wrapped around an old farmhouse are two walled gardens planted in contemporary cottage style, roses and clematis on walls and unusual perennials in deep borders give interest all seasons. South garden has exceptional colourist design and the ever expanding insect friendly planting in the gravel of the old farmyard creates an interesting display of form and colour often with self-seeded surprises! Featured in Wells Life, Fosseway Magazine, Country Gardener, regional press with Radio Bristol, Somerset, and Glastonbury fm. Gravel forecourt, 2 shallow steps.

   🚫 🏠

GROUP OPENING

18 CONGRESBURY GARDENS

Congresbury, Bristol BS49 5DN. *Approx halfway between Bristol and Weston-super-Mare. 12m S of Bristol on A370. At T-lights in Congresbury look for signs.* **Home-made teas at Fernbank, Middlecombe Nursery and Church House. Combined adm £5, chd free. Sun 7 June (10.30-4.30).**

NEW CHURCH HOUSE

Broad Street. Mrs Lorraine Coles.
Cross bridge to T-lights. Turn L at T-lights and immed R into Broad Street. Garden is 150 metres on R. Park in side streets or car park N of river

FERNBANK

High Street. Julia Thyer.
From T-lights on A370 at Ship & Castle, turn into High St (B3133). Garden 100yds on R, park in side streets or car park N of river
http://juliathyer.blogspot.co.uk

MIDDLECOMBE NURSERY

Wrington Rd, Congresbury.
Nigel J North.
On edge of Congresbury, on Bristol side, turn to Wrington along Wrington Rd off A370 Weston to Bristol rd. Garden 250yds on L
www.middlecombenursery.co.uk

NEW 18 STONEWELL LANE

Mr Nigel Jarvis.
Stonewell Lane is after PO and shops in Brinsea Rd, continue to bottom, 18 is on R at Xrds at bottom of lane

29 STONEWELL LANE

Mike & Janet Sweeting.
See 18 Stonewell Lane, 29 is bungalow with 2 odd chimney pots, in front of you as you come down lane

Village group of 5 strikingly contrasting gardens. Fernbank: romantic haven for wildlife. Follow paths to surprises, explore the potager and picturesque greenhouse, potter in the potting shed, discover the lily ponds with trickling water, be inspired by banks of potted plants and a furnished Wendy house. Church House: courtyard garden that shows what you can do with an enclosed space within the confines of the village. Middlecombe Nursery: 3 acre nursery site in country setting with series of different gardens, owned by Nigel North, a regular contributor to BBC Radio Bristol. 29 Stonewell Lane: garden to encourage wildlife with a cottage garden feel with borders, mature trees, a pond and herbaceous perennials. 18 Stonewell Lane: modern garden divided into a number of rooms designed to attract wildlife, provide outdoor living areas and seclusion along with space for children and pets to play. No wheelchair access at Church House.

   🚫 🐕 🚫 ☕

---

19 ◆ COTHAY MANOR & GARDENS

Greenham, nr Wellington TA21 0JR. Mr & Mrs Alastair Robb, 01823 672283, www.cothaymanor.co.uk. *5m SW of Wellington. 7m off M5 via A38, signed Greenham, follow Brown Signs for Cothay Manor & Gardens. See website for more detailed directions.* **Cream teas. Adm £7.50, chd £3.75. For NGS: Sun 26 July (2-5). For** other opening times and information, please phone or see garden website.

Few gardens are as evocatively romantic as Cothay. Laid out in 1920s and replanted in 1990s within the original framework, Cothay encompasses a rare blend of old and new. Plantsman's paradise set in 12 acres of magical gardens. Antiques, garden shop, tea room. Sorry no dogs or picnicking in gardens. Sunday house tours 11:45 and 2:15. £14.25 (ticket price includes garden), advance booking recommended. Partial wheelchair access, gravel paths.

   ♿ 🚫 🚐 ☕

Home-made teas in Great Hall of house . . .

---

20 ◆ COURT HOUSE

East Quantoxhead TA5 1EJ. East Quantoxhead Estate (Hugh Luttrell Esq), 01278 741271, hugh_luttrell@yahoo.co.uk. *12m W of Bridgwater. Off A39, house at end of village past duck pond. Enter by Frog Lane (Bridgwater/Kilve side from A39). Car park 50p in aid of church. Tea in Village Hall or in Kilve.* **Adm £4, chd free. For NGS: Sun 10 May, Sun 19 July (1-5). For other opening times and information, please phone.**

Lovely 5 acre garden, trees, shrubs, many rare and tender, herbaceous and 3 acre woodland garden with spring interest and late summer borders. Traditional kitchen garden (all chemical free). Views to sea and Quantocks. Gravel, stone and some mown grass paths.

   ♿ 🐕 🚫 ☕

---

21 CROWCOMBE COURT

Crowcombe, Taunton TA4 4AD. Mr & Mrs David Kenyon. *W of Taunton. On A358.* **Home-made teas in Great Hall of house. Adm by donation. Sun 12 Apr, Sun 26 July, Sun 13 Sept (2-6).**

Magnificent Grade 1 listed house (not open) which has benefitted from extensive refurbishment. The 10 acres of gardens, previously sadly neglected, are now being rejuvenated under new ownership. Woodland

garden, lake, walled garden, all undergoing a rescue mission! Wheelchair access through most of garden.

22 DAGGS ALLOTMENTS
High Street, Thornbury BS35 2AW, 01454 418736, annehenley@yahoo.co.uk, www.thornburyallotments.com. *Park in free car park off Chapel St.* Adm £4, chd free. Visitors welcome by arrangement June to Aug for groups of 8 - 20.
Thornbury is a historic market town and has been a regular winner of awards in the RHS Britain in Bloom competition. 105 plots, all in cultivation, many organic, incl vegetables, soft fruit, herbs and flowers for cutting. Narrow, steep, grass paths between plots. Many plot holders will be available to answer any questions you may have about the plots, cultivation techniques and varieties grown. Short talk on the history of Daggs since 1546.

23 NEW THE DAIRY
Clevedon Road, Weston-in-Gordano, Bristol BS20 8PZ. Mrs Christine Lewis. *Weston in Gordano is on B3124 Portishead to Clevedon road. Find Parish Church on main road and take lane down side of churchyard for 200m.* Home-made teas. Adm £4, chd free. Sun 21 June, Sun 2 Aug (2-6).
1 acre garden surrounded by wildlife reserve, with extensive views over the Gordano Valley. Developed over 11 years from concrete cattle yards and tipped land, and not yet complete. North and south courtyards planted for winter and summer interest. Lower garden has large pond and is planted to peak from midsummer to autumn. Separate fruit and vegetable garden.

24 ◆ DUNSTER CASTLE GARDENS
Dunster TA24 6SL. National Trust, 01643 821314, www.nationaltrust.org.uk. *3m SE of Minehead. NT car park approached direct from A39 Minehead to Bridgwater rd, nr to A396 turning. Car park charge to non-NT members.* Light refreshments at the camellia house on the south terrace. Adm £5.60, chd £2.80. For NGS: Sun 5 July (11-5). For other opening

times and information, please phone or see garden website.
Hillside woodland garden surrounding fortified mansion, previously home to the Luttrell family for 600yrs. Terraced areas, interlinked by old carriage drives and paths, feature tender plants. Fine views over polo lawns and landscape with C18 features. Winter interest border. Dream garden with dahlia displays in main season. Play elements within the river gardens.

25 ◆ DYRHAM PARK
Bath SN14 8ER. National Trust, 01179 371330, www.nationaltrust.org.uk/dyrham-park. *8m N of Bath, 12m E of Bristol. On Bath to Stroud rd (A46), 2m S of Tormarton interchange with M4, J18. SatNav use SN14 8HY.* Adm £5.20, chd £2.60. For NGS: Fri 26, Sat 27 June (10-7). For other opening times and information, please phone or see garden website.
C17 mansion with formal gardens on W side, lawns, herbaceous borders, fine yew hedges, ponds and cascade. Nichols orchard with perry pear trees. Continuing project to refresh new areas. On E side of house is C17 orangery traditionally used for citrus plants. Garden tours, including a look at the historic pear orchard, at various times during both days. Please see NT website for times. Special tours for NGS opening, ask at Visitor Reception on the day. Steep slopes in park, cobbles in courtyard. Disabled WC.

26 EAST BURFORD HOUSE
Summer Hill Lane, West Compton, Pilton, Shepton Mallet BA4 4PA. Christopher & Lindsay Bond, 01749 890352, bondchristopher@btconnect.com. *3m W of Shepton Mallet. Xrds at bottom of hill in Pilton on A361 go uphill between PH and former shop for ¹/₂ m into bottom of valley, black gates on L beyond turn to farm.* Tea. Adm £4.50, chd free. Visitors welcome by arrangement 15 May to 15 June.
Garden full of surprises. 3 acres surround fine country house (not open) set in isolated Mendip valley. Formal walled and wild gardens, different areas incl herbaceous, bog, woodland, gravel, wisteria, pergola, desert and raised strawberry beds, lake with shell beach, rills, pagoda,

pavilion, sculptures and children's playground. Hillside woodland walk, bring own picnic, dogs welcome. Stout shoes advised. Garden sculptures and water features. Featured in Mendip Times, Western Daily Press, Bath magazines, regional press with Radio Bristol, Somerset and Glastonbury fm. Wheelchair access limited to formal garden.

1 acre garden surrounded by wildlife reserve . . .

27 EAST END FARM
Pitney, Langport TA10 9AL. Mrs A M Wray, 01458 250598. *2m E of Langport. Please telephone for directions.* Adm £3, chd free. Visitors welcome by arrangement June.
Approx ¹/₃ acre. Timeless small garden of many old-fashioned roses in beautiful herbaceous borders set amongst ancient listed farm buildings. Mostly wheelchair access.

28 ◆ EAST LAMBROOK MANOR GARDENS
East Lambrook TA13 5HH. Mike & Gail Werkmeister, 01460 240328, www.eastlambrook.com. *2m N of South Petherton. Follow brown tourist signs from A303 South Petherton r'about or B3165 Xrd with lights N of Martock.* Teas. Adm £5.75, chd free. For NGS: Sun 8 Feb, Sun 10 May, Sat 6 June, Sun 7 Feb 2016 (10-5). For other opening times see below.
The quintessential English cottage garden created by C20 gardening legend Margery Fish. Plantsman's paradise with old-fashioned and contemporary plants grown in a relaxed and informal manner to create an extraordinary garden of great beauty and charm. With noted collections of snowdrops, hellebores and geraniums and the excellent specialist Margery Fish Plant Nursery. Moish Sokal watercolour exhibition June. Also open Feb and May to July Tues to Sun & BH Mons; Mar, Apr and Aug to Oct Tues to Sat and BH Mons; (10-5). Featured in The Garden, Garden News, The Oldie, Country Gardener and local press. Partial wheelchair access only due to narrow gravel paths and steps.

29 ◆ ELWORTHY COTTAGE
Elworthy, Taunton TA4 3PX. Mike & Jenny Spiller, 01984 656427, www.elworthy-cottage.co.uk. *12m NW of Taunton. On B3188 between Wiveliscombe and Watchet.* **Adm £3, chd free. For NGS: Thur 2, Mon 6, Thur 16 Apr, Thurs 14, 21, Sun 24, Thur 28 May, Thurs 4, 11 June, Thur 27, Mon 31 Aug, Thur 3 Sept (11-5). For other opening times and information, please phone or see garden website.**
1 acre plantsman's garden in tranquil setting. Island beds, scented plants, clematis, unusual perennials and ornamental trees and shrubs to provide yr round interest. In spring pulmonarias, hellebores and more than 200 varieties of snowdrops. Planted to encourage birds, bees and butterflies, lots of birdsong. Wild flower areas, decorative vegetable garden, living willow screen. Stone ex privy and pigsty feature. Adjoining nursery. Also open Thurs Apr - Aug incl (10-5). All fees for visits by arrangement incl groups and coach parties to be donated to NGS.

30 ESOTERA
Foddington, nr Babcary TA11 7EL. Andrew & Shirley Harvey. *6m E of Somerton, 6m SW of Castle Cary. Signs to garden off A37 Ilchester to Shepton Mallet and B3153 Somerton to Castle Cary. (Old) A303 from Sparkford.* Home-made teas. **Adm £4, chd free. Sat 30, Sun 31 May, Sat 20, Sun 21 June (11-5).**
2 acre established cottage garden housing wildlife ponds, large prairie border, contemporary potting shed surrounded by large herbaceous borders. Avenue of Malus Huphensis underplanted with meadow flowers leads to working kitchen garden and wildlife area with shepherd hut. Courtyard takes you to tea room with our wide selection of home-made cakes. Children must be supervised at all times.

31 22 EXETER ROAD
Weston-super-Mare BS23 4DB. Mrs P A Williams. *Weston-super-Mare. M5 J21, A370 towards town centre, L into Drove Rd. Over rail bridge, R into Quantock Rd, R into Malvern Rd then R then R. Use rear entrance between nos 20 & 21.* Home-made teas. **Adm £3, chd free. Sun 19, Sun 26 July (11-4.30).**
Small rear garden behind Victorian

terraced house. Jungle-like appearance, packed with plants, some unusual or exotic - palms, bananas, elephant ears, bamboo, Australian tree fern, olive tree and Indian bean tree. Featured in Amateur Gardening magazine.

Even on a hazy day this 5 acre garden offers plenty of interest . . .

32 FAIRFIELD
Stogursey, Bridgwater TA5 1PU. Lady Acland Hood Gass. *7m E of Williton. 11m W of Bridgwater. From A39 Bridgwater to Minehead rd turn N. Garden 1½ m W of Sturgursey on Stringston rd. No coaches.* Tea. **Adm £4, chd free. Sun 29 Mar (2-5).**
Woodland garden with bulbs, shrubs and fine trees. Paved maze. Views of Quantocks and sea.

33 FERNHILL
Whiteball, nr Wellington TA21 0LU. Peter & Audrey Bowler, 01823 672423, muldoni@hotmail.co.uk, www.sampfordarundel.org.uk/fernhill/. *3m W of Wellington. At top of Whiteball hill on A38 on L going W just before dual carriageway, parking on site.* Tea. **Adm £3.50, chd free. Sun 28 June, Sun 26 July, Sun 23 Aug (2-5). Visitors also welcome by arrangement June to Aug no less than 10 people.**
In approx 2 acres, a delightful garden to stir your senses, with a myriad of unusual plants and features. Intriguing almost hidden paths leading through English roses and banks of hydrangeas. Scenic views stretching up to the Blackdowns and its famous monument. Truly a Hide and Seek garden..... for all ages. Well stocked herbaceous borders, octagonal pergola and water garden with slightly wild boggy area. Wheelchair access to terrace and other parts of garden from drive.

34 1 FROBISHER ROAD
Ashton Gate, Bristol BS3 2AU. Karen Thomas. *2m SW of city centre. Bristol City FC on R, next R Duckmoor Rd, 5th turning L before bollards.* Home-made teas. **Adm £3, chd free. Sun 31 May, Sun 16 Aug (2-5).**
Cheek by jowl planting, arches, obelisks, hanging baskets, containers, 2 metal deer sculptures, hidden paths, seating areas, metal Victorian scroll gazebo, 3.4metres high, 3 water features, one solar powered, two small ponds. Home-made cakes in conservatory with a drink £2. Daffodil design metal gates to house and driveway, leading to compact city garden.

GROUP OPENING

35 FROME GARDENS
Frome BA11 4HR. *15m S of Bath. The Bastion Garden is in town centre on Cork St. 9 Catherston Close signed from Sainsbury r'about, W side of town, towards Shepton Mallet A361.* Home-made teas at The Bastion Garden. **Combined adm £4, chd free. Sun 14 June (12-5).**

◆ THE BASTION GARDEN
Cork Street. Mrs Karen Harvey-Lloyd.
Access to garden via Zion Path next to Care Home opp Cork St car park
www.bastiongarden.com

9 CATHERSTON CLOSE
Dave & Prue Moon
(See separate entry)

2 varied gardens. The Bastion Garden: C18 extensively restored but still a work in progress. Features reveted banks, raised platforms, yew hedges and unusual shaped pond. The emphasis is on shape and form not extensive floral planting. Colourful 50-metre curved border of David Austin roses with low box hedging. 9 Catherston Close: A town garden which has grown over the years to ⅓ acre! Colour-themed shrub and herbaceous borders, pond, patios, pergolas and wild meadow areas lead to wonderful far reaching views. Productive vegetable and fruit garden with greenhouse. Exhibition of garden photography, from near and far, by garden owner is displayed in summerhouse. Featured in Fosseway

and Country Gardener magazines, regional press with Radio Bristol, Somerset and Glastonbury fm. Some gravel, slopes and small steps.

& & &

---

36 GANTS MILL & GARDEN
Gants Mill Lane, Bruton BA10 0DB. Elaine & Greg Beedle, www.gantsmill.co.uk. *½ m SW of Bruton. From Bruton centre take Yeovil rd, A359, under railway bridge, 100yds uphill, fork R down Gants Mill Lane. Parking for wheelchair users.* Home-made teas. **Adm £6, chd free. Sun 5 July (2-7).**
³/₄ acre garden. Clematis, rose arches and pergolas, streams, ponds, waterfalls. Riverside walk to top weir, delphiniums, day lilies, 100+ dahlia varieties, vegetable, soft fruit and cutting flower garden. Garden is overlooked by the historic watermill, open on NGS day. Firm wide paths round the garden. Narrow entrance to mill not accessible to wheelchairs. WC.

& &

GROUP OPENING

37 GLASTONBURY SECRET GARDENS
Glastonbury BA6 9JJ. *100yds from Glastonbury Mkt Cross in Northload St (Pedestrian Area). Off A39 at Beckery r'about into Sedgemoor Way then take 2nd R into Northload West meter C/P. Garden entrances are clearly signed.* Teas and cupcakes. **Combined adm £4, chd free. Sun 5 July (1-4).**

JACOB'S LOFT
7/9 Northload Street. William Knight
01458 835144
info@glastonburyholidayhomes.com
www.glastonburyholidayhomes.com

SAINT MARGARET'S CHAPEL GARDEN
Magdalen Street. Ms Sandra Booth.
The garden is behind 38 Magdalene Street.
http://stmargaretschapel.org.uk/

Jacob's Loft: 100 yds from Glastonbury Market Cross in Northload St. Inner town courtyard garden, example of what can be

achieved in urban environment. Formerly rear gardens of inner town commercial properties and a Victorian/Georgian Terrace. Collection of Agricultural and Horticultural tools and artefacts. St Margaret's Chapel garden (Best Community Entry - Gold - in Mendip in Bloom) is accessed down a rather small alleyway, but in turning the corner everyone, without exception, gasps at the calm splendour of the garden, the peace of the C11 chapel and the ancient almshouses. Whether you are a pilgrim or a garden lover or both, we welcome you to these havens of peace, beauty, and tranquillity. While in bohemian Glastonbury visit our curious/quirky range of shops, our famous Abbey and if you feel energetic climb Glastonbury Tor.

---

38 GLEBE COURT
West Monkton, Taunton TA2 8QT. Mr and Mrs Anthony Pugh-Thomas. *2m NE of Taunton. Follow signs to West Monkton off A38. In village take driveway (entrance marked by two large 5 mph signs) leading to church. Cream teas locally available.* **Adm £5, chd free. Sat 30, Sun 31 May (2-5.30).**
Walled garden with greenhouses, orchard, vegetable plots, fruit tree

cages and flower beds; herbaceous and shrub borders; copse and paddocks with some unusual trees; series of ponds. 11 acres in all surrounding Georgian Rectory. (House not open to the public). Dogs must be on leads. Partial wheelchair access: some uneven steps. Access to walled garden up slope and through gate with couple of low steps.

---

39 NEW GLEBE FARMHOUSE
Lower Street, Buckland Dinham, Frome BA11 2QN. Marie & Andrew Gilchrist. *1m NE of Frome on A362. On A362, from Frome, 1st L into Lower St; from Radstock, take last R at bottom of hill. Parking in centre of village close to church, can drop off at farmhouse prior to parking near church.* Home-made teas. **Adm £4, chd free. Sat 18 July (9.30-6).**
At edge of village with extensive views of surrounding countryside lies this ½ acre garden surrounding Georgian farmhouse. Landscaped by present owners into separate planting areas consisting of terrace garden, parterre with charming cottage, shade walk and two further traditional gardens of attractive mixed and herbaceous colour themed borders.

Tranby House

40 GOBLIN COMBE HOUSE

Plunder Street, Cleeve, Bristol
BS49 4PQ. Mrs H R Burn, 01934
838599, hilaryburn@live.co.uk. *10m
S of Bristol. A370, turn L onto Cleeve
Hill Rd before Lord Nelson Inn; 300m
L onto Plunder St, 1st drive on R.
Parking just beyond Plunder St
turning.* Tea. **Adm £3.50, chd free.
Wed 10, Wed 17, Wed 24 June
(2-5). Visitors also welcome by
arrangement May to June.**
2 acre terraced garden with lovely
views. Interesting collection of trees,
mixed shrubs and herbaceous
borders, surrounded by orchards,
fields and woodlands. Home to the
rare plant purple gromwell found on
woodland edges with alkaline soils.
The garden contains uneven and
steep paths which are very slippery
when wet. Highly recommended by
Trevor Fry from Radio Bristol. Wide
range of plants on sale.

41 HANGERIDGE FARMHOUSE

Wrangway, Wellington TA21 9QG.
Mrs J M Chave, 01823 662339,
hangeridge@hotmail.co.uk. *2m S of
Wellington. 1m off A38 bypass signed
Wrangway. 1st L towards Wellington
Monument, over mway bridge 1st R.*
Home-made teas. **Adm £3, chd free.
Suns 19 Apr, 17 May, 28 June, Sun
5, Wed 15, Sun 19 July, Sun 16
Aug, Mon 7 Sept (2-5). Groups of
10+ also welcome by arrangement
Apr to Aug.**
Informal, relaxing, mature family
garden set under Blackdown Hills.
Seats to enjoy views across
Somerset landscape. Atmospheric
mix of herbaceous borders and this
lovely and still-evolving garden
contains wonderful flowering shrubs,
heathers, mature trees, rambling
climbers and seasonal bulbs. Content
and design belie its 1 acre size.
Garden not to be missed.

42 HARTWOOD HOUSE

Crowcombe Heathfield, Taunton
TA4 4BS. Cdr & Mrs David
Freemantle, 01984 667202,
hartwoodhouse@hotmail.com,
hartwoodhousebandb.co.uk.
*Approx 10m from Taunton, 5m from
Williton. Clearly signed from A358.
Situated in quiet tree-lined lane
known locally as the Avenue.* Cream
teas. **Adm £3, chd free. Sun 12 Apr,
Sun 10 May, Sun 14 June (2-5.30).
Visitors also welcome by
arrangement Mar to Oct.**

2 acre garden surrounded by
magnificent oak and beech trees.
Wide range of specimen trees and
flowering shrubs provide colour and
scent all yr. The formal garden has a
circular theme and colour coded
borders. Extensive vegetable and fruit
garden laid out in potager style,
further on, grassy paths lead into an
ancient cider apple orchard being
replanted with native trees. Garden
is generally flat, firm underfoot with
wide gateways. Teas and toilet
facilities are easily accessed by
wheelchair users.

A garden which
could be created in
many new homes
with a little love . . .

43 HENLEY MILL

Henley Lane, Wookey BA5 1AW.
Peter & Sally Gregson,
01749 676966,
millcottageplants@gmail.com,
www.millcottageplants.co.uk. *2m
W of Wells, off A371 towards
Cheddar. Turn L into Henley Lane,
driveway 50yds on L through stone
pillars to end of drive.* Home-made
teas. **Adm £4.50, chd free. Visitors
welcome by arrangement Apr to
Sept, teas/home-made cake by
arrangement.**
2½ acres beside R Axe. Scented
garden with roses, hydrangea
borders, shady folly garden and late
summer borders with grasses and
perennials. Zig-zag boardwalk at river
level. Kitchen and cutting garden.
Rare Japanese hydrangeas. Garden
is on one level, but paths can get a
bit muddy after heavy rain.

44 ◆ HESTERCOMBE GARDENS

Cheddon Fitzpaine TA2 8LG.
Hestercombe Gardens Trust,
01823 413923,
www.hestercombe.com. *4m N of
Taunton. Follow brown tourist signs
rather than SatNav.* **Adm £9.70, chd
£3.70. For NGS: Tue 17 Mar, Tue 9
June (10-5).** For other opening
times and information, please
phone or see garden website.
Georgian landscape garden designed
by Coplestone Warre Bampfylde,

Victorian terrace/shrubbery and
stunning Edwardian Lutyens/Jekyll
formal gardens together make up 50
acres of woodland walks, temples,
terraces, pergolas, lakes and
cascades. Hestercombe House is
also now open. Special features:
restored watermill and barn, lesser
horseshoe bats, historic house
comprising contemporary gallery,
family garden trails. Gravel paths,
steep slopes, steps. All abilities route
marked.

45 NEW HILLCREST

Curload, Stoke St. Gregory,
Taunton TA3 6JA. Charles &
Charlotte Sundquist. *At top of
Curload. From A358 turn L along
A378, then branch L to North Curry
and Stoke St. Gregory. L ½ m after
Willows & Wetlands centre. Hillcrest is
1st on R with parking directions.*
Home-made teas. **Adm £4, chd free.
Sat 9, Sun 10 May (2-5).**
The garden boasts stunning views of
the Somerset Levels, Burrow Mump
and Glastonbury Tor, but even on a
hazy day this 5 acre garden offers
plenty of interest. Woodland walks,
varied borders, flowering meadow
and several ponds, as well as a
kitchen garden, greenhouses,
orchards, and a unique standing
stone as a focal point. Most of garden
is level. Path through flower meadow
to lower pond and wood has gentle
but quite long slope.

GROUP OPENING

46 HINTON ST GEORGE GARDENS

High Street, nr Crewkerne
TA17 8SE. *3m N of Crewkerne. N of
A30 Crewkerne-Chard; S of A303
Ilminster Town Rd, at r'about signed
Lopen & Merriott, then R to Hinton St
George. Coaches must park on High
St.* Home-made teas at Hooper's
Holding. **Combined adm £5, chd
free. Sun 12, Mon 13 July (2-5.30).**

END HOUSE
West Street. Helen Newman

HOOPER'S HOLDING
Ken & Lyn Spencer-Mills
Visitors also welcome by
arrangement May to Aug. Tea
and cakes by prior
arrangement.
01460 76389
kenlyn@devonrex.demon.co.uk

THE OLIVE GARDEN
12 Lopen Road. Pat Read

Gardens varying in size and style in beautiful hamstone village. C15 church. Country seat of the Earls of Poullett for 600yrs until 1973. Hooper's Holding has a ½ acre garden in colour compartments. Rare plants, many exotics, garden mosaics and sculptures. End House has sweeping lawns, gravel gardens and interesting trees and shrubs including colourful azaleas (approx ½ acre). The Olive Garden is a loving restoration of a site which had been neglected for decades, maturing well. Wheelchair access to End House and Hooper's Holding.

♿ 🐕 ❀ 🚐 ☕

In 2014 NGS jointly funded a Cancer Wellbeing Centre in Bristol

47 HONEYHURST FARM
Honeyhurst Lane, Rodney Stoke, Cheddar BS27 3UJ. Don & Kathy Longhurst, 01749 870322, donlonghurst@btinternet.com. *4m E of Cheddar. From A371 between Wells and Cheddar, turn into Rodney Stoke signed Wedmore. Pass church on L and continue for almost 1m.* Cream teas. **Adm £3.50, chd free. Sun 19 July (2-5). Groups of 10 to 40 also welcome by arrangement Apr to Sept.**

⅔ acre part walled rural garden with babbling brook and 4 acre traditional cider orchard, with views. Specimen hollies, copper beech, paulownia, yew and poplar. Pergolas, arbour and numerous seats. Mixed informal shrub and perennial beds with many unusual plants. Many pots planted with shrubs, hardy and half-hardy perennials. Level, grass and some shingle.

♿ 🐕 ❀ 🚐 🛏 ☕

48 JASMINE COTTAGE
26 Channel Road, Clevedon BS21 7BY. Margaret & Michael Redgrave, 01275 871850, margaret@bologrew.net, http://jasminecottage.bologrew.net. *12m W of Bristol. M5 J20 from Clevedon seafront travel N (0.8m), via Wellington Terrace, follow winding rd to St Mary's Church, R into Channel Rd, approx 100yds on L.* **Adm £3, chd free. Thurs 11, 25 June, 9, 23 July (2-5). Visitors also welcome by arrangement June & July.**

A mature peaceful cottage garden covering ⅓ acre with a wide variety of plants chosen for their form, scent and colour. We are enthusiastic growers and many examples will be on our plant stall.

❀ 🚐

49 ◆ JEKKA'S HERBETUM
Shellards Lane, Alveston, Bristol BS35 3SY. Mrs Jekka McVicar, 01454 418878, www.jekkasherbfarm.com. *7m N of M5 J16, or 6m S from J14 of M5. 1m off A38 signed Itchington. From M5 J16, A38 to Alveston, past church turn R at junction signed Itchington. M5 J14 on A38 turn L after T-lights to Itchington.* Home-made teas. **Adm £5, chd free. For NGS: Sun 31 May, Sun 12 July, Sun 9 Aug (10-4.30). For other opening times and information, please phone or see garden website.**

Jekka's Herbetum is a living herb encyclopaedia displaying the largest collection of culinary herbs in the UK. A wonderful resource for plant identification for the gardener and a gastronomic experience for chefs and cooks. The dates chosen to be open coincide with the flowering times of the herbs. 31 May thymes, 12 July lavender, 9 Aug, mint and oregano. Wheelchair access possible however terrain is rough from car park to Herbetum.

♿ ❀ ☕

50 ◆ KILVER COURT SECRET GARDENS
Kilver Street, Shepton Mallet BA4 5NF. Roger Saul, 01749 340417, www.kilvercourt.com. *Directly off A37 road to Bath, opp Cider factory in Shepton Mallet.* **Adm £5, chd £2.50. For NGS: Wed 15 Apr, Thur 28 May, Mon 14 Sept (10-4). For other opening times and information, please phone or see garden website.**

Created in 1800s and restored, early1960's, by the Showering family, who commissioned George Whiteleg to recreate his gold medal winning Chelsea garden. The garden, which has recently been featured on BBC Gardeners' World, showcases a millpond, herbaceous borders and formal parterre with the most stunning backdrop, the Grade II listed viaduct built for the historical Somerset and Dorset railway. Some slopes and rockery not accessible for wheelchairs but can be viewed. Disabled parking in lower car park.

♿ ❀ 🚐 ☕

51 NEW LINDEN
6 Longmead Close, Norton St Philip BA2 7NS. Alistair Bell, alistair_bell759@hotmail.com. *6m S of Bath on B3110. Follow yellow signs from B3110 and A366 Xrds in centre of village. Directly at end of Longmead Close if approaching on A366 from E.* Disabled parking on drive. Tea. **Combined adm £4, chd free. Combined with 8 Upper Farm Close. Sat 25, Sun 26 July (1-5).**

Compact new garden created in modern development, featuring a tapestry of herbaceous colour, roses, shrubs and raised borders in an easy to live with arrangement. An example of a garden which could be created in many new homes with a little love and enthusiasm. Parking either on drive (room for 5 cars) or in road close by. Level paved access.

♿ 🐕 ☕

52 LITTLE GARTH
Dowlish Wake, Ilminster TA19 0NX. Roger & Marion Pollard, 01460 52594. *2m S of Ilminster. R off Ilminster to Crewkerne rd at Kingstone Cross, then L, follow Dowlish Wake sign. L at white cottage before reaching church. Turn R, follow signs. Park in front of nearby church.* **Adm £3, chd free. Sats 2 May, 6 June, 4 July, 1 Aug, 5 Sept (10.30-5). Visitors also welcome by arrangement May to Sept.**

½ acre plantsman's garden for all seasons with many interesting and unusual perennials. Although essentially cottage style, emphasis is placed on the artistic arrangement of plants, using foliage, grasses and colour themes. Refreshments and public toilets at nearby Cider Mill, proceeds to Cider Mill. Mostly wheelchair access.

♿ 🐕 ❀ 🚐 ☕

© Christina Santa Ana

The Old Rectory, Limington

53 LITTLE YARFORD FARMHOUSE

Kingston St Mary, Taunton TA2 8AN. Brian Bradley, 01823 451350, yarford@ic24.net. *3½ m N of Taunton. From Taunton on Kingston St Mary rd. At 30mph sign turn L at Parsonage Lane. Continue 1¼ m W, to Yarford sign. Continue 400yds. Turn R up concrete rd.* Light refreshments. **Adm £4.50, chd free. Fri 8 May (11-5); Sat 9, Sun 10 May (2-5.30); Mon 11 May (11-5).** Visitors also welcome by arrangement day or eve, Apr to Sept, guided tours of trees at 2 & 3.30.

This unusual garden embraces a C17 house (not open) overgrown with a tapestry of climbing plants. The 3 ponds exhibit a wide range of aquatic gems. Of special interest is the collection of 300 trees, listed on website of rare and unusual cultivars, both broad leaf and conifer, all differing in form and colour incl weeping and fastigiate: a tree for every place and occasion. The 5 acres are a delight to both artist and plantsman. 'An inspirational, magical experience'. It is an exercise in landscaping and creating views both within the garden and without to the vale and the Quantock Hills. Mostly wheelchair access.

 ♿ 🐕 🐝 🚐 ☕

54 LUCOMBE HOUSE

12 Druid Stoke Ave, Stoke Bishop, Bristol BS9 1DD. Malcolm Ravenscroft, 01179 682494, famrave@gmail.com. *4m NW of Bristol centre. On L at top of Druid Hill. Garden on R 200m from junction.* Tea. **Adm £3, chd free. Sun 10 May, Sun 7 June (2-6). Also open 1 Sunnyside on 7 June only.** Visitors also welcome by arrangement May to Sept.

Woodland area with over 30 mature trees planted in last 5 yrs underplanted with ferns, bluebells and white foxgloves. Front garden to be redesigned in 2015 to include formal parterre. Separate semi-formal area and untouched wild area under 220yr-old Lucombe oak. Landscape gardener will be on site and happy to answer questions. Rough paths in woodland area, 2 steps to patio.

 ♿ 🐝 ☕

55 LYDEARD HOUSE

West Street, Bishops Lydeard, Taunton TA4 3AU. Mrs Colin Wilkins. *5m NW of Taunton. A358 Taunton to Minehead, do not take 1st 3 R turnings to Bishops Lydeard but 4th signed to Cedar Falls. Follow signs to Lydeard House.* Home-made teas. **Adm £4, chd free. Sun 21 June (2-5.30).**

4 acre garden with C18 origins and many later additions. Sweeping lawns, lake overhung with willows, canal running parallel to Victorian rose-covered pergola, along with box parterre, chinoiserie-style garden, recent temple folly and walled vegetable garden plus wonderful mature trees. Plants for sale from local nursery. Children must be supervised because of very deep water. Deep gravel paths and steps may cause difficulty but most features accessible by lawn.

 ♿ 🐝 ☕

GROUP OPENING

56 LYMPSHAM GARDENS

Church Road, Lympsham, Weston-super-Mare BS24 0DT. *5m S of Weston-super-Mare and 5m N of Burnham on Sea. 2m M5 J22. Entrance to both gardens from main gates of Manor at junction of Church Rd and Lympsham Rd.* Cream teas. **Combined adm £4 £5, chd free. Sat 20, Sun 21 June (2-5).**

NEW **CHURCH FARM**
Church Lane. Andy & Rosemary Carr

LYMPSHAM MANOR
James & Lisa Counsell

At heart of stunning village of Lympsham is C15 church of St Christopher. The Manor, built as the rectory exactly 200 years ago, and C17 Church Farm are by the church and connected to each other by side gate. The Manor is a gothic pinnacled, castellated rectory manor house with 2 octagonal towers, set in 10 acres of formal and semi-formal garden, surrounded by paddocks and farmland. Main features are its carefully preserved, fully working Victorian kitchen garden and greenhouse, arboretum of trees from all parts of the world, large stocked

fish pond and beautiful old rose garden. Church Farm: ³/₄ acre informal country garden surrounding farmhouse. Well-stocked herbaceous border, shrub lined paths, raised vegetable beds and small courtyard herb garden. Old outside Victorian privy in Manor garden.

57 ◆ LYTES CARY MANOR

Kingsdon, nr Somerton TA11 7HU. National Trust, 01458 224471, www.nationaltrust.org.uk/lytes-cary-manor. *3m SE of Somerton. Signed from Podimore r'about at junction of A303, A37, take A372.* Light refreshments, sandwiches, soup, cream teas, hot and cold drinks. **Adm £9, chd £4.50. For NGS: Thur 11 June (10.30-5). For other opening times and information, please phone or see garden website.**
Arts and Crafts style garden with many contrasts, topiary and mixed borders. Home of medieval herbalist Henry Lyte. Estate walks: Garden and Behind the Scenes tour at 2pm. Uneven paths.

GROUP OPENING

58 MARSHFIELD GARDENS

Marshfield SN14 8LR. *7m NE of Bath. From Bath A46 to Cold Ashton r'about, turn R onto A420. From M4 J18 turn onto A46 and L at Cold Ashton r'about. From Chippenham A420 going W. Follow yellow signs into village.* Home-made teas. **Combined adm £5 May, £3.50 July, chd free. Sat 23, Sun 24 May, Sat 4 July (1-5).**

BRAMLEY COTTAGE
Sheepfair Lane. Mr & Mrs Glyn Watkins.
open all dates

42 HIGH STREET
Mary & Simon Turner.
open May weekend. Rear access from Back Lane via Touching End Lane or Britton's Passage

43 HIGH STREET
Marshfield. Linda & Denis Beazer.
open all dates

111 HIGH STREET
Joy & Mervyn Pierce.
open May weekend. Bristol end of village, from Bristol on R just past turning for Colerne

116 HIGH STREET
Mr Doug Bond.
open all dates

3 OLD SCHOOL COURT
Mrs R Crew.
open May weekend

WEIR COTTAGE
Weir Lane. Ian & Margaret Jones.
open all dates

YEELES HOUSE
24 Back Lane. Kay and Peter Little.
open May weekend. Entry halfway down Back Lane

8 gardens incl cottage gardens, courtyard gardens, walled garden and bog garden. Summerhouse with green sedum roof. Flower borders, fruit trees and vegetables grown for exhibiting in village show. Raised beds. Focus on year round interest and colour. Interesting village with C13 church, High St with shops and PHs. 23 & 24 May: 111 High St open for lunches and teas 12 noon (proceeds to Marshfield Almshouses). Gardens open 1 - 5pm. 4 July: 4 gardens. Same as above but teas at Weir Cottage. 23 May guided walk by Cotswold Wardens around Marshfield Access Trail. Meet 10.30am Market Place. Boots recommended. No dogs. 01225 891229 for info.

> This garden demonstrates the resilience of nature . . .

59 ◆ MIDNEY GARDENS

Mill Lane, Midney, Somerton TA11 7HR. David Chase & Alison Hoghton, 01458 274250, www.midneygardens.co.uk. *1m SE of Somerton. 100yds off B3151. From Podimore r'about on A303 take A372. After 1m R on B3151 towards Street. After 2m L on bend into Mill Lane.* Home-made teas. **Adm £4.50, chd free. For NGS: Sun 10 May, Fri 18 Sept (11-5). For other opening times and information, please phone or see garden website.**
1 acre plantsmanís garden, where unusual planting combinations,

interesting use of colour, subtle themes and a natural flowing style create a garden full of variety and inspiring ideas. Increasingly known for it's wildlife friendly planting it includes a seaside garden, Clarice Cliff inspired garden, white garden, kitchen garden, woodland walk and wildlife pond. Nursery offers herbaceous perennials, alpines, herbs and grasses.

60 ◆ MILTON LODGE

Old Bristol Road, Wells BA5 3AQ. Simon Tudway Quilter, 01749 672168, www.miltonlodgegardens.co.uk. *½ m N of Wells. From A39 Bristol-Wells, turn N up Old Bristol Rd; car park first gate on L signed.* Tea. **Adm £5, chd free. For NGS: Sun 17 May, Sun 7 June, Sun 5 July (2-5). For other opening times and information, please phone or see garden website.**
Mature Grade II, terraced garden conceived c1900. Sloping ground transformed into architectural terraces with profusion of plants, capitalising on views of Wells Cathedral and Vale of Avalon. 1960, garden lovingly restored to former glory, orchard replaced with raised collection of ornamental trees. Cross Old Bristol Rd to 7 acre woodland garden, the Combe, natural peaceful contrast to formal garden at Milton Lodge. First opened for NGS 1962. Also open Tues, Weds, Suns, BHs, Easter - 31 Oct (2-5). Featured in The County and Country Gardener magazines, regional press with Radio Bristol, Somerset and Glastonbury fm.

61 ◆ MONTACUTE HOUSE

Montacute TA15 6XP. National Trust, 01935 823289, www.nationaltrust.org.uk/montacute-house. *4m W of Yeovil. NT signs off A3088 & A303.* Light refreshments in courtyard café. **Adm £12.40, chd £6.20. For NGS: Sun 7 June (10-4.30). For other opening times and information, please phone or see garden website.**
Magnificent Elizabethan house with contemporary garden layout. Fine stonework provides setting for informally planted mixed borders and old roses; range of garden features illustrates its long history. 80% wheelchair access.

GROUP OPENING

62 NUNNEY GARDENS

Nunney, nr Frome BA11 4NP. *3m S of Frome. Nunney Catch, A361 between Frome and Shepton Mallet, follow signs to Nunney (1m). In market sq, follow car park signs then NGS arrows.* Home-made teas at Sunny Bank. **Combined adm £5, chd free. Sun 14 June (11-4).**

THE MILLER'S HOUSE
17 Horn Street. Caroline Toll

SUNNY BANK
High Street. Mr & Mrs S Thomas

Picturesque village clustered around C15 church, duck pond fed by Nunney Brook, ruined medieval castle with moat and market sq. 2 contrasting gardens. Miller's House: garden of person who considers herself to be an untidy planter! Mostly perennial garden terraced borders, rockeries, large, romantic mill pond and wild section between leat and Nunney Brook. Planting designed for butterfly attraction and perfume. Many areas to sit and enjoy views of garden. Be sure to look at terraced vegetable patch and small modern sculptures around garden. Caution with children and on steps and path around mill pond. Sunny Bank has been transformed from former vegetable plot into intriguing ½ acre garden providing variety and interest in numerous sections. 2 subtropical houses containing cacti and succulents, featured in Amateur Gardening Magazine, are interspersed with fossils and unusual natural objects. In contrast to this are damp shaded areas containing hostas, ferns and woodland plants leading to raised carp pond and herbaceous borders. Plants for sale at Sunny Bank. Featured in Somerset Life and regional press with Radio Bristol, Somerset and Glastonbury fm. The Miller's House - 2 steps to garden, access to top lawn, millpond view below. Sunny Bank - slope up drive to garden, outside view of tropical house.

  ♿ ❀ ☕

63 NYNEHEAD COURT

Nynehead, Wellington TA21 0BN. Nynehead Care Ltd, 01823 662481/07834 773441, nyneheadcare@aol.com. *2m N of Wellington. M5 J26 B3187 towards Wellington. R on r'about marked Nynehead & Poole, follow lane for 1m, take Milverton turning at fork.* Home-made teas in orangery. **Adm £3.50, chd free. Sun 17 May, Sun 14 June (2-5). Visitors also welcome by arrangement please telephone for details.**
Nynehead Court Gardens are on English Heritage's list of gardens of historic interest. Once the ancestral home of the Sanford family. Gardens laid out during the Victorian period, points of interest - pinetum, ice house, parterre and extended walks within parkland of old estate. Garden tours by head gardener, Justin Cole, start 2pm prompt (tour lasts 1 hr approx). Limited wheelchair access, cobbled yards/gentle slopes.

  ♿ ☕

hospice UK

The NGS funds vital hospice care projects

64 THE OLD RECTORY, DOYNTON

18 Toghill Lane, Doynton, Bristol BS30 5SY. Edwina & Clive Humby, http://doyntongardens.tumblr.com. *At heart of village of Doynton, between Bath and Bristol. Follow Toghill Lane up from The Holy Trinity Church about 500 metres, around cricket field to car park field. Signs to garden.* Cream teas. **Adm £4, chd free. Sat 13 June (11-4).**
Doynton's Grade II-listed Georgian Rectory's walled garden and extended 15 acre estate. Renovated over 12 yrs, it sits within AONB. Garden has diversity of modern and traditional elements, fused to create an atmospheric series of garden rooms. It is both a landscaped and large kitchen garden, featuring a canal, vegetable plots, fruit cages and tree house. Partial wheelchair access, some narrow gates and uneven surfaces.

  🐕 ☕

65 THE OLD RECTORY, LIMINGTON

Church St, Limington, nr Yeovil BA22 8EQ. John Langdon & Paul Vintner, 01935 840127, jdlpv@aol.com. *2m E of Ilchester. From A303 exit on A37 to Yeovil/Ilchester. At 1st r'about L to Ilchester/Limington. 2nd R to Limington. Continue 1½ m.* Tea and coffee, cold drinks and cream teas. Wine available for evening group visits by prior arrangement. **Adm £4, chd free. Sat 6, Sun 7 June (2.30-5.30). Group visits also welcome by arrangement Apr to Sept day or eve.**
Romantic walled gardens of 1½ acres. Formal parterres, herbaceous borders. Many unusual shrubs and trees incl 200 yr-old lucombe oak, liriodendron, paulownia, laburnocytisus, leycesteria and poncirus. Extensive planting of bulbs incl galanthus, anemone blanda, winter aconites, tulips and alliums. A variety of peaceful seating areas. Featured in Somerset County Gardener, Somerset Life and Mendip Times. Gravel drive, one gentle slope only.

  ♿ 🐕 ❀ ☕

66 ORCHARD WYNDHAM

nr Williton TA4 4HH. The Wyndham Trustees. *7m SE of Minehead, 16m from Taunton. Out of Williton take A39 towards Minehead then signed L and up long drive to house. Exit past Bakelite Museum.* Cream teas at Bakelite Museum, just at the bottom of drive. **Adm £3, chd free. Sun 21 June (2-4.30).**
Garden of historic house (not open on NGS days) in parkland setting: woods, interesting old trees, borders, rose walk, 2 small lakes, wild garden.

  ☕

67 PEN MILL FARM

Pen Selwood, Wincanton BA9 8NF. Mr & Mrs Peter FitzGerald, 01747 840895, fitzgeraldatpen@aol.com, www.penmillcottage.co.uk. *1m from Stourhead, off A303 between Mere and Wincanton. Leave A303 on A3081 (Bruton exit). Turn off old A303 to Penselwood. 2nd L fork up narrow unsigned lane. R at grass triangle to Zeals down steep hill. Pen Mill Farm is on the R.* Home-made teas. Delicious home made cakes and scones both days. Ploughmans lunches available Sun. **Adm £4, chd free. Sat 5 Sept (2-5); Sun 6 Sept (12-5). Groups of 10+ also very**

welcome by arrangement May to Oct.

Romantic garden with acid-loving mature trees and shrubs in secluded valley on Dorset, Somerset and Wiltshire border where tributary of R Stour cascades into the lake. Late summer herbaceous borders with abundant colour and over 40 salvias. Enjoy the peace and quiet of this lovely setting. Plant stall with many unusual salvias and other plants. Filmed for Visit Britain. Mostly wheelchair access. No dogs in garden but car park has shade and dogs can run in the fields.

68 PENNY BROHN CANCER CARE

Chapel Pill Lane, Pill, North Somerset BS20 0HH. Penny Brohn Cancer Care, www.pennybrohncancercare.org. *4m W of Bristol. Off A369. Clifton Suspension Bridge to M5 (J19 Gordano Services). Follow signs to Penny Brohn Cancer Care and to Pill and Ham Green.* Home-made teas. Adm £4, chd free. **Sun 21 June (11-4).**

3½ acre tranquil garden surrounds Georgian mansion with many mature trees, wild flower meadow, flower garden, cedar summerhouse, fine views from historic gazebo overlooking R Avon, courtyard gardens with water features. Garden is maintained by volunteers and plays an active role in the Charity's Living Well with Cancer approach. Plants, teas, music and plenty of space to enjoy a picnic. Gift shop. Tours of centre to find out more about the work of Penny Brohn Cancer Care. Some gravel and grass paths.

69 ◆ PRIOR PARK LANDSCAPE GARDEN

Ralph Allen Drive, Bath BA2 5AH. National Trust, 01225 833422, www.nationaltrust.org.uk/prior-park. *1m S of Bath. Visitors are advised to use public transport as there is no parking at Prior Park or nearby, except for disabled visitors.* Light refreshments by the lakes. Adm £7, chd £3.50. **For NGS: Sun 10 May (10-5.30).** For other opening times and information, please phone or see garden website.

Beautiful and intimate C18 landscape garden created by Bath entrepreneur Ralph Allen (1693-1764) with advice from the poet Alexander Pope and

Capability Brown. Sweeping valley with magnificent views of city. Palladian bridge and lakes. Wilderness restoration, completed in 2007, involved reinstating the serpentine lake, cascade and cabinet to their former glory. Drifts of wild garlic carpeting the woodlands. Limited wheelchair access (the wilderness and view point are accessible, steep slopes, gravel paths and steps in rest of garden).

70 NEW RENDY FARM

Oake, Taunton TA4 1BB. Mr & Mrs N Popplewell. *1m from Oake PO and shop on road from Oake to Nynehead.* Home-made teas. Adm £4, chd free. **Sun 24, Mon 25 May (2-5).**

3 acre garden with formal walled front garden, raised vegetable beds, greenhouse and polytunnel enclosed by hornbeam and yew hedging. Decorative fruit and cut flower beds, meadow with large wild pond and orchard with stream running through.

71 ROCK HOUSE

Elberton BS35 4AQ. Mr & Mrs John Gunnery, 01454 413225. *10m N of Bristol. 3½ m SW Thornbury. From Old Severn Bridge on M48 take B4461 to Alveston. In Elberton, take 1st turning L to Littleton-on-Severn and turn immed R.* Adm £3, chd free. **Sun 1, Sun 8 Feb 2015, Sun 7, Sun 14 Feb 2016 (11-4).** Visitors also welcome by arrangement Jan to Sept.

2 acre garden. Pretty woodland with snowdrops, hellebores and spring bulbs. Cottage garden plants, roses, iris and many interesting varieties of trees. Limited wheelchair access.

72 ROSE COTTAGE

Smithams Hill, East Harptree, Bristol BS40 6BY. Bev & Jenny Cruse, 01761 221627, bandjcruse@gmail.com. *5m N of Wells, 15m S of Bristol. From B3114 turn into High St in EH. L at Clock Tower and immed R into Middle St, up hill for 1m. From B3134 take EH road opp Castle of Comfort continue 1½ m. Car parking in field opp cottage.* Home-made teas. Adm £4.50, chd free. **Sun 19 Apr (2-5).** Visitors also welcome by arrangement Apr to July.

1-acre hillside cottage garden with panoramic views over Chew Valley.

Garden carpeted with primroses, spring bulbs and hellebores, in the summer with roses and hardy geranium. Bordered by stream and established mixed hedges. Plenty of seating areas to enjoy the views and teas, as well as the music of the Congresbury Brass Band. Wildlife area and pond in corner of car park field. Award winner Bath in Bloom. New scented arbour and gravel garden. Featured in Mendip Times and regional press with Radio Bristol, Somerset and Glastonbury fm.

> Decorative fruit and cut flower beds . . . orchard with stream running through . . .

73 RUGG FARM

Church Street, Limington, nr Yeovil BA22 8EQ. Morene Griggs, Peter Thomas & Christine Sullivan, 01935 840503, griggsandthomas@btinternet.com. *2m E of Ilchester. From A303 exit on A37 to Yeovil/ Ilchester. At 1st r'about L to Ilchester/Limington, 2nd R to Limington, continue 1½ m.* Home-made teas. Adm £4, chd free. **Sun 19 July (11-5).** Groups of 8+ also welcome by arrangement June to Aug.

2-acre garden created since 2007 around former farmhouse and farm buildings. Diverse areas of interest. Ornamental, kitchen and cottage gardens, lawn and borders, courtyard container planting, orchard, wildlife meadows and pond, developing shrubberies, woodland plantings and walk (unsuitable for wheelchairs). Exuberant annuals and perennials throughout. Compost Champion in residence. Metalwork designs by Andy Stevenson Garden Sculptures. Featured in Somerset Life and County magazines. Some gravel paths.

74 **ST PETER'S HOSPICE**
Charlton Road, Brentry, Bristol
BS10 6NL. *4m N of Bristol. From Durdham Downs follow A4018 N towards M5, follow signs for St Peter's Hospice onto Charlton Rd. Enter car park on L.* Home-made teas. Salads, soup, sandwiches and cakes all made by St Peter's Hospice chefs and ice creams are available. **Adm £3.50, chd free. Sat 13, Sun 14 June (10-4.30).**
Spacious, tranquil garden for patients and visitors. Historically a remnant of nearby Repton House grounds. Distant view across Severn Estuary. Lawns with mature and maturing trees, wild flower area and fruit trees, gravel garden, herbaceous borders, sensory labyrinth, formal bedding display, tubs and baskets. Plenty of seating for resting and picnics, and room to run around. Most of garden is accessible by wheelchair.

75 **SERRIDGE HOUSE**
Henfield Rd, Coalpit Heath
BS36 2UY. Mrs J Manning, 01454 773188. *9m N of Bristol. On A432 at Coalpit Heath T-lights (opp church), turn into Henfield Rd. R at PH, ½ m small Xrds, garden on corner with Ruffet Rd, park on Henfield Rd.* Cream teas. **Adm £4.50, chd free. Visitors welcome by arrangement July to Aug for groups of 10 - 40.**
2½ acre garden with mature trees, heather and conifer beds, island beds mostly of perennials, woodland area with pond. Colourful courtyard with old farm implements. Lake views and lakeside walks. Unique tree carvings. Mostly flat grass and driveway. Wheelchair access to lake difficult.

76 ◆ **SHERBORNE GARDEN**
Litton, Radstock, Somerset
BA3 4PP. Mr & Mrs John
Southwell, 01761 241220. *15m S of Bristol. 15m W of Bath, 7m N of Wells. On B3114 Chewton Mendip to Harptree rd, ½ m past The Kings Arms.* Tea. **Adm £4, chd free. For NGS: Sun 15, Mon 16 Feb, Sun 19 July, Sun 14, Mon 15 Feb 2016 (11-4). For other opening times and information, please phone.**
4½ acre gently sloping garden with small pinetum, holly wood and many unusual trees and shrubs. Cottage garden leading to privy. 3 ponds linked by wadi and rills with stone and wooden bridges. Snowdrops and hellibores. Hosta walk leading to pear

and nut wood. Rondel and gravel gardens with grasses and phormiums. Collections of day lilies, rambling and rose species. Good labelling. Plenty of seats. Grass and gentle slopes.

New 7 acre hillside garden . . .

77 **SOLE RETREAT**
Haydon Drove, Haydon, West
Horrington, Wells BA5 3EH. Jane Clisby, 01749 672648/07790 602906, janeclisby@aol.com, www.soleretreat.co.uk. *3m NE of Wells. From Wells take B3139 towards the Horringtons. Keep on main road. after 3m L for Sole Retreat Reflexology, signed, garden 50yds on L.* Home-made teas. **Adm £3.50, chd free. Sun 19 July, Sun 30 Aug (11-5). Visitors also welcome by arrangement July to Aug please book teas in advance, car sharing advised.**
It is a challenge to garden at almost 1000ft on the Mendip Hills AONB. Laid out with tranquillity and healing in mind, the garden is full of old garden favourites set in ⅓ acre. Within dry stone walls and raw face bedrock are 9 differing areas incl sun terrace, herbaceous borders, water feature and pool, contemplation garden, fernery and vegetable plot. Contemplation garden. Featured in Mendip Times, Wells Life, regional press with Radio Bristol, Somerset and Glastonbury fm. Some gravel.

78 NEW **SOUTH KELDING**
Brewery Hill, Upton Cheyney,
Bristol BS30 6LY. Barry & Wendy Smale, 01179 325145, wendy.smale@yahoo.com. *Halfway between Bristol and Bath off A431. Upton Cheyney lies ½ m up Brewery Hill off A431 just outside Bitton. Detailed directions and parking arrangements given when appt*

made. Restricted access means pre-booking essential. Home-made teas. **Adm £4, chd free. Visitors welcome by arrangement May to Sept for groups of 8+.**
This new 7 acre hillside garden offers panoramic views from its upper levels, with herbaceous and shrub beds, prairie-style scree beds, orchard, native copses and small arboretum grouped by continents. Beyond this lie a large wildlife pond, boundary stream and wooded area featuring shade and moisture-loving plants. In view of slopes and uneven terrain this garden is unsuitable for disabled access.

79 **SOUTH MEADE**
Meade Lane, Seavington St Mary
TA19 0QL. Charo & Robin Ritchie. *3m E of Ilminster. Via B3168 to Seavington St Michael, near PH turn down Water Street to Seavington Millenneum Hall, shop and café and see parking signs and map.* **Adm £3, chd free. Daily Mon 15 June to Fri 19 June incl (2-5.30). Daily Mon 31 Aug to Fri 4 Sept incl (2-5.30).**
Beautiful country views all around. Mix of herbaceous, shrubs, roses and over 100 clematis are dotted around the garden. Absorb nature sitting in the Mediterranean patio and special Japanese pond areas. The searching for garden perfection is what fills my heart with joy. Exhibition of watercolour floral art.

80 **SOUTHFIELD FARM**
Farleigh Rd, Backwell, Bristol
BS48 3PE. Pamela & Alan Lewis. *6m S of Bristol. On A370, 500yds after George Inn towards WsM. Farm directly off main rd on R with parking. Large car park.* Home-made teas. **Adm £4, chd free. Sun 14 June (2-5).**
2 acre owner-designed garden of rooms with views. Mixed shrub and herbaceous borders, perennials, bulbs and blossom. Roses, climbers, pergolas and seating. Formal ponds. Orchard, vegetable garden, summerhouse, terracing and courtyards. Path through native meadow to woodland garden and to large wildlife pond with paths, seating and bird hide. Tearooms in old stable courtyard. Wheelchair access to most areas. Some gravel. Small courtyard and terrace only accessible by steps.

81 ◆ SPECIAL PLANTS
Greenways Lane, nr Cold Ashton SN14 8LA. Derry Watkins, 01225 891686, derry@specialplants.net, www.specialplants.net. *6m N of Bath. From Bath on A46, turn L into Greenways Lane just before r'about with A420*. Home-made teas. **Adm £4.50, chd free. For NGS: Thurs 18 June, 16 July, 20 Aug, 17 Sept, 15 Oct (11-5). For other opening times and information, please phone or see garden website.**
Architect-designed 3/4 acre hillside garden with stunning views. Started autumn 1996. Exotic plants. Gravel gardens for borderline hardy plants. Black and white (purple and silver) garden. Vegetable garden and orchard. Hot border. Lemon and lime bank. Annual, biennial and tender plants for late summer colour. Spring fed ponds. Bog garden. Woodland walk. Allium alley. Free list of plants in garden. New wavy bridge linking field and woods. Featured in RHS The Garden.

82 STANTON COURT NURSING HOME
Stanton Drew BS39 4ER. Pam Townsend, stantoncourtnh.net. *5m S of Bristol. From Bristol on A37, R onto B3130 signed Chew Magna. Approx 1 1/2 m, L at old thatched toll house into Stanton Drew, 1st property on L*. Delicious light lunches and cream teas served from conservatory. **Adm £3, chd free. Sun 29 Mar, Sun 13 Sept (1-4).**
2 acres of tranquil gardens around gracious Georgian House (grade II listed). Mature trees, extensive herbaceous borders with many interesting plants and spring bulbs. Large vegetable garden, fruit trees and soft fruit bushes. Gardener Judith Chubb Whittle keeps this lovely garden interesting in all seasons. Set in beautiful countryside. Stanton Drew's Ancient Stone Circle can be seen from the end of the garden - it is just a short walk from Stanton Court. Paved, level footpaths allow access to all parts of the garden.

83 STOBERRY GARDEN
Stoberry Park, Wells BA5 3LD. Frances & Tim Young, 01749 672906, stay@stoberry-park.co.uk, www.stoberry-park.co.uk. *1/2 m N of Wells. From Bristol - Wells on A39, L into College Rd and immed L through Stoberry Park, signed*. Tea. **Adm £5, chd free. Sun 31 May, Mon 31 Aug (2-5.30).**
With breathtaking views over Wells and the Vale of Avalon, this 6 acre family garden planted sympathetically within its landscape provides a stunning combination of vistas accented with wildlife ponds, water features, sculpture, 1 1/2 acre walled garden, gazebo, lime walk. Colour and interest in every season; spring bulbs, irises, acer glade, salvias; new features - wild flower circles, rose garden. Featured in The Visitor, Fosseway magazine, regional press with Radio Bristol, Somerset and Glastonbury fm. Gravel paths, steep slopes.

Kilver Court Secret Gardens
© Val Corbett

GROUP OPENING

84 STOGUMBER GARDENS
Station Road, Stogumber TA4 3TQ. *11m NW of Taunton. 3m W of A358. Signed to Stogumber, W of Crowcombe. Maps given to all visitors*. Cream teas in village hall. **Combined adm £5, chd free. Sun 21 June (2-6).**

BRAGLANDS BARN
TA4 3TP. Simon & Sue Youell www.braglandsbarn.com

BROOK HOUSE
TA4 3SZ. Jan & Jonathan Secker-Walker

CRIDLANDS STEEP
TA4 3TL. Audrey Leitch

HIGHER KINGSWOOD
TA4 3TN. Fran & Tom Vesey

KNOLL COTTAGE
Elaine & John Leech
Visitors also welcome by arrangement May to Oct. 01984 656689 john@knoll-cottage.co.uk www.knoll-cottage.co.uk

POUND HOUSE
TA4 3SZ. Barry & Jenny Hibbert

6 delightful and very varied gardens in picturesque village at edge of Quantocks. 2 surprisingly large gardens in village centre, one semi-wild garden, and 3 very large gardens on outskirts of village, with many rare and unusual plants. Conditions range from waterlogged clay to well-drained sand. Features include a walled garden, ponds, bog gardens, rockery, vegetable and fruit gardens, a collection of over 80 different roses, even a cider-apple orchard. Fine views of surrounding countryside. Dogs on leads allowed in 5 gardens. Wheelchair access to main features of all gardens.

GROUP OPENING

85 **NEW** **STOKE BISHOP GARDENS**
BS9 3UW/BS9 1JB. WEST BRISTOL. *2m N of Bristol city centre, 3m S of J16 M5. please see individual gardens for directions.* Teas at Crete Hill House. **Combined adm £5, chd free.** Sun 14 June (1-5).

NEW **CRETE HILL HOUSE**
Cote House Lane, Durdham Down BS9 3UW. John Burgess. *A4018 Westbury Rd, L at White Tree r'about, R into Cote Rd, continue into Cote House Lane. Narrow lane, parking limited, recommended to park in Saville Rd and walk to both gardens*

NEW **GREYSTONES**
Hollybush Lane, BS9 1JB. Mr & Mrs P Townsend. *A4018 Westbury Rd, L at White Tree r'about, L into Saville Rd, Hollybush Lane 2nd on R. Narrow lane, parking limited, recommended to park in Saville Rd and walk to both gardens*

Pair of interesting gardens both located adjacent to the Downs. Crete Hill House: C18 house, hidden corner of Bristol, 80' x 40' garden, mainly SW facing, shaped lawn, heavily planted traditional mixed shrub, rose and herbaceous borders, pergola, camellia bed, small terrace with pond. Greystones: peaceful garden with places to sit and enjoy a quiet corner of Bristol. Interesting courtyard with raised beds and large variety of conifers and shrubs leads to secluded garden of contrasts - from sun drenched beds with olive tree and brightly coloured flowers to shady spots, with acers, hostas and fern walk, small apple orchard, espaliered pears and koi pond. Paved footpaths provide level access to all areas.

86 ♦ **STON EASTON PARK**
Ston Easton, Radstock BA3 4DF. Ston Easton Ltd, 01761 241631, www.stoneaston.co.uk. *On A37 between Bath & Wells. Entrance to Park through high metal gates set back from main road, A37, in centre of village, opp bus shelter.* Light refreshments in the Yellow Dining Room. Advance booking required for lunch and full afternoon tea, please phone to make reservation. **Adm £4, chd free.** For NGS: Thur 21 May,

Wed 15 July, Wed 2 Sept (10.30-4). For other opening times and information, please phone or see garden website.
A hidden treasure in the heart of the Mendips. Walk through the glorious parkland of the historic 36 acres of Repton landscape, alongside the quietly cascading River Norr, to the productive walled Victorian kitchen garden. Visit the octagonal rose garden, stunning herbaceous border, colourful flowerbeds, fruit cage and orchard. The parkland at Ston Easton Park is now the only remaining Humphry Repton landscape in Somerset. His Red Book, a facsimile demonstrating his plans in before and after stages, illustrated in wonderful watercolours, can be found in the hotel reception. Featured in Fosseway Magazine, Country Gardener, Western Daily Press, Somerset Life and regional press with Radio Bristol, Somerset and Glastonbury fm. Gravel paths, steep slopes, shallow steps.

GROUP OPENING

87 **STONE ALLERTON GARDENS**
Stone Allerton BS26 2NW. *Near Wedmore. 2m from A38, signed from Lower Weare.* Home-made teas at Greenfield House. **Combined adm £6, chd free.** Sun 3, Mon 4 May (2-5.30).

BADGERS ACRE
Lucy Hetherington & Jim Mathers
Visitors also welcome by arrangement Apr to July adm £4. Please request teas when booking.
01934 713159
lucyhetherington@btinternet.com

GREENFIELD HOUSE
BS26 2NH. Mr & Mrs Bull

Two beautiful gardens on edge of Somerset levels. Badgers Acre: 1-acre garden. Colour themed mixed borders. Secret walk, pond and colourful rockery. Semi-circular tulip and allium bed surrounded by box. Vegetable potager with pergola draped in rambling roses and clematis. Greenfield House: 4 main gardens all manageable size. Grass and shrub border, colour garden, cottage garden. Large range of shrubs, perennial plants, bulbs, many unusual. How to make a garden

using garden centre bargains. Various ponds for fish and wildlife. Chicken area. Plants changed since last year.

STOURHEAD GARDEN
See Wiltshire.

Continually evolving to provide colour and interest from spring to autumn. Plants for sale in aid of Wildlife Trust . . .

GROUP OPENING

88 **STOWEY GARDENS**
Stowey, Bishop Sutton, Bristol BS39 5TL. *10m W of Bath. Stowey Village A368 between Bishop Sutton and Chelwood. From Chelwood r'about take Weston-s-Mare rd A368. At Stowey Xrds turn R for car park, 150 yards down lane. Ample parking available opp Dormers.* Delicious home-made teas at Stowey Mead. **Combined adm £6, chd free.** Sun 21 June (2-6).

DORMERS
Stowey Bottom. Mr & Mrs G Nicol

2 STOWEY CROSS COTTAGE
Stowey Crossroads. Viv & Roger Hodge

1 STOWEY CROSS COTTAGE
Stowey Crossroads. Deborah & Kim Heath

STOWEY MEAD
Stowey. Mr Victor Pritchard

VICARAGE COTTAGE
Stowey. Mr & Mrs P Haggett

5 gardens opening for 3rd yr for NGS provide a varied and interesting afternoon's viewing. From some large, informal and interesting planting to designer-planned and loved

smaller gardens there is something of interest for everyone. All within 10 minutes walk of parking area, natural progression from one to another. Plants for sale at Dormers.

89 ▶ 1 SUNNYSIDE
Stoke Bishop, Bristol BS9 1BQ. Mrs Magda Goss. *Approach via Stoke Hill or Druid Hill,near shops. Parking on Druid Hill, gate with sloping gravel drive.* **Adm £2.50, chd free. Sun 7 June (2-6). Also open Lucombe House.**
C17 cottage in heart of Stoke Bishop with part walled, cottage style front garden. Garden sculptures dominated by large magnolia, perennials, roses and spring bulbs. Courtyard garden with open studio at rear.

90 ▶ SUTTON HOSEY MANOR
Long Sutton TA10 9NA. Roger Bramble, 0207 3906700, rbramble@bdbltd.co.uk. *2m E of Langport, on A372. Gates N of A372 at E end of Long Sutton.* Home-made teas. **Adm £4, chd £2. Sun 19 July (2.30-6). Groups also welcome by arrangement Aug to Sept.**
3 acres, of which 2 walled. Lily canal through pleached limes leading to amelanchier walk past duck pond; rose and juniper walk from Italian terrace; judas tree avenue; ptelea walk. Ornamental potager. Drive-side shrubbery. Music by musicians of the Young Musicians Symphony Orchestra.

91 ▶ ◆ TINTINHULL
nr Yeovil BA22 8PZ. National Trust, 01935 823289, www.nationaltrust.org.uk/tintinhull-garden. *5m NW of Yeovil. Tintinhull village. Signs on A303, W of Ilchester.* Cream teas. **Adm £7.50, chd £3.75. For NGS: Sun 7 June (11-4.30). For other opening times and information, please phone or see garden website.**
C17 and C18 house (part open). Famous 2-acre garden in compartments, developed 1900 to present day, influenced by Hidcote; many good and uncommon plants. Wheelchair access with care, uneven paths.

92 ▶ TORMARTON COURT
Church Rd, Tormarton GL9 1HT. Noreen & Bruce Finnamore, 01454 218236, home@thefinnamores.com. *3m E of Chipping Sodbury, off A46 J to M4. Follow signs to Tormarton from A46 then follow signs for car parking.* Home-made teas. Refreshments by prior arrangement. **Adm £5, chd free. Visitors welcome by arrangement Mar to July for groups of 20+.**
11 acres of formal and natural gardens in stunning Cotswold setting. Features incl roses, herbaceous, kitchen garden, Mediterranean garden, mound and natural pond. Extensive walled garden, spring glade and meadows with young and mature trees.

93 ▶ TRANBY HOUSE
Norton Lane, Whitchurch, Bristol BS14 0BT. Jan Barkworth. *5m S of Bristol. 1/2 m S of Whitchurch. Leave Bristol on A37 Wells Rd, through Whitchurch village, 1st turning on R signed Norton Malreward.* Tea. **Adm £3.50, chd free. Suns 7 June, 19 July, 16 Aug, 6 Sept (2-5).**
1 1/4 -acre well-established informal garden, designed and planted to encourage wildlife. Wide variety of trees, shrubs and cottage garden plants; pond and wild flower meadow. Garden is divided into smaller areas, each with its own characteristics. Continually evolving to provide colour and interest from spring to autumn. Plants for sale in aid of Wildlife Trust.

94 ▶ NEW TROYTES FARMSTEAD
Tivington, Minehead TA24 8SU. Mr Theodore Stone, 01643 704 531, info@mineheadcottage.com. *Take A39 from Minehead to Porlock. L at 1st Xrds for Wooton Courteney, garden 1/2 m on R.* Light refreshments. **Adm by donation. Visitors welcome by arrangement May to Sept, refreshments by arrangement.**
Garden now 22yrs old. 2 acres originally neglected farmland has 2 small water courses incl ancient C12 sheep wash. Main feature some very fine trees well placed to view and photograph.

95 ▶ TRUFFLES
Church Lane, Bishop Sutton, Bristol BS39 5UP. Sally Monkhouse, 01275 333665, sallymonkhouse961@btinternet.com. *10m W of Bath. On A368 Bath to Weston-super-Mare rd. Take rd opp PO/stores uphill towards Hinton Blewett. 1st R into Church Lane.* Home-made teas. **Adm £4, chd free. Sat 4, Sun 5 July (1.30-5.30). Groups of 10+ also welcome by arrangement July.**
2 acres, a different and surprising, relaxing garden with views. Formal and wildlife planting linked with meandering paths, lots of seating. Hidden valley, small stream, wildlife pond, flower meadows, varied flower beds. Unique 1/4 acre kitchen garden with several 21ft long x 4ft wide large waist high raised beds. Grass and gravel paths, part of garden accessible to wheelchair users.

96 ▶ ◆ TYNTESFIELD
Wraxall BS48 1NX. National Trust, 01275 461900, www.nationaltrust.org.uk/tyntesfield. *7m SW of Bristol. Nr Nailsea, entrance off B3128. Follow the brown signs.* **Adm £9.45, chd £4.75. For NGS: Sun 19 July (10-6). For other opening times and information, please phone or see garden website.**
Remarkably intact Victorian garden with formal bedding displays and a productive walled kitchen garden which offers produce for sale to the public, and supplies the Cow Barn Kitchen on site. The grounds also include an arboretum, wild flower meadows and an orangery. Talks and demonstrations throughout the day. Steep slopes, steps and gravel paths throughout garden. Courtesy bus from visitor centre to kitchen garden.

Yews Farm

97 ◆ UNIVERSITY OF BRISTOL BOTANIC GARDEN

Stoke Park Rd, Stoke Bishop, Bristol BS9 1JG. University of Bristol, 0117 3314906, www.bristol.ac.uk/Botanic-Garden. ¼ m W of Durdham Downs. Located in Stoke Bishop next to Durdham Downs 1m from city centre. After crossing the Downs to Stoke Hill, Stoke Park Rd is first on R. Tea. **Adm £4.50, chd free. For NGS: Sun 7 June (10-5). For other opening times and information, please phone or see garden website.** Exciting contemporary botanic garden with organic flowing network of paths which lead visitors through collections of Mediterranean flora, rare native, useful plants (incl. European and Chinese herbs) and those that illustrate plant evolution. Large floral displays illustrating pollination/flowering plant evolution. Glasshouses, home to giant Amazon waterlily, tropical fruit and medicine plants, orchids, cacti and unique sacred lotus collection. Open at other times by arrangement. Special tours of garden throughout day. Featured on BBC Radio 4 Food Programme. Wheelchair available to borrow from Welcome Lodge. Wheelchair friendly route through garden available upon request, also accessible WC.

98 NEW 8 UPPER FARM CLOSE

Norton St Philip BA2 7NA. Linda and John Oliver. *Between Frome and Bath, approx 7m from each. Next turning after Longmead Close going into Norton St Philips.* Home-made teas. **Combined with Linden, combined adm £4, chd free.**

Sat 25, Sun 26 July (1-5). A feast for lovers of textures and foliage, strong on evergreen structure. A traditional cottage rose garden greets visitors but behind the house a terrace with lavishly planted pots looks over a naturalistic pond and a pretty potager. There are plenty of ideas for shade loving planting with much use of bold heucheras and grasses and gravel garden is crammed with airy contemporary planting. Limited wheelchair access.

99 VELLACOTT

Lawford, Crowcombe TA4 4AL. Kevin & Pat Chittenden, 01984 618249, kevinchit@hotmail.co.uk. *9m NW of Taunton. Off A358, signed Lawford. For directions please phone.* Home-made teas. **Adm £3, chd free. Sat 6, Sun 7 June (12-5). Visitors also welcome by arrangement May to Sept, max 20.** 1-acre informal garden on S-facing slope with lovely views of the Quantock and Brendon Hills. Profusely stocked with wide selection of herbaceous plants, shrubs and trees. Other features include ponds, ruin and potager. Plenty of places to sit and enjoy the surroundings.

VENN CROSS RAILWAY GARDENS

See Devon.

100 ◆ THE WALLED GARDENS OF CANNINGTON

Church Street, Cannington TA5 2HA. Bridgwater College, 01278 655042, canningtonwalledgardens.co.uk. *3m NW of Bridgwater. On A39*

Bridgwater-Minehead rd - at 1st r'about in Cannington 2nd exit, through village. War memorial, 1st L into Church Street then 1st L. Light refreshments. **Adm £3.50, chd free. For NGS: Sat 26, Sun 27 Sept (10-4). For other opening times and information, please phone or see garden website.** Within the grounds of a medieval Priory, the Gardens have undergone extensive redevelopment over the last few years. Classic and contemporary features include a National Collection in progress, stunning blue garden, sub-tropical walk, Victorian-style fernery and large botanical glasshouse. Gravel paths. A motorised scooter can be borrowed free of charge (only one available).

101 WATCOMBE

92 Church Road, Winscombe BS25 1BP. Peter & Ann Owen, 01934 842666, peter.o@which.net. *12 m SW of Bristol, 3m N of Axbridge. 100 yds after signs on A38 turn L (from S), R (from N) into Winscombe Hill. After 1m reach The Square. Pink house on L after further 150yds.* Cream teas. Home made cakes, some gluten free. Gluten free scones. **Adm £3.50, chd free. Sun 26 Apr, Sun 17 May, Thur 11 June (2-5.30). Groups of 2+ also welcome by arrangement Apr to July.** ¾ -acre mature Edwardian garden with colour-themed, informally planted herbaceous borders. Topiary, box hedging, lime walk, pleached hornbeams, cordon fruit trees, vegetable plot, 2 small formal ponds, many unusual trees and shrubs. Strong framework separating several different areas of the garden, pergola with varied wisteria, lime walk, unusual topiary, growing collection of approx 80 clematis! Some steps but most areas accessible by wheelchair with minimal assistance.

102 NEW WAVERLEY

Moorland, Bridgwater TA7 0AT. Ash & Alison Warne. *3m from J24 M5. Moorland is on minor rd between Burrowbridge and Huntworth. Garden opp church. Park village hall car park - 300 mtrs W of garden. Limited disabled parking in drive - tel 07548 889705 to book space.* Home-made teas. **Adm £3, chd free. Sat 13, Sun 14, Sat 27, Sun 28 June (11-4.30).**

Look out for exciting Designer Gardens D

Started in 2010, ¹/₃ acre garden is packed with informal arrangements of shrubs, trees and perennials. Flooded to a depth of 1 mtr for 3 weeks in Feb 2014, this garden demonstrates the resilience of nature. Over 40 roses and 20 clematis vie for space amongst 20 different young trees. Bamboo lovers will enjoy 10 different species. Paths allow access to all areas. Secluded seats to enjoy teas. No steps, gravel drive. Paths all level.

103 WAYFORD MANOR
Wayford, Crewkerne TA18 8QG. Wayford Manor. *3m SW of Crewkerne. Turning N off B3165 at Clapton; or S off A30 Chard to Crewkerne rd.* Home-made teas. **Adm £5, chd £2.50. Sun 26 Apr (2-5).**
The mainly Elizabethan manor (not open) mentioned in C17 for its 'fair and pleasant' garden was redesigned by Harold Peto in 1902. Formal terraces with yew hedges and topiary have fine views over W Dorset. Steps down between spring-fed ponds past mature and new plantings of magnolia, rhododendron, maples, cornus and, in season, spring bulbs, cyclamen, giant echium. Primula candelabra, arum lily, gunnera around lower ponds.

104 WELLFIELD BARN
Walcombe Lane, Wells BA5 3AG. David & Virginia Nasmyth, 01749 675129, david.nasmyth@talktalk.net. *¹/₂ m N of Wells. From A39 Bristol to Wells rd turn R at 30 mph sign into Walcombe Lane. Entrance at 1st cottage on R, parking signed.* Home-made teas. **Adm £4, chd free. Tue 26 May (11-5). Visitors also welcome by arrangement June to July, max 29 seat coach on site.**
1¹/₂ -acre gardens, made by owners over the past 18yrs from concrete farmyard. Ha-ha, wonderful views, pond, lawn, mixed borders, formal sunken garden, hydrangea bed, grass walks and interesting young and semi-mature trees. Structured design integrates house and garden with landscape. New areas under development. Special interest plants are the hardy geranium family. Featured in regional and gardening magazines, regional press with local radio. Moderate slopes in places, some gravel paths.

GROUP OPENING

105 WEST BRISTOL GARDENS
BS9 2LR/BS9 2PY, Bristol BS9 2LR, 07779 203626, p.l.prior@gmail.com. *3m NW of Bristol city centre. Please see individual gardens for directions.* Home-made teas at 159 Westbury Lane. **Combined adm £5, chd free. Sun 14 June (2-5.30). Visitors also welcome by arrangement Apr to Sept for groups 10-30.**

4 HAYTOR PARK
Mr & Mrs C J Prior.
From A4162 Inner Ring Rd take turning into Coombe Bridge Ave, Haytor Park is 1st on L. Please no Parking in Haytor Park
Visitors also welcome by arrangement Apr to Sept for groups 10 to 30.
07779 203626
p.l.prior@gmail.com

159 WESTBURY LANE
Coombe Dingle BS9 2PY.
Maureen Dickens.
L A4162/Sylvan Way, B4054/Shirehampton Rd, R to Westbury Lane. 1st house on R
Visitors also welcome by arrangement Apr to Sept for groups 10-30.
01179 043008
159jmd@gmail.com

Pair of interesting and contrasting gardens. 4 Haytor Park: enter past the sun baked, pot laden patio seeking dragons through a tracery of arches and cascading climbers. Along meandering paths to plant packed secret spaces. Discover hidden seats to dream upon. Search for the rare shoe tree and arty paraphernalia via ponds and a veritable plethora of plants. 159 Westbury Lane: lovely quiet garden, barely overlooked on edge of city. Planted to owner's design from scratch in cottage garden style. Full of interesting and many unusual plants bought from specialist nurseries. Primarily an early summer garden but being developed to show flowers all yr. Quirky touch with garden artifacts in many places. Many interesting visiting birds. A garden full of interesting plants full of colour and leaf structure with lots of hidden artefacts to find.

106 WOODLEA BOTTOM
Greyfield Road, High Littleton, Bristol BS39 6YA. Adrian & Jane Neech, 01761 479794, jane.neech@btinternet.com. *Follow A39 to High Littleton. Turn into Greyfield Rd, opp Dando's Stores. Garden 400 yds on L. Limited parking on Greyfield Rd.* **Adm £3, chd free. Sat 30, Sun 31 May (10-4). Visitors also welcome by arrangement May, adm £4, refreshments to be booked in advance.**
A garden of rooms, each with a different theme. A balance of naturalised planting and herbaceous borders alongside productive greenhouses and fruit and vegetable areas. Interesting specimen trees and roses, don't forget to look up and through the hedge windows! Summerhouse and attractive garden pots. No dogs please. Featured in regional press with Radio Bristol, Somerset and Glastonbury fm.

107 YEWS FARM
East Street, Martock TA12 6NF. Louise & Fergus Dowding, 01935 822202, fergus.dowding@btinternet.com, www.louisedowding.co.uk. *Turn off main road through village at Market House, onto East St, past PO, garden 150 yards on R, 50 yards before Nag's Head.* Home-made teas. Free glass of fine home-made cider to all with a healthy constitution and aged over 18. **Adm £4.50, chd free. Sun 28, Mon 29 June (2-7). Groups of 20-50 also welcome by arrangement June to July.**
1 acre theatrical planting in large walled garden. Outsized plants in jungle garden. Sculptural planting for height, shape, leaf and texture. Self-seeded gravel garden, box and bay ball border, espalier apples, eclectic cloud pruning, much block planting. Working organic kitchen garden. Hens, pigs, orchard and active cider barn - the full monty! We grow the Martock broad bean, the only known survivor of a mediaeval variety of broad bean. Visitors may throw Beauty of Bath apples to the pigs. Child friendly garden, with hammocks, swing etc. Featured in Geheimer Garten England (Secret Gardens of England) by Heidi Gildemeister. Mostly wheelchair access.

Lemon drizzle cake, Victoria sponge … yummy!

STAFFORDSHIRE

Birmingham & West Midlands

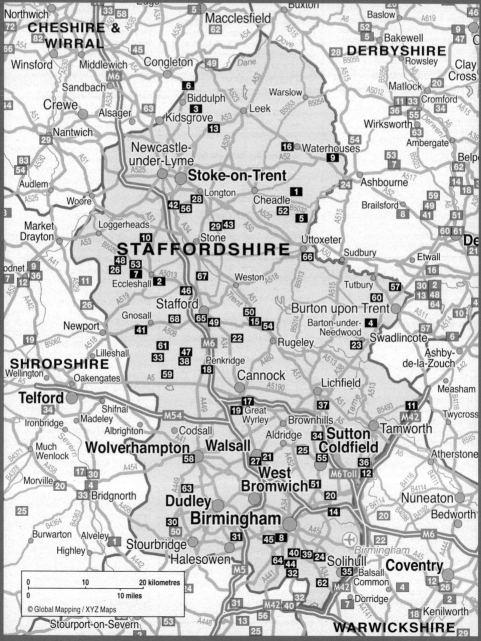

Staffordshire, Birmingham & West Midlands

Staffordshire, Birmingham and part of the West Midlands is a landlocked 'county', one of the furthest from the sea in England and Wales.

It is an NGS county of surprising contrasts, from the 'Moorlands' in the North East, the 'Woodland Quarter' in the North West, the 'Staffordshire Potteries' and England's 'Second City' in the South East, with much of the rest of the land devoted to agriculture, both dairy and arable.

The garden owners enthusiastically embraced the NGS from the very beginning, with seven gardens opening in the inaugural year of 1927, and a further thirteen the following year.

The county is the home of the National Memorial Arboretum, the Cannock Chase Area of Outstanding Natural Beauty and part of the new National Forest.

There are many large country houses and gardens throughout the county with a long history of garden-making and with the input of many of the well known landscape.

Today, the majority of NGS gardens are privately owned and of modest size. However, a few of the large country house gardens still open their gates for NGS visitors.

Below: Four Seasons

Staffordshire, Birmingham & West Midlands Volunteers

County Organiser
John & Susan Weston
01785 850448
johnweston123@btinternet.com

County Treasurer
John Weston
(as above)

Publicity
Graham & Judy White
01889 563930
cityofgold@lineone.net

Booklet Coordinator
Graham & Judy White
(as above)

Assistant County Organisers
Jane Cerone
01827 873205
janecerone@btinternet.com

Ken & Joy Sutton
01889 590631
suttonjoy2@gmail.com

Sheila Thacker
01782 791244
metbowers@gmail.com

Since our foundation we have donated more than £42.5 million to charity

Opening Dates

All entries subject to change.
For latest information check www.ngs.org.uk

January

Wednesday 21
`56` The Trentham Estate

March

Sunday 29
`49` St John's Gardens

April

Saturday 4
`9` NEW Blore Hall
Sunday 12
`37` Millennium Garden
Sunday 19
`52` Stonehill Quarry Garden
Sunday 26
`45` Pereira Road Gardens

May

Sunday 3
`24` Hall Green Gardens
`68` Yew Tree Cottage
Monday 4
`62` Wits End
Thursday 7
`68` Yew Tree Cottage
Sunday 10
`50` The Secret Garden
Wednesday 13
`8` Birmingham Botanical Gardens
Friday 15
`49` St John's Gardens (Evening)
Sunday 17
`5` The Beeches
`14` Castle Bromwich Hall Gardens Trust
`19` Dorset House
`54` Tanglewood Cottage
`57` 41 Twentylands
Wednesday 20
`28` High Trees
Sunday 24
`21` Four Seasons
`25` Hamilton House
`42` The Old Dairy House
Monday 25
`12` Bridge House
`21` Four Seasons
`42` The Old Dairy House

Sunday 31
`62` Wits End

June

Wednesday 3
`28` High Trees
Friday 5
`15` Coley Cottage
`50` The Secret Garden

Festival Weekend

Saturday 6
`6` Biddulph Grange Garden
Sunday 7
`2` Ashcroft and Claremont
`22` The Garth
`35` 89 Marsh Lane
`46` The Pintles
`47` Priory Farm
`55` 91 Tower Road
`58` 19 Waterdale
Thursday 11
`68` Yew Tree Cottage
Sunday 14
`31` 13 Lansdowne Road
`49` St John's Gardens
`60` NEW Wild Wood Lodge
Monday 15
`1` Alton Towers Gardens
Wednesday 17
`4` Bankcroft Farm
Sunday 21
`5` The Beeches
`11` NEW Breakmills
`15` Coley Cottage
`34` NEW 3 Marlows Cottages
`36` Middleton Hall
`40` Moseley Gardens South
`41` The Mount, Coton, Gnosall
`50` The Secret Garden
`64` Woodbrooke Quaker Study Centre
Wednesday 24
`4` Bankcroft Farm
`34` NEW 3 Marlows Cottages
Friday 26
`62` Wits End
Saturday 27
`16` Colour Mill
Sunday 28
`13` Brooklyn
`22` The Garth
`23` Grafton Cottage
`33` NEW Little Onn Hall

`62` Wits End
`65` Woodland Grange Gardens

July

Wednesday 1
`56` The Trentham Estate (Evening)
Sunday 5
`18` 4 Dene Close
`24` Hall Green Gardens
`37` Millennium Garden
`38` Mitton Manor
`39` Moseley Corner, The Art of Gardens
`45` Pereira Road Gardens
`51` 190 Station Road
`59` The Wickets
Wednesday 8
`53` Sugnall Walled Garden
`56` The Trentham Estate (Evening)
`59` The Wickets
Thursday 9
`68` Yew Tree Cottage
Friday 10
`67` Yarlet House
Saturday 11
`66` Woodleighton Grove Gardens
Sunday 12
`7` Birch Trees
`19` Dorset House
`58` 19 Waterdale
`66` Woodleighton Grove Gardens
Saturday 18
`9` NEW Blore Hall
`43` The Old Vicarage
Sunday 19
`23` Grafton Cottage
`43` The Old Vicarage
`68` Yew Tree Cottage
Sunday 26
`5` The Beeches
`10` The Bowers
`20` 198 Eachelhurst Road
`27` Hidden Gem
`32` NEW Little Indonesia

August

Sunday 2
`23` Grafton Cottage
`62` Wits End
Thursday 6
`16` Colour Mill
Sunday 9
`23` Grafton Cottage
Wednesday 12
`15` Coley Cottage
`50` The Secret Garden

Sunday 16
`60` NEW Wild Wood Lodge
Saturday 22
`25` Hamilton House (Evening)
Sunday 23
`29` Idlerocks Farm
`30` 'John's Garden' at Ashwood Nurseries
Sunday 30
`5` The Beeches
`7` Birch Trees
`59` The Wickets
`62` Wits End
Monday 31
`7` Birch Trees
`12` Bridge House

Gently sloping cottage style garden . . .

September

Wednesday 9
`53` Sugnall Walled Garden
Sunday 13
`48` Rowley House Farm

October

Saturday 24
`21` Four Seasons
Sunday 25
`21` Four Seasons

Gardens open to the public

`1` Alton Towers Gardens
`6` Biddulph Grange Garden
`8` Birmingham Botanical Gardens
`14` Castle Bromwich Hall Gardens Trust
`36` Middleton Hall
`53` Sugnall Walled Garden
`56` The Trentham Estate

By arrangement only

`3` Badger Hill
`17` 12 Darges Lane
`26` Heath House
`44` Paul's Oasis of Calm
`61` Willow Cottage
`63` The Wombourne Wodehouse

Over 400 Volunteers help run the NGS – why not become one too?

Also open by arrangement

5 The Beeches
7 Birch Trees
10 The Bowers
12 Bridge House
15 Coley Cottage
16 Colour Mill
18 4 Dene Close

19 Dorset House
22 The Garth
23 Grafton Cottage
24 16 Burnaston Road, Hall Green Gardens
24 37 Burnaston Road, Hall Green Gardens
24 36 Ferndale Road, Hall Green Gardens
24 Hall Green Gardens

24 120 Russell Road, Hall Green Gardens
27 Hidden Gem
29 Idlerocks Farm
32 Little Indonesia
38 Mitton Manor
41 The Mount, Coton, Gnosall
47 Priory Farm
48 Rowley House Farm

49 St John's Gardens
51 190 Station Road
54 Tanglewood Cottage
57 41 Twentylands
58 19 Waterdale
59 The Wickets
62 Wits End
66 Woodleighton Grove Gardens
68 Yew Tree Cottage

The Gardens

1 ◆ ALTON TOWERS GARDENS

Alton, Stoke on Trent ST10 4DB. Alton Towers Resort, 01538 703344, www.altontowers.com. *6m N of Uttoxeter. From A50, follow 'brown signs' for Alton Towers. At the theme park follow signs for Alton Towers Hotel. Enter garden through the Alton Towers Hotel.* **Adm £4, chd free. For NGS: Mon 15 June (3.30-6). For other opening times and information, please phone or see garden website.**

Alton Tower's magnificent early C19 gardens, designed by the flamboyant 15th Earl of Shrewsbury, feature pools, pagoda fountain, statues, mature trees, shrubs, rhododendrons and azaleas set in a steep sided valley with steep walks and viewing terraces. Access via the 1m long 'woodland walk' from the Alton Towers Hotel. Refreshments in hotel. One of the first gardens in Staffordshire to 'Open' for the NGS in 1932. Unfortunately the historic nature of the gardens makes them unsuitable for wheelchair users or those with limited mobility.

GROUP OPENING

2 ASHCROFT AND CLAREMONT

Eccleshall ST21 6JP. *7m W of Stafford. J14 M6. At Eccleshall end of A5013 the garden is 100 metres before junction with A518. On street parking nearby.* Home-made teas at Ashcroft. **Combined adm £4, chd free. Sun 7 June (2-5).**

ASHCROFT
1 Stafford Road. Peter & Gillian Bertram

CLAREMONT
26 Claremont Road. Maria Edwards

Birch Trees
© Julia Stanley

Two gardens as different as Monet's soft pastel colours are to Vincent's bright sunflowers. Ashcroft is a 1-acre wildlife-friendly garden, pond and covered courtyard. Rooms flow seamlessly around the Edwardian house. Herb bed, treillage, greenhouse with raised beds. Find the topiary peacock that struts in the gravel bed. In the woodland area Gollum lurks in the steps of the ruin. Claremont is a small town garden its design based on feng shui principles. Manicured lawns, herbaceous borders, shrubs, perennials and annuals. Constantly evolving with colour and new features, maintaining interest throughout the year. Come and be inspired! Maria is happy to explain the principles of Feng Shui in garden layout. Tickets & plants available at Ashcroft. Wheelchair access at Ashcroft only.

3 BADGER HILL

Rock End, Biddulph Moor, Stoke-on-Trent ST8 7NP. Mr & Mrs Shirley & Michael Bligh-Smith, 01782 519203. *1½ m SE of Biddulph. Off A527 Stoke to Congleton Rd. At Knypersley T-lights turn onto Park Lane signed Biddulph Moor. Rock End & driveway to garden is approx 1m. Parking at Booth's Garage.* Home-made teas. **Adm £4, chd free. Visitors welcome by arrangement** This 1 acre terraced garden, in a unique country setting, approached along a drive with a steep bank on one side where native trees, shrubs and plants grow among rocky outcrops. In the main garden, gravel paths link herbaceous borders, island beds, rockeries and several water features incl a wildlife pool. Trees and colourful foliage separate tranquil seating areas. The garden has been planted for all year round interest. Featured in Amateur Gardening.

4 BANKCROFT FARM

Tatenhill, Burton-on-Trent
DE13 9SA. Mrs Penelope Adkins.
2m SW of Burton-on-Trent. Take Tatenhill Rd off A38 Burton-Branston flyover. 1m, 1st house on L approaching village. Parking on farm. Adm £3, chd free. **Wed 17, Wed 24 June (2-5).**
Lose yourself for an afternoon in our 1½ -acre organic country garden. Arbour, gazebo and many other seating areas to view ponds and herbaceous borders, backed with shrubs and trees with emphasis on structure, foliage and colour. Productive fruit and vegetable gardens, wildlife areas and adjoining 12-acre native woodland walk. Picnics welcome. Many gravel paths.

5 THE BEECHES

Mill Street, Rocester ST14 5JX.
Ken & Joy Sutton, 01889 590631,
suttonjoy2@gmail.com. *5m N of Uttoxeter. On B5030 from Uttoxeter turn R at 2nd r'about into village by JCB factory. At Red Lion PH & mini r'about take rd signed Mill Street. Garden 250 yds on R. Car park at JCB academy.* Home-made teas. Adm £3, chd free. **Suns 17 May, 21 June, 26 July, 30 Aug (1.30-5). Visitors also welcome by arrangement May to Aug min adm £60 if less than 20 people.**
Stroll along the driveway containing island beds planted with mixed shrubs and perennials, and enter a stunning plant lover's garden of approx ⅔ acre, enjoying views of surrounding countryside. Box garden, mixed shrubs incl rhododendrons and azaleas, vibrant colour-themed herbaceous borders, roses, clematis and climbing plants, fruit trees, pools and late flowering perennials also raised vegetable and soft fruit garden, yr-round garden. Partial wheelchair access.

6 ◆ BIDDULPH GRANGE GARDEN

Grange Road, Biddulph ST8 7SD.
National Trust, 01782 375 533,
www.nationaltrust.org.uk. *3½ m SE of Congleton. 7m N of Stoke-on-Trent off A527, Congleton to Biddulph rd.* Adm £8.10, chd £4.05. **For NGS: Sat 6 June (11-5.30). For other opening times and information, please phone or see garden website.**
Amazing Victorian garden created by Darwin contemporary and correspondent James Bateman as an extension of his beliefs, scientific interests and collection of plants. Visit the Italian terrace, Chinese inspired garden, dahlia walk and the oldest surviving golden larch in Britain brought from China by the great plant hunter Robert Fortune.

NGS & Perennial; giving support where it's needed

7 BIRCH TREES

Copmere End, Eccleshall
ST21 6HH. Susan & John Weston,
01785 850448,
johnweston123@btinternet.com.
1½ m W of Eccleshall. On B5026, turn at junction signed Copmere End. After ½ m straight across Xrds by Star Inn. Home-made teas. Adm £3, chd free. **Sun 12 July, Sun 30, Mon 31 Aug (1.30-5.30). Visitors also welcome by arrangement June to Aug, groups of 10 - 30.**
Surprising ½ acre SW-facing sun trap which takes advantage of the 'borrowed landscape' of the surrounding countryside. Take time to explore the pathways between the island beds which contain many unusual herbaceous plants, grasses and shrubs; also vegetable patch, stump bed, alpine house, orchard and water features.

8 ◆ BIRMINGHAM BOTANICAL GARDENS

Westbourne Road, Edgbaston B15
3TR. Birmingham Botanical & Horticultural Society,
0121 454 1860,
www.birminghambotanicalgardens
.org.uk. *1½ m SW of the centre of Birmingham. From J6 M6 take A38(M) to city centre. Follow underpasses signed Birmingham West to A456. At Fiveways island turn L onto B4217 (Calthorpe Rd) signed Botanical Gardens.* In our Terrace pavilion tearoom which overlooks stunning views of the gardens, you can enjoy light snacks and refreshments. Adm £7, chd free. **For NGS: Wed 13 May (10-6). For other opening times and information, please phone or see garden website.**
Extensive botanical garden set in a green urban environment with a comprehensive collection of plants from throughout the world growing in the glasshouses and outside. Four stunning glasshouses take you from tropical rainforest to arid desert. Fifteen acres of beautiful landscaped gardens. Roses, alpines, perennials, rare trees and shrubs. Playground, Children's Discovery Garden, Gallery. Birmingham Botanical Gardens are open every day of the year except Christmas Day and Boxing Day.

9 NEW BLORE HALL

Blore, Ashbourne DE6 2BS.
Mr Chris Green. *Leaving Ashbourne head towards Leek on the A52. Take the 1st turn on your R to Mappleton/Okeover & continue to the end of the rd & then turn L heading towards Blore.* Adm £5, chd free. **Sat 4 Apr, Sat 18 July (10.30-3).**
Set just outside the peak district Blore Hall dates back to the 1400 and is set in three acres of well established and mature gardens. Take a walk around our koi carp ponds while taking in the glorious views over Dove Dale or just enjoy the densely planted borders which surround our old hall. The gardens also attract a wide range of wildlife, and birdlife has certainly been encouraged. All of the gardens can be accessed with a wheelchair, disabled WC facilities located in the swimming pool.

10 THE BOWERS

Church Lane, Standon, nr
Eccleshall ST21 6RW. Maurice &
Sheila Thacker, 01782 791244,
metbowers@gmail.com. *5m N of Eccleshall. Take A519 & at Cotes Heath turn L signed Standon. After 1m turn R at Xrds by church, into Church Lane ½ m on L.* Home-made teas. Adm £3, chd free. **Sun 26 July (1.30-4.30). Visitors also welcome by arrangement July to Aug.**
Come and share our tranquil ⅓ acre cottage style garden. Meander around the grass paths which enclose colour -themed borders

containing over 200 clematis and many hardy geraniums and hostas. You will see height, blossom and flowers in abundance. Our garden is always evolving with new features each year. Small water feature, obelisks, arches and trellising. Many unusual and rare clematis. Some gravel paths may prove difficult.

11 NEW BREAKMILLS

Hames Lane, Newton Regis, Tamworth B79 0NH. Mr Paul Horobin. *Approx 5m N of Tamworth & 3m S of M42 J11. Signed from B5493, Hames Lane is a single track lane near the Queens Head PH. Disabled parking at the house, other visitors please follow parking signs or park in village centre.* Teas and home made cakes. **Adm £3.50, chd free. Sun 21 June (11-5).**
Just under 2 acres of low maintenance garden featuring small tropical area, island beds, shale area for grasses. Pond, man made stream, vegetable patch and mature trees. Originally a paddock area, trees planted some 15-20 yrs ago but garden really developed over the last 5yrs and still a work in progress. Lots of seating areas to enjoy both the fun aspects of our garden and the surrounding countryside. Larger grassed area may be difficult for wheelchairs on very wet days but access to long drive and eating area in all conditions.

12 BRIDGE HOUSE

Dog Lane, Bodymoor Heath B76 9JF. Mr & Mrs J Cerone, 01827 873205, janecerone@btinternet.com. *5m S of Tamworth. From A446 at Belfry Island take A4091 after 1m turn R onto Bodymoor Heath Lane & continue 1m into village, parking in field opp garden.* Home-made teas. **Adm £3.50, chd free. Mon 25 May, Mon 31 Aug (2-5). Visitors also welcome by arrangement May to Sept for groups 5-30.**
1-acre garden surrounding converted public house. Divided into smaller areas with a mix of shrub borders, azalea and fuchsia, herbaceous and bedding, orchard, kitchen garden and wild flower meadow. Pergola walk, formal fish pool, pond, bog garden and lawns. Kingsbury Water Park and RSPB Middleton Lakes Reserve located within a mile.

13 BROOKLYN

Gratton Lane, Endon, Stoke-on-Trent ST9 9AA. Janet & Steve Howell. *4m W of Leek. 6m from Stoke-on-Trent on A53 turn at Black Horse PH into centre of village, R into Gratton Lane 1st house on R. Parking signed in village.* Home-made teas. **Adm £3, chd free. Sun 28 June (12-5).**
A plant lovers country cottage garden in the heart of the old village of Endon. Small pretty front garden, borders overflowing with geraniums, astrantia, alliums and roses. Rear garden features shady area with hostas and ferns, small waterfall and pond. Steps to lawn surrounded by well-stocked borders, summerhouse, seating areas with village and rural views. Enjoy tea and cake in the potting shed.

Lots of seating areas to enjoy the fun aspects of our garden . . .

14 ♦ CASTLE BROMWICH HALL GARDENS TRUST

Chester Road, Castle Bromwich, Birmingham B36 9BT. Castle Bromwich Hall & Gardens Trust, 0121 749 4100, www.cbhgt.org.uk. *4m E of Birmingham. 1m J5 M6 (exit N only).* Light refreshments. **Adm £4.50, chd £1. For NGS: Sun 17 May (12.30-4.30).** For other opening times and information, please phone or see garden website.
A delightful 10-acre English formal walled garden. Comprising orchards, formal period planting schemes and a unique kitchen garden of the C17 and early C18. An all-season garden incl a recently restored C18 Mirror Pond.

15 COLEY COTTAGE

Coley Lane, Little Haywood ST18 0UU. Yvonne Branson, 01889 882715, yvonnebranson0uu@btinternet.com. *5m SE of Stafford. A51 from Rugeley or Weston signed Little Haywood. 1/2 m from Seven Springs. A513 Coley Lane from Red Lion PH past Back Lane, 100yds on L opp red post box.* Home-made teas. **Adm £2.50, chd free. Fri 5, Sun 21 June, Wed 12 Aug (11-4).** Also open The

Secret Garden. Visitors also welcome by arrangement June to Aug pre bookings for more than 10 persons.
A plant lover's cottage garden, full of subtle colours and perfume, every inch packed with plants. Clematis and old roses covering arches, many hostas and agapanthus, a wildlife pool, all designed to attract birds and butterflies. This garden is now 8yrs old, trees, roses and herbaceous planting has become well established.

16 COLOUR MILL

Winkhill, Leek, Staffs ST13 7PR. Bob & Jackie Pakes, 01538 308680, robert.pakes@virgin.net, colourmill.webplus.net. *7m E of Leek. Follow A523 from either Leek or Ashbourne, look for NGS signs on the side of the main rd which will direct you down to Colour Mill.* Home-made teas. **Adm £3, chd free. Sat 27 June, Thur 6 Aug (1.30-5). Visitors also welcome by arrangement May to Aug.**
3/4 -acre S-facing garden, created in the shadow of a former iron foundry, set beside the delightful R Hamps frequented by kingfisher and dipper. Informal planting in a variety of rooms surrounded by beautiful 7ft beech hedges. Large organic vegetable patch complete with greenhouse. Maturing trees provide shade for the interesting seating areas.

17 12 DARGES LANE

Great Wyrley WS6 6LE. Mrs A Hackett, 01922 415064, annofdarges@orange.net. *2m SE of Cannock. From A5 take A34 towards Walsall. Darges Lane is 1st turning on R (over brow of hill). House on R on corner of Cherrington Drive.* Home-made teas. **Adm £3, chd free. Visitors welcome by arrangement May to Sept.**
1/4 -acre well-stocked enthusiastic plantsman's garden on two levels. Foliage plants are a special feature, together with shrubaceous borders containing rare and unusual plants, divided into areas that link with each other. The use of an extensive collection of clematis gives height in small spaces. Objects of art are eased into every corner, and the owner's own artwork is available to view. Constant updating gives fresh interest to both owner and visitors.

Karibu, Woodleighton Grove Gardens

 4 DENE CLOSE

Penkridge ST19 5HL. David & Anne Smith, 01785 712580. *6m S of Stafford. On A449 from Stafford. At far end of Penkridge turn L into Boscomoor Lane, 2nd L into Filance Lane, 3rd R Dene Close. Please park with consideration in Filance Lane. Disabled only in Dene Close.* Home-made teas. **Adm £3, chd free. Sun 5 July (11-5). Visitors also welcome by arrangement June to July coaches permitted.**

A medium-sized garden of many surprises. Vibrant colour-themed herbaceous areas. Many different grasses and bamboos creating texture and interest in the garden. Attractive display of many unusual hostas shown for great effect 'theatre style'. Shady area for ferns etc. Water feature. Summerhouse and quiet seating areas within the garden. Featured in local press.

19 DORSET HOUSE

68 Station Street, Cheslyn Hay WS6 7EE. Mary & David Blundell, 01922 419437, david.blundell@talktalk.net. *2m SE of Cannock J11 M6 A462 towards Willenhall. L at island. At next island R into 1-way system (Low St), at T junction L into Station St. A5 Bridgetown L to island, L Coppice St. R into Station St.* Home-made teas and cakes. **Adm £3, chd free. Sun 17 May, Sun 12 July (11-5). Visitors also welcome by**

arrangement May to July groups of 10+.

Step back in time with a visit to this inspirational 1/2 -acre garden which incorporates country cottage planting at its very best. Unusual rhododendrons, acers, shrubs and perennials planted in mixed borders. Clematis-covered arches and hidden corners with water features including stream and wildlife pool all come together to create a haven of peace and tranquillity. Featured regulary in the local press.

20 198 EACHELHURST ROAD

Walmley, Sutton Coldfield B76 1EW. Jacqui & Jamie Whitmore. *5mins N of Birmingham. M6 J6, A38 Tyburn Rd to Lichfield, continue to T-lights at Lidl and continue on Tyburn Rd, at island take 2nd exit to destination rd.* Home-made teas. **Adm £3, chd free. Sun 26 July (12.30-4.30).**

A long garden approx 210ft x 30ft divided by arches and pathways. Plenty to explore incl wildlife pond, cottage garden and hanging baskets leading to formal garden with box-lined pathways, well, stocked borders, willow gazebo and chicken house then through to raised decking area, overlooking Pype Hayes golf course, with summer house and bar and Mediterranean plants. Featured in the Sutton Observer and 1st prize in Best Back Garden (The Sun).

21 FOUR SEASONS

26 Buchanan Road, Walsall WS4 2EN. Marie & Tony Newton, www.fourseasonsgarden.co.uk. *Adjacent to Walsall Arboretum. From Ring Rd A4148 near Walsall town centre. At large junction take A461 to Lichfield. At 1st island 3rd exit Buchanan Ave, fork R into Buchanan Rd.* **Adm £3.50, chd free. Sun 24, Mon 25 May, Sat 24, Sun 25 Oct (10-5).**

Stunning in all seasons. Suburban, S-facing 1/3 acre, gently sloping to arboretum. 180 acers, 350 azaleas, bulbs, hellebores, camellias, perennials, begonias, bright conifers, topiary and shrubs. Beautiful autumn colours, bark and berries. Many 'rooms'. Themes incl contrast of red, blue and yellow. Jungle, oriental pagoda, bridges, water features and stone ornaments. Some steps. WC. Featured in local and international publications and in BBC 'Great British Garden Revival'. Filmed for Alan Titchmarsh's forthcoming ITV series about Britain's best gardens.

22 THE GARTH

2 Broc Hill Way, Milford, Stafford ST17 0UB. Mr & Mrs David Wright, 01785 661182, anitawright1@yahoo.co.uk, www.anitawright.co.uk. *4 1/2 m SE of Stafford. A513 Stafford to Rugeley rd; at Barley Mow turn R (S) to Brocton; L after 1/2 m.* Cream teas. **Adm £3, chd free. Sun 7, Sun 28 June (2-6).**

Visitors also welcome by arrangement.
½ -acre garden of many levels on Cannock Chase AONB. Acid soil loving plants. Series of small gardens, water features, raised beds. Rare trees, island beds of unusual shrubs and perennials, many varieties of hosta and ferns. Varied and colourful foliage, summerhouse, arbours and quiet seating to enjoy the garden. Ancient sandstone caves. Featured on Radio Stoke.

Look around
our koi carp ponds
while taking in the
glorious views
over Dove Dale . . .

23 GRAFTON COTTAGE

Barton-under-Needwood DE13 8AL. Margaret & Peter Hargreaves, 01283 713639, marpeter1@btinternet.com. *6m N of Lichfield. Leave A38 for Catholme S of Barton, follow sign to Barton Green, L at Royal Oak, ¼ m.* Home-made teas. **Adm £3, chd free. Share to Alzheimer's Research Trust. Suns 28 June, 19 July, 2, 9 Aug (11.30-5).** Visitors also welcome by arrangement June to Aug min adm £60 per group.

This is where the bees and owners work overtime producing a traditional cottage garden, admired over the years. A visitor commented it's like indulging in a memorable meal which lingers on the palate'. Coloured themed borders with unusual herbaceous plants and perfume from old fashioned roses, sweet peas, violas, dianthus, phlox and lilies. Particular interests are viticella clematis, delphiniums, cottage garden annuals and use of foliage plants. Stream and small vegetable plot. Featured in English Garden magazine.

GROUP OPENING

24 HALL GREEN GARDENS

Hall Green, Birmingham B28 8SQ. *Off A34, 3m city centre, 6m from M42 J4. Off A34 Stratford Rd 3m City Centre & 6m M42 J4. Russell Rd B28 8SQ & Boden Rd B28 9DL, Hall Green.* Home-made teas at 16 Burnaston Rd & 120 Russell Road. **Combined adm £4, chd free. Sun 3 May, Sun 5 July (1.30-5.30).** Visitors also welcome by arrangement May to July.

42 BODEN ROAD
Mrs Helen Lycett.
At the large Robin Hood Island (on L you will see The China Garden restaurant as you enter island) take 4th turning into Shirley Rd. Take 5th L Boden Rd

16 BURNASTON ROAD
Howard Hemmings & Sandra Hateley
Visitors also welcome by arrangement May to Sept.
0121 624 1488
howard.hemmings@blueyonder.co.uk

37 BURNASTON ROAD
Mrs Carolyn Wynne-Jones.
At T-lights by South Birmingham City College turn into Colebank Rd then 1st R into Southam Rd, then 1st L
Visitors also welcome by arrangement May to July.
0121 608 2397
markwynne-jones@blueyonder.co.uk

36 FERNDALE ROAD
Mrs E A Nicholson
Visitors also welcome by arrangement Mar to Sept.
0121 777 4921

120 RUSSELL ROAD
Mr David Worthington.
Follow signs for Stratford from city centre. Fork L at Shaftmoor Lane; Russell Rd is at top of hill on R
Visitors also welcome by arrangement Mar to Sept groups up to 30.
0121 624 7906
hildave@hotmail.com

19 STAPLEHURST ROAD
Mrs Sheena Terrace.
Opening in May only. Off A34 Stratford Rd Hall Green, between junctions of Fox Hollies Rd/Highfield Rd & School Rd/Colebank Rd B28 9AR

A group of 6 suburban gardens, each unique in style. A S-facing lawned and border garden with interesting features incl a log display, conifers, water feature and various artefacts. 'Find IT' quiz for children. A tranquil garden with curving borders containing different perennials, shade areas, soft fruit and vegetables. Plantsman's garden featuring formal raised pool and hosta collection with unusual perennials and container planting. A shady garden with mature trees, pond, cottage style borders and vegetable area, a large restful garden with mature trees, 2 lawns, cottage style borders, seating area and re-opening florist large suburban garden with many unusual plants giving year round interest, the garden is divided into distinct areas, large ornamental garden with pool and waterfalls, tree and soft fruit garden. Partial wheelchair access. Steps in garden 19 Staplehurst Rd, 16 Burnaston Rd 1 step, ramp available, 42 Boden Rd patio viewing area only, Russell Rd deep door sill at entry.

25 HAMILTON HOUSE

Roman Grange, Roman Road, Little Aston Park, Sutton Coldfield B74 3GA. Philip & Diana Berry, www.hamiltonhousegarden.co.uk. *3m N of Sutton Coldfield. Follow A454 (Walsall Rd) & enter Roman Rd, Little Aston Park. Roman Grange is 1st L after church but enter rd via pedestrian gate.* Home-made teas. 22 Aug wine & canapes, not incl in adm. **Adm £3.50, chd free. Sun 24 May (2-5). Evening Opening Sat 22 Aug (7-10).**
½ -acre N-facing English woodland garden in tranquil setting, making the most of challenging shade, providing haven for birds and other wildlife. Large pond with stone bridge, pergolas, water features, box garden with a variety of roses and herbs. Interesting collection of rhododendrons,clematis, hostas, ferns and old English roses. Join us either for afternoon tea, listening to music from a string quartet and admire the art of our garden. Alternatively in the evening listen to the elegant vocals of Simon Partridge whilst enjoying wine, canapés and candle light. Featured on BBC 2's The Great British Garden Revival, The Journal and Sutton Coldfield Observer.

26 HEATH HOUSE

Offley Brook, nr Eccleshall ST21 6HA. Dr D W Eyre-Walker, 01785 280318, neyrewalker@btinternet.com. *3m W of Eccleshall. From Eccleshall take B5026 towards Woore. At Sugnall turn L, after 1¹/₂ m turn R immed by stone garden wall. After 1m straight across Xrds.* Refreshments available for small numbers. **Adm £5, chd free. Visitors welcome by arrangement Apr to Aug use Satnav, mobile phones do not work locally.** 1¹/₂ -acre country garden of C18 miller's house in lovely valley setting, overlooking mill pool. Plantsman's garden containing many rare and unusual plants in borders, bog garden, woodland, alpine house, raised bed and shrubberies and incl slowly expanding collection of hardy terrestrial orchids.

27 HIDDEN GEM

15 St Johns Road, Pleck, Walsall WS2 9TJ. Maureen & Sid Allen, 07825 804670, hsallen@virginmedia.com. *2m W of Walsall. Off J10 M6. Head for Walsall on A454 Wolverhampton Rd. Turn R into Pleck Rd A4148 then 4th R into St Johns Rd.* Tea. **Adm £3, chd free. Sun 26 July (12.30-4). Visitors also welcome by arrangement June to Aug groups of 10+.** Situated between two busy motorway junctions. Come and visit our 'Hidden Gem.' What a surprise! A long narrow pretty garden, lovely foliage in June, pretty perennials, shrubs, trees, lush tropical plants from July onwards. Japanese area with stream. Shady walk with ferns,into pretty gravel garden lots of wildlife. Very relaxing atmosphere. WHAT A GEM! Featured on Britains Best Gardens with Alan Titchmarsh to be shown summer 2015 and in local press.

28 HIGH TREES

18 Drubbery Lane, nr Longton Park ST3 4BA. Peter & Pat Teggin. *5m S of Stoke-on-Trent. Off A5035, midway between Trentham Gardens & Longton. Opp Longton Park.* Cream teas. **Adm £3, chd free. Wed 20 May, Wed 3 June (1-4).** Garden designer's pretty, perfumed hidden garden. Colourful herbaceous plants juxtapose to create a rich woven tapestry of spires, flats and fluffs interwoven with structure

planting and focal points. An ideas garden continuing to inspire, evoking orderly diversity. All within two minutes walk of a Victorian park. Featured in the local press.

29 IDLEROCKS FARM

Hilderstone Road, Spot Acre, nr Stone ST15 8RP. Barbara Dixon, 01889 505450. *3m E of Stone. From Stone take the A520 to Meir Heath, turn R onto B5066 towards Hilderstone, farm 1¹/₂ m on R. ¹/₂ m drive with parking in the field by the house.* Home-made tea, cakes and coffee. **Adm £3, chd free. Sun 23 Aug (1.30-4.30). Visitors also welcome by arrangement Feb (see small collection of snowdrops).** Medium sized garden set in farmland and woodland, 800ft above sea level. Long herbaceous border, wildlife pond, views across the Trent Valley to the Wrekin and Clee Hills.

30 'JOHN'S GARDEN' AT ASHWOOD NURSERIES

Ashwood Lower Lane, Ashwood, nr Kingswinford DY6 0AE. John Massey, www.ashwoodnurseries.com. *5m S of Wolverhampton. 1m past Wall Heath on A449 turn R to Ashwood along Doctor's Lane. At T-junction turn L. Park at Ashwood Nurseries.* Home-made teas at adjacent tea room at Ashwood Nurseries. **Adm £5, chd free. Sun 23 Aug (10-4).** A stunning private garden adjacent to Ashwood Nurseries, it has a huge plant collection and many innovative design features in a beautiful canal-side setting. There are informal beds, woodland dells, a South African border, a rock garden and a unique succulent garden. Summer sees fine displays of grasses, herbaceous perennials, daphnes and clematis together with a notable collection of hydrangeas. Tea Room, Garden Centre and Gift Shop at adjacent Ashwood Nurseries. Coaches are by arrangement only. Disabled access difficult if very wet.

31 13 LANSDOWNE ROAD

Hurst Green, Halesowen B62 9QT. Mr Peter Bridgens & Mr Michael King. *7m W of Birmingham. A458 Hagley Rd out of Birmingham, towards Stourbridge. From M5 J2 take 1st exit A4123 towards*

Birmingham. Home-made teas. **Adm £3.50, chd free. Sun 14 June (2-5.30).** A plantsman's suburban garden designed to ensure maximum use of space. The garden features rare and unusual plants, incl Meconopsis, Buddleia agathosma, Stewartia, Halesia, Schizandra. Water features and bog area. The mixed borders are planted giving a long season of interest. Attention paid to plant association and colour themes. The garden presents a softly planted look with a tropical twist.

Summer House and some woodland planting by old Saxon moat . . .

32 NEW LITTLE INDONESIA

20 Poston Croft, Kings Heath B14 5AB. Dave & Pat McKenna, 0121 628 1397, patanddave76@yahoo.co.uk, www.littleindonesia.wordpress. com. *1¹/₂ m from Kings Heath High St. Poston Croft is 6th L off Broad Lane, off A435 Alcester Rd, parking limited in the cul-de-sac but more parking available on service rd on Broad Lane opp Poston Croft.* Home-made teas. **Adm £3.50, chd free. Sun 26 July (11-4). Visitors also welcome by arrangement June to Sept. Mon, Tue & Sun afternoons only.** A garden that is the realisation of my dreams. An amazing plant paradise with the feel of entering a jungle, even though we are in the heart of Birmingham. Planted so that it seems to go on for ever. Plants of unusual leaf shapes and textures. Bananas, cannas and grasses jostle with one another for space. A plantaholic's paradise. Steps down to garden, stepping stone pathways leading to lawns.

33 NEW LITTLE ONN HALL

Little Onn, Church Eaton ST20 0AU. David & Caroline Bradshaw. *6m SW of Stafford. A449 Wolverhampton to Stafford; at Gailey r'about turn W onto A5 for 1¹/₄ m; turn R to Stretton, 200 yds turn L for*

Church Eaton. Follow signs. Home-made teas. **Adm £4.50, chd free. Sun 28 June (12-4.30).**
6-acre garden; herbaceous lined drive, terraces, Summer House and some woodland planting by old Saxon moat. The gates and gardens were designed by Thomas Mawson who in 1870 was a leading designer of the period. Present owners are working to restore the gardens to their former glory. Area for picnics.

MARLBROOK GARDENS
See Worcestershire.

34 NEW 3 MARLOWS COTTAGES
Little Hay Lane, Little Hay WS14 0QD. Phyllis Davies. *4m S of Lichfield. Take A5127, Birmingham Rd. Turn L at Park Lane (opp Tesco Express) then R at T junction into Little Hay Lane, ¹/₂ m on L.* Home-made teas. **Adm £3, chd free. Sun 21, Wed 24 June (11-4).**
Very long, narrow, gently sloping cottage style garden with borders and beds contain abundant herbaceous perennials and shrubs leading to vegetable patch.

35 89 MARSH LANE
Solihull B91 2PE. Mrs Gail Wyldes. *¹/₂ m from Solihull town centre. A41 from M42 J5. Turn sharp L at first T-lights. Garden on R. Parking 400 metres further along Marsh Lane at Solihull Cricket Club by mini r'about.* Home-made teas. **Adm £3.50, chd free. Sun 7 June (2-5).**
Suburban Oasis. Trees, shrubs and herbaceous planting for all year interest with emphasis on leaf shape and structure. Wildlife pond, bog garden, water features, african style gazebo, gravel gardens, shady places and sunny seating areas. Patio with pergola and raised beds. Hostas and ferns abound. The garden is continually evolving with new plants and features. Small step from patio to the main back garden and paths may be a little narrow.

36 ◆ MIDDLETON HALL
Tamworth B78 2AE. Middleton Hall Trust, 01827 283095, www.middleton-hall.org.uk. *4m S of Tamworth, 2m N J9 M42. On A4091 between The Belfry & Drayton Manor.* Light refreshments. **Adm £4, chd £1. For NGS: Sun 21 June (11-4).** For other opening times and

information, please phone or see garden website.
Two walled gardens set in 40 acres of grounds surrounding Grade 2 Middleton Hall, the C17 home of naturalists Sir Francis Willoughby and John Ray. Large colour-themed herbaceous borders radiating from a central pond, restored gazebo, pergola planted with roses, clematis and wisteria. Courtyard garden with raised beds. Musical entertainment in the Hall.

37 MILLENNIUM GARDEN
London Road, Lichfield WS14 9RB. Carol Cooper. *1m S of Lichfield. Off A38 along A5206 towards Lichfield ¹/₄ m past A38 island towards Lichfield. Park in field on L.* Yellow signs on field gate. Tea. **Adm £3.50, chd free. Sun 12 Apr, Sun 5 July (1-5).**
2-acre garden with mixed spring bulbs in the woodland garden and with host of golden daffodils fade slowly into the summer borders in this English country garden. Designed with a naturalistic edge and with the environment in mind. A relaxed approach creates a garden of quiet sanctuary with the millennium bridge sitting comfortably, its surroundings of lush planting and mature trees. Well stocked summer borders give shots of colour to lift the spirit and the air fills with the scent of wisterias and climbing roses. A stress free environment awaits you at the Millennium Garden.

38 MITTON MANOR
Mitton, Penkridge, Stafford ST19 5QW. Mrs E A Gooch, 07970 457457, eag@eguk.co.uk. *2m W of Penkridge. Property is on Whiston Rd. Parking in field before house. No parking for coaches.* Cream teas. **Adm £5, chd free. Sun 5 July (11.30-4.30). Visitors also welcome by arrangement May to Aug.**
This 7-acre country garden was started in 2001 and has been developed from an overgrown wilderness. The garden surrounds a Victorian manor (not open) and contains rooms of different styles, formal box/topiary, prairie planting and natural woodland bordered by a stream. Stunning vistas, water features and sculpture. Live music. Many levels, narrow and gravel paths.

GROUP OPENING

39 MOSELEY CORNER, THE ART OF GARDENS
Birmingham B13 9PN. *3m S of city centre. From Moseley take St Mary's Row which becomes Wake Green Rd. After ¹/₂ m turn R into St Agnes Rd and L at the church, park here for all gardens.* Home-made teas at 56 St Agnes Road. **Combined adm £3.50, chd free. Sun 5 July (1-5.30).**

     NEW 48 ST AGNES ROAD
Mrs Judy Wenban-Smith

     56 ST AGNES ROAD
Michael & Alison Cullen

     269 YARDLEY WOOD ROAD
Miss Marion Stoddart.
1 min walk from St Agnes Rd

The gardens are all on the corner of Yardley Wood Rd and St Agnes Rd in Moseley. They demonstrate unique design, each expressing the garden owners' creative vision and endeavour. 56 St Agnes Road is immaculately maintained with curving borders around a formal lawn with delicate acers and contemporary sculpture. The tranquillity of this elegant garden is enhanced by a Victorian style fish pond with fountain and waterfall. 269 Yardley Wood Road has 3 rooms with a terrace and pergola adorned with hops, clematis, roses, jasmine and solanum leading up steps to a lawn with gazebo, many shrubs and herbaceous borders. The hidden top garden is tranquil with stream, pond and architectural planting.
48 St Agnes Road has a courtyard leading to a pond with frogs, newts and water lilies. There are mature herbaceous borders with perennial and annual planting and poles for climbing roses and clematis, some unusual plants as well as fruit trees, currant bushes and vegetables.

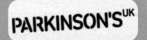

From tiny back plots to country estates …

Courtyard leading to a pond with frogs, newts and water lilies . . .

GROUP OPENING

40 MOSELEY GARDENS SOUTH

Moseley/Kings Heath, Birmingham B13 9TF. *3m city centre. Halfway between Kings Heath & Moseley village. Our gardens can be found between the A435 (Alcester Rd) & B4217 (Wake Green Rd) in S Birmingham.* Home-made teas at 51 Valentine Road. Lovely selection of cakes, mostly home-made by our gardeners, friends and family. Indoor seating available in inclement weather. **Combined adm £4, chd free. Sun 21 June (2-6).**

7 ASHFIELD ROAD
Hilary Bartlett

19 PROSPECT ROAD
Tony White

65 SCHOOL ROAD
Wendy Weston

51 VALENTINE ROAD
Kings Heath. Clare Goulder

34 WOODFIELD ROAD
Rosemary Chatfield

NEW 10 WOODFIELD ROAD
Kings Heath. Dr & Mrs Mark Piney

Come and explore our 6 beautiful and varied urban plots, from small city gardens to a ¹/₂ acre of spreading lawns with mature trees. Moseley has many fine Edwardian and Victorian villas hiding wonderful secret gardens. Some of our front gardens are worth seeing too! The street containers and hanging baskets of award-winning Moseley in Bloom enhance the area. We have wildlife and koi ponds, other water features, fruit and vegetable cultivation, outdoor artworks, chickens in a fox-proof run and as many different design ideas as gardeners. These incl wildlife, child-friendly, and easy

maintenance gardens. Our excellent plants and preserves stall is a big attraction, and there will be a quiz or treasure trail for children in at least one garden. Meet our gardeners, and enjoy tea and home-made cakes in a quintessentially English setting. Well-stocked, mature borders, a variety of seating areas and water features, excellent plants and preserves for sale, and teas with home-made cakes. We get advance publicity in the following local interest publications: B13 magazine Moseley Society Newsletter My Moseley and Kings Heath magazine.

41 THE MOUNT, COTON, GNOSALL

Stafford ST20 0EQ. Andrew & Celia Payne, 01785 822253, ac.payne@waitrose.com. *8m W of Stafford. From Stafford take A518 W towards Newport/Telford. Go through Gnosall, over canal. Garden on edge of Gnosall Village on L of A518.* Home-made teas. **Adm £3, chd free. Sun 21 June (2-5.30). Visitors also welcome by arrangement June.** Richly planted wildlife friendly garden with large collection of unusual plants set in ³/₄ acre. Divided into areas, incl a wild flower meadow, cottage garden and vegetable plot, highlights consist of over 100 different hosta varieties, many colourful hardy geraniums, bamboos and a huge Kiftsgate rose. The plant stall will have over 40+ varieties of hosta for sale plus other interesting plants.

42 THE OLD DAIRY HOUSE

Trentham Park, Stoke-on-Trent ST4 8AE. Philip & Michelle Moore. *S edge of Stoke-on-Trent. Next to Trentham Gardens. Off Whitmore Rd. Please follow NGS signs or signs for Trentham Park Golf Club. Parking in church car park.* Home-made teas. **Adm £3, chd free. Sun 24, Mon 25 May (1-5).** Grade 2 listed house (not open) designed by Sir Charles Barry forms backdrop to this 2-acre garden in parkland setting. Shaded area for rhododendrons, azaleas plus expanding hosta and fern collection. Mature trees, 'cottage garden' and long borders. Narrow brick paths in vegetable plot. Large courtyard area for teas. Some gravel paths but lawns are an option.

43 THE OLD VICARAGE

Fulford, nr Stone ST11 9QS. Mike & Cherry Dodson. *4m N of Stone. From Stone A520 (Leek). 1m R turn to Spot Acre & Fulford, turn L down Post Office Terrace, past village green/PH towards church. Parking in signed field on L.* Home-made teas. **Adm £3.50, chd free. Sat 18, Sun 19 July (2-5).** On edge of attractive village, 1¹/₂ acres of formal garden on a sloping site around Victorian house (not open). Relaxed herbaceous borders, roses, pretty small pond with seating area, summerhouse and planting for light and shade among the mature trees. Organic vegetables in raised beds, greenhouse, chickens and fruit cage to keep the kitchen well supplied. A lovely scenic walk around 2-acre reclaimed lake with a 'wilder' feel with native species planted to encourage wildlife. Waterfall, new arboretum, acer and fern glade, jetty and fishing hut to sit and enjoy (managed!) nature. Wheelchair access to most areas.

44 PAUL'S OASIS OF CALM

18 Kings Close, Kings Heath, Birmingham B14 6TP. Mr Paul Doogan, 0121 444 6943, gardengreen18@hotmail.co.uk. *4m from city centre. 5m from the M42 J4. Take A345 to Kings Heath High St then B4122 Vicarage Rd. Turn L onto Kings Rd then R to Kings Close.* Tea. **Adm £2.50, chd free. Visitors welcome by arrangement May to Aug.** Garden cultivated from nothing into a little oasis. Measuring 18ft x 70ft. It's small but packed with interesting and unusual plants, water features and 7 seating areas. It's my piece of heaven. Photographed for Garden News magazine, short listed and filmed for ITV's Britains best Gardens with Alan Titchmarsh.

GROUP OPENING

45 PEREIRA ROAD GARDENS

Harborne, Birmingham B17 9JN. *¹/₂ m N of Harborne High Street. Between Gillhurst Rd & Margaret Grove. ¼ m from Hagley Rd or ¹/₂ m from Harborne High St.* Home-made teas. **Combined adm £2.50 (Apr) £4 (July), chd free. Sun 26 Apr, Sun 5 July (2-5).**

Alton Towers Gardens

14 PEREIRA ROAD
Mike Foster.
Not open 26th April

50 PEREIRA ROAD
Peg Peil

55 PEREIRA ROAD
Emma Davies & Martin
Commander.
Not open 26th April

Group of 3 different urban gardens.
No.14 is a well established suburban
garden with mixed herbaceous and
shrub borders. Wildlife-friendly with 2
ponds and wild flower area. Ongoing
alterations provide new areas of
interest each year. No. 50 is a
plantaholic's paradise with over 1000
varieties, many rare, incl fruits,
vegetables, herbs, grasses and large
bed of plants with African
connections. Over 100 varieties on
sale - see how they grow. No. 55 is a
sloping garden, incl gravelled beds
with mixed planting, grasses and a
small pond. All gardens have steps.
Please note that Nos 14 and 55 are
open July only. In July, free admission
to Harborne Nature Reserve and
Pereira Road allotments incl.

46 THE PINTLES
18 Newport Road, Great
Bridgeford, Stafford ST18 9PR.
Peter & Leslie Longstaff. *J14 M6
take A5013 towards Eccleshall. In
Great Bridgeford turn L onto B5405.
Car park on L after ¹/₂ m in front of
Village Hall.* Home-made teas. Tea,
coffee and soft drinks, selection of
home made cakes. **Adm £3, chd
free. Sun 7 June (1-5).**
Located in the village of Great
Bridgeford this traditional semi-
detached house has a medium sized
wildlife friendly garden designed to
appeal to many interests. There are
two greenhouses, over 200 cacti and
succulents, vegetable and fruit plot,
wildlife pond, weather station, orchid
collection and hidden woodland
shady garden. Plenty of outside
seating to enjoy the home made
cakes and refreshments. Featured in
Amateur Gardening. Steps or small
ramp into main garden.

47 PRIORY FARM
Mitton Road, Bradley, Stafford
ST18 9ED. Debbie Farmer,
debbie_farmer@live.co.uk. *3¹/₂ m W
Penkridge. At Texaco island on A449
in Penridge take Bungham Lane.
Cont for 2¹/₂ m past Swan & Whiston
Hall to Mitton. Turn R to Bradley, cont
1m to Priory Farm on L.* Home-made

teas. BBQ food also available. **Adm
£4, chd free. Sun 7 June (11-4).
Visitors also welcome by
arrangement June to Aug for
groups of 10+.**
A hidden gem. Delightful 120yr old
cottage with own lake set in mature
gardens and grounds. Wildlife in
abundance, stables, wonderful wood
and walks, dells and orchard. A truly
unique country hideaway. Step back
in time.

48 ROWLEY HOUSE FARM
Croxton, Stafford ST21 6PJ. Tony &
Beryl Roe, 01630 620248. *4m W of
Eccleshall. Between Eccleshall &
Loggerheads on B5026. At Wetwood
Xrds turn for Fairoak. Take 1st L turn
& continue for ³/₄ m.* Home-made
teas. **Adm £3.50, chd free. Sun 13
Sept (2-5). Visitors also welcome
by arrangement June to July.**
Quiet country garden, part reclaimed
from farm rick-yard. Shrub roses in
orchard, soft fruits, vegetables and
water feature incl. Extensive views
towards the Wrekin and Welsh hills
from adjacent land at 570ft, with
plantings of 95 varieties of 7 species
of ilex, various corylus and specimen
trees. Small water feature. Gravel
paths.

Former farm yard and buildings with extensive views of the Staffordshire countryside towards Needwood Forest . . .

GROUP OPENING

49 ST JOHN'S GARDENS
St Johns Road, Stafford ST17 9AS. Fiona Horwath, 01785 258923, fiona_horwath@yahoo.co.uk. *1/2 m S of Stafford town centre. Just a few mins from J13 M6 off A449 just after Rising Brook. Through entrance to private park. Please park considerately.* Home-made teas at No 29. **Combined adm £4, chd free. Sun 29 Mar (2-5). Evening Opening £5, chd free, wine, Fri 15 May (6.30-9). Sun 14 June (2-5). Visitors also welcome by arrangement Mar to Sept.**

23 ST JOHNS ROAD
Rowley Park, Stafford. Fiona Horwath

29 ST JOHN'S ROAD
Mrs Carol Shanahan

Two near neighbours who share a passion for all things horticultural - we are lucky that our respective gardens enjoy a southerly aspect which we use to its full advantage. However, you will also find plenty of ideas for dry shade and challenging areas. You are most welcome to sit and relax with home-made tea and cake whilst being inspired by the well-stocked beds that surround you. No.23 is a Victorian house (not open) and as you pass through the black and white gate you enter a part-walled plant lover's haven. There are bulbs and shady woodlanders in spring and a plethora of herbaceous plants and climbers. At no.29, against a backdrop of mature Hornbeams there are 2 acres of informal garden made up of many complementary areas.

View the wooded 'dingly dell', colourful terraces, abundant kitchen garden, bronze armillary, water features, circular lawns plus the roses and clematis that scramble through the trees. Don't miss the working area of the garden for the most upmarket compost bins - all made from decking. As both gardeners are keen hardy planters and sow far too many seeds there is always something good for sale. Wheelchair access only at no 29.

50 THE SECRET GARDEN
3 Banktop Cottages, Little Haywood ST18 0UL. Derek Higgott & David Aston, 01889 883473, poshanddeks@yahoo.co.uk. *5m SE of Stafford. A51 from Rugeley or Weston signed Little Haywood A513 Stafford Coley Lane, Back Lane R into Coley Grove. Entrance 50 metres on L.* Home-made teas. **Adm £3, chd free. Sun 10 May, Fri 5, Sun 21 June, Wed 12 Aug (11-4). Also open Coley Cottage.**
Wander past the other cottage gardens and through the evergreen arch and there before you a fantasy for the eyes and soul. Stunning garden approx 1/2 acre, created over the last 30yrs. Strong colour theme of trees and shrubs, underplanted with perennials, 1000 bulbs and laced with clematis; other features incl water, laburnum and rose tunnel and unique buildings. Is this the jewel in the crown? Raised gazebo with wonderful views over untouched meadows and Cannock Chase. Featured in Daily Telegraph. Some slopes.

51 190 STATION ROAD
Boldmere, Sutton Coldfield B73 5LH. Jenny & Bill Baker, 0121 244 2916, furfuls2000@yahoo.co.uk. *Leave M6 at J6 following signs for Birmingham NE A38. Then take A5127 signed to Sutton Coldfield. Turn L into Station Rd after 3m.* Home-made teas in adjoining garden. **Adm £3, chd free. Sun 5 July (11-5). Visitors also welcome by arrangement July to Sept groups no larger than 10 welcomed at the weekends.**
Medium-sized suburban garden designed for visual impact with colour and interest provided predominantly by foliage. Many different acers, ferns and hostas grown in containers.

Mints, herbs, shrubs, trees and bedding also grown in pots. Greenhouse, pond, rockery and tortoise enclosure. Home made teas and plant sale in adjoining garden.

52 STONEHILL QUARRY GARDEN
Great Gate, Croxden, nr Uttoxeter ST10 4HF. Mrs Caroline Raymont. *6m NW of Uttoxeter. From A50 at Uttoxeter take B5030 to JCB Rocester, turn L to Hollington. Take 3rd R Croxden Abbey. At Great Gate turn L at T junction to Stonehill.* Tea. **Adm £3. Sun 19 Apr (2-5).**
6 acre plantsman's landscape garden set in a historical quarry with bamboo jungle, rock garden with wildlife pond. Features rhododendrons, azaleas and ornamental trees under planted with spring bulbs, asiatic and US woodland plants (Trilliums and Erythroniums). C12 Cistercian Abbey ruins (adm free) 1/2 kilometre away. Churnet Valley walks and Alton Towers 10mins away. Featured on BBC Gardeners World Joe Swift showing quarry garden. Disabled parking only at house. Wheelchair access to main terrace and main lawn only. Garden unsuitable for children.

53 ◆ SUGNALL WALLED GARDEN
Sugnall, Eccleshall, Stafford ST21 6NF. Dr & Mrs David Jacques, 01785 850820, www.sugnall.co.uk. *21/2 m NW of Eccleshall. Just off B5026 Eccleshall to Loggerheads Rd. Turn at the Sugnall Xrds & use the Sugnall Business Centre car park.* Home-made teas. Light lunches, teas, wine & beer available. **Adm £2, chd free. For NGS: Wed 8 July, Wed 9 Sept (12-4). For other opening times and information, please phone or see garden website.**
Historic walled kitchen garden of 1737, renovated for today. Work in progress, e.g. glass houses still to be repaired, but most of the 2 acres is under cultivation with 200 apple and pear dwarf pyramids, 50 fan-trained wall fruit and a wide variety of produce within the quarters. Flower borders around marquee and events area. Tearoom serving light lunches made from produce in the garden. Garden shop. Accessable WC.

54 TANGLEWOOD COTTAGE
Crossheads, Colwich, Stafford
ST18 0UG. Dennis & Helen Wood,
01889 882857,
shuvitdog@hotmail.com,
Tanglewood cottage, Facebook.
*5m SE of Stafford. A51
Rugeley/Weston R into Colwich.
Church on L school on R, under
bridge R into Crossheads Lane follow
railway approx 1/4 m (it does lead
somewhere). Parking signed.* Home-
made teas. **Adm £3, chd free. Sun
17 May (10.30-2.30).** Visitors also
welcome by arrangement May to
Sept for groups 15+. Catering
requirements on request.
A country cottage garden. Mixed
borders, koi carp pool, tranquil
seated areas, courtyard, vegetables
and fruit, chickens and aviary. An
array of wonderful perennials. A
garden of peace and tranquillity,
different rooms and variety. Year on
year people spend many hours
relaxing with us. Art and jewellery
display and sales. HPS Plant Fair in
village hall Sun 17 May. Lots of gravel
paths, people with walking sticks
seem to manage quite well.
Wheelchairs would have difficulty.

55 91 TOWER ROAD
Four Oaks, Sutton Coldfield B75
5EQ. Heather & Gary Hawkins. *3m
N Sutton Coldfield. From A5127 at
Mere Green island, turn onto Mere
Green Rd, L at St James Church, L
again onto Tower Road.* Home-made
teas. **Adm £3, chd free. Sun 7 June
(1.30-5.30).**
163ft S-facing garden with sweeping
borders and island beds planted with
an eclectic mix of shrubs and
perennials. A well stocked fishpond,
imposing cast iron water feature and
a hiding griffin enhance your journey
around the garden. A vast array of
home made cakes to tempt you
during your visit. The ideal setting for
sunbathing, children's hide and seek
and lively garden parties. Amazing
selection of home-made cream teas
to eat in the garden or take away.
More than just an Open Garden, we
like to think of it as a garden party!

56 ◆ THE TRENTHAM ESTATE
Stone Road, Stoke-on-Trent
ST4 8JG. Michael Walker, 01782
646646, www.trentham.co.uk. *M6
J15. Well signed on r'about, A34 with
A5035.* Home-made teas in the
gardens. **Adm £4.20, chd £4.20. For**

NGS: **Wed 21 Jan (12-3). Evening
Openings £5, chd £5,** Home-made
teas, **Wed 1, Wed 8 July (5-8).** For
other opening times and
information, please phone or see
garden website.
One of the largest garden
regeneration projects in Britain, using
award winning designers Tom Stuart-
Smith and Piet Oudolf, who have
introduced vast contemporary
plantings, using over 300,000 choice
perennials and bulbs. Major
programme of restoration has
recently been undertaken to reveal,
restore and replenish the landscape
designed by Capability Brown. NGS
Special Evening Opening. Trenthams'
Head of Garden and Estate, Michael
Walker, will provide a complimentary
tour of the garden starting at 6pm on
both evening openings.

57 41 TWENTYLANDS
Rolleston-on-Dove, Burton-on-
Trent DE13 9AJ. Maureen & Joe
Martin, 01283 520208,
joe.martin11@btinternet.com. *3m E
of Tutbury. At r'about on Tutbury bypass A511 take Rolleston Lane.
Continue through Rolleston-on-Dove,
past Scout HQ. Twentylands on R,
opp the Jinny Inn.* Home-made teas.
**Adm £3, chd free. Sun 17 May
(12-5).** Visitors also welcome by
arrangement May to Sept min 6
max 20.
Small back garden. Every corner
used and packed with plants.
Herbaceous borders with fruit trees
and shrubs. Herb corner, fernery, bog
garden with many candelabra
primula, in Spring, and other bog
plants. Chinese garden with chess
pavilion and bonsai, water features,
small pond with lilys, wood carvings,
greenhouses, Water harvesting and
composting systems. Many plants
raised from seed. Tutbury Castle and
Blue Cross Horse Sanctuary near by.

58 19 WATERDALE
Compton, Wolverhampton
WV3 9DY. Anne & Brian Bailey,
01902 424867,
m.bailey1234@btinternet.com,
www.facebook.com/pages/Garden
-of-Surprises/165745816926408.
*1 1/2 m W of Wolverhampton city
centre. From Wolverhampton Ring Rd
take A454 towards Bridgnorth for 1m.
Waterdale is on the L off A454
Compton Rd West.* Home-made
teas. **Adm £3.50, chd free. Sun 7**

June, **Sun 12 July (1.30-5.30).**
Visitors also welcome by
arrangement May to Aug for
groups of 10-35.
Secluded town garden which
gradually reveals itself in a journey
through deep, lush planting, full of
unusual plants, with a surprise round
every corner. From the sunny, flower
filled terrace, a ruined folly emerges
from a luxuriant fernery and leads into
an oriental garden, complete with
teahouse. Towering bamboos hide
the way to the gothic summerhouse
and mysterious shell grotto. Featured
in the Express and Star and George
Clarke's 'Amazing Spaces - Shed of
the Year'.

WESTACRES
See Worcestershire.

59 THE WICKETS
47 Long Street, Wheaton Aston
ST19 9NF. Tony & Kate Bennett,
01785 840233,
ajtonyb@talktalk.net. *8m W of
Cannock, 10m N of Wolverhampton,
10m E of Telford. M6 J12 W towards
Telford on A5; 3m R signed Stretton;
150yds L signed Wheaton Aston; 2m
L; over canal, garden on R or at
Bradford Arms on A5 follow signs.*
Tea. **Adm £3, chd free. Sun 5, Wed
8 July, Sun 30 Aug (1.30-5).**
Visitors also welcome by
arrangement June to Aug.
This quirky garden is full of humour
and surprises. If you are looking for
new and original ideas for your own
garden then this is the garden to visit.
Its interlocking themed areas incl a
fernery, grasses bed, herbaceous
islands, dry stream, many pots, tubs
and baskets and a cricket match! It
will stimulate your imagination as you
sit and enjoy our acclaimed tea and
cake. 2 steps in garden.

© Marianne Majerus

Grafton Cottage

60 NEW WILD WOOD LODGE
Bushton Lane, Anslow, Burton-On-Trent DE13 9QL. Mr & Mrs Richard & Dorothy Ward. *Bushton Lane is signed in centre of village. Wild Wood Lodge is 1/4 m down Bushton Lane.* Home-made teas. **Adm £3, chd free. Sun 14 June, Sun 16 Aug (1.30-5).**
The garden established over the last few years much of which was a former farm yard and buildings with extensive views of the Staffordshire countryside towards Needwood Forest. Covering approx 1 acre it consists of a productive orchard, raised vegetable beds, colourful herbaceous borders, shrubs, ornamental trees, a wild life pond and a fishing lake. Level garden, wide paths.

61 WILLOW COTTAGE
High Street, Church Eaton ST20 0AG. Sue & Jeremy Bach, 01785 823085, jeremy.bach@btinternet.com. *7 1/2 m SW of Stafford. A518. At Haughton tn L for Church Eaton. At T-junction, turn R down High St to Royal Oak PH car park. Walk back to Cottage.* **Adm £3, chd free. Visitors welcome by arrangement.**
Behind the country cottage frontage is an oasis of flower and colour. The gentle sound of water welcomes you to walk amongst the herbaceous beds, water features, ponds and vegetable plot. Sit in some of the quiet corners of this garden and enjoy the passing wildlife.

62 WITS END
59 Tanworth Lane, Shirley B90 4DQ. Sue Mansell, 0121 744 4337, wits-end@hotmail.co.uk. *2m SW of Solihull. Take B4102 from Solihull for 2m. R at island onto A34. After next island (Sainsbury's) Tanworth Lane 1st L off A34.* Home-made teas. **Adm £3, chd free. Mon 4 May (11.30-4.30); Sun 31 May (2-5); Fri 26 June (11.30-4.30); Sun 28 June, Sun 2, Sun 30 Aug (2-5). Visitors also welcome by arrangement June to Aug groups 10+.**
Interesting all-yr-round plantaholic's cottage-style garden. Perennials and shrubs, many unusual in various shaped beds (some colour co-ordinated) plus spectacular late summer border. Various containers displaying an array of sempervivum and jovibarba. New water features, scree and design changes planned for 2015.

63 THE WOMBOURNE WODEHOUSE
Wolverhampton WV5 9BW. Mr & Mrs J Phillips, 01902 892202. *4m S of Wolverhampton. Just off A449 on A463 to Sedgley.* **Adm £5, chd free. Visitors welcome by arrangement Apr to July small or large groups welcome preferably weekdays.**
18-acre garden laid out in 1750. Rhododendrons, azaleas, woodland walk and 180 different varieties of tall bearded irises in walled kitchen garden (mid May to early June), 66yd herbaceous border, also 2 small borders and water garden (June and July). Partial wheelchair access.

64 WOODBROOKE QUAKER STUDY CENTRE
1046 Bristol Road, Selly Oak B29 6LJ. Woodbrooke Quaker Study Centre, 0121 472 5171, enquiries@woodbrooke.org.uk, www.woodbrooke.org.uk. *4m SW of Birmingham. On A38 Bristol Rd, S of Selly Oak, opp Witherford Way.* Cream teas. **Adm £4, chd free. Sun 21 June (2.30-5.30).**
10 acres of organically-managed garden and grounds. Grade II listed house (not open), former home of George Cadbury. Herbaceous and

shrub borders, walled garden with herb garden, potager and cutting beds, Chinese garden, orchard, arboretum, Victorian boat house, lake and extensive woodland walks. Very fine variety of trees. Our Garden Manager and other staff will be on hand to help visitors to identify the key garden features and make the most of their visit. Garden tours and short talks will be available. Freshly baked cakes and hot drinks will be available to purchase. Some paths may be unsuitable for wheelchair access depending on the weather.

GROUP OPENING

65 WOODLAND GRANGE GARDENS
Rowley Hall Drive, Stafford ST17 9FF. *1m SW of Stafford town centre. Off A518 Newport Rd. Turn into Rowley Ave, signed Rowley Hall Hospital. Continue through the white gates following the lane straight on. Park in the hospital car park. No access from A449.* Home-made teas. **Combined adm £4, chd free. Sun 28 June (1-5).**

> **7 ROWLEY HALL DRIVE**
> Mr Paul Brett & Mr John McEvoy
>
> **10 ROWLEY HALL DRIVE**
> Mr & Mrs Wootton
>
> **12 ROWLEY HALL DRIVE**
> Jane & Chris Whitney-Cooper

A trio of smaller-scale suburban 'real-life' gardens to spark the imagination. Three suburban gardens established over the past 20 years on a site that was once part of the grounds of Rowley Hall. They are planted in contrasting styles, but all draw on features of the parkland that still surrounds these modern houses. No. 10 is a villa-style garden, open and spacious, with formal lawns surrounded by professionally laid-out borders for year-round colour and interest. No.12 is a country/cottage style garden, combining productive vegetable areas as well as attractive borders and mixed planting. The owners use organic principles and have completed their country-style 'Good Life' with a brood of hens. No.7 is an edge of woodland style garden with a feel of peace, calm and tranquillity. It uses focal points and perspective principles to enhance this effect. Shrubs and foliage plants,

rather than flowers are used to create a naturalistic setting attractive to wildlife. Ice-creams together with strawberries and cream will be available at No.10, tea and cakes at No.12 and plants from the gardens will be on sale at No.7 for you to take home to your own 'earthly paradise'. Parking at Rowley Hall, short walk down drive to Rowley Hall Drive. Gardens will be signed. Tickets available at 10 Rowley Hall Drive..

> *Owners use organic principles and have completed their country-style 'Good Life' with a brood of hens . . .*

GROUP OPENING

66 WOODLEIGHTON GROVE GARDENS
Woodleighton Grove, Uttoxeter ST14 8BX, 01889 563930, cityofgold@lineone.net. *SE of Uttoxeter. From Uttoxeter take B5017 (Marchington). Go over Town Bridge, 1st exit at r'about, then 3rd exit at r'about into Highwood Rd, After ¼ m turn R.* Home-made teas. **Combined adm £3.50, chd free. Sat 11 July (11-5); Sun 12 July (1-5). Visitors also welcome by arrangement June to July min 12, adm £6 incl home-made teas. WC.**

> **APOLLONIA**
> Helen & David Loughton
>
> **KARIBU**
> Graham & Judy White

These two adjacent gardens demonstrate varied and fascinating approaches to garden design, layout and planting, and have inspired and given many visitors ideas for their own gardens. Apollonia is a Plantaholics Garden, strong structure on several levels; summerhouse, greenhouse, fruit arch under development, natural stream, some

steep steps. Unusual and interesting planting including bamboos, bananas, hostas and agaves. A place to relax and enjoy. Karibu is a distinctive and intriguing garden with a number of absorbing features. Informally planted on two levels, with a natural stream, summerhouse, greenhouse, folly, gazebo and stumpery. Archways, bridges, steps and a boardwalk lead to a selection of tranquil resting places. The garden discreetly houses many fascinating artefacts, plus a collection of antique horticultural and agricultural hand tools. The greenhouse contains nearly 400 cacti and succulents.

67 YARLET HOUSE
Yarlet, Stafford ST18 9SU. Mr & Mrs Nikolas Tarling. *2m S of Stone. Take A34 from Stone towards Stafford, turn L into Yarlet School & L again into car park.* Home-made teas. **Adm £4, chd free. Share to Staffordshire Wildlife Trust. Fri 10 July (10-2).**
4 acre garden with extensive lawns, walks, lengthy herbaceous borders and traditional Victorian box hedge. Water gardens with fountain and rare lilies. Sweeping views across Trent Valley to Sandon. Victorian School Chapel. 9 hole putting course. Boules pitch. Yarlet School Art Display. Gravel paths.

68 YEW TREE COTTAGE
Podmores Corner, Long Lane, nr White Cross, Haughton, Stafford ST18 9JR. Clive & Ruth Plant, 01785 282516, pottyplantz@aol.com. *4m W of Stafford. Take A518 W Haughton, turn R Station Rd (signed Ranton) 1m, then turn R at Xrds ¼ m on R.* Home-made teas. **Adm £3, chd free. Sun 3 May (2-5); Thur 7 May, Thur 11 June, Thur 9 July (11-5); Sun 19 July (2-5). Visitors also welcome by arrangement May to Aug.**
Hardy Planter's garden brimming with unusual plants. All-yr-round interest incl meconopsis, trillium, arisaema and dierama. ½ -acre incl pond, gravel garden, herbaceous borders, vegetable garden and plant sales area. Covered courtyard with oak-timbered vinery to take tea in if the weather is unkind, and seats in the garden for lingering on sunny days.

SUFFOLK

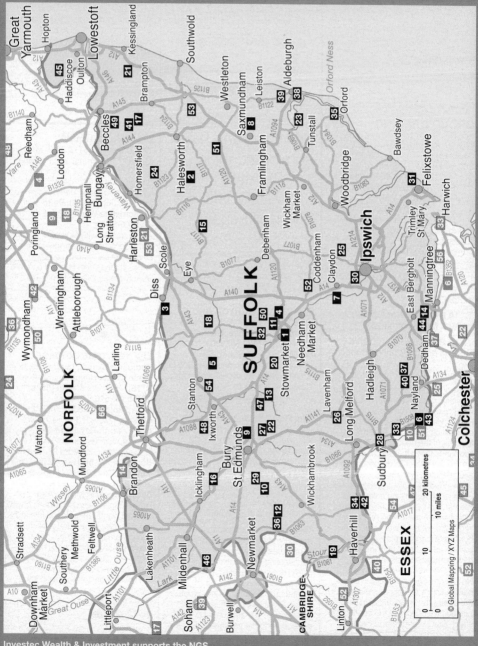

Suffolk

Suffolk has so much to offer – from charming coastal villages, ancient woodlands and picturesque valleys – there is a landscape to suit all tastes.

Keen walkers and cyclists will enjoy Suffolk's low-lying, gentle countryside, where fields of farm animals and crops reflect the county's agricultural roots.

Stretching north from Felixstowe, the county has miles of Heritage Coast set in an Area of Outstanding Natural Beauty. The Suffolk coast was the inspiration for composer Benjamin Britten's celebrated work, and it is easy to see why.

To the west and north of the county are The Brecks, a striking canvas of pine forest and open heathland, famous for its chalky and sandy soils - and one of the most important wildlife areas in Britain.

A variety of gardens to please everyone open for Suffolk NGS, so come along on an open day and enjoy the double benefit of a beautiful setting and supporting wonderful charities.

Suffolk Volunteers

County Organiser
Jenny Reeve
01638 715289
j.reeve05@tiscali.co.uk

County Treasurer
David Reeve
01638 715289
dreeve43@gmail.com

Publicity
Jenny Reeve
(as above)

Booklet Coordinator
Adrian Simpson-James
01502 710555
sjs@megenna.freeserve.co.uk

Assistant County Organisers
Gilly Beddard
01394 450468
gbedd@btinternet.com

Frances Boscawen
01728 638768
francesboscawen@gmail.com

Catherine Horwood Barwise
01787 279315
catherine@richmondhouse-clare.com

Yvonne Leonard
01638 712742
yj.leonard@btinternet.com

Barbara Segall
01787 312046
barbara@bsegall.com

Adrian Simpson-James
(as above)

Dick Soper
01284 850678
soperdoc@gmail.com

Left: Great Thurlow Hall

Currently the NGS donates around £2.5 million every year

Opening Dates

All entries subject to change.
For latest information check www.ngs.org.uk

February

Sunday 15
17 Gable House

March

Saturday 28
24 The Laburnums

Sunday 29
19 Great Thurlow Hall

April

53 **The Woottens (every day except Mondays)**

Sunday 5
52 Woodwards

Sunday 12
4 Bays Farm
5 The Beeches
14 East Bergholt Place - The Place for Plants

May

53 **The Woottens (every day except Mondays)**

Friday 1
45 Somerleyton Hall & Gardens

Monday 4
6 Bevills

Saturday 9
25 Larks' Hill

Sunday 10
4 Bays Farm
7 Blakenham Woodland Garden
11 Columbine Hall
29 Moat House
46 Street Farm

Sunday 17
28 NEW 22 Melford Road
40 The Priory
43 Rosedale

Sunday 24
2 NEW Appleacre
26 Lavenham Hall
52 Woodwards

Monday 25
47 NEW Trinity House

Saturday 30
50 NEW Wood Farm, Gipping

Sunday 31
13 Drinkstone Park
31 Old Felixstowe Gardens
34 Orchard House
36 NEW Ousden House
42 Richmond House

June

53 **The Woottens (every day except Mondays)**

Festival Weekend

Saturday 6
52 Woodwards
54 Wyken Hall

Sunday 7
17 Gable House
30 428 Norwich Road
35 Orford Gardens
44 Rosemary
54 Wyken Hall

Sunday 14
4 Bays Farm
13 Drinkstone Park
32 NEW Old Newton Gardens

Saturday 20
33 Old Rectory House

Sunday 21
9 NEW Cattishall Farmhouse
23 Iken Gardens

Saturday 27
49 White House Farm

Sunday 28
39 Priors Oak

July

53 **The Woottens (every day except Mondays)**

Sunday 5
13 Drinkstone Park
15 Frythe Barn
51 Wood Farm, Sibton

Tuesday 7
52 Woodwards

Saturday 11
25 Larks' Hill

Sunday 12
1 NEW Abbot's Hall Walled Garden
3 Batteleys Cottage
4 Bays Farm
41 Redisham Hall

Sunday 19
13 Drinkstone Park

Sunday 26
43 Rosedale
48 NEW Troston Gardens
52 Woodwards

August

53 **The Woottens (every day except Mondays)**

Saturday 8
18 Gislingham Gardens

Sunday 9
4 Bays Farm
16 Fullers Mill Garden
18 Gislingham Gardens

Tuesday 11
52 Woodwards

Sunday 16
10 Cobbs Hall

Sunday 30
42 Richmond House
52 Woodwards

September

53 **The Woottens (every day except Mondays)**

Sunday 13
4 Bays Farm
8 NEW By the Crossways
22 Home Farm House
27 The Lucy Redman Garden
38 Priors Hill, Aldeburgh

Sunday 20
21 Henstead Exotic Garden

October

53 **The Woottens (every day except Mondays)**

February 2016

Sunday 14
17 Gable House

A country garden covering an acre that has evolved over thirty years . . .

Gardens open to the public

7 Blakenham Woodland Garden
14 East Bergholt Place - The Place for Plants
16 Fullers Mill Garden
45 Somerleyton Hall & Gardens
53 Woottens
54 Wyken Hall

By arrangement only

12 Dip-on-the-Hill
20 Green Farmhouse
37 Polstead Mill

Also open by arrangement

3 Batteleys Cottage
4 Bays Farm
8 NEW By the Crossways
10 Cobbs Hall
13 Drinkstone Park
15 Frythe Barn
17 Gable House
25 Larks' Hill
26 Lavenham Hall
28 NEW 22 Melford Road
29 Moat House
30 428 Norwich Road
31 41 Westmorland Road, Old Felixstowe Gardens
38 Heron House, Priors Hill, Aldeburgh
39 Priors Oak
42 Richmond House
43 Rosedale
48 NEW Church Cottage, Troston Gardens
49 White House Farm
52 Woodwards

The Gardens

1 NEW ABBOT'S HALL WALLED GARDEN

Museum of East Anglian Life, Iliffe Way, Stowmarket IP14 1DE, www.eastanglianlife.org.uk. *The Museum of East Anglian Life is adjacent to ASDA supermarket in Stowmarket. The Museum is signed from the main A14 trunk rd & B1115 to Great Finborough. For SatNav users please search for 'Iliffe Way' or IP14 1DE.* Home-made teas. **Adm £2.50, chd free. Sun 12 July (11-5).** An oasis in the heart of Stowmarket this ½ acre walled Victorian kitchen garden has been restored and replanted since 2012. Showcasing many heritage vegetable varieties as well as trained fruit trees, herb bed, cut flower border, old roses and apple tunnel. It also boasts a renovated greenhouse, potting shed and conservatory. Good wheelchair access, gravel paths. A small car park is located in the grounds of Abbot's Hall for visitors with access needs only.

2 NEW APPLEACRE

Bell Green, Cratfield, Halesworth IP19 0DH. Mr & Mrs T Shaw. *7m W of Halesworth. B1123 to Harleston. At Linstead Parva, turn L up Godfrey's Hill. After approx 1m turn L onto Mary's Lane & follow NGS signs. 50 metres W of the Poacher PH.* Home-made teas. **Adm £3.50, chd free. Sun 24 May (11-5).** A country garden covering an acre that has evolved over thirty years. A garden full of secrets waiting to be revealed, with open vistas over the Suffolk countryside. Explore a variety of large herbaceous borders, box topiary, mature trees, lily pond, greenhouse, lawns and raised vegetable beds. Wild plant areas bring developed for 2015. Partial wheelchair access, but caution needed in some areas.

3 BATTELEYS COTTAGE

The Ling, Wortham, Diss IP22 1ST. Mr & Mrs Andy & Linda Simpson, 07949 204820, lindaruth11@gmail.com. *3m W of Diss. Turn signed from A143 Diss/Bury Rd at Wortham. By church turn R at T-junction. At top of hill turn L. Go down hill & round sharp L corner.* Home-made teas. **Adm £4,**

chd free. **Sun 12 July (1-5.30). Visitors also welcome by arrangement May to Sept refreshments available for groups by arrrangement.**
1 acre plantsman's garden of both mature and newer mixed plantings incl many different perennials and grasses. Ponds and stream, potager garden, fruit and vegetable garden, orchard and meadow area. New features being planned for 2015. Varied local habitat and mixed planting in the garden makes this a haven for birds. Lots of corners to sit in and view over open countryside. Wheelchair access to most parts of the garden, gravel, grass and bark paths.

4 BAYS FARM

Forward Green, Earl Stonham, Stowmarket IP14 5HU. Richard & Stephanie Challinor, 01449 711286, stephanie@baysfarmsuffolk.co.uk, www.baysfarmgardens.co.uk. *3½ m E of Stowmarket. J50 A14, take A1120 direction Stowupland. Proceed through Stowupland on A1120 for 1m, at sharp L bend turn R signed Broad Green. 1st house on R.* Home-made teas. **Adm £3.50, chd free. Suns 12 Apr, 10 May, 14 June, 12 July, 9 Aug, 13 Sept (2-5.30). Visitors also welcome by**

arrangement Mar to Sept.
A true 2-acre plantsman's garden with all year round interest with regular monthly openings to reflect the ever changing seasons. Formal gardens comprising shady borders, scented and sun-loving beds with woodland and butterfly planting. Large kitchen gardens, greenhouse, orchard, wild flower area and herb garden. NEW extensive borders and planting for 2015. Home-made teas and savouries. Formal gardens designed by Chelsea Gold Medal winner, Xa Tollemache of Helmingham Hall. Gravel paths.

5 THE BEECHES

Grove Road, Walsham-le-Willows IP31 3AD. Dr A J Russell. *11m E of Bury St Edmunds. A143 to Diss. Turn R to Walsham-le-Willows. 1st Xrds in village turn R. Church on L. After 100yds turn L. Beeches on L.* Home-made teas. **Adm £4, chd free. Share to St Marys Church, Walsham-le-Willows. Sun 12 Apr (2-5).** 150yr-old, 3-acre garden, which incl specimen trees, pond, stream, potager, memorial garden, lawns and a variety of beds. Stream area landscaped. Mediterranean bed and camellia bed. Gravel paths.

Cattishall Farmhouse

6 BEVILLS
Sudbury Road, Bures CO8 5JW.
Mr & Mrs G T C Probert. *4m S of Sudbury. Just N of Bures on the Sudbury rd B1508.* Home-made teas. **Adm £4, chd free. Mon 4 May (2-5.30).**
A beautiful house (not open) overlooking the Stour Valley with parkland trees, hills and woodland. The gardens are formal and Italianate in style with hedges and lawns flanked by Irish yews and mature specimen trees. Terraces, borders, ponds, vistas and woodland walks. Spring bulbs and bluebell wood. Gravel paths.

7 ◆ BLAKENHAM WOODLAND GARDEN
Little Blakenham, Ipswich IP8 4LZ. Lord & Lady Blakenham, www.blakenhamwoodlandgarden. org.uk. *4m NW of Ipswich. Follow signs at Little Blakenham, 1m off B1113.* Home-made teas. **Adm £3, chd £1.50. For NGS: Sun 10 May (10-5). For other opening times and information, please see garden website.**
Beautiful 6-acre woodland garden with variety of rare trees and shrubs. Chinese rocks and a landscape sculpture. Especially lovely in spring with snowdrops, daffodils, camellias, magnolias and bluebells followed by roses in early summer. Special bluebell opening 10 May. Partial wheelchair access.

8 NEW BY THE CROSSWAYS
Kelsale, Saxmundham IP17 2PL. Mr & Mrs William Kendall, 077678 24923, miranda@bythecrossways.co.uk. *2m NE of Saxmundham, just off Clayhills Rd. ¹/₂ m N of town centre, turn R to Theberton on Clayhills Rd. After 1¹/₂ m, 1st L to Kelsale, then turn L immed after white cottage.* Tea. **Adm £4, chd free. Sun 13 Sept (11-5). Visitors also welcome by arrangement Mar to Dec for groups of 10 during the week.**
3-acre wildlife garden designed as a garden within an organic farm, where wilderness areas lie next to productive beds. Large semi-walled vegetable and cutting garden, a spectacular crinkle-crankle wall. Extensive perennial planting, grasses and wild areas. Set around the owner's Edwardian family home built by suffragist ancestor. The garden is

mostly flat, with paved or gravel pathways around the main house, a few low steps and extensive grass paths and lawns.

WE ARE MACMILLAN. CANCER SUPPORT

2015 sees the NGS total to Macmillan pass £15 million

9 NEW CATTISHALL FARMHOUSE
Cattishall, Great Barton, Bury St. Edmunds IP31 2QT. Mrs J Mayer. *3m NE of Bury St Edmunds. Approaching Great Barton from Bury on A143 take 1st R turn to church. If travelling towards Bury take last L turn to church as you leave the village. At church bear R and follow lane to Farmhouse on R.* Home-made teas. **Adm £4, chd free. Sun 21 June (1-5).**
Approx 2 acre farmhouse garden enclosed by a flint wall and mature beech hedge laid mainly to lawns with both formal and informal planting and a large herbaceous border. There is an abundance of roses and a recently developed kitchen garden incl a wild flower area and fruit cages. Chickens, bees and a boisterous Labrador also live here. Generally flat with some gravel paths. The occasional small step.

10 COBBS HALL
Great Saxham IP29 5JN. Dick & Sue Soper, 01284 850678, soperdoc@gmail.com. *4¹/₂ m W of Bury St Edmunds. A14 exit to Westley. R at Westley Xrds. L fork at Lt.Saxham towards Chevington. 1.4m to sign on R. Mustard coloured house 300yds on L.* Home-made teas. **Adm £4, chd free.** Share to St Andrews Church, Gt Saxham. **Sun 16 Aug (2-5.30). Visitors also welcome by arrangement June to Sept.**

2 acres of lawns and borders, ornamental trees, large fish and lily pond. Parterre, folly, walled kitchen garden, fernery/stumpery, grass tennis court and pretty courtyard. New cascade water feature. Generally flat with a few gentle slopes and some gravel paths.

11 COLUMBINE HALL
Gipping Road, Stowupland, Stowmarket IP14 4AT. Hew Stevenson & Leslie Geddes-Brown, www.columbinehall.co.uk. *1¹/₂ m NE of Stowmarket. Turn N off A1120 opp Total garage across village green, then R at T-junction into Gipping Rd. Garden on L just beyond derestriction sign.* Home-made teas. **Adm £4, chd free. Sun 10 May (2.30-6).**
George Carter's formal garden and herb garden surround moated medieval manor (not open). Outside the moat, vistas, stream, ponds and bog garden, Mediterranean garden, colour-themed vegetable garden, cutting garden, orchards and parkland. Gardens developed since 1994 with constant work-in-progress, incl transformed farm buildings and eyecatchers. Incl disabled WC.

12 DIP-ON-THE-HILL
Ousden, Newmarket CB8 8TW. Dr & Mrs. Geoffrey Ingham, 01638 500329, gki1000@cam.ac.uk. *5m E of Newmarket; 7m W of Bury St Edmunds. From Newmarket: 1m from junction of B1063 & B1085. From Bury St Edmunds follow signs for Hargrave. Parking at village hall.* Tea. **Adm £3.50, chd free. Visitors welcome by arrangement** July to Sept.
Approx one acre in a dip on a S-facing hill based on a wide range of architectural/sculptural evergreen trees, shrubs and groundcover: pines; grove of Phillyrea latifolia; 'cloud pruned' hedges; palms; large bamboo; ferns; range of kniphofia and croscosmia. Visitors may wish to make an arrangement when visiting gardens nearby.

13 DRINKSTONE PARK
Park Road, Drinkstone, Bury St. Edmunds IP30 9ST. Michael & Christine Lambert, 01359 272513, chris@drinkstonepark.co.uk, www.drinkstonepark.co.uk. *6m from Bury St Edmunds. E on A14 J46*

You are always welcome at an NGS garden!

turn R & head for Drinkstone. W on A14 J46 take R next junction turn L and immed R to Drinkstone. Home-made teas. **Adm £3.50, chd free. Suns 31 May, 14 June, Suns 5, 19 July (1-5).** Visitors also welcome by arrangement May to Aug, refreshments can be arrange to suit group.

Three acre garden with wildlife pond formal Koi pond, herbaceous borders, orchard, woodland and wildlife area, large productive vegetable plot with poly tunnel and greenhouses. Some gravel paths.

An organic farm, where wilderness areas lie next to productive beds . . .

14 ◆ EAST BERGHOLT PLACE - THE PLACE FOR PLANTS
East Bergholt CO7 6UP. Mr & Mrs Rupert Eley, 01206 299224, www.placeforplants.co.uk. *2m E of A12, 7m S of Ipswich. On B1070 towards Manningtree, 2m E of A12. Situated on the edge of East Bergholt.* Home-made teas. **Adm £6, chd free. For NGS: Sun 12 Apr (1-5).** For other opening times and information, please see garden website.

20-acre garden originally laid out at the turn of the last century by the present owner's great grandfather. Full of many fine trees and shrubs, many seldom seen in East Anglia. A fine collection of camellias, magnolias and rhododendrons, topiary, and the National Collection of deciduous Euonymus.

 NCH ☕

15 FRYTHE BARN
Wilby Road, Stradbroke, Eye IP21 5JP. Don & Carol Darling, 01379 388098, caroldon01@gmail.com. *11m SE of Diss, 10m N of Framlingham. From Framlingham B1118 to Stradbroke. Through Wilby past Neaves Lane on*

R 2nd driveway on R From Diss B1118 to Stradbroke, R church, immed L. Home-made teas. Gluten and Dairy free options available. **Adm £4, chd free. Sun 5 July (12-5).** Visitors also welcome by arrangement Apr to Oct groups of up to 30.

A maze of concrete and brick buildings transformed in 7yrs into a delightfully relaxing 2 acre garden. Take a stroll via a willow tunnel, spinney with bee hives and bog garden through the orchard to a leafy arbour, surrounded by flowing grasses. View from here the large pond and stream to the left, sensitively planted borders to the right and Italian style patio in front of the renovated barn. Wildlife area, large grass beds, pond, mixed borders, roses. No wheelchair access to spinney/wild flower meadow.

16 ◆ FULLERS MILL GARDEN
West Stow IP28 6HD. Perennial - The Gardeners Royal Benevolent Society, www.fullersmillgarden.org.uk. *6m NW of Bury St Edmunds. Turn off A1101 Bury to Mildenhall Rd, signed West Stow Country Park, go past Country Park continue for ¹/₄ m, garden entrance on R. Sign at entrance.* Home-made teas. **Adm £4, chd free. For NGS: Sun 9 Aug (2-5).** For other opening times and information, please see garden website.

An enchanting 7 acre garden on the banks of R Lark. A beautiful site of light, dappled woodland with a plantsman's paradise of rare and unusual shrubs, perennials and marginals planted with great natural charm. Euphorbias and lilies are a particular feature. A garden with interest in every season. In late Sept colchicums in flower incl outstanding white variety. Also yellow crocus-like Sternbergia should be in bloom. Featured in Country Life, Suffolk Magazine, Cambridge Evening News and BBC Chelsea coverage. Partial wheelchair access around garden.

17 GABLE HOUSE
Halesworth Road, Redisham,, Beccles NR34 8NE. John & Brenda Foster, 01502 575298, gablehouse@btinternet.com. *5m S of Beccles. A144 S from Bungay, L at St Lawrence School, 2m to Gable House. Or A12 Blythburgh, A145 to*

Beccles, Brampton Xrd L to Station Rd. 3m on is garden. Light refreshments. **Adm £3.50, chd free. Share to St Peter's Church, Redisham. Sun 15 Feb (11-4); Sun 7 June (11-5); Sun 14 Feb 2016.** Visitors also welcome by arrangement Feb to Sept max of 50 visitors.

One acre Plantsman's garden of all year interest. Vast collection of snowdrops, cyclamen, hellebores etc for the February opening. The June open day brings colour and variety from shrub roses, perennials and interesting trees and shrubs. Greenhouses contain rare bulbs and tender plants. Many unusual trees and shrubs. Featured in Suffolk Magazine.

GROUP OPENING

18 GISLINGHAM GARDENS
Mill Street, Gislingham IP23 8JT. *4m W of Eye. Gislingham 2¹/₂ m W of A140. 9m N of Stowmarket, 8m S of Diss. Disabled parking at Ivy Chimneys.* Tea at Ivy Chimneys. Teas cakes and soft drinks if hot. **Combined adm £3.50, chd free. Sat 8, Sun 9 Aug (11-4.30).**

NEW HAREBELLS
Mill Street. Mr & Mrs Darrel Charles

IVY CHIMNEYS
Iris & Alan Stanley

2 varied gardens in a picturesque village with a number of Suffolk timbered houses. Ivy Chimneys is planted for yr round interest with ornamental trees, some topiary, exotic borders and fishpond set in an area of Japanese style. Wisteria draped pergola supports a productive vine. Also a separate ornamental vegetable garden. New for 2014 fruit trees in the front garden. Harebells, 150 yards further down Mill Street from Ivy Chimneys, was a new build property in 2013 and the garden has since been developed from scratch. The garden has a feature round lawn edged by colour themed borders. A walk through pergola leads to a productive area incl a greenhouse and raised vegetables beds, a wildlife pond and views over open countryside.

© Stuart Kirk

Lavenham Hall

19 GREAT THURLOW HALL

Great Thurlow, Haverhill CB9 7LF.
Mr & Mrs George Vestey. *12m S of
Bury St Edmunds, 4m N of Haverhill.
Great Thurlow village on B1061 from
Newmarket; 3½ m N of junction with
A143 Haverhill/Bury St Edmunds rd.*
Home-made teas. **Adm £4, chd free.
Sun 29 Mar (2-5).**
River walk newly restored and trout
lake with extensive display of daffodils
and blossom. Spacious lawns,
shrubberies and roses. Walled
kitchen garden.

20 GREEN FARMHOUSE

The Green, Shelland, Stowmarket
IP14 3JE. Miss Rosemary Roe,
01449 736591. *4m NW of
Stowmarket, 10m SE of Bury St
Edmunds. A14 W-bound. A1308-
signed Wetherden, L to Harleston,
follow NGS signs. A14 E-bound take
Wetherden/Haughley Park turn, then
R signed Buxhall. Follow NGS signs.*
Light refreshments. **Visitors
welcome by arrangement** Mar
to Aug adm £5 incl refreshments,
chd free.
2 acre garden created around a

thatched cottage commanding
wonderful view of Mid-Suffolk
countryside. A garden with all-year
interest and wide variety of plants.
Easy walks through garden rooms
with shrubs, herbaceous borders,
lawns and vistas, courtyard and
gravel gardens, stumpery, natural
pond and developing wild flower
meadow. Garden would be a good
subject for photographic/art groups.
Featured in the Peggy Cole column in
East Anglian Daily Times. Partial
wheelchair access.

21 HENSTEAD EXOTIC GARDEN

Church Road, Henstead, Beccles,
Suffolk NR34 7LD. Andrew Brogan,
www.hensteadexoticgarden.co.uk.
*Equal distance between Beccles,
Southwold & Lowestoft approx 5m.
1m from A12 turning after Wrentham
(signed Henstead) very close to
B1127.* Home-made teas. **Adm
£3.50, chd free. Sun 20 Sept (11-4).**
2-acre exotic garden featuring 100
large palms, 20+ bananas and 200
bamboo plants. 2 streams, 20ft
tiered walkway leading to Thai style

wooden covered pavilion.
Mediterranean and jungle plants
around 3 large ponds with fish.
Suffolk's most exotic garden. Newly
extended this year.

22 HOME FARM HOUSE

Rushbrooke IP30 0EP. Anita Wigan.
*3m SE of Bury St Edmunds. A14 J44,
proceed towards town centre, after
50yds 1st exit from r'about then
immed R. Proceed ¾ m to T-junction,
turn L, follow rd for 2m Rushbrooke
Church on L, turn R into drive opp
church.* Home-made teas. **Adm £4,
chd free. Sun 13 Sept (2-5). Also
open The Lucy Redman Garden.**
3 acre walled garden with mixed
shrubs and herbaceous borders,
roses and formal lawns. 1-acre
kitchen garden plus glasshouses with
peaches, apricots, nectarines, grapes
and figs etc. 5-acre parkland with
moat garden, specimen trees and
orchard. Small cottage garden
alongside moat.

GROUP OPENING

23 IKEN GARDENS

Tunstall Road, Iken, Woodbridge
IP12 2ER. *3m from Tunstall & Snape.
From A12 take A1094 towards
Aldeburgh. At Snape Church turn R
to Snape. Past Snape Maltings turn L
signed Orford. At next Xrds turn L
signed Iken. After 1m Church Farm &
Decoy Cottage on R.* Home-made
teas at Church Farm. **Combined
adm £3.50, chd free. Sun 21 June
(2-5).**

CHURCH FARM
Mrs Caroline Erskine

DECOY COTTAGE
Sir Thomas Hughes-Hallett

Two adjoining gardens in a charming
Suffolk village. Decoy Cottage is a
twenty acre country garden with
woods orchard, lake and highland
cattle on show. Church Farm is a two
acre area surrounded by mature
alders and pines. Many young
specimen trees and shrubs planted
over the last six years. Mixed planting
of perennials, grasses and smaller
shrubs. Wheelchair access is fine for
garden but not for woods etc. No
access for wheelchairs through
Church Farm garden.

24 THE LABURNUMS

St. James South Elmham, Halesworth IP19 0HN. Mrs Jane Bastow, 01986 782413. *6m W of Halesworth, 7m E of Harleston & 6m S of Bungay. Parking at nearby village hall. For disabled parking please phone to arrange.* Home-made teas. If the weather is cold there will be hot soup as well as the usual fare. **Adm £4, chd free.** Sat 28 Mar (11-5).
1-acre garden is 20+ years old and is packed with annuals, perennials, flowering shrubs and trees and areas dedicated to wild flowers. The spring garden is awash with colour-snowdrops, aconites, hellebores, daffodils and much more. There are three ponds, a sunken garden and two glasshouses 2015 sees the new larger conservatory where the refreshments will be served surrounded by citrus plants etc. Plant stall with a variety of plants and bulbs. Gravel drive. Partial access to front garden. Steps to sunken garden. Concrete path in back garden.

Mature shrubs provide the perfect backdrop for the various colourful seating areas to enjoy light refreshments . . .

25 LARKS' HILL

Clopton Road, Tuddenham St Martin IP6 9BY. Mr John Lambert, 01473 785248, jrlambert@talktalk.net. *3m NE of Ipswich. From Ipswich take B1077, go through village, take the Clopton Rd.* Home-made teas. **Adm £5, chd free.** Sat 9 May, Sat 11 July (1.30-5). **Visitors also welcome by arrangement May to Aug groups of 15+.**
The gardens of eight acres comprise woodland, field and formal areas, and fall away from the house to the valley floor. A hill within a garden and in Suffolk at that! Hilly garden with a modern castle keep with an interesting and beautiful site

overlooking the gentle Fynn valley and the village beyond. A garden worthy of supporting the House, its family members and its visitors. A fossil of a limb bone from a Pliosaur that lived at least sixty million years ago was found in the garden in 2013. The discovery was reported in the national press but its importance has been recognised world-wide. A booklet is available to purchase giving all the details.

26 LAVENHAM HALL

Hall Road, Lavenham, Sudbury CO10 9QX. Mr & Mrs Anthony Faulkner, 01787 249841, adhfaulkner@aol.com. *Next to Lavenham's iconic church & close to High St. From church turn off the main rd down the side of church (Potland Rd). Go down hill. Car Park on R after 100 metres.* **Adm £4, chd free.** Sun 24 May (11-5). **Visitors also welcome by arrangement Apr to Sept groups of 10+. Painting/photo groups welcome.**
5-acre garden built around the ruins of the original ecclesiastical buildings on the site and the village's 1-acre fishpond. The garden incl deep borders of herbaceous planting with sweeping vistas and provides the perfect setting for the sculptures which Kate makes in her studio at the Hall and exhibits both nationally and internationally. 40 garden sculptures on display. There is a gallery in the grounds which displays a similar number of indoor sculptures. Note large number of gravel paths and slopes within the garden.

27 THE LUCY REDMAN GARDEN

6 The Village, Rushbrooke, Bury St Edmunds IP30 0ER. Lucy Redman & Dominic Watts, 07503 633671, lucyredman7@gmail.com, www.lucyredman.co.uk and www.metallurgi.co.uk. *3m E of Bury St Edmunds. A14 take Exit 44(BSE east) 1st exit off r'about towards BSE. 2nd r'about L then R down Rushbrooke Lane. T-junction L for 2m. Turn R at white houses, thatched house on L.* **Adm £3.50, chd free.** Sun 13 Sept (2-5). **Also open Home Farm House where tea /coffee and cake is available.**
Thatched cottage with 3/4 -acre quirky plantsman's family garden where unusual plants blend with sculptures and staged reclamation. Pebble

parterre in lawn, decorative vegetable garden. 20m Celtic water sculpture inc. 250 alpines. Woven metal turf tree seat / fencing and lawn edging by Dominic's business, Metallurgi. Stipa gigantea walkway up to woven metal basket. Garden visited by Beth Chatto. Featured in Landscape magazine and Suffolk magazine. Woven metal turf tree seat made by Dominic Watts shown at The Chelsea Flower Show. Gravel paths.

28 NEW 22 MELFORD ROAD

Sudbury CO10 1LS. Mr & Mrs C Bentley, 01787 374249, colette@ceebees.demon.co.uk. *Outskirts of town - 500 metres from town centre. Located on A134 Sudbury to Long Melford rd opp the Bay Horse PH. Parking is possible at the rear of the garden in Queens Rd. Town centre car park (free) 300 metres from the garden.* Light refreshments. **Adm £3.50, chd free.** Sun 17 May (11-5). **Visitors also welcome by arrangement June to Sept.**
An unusual compact Victorian town garden with large fish pond and waterfall. It has been divided into several areas to create the illusion of space and individuality. Mature shrubs provide the perfect backdrop for the various colourful seating areas to enjoy light refreshments. Partial wheelchair access as majority of garden is viewed by ascending steps.

29 MOAT HOUSE

Little Saxham, Bury St. Edmunds IP29 5LE. Mr & Mrs Richard Mason, 01284 810941, rnm333@live.com. *2m SW of Bury St Edmunds. Leave A14 at J42 - through Westley Village, at Xrds R towards Barrow/Saxham 1.3m L (follow signs).* Home-made teas. **Adm £4, chd free.** Sun 10 May (2-6). **Visitors also welcome by arrangement May to Aug groups between 20 & 40.**
Set in a 2 acre historic and partially moated site. This tranquil mature garden has been developed by the present owners over 20yrs. Bordered by mature trees the garden is in various sections incl a sunken garden, rose and clematis arbours, herbaceous borders surrounded by box hedging, small arboretum. Featured in Country Homes and Interiors and the Suffolk Magazine.

30▶ 428 NORWICH ROAD
Ipswich IP1 5DU. Robert & Gloria
Lawrence, 01473 743673,
globoblaw@talktalk.net. *1¹/₂ m W of
Ipswich town centre. On A1156
Norwich Rd garden is 200yds W of
railway bridge.* Cream teas. **Adm
£2.50, chd free.** Sun 7 June (2-5).
**Visitors also welcome by
arrangement 15 June to 7 July.**
Front garden of roses and large tubs
of bedding plants. Rear ¹/₃ acre
garden with sunken terrace leading
up to lawn with rose beds,
herbaceous border and dry stone
garden. Lawn leads to bog garden,
island mixed bed and on to orchard
(17 fruit trees), asparagus bed, small
vegetable plot with composting area
and greenhouse. Strawberry Cream
Teas. Wheelchair access is limited to
the front and terrace area because of
steps leading to lawn area and
orchard.

GROUP OPENING

**31▶ OLD FELIXSTOWE
GARDENS**
41 Westmorland Road, Felixstowe
IP11 9TJ. Mrs Diane Elmes. *Corner
of Wrens Park & Westmorland Road.
Enter Felixstowe on A154. At r'about
take 1st exit then turn R - into
Beatrice Av. L to High Road East.
Proceed to Clifflands Car Park. Follow
signs.* Light refreshments. **Combined
adm £4, chd free.** Sun 31 May
(11-5).

33 FERRY ROAD
Peter & Monica Smith

FERRYFIELDS
206 Ferry Road. Mr & Mrs Paul
Smith.
*Follow signs to Felixstowe Golf
Club. Ferry Rd is opp Golf Club.
Ferryfields (206 Ferry Rd) is about
¹/₄ m on L*

41 WESTMORLAND ROAD
Mrs Diane Elmes.
*No. 41 is on the corner of Wrens
Park*
**Visitors also welcome by
arrangement Apr to Sept for
groups up to 10.**
01394 284647
dianeelmes@talktalk.net

Three very different gardens either
close to the sea or the R Deben.
33 Ferry Road is a large irregular
shaped garden with established
trees, shrubs, herbaceous borders

and vegetables. It is well established
but is constantly evolving. Ferryfields
has mature gardens of ¹/₃ acre with
lawns, borders and informal island
beds with shrubs, perennials,
greenhouses, pond and gazebo with
views across the Deben Estuary. The
owners of 41 Westmorland Road
moved into their house five years ago,
since when they have recovered the
garden by taking down 21 leylandii
trees and various other dead trees. It
is now full of perennials and has
interesting and eclectic features.

&♿ 🐕 ❀ ☕

Clematis and
roses scramble
through trees and
pergola . . .

GROUP OPENING

32▶ NEW **OLD NEWTON
GARDENS**
Church Road, Old Newton,
Stowmarket IP14 4ED. *2¹/₂ m N of
Stowmarket. From B1113 R at
Shoulder of Mutton in Old Newton.
Parking 150yds on L at village hall.*
Light refreshments at Hill House.
Homemade teas and savouries.
Combined adm £4, chd free.
Sun 14 June (11-5).

NEW **HILL HOUSE**
Church Road, Old Newton,
Stowmarket. Sue and Phill
Bowler.
*From car park L on Church Rd
then R before going down hill.
Limited parking along Whitehall
Rd*

NEW **THE OLD VICARAGE**
Silver Street, Old Newton,
Stowmarket. Mr & Mrs R M
Brooks.
*From car park R on Church Rd,
straight across Xrds into Station
Rd then R into Silver St. The Old
Vicarage is L on corner of Elm
Tree Close*

Hill House is a thatched cottage with
1¹/₂ acre garden. Lots of flowers and
flowering shrubs, much appreciated
by bees and butterflies. Also roses, a

natural pond, mature trees, an
orchard (about 36 trees), soft fruit and
vegetable garden. Some of the
ground can be uneven, especially in
the orchard. The Old Vicarage's small
garden is for plant enthusiasts. It has
been extensively developed since
2006. There are many interesting
ornamental trees and shrubs. The
informal beds are packed with
herbaceous perennials. Clematis and
roses scramble through trees and
pergola.

❀ ☕

33▶ OLD RECTORY HOUSE
Kedington Hill, Little Cornard,
Sudbury CO10 0PD. Mrs Jane
Mann. *2¹/₂ m outside Sudbury off
B1508 Bures Rd. From Bures Rd
follow signs to Little Cornard Parish
Church. Garden is approx ¹/₂ m up
the lane on L. Parking opp.* Home-
made teas. **Adm £4, chd free.**
Sat 20 June (11-5).
Large country garden surrounded by
meadows. Approx 3 acres of garden
with some large specimen trees and
interesting recent tree planting.
Walled ornamental fruit and vegetable
garden, greenhouse, herbaceous
beds and bank. Roses, cottage
garden, parterre, three ponds with
waterside planting and woodland
walk. Some slopes and uneven
ground. Loose gravel in places.

&♿ ❀ ☕

34▶ ORCHARD HOUSE
22 Nethergate Street, Clare
CO10 8NP. Gillian & Geoffrey Bray.
*100yds from centre of Clare. On L of
Nethergate St (A1092) from direction
of Stoke-by-Clare. Limited on-street
parking. Please use Country Park car
park off Well Lane.* Home-made teas.
**Combined adm with Richmond
House, 20 Nethergate Street £6,
chd free.** Sun 31 May (2-5).
A surprisingly large garden for a town
house. Redesigned, re-landscaped
and replanted by the owners in 2008.
Still an on-going project! The long
garden is terraced and divided into
areas of different interest. A herb
garden, colour-themed mixed
borders, a tranquil pond garden and
productive kitchen garden and wild
meadow. All maintained entirely by
the owners. Sloping gravel path from
bottom to top allows viewing of most
areas without using the steps.
Garden divided into flat terraced
areas.

&♿ ❀ ☕

Abbot's Hall Walled Garden

Sign up to our eNewsletter for news and updates

Created from a blank canvas in 2011 with the idea of establishing a traditional cottage garden with a slightly quirky twist . . .

GROUP OPENING

35 ORFORD GARDENS

High Street, Orford, Woodbridge IP12 2NW. *8m from Woodbridge. In Orford, follow B1084 past Kings Head bear L. L into High Street follow Yellow Signs.* Tea at Brundish Lodge. **Combined adm £5, chd free.** Sun 7 June (2-6).

BELL HOUSE
Quay Street. Tim & Jane Allen.
Leaving Wayside, turn R down Burnt Lane, R into Daphne Rd. Gate & drive into Bell House on L next to No 34

BRUNDISH LODGE D
High Street. Mrs Elizabeth Spinney.
In Orford, follow main rd to L keep going along church railings. Garden 3rd on R. Do not go down to the Quay

WAYSIDE
Burnt Lane. Geoffrey & Anne Smeed.
From Market Sq, down Quay St approx 300yds; turn L at Xrds into Daphne Rd; approx 200yds Wayside on L

Three very different gardens with varied planting situated in the picturesque village of Orford. Bell House: a small, sheltered, cottage garden with a rill, planned to give year-round interest. approx one third newly planted following building work in 2013. No lawn so as to give maximum room for plants.

Wheelchair accessible.
Brundish Lodge: is a garden of approx one third of an acre. It was completely redesigned, reconstructed and replanted in 2005. It has beds which are a mixture of shrubs, herbaceous plants and grasses grouped around a central lawn.
Wayside: a village garden of apprpox ¼ acre, comprising a series of 'rooms' surrounding the house (not open).
A mixture of shrubs and perennials, chosen to suit the light, dry soil, and to cope with the cold easterly winds.

&♿ ☕

36 NEW OUSDEN HOUSE

Ousden, Newmarket CB8 8TN. Mr & Mrs Alastair Robinson.
Newmarket 6m, Bury St Edmunds 8m. Ousden House stands at the west end of the village next to the Church. Home-made teas. **Adm £6, chd free.** Sun 31 May (2-6).
A 12 acre garden with several changes of level and spectacular views created over the past twenty years from paddocks and woodland surrounding the site of Ousden Hall, demolished in 1955. Now focused on Ousden House, the former stable block, there are herbaceous borders, rose garden, formal courtyard, long double crinkle-crankle hedge, extensive water garden, ornamental woodland garden and lake. Featured in Suffolk Magazine, East Anglian Daily Times.

✿ ☕

37 POLSTEAD MILL

Mill Lane, Polstead, Colchester CO6 5AB. Mrs Lucinda Bartlett, 01206 265969, lucyofleisure@hotmail.com.
Between Stoke by Nayland & Polstead on the R Box. From Stoke by Nayland take rd to Polstead - Mill Lane is 1st on L & Polstead Mill is 1st house on R. Home-made teas. **Adm £5, chd £3. Visitors welcome by arrangement** June to Sept for groups of 10+.
The garden has formal and informal areas, a wild flower meadow and a large kitchen garden. The R Box runs through the garden and there is a mill pond, which gives opportunity for damp gardening, while much of the rest of the garden is arid and is planted to minimise the need for watering.

✿ ☕

GROUP OPENING

38 PRIORS HILL, ALDEBURGH

Priors Hill Road, Aldeburgh IP15 5EP. *Turn R off A1094 into Park Rd 100yds after r'about with B1122. After 400yds, turn R into Priors Hill Rd.* Tea. **Combined adm £5, chd free.** Sun 13 Sept (2-5).

HERON HOUSE
Aldeburgh. Mr & Mrs Jonathan Hale.
Last house on Priors Hill Rd on R, at the junction where it rejoins Park Rd
Visitors also welcome by arrangement Apr to Oct.
01728 452200
jonathanrhhale@aol.com

STANNY
Kimberley & Angus Robertson

Two gardens, both south-facing, situated in Priors Hill Road with enviable views over the R Alde and the sea. Both gardens are on a slope which gives the opportunity for terracing and associated planting. Heron House consists of two acres with views over coastline, river and marshes. Unusual trees, herbaceous beds, shrubs and ponds with waterfall in large rock garden, stream and bog garden. Stanny is terraced over three levels. There are many established camellias, hydrangea, grasses and mature trees, which include Holm Oaks, Scots Pine, Japanese Maples and Strawberry Trees. There is a waterfall, a large natural pond and a wild flower meadow along with some exotic planting. Please note both gardens have ponds and children must be supervised. Lovely views. Wheelchair access with difficulty in some instances.

&♿ ☕

39 PRIORS OAK

Leiston Road, Aldeburgh IP15 5QE. Mrs Trudie Willis, 01728 452580, trudie.willis@dinkum.free-online.co.uk, priorsoak butterfly garden (see google). *1m N of Aldeburgh on B1122. Garden on L opp RSPB Reserve.* Tea. **Adm £5, chd free.** Sun 28 June (2-6). Visitors also welcome by arrangement Apr to Oct.
10-acre wildlife and butterfly garden. Ornamental salad and vegetable gardens with companion planting. Herbaceous borders, ferns and

Mediterranean plants. Pond and wild flower acid grassland with a small wood. Skirting the wood are 100 buddleia in excess of 30 varieties forming a perfumed tunnel. Very tranquil and fragrant garden with grass paths and yearly interest. Rich in animal and bird life. Specialist butterfly garden, as seen in SAGA magazine, renovated railway carriages, tortoise breeding, wildlife walks. Coaches or private visits by arrangement only.

40 THE PRIORY
Stoke by Nayland, Colchester CO6 4RL. Mr & Mrs H F A Engleheart. *5m SW of Hadleigh. Entrance on B1068 to Sudbury (NW of Stoke by Nayland).* Home-made teas. **Adm £5, chd free. Sun 17 May (2-5).**
Interesting 9-acre garden with fine views over Constable countryside; lawns sloping down to small lakes and water garden; fine trees, rhododendrons and azaleas; walled garden; mixed borders and ornamental greenhouse. Wide variety of plants. Access over most of garden. Some steps.

41 REDISHAM HALL
nr Beccles NR34 8LZ. The Palgrave Brown Family. *5m S of Beccles. From A145, turn W on to Ringsfield-Bungay rd. Beccles, Halesworth or Bungay, all within 5m.* Home-made teas. **Adm £4, chd free. Sun 12 July (2-6).**
C18 Georgian house (not open). 5-acre garden set in 400 acres parkland and woods. Incl 2-acre walled kitchen garden (in full production) with peach house, vinery and glasshouses. Lawns, herbaceous borders, shrubberies, ponds and mature trees. 2015 will be our 50th annual opening for the NGS. During this time we have only been closed once due to an outbreak of foot and mouth. The garden has lots of gravel paths and there are lawned slopes. Wheelchair access is possible with assistance. Parking is on uneven parkland.

42 RICHMOND HOUSE
20 Nethergate Street, Clare CO10 8NP. Dr Catherine Horwood Barwise, 07961 838598, cbarwise@gmail.com, www.facebook.com/richmondhous egarden. *100 metres from centre of*

Clare. On L of Nethergate St (A1092) *from direction of Stoke-by-Clare. Limited on-street parking. Please use Country Park car park off Well Lane.* **Adm £3.50, chd free. Sun 31 May, Sun 30 Aug (2-5). Combined adm with Orchard House, 22 Nethergate Street, Sun 31 May, £6. Visitors also welcome by arrangement June to Sept for groups of 10+ (not July).**
Romantic walled garden with emphasis on scented plants. Pleached-tree-framed steps lead to formal 'new perennial' parterre; Med. terrace by swimming pool; informal garden area with species roses, peonies and spring bulbs; mini meadow; vegetable/cutting garden, chickens, trained fruit trees, greenhouse; tulips; dahlias; hellebore/fern path. Over 40 small-flowered clematis and 50+ roses. Featured in House & Garden and Daily Telegraph.

43 ROSEDALE
40 Colchester Road, Bures CO8 5AE. Mr & Mrs Colin Lorking, 01787 227619, rosedale40@btinternet.com. *6m SE of Sudbury. From Colchester take B1508. After 10m garden on L as you enter the village, from Sudbury B1508 after 5m garden on R.* Home-made teas. **Adm £3, chd free. Sun 17 May, Sun 26 July (12-5). Visitors also welcome by arrangement preferably evenings and weekends.**
Approx ⅓ acre plantsman's garden developed over the last 21yrs, containing many unusual plants, herbaceous borders and pond. For the May opening see a super collection of peonies and for the July opening a stunning collection of approx 60 Agapanthus in full flower. Featured in Suffolk Magazine.

44 ROSEMARY
Rectory Hill, East Bergholt CO7 6TH. Mrs N E M Finch, 01206 298241, www.rosemarybnb.co.uk. *9m NE of Colchester. From A12 take B1070 to East Bergholt, first R Hadleigh Rd. At junction with village St turn R, past Red Lion PH, PO & Church. Garden 100 yards on L.* Home-made teas. **Adm £4, chd free. Sun 7 June (2-5.30).**
This romantic garden, which appeals particularly to artists, has been developed over 35yrs. Planted to

reveal paths and vistas. Many flowering trees and shrubs, much admired 'tapestry' bed with mixed hellebores, bulbs and appropriate ground cover. 2 bog beds, and unusual trees. Planted for all seasons. Over 100 old-fashioned roses.

45 ◆ SOMERLEYTON HALL & GARDENS
Lovingland NR32 5QQ. Lord Somerleyton, 01502 734901, www.somerleyton.co.uk. *5m NW of Lowestoft. From Norwich (30mins) - on the B1074, 7m SE of Great Yarmouth (A143). Coaches should follow signs to the rear west gate entrance.* Light refreshments. Kitchen Garden Restaurant open for delicious light lunches, home-bakes cakes and cream teas. **Adm £6.45, chd £4.45. For NGS: Fri 1 May (10-5). For other opening times and information, please phone or see garden website.**
12½ acres of beautiful gardens contain a wide variety of magnificent specimen trees, shrubs, borders and plants providing colour and interest throughout the yr. Sweeping lawns and formal gardens combine with majestic statuary and original Victorian ornamentation. Highlights incl the Paxton glasshouses, pergola, walled garden and famous yew hedge maze. House and gardens remodelled in 1840s by Sir Morton Peto. House created in Anglo-Italian style with lavish architectural features and fine state rooms. All areas of the gardens are accessible, path surfaces are gravel and can be a little difficult after heavy rain. Wheelchairs available on request.

Wood Farm, Gipping

---

46 STREET FARM
North Street, Freckenham
IP28 8HY. David & Clodagh
Dugdale. *3m W of Mildenhall. From
Newmarket, follow signs to Snailwell,
& Chippenham & then onto
Freckenham.* Light refreshments.
**Adm £4, chd free. Sun 10 May
(11-5).**
Approx 1 acre of landscaped garden,
with several mature trees. The garden
includes a water cascade, pond with
island and a number of bridges.
Formal rose garden, rose pergola,
herbaceous borders and hornbeam
walk. Gravel paths with steps and
slopes.

47 NEW TRINITY HOUSE
Rectory Gardens, Beyton, Bury St.
Edmunds IP30 9UZ. Barbara &
Graham Jones. *6m E of Bury St
Edmunds. A14 exit J46 to Beyton.R
at bottom of slip rd, continue to top
of Green and turn R. Turn L at White
Horse PH, into Church Rd. After 1/2 m
park at Church on L. Follow signs for
garden.* Home-made teas in Church
Hall adjacent to Car Park. Tea, Coffee

and soft drinks with home made
cakes and biscuits. **Adm £2.50, chd
free. Mon 25 May (11-5).**
Peaceful village garden surrounded
by mature trees. Meandering paths
wind around beds of hydrangea,
ferns and not-often seen perennials,
along with several unusual trees.
Fruiting Kiwi vine and climbing
hydrangeas adorn the house walls.
Lily Pond with rill, bog bed and small
tucked away 'frog' pond.
Summerhouse, conservatory with
exotic plants, and many seating areas
offer vistas over the garden. Main
entrance to garden from car-park a
little uneven. Access also available
through Rectory Gardens, follow
signs but care needed - no path on
road.

GROUP OPENING

48 NEW TROSTON GARDENS
The Street, Troston, Bury St.
Edmunds IP31 1EW. *5m NE of Bury
St Edmunds. From the A143 turn at
the Bunbury Arms, signed Troston &*
*Gt Livermere. Follow the rd through
Gt Livermere, signed to Troston. Car
parking in The Bull car park or along
the lane.* Tea. **Combined adm £4,
chd free. Sun 26 July (2-5.30).**

NEW CHURCH COTTAGE
Graeme & Marysa Norris
Visitors also welcome by
arrangement May to Sept.
marysa.i@lmrinternational.
co.uk

NEW TROSTON LODGE
The Street. Jane Nelson &
Roger Anderson.
*From The Bull PH in the centre of
Troston. Troston Lodge is on L
200yds down the rd, almost opp
Street Farm*

A charming period cottage opp St
Mary's church and an elegant
'country ' Georgian village house in
the small village of Troston.
Church Cottage is a well established
3/4 acre garden, with new owners who
have made many changes and who
are still developing the garden. It has
raised vegetable beds, a yew allee, a
wildlife pond and newly developed
'new wave' perennial beds. Troston

Lodge is set within an acre. The walled garden has formal lawns, mixed beds and mature trees, with an adjacent productive vegetable plot, and leisure garden with swimming pool. The church with its medieval wall paintings and graffiti will also be open. Both gardens have some gravel paths and level changes with steps.

---

49 **WHITE HOUSE FARM**
Ringsfield, Beccles NR34 8JU. James & Jan Barlow, (gardener) 07780 901233, coppertops707@aol.com. *2m SW of Beccles. From Beccles take B1062 to Bungay, after 1¼ m turn L signed Ringsfield. Continue for approx 1m. Parking opp church. Garden 300yds on L.* Home-made teas. Cakes and savoury flans. **Adm £4, chd free. Sat 27 June (10.30-4.30). Visitors also welcome by arrangement Mar to Oct Tues - Friday, daytime or evening, not w/ends.**
Tranquil park-type garden approx 30 acres, bordered by farmland and with fine views. Comprising formal areas, copses, natural pond, ornamental pond, woodland walk, vegetable garden and orchard. Picnickers welcome. NB The ponds and beck are unfenced. Partial wheelchair access to the areas around the house.

---

50 **NEW** **WOOD FARM, GIPPING**
Back Lane, Gipping, Stowmarket IP14 4RN. Mr & Mrs R Shelley. *Gipping. From A14 take A1120 through Stowupland, turn L by Plain English Kitchens, follow for approx 1m take 1st turning R marked By Road & follow for exactly 1m along country lane. Wood Farm is on L.* Home-made teas. **Adm £3.50, chd free. Sat 30 May (2-6).**
Wood Farm is an old Suffolk homestead of 11 acres with barns, ponds, orchard and a hay meadow bordered with established hedging, trees and woodland. The 8 acres of hay meadow were sown in 1999 and paths are mown to walk through it. The flower and vegetable gardens were created from a blank canvas in 2011 with the idea of establishing a traditional cottage garden with a slightly quirky twist. Partial wheelchair access.

---

51 **WOOD FARM, SIBTON**
Halesworth Road, Sibton, Saxmundham IP17 2JL. Andrew & Amelia Singleton. *4m S of Halesworth. Turn off A12 at Yoxford onto A1120. Turn R after Sibton Nursery towards Halesworth. Take the 2nd drive on R after the White Horse PH.* Home-made teas. **Adm £4, chd free. Sun 5 July (2-6).**
Country garden surrounding old farmhouse, divided into colour themed areas, incl white garden, hot courtyard and blue and yellow border. Large (unfenced) ponds, vegetable garden, wild white flowering shrub area and mown walks. Garden designer owner. Some gravel paths which are not suitable for wheelchairs but which can be easily avoided by using alternative routes.

---

52 **WOODWARDS**
Blacksmiths Lane, Coddenham, Ipswich IP6 9TX. Marion & Richard Kenward, 01449 760639, richardwoodwards@btinternet.com . *7m N of Ipswich. From A14 turn onto A140, after ¼ m take B1078 towards Wickham Market, Coddenham is on route. Coaches please use postcode IP6 9PS. Ample parking for coaches.* Home-made teas. **Adm £2.50, chd free. Sun 5 Apr, Sun 24 May, Sat 6 June, Tue 7, Sun 26 July, Tue 11, Sun 30 Aug (10.30-5.30). Visitors also welcome by arrangement Mar to Aug groups 2-100+.**
Award winning S-facing gently sloping garden of 1½ acres, overlooking the rolling Suffolk countryside. Designed and maintained by owners for yr-round colour and interest, lots of island beds, well stocked with 1000s of bulbs, shrubs and perennials, vegetable plot, display of 100+ hanging baskets for spring and summer. Well kept lawns, with large mature trees. More than 25000 bulbs have been planted over the last 3yrs for our spring display. Featured in Garden News, East Anglian Daily Times Weekend supplement, Suffolk Magazine and the W.I. News.

---

53 ◆ **WOOTTENS**
Blackheath Road, Wenhaston IP19 9HD. Mrs E Loftus, 01502 478258, info@woottensplants.co.uk, www.woottensplants.co.uk. *18m S of Lowestoft. On A12 & B1123, follow signs to Wenhaston.* Light refreshments in Summer House. **Adm by donation. For NGS: Every Tue, Wed, Thur, Fri, Sat & Sun 1 Apr to 30 Oct (10-4). For other opening times and information, please phone or see garden website.**
Woottens Display Garden was redesigned in 2003 and consists of 27 raised display areas overflowing with hardy perennials to admire and inspire. The garden is inhabited with many rare and unusual cultivars and some of our traditional favourites. Spring Fair Early May. Displays of auriculas, irises, pelargoniums, hemerocallis through the year. Courses and Open Days run throughout the year.

---

54 ◆ **WYKEN HALL**
Stanton IP31 2DW. Sir Kenneth & Lady Carlisle, 01359 250287, www.wykenvineyards.co.uk. *9m NE of Bury St Edmunds. Along A143. Follow signs to Wyken Vineyards on A143 between Ixworth & Stanton.* Wine and teas. **Adm £4, chd free. For NGS: Sat 6, Sun 7 June (10-6). For other opening times and information, please phone or see garden website.**
4-acre garden much developed recently; knot and herb garden; old-fashioned rose garden, wild garden, nuttery, pond, gazebo and maze; herbaceous borders and old orchard. Woodland walk, vineyard. Restaurant and shop. Vineyard. Farmers' Market on Saturdays 9-1.

Share your day out on Facebook and Twitter

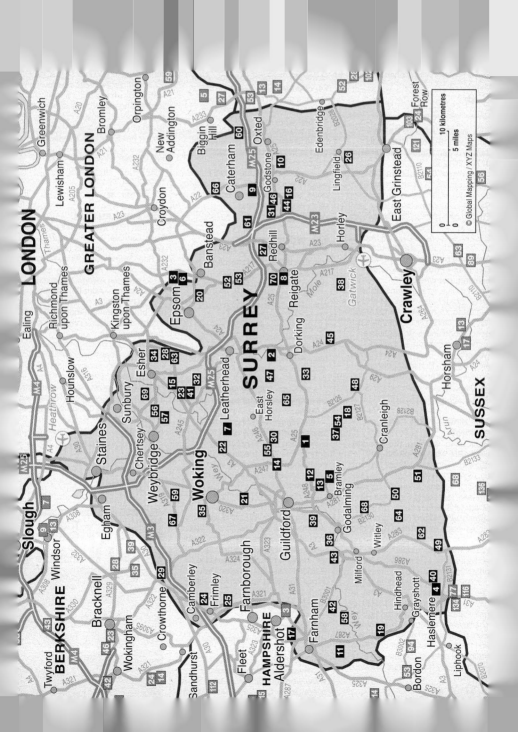

Surrey

As a designated Area of Outstanding Natural Beauty, it's no surprise that Surrey has a wealth of gardens on offer.

With its historic market towns, lush meadows and scenic rivers, Surrey provides the ideal escape from the bustle of nearby London.

Set against the rolling chalk uplands of the unspoilt North Downs, the county prides itself on extensive country estates with historic houses and ancient manors. Visitors are inspired by the breathtaking panorama from Polesden Lacey, lakeside views at The Old Croft or timeless terraces at Albury Park.

Surrey is the heartland of the NGS at Hatchlands Park and the RHS at Wisley, both promoting a precious interest in horticulture. Surrey celebrates a landscape coaxed into wonderful vistas by great gardeners such as John Evelyn, Capability Brown and Gertrude Jekyll.

With many eclectic gardens to visit, there's certainly plenty to treasure in Surrey.

Below: Bardsey

Surrey Volunteers

County Organiser
Maggie Boyd
01428 652283
maggie.boyd@live.co.uk

County Treasurer
David Boyd
01428 652283
dhboyd@live.co.uk

Publicity
Annie Keighley
01252 838660
annie.keighley12@btinternet.com

Booklet Coordinator
Keith Lewis
01737 210707
kandelewis@ntlworld.com

**Booklet Production
& Group Tours**
David Boyd
(as above)

Assistant County Organisers
David Boyd
(as above)

Margaret Arnott
01372 842459
m.a.arnott@btinternet.com

Anne Barnes
01306 730196
spurfold@btinternet.com

Di Grose
01883 742983
di.grose@godstone.net

Annie Keighley
(as above)

Keith Lewis
(as above)

Caroline Shuldham
01932 596960
cshuldham@yahoo.co.uk

Shirley Stoneley
01737 244235
woodburycottage@gmail.com

Jean Thompson
01483 425633
norney.wood@btinternet.com

Since our foundation we have donated more than £42.5 million to charity

Opening Dates

All entries subject to change.
For latest information check www.ngs.org.uk

February

Sunday 15
27 Gatton Park

March

Sunday 22
1 Albury Park
14 Clandon Park

Sunday 29
9 The Chalet
64 Vann

Monday 30
64 Vann

Tuesday 31
64 Vann

April

Wednesday 1
64 Vann

Thursday 2
64 Vann

Friday 3
64 Vann

Saturday 4
64 Vann

Sunday 5
8 Caxton House
9 The Chalet

Monday 6
59 Timber Hill

Sunday 12
18 Coverwood Lakes

Sunday 19
18 Coverwood Lakes
52 41 Shelvers Way

Sunday 26
18 Coverwood Lakes
59 Timber Hill

Thursday 30
22 Dunsborough Park

May

10 **Chauffer's Flat**
(daily from May 18 to May 24)
64 **Vann** (daily from May 4 to May 10)

Sunday 3
11 Chestnut Cottage
19 Crosswater Farm
51 NEW Saffron Gate

Monday 4
18 Coverwood Lakes
19 Crosswater Farm
51 NEW Saffron Gate
53 Shieling
65 Walton Poor House

Saturday 9
26 The Garth Pleasure Grounds
29 Hall Grove School

Sunday 10
15 Claremont Landscape Garden
26 The Garth Pleasure Grounds
56 NEW Stuartfield
67 Westways Farm

Saturday 16
17 56 Copse Avenue
54 Spurfold

Sunday 17
12 Chilworth Manor
17 56 Copse Avenue
18 Coverwood Lakes
24 26 The Fairway
30 Hatchlands Park
37 Knowle Grange
54 Spurfold
60 Titsey Place Gardens
62 NEW Upper Sydenhurst

Friday 22
49 Ramster

Saturday 23
31 The Hawthorns

Sunday 24
3 NEW 15 The Avenue
11 Chestnut Cottage
18 Coverwood Lakes
22 Dunsborough Park
45 The Old Croft
66 57 Westhall Road

Monday 25
3 NEW 15 The Avenue
45 The Old Croft
66 57 Westhall Road

Sunday 31
7 Bridge End Cottage
20 Culverkeys
24 26 The Fairway

100 hosta's hug the house . . .

25 Frimley Green Gardens

June

10 **Chauffeur's Flat**
(daily from June 22 to June 28)
64 **Vann** (daily from June 7 to June 13)

Wednesday 3
25 Frimley Green Gardens

Festival Weekend

Saturday 6
25 Frimley Green Gardens

Sunday 7
39 Loseley Park
51 NEW Saffron Gate
68 Winkworth Arboretum

Friday 12
53 Shieling (Evening)

Sunday 14
53 Shieling
60 Titsey Place Gardens
61 Tollsworth Manor

Friday 19
2 Ashleigh Grange (Evening)

Saturday 20
38 Little Mynthurst Farm
42 Monksfield (Evening)

Sunday 21
2 Ashleigh Grange
13 Chinthurst Lodge
35 Horsell Group Gardens
38 Little Mynthurst Farm
40 The Manor House
51 NEW Saffron Gate

Wednesday 24
2 Ashleigh Grange
13 Chinthurst Lodge

Friday 26
47 Polesden Lacey

Saturday 27
4 Bardsey
57 Sunrise of Weybridge
69 NEW 51 Wolsey Drive

Sunday 28
4 Bardsey
23 Fairmile Lea
41 Moleshill House
46 The Old Rectory

July

Saturday 4
48 Pratsham Grange

Sunday 5
34 NEW 45 Hillcrest Gardens
36 NEW 16 Hurtmore

Chase
42 Monksfield
48 Pratsham Grange
63 NEW 72 Vale Road

Saturday 11
70 Woodbury Cottage

Sunday 12
20 Culverkeys
60 Titsey Place Gardens
70 Woodbury Cottage

Saturday 18
4 Bardsey

Sunday 19
4 Bardsey
52 41 Shelvers Way
55 Stuart Cottage

Sunday 26
32 Heathside

August

Saturday 8
6 Bethany
45 The Old Croft

Sunday 9
5 NEW Barnett Hill
6 Bethany
45 The Old Croft

Saturday 15
48 Pratsham Grange

Sunday 16
48 Pratsham Grange
60 Titsey Place Gardens

Sunday 30
55 Stuart Cottage

September

Saturday 5
16 Coldharbour House
70 Woodbury Cottage

Sunday 6
16 Coldharbour House
70 Woodbury Cottage

Wednesday 9
70 Woodbury Cottage

Saturday 12
22 Dunsborough Park

Sunday 13
33 Hill Farm
37 Knowle Grange

October

Sunday 4
1 Albury Park
68 Winkworth Arboretum

Sunday 11
15 Claremont Landscape Garden

Sunday 18
18 Coverwood Lakes

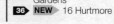

Over 400 Volunteers help run the NGS – why not become one too?

The Gardens

1 ALBURY PARK

Albury GU5 9BH. Trustees of Albury Estate. *5m SE of Guildford. From A25 take A248 towards Albury for ¼ m, then up New Rd, entrance to Albury Park immed on L.* Home-made teas. **Adm £4, chd free. Sun 22 Mar, Sun 4 Oct (2-5).**
14 acre pleasure grounds laid out in 1670s by John Evelyn for Henry Howard, later 6th Duke of Norfolk. ¼ m terraces, fine collection of trees, lake and river. Gravel path and slight slope.

2 ASHLEIGH GRANGE

Off Chapel Lane, Westhumble RH5 6AY. Clive & Angela Gilchrist, 01306 884613, ar.gilchrist@btinternet.com. *2m N of Dorking. From A24 at Boxhill/Burford Bridge follow signs to Westhumble. Through village & L up drive by ruined chapel (1m from A24).* Home-made teas. **Adm £4, chd free. Share to Barnardo's. Evening Opening £5.50, chd free, wine, Fri 19 June (6-8). Sun 21, Wed 24 June (2-5.30). Visitors also welcome by arrangement May to July.**
Plant lover's chalk garden on 3½ acre sloping site in charming rural setting with delightful views. Many areas of interest incl rockery and water feature, raised ericaceous bed, prairie style bank, foliage plants, woodland walk, fernery and folly. Large mixed herbaceous and shrub borders planted for dry alkaline soil and widespread interest.

3 NEW 15 THE AVENUE

Cheam, Sutton SM2 7QA. Mr & Mrs N Brandon. *1m SW of Sutton. By car exit A217 onto Northey Av, 2nd R into The Avenue. By train 10 mins walk from Cheam station. By bus use 470.* Home-made teas. **Adm £4, chd free. Sun 24, Mon 25 May (1-5).**
A contemporary garden designed by RHS Chelsea Gold Medal Winner. 4 levels with steps and gravel paths. Divided into rooms by beech hedging and columns; formal entertaining area, lawn and wild flower meadow. Over 100 hostas hug the house. Silver birch, cloud pruned box, ferns, grasses, tall bearded irises, contemporary sculptures. Featured on ITVs Alan Titchmarsh Show. Partial wheelchair access, terraced with steps; sloping path provides view of whole garden but not all accessible.

41 Shelvers Way

Take your Group to an NGS garden

4 ► BARDSEY
11 Derby Road, Haslemere
GU27 1BS. Maggie & David Boyd,
01428 652283,
maggie.boyd@live.co.uk,
www.bardseygarden.co.uk. ¼ m N
of Haslemere station. Turn off B2131
(which links A287 to A286 through
town) 400yds W of station into
Weydown Rd, 3rd R into Derby Rd,
garden 400yds on R. Home-made
teas. Adm £4.50, chd free. Sat 27,
Sun 28 June, Sat 18, Sun 19 July
(11-5). Visitors also welcome by
arrangement June to July for
groups 10+.
Unexpected 2 acre garden in the
heart of Haslemere. Several distinct
areas containing scent, colour, texture
and movement. Stunning pictorial
meadow within a parterre. Prairie
planted border provides a modern
twist. Large productive fruit and
vegetable garden. Natural ponds and
bog gardens. Several unusual
sculptures. Ducks and chickens
supply the eggs for cakes. Classic
MGs on parade. Featured in both
Period Homes & Interiors and Surrey
Life. First third of garden level, other
two thirds sloping.

5 ► NEW ► BARNETT HILL
Blackheath Lane, Wonersh,
Guildford GU5 0RF. The Sundial
Group, 01483 893361,
www.sundialgroup.com. Between
Guildford & Cranleigh. From Guildford
take A281 Shalford. At r'about 1st
exit A248 Dorking. After 1m, just past
30mph & Wonersh signs go L into
Blackheath Ln. Cont up narrow lane,
turn R at top of hill. Cream teas and
Sunday lunches served in the house.
Please book in advance. Adm £6,

chd free. Sun 9 Aug (11-5.30).
This 26 acre hill top estate is lavishly
planted to impress visitors with all
kinds of tastes. The sheltered walls
adorned with magnificent specimens,
formal bedding in all its summer finery
and herbaceous borders to die for are
only part of the experience. Exotic
beds with majestic bananas and
sumptuous brugmansias edge lawns
leading to paths that wind down the
hill to cool woodland walks. Good
wheelchair access but some steps
and steep pathways in places off
main lawns.

6 ► BETHANY
87 Sandy Lane, South Cheam
SM2 7EP. Brian & Pam West & Mrs
D West. 2m W of Sutton. Approx 1m
S of Cheam village, or from A217 turn
into Northey Ave. At small r'about L
into Sandy Lane, then approx 100yds
on L. Home-made teas. Adm £4,
chd free. Sat 8, Sun 9 Aug (1-5.30).
⅓ acre plantsman's garden with a
subtropical feel where palm trees,
tree ferns, banana trees, agave and
bamboo surround the wide lawn.
Vibrant coloured dahlias and a large
collection of cannas make this an
exciting August garden. Behind pretty
summerhouse is vegetable garden
and greenhouses.

7 ► BRIDGE END COTTAGE
Ockham Lane, Ockham GU23 6NR.
Clare & Peter Bevan, 01483
479963, c.fowler@ucl.ac.uk. Nr
RHS Gardens, Wisley. At Wisley
r'about turn L onto B2039 to
Ockham/Horsley. After ½ m turn L
into Ockham Lane. House ½ m on R.
From Cobham go to Blackswan Xrds.
Home-made teas. Adm £4, chd free.
Sun 31 May (11.30-4.30). Visitors
also welcome by arrangement May
to July.
A 2 acre country garden with different
areas of interest, incl perennial
borders, mature trees, pond and
streams, small herb parterre, fruit
trees and a vegetable patch. An
adjacent 2 acre field was sown with
perennial wild flower seed in May
2013, and flowered well last year.
There is a new project underway to
plant up a long stream walk
according to Culpeper's - The
English Physitian. Large perennial wild
flower meadow. Partial wheelchair
access.

8 ► CAXTON HOUSE
67 West Street, Reigate RH2 9DA.
Bob Bushby, 01737 243158,
Bob.bushby@sky.com. On A25
towards Dorking, approx ¼ m W of
Reigate on L. Parking on rd or past
Black Horse PH on Flanchford rd.
Home-made teas. Adm £5, chd free.
Sun 5 Apr (2-5). Visitors also
welcome by arrangement Apr to
Sept for groups 10+.
Lovely large spring garden with
Arboretum, 2 well stocked ponds,
large collection of hellebores and
spring flowers. Pots planted with
colourful displays. Interesting plants in
conservatory. Small Gothic folly built
by owner. Herbaceous borders with
grasses, perennials, spring bulbs and
parterre. New bed with wild daffodils
and wild flower meadow in summer.
Antique dog cart completes the
picture.

9 ► THE CHALET
Tupwood Lane, Caterham
CR3 6ET. Miss Lesley Manning &
Mr David Gold. ½ m N of M25 J6.
Exit J6 off M25 onto A22 to N. After
½ m take sharp 1st L, or follow signs
from Caterham. Ample free parking.
Disabled access via top gate. Home-
made teas. Adm £5, chd free. Share
to St Catherine's Hospice. Sun 29
Mar, Sun 5 Apr (11-4.30).
55 acres. Carpets of tens of
thousands of daffodils; lakes,
ornamental ponds, koi pond and
waterfall. Ancient woodlands,
grasslands and formal garden. Large
planted terraces. Beautiful Victorian
mansion (not open). Woodland and
garden trail. On view, a limited edition
Blue Train Bentley, and a Silver
Phantom Rolls Royce. Partial
wheelchair access, some steep
slopes. 3 large unfenced ponds.

10 ► CHAUFFEUR'S FLAT
Tandridge Lane, Tandridge
RH8 9NJ. Mr & Mrs Richins. 2m E
of Godstone. 2m W of Oxted. Turn off
A25 for Tandridge. Take drive on L
past church. Follow arrows to circular
courtyard. Home-made teas (Sat and
Sun only). Adm £4, chd free. Share
to Sutton & Croydon MS Therapy
Centre. Daily Mon 18 May to Sun
24 May and Mon 22 June to Sun
28 June (10-5).
Enter a 1 acre tapestry of magical
secret gardens with magnificent
views. Touching the senses, all sure
footed visitors may explore the many

surprises on this constantly evolving exuberant escape from reality. Imaginative use of recycled materials creates an inspired variety of ideas, while wild and specimen plants reveal an ecological haven.

11 CHESTNUT COTTAGE
15 Jubilee Lane, Boundstone, Farnham GU10 4SZ. Mr & Mrs David Wingent. *2¹/₂ m SW of Farnham. At A31 r'about take A325 - Petersfield, ¹/₂ m bear L. At r'about into School Hill, ¹/₂ m over staggered X'rds into Sandrock Hill Rd, 4th turn R after PH.* Home-made teas. **Adm £3.50, chd free. Sun 3, Sun 24 May (2-5.30).**
¹/₂ acre garden created by owners on different levels. Rhododendrons, azaleas, acers and conifers. Long pergola with wisteria and roses, attractive gazebo copied from the original at NT Hunting Lodge in Odiham. Peaceful setting. Plant expert John Negus will be in attendance.

12 CHILWORTH MANOR
Halfpenny Lane, Chilworth, Guildford GU4 8NN. Mia & Graham Wrigley. *3¹/₂ m SE of Guildford. From centre of Chilworth village turn into Blacksmith Lane. 1st drive on R on Halfpenny Lane.* Home-made teas. **Adm £6, chd free. Sun 17 May (11-5).**
Extensive grounds of lawns and mature trees around C17/C18 manor on C11 monastic site. Substantial C18 terraced walled garden laid out by Sarah, Duchess of Marlborough, with herbaceous borders, topiary and fruit trees. Original stewponds integrated with new Japanese themed garden and woodland garden and walk. Paddock home to alpacas. Ongoing restoration project aims to create a contemporary and practical garden sensitive to its historic context. Garden and tree walks at 12 noon, 1.30 pm, 2.30pm and 4pm.

13 CHINTHURST LODGE
Wonersh Common, Wonersh, Guildford GU5 0PR. Mr & Mrs M R Goodridge, 01483 535108, michaelgoodridge@ymail.com. *4m S of Guildford. From A281 at Shalford turn E onto B2128 towards Wonersh. Just after Waverley sign, before village, garden on R.* Home-made teas. **Adm £5, chd free. Sun 21,**

Wed 24 June (11-5.30). Visitors also welcome by arrangement May to July.
1 acre yr-round enthusiast's atmospheric garden, divided into rooms. Herbaceous borders, white garden, specimen trees and shrubs, gravel garden with water feature, small kitchen garden, fruit cage, 2 wells, ornamental ponds, herb parterre and millennium parterre garden. Some gravel paths, which can be avoided.

14 ♦ CLANDON PARK
West Clandon, Guildford GU4 7RQ. National Trust, 01483 222482, www.nationaltrust.org.uk. *3m E of Guildford on A247. From A3 follow signs to Ripley to join A247 via B2215.* Light refreshments. **Adm £5, chd £2.50. For NGS: Sun 22 Mar (10.30-5). For other opening times and information, please phone or see garden website.**
Garden around the house laid out informally, apart from parterre beneath South front. To the South a mid C18 grotto. Principal front faces parkland, laid out in the style of Capability Brown around 1770. Created in 1901, Dutch garden modelled on the No.1 pond garden at Hampton Court Palace. Large bulb and daffodil field looks stunning in spring.

15 ♦ CLAREMONT LANDSCAPE GARDEN
Portsmouth Road, Esher KT10 9JG. National Trust, 01372 467806, www.nationaltrust.org.uk. *1m SW of Esher. On E side of A307 (no access from A3 bypass).* Light refreshments. **Adm £8, chd £4. For NGS: Sun 10 May, Sun 11 Oct (10-6). For other opening times and information, please phone or see garden website.**
One of the earliest surviving English landscape gardens, begun by Vanbrugh and Bridgeman before 1720 and extended and naturalised by Kent and Capability Brown. Lake, island with pavilion; grotto and turf amphitheatre; viewpoints and avenues. Free guided walk at 2pm both NGS days with member of the gardening team. Cafe serving homemade cakes, light lunches and afternoon teas. Access maps available with recommended route.

16 COLDHARBOUR HOUSE
Coldharbour Lane, Bletchingley, Redhill RH1 4NA. Mr Tony Elias, 01883 742685. *Coldharbour Lane off Rabies Heath Rd ¹/₂ m from A25 at Bletchingley and 0.9m from Tilburstow Hill Rd. Park in field & walk down to house.* Tea. **Adm £4.50, chd free. Sat 5, Sun 6 Sept (1-5). Visitors also welcome by arrangement Apr to Oct for groups 10+.**
This 1¹/₂ acre garden offers breathtaking views to the South Downs. Originally planted in the 1920's, it has since been adapted and enhanced. Several mature trees and shrubs incl a copper beech, a Canadian maple, magnolias, azaleas, rhododendrons, camellias, wisterias, fuschias, hibiscus, potentillas, mahonias, a fig tree and a walnut tree.

Romantic somewhat secret garden on the edge of Epsom Downs . . .

17 56 COPSE AVENUE
Farnham GU9 9EA. Lyn & Jimmy James, 01252 323473, lynandjimmy@virginmedia.com. *Approx 1¹/₂ m N of Farnham. At Shepherd & Flock r'about take A325 to Farnborough. At 2nd r'about take Weybourne exit. At 2nd turn L. Take 2nd R at end of rd L.* Home-made teas. **Adm £4, chd free. Sat 16, Sun 17 May (12-5). Visitors also welcome by arrangement May to June for groups 10+.**
A fascinating and unusual 1 acre garden in a residential area. The garden was originally landscaped in the late 1960s following the plans of a Chelsea Flower Show garden, but was subsequently allowed to become very overgrown. The present owners have restored many of the original features and are adding innovative areas of planting and interest. Accessible for wheelchairs but some steep steps and uneven paths.

Monksfield

18 COVERWOOD LAKES

Peaslake Road, Ewhurst GU6 7NT. The Metson Family, 01306 731101, coverwoodfarm@coverwoodlakes. co.uk, www.coverwoodlakes.co.uk. *7m SW of Dorking. From A25 follow signs for Peaslake; garden ½ m beyond Peaslake on Ewhurst rd.* Light refreshments incl home produced Hereford burgers, bacon rolls, etc. **Adm £5, chd free. Sun 12, Sun 19, Sun 26 Apr, Mon 4, Sun 17, Sun 24 May (11-5); Sun 18 Oct (11-4.30).** 14 acre landscaped garden in stunning position high in the Surrey Hills with 4 lakes and bog garden. Extensive rhododendrons, azaleas and fine trees. 3½ acre lakeside arboretum. Marked trail through the 180 acre working farm with Hereford cows and calves, sheep and horses, extensive views of the surrounding hills.

  🚽 🚐 🛏 ☕

19 ◆ CROSSWATER FARM

Crosswater Lane, Churt, Farnham GU10 2JN. The Millais family, 01252 792698, www.rhododendrons.co.uk. *6m S of Farnham, 6m NW of Haslemere. From A287 turn E into Jumps Rd ½ m N of Churt village centre. After*

¼ m turn acute L into Crosswater Lane & follow signs for Millais Nurseries. Home-made teas. **Adm £4, chd free. For NGS: Sun 3, Mon 4 May (10-5). For other opening times and information, please phone or see garden website.** Idyllic 6 acre woodland garden. Plantsman's collection of rhododendrons and azaleas, incl rare species collected in the Himalayas, hybrids raised by the owners. Everything from alpine dwarfs to architectural large leaved trees. Ponds, stream and companion plantings incl Sorbus, Magnolias and Japanese Acers. Trial gardens of new varieties. Woodland garden and specialist plant centre. Feature on organic compost tea sprays. Featured in Gardening Which. Grass paths may be difficult for wheelchairs after rain.

  🚽 ✿ 🚐 ☕

20 CULVERKEYS

20A Longdown Lane North, Ewell, Epsom KT17 3JQ. Anne Salt, 020 8393 6861. *1m E of Epsom, 1m S of Ewell Village. Leave Ewell bypass (A24) by Reigate Rd (A240) to pass Nescot on L. Turn R in ¼ m.* Tea. **Adm £3, chd free. Sun 31 May, Sun**

12 July (2-5). Visitors also welcome by arrangement May to Sept. Groups min 10, max 20.
A romantic somewhat secret garden on the edge of Epsom Downs. Meandering paths pass borders planted to capacity with interesting and unusual plants. Arches smothered in climbers reveal secluded corners and running water soothes the spirit. Designed for yr-round interest, shrubs and trees play host to many clematis.

  ☕

21 DRYBRIDGE HOUSE

Pyle Hill, Woking GU22 0SR. Liz & Richard Summers, 01483 763264, lizsummers4@gmail.com. *From Guildford, A3, take A320 to Woking. After 2.6m pass PYO & take next R turn. Turn immed R into Pyle Hill.* Home-made teas. **Adm £5, chd free. Visitors welcome by arrangement Aug to Sept for groups 10+.** Plantsman's garden with an extensive and colourful range of late summer perennials and grasses. 1½ acres incl formal areas, vegetable garden and courtyard. Featured in Period Homes & Interiors.

  🚽 🐕 ☕

Every garden visit makes a difference

© Daniel Pullen

22 ◆ DUNSBOROUGH PARK

Ripley GU23 6AL. Baron &
Baroness Sweerts de Landas
Wyborgh, 01483 225366,
www.dunsboroughpark.com. *6m
NE of Guildford. Entrance across
Ripley Green via The Milkway past
cricket green on R & playground on L,
round corner to double brown
wooden gates.* Home-made teas.
**Adm £6, chd free. For NGS:Thur 30
Apr (1-7); Sun 24 May, Sat 12 Sept
(1-5). For other opening times and
information (incl private tours)
please phone or see garden
website.**
Extensive walled gardens of 6 acres
redesigned by Penelope Hobhouse
and Rupert Golby, structured with
box hedging creating different garden
rooms. Exciting herbaceous borders
with beautiful standard wisterias. 70ft
ginkgo hedge and ancient mulberry
tree. Atmospheric water garden with
life size gunnera/rhododendrons.
Festival of Tulips 20,000 new
bulbs/15,000 1yr old bulbs planted in
wild meadow, Sat 18, Sat 25 and
Sun 26 Apr (not for NGS), 30 Apr for
NGS (1-7). Roses/peonies in June
(Sat 13 June, not for NGS) and
dahlias in September.

♿ ❀ 🚐 ☕

23 FAIRMILE LEA

Portsmouth Road, Cobham
KT11 1BG. Steven Kay. *2m NE of
Cobham. On Cobham to Esher rd.
Access by lane adjacent to Moleshill
House & car park for Fairmile
Common woods.* Home-made teas.
**Combined adm £6, chd free. Sun
28 June (2-5). Combined with
Moleshill House.**
Large Victorian sunken garden with
pond. An old acacia tree stands in
the midst of the lawn. Interesting
planting on a large mound
camouflages an old underground air
raid shelter. Caged vegetable garden.
Formality adjacent to wilderness.

🎫 ☕

24 26 THE FAIRWAY

Camberley GU15 1EF. Jacky
Sheppard. *1½ m from M3 J4. Follow
signs to Frimley Pk Hosp. At r'about
take 3rd exit B311 Chobham Rd.
Cont on B311 L at 2nd r'about. 1st L
into Fairway.* Home-made teas. **Adm
£3.50, chd free. Sun 17, Sun 31
May (11-4).**
Spring and summer is the ideal time
to see the azaleas, rhododendrons
and heathers that surround the
house. The hundreds of bulbs,

primroses and winter anemones give
ground cover beneath the shrubs.
Climbers and a variety of plants
continue a theme to make way for
summer flowering.

☕

Stunning colour
combinations
excite . . .

GROUP OPENING

25 FRIMLEY GREEN GARDENS

Frimley Green GU16 6HE. *3m S of
Camberley. M3 J4 follow A325 to
Frimley Centre, towards Frimley
Green for 1m.Turn R by the green, R
into The Hatches for on street
parking. Some parking also opp
Elmcroft at Recreation Ground on
B3411.Tickets & map available at all
gardens.* Home-made teas at
Wildwood. **Combined adm £5, chd
free. Sun 31 May, Wed 3, Sat 6
June (2-5).**

ELMCROFT
Mrs Geraldine Huggon

OAKLEIGH
Mrs Angela O'Connell

TABOR
Susan Filbin

WILDWOOD
Annie Keighley

Visit four very different gardens in the
friendly village of Frimley Green. Be
inspired by designer chic and how to
get the best from a small space at
Tabor. Here you can admire a riot of
hostas, colourful pots and an unusual
water feature. Experience a secret
cottage garden at Wildwood with its
tumbling roses, pond and ornamental
potager. At Elmcroft, where no space
is wasted, a huge *Buddleia alternifolia*
forms a stunning backdrop for self
sown varieties of cottage classics,
incl hardy geraniums and aquilegias.
Look for surprises at winding
Oakleigh, with a variety of plants
creating a bright palette of colour.
Some old favourites and unusual
plants for sale at Elmcroft. Featured in
Surrey Life.

❀ ☕

26 THE GARTH PLEASURE GROUNDS

Newchapel Road, Lingfield
RH7 6BJ. Mr Sherlock & Mrs
Stanley, ab_post@yahoo.com,
www.oldworkhouse.webs.com.
*From A22 take B2028 by Mormon
Temple to Lingfield. The Garth is on L
after 1½ m, opp Barge Tiles. Parking:
Barge Tiles or Gunpit Rd.* Home-
made teas. **Adm £5, chd free. Sat 9,
Sun 10 May (2-5.30). Visitors also
welcome by arrangement May to
Aug. Please email 2 weeks in
advance.**
Mature 9 acre Pleasure Grounds
created by Walter Godfrey in 1919
present an idyllic setting surrounding
the former parish workhouse
refurbished in Edwardian style. The
formal gardens, enchanting nuttery, a
spinney with many mature trees and
a pond attract wildlife. Wonderful
bluebells in spring. The woodland
gardens and beautiful borders full of
colour and fragrance for yr-round
pleasure. Many areas of interest incl
pond, woodland garden, formal
gardens, spinney with large specimen
plants incl 500yr old oak and many
architectural features designed by
Walter H Godfrey. Partial wheelchair
access in woodland, Iris and Secret
gardens.

♿ 🎫 ❀ 🚐 ☕

27 ◆ GATTON PARK

Rocky Lane, Merstham RH2 0TW.
Royal Alexandra & Albert School,
01737 649068,
www.gattonpark.com. *3m NE of
Reigate. 5 mins from M25 J8 (A217)
or from top of Reigate Hill, over M25
then follow sign to Merstham.
Entrance is off Rocky Lane accessible
from Gatton Bottom or A23
Merstham.* Light refreshments. **Adm
£4, chd free. For NGS: Sun 15 Feb
(11-4), Sun 14 Feb 2016. For other
opening times and information,
please phone or see garden
website.**
Gatton Park is the core 250 acres of
the estate originally laid out by
Capability Brown. Gatton also boasts
a Japanese garden, rock and water
garden and Victorian parterre nestled
within the sweeping parkland.
Stunning displays of snowdrops and
aconites in February and March. Free
activities for children. Partial
wheelchair access.

♿ 🎫 ❀ ☕

Find a garden near you – download our free iOS app

28 **21 GLENAVON CLOSE**
Claygate, Esher KT10 0HP. Selina &
Simon Botham, 01372 210570,
selina@designsforallseasons.co.uk,
www.designsforallseasons.co.uk.
*2m SE of Esher. from A3 S exit Esher,
R at T-lights. Cont straight through
Claygate village bear R at two mini
r'bouts, Church and rec. Turn L at
bollards into Causeway. At end
straight over to Glenavon Close.* Tea.
Visitors welcome by arrangement
Mar to Oct with guided tours by
award winning garden designer.
A relaxing 66ft x 92ft secluded garden
created by garden designer Selina
Botham and her husband Simon.
Swathes of grasses and perennials
surround a spacious lawn. Curving
paths invite exploration. New in 2013
curved seating area and secret fruit
garden. A magnificent willow is the
setting for a pond, deck and garden
office. Sculpted silverbirch path. New
sculpted bug hotels and bird houses.
Guided tours by RHS Gold medal
winning designer, exhibit of private
garden design work and RHS show
garden concepts. Featured in The
Guardian Magazine and on BBC
Gardener's World.

The garden
has a wealth of
different natural
habitats to
encourage
wildlife . . .

29 **HALL GROVE SCHOOL**
London Road (A30), Bagshot
GU19 5HZ. Mr & Mrs A R Graham.
*6m SW of Egham. M3 J3, follow
A322 1m until sign for Sunningdale
A30, 1m E of Bagshot, opp Long
Acres garden centre, entrance at
footbridge. Ample car park.* Home-
made teas. Adm £5, chd free.
Sat 9 May (2-5).
Formerly small Georgian country
estate, now co-educational
preparatory school. Grade II listed
house (not open). Mature parkland

with specimen trees. Historical
features incl ice house, old walled
garden, heated peach wall. New lake,
woodland walks, rhododendrons and
azaleas. Live music at 3pm.

30 ◆ **HATCHLANDS PARK**
East Clandon, Guildford GU4 7RT.
National Trust, 01483 222482,
www.nationaltrust.org.uk. *4m E of
Guildford. Follow brown signs to
Hatchlands Park (NT).* Light
refreshments. Adm £4.20, chd £2.
For NGS: Sun 17 May (10.30-6).
For other opening times and
information, please phone or see
garden website.
Garden and park designed by Repton
in 1800. Follow one of the park walks
to the stunning bluebell wood in
spring (2.5km/1.7m round walk over
rough and sometimes muddy
ground). South of the house, a small
parterre designed by Gertrude Jekyll
in 1913 to flower in early June. In
autumn enjoy the changing colours
on the long walk. Partial wheelchair
access to parkland, rough, undulating
terrain, grass and gravel paths, dirt
tracks, cobbled courtyard. Tramper
booking essential.

31 **THE HAWTHORNS**
Pendell Road, Bletchingley
RH1 4QJ. The Hawthorns School.
*1m N of Bletchingley. Turn off A25 by
Red Lion in Bletchingley along Little
Common Lane. School over Xrds at
bottom of hill.* Light refreshments.
Adm £3, chd free. Sat 23 May
(1-5).
A woodland heritage trail leads
visitors through the remnants of what
was once one of the most famous
late Victorian gardens in Surrey.
Pendell Court is now home to The
Hawthorns School, the pupils of
which are actively engaged in
conserving what remains of Sir
George Macleay's arboretum. Trail
incl muddy and uneven ground.

32 **HEATHSIDE**
10 Links Green Way, Cobham
KT11 2QH. Miss Margaret Arnott &
Mr Terry Bartholomew, 01372
842459,
m.a.arnott@btinternet.com. *1¹/₂ m E
of Cobham. Through Cobham A245,
4th L after Esso garage into Fairmile
Lane. Straight on into Water Lane.
Links Green Way 3rd turning on L.*
Home-made teas. Adm £4, chd free.

Sun 26 July (11-5). Visitors also
welcome by arrangement.
Afternoon tea, or wine & canapes
(evening) available.
¹/₃ acre terraced, plantsman's garden,
designed for yr-round interest. There
is a sumptuous collection of
wonderful plants, all set off by
harmonious landscaping. Many urns
and obelisks aid the display. Two
ponds and two water features add
tranquil sound. A parterre and various
topiary shapes add formality.
Stunning colour combinations excite.
Many inspirational ideas. 5m from
RHS Wisley. Featured in Surrey Life,
Real Homes and Country Homes &
Interiors.

33 **HILL FARM**
Logmore Lane, Westcott, Dorking
RH4 3JY. Helen Thomas. *1m W of
Dorking. Parking on Westcott Heath
just past Church. Entry to garden just
opp.* Home-made teas. Adm £3.50,
chd free. Sun 13 Sept (11.30-4.30).
1³/₄ acre recently redesigned garden
set in the magnificent Surrey Hills
landscape. The garden has a wealth
of different natural habitats to
encourage wildlife, and planting areas
which come alive through the different
seasons. A wildlife pond, woodland
walk, a tapestry of heathers and
glorious late summer grasses and
perennials. A garden to be enjoyed by
all. Everyone welcome. Pond dipping,
nature trail and drawing competition.
Working excavation and restoration of
lime kiln, display of drawings, planting
plans, and photos of redesign.
Sloping garden, most areas are
accessible to wheelchair users. Most
paths are grass so care needed if
very wet.

34 **NEW** **45 HILLCREST
GARDENS**
Esher KT10 0BU. Mr & Mrs C
Robertson. *1m E of Esher. A307 to
Scilly Isles r'about, then R onto the
A309. Over lights & immed R into
central reservation gap into Hillcrest
Gardens. Bear R up the hill then L.*
Home-made teas. Combined adm
£5, chd free. Sun 5 July (11-5).
Combined with 72 Vale Road.
Small (85' x 45') 1930's style family
garden with colourful borders of
cottage garden plants, lawns, pond,
vegetable plot and relaxed patio area.
Lots of interesting little features.

NGS funding helps us support more carers

GROUP OPENING

35 HORSELL GROUP GARDENS

Horsell, Woking GU21 4XA. *1¹/₂ m W of Woking in Village of Horsell. Leave M25 at junction 11. Take A320 signed Woking then A3046 signed Chobham after approx 1m at r'about turn L signed Horsell, with parking on Village Green outside Cricketers PH.* Home-made teas. **Combined adm £5, chd free. Sun 21 June (12-6).**

BIRCH COTTAGE
Celia & Mel Keenan

3-4 BIRCH COTTAGES
Mr & Mrs Freeman

NEW 115 HIGH STREET
Mrs Pamela Barden

HORSELL ALLOTMENTS
Horsell Allotments Association
www.horsellalots.wordpress.com

3 gardens and an award winning allotment in the village of Horsell which is on the edge of the Common, famously mentioned in HG Wells's, War of the Worlds. 3-4 Birch Cottages is full of charm with an interesting courtyard with rill. Walk down this long garden through into a series of rooms with topiary and attractive planting and many specimen roses. Birch Cottage is a grade II listed cottage with a box hedge style knot garden, a chinese slate courtyard with planted pots and hanging baskets, a canal water feature and an active white dove dovecote, surrounded with an abundance of planting. Horsell Allotments have over 100 individual plots growing a variety of unusual flowers and vegetables, many not seen in supermarkets, 2 working beehives with informative talks from their owners. 115 High Street is a plant lover's garden designed and created by owners for yr-round interest, with ideas for planting

woodland dry shade and many rare and unusual plants. Allotments and 3-4 Birch Cottage are flat, Birch Cottage, has gravel and steps but wheelchair visitors can see main garden. No wheelchair access at 115 High Street.

♿ 🕺 ★ ☕

36 NEW 16 HURTMORE CHASE

Hurtmore, Godalming GU7 2RT. Mrs Ann Bellamy, 01483 421274. *4m SW of Guildford. From Godalming follow signs to Charterhouse & cont about ¹/₄ m beyond Charterhouse School. Or from A3 take Norney, Shackleford & Hurtmore turn off & proceed E for ¹/₂ m.* Home-made teas. **Adm £3.50, chd free. Sun 5 July (11-5). Visitors also welcome by arrangement June and July.**
A secluded medium sized (approx ¹/₄ acre) garden comprised mainly of a large lawn divided into discrete areas by shrubs, trees and flowerbeds with a high degree of colour. On the bungalow side of the lawn there is a patio area with hanging baskets, troughs and planted pots with fuchsias being a speciality. In the opposite corner there is a shaded arbour bordered by hostas. Kerb height step up from patio to lawn so minor assistance may be required for wheelchairs.

♿ ★ ☕

37 KNOWLE GRANGE

Hound House Road, Shere, Guildford GU5 9JH. Mr P R & Mrs M E Wood, 01483 202108, prmewood@hotmail.com. *8m S of Guildford. From Shere (off A25), through village for ³/₄ m. After railway bridge, cont 1¹/₂ m past Hound House on R (stone dogs on gatepost). After 100yds turn R at Knowle Grange sign, go to end of lane.* Home-made teas. **Adm £6, chd free. Sun 17 May, Sun 13 Sept 11-5). Visitors also welcome by arrangement May to Sept. Mini buses only.**
80 acre idyllic hilltop position. Extraordinary and exciting 7 acre gardens, created from scratch since 1990 by Marie-Elisabeth Wood, blend the free romantic style with the strong architectural frame of the classical tradition. Walk the rural one mile Bluebell Valley Unicursal Path of Life and discover its secret allegory. Deep unfenced pools, high unfenced drops.

☕

38 LITTLE MYNTHURST FARM

Norwood Hill, Nr Horley RH6 0HR. Mr Ghasan Al Nemar. *4m SW of Reigate. Take A217 towards Horley; after 2m turn R down Irons Bottom Lane (just after Sidlow Bridge). 1st R Dean Oak Lane, then L at T-junction.* Disabled drop off & parking. Tea. **Adm £5, chd free. Sat 20, Sun 21 June (12-5).**
The house where Lord Baden-Powell lived. 12 acre garden in lake setting around old farmhouse (not open). Walled garden, old fashioned roses, shrubs, herbaceous. Tudor courtyard and orchard. Bird and butterfly garden. Kitchen garden with large greenhouses. Secret garden, parterre with box hedging. Many areas of the garden are easily accessible for wheelchair users.

♿ ★ 🚌 ☕

39 ◆ LOSELEY PARK

Guildford GU3 1HS. Mr & Mrs M G More-Molyneux, 01483 304440/405112, www.loseley-park.com. *4m SW of Guildford. For SatNav please use GU3 1HS Stakescorner Lane.* Tea. **Adm £5, chd £2.50. For NGS: Sun 7 June (11-5). For other opening times and information, please phone or see garden website.**
Delightful 2¹/₂ acre walled garden. Award winning rose garden (over 1,000 bushes, mainly old fashioned varieties), extensive herb garden, fruit/flower garden, white garden with fountains, and spectacular organic vegetable garden. Magnificent vine walk, herbaceous borders, moat walk, ancient wisteria and mulberry trees.

♿ ★ 🚌 ☕

40 THE MANOR HOUSE

Three Gates Lane, Haslemere GU27 2ES. Mr & Mrs Gerard Ralfe. *1m NE of Haslemere. From Haslemere centre take A286 towards Milford. Turn R after Museum into Three Gates Lane. At T-Junction turn R into Holdfast Lane. Car park on R.* Home-made teas. **Adm £5, chd free. Sun 21 June (12-5).**
Described by Country Life as 'The hanging gardens of Haslemere', The Manor House gardens are in a valley of the Surrey Hills. One of Surrey's inaugural NGS gardens, they are still under restoration. Fine views, six acres, water gardens.

☕

41 MOLESHILL HOUSE

The Fairmile, Cobham KT11 1BG.
Penny Snell,
pennysnellflowers@btinternet.com,
www.pennysnellflowers.co.uk. *2m
NE of Cobham. On A307 Esher to
Cobham Rd next to free car park by
A3 bridge, at entrance to Waterford
Close.* **Combined adm £6, chd free.
Share to The Garden Museum.
Sun 28 June (2-5). Combined with
Fairmile Lea. Visitors also welcome
by arrangement Apr to Sept for
groups 15+.**
Romantic garden. Short woodland
path leads from dovecote to
beehives. Informal planting contrasts
with formal topiary box and garlanded
cisterns. Colourful courtyard and
pots, conservatory, fountains, bog
garden. Pleached avenue, new
circular gravel garden replacing most
of the lawn. Gypsy caravan garden
and a new mystery feature for 2015.
Music at Moleshill House, teas at
Fairmile Lea. Garden 5 mins from
Claremont Landscape Garden,
Painshill Park and Wisley, also
adjacent excellent dog walking
woods. Featured in German and
Austrian Gardening magazines.

42 MONKSFIELD

Charles Hill (B3001), Tilford,
Farnham GU10 2AL. Mr & Mrs
Mark Reynolds, 07734 155298,
Monksfieldhouse@gmail.com. *On
B3001 Farnham to Elstead Rd,
approx 800 metres S of junction with
Crooksbury Rd. Car parking is opp
house in the field.* **Adm £5, chd free.
Evening Opening £5, chd free, Sat
20 June (6-10.30). Sun 5 July
(10.30-5.30). Visitors also welcome
by arrangement May to Aug for
groups 15+.**
10^1/$_2$ acre varied family garden. With
Hampton Court show garden,
orchard/walled garden, 300ft long
border and formal garden to the
south of the house, incl large
sculptures, cottage garden, ^{1}/$_2$ acre
wildlife pond and large selection of
mature and newly planted specimen
trees. Pimms evening with music (Sat
20 June) and cream teas (Sun 5 July).
Internal road allowing wheelchair
access to many parts of grounds.

43 NORNEY WOOD

Elstead Road, Shackleford,
Godalming GU8 6AY. Mr & Mrs R
Thompson,
norney.wood@btinternet.com. *5m*

*SW of Guildford. At Xrds of Elstead rd
& Shackleford rd, ^{1}/$_2$ m towards
Elstead from A3
Hurtmore/Shackleford junction.* Light
refreshments. **Adm £8, chd free.
Visitors welcome by arrangement
May to July for groups 10+.**
The garden, in the style of Gertrude
Jekyll, created over a period of 5yrs,
is set against a backdrop of mature
trees and rhododendrons. The formal
lawn terrace garden is surrounded by
rose and herbaceous borders.
Gertrude Jekyll's love of structures
has been recreated with a Thunder
house and paths linking the upper
lawn terrace with the Tranquility water
garden and pleached Lime tree walk.
Long mixed herbaceous and rose
borders; Multiple water features in the
form of structured ponds and natural
ponds; Woodland backdrop with
mature trees and open grassland
area; Kitchen garden; wild flower
bank. Garden pavilions and
structured landscapes. Featured in
Country Life Magazine and various
Surrey publications. Wheelchair
access possible on upper level only.

44 ODSTOCK

Castle Square, Bletchingley
RH1 4LB. Averil & John Trott,
01883 743100. *3m W of Godstone.
Castle Square - Just off A25 in
Bletchingley. At top of village nr Red
Lion PH.* Home-made teas. **Adm £4,
chd free. Visitors welcome by
arrangement May to Sept for
groups 10+.**
^{2}/$_3$ acre plantsman's garden
maintained by owners and developed
for yr-round interest. Special interest
in grasses, climbers and dahlias. A no
dig, low maintenance vegetable
garden. Short gravel drive. Main lawn
suitable for wheelchairs but some
paths maybe too narrow.

45 THE OLD CROFT

South Holmwood, Dorking
RH5 4NT. David & Virginia Lardner-
Burke, www.lardner-burke.org.uk.
*2m S of Dorking. From Dorking A24 S
for 2m, L to Leigh/Brockham into Mill
Rd. ^{1}/$_2$ m on L, 2 free NT car parks on
Holmwood Com. Access 500yds
along woodland walk.* Home-made
teas. **Adm £5, chd free. Sun 24,
Mon 25 May, Sat 8, Sun 9 Aug
(2-6).**
Beautiful 5 acre garden with many
diverse areas of natural beauty, giving
a sense of peace and tranquillity.

Stunning vistas incl lake, bridge, pond
fed by natural stream running over
rocky weirs, bog gardens, roses,
perennial borders, elevated viewing
hide, tropical bamboo maze, curved
pergola of rambling roses, unique
topiary buttress hedge, many
specimen trees and shrubs. Visitors
return again and again. Featured in
Period Living. **For direct access for
disabled and elderly visitors
please phone 01306 888224.**

> Short woodland
> path leads from
> dovecote to
> beehives . . .

46 THE OLD RECTORY

Sandy Lane, Brewer Street,
Bletchingley RH1 4QW. Mr & Mrs A
Procter, 01883 743388/07515
394506,
trudie.y.procter@googlemail.com.
*Top of village nr Red Lion PH, turn R
into Little Common Lane then R
Cross Rd into Sandy Lane. Parking nr
house, disabled parking in courtyard.*
Home-made teas. **Adm £5, chd free.
Sun 28 June (11-4). Visitors also
welcome by arrangement Mar to
Sept. Please phone/email for
arrangements.**
Georgian Manor House (not open).
Quintessential Italianate topiary
garden, statuary, box parterres,
courtyard with columns, water
features, antique terracotta pots.
Much of the 4 acre garden is the
subject of ongoing reclamation. This
incl the ancient moat, woodland with
fine specimen trees and walled
kitchen garden. Rill, sunken and
exotic garden under construction.
Featured on BBC Emma, in Country
Living and Vogue. Gravel paths.

47 ◆ POLESDEN LACEY

Great Bookham, Dorking RH5 6BD.
National Trust, 01372 452048,
www.nationaltrust.org.uk. *Nr
Dorking, off A246 Leatherhead to
Guildford rd. 1^1/$_2$ m S of Great
Bookham, well signed.* **Adm £8.50,
chd £4.30. For NGS: Fri 26 June**

Ashleigh Grange

(10-4.30). For other opening times and information, please phone or see garden website.
Designed as the perfect setting for Mrs Greville, a famous Edwardian hostess, to entertain royalty and the best of society, Polesden Lacey has beautiful formal gardens with something to offer for every season, as well as glorious views over the rolling Surrey Hills. Wheelchairs and battery cars available from Visitor Reception, it is advisable to pre-book.

48 PRATSHAM GRANGE
Tanhurst Lane, Holmbury St Mary RH5 6LZ. Alan & Felicity Comber, 01306 621116, alancomber@aol.com. *12m SE of Guildford, 8m SW of Dorking. From A25 take B2126. After 4m turn L into Tanhurst Lane. From A29 take B2126. Before Forest Green turn R*

on B2126 then 1st R to Tanhurst Lane. Home-made teas. **Adm £5, chd free. Sat 4, Sun 5 July, Sat 15, Sun 16 Aug (12-5).** Visitors also welcome by arrangement June to Aug.
4 acre garden overlooked by Holmbury Hill and Leith Hill. Features incl herbaceous borders, cutting flower garden, 2 ponds joined by cascading stream and rose, hydrangea and dahlia beds. New areas incl white and yellow beds and alstroemeria and heathers incorporated in geometric beds. Featured in Surrey Life magazine. Some slopes and gravel paths. Deep ponds.

49 ◆ RAMSTER
Chiddingfold, Surrey GU8 4SN. Mr & Mrs Paul Gunn, 01428 654167, www.ramsterevents.com. *On A283*

1¹⁄₂ m S of Chiddingfold; large iron gates on R, signed from rd. Light refreshments. **Adm £6, chd free. For NGS: Fri 22 May (10-5).** For other opening times and information, please phone or see garden website.
A stunning, mature woodland garden set in over 20 acres, famous for its rhododendron and azalea collection and its carpets of bluebells in Spring. Enjoy a peaceful wander down the woodland walk, explore the bog garden with its stepping stones, or relax in the tranquil enclosed Tennis Court Garden. Tea house open every day while the garden is open, serving delicious cakes and sandwiches. Teahouse and WC wheelchair accessible, some paths in garden suitable for wheelchairs.

Lemon drizzle cake, Victoria sponge … yummy!

50 THE ROUND HOUSE

Dunsfold Road, Loxhill GU8 4BL.
Mrs Sue Lawson, 01483 200375,
roundhouseloxhill@gmail.com. *4m
S of Bramley. Off A281, at
Smithbrook Kilns turn R to Dunsfold.
Follow to T-junction. Go R (B2130).
After 1.2m Park Hatch on R, enter
park, follow drive to garden.* Home-
made teas. **Adm £4, chd free.
Visitors welcome by arrangement
May to Aug. Occasional visits in
September.**

2¹/₂ acre walled Victorian garden with
far reaching views from the top of the
garden. Continuing renewal
programme since 2002. Colourful
mixed beds with perennials, roses
and interesting statuary. Water
cascades. Apple and plum orchard.
Serpentine paths between shrubs
and wild flowers. 75 metre lavender
walk. Ornamental fish pond and wild
flower orchard. Gravel paths and
steep slopes.

51 NEW SAFFRON GATE

Tickners Heath, Alfold, Cranleigh
GU6 8HU. Mr & Mrs D Gibbison,
01483 200219,
clematis@talk21.com. *Between
Alfold & Dunsfold. A281 between
Guildford & Horsham approx 8m turn
at Alfold crossways follow signs for
Dunsfold. Do not turn at A281 t-lights
for Dunsfold (wrong road).* Home-
made teas. **Adm £3.50, chd free.
Sun 3, Mon 4 May, Sun 7, Sun 21
June (11-4). Visitors also welcome
by arrangement Apr to Aug.**

1 acre garden with many rare plants,
designed and planted by current
owners plus a well maintanted
vegetable garden. Cottage style with
a pleasing mixture of perennials. Seek
out the unusual clematis at least 120
different varieties which add height
and interest. An arbor is planted with
climbers and a river of blue
geraniums beneath. Also incl are
spring bulbs and yr-round foliage and
colour. Disabled drop off point.

52 41 SHELVERS WAY

Tadworth KT20 5QJ. Keith &
Elizabeth Lewis, 01737 210707,
kandelewis@ntlworld.com. *6m S of
Sutton off A217. 1st turning on R
after Burgh Heath T-lights heading S
on A217. 400yds down Shelvers Way
on L.* Home-made teas. **Adm £3.50,
chd free. Sun 19 Apr, Sun 19 July
(2-5.30). Visitors also welcome by**

arrangement Apr to July for groups
10+.
Visitors say 'one of the most colourful
back gardens in Surrey'. In spring, a
myriad of small bulbs with specialist
daffodils and many pots of colourful
tulips. Choice perennials follow, with
rhododendrons and azaleas. Cobbles
and shingle support grasses and self
sown plants with a bubble fountain.
Annuals, phlox and herbaceous
plants ensure colour well into
September. A garden for all seasons.

53 SHIELING

The Warren, Kingswood, Tadworth
KT20 6PQ. Dr Sarah Wilson,
01737 833370,
sarahwilson@doctors.org.uk.
*Kingswood Warren Estate. Off A217,
gated entrance just before church on
southbound side of dual carriageway
after Tadworth r'about. ³/₄ m walk
from Station. Parking on Warren or by
church on A217.* Tea. **Adm £5, chd
free. Mon 4 May (2-6). Evening
Opening £7, chd free, wine, Fri 12
June (5.30-9). Sun 14 June (2-5).
Visitors also welcome by
arrangement Apr to Aug.**

A one acre garden restored to its
original 1920's design. The front is a
formal garden with island beds and
shrub borders At the back there is a
surprise with a large rock garden
planted with bulbs, perennials and
shrubs. The rest is a woodland
garden with acid loving plants and
some old and interesting trees and
shrubs. Articles in local village
magazine, Gardeners World and
Surrey Life. Gravel drive and some
narrow paths in back garden
otherwise grass and paths easy for
wheelchairs.

54 SPURFOLD

Radnor Road, Peaslake, Guildford
GU5 9SZ. Mr & Mrs A Barnes,
01306 730196,
spurfold@btinternet.com. *8m SE of
Guildford. A25 to Shere then through
to Peaslake. Pass Village stores & L
up Radnor Road.* Home-made teas.
**Adm £5, chd free. Sat 16, Sun 17
May (12-5.30). Visitors also
welcome by arrangement May to
Aug, groups 15+. Home-made teas
(day), glass of wine (eve).**

4 acres, large herbaceous and shrub
borders, formal pond with
Cambodian Buddha head, sunken
gravel garden with topiary box and

water feature, terraces, beautiful
lawns, mature rhododendrons and
azaleas, woodland paths, and
gazebos. Garden contains a
collection of Indian elephants and
other objets d'art. Topiary garden
created 2010 and new formal lawn
area created in 2012.

Tea house open
serving delicious
cakes and
sandwiches . . .

55 STUART COTTAGE

Ripley Road, East Clandon
GU4 7SF. John & Gayle Leader,
01483 222689,
gayle@stuartcottage.com,
www.stuartcottage.com. *4m E of
Guildford. Off A246 or from A3
through Ripley until r'about, turn L &
cont through West Clandon until T-
lights, then L onto A246. East
Clandon 1st L.* Home-made teas.
**Adm £4, chd free. Sun 19 July, Sun
30 Aug (2-5). Visitors also welcome
by arrangement June to Sept for
groups 15+ (no upper limit).**

This much visited ¹/₂ acre garden
seems to please many, being planted
to offer floral continuity through the
seasons. In June, the romance of the
rose walk combines with the sound of
water, in July, flowerbeds are
floriferous with soft coordinated
colours and scented plants, in
August, vibrant colours will lift the
spirits and in September, tender
perennials reach their zenith. Access
to all the garden for wheelchairs.

56 NEW STUARTFIELD

113 Silverdale Avenue, Walton-on-
Thames MBE & Kevin Ingram. *1.3m
S of Walton-on-Thames. From A3,
A245 to Walton. R B365 Seven Hills
Rd. At 2nd r'about A317 to Walton. L
next r'about B365 Ashley Rd.
Silverdale Av 2nd on L.* Home-made
teas. **Adm £3.50, chd free. Sun 10
May (11-5).**

An inspiring garden that takes you to different parts of the world, whether through New Zealand tree ferns, Japanese acers, or Moroccan inspired summerhouse. A mature garden with beautiful rhododendrons, extensively redesigned 15yrs ago by Joe Swift of Gardener's World fame. There is also a pond and many sculptural features to enjoy.

☕

57 ▶ SUNRISE OF WEYBRIDGE
Ellesmere Road, Weybridge KT13 0HY. Mr Will Burke, www.sunrise-care.co.uk/communities/weybridge. *1m E of Weybridge. From A3, 2¹/₂ m from Painshill r'about or M25 J11, approx 4m.* Light refreshments. **Adm £4, chd free. Sat 27 June (12-4).**
Situated on the outskirts of the town of Weybridge, Sunrise Senior living of Weybridge is a beautifully appointed purpose built care residence. The community possesses extensive award winning private gardens with unique features, a beautiful lawn where garden parties and barbeques are held in the summer and a paved walkway surrounds the buildings under the mature trees overhead. Tea, coffee, soft drinks and patiseries will be served in the garden. Fully compatible and accessible to all models of wheelchair and mobility devices.

& 🥾 🚌 ☕

58 ▶ TILFORD COTTAGE
Tilford Road, Tilford GU10 2BX. Mr & Mrs R Burn, 01252 795423, rodburn@tiscali.co.uk, www.tilfordcottagegarden.co.uk. *3m SE of Farnham. From Farnham station along Tilford Rd. Tilford Cottage opp Tilford House. Parking by village green.* **Adm £6, chd free. Visitors welcome by arrangement all year. Refreshments available on request.**
Artist's garden designed to surprise, delight and amuse. Formal planting, herb and knot garden. Numerous examples of topiary combine beautifully with the wild flower river walk. Japanese and water gardens, hosta beds, rose, apple and willow arches, treehouse and fairy grotto all continue the playful quality especially enjoyed by children. Dogs on lead please! Holistic centre open for taster sessions. Art studio open for viewing. Some gravel paths and steep slopes.

& 🥾 ❀ ☕

59 ▶ TIMBER HILL
Chertsey Road, Chobham GU24 8JF. Mr & Mrs Nick Sealy, 01932 873875, nicksealy@chobham.net, www.timberhillgarden.co.uk. *4m N of Woking. 2¹/₂ m E of Chobham and ¹/₃ m E of Fairoaks aerodrome on A319 (N side). 1¹/₄ m W of Ottershaw, J11 M25.* Home made light lunches & teas in old Surrey barn. Preferably book for lunch or take pot luck! **Adm £4.50, chd free. Mon 6, Sun 26 Apr (11.30-4.30). Visitors also welcome by arrangement Jan to May - see website for spring openings.**
Beautifully situated 15 acre garden and woodland with views to N Downs. Fine specimens of oaks, liquidambar and liriodendron. Early witch hazel walk and crocuses; new plantings of beech, cherry, maples. camellias and magnolias shelter behind banks of rhododendron ponticum. Drifts of spring narcissi, daffodils and camassia, tulips in borders; bluebells/azaleas in May; old roses in June. Excellent help (buggy) for disabled.

& 🥾 ❀ ☕

60 ▶ ◆ TITSEY PLACE GARDENS
Titsey Hill, Oxted RH8 0SD. The Trustees of the Titsey Foundation, 01273 715356, www.titsey.org. *3m N of Oxted. A25 between Oxted & Westerham. Follow brown signs to Titsey Estate from A25 at Limpsfield or see website directions.* Cream teas. **Adm £4.50, chd £1. For NGS: Suns 17 May, 14 June, 12 July, 16 Aug (1-5). For other opening times and information, please phone or see garden website.**
One of the largest surviving historic estates in Surrey. Magnificent ancestral home and gardens of the Gresham family since 1534. Walled kitchen garden restored early 1990s. Golden Jubilee rose garden. Etruscan summer house adjoining picturesque lakes and fountains. 15 acres of formal and informal gardens in idyllic setting within the M25. Tearooms with delicious home-made teas served between 12:30-5 on open days. Last admissions to gardens at 4pm, gardens close at 5pm. Dogs allowed in picnic area, car park and woodland walks. Good wheelchair access and disabled car park alongside tearooms.

& ☕

61 ▶ TOLLSWORTH MANOR
Rook Lane, Chaldon, Caterham CR3 5BQ. Carol & Gordon Gillett. *2m W of Caterham. From Caterham-on-the-Hill, take B2031 through Chaldon. 300yds out of Chaldon take concrete farm track on L. Parking in farmyard beyond house.* Home-made teas. **Adm £4, chd free. Sun 14 June (2-6).**
Surrounding a C14 rose/clematis covered house, an old fashioned country garden, created from derelict site over 31yrs by present owners. Well stocked herbaceous borders with old fashioned roses, peonies, delphiniums. Wildlife pond and duck pond with ducks. Lovely views over surrounding farmland. Shetland pony. Friendly atmosphere. Some uneven paths.

& ❀ ☕

62 ▶ NEW ▶ UPPER SYDENHURST
Mill Lane, Chiddingfold, Godalming GU8 4SJ. Bridget & Robin Pinchbeck. *Turn into Mill Lane by St Mary's Church. Cont up Mill Lane for approx ¹/₂ m. Go past Upper Sydenhurst on L into field for parking, also on L.* Home-made teas in barn. **Adm £4, chd free. Sun 17 May (2-5).**
17 acre garden surrounding part C16 house (not open). Small parterre, courtyard and vegetable garden. Series of ponds leading to woodland walk. Wisteria covered pergola. Recent hedges and herbaceous borders planted to encourage pollinators. Italian garden. New black and white border, orchard and wildflower meadow. Italian products and local artwork for sale.

❀ ☕

63 NEW 72 VALE ROAD
Claygate, Esher KT10 0NL. Mrs
Janet Watkins. *A3 - A244 towards
Esher. At T-lights turn R into
Milbourne Lane, cont to Claygate.
Turn R at Foley Arms and keep
straight on taking 2nd L onto
Beaconsfield Rd. Park on R before
T junc.* Home-made teas. **Combined
adm £5, chd free. Sun 5 July
(11-5). Combined with 45 Hillcrest
Gardens.**
The contemporary gravel garden at
the front (Feb 2013) is planted out in
blocks with a pathway designed to
lead visitors to the side front door.
The back garden (May 2011) is curvy
to create a sense of gentle enclosure
and is planted with swathes of
grasses and perennials. Design
drawings available plus before and
after photos. Wheelchair access to
patio in back garden.

64 ◆ VANN
Hambledon GU8 4EF. Mrs M
Caroe, 01428 683413,
www.vanngarden.co.uk. *6m S of
Godalming. A283 to Wormley. Turn L
at Hambledon. On NGS days only,
follow yellow Vann signs for 2m.
Please park in field, not in rd.*
Refreshments for pre booked parties
only. **Adm £6, chd free. For NGS:
Daily Sun 29 Mar to Sat 4 Apr;
Mon 4 May to Sun 10 May; Sun 7
June to Sat 13 June (11-6). For
other opening times and
information, please phone or see
garden website.**
5 acre English Heritage registered
garden surrounding Tudor and
William and Mary house (not open)
with Arts and Crafts additions by W D
Caröe incl a Bargate stone pergola.
At the front, brick paved original
cottage garden; to the rear, ¼ acre
pond, yew walk with rill and Gertrude
Jekyll water garden. Snowdrops and
hellebores, spring bulbs, Fritillaria in
Feb/March. Island beds, crinkle
crankle wall, orchard with wild
flowers, vegetable garden.
Centenary garden and woodland.
Featured in Country Life, Daily
Telegraph Magazine, Groei & Bloei
(Belgium) and Period Homes and
Interiors. Deep water. Water garden
paths not suitable for wheelchairs,
but many others are. Please ring
prior to visit to request disabled
parking.

65 ◆ WALTON POOR HOUSE
Ranmore RH5 6SX. Prue Calvert,
01483 282273,
wnscalvert@btinternet.com. *6m
NW of Dorking. From Dorking take rd
to Ranmore, cont for approx 4m,
after Xrds 1m on L. From A246 at E
Horsley go S into Greendene, 1st L
Crocknorth Rd, 1m on R.* Home-
made teas. **Adm £3.50, chd free.
Mon 4 May (12-5). Visitors also
welcome by arrangement May to
Oct for groups 10+.**
Tranquil, almost secretive, 4 acre
mostly wooded garden in North
Downs AONB, planted to show
contrast between colourful shrubs
and mature trees. Paths wind through
garden to pond, hideaway dell and
herb garden, planted to show the use
of aromatic plants and shrubs.
Specialist nursery with wide variety of
herbs, shrubs and aromatic plants.
Herb talks, recipe leaflets and
refreshments available for groups by
appt. Grass paths.

66 57 WESTHALL ROAD
Warlingham CR6 9BG. Robert &
Wendy Baston. *3m N of M25. M25,
J6, A22 London, at Whyteleafe
r'about, take 3rd R, under railway
bridge, turn immed R into Westhall
Rd.* Home-made teas. **Adm £3.50,
chd free. Share to Warlingham
Methodist Church. Sun 24, Mon 25
May (2-5). Also open Elm Tree
Cottage (see London).**
Reward for the sure footed - many
steep steps to 3 levels! Swathes of
tulips and alliums. Mature kiwi and
grape vines. Mixed borders. Raised
vegetable beds. Box, bay, cork oak
and yew topiaries. Amphitheatre of
potted plants on lower steps.
Stunning views of Caterham and
Whyteleafe from top garden.

67 ◆ WESTWAYS FARM
Gracious Pond Road, Chobham
GU24 8HH. Paul & Nicky Biddle,
01276 856163,
nicolabiddle@rocketmail.com. *4m
N of Woking. From Chobham Church
proceed over r'about towards
Sunningdale, 1st Xrds R into Red
Lion Rd to junction with Mincing
Lane.* Home-made teas. **Adm £4,
chd free. Sun 10 May (10-5).
Visitors also welcome by
arrangement Apr to June for
groups 10 min, 50 max.**
Open 6 acre garden surrounded by
woodlands planted in 1930s with

mature and some rare
rhododendrons, azaleas, camellias
and magnolias, underplanted with
bluebells, lilies and dogwood;
extensive lawns and sunken pond
garden. Working stables and
sandschool. Lovely Queen Anne
House (not open) covered with listed
Magnolia grandiflora. Victorian design
glasshouse. New planting round
garden room.

> Impressive
> displays of
> daffodils,
> bluebells and
> azaleas await
> in spring . . .

68 ◆ WINKWORTH ARBORETUM
Hascombe Road, Godalming
GU8 4AD. National Trust, 01483
208477, www.nationaltrust.org.uk.
*2m SE of Godalming on B2130. Car:
nr Hascombe, 2m SE of Godalming
on E side of B2130. Bus: 42/44
Guildford to Cranleigh (stops at
Arboretum).* Light refreshments. **Adm
£7.50, chd £3.75. For NGS: Sun 7
June, Sun 4 Oct (10-5.30). For
other opening times and
information, please phone or see
garden website.**
This dramatic hillside Arboretum
perfectly demonstrates what Dr Fox,
the Arboretum's creator, described as
'using trees and shrubs to paint a
picture'. Impressive displays of
daffodils, bluebells and azaleas await
in spring. Picnic by the lake in
summer. Don't miss the stunning
autumnal display created by maples,
cherries and tupelos. Guided walk
with member of the garden team.
Steep slopes.

69 **NEW** **51 WOLSEY DRIVE**
Walton-on-Thames KT12 3BB. Ms
Daphne Tonna-Barthet. *From
Rydens Rd, turn onto Tudor Dr, then
L at end onto Wolsey Dr.* Home-
made teas. **Adm £3, chd free.**
Sat 27 June (10-6).
This is an attractively landscaped
garden in the middle of suburbia. A
medium sized plot (20x16m)
designed with differing areas with
plenty of seating and incorporating
several modern sculptures. Whilst incl
raised beds for growing vegetables it
still looks pretty and maintains an air
of tranquillity. An unusual construction
located at the back of the garden

holds a nice surprise. In addition to
light refreshments, the host is a keen
crafter and there will also be home-
made soap for sale with all proceeds
donated to the NGS.
☕

70 **WOODBURY COTTAGE**
Colley Lane, Reigate RH2 9JJ.
Shirley & Bob Stoneley, 01737
244235. *1m W of Reigate. M25 J8,
A217 (Reigate). Immed before level
Xing turn R into Somers Rd, cont as
Manor Rd. At end turn R into
Coppice Lane & follow signs to car
park.* Home-made teas. **Adm £3.50,
chd free. Sat 11, Sun 12 July, Sat**

5, Sun 6, Wed 9 Sept (1-5). Visitors
also welcome by arrangement July
to Sept for groups 10+.
Cottage garden just under ¼ acre. It
is stepped on a slope, enhanced by
it's setting under Colley Hill and the
North Downs. We grow a colourful
diversity of plants incl perennials,
annuals and tender ones. A particular
feature throughout the garden is the
use of groups of pots containing
unusual and interesting plants. The
garden is colour themed and is still
rich and vibrant in September.

Spurfold

SUSSEX

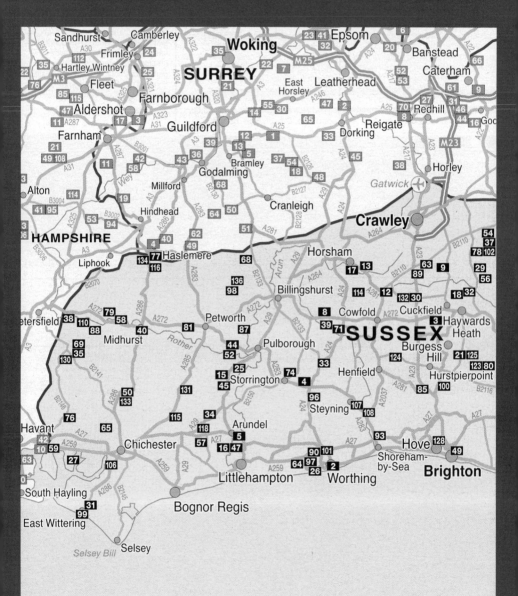

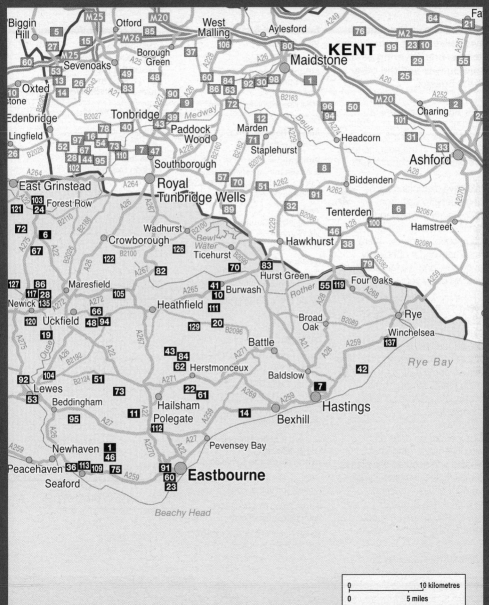

© Global Mapping / XYZ Maps

Sussex

Sussex is a vast county of two halves with two county teams, one covering east & mid Sussex and the other in west Sussex.

The county stretches from Havant in the west up to East Grinstead in the north and Winchelsea in the east, so there are plenty of gardens to see.

We have a stunning range of gardens to visit, from rolling acres of parkland, small courtyards, village trails and school gardens – there is something for absolutely everyone, and we feel sure that you will enjoy your visit.

Many of our gardens are located within the South Downs National Park, and there is also the added bonus of delicious home-made cakes and tea served at most of them, and often plants for sale, many propagated by the owners themselves.

Many of our gardens are also open by arrangement. Should you need advice please e-mail ngseastsussex@gmail. com for anything related to east & mid Sussex, or ngswestsussex@gmail.com for anything in west Sussex.

Below: Sheffield Park and Garden

East & Mid Sussex Volunteers

County Organiser & Booklet Coordinator
Irene Eltringham-Willson
01323 833770
irene.willson@btinternet.com

County Treasurer
Andrew Ratcliffe 01435 873310
anratcliffe@gmail.com

Publicity & Assistant County Organiser
Geoff Stonebanks 01323 899296
ngseastsussex@gmail.com

Twitter & Assistant County Organiser
Liz Warner 01273 586050
lizwarner69@outlook.com

Assistant County Organisers
Jane Baker 01273 842805
jane.baker47@btinternet.com

Lynne Brown 01273 556439
brown.lynne@ntlworld.com

Emma Burnett 01273 400606
emmaburnett16@btinternet.com

Diane Gould 01825 732253
heron.brook@btinternet.com

Jasmine Hart 01273 400427
jasminehart111@yahoo.co.uk

Peggy Harvey 01424 532093
chantry@talktalk.net

Richard & Matty Holmes
01797 223055
mrholmes123@btinternet.com

Philippa Hopkins 01342 822090
piphop@btinternet.com

Susan Laing 01444 892500
splaing@btinternet.com

Sarah Ratcliffe 01435 873310
sallyrat@btinternet.com

West Sussex Volunteers

County Organiser & Booklet Coordinator
Teresa Barttelot
01798 865690
teresabarttelot@btinternet.com

County Treasurer
Liz Collison
01903 719245
lizcollison@yahoo.com

Publicity
Adrian Skeates
07743 505392
as13cs@btinternet.com

Social Media
Claudia Pearce 07985 648216
claudiapearce17@gmail.com

Assistant County Organisers
Sanda Belcher 01428 723259
sandambelcher@gmail.com

Jane Burton 01243 527822

Lesley Chamberlain
chamberlain_lesley@hotmail.com

Patty Christie 01730 813323
patty@christieuk.co.uk

Sue Foley 01243 814452
suefoley@mac.com

Jane Lywood 01403 820225
jmlywood@aol.com

Carrie McArdle 01403 820272
carrie.mcardle@btinternet.com

Claudia Pearce 07985 648216
claudiapearce17@gmail.com

Fiona Phillips 01273 462285
fiona.h.phillips@btinternet.com

Susan Pinder 01403 820430
nasus.rednip@gmail.com

Caroline & Adrian Skeates
07743 505392
as13cs@btinternet.com

Currently the NGS donates around £2.5 million every year

Opening Dates

All entries subject to change.
For latest information check www.ngs.org.uk

February

Tuesday 10
100 Pembury House

Wednesday 11
100 Pembury House

Thursday 12
100 Pembury House

Sunday 15
81 Manor of Dean

Tuesday 17
100 Pembury House

Wednesday 18
100 Pembury House

Thursday 19
100 Pembury House

March

Sunday 1
96 The Old Vicarage

Monday 2
100 Pembury House

Thursday 5
100 Pembury House

Friday 6
100 Pembury House

Sunday 8
81 Manor of Dean

Sunday 15
70 King John's Lodge
110 Sandhill Farm House

Wednesday 18
126 Tidebrook Manor

Saturday 21
101 6 Plantation Rise

Saturday 28
76 Lordington House
101 6 Plantation Rise

Sunday 29
33 Dachs
76 Lordington House

April

Sunday 5
97 Palatine School Gardens

Monday 6
96 The Old Vicarage

Thursday 9
137 Winchelsea's Secret Gardens

Saturday 11
22 Butlers Farmhouse
52 The Grange
106 Rymans
110 Sandhill Farm House

Sunday 12
22 Butlers Farmhouse
33 Dachs
52 The Grange
106 Rymans
162 Sandhill Farm House
116 Shalford House

Sunday 19
81 Manor of Dean
85 Newtimber Place

Thursday 23
83 Merriments

Saturday 25
35 Down Place
130 Uppark

Sunday 26
15 Bignor Park
17 Blue Jays
28 Clinton Lodge
35 Down Place
49 The Garden House
79 Malt House
92 Offham House
96 The Old Vicarage

May

44 Fittleworth House (every Wednesday)

Saturday 2
43 Fineoaks

Sunday 3
16 4 Birch Close
31 Cookscroft
43 Fineoaks
58 Hammerwood House
79 Malt House

Monday 4
16 4 Birch Close
79 Malt House

Wednesday 6
10 Bateman's

Saturday 9
121 Standen
122 Stone Cross House

Sunday 10
3 Ansty Gardens
47 70 Ford Road
48 Framfield Grange
58 Hammerwood House
122 Stone Cross House

Wednesday 13
9 Balcombe Gardens
133 West Dean Gardens

Friday 15
24 Caxton Manor
73 NEW Limekiln Farm
103 2 Quarry Cottages

Saturday 16
17 Blue Jays
24 Caxton Manor
67 Holly House
73 NEW Limekiln Farm
103 2 Quarry Cottages
128 11 Tredcroft Road

Sunday 17
12 Beedinglee
17 Blue Jays
67 Holly House
72 Legsheath Farm
123 Stonehealed Farm
128 11 Tredcroft Road

Wednesday 20
114 Sedgwick Park House

Saturday 23
7 96 Ashford Road
37 Duckyls Holt
102 The Priest House

Sunday 24
8 Bakers House
37 Duckyls Holt
50 Gardeners' Cottage
64 Highdown Gardens
70 King John's Lodge
104 Ringmer Park
105 Rose Cottage
114 Sedgwick Park House
116 Shalford House
131 Upwaltham Barns

Monday 25
37 Duckyls Holt
70 King John's Lodge
131 Upwaltham Barns

Saturday 30
7 96 Ashford Road
23 51 Carlisle Road
77 Lowder Mill

Sunday 31
23 51 Carlisle Road
53 NEW 6 Grange Road
56 Great Lywood Farmhouse
57 Halfpenny Cottage
77 Lowder Mill
81 Manor of Dean
92 Offham House

Home-made organic jams and marmalades for sale . . .

June

44 Fittleworth House (every Wednesday)

Wednesday 3
120 Sparrow Hatch

Thursday 4
64 Highdown Gardens
120 Sparrow Hatch

Friday 5
56 Great Lywood Farmhouse

Festival Weekend

Saturday 6
40 54 Elmleigh
66 Hobbs Barton
88 Nyewood House
106 Rymans
117 Sheffield Park and Garden
121 Standen
137 Winchelsea's Secret Gardens

Sunday 7
14 Bexhill Gardens
15 Bignor Park
34 Dale Park House
40 54 Elmleigh
56 Great Lywood Farmhouse
63 High Beeches Woodland and Water Garden
65 4 Hillside Cottages
66 Hobbs Barton
84 NEW Moieties Farm & Barn
88 Nyewood House
96 The Old Vicarage
106 Rymans
112 Sayerland House

Tuesday 9
36 Driftwood

Wednesday 10
52 The Grange
126 Tidebrook Manor

Thursday 11
118 Slindon Gardens Group
134 NEW Whitehanger (Evening)

Friday 12
98 Parsonage Farm

Saturday 13
9 Balcombe Gardens
19 Bradness Gallery
35 Down Place
67 Holly House
130 Uppark

Visit a garden on National Gardens Festival Weekend 6 & 7 June

© Abigail Rex

33 Peerley Road

Sunday 14
- **2** Ambrose Place Back Gardens
- **12** Beedinglee
- **19** Bradness Gallery
- **35** Down Place
- **60** Hardwycke
- **67** Holly House
- **82** Mayfield Gardens
- **87** North Springs
- **89** Nymans
- **118** Slindon Gardens Group
- **127** Town Place

Monday 15
- **28** Clinton Lodge

Tuesday 16
- **1** Alfriston Clergy House

Thursday 18
- **6** Ashdown Park Hotel
- **41** NEW Elphicks Cottage
- **127** Town Place
- **134** NEW Whitehanger (Evening)

Friday 19
- **13** 4 Ben's Acre
- **41** NEW Elphicks Cottage

Saturday 20
- **40** 54 Elmleigh
- **42** Fairlight End
- **62** Herstmonceux Parish Trail
- **70** King John's Lodge
- **74** Little Wantley
- **95** Old Vicarage
- **110** Sandhill Farm House

Sunday 21
- **3** Ansty Gardens
- **8** Bakers House
- **40** 54 Elmleigh

- **42** Fairlight End
- **62** Herstmonceux Parish Trail
- **70** King John's Lodge
- **74** Little Wantley
- **90** Oak Grove College
- **97** Palatine School Gardens
- **105** Rose Cottage
- **110** Sandhill Farm House
- **115** NEW Selhurst Park

Tuesday 23
- **78** NEW Luctons

Thursday 25
- **36** Driftwood

Saturday 27
- **26** Channel View
- **31** Cookscroft (Evening)
- **78** NEW Luctons
- **86** North Hall
- **102** The Priest House
- **135** 1 Whites Cottages

Sunday 28
- **26** Channel View
- **71** Knepp Castle
- **86** North Hall
- **113** Seaford Group
- **127** Town Place
- **132** Warninglid Gardens
- **135** 1 Whites Cottages

July

- **44** **Fittleworth House (every Wednesday)**

Wednesday 1
- **75** The Long House

Thursday 2
- **78** NEW Luctons

Friday 3
- **68** Jacaranda (Evening)

Saturday 4
- **43** Fineoaks
- **46** Follers Manor

Sunday 5
- **43** Fineoaks
- **46** Follers Manor
- **47** 70 Ford Road
- **116** Shalford House
- **127** Town Place

Tuesday 7
- **36** Driftwood

Friday 10
- **108** St Mary's House Gardens

Saturday 11
- **29** Cobb Cottage North
- **40** 54 Elmleigh
- **108** St Mary's House Gardens

Sunday 12
- **40** 54 Elmleigh

Wednesday 15
- **52** The Grange
- **119** South Grange

Thursday 16
- **61** Gardens & Grounds of Herstmonceux Castle

Saturday 18
- **101** 6 Plantation Rise
- **136** NEW Whithurst Park

Sunday 19
- **29** Cobb Cottage North

Wednesday 22
- **107** Saffrons

Saturday 25
- **101** 6 Plantation Rise

Sunday 26
- **21** Burgess Hill Gardens
- **53** NEW 6 Grange Road
- **65** 4 Hillside Cottages
- **94** Old Pound Farm
- **99** 33 Peerley Road
- **107** Saffrons

Monday 27
- **21** Burgess Hill Gardens

August

Saturday 1
- **136** NEW Whithurst Park

Monday 3
- **28** Clinton Lodge
- **51** NEW Golden Cross & Laughton Duo

Tuesday 4
- **111** Sarah Raven's Cutting Garden

Saturday 8
- **22** Butlers Farmhouse

Sunday 9
- **22** Butlers Farmhouse
- **36** Driftwood
- **81** Manor of Dean

Saturday 15
- **54** Gravetye Manor

Sunday 16
- **47** 70 Ford Road
- **80** Malthouse Farm

Tuesday 18
- **80** Malthouse Farm

Saturday 22
- **67** Holly House
- **119** South Grange

Sunday 23
- **60** Hardwycke
- **67** Holly House
- **96** The Old Vicarage
- **119** South Grange

Saturday 29
- **13** 4 Ben's Acre

Sunday 30
- **39** Durrance Manor

Monday 31
- **124** Sussex Prairies

September

Friday 4
- **125** 30 Sycamore Drive (Evening)

Saturday 5
- **106** Rymans

Sunday 6
- **98** Parsonage Farm
- **106** Rymans
- **116** Shalford House

Tuesday 8
- **18** Borde Hill Garden

Sunday 13
- **68** Jacaranda
- **104** Ringmer Park

Wednesday 16
- **117** Sheffield Park and Garden
- **126** Tidebrook Manor

Sunday 20
- **15** Bignor Park
- **70** King John's Lodge

Sunday 27
- **63** High Beeches Woodland and Water Garden

October

Saturday 17
- **121** Standen

Sunday 18
- **96** The Old Vicarage

Gardens open to the public

- **1** Alfriston Clergy House
- **5** Arundel Castle & Gardens - The Collector Earl's Garden

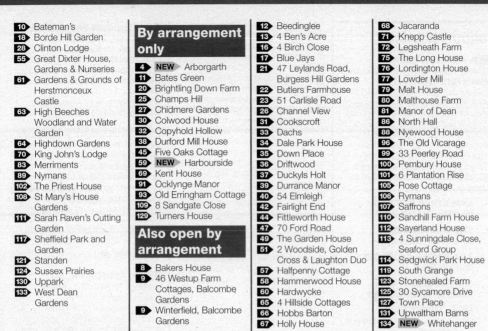

The Gardens

1 ◆ ALFRISTON CLERGY HOUSE

Alfriston BN26 5TL. National Trust, 01323 871961, www.nationaltrust.org.uk/alfriston. *4m NE of Seaford. Just E of B2108, in Alfriston Village, adjoining The Tye & St Andrew's Church. Bus: RDH 125 from Lewes, Autopoint 126 from Eastbourne & Seaford.* **Adm £5, chd £2.50. For NGS: Tue 16 June (10.30-4.30). For other opening times and information, please phone or see garden website.** Enjoy the scent of roses, admire the vegetable garden and orchard in a tranquil setting with views across the R Cuckmere. Visit this C14 thatched Wealden hall house, the first building to be acquired by the NT in 1896. Our gardener will be available to talk to you about this peaceful cottage garden. Partial wheelchair access.
♿ ❀

GROUP OPENING

2 AMBROSE PLACE BACK GARDENS

Richmond Road, Worthing BN11 1PZ. *Worthing Town Centre. Entry points: Ambrose Villa, corner*

Portland Rd & Richmond Rd; No 1, next to St Paul's Church; No 10, opp Worthing Library. Light refreshments available at some of the gardens. **Combined adm £5, chd free. Sun 14 June (11-1 & 2-5).**

1 AMBROSE PLACE
Tom & Helen Watson.
Entry point for visitors

3 AMBROSE PLACE
Graham & Bette Swindon

4 AMBROSE PLACE
Graham & Terri Heald

5 AMBROSE PLACE
Pat & Sue Owen

6 AMBROSE PLACE
Sue Swanborough

7 AMBROSE PLACE
Mark & Susan Frost

8 AMBROSE PLACE
Steve & Claire Hughes

9 AMBROSE PLACE
Derek & Anna Irvine

10 AMBROSE PLACE
Alan & Marie Pringle.
Entry point for visitors

11 AMBROSE PLACE
Steve & Carolyn Bailey

12 AMBROSE PLACE
Peter & Nina May

13 AMBROSE PLACE
Malcolm & Hilary Leeves

14 AMBROSE PLACE
Mr & Mrs A Marks

AMBROSE VILLA
122 Portland Road. Mark & Christine Potter.
Entry point for visitors

The highly acclaimed back gardens of Ambrose Place have been described as a 'horticultural phenomenon', and have a rich panoply of styles, plantings and layouts. Behind a classic Regency terrace, itself the architectural jewel of Worthing, the gardens draw inspiration from such exotic diversity as Morocco, Provence and the Alhambra to the more traditional sources of the English cottage and Victorian gardens. All within the typically limited space of a terrace (seriously restricted disabled access), a variety of imaginative water features add to the charm and attraction for all gardeners and prove that small can be beautiful. Do come and enjoy our special spaces, we have 14 gardens open this year. Featured on BBC Sussex Radio Dig-it programme, Worthing Herald, West Sussex Gazette and other local media.
❀

You are always welcome at an NGS garden!

GROUP OPENING

3 **ANSTY GARDENS**
Bolney Road, Ansty, nr Haywards
Heath RH17 5AW. *3m W of
Haywards Heath on A272. 1m E of
A23. Park on L of A272 300yds W of
r'about at junction of A272 & B2036,
or if too wet try Council car park at
Ansty end of Deaks Lane, just W of
r'about (RH17 5AS).* Home-made
teas at The Barn House (May) &
Whydown (June). **Combined adm
£5, chd free. Sun 10 May, Sun 21
June (1.30-6).**

APPLETREE COTTAGE
Mr & Mrs G J Longfield

THE BARN HOUSE
Mr & Mrs Michael Dykes

3 LAVENDER COTTAGES
Derry Baillieux

SPRINGFIELD
Deaks Lane. David Pyrah

NEW **THICKETS**
Deaks Lane. Mr & Mrs Jamie &
Pia Campbell.
Open May only

WHYDOWN COTTAGE
Bolney Road. Mrs M Gibson &
Lance Gibson

Ansty's gardens offer interesting
contrast. Whydown Cottage covers
an acre with water features and an
atmospheric woodland incl an
Embothrium. 3 Lavender Cottages
has an attractive garden to the front
and pretty brick courtyard to the rear
with cottage flowers. While strolling
along, do look at a garden in the
making, the front garden at Thickets
is open this year. Close by is
picturesque C16 Appletree Cottage
set in 2 acres with herbaceous beds,
vegetable garden and fruit cage with
wonderful views. Springfield's 1 acre
offers mature trees and large pond,
also camellias, azaleas,
rhododendrons, and herbaceous
border. Finally the group incl The Barn
House with approx an acre walled
garden and pretty pond. Wheelchair
access at Whydown unless very wet,
partial access at 3 Lavender Cottages
and no access at Springfield.

4 **NEW** **ARBORGARTH**
Bracken Lane, Storrington,
Pulborough RH20 3HS. Ted & Syb
Hickford, syb.hickford@sky.com.

*1½ m from centre of Storrington
Village. Travel N from S coast on A24.
After Washington r'about, L into Rock
Rd signed Thakeham & West
Chiltington. Bracken Lane is 5th
turning on L, drive on R just past
Bunbury Close.* **Adm £5, chd free.
Visitors welcome by arrangement
Mar to Sept for groups of 10-20
max with refreshments on request.**
1 acre terraced garden, designed,
developed and maintained over 30
yrs by current owners giving three
seasons of colour and interest from
mid Mar to end of Sept. The garden
incl spring bulbs, camellias, azaleas,
bluebells, unusual trees, wide thyme
bed, herbaceous borders, box
hedging, stream, pond, waterfall, bog
garden, and some topiary, all
surrounded by high yew and beech
hedging. Wheelchair access to two
levels only but with views over the
garden. Access limited as wide steps
and sloping grass paths to lower
level.

Working walled kitchen garden growing a wide range of fruit, vegetables and flowers . . .

5 **♦ ARUNDEL CASTLE &
GARDENS - THE COLLECTOR
EARL'S GARDEN**
Arundel BN18 9AB. Arundel Castle
Trustees Ltd, 01903 882173,
www.arundelcastle.org. *In the
centre of Arundel, N of A27.* **For
opening times and information,
please phone or see garden
website.**
Ancient castle. Family home of the
Duke of Norfolk. 40 acres of grounds
and gardens. The Collector Earl's
Garden with hot subtropical borders
and wild flowers. English herbaceous
borders. 2 restored Victorian
glasshouses with exotic fruit and
vegetables. Walled flower and organic
kitchen gardens. C14 Fitzalan Chapel
white garden.

6 **ASHDOWN PARK HOTEL**
Wych Cross, East Grinstead
RH18 5JR. Mr Kevin Sweet,
01342 824988,
reservations@ashdownpark.co.uk,
www.elitehotels.co.uk. *6m S of East
Grinstead. Turn off A22 at Wych
Cross T-lights.* Light refreshments.
**Adm £5, chd free. Thur 18 June
(1-5).**
186 acres of parkland, grounds and
gardens surrounding Ashdown Park
Hotel. Our Secret Garden is well
worth a visit with many new plantings.
Large number of deer roam the
estate and can often be seen during
the day. Enjoy and explore the
woodland paths, quiet areas and
views. Featured in Sussex Life and
local press. Some gravel paths and
uneven ground with steps.

7 **96 ASHFORD ROAD**
Hastings TN34 2HZ. Lynda &
Andrew Hayler. *From A21
(Sedlescombe Rd N) towards
Hastings take 1st exit on r'about
A2101, then 3rd on L.* **Adm £3, chd
free. Sat 23, Sat 30 May (1-5).**
Small (100ft x 52ft) Japanese inspired
front and back garden. Full of
interesting planting. Many acers,
azaleas and bamboos. Over 100
different hostas, many miniature.
Lower garden with greenhouse and
raised beds. New for 2015 a
Japanese Tea House. Featured in
Hastings Observer.
❀

8 **BAKERS HOUSE**
Bakers Lane, Shipley RH13 8GJ.
Mr & Mrs Mark Burrell, 01403
741215, margot@dragons.me.uk.
*5m S of Horsham. Take A24 to
Worthing, then A272 W, 2nd turn to
Dragon's Green. L at George &
Dragon PH, Bakers Lane then
300yds on L.* Home-made teas. **Adm
£5, chd free. Sun 24 May, Sun 21
June (2-6). Visitors also welcome
by arrangement May to June.**
There is so much to see in this large
parkland garden incl great oaks, lake,
laburnum tunnel, rose walks with old
fashioned roses, scented knot
garden, olive and lemon walk, bog
gardens and a big kitchen garden
with potager. Featured in Sussex Life
(May 2014) as one of the 25 top
gardens to visit in Sussex. Partial
wheelchair access, garden has gravel
paths.

GROUP OPENING

9 BALCOMBE GARDENS
Balcombe. *3m N of Cuckfield on B2036. From J10A on M23, follow B2036 S for 2¹/₂ m.* Home-made teas at Krawden. **Combined adm £5, chd free. Wed 13 May, Sat 13 June (12-5).**

KRAWDEN
Victoria Road, RH17 6LJ. Ann & Eddie Bryant

46 WESTUP FARM COTTAGES
RH17 6JJ. Chris & Sarah Cornwell.
¹/₄ m N of station, turn L off B2036 immed before Balcombe Primary School (signed) ³/₄ m
Visitors also welcome by arrangement Apr to Sept for groups of 4+.
01444 811891
chris.westup@btinternet.com

WINTERFIELD
RH17 6LP. Sue & Sarah Howe.
Just N of station, R into Newlands, follow road uphill. Garden on R once road has become Oldlands Ave
Visitors also welcome by arrangement May to July.
01444 811380
sarahjhowe_uk@yahoo.co.uk

Balcombe is in a designated AONB. Traceable back to the Saxons, the village contains 55 listed buildings incl C15 parish church of St Mary's. Nearby is the famous Ouse Valley Viaduct, ancient woodlands, lake, millpond and reservoir. The three gardens opening for the NGS will especially appeal to plant lovers and are full of variety and interest. Hidden in the countryside of the High Weald, Westup Farm Cottages' garden contains unique and traditional features linked by intimate paths through lush and subtle planting. Winterfield contains as many trees and shrubs as can be crammed into ¹/₂ acre with wild flowers, gravelled areas, alpine troughs, a secret garden, pond and borders. Krawden offers roses, herbaceous borders, fruit and vegetables, a Mediterranean area with gravel and water feature and provides the venue for teas. Wheelchair access at Winterfield and Krawden only.

♿ ⊛ 🚐 ☕

10 ◆ BATEMAN'S
Bateman's Lane, Burwash TN19 7DS. National Trust, 01435 882302, www.nationaltrust.org.uk. *6m E of Heathfield. ¹/₂ m S of A265 on road leading S at W end of Burwash, or N from Woods Corner (B2096). Pick up & drop off point available.* **Adm £9.50, chd £4.75. For NGS: Wed 6 May (10-5.30). For other opening times and information, please phone or see garden website.**
Bateman's is an idyllic spot; a family home loved by Rudyard Kipling. Nestled in a shallow valley, the house and garden were a joy and an inspiration to him, from the formal lawns and clipped yew hedges to the romantic meadow with the meandering river flowing through it. Highlights incl Wild Garden carpeted with spring bulbs below flowering trees and shrubs, Orchard, Vegetable Garden and Watermill. Most of the garden is accessible. There are some slopes and uneven paths.

♿ ⊛ 🚐 ☕

Great variety of home-grown plants for sale . . .

11 ◆ BATES GREEN
Tye Hill Road, Arlington BN26 6SH. Carolyn & John McCutchan, 01323 485152, www.batesgreen.co.uk. *3¹/₂ m SW of Hailsham & A22. Midway between the A22 & A27, 2m S of Michelham Priory. Bates Green is in Tye Hill Rd (N of Arlington Village), 350yds S of Old Oak Inn.* **Adm £5, chd free. For NGS: Visitors welcome by arrangement Mar to Oct excl Aug. Refreshments on request.**
Plantsman's 2 acre tranquil garden, of interest through the seasons. Springtime incl narcissi, primroses, violets, early tulips and coloured stems of cornus. Summer progresses with alliums, hardy geraniums, kniphofias, hemerocallis, grasses, crocosmias and organic vegetables. Autumn peaks with asters, cyclamen, colchicum, dahlias, heleniums, miscanthus, and verbenas. Featured in Sussex Life (May 2014). Wheelchair access to most areas.

♿ 🏠 ⊛ 🚐 ☕

12 BEEDINGLEE
Brighton Road, Lower Beeding, Horsham RH13 6NQ. Mrs Jo Longley, 01403 891251, joslongley@gmail.com. *4m SE of Horsham on A281 to Cowfold. Approx ¹/₂ m N of South Lodge Hotel on A281 from Cowfold to Horsham. The entrance is almost opp a red post box on a stalk.* Light refreshments, cream teas & home-made cakes. **Adm £4, chd free. Sun 17 May, Sun 14 June (11-5). Visitors also welcome by arrangement May to Oct for groups of 25 max.**
Originally part of the Leonardslee Estate, the planting of the 6 acre Victorian/Edwardian garden disappeared during the hurricane of 1987, when over 100 mature trees blew down. The present garden has evolved since then with many interesting and unusual trees and shrubs. Still an informal garden, there are hidden paths, a secret garden, lawns and a wild flower garden.

🏠 ⊛ ☕

13 4 BEN'S ACRE
Horsham RH13 6LW. Pauline Clark, 01403 266912, brian.clark8850@yahoo.co.uk, www.youtube.com, search Pauline & Brian's Sussex Garden. *NE of Horsham. From A281 via Cowfold after Hilliers Garden Centre, take 2nd R by Tesco, St Leonards Rd, then into Comptons Lane. 5th R Heron Way after mini-r'about, 2nd L Glebe Crescent, 1st L Ben's Acre (avoid Brambling Rd, past a school in June).* Home-made teas. **Adm £4, chd free. Fri 19 June (12-2.30 & 3.30-6); Sat 29 Aug (1-5). Visitors also welcome by arrangement late June to early Sept for groups of 15-35.**
A keen Hardy Plant Society member's garden, that is said to have the wow effect and with surprises and delights for the visitor. On the edge of St Leonards Forest and riverside walk, 100ft x 45ft using steps and terraces to take you to borders planted to capacity with interesting potpourri of colour, texture and form. Featuring arbours, summerhouse, and ponds with waterfall, topiary, and pots of succulents. Many seats around the garden while having one of our delicious teas. Come, enjoy and take home some ideas for your garden. Featured in Real Homes (2014).

🏠 ⊛ ☕

GROUP OPENING

14 BEXHILL GARDENS
Bexhill. *Bexhill & Little Common. Proceed to Little Common r'about on A259, then see directions for each garden. Tickets available on the day from any of the gardens.* Home-made teas at Clare Cottage. **Combined adm £5, chd free. Sun 7 June (11-5).**

NEW 14 CHANTRY AVENUE
TN40 2EA. Peggy Harvey.
From A259 r'about by Ravenside Retail Park, follow Battle & Ninfield sign on A2036, passing through T-lights. 1m on take 3rd turning on L into Chantry Ave. Property on L nr bottom of road

NEW CLARE COTTAGE
Collington Lane East, TN39 3RG. Mr Terry Johns

NEW 147 DORSET ROAD
TN40 2HU. Anita Jones.
From the A259 by Ravenside Retail Park r'about take A2036 to Ninfield. Proceed to T-lights, turn L into Penland Rd. No 147 is 100yds on the R corner of Penland & Dorset Rd

6 KINGSWOOD AVENUE
TN39 4EJ. Mr & Mrs Lal & Gloria Ratnayake.
Exit r'about E towards Hastings. After ¾ m turn L into Warwick Rd, at end of road turn R at T-junction, then immed L into Broad View, 2nd R Glenleigh Ave, 1st L Kingswood Ave

ORCHARD COTTAGE
22 Gatelands Drive, TN39 4DP. Pat McCarthy.
From Little Common keep on A259 for approx 1¼ m towards Hastings. Turn L at T-lights (Viking Chip Bar) onto A269 London. Take 1st L into Woodsgate Park, then 4th R into Gatelands Drive

An attractive Edwardian residential seaside town famous for its De la Warr Pavilion Arts Centre. Also noted for the enthusiastic gardeners who open to the public. 14 Chantry Avenue is an unusual Chinese inspired garden, while 147 Dorset Road is newly created in tropical & Mediterranean style. Kingswood Avenue has mature trees, shrubs and herbaceous borders, also bonsai plants, fuschias and pelargoniums. Small pond with frogs and dragonflies. Plants for sale. Clare

Cottage has a restful atmosphere with herbaceous borders and a log cabin. Orchard Cottage is a plantswoman's recently designed small garden, with a wonderful variety of plants for sale. Wheelchair access to some gardens.

The garden makes clever use of grasses and is set amongst woodland, with stunning countryside views . . .

15 BIGNOR PARK
Pulborough RH20 1HG.
The Mersey Family,
www.bignorpark.co.uk. *5m S of Petworth & Pulborough. Well signed from B2138. Nearest villages Sutton, Bignor & West Burton. Approach from the E, directions & map available on website.* Home-made teas. **Adm £5, chd free. Sun 26 Apr, Sun 7 June, Sun 20 Sept (2-5).**
11 acres of peaceful garden to explore, with magnificent views of the South Downs. Interesting trees, shrubs, wild flower areas, with swathes of daffodils in spring. The walled flower garden has been replanted with herbaceous borders. Temple, Greek loggia, Zen pond and unusual sculptures. Former home of romantic poet Charlotte Smith, whose sonnets were inspired by Bignor Park. Spectacular Cedars of Lebanon and rare Holm Oak. Featured in Daily Telegraph, Sunday Times, The Lady and a number of local publications. Wheelchair access to shrubbery and croquet lawn, gravel paths in rest of garden and steps in stables quadrangle.

16 4 BIRCH CLOSE
Arundel BN18 9HN. Elizabeth & Mike Gammon, 01903 882722, e.gammon@toucansurf.com. *1m S of Arundel. From A27 & A284 r'about at W end of Arundel take Ford Rd. After ½ m turn R into Maxwell Rd &

follow signs. Home-made teas. **Adm £3, chd free. Sun 3, Mon 4 May (2-5).** Visitors also welcome by arrangement May to June for groups of 10+.
⅓ acre of woodland garden on edge of Arundel. Wide range of mature trees and shrubs with many hardy perennials. Emphasis on extensive selection of spring flowers and clematis (over 100 incl 11 montana). All in a tranquil setting with secluded corners, meandering paths and plenty of seating. Partial wheelchair access to approx half of garden.
&. ⊗ ☕

17 BLUE JAYS
Chesworth Close, Horsham RH13 5AL. Stella & Mike Schofield, 01403 251065. *5 mins walk SE of St Mary's Church Horsham. From A281 (East St) L down Denne Rd, L to Chesworth Lane, R to Chesworth Close. Garden at end of close. 4 disabled spaces, other parking in local streets & Denne Rd car park (free on Suns).* Home-made teas. **Adm £3.50, chd free. Share to The Badger Trust. Sun 26 Apr, Sat 16, Sun 17 May (12.30-5).** Visitors also welcome by arrangement Apr to Sept for groups of 8+ with refreshments on request.
Wooded 1 acre garden with rhododendrons, camellias and azaleas. Candelabra primulas and ferns edge the R Arun. Primroses and spring bulbs border woodland path and stream. Cordylines, gunneras, flower beds, a pond, a fountain and new formal rose garden set in open lawns. Arch leads to a vegetable plot and orchard bounded by the river. Large WW2 pill box in the orchard; visits inside with short talk are available. Wheelchair access to most areas.

18 ◆ BORDE HILL GARDEN
Borde Hill Lane, Haywards Heath RH16 1XP. Borde Hill Garden Ltd, 01444 450326, www.bordehill.co.uk. *1½ m N of Haywards Heath. 20 mins N of Brighton, or S of Gatwick on A23 taking exit 10a via Balcombe.* **Adm £8, chd £5. For NGS: Tue 8 Sept (10-6).** For other opening times and information, please phone or see garden website.
Fascinating heritage garden in stunning landscapes with twisting trails ensure Borde Hill Garden provides entertainment and

4 Birch Close

© Jonathan Need

enjoyment for horticulture enthusiasts, country lovers and families. Nestled in 200 acres of English Heritage listed parkland and woodland with panoramic views overlooking the Sussex Weald. Nationally important collection of rare shrubs and champion trees, outdoor rooms including the Rose and Italian gardens, makes Borde Hill the perfect day out destination. 2015 is the 50th anniversary of Borde Hill as a charity. Wheelchair access to formal garden (17 acres). Dogs welcome on leads.

♿ 🐕 ⛱ 🚐 ☕

19 BRADNESS GALLERY
Spithurst Road, Spithurst, Barcombe BN8 5EB. Michael Cruickshank & Emma Burnett, 01273 400606, emmaburnett16@btinternet.com, www.emmaburnett.co.uk. *5m N of Lewes. Bradness Gallery lies midway between Barcombe & Newick in Spithurst. Free parking in field.*

Disabled parking will be available outside the gallery. Home-made teas. **Adm £4, chd free. Sat 13, Sun 14 June (11-5.30).**
Delightful and tranquil mature, organic, wildlife garden with trees, scented shrubs, old roses, herbaceous borders and wild garden planting. A wooded stream flows along the bottom and two large ponds are home to wild ducks, dragonflies and frogs. Also raised beds for vegetables and cut flowers. Courtyard. Delicious home-made teas and cakes and a lovely new tearoom for rainy days. Surrounded by fields and cows. The gallery will be open showing original paintings, prints and cards by the owners. Featured in Prima Magazine entitled 'Our wild and romantic garden' (Sept 2014). Wheelchair access to the upper part of the garden, but the garden does slope down to the ponds and stream and the ground is uneven.

♿ 🚐 ☕

20 BRIGHTLING DOWN FARM
Observatory Road, Dallington TN21 9LN. Mr & Mrs P Stephens, 07770 807060 / 01435 831118, valstephens@icloud.com. *1m from Woods Corner. At Swan PH at Woods Corner, take road opp signed Brightling. Take 1st L, signed Burwash. Almost immed, turn into 1st driveway on L.* Home-made teas. **Adm £7.50, chd free. Visitors welcome by arrangement May to Oct for groups 10-30.**
The garden has several different areas incl a Zen garden, water garden, walled vegetable garden with 2 large greenhouses, herb garden and herbaceous borders. The garden makes clever use of grasses and is set amongst woodland, with stunning countryside views. Winner of the Society of Garden Designers award.

🅳 ☕

GROUP OPENING

BURGESS HILL GARDENS

Burgess Hill. *10m N of Brighton. 3 gardens in town centre, 4 gardens off Folders Lane & 1 in Janes Lane. Tickets & maps from any garden.* Home-made teas. Combined adm £5, chd free. Sun 26, Mon 27 July (1-5).

14 BARNSIDE AVENUE
RH15 0JU. Brian & Sue Knight. *From Folders Lane (B2113) take Kings Way & Barnside is on R*

NEW CHESTNUT HOUSE
66 Janes Lane, RH15 0QR. Liz Gordon. *Janes Lane is off the B2112 & runs through to Valebridge Rd, which is nr Wivelfield Station & 47 Leylands Rd*

41 FAIRFIELD ROAD
RH15 8QB. Mrs Catriona Arnold. *Fairfield Rd runs parallel to London Rd. Park in road*

47 LEYLANDS ROAD
RH15 8AF. Diane & Stephen Rabson. *Leylands Rd lies between London Rd (B2036) & Wivelsfield Station* Visitors also welcome by arrangement July to Aug. 01444 247937

9 SYCAMORE DRIVE
RH15 0GG. Peter Machin & Martin Savage. *Off Folders Lane 1st house on LH-side at entrance to Sycamore Drive. Walk over gated bridge & follow signs*

30 SYCAMORE DRIVE
RH15 0GH. John Smith & Kieran O'Regan (See separate entry)

59 SYCAMORE DRIVE
RH15 0GG. Steve & Debby Gill

This diverse group of seven is a mixture of established and small new gardens. Three of the group are a great example of what can be achieved over a 6 yr period from a blank canvas in a new development (Sycamore Drive) while close by is 14 Barnside Avenue, a wisteria clad house (pruning advice given) with a family lawn and borders. 47 Leylands Road is a garden packed with an array of plants and a wildlife pond. At nearby 41 Fairfield Road the award-winning back garden is home to free range bantams! Our new addition in Janes Lane is an established, medium sized garden with a lawn flanked by borders, a wild flower area and plenty of space for teas. Many useful ideas for people living in new build properties with small gardens and heavy clay soil. Partial wheelchair access to some gardens.

&♿ 🐕 ❀ ☕

Wander along the paths and over the bridges among the flowers, shrubs and beautiful trees . . .

---

22 BUTLERS FARMHOUSE

Butlers Lane, Herstmonceux BN27 1QH. Irene Eltringham-Willson, 01323 833770, irene.willson@btinternet.com. *3m E of Hailsham.* Take A271 from Hailsham, go through village of Herstmonceux, turn R signed Church Rd then approx 1m turn R. Do not use SatNav! Home-made teas. Adm £3.50 (Apr), £5 (Aug), chd free. Sat 11, Sun 12 Apr, Sat 8, Sun 9 Aug (2-5). Visitors also welcome by arrangement Mar to Oct with refreshments provided.
Lovely rural setting for 1 acre garden surrounding C16 farmhouse (not open) with views of South Downs. Pretty in spring with primroses and hellebores. Mainly herbaceous with rainbow border, small pond with dribbling frogs and Cornish inspired beach corners. Restored to former glory, as shown in old photographs, but with a few quirky twists such as a poison garden and a secret jungle garden. Relax and listen to live jazz in the garden in August. Featured in Period Homes & Interiors (March 2014). Listed in Sussex Life as one of top 25 gardens to visit. Most of garden accessible by wheelchair.

&♿ ❀ 🚐 🛏 ☕

---

23 51 CARLISLE ROAD

Eastbourne BN21 4JR. Mr & Mrs N Fraser-Gausden, 01323 722545, n.fg@sky.com. *200yds inland from seafront (Wish Tower), close to Congress Theatre.* Home-made teas. Adm £3, chd free. Sat 30, Sun 31 May (2-5). Visitors also welcome by arrangement May to June.
Walled, S-facing garden (82ft sq) with mixed beds intersected by stone paths and incl small pool. Profuse and diverse planting. Wide selection of shrubs, old roses, herbaceous plants and perennials mingle with specimen trees and climbers. Constantly revised planting to maintain the magical and secluded atmosphere. Has been featured in many gardening magazines over the yrs.

❀ ☕

24 CAXTON MANOR

Wall Hill, Forest Row RH18 5EG. Adele & Jules Speelman. *1m N of Forest Row, 2m S of E Grinstead.* From A22 take turning to Ashurstwood, entrance on L after 1/3 m, or 1m on R from N. Home-made teas. Adm £5, chd free. Share to St Catherine's Hospice, Crawley. Fri 15, Sat 16 May (2-5).
Delightful 5 acre Japanese inspired gardens planted with mature rhododendrons, azaleas and acers, surrounding large pond with boathouse, massive rockery and waterfall, beneath the home of the late Sir Archibald McIndoe (house not open). Japanese tea house and Japanese style courtyard. **Also open 2 Quarry Cottages (separate admission)**.

&♿ ❀ 🚐 ☕

25 CHAMPS HILL

Waltham Park Road, Coldwaltham, Pulborough RH20 1LY. Mr & Mrs David Bowerman, 01798 831205, mary@thebct.org.uk. *3m S of Pulborough.* On A29, turn R to Fittleworth into Waltham Park Rd, garden 400 metres on R. Tea. Adm by donation. Visitors welcome by arrangement Mar to Oct for groups of 10+.
Champs Hill has been developed around three disused sand quarries since 1960. The woodlands are full of beautiful rhododendrons and azaleas, but the most striking feature is the collection of heathers, over 300 cultivars. The garden also has some interesting sculptures, and stupendous views.

&♿ 🚐 ☕

26 CHANNEL VIEW

52 Brook Barn Way, Goring-by-Sea, Worthing BN12 4DW. Jennie & Trevor Rollings, 01903 242431, tjrollings@gmail.com. *1m W of Worthing near seafront. Turn S off A259 into Parklands Ave, L at T-junction into Alinora Crescent. Brook Barn Way is immed on L.* Home-made teas. **Adm £4, chd free. Sat 27, Sun 28 June (2-5). Visitors also welcome by arrangement May to Sept.**

Mature owner designed garden by the sea, imaginatively blending traditional Tudor cottage garden with subtropical, Mediterranean and antipodean planting. Unusually designed structures, paths, arches and pond combine dense planting with shady viewpoints and sunny patios. Interconnecting garden rooms ensure multiple perspectives and hidden vistas. Great variety of home-grown plants for sale. Featured in West Sussex Gazette and Worthing Herald. Partial wheelchair access.

  ♿ 🐕 ✿ 🚐 ☕ 🍵

27 CHIDMERE GARDENS

Chidham Lane, Chidham, Chichester PO18 8TD. Jackie & David Russell, 01243 572287, info@chidmere.com, www.chidmerefarm.com. *6m W of Chichester at SE end of Chidham Lane by pond in village.* Home-made teas. **Adm £5, chd free. Visitors welcome by arrangement Mar to Sept for groups of 10-20. Adm incl a cup of tea or coffee.**

Wisteria clad C15 house (not open) surrounded by yew and hornbeam hedges situated next to Chidmere pond; a natural wildlife preserve (approx 5 acres). Garden incl white garden, formal rose garden, well stocked herbaceous borders and springtime woods. 8 acres of orchards with wide selection of heritage and modern varieties of apples, pears and plums incl 200 yr old varieties of Blenheim Orange and Bramley Seedling. Partial wheelchair access.

  ♿ ☕ 🍵

28 ♦ CLINTON LODGE

Fletching, Uckfield TN22 3ST. Lady Collum, 01825 722952, www.clintonlodgegardens.co.uk. *4m NW of Uckfield. Clinton Lodge is situated in Fletching High St, N of Rose & Crown PH. Off road parking provided. It is important visitors do not park in street. Parking available*

from 1pm. Home-made teas. **Adm £5, chd free. Share to local charities. For NGS: Sun 26 Apr, Mon 15 June, Mon 3 Aug (2-5.30). For other opening times and information, please phone or see garden website.**

6 acre formal and romantic garden, overlooking parkland, with old roses, William Pye water feature, double white and blue herbaceous borders, yew hedges, pleached lime walks, copy of C17 scented herb garden, Medieval style potager, vine and rose allée, wild flower garden. Canal garden, small knot garden, shady glade and orchard. Caroline and Georgian house (not open).

  ✿ ☕ 🍵

29 COBB COTTAGE NORTH

Selsfield Rd, Ardingly, Haywards Heath RH17 6TH. Peter & Marlene Holter. *B2028 N of Village. Opp S gate of South of England showground, 1m S of Wakehurst Place (National Trust). Gravel car park.* Home-made teas. **Adm £3.50, chd free. Sat 11, Sun 19 July (11-5).**

½ acre edge of village garden with shrubs, perennials, and annuals set off by lawns, several interesting trees 3 wildlife ponds with cascades, patio with seating, terracotta pots and hanging baskets. Marvel at Peter's giant show onions in raised beds along with an extensive range of other vegetables, soft fruit, and full greenhouse. Plants and soft fruit for sale. Public WC 150yds away in village. The garden is mostly accessible by wheelchair, but sloping site and grass paths.

  ♿ 🐕 ✿ ☕ 🍵

30 COLWOOD HOUSE

Cuckfield Lane, Warninglid RH17 5SP. Mr & Mrs Patrick Brenan, 01444 461831, rbrenan@me.com. *6m W of Haywards Heath, 6m SE of Horsham. Entrance on B2115 (Cuckfield Lane). From E, N & S, turn W off A23, towards Warninglid for ¾ m. From W come through Warninglid Village.* Tea. **Share to Seaforth Hall. Visitors welcome by arrangement Apr to Sept for groups of 10+.**

12 acres of garden with mature and specimen trees from the late 1800s, lawns and woodland edge. Formal parterre, rose and herb gardens. 100ft terrace and herbaceous border overlooking flower rimmed croquet lawn. Cut turf labyrinth and forsythia

tunnel. Water features, statues and gazebos. Pets' cemetery. Giant chessboard. Lake with island and temple. The garden has gravel paths and some slopes.

  ♿ 🐕 ☕ 🍵

> Viewing platform between two oak trees affording far reaching views of garden and countryside . . .

31 COOKSCROFT

Bookers Lane, Earnley, nr Chichester PO20 7JG. Mr & Mrs J Williams, 01243 513671, williams.cookscroft330@btinternet.com, www.cookscroft.co.uk. *6m S of Chichester. At end of Birdham Straight A286 from Chichester, take L fork to E Wittering B2198. 1m on, before sharp bend, turn L into Bookers Lane. 2nd house on L. Parking available.* Cream teas in the garden. **Adm £4, chd free. Sun 3 May (1-5). Evening Opening, wine, Sat 27 June (5-9). Visitors also welcome by arrangement Apr to Sept, groups welcome, ample parking.**

This is a garden for all seasons which delights the visitor. Started in 1988, it features cottage, woodland cottage and Japanese style gardens, water features and borders of perennials, with a particular emphasis on S Hemisphere plants. Unusual plants for the plantsman to enjoy, many grown from seed. Extensive open borders with correas, corokias, leptospermum and prostatheras and trees from down under. Featured in Chichester Observer (May 2014). The garden has grass paths and unfenced ponds.

  ♿ 🐕 ✿ 🚐 ☕ 🍵

© Leigh Clapp

Sandhill Farm House

32 COPYHOLD HOLLOW

Copyhold Lane, Borde Hill, Haywards Heath RH16 1XU. Frances Druce, 01444 413265, ngs@copyholdhollow.co.uk, www.copyholdhollow.co.uk. *2m N of Haywards Heath. Follow signs for Borde Hill Gardens. With Borde Hill Gardens on L, over brow of hill, take 1st R signed Ardingly. Garden ¹/₂ m.* Home-made teas. **Adm £4, chd free. Visitors welcome by arrangement most Thurs May to Aug from 12-3pm. Please phone or email to book time slot as parking is limited.**
Cottage garden in a hollow, with woodland garden above. Spring fed pond with dam and waterfall edged with damp loving perennials. The oak stumpery gives way to a rock garden on the way to the crow's nest and the whole garden is planted for yr-round interest. Crow's nest viewing platform slung between two oak trees affording far reaching views of garden and countryside. Featured in Country Living (April 2014) and Sussex Society (June 2014).

🌸 🛏 ☕

33 DACHS

Spear Hill, Ashington RH20 3BA. Bruce Wallace, 01903 892466, wallacebuk@aol.com. *Approx 6m N of Worthing. From A24 at Ashington onto B2133 Billingshurst Rd, R into Spear Hill. We are the 1st house, garden runs along Billingshurst Rd.* Home-made teas. **Adm £4, chd free. Sun 29 Mar, Sun 12 Apr (2-5.30). Visitors also welcome by arrangement Mar to Oct for day or evening visits.**
A waterlogged field turned into a beautiful garden of about 2 acres. Incl white garden, bog area, stream and unusual design of bridges. Several other themed beds with perennials of different textures and colours. Over 200 varieties of daffodils (100 new this yr) and narcissi, some snowdrops, fritillaria and iris in spring. Free gifts for children to encourage them to grow things. Featured in Sussex Life.

♿ 🎒 🌸 🚌 ☕

34 DALE PARK HOUSE

Madehurst, Arundel BN18 0NP. Robert & Jane Green, 01243 814260, robertgreen@farming.co.uk.

4m W of Arundel. Take A27 E from Chichester or W from Arundel, then A29 (London) for 2m, turn L to Madehurst and follow red arrows. Home-made teas. **Adm £4, chd free. Sun 7 June (2-5). Visitors also welcome by arrangement May to Aug.**
Set in parkland within the South Downs National Park, enjoying magnificent views to the sea. Come and relax in the large walled garden, which features an impressive 200ft herbaceous border. There is also a sunken gravel garden, mixed borders, a small rose garden, dreamy rose and clematis arches, interesting collection of hostas, foliage plants and shrubs, an orchard and kitchen garden.

🌸 🚌 ☕

35 DOWN PLACE

South Harting, Petersfield GU31 5PN. Mr & Mrs D M Thistleton-Smith, 01730 825374, selina@downplace.co.uk. *1m SE of South Harting. B2141 to Chichester, turn L down unmarked lane below top of hill.* Cream teas. **Adm £4, chd free. Share to Friends of Harting Church. Sat 25, Sun 26 Apr, Sat 13, Sun 14 June (2-6). Visitors also welcome by arrangement Apr to July for groups of 15+.**
7 acre hillside, chalk garden on the north side of South Downs with fine views of surrounding countryside. Extensive herbaceous, shrub and rose borders on different levels merging into natural wild flower meadow renowned for its collection of native orchids. Fully stocked vegetable garden and greenhouses. Spring flowers and blossom. Substantial top terrace and borders accessible to wheelchairs.

♿ 🌸 ☕

36 DRIFTWOOD

4 Marine Drive, Bishopstone, Seaford BN25 2RS. Geoff Stonebanks & Mark Glassman, 01323 899296, geoffstonebanks@gmail.com, www.driftwoodbysea.co.uk. *A259 between Seaford & Newhaven. Turn L into Marine Drive from Bishopstone Rd, 2nd on R. Please park carefully in road but not on bend beyond house.* Light refreshments. **Adm £4, chd free. Tue 9, Thur 25 June, Tue 7 July, Sun 9 Aug (11-5). Visitors also welcome by arrangement June to Aug for groups of 4-20.**
A 2014 visitor said, it's the most staggering and inspirational garden to

show what can be achieved without possessing rolling acres but having an eye, imagination, a love of plants and great energy and enthusiasm. An exuberant yet immaculate seaside garden (112ft x 48ft). The heavy, dense plantings with no lawn and no exposed soil create an illusion of a much bigger garden. This is a real must see garden! Large selection of home-made cakes and savoury items available, all served on vintage china on trays in the garden. Jean Griffin, BBC Sussex Gardening expert from Dig It will be offering advice in my garden for visitors on 7 July. In 2014 featured live on ITV's Good Morning Britain, listed as one of 25 Sussex Gardens to see by Sussex Life, featured in Garden Answers, Etc Magazine, 100 Idées Jardin, & referenced in both The Sunday Times & Daily Mail Weekend Magazine. Steep drive, narrow paths and many levels, but help readily available on-site or call ahead before visit.

37 DUCKYLS HOLT
Selsfield Road, West Hoathly RH19 4QN. Mrs Diana Hill & Miss Sophie Hill, 01342 810282, sophie@duckylsholt.fsnet.co.uk. *4m SW of East Grinstead, 6m E of Crawley. At Turners Hill take B2028. After 1m fork L to West Hoathly. Garden on R immed beyond 30mph sign. Some parking at garden, other parking in village.* Home-made teas & cakes. **Adm £3.50, chd free. Sat 23, Sun 24, Mon 25 May (11-5.30). Combined adm with The Priest House on 23 May only £4, chd free. Visitors also welcome by arrangement May to June with refreshments on request.**
Delightful cottage garden of approx 2 acres on many different levels with a naturalistic feel. Small herb garden, colourful formal and informal plantings, herbaceous borders, rose border and formal rose garden. Lots of pots and baskets, a riot of colour, and mature azaleas and rhododendrons in season. Featured in Sussex Living magazine (2014).

38 DURFORD MILL HOUSE
West Harting, Petersfield GU31 5AZ. Mrs Sue Jones, 01730 821125, sdurford@btinternet.com. *3m E of Petersfield. Just off A272 between Petersfield & Rogate, signed Durford Mill & the Hartings. From S Harting past village shop, 1st L to West Harting.* Light refreshments. **Adm £7, chd free. Visitors welcome by arrangement May to June.**
Come and relax in our peaceful mill garden with its meandering stream and quiet places to sit. Wander along the paths and over the bridges among the flowers, shrubs and beautiful trees. Finishing up with delicious home-made cakes and tea. Wheelchair access to main garden and tea area.

Uninterrupted views, over a ha-ha of the South Downs . . .

39 DURRANCE MANOR
Smithers Hill Lane, Shipley RH13 8PE. Gordon & Joan Lindsay, 01403 741577, jlindsay@dsl.pipex.com. *7m SW of Horsham. A24 to A272 (S from Horsham, N from Worthing), turn W towards Billingshurst. Approx 1¾ m, 2nd L Smithers Hill Lane signed to Countryman PH. Garden 2nd on L.* Tea. **Adm £4.50, chd free. Sun 30 Aug (2-6). Visitors also welcome by arrangement Apr to Sept.**
This 2 acre garden, surrounding a Medieval hall house (not open) with Horsham stone roof enjoys uninterrupted views, over a ha-ha of the South Downs and Chanctonbury Ring. There are many different gardens here, incl colourful long borders, Japanese inspired gardens, a large pond, wild flower meadow and orchard, shade gardens, greenhouse and vegetable garden.

40 54 ELMLEIGH
Midhurst GU29 9HA. Wendy Liddle, 07796 562275, wendyliddle@btconnect.com. *¼ m W of Midhurst, off A272. Wheelchair users please use designated parking spaces at top of drive, phone on arrival for assistance.* Home-made teas, cream teas & cakes. **Adm £3, chd free. Sat 6, Sun 7, Sat 20, Sun 21 June, Sat 11, Sun 12 July (10-5). Visitors also welcome by arrangement May to Sept.**

Come and walk around this beautiful, award-winning garden on the edge of Midhurst. Planted with majestic Scots pines, shrubs, perennials and annuals, packed with interest, a tapestry of unusual plants giving all season colour. Many raised beds and numerous statues. A child-friendly garden. New wildlife pond, bog garden and stumpery.

41 NEW ELPHICKS COTTAGE
Spring Lane, Burwash TN19 7HU. Lorna Chernajosvky. *200yds L down Spring Lane from Burwash High St. 6m E of Heathfield on A265, Spring Lane 1st L after petrol station. From Hurst Green take A265 4m W through Burwash village passing shops & PH. Turn R 200yds after car sales rooms into Spring Lane.* Home-made teas. **Adm £3.50, chd free. Thur 18, Fri 19 June (2-5).**
2 acre site surrounding 300 yr old cottage (not open). Formal front garden with knot garden contrasts with areas of naturalistic planting. On different levels with steep paths in places. A tranquil unfenced ¼ acre lake with island is stocked with carp and rudd. Woodland was cleared of 200 Scots pine trees in 2013 and replanting is currently underway.

42 FAIRLIGHT END
Pett Road, Pett, Hastings TN35 4HB. Chris & Robin Hutt, 07774 863750, chrishutt@btopenworld.com. *4m E of Hastings. From Hastings take A259 to Rye. At White Hart Beefeater turn R into Friars Hill. Descend into Pett Village. Park in village hall car park, opp house.* Home-made teas, light lunches & Pimms (in village hall if wet). **Adm £4.50, chd free. Share to Pett Village Hall. Sat 20, Sun 21 June (11-5). Visitors also welcome by arrangement May to Sept for groups of 10+.**
3 acre sloping garden with lovely views. Model kitchen garden with 30 raised beds. Wild flower meadow with mown paths, large orchard, two natural ponds joined by a stream and terraced herbaceous borders. Ian Kitson designed split level garden in front of house with corten steel wall and plant supports, topiary, and decking, all around ancient cherry tree. Fine hay and wildflower meadows. Steep paths, gravelled areas, unfenced ponds.

 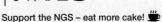

43 FINEOAKS

Hammer Lane, Cowbeech, Nr
Hailsham TN21 9HF. Brian &
Brenda Taylor. *5m S of Heathfield,
5m N of Hailsham. From Cowbeech
1m on LH-side, or from A22 Boship
r'about take A271 Bexhill Rd for
5 mins, then follow signs for
Cowbeech.* Home-made teas.
**Adm £4, chd free. Sat 2, Sun 3
May, Sat 4, Sun 5 July (12-5).**
An immaculate 3½ acre garden in
idyllic countryside. A rural farming
setting with a trout stream that flows in
spring, trickling in summer. The lawns
are punctuated with island beds
planted idiosyncratically with a mix of
shrubs, herbaceous and bedding
plants. Further afield an orchard, large
vegetable and fruit garden,
greenhouse and ancient woodland.
Nearer the house a pond, fountain and
pretty rockery. Ancient woodland with
bluebells in early May, ideal for little
explorers! Home-made organic jams
and marmalades for sale.

44 FITTLEWORTH HOUSE

Bedham Lane, Fittleworth,
Pulborough RH20 1JH. Edward &
Isabel Braham, 01798 865074,
www.marksaunders66.com. *2m E,
SE of Petworth. Midway between
Petworth & Pulborough on the A283
in Fittleworth, turn into lane signed
Bedham. 50yds along on L.* Tea.
**Adm £5, chd free. Every Wed 6
May to 29 July (2-5). Visitors also
welcome by arrangement Apr to
July for groups of 5+.**
3 acre tranquil garden with working
walled kitchen garden growing a wide
range of fruit, vegetables and flowers.
Large glasshouse and old potting
shed. Rhododendrons, roses,
fountain, mixed borders. Magnificent
cedar overlooks wisteria covered
Georgian house (not open) and
croquet lawn. Wild garden, long grass
areas, wildlife pond, spring bulbs.
Head gardener with 30 yrs
experience on hand to answer
questions. The garden sits on a
gentle slope but is accessible for
wheelchairs and buggies.

45 FIVE OAKS COTTAGE

Nr Petworth RH20 1HD. Jean &
Steve Jackman, 07939 272443,
jeanjackman@hotmail.com. *5m S of
Pulborough. To ensure best route
please ring or email and printed
directions will be provided. SatNav
does not work.* **Adm £5, chd free.**

Visitors welcome by arrangement
July and Sept for individuals or
groups of 20 max.
An acre of delicate jungle surrounding
Arts and Crafts style cottage, owned
by artists and founders of The Floral
Fringe Wildlife Fair. Stunning views of
the South Downs, wildlife
encouraged. Naturalistic new
perennial style planting, much new for
2015. Creative clashes of colour and
use of shrubs. Knapweed meadow
attracting clouds of butterflies in July.
Award-winning wildlife garden and
two small ponds. Featured in Country
Living, Country Homes & Interiors,
local press and Dutch and French
publications.

46 FOLLERS MANOR

Seaford Road, Alfriston BN26 5TT.
Geoff & Anne Shaw,
www.follersmanor.co.uk. *½ m S of
Alfriston. From Alfriston uphill towards
Seaford. Park on L in paddock before
garden. Garden next door to Alfriston
Youth Hostel immed before road
narrows.* Home-made teas. **Adm £5,
chd free. Sat 4, Sun 5 July (2-5.30).**
Contemporary garden designed by
Ian Kitson attached to C17 listed
historic farmhouse. Entrance
courtyard, sunken garden,
herbaceous displays, wildlife pond,
wild flower meadows, woodland area
and beautiful views of the South
Downs. Winner of Sussex Heritage
Trust Award and three awards from
the Society of Garden Designers;
Best Medium Residential Garden,
Hard Landscaping and, most
prestigious, the Judges Award.
Featured in Financial Times and
inclusion in new Alan Titchmarsh
programme 2015. Partial wheelchair
access to some areas.

47 70 FORD ROAD

Arundel BN18 9EX. Tony & Lizzie
Gilks, 01903 884981,
timespan70@tiscali.co.uk. *1m S of
Arundel. At Chichester r'about take
exit to Ford & Bognor Regis.* Home-
made teas, cakes, selection of
sandwiches & scones. **Adm £3.50,
chd free. Sun 10 May, Sun 5 July,
Sun 16 Aug (2-5). Visitors also
welcome by arrangement Apr to
Sept for groups of 2-30.**
An immaculate and stunningly laid out
town garden with ingenious ideas of
how to incorporate well stocked
flower beds with yr-round colour and
texture, herbs, fruit and vegetable
beds. In all a wonderfully lush
sanctuary in which to relax.

48 FRAMFIELD GRANGE

Framfield, Uckfield TN22 5PN. Mr
& Mrs Jack Gore. *3m E of Uckfield.
From Uckfield take B2102 to
Framfield 2½ m. Continue through
Framfield on B2102. The Grange
approx ¼ m E on R.* Tea. **Adm £5,
chd free. Sun 10 May (2-5).**
10 acres of garden with shrub
borders, lake and wild flower
meadow with orchids. Woodland
walks, bluebell glades. Many hybrids
and species of rhododendron and
azaleas. Beautifully kept walled
kitchen garden. Wheelchair access
via main gate and restricted to main
part of garden only.

49 THE GARDEN HOUSE

5 Warleigh Road, Brighton
BN1 4NT. Bridgette Saunders &
Graham Lee, 07729 037182 or
01273 702840,
contact@gardenhousebrighton.
co.uk,
www.gardenhousebrighton.co.uk.
*1½ m N of Brighton Pier. The Garden
House can be found 1½ m N of
seafront, 1st L off Ditching Rd, past
T-lights. Street paid parking available.*
Home-made teas. **Adm £3.50, chd
free. Sun 26 Apr (11-4). Visitors
also welcome by arrangement Feb
to Sept for groups of 10+.**
Tucked away in the heart of the city
this really is a secret garden, in
Victorian times a market garden. The
garden is organic and gives interest
all yr, supporting cut flowers,
vegetables, fruit, old climbing roses
and a pond. Many of the plants have
been propagated by the garden
owner, and the garden has unique
features using many recycled
materials. Features incl garden
produce and plants for sale.

50 GARDENERS' COTTAGE
West Dean, nr Chichester
PO18 0RX. Jim Buckland & Sarah
Wain. *6m N of Chichester. Off A286,
follow signs to West Dean Gardens &
park in car park. Follow signs to
cottage.* Home-made teas. **Adm £3,
chd free. Sun 24 May (11-5).**
Small, serene and secluded theatrical
retreat with strong emphasis on
texture, foliage and good structure
created by trees, topiary, labyrinthine
paths, interesting spaces. Separate
courtyard garden with pond.

GROUP OPENING

51 NEW GOLDEN CROSS &
LAUGHTON DUO
Golden Cross BN27 3SS &
Laughton BN8 6BL. *About 6m E of
Lewes on B2124 through Laughton,
E of Roebuck PH (2 Woodside).
Approx 11m N of Eastbourne, just off
A22, turn into Chalvington Rd immed
S of Golden Cross PH (1 Rose
Cottage).* Home-made teas.
**Combined adm £5, chd free. Mon
3 Aug (11-5).**

NEW 1 ROSE COTTAGE
Chris & Jackie Burgess

2 WOODSIDE
Dick & Kathy Boland
Visitors also welcome by
arrangement June to July.
01323 811507
kathy.boland01@btinternet.com

Two gardens of similar size and
component parts. Both have
herbaceous borders, lawns, shade
areas, fruit and vegetables and
summerhouses but are very different
in character. 2 Woodside is a garden
divided into distinct rooms with
glimpses between them. 1 Rose
Cottage is a densely planted garden
crammed with cottage garden plants
viewed from winding paths taking you
round corners to find new surprises.

52 THE GRANGE
Hesworth Lane, Fittleworth,
Pulborough RH20 1EW. Mr & Mrs
W Caldwell. *3m W of Pulborough.
In Fittleworth turn S onto B2138
then W at Swan PH. From S turn
L off A29 onto B2138 at Bury Gate,
then L again at Swan PH. Please
do not use SatNav.* Home-made
teas. **Adm £4, chd free.**

Sat 11, Sun 12 Apr, Wed 10 June,
Wed 15 July (2-5.30).
3 acre garden gently sloping to R
Rother. Formal areas enclosed by
yew hedges comprising colour
themed beds and herbaceous
borders around pretty C18 house (not
open). Small potager and
orchard.Tulips and other spring
flowering bulbs and snakeshead
fritillaries a feature in April. Featured in
The English Garden (April 2014). The
garden has gravel paths.

Formal and knot
garden contrasts
with areas of
naturalistic
planting . . .

53 NEW 6 GRANGE ROAD
Lewes BN7 1TR. Bridget Millmore.
*Gate between 2 & 3 Grange Rd. 350
metres W of Southover Grange
Gardens & the historic cobbled Keere
St.* Home-made teas. **Adm £3.50,
chd free. Sun 31 May, Sun 26 July
(2-5.30).**
Hidden historic town garden
established in the 1930s by the
Martin sisters and developed since
the 1980s by the late Paul Millmore.
Accessed via steps to a narrow
cobbled passageway which opens
out to reveal a truly secret garden.
$1/2$ acre in size, laid out formally with
brick paviour paths, perennial
borders, pond, mature trees and
topiary. Stone seats offer different
places to pause and enjoy views of
this unique garden.

54 GRAVETYE MANOR
West Hoathly RH19 4LJ.
Jeremy & Elizabeth Hosking,
www.gravetyemanor.co.uk. *From
M23, J10 E Grinstead, A264 Dukes
Head, B2028 Turner's Hill. After
Turner's Hill take L fork for
Sharpthorne, then take first L
into Vowels Lane.* **Adm £20 incl
tea & home-made cake.
Sat 15 Aug (2-5).**

Pre-booking essential. For tickets
please phone 01483 211535 or visit
www.ngs.org.uk.
The gardens at Gravetye Manor can
be considered amongst the most
influential in English gardening history.
The manor was the home of
revolutionary gardener, William
Robinson from 1884-1935. Thanks to
the backing of new owners, a major
restoration project is under way.
Overseeing the project is head
gardener, Tom Coward, who has
come from working 3 years alongside
Fergus Garrett at Great Dixter. Parts of
the garden are accessible via ramps.

55 ♦ GREAT DIXTER HOUSE,
GARDENS & NURSERIES
Northiam TN31 6PH. Great Dixter
Charitable Trust, 01797 252878,
www.greatdixter.co.uk. *8m N of
Rye. $1/2$ m NW of Northiam off A28.*
**For opening times and information,
please phone or see garden
website.**
Designed by Edwin Lutyens and
Nathaniel Lloyd whose son,
Christopher, officiated over these
gardens for 55 yrs, creating one of
the most experimental and constantly
changing gardens of our time. Wide
variety of interest from clipped topiary,
wild meadow flowers, natural ponds,
formal pool and the famous long
border and exotic garden. A long and
varied season is aimed for. A wide
range of educational study days and
workshops held. Some areas of the
garden are accessible for
wheelchairs; a map is available from
the ticket kiosk.

56 GREAT LYWOOD
FARMHOUSE
Lindfield Road, Ardingly
RH17 6SW. Richard & Susan Laing.
*$2^{1}/_{2}$ m N of Haywards Heath.
Between Lindfield & Ardingly on
B2028. 2m N of Lindfield, turn L (W)
down paved track. 1st house on R,
car park beyond house.* Home-made
teas. **Adm £5, chd free. Sun 31
May, Fri 5, Sun 7 June (2-6).**
Approx $1^{1}/_{2}$ acre terraced garden
surrounding C17 Sussex farmhouse
(not open). Terracing and lovely views
to South Downs. Featuring lawns and
grass walks, mixed borders, rose
garden, kitchen garden and orchard,
walled garden with dovecote.
Wheelchair access possible, some
slopes and short grass.

---

57 **HALFPENNY COTTAGE**
Copse Lane, Walberton BN18 0QH.
Sue & Dave Settle, 01243 542399,
dave.settle@talktalk.net. *5m from
Chichester & Arundel. Off A27 at
Fontwell r'about, past petrol station
to end of village. At last mini-r'about
turn R onto West Walberton Lane,
Copse Lane next L.* Home-made
teas. **Adm £4, chd free. Sun 31 May
(1.30-5.30). Visitors also welcome
by arrangement May to June.**
Delightful ¹⁄₂ acre garden designed and
planted by the present owners in a
romantic cottage style with different
colour themed borders using a palette
of soft colours, winding brick paths
and rose pergola. Mediterranean
garden, green oak gazebo and
enclosed kitchen garden. Lots of
interesting perennial planting
combinations.

58 **HAMMERWOOD HOUSE**
Iping, Midhurst GU29 0PF. Mr &
Mrs M Lakin, 07785 776222,
amandalakin@me.com. *3m W of
Midhurst. Take A272 from Midhurst,
approx 2m outside Midhurst, turn R
for Iping. From A3, leave for Liphook,
follow B2070. Turn L for Iping.* Home-
made teas. **Adm £5, chd free. Share
to Iping Church. Sun 3, Sun 10
May (1.30-5). Visitors also
welcome by arrangement in May
for groups of 10+.**
Large s-facing garden with lots of
mature shrubs, incl camellias,
rhododendrons and azaleas. An
arboretum with a variety of flowering
and fruit trees. The old yew and
beech hedges give a certain amount
of formality to this traditional English
garden. Tea on the terrace is a must
with the most beautiful view of the
South Downs. For the more energetic
there is a woodland walk. Partial
wheelchair access as garden is set
on a slope.

59 **NEW** **HARBOURSIDE**
Prinsted Lane, Prinsted,
Emsworth PO10 8HS. Ann Moss,
01243 370048,
ann.moss8@btinternet.com. *6m E
of Chichester. Turn off A27 Tesco
r'about onto A259 W, after 2nd
r'about take 2nd turning on L.
Chinese takeaway on corner, follow
road until forced to turn R at Scout
Hut. House next door with boat in
front garden.* **Adm £4.50, chd free.
Visitors welcome by arrangement
for groups of 12-24 with light
refreshments on request.**

Award-winning coastal garden takes
you on a journey through garden
styles from around the world. Visit
France, Holland, Spain, New Zealand
and Japan. View and enjoy tree ferns,
topiary, shady area, secret woodland
parlor, potager, containers, unusual
shrubs, silver birch walk and
herbaceous borders for yr-round
interest. Wide variety of plants, music
and seating. Boat and seaside
memorabilia in the front garden with
themed garden art throughout.
Wheelchair access to most of the
garden, after 10ft of gravel at the
garden entrance.

60 **HARDWYCKE**
Southfields Road, Eastbourne
BN21 1BZ. Lois Machin,
01323 729391,
loisandpeter@yahoo.co.uk. *Centre
of Eastbourne, Upperton. A259
towards Eastbourne, Southfields Rd
on R just before junction with A2270
(Upperton Rd). Limited parking,
public car park (pay) in Southfields
Rd.* Home-made teas. **Adm £3.50,
chd free. Sun 14 June, Sun 23 Aug
(11-5). Visitors also welcome by
arrangement May to Sept for 15
max.**
Delightful S-facing town garden
mainly of chalky soil, with many usual
and unusual plants. Separate
vegetable garden with restored
1920's summerhouse. Wide selection
of shrubs incl 50 types of clematis. L
shaped garden that has 2 spaces
70ft x 50ft and 18ft x 50ft. 2 slight
steps to rear garden area, accessible
with care.

61 **◆ GARDENS & GROUNDS
OF HERSTMONCEUX CASTLE**
Herstmonceux, Hailsham
BN27 1RN. Bader International
Study Centre, Queen's University
(Canada), 01323 833816,
www.herstmonceux-castle.com.
*Located between Herstmonceux &
Pevensey on the Wartling Rd. From
Herstmonceux take A271 to Bexhill,
2nd R signed Castle. Do not use
SatNav.* Light lunches, hot & cold
beverages & cream teas in Chestnuts
Tearoom. **Adm £6, chd free. For
NGS: Thur 16 July (10-6). For other
opening times and information,
please phone or see garden
website.**
Herstmonceux is renowned for its
magnificent moated castle set in
beautiful parkland and superb

Elizabethan walled gardens, leading
to delightful discoveries such as our
rhododendron, rose and herb
gardens and onto our woodland
trails. Take a slow stroll past the lily
covered lakes to the 1930s folly and
admire the sheer magnificence of the
castle. The Gardens & Grounds first
opened for the NGS in 1927. Partial
wheelchair access to formal gardens.

> A narrow
> cobbled
> passageway
> which opens
> out to reveal
> a truly secret
> garden . . .

GROUP OPENING

62 **HERSTMONCEUX PARISH
TRAIL**
Hailsham BN27 4JF. *2m N of
Herstmonceux Village off A271. See
directions for each garden.* Cream
teas in the café at Lime Cross
Nursery (close at 4.30pm) & teas at
Cowbeech House (2-5). **Combined
adm £4, chd free. Sat 20, Sun 21
June (10-5).**

2 ACRES
Di Tate.
*1 min E of Herstmonceux Village
(A271) on LH-side*

THE ALLOTMENTS - STUNTS
GREEN
George Taylor.
*E on A271, take L at Woolpack
PH onto West End Rd, then next
R towards Cowbeech Village.
Allotments on RH-side*

COWBEECH HOUSE
Mr Anthony Hepburn.
*In the centre of Cowbeech Village
opp the Merrie Harriers PH*

LIME CROSS NURSERY
PINETUM
Vicky and Helen Tate.
*1 min E of Herstmonceux Village
A271 on LH-side*
www.limecross.co.uk

Herstmonceux Parish Trail starts at Cowbeech House at Cowbeech with its tranquil setting, relaxing water features and maybe a few stunning surprises. The next part of the trail is the 54 allotments set in a picturesque fruit farm at Stunts Green showing community spirit aplenty. The final part of the trail takes you to Herstmonceux where you will find Two Acres, with its splendid selection of trees and shrubs sloping to the beautiful garden pond adjacent to Lime Cross Nursery. Delicious cream teas are available in the cafe at Lime Cross Nursery which can be enjoyed in the surrounding garden areas especially overlooking the Pinetum. This will give you a chance to sit down, relax and take in the beauty of the gardens. Partial wheelchair access to some gardens.

&. ⊛ 👜

Sedgwick Park House
© Leigh Clapp

63 ◆ HIGH BEECHES WOODLAND AND WATER GARDEN
High Beeches Lane, Handcross, Haywards Heath RH17 6HQ. High Beeches Gardens Conservation Trust, 01444 400589, www.highbeeches.com. *5m NW of Cuckfield. On B2110, 1m E of A23 at Handcross.* Light refreshments. **Adm £7, chd free. For NGS: Sun 7 June, Sun 27 Sept (1-5). For other opening times and information, please phone or see garden website.**
25 acres of enchanting landscaped woodland and water gardens with spring daffodils, bluebells and azalea walks, many rare and beautiful plants, an ancient wild flower meadow and glorious autumn colours. Picnic area. National Collection of Stewartias. Article in etc magazine.

 NCH 👜

64 ◆ HIGHDOWN GARDENS
33 Highdown Rise, Littlehampton Road, Goring-by-Sea, Worthing BN12 6FB. Worthing Borough Council, 01903 501054, www.highdowngardens.co.uk. *3m W of Worthing. Off A259. Approx 1m from Goring-by-Sea Railway Station.* Adm by donation. **For NGS: Sun 24 May, Thur 4 June (10-6). For other opening times and information, please phone or see garden website.**
Famous garden created by Sir Frederick Stern situated on downland countryside in a chalk pit. The garden

contains a wide collection of plants, many were raised from seed brought from China by great collectors like Wilson, Farrer and Kingdon-Ward. Winner Silver Gilt SE in Bloom Heritage Section 2014. Hillside garden with mainly grass paths, partial wheelchair access.

&. NCH

65 ◆ 4 HILLSIDE COTTAGES
Downs Road, West Stoke, Chichester PO18 9BL. Heather & Chris Lock, 01243 574802, chlock@btinternet.com. *3m NW of Chichester. From A286 at Lavant, head W for 1½ m, nr Kingley Vale.* Tea. **Adm £3, chd free. Sun 7 June, Sun 26 July (2-5). Visitors also welcome by arrangement June to Aug.**
Garden 120ft x 27ft in a rural setting. Densely planted with mixed borders and shrubs. Large collection of roses, mainly New English shrub roses; walls, fences and arches covered with mid and late season clematis; baskets overflowing with fuchsias. A profusion of colour and scent in a well maintained small garden.

👜

66 ◆ HOBBS BARTON
Streele Lane, Framfield, Nr Uckfield TN22 5RY. Mr & Mrs Jeremy Clark, 01825 732259, hobbsbarton@btinternet.com. *3m E of Uckfield. Signed from Framfield (nr church) & Buxted (A272 mini-r'about nr train station).* Home-made teas in C17 Barn Room. **Adm £5, chd free. Share to The Friends of Sussex Hospices. Sat 6, Sun 7 June (2-5.30). Visitors also welcome by arrangement June to July for groups of 10+.**
Peaceful pastoral setting, typical of rural Sussex. Far from traffic noise, this is a mature garden of 2¾ acres developed by present owners over the past 41 yrs. Sweeping lawns lead to areas with many types of rose, shrubberies and herbaceous borders; numerous specimen trees incl *Metasequoia Glyptostroboides*, liriodendron, giant prostrate junipers; water features; part walled vegetable and fruit garden. Developing woodland garden. Delightful 15 min circular lakeside stroll. Picnics and dogs in car park field only (some shady areas).

&. ⊛ 👜

67 HOLLY HOUSE

Beaconsfield Road, Chelwood Gate, Haywards Heath RH17 7LF. Mrs Deirdre Birchell, 01825 740484, db@hollyhousebnb.demon.co.uk, www.hollyhousebnb.co.uk. *7m E of Haywards Heath. From Nutley Village on A22 turn off at RajRani signed Chelwood Gate 2m. Chelwood Gate Village Hall on R, Holly House is opp.* Home-made teas. **Adm £3.50, chd free. Sat 16, Sun 17 May, Sat 13, Sun 14 June, Sat 22, Sun 23 Aug (2-5). Visitors also welcome by arrangement May to Aug.**
An acre of English garden providing views and cameos of plants and trees round every corner with many different areas giving constant interest. A fish pond and a wildlife pond beside a grassy area with many shrubs and flower beds. Among the trees and winding paths there is a cottage garden which is a profusion of colour and peace. Exhibition of paintings and cards by owner. Garden accessible by wheelchair in good weather, but it is not easy.

&♿ 🛏 🍵

68 JACARANDA

Chalk Road, Ifold RH14 0UE. Brian & Barbara McNulty, 01403 751532, bam101@btinternet.com. *1m S of Loxwood. From A272/A281 take B2133 (Loxwood). 1/2 m S of Loxwood take Plaistow Rd. 3rd R into Chalk Rd. Follow signs for parking & garden. Wheelchair users can park in driveway.* Home-made teas. **Adm £3, chd free. Evening Opening £5, chd free, wine, Fri 3 July (6-9). Sun 13 Sept (2-5). Visitors also welcome by arrangement May to Oct for groups of 30 max.**
A tranquil garden of 1/4 acre created from scratch over past 15 yrs. The sweeping borders are packed with trees, shrubs, bulbs, perennials, roses and climbers. A plant lover's paradise. Many pots incl almost 100 hostas displayed beneath a lovely walnut tree. Very productive kitchen garden with raised bed and greenhouse. Compost area and unusual potting bench.

&♿ 🍵

69 KENT HOUSE

East Harting, nr Petersfield GU31 5LS. Mr & Mrs David Gault, 01730 825206. *4m SE of Petersfield. On B2146 at South Harting take Elsted to Midhurst road E for 1/2 m. Just W of Turkey Island, turn N up no*

through road for 400yds. Tea. **Adm £4, chd free. Visitors welcome by arrangement May to Aug.**
The garden of about 1½ acres is designed around 4 areas, each with quite a different feeling. A shaded garden for spring with bulbs and woodlanders, 2 summer gardens; 1 based on the square, and the other on the circle, and an area of open spaces bringing in lovely views of the Downs and surrounding countryside.

&♿ 🍵

PERENNIAL
GARDENERS' ROYAL BENEVOLENT SOCIETY

NGS & Perennial; over 30 years of caring for horticulturists

70 ◆ KING JOHN'S LODGE

Sheepstreet Lane, Etchingham TN19 7AZ. Jill Cunningham, 01580 819232, www.kingjohnsnursery.co.uk. *2m W of Hurst Green. A265 Burwash to Etchingham. Turn L before Etchingham Church into Church Lane which leads into Sheepstreet Lane after 1/2 m. L after 1m.* Home-made teas in the tearoom of King John's Nursery. **Adm £4, chd free. For NGS: Sun 15 Mar, Sun 24, Mon 25 May, Sat 20 June (2-5); Sun 21 June (11-5); Sun 20 Sept (2-5). For other opening times and information, please phone or see garden website.**
4 acre romantic garden for all seasons surrounding an historic listed house (not open). Formal garden with water features, rose walk and wild garden and pond. Rustic bridge to shaded ivy garden, large herbaceous borders, old shrub roses and secret garden. Further 4 acres of meadows, fine trees and grazing sheep. Nursery and shop. Garden is mainly flat. Stepped areas can usually be accessed from other areas. No disabled WC.

&♿ 🛏 🍵

71 KNEPP CASTLE

Knepp Castle, West Grinstead, Horsham RH13 8LJ. Sir Charles & Lady Burrell, 07786 241413, gm-hf.butler@hotmail.com. *8m S of Horsham. Turning to Shipley off the A272. 1/2 m to entrance on L. Follow driveway through the parkland.* Home-made teas. **Adm £5, chd free. Sun 28 June (11-5). Visitors also welcome by arrangement.**
Recently designed and replanted garden surrounding Knepp Castle (not open). Main garden dominated by three old Cedar of Lebanon, clipped yew, box and a ha-ha overlooking the spectacular lake and Repton Park with free roaming deer, cattle and Exmoor ponies. Sympathetic planting to reflect the landscape, 2 acre walled garden containing vegetables, fruit, flowers, herbs and pool.

&♿ 🍵

72 LEGSHEATH FARM

Legsheath Lane, nr Forest Row RH19 4JN. Mr & Mrs M Neal, 01342 810230, legsheath@btinternet.com. *4m S of East Grinstead. 2m W of Forest Row, 1m S of Weirwood Reservoir.* Home-made teas. **Adm £5, chd free. Share to Holy Trinity Church, Forest Row. Sun 17 May (2-5.30). Visitors also welcome by arrangement Apr to Sept.**
Panoramic views over Weirwood Reservoir. Exciting 10 acre garden with woodland walks, water gardens and formal borders. Of particular interest, clumps of wild orchids, fine davidia, acers, eucryphia and rhododendrons. Mass planting of different species of meconopsis on the way to ponds. Featured in Period Homes & Interiors (May 2014).

&♿ 🍵

73 NEW LIMEKILN FARM

Chalvington Road, Chalvington, Hailsham BN27 3TA. Dr J Hester and Mr M Royle. *10m N of Eastbourne. Nr Hailsham. Turn S off the A22 at Golden Cross & follow the Chalvington road for 1m. The entrance has white gates on the LH-side of the road, car parking 100 metres further on.* Home-made teas in the Oast House. **Adm £4, chd free. Fri 15, Sat 16 May (2-5.30).**
The garden was designed in the 1930s when the house was owned by Charles Stewart Taylor, MP for Eastbourne. It has not changed in basic layout since then. The house and garden are mentioned in Virginia

Woolf's diaries of 1929, depicting a dilapidated charm that still exists today. Flint walls enclose the main lawn, herbaceous borders and rose garden. There is a vegetable garden, informal pond, secret garden, mature and newly planted specimen trees.

&♿ ❀ ☕

Come along to one of our themed open days; Rhubarb, Asparagus or Dahlia Sundays . . .

74 ► LITTLE WANTLEY
Fryern Road, Storrington RH20 4BJ. Brian Barnes. *1m N of Storrington. From Storrington follow signs to West Chiltington. Entrance approx 1m on R in Fryern Rd. Parking in field*. Home-made teas. **Adm £5, chd free. Share to Macmillan Cancer Support. Sat 20, Sun 21 June (2-5.30).**
Hilary Barnes, owner and designer of this 4½ acre garden sadly died in July 2014. She spent many hours each day deciding where every plant should be placed for best effect. Award-winning garden incl a lake incorporating 2 islands, a cantilevered jetty with pergola and impressive marginal planting, deep herbaceous borders, rose and nut walks, secret garden and stumpery. Deep water: children must be strictly supervised. No disabled WC available.

♿ ☕

75 ► THE LONG HOUSE
The Lane, Westdean, Nr Seaford BN25 4AL. Robin & Rosie Lloyd, 01323 870432, rosiemlloyd@gmail.com. *3m E of Seaford, 6m W of Eastbourne. From A27 follow signs to Alfriston then Litlington, Westdean 1m on L. From A259 at Exceat, L on Litlington Rd, ¼ m on R*. Home-made teas. **Adm £4, chd free. Wed 1 July (2-5). Visitors also welcome by arrangement May to July for groups of 10+.**
If you enjoyed Bankton Cottage in Crawley Down, we hope you like our new garden here in the tiny hamlet of Westdean; a cottage garden with colour themes on a chalk slope. Hollyhocks, roses and lavenders abound, and there's a perennial border the entire length of the house at the rear, a paddock of wild flowers and many rooms with slopes and steps surrounding our C17 flint cottage. Situated on The South Downs Way. Gravel forecourt at entrance, some slopes and steps.

♿ ❀ ☕

76 ► LORDINGTON HOUSE
Lordington, Chichester PO18 9DX. Mr & Mrs John Hamilton, 01243 375862. *7m W of Chichester. On W side of B2146, ½ m S of Walderton, 6m S of South Harting. Enter through white railings*. Home-made teas. **Adm £4, chd free. Sat 28, Sun 29 Mar (1.30-4.30). Visitors also welcome by arrangement June to July. Regret no coaches.**
Early C17 house (not open) and walled gardens in South Downs National Park. Clipped yew and box, lawns, borders and fine views. Vegetables, fruit and poultry in old kitchen garden. Carpet of daffodils in spring. Nearly 100 roses planted since 2008. Various trees both mature and young. Lime avenue planted in 1973 to replace elms. Overlooks farmland, Ems Valley and wooded slopes of South Downs, all in AONB. Featured in Chichester Observer. Gravel paths, some uneven paving and slopes.

♿ 🐕 ❀ 🛏 ☕

77 ► LOWDER MILL
Bell Vale Lane, Fernhurst, Haslemere GU27 3DJ. Anne & John Denning, 01428 644822, anne@denningconsultancy.co.uk, www.lowdermill.com. *1½ m S of Haslemere. Follow A286 out of Midhurst towards Haslemere, through Fernhurst and take 2nd R after Kingsley Green into Bell Vale Lane*. Home-made teas. **Adm £3.50, chd £1.50. Sat 30 May (11-5.30); Sun 31 May (10.30-5.30). Visitors also welcome by arrangement close to garden open days.**
C17 mill house and former mill set in 3 acre garden. The garden has been restored with the help of Bunny Guinness. Interesting assortment of container planting forming a stunning courtyard between house and mill. Streams, waterfalls, innovative and quirky container planting around the potting shed and restored greenhouse. Raised vegetable garden. Rare breed chicken and ducks, as well as resident kingfishers. Renowned for superb home-made teas, served overlooking the mill lake. Extensive plant stall, mainly home propagated. Choir singing on Sun 31 May at 11am. Featured in Country Life, County Living, Sussex Life and Chichester Observer.

❀ ☕

78 ► NEW ► LUCTONS
North Lane, West Hoathly, East Grinstead RH19 4PP. Drs Hans & Ingrid Sethi. *4m SW of East Grinstead, 6m E of Crawley. Off minor road between Turners Hill & Forest Row. Nr church & Priest House. Car parks in village*. Cream teas. **Adm £5, chd free. Tue 23, Sat 27 June, Thur 2 July (1.30-5.30). Combined adm with The Priest House on 27 June only.**
A 2 acre garden, allegedly in Gertrude Jekyll style, with small box parterre, lawns, yew topiary, shrubberies, pond, much loved herbaceous borders, large fruit and vegetable garden, chickens, compost complex, vine, peach and green houses, and wild flower orchard with meadow flowers and spotted orchids.

❀ ☕

79 ► MALT HOUSE
Chithurst Lane, Rogate, Petersfield GU31 5EZ. Mr & Mrs G Ferguson, 01730 821433, g.ferguson34@btinternet.com. *3m W of Midhurst. On A272, turn N signed Chithurst for 1½ m, narrow lane; or off A3 at Liphook to old A3 (B2070) for 2m, L to Milland following signs to Chithurst for 1½ m*. Home-made teas. **Adm £5, chd free. Sun 26 Apr, Sun 3, Mon 4 May (2-6). Visitors also welcome by arrangement Apr to June.**
6 acres; flowering shrubs incl exceptional rhododendrons and azaleas, leading to 50 acres of arboretum and lovely woodland walks, plus many rare plants and trees. On the South Downs. Partial wheelchair access only.

♿ 🐕 ☕

© Jonathan Need

Durrance Manor

80 MALTHOUSE FARM

Streat Lane, Streat, Hassocks BN6 8SA. Richard & Helen Keys, 01273 890356, helen.k.keys@btinternet.com. *2m SE of Burgess Hill. From r'about between B2113 & B2112 take Folders Lane & Middleton Common Lane E; after 1m, R into Streat Lane, garden is ½ m on R.* Home-made teas. **Adm £4, chd free. Sun 16, Tue 18 Aug (2-5.30).** Visitors also welcome by arrangement Apr to Sept. Adm £8 incl tea, coffee & cake.

Rural 5 acre garden with stunning views to South Downs. Garden divided into separate rooms, box parterre, recently planted border with glass sculpture, herbaceous and shrub borders, kitchen garden. Orchard leading to partitioned areas with grass walks, stream of summer flowers, snail mound, birch maze. Wildlife farm pond. Featured in Period Living (July 2014). Wheelchair access possible although some steps. Caution if wet as much access is across grass.

81 MANOR OF DEAN

Tillington, Petworth GU28 9AP. Mr & Mrs James Mitford, 07887 992349, emma@mitford.uk.com. *3m W of Petworth. From Petworth go through Tillington & follow yellow signs N from A272.* Home-made teas. **Adm £4, chd free. Sun 15 Feb (2-4); Suns 8 Mar, 19 Apr, 31 May, 9 Aug (2-5).** Visitors also welcome by arrangement Feb to Sept for groups of 10+. Regret no coaches.
Traditional English garden, approx 3

acres, with herbaceous borders, a variety of early flowering bulbs, snowdrops, spring bulbs, grass walks and grass steps. Walled kitchen garden with fruit, vegetables and cutting flowers. Lawns, rose garden and informal areas with views of the South Downs. Garden under a long-term programme of improvements. Come along to one of our themed open days: Rhubarb Sunday (19 Apr), Asparagus Sunday (31 May) and Dahlia Sunday (9 Aug) when you can see how they are grown, buy some to take home and enjoy the productive walled garden. Come early to avoid disappointment.

GROUP OPENING

82 MAYFIELD GARDENS

Mayfield TN20 6TE. *10m S of Tunbridge Wells. Turn off A267 into Mayfield. Parking available in village & a detailed map will be available from each of the gardens.* Home-made teas. **Combined adm £5, chd free. Sun 14 June (11-5).**

HOOPERS FARM
Andrew & Sarah Ratcliffe

MAY COTTAGE
Fletching Street. M Prall

THE MIDDLE HOUSE
High Street. Mr Johnny Marsh 01435 872146 info@themiddlehousemayfield. co.uk

NEW MULBERRY
Fletching Street. M Vernon

NEW SOUTH STREET GARDEN PLOTS
Fletching Street. Mrs Val Buddle

WARREN HOUSE
Chris Lyle & Pat Robson

Mayfield is a beautiful Wealden village with tearooms, old PH and interesting historical connections. The gardens to visit are all within walking distance of the village centre. They vary in size and style, incl colour themed and cottage style planting, a wild flower meadow, woodland and vegetables. There are far reaching, panoramic views over beautiful countryside.

83 ◆ MERRIMENTS

Hawkhurst Road, Hurst Green TN19 7RA. Peggy & David Weeks, 01580 860666, www.merriments.co.uk. *Off A21, 1m N of Hurst Green. On A229 Hawkhurst Rd. Situated between Hurst Green & Hawkhurst.* Home-made teas. **Adm £5, chd free. For NGS: Thur 23 Apr (10-5). For other opening times and information, please phone or see garden website.**

A well kept secret awaits you in this stunning garden, the South East's hidden gem. In April the wide sweeping borders are filled with thousands of jewel coloured tulips. Delicate cherry blossoms add romance to the garden and beautifully frame the pond. The Spring Garden will be a patchwork of pretty soft colours from hellebores, wood anemones, snakeheads fritillaries, and ferns springing to life. There are a number of benches in the garden to allow visitors to enjoy the atmosphere of this special ever-evolving garden. There are many unusual plants most of which are sold in the nursery; there is also a great shop, restaurant serving home-made lunches and teas. Featured in Sussex Life and Country Living.

84 NEW MOIETIES FARM & BARN

Foul Mile, Cowbeech, Hailsham BN27 4JJ. Eleanor Gay and Nic Gleadow. *3m S of Heathfield signed from Rushlake Green. 3m N of Hailsham signed from Cowbeech. Off road parking in field.* Tea. **Adm £3.50, chd free. Sun 7 June (2-5.30).**
2 acre informal country garden

surrounding C18 farmhouse and recently converted barn (not open). Mixed borders with ancient apple trees, kitchen garden, cut flower plot, meadow with mown paths to ¹/₂ acre farm pond overlooking woodland plantations and pasture. Partial wheelchair access, gravel paths.

85 ► NEWTIMBER PLACE
Newtimber BN6 9BU. Mr & Mrs Andrew Clay, 01273 833104, andy@newtimberholidaycottages. co.uk, www.newtimberplace.co.uk. *7m N of Brighton. From A23, take A281 towards Henfield. Turn R at small Xrds signed Newtimber in approx ¹/₂ m. Go down Church Lane, garden is at end of lane on L.* Home-made teas. **Adm £4, chd free. Sun 19 Apr (2-5.30).**
Beautiful C17 moated house (not open). Gardens and woods full of bulbs and wild flowers in spring. Herbaceous border and lawns. Moat flanked by water plants. Mature trees, wild garden, ducks, chickens and fish. Wheelchair access across lawn to some of garden, tearoom and WC.

86 ► NORTH HALL
North Hall Lane, Sheffield Green, Uckfield TN22 3SA. Celia & Les Everard, 01825 791103, indigodogs@yahoo.co.uk. *1¹/₂ m NW of Fletching Village. 6m N Uckfield. From A272 turn N at Piltdown or N Chailey. From A275 turn E at Sheffield Green into North Hall Lane.* Home-made teas. **Combined adm with 1 Whites Cottages £4.50, chd free. Sat 27, Sun 28 June (2-5.30). Visitors also welcome by arrangement June to July for groups of 10+.**
A romantic garden surrounding a C16 house (not open) planted to please the senses. Roses tumble, clematis scramble and the dense and varied planting needs little support, a palette of soft colours and heady scent. Themed island beds and a moated terrace add to the many cottage garden features. Wildlife and self seeding encouraged. Home grown plants and delicious teas.

87 ► NORTH SPRINGS
Bedham, nr Fittleworth RH20 1JP. Mr & Mrs R Haythornthwaite. *Between Fittleworth & Wisborough Green. From Wisborough Green take A272 towards Petworth. Turn L into*

Fittleworth Rd signed Coldharbour. Proceed 1¹/₂ m. From Fittleworth take Bedham Lane off A283 & proceed for approx 3m NE. Limited parking. Home-made teas. **Adm £4, chd free. Sun 14 June (1-6).**
Hillside garden with beautiful views surrounded by mixed woodland. Focus on structure with a wide range of mature trees and shrubs. Stream, pond and bog area. Abundance of roses, clematis, hostas, rhododendrons and azaleas.

Wildlife and self seeding encouraged . . .

88 ► NYEWOOD HOUSE
Nyewood, nr Rogate GU31 5JL. Mr & Mrs C J Wright, 01730 821563, s.warren.wright@gmail.com. *4m E of Petersfield. From A272 at Rogate take South Harting Rd for 1¹/₂ m. Turn L at pylon towards South Downs Manor. Nyewood House 2nd on R over cattle grid.* Cream teas & home-made teas. **Adm £4, chd free. Sat 6, Sun 7 June (2-5.30). Visitors also welcome by arrangement May to June for groups of 15+.**
Victorian country house garden with stunning views of South Downs. 3 acres comprising formal gardens with rose walk and arbours, pleached hornbeam, colour themed herbaceous borders, shrub borders, lily pond and fully stocked kitchen garden with greenhouse. Wooded area featuring spring flowers followed by wild orchids and wild flowers. Featured in Sussex Life and Chichester Observer. Gravel drive.

89 ► ♦ NYMANS
Handcross RH17 6EB. National Trust, www.nationaltrust.org.uk/nymans. *4m S of Crawley. On B2114 at Handcross signed off M23/A23 London-Brighton road. Metrobus 271 & 273 stop nearby.* Light refreshments. **Adm £12.20, chd £6.60. For NGS: Sun 14 June (10-5).**

For other opening times and information, please see garden website.
In the late 1800's Ludwig Messel bought Nymans estate in the Sussex High Weald to make a dream country house. Inspired by its woodland setting he created a garden with plants collected from around the world. Here he entertained family and friends and enjoyed relaxing and picnicking in the garden and woods. Today Nymans is still a garden lovers' home, a place to relax in a peaceful country garden.

90 ► OAK GROVE COLLEGE
The Boulevard, Worthing BN13 1JX. *1m W of Worthing. Turn S off A2032 at r'about onto The Boulevard, signed Goring. School entrance 1st L (shared entrance with Durrington High School).* Light refreshments, lunches & wine. **Combined adm with Palatine School Gardens £4, chd free. Sun 21 June (11-5).**
An inspiring example of how special needs children have transformed their school grounds into a green oasis. Extensive and unusual planting, sculptures, herb garden, large courtyard, sculptures, mosaics, and vegetable growing area. Living willow, reclaimed woodland, camera obscura, outdoor performance and cooking areas.

91 ► OCKLYNGE MANOR
Mill Road, Eastbourne BN21 2PG. Wendy & David Dugdill, 01323 734121, ocklyngemanor@hotmail.com, www.ocklyngemanor.co.uk. *Close to Eastbourne District General Hospital. Take A22 (Willingdon Rd) towards Old Town, turn L into Mill Rd just before parade of shops.* **Adm £3.50, chd free. Visitors welcome by arrangement May to Aug for groups of 10-50.**
Hidden oasis behind an ancient, flint wall. Informal and tranquil, ¹/₂ acre chalk garden with sunny and shaded places to sit. Use of architectural and unusual trees. Rhododendrons, azaleas and acers in containers. Garden evolved over 20 yrs, maintained by owners. Georgian house (not open), former home of Mabel Lucie Attwell. Short gravel path before entering garden. Brick path around perimeter.

Look out for the NGS yellow arrows …

92 OFFHAM HOUSE

The Street, Offham, Lewes BN7 3QE. Mr S Goodman and Mr & Mrs P Carminger. *2m N of Lewes on A275. Offham House is on the main road (A275) through Offham between the filling station & the Blacksmiths Arms.* Home-made teas. **Adm £5, chd free. Sun 26 Apr, Sun 31 May (1-5).**
Romantic garden with fountains, flowering trees, double herbaceous border, long peony bed. 1676 Queen Anne house (not open) with well knapped flint facade. Herb garden and walled kitchen garden with glasshouses, coldframes, chickens, guinea fowl and friendly pigs. Teas on the lawn, or in the conservatory.

93 OLD ERRINGHAM COTTAGE

Steyning Road, Shoreham-By-Sea BN43 5FD. Fiona & Martin Phillips, 01273 462285, fiona.h.phillips@btinternet.com. *2m N of Shoreham by Sea. From A27 Shoreham flyover take A283 towards Steyning. Take 2nd R into private lane. Follow sharp LH-bend at top, house on L. Limited parking.* Home-made teas. **Adm £4.50, chd free. Visitors welcome by arrangement May to June for groups of 10+.**
In South Downs National Park over 1 acre plantsman's garden with mixed borders, pond, meadow and panoramic views. At back divided by yew hedging with stream, parterre and paths leading through wide variety of perennials. Many plants grown from seed and coastal climate allows for success with unusual tender plants. Greenhouses for melon, peach, fig, persimmon and highly productive fruit and vegetable area.

94 OLD POUND FARM

Pound Lane, Framfield, East Sussex TN22 5RT. Alan & Beryl Henderson. *4m E of Uckfield take B2102 through Framfield. 1m from centre of village turn L into Pound Lane. Parking in field behind Pound Cottage next door.* Home-made teas. **Adm £4, chd free. Sun 26 July (2-5).**
Typical Sussex farmhouse, part dating back to 1480, with attractive terrace and 2 acre garden consisting of long herbaceous perennial border; area with many ancient rhododendrons and fruit trees; attractive hedges and trees; pond

area which incl an ancient cattle watering hole. Wheelchair access to most areas.

95 OLD VICARAGE

The Street, Firle, Lewes BN8 6NR. Mr & Mrs Charlie Bridge. *Off A27 5m E of Lewes. Signed from main road.* Cream teas. **Adm £4, chd free. Sat 20 June (2-5).**
Garden originally designed by Lanning Roper in the 1960's. 4 acre garden set around a Regency vicarage (not open) with wonderful Downland views. Features a walled garden with vegetable parterre and flower borders, wild flower meadow, pond, pleached limes and over 100 roses. Partial wheelchair access as some areas may be difficult.

96 THE OLD VICARAGE

The Street, Washington RH20 4AS. Sir Peter & Lady Walters, 07766 761926, meryl.walters@me.com. *2½ m E of Storrington, 4m W of Steyning. From Washington r'about on A24 take A283 to Steyning. 500yds R to Washington. Pass Frankland Arms, R to St Mary's Church.* Home-made teas. Some gluten free cakes and biscuits available. **Adm £4.50, chd free. Sun 1 Mar, Mon 6, Sun 26 Apr, Sun 7 June, Sun 23 Aug, Sun 18 Oct (10.30-4.30). Visitors also welcome by arrangement Mar to Oct for groups of 10+.**
3½ acre garden, set around 1832 Regency style house (not open). Front is formally laid out with topiary, a large lawn and mixed border. To the rear some mature trees dating back to C19, herbaceous border, new large pond and stunning uninterrupted 20m view to the North Downs. Stream and woodland area with log cabin. Featured in Country Living (April 2014) and Daily Telegraph.

97 PALATINE SCHOOL GARDENS

Palatine Road, Worthing BN12 6JP. Mrs N Hawkins, www.palatineschool.org. *Turn S off A2032 at r'about onto The Boulevard, signed Goring. Take R at next r'about into Palatine Rd. School approx 100yds on R.* Home-made teas. **Adm £3.50, chd free. Sun 5 Apr (2-5); Sun 21 June (11-5).** Combined adm with Oak Grove College on Sun 21 June only £4, chd free.

This is a many roomed mature garden with varied planting. Constructed by teachers, volunteers and children with special needs, it never ceases to surprise visitors. Wildlife corner, large and small ponds, themed gardens and children's outdoor art features, along with rockeries, living willow, labyrinth, mosaics and interesting tree collection.

98 PARSONAGE FARM

Kirdford RH14 0NH. David & Victoria Thomas. *5m NE of Petworth. From centre of Kirdford (before church) turn R, through village, past Foresters PH on R. Entrance on L, just past R turn to Plaistow.* Home-made teas. **Adm £5, chd free. Share to Churchers College - Sudden Death in Epilepsy (SUDEP). Fri 12 June, Sun 6 Sept (2-6).**
Major garden in beautiful setting developed over 20 yrs with fruit theme and many unusual plants. Formally laid out on grand scale with long vistas; C18 walled garden with borders in apricot, orange, scarlet and crimson; topiary walk; pleached lime allée; tulip tree avenue; rose borders; large vegetable garden with trained fruit; turf amphitheatre; lake; informal autumn shrubbery and jungle walk.

99 33 PEERLEY ROAD

East Wittering PO20 8PD. Paul & Trudi Harrison, 01243 673215, stixandme@aol.com. *7m S of Chichester. From A286 take B2198 to Bracklesham. Turn R into Stocks Lane, L at Royal British Legion into Legion Way. Follow road round to Peerley Rd ½ way along.* **Adm £2.50, chd free. Sun 26 July (1-4). Visitors also welcome by arrangement May to Sept.**

Small seaside garden 65ft x 32ft, 110yds from sea. Packed full of ideas and interesting plants using every inch of space to create rooms and places for adults and children to play. A must for any suburban gardener. Specialising in unusual plants that grow well in seaside conditions with advice on coastal gardening.

❀

100 PEMBURY HOUSE
Ditchling Road (New Road), Clayton, nr Hassocks BN6 9PH. Nick & Jane Baker, 01273 842805, jane.baker47@btinternet.com, www.pemburyhouse.co.uk. *6m N of Brighton, off A23. On B2112, 110 metres from A273. Disabled parking at the house, otherwise parking at village green (BN6 9PJ) clearly signed. Good public transport service.* Light refreshments & home-made teas. **Adm £5, chd free. Tue 10, Wed 11, Thur 12, Tue 17, Wed 18, Thur 19 Feb, Mon 2, Thur 5, Fri 6 Mar (11-4). Visitors also welcome by arrangement Feb to Mar for groups of 15+.**

This is the last year that the garden will be open for snowdrops and hellebores. Depending on the vagaries of the season, winter flowering shrubs, hellebores and drifts of snowdrops are at their best in February, with the hellebores still going strong in March. Winding paths give a choice of walks through over 2 acres of garden, which is in, and enjoys views of the South Downs National Park. Small 30 yr old woodland. Wellies, macs and winter woollies advised. Hellebores and snowdrops for sale. Limited disabled access in wet weather.

 ♿ 🐾 ❀ 🚐 ☕

101 6 PLANTATION RISE
Worthing BN13 2AH. Nigel & Trixie Hall, 01903 262206, trixiehall@btinternet.com. *2m from seafront on outskirts of Worthing. A24 meets A27 at Offington r'about. Turn into Offington Lane, 1st R into The Plantation, 1st R again into Plantation Rise.* Light refreshments. **Adm £4, chd free. Sats 21, 28 Mar, 18, 25 July (2-5). Visitors also welcome by arrangement May to Oct for groups of 4-30.**

Our garden is 70' x 80' with pond, summerhouse, folly, flower decked pergolas over patios, 9 silver birches, plus evergreen shrubs, azaleas, rhododendrons and acers. Heathers in spring, and a profusion of roses,

clematis and perennials in August, all to ensure yr-round colour and interest. WC available on request. The garden has some steps.

 ♿ 🚐 ☕

Coastal garden takes you on a journey through garden styles from around the world . . .

102 ◆ THE PRIEST HOUSE
North Lane, West Hoathly RH19 4PP. Sussex Archaeological Society, 01342 810479, www.sussexpast.co.uk. *4m SW of East Grinstead. Turn E to West Hoathly, 1m S of Turners Hill at Selsfield Common junction on B2028. 2m S turn R into North Lane, garden ¼ m.* **Adm £2, chd free. For NGS: Sat 23 May, Sat 27 June (10.30-5.30). For other opening times and information, please phone or see garden website.**

C15 timber framed farmhouse with cottage garden on fertile acid clay. Large collection of culinary and medicinal herbs in a small formal garden and mixed with perennials and shrubs in exuberant borders. Long established yew topiary, box hedges and espalier apple trees provide structural elements. Traditional fernery and small secluded shrubbery. Adm to Priest House Museum £1 for NGS visitors. Featured in Dutch gardening magazine Tuinieren.

 🐾 ❀

103 2 QUARRY COTTAGES
Wall Hill Road, Ashurst Wood, East Grinstead RH19 3TQ. Mrs Hazel Anne Archibald. *1m S of East Grinstead. From N turn L off A22 from East Grinstead, garden adjoining John Pears Memorial Ground. From S turn R off A22 from Forest Row, garden on R at top of hill.*

Home-made teas. **Adm £3, chd free. Fri 15, Sat 16 May (2-5).**
Peaceful little garden that has evolved over 40 yrs in the present ownership. A natural sandstone outcrop hangs over an ornamental pond; mixed borders of perennials and shrubs with specimen trees. Many seating areas tucked into corners. Highly productive vegetable plot. Terrace round house revamped 2013. Florist and gift shop in barn. Featured in Womans Weekly Garden magazine. **Also open Caxton Manor (separate admission).**

 ❀ ☕

104 ▸ RINGMER PARK
Ringmer, Lewes BN8 5RW. Deborah & Michael Bedford, www.ringmerpark.com. *On A26 Lewes to Uckfield road. 1½ m NE of Lewes, 5m S of Uckfield.* Home-made teas. **Adm £5, chd free. Sun 24 May, Sun 13 Sept (2-5).**
Situated below the South Downs, outside Lewes in East Sussex, lies near 8 acres of garden built up over the past 30 yrs by gardener, Michael Bedford. He has created a series of gardens and borders differentiated in terms of plants types, structure and colour palette. Superb Downland views and featured in various publications over last few yrs. Further details available on the Ringmer Park website.

 ♿ 🐾 🚐 ☕

105 ▸ ROSE COTTAGE
Hall Lane, Hadlow Down TN22 4HJ. Ken & Heather Mines, 01825 830314, kenmines@hotmail.com. *6m NE of Uckfield. After entering village on A272, turn into Hut Lane (signed Village Hall) just by the New Inn. Follow signs.* Home-made teas. **Adm £4, chd free. Sun 24 May, Sun 21 June (2-5). Visitors also welcome by arrangement May to July.**
Plantsman's ⅔ acre garden with views across an AONB. Old roses, exuberant planting and luxuriance within a strong design create a garden that visitors refer to as harmonious, tranquil and evoking memories of childhood. Self-seeding is encouraged, so constantly changing. David Newman sculptures are integral to the design, further enhanced by Victorian church stonework. Bug hunt and fact sheet for children.

 ❀ 🚐 ☕

106 RYMANS

Apuldram, Chichester PO20 7EG.
Mrs Michael Gayford,
01243 783147,
suzanna.gayford@btinternet.com.
*1m S of Chichester. Take Witterings
Rd, at 1¹/₂ m SW turn R signed Dell
Quay. Turn 1st R, garden ¹/₂ m on L.*
Home-made teas. **Adm £5, chd free.
Sat 11, Sun 12 Apr, Sat 6, Sun 7
June, Sat 5, Sun 6 Sept (2-5).
Visitors also welcome by
arrangement Apr to Sept for
groups of 8+.**
Walled and other gardens
surrounding lovely C15 stone house
(not open); bulbs, flowering shrubs,
roses, ponds, potager. Many unusual
and rare trees and shrubs. In late
spring the wisterias are spectacular.
The heady scent of hybrid musk
roses fills the walled garden in June.
In late summer the garden is ablaze
with dahlias, sedums, late roses,
sages and Japanese anemones.

107 SAFFRONS

Holland Road, Steyning BN44 3GJ.
Tim Melton & Bernardean Carey,
01903 810082,
tim.melton@btinternet.com. *6m NE
of Worthing. Exit r'about on A283 at
S-end of Steyning bypass into Clays
Hill Rd. 1st R into Goring Rd, 4th L
into Holland Rd. Park in Goring Rd &
Holland Rd.* Home-made teas. **Adm
£4, chd free. Wed 22, Sun 26 July
(2-5.30). Visitors also welcome by
arrangement in July for groups of
10+.**
A stylish garden of textural contrasts
and rich colour. The herbaceous beds
are filled with agapanthus, spiky
eryngium and fragrant lilies, alliums
and salvias. A broad lawn is
surrounded by borders of Japanese
Maples, rhododendrons, hydrangeas
and specimen trees interspersed with
ferns and grasses. Fruit cage,
vegetable beds and fruit trees.
Featured in Sussex Life (May 2014)
as one of 25 glorious gardens to visit.

108 ◆ ST MARY'S HOUSE GARDENS

Bramber BN44 3WE. Peter
Thorogood & Roger Linton,
01903 816205,
www.stmarysbramber.co.uk. *1m E
of Steyning. 10m NW of Brighton in
Bramber Village off A283.* Home-
made teas. **Adm £4, chd free. For
NGS: Fri 10, Sat 11 July (2-5.30).**

For other opening times and
information, please phone or see
garden website.
5 acres incl charming formal topiary,
large prehistoric *Ginkgo biloba*, and
magnificent *Magnolia grandiflora*
around enchanting timber framed
Medieval house (not open). Victorian
Secret gardens incl splendid 140ft
fruit wall with pineapple pits, Rural
Museum, Terracotta Garden, Jubilee
Rose Garden, King's Garden and
unusual Circular Poetry Garden.
Woodland walk with wildlife pond. In
the heart of the South Downs
National Park.

109 8 SANDGATE CLOSE

Seaford BN25 3LL. Mr & Mrs
Jones, 01323 899452,
sweetpeasa52@gmail.com,
www.sandgateclosegarden.co.uk.
*From A259 follow signs to Alfriston, E
of Seaford. Turn R into Hillside Ave, L
into Hastings Ave, R into Deal Close
& R into Sandgate Close.* Light
refreshments, a range of gluten free
cakes or lunch provided on request.
**Adm £4, chd free. Visitors
welcome by arrangement June to
Aug. Adm reduced to £3.50 for
groups of 10+.**
8 Sandgate Close is a green and
tranquil haven, with a delightful mix of
trees, shrubs and perennial borders in
different themed beds. Courtyard
garden, gazebo, summerhouse,
water features, sweet pea arches,
huge range of plants in all seasons,
plenty of places to sit and enjoy.
Plants, jams and books for sale.
Featured in Sussex Life (July 2014).
Mostly flat but with a small number of
steps into the courtyard and WC.

110 SANDHILL FARM HOUSE

Nyewood Road, Rogate,
Petersfield GU31 5HU. Rosemary
Alexander, 01730 818373,
www.rosemaryalexander.co.uk. *4m
SE of Petersfield. From A272 Xrds in
Rogate, take road S signed Nyewood
& Harting. Follow road for approx 1m
over small bridge. Sandhill Farm
House on R, over cattle grid.* Home-
made teas. **Adm £3.50, chd free.
Sun 15 Mar, Sun 8, Sun 11, Sun 12 Apr,
Sat 20, Sun 21 June (2-5). Visitors
also welcome by arrangement Mar
to Sept for groups of 10+.
Gardening Club bookings
welcome.**
Front and rear gardens are broken up
into garden rooms, incl small kitchen

garden. Front garden incl small
woodland area planted with early
spring flowering shrubs and bulbs,
white garden and hot dry terraced
area. Rear garden has mirror borders,
small decorative vegetable garden
and red border. Grit and grasses
garden. Organic and environmentally
friendly. Home of author and Principal
of The English Gardening School.
Featured in many magazine incl
Period Living (Oct 2014). The garden
has gravel paths and a few steps.

> Colour themed
> borders using a
> palette of soft
> colours, winding
> brick paths and
> rose pergola . . .

111 ◆ SARAH RAVEN'S CUTTING GARDEN

Perch Hill Farm, Willingford Lane,
Robertsbridge, Brightling
TN32 5HP. Sarah Raven,
www.sarahraven.com. *7m SW of
Hurst Green. From Burwash turn off
A265 by church & memorial, follow
road for 3m. From Woods Corner
take road opp Swan Inn, take 1st L,
go uphill & take 1st L again. Parking is
in a field (uneven ground possible).*
We serve tea, coffee & cakes all day.
Lunch available from 12.15. **Adm £5,
chd free. For NGS: Tue 4 Aug
(9.30-4). For other opening times
and information, please phone or
see garden website.**
Sarah's inspirational, productive 2
acre working garden with different
garden rooms incl large cut flower
garden, vegetable and fruit garden,
salads and herbs area plus two
ornamental gardens. We have some
steps and gravel paths so wheelchair
access is difficult in these areas.

112 SAYERLAND HOUSE

Sayerland Lane, Polegate
BN26 6QP. Penny & Kevin Jenden,
07789 992348, penny@jenden.net.
*2m S of Hailsham, 1m N of Polegate.
At Cophall r'about on A27 take A22,
turn L at 1st turning (100yds). Follow
through Bay Tree Lane, turn sharp L*

*into Sayerland Lane. From N on A22
turn L into Bay Tree Lane before
r'about.* Home-made teas & light
refreshments. **Adm £5, chd free.
Sun 7 June (2-6). Visitors also
welcome by arrangement.**
5 acre garden surrounding listed C15
house (not open). Several distinct
garden areas. Walled garden with
colour themed borders, rose garden,
ponds, organic kitchen and cutting
garden, tropical beds and shade
beds. Wild woodland areas. Many
mature shrubs and specimen trees.

❀ ☕

GROUP OPENING

113 SEAFORD GROUP
Seaford. *Start at either garden, both
gardens will have maps to direct you
to the next garden. Both properties
are within a 5-10 min walk of the
coastal bus route.* Home-made teas.
**Combined adm £5, chd free. Sun
28 June (11-5).**

NEW HIGH TREES
83 Firle Road, BN25 2JA. Tony
& Sue Luckin.
*Top end of Firle Rd from centre of
Seaford, opp Bowden House
School*

4 SUNNINGDALE CLOSE
BN25 4PF. Mick & Debbie
Hibberd.
*From E or W use A259 coast
road, follow NGS signs, turn R or
L down Southdown Rd*
**Visitors also welcome by
arrangement June to Aug.**
01323 899385
sunningdale.garden4thof9@
gmail.com

2 unique gardens are opening
for the Seaford Group this year.
4 Sunningdale Close has a delightful
mix of plants, colour and exceptional
planting. High Trees, new for 2015, is
a beautiful garden, with numerous
interesting plants, ferns and grasses.
Woodland garden accessed through
a beautiful pergola. Wheelchair
access at 4 Sunningdale Close only.

♿ ❀ ☕

114 SEDGWICK PARK HOUSE
Sedgwick Park, Horsham
RH13 6QQ. John & Clare Davison,
01403 734930,
clare@sedgwickpark.com,
www.sedgwickpark.co.uk.
1m S of Horsham off A281. A281

8 Sandgate Close
© Leigh Clapp

*towards Cowfold, Hillier Garden
Center on R, then 1st R into
Sedgwick Lane. At end of lane
enter N gates of Sedgwick Park or
W gate via Broadwater Lane, from
Copsale or Southwater off A24.*
Home-made teas. **Adm £5, chd
free. Wed 20 May (2-6.30);
Sun 24 May (1-5). Visitors also
welcome by arrangement May to
Oct for tours of house and
gardens.**
Parkland, meadows and woodland.
Formal gardens by Harold Peto
featuring 20 interlinking ponds,
impressive water garden known as
The White Sea. Large Horsham stone
terraces and lawns look out onto
clipped yew hedging and specimen
trees. Well stocked herbaceous
borders, set in the grounds of Grade
II listed Ernest George Mansion. One
of the finest views of South Downs,
Chanctonbury Ring and Lancing
Chapel. Turf labyrinth and organic
vegetable garden with chickens.

Garden has uneven paving, slippery
when wet; unfenced ponds and
swimming pool.

♿ 🏡 ❀ 🚐 ☕

115 NEW SELHURST PARK
Halnaker, Chichester PO18 0LX.
Richard & Sarah Green. *8m S of
Petworth. 4m N of Chichester on
A285.* Home-made teas. **Adm £4,
chd free. Sun 21 June (2-5).**
Large flint walled garden with
interesting planting in 160ft south and
east facing herbaceous border. Rose,
hellebore and hydrangea borders
overlooked by a conservatory at one
end. Knot and herb garden. Pool
border with exotic palms and
grasses. Vegetable and cutting
garden with rose arches. New fruit
garden with espaliers. Featured in
Chichester Observer. Walled garden
accessible to wheelchairs. Partial
access to other areas.

♿ ❀ ☕

116 **SHALFORD HOUSE**
Square Drive, Kingsley Green
GU27 3LW. Sir Vernon & Lady Ellis.
*2m S of Haslemere. Just S of border
with Surrey on A286. Square Drive is
at brow of hill to the E. Turn L after
approx ¼ m & follow road to R at
bottom of hill.* Home-made teas.
**Adm £5, chd free. Sun 12 Apr (2-5);
Suns 24 May, 5 July, 6 Sept
(2-5.30).**
Highly regarded 10 acre garden
designed and created from scratch
over last 24 yrs. Beautiful hilly setting
with streams, ponds, waterfall,
sunken garden, good late borders,
azaleas, and walled kitchen garden.
Wild flower meadow with orchids,
prairie style plantation and stumpery
merging into further 7 acre woodland.
Additional 30 acre arboretum with
beech, rhododendrons, bluebells,
ponds and specimen trees.

D ☕

117 ◆ **SHEFFIELD PARK AND GARDEN**
Sheffield Park TN22 3QX. National
Trust, 01825 790231,
www.nationaltrust.org.uk. *10m S of
East Grinstead. 5m NW of Uckfield; E
of A275.* **Adm £8.75, chd £4.40. For
NGS: Sat 6 June, Wed 16 Sept (10-
5). For other opening times and
information, please phone or see
garden website.**
Magnificent 120 acres (40 hectares)
landscaped garden laid out in C18 by
Capability Brown and Humphry
Repton. Further development in early
yrs of this century by its owner Arthur
G Soames. Centrepiece is original
lakes, with many rare trees and
shrubs. Beautiful at all times of the yr,
but noted for its spring and autumn
colours. National Collection of Ghent
azaleas. Natural play trail for families
on South Park. Large number of
Champion Trees, 87 in total. Garden
largely accessible for wheelchairs,
please call for information.

& ⊗ 🚐 NCH ☕

GROUP OPENING

118 **SLINDON GARDENS GROUP**
Slindon, nr Arundel BN18 0RE. *4m
W of Arundel. From Slindon Xrds on
A29 turn N into village. Follow road
up village for approx ½ m. The Well
House on L just past Church Hill, park
in farm opp.* Home-made teas.
**Combined adm £4.50, chd free.
Thur 11, Sun 14 June (2-5).**

COURT COTTAGE
Mark & Clare Bacchus

MANCHESTER HOUSE
Niki Adamson

THE WELL HOUSE
Sue & Patrick Foley

The pretty NT village of Slindon has
many fine listed buildings and lovely
walks on the Downs. Enjoy three
contrasting gardens, within a short
stroll of each other. Court Cottage
features hot and cool island borders,
linked by an arch of roses and
clematis, and a splendid, mature
beech hedge. There is a small
orchard and raised vegetable beds.
Manchester House has a small formal
garden, laid out with box hedging
enclosing beds stocked with many
scented roses and perennials. Enjoy a
delicious home-made tea in the
delightful romantic setting of the old,
walled garden at The Well House,
where there is much to delight incl
traditional herbaceous beds stocked
with mixed perennials, shrubs and
roses. Also a small vegetable and
cutting garden and side garden
designed around a pool. Interesting
plants propagated from our gardens
for sale. Dogs welcome at Court
Cottage only. Featured in Bognor and
Chichester Observers. Only partial
wheelchair access at Manchester
House.

& ⊗ ☕

---

119 **SOUTH GRANGE**
Quickbourne Lane, Northiam, Rye
TN31 6QY. Linda & Michael Belton,
01797 252984,
belton.northiam@virgin.net.
*Between A268 & A28, approx ½ m E
of Northiam. From Northiam centre
follow Beales Lane into Quickbourne
Lane, or Quickbourne Lane leaves
A286 approx 1¾ m S of A28/A286
junction.* Light refreshments & home-
made teas. **Adm £3.50, chd free.
Wed 15 July (2-5); Sat 22, Sun 23
Aug (11-5). Visitors also welcome
by arrangement May to Oct for
groups of 20 max.**
Hardy Plant Society members'
garden for all yr interest combining
grasses, herbaceous perennials,
shrubs, trees, raised beds, wildlife
pond, vegetable plot. Orchard incl
meadow flowers, fruit cage with
willow windbreak, rose arbour,
polytunnel. Woodland is left wild.
House roof runoff diverted to pond
and bulk storage. Home propagated
plants for sale. We are becoming

older folk who garden without
assistance and like to think that
visitors can see what they too might
achieve. We try to maintain varied
habitats for most of the creatures that
we share the garden with.

& ⊗ 🚐 🛏 ☕

Visit a garden and
support hospice
care

120 **SPARROW HATCH**
Cornwell's Bank, Newick BN8 4RD.
Tony & Jane Welfare. *5m E of
Haywards Heath. From A272 turn R
into Oxbottom Lane (signed
Barcombe), ½ m fork L into Narrow
Rd, continue to T-junction & park in
Chailey Lane (no parking at house).*
Cold drinks available only. **Adm £3,
chd free. Wed 3, Thur 4 June (2-5).**
Delightful ⅓ acre plantsman's cottage
garden, wholly designed, made and
maintained by owners. Many features
incl 2 ponds, formal and wildlife,
herbaceous borders, shady dell,
vegetables, herbs, alpines. Planned
for owners' enjoyment and love of
growing plants, both usual and
unusual. Plants for sale, propagated
and grown by garden owner.
Featured in Garden News. Dogs on
leads only.

 ⊗ ☕

121 ◆ **STANDEN**
West Hoathly Road, East Grinstead
RH19 4NE. National Trust,
01342 323029,
www.nationaltrust.org.uk/standen.
*2m S of East Grinstead. Signed from
B2110 Turners Hill Rd & from East
Grinstead Town Centre.* **Adm £9.50,
chd £4.75. For NGS: Sat 9 May,
Sat 6 June, Sat 17 Oct (10-5). For
other opening times and
information, please phone or see
garden website.**
This arts and crafts inspired garden,
with spectacular views across
Weirwood Reservoir to Ashdown
Forest beyond, was created by Mrs
Margaret Beale at the end of the C19.
The collection of plants that she
gathered here were of horticultural
significance and incl many unique

plants brought back from the family's travels abroad and also collected by plant hunters of that day. Plant sales area. Kitchen garden produce available to buy. Specialist garden tours available on NGS days in spring and autumn (proceeds to NGS). Hillside garden with steps, slopes and gravel paths; wheelchair map available.

122 STONE CROSS HOUSE

Alice Bright Lane, Crowborough TN6 3SH. Mr & Mrs D A Tate. *1½ m S of Crowborough Cross. At Crowborough T-lights (A26) turn S in to High St & shortly R on to Croft Rd. Over 3 mini-r'abouts to Alice Bright Lane. Garden on L at next Xrds.* Home-made teas. **Adm £5, chd free. Sat 9, Sun 10 May (2-5).**
Beautiful 9 acre country property with gardens containing a delightful array of azaleas, acers, rhododendrons and camellias, interplanted with an abundance of spring bulbs. The very pretty cottage garden has interesting examples of topiary and unusual plants. Jacob sheep graze the surrounding pastures. Mainly flat, no steps. Gravel drive.

Beehives, bee border and bee wildflower meadow . . .

123 STONEHEALED FARM

Streat Lane, Streat BN6 8SA. Lance & Fiona Smith, 01273 891145, afionasmith@hotmail.com. *2m SE of Burgess Hill. From Ditchling B2116, 1m E of Westmeston, turn L (N) signed Streat, 2m on R immed after railway bridge.* Home-made teas. **Adm £4, chd free. Share to St Peter & St James Hospice. Sun 17 May (2-5.30). Visitors also welcome by arrangement Apr to Oct for groups of 10+.**
C17 house (not open) in beautiful rural setting. Sheltered garden rooms link with areas open to views of the South Downs. Paths wind through relaxed informal planting of trees, shrubs, climbers and unusual perennials, around ponds, through a vegetable garden and extending out

into surrounding fields. Wonderful overview from a raised platform in an ancient oak tree. Delicious home-made teas served under cover. Some gravel paths and steps.

124 ◆ SUSSEX PRAIRIES

Morlands Farm, Wheatsheaf Road, Nr Henfield BN5 9AT. Paul & Pauline McBride, 01273 495902, www.sussexprairies.co.uk. *2m NE of Henfield on B2116 Wheatsheaf Rd (also known as Albourne Rd). Follow Sussex Prairie signs.* Home-made teas. **Adm £6, chd free. For NGS: Mon 31 Aug (11-5). For other opening times and information, please phone or see garden website.**
Exciting prairie garden of approx 6 acres planted in the naturalistic style using 30,000 plants and over 600 different varieties. A colourful garden featuring a huge variety of unusual ornamental grasses. Expect layers of colour, texture and architectural splendour. Surrounded by mature oak trees with views of Chanctonbury Ring and Devil's Dyke on the South Downs. Permanent sculpture collection and exhibited sculpture throughout the season. Rare breed sheep and pigs. Featured in Homes & Gardens (July 2014). Woodchip paths may be difficult for wheelchairs. Disabled WC.

125 30 SYCAMORE DRIVE

RH15 0GH. John Smith & Kieran O'Regan, 01444 871888, jsarastroo@aol.com. *8m N of Brighton. Sycamore Drive is off Folders Lane (B2113) in Burgess Hill at Ditchling Common end.* **Evening Opening £5, wine, Fri 4 Sept (7-9.30). Visitors also welcome by arrangement June to Sept for 10 max.** Home-made teas.
See this garden transform at night into a candlelit calm oasis. Have a glass of wine and canapés as you enjoy this magical space. Licenced bar available. Adm includes wine & canapés, no concessions. Please register your intention to visit in advance. Featured in Saturday Daily Mail and Sussex Living. Partial wheelchair access only.

126 TIDEBROOK MANOR

Tidebrook, Wadhurst TN5 6PD. Edward Flint, Head Gardener. *Between Wadhurst & Mayfield. From*

Wadhurst take B2100 towards Mark Cross, L at Best Beech PH, downhill 200 metres past church on R, then a drive on L. **Adm £5, chd free. Wed 18 Mar, Wed 10 June, Wed 16 Sept (10-4).**
4 acre garden developed over the last decade with outstanding views of the Sussex countryside. In the Arts and Crafts tradition the garden features large mixed borders, intimate courtyards, meadows, hydrangea walk, kitchen garden with raised beds, a willow platt and a wild woodland of particular interest in the spring. A lively and stimulating garden throughout the yr. At the June and Sept opening there will be tours with Edward Flint, Head Gardener at 11am and 2pm (£2 additional charge), and plants for sale. Refreshments available in nearby Mayfield. No wheelchair access to woodland area.

127 TOWN PLACE

Ketches Lane, Freshfield, nr Sheffield Park RH17 7NR. Dr & Mrs Anthony McGrath, 01825 790221, mcgrathsussex@hotmail.com, www.townplacegarden.org.uk. *5m E of Haywards Heath. From A275 turn W at Sheffield Green into Ketches Lane for Lindfield. 1¾ m on L.* Cream teas. **Adm £5, chd free. Sun 14, Thur 18, Sun 28 June, Sun 5 July (2-6). Visitors also welcome by arrangement June to July for groups of 20+.**
3 acres with over 600 roses, 150ft herbaceous border, walled herb garden, ornamental grasses, ancient hollow oak, orchard and potager. Green Priory Church and Cloisters. C17 Sussex farmhouse (not open).

128 11 TREDCROFT ROAD

Hove BN3 6UH. Barbara Kennington. *E of Hove Park. Tredcroft Rd runs between Woodruff Ave & Shirley Drive. Free street parking.* Home-made teas. **Adm £3, chd free. Sat 16, Sun 17 May (11-5).**
Town garden on 4 levels facing NW, on clay soil. Designed and landscaped in 2007, the garden is now well established and boasts many creative features incl sculptures, a pebble mosaic, an exotic pool garden, shaded walk, many perennials and grasses and a working vegetable garden.

© Marianne Majerus

Lowder Mill

129 TURNERS HOUSE

Turners Green, Heathfield TN21 9RB. Christopher Miscampbell & Julia Padbury, 01435 831191, chris-joolz@zen.co.uk. *4m E of Heathfield. S off B2096 at Middle Lane, 3 Cups Corner signed Rushlake Green, Hailsham, for ¹/₃ m. Look for big clock face on L. Park on green, not roads.* Adm £4, chd free. **Visitors welcome by arrangement** Apr to July for individuals and groups of 15 max. Refreshments by prior request.

²/₃ acre country garden of lush, densely planted, colour themed shrubaceous borders, developed and maintained by owners battling against the combined challenges of exposure and drought. Catenary rose walk leading to summerhouse, displaying photos showing the development of the garden. Scrubbed birch grove, small underplanted orchard. Partial wheelchair access following wet weather. Grass, old brick paths, stepping stones, and some gravel. WC on request (not disabled WC).

130 ◆ UPPARK

South Harting GU31 5QR. National Trust, 01730 825415, www.nationaltrust.org.uk/uppark. *1¹/₂ m S of South Harting. 5m SE of Petersfield on B2146.* Adm £10, chd £5. **For NGS: Sat 25 Apr, Sat 13 June (11-5).** For other opening times and information, please phone or see garden website.

A late C18 garden, initially shaped by Lancelot Capability Brown, well maintained garden with fine lawns and a number of specimen trees. Island beds stocked with herbaceous plants and many fragrant shrubs are the key feature of the main garden. Humphry Repton's architectural features of the game larder and dairy create some interesting focal points. The recently restored Gothic seat is a great place to relax and take in the views of the south meadow and South Downs National Park beyond. Refreshments can be enjoyed on the lawn outside the Orangery café. Wheelchair access to the formal garden except in very wet weather.

131 UPWALTHAM BARNS

Upwaltham GU28 0LX. Roger & Sue Kearsey, 01798 343145. *6m S of Petworth. 6m N of Chichester on A285.* Home-made teas, wine. Adm £4.50, chd free. **Share to St Mary's Church. Sun 24, Mon 25 May (2-6). Visitors also welcome by arrangement May to Sept.**

Unique farm setting transformed into a garden of many rooms. Entrance is a tapestry of perennial planting to set off C17 flint barns. At the rear is a walled, terraced garden redeveloped and planted with an abundance of unusual plants. Extensive vegetable garden. Landscaping in walled garden in progress. Roam at leisure, relax and enjoy in all seasons. Lovely views of the South Downs and C12 Shepherds Church (open to visitors). The grounds have some gravel paths.

GROUP OPENING

132 WARNINGLID GARDENS

Warninglid, Haywards Heath RH17 5TR. *Midway between Haywards Heath & Horsham, both 6m. From A23 W towards Warninglid for ³/₄ m. S at B2115 Xrds (Cuckfield/Warninglid Lane). From W through Warninglid. Park at recreation ground. Road parking limited for disabled access, drop off for elderly. Cream teas in Cricket Pavilion adjoining parking.* Combined adm £5, chd free. Sun 28 June (2-5).

BEECHES
Mr & Mrs C Steel

HAY HOUSE
David Brewerton

1 HERRINGS COTTAGES
Mr A L Brown

OLD BARN COTTAGE
Alison & David Livesley

OLD POST
Mariola & Bob Clark

7 THE STREET
Mrs Angela Buckton

YEOVENENY HOUSE
Mr & Mrs Bill & Joan Hill

Warninglid is a pretty Medieval village set in a conservation area of outstanding natural beauty. The village architecture provides a perfect back drop to the gardens on view. Several of the gardens are sited in The Street and on Spronketts Lane; part of the old coach and horses smuggling route along the south coast towards Shoreham, through Wineham. The gardens are of remarkable variety and in different ways reflect the distinctive approach of each gardener. Terraces, shrubs and water features are used to enhance the natural landscapes and offer variety and contrast stimulating thoughts and ideas for you as the visitor. We have many gardening ideas to take away for everyone! Partial wheelchair access.

133 ◆ WEST DEAN GARDENS

West Dean PO18 0QZ. Edward James Foundation, 01243 818221, www.westdean.org.uk. *5m N of Chichester. On A286, midway between Chichester & Midhurst.* Light refreshments. Adm £7.70, chd

free. **For NGS: Wed 13 May (10.30-5). For other opening times and information, please phone or see garden website.**

35 acre historic garden in tranquil downland setting. 300ft long Harold Peto pergola, mixed and herbaceous borders, rustic summerhouses, water and spring garden, and specimen trees. 2½ acre walled garden contains fruit collection, 13 Victorian glasshouses, apple store, large working kitchen garden and extensive plant collection. Circuit walk (2¼ m) climbs through parkland to 45 acre St Roche's Arboretum. Most areas of the walled garden and grounds are accessible.

&. ⊛ 🚐 ⊨ ☕

134 **NEW** **WHITEHANGER**
Marley Lane, Haslemere GU27 3PY. David & Lynn Paynter, 01428 653273, l.paynter@btopenworld.com. *3m S of Haslemere. Take the A286 Midhurst road from Haslemere & after approx 2m turn R into Marley Lane (opp Hatch Lane). After 1m turn into drive shared with Rosemary Park Nursing Home.* **Evening Openings £5, chd £2.50, wine, Thur 11, Thur 18 June (5.30-8.30). Visitors are welcome by arrangement in June for groups of 10+.**
Set in 6 acres, on the edge of the South Downs National Park, surrounded by NT woodland, this rural garden was started in 2012 when a new Huf house was built on a derelict site. Now there are lawned areas with beds of perennials; a serenity pool with Koi carp, and a wild flower meadow. Added in 2014 are a Japanese garden and a sculpture garden. Planned for 2015 is a woodland walk. Surrey Artists Open Studio exhibition.

&. ☕

135 **1 WHITES COTTAGES**
Fletching, Uckfield TN22 3SP. Gillian & Colin Smith. *4m NW of Uckfield. From A272 turn N at Piltdown or North Chailey 1m. From A275 turn E at Sheffield Green 2m.* Home-made teas at North Hall. **Combined adm with North Hall £4.50, chd free. Sat 27, Sun 28 June (2-5.30).**
Located in the picturesque village of Fletching, this enchanting little garden is delightfully crammed with everything synonymous with a true cottage garden. Small in space but huge in interest it features amongst

the lovely perennial planting and unique paths, a child's gipsy caravan and free running ducks. Reasonably priced home propagated plants for sale.

⊛ ☕

136 **NEW** **WHITHURST PARK**
Plaistow Road, Kirdford, Billingshurst RH14 0JW. Mr Richard Taylor & Mr Rick Englert, www.whithurst.com. *7m NW of Billingshurst. A272 to Wisborough Green, follow signs to Kirdford village, turn R at 1st T-junction through village, then R onto Plaistow Rd, 1m to Whithurst Park sign, then L uphill to garden.* Home-made teas. **Adm £5, chd free. Sat 18 July, Sat 1 Aug (10-6).**
5 yr old walled kitchen garden with many espaliered fruit trees within and without. Herb beds, vegetable beds, flower borders and cutting beds. Central greenhouse and potting shed with interesting behind the wall support buildings incl extensive compost area close to beehives and the bee border and bee wildflower meadow. Sustainability through permaculture principles. Ramp up 3 inch step onto garden paths.

&. ⊛ ☕

GROUP OPENING

137 **WINCHELSEA'S SECRET GARDENS**
Winchelsea TN36 4EJ. *2m W of Rye, 8m E of Hastings. Purchase ticket for all gardens at first garden visited; a map will be provided showing gardens and location of teas.* Home-made teas in village hall (2-4.45pm). **Combined adm £5 (April), £6 (June), chd free. Thur 9 Apr, Sat 6 June (1-5.30).**

ALARDS
Vicky Jessup.
Open April only

THE ARMOURY
Mr & Mrs A Jasper.
Open June only

1 BARRACK SQUARE
Andy & Maureen Pemble.
Open June only

2 BARRACK SQUARE
Melvyn & Jan Pett.
Open June only

3 BARRACK SQUARE
Ms Deborah Upton.
Open June only

CLEVELAND HOUSE
Mr & Mrs J Jempson

CLEVELAND PLACE
Sally & Graham Rhodda

FIVE CHIMNEYS
Tony & Sue Davis.
Open June only

KING'S LEAP
Philip Kent.
Open April only

PERITEAU HOUSE
Dr & Mrs Lawrence Youlten

RYE VIEW
Howard Norton & David Page

SOUTH MARITEAU
Robert & Sheila Holland.
Open June only

2 STRAND PLAT
Rookery Lane. Mr & Mrs Anthony and Gillian Tugman.
Open June only

THE WELL HOUSE
Alice Kenyon.
Open April only

Seven spring gardens and eleven summer gardens in the beautiful Cinque Port town of Winchelsea. Many styles, large and small, hilltop and riverside, gardens with commanding views and secret walled gardens, spring bulbs, herbaceous borders and more. See the gardens and explore the town with its magnificent church and famous Medieval merchants' cellars. Guided tours of cellars both dates at 11am, see winchelseacellars.com, booking essential 01797 222629. Town information at winchelsea.net and winchelsea.com. Enquiries to david@ryeview.net. If you are bringing a coach, please let us know. Wheelchair access to over half of the gardens; see map for details.

&. ⊛ 🚐 ☕

Superb home-made teas overlooking the mill lake . . .

WARWICKSHIRE

(for Birmingham & West Midlands see Staffordshire

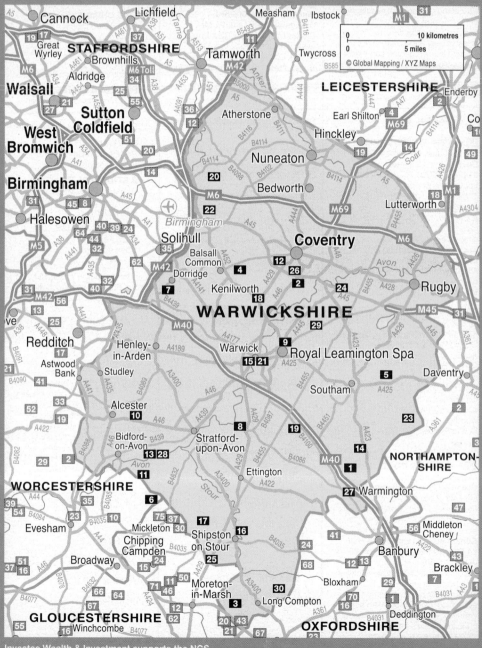

Warwickshire

Warwickshire is a landlocked county, with no city of its own, but with two big cities on the doorstep.

There are nearly twenty bustling and fashionable towns, quintessentially English villages and plenty of welcoming Tudor beam 'foodie' pubs, plus flowers all year round. This county – say it Worrick-sher – has experienced much change, with manufacture and small industry (such as needles) all gone.

Today motorways run through, but it is still leafy Warwickshire. Undulating country miles take you to Regency Leamington, castles at Kenilworth and Warwick, and that school at Rugby.

Today Warwickshire has a new theme for a new century –Tourism. Inspired by our old poacher William Shakespeare at Stratford-upon-Avon, the Bard's fans flock to Warwickshire from all over the world to roam the towns, from Alcester to Atherstone, and enjoy their beautiful flowers and magnificent trees.

For your eyes only, the NGS in Warwickshire offers a stunning display of flower-power week on week, thanks to the generous garden owners.

Warwickshire Volunteers

County Organiser
Julia Sewell
01295 680234
sewelljulia@btinternet.com

County Treasurer
Susan Solomon
01789 740183
SS@follylodge.eclipse.co.uk

Publicity
Lily Farrah
01789 204858
dipsy25@hotmail.com

Elspeth Napier
01608 666278
elspeth@cherryvilla.demon.co.uk

Peter Pashley
01789 294932
peter@peterpash.mail1.co.uk

Jane Robbins
01926 409266
jane@jrpromotions.biz

Booklet Coordinators
Janet Neale
01295 690515
janetneale5@gmail.com

Hugh Thomas
01926 423063
hugh@charityview.co.uk

Assistant County Organisers
Emma Burbidge
01789 842650
emmaburbidge@hotmail.co.uk

Sue Herbert
07862 647147
suemherbert@icloud.com

Elspeth Napier
01608 666278
elspeth@cherryvilla.demon.co.uk

Sal Renwick
01564 770215
sal.renwick@blueyonder.co.uk

Eleni Tovey
02476 419049
elenitovey@aol.com

Left: Old Beams, Stretton-on-Fosse Gardens

Since our foundation we have donated more than £42.5 million to charity

Opening Dates

All entries subject to change.
For latest information check www.ngs.org.uk

February

Saturday 21
15 Hill Close Gardens

April

5 Bridge Nursery (every day from Apr 11)

Sunday 12
25 Stretton-on-Fosse Gardens

Sunday 19
7 Broadacre

May

5 Bridge Nursery (every day)

Monday 4
12 Earlsdon Gardens

Sunday 17
22 Packington Hall

Sunday 24
3 Barton House
6 Broad Marston & Pebworth Gardens

Monday 25
6 Broad Marston & Pebworth Gardens

June

5 Bridge Nursery (every day)

Festival Weekend

Saturday 6
29 Weston-under-Wetherley Gardens

Sunday 7
10 The Croft House
29 Weston-under-Wetherley Gardens

Saturday 13
8 Charlecote Park (Evening)

Sunday 14
11 Dorsington Gardens
16 Honington Village Gardens
19 Lighthorne Gardens
20 Maxstoke Castle
26 Styvechale Gardens
30 Whichford & Ascott Gardens

Sunday 21
18 Kenilworth Gardens
27 Warmington Village Gardens

Saturday 27
17 Ilmington Gardens
28 Welford-on-Avon & District Gardens

Sunday 28
4 NEW Berkswell Gardens
17 Ilmington Gardens
23 Priors Marston Manor

28 Welford-on-Avon & District Gardens

July

5 Bridge Nursery (every day)

Sunday 5
1 Avon Dassett Gardens

Wednesday 22
25 Stretton-on-Fosse Gardens

Saturday 25
24 Ryton Organic Gardens

Sunday 26
2 Avondale Nursery
24 Ryton Organic Gardens

August

5 Bridge Nursery (every day)

Saturday 8
8 Charlecote Park (Evening)

Sunday 23
2 Avondale Nursery

Sunday 30
14 The Granary

Monday 31
14 The Granary

September

5 Bridge Nursery (every day until Sep 20)

Saturday 5
24 Ryton Organic Gardens

Sunday 6
24 Ryton Organic Gardens

Saturday 26
15 Hill Close Gardens

Gardens open to the public

2 Avondale Nursery
5 Bridge Nursery
8 Charlecote Park
15 Hill Close Gardens
21 The Mill Garden
24 Ryton Organic Gardens

By arrangement only

9 19 Church Lane
13 Elm Close

Also open by arrangement

3 Barton House
7 Broadacre
10 The Croft House
12 43 Armorial Road, Earlsdon Gardens
14 The Granary
23 Priors Marston Manor
25 Court House, Stretton-on-Fosse Gardens
26 43 Armorial Road, Styvechale Gardens
26 16 Delaware Road, Styvechale Gardens
26 2 The Hiron, Styvechale Gardens

The Gardens

GROUP OPENING

1 AVON DASSETT GARDENS
Southam CV47 2AE. Mike & Jill Lewis. *7m N of Banbury. From M40 J12 turn L, & L again B4100. 2nd L into village. Park in village & at top of hill.* Home-made teas at Old Mill Cottage. **Combined adm £5, chd free. Sun 5 July (2-6).**

NEW **10 AVON CARROW**
Anna Prosser

NEW **11 AVON CARROW**
Mick & Avis Forbes

THE COACH HOUSE
Diana & Peter Biddlestone

NEW **THE EAST WING, AVON CARROW**
Christine Fisher & Terry Gladwin

HILL TOP FARM
Mrs N & Mr D Hicks

OLD MILL COTTAGE
Mike & Jill Lewis

THE OLD RECTORY
Lily Hope-Frost

POPPY COTTAGE
Bob & Audrey Butler

NEW **THE THATCHES**
Trevor & Michele Gill

Pretty Hornton stone village sheltering in the lee of the Burton Dassett hills, well wooded with parkland setting, and The Old Rectory mentioned in Domesday Book. Wide variety of gardens incl kitchen gardens, gravel and tropical gardens. Range of plants incl alpines, herbaceous, perennials, roses, climbers and shrubs. Features incl Art Exhibition, book sale, plant tombola and two churches open. Wheelchair access to most properties.

♿ 🐕 ⊗ 🚐 ☕

Delicious home-made teas on the terrace . . .

The Whichford Pottery, Whichford & Ascott Gardens

© Andrew Lawson

Take your Group to an NGS garden 🚌

2 ◆ **AVONDALE NURSERY**
at Russell's Nursery, Mill Hill, Baginton CV8 3AG. Mr Brian Ellis, 02476 673662, www.avondalenursery. co.uk. *3m S Coventry. At junction of A45 & A46 take slip road to Baginton, 1st L to Mill Hill. Opp Old Mill Inn.* Light refreshments in Potting Shed Cafe at Russell's Nursery. **Adm £3, chd free.** For NGS: Sun 26 July, Sun 23 Aug (11-4). For other opening times and information, please phone or see garden website.
Vast array of flowers and ornamental grasses, incl National Collections of *Anemone nemorosa*, *Sanguisorba* and *Aster novae-angliae*. Choc-a-bloc with plants, our Library Garden is a well labelled reference book illustrating the unusual, exciting and even some long-lost treasures. Adjacent nursery is a plantaholic's delight! On Sun 26 July (2-3), Brian hopes you will join him for an enthusiastic Talk Around the Library Garden, when he will show you all of his current late flowering plant obsessions, incl big collections of *Helenium*, *Crocosmia*, *Sanguisorba* and ornamental grasses, and the garden will be looking at its best! Adm £5 incl tea, coffee and biscuits (all proceeds to NGS). Featured on Gardener's World, in House & Garden, The English Garden and RHS Garden magazine.
& 🐾 ❀ � **NCH** ☕

WE ARE
MACMILLAN.
CANCER SUPPORT

The NGS has funded 147 different Macmillan projects

3 ◆ **BARTON HOUSE**
Barton-on-the-Heath GL56 0PJ. Mr & Mrs I H B Cathie, 01608 674303, hamish.cathie@thebartonfarms. com. *2m W of Long Compton. 2m W off A3400 Stratford-upon-Avon to Oxford road; 1¹/₄ m N off A44 Chipping Norton to Moreton-in-Marsh road.* Home-made teas. **Adm £5, chd free. Sun 24 May (2-6).** Visitors also welcome by arrangement spring to autumn.
6¹/₂ acres with mature trees, azaleas,

species and hybrid rhododendrons, magnolias, moutan tree peonies. National collections of *Arbutus* and *Catalpa*. Japanese garden, rose garden, secret garden and many rare and exotic plants. Victorian kitchen garden. Exotic garden with palms, cypresses and olive trees established 2002. Vineyard planted in 2000 - free wine tasting. Manor house by Inigo Jones (not open). Some gravel paths and steps. Can be slippery but generally wheelchair friendly. Dogs strictly on leads only.
& ❀ � **NCH** ☕

GROUP OPENING

4 NEW **BERKSWELL GARDENS**
Berkswell, Coventry CV7 7GG. *A452 to Balsall Common & follow signs to Berkswell. Tickets & maps available at each garden. Car necessary to visit all gardens.* Light refreshments at Yew Tree Barn, Holly Oak, The Tower House & Eardley Cottage. **Combined adm £5, chd free. Sun 28 June (11-5).**

> NEW **BATAVIA**
> Waste Lane. John & Win Furber.
> *Appox ¹/₄ m from Nailcote Hall*

> NEW **BROOKSIDE HOUSE**
> Truggist Lane. Shirley & Frank Rounthwaite.
> *Nr junction of Truggist Lane & Spencers Lane, Carol Green*

> NEW **145 DUGGINS LANE**
> Mary & Edward Cotterrell

> NEW **EARDLEY COTTAGE**
> Meriden Road. June & Bob Smitten.
> *Approx ³/₄ m towards Meriden from Berkswell*

> NEW **FAIRWAYS**
> Waste Lane. Tom Bunt & Janet Lloyd-Bunt.
> *On B4101 nr junction of Hodgetts Lane & Waste Lane*

> NEW **FERN COTTAGE**
> Hob Lane. Jean Mauger.
> *A452 to Balsall Common, at T-light R into Kelsey Lane, after ¹/₂ m R into Windmill Lane, 150yds L into Hob Lane, garden on R*

> **FIRS FARM**
> Windmill Lane. Mr & Mrs C Ellis

> NEW **HOLLY OAK**
> Shirley Lane, Meriden. Jane Bostock

> NEW **OLD HALL**
> Waste Lane. John Morris.
> *On B4101 nr junction of Hodgetts Lane & Waste Lane*

> **THE PINES**
> Hodgetts Lane. Mr & Mrs C Davis

> NEW **SQUIRRELS JUMP**
> Waste Lane. Brian & Jenny Harris.
> *On B4101, 1m E of junction with A452 at Balsall Common. Garden on L approx 200 metres from humped back bridge*

> NEW **THE TOWER HOUSE**
> Spencers Lane. Penny & David Stableforth.
> *1m from Berkswell towards Tile Hill & 1m from Balsall Common*

> NEW **YEW TREE BARN**
> Baulk Lane. Angela & Ken Shaw.
> *At Xrd in Berkswell take Spencers Lane for 1¹/₂ m. R into Baulk Lane. Garden 50yds on L. Parking on Baulk Lane or preferably Spencers Lane*

Berkswell is a beautiful village dating back to Saxon times with a C12 Norman church and has several C16 and C17 buildings incl the village PH. In 2014 the village was awarded Gold in the RHS Britain in Bloom campaign plus a special award for the Best Large Village in the Heart of England. The gardens provide great variety with fine examples of small and large, formal and informal, wild, imaginatively planted herbaceous borders and productive vegetable gardens. Something for everyone and plenty of ideas to take home. Plants for sale at some gardens. Also open to visitors is the C12 Norman church with a garden, and a themed art exhibition at the gallery at Fern Cottage. Wheelchair access to some gardens.
🐾 ❀ ☕

---

5 ◆ **BRIDGE NURSERY**
Tomlow Road, Napton, nr Southam CV47 8HX. Christine Dakin & Philip Martino, 01926 812737, www.bridge-nursery.co.uk. *3m E of Southam. Brown tourist sign at Napton Xrds on A425 Southam to Daventry road.* Tea. **Adm £2.50, chd free. For NGS: Daily Sat 11 Apr to Sun 20 Sept (10-4).** For other opening times and information, please phone or see garden website.

Clay soil? Don't despair. Here is a garden full of an exciting range of plants which thrive in hostile conditions. Grass paths lead you round borders filled with many unusual plants. Features incl a pond and a bamboo grove complete with panda! A peaceful haven for wildlife and visitors.

Canal-side garden with views of the Oxford canal and Dassett Hills . . .

GROUP OPENING

6 ▶ BROAD MARSTON & PEBWORTH GARDENS
Stratford-upon-Avon CV37 8XZ. *9m SW of Stratford-upon-Avon. On B439 at Bidford turn S towards Honeybourne, after 3m turn L at Xrds signed Pebworth.* Home-made teas at Pebworth Village Hall. **Combined adm £6, chd free. Sun 24, Mon 25 May (2-6).**

ASHLOW
Rachel & Dudley Jarrett

BANK HOUSE
Clive & Caroline Warren

1 ELM CLOSE
Mr & Mrs G Keyte

FELLY LODGE
Maz & Barrie Clatworthy

ICKNIELD BARN
Sheila Davies

JASMINE COTTAGE
Ted & Veronica Watson

THE KNOLL
Mr & Mrs K Wood

NOLAN COTTAGE
Gill & Ron Thomas

PETTIFER HOUSE
Mr & Mrs Michael Veal

Broad Marston, a small hamlet with a priory and manor (not open), modern houses and thatched cottages, lies at the lowest point of the parish and the gardens are all on the level. Pebworth

received a Silver-gilt in the Heart of England in Bloom. The gardens in Pebworth, run down the hill topped by St. Peter's C13 church (open). At the bottom of the hill lies the primary school with a thriving garden. The children grow vegetables and then cook them. Among the houses here you will find the village hall and two small but interesting gardens very different in character. This is another area with old thatched cottages, and properties of various ages, and a variety of garden styles. No wheelchair access to The Knoll.

7 ▶ BROADACRE
Grange Road, Dorridge, Solihull B93 8QA. Mr John Woolman, 07818 082885, jw234567@gmail.com, www.broadacregarden.org. *Approx 3m SE of Solihull. On B4101 opp Railway PH.* Home-made teas. **Adm £3, chd free. Sun 19 Apr (2-6). Visitors also welcome by arrangement.**
Broadacre is a semi-wild garden attractively landscaped with pools, lawns and trees and with two adjoining wild flower meadows. The garden is at its best when the fruit trees are blossoming in the spring. Bring stout footwear to follow the nature trail around the meadows. Lovely venue for a spring picnic. Pets welcome. Dorridge Cricket Club is in the grounds.

8 ▶ ◆ CHARLECOTE PARK
Wellesbourne, Warwick CV35 9ER. National Trust, 01789 470277, www.nationaltrust.org.uk/ charlecote. *5m E of Stratford-upon-Avon, 6m S of Warwick, 1m W of Wellesbourne. J15 of M40 take A429 towards Cirencester, then signs for Charlecote Park. From Stratford-upon-Avon B4086 towards Wellesbourne, then signs for Charlecote Park.* **For NGS: Evening Openings £10, chd free, wine, Sat 13 June, Sat 8 Aug (6-8). 25 places for each opening incl private tour of the gardens lead by the senior gardener and the park & garden manager. Pre-booking essential, please phone to book. For other opening times and information, please phone or see garden website.**
Charlecote Park has been home to the Lucy family for more than 800 yrs.

The gardens incl a formal parterre, woodland walk, herbaceous border and wider parkland which is a Capability Brown landscape offering picturesque views across the R Avon. A herd of fallow deer has been in the park since Tudor times. Charlecote Park was one of the first gardens to open in support of NGS back in 1927. House not open. Gravel paths around the grounds.

9 ▶ 19 CHURCH LANE
Lillington, Leamington Spa CV32 7RG. David & Judy Hirst, 01926 422591. *1½ m NE of Leamington Spa. Take A445 towards Rugby. Church Lane on R just beyond r'about junction with B4453. Garden on corner of Hill Close. Enter via gate in brick archway in Hill Close.* **Adm £3, chd free. Visitors welcome by arrangement Feb to Aug for groups of 16 max.**
Camellias, spring bulbs and hellebores greet the early visitor to this plantsperson's cottage style garden. Many unusual plants in all seasons, with pleasingly combined herbaceous areas, clematis, raised beds and alpine containers. A country atmosphere, satisfying to the horticultural connoisseur as well as to the general gardener.

10 ▶ THE CROFT HOUSE
Haselor, Alcester B49 6LU. Isobel & Patrick Somers, 01789 488881, ifas1010@aol.com. *6m W of Stratford-upon-Avon, 2m E of Alcester, off A46. From A46 take Haselor turn. From Alcester take old Stratford Rd, L turn for Haselor then R at Xrds. Garden in centre of village. Please park considerately.* Tea. **Adm £3, chd free. Sun 7 June (12-5). Visitors also welcome by arrangement May to July for individuals or groups.**
Wander through an acre of trees, shrubs and herbaceous borders densely planted with a designer's passion for colour and texture. Hidden areas invite you to linger. Gorgeous scented wisteria on two sides of the house. Organically managed, providing a haven for birds and other wildlife. Frog pond, treehouse, small vegetable plot and a few venerable old fruit trees from its days as a market garden. Art & Crafts Exhibition in the garden studio, donating to NGS.

Bridge Nursery

6 DINGLE END
See Worcestershire.

GROUP OPENING

11 DORSINGTON GARDENS
Dorsington CV37 8AR. *6m SW of Stratford-upon-Avon. On B439 from Stratford turn L to Welford-on-Avon, then R to Dorsington.* Home-made teas in the village (signed on the day). **Combined adm £5, chd free.** Sun 14 June (1-5).

THE BARN
Mr & Mrs P Reeve

CRABTREE FARM COTTAGE
Mr & Mrs David Boulton

NEW CRABTREE FARM HOUSE
Jane Davies

2 DORSINGTON MANOR
Mr & Mrs C James

3 DORSINGTON MANOR
Mr & Mrs E Rusling

1 GLEBE COTTAGES
Mr & Mrs A Brough

The village is a tranquil hamlet mentioned in the Domesday Book, featuring a conservation area with many diverse gardens in and around the village. Ranging from small cottage gardens, to newly created gardens, featuring roses, vegetables, gurgling brooks and more. Mr Felix Dennis sadly died in June 2014 so his gardens and attractions will no longer be open and Dorsington is returning to a simple display of village gardens in a rural setting.

&♿ ❀ ☕

GROUP OPENING

12 EARLSDON GARDENS
Coventry CV5 6FS. *Turn towards Coventry at A45 & A429 T-lights. Take 3rd L into Beechwood Ave, continue ¹/₂ m to St. Barbara's Church at Xrds with Rochester Rd. Maps & tickets at St Barbara's Church Hall.* Light refreshments at St Barbara's Church Hall. **Combined adm £3.50, chd free.** Mon 4 May (11-4).

43 ARMORIAL ROAD
Gary & Jane Flanagan
Visitors also welcome by arrangement May to Sept with other Styvechale gardens.
07739 884098
garyflanagan@hotmail.co.uk

3 BATES ROAD
Victor Keene MBE

40 HARTINGTON CRESCENT
Viv & George Buss

114 HARTINGTON CRESCENT
Liz Campbell & Denis Crowley

54 SALISBURY AVENUE
Peter & Pam Moffit

2 SHAFTESBURY ROAD
Ann Thomson & Bruce Walker

23 SPENCER AVENUE
Susan & Keith Darwood

Varied selection of town gardens from small to more formal with interest for all tastes incl a mature garden with deep borders bursting with spring colour, a large garden with extensive lawns and an array of rhododendrons, azaleas and large mature trees; densely planted town garden with sheltered patio area and wilder woodland and surprisingly large garden offering interest to all ages! There is also a pretty garden set on several levels with hidden aspects, large peaceful garden with water features and vegetable plot and a large mature garden in a peaceful surrounding. Plantaholic's garden with a large variety of plants, clematis and small trees, some unusual and a woodland setting providing the backdrop to a garden of many contrasts incl a terrace of subtropical plants.

🐶 ❀ ☕

13 ELM CLOSE
Welford on Avon CV37 8PT. Eric & Glenis Dyer, 01789 750793, glenisdyer@gmail.com. *5m SW of Stratford, off B4390. Elm Close is between Welford Garage & The Bell Inn.* **Adm £3, chd free. Visitors welcome by arrangement Feb to July for groups of 15-50.** Refreshments on request.
Drifts of snowdrops, aconites, erythroniums and hellebores in spring are followed by species peonies, sumptuous tree peonies, herbaceous peonies and delphiniums. Colourful Japanese maples, daphnes and cornus are underplanted with hostas, heucheras, and brunneras. Then agapanthus, salvias and hydrangeas extend the seasons, with hundreds of clematis providing yr-round colour. Sloping gravel front drive.

&♿ ❀ 🚐 ☕

14 ▶ THE GRANARY
Fenny Compton Wharf, Fenny Compton, Southam CV47 2FE.
Lucy & Mike Davies, 01295 770033, bookings@the-granary.co.uk, www.the-granary.co.uk. *7m S of Southam. On A423 Southam to Banbury road. 200yds S of turning to Fenny Compton turn R into service road signed Fenny Compton Wharf. Follow NGS signs.* Light refreshments & lunches. **Adm £4, chd free.** Sun 30, Mon 31 Aug (11-4.30). Visitors also welcome by arrangement June to Sept for groups of 10-30.
Attractive 1 acre canal-side garden with views of the Oxford canal and Dassett Hills. Recent additions incl herbaceous beds, water feature and herb garden. Beyond is a ¹/₃ acre kitchen plot comprising a vegetable area (grown on organic principles), a polytunnel for propagation and salad crops, fruit cage and orchard. There is also a copse of native British trees in the 3 acre paddock. Gravel paths with steps down to the herb garden and up to the vegetable area.

🌾 ⊕ ⊨ ☕

15 ▶ ◆ HILL CLOSE GARDENS
Bread and Meat Close, Warwick CV34 6HF. Hill Close Gardens Trust, 01926 493339, www.hillclosegardens.com. *Town centre. Entry from Friars St on Bread & Meat Close. Car park by entrance next to racecourse. 2hrs free parking. Disabled parking outside the gates.* Light refreshments in Visitor Centre. **Adm £3.50, chd £1.** For NGS: Sat 21 Feb (11-4); Sat 26 Sept (11-5). For other opening times and information, please phone or see garden website.
Restored Grade II* Victorian leisure gardens comprising 16 individual hedged gardens, 8 brick summerhouses. Herbaceous borders, heritage apple and pear trees, C19 daffodils, over 100 varieties of snowdrops, many varieties of asters and chrysanthemums. Heritage vegetables. Plant Heritage border, auricula theatre, Victorian style glasshouse. Children's garden. Wheelchair available which can be booked in advance by phone. Access route indicated on plan of the gardens.

♿ ⊕ 🚐 ☕

GROUP OPENING

16 ▶ HONINGTON VILLAGE GARDENS
Shipston-on-Stour CV36 5AA.
1¹/₂ m N of Shipston-on-Stour. Take A3400 towards Stratford-upon-Avon then turn R signed Honington. Home-made teas. **Combined adm £5, chd free.** Sun 14 June (2-6).

HONINGTON GLEBE
Mr & Mrs J C Orchard

HONINGTON HALL
B H E Wiggin

THE OLD COTTAGE
Liz Davenport

THE OLD HOUSE
Mr & Mrs I F Beaumont

ORCHARD HOUSE
Mr & Mrs Monnington

SHOEMAKERS COTTAGE
Christopher & Anne Jordan

C17 village, recorded in Domesday, entered by old toll gate. Ornamental stone bridge over the R Stour and interesting church with C13 tower and late C17 nave after Wren. Six super gardens. 2 acre plantsman's garden consisting of rooms planted informally with yr-round interest in contrasting foliage, texture, lily pool and parterre. Extensive lawns and fine mature trees with river and garden monuments. Small garden that is well stocked with interesting established shrubs and container plants, and a structured cottage garden formally laid out with box hedging and small fountain. Small, developing garden created by the owners with informal mixed beds and borders. Wheelchair access to most gardens.

♿ 🌾 🚐 ☕

GROUP OPENING

17 ▶ ILMINGTON GARDENS
Ilmington CV36 4LA, 01608 682230. *8m S of Stratford-upon-Avon. 8m N of Moreton in Marsh. 4m NW of Shipston-on-Stour off A3400. 3m NE of Chipping Campden.* Cream teas at Ilmington Village Hall. **Combined adm £6, chd free.** Share to Warwickshire and Northamptonshire Air Ambulance. Sat 27, Sun 28 June (2-6).

CHERRY ORCHARD
Mr Angus Chambers

COMPTON SCORPION FARM
Mrs Karlsen.
Take Featherbed Lane, opp Red Lion PH; after 200yds turn R. Garden on R after approx 2m as road ascends steeply

CRAB MILL
Mr & Mrs D Brown

NEW ▶ THE DOWER HOUSE
Mr & Mrs M Tremellen

FOXCOTE HILL
Mr & Mrs Michael Dingley

FROG ORCHARD
Mr & Mrs Jeremy Snowden

GRUMP COTTAGE
Mr & Mrs Martin Underwood

ILMINGTON MANOR
Mr Martin Taylor

PARK FARM HOUSE
Mike & Lesley Lane

RAVENSCROFT
Mr & Mrs Clasper

Ilmington is an ancient hillside Cotswold village 2m from the Fosse Way with two good PH and splendid teas at the village hall. Buy your ticket at Ilmington Manor (next to the Red Lion PH), wander the 3 acre gardens with fish pond. Then to the delightfully planted large gardens of Foxcote Hill. Walk 100yds to tiny Grump Cottage's small stone terraced suntrap. Up Grump Street to Crab Mill's hillside gardens, then up to Ravenscroft's large sculpture filled sloping vistas commanding the hilltop. Walk to nearby Frog Lane, view cottage gardens at Park Farm House, Cherry Orchard and Frog Orchard. Cross the village to The Dower House, a newly opened garden overlooking the Manor ponds and the Norman church. Drive 2m to isolated bliss at beautiful Compton Scorpion Farm. Ilmington Morris Men performing round the village on Sunday only.

☕

Demonstration gardens from modest to expansive, showcasing a range of organic best practice . . .

Find a garden near you – download our free iOS app

GROUP OPENING

🔟 KENILWORTH GARDENS
Kenilworth CV8 1BT. *Fieldgate Lane off A452. Tickets & maps available at all gardens. Parking available at Abbey Fields, & street parking at Fieldgate Lane (limited), Malthouse Lane & Beehive Hill.* Home-made teas at St Nicholas Parochial Hall. Combined adm £5, chd free. Sun 21 June (1-5).

BEEHIVE HILL ALLOTMENTS
Mr Keith Rocket

FIELDGATE
Liz & Bob Watson

14C FIELDGATE LANE
Mrs Sandra Aulton

7 FIELDGATE LAWN
Mr Simon Cockell

25 MALTHOUSE LANE
David & Linda Pettifor

NEW ST NICHOLAS PAROCHIAL HALL
St Nicholas Church

Kenilworth was historically a very important town in Warwickshire, which now has one of England's best castle ruins and plenty of PH and good restaurants. This year we welcome another new garden, St Nicholas Parochial Hall garden to the group. This makes six in all, providing great variety; the group incl small and large gardens, formal and informal, and floral and vegetable gardening. All the gardens have won gold awards in the Kenilworth in Bloom garden competition with four attaining Best in Class.

🎭 ❀ 🚐 ☕

GROUP OPENING

🔟 LIGHTHORNE GARDENS
Lighthorne, Warwick CV35 0AR. *10m S of Warwick. Lighthorne will be signed from the Fosse Way & B4100.* Home-made teas at the village hall. Combined adm £6, chd free. Sun 14 June (2-6).

1 CHURCH HILL COURT
Irene Proudman

4 CHURCH HILL COURT
Carol Schofield

NEW ELMHURST
Mr & Mrs Nigel & Sally Dick

NEW 16 MOUNTFORD DRIVE
Mr Michael Kerr

THE OLD RECTORY
The Hon Lady Butler

THE PADDOCK
Martin & Lesley Thornton

ROBIN COTTAGE
Martin & Mel Ryan

ROSEMARY COTTAGE
Jane & Edward Stroud

TAWTON
David Copson & Maureen Thomson

Lighthorne is a compact, pretty village between the Fosse Way and the B4100, with a charming church (open), PH and village hall. The nine gardens opening are within easy reach on foot. At The Old Rectory the garden is sheltered by old stone walls clothed with roses and dominated by two magnificent copper beeches. Some gardens are very small, particularly the tiny one beside the village green 12ft by 6ft, but all are interesting and different. Partial wheelchair access.

☕

Walk amongst the trees and wildlife with stunning views up to the house and garden aviary . . .

THE MANOR
See Gloucestershire.

🔟 MAXSTOKE CASTLE
Coleshill B46 2RD. Mr & Mrs M C Fetherston-Dilke. *2½ m E of Coleshill. E of Birmingham, on B4114. Take R turn down Castle Lane, Castle Drive 1¼ m on R.* Tea. **Adm £7, chd £4.50.** Sun 14 June (11-5). Approx 5 acres of garden and grounds with herbaceous, shrubs and trees in the immed surroundings of this C14 moated castle. No wheelchair access to house.

♿ ❀ ☕

74 MEADOW ROAD
See Worcestershire.

🔟 ◆ THE MILL GARDEN
55 Mill Street, Warwick CV34 4HB. Julia (née Measures) Russell & David Russell, www.ngs.org.uk. *Off A425 beside old castle gate, at the bottom of Mill St. Use St Nicholas car park.* **For opening times and information, please see website.** This garden lies in a magical setting on the banks of the R Avon beneath the walls of Warwick Castle. Winding paths lead round every corner to dramatic views of the castle and ruined Medieval bridge. This informal cottage garden is a profusion of plants, shrubs and trees. Beautiful all year. Open daily from Apr to Oct (9-6). Partial wheelchair access. Unsuitable for electric wheelchairs.

♿ ❀

MORTON HALL
See Worcestershire.

🔟 PACKINGTON HALL
Meriden, nr Coventry CV7 7HF. Lord & Lady Aylesford. *Midway between Coventry & Birmingham on A45. Entrance 400yds from Stonebridge island towards Coventry. CV7 7HE for SatNav.* Home-made teas. **Adm £5, chd free.** Sun 17 May (2-5). Packington is the setting for an elegant Capability Brown landscape. Designed from 1750 in 100 acres of parkland which sweeps down to a lake incl 1762 Japanese bridge. Mirrored terrace beds glow with perennials. Nearby is the Millennium Rose Garden planted with old fashioned roses complete with flowers, hips and haws. Delicious WI teas on the terrace.

☕

23 PRIORS MARSTON MANOR
The Green, Priors Marston
CV47 7RH. Dr & Mrs Mark Cecil,
01788 891439,
whewitt15@yahoo.co.uk. *8m SW of
Daventry. Off A361 between Daventry
& Banbury at Charwelton. Follow sign
to Priors Marston approx 2m. Arrive
at T-junction with war memorial on R
& follow yellow signs to car parking.*
Home-made teas. **Adm £4.50, chd
free. Sun 28 June (2-6). Visitors
also welcome by arrangement
June to Aug on Mon, Tue, Thur or
Fri only.**
Arrive through the woodland rotunda
garden and explore the manor
gardens. Greatly enhanced by
present owners to relate back to a
Georgian manor garden and pleasure
grounds. Wonderful walled kitchen
garden provides seasonal produce
and cut flowers for the house.
Herbaceous flower beds and a
sunken terrace with water feature by
William Pye. Lawns lead down to the
lake around which you can walk
amongst the trees and wildlife with
stunning views up to the house and
garden aviary. Sculpture. Partial
wheelchair access.

Marie Curie Cancer Care

Marie Curie's hospice gardens provide tranquillity for patients

PUMP COTTAGE
See Worcestershire.

24 ◆ RYTON ORGANIC GARDENS
Wolston Lane, Ryton on
Dunsmore, Coventry CV8 3LG.
Garden Organic, 02476 303517,
www.rytongardens.org.uk. *5m SE
of Coventry. From A45 take N exit
signed Wolston with brown tourist
signs for Ryton Gardens.* Light
refreshments with vegetarian, vegan
and exciting street food. **Adm £5.50,
chd free. For NGS: Sat 25, Sun 26
July, Sat 5, Sun 6 Sept (10-5).**

Guided tours at 11am and 2pm by
professional organic growers
highlighting the seasonal aspects
of the organic gardens. For other
opening times and information,
please phone or see garden
website.
The UK's national centre for organic
gardening offers visitors approx 8
acres of beautiful organic
demonstration gardens from modest
to expansive, showcasing a range of
organic best practice. The Organic
Way is an introduction to the history
and practice of organic growing,
leading to a series of demonstration
areas highlighting soil management,
composting and natural feeds.
Children's play area and
greenhouses. Featured across a
range of media incl Channel 4's All
Muck and Magic and Gardeners'
World magazine.

GROUP OPENING
25 STRETTON-ON-FOSSE GARDENS
Stretton on Fosse, Moreton-in-
Marsh GL56 9SD. *Off A429 between
Moreton-in-Marsh & Shipston-on-
Stour. Two gardens in the centre of
the village. Court House is next to the
church, Old Beams a few doors
away.* Home-made teas at Court
House. **Combined adm £5, chd
free. Sun 12 Apr, Wed 22 July
(2-6).**

COURT HOUSE
Christopher White
Visitors also welcome by
arrangement Jan to Dec.
01608 663811
mum@star.co.uk

OLD BEAMS
Mrs Hilary Fossey

Court House is a continually evolving,
4 acre garden with yr-round interest
and colour. Extensive and varied
spring bulbs. Herbaceous borders,
fernery, recently redesigned and
restored walled kitchen garden. Rose
garden, newly planted winter garden,
pond area and paddocks which are
gradually being established with wild
flowers. Old Beams is a walled
cottage garden on a slope with
traditional cottage garden plants,
small lawn, rockery, fruit cage and
vegetable garden.

GROUP OPENING
26 STYVECHALE GARDENS
Baginton Road, Coventry CV3 6FP.
*The gardens are located on the S-
side of Coventry close to A45. Tickets
& map available on the day from West
Orchard United Reformed Church,
The Chesils, CV3 6FP. Advance
tickets available from
suepountney@btinternet.com.* Home-
made teas. **Combined adm £3.50,
chd free.** Share to Warwickshire
and Northamptonshire Air
Ambulance Service. **Sun 14 June
(11-5).**

43 ARMORIAL ROAD
CV3 6GH. Gary & Jane
Flanagan
Visitors also welcome by
arrangement May to Sept with
other Styvechale gardens.
07739 884098
garyflanagan@hotmail.co.uk

164 BAGINTON ROAD
Fran & Jeff Gaught

166 BAGINTON ROAD
Wilf & Ann Hawes

16 DELAWARE ROAD
CV3 6LX. Val & Roy Howells
Visitors also welcome by
arrangement May to Sept with
other Styvechale gardens.
02476 419485
valshouse@hotmail.co.uk

2 THE HIRON
CV3 6HT. Sue & Graham
Pountney
Visitors also welcome by
arrangement May to Sept with
other Styvechale gardens.
02476 502044
suepountney@btinternet.com

A collection of lovely, mature,
suburban gardens, each one different
in style and size. Come and enjoy the
imaginatively planted herbaceous
borders, spectacular roses, water
features, fruit and vegetable patches,
cottage garden planting and shady
areas, something for everyone and
plenty of ideas for you to take home.
Relax in the gardens and enjoy the
warm, friendly welcome you will
receive from us all. There will be
refreshments available and plants for
sale in some of the gardens. Other
gardens will be open on the day.

Mirrored terrace
beds glow with
perennials . . .

GROUP OPENING

27 WARMINGTON VILLAGE GARDENS

Banbury OX17 1BU. *5m NW of Banbury. Take B4100 N from Banbury, after 5m turn R across short dual carriageway into Warmington. From N take J12 off M40 onto B4100.* Home-made teas at village hall. **Combined adm £5, chd free.** Sun 21 June (2-5.30).

GROVE FARM HOUSE
Richard & Kate Lister

KIRK LEE
Mr & Mrs L Albrighton

NEW THE MANOR COTTAGE
Mr & Mrs T Hall

THE MANOR HOUSE
Mr & Mrs G Lewis

OLD RECTORY FARMHOUSE
Dr & Mrs J Deakin

SPRINGFIELD HOUSE
Jenny & Roger Handscombe
01295 690286
jenny.handscombe@virgin.net

WESTERING
Mr & Mrs R Neale

1 THE WHEELWRIGHTS
Ms E Bunn

2 THE WHEELWRIGHTS
Mrs C Hunter

NEW WOODCOTE
Ruth Warrior

Warmington, at the edge of the Cotswolds is an exceptionally attractive village with its C17 Hornton stone houses set around the village green. In front of the pond is The Manor House with its Elizabethan knot garden, and topiary. Kirk Lee on 3 levels has panoramic views across the valley. 1 and 2 The Wheelwrights are adjacent courtyard gardens with

very different and attractive characters. Springfield House with its gravel garden is terraced and informal. A garden of many parts is to be found at Old Rectory Farmhouse, incl a slate and heather garden and a wooded area. A knot garden and a pleached hornbeam pathway are to be found in the lovely garden at Grove Farm and Manor Cottage is conspicuous on The Green for its beautiful lavender border. Westering and Woodcote have colourful herbaceous beds with many unusual plants. Do visit St Michael's Church at the top of the village containing the Millennium Tapestry.

GROUP OPENING

28 WELFORD-ON-AVON & DISTRICT GARDENS

Welford-on-Avon CV37 8PT. *5m SW of Stratford-upon-Avon. Off B4390.* Home-made teas in the village hall. **Combined adm £5, chd free.** Sat 27, Sun 28 June (2-6).

ARDENCOTE
Mike & Sally Luntley

NEW ASH COTTAGE
Mr & Mrs Peter & Sue Hook

AVONCOT
Emma & Shaun Baker

2 CHAPEL STREET
Mr Rod Scarrott

NEW CHERRY TREES
John & Norma Sweeney

6 QUINEYS LEYS
Mr & Mrs Gordon & Penny Whitehead

9 QUINEYS LEYS
Ann Raff

SOUTHLAWNS
Mr & Mrs Guy & Amanda Kitteringham

In addition to its superb position on the river, with serene swans, dabbling ducks and resident herons, Welford-on-Avon has a beautiful church, an excellent family butcher's shop, a very convenient general store and selection of PH serving great food. Just down the road is a highly popular farm shop where seasonal fruit and vegetables are much in demand. With its great variety of house styles, incl an abundance of beautiful cottages with thatched roofs and chocolate-box charisma, Welford also has an army of keen gardeners

(garden club has over 100 members!). The gardens open for the NGS range from a plot with fantastic topiary, herb knot and live willow weaving, to those with water features, gardens featuring pot plants, plots with chickens and vegetables, all with a glorious array of containers and hanging baskets. Fruit and vegetable areas are also integral to these gardens for all seasons.

GROUP OPENING

29 WESTON-UNDER-WETHERLEY GARDENS

Leamington Spa CV33 9BW. *3m NE of Leamington Spa on B4453. Park at village hall & nr church. Disabled parking at some gardens. All gardens well signed & a guide to gardens available from village hall.* Home-made teas at Weston-under-Wetherley Village Hall. **Combined adm £4, chd free.** Sat 6, Sun 7 June (12.30-5).

4 ALDERMAN WAY
Mr Paddy Taylor

8 ALDERMAN WAY
Tracy & Bill Byrne

10 ALDERMAN WAY
Alastair Rodda

23 ALDERMAN WAY
Lynne Williams

GLEBE COTTAGE
Stephen Evans

THE OLD FORGE
Sarah & Peter Haine

5 RUGBY ROAD
Mrs Brenda Boardman
www.brenboardman.com

13 RUGBY ROAD
Jean Smith

12 SIMPKINS CLOSE
Sue & Chris Garden

Nine village gardens showing a variety of styles, sizes and purpose; pergolas and patios, water features, ponds, vegetable gardens, raised beds, packed herbaceous borders and field views. The village has a C12 parish church, St Michael's; a recently built village hall where tea and home-made cakes are served. Also enjoy the artists studio, craft stalls, plant stalls and a raffle.

Broadacre

GROUP OPENING

30 **WHICHFORD & ASCOTT GARDENS**

Whichford & Ascott, Shipston-on-Stour CV36 5PP. *6m SE of Shipston-on-Stour. Take A3400 between Chipping Norton & Shipston-on-Stour. The road off this to Whichford & Ascott is equidistant between these two towns. Car park opp church. Disabled parking at Murton Cottage, Ascott.* Home-made teas at Whichford House, with jazz entertainment. **Combined adm £6, chd free.** Sun 14 June (2-5.30).

ASCOTT LODGE
Charlotte Copley

KNIGHT'S PLACE
Mr & Mrs Derek Atkins

MURTON COTTAGE
Hilary & David Blakemore

THE OLD RECTORY
Peter & Caroline O'Kane

PLUM TREE COTTAGE
Janet Knight

WHICHFORD HILL HOUSE
Mr & Mrs John Melvin

WHICHFORD HOUSE
Bridget & Simon Herrtage

THE WHICHFORD POTTERY
Jim & Dominique Keeling

This group of gardens reflects a range of several garden types and sizes. The two villages are in an area of outstanding natural beauty. They nestle within a dramatic landscape of hills, pasture and woodland, which is used to picturesque effect by the garden owners. Fine lawns, mature shrub planting and much interest to plantsmen provide a peaceful visit to a series of beautiful gardens. Many incorporate the inventive use of natural springs, forming ponds, pools and other water features. Classic cottage gardens contrast with other larger gardens which adopt variations on the traditional English garden of herbaceous borders, climbing roses, yew hedges and walled enclosures. A children's quiz will link the gardens. Other amenities are the C12 church, the internationally renowned pottery, and a PH serving meals. Partial wheelchair access as some gardens are on sloping sites.

  🚫 🐕 ❀ ☕

Lemon drizzle cake, Victoria sponge ... yummy! ☕

WILTSHIRE

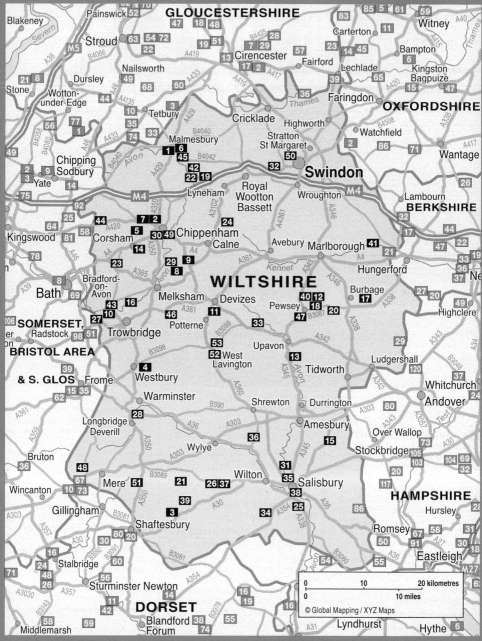

Wiltshire

Wiltshire, a predominantly rural county, covers 1346 square miles and has a rich diversity of landscapes, including downland, wooded river valleys and Salisbury Plain.

Chalk lies under two-thirds of the county, with limestone to the north, which includes part of the Cotswolds Area of Outstanding Natural Beauty.

The county's gardens reflect its rich history and wide variety of environments. Gardens opening for the NGS include the celebrated landscape garden of Stourhead and other National Trust properties, large privately owned gems such as Broadleas, Little Durnford Manor and Iford Manor, and more modest properties lovingly maintained by the owners such as Ridleys Cheer and Priory House.

The season opens in Wiltshire with the snowdrops at Lacock Abbey, continues with fine spring gardens like Corsham Court and Allington Grange. A wide selection of gardens, large and small, are at their peak in the summer; gardens like Sharcott Manor open throughout the season until September. There are also town gardens, village openings and a Chinese garden at Beggars Knoll.

The county's gardens are all delightful and have many loyal followers.

Wiltshire Volunteers

County Organiser
Sean & Kena Magee
01666 880009
spbmagee@googlemail.com

County Treasurer
Sean & Kena Magee
(as above)

Publicity
& Booklet Coordinator
Tricia Duncan
01672 810443
tricia@windward.biz

Social Media
Marian Jones
01249 657400
Marian@marianjones.orangehome.co.uk

Assistant County Organisers
Suzie Breakwell
01985 850297
suzievb@me.com

Sarah Coate
01722 782365

Jo Hankey
01722 742472
rbhankey@gmail.com

Shirley Heywood
01985 844486

Diana Robertson
01672 810515
diana@broomsgrovelodge.co.uk

Left: Priory House © Heather Edwards

Since our foundation we have donated more than £42.5 million to charity

Opening Dates

All entries subject to change.
For latest information check www.ngs.org.uk

February

Wednesday 25
29 Lacock Abbey Gardens
Saturday 28
29 Lacock Abbey Gardens

March

Sunday 15
1 Abbey House Gardens
Sunday 22
21 Fonthill House
Sunday 29
37 NEW Mitre Cottage

April

Wednesday 1
47 Sharcott Manor
Sunday 12
11 Broadleas House Gardens
14 Corsham Court
47 Sharcott Manor
Thursday 16
33 Mallards
Sunday 19
31 Little Durnford Manor
43 Priory House
Wednesday 22
23 Hazelbury Manor Gardens
Saturday 25
28 Job's Mill
Sunday 26
27 Iford Manor
40 Oare House

May

Sunday 3
2 Allington Grange
15 Cottage in the Trees
51 Waterdale House
Monday 4
2 Allington Grange
Wednesday 6
47 Sharcott Manor
Sunday 10
5 Biddestone Manor
11 Broadleas House Gardens
12 Broomsgrove Lodge

14 Corsham Court
Wednesday 13
8 Bowden Park
Thursday 14
33 Mallards
Friday 15
38 Mompesson House
Saturday 16
10 Bradford on Avon Gardens
Sunday 17
3 NEW Ark Farm
45 River Barn
50 Twigs Community Garden
Monday 18
16 The Courts Garden
Wednesday 20
23 Hazelbury Manor Gardens
Friday 22
53 Windmill Cottage
Sunday 24
26 Hyde's House
39 North Cottage
41 The Old Mill

June

Wednesday 3
47 Sharcott Manor
Thursday 4
53 Windmill Cottage
Friday 5
53 Windmill Cottage

Festival Weekend

Saturday 6
28 Job's Mill
48 Stourhead Garden
Sunday 7
17 Crofton Lock House
31 Little Durnford Manor
Thursday 11
33 Mallards
Saturday 13
52 West Lavington Manor
Sunday 14
11 Broadleas House Gardens
13 Chisenbury Priory
17 Crofton Lock House
19 Dauntsey Gardens
23 Hazelbury Manor Gardens
39 North Cottage
44 Ridleys Cheer
Thursday 18
53 Windmill Cottage

Friday 19
53 Windmill Cottage
Saturday 20
22 Great Somerford Gardens
Sunday 21
7 Bolehyde Manor
15 Cottage in the Trees
22 Great Somerford Gardens
Saturday 27
18 Dane Brook
Sunday 28
18 Dane Brook
35 Mawarden Court
36 The Mill House
40 Oare House

July

Wednesday 1
47 Sharcott Manor
Friday 3
53 Windmill Cottage
Sunday 5
6 Blicks Hill House
24 Hilmarton Group Gardens
37 NEW Mitre Cottage
39 North Cottage
Saturday 11
18 Dane Brook
Sunday 12
18 Dane Brook
25 Horatio's Garden
Friday 17
53 Windmill Cottage
Saturday 18
4 Beggars Knoll Chinese Garden
Sunday 19
4 Beggars Knoll Chinese Garden
11 Broadleas House Gardens
20 Easton Royal Gardens
32 Lydiard Park Walled Garden
50 Twigs Community Garden
Sunday 26
30 130 Ladyfield Road and Allotments
49 Sweet Briar Cottage

August

Sunday 2
15 Cottage in the Trees
43 Priory House
Wednesday 5
47 Sharcott Manor
Sunday 9

17 Crofton Lock House
46 NEW Seend Head House

September

Wednesday 2
47 Sharcott Manor
Sunday 6
45 River Barn
47 Sharcott Manor
Wednesday 9
34 Manor House
Wednesday 16
23 Hazelbury Manor Gardens

February 2016

Wednesday 24
29 Lacock Abbey Gardens
Saturday 27
29 Lacock Abbey Gardens

Gardens open to the public

1 Abbey House Gardens
9 Bowood Rhododendron Walks
14 Corsham Court
16 The Courts Garden
27 Iford Manor
29 Lacock Abbey Gardens
32 Lydiard Park Walled Garden
36 The Mill House
38 Mompesson House
45 River Barn
48 Stourhead Garden
50 Twigs Community Garden
51 Waterdale House

By arrangement only

42 The Pound House

Bee garden and orchard stuffed with good plants . . .

Also open by arrangement

- **2** Allington Grange
- **4** Beggars Knoll Chinese Garden
- **6** Blicks Hill House
- **7** Bolehyde Manor
- **13** Chisenbury Priory
- **15** Cottage in the Trees
- **17** Crofton Lock House
- **33** Mallards
- **34** Manor House
- **39** North Cottage
- **43** Priory House
- **45** River Barn
- **49** Sweet Briar Cottage
- **52** West Lavington Manor
- **53** Windmill Cottage

Iford Manor

© Heather Edwards

The Gardens

1 ◆ **ABBEY HOUSE GARDENS**
Malmesbury Town Centre
SN16 9AS. Ian & Barbara Pollard,
01666 827650,
www.abbeyhousegardens.co.uk.
*5m N of J17 M4. Beside C12 Abbey.
Parking in town centre (short stay) or
follow brown signs to long stay (via
steps to gardens).* Tea. **Adm £8, chd
free. For NGS: Sun 15 Mar (11-
5.30).** For other opening times and
information, please phone or see
garden website.
With 1300 years of history, the first
King of all England buried somewhere
in the garden, two saints thrown
down the well, and now one of the
great gardens of the world. The spirit
of the place shines through and could
be the best garden visit you ever
make. Featured on many television
programmes such as Gardeners
World, Countryfile, The One Show to
name but a few. Wheelchair access
to at least 60% of gardens.

♿ ☯ 🚌 ☕

2 **ALLINGTON GRANGE**
Allington, Chippenham
SN14 6LW. Mrs Rhyddian Roper,
01249 447436,
rhyddianroper@hotmail.co.uk,
www.allingtongrange.com. *2m W of
Chippenham. Take A420 W from
Chippenham. 1st R signed Allington
Village, entrance 1m up lane on L.*
Home-made teas. **Adm £4, chd free.
Sun 3, Mon 4 May (2-5).** Visitors

also welcome by arrangement.
Informal country garden of approx 1½
acres, around C17 farmhouse (not
open) with a diverse range of plants.
Mixed and herbaceous borders,
colour themed; white garden with
water fountain. Pergola lined with
clematis and roses. Walled potager.
Small orchard with chickens. Wildlife
pond with natural planting. Many
spring bulbs. Mainly level with ramp
into potager. Dogs on leads.

♿ 🌸 ☯ ☕

3 NEW ► **ARK FARM**
Old Wardour, Tisbury, Salisbury
SP3 6RP. Mrs Miranda Thomas.
*Old Wardour is 2m from Tisbury.
Drive down High Street and on, past
station, take 1st R. Follow signs to
Old Wardour Castle.* Tea. **Adm £3,
chd free. Sun 17 May (2-5).**
Informal hidden gardens in beautiful
setting with small wooded area,
pond, water plants, lakeside walk,
views of Old Wardour castle. This is a
very difficult garden for wheelchairs.
Not advised!

☕

4 **BEGGARS KNOLL CHINESE
GARDEN**
Newtown, Westbury BA13 3ED.
Colin Little & Penny Stirling,
01373 823383,
silkendalliance@talktalk.net. *1m SE
of Westbury. Turn off B3098 at White
Horse Pottery, up hill towards the
White Horse for ¾ m. Disabled
parking at end of drive. Main parking*

*300 yds up hill, shuttle service for
return.* Home-made teas. **Adm
£3.50, chd free. Sat 18, Sun 19
July (2-6).** Visitors also welcome
by arrangement June & July.
This inspirational 1-acre garden is
filled with colourful plantings set
against a backdrop of Chinese
pavilions, gateways, statues and
dragons. Intricate Chinese mosaic
pavements wind around ponds and
rocks. Rare Chinese shrubs, mature
trees, and flower filled borders form a
haven of serenity. A large potager
houses chickens, and pigs live in the
woods. Spectacular views too!

☯ ☕

5 **BIDDESTONE MANOR**
Chippenham Lane, Biddestone
SN14 7DJ. Rosie Harris, Head
Gardener. *5m W of Chippenham. On
A4 between Chippenham & Corsham
turn N. From A420, 5m W of
Chippenham, turn S. Use car park.*
Home-made teas. **Adm £5, chd free.
Sun 10 May (2-5).**
Stroll through our 8 peaceful acres of
wide lawns, lake and ponds,
arboretum and roses. Kitchen cutting
gardens and orchard. Then join us for
tea in the formal front garden.
Beautiful C17 Manor House (not
open) with ancient dovecote. Maybe
spot the bee orchids and kingfisher.
Garden photography for sale.
Wheelchair access to most parts, a
few steps, help always available.

♿ 🐶 ☯ ☕

6 BLICKS HILL HOUSE

Blicks Hill, Malmesbury SN16 9HZ. Alan & Valerie Trotman, 01666 829669, vat@timberwright.co.uk. *1/2 m E of Malmesbury. On A429 Malmesbury bypass, turn off 1/2 way between r'abouts*. Home-made teas. Adm £4, chd free. **Sun 5 July (11-5.30).** Visitors also welcome by arrangement May to July for groups of 10+.

Stunning, and having the wow factor is how visitors describe this garden situated on a 1 acre stepped and sloping site. Mature trees give a backdrop to the colourful beds and borders which have all been created since 2004 for yr-round interest. Unique pergola leading to a woodland glade, water feature and stream constructed in green slate, hanging baskets, tubs and bedding plants add extra impact. Very much a plantsman's garden containing many unusual and special plants. Gradual slope.

7 BOLEHYDE MANOR

Allington SN14 6LW. The Earl & Countess Cairns, 01249 443056, amandamcairns@gmail.com. *1 1/2 m W of Chippenham. On Bristol Rd (A420). Turn N at Allington Xrds. 1/2 m on R. Parking in field*. Home-made teas. Adm £4, chd free. **Sun 21 June (2.30-6).** Visitors also welcome by arrangement May & June, weekdays preferred.

Series of gardens around C16 manor house (not open), enclosed by walls and topiary. Formal framework densely planted with many interesting shrubs and climbers, especially roses. Mixed borders. Blue walk of alliums and agapanthus. Inner courtyard with troughs full of tender plants. Collection of tender pelargoniums. Vegetable/fruit garden and greenhouse.

8 BOWDEN PARK

Lacock, Chippenham SN15 2PP. Bowden Park Estate. *10 mins from Chippenham. Entrance via Top Lodge at top of Bowden Hill, between A342 at Sandy Lane and A350 in Lacock*. Home-made teas. Adm £5, chd free. **Wed 13 May (1-5).**

22 acre private garden within surrounding parkland. Pleasure garden, water garden, working kitchen garden with formal lawns and grotto. Rhododendrons and azaleas in flower.

9 ◆ BOWOOD RHODODENDRON WALKS

Calne SN11 9PG. The Marquis of Lansdowne, 01249 812102, www.bowood.org. *3 1/2 m SE of Chippenham. Located off J17 M4 nr Bath & Chippenham. Entrance off A342 between Sandy Lane & Derry Hill Villages. Follow brown signs*. **For opening times and information, please phone or see garden website.**

This 60 acre woodland garden of azaleas and rhododendrons is one of the most exciting of its type in the country. From the individual flowers to the breathtaking sweep of colour formed by hundreds of shrubs, surrounded by carpets of bluebells, this is a garden not to be missed. Planting began in 1850 and some of the earliest known hybrids feature among the collection. The Rhododendron Walks are located 2m from Bowood House and Gardens.

Informal hidden gardens in beautiful setting . . .

GROUP OPENING

10 BRADFORD ON AVON GARDENS

Bradford on Avon BA15 1LF. *nr centre of Bradford on Avon. See individual gardens for directions*. Home-made teas at Horton's House. Combined adm £5, chd free. **Sat 16 May (2-6).**

BARTON FARM
Pound Lane. Simon & Amanda Relph.
From centre take B3109 Frome road. Pound Lane is on R signed Tythe Barn or on L coming from Frome. Parking near house very limited but OK for drop off, park at station

HORTON'S HOUSE
15 Church Street. Annette Seekings.
Park in station car park, walk down to river, turn R and follow to footbridge. Over footbridge and Hortons House is in front of you and Rosemary Walk is next door

NEW LYNCHETTS

15 Woolley Street. Professor & Mrs George Lunt.
The garden is accessed from the rear. Go past front of house on Woolley St and after 100m take the L fork, signed Woolley St. Enter the drive after a further 100m & walk to top

1 ROSEMARY WALK
Penny Hopwood & Sally Wilson.
see Horton's House for directions

Barton Farm: C14 home which looks across to tythe barn. Walled garden at rear planted principally with flowering shrubs and underplanted with bulbs, primroses and herbaceous plants, particularly those tolerant of dry shade. Recently re-planted. Horton's House (1496): The steeply sloping land of approx 1 acre is now terraced and planted by owners with orchard and fig trees, roses and plants that love sunny S-facing aspect. 1 Rosemary Walk: Walled, terraced garden, landscaped and planted in 2008. Colour themed beds with a variety of plants and shrubs. Lynchetts garden extends to almost 2 acres and slopes up hillside. An old tennis court provides a large central level lawn. Few of the original fruit trees remain but many new plantings of old varieties of apples have been made. Among the older trees are mulberry and medlar and more recently quince and figs have been established. Nearer the house is a herbaceous border and small terraced beds.

11 BROADLEAS HOUSE GARDENS

Devizes SN10 5JQ. Mr & Mrs Cardiff. *1m S of Devizes. From Hartmoor Rd turn into Broadleas Park, follow rd for 350 metres then turn R into estate. Please note, there is no access from A360 Potterne Rd*. Home-made teas. Adm £5, chd free. **Suns 12 Apr, 10 May, 14 June, 19 July (2-5.30).**

6 acre garden of hedges, herbaceous borders, rose arches, bee garden and orchard stuffed with good plants. It is overlooked by the house and arranged above the small valley garden which is crowded with magnolias and rhododendrons, cornus and hydrangeas.

12 BROOMSGROVE LODGE

New Mill, Pewsey SN9 5LE. Diana Robertson, 01672 810515, Diana@broomsgrovelodge.co.uk. *2m E of Pewsey. From A345 take B3087 Burbage Rd, after 1¹/₂ m L to New Mill, through village & past canal. Park in field.* Home-made teas. **Adm £3.50, chd free. Sun 10 May (2-6).** Alongside stunning views of Martinsell Hill discover the imaginatively planted herbaceous borders, in spring full of tulips and forget-me-nots. Large vegetable garden, greenhouse and tunnel. Sunken terrace full of vibrantly planted pots where tea is served and a 4 acre field to wander around, admire the views and enjoy a picnic.

🚬 ✿ 🚐 🛏 ☕

13 CHISENBURY PRIORY

East Chisenbury SN9 6AQ. Mr & Mrs John Manser, john.peter.manser@live.com. *3m SW of Pewsey. Turn E from A345 at Enford then N to E Chisenbury, main gates 1m on R.* Home-made teas. **Adm £5, chd free. Sun 14 June (2-6).** Visitors also welcome by arrangement May to July.
Medieval Priory with Queen Anne face and early C17 rear (not open) in middle of 5 acre garden on chalk. Mature garden with fine trees within clump and flint walls, herbaceous borders, shrubs, roses. Moisture loving plants along mill leat, carp pond, orchard and wild garden, many unusual plants. Front borders redesigned in 2009 by Tom Stuart-Smith.

🚬 ✿ ☕

14 ◆ CORSHAM COURT

Corsham SN13 0BZ. Mr James Methuen-Campbell, 01249 701610, www.corsham-court.co.uk. *4m W of Chippenham. Signed off A4 at Corsham.* **Adm £5, chd £2.50. For NGS: Sun 12 Apr, Sun 10 May (2-5). For other opening times and information, please phone or see garden website.**
Park and gardens laid out by Capability Brown and Repton. Large lawns with fine specimens of ornamental trees surround the Elizabethan mansion. C18 bath house hidden in the grounds. Spring bulbs, beautiful lily pond with Indian bean trees, young arboretum and stunning collection of magnolias. Wheelchair (not motorised) access to house, gravel paths in garden.

🚬

15 COTTAGE IN THE TREES

Tidworth Rd, Boscombe Village, nr Salisbury SP4 0AD. Karen & Richard Robertson, 01980 610921, robertson909@btinternet.com. *7m N of Salisbury. Turn L of A338 just before Social Club. Continue past church, turn R after bridge to Queen Manor, cottage 150yds on R.* Cream teas. **Adm £2.50, chd free. Sun 3 May, Sun 21 June, Sun 2 Aug (2-5).** Visitors also welcome by arrangement Mar to Sept for groups of 10+.
Enchanting ¹/₂ acre cottage garden, immaculately planted with water feature, raised vegetable beds, small wildlife pond and gravel garden. Spring bulbs, hellebores and pulmonarias give a welcome start to the season, with pots and baskets, roses and clematis. Mixed borders of herbaceous plants, dahlias, grasses and shrubs giving all-yr interest.

✿ ☕

16 ◆ THE COURTS GARDEN

Holt, Trowbridge BA14 6RR. National Trust, 01225 782875, www.nationaltrust.org.uk/courts-garden/. *2m E of Bradford-on-Avon. S of B3107 to Melksham. In Holt follow NT signs, park at village hall and at overflow car park when signed.* Cream teas. The Rose Garden Tea room (not NT), situated within the garden, offers a selection of light refreshments and hot and cold lunches. **Adm £6.75, chd £3.40. For NGS: Mon 18 May (11-5.30). For other opening times and information, please phone or see garden website.**
Beautifully kept but eclectic garden. Yew hedges divide garden compartments with colour themed borders and organically shaped topiary. Water garden with 2 pools, temple, conservatory and small kitchen garden split by an apple allée, all surrounded by 3¹/₂ acres of arboretum with specimen trees. Wheelchair access map available.

🚬 ✿ 🚐 ☕

17 CROFTON LOCK HOUSE

Crofton, Great Bedwyn, Marlborough SN8 3DW. Michael & Jenny Trussell, 01672 870674, jennytrussell@hotmail.com. *Lock 62, K&A Canal, Crofton, 1m W of Great Bedwyn. 4m W of Hungerford. Signs from A4 at Great Bedwyn turning, and from A338 at East Grafton. Limited parking. Garden 8 - 10 mins walk along towpath.* Home-made teas. **Adm £3, chd free. Share to Wiltshire Air Ambulance. Sun 7, Sun 14 June, Sun 9 Aug (1.30-5.30).** Visitors also welcome by arrangement June to Aug for groups of 20 max.
³/₄ acre garden in idyllic setting around 200 yr old lock keeper's cottage. Garden comprises herbaceous beds designed with a painter's eye to provide riotous colour, sculptural form, and an abundance of wildlife from spring to autumn; at rear a small orchard, collection of apple and soft fruit trees and raised vegetable beds. Artist's studio open. Off grid house relying on sun and wind for electricity, own water supply. Plants for sale. Crofton steam pumping station and Wilton Windmill close by.

✿ ☕

18 DANE BROOK

Milkhouse Water, Pewsey SN9 5JX. Mr & Mrs P Sharpe, www.danebrook.co.uk. *1m NE of Pewsey. From Pewsey take B3087 Burbage Rd. After approx ³/₄ m turn L to Milkhouse Water. Dane Brook is 1st on R after railway bridge.* Home-made teas. Gluten free available. **Adm £4, chd free. Share to SSAFA. Sat 27, Sun 28 June, Sat 11, Sun 12 July (1-5).**
Approx 1 acre of gardens, incl herbaceous beds, shrubs, trees, semi formal garden, roses, oxbow pond with planted banks and thatched summerhouse. Tree lined river walk runs the length of the garden, leading to shrubbery. Also lawns and paved areas with planted containers. Far reaching views from paddocks. Craft shop with handmade gifts and accessories, home-made sweets, jams, chutney, rare breed sheep, vintage tractor, horses. Wheelchair accessible in dry weather with exception of pond and stream areas.

🚬 🐾 ✿ ☕

Seend Head House

GROUP OPENING

 DAUNTSEY GARDENS
Chippenham SN15 4HW. *5m SE of Malmesbury. Approach via Dauntsey Rd from Gt Somerford, 1¼ m from Volunteer Inn*. Home-made teas at Idover House. **Combined adm £5, chd free.** Sun 14 June (1.30-5).

THE COACH HOUSE
Col & Mrs J Seddon-Brown

DAUNTSEY PARK
Mr & Mrs Giovanni Amati
01249 721777
enquiries@dauntseyparkhouse.
co.uk

THE GARDEN COTTAGE
Miss Ann Sturgis

IDOVER HOUSE
Mr & Mrs Christopher Jerram

THE OLD POND HOUSE
Mr & Mrs Stephen Love

This group of 5 gardens, centred around the historic Dauntsey Park Estate, ranges from the Classical C18 country house setting of Dauntsey Park, with spacious lawns, old trees and views over the R Avon, to mature country house gardens and traditional walled gardens. Enjoy the formal rose garden in pink and white, old fashioned borders and duck ponds at Idover House, and the quiet seclusion of The Coach House with its thyme terrace and gazebos, climbing roses and clematis. Here, mop-headed pruned crataegus prunifolia line the drive. The Garden Cottage has a traditional walled kitchen garden with organic vegetables, apple orchard, woodland walk and yew topiary. Meanwhile the 2 acres at The Old Pond House are both clipped and unclipped! Large pond with lilies and fat carp, and look out for the giraffe and turtle.
&♿ ✿ ☕

GROUP OPENING

 EASTON ROYAL GARDENS
Easton Royal, Pewsey SN9 5LY.
Tricia Duncan 01672 810443. *4m E of Pewsey, 1m W of Burbage. From Burbage r'about on A338 follow B3087 for Pewsey for lm to village Xrds. From Pewsey take B3087 for Burbage for 4m to Easton Royal Xrds*. Park in the playing field at Xrds. Home-made teas at village hall. **Combined adm £5, chd free.** Sun 19 July (1.30-5.30).

CHAPEL COTTAGE
Tricia & Allan Duncan

COPES COTTAGE
Sarah Townsend-Rose & Colin Sibun

Two lovely gardens set in this historic conservation village. The gardens are tucked under The Salisbury Plain with distant views of The Vale of Pewsey for you to enjoy. Chapel Cottage has colourful, wide mixed borders, clematis, roses, small vegetable patch, mini meadow, mature trees and sitooterie with distant views. Copes Cottage has a delightful cottage garden with a stunning gravel garden, pool area, vegetables, cutting garden, and meadow with distant views. The soil in both gardens is greensand and both are exposed to the winds. Mini market of gardening and goody stalls in playing field and a chance to see an orchard of fruit trees and a woodland walk, planted 2 yrs ago by villagers in playing field. Copes Cottage has limited wheelchair access.
&♿ ✿ ☕

21 FONTHILL HOUSE
nr Tisbury. SP3 5SA. The Lord Margadale of Islay,
www.fonthill.co.uk/gardens. *13m W of Salisbury. Via B3089 in Fonthill Bishop. 3m N of Tisbury*. Home-made teas. **Adm £6, chd free.** Sun 22 Mar (2-6).
Large woodland garden. Daffodils, rhododendrons, azaleas, shrubs, bulbs; magnificent views; formal gardens. The gardens have been

extensively redeveloped recently under the direction of Tania Compton and Marie-Louise Agius. The formal gardens are being continuously improved with new designs, exciting trees, shrubs and plants. Partial wheelchair access.

GROUP OPENING

22 GREAT SOMERFORD GARDENS

Great Somerford, Chippenham SN15 5JB. Doreen Jevons. *4m SE of Malmesbury. 4m N of M4 between J16 & J17. 2m S of B4042 Malmesbury to Royal Wootton Basset. 3 m E of A4209 Cirencester to Chippenham road. Cross river bridge in Great Somerford. Park opp The Mount, additional parking on Dauntsey Road opp allotments and West St opp Manor House.* Home-made teas at The Mount. Ice creams. **Combined adm £5, chd free.** Sat 20, Sun 21 June (1.30-5.30).

> **GREAT SOMERFORD'S FREE GARDENS & ALLOTMENTS**
> In trust to Great Somerford Parish Council
>
> **MANOR HOUSE**
> West Street. Mr & Mrs Davis
>
> **THE MOUNT**
> Mr & Mrs McGrath.
> *Proceed up drive towards church*
>
> **THE OLD POLICE HOUSE**
> Diane Hunt
>
> **SOMERFORD HOUSE**
> Dr & Mrs Hyde.
> *Opening on Sat 20 Jun only*

Great Somerford is a medium-sized village, with a lovely walk by R Avon. Maintained by very active gardeners, there are three well-established large gardens and a charming smaller one and Gt Somerford's Free Gardens and Allotments. Partial wheelchair access.

23 HAZELBURY MANOR GARDENS

Wadswick, Box SN13 8HX. Mr L Lacroix. *5m SW of Chippenham, 5m NE of Bath. From A4 at Box, A365 to Melksham, at Five Ways junction L onto B3109 toward Corsham, 1st L at top of hill, drive immed on R.* **Adm £5, chd free.** Wed 22 Apr, Wed 20 May (11-3); Sun 14 June (2-5.30);

Wed 16 Sept (11-3).
8 Acres of Grade II landscaped organic gardens around C15 fortified manor (not open). Edwardian garden with yew hedges and topiary, beech stilt hedges, laburnum tunnel and pleached lime avenue. Large variety of plants, shrubs fill 5000 sq metres of planting, many herbal and native species. Productive vegetable gardens, orchards and a circle of megaliths. Wild flower drive from butterfly rich common.

5 gardens,
all with their
own individual
charm . . .

GROUP OPENING

24 HILMARTON GROUP GARDENS

Hilmarton, Calne SN11 8SE. *On A3102 between Calne and Lyneham. Turn off A3102, opp The Duke PH, into village, follow signs to car park. Directions to gardens will be provided.* Home-made teas in the Hilmarton Community Room, Poynder Place. **Combined adm £5, chd free.** Sun 5 July (12-5).

> **NEW BRIDLEWAY**
> Mr & Mrs George Blackburn
>
> **NEW 21 COMPTON ROAD**
> Mr Peter Delamere
>
> **NEW MANOR FARM**
> Mr Rodney & Miss Shirley Yeatman
>
> **NEW POYNDER ALMSHOUSE ALLOTMENTS**
> Poynder Almshouse Trustees
>
> **WEAVERS**
> Sheron & Mel Wilkins

5 gardens, all with their own individual charm and interest and all within easy walking distance of each other. A multi level garden with interesting features. A typical farmhouse garden with old and new designs. A delightful village garden recently rejuvenated by present owner. A group of five small allotments, tended by individual

gardeners. A cottage garden set out into lawned borders linked by leafy pergola. Wheelchair access is possible to the majority of garden areas although some have gravelled driveways.

25 HORATIO'S GARDEN

Duke of Cornwall Spinal Treatment Centre, Salisbury Hospital NHS Foundation Trust, Odstock Road, Salisbury SP2 8BJ. Tina Crossley, www.horatiosgarden.org.uk. *Please park in car park 8 or 10.* Home-made teas. Delicious cakes made by Horatio's Garden volunteers. **Adm £4, chd free. Share to Horatio's Garden.** Sun 12 July (2-5).
Small garden which opened in Sept 2012 and was designed by Cleve West for patients with spinal cord injury at the Duke of Cornwall Spinal Treatment Centre. Built from donations given in memory of Horatio Chapple who was a volunteer at the centre in his school holidays. Low limestone walls, which represent the form of the spine, divide densely planted beds and double as seating. Everything in the garden has been designed to benefit patients during their long stays in hospital. Garden is run by Head Gardener Tina Crossley and team of volunteers, called Horatio's Garden Friends. Cleve West has 8 RHS gold medals, incl Best in Show at Chelsea Flower Show in 2011 and 2012. Featured in Daily Mail, Evening Standard, BBC Gardeners World & English Garden Magazine.

26 HYDE'S HOUSE

Dinton SP3 5HH. Mr George Cruddas. *9m W of Salisbury. Off B3089 nr Dinton Church on St Mary's Rd.* Home-made teas at Thatched Old School Room with outside tea tables. **Adm £5, chd free.** Sun 24 May (2-5).
3 acres of wild and formal garden in beautiful situation with series of hedged garden rooms. Numerous shrubs, flowers and borders, all allowing tolerated wild flowers and preferred weeds. Large walled kitchen garden, herb garden and C13 dovecote (open). Charming C16/18 Grade I listed house (not open), with lovely courtyard. Free walks around park and lake. Steps, slopes and gravel paths.

27 ◆ IFORD MANOR
Lower Westwood, Bradford-on-Avon BA15 2BA. Mrs Cartwright-Hignett, 01225 863146, www.ifordmanor.co.uk. *7m S of Bath. Off A36, brown tourist sign to Iford 1m. Or from Bradford-on-Avon or Trowbridge via Lower Westwood Village (brown signs).* Home-made teas. **Adm £5, chd over 10 £4.50, under 10 free. For NGS: Sun 26 Apr (2-5).** For other opening times and information, please phone or see garden website.
Very romantic award-winning, Grade I listed Italianate garden famous for its tranquil beauty. Home to the Edwardian architect and designer Harold Peto 1899-1933. The garden is characterised by steps, terraces, sculpture and magnificent rural views. (House not open). Housekeeper's cream teas and home made cakes. Please see website for wheelchair access details.

28 JOB'S MILL
Five Ash Lane, Crockerton, Warminster BA12 8BB. Lady Silvy McQuiston. *1½ m S of Warminster. Down lane E of A350, S of A36 r'about.* Home-made teas. **Adm £3.50, chd free. Sat 25 Apr (2-5); Sat 6 June (2-6).**
Surrounding an old converted water mill, a delightful terraced garden through which the R Wylye flows. Riverside and woodland walks, vegetable garden, orchard, herbaceous border and water garden.

29 ◆ LACOCK ABBEY GARDENS
High street, Lacock, Chippenham SN15 2LG. National Trust, 01249 730459, www.nationaltrust.org.uk/lacock. *3m S of Chippenham. Off A350. Follow NT signs. Use public car park just outside Abbey.* **Adm £5.50, chd £2.75. For NGS: Wed 25, Sat 28 Feb 2015, Wed 24, Sat 27 Feb 2016 (10.30-5.30).** For other opening times and information, please phone or see garden website.
Woodland garden with carpets of aconites, snowdrops, crocuses and daffodils. Botanic garden with greenhouse, medieval cloisters and magnificent trees. Mostly level site, some gravel paths.

30 130 LADYFIELD ROAD AND ALLOTMENTS
Ladyfield Road, Chippenham SN14 0AP. Philip & Pat Canter and Chippenham Town Council. *1m SW of Chippenham. Between A4 Bath and A420 Bristol rds. Signed off B4528 Hungerdown Lane which runs between A4 & A420.* Home-made teas. **Adm £3, chd free. Sun 26 July (1.30-5.30).**
Very pretty small garden with more than 30 clematis, climbing roses and small fish pond. Curved neat edges packed with colourful herbaceous plants and small trees. 2 patio areas with lush lawn, pagoda and garden arbour. Also Hungerdown Allotments, 15 allotments owned by Chippenham Town Council. Wheelchair access to garden and to allotments on main drive only.

It could be called a plantsman's garden . . .

31 LITTLE DURNFORD MANOR
Little Durnford, Salisbury SP4 6AH. The Earl & Countess of Chichester. *3m N of Salisbury. Just north beyond Stratford-sub-Castle. Remain to E of R Avon at road junction at Stratford Bridge and continue towards Salterton for ¹/₂ m heading N.* Teas and home-made cakes in cricket pavilion. **Adm £3.50, chd free. Sun 19 Apr, Sun 7 June (2-5).**
Extensive lawns with cedars, walled gardens, fruit trees, large vegetable garden, small knot and herb gardens. Terraces, borders, sunken garden, water garden, lake with islands, river walks, labyrinth walk. Little Durnford Manor is a substantial grade II listed, C18 private country residence (not open) built of an attractive mix of Chilmark stone and flint. Camels, alpacas, llama, pigs, donkeys and sheep are all grazing next to the gardens. Gravel paths, some narrow. Steep slope and some steps.

32 ◆ LYDIARD PARK WALLED GARDEN
Lydiard Tregoze, Swindon SN5 3PA. Swindon Borough Council, 01793 466664, www.lydiardpark.org.uk. *3m W Swindon, 1m from J16 M4. Follow brown signs from W Swindon.* Light refreshments in tearooms by walled garden. **Adm £2, chd £1. For NGS: Sun 19 July (11-5).** For other opening times and information, please phone or see garden website.
Beautiful ornamental C18 walled garden. Trimmed shrubs alternating with individually planted flowers and bulbs incl rare daffodils and tulips, sweet peas, annuals and wall-trained fruit trees. Park and children's playground. Unique features including well and sundial. Wide level paths, no steps.

33 MALLARDS
Chirton SN10 3QX. Tim & Jenny Papé, 01380 840593, jennypape@tiscali.co.uk. *4¹/₂ m SE of Devizes. 1m N of A342 at Chirton on road to Patney.* Light refreshments. **Adm £3, chd free. Thur 16 Apr, Thur 14 May, Thur 11 June (11-5).** Visitors also welcome by arrangement Apr to July.
1 acre hidden garden sloping gently down to woodland beside the upper R Avon. Colourful sunny gravel bed, mixed borders, woodland glade, miniature dell and waterside, all informally planted for yr-round interest. Vegetable garden and woodland walk. Most of garden and wood wheelchair accessible. No disabled WC.

34 MANOR HOUSE
Stratford Tony, Salisbury SP5 4AT. Mr & Mrs Hugh Cookson, 01722 718496, lucindacookson@stratfordtony.co.uk, www.stratfordtony.co.uk. *4m SW of Salisbury. Take minor rd W off A354 at Coombe Bissett. Garden on S after 1m. Or take minor rd off A3094 from Wilton signed Stratford Tony and racecourse.* Home-made teas. **Adm £4, chd free. Wed 9 Sept (2-5).** Visitors also welcome by arrangement adm £5.
Varied 4 acre garden with all yr interest. Formal and informal areas. Small lake fed from R Ebble, waterside planting, herbaceous borders with colour from spring to

late autumn. Pergola-covered vegetable garden, formal parterre garden, orchard, shrubberies, roses, specimen trees, winter colour and structure, many original contemporary features and places to sit and enjoy the downland views. Some gravel.

♿ ❀ 🚐 ☕

35 **MAWARDEN COURT**
Stratford Road, Stratford sub Castle SP1 3LL. Alastair and Natasha McBain. *2m WNW Salisbury. A345 from Salisbury, L at T-lights, opp St Lawrence Church.* Tea in pool pavilion. Cakes, biscuits etc. **Adm £5, chd free. Share to Friends of St Lawrence. Sun 28 June (2-6).**
Mixed herbaceous and rose garden set around C17 house (not open). Pergola walk down through white beam avenue to R Avon and pond pontoon with walk through poplar wood and along river.

♿ ❀ ☕

36 ◆ **THE MILL HOUSE**
Berwick St James, Salisbury SP3 4TS. Diana Gifford Mead, 01722 790331, www.millhouse.org.uk. *8m NW of Salisbury. S of A303, N of A36, on B3083, S end of village.* Home-made teas in village hall. **Adm £3, chd free. For NGS: Sun 28 June (2-6). For other opening times and information, please phone or see garden website.**
Surrounded by the R Till, millstream and 10 acre traditional wet water meadow, this garden of wildness supports over 300 species of old fashioned roses rambling from the many trees. It is filled with butterflies, moths and insects. Birdsong is phenomenal in spring and summer. Herbaceous borders crammed with plants of yesteryear, unforgettable scents. Glorious spring bulbs. SSSI. Open all yr-round.

♿ 🏡 🚐 🛏 ☕

37 **NEW** **MITRE COTTAGE**
snow hill, Dinton SP3 5HN. Mrs Beck. *9m W of Salisbury. From B3089 turn up Snow Hill by shop. From Wylye bear L at fork by church.* **Adm £3.50, chd free. Sun 29 Mar (2-5); Sun 5 July (2-6).**
Cottage style garden of ³/₄ acre with a wide variety of plants and shrubs and winding paths down a slight slope. Many hellebores and bulbs in spring and old fashioned roses. Mature garden with a wide variety of bulbs,

shrubs and trees for yr-round interest. Paths wander down slight hillside from one part to another. It could be called a plantsman's garden I am told.

🏡 ❀

38 ◆ **MOMPESSON HOUSE**
The Close, Salisbury SP1 2EL. National Trust, 01722 335659, www.nationaltrust.org.uk. *Central Salisbury. Enter Cathedral Close via High St Gate, Mompesson House on R.* Light refreshments. **Adm £1, chd free. For NGS: Fri 15 May (11-4). For other opening times and information, please phone or see garden website.**
The appeal of this comparatively small but attractive garden is the lovely setting in Salisbury Cathedral Close, with a well known Queen Anne house (not open). Planting as for an old English garden with raised rose and herbaceous beds around the lawn. Climbers on pergola and walls, shrubs and small lavender walk. Cake stall.

♿ ❀ ☕

Visit a garden and support hospice care

39 **NORTH COTTAGE**
Tisbury Row, Tisbury SP3 6RZ. Jacqueline & Robert Baker, 01747 870019, robert.baker@pearceseeds.co.uk. *12m W of Salisbury. From A30 turn N through Ansty, L at T-junction, towards Tisbury. From Tisbury take Ansty road. Car park entrance nr junction signed Tisbury Row.* Home-made teas. Light lunches. **Adm £3, chd free. Sun 24 May, Sun 14 June, Sun 5 July (11.30-5). Visitors also welcome by arrangement June & July.**
Cottage garden and smallholding set in quiet vale in a beautiful part of South Wiltshire. Views over meadow towards Castle Ditches. Visitors have compared the garden favourably to that of Margery Fish. Of course it's lovely, so there is no need to wax lyrically about the intriguing beauty therein! It will be a memorable visit

and we provide scrumptious home-made food. Pottery and handicrafts all made by garden owners. Ceramics featured in garden, which is part of the Wylye Valley Arts Trail.

🏡 ❀ 🚐 ☕

40 **OARE HOUSE**
Rudge Lane, Oare, nr Pewsey SN8 4JQ. Sir Henry Keswick. *2m N of Pewsey. On Marlborough Rd (A345).* Teas, coffee, soft drinks, home-made cakes. **Adm £5, chd free. Share to The Order of St John. Sun 26 Apr, Sun 28 June (2-6).**
1740s mansion house later extended by William Clough Ellis in 1920s (not open). The formal gardens originally created around the house have been developed over the years to create a wonderful garden full of many unusual plants. Current owner is very passionate and has developed a fine collection of rarities. Garden is undergoing a renaissance but still maintains split compartments each with its own individual charm; traditional walled garden with fine herbaceous borders, vegetable areas, trained fruit, roses and grand mixed borders surrounding formal lawns. The Magnolia garden is wonderful in spring with some trees dating from 1920s, together with strong bulb plantings. Large arboretum and woodland walks with many unusual and champion trees. In spring and summer there is always something of interest, with the glorious Pewsey Vale as a backdrop. Partial wheelchair access.

♿ 🏡 ❀ ☕

41 **THE OLD MILL**
Ramsbury SN8 2PN. Annabel & James Dallas. *8m NE of Marlborough. From Marlborough head to Ramsbury. At The Bell PH follow sign to Hungerford. Garden behind yew hedge on R 100yds beyond The Bell.* Home-made teas. **Adm £5, chd free. Sun 24 May (2-6).**
Water running through multitude of channels no longer drives the mill but provides backdrop for whimsical garden of pollarded limes, colour themed borders and naturalistic planting. Paths meander by streams and over small bridges. Vistas give dramatic views of downs beyond. New kitchen/herb garden and cutting bed give added interest.

☕

PEN MILL FARM
See Somerset, Bristol & South
Gloucestershire.

42 ▸ THE POUND HOUSE
Little Somerford SN15 5JW. Mr &
Mrs Michael Baines, 01666 823212,
squeezebaines@yahoo.com. *2m E
of Malmesbury on B4024. In village
turn S, leave church on R. Car park
on R before railway bridge.* Home-
made teas. **Adm £4, chd free.**
Visitors welcome by arrangement
Apr to Oct.
Large well planted garden
surrounding former rectory attached
to C17 house. Mature trees, hedges
and spacious lawns. Well stocked
herbaceous borders, roses, shrubs,
pergola, parterre, swimming pool
garden, water, ducks, chickens,
alpacas and horses. Raised
vegetable garden and lots of places
to sit. A very beautiful English garden!

43 ▸ PRIORY HOUSE
Market Street, Bradford-on-Avon
BA15 1LH. Mr & Mrs Tim Woodall,
trwwoodall@yahoo.com. *Town
centre. Park in town centre. Take
A363 signed Bath up Market St.
House 500yds.* Home-made teas.
Adm £4, chd free. Sun 19 Apr, Sun
2 Aug (2-5.30). Visitors also
welcome by arrangement Apr to
Aug, conducted tours of 10+.
³/₄ -acre town garden, mostly formal.
Spring garden of narcissi, tulips and
hellebores. Late summer borders
planted in traditional manner using
asters, heleniums, dahlias, daylilies
and others, but with a modern twist
using grasses. Knot garden in front of
part Georgian house is an
interpretation of the sash windows.
Featured in Gardens Illustrated. Steep
slopes and steps at bottom of
garden.

44 ▸ RIDLEYS CHEER
Mountain Bower SN14 7AJ. Mr &
Mrs A J Young,
www.ridleyscheer.co.uk. *9m WNW
of Chippenham. At The Shoe, on
A420 8m W of Chippenham, turn N
then take 2nd L & 1st R.* Home-made
teas. **Adm £4, chd free.** Sun 14
June (2-5).
Largely informal garden; mixed
borders, lawns, extensive collection
of shrubs and trees incl acers,
magnolias, liriodendrons, tree
peonies, deutzias, daphnes, oaks,
beech, birch and hollies. Some 130

rose varieties; old-fashioned and
modern shrub roses, and magnificent
tree ramblers. Potager, miniature box
garden, arboretum, 3 acre wild flower
meadow, plus new ¹/₂ acre flower
meadow. Dew pond. One of the main
features of the garden in June is the
collection of old fashioned shrub rose
and tree ramblers. Mixed borders in
full bloom as well as tulip trees and
the early flowers in the wildflower
meadows. Featured in Country Living.
Wheelchair access from car park in
meadow.

> Stroll along
> the river or
> through the
> field with young
> trees . . .

45 ▸ ◆ RIVER BARN
Cowbridge Farm, Swindon Road,
Malmesbury SN16 9LZ. Finn and
Nicki Spicer, 01666 825670,
www.riverbarn.org.uk. *1m SE of
Malmesbury. From Malmesbury
r'about, take Wootton Bassett road
(B4042) for approx ¹/₂ m. L immed
after Sir Bernard Lovell turning.*
Home-made teas. **Adm £4.50, chd
free.** For NGS: Sun 17 May, Sun 6
Sept (11-5.30). For other opening
times and information, please
phone or see garden website.
3 acre garden in a sublime river
setting as part of former model farm.
Planting commenced 2007 to create
an arboretum with wild flower areas
and wildlife pond. Colourful walled
courtyard garden with koi pond, rose
pergola, mosaics and rich planting.
Formal terraced lawn overlooking
Avon, pygmy pinetum with prairie
style planting, stone circle, fruit and
vegetable garden. Dragonflies
breeding in wildlife pond. Wildflower
areas teeming with butterflies, moths,
honey bees, solitary bees and
bumblebees. R Avon with swans,
ducks, moorhens, dabchicks and
kingfishers..

46 ▸ NEW ▸ SEEND HEAD HOUSE
Row Lane, Seend Head, Melksham
SN12 6PP. Mr & Mrs George &
Isabel Clarke. *Turning off A361 5m
W of Devizes. Turn into Row Lane
(signposted Seend Head on nasty
bend) off A361, 5m W of Devizes and
4.5 S of Melksham.* Tea. **Adm £4,
chd free.** Sun 9 Aug (2-5).
S-facing mill owner's house looking
over extensive lawns sloping down to
river. 13 acre plot under renovation. 3
yr old flowerbeds, colour themed,
with mix of shrubs and herbaceous
plants bringing colour up to the C18
house. Stroll along the river or
through the field with young trees
gradually becoming parkland. Young
orchard. Vegetable garden being
usurped for cutting garden.

47 ▸ SHARCOTT MANOR
Pewsey SN9 5PA. Captain & Mrs D
Armytage. *1m SW of Pewsey. Via
A345 from Pewsey towards Salisbury.
Turn R signed Sharcott at grass
triangle. 400yds up lane, garden on L
over cattle-grid.* Home-made teas.
Adm £4, chd free. Wed 1 Apr
(11-5); Sun 12 Apr (2-6); Wed 6
May, Wed 3 June, Wed 1 July, Wed
5 Aug, Wed 2 Sept (11-5); Sun 6
Sept (2-6).
6 acre plantsman's garden on
greensand, planted for yr-round
interest. Wide range of trees and
shrubs, densely planted mixed
borders with many unusual plants
and climbers. Magnificent tree
ramblers. Woodland walk carpeted
with spring bulbs around ¹/₂ acre
lake. Good autumn colour. Small
collection of ornamental water fowl.
Gravel and narrow grass paths, grass
slope.

48 ▸ ◆ STOURHEAD GARDEN
Stourton, Warminster BA12 6QD.
National Trust, 01747 841152,
www.nationaltrust.org.uk/
stourhead. *3m NW of Mere on
B3092. Follow NT signs, the property
is very well signed from all main roads
incl A303.* **Adm £8.30, chd £4.50.**
For NGS: Sat 6 June (9-7). For
other opening times and
information, please phone or see
garden website.
One of the earliest and greatest
landscape gardens in the world,
creation of banker Henry Hoare in
1740s on his return from the Grand
Tour, inspired by paintings of Claude

and Poussin. Planted with rare trees, rhododendrons and azaleas over last 250yrs. Wheelchair access and buggy available.

49 ▶ SWEET BRIAR COTTAGE

19 Gladstone Road, Chippenham, Wiltshire SN15 3BW. Paul & Joy Gough, 01249 656005, paulgough@btopenworld.com. *Chippenham town centre. In town centre, turn off A4 Ave La Fleche into Gladstone Rd. Park in Borough Parade car parks. Garden just above car park opp Angel Hotel.* Home-made teas. **Adm £3.50, chd free. Sun 26 July (1.30-5).** Visitors also welcome by arrangement May to Sept.

Nearly an acre of walled garden restored in 2006, visitors are still amazed that such a large garden can exist within a town centre location. Low box-edged herbaceous borders planted to encourage wildlife. Slate paths. Vegetables grown organically in 4ft beds. Large collection of roses, ornamental and fruit trees. Featured in Western Daily Press.

50 ▶ ◆ TWIGS COMMUNITY GARDEN

Manor Garden Centre, Cheney Manor, Swindon SN2 2QJ. TWIGS, 01793 523294, www.twigscommunitygardens.org. uk. *From Gt Western Way, under Bruce St Bridges onto Rodbourne Rd. 1st L at r'about, Cheney Manor Industrial Est. Through estate, 2nd exit at r'about. Opp Pitch & Putt. Signs on R to Manor Garden Centre.* Home-made teas. Excellent hot and cold lunches available at Olive Tree café within the Manor Garden centre adj to Twigs. **Adm £3, chd free. For NGS: Sun 17 May, Sun 19 July (1-5).** For other opening times and information, please phone or see garden website.

Twigs is a delightful 2 acre community garden, created and maintained by volunteers. Features incl 7 individual display gardens, ornamental pond, plant nursery, Iron Age round house, artwork, fitness trail, separate kitchen garden site, Swindon beekeepers and the haven, overflowing with wild flowers. Most areas wheelchair accessible. Disabled WC.

Beggars Knoll Chinese Garden

51 ▶ ◆ WATERDALE HOUSE

East Knoyle SP3 6BL. Mr & Mrs Julian Seymour, 01747 830262. *8m S of Warminster. N of East Knoyle, garden signed from A350. Do not use SatNav.* Home-made teas. **Adm £5, chd free. For NGS: Sun 3 May (2-6).** For other opening times and information, please phone.

4 acre mature woodland garden with rhododendrons, azaleas, camellias, maples, magnolias, ornamental water, bog garden, herbaceous borders. Bluebell walk. Shrub border created by storm damage mixed with agapanthus and half hardy salvias. Waterproof footwear is essential as parts of the garden are very wet. Limited wheelchair access.

52 ▶ WEST LAVINGTON MANOR

1 Church Street, West Lavington SN10 4LA. Mr & Mrs Andrew Doman, andrewdoman01@gmail.com. *6m S of Devizes, on A360. House opp White St, where parking available.* Home-made teas provided by West Lavington Youth Club. **Adm £6, chd free. Share to West Lavington Youth Club. Sat 13 June (11-6).** Visitors also welcome by arrangement for groups of 10+ any weekday.

5 acre walled garden first established

in C17 by John Danvers who brought Italianate gardens to the UK. Herbaceous border, Japanese garden, rose garden, orchard and arboretum with some outstanding specimen trees all centered around a trout stream and duck pond. This year our new bog garden will be fully developed.

53 ▶ WINDMILL COTTAGE

Kings Road, Market Lavington SN10 4QB. Rupert & Gill Wade, 01380 813527. *5m S of Devizes. Turn E off A360 1m N of West Lavington, 2m S of Potterne. At top of hill turn L into Kings Rd, L into Windmill Lane after 200yds. Limited parking.* Home-made teas. **Adm £3, chd free. Fri 22 May, Thur 4, Fri 5, Thur 18, Fri 19 June, Fri 3, Fri 17 July (2-5).** Visitors also welcome by arrangement May to July.

1 acre cottage style, wildlife friendly garden on greensand. Mixed beds and borders with long season of interest. Roses on pagoda, large vegetable patch for kitchen and exhibition at local shows, polytunnel and greenhouse. Whole garden virtually pesticide free for last 19yrs. Small bog garden by wildlife pond. Secret glade with prairie.

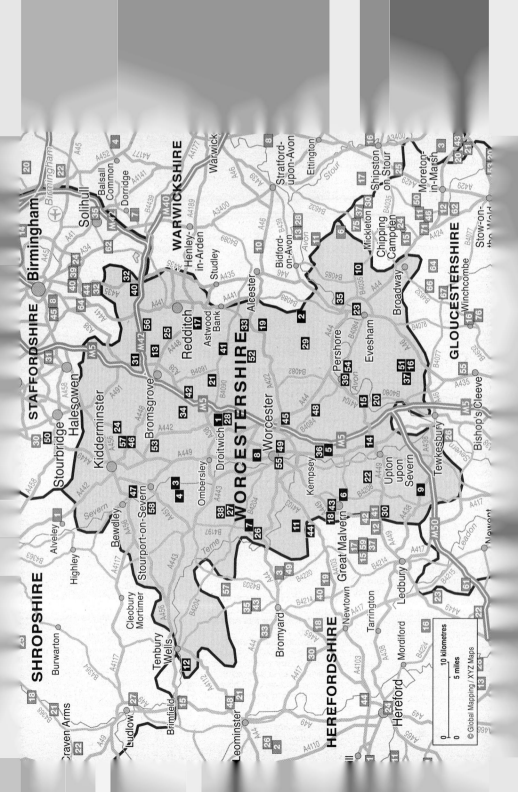

Worcestershire

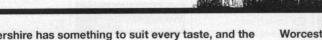

Worcestershire has something to suit every taste, and the same applies to its gardens.

From the magnificent Malvern Hills, the inspiration for Edward Elgar, to the fruit orchards of Evesham which produce wonderful blossom trails in the spring, and from the historic city of Worcester, with its 11th century cathedral and links to the Civil War, to the numerous villages and hamlets that are scattered throughout the county, there is so much to enjoy in this historic county.

Worcestershire is blessed with gardens created by celebrated gardeners such as Capability Brown to ordinary amateur gardeners, and the county can boast properties with grounds of over one hundred acres to small back gardens of less than half an acre, but all have something special to offer.

Visitors to Worcestershire's NGS gardens will find some with wonderful arrays of plants, trees and vegetables, while others show the owners' creativity or sense of fun – there is even one garden with a miniature railway and another in the grounds of a prison!

Worcestershire's garden owners guarantee visitors beautiful gardens, some real surprises and a warm welcome.

Below: Birtsmorton Court

Worcestershire Volunteers

County Organiser
David Morgan
01214 453595
meandi@btinternet.com

County Treasurer
Cliff Woodward
01562 886349

Publicity
Pamela Thompson
01886 888295
peartree.pam@gmail.com

Booklet Advertising & Coordinator
Alan Nokes
01214 455520
alyn.nokes@btinternet.com

Assistant County Organisers
Mike George
01905 427567

Lynn Glaze
01386 751924
lynnglaze@cmail.co.uk

Opening Dates

All entries subject to change.
For latest information check www.ngs.org.uk

February

Saturday 14
53 Whitlenge Gardens
Sunday 15
53 Whitlenge Gardens

March

Thursday 5
41 Red House Farm
Sunday 22
30 Little Malvern Court
Sunday 29
51 Whitcombe House

April

Thursday 2
41 Red House Farm
Friday 3
45 Spetchley Park Gardens
Sunday 5
52 White Cottage
Monday 6
52 White Cottage
Saturday 11
53 Whitlenge Gardens
Sunday 12
53 Whitlenge Gardens
Saturday 18
49 The Walled Garden
Wednesday 22
49 The Walled Garden
Saturday 25
44 Shuttifield Cottage
Sunday 26
1 24 Alexander Avenue

May

Saturday 2
15 1 Church Cottage
44 Shuttifield Cottage
Sunday 3
15 1 Church Cottage
Monday 4
15 1 Church Cottage
30 Little Malvern Court
Thursday 7
41 Red House Farm
Saturday 9
34 New House Farm, Elmbridge

Sunday 10
29 Jasmine Cottage
34 New House Farm, Elmbridge
51 Whitcombe House
Saturday 16
25 Hewell Grange
Sunday 17
25 Hewell Grange
52 White Cottage
Wednesday 20
8 5 Beckett Drive
Thursday 21
23 Harrells Hardy Plants Nursery Garden
Saturday 23
44 Shuttifield Cottage
55 68 Windsor Avenue
Sunday 24
2 Ashley
6 Barnard's Green House
15 1 Church Cottage
29 Jasmine Cottage
31 Marlbrook Gardens
47 Toll House Cottage
55 68 Windsor Avenue
Monday 25
2 Ashley
15 1 Church Cottage
Friday 29
13 NEW Burcot Gardens
Saturday 30
13 NEW Burcot Gardens
22 NEW Hanley Swan NGS Gardens
38 Pear Tree Cottage
53 Whitlenge Gardens
Sunday 31
14 Bylane
22 NEW Hanley Swan NGS Gardens
23 Harrells Hardy Plants Nursery Garden
38 Pear Tree Cottage
53 Whitlenge Gardens

Sit and enjoy a cup of tea or coffee in the cosy summer house . . .

June

Thursday 4
23 Harrells Hardy Plants Nursery Garden
41 Red House Farm

Festival Weekend

Saturday 6
7 The Barton
20 Eckington Gardens
39 Pershore Gardens
Sunday 7
7 The Barton
9 Birtsmorton Court
20 Eckington Gardens
28 Hiraeth
39 Pershore Gardens
Saturday 13
8 5 Beckett Drive
58 NEW Worralls Mill
Sunday 14
8 5 Beckett Drive
51 Whitcombe House
58 NEW Worralls Mill
Thursday 18
23 Harrells Hardy Plants Nursery Garden
Saturday 20
10 Bretforton Manor
18 NEW Cowleigh Lodge
43 NEW Rothbury
44 Shuttifield Cottage
Sunday 21
5 NEW Bannut Hill Gardens
18 NEW Cowleigh Lodge
52 White Cottage
56 Withybed Green
Saturday 27
3 Astley Country Gardens
Sunday 28
3 Astley Country Gardens
6 Barnard's Green House
12 Brook Farm
27 Highfield Cottage

July

Wednesday 1
28 Hiraeth
Thursday 2
41 Red House Farm
Saturday 4
24 Harvington Hall
Sunday 5
24 Harvington Hall

27 Highfield Cottage
45 Spetchley Park Gardens
54 Wick Village
Thursday 9
23 Harrells Hardy Plants Nursery Garden
Saturday 11
21 Hanbury Hall & Gardens
44 Shuttifield Cottage
Sunday 12
14 Bylane
21 Hanbury Hall & Gardens
Thursday 16
23 Harrells Hardy Plants Nursery Garden
Saturday 18
50 Westacres
Sunday 19
1 24 Alexander Avenue
23 Harrells Hardy Plants Nursery Garden
47 Toll House Cottage
50 Westacres
52 White Cottage
Saturday 25
17 The Cottage, 3 Crumpfields Lane
43 NEW Rothbury
Sunday 26
4 Astley Towne House
17 The Cottage, 3 Crumpfields Lane
43 NEW Rothbury
Friday 31
36 NEW 9 Old Road South

August

Saturday 1
36 NEW 9 Old Road South
Sunday 2
28 Hiraeth
Thursday 6
8 5 Beckett Drive (Evening)
41 Red House Farm
Saturday 8
58 NEW Worralls Mill
Sunday 9
11 Bridges Stone Mill
58 NEW Worralls Mill
Saturday 15
35 Offenham Gardens
Sunday 16
35 Offenham Gardens
Sunday 23
14 Bylane

Over 400 Volunteers help run the NGS – why not become one too?

Saturday 29
44 Shuttifield Cottage
Sunday 30
4 Astley Towne House
19 6 Dingle End
31 Marlbrook Gardens
Monday 31
19 6 Dingle End
38 Pear Tree Cottage (Evening)

September

Thursday 3
41 Red House Farm
Saturday 5
34 New House Farm, Elmbridge
53 Whitlenge Gardens
Sunday 6
34 New House Farm, Elmbridge
52 White Cottage

---

53 Whitlenge Gardens
Sunday 20
6 Barnard's Green House

October

Sunday 11
52 White Cottage

Gardens open to the public

12 Brook Farm
21 Hanbury Hall & Gardens
23 Harrells Hardy Plants Nursery Garden
24 Harvington Hall
30 Little Malvern Court
41 Red House Farm
42 Riverside Gardens at Webbs

---

45 Spetchley Park Gardens
46 Stone House Cottage Gardens
53 Whitlenge Gardens

By arrangement only

16 Conderton Manor
26 High View
32 74 Meadow Road
33 Morton Hall
37 Overbury Court
40 Pump Cottage
48 The Tynings
57 The Woodlands

Also open by arrangement

1 24 Alexander Avenue
6 Barnard's Green House

---

8 5 Beckett Drive
14 Bylane
15 1 Church Cottage
17 The Cottage, 3 Crumpfields Lane
20 Eckington Gardens
20 Mantoft, Eckington Gardens
28 Hiraeth
31 Marlbrook Gardens
31 Oak Tree House, Marlbrook Gardens
31 Round Hill Garden, Marlbrook Gardens
34 New House Farm, Elmbridge
38 Pear Tree Cottage
44 Shuttifield Cottage
47 Toll House Cottage
50 Westacres
51 Whitcombe House
52 White Cottage

The Gardens

1 24 ALEXANDER AVENUE
Droitwich Spa WR9 8NH. Malley & David Terry, 01905 774907, terrydroit@aol.com. *1m S of Droitwich. Droitwich Spa towards Worcester A38. Or from M5 J6 to Droitwich Town centre.* Adm £3.50, chd free. Sun 26 Apr, Sun 19 July (2-5.30). Visitors also welcome by arrangement Apr to Sept.
Beautifully designed giving feeling of space and tranquillity. 100+ clematis varieties interlacing high hedges. Borders with rare plants and shrubs. Sweeping curves of lawns and paths to woodland area with shade-loving plants. Drought-tolerant plants in S-facing gravel front garden. Alpine filled troughs. April spring bulbs, July clematis. Featured in Worcestershire Now. Partial wheelchair access.

2 ASHLEY
Low Road, Church Lench, Evesham WR11 4UH. Roy & Betty Bowron, 01386 871347, bettybowz@gmail.com. *6m N of Evesham. In centre of Church Lench take Low Rd N at junction with Main Street. Ashley is 4th property on R.* Home-made teas. Adm £3, chd free. Sun 24, Mon 25 May (2-6).
Sloping garden with steps down to lawn, garden pond with plants and fish. Mixed flower beds, greenhouse and vegetable garden. Large pergola with climbing roses, and shaded section with semi-exotic plants which incl tree ferns, other ferns, banana plants, etc. Plants on the large patio incl sago palms, bird of paradise (strelitzia), Hawaiian Palm, agarves and various other plants.

GROUP OPENING

3 ASTLEY COUNTRY GARDENS
Group Co-ordinator Roger Russell, Astley, nr Stourport-on-Severn DY13 0SG, 01299 823769, rogchrisrussell@btinternet.com. *3m SW of Stourport-on-Severn. Start at Village Hall. Situated off B4196 - accessed via Ridleys Cross in centre of Astley (DY13 0RE). Light refreshments. at Astley Towne House and Longmore Hill Farmhouse.* Combined adm £5, chd free. Sat 27, Sun 28 June (1-6).

ASTLEY TOWNE HOUSE
Tim & Lesley Smith.
On B4196 Worcester to Bewdley Rd
www.astleytownehousesubtropicalgarden.co.uk

LITTLE LARFORD
Seedgreen Lane. Lin & Derek Walker.
Turn L signed Larford Lakes. Garden approx 1¹/₂ m further on. Access via Larford Lane or Seedgreen Lane

---

LONGMORE HILL FARMHOUSE
Larford Lane. Roger & Christine Russell.
Turn off B4196 at Astley signed Larford Lakes. Garden approx 300yds on L

THE WHITE HOUSE
Dunley. Tony & Linda Tidmarsh.
Turn L off A451 opp garage in Dunley. Access to the garden approx. 50yds on L

THE WHITE HOUSE
Seedgreen Lane. John & Joanna Daniels.
Off B4196 Holt Heath to Stourport Rd

A wonderful range of 5 country gardens of great variety, in picturesque, peaceful and colourful settings. These incl the garden of a Grade II listed half timbered house with sub tropical planting, stumpery with tree ferns and woodland temple, underground grotto and water features; classical style garden with a variety of features celebrating events in the owner's family; ¹/₂ acre garden with mixed borders, 'wheel' herbery and large paddock with specimen trees overlooking the Severn Valley; a Grade II listed C16 farmhouse garden with mixed borders, small feature courtyard leading to a part-walled terrace and lily pond; thatched cottage surrounded by mixed borders, bedding displays and woodland.

4 ▶ ASTLEY TOWNE HOUSE

Astley DY13 0RH. Tim & Lesley Smith, www.astleytownehousesubtropicalgarden.co.uk. *3m W of Stourport-on-Severn. On B4196 Worcester to Bewdley Road.* Home-made teas. **Adm £4, chd free. Sun 26 July, Sun 30 Aug (1-5).**
2¹/₂ acres garden of a Grade II listed timber building (not open) incl subtropical planting. Stumpery garden with tree ferns and woodland temple. Mediterranean garden, tree house, revolving summerhouse and underground grotto with shell mosaics and water features. A recent addition is 'Mr McGregor's' vegetable garden. Teas/cakes and plant stall within the garden. Featured on Gardeners' World and various gardening publications. Partial wheelchair access.

&♿ 🐾 ✿ ☕

GROUP OPENING

5 ▶ NEW ▶ BANNUT HILL GARDENS

Kempsey, Worcester WR5 3NG. Group Co-ordinator Gail Brookes, 01905 821823. *4m SW M5 J7, 4m S Worcester city centre. South side of Kempsey village, off A38, Take Plovers Rise opp the Lawns Nursing home. Follow Yellow NGS signs to direct you to the gardens.* Home-made teas at Orchard Cottage. **Combined adm £3.50, chd free. Sun 21 June (10-5).**

NEW ▶ 35 BANNUT HILL
Gail Brookes

NEW ▶ ORCHARD COTTAGE
Bannut Hill. Mrs Susan Hardaker.
Follow yellow signs from Plovers Rise pointing to direction of the two gardens

Two gardens, 35 Bannut Hill (top of hill), this small garden with many interesting and quirky ideas incl wildlife pond, hexagonal greenhouse, 7 fruit trees, pixie house and lots of homes for wildlife. There is also an unusual water feature in the courtyard back garden but look out for the giant Ants!!! Orchard Cottage (bottom of hill), a garden which hosts a number of well designed features with its mature fruit trees over a wrought iron arch, wildlife pond, raised vegetable area. Sit and enjoy a cup of tea or coffee in the cosy summer house,

there are plenty of seats around the garden. A path down the side of the house to a delightful quaint front garden with another seating area surrounded with its lush white borders. Games and quiz for the children in Orchard Cottage.

☕

6 ▶ BARNARD'S GREEN HOUSE

Hastings Pool, Poolbrook Road, Malvern WR14 3NQ. Mrs Sue Nicholls, 01684 574446. *1m E of Malvern. At junction of B4211 & B4208.* Home-made teas. **Adm £4, chd free. Sun 24 May, Sun 28 June, Sun 20 Sept (2-6). Visitors also welcome by arrangement Apr to Sept.**
With a magnificent backdrop of the Malvern Hills, this 1¹/₂ acre old-fashioned garden is a plantsman's paradise. The main feature is a magnificent cedar. 3 herbaceous and 2 shrub borders, rose garden, red and white and yellow borders, an evergreen and hydrangea bed, 2 rockeries, pond, sculptures and vegetable garden. Good garden colour throughout the year. Dogs on leads.

&♿ 🐾 ✿ 🚐 ☕

WE ARE MACMILLAN.
CANCER SUPPORT

The NGS has given over £14 million to Macmillan

7 ▶ THE BARTON

Berrow Green, Martley WR6 6PL. David & Vanessa Piggott. *1m S of Martley. On B4197 between Martley & A44 at Knightwick, corner of lane to Broadheath. Parking & lunches (12.30 to 2.30) at Admiral Rodney PH opp.* Home-made teas. **Adm £3.50, chd free. Sat 6, Sun 7 June (1-5).**
This ¹/₂ acre cottagey garden full of colour and texture contains unusual shrubs and billowing herbaceous planting. Paths wind through colour-themed gardens, gravel and grass beds. Roses, clematis and unusual

climbers decorate pergolas and trellises. Terracotta-decorated walls enclose a vegetable plot and new tender bed. Visitors comments 'Best private garden I've seen.' ' So unusual and beautiful.'. Book sale.

&♿ ✿ 🚐 ☕

8 ▶ 5 BECKETT DRIVE

Northwick, Worcester WR3 7BZ. Jacki & Pete Ager, 01905 451108, peteandjacki@tiscali.co.uk. *1¹/₂ m N of Worcester city centre. Cul-de-sac off A449 Ombersley Rd directly opp Grantham's garage, 1m S of Claines r'about on A449.* Home-made teas. **Adm £3, chd free. Wed 20 May, Sat 13, Sun 14 June (2-5). Evening Opening £4, chd free, wine, Thur 6 Aug (6-9). Visitors also welcome by arrangement May to Aug groups or societies between 10 & 30 people.**
A plantsman's garden with a wide variety of colourful planting in distinctly different settings. Hot borders give way to a raised alpine area and sun-loving bed before moving into a shade garden with a wide variety of hostas and ferns. A walk through this long, narrow garden reveals a number of surprising features, a recent garden visitor describing it as 'a magical mystery tour'. Compost advisors in attendance.

🐾 ✿ ☕

9 ▶ BIRTSMORTON COURT

Birtsmorton, nr Malvern WR13 6JS. Mr & Mrs N G K Dawes. *7m E of Ledbury. Off A438 Ledbury/Tewkesbury rd.* Tea. **Adm £5, chd free. Sun 7 June (2-5).**
Fortified manor house (not open) dating from C12; moat; Westminster pool laid down in Henry VII's reign at time of consecration of Westminster Abbey. Large tree under which Cardinal Wolsey reputedly slept in shadow of ragged stone. White garden, potager; topiary.

&♿ ✿ ☕

10 ▶ BRETFORTON MANOR

Main Street, Bretforton, Evesham WR11 7JH. Mr & Mrs M L Chambers. *4m E of Evesham, 6¹/₂ m N of Broadway. Centre of Bretforton village, next to the church.* **Adm £6, chd free. Sat 20 June (11-5).**
An outstanding garden of 5 acres recently redesigned and replanted. The immaculately maintained garden contains mixed and herbaceous borders, an exotic border, scented

Brook Farm

walk and many tender and unusual plants. Hedges and topiary both old and new, several water features and many listed buildings and structures. The orchard has been extended and now contains a wide variety of fruit and specimen trees. The dovecote, aviary, apiary, cider barn and old village stocks are all listed. Beautiful walled garden, waterfall and ponds. Glasshouses and small kitchen garden with cut flower borders. Featured in Cotswold Life, Cotswold Gardens Section 'Maintaining Standards'; The English Garden, Worcestershire Gardens 'Beauty reborn'; Landscape In the garden 'Late border colour'. Gravel paths, unfenced ponds.

&. ✿

11 ▶ BRIDGES STONE MILL

Alfrick Pound WR6 5HR. **Sir Michael & Lady Perry.** *6m NW of Malvern. A4103 from Worcester to Bransford r'about, then Suckley Rd*

for 3m to Alfrick Pound. Home-made teas. **Adm £5, chd free. Sun 9 Aug (2-5.30).**
Formerly a cherry orchard adjoining the mainly C19 water mill, this is now a 2¹/₂ -acre garden laid out with trees, shrubs, mixed beds and borders. Small lake, stream and brook. The garden is bounded by 200yd stretch of Leigh Brook (an SSSI), and a mill stream from the mill's own weir. Extensive all-yr round planting. Ornamental vegetable parterre completes the picture. Wheelchair access by car to courtyard.

&. ✿ ☕

12 ◆ BROOK FARM

Hayes Lane, Berrington, nr Tenbury Wells WR15 8TJ. **Sarah & William Wint,** 01584 819868 www.brookfarmberrington.com. *2m W of Tenbury Wells. From A49, A456 to Tenbury until big bridge over River at Little Hereford. L, after 50yds L. Follow for 1¹/₂ m, until*

humpbacked bridge at bottom of hill. Brook Farm on R. Home-made teas on NGS days in Conservatory. **Adm £3.50, chd free. For NGS: Sun 28 June (12.30-6).** For other opening times and information, please phone or see garden website.
A relaxed country garden. It's been described as a cottage garden, wildlife garden and chaotic garden. To paraphrase the lovely Eric Morecambe 'They're all the right plants, just not necessarily in the right order'. 1¹/₂ -acre garden, 7 acres woodland and wilderness. Garden guides. We have welcomed Roise and her Sound Therapy to the Sound Sanctuary in the Old Hopkiln. Tea and Cake, some weeds. Featured in English Garden, and various local newspapers. Partial wheelchair access over gravel and grass, which is passable unless it's very wet.

&. 🐕 ✿ 🛏 ☕

New House Farm, Elmbridge

NGS admission ticket (limited to one per ticket holder) a donation to the NGS for all plants sold to NGS visitors.

14 BYLANE
Worcester Road, Earls Croome WR8 9DA. Shirley & Fred Bloxsome, 01684 592489, shirleymay70@hotmail.co.uk. *1m N of Upton on Severn turning. On main A38 directly past Earls Croome Garden Centre, signed Bridle Way. Directly behind Earls Croome Garden Centre, turn down bridle way to park.* Home-made teas. **Adm £3, chd free. Sun 31 May, Sun 12 July, Sun 23 Aug (1-5). Visitors also welcome by arrangement May to Sept, adm £5 incl teas. Please give one months notice.**
Herbaceous garden, paddock with wildlife pond, vegetable garden chickens, wood with mature trees and bluebells. Approximatley 2 acres in all, Picnic area, private parties welcome. Plenty of seating areas and shelter if needed, very quiet and secluded.

15 1 CHURCH COTTAGE
Church Road, Defford WR8 9BJ. John Taylor & Ann Sheppard, 01386 750863, ann98sheppard@btinternet.com. *3m SW of Pershore. A4104 Pershore to Upton rd, turn into Harpley Rd, Defford, black & white cottage at side of church. Parking in village hall car park.* Home-made teas. **Adm £3, chd free. Sat 2, Sun 3, Mon 4, Sun 24, Mon 25 May (11-5). Visitors also welcome by arrangement May to July groups of 10 - 40.**
True countryman's ⅓-acre garden. Interesting layout. Japanese -style feature with new 'dragons den'. Specimen trees; water features; vegetable garden; poultry and cider making. Perennial garden under construction. Featured in Amateur Gardening and Practical Gardener. Wheelchair access to most areas.

16 CONDERTON MANOR
Conderton, nr Tewkesbury GL20 7PR. Mr & Mrs W Carr, 01386 725389, carrs@conderton.com. *5½ m NE of Tewkesbury. From M5 - A46 to Beckford - L for Overbury/ Conderton From Tewkesbury B4079 to Bredon - then follow signs to*

GROUP OPENING

13 NEW BURCOT GARDENS
Bromsgrove B60 1LJ. *2m N from Bromsgrove, 1m W from Tardebigge, 1m SE from J1 of M42, 2m SE from J4 of M5. On B4096 approx 1m S of J1 of M42 towards Burcot. Park at Fresh@ Burcot Garden Centre, Alcester Rd just past 1st r'about on R. Both gardens a short walk away & signed. For SatNav - B60 1PW.* Light refreshments at Fresh @ Burcot Garden Centre. Fresh will be donating profits from refreshment sales to NGS - please show your NGS ticket to ensure this happens. **Combined adm £3.50, chd free. Fri 29, Sat 30 May (12-5).**

NEW APPLETREEWICK
9a Pikes Pool Lane. Mrs Ruth Edwards.
From Fresh, short walk turn R out of entry & R up Pikes Pool Lane. Appletreewick (9a) on L. Caution: no footpath in Pikes Pool Lane

NEW 16 GREEN HILL
Mr Chris Franklin.
From Fresh short walk L out of gate & R at r'about up Green Hill. House on R. Caution: part of Green Hill has no footpath. Space for 2 vehicles on front drive for those with walking difficulties

Two contrasting gardens in the small village of Burcot near Bromsgrove. 16 Green Hill, A small garden created by owner over last 3yrs. Designed for minimum maintenance and all year round colour mainly with trees and shrubs. A good example of what can be achieved with a small garden. Appletreewick is a long, sloping, natural garden recently redesigned and still developing to encourage local wildlife. Small natural swimming pond (not for public use), sculptures, artefacts, seating and with a view of the Clent Hills from the top orchard. Plants and refreshments at Fresh@Burcot Garden Centre (where you park the car) who are offering a special deal - buy 1 outdoor plant and get 1 free when you show your

Overbury. Conderton from B4077 follow A46 directions from Teddington r'about. Tea. **Visitors welcome by arrangement Mar to Nov individuals and groups welcome. Max 30.**

7-acre garden, recently replanted in a contemporary style with magnificent views of Cotswolds. Flowering cherries and bulbs in spring. Formal terrace with clipped box parterre; huge rose and clematis arches, mixed borders of roses and herbaceous plants, bog bank and quarry garden. Many unusual trees and shrubs make this a garden to visit at all seasons. Visitors are particularly encouraged to come in spring and autumn. This is a garden/small arboretum of particular interest for tree lovers. The views towards the Cotswolds are spectacular. Some gravel paths and steps - no disabled WC.

& 🚐 ☕

17 THE COTTAGE, 3 CRUMPFIELDS LANE
Webheath, Redditch B97 5PN. Victor Johnson, pjohnson889@btinternet.com. *From A448 through Redditch take slip rds signed to Headless Cross, at r'about take 3rd exit then follow NGS signs.* Home-made teas, cakes and soft drinks. **Adm £4, chd free. Sat 25, Sun 26 July (10.30-4). Visitors also welcome by arrangement June to Aug for groups from 2 to 20.**

Newly established 1½ - acre garden landscaped to provide 5 rooms on 4 levels stepped into a hillside. From the 2nd level are stunning views over Vale of Evesham. 2 water features, (1 in a cave) and places to sit and enjoy the wildlife. Wonderland can be found in meadow area of wild flowers. Partial wheelchair access to levels 2 and 3 are accessible with able body escort (help available).

& ❀ ☕

18 NEW COWLEIGH LODGE
16 Cowleigh Bank, Malvern WR14 1QP. Jane & Mic Schuster. *7m SW from Worcester, on the slopes of the Malvern Hills. From Worcester or Ledbury follow the A449 to Link Top. Take North Malvern Rd (behind Holy Trinity church), follow yelllow signs. From Hereford take B4219 after Storridge church, follow yellow signs.* Home-made teas. **Adm £3.50, chd free. Sat 20, Sun 21 June (11-5).**

Just under an acre this is a developing garden now in its 3rd year

with lots of interesting features to be seen as you stroll past the rose garden, grass beds and bamboos coming to the wildlife pond, or take the wildlife path passing the bee hotel and bog garden on the way. Formal and informal planting, colour themed beds, apple trees and vegetable garden topped off with wonderful views from the top.

❀ ☕

19 6 DINGLE END
Inkberrow, Worcester WR7 4EY. Mr & Mrs Glenn & Gabriel Allison. *12m E of Worcester. A422 from Worcester. At the 30 sign in Inkberrow turn R down Appletree Lane then 1st L up Pepper St. Dingle End is 4th on R of Pepper St. Limited parking in Dingle End but street parking on Pepper St.* Light refreshments. Home made teas. Also soup and home bred beefburgers at lunchtime. **Adm £3, chd free. Sun 30, Mon 31 Aug (11-5).**

Over 1 acre garden with formal area close to the house opening into a flat area featuring a large pond, stream and weir with apple orchard and woodland area. Large vegetable garden incl an interesting variety of fruits. Garden designed for wildlife. Giant Redwood Tree. Large pond and stream with many ducks and moorhens. Slopes alongside every terrace.

& 🐾 ☕

GROUP OPENING

20 ECKINGTON GROUP GARDENS
Eckington WR10 3BH. Group Coordinator Lynn Glaze, 01386 751924, lynnglaze@cmail.co.uk. *4 gardens - 2 in Manor Rd, 2 in or close to New Rd/Nafford Rd. A4104 Pershore to Upton & Defford, L turn B4080 to Eckington. In centre, by war memorial turn R for Brook House & turn L for other gardens.* Home-made teas at Brook House. Mantoft - wine & soft drinks. **Combined adm £5, chd free. Sat 6, Sun 7 June (11-5). Visitors also welcome by arrangement Apr to Sept.**

BROOK HOUSE
Manor Road. George & Lynn Glaze

COURT GATE COTTAGE
Manor Road. Mr & Mrs David & Yvonne Walton.
200yds from Brook House

MANTOFT
Mr & Mrs M J Tupper.
Park on rd - garden has electric gates, admission requires pressing a button on a VDU screen to obtain entrance **Visitors also welcome by arrangement Apr to Sept please phone for further info.** 01386 750819

NAFFORD HOUSE 🛏
Nafford Road. Janet & John Wheatley, 01386 750233.
1m from Mantoft along Nafford Rd

4 very diverse gardens; traditional open cottage garden with koi pond; cottage garden broken into smaller areas; formal and structured walled garden with topiary; natural wooded garden sloping down to the riverside. Set in/close to lovely village of Eckington with riverside parking and picnic site. Brook House 1 acre cottage garden with herbaceous beds and koi pond surrounded by rockery. Court Gate Cottage ⅔ acre cottage garden, broken into 'rooms', with wildlife pond, summer house and vegetable garden. Mantoft - formal walled garden with fish pond, topiary and dew pond, with ducks and geese. Hedges and stone paths, gazebo overlooking garden and new dovecote. Nafford House 2 acre mature natural garden/wood with slopes to R Avon, formal gardens, magnificent wisteria and orangery planned. Partial wheelchair access at Nafford House to wooded area and slopes to river.

& ❀ ☕

Take the wildlife path passing the bee hotel and bog garden on the way . . .

21 ◆ HANBURY HALL & GARDENS

School Road, Hanbury, Droitwich WR9 7EA. National Trust, 01527 821214, www.nationaltrust.org.uk/ hanburyhall. *4m E of Droitwich. From M5 exit 5 follow A38 to Droitwich; from Droitwich 4m along B4090.* Adm £7.50, chd £3.75. For NGS: Sat 11, Sun 12 July (10.30-5). For other opening times and information, please phone or see garden website.
Re-creation of early C18 formal garden by George London. Parterre, fruit garden and wilderness. Mushroom house, orangery and ice house, William and Mary style house dating from 1701. Opportunity to meet the gardeners and to see behind the scenes in the Walled Garden. Buggy available to bring visitors from the car park to the front of the property and wheelchairs are available from the Hall.

♧ ❀ 🚚 ☕

Plants for all seasons enclosed with climbing roses, a white wisteria covers an entrance to a small oriental garden . . .

GROUP OPENING

22 NEW HANLEY SWAN NGS GARDENS

Hanley Swan, Worcester WR8 0DJ. Group Co-ordinator Brian Skeys, 01684 311297, brimfields@icloud.com. *5m E of Malvern, 3m NW of Upton upon Severn, 9m S of Worcester. From Worcester/Callow End take B4424 to Hanley Castle then turn R. From Upton upon Severn B4211 to Hanley Castle turn L. From Malvern/Ledbury from A449 take B4209. Gardens signed from village.* Cream teas at 19 Winnington Gardens. Combined adm £5, chd free. Sat 30, Sun 31 May (1-5).

BLACKMORE GRANGE

Blackmore End. Mr & Mrs D Robertson.
From village centre of Hanley Swan on B4209 take Worcester Rd past Butcher's shop on R, RC church on L for ³/₄ m. Parking in field just before Rd bends to R

NEW CHASEWOOD

Picken End. Mrs Sydney Harrison.
From centre of village on B4209 take Welland Rd, then 2nd L into Picken End & Winnington Gds. Parking in field at the end of Picken End, Chasewood is in Picken End
01684 310527
sydney.harrison@cmail.co.uk

NEW 19 WINNINGTON GARDENS

Brian & Irene Skeys.
2mins walk from Chasewood

3 gardens different in size and style in Hanley Swan. Blackmore Grange, a 2 acre informal garden packed with plants, shrubs and trees. A swimming pool has been transformed into the stable yard garden, with traditional cottage-style planting. There's a woodland walk, wild area, orchard, kitchen garden and mixed borders. Chasewood has lavender and old fashioned roses alongside clematis and honeysuckle. A gravel garden with an Iris and Thyme walk and seating by a small bog garden. Shrubs and climbers cover the boundaries. A collection of Bonsai and Coach Built Prams.
19 Winnington Gardens is a garden of rooms. Roses and vines cover an archway to mixed borders of plants for all seasons enclosed with climbing roses, a white wisteria covers an entrance to a small oriental garden, raised beds, trained fruit trees, a raised herb bed with a special standard gooseberry bush, greenhouses, a potting shed with a small collection of vintage garden tools. A garden room has a display of botanic art.

❀ ☕

---

23 ◆ HARRELLS HARDY PLANTS NURSERY GARDEN

Rudge Road, Evesham WR11 4JR. Liz Nicklin & Kate Phillips, 01386 443077, www.harrellshardyplants.co.uk. *¹/₄ m from centre of Evesham. From A4184 turn into Queens Rd R at end, then L, Rudge Rd. 150 yds on R*

down lane. SatNav WR11 4LA. Home-made teas. Homemade cakes. Adm £3, chd free. For NGS: Thur 21, Sun 31 May, Thurs 4, 18 June, Thurs 9, 16, Sun 19 July (2-5). For other opening times and information, please phone or see garden website.
This garden is naturalistic in style and informally planted with a glorious array of hardy perennials, grasses and a large range of hemerocallis. The 1-acre site consists of beds and borders accessed by bark paths, with several seating areas giving views over the garden. 'Harrell's Hardy Plants is an absolute gem! The garden is absolutely breathtaking- the web site gives you a hint, you really do need to visit to appreciate the wonderful planting scheme, and learn the story behind the garden'.
Featured in Evesham Journal.

❀ ☕

---

24 ◆ HARVINGTON HALL

Harvington, Kidderminster DY10 4LR. The Roman Catholic Archdiocese of Birmingham, 01562 777846, www.harvingtonhall.com. *3m SE of Kidderminster. ¹/₂ m E of A450 Birmingham to Worcester Rd & approx ¹/₂ m N of A448 from Kidderminster to Bromsgrove.* Light refreshments. Adm £3.50, chd £1.50. For NGS: Sat 4, Sun 5 July (11.30-4). For other opening times and information, please phone or see garden website.
Romantic Elizabethan moated manor house with island gardens, small Elizabethan-style herb garden, all tended by volunteers. Tours of the Hall, which contains secret hiding places and rare wall paintings, are also available. Access to gardens, Malt House Visitor Centre, tea room, shop and WC.

♧ ❀ 🚚 ☕

---

25 HEWELL GRANGE

Hewell Lane, Tardebigge, Redditch B97 6QS. HMP Hewell, 01527 785050, helen.cartwright@hmps.gsi.gov.uk. *2m NW of Redditch. HMP Hewell is situated on B4096. For SatNav use B97 6QQ. Follow signs to Grange Resettlement Unit. Visitors must book in advance via email (address above). This is a prison and there are booking and security procedures to be followed.* Home-made teas. Adm £5, chd free. Sat 16, Sun 17 May (9.30-4). Visitors by arrangement only on specified days and times.

All visitors must follow a booking procedure and due to prison environment, must follow security procedures. Booking via email only to Helen Cartwright helen.cartwright@hmps.gsi.gov.uk. Hewell Grange is an C18 landscape park and lake laid out by Lancelot Brown and modified around 1812 by Humphery Repton. The grounds of this prison feature rhododendrons and azaleas, restored Repton bridge, formal garden, water tower, and rock garden. Grounds have mature woodland. Not a flower garden. Please note - Visitors to the garden will be shown the garden features in escorted small groups. The garden tour may be over 60 minutes. Therefore, visitors must be physically able to walk for this length of time. There are uneven surfaces in the grounds so sensible walking footwear is essential. Lakeside walk and bluebell walk Please Note - All visits have to have been booked prior to date.

26 ▶ HIGH VIEW

Martley WR6 6PW. Mike & Carole Dunnett, 01886 821559, mike.dunnett@btinternet.com. *1m S of Martley. On B4197 between Martley & A44 at Knightwick.* Home-made teas. **Adm £4.50, chd free. Visitors welcome by arrangement June to Aug group of 10+.**
Intriguing and mature 2½ acre garden developed over 40yrs. Visitors have described the garden as magical, inspirational and one of the best kept horticultural secrets of Worcestershire! With its superb views over the Teme valley, vast range of plants and many interesting features, it is a garden not to be missed. Steps and steep slopes so appropriate foot wear required.

27 ▶ HIGHFIELD COTTAGE

Kings Green, Wichenford, Worcester WR6 6YG. Valerie Mills. *7m from Worcester. Take B4204 from Worcester to Martley turn R at the Masons Arms PH. Follow yellow NGS signs from here. Parking available.* Home-made teas. **Adm £3.50, chd free. Sun 28 June, Sun 5 July (2-6).**
An ever evolving, real picture book cottage garden with traditional borders overflowing with delphiniums, roses, geraniums and many other perennials. Mature trees, shrubs and large water garden. Raised vegetable

Oak Tree House, Marlbrook Gardens

beds, gravel paths and seating areas. Small woodland with live ornamental pheasants. Exhibition of local artists' paintings and sculptures.

28 ▶ HIRAETH

30 Showell Road, Droitwich WR9 8UY. Sue & John Fletcher, 07752 717243/01905 778390, jfletcher@inductotherm.co.uk. *1m S of Droitwich. On The Ridings estate. Turn off A38 r'about into Addyes Way, 2nd R into Showell Rd, 500yds on R. Follow the yellow signs!* Home-made teas. Tea, coffee, cold drinks, home-made cakes and scones available served with china cups, saucers, plates, tea-pots and coffee-pots! **Adm £3, chd free. Sun 7 June (2-5.30); Wed 1 July (1.30-5); Sun 2 Aug (2-5.30). Visitors also welcome by arrangement June to Aug for groups of 10-30.**
'A haven on the way to heaven' - description in Visitors Book. Front, rear gardens contain unusual plants, traditional cottage garden, herbaceous, hostas, ferns, 300yr-old Olive Tree, arches, pool, waterfall, 200yr-old stile, oak sculptures, metal animals, birds etc incl, giraffes,

elephant. An oasis of colours in a garden not to be missed. Featured on Local Radio. Partial wheelchair access.

29 ▶ JASMINE COTTAGE

Broad Lane, Bishampton, Pershore WR10 2LY. David & Lesley Miller. *4m S of Inkberrow, 4m NE of Pershore. At Bishampton join Broad Lane after 200yds track on L, property on L up track. Parking at Villages Hall, Broad Lane 200 yards further down on R (WR10 2LY).* Home-made teas. Tea/coffee/squash. Delicious selection of home-made cakes. **Adm £3, chd free. Sun 10, Sun 24 May (11-3).**
A haven of delight nestled in this rural Worcestershire village, a pretty ⅓ acre garden, packed with interest to complement the Grade II listed black and white cottage. The plot has been transformed in the past three years from a plain lawn to include ponds, colourful mixed borders, arbours, trees, and vegetable patch, and is testimony to what can be achieved in a relatively small space. Gravel drive, and some steps in the garden.

30 ◆ LITTLE MALVERN COURT

Little Malvern WR14 4JN. Mrs T M Berington, 01684 892988, www.littlemalverncourt.co.uk. *3m S of Malvern. On A4104 S of junction with A449.* Home-made teas. **Adm £6, chd £0.50. For NGS: Sun 22 Mar, Mon 4 May (2-5). For other opening times and information, please phone or see garden website.**

10 acres attached to former Benedictine Priory, magnificent views over Severn valley. Garden rooms and terrace around house designed and planted in early 1980s; chain of lakes; wide variety of spring bulbs, flowering trees and shrubs. Notable collection of old-fashioned roses. Topiary hedge and fine trees. The May Bank Holiday - Flower Festival in the Priory Church. Partial wheelchair access.

♿ ❀ ☕

GROUP OPENING

31 MARLBROOK GARDENS

Braces Lane, Marlbrook, Bromsgrove B60 1DY. Group Co-ordinator Alan Nokes, 0121 445 5520, alyn.nokes@btinternet.com. *2m N of Bromsgrove. 1m N of M42 J1, follow B4096 signed Rednal, turn L at Xrds into Braces Lane. 1m S of M5 J4, follow A38 signed Bromsgove, turn L at T-lights into Braces Lane. Parking available.* Home-made teas. **Combined adm £5, chd free. Sun 24 May, Sun 30 Aug (1.30-5.30). Visitors also welcome by arrangement June to Aug for groups of 10+ Viewing for one or both gardens.**

OAK TREE HOUSE
Di & Dave Morgan.
500 yds from car park
Visitors also welcome by arrangement June to Aug groups of 10+.
0121 445 3595
meandi@btinternet.com

ROUND HILL GARDEN
Lynn & Alan Nokes
Visitors also welcome by arrangement June to Sept groups of 10+.
0121 445 5520
alyn.nokes@btinternet.com
www.roundhillgarden.weebly.com

Two unique and stunning gardens, each capable of opening individually in their own right. Together they're a wonderful experience of contrasting styles, Round Hill Garden a traditional garden with a twist into the exotic and unusual and Oak Tree House a plantswoman's cottage garden with views over open fields. Both gardens overflowing with plants for sun and shade, and with vegetables areas. Streams, ponds, water features (incl new water feature at Oak Tree House), patios, artefacts, sculptures, glasshouses and special collections add to the individuality. Recognised for excellence, with many articles published in national papers/gardening magazines. Continually evolving, many repeat visitors enjoy sharing with us their new discoveries. Art displays at both gardens by garden owners. Garden Quiz for children.

❀ 🚌 ☕

PERENNIAL
GARDENERS' ROYAL BENEVOLENT SOCIETY

NGS & Perennial; over 30 years of caring for horticulturists

32 74 MEADOW ROAD

Wythall B47 6EQ. Joe Manchester, 01564 829589, joe@cogentscreenprint.co.uk. *4m E of Alvechurch. 2m N from J3 M42. On A435 at Beckets Farm r'about take rd signed Earlswood/Solihull. Approx 250 metres turn L into School Drive, then L into Meadow Rd.* Home-made teas. **Adm £2.50, chd free. Visitors welcome by arrangement May to Sept.**

Has been described one of the most unusual urban garden dedicated to woodland, shade-loving plants. 'Expect the unexpected' in a few tropical and foreign species. Meander through the garden under the majestic pine, eucalyptus and silver birch. Sit and enjoy the peaceful surroundings and see how many different ferns and hostas you can find.

❀ 🚌 ☕

33 MORTON HALL

Morton Hall Lane, Holberrow Green, Redditch B96 6SJ. Mrs A Olivieri, 01386 791820, morton.garden@mhcom.co.uk, www.mortonhallgardens.co.uk. *In the centre of Holberrow Green, at a wooden bench around a tree, turn up Morton Hall Lane. You will reach the main gates to Morton Hall on your R. Press intercom to be admitted.* Home-made teas. Tea/coffee & savoury snack for morning visits, tea/coffee & cake for afternoon visits. Unable to cater for special dietary requirements. **Adm £8, chd free. Visitors welcome by arrangement Apr to Sept for groups of 10-20. Adm incl refreshments.**

An elegant stroll garden around a late Georgian house (not open), with potager, hot coloured borders, formalised flower garden, wisteria arbour, large rock garden leading to soft plantings around pools and teahouse, into fritillary meadows with wild roses and towering redwoods. Living roof, Mediterranean plantings, and Ha-Ha with views over vale of Evesham'.

☕

34 NEW HOUSE FARM, ELMBRIDGE

Elmbridge Lane, Elmbridge WR9 0DA. Charles & Carlo Caddick, 01299 851249, Carlocaddick@hotmail.com. *2½ m N of Droitwich Spa. A442 from Droitwich to Cutnall Green. Take lane opp Chequers PH. Go 1m to T-junction. Turn L towards Elmbridge Green/Elmbridge (past church & hall). At T-junction go R into Elmbridge Lane, garden on L.* Home-made teas. **Adm £4, chd free. Sat 9, Sun 10 May, Sat 5, Sun 6 Sept (2-4.30). Visitors also welcome by arrangement May to Sept.**

This charming garden surrounding an early C19 red brick house (not open), has a wealth of rare trees and shrubs under planted with unusual bulbs and herbaceous plants. Special features are the 'perry wheel', ornamental vegetable gardens. Water garden, dry garden, rose garden, mews, the retreat, potager and greenhouse. Topiary and tropical. plants complete the effect. Plant nursery with many exotics for sun and shade. Plant clearance sale. Mews garden not accessible to wheelchairs.

♿ 🏠 ❀ 🚌 ☕

GROUP OPENING

35 **OFFENHAM GARDENS**
Main Street, Offenham WR11 8QD,
01386 424880,
asjames@btinternet.com.
*Approaching Offenham on B4510
from Evesham, L into village signed
Offenham & ferry ¾ m. Follow rd
round into village. Park in village hall
car park opp Church, WR11 8QD.*
Home-made teas. **Combined adm
£4, chd free. Sat 15, Sun 16 Aug
(11-5).**

> **NEW** **DECHMONT**
> Angela & Paul Gash
>
> **LANGDALE**
> Sheila & Adrian James
> www.adrianjames.org.uk
>
> **WILLOWAY**
> Stephen & Linda Pitts

Offenham is a picturesque village in
the heart of the Vale of Evesham, with
thatched cottages and traditional
maypole. Three gardens of diverse
interests from woodland and wildlife
to topiary, herbaceous and exotic.
Langdale is a plant lovers garden
designed for all year round interest.
Surrounding a formal rill are relaxed
lawns and borders in a variety of
styles, from woodland to hot exotic,
leading down to a productive
vegetable garden. Willoway, an oasis
of sound and colour, is initially hidden
by the traditional front garden. A
corridor of Hostas leads the visitor to
the patio, a lush carpet of lawn, and
then, via the bamboo curtain, to the
oriental area. A streptocarpus
collection contains varieties from
Eastern Europe and Japan.
Dechmont is a new addition for 2015.
With a mature walnut tree it features
box topiary, patio areas, year round
interest from conifers, shrubs and
acers, colour from bulbs, perennials,
annuals, clematis and roses set within
curved borders.

❀ ☕

---

36 **NEW** **9 OLD ROAD SOUTH**
Kempsey, Worcester WR5 3NJ.
Anne Potter. *2m S of A4440 jct with
A38. Old Road South can be
accessed off A38 & Squires Walk in
village. Garden is located off a narrow
lane with restricted parking. Please
leave small layby immed opp for Blue
Badge holders.* Home-made teas.
Teas, coffees and cold drinks plus
home made cakes, some made with

home grown ingredients. **Adm £3,
chd free. Fri 31 July, Sat 1 Aug
(10.30-4).**
Third of an acre garden with
expansive views of the Malvern Hills
and open countryside. Established
during the last 6yrs it is a
rustic/country garden with some
modern sculpture. Developed by
plantaholic owner - it has been
described as quirky! Seating area
within young mixed orchard. Flat but
somewhat uneven paths.

🐕 ☕

37 **OVERBURY COURT**
nr Tewkesbury GL20 7NP.
Mr & Mrs Bruce Bossom,
01386 725111(office),
gardens@overburyestate.co.uk. *5m
NE of Tewkesbury. Village signed off
A46, Turn off village rd beside the
church. Park by gates & walk up
drive.* **Adm £4, chd free. Visitors
welcome by arrangement Mar to
Aug for groups of 10+.**
Georgian house 1740 (not open);
landscape garden of same date with
stream and pools; daffodil bank and
grotto. Plane trees; yew hedges;
shrubs; cut flowers; coloured foliage;
gold and silver, shrub rose borders.
Norman church adjoins garden. Close
to Whitcombe and Conderton Manor.
Some slopes, while all the garden can
be viewed, parts are not accessible to
wheelchairs.

♿ 🐕 🚌

38 **PEAR TREE COTTAGE**
Witton Hill, Wichenford, Worcester
WR6 6YX. Pamela & Alistair
Thompson, 01886 888295,
peartree.pam@gmail.com,
www.peartreecottage.me. *13m NW
of Worcester & 2m NE of Martley.
From Martley, take B4197. Turn R into
Horn Lane then first L signed Prickley
Green. Keep R & Pear Tree Cottage is
on L at top of hill.* Home-made teas.
31 Aug - a glass of wine is incl with
adm. **Adm £4, chd free. Sat 30, Sun
31 May (11-6). Evening Opening
£4.50, chd free, wine, Mon 31 Aug
(6-10). Visitors also welcome by
arrangement May to Aug all
visitors VERY welcome!**
A Grade II listed black and white
cottage (not open) with SW-facing
gardens and far reaching views
across orchards to Abberley clock
tower. The gardens extend to approx
¾ acre and comprise of gently
sloping lawns with mixed and
woodland borders, shade and plenty
of strategically placed seating. The

garden exudes a quirky and
humorous character with the odd
surprise! The 'Gardeners' Loo' is
available to visitors. Featured in
Worcestershire Life Magazine. Partial
wheelchair access.

♿ ☕

39 **PERSHORE GARDENS**
Pershore WR10 1BG. Group Coordinator Jan Garratt, 01386
553197, jangarratt@btinternet.com,
www.visitpershore.co.uk. *On
B4084 between Worcester &
Evesham, & 6m from exit 7 on M5.
There is also a train station to the
north of the town.* **Combined adm
£5, chd free. Sat 6, Sun 7 June
(1-5).**
Tickets valid both days. Tickets
available in advance from Tourist
Information and 'Blue' in Broad Street
and on the day at Number 8
Community Arts Centre in the High
Street and any open garden. Explore
20 large and small gardens in the
attractive market town of Pershore.
These incl gardens tucked away
behind Georgian town houses,
gardens which sweep down to the
River Avon, tiny courtyards and
walled gardens and a Primary School
garden. Wheelchair access to some
gardens.

🐕 ❀ 🚌 ☕

Sit and
enjoy the
peaceful
surroundings
and see
how many
different
ferns and
hostas you
can find . . .

The Walled Garden

40 ▶ PUMP COTTAGE
Hill Lane, Weatheroak, nr
Alvechurch B48 7EQ. Barry Knee &
Sue Hunstone, 01564 826250,
barryknee.1947@btinternet.com,
www.pumpcottage.org.uk. *3m E of
Alvechurch. 1¹/₂ m from J3 M42 off
N-bound c'way of A435 (signed
Alvechurch). Parking in adjacent field.*
Home-made teas. Homemade cakes
incl gluten free. **Visitors welcome
by arrangement June only,
individuals or groups are welcome.**
Described by visitors as 'A secret
wonderland, surprises at every turn'.
C19 cottage, rural setting.
Enchanting, romantic 1 acre
plantaholic's garden with yr-round
interest. Colourful borders, roses,
rockery, fernery, water features,
natural pond, and wildlife area.
Creative features, artefacts and
ornaments. Continually evolving,
creation of new bog area and
replanted borders for 2015. Partial
wheelchair access.

41 ◆ RED HOUSE FARM
Flying Horse Lane, Bradley Green,
nr Redditch B96 6QT. Mrs M M
Weaver, 01527 821269,
www.redhousefarmgardenandnurs
ery.co.uk. *7m W of Redditch, 7m E
of Droitwich. On B4090 Alcester to
Droitwich Spa. Ignore sign to Bradley*

Green. Turn opp The Red Lion PH.
Adm £2.50, chd free. **For NGS:
Thurs 5 Mar, 2 Apr, 7 May, 4 June,
2 July, 6 Aug, 3 Sept (12-5).** For
other opening times and
information, please phone or see
garden website.
Created as a peaceful haven from its
working farm environment, this
mature ¹/₂ acre country garden offers
yr-round interest. In densely planted
borders accessed by winding paths a
wide range of traditional favourites
rub shoulders with the newest of
introductions and make each visit a
pleasurable and rewarding
experience. Adjacent nursery open
daily 10-5.

**42 ▶ ◆ RIVERSIDE GARDENS AT
WEBBS**
Wychbold, nr Droitwich WR9 0DG.
Webbs of Wychbold, 01527
860000, www.webbsdirect.co.uk.
*2m N of Droitwich Spa. 1m N of M5
J5 on A38. Follow tourism signs from
M5.* For opening times and
information, please phone or see
garden website.
2¹/₂ acres. Themed gardens incl
Colour spectrum, tropical and dry
garden, New David Austin Rose
collection, new vegetable garden
area, grassery, bamboozelum
Contemplation and self sufficient

Garden. New Wave gardens opened
2004, designer Noel Kingsbury, to
create natural seasonal interest with
grasses and perennials.This area is
now home to beehives which
produce honey for our own food hall.
The New Wave Garden was slightly
changed over 2014 to become more
of a natural wildlife area. There are
willow wigwams made for children to
play in. Open all yr except Christmas,
Boxing Day and Easter Sunday. Our
New Wave Gardens area has grass
paths which are underlaid with mesh
so people with heavy duty
wheelchairs can be taken around.

43 NEW ▶ ROTHBURY
5 St Peters Road, North Malvern
WR14 1QS. John Bryson &
Philippa Lowe. *7m W of M5 J7
(Worcester). Turn off A449 Worcester
to Ledbury Rd at B4503, signed
Leigh Sinton. Almost immed take the
middle rd (Hornyold Rd). St Peter's
Rd is ¹/₄ m uphill, 2nd R.* Light
refreshments. Homemade light
lunches (12-2), cakes and teas. **Adm
£3, chd free. Sat 20 June, Sat 25,
Sun 26 July (11-5.30).**
Set on slopes of Malvern Hills, ¹/₃ acre
garden surrounding Arts and Crafts
house (not open), created by owners
since 1999. Herbaceous borders,
rockery with thyme walk, wildlife

pond, vegetable patch, small orchard, containers. A series of hand-excavated terraces accessed by sloping paths and steps. Views to Lickey Hills and Worcester and of the Malverns. Seats. Mostly accessible. One very low step at entry, one standard step to main lawn and one to WC. Decking slope to top lawn.

44 SHUTTIFIELD COTTAGE

Birchwood, Storridge WR13 5HA. Mr & Mrs David Judge, 01886 884243, judge.shutti@btinternet.com. *8m W of Worcester. Turn R off A4103 opp Storridge Church to Birchwood. After 1¼ m L down steep tarmac drive. Please park on roadside but drive down if walking is difficult (150 yards).* Tea. **Adm £5, chd free. Sats 25 Apr, 2, 23 May, 20 June, 11 July, 29 Aug (1.30-5). Visitors also welcome by arrangement Apr to Oct.**
Superb position and views. Unexpected 3-acre plantsman's garden, extensive herbaceous borders, primula and stump bed, many unusual trees, shrubs, perennials, colour-themed for all-yr interest. Walks in 20-acre wood with ponds, natural wild areas, anemones, bluebells, rhododendrons, azaleas are a particular spring feature. Large old rose garden with many spectacular mature climbers. Good garden colour throughout the yr. Small deer park, vegetable garden. Wildlife ponds, wild flowers and walks in 20 acres of ancient woodland. Featured on Gardeners World and many publications.

45 ◆ SPETCHLEY PARK GARDENS

Spetchley WR5 1RS. Mr John Berkeley, www.spetchleygardens.co.uk. *2m E of Worcester. On A44, follow brown signs.* Light refreshments. and afternoon teas available. **Adm £6.50, chd £2. For NGS: Fri 3 Apr, Sun 5 July (11-6). For other opening times and information, please see garden website.**
Surrounded by glorious countryside lays one of Britain's best-kept secrets. Spetchley is a garden for all tastes containing one of the biggest private collections of plant varieties outside the major botanical gardens. Spetchley is not a formal paradise of neatly manicured lawns or beds but rather a wondrous display of plants,

shrubs and trees woven into a garden of many rooms and vistas. Spetchley hosts 2 Specialist plant fairs in April and Sept. We have received recent press coverage for the Spetchley Revival Project which has received funding from both DEFRA and HLF for projects designed to improve the visitor experience. Gravel paths.

The Queen's Nursing Institute

We help improve patient care in the community

46 ◆ STONE HOUSE COTTAGE GARDENS

Stone DY10 4BG. James & Louisa Arbuthnott, 07817 921146, www.shcn.co.uk. *2m SE of Kidderminster. Via A448 towards Bromsgrove, next to church, turn up drive.* **For opening times and information, please phone or see garden website.**
A beautiful and romantic walled garden adorned with unusual brick follies. This acclaimed garden is exuberantly planted and holds one of the largest collections of rare plants in the country. It acts as a shop window for the adjoining nursery. Open Wed to Sat late March to early Sept 10-5. Partial wheelchair access.

47 TOLL HOUSE COTTAGE

Stourport Road, Bewdley DY12 1PU. Joan & Rob Roberts, 01299 402331, joanroberts7@live.co.uk. *1m S of Bewdley, 2m N of Stourport, 3m W of Kidderminster. On A456 between Bewdley & Stourport, Opp Blackstone car park & picnic site (free parking). Disabled parking on drive.* Home-made teas. **Adm £3.50, chd free. Sun 24 May (10-4.30); Sun 19 July (10-5). Visitors also welcome by arrangement 18 May to end Aug min 10 max 30.**
Developing ½ acre garden started in 2008 in 2 sections. Cottage garden

with a collection of bulbs, herbaceous and shrubs for year round colour incl lawn. A small arboretum with grass walkways and summerhouse. A large pool with waterfall and beach for wildlife. Vegetable garden with raised beds in large fruit cage. A painters garden. Gallery for Woodturning and Paintings also open for viewing.

48 THE TYNINGS

Church Lane, Stoulton, nr Worcester WR7 4RE. John & Leslie Bryant, 01905 840189, johnlesbryant@btinternet.com. *5m S of Worcester; 3m N of Pershore. On the B4084 (formerly A44) between M5 J7 & Pershore. The Tynings lies beyond the church at the extreme end of Church Lane. Ample parking.* Light refreshments. **Adm £3, chd free. Visitors welcome by arrangement July to Sept.**
Acclaimed plantsman's ½ -acre garden, generously planted with a large selection of rare trees and shrubs. Features incl specialist collection of lilies, many unusual climbers and rare ferns. The colour continues into late summer with dahlia, berberis, euonymus and tree colour. Surprises around every corner. You will not be disappointed. Lovely views of adjacent Norman Church and surrounding countryside. Plants labelled and plant lists available. Further info and photos on NGS website.

49 THE WALLED GARDEN

6 Rose Terrace, off Fort Royal Hill, Worcester WR5 1BU. William & Julia Scott. *Close to the City centre. ½ m from Cathedral. Via Fort Royal Hill, off London Rd (A44). Park on 1st section of Rose Terrace & walk the last 20yds down track.* Tea. **Adm £3.50, chd free. Sat 18, Wed 22 Apr (1-5).**
In this peaceful oasis of scent and colour, a tapestry of culinary and medicinal herbs, vegetables, flowers and fruit grow organically. History, symmetry and historic references are the foundation of this C19 walled kitchen garden which is seasonally evolving with new projects and planting schemes. Common and rare herbs, maturing fruit trees incl Mulberry, Medlar and Quince. Featured in Cotswold Life, Worcestershire Now.

50 WESTACRES
Wolverhampton Road, Prestwood, Stourbridge DY7 5AN. Mrs Joyce Williams, 01384 877496. *3m W of Stourbridge. A449 in between Wall Heath (2m) & Kidderminster (6m). Ample parking Prestwood Nurseries (next door).* **Adm £4, chd free. Sat 18, Sun 19 July (11-4). Visitors also welcome by arrangement June to Aug.**
³/₄-acre plant collector's garden with unusual plants and many different varieties of acers, hostas, shrubs. Woodland walk, large koi pool. Covered tea area with home-made cakes. Come and see for yourselves, you won't be disappointed. Described by a visitor in the visitors book as 'A garden which we all wished we could have, at least once in our lifetime'. Plants for Sale. Garden split up into different areas. Garden is flat. Disabled parking.

 ♿ 🐕 🌼 ☕

Developed by plantaholic owner - it has been described as quirky . . . !

51 WHITCOMBE HOUSE
Overbury, nr Tewkesbury GL20 7NZ. Faith & Anthony Hallett, 01386 725206, faith.hallett1@gmail.com. *9m S of Evesham, 5m NE Tewkesbury. Leave A46 at Beckford to Overbury (2m). Or B4080 from Tewkesbury through Bredon/Kemerton (5m). Or small lane signed Overbury at roundabout junction A46, A435 and B4077. Approx 5m from J9 on M5.* Tea. **Adm £3.50, chd free. Sun 29 Mar, Sun 10 May, Sun 14 June (2-5). Visitors also welcome by arrangement Mar to Sept evening visits (with wine) also possible.**
1 acre planted for every season in an idyllic Cotswold stone setting. Spring

bulbs give way to cool blue and white, allium and flowering shrubs are followed by cascading roses, summer pastels and fiery oranges, red and yellows. The spring-fed stream flows through colourful moisture loving plants. Asters, cosmos and yet more roses provide late summer colour. Lots of seats for relaxation. For easiest wheelchair access please contact us in advance for details.

 ♿ 🐕 🌼 🚐 ☕

52 WHITE COTTAGE
Earls Common Road, Stock Green, nr Inkberrow B96 6SZ. Mr & Mrs S M Bates, 01386 792414, smandjbates@aol.com. *2m W of Inkberrow, 2m E of Upton Snodsbury. A422 Worcester to Alcester, turn at sign for Stock Green by Red Hart PH, 1¹/₂ m to T- junction, turn L 500 yds on the L.* **Adm £3, chd free. Sun 5, Mon 6 Apr, Suns 17 May, 21 June, 19 July, 6 Sept, 11 Oct (11-4.30). Visitors also welcome by arrangement Apr to Oct groups up to 10+.**
2 acre garden with large herbaceous and shrub borders, island beds, stream and bog area. Spring meadow with 100's of snakes head fritillaries. Formal area with lily pond and circular rose garden. Alpine rockery and new fern area. Large collection of interesting trees incl Nyssa Sylvatica, Parrotia persica, and Acer 'October Glory' for magnificent Autumn colour and many others. Gravel drive to the gate but it is manageable.

 ♿ 🌼 🚐

53 ◆ WHITLENGE GARDENS
Whitlenge Lane, Hartlebury DY10 4HD. Mr & Mrs K J Southall, 01299 250720, www.whitlenge.co.uk. *5m S of Kidderminster, on A442. A449 Kidderminster to Worcester L at T-lights, A442 signed Droitwich, over island, ¹/₄ m, 1st R into Whitlenge Lane. Follow brown signs.* Light refreshments. **Adm £4, chd free. For NGS: Sats, Suns 14, 15 Feb, 11, 12 Apr, 30, 31 May, 5, 6 Sept (10-5). For other opening times and information, please phone or see garden website.**
3 acre show garden of professional designer with over 800 varieties of trees, shrubs etc. Twisted pillar pergola, camomile lawn, waterfalls and pools. Mystic features of the Green Man, 'Sword in the Stone' and cave fernery. Walk the labyrinth and

take refreshments in The Garden 'Design Studio' tearoom. 400 sq metre grass labyrinth, 2¹/₂ metre high brick and oak moongate with 4 cascading waterfalls, deck walk through giant gunnera leaves, camomile paths through herb gardens, childrens play and pet corner. Locally sourced homemade food in tearoom, plant nursery.

 ♿ 🌼 🚐 ☕

GROUP OPENING

54 WICK VILLAGE
Pershore WR10 3NU. Co-ordinator Kate Smart, 01386 550007, kate.tudorhall@gmail.com. *1m E of Pershore on B4084. Signed to Wick is almost opp Pershore Horticultural College.* Home-made teas at Aalsmeer. Ice creams and cold drinks available at 'The Barn'. **Combined adm £5, chd free. Sun 5 July (1.30-6).**

AALSMEER
Main Street. Peter Edmunds

THE BARN
Main Street. Alison & David Scott

CONFETTI FIELD
Yock Lane. Charles Hudson www.confettidirect.co.uk

NEW **THE COTTAGE**
Cooks Hill. Mr & Mrs Lindsey & Giovanni Wilkes

LAMBOURNE HOUSE
Main Street. Mr & Mrs G Power

THE OLD FORGE
Main Street. Sean & Elaine Young

RYECOT
Owletts Lane. Margaret & Michael Williams

TUDOR HALL Ⓓ
Main Street. Mr D & Mrs A Smart

VENEDIGER
Wick House Close. Alan & Barbara de Ville

5 WICK HOUSE CLOSE
Jill & Martin Willams

WILLOW CORNER
Wick House Close. Marjorie Donaldson

NEW **WOODBINE COTTAGES**
Main Street. Mr & Mrs Raymond Day

WYKE MANOR
Main Street. Charles Hudson

Our gardens for 2015 offer the visitor a range of delightful garden experiences from the spectacle of 25 acres of confetti fields to compact and colourful, cottage gardens incl delicious vegetables. As we open every other year, regular visitors will notice we have some new gardens open for the first time as well as some 'unexpected gems' that we know you'll love to explore again. You can visit the romantic and picturesque Wyke Manor gardens, gardens with plenty of well-stocked herbaceous borders, productive fruit and vegetable plots and magical ponds teeming with wildlife. You can also visit gardens that have been recently redesigned to meet familiar horticultural challenges proving that 'low maintenance' gardening is not synonymous with a lack of creativity or beautiful planting. To make your visit more leisurely we are also running a free minibus service up and down the village to save your feet for those well-tended lawns. Wick is the home of The Real Flower Petal Company. As seen on Michael Portillo's 'Great Railway Journeys'. Many of the gardens are suitable for wheelchair access.

& 🎍 ⊛ 🚐 ☕

---

55 68 WINDSOR AVENUE
St Johns, Worcester WR2 5NB. Roger & Barbara Parker. *W area of Worcester, W side of R Severn. Off the A44 to Bromyard Rd into Comer Rd, 3rd L into Laugherne Rd, 3rd L into Windsor Ave, at bottom in Cul-de-sac. Limited parking, please park courteously on road side, car share if possible.* Home-made teas. Soft drinks also available. **Adm £4, chd free. Sat 23, Sun 24 May (11-4).**
Almost one acre garden divided into three areas, situated behind a 1930's semi detached house in a cul-de-sac, visitors are amazed and often comment on size of garden. Garden incl bog garden, flower beds, oriental area, vegetable patch, four greenhouses and four ponds each in very different styles. If that is not enough we have Chickens, Quayle, ornamental Pheasants and Finches. Gravel paths are everywhere.

⊛ ☕

GROUP OPENING

56 WITHYBED GREEN
Alvechurch B48 7PP. *3m N of Redditch, 11m SW of Birmingham. 6mins from J2 of M42. From Alvechurch centre take Tanyard Lane or Bear Hill. Follow NGS signs along Snake Lane & Withybed Lane. Rail Alvechurch Stn.* Home-made teas on Parking Field. **Combined adm £5, chd free. Sun 21 June (1-6).**

FAIRVIEW
Birches Lane. Bryan & Angela Haycocks

2 FRONT COTTAGES
Ann & Clive Southern

NEW 3 FRONT COTTAGES
Andy & Annie Fincham

6 FRONT COTTAGES
Mr & Mrs Horne

THE MOUSEHOLE
4 Forward Cottages. David & Lucy Hastie

6 REAR COTTAGES
John Adams & Amelda Brown

SELVAS COTTAGE
Birches Lane. Mr & Mrs J L Plewes

7 varied gardens (one new this year) opening biennially. Withybed Green is a secret hamlet to the W of Alvechurch set between semi-wooded hillsides and the Birmingham Worcester Canal. The gardens include a rose garden, ancient woodland, allotments, small cottage gardens and a stream-side walk. Withybed Green is compact and in a charming environment and you can easily walk round all seven gardens. The houses and cottages mostly date from C19, built for farm workers, nail makers, canal and railway builders. Withybed has its own canal-side PH, The Crown.

🎍 ⊛ ☕

---

57 THE WOODLANDS
Dunclent, Stone, Kidderminster DY10 4AY. Pat & Phil Gaskin, 01562 740795, thewoodlands1@yahoo.co.uk. *2m SE of Kidderminster. A448 Bromsgrove Rd. Turn into Dunclent Lane, follow signs down narrow lane onto unadopted rd, short distance. Parking in adjoining field.* Home-made teas. **Adm £6, chd free. Visitors welcome by arrangement** June to July groups of 8 +. (adm incl refreshments).

Intriguing approx ¾ -acre garden in rural woodland, open fields haven. Developed last 9yrs, designed on various levels, with secret winding paths, steps to coloured themed herbaceous/shrub borders, large vegetable garden, tomato/cucumber greenhouses. Courtyard, waterfall, pergola walk, pond, swimming pool, hanging baskets and tubs of flowers, a very attractive colourful garden. Attractive and unusual waterfall linking one level of the garden to another. Interesting garden on many levels. Featured in Kidderminster Shuttle. Partial wheelchair access to lower level of garden would be able to access refreshment area.

& ⊛ ☕

Old water mill, brook runs through garden . . .

---

58 NEW WORRALLS MILL
Netherton Lane, Abberley DY13 0UL. Mr & Mrs B J Merriman. *3m SW of Stourport-on-Severn. From Stourport-on-Severn take Gt Witley rd over R Severn. Continue to sign for Dunley on L, take 2nd turn on R Heightington tel box on corner, top of lane, turn L Abberley into Netherton Lane, along over bridge 1st R. Park in lane, parking by house for less abled visitors.* Home-made teas. **Adm £5, chd free. Sat 13, Sun 14 June, Sat 8, Sun 9 Aug (11-5).**
Old water mill, brook runs through garden. Large trees, oak, ash, shrubs and red bridge at front of house. Back of house, terracing, hot bed, mixed borders, pergola to 'jungle', bamboo, fatsia etc. Fish pond; large pool (wildlife) in what was once mill race bog; garden stream; old woodland. Approx ¼ m long, 2 acres. Gravel paths and some steps.

& ☕

YORKSHIRE

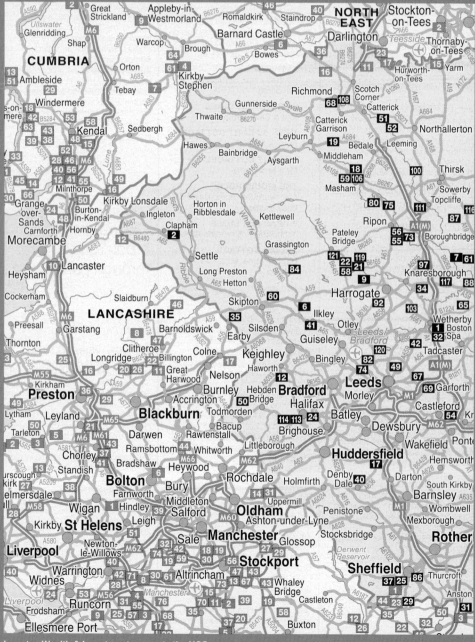

Yorkshire

Yorkshire, England's largest county, stretches from the Pennines in the west to the rugged coast and sandy beaches of the east: a rural landscape of moors, dales, vales and rolling wolds.

Nestling on riverbanks lie many historic market towns, and in the deep valleys of the west and south others retain their 19th century industrial heritage of coal, steel and textiles.

The wealth generated by these industries supported the many great estates, houses and gardens throughout the county. From Hull in the east, a complex network of canals weaves its way across the county, connecting cities to the sea and beyond.

The Victorian spa town of Harrogate with the RHS garden at Harlow Carr, or the historic city of York with a minster encircled by Roman walls, are both ideal centres from which to explore the gardens and cultural heritage of the county.

There are many NGS gardens to choose from, the majority of which enjoy visits from groups – Parcevall Hall in the west, Newby Hall near Ripon, Scampston Hall with a Piet Oudolf designed walled garden, and Burton Agnes Hall in the east are gardens for all seasons and are among the finest of all English gardens.

Yorkshire Volunteers

County Organisers

East Yorks
Louise Martin
01430 422266
louisem200@hotmail.co.uk

North Yorks – Cleveland, Hambleton, Richmond, Rydale & Scarborough
Josephine Marks
01845 501626
jlmarks60@gmail.com

West & South Yorks & North Yorks - Craven, Harrogate, Selby & York
Bridget Marshall
01423 330474
biddymarshall@btopenworld.com

County Treasurer
Angela Pugh
01423 330456
amjopugh@clannet.co.uk

Publicity
Jane Cooper 01484 604232
coopers_shepley@btinternet.com

Booklet Advertising
John Plant
01347 888125
plantjohnsgarden@btinternet.com

Assistant County Organisers

Clubs & Societies
John Plant
(as above)

East Yorks
Kirstin de Morgan 01759 369653
k.demorgan@btinternet.com

Helen Marsden 01430 860222
jerryhelen@btinternet.com

Ian & Linda McGowan 01482 896492
adnil_magoo@yahoo.com

Natalie Verow 01759 368444
natalieverow@aol.com

Kate Willans 01964 534502
kwkatewillans32@gmail.com

North Yorks
Gillian Mellor 01723 891636
gill.mellor@btconnect.com

Hugh Norton 01653 628604
hughnorton0@gmail.com

Judi Smith 01765 688565
lowsutton@hotmail.co.uk

West & South Yorks
Deborah Bigley 01609 748915
debsandbobbigley@btinternet.com

Felicity Bowring 01729 823551
diss@austwick.org

Veronica Brook 01423 340875
veronicabowring@me.com

Rosie Hamlin 01302 535135
rosiehamlin@aol.com

Jane Hudson 01924 840980
janehudson42@btinternet.com

Right: Burton Agnes Hall & Gardens

Currently the NGS donates around £2.5 million every year

Opening Dates

All entries subject to change.
For latest information check www.ngs.org.uk

February

Sunday 22
23 Devonshire Mill

Wednesday 25
2 Austwick Hall

March

Saturday 21
28 Fawley House

Sunday 22
28 Fawley House
34 Goldsborough Hall
40 Highfields

April

Thursday 2
46 Hotham Hall

Thursday 9
46 Hotham Hall

Sunday 12
18 Clifton Castle

Sunday 19
1 Acorn Cottage
27 Ellerker House
32 Four Gables
40 Highfields
48 Jackson's Wold

Wednesday 22
7 NEW Beechcroft Farmhouse

Sunday 26
17 The Circles Garden
51 Langton Farm
92 RHS Garden Harlow Carr

May

Sunday 3
53 Linden Lodge
91 Rewela Cottage
117 Whixley Gardens

Monday 4
53 Linden Lodge
117 Whixley Gardens

Saturday 9
115 Weathervane House

Sunday 10
58 Low Hall
105 Stillingfleet Lodge
110 Terrington House
113 Warley House Garden
119 Woodlands Cottage

Wednesday 13
6 Beacon Hill House
113 Warley House Garden

Saturday 16
90 The Red House

Sunday 17
42 Hillbark
78 NEW Oakley Garth
90 The Red House
94 NEW Rosebank

Wednesday 20
84 Parcevall Hall Gardens

Sunday 24
5 Beacon Garth
93 The Ridings

Saturday 30
80 Old Sleningford Hall
122 The Yorkshire Arboretum

Sunday 31
12 Brookfield
20 The Court
37 16 Hallam Grange Croft
69 Millrace Nursery
77 Nutkins & New House, Hornsea
80 Old Sleningford Hall

June

24 **Dove Cottage Nursery Garden (every Friday)**

Wednesday 3
12 Brookfield
41 5 Hill Top

Thursday 4
101 Skipwith Hall

Friday 5
98 Shandy Hall Gardens (Evening)

Festival Weekend

Saturday 6
14 Burton Agnes Hall & Gardens
47 Hunmanby Grange
99 Shiptonthorpe Gardens

Sunday 7
14 Burton Agnes Hall & Gardens
41 5 Hill Top
47 Hunmanby Grange
57 Lockington Gardens
65 Marston Grange
70 NEW 23 Molescroft Road
99 Shiptonthorpe Gardens

Wednesday 10
87 Pilmoor Cottages

Friday 12
28 Fawley House

Saturday 13
28 Fawley House
52 NEW Langton Hall

Sunday 14
28 Fawley House
63 NEW The Manor House
64 Mansion Cottage
68 Millgate House
75 Norton Conyers
85 NEW Penny Piece Cottages
103 NEW Spofforth Gardens
108 Swale Cottage

Wednesday 17
87 Pilmoor Cottages

Friday 19
98 Shandy Hall Gardens (Evening)
112 Tickton CE Primary

Saturday 20
45 Holmfield
81 Omega
100 NEW Sion Hill
121 Yorke House

Sunday 21
9 Birstwith Hall
26 Dowthorpe Hall & Horse Pasture Cottage
45 Holmfield
48 Jackson's Wold
54 Little Eden
59 Low Sutton
61 Maidens Folly
78 NEW Oakley Garth
81 Omega
88 The Priory, Nun Monkton & Village Gardens
94 NEW Rosebank
100 NEW Sion Hill
106 Sutton Grange
121 Yorke House

Lawns and seating areas providing different aspects of the garden . . .

Wednesday 24
35 The Grange

Friday 26
16 Churchside

Saturday 27
16 Churchside

Sunday 28
7 NEW Beechcroft Farmhouse
8 Beverley Hidden Town Gardens
16 Churchside
25 34 Dover Road
29 Fernleigh
43 NEW 2 Hollin Close
68 Millgate House
71 Neakins House
72 Ness Hall
82 The Orchard
109 NEW Tamarind

July

24 **Dove Cottage Nursery Garden (every Friday)**

Friday 3
86 NEW Pictorial Meadows
98 Shandy Hall Gardens (Evening)

Saturday 4
86 NEW Pictorial Meadows
102 Sleightholmedale Lodge

Sunday 5
22 Dacre Banks & Summerbridge Gardens
30 Fernwood
34 Goldsborough Hall
38 Havoc Hall
42 Hillbark
44 54 Hollym Road
93 The Ridings
95 Rustic Cottage
102 Sleightholmedale Lodge

Saturday 11
13 Bugthorpe Gardens
15 Cawood Gardens
107 NEW Sutton upon Derwent School
118 NEW Whyncrest

Sunday 12
13 Bugthorpe Gardens
15 Cawood Gardens
114 NEW Warley Village
118 NEW Whyncrest

Sunday 19
39 NEW 20 Highfield Road
76 The Nursery
79 Oatmill Cottage

Visit a garden on National Gardens Festival Weekend 6 & 7 June

111 NEW Thornycroft

Wednesday 22
76 The Nursery

Friday 24
67 Mere'stead (Evening)

Sunday 26
21 Cow Close Cottage
29 Fernleigh
49 The Jungle Garden
89 Queensgate & Kitchen Lane Allotments
91 Rewela Cottage

August

24 Dove Cottage Nursery Garden (every Friday)

Sunday 2
55 Littlethorpe Gardens
69 Millrace Nursery
104 Stamford Bridge Gardens

Wednesday 5
97 NEW Serenity

Saturday 8
64 Mansion Cottage

Sunday 9
64 Mansion Cottage
97 NEW Serenity

Wednesday 12
35 The Grange
74 2 Newlay Grove

Sunday 23
36 NEW Greenwick Farm
54 Little Eden

Sunday 30
29 Fernleigh
87 Pilmoor Cottages

Monday 31
10 Bridge Farm House

September

Sunday 6
62 Manor Farm
105 Stillingfleet Lodge

Saturday 12
53 Linden Lodge

Sunday 13
53 Linden Lodge

October

Sunday 4
66 Maspin House

Sunday 11
66 Maspin House

February 2016

Sunday 21
23 Devonshire Mill

Wednesday 24
2 Austwick Hall

Gardens open to the public

14 Burton Agnes Hall & Gardens
19 Constable Burton Hall Gardens
48 Jackson's Wold
50 Land Farm
73 Newby Hall & Gardens
75 Norton Conyers
84 Parcevall Hall Gardens
86 NEW Pictorial Meadows
92 RHS Garden Harlow Carr
96 Scampston Walled Garden
98 Shandy Hall Gardens
105 Stillingfleet Lodge
111 NEW Thornycroft
120 York Gate
122 The Yorkshire Arboretum

By arrangement only

3 3 Bainton Close
4 Basin Howe Farm
11 Brook Farm
31 Firvale Allotment Garden
33 Friars Hill
56 Littlethorpe Manor
60 Lower Heugh Cottage Garden
83 Orchard House
116 The White House

Also open by arrangement

5 Beacon Garth
9 Birstwith Hall
10 Bridge Farm House
12 Brookfield
13 3 Church Walk, Bugthorpe Gardens
13 The Old Rectory, Bugthorpe Gardens
15 9 Anson Grove, Cawood Gardens
15 21 Great Close, Cawood Gardens
15 The Pigeoncote, Cawood Gardens
20 The Court
21 Cow Close Cottage
22 Dacre Banks & Summerbridge Gardens
23 Devonshire Mill
25 34 Dover Road
26 Dowthorpe Hall & Horse Pasture Cottage
28 Fawley House
29 Fernleigh
30 Fernwood
34 Goldsborough Hall
35 The Grange
37 16 Hallam Grange Croft
45 Holmfield
46 Hotham Hall
49 The Jungle Garden
51 Langton Farm
53 Linden Lodge
54 Little Eden
55 Greencroft, Littlethorpe Gardens
58 Low Hall
64 Mansion Cottage
66 Maspin House
69 Millrace Nursery
72 Ness Hall
77 Nutkins & New House, Hornsea
79 Oatmill Cottage
81 Omega
82 The Orchard
85 NEW Penny Piece Cottages
87 Pilmoor Cottages
91 Rewela Cottage
93 The Ridings
95 Rustic Cottage
97 NEW Serenity
99 Field View, Shiptonthorpe Gardens
102 Sleightholmedale Lodge
104 Stamford Bridge Gardens
113 Warley House Garden
117 Cobble Cottage, Whixley Gardens
117 The Old Vicarage, Whixley Gardens
118 NEW Whyncrest
119 Woodlands Cottage
121 Yorke House

Hunmanby Grange

Find a garden near you – download our free Android app

The Gardens

1 ACORN COTTAGE

50 Church Street, Boston Spa LS23 6DN. Andrew Froggatt & Tim Froggatt. *1m SE of Wetherby. Off A1 on A659 Church St opp Central Garage.* **Combined adm with Four Gables £4, chd free. Sun 19 Apr (12.30-5).**
Small, well-established alpine garden full of spring delights. Three generations of the family have collected the plants and bulbs, and these have recently been rearranged and the garden significantly altered for ease of maintenance and access without losing the character and uniqueness of this fine collection.

2 AUSTWICK HALL

Town Head Lane, Austwick, nr Settle LA2 8BS. James E Culley & Michael Pearson, 015242 51794, austwickhall@austwick.org, www.austwickhall.co.uk. *5m W of Settle. Leave the A65 to Austwick. Pass the PO on R, Gamecock Inn on L. Take first L onto Town Head Lane. Parking on Town Head Lane.* Home-made teas. **Adm £4, chd free. Wed 25 Feb, Wed 24 Feb 2016 (12-4).**
Set in the dramatic limestone scenery of the Dales the garden nestles into a steeply wooded hillside. Extensive drifts of common single and double snowdrops are an impressive sight with examples of over 50 other varieties. Sculptures along the trail add further interest. Woodland paths may be slippery in wet weather so sensible footwear is recommended.

3 3 BAINTON CLOSE

Beverley HU17 7DL. Mrs Elaine Thornton, 01482 861643. *Located off New Walk opp Police Station. Please use address at 'final destination', as SatNav takes you to next lane.* **Adm £2.50, chd free. Visitors welcome by arrangement Feb 15 to 22 Feb 10.30-3 for groups of 1-10.**
Small town garden with a variety of spring flowers incl hellebores and a collection of approx 150 varieties of snowdrop which will be of particular interest to 'Galanthophiles'.

Winding paths lead through series of smaller gardens with different planting themes . . .

4 BASIN HOWE FARM

Cockmoor Road, Sawdon, Scarborough YO13 9EG. Mr & Mrs Richard & Heather Mullin, 01723 850180, info@basinhowefarm.co.uk, www.basinhowefarm.co.uk. *Turn off A170 between Scarborough & Pickering at Brompton by Sawdon follow sign to Sawdon. Basin Howe Farm 1 1/2 m above Sawdon village on the L.* Home-made teas. Refreshments by arrangement for a small charge. **Adm £5, chd free. Visitors welcome by arrangement May to Aug (not Sats).**
These gardens have a lovely atmosphere. 3 acres of garden with rose garden, box parterre with seasonal planting and koi pond, herbaceous borders, wildlife ponds and elevated viewing deck with Pod summer house. Orchard and woodland shelter belt, lawns and shrubs. Paved seating areas but gravel paths. Basin Howe is high above the Wolds and has a Bronze Age Burial Mound. Maintained by owners. Winners of Gold and Overall Category Winners for Yorkshire in Bloom 2014, and Garden of the Year in Scarborough in Bloom 2014. Wheelchair Access is possible to most areas but a helper is required. Paths are gravel and grass.

5 BEACON GARTH

Redcliff Road, Hessle, Hull HU13 0HA. Ivor & June Innes, 01482 646140, ivorinnes@mac.com. *4 1/2 m W of Hull. Follow signs for Hessle Foreshore.* Home-made teas. **Adm £4, chd free. Sun 24 May (12-5). Visitors also welcome by arrangement Apr to July.**
Edwardian, Arts & Crafts House (mentioned in Peysner's Guide to Hull) and S-facing garden set in 3 1/2 acres, in an elevated position overlooking the Humber. Stunning sunken rock garden with bulbs and specimen trees, hostas and ferns. Mature trees, large lawns and herbaceous borders. Gravel paths, haha, box hedges and topiary. Child friendly; children's play area. Teas served in main hallway of house. Partial wheelchair access.

6 BEACON HILL HOUSE

Langbar, nr Ilkley LS29 0EU. Mr & Mrs H Boyle. *4m NW of Ilkley. 1 1/4 m SE of A59 at Bolton Bridge.* Home-made teas. **Adm £4, chd free. Share to Riding for the Disabled. Wed 13 May (1.30-5).**
Look over the garden wall onto a grouse moor. This 7-acre 'intake', steeply sloping but gardened since 1848, is a spring paradise with early rhododendrons, magnolias and bulbs. Roses, large scented rhododendrons and borders take over, some unusual trees, an established liriodendron, pterostyrax, hoherias and several species of eucryphia. Small kitchen garden, orchard and pond.

7 NEW BEECHCROFT FARMHOUSE

Aldwark, nr Alne, York YO61 1UB. Alison Pollock. *14m NW of York, 17m E of Harrogate, 7m SW of Easingwold. Follow signs for Aldwark Manor hotel & golf course for village. Approach from A1(M) and W is via Aldwark Toll Bridge (40p toll for cars).* Home-made teas. **Adm £3.50, chd free. Wed 22 Apr, Sun 28 June (1-5).**
Country garden surrounding Georgian farmhouse (not open). All yr interest starts with rare snowdrops, hellebores and borders for winter colour. Winding paths lead through series of smaller gardens with different planting themes. Cottage borders with old roses, tulips, clematis. Hidden areas with seating give a secluded feel. Gravel courtyard with small formal pool, late and unusual perennials and grasses.

GROUP OPENING

8 BEVERLEY HIDDEN TOWN GARDENS

Beverley HU17 8JH. *Centre of Beverley. Starting from the West Towers of Beverley Minster, proceed to Minster Moorgate, continue 50yds & enter L St Matthews Court, Railway St HU17 0DX is short walk away.* **Combined adm £4, chd free.** Sun 28 June (11-4).

30 RAILWAY STREET
Wendy Munday

32 RAILWAY STREET
M Williamson

34 RAILWAY STREET
S Clay

16 ST MATTHEWS COURT
off Minster Moorgate. Annegret Aveyard

Four town gardens. 16 St Matthews Court: front garden overlooking spectacular West Towers of Beverley Minster. A rich collection of hellebores, tulips, grasses and other spring flowers. Hidden garden at back features many perennials, roses, climbers, annuals and grasses, Mediterranean area with different succulents and small pond with water plants. Has been described as giving a Continental feel with its modern art work. 30 Railway Street: through spectacular 'triumphal arch' is an amazing display of climbers, pots and water feature. 32 Railway Street: a relatively new courtyard garden extensively planted with a variety of ferns, shrubs and climbers - a predominantly white and green colour scheme provides a calm, tranquil and relaxing atmosphere.
34 Railway Street: paved, creatively planted courtyard. All 3 Railway Street gardens have a S aspect and tender plants thrive. In 'Beverley in Bloom' 32 Railway St won the Gold medal for individual gardens, and the 3 other gardens in the group won Silver Gilt medals.

9 BIRSTWITH HALL

High Birstwith, Harrogate HG3 2JW. Sir James & Lady Aykroyd, 01423 770250, info@birstwithhall.co.uk. *5m NW of Harrogate. Between Hampsthwaite & Birstwith villages, close to A59 Harrogate/Skipton Rd.* Home-made teas. **Adm £4, chd free.** Sun 21 June (2-5). **Visitors also welcome**

by arrangement May to July groups and coaches welcome. Large 8 acre garden nestling in secluded Yorkshire dale with formal garden and ornamental orchard, extensive lawns, picturesque stream, large pond and Victorian greenhouse.

Picnics welcome so bring your Teddy Bears down to our woodland area . . .

10 BRIDGE FARM HOUSE

Long Lane, Great Heck, nr Selby DN14 0BE. Barbara & Richard Ferrari, 01977 661277, barbaraferrari@mypostoffice.co.uk. *6m S of Selby, 3m E M62 J34. At M62 J34 take A19 to Selby, at r'about turn E to Snaith on A645. R at T-lights, L at T-junction onto Main St, past Church, to T-junction, cross to car park (opp).* **Adm £3, chd free.** Mon 31 Aug (12-4.30). **Visitors also welcome by arrangement. Snowdrop enthusiasts mid Feb-mid March.**
2-acre garden on sandy soil, divided by hedges to house a varied collection of plants: many unusual and rarely seen elsewhere, providing year round colour and interest, starting in Spring with a collection of named snowdrops. Including mature trees, bog, gravel, ponds, long double mixed borders, hens, compost heaps and wildlife. Come and see - not featured in any publications!

11 BROOK FARM

Elstronwick, Hull HU12 9BP. Mrs Janet Dolling, 01964 670191. *10m E of Hull city centre. Go N on Hedon to Withernsea Rd. Turn off L before Burton Pidsea. Go down Back Lane. Garden at junction of Elstronwick & Danthorpe, next to beck bridge.* **Adm £3, chd free. Visitors welcome by arrangement** Feb to May for groups of 2 - 25.
Plantsman's garden with large collection of Hellebores. ³/₄ acre with borders, gravel and formal areas.

Many species of snowdrops, hellebores and narcissus, tulips and peonies. Large vegetable and fruit garden. Wooded area with large collection of woodland plants. Flowering and ornamental trees.

12 BROOKFIELD

Jew Lane, Oxenhope, nr Keighley BD22 9HS. Mrs R L Belsey, 01535 643070. *5m SW of Keighley. From Keighley take A629 (Halifax) Fork R A6033 towards Haworth & Oxenhope turn L at Xrds into village. Turn R (Jew Lane) at bottom of hill.* Home-made teas. Biscuits. **Adm £4, chd free.** Sun 31 May, Wed 3 June (1.30-5.30). **Visitors also welcome by arrangement May to Aug.**
1-acre, intimate garden, incl large pond with an island, mallards and wild geese also greylags. Many varieties of primula, candelabra and florindae; azaleas and rhododendrons. Unusual trees and shrubs, screes, greenhouses and conservatory. Series of island beds. Children's quiz and garden notes. Featured in Yorkshire Ridings Magazine. Partial wheelchair access - steep slope and steps.

GROUP OPENING

13 BUGTHORPE GARDENS

York YO41 1QG. *4m E of Stamford Bridge, A166, village of Bugthorpe.* Tea at The Old Rectory. Toilets in Village Hall. **Combined adm £5, chd free.** Sat 11, Sun 12 July (10.30-4.30).

3 CHURCH WALK
York. Barrie Creaser & David Fielding
Visitors also welcome by arrangement for 15 max.
01759 368152
barriecreaser@gmail.com

THE OLD RECTORY
Dr & Mrs P W Verow.
House 1st on R from A166 (York direction)
Visitors also welcome by arrangement July, near weekend of opening, max 15.
01759 368444
natalieverow@aol.com

Two contrasting gardens situated in the small village of Bugthorpe. The Old Rectory is a ³/₄ acre garden with views of the Yorkshire Wolds.

Mixed borders, ponds, stumpery, terrace, summerhouse, courtyard and many mature trees. Raised vegetable beds. Artist in the garden and herbaceous perennials for sale. 3 Church Walk a cottage garden with herbaceous borders, wildlife pond, trees, shrubs and kitchen garden designed by the current owners.

14 ◆ **BURTON AGNES HALL & GARDENS**
Burton Agnes, Driffield YO25 4NB. Mrs S Cunliffe-Lister, 01262 490324, www.burtonagnes.com. *Between Driffield & Bridlington on A614 in village of Burton Agnes. Parking signed.* **Adm to Gardeners Fair incls adm to gardens. Donation to NGS from admissions.** For NGS: Sat 6, Sun 7 June (11-5) Gardener's Fair. **For other opening times and information, please phone or see garden website.** Beautiful award-winning gardens of Burton Agnes Hall are home to 3,000 different plant species, herbaceous borders, jungle garden, potager, coloured gardens, giant games, maze and collection of campanulas. Surrounded by lawns, topiary yews, fountains and woodland walk. Collections of hardy geraniums, clematis, penstemons and unusual perennials. Gardener's Fair.

GROUP OPENING

15 **CAWOOD GARDENS**
Cawood, nr Selby YO8 3UG. *On B1223 5m N of Selby & 7m SE of Tadcaster. Between York & A1 on B1222. Village maps given at all gardens.* Home-made teas at 9 Anson Grove & 21 Great Close. **Combined adm £5, chd free.** Sat 11, Sun 12 July (12-5).

9 ANSON GROVE
Tony & Brenda Finnigan
Visitors also welcome by arrangement May to Aug.
01757 268888
beeart@ansongrove.co.uk

21 GREAT CLOSE
David & Judy Jones
Visitors also welcome by arrangement May to Aug.
01757 268571
dave-judyjones@hotmail.co.uk

Ash Tree House, Whixley Gardens

THE PIGEONCOTE
2a Wistowgate. Maria Parks & Angela Darlington
Visitors also welcome by arrangement May to Aug.
01757 268661
mariaparks@gmail.com

These three contrasting gardens in an attractive historic village are linked by a pretty riverside walk to the C11 church and Memorial garden and across the Castle Garth to the remains of Cawood Castle. 9 Anson Grove is a small garden with tranquil pools and secluded sitting places. Narrow winding paths and raised areas give views over oriental-style pagoda, bridge and Zen garden. 21 Great Close is a flower arranger's garden, designed and built by the owners. Interesting trees and shrubs combine with herbaceous borders incl many grasses. Two ponds are joined by a stream, winding paths take you to the vegetable garden and summerhouse, then back to the colourful terrace for views across the garden and countryside beyond. The small walled garden, Pigeoncote at 2 Wistowgate is surrounded by historic C17 buildings. A balanced design of formal box hedging, cottage garden planting and creative use of grasses. Angled brick

pathways lead to shaded seating areas with all day sunny views. Crafts and paintings on sale at 9 Anson Grove.

16 **CHURCHSIDE**
41 Station Road, Wressle, Selby YO8 6ES. Suzanne York. *5m from J37 M62, 6¹/₂ m from A19/A63 junction. From the A63 Loftsome Bridge Coaching House, travel towards Wressle/Breighton. Churchside is directly in front on 1st sharp RH-bend.* Cream teas. **Adm £3, chd free.** Fri 26, Sat 27, Sun 28 June (1-5). Five yr old cottage garden. ¹/₄ acre full of herbaceous perennials and several garden areas to create interest for every family member. Rose rope, large front cottage garden, raised vegetable beds, small wildlife pond and a raised fish pond. Wooded retreat planted with yellow and white scheme. Summerhouse, Wendy house and sitting areas. A relaxing haven. The path amongst the front flower border cannot be accessed by wheelchair users. WC facilities are across a 20cm step and with limited space.

17 ► THE CIRCLES GARDEN

8 Stocksmoor Road, Midgley, nr Wakefield WF4 4JQ. Joan Gaunt. *Equidistant from Huddersfield, Wakefield & Barnsley, W of M1. Turn off A637 in Midgley at the Black Bull PH (sharp bend) onto B6117 (Stocksmoor Rd). Please park on L adjacent to houses.* Home-made teas. **Adm £3, chd free. Sun 26 Apr (1.30-5).**
An organic and self-sustaining plantswoman's ¹⁄₂-acre garden on gently sloping site overlooking fields, woods and nature reserve opposite. Designed and maintained by owner. Interesting herbaceous, bulb and shrub plantings linked by grass and gravel paths, a woodland area with mature trees, spring and summer meadows, fernery, greenhouse, fruit trees, viewing terrace with pots. Also, around 100 hellebores grown from my seed. South African plants, hollies, small bulbs are particular interests.

18 ► CLIFTON CASTLE

Ripon HG4 4AB. Lord & Lady Downshire. *2m N of Masham. On rd to Newton-le-Willows & Richmond. Gates on L next to red telephone box.* Home-made teas. **Adm £4, chd free. Sun 12 Apr (2-5).**
Fine views, river walks, wooded pleasure grounds with bridges and follies. Cascades, wild flower meadow and C19 walled kitchen garden. Gravel paths and steep slopes to river.

19 ► ◆ CONSTABLE BURTON HALL GARDENS

Constable Burton, nr Leyburn DL8 5LJ. Mr Charles Wyvill, 01677 450428, www.constableburton.com. *3m E of Leyburn. Constable Burton Village. On A684, 6m W of A1.* **For opening times and information, please phone or see garden website.**
Large romantic garden with terraced woodland walks. Garden trails, shrubs, roses and water garden. Display of daffodils and over 6,500 tulips planted annually amongst extensive borders. Fine John Carr house (not open) set in splendour of Wensleydale countryside. Tulip Festival each year on the first May Bank Holiday weekend, Constable Burton Hall Gardens plays host to a magnificent Tulip Festival. Sponsored by Chelsea award winning nursery

Bloms Bulbs, over 6,500 traditional and new variant tulips are planted throughout the gardens. Featured on BBC Gardeners World.

20 ► THE COURT

Humber Road, North Ferriby HU14 3DW. Guy & Liz Slater, 01482 633609, liz@guyslater.karoo.co.uk. *7m W of Hull. Travelling E on A63 to Hull, follow sign for N Ferriby. Through village to Xrds with war memorial, turn R & follow rd to T-junction with Humber Rd. Turn L & immed R into cul-de-sac, last house on L.* Home-made teas. **Adm £3, chd free. Sun 31 May (1-5).** Visitors also welcome by arrangement Feb to Aug groups of 10+.
Romantic and restful, with hidden seating areas offering different vistas. Roses and clematis scrambling up walls and trees. 2 summerhouses, small pond and waterfall with secluded arbours and historical items. A long tunnel of wisteria, clematis and laburnum leads to a little path with Betula jacquemontii, small stumpery, and grown up swing.

Situated 5mins from cliff top and beach, a garden with variety of plants . . .

21 ► COW CLOSE COTTAGE

Stripe Lane, Hartwith, Harrogate HG3 3EY. William Moore & John Wilson, 01423 779813, cowclose1@btinternet.com. *8m NW of Harrogate. From A61(Harrogate-Ripon) at Ripley take B6165 to Pateley Bridge. 1m beyond Burnt Yates turn R signed Hartwith onto Stripe Lane. Parking available.* Home-made teas. **Adm £3, chd free. Sun 26 July (11-4.30).** Visitors also welcome by arrangement June to Aug adm £5, incl refreshments available on request.
²⁄₃-acre recently redeveloped country garden on sloping site with stream

and far reaching views. Large borders with drifts of interesting, well-chosen, later flowering summer perennials and some grasses contrasting with woodland shade and streamside plantings. Gravel path leading to vegetable area. Terrace and seating with views of the garden and beyond. Orchard and newly constructed ha-ha with steps leading to meadow below.

GROUP OPENING

22 ► DACRE BANKS & SUMMERBRIDGE GARDENS

Nidderdale HG3 4EW, 01423 780456, pat@yorkehouse.co.uk. *4m SE of Pateley Bridge, 10m NW of Harrogate, 10m SW of Ripon, 10m N of Otley on B6451 & B6165. Parking at each garden. Maps available to show garden locations.* Cream teas at Yorke House, Low Hall and Woodlands Cottage. **Combined adm £7, chd free. Sun 5 July (11-5).** Visitors also welcome by arrangement June to July for groups of 10+ minimum.

LOW HALL ⊨
Mrs P A Holliday
(See separate entry)

RIVERSIDE HOUSE
Riverside Lane, Summerbridge, HG3 4JP. Joy Stanton.
Please park in the sawmill or woodmill & walk across the bridge, turn L into Riverside Lane. Advise against travelling down Riverside Lane in a car

WOODLANDS COTTAGE
Mr & Mrs Stark
(See separate entry)

YORKE HOUSE
Tony & Pat Hutchinson
(See separate entry)

Dacre Banks and Summerbridge Gardens are situated in the beautiful countryside of Nidderdale and designed to take advantage of the scenic Dales landscape. The gardens are linked by an attractive walk along the valley and may be accessed individually by car. Low Hall has a romantic walled garden set on different levels around the historic C17 family home (not open) with extensive herbaceous borders, shrubs, climbing roses and tranquil water garden. Riverside House is a mysterious waterside garden on many levels, supporting shade-loving plants and incorporates a Victorian

folly, fernery, courtyard and naturalistic riverside plantings. Woodlands Cottage is designed to harmonise with boulder-strewn woodland whilst also having varied areas of formal and informal planting, a wild flower meadow and productive fruit and vegetable garden.
Yorke House has colour-themed borders, attractive waterside plantings and secluded millennium garden full of fragrant plants and rambling roses. Visitors welcome to use orchard picnic area at Yorke House. Featured in Harrogate Advertiser. Partial wheelchair access at some gardens.

🐾 🌸 🚐 ☕

23 DEVONSHIRE MILL
Canal Lane, Pocklington, York YO42 1NN. Sue & Chris Bond, 01759 302147, chris.bond.dm@btinternet.com, www.devonshiremill.co.uk. *1m S of Pocklington. Situated on Canal Lane, Pocklington off A1079 at The Wellington Oak PH.* Home-made teas. Adm £3, chd free. Sun 22 Feb 2015 (11-4.30), Sun 21 Feb 2016. Visitors also welcome by arrangement Feb to Aug.
Early spring features double snowdrops (mainly galanthus flore pleno) in old orchards, hellebores and ferns in a woodland setting. The house (not open) is a 200yr old Grade II listed watermill. An intimate garden with different areas and mill stream. Organic principles used to encourage wildlife. Productive vegetable gardens with raised beds, polytunnel, greenhouses, hen run and well-stocked herbaceous borders.

🐾 🛏 ☕

24 DOVE COTTAGE NURSERY GARDEN
Shibden Hall Road, nr Halifax HX3 9XA. Kim & Stephen Rogers, www.dovecottagenursery.co.uk. *1m E Halifax. From Halifax take A58 turn L signed Claremount, cont over bridge, cont ¹/₂ m. J26 M62- A58 Halifax. Drive 4m. L turn at pet shop down Tanhouse Hill, cont ¹/₂ m.* Tea. Adm £3, chd free. Every Fri 5 June to 28 Aug (10-5).
Hedges and green oak gates enclose ¹/₃ -acre sloping garden, generously planted by nursery owners over 17yrs. A beautiful mix of late summer perennials and grasses. Winding paths and plenty of seats incl a romantic tulip arbour. Plants for sale

in nursery. Wildlife friendly. 'Considered good example of cottage garden' (- Carole Klein thought so!). Featured on the BBC Great British Garden Revival.

🌸 🚐 ☕

NGS funding helps us support more carers

25 34 DOVER ROAD
Hunters Bar, Sheffield S11 8RH. Marian Simpson, 079575 36248, marian@mjsimpson.plus.com. *1¹/₂ m SW of city centre. From A61 (ring rd) A625 Moore St/Eccleshall Rd for approx 1m. Dover Rd on R.* Home-made teas. Wide range of home-made drinks and cakes. Adm £3, chd free. Sun 28 June (11-4.30). Visitors also welcome by arrangement May to Aug.
Colourful, small town garden packed with interest and drama, combining formality with exotic exuberance. Attractive alpine area replacing old driveway, many interesting containers and well-stocked borders. Conservatory, seating areas and lawns complement unusual plants and planting combinations. Featured in Yorkshire Post, Sheffield Telegraph and on BBC Radio Sheffield.

🐾 🌸 ☕

26 DOWTHORPE HALL & HORSE PASTURE COTTAGE
Skirlaugh, Hull HU11 5AE. Mr & Mrs J Holtby, 01964 562235, john.holtby@farming.co.uk, www.dowthorpehall.com. *6m N of Hull, 8m E of Beverley. From Hull A165 towards Bridlington. Through Ganstead & Coniston. 1m S of Skirlaugh on R, (long drive white railings & sign at drive end).* Adm £5, chd free. Sun 21 June (11-5). Visitors also welcome by arrangement Apr to July.
Dowthorpe Hall: 3¹/₂ acres, large herbaceous borders, lawns, shady area, pond with bridge, scree garden, hardy garden, orchards and vegetable potager. Horse Pasture

Cottage: small cottage garden, herbaceous border and woodland water feature. Gravel, lawns, no steps.

♿ 🐾 🛏

27 ELLERKER HOUSE
Everingham, York YO42 4JA. Mrs R Los & Mr M Wright, www.ellerkerhouse.weebly.com. *15m SE of York. 5¹/₂ m from Pocklington. On rd towards Harswell on R.* Home-made teas. Adm £4.50, chd free. Sun 19 Apr (10-4).
5 acres of garden on sandy soil. Lots of spring bulbs, mature trees, formal lawn and extensive grass area. Woodland walkway around lake. Traditional oak and thatched breeze hut. Several seating areas with views of the garden. Rose archway, herbaceous borders. RARE PLANT FAIR (Many different stalls selling a variety of plants).

♿ 🌸 ☕

28 FAWLEY HOUSE
7 Nordham, North Cave, Brough, Hull HU15 2LT. Mr & Mrs T Martin, 01430 422266, louisem200@hotmail.co.uk, www.nordhamcottages.co.uk. *15m W of Hull. M62 E, J38 turn L towards North Cave Wetlands, then R where rd bends to L. Fawley House, is tall house on R, ¹/₂ m along Nordham.* Tea. Adm £4, chd free. Sat 21, Sun 22 Mar (12-4); Fri 12 June (2-7); Sat 13, Sun 14 June (1-5). Visitors also welcome by arrangement Feb to Oct for groups of 10+.
Tiered, 2¹/₂ -acre garden with lawns, mature trees, formal hedging and gravel pathways. Lavender beds, mixed shrub/herbaceous borders, hot coloured borders. Apple espaliers, pears, soft fruit, vegetable and herb gardens. Terrace with pergola and vines. Sunken garden with white border. Woodland with naturalistic planting and spring bulbs. Quaker well, stream and spring area. New fern and Hellebore bed near the stream. Beautiful snowdrops and aconites early in year and stunning Autumn colours. Exhibition of art from East Riding Artists in June, with art displayed from some NGS East Yorkshire gardens from 2014. For accommodation, please see website. Art exhibition in Fri 12, Sat 13, Sun 14 June Treasure Hunt for children in March and June. Partial wheelchair access to top of garden and terrace on pea gravel.

♿ 🌸 🛏 ☕

© Nicola Stocken Tomkins

Highfields

29 FERNLEIGH

9 Meadowhead Avenue, Meadowhead, Sheffield S8 7RT. Mr & Mrs C Littlewood, 01142 747234, littlewoodchristine@gmail.com. *4m S of Sheffield city centre. From Sheffield city centre. A61, A6102, B6054 r'about, exit B6054. 1st R Greenhill Ave, 2nd R. From M1 J33, A630 to A6102, then as above.* Home-made teas. **Adm £2.50, chd free. Sun 28 June, Sun 26 July, Sun 30 Aug (1-5).** Visitors also welcome by arrangement May to Aug, coach drop-off only. Plantswoman's ⅓ acre cottage style garden. Large variety of unusual plants set in differently planted sections to provide all-yr interest. Auricula theatre and paved area for drought resistant plants in pots. Seating areas to view different aspects of garden. Patio, gazebo and greenhouse. Miniature log cabin with living roof. Sempervivum, alpine displays and wildlife 'hotel'. 'Animal Search' for children. Featured in Sheffield Star Active 8 magazine.

❀ 🚌 ☕

30 FERNWOOD

Cropton YO18 8HL. Dick & Jean Feaster, 01751 417692, adrian.feaster@btinternet.com. *4m NW of Pickering. From A170 turn at Wrelton signed Cropton.* **Adm £3.50, chd free. Sun 5 July (1-5).** Visitors also welcome by arrangement May to July groups of 10+.
A hidden garden on edge of the North Yorkshire moors will delight visitors. Over 1 acre in size, garden incl number of colourful herbaceous borders, island beds, theme areas, delphiniums and spectacular tropaeolum speciosum covering 12ft Korean fir. Plantsperson's garden. Gravel paths.

♿ ❀ 🚌

31 FIRVALE ALLOTMENT GARDEN

Winney Hill, Harthill, nr Worksop S26 7YN. Don & Dot Witton, 01909 771366, donshardyeuphorbias@btopenworld.com, www.euphorbias.co.uk. *12m SE of Sheffield, 6m W of Worksop. M1 J31 A57 to Worksop. Turn R to Harthill. Allotments at S end of village, 26 Casson Drive at N end on Northlands Estate.* Home-made teas at 26 Casson Drive (S26 7WA). **Adm £3, chd free.** Visitors welcome by arrangement Mar to July.
Large allotment containing 13 island beds displaying 500+ herbaceous

perennials incl the National Collection of hardy Euphorbias with over 100 varieties flowering between March and October. Organic vegetable garden. Refreshments, WC, plant sales at 26 Casson Drive - small garden with mixed borders, shade and seaside garden.

❀ 🚌 **NCH** ☕

32 FOUR GABLES

Oaks Lane, Boston Spa, nr Wetherby LS23 6DS. David & Anne Watts, 01937 845592, info@fourgables.co.uk, www.fourgables.co.uk. *2m SE of Wetherby off A659 in Boston Spa 200yds before the Church. Park at the Church car park midway for both gardens. Do not park on main rd or Oaks Lane.* Home-made teas. Refreshments inside if raining. **Combined with Acorn Cottage £4, chd free. Sun 19 Apr (12.30-5).** Many surprises in this ½ -acre garden surrounding Grade II listed Arts and Crafts home (not open). View 7 different gardens in one visit. Fine specimen trees, hellebores, wood anemone, dicentra, tree peony, aquilegia and fritillaria. Ponds, deep well, 30ft wood sculpture and various garden features. Teas indoors if raining. Attractive courtyard with seating areas and raised beds.

🏡 ❀ 🛏 ☕

33 FRIARS HILL

Sinnington YO62 6SL. Mr & Mrs C J Baldwin, 01751 432179, friars.hill@abelgratis.co.uk. *4m W of Pickering. On A170.* Tea. **Adm £3.50, chd free.** Visitors welcome by arrangement Mar to July.
Plantswoman's 1¾-acre garden containing over 2500 varieties of perennials and bulbs, with yr-round colour. Early interest with hellebores, bulbs and woodland plants. Herbaceous beds. Hostas, delphiniums, old roses and stone troughs. Excellent Autumn colour.

🏡 ❀ 🚌 **NCH** ☕

34 GOLDSBOROUGH HALL

Church Street, Goldsborough HG5 8NR. Mr & Mrs M Oglesby, 01423 867321, info@goldsboroughhall.com, www.goldsboroughhall.com. *2m SE of Knaresborough. 3m W of A1M. Off A59 (York-Harrogate) carpark 300yds past PH on R.* Light lunches, sandwiches, cakes and cream teas. **Adm £5, chd free. Share to St Mary's Church, Goldsborough.**

Sun 22 Mar (12-4); Sun 5 July (12-5). Visitors also welcome by arrangement Feb to Oct groups of 10+.
Previously opened for NGS from 1928-30 and now beautifully restored by present owners (re-opened in 2010). 12-acre garden and formal landscaped grounds in parkland setting and Grade II*, C17 house, former residence of the late HRH Princess Mary, daughter of George V and Queen Mary. Gertrude Jekyll inspired replanted 120ft double herbaceous borders and rose garden. Quarter-mile Lime Tree Walk planted by royalty in the 1920s and a new flower border featuring 'Yorkshire Princess' rose, named after Princess Mary. Featured in local and national press, magazines and TV. Gravel paths and some steep slopes.

35 THE GRANGE

Carla Beck Lane, Carleton in Craven, Skipton BD23 3BU. Mr & Mrs R N Wooler, 07740 639135, margaret.wooler@hotmail.com. 1½ m SW of Skipton. Turn off A56 (Skipton-Clitheroe) into Carleton. Keep L at Swan PH, continue to end of village then turn R into Carla Beck Lane. Cream teas. £2.50. **Adm £5, chd free. Share to Sue Ryder Care Manorlands Hospice.** Wed 24 June, Wed 12 Aug (12-4.30). Visitors also welcome by arrangement July to Aug, groups 30+.
Over 4 acres set in the grounds of Victorian house (not open) with mature trees and panoramic views towards The Gateway to the Dales. The garden has been restored by the owners over the last 2 decades with many areas of interest being added to the original footprint. Bountiful herbaceous borders with many unusual species, rose walk, parterre, mini-meadows and water features. Large greenhouse and raised vegetable beds. Oak seating placed throughout the garden invites quiet contemplation, a place to 'lift the spirit'. Gravel paths and steps.

36 NEW GREENWICK FARM

Huggate, York, East Yorkshire YO42 1YR. Fran & Owen Pearson, 01377 288122, greenwickfarm@hotmail.com. From York on A166, turn R lm after Garrowby Hill, at brown sign for picnic area & scenic route. 2m W of Huggate. White wind turbine on drive. Home-made teas. **Adm £3.50, chd free.** Sun 23 Aug (1-5).
1 acre woodland garden created 5yrs ago from disused farm waste area. Set in a large dell with many mature trees incl Elm. Interesting planting of shrubs, unusual trees, herbaceous/mixed borders and island beds. Paths lead up through planting to give spectacular views across wooded valley and the Wolds. Access for wheelchairs difficult, but good view of garden from hard standing outside house/tea area.

Paths lead up through planting to give spectacular views across wooded valley and the Wolds . . .

37 16 HALLAM GRANGE CROFT

Fulwood, Sheffield S10 4BP. Tricia & Alistair Fraser, 0114 230 6508, tricia.fraser@talktalk.net. Approx 4m SW of Sheffield city centre. Follow A57 (Glossop). 1½ m after University turn L after petrol station. After 1m turn L at top of hill & follow signs. Home-made teas. **Adm £2.50, chd free.** Sun 31 May (12.30-4.30). Visitors also welcome by arrangement May to Sept min entry charge for 10 people applies.
Developed over 20yrs, a plantswoman's SE-facing sloping wildlife-friendly garden. Backed by mature trees with established perennial and shrub planting incl many unusual hardy geraniums. Shady areas, pond, summerhouse, greenhouse and vegetable plots. Raised bed, rockery and decking area feature alpines and sun-loving perennials. Plants propagated by the owners on sale. Featured in Sheffield Telegraph.

38 HAVOC HALL

York Rd, Oswaldkirk, York YO62 5XY. David & Maggie Lis, www.havochall.co.uk. 21m N of York. On B1363, 1st house on R as you enter Oswaldkirk from S & last house on L as you leave village from N. Home-made teas. **Adm £4, chd free.** Sun 5 July (1-5.30).
Started in 2009, comprising 8 areas incl knot, herbaceous, mixed shrub and flower gardens, courtyard, vegetable area and orchard, woodland walk and large lawned area with hornbeam trees and hedging. To the S is a 2-acre wild flower meadow and small lake. Extensive collection of roses, herbaceous perennials and grasses. See website for other opening times. Some steps but these can be avoided.

39 NEW 20 HIGHFIELD ROAD

Whitby YO21 3LW. Mr & Mrs Les & Ann Spedding. From York/Middlesbrough at r'about adjacent to park & ride take 1st exit onto B1460 after garage turn L onto Love Lane B1416 turn R onto Highfield R. Home-made teas. Sweet & savoury homemade refreshments. **Adm £3, chd free.** Sun 19 July (1-4).
Situated 5mins from cliff top and beach, a garden with variety of plants. Gravel paths lead to herbaceous borders some shady with mature trees contrasting to sun loving plants. 2 raised timber framed ponds with running water largest formal containing water lilies. Many pots some with specimen plants and tropical. Collection of succulents, perennial pelargoniums and dahlias. Greenhouse and seating areas. Winner: Whitby in Bloom Gold award and best in Caregory.

40 HIGHFIELDS

Manorstead, Skelmanthorpe, Huddersfield HD8 9DW. Julie & Tony Peckham. 8m SE of Huddersfield. M1 (J39) A636 towards Denby Dale. Turn R in Scissett village (B6116). Turn L (Barrowstead) just before zebra crossing. Teas. **Adm £2.50, chd free.** Sun 22 Mar, Sun 19 Apr (1-4).
Small garden which shows creativity within metres rather than acres. Focuses on early spring/summer plants. First opening this year in March for Hellebore and early bulbs. Incl two ponds, rock gardens, alpine beds, woodland plants and small alpine display in greenhouse. Summerhouse and lots of intimate seating areas.

41 5 HILL TOP

Westwood Drive, Ilkley LS29 9RS.
Lyn & Phil Short. *½ m S of Ilkley.
Turn S at town centre T-lights up
Brook St, cross The Grove taking
Wells Rd up to the Moors and follow
NGS signs.* Home-made teas. **Adm
£3, chd free. Wed 3, Sun 7 June
(11-4.30).**
Delightful ⅔ acre steep garden on
edge of Ilkley Moor. Sheltered
woodland underplanted with
naturalistic, flowing tapestry of
foliage, shade-loving flowers, shrubs
and ferns amongst large moss
covered boulders. Natural stream,
bridges, meandering gravel paths and
steps lend magic to 'Dingley Dell'.
Lawns, large rockery and
summerhouse with stunning views.
Steep steps, slopes and gravel paths.

Perennial; supporting
horticulturists
since 1839

42 HILLBARK

Church Lane, Bardsey, nr Leeds
LS17 9DH. Tim Gittins & Malcolm
Simm, www.hillbark.co.uk. *4m SW
of Wetherby. Turn W off A58 into
Church Lane, garden on L before
church.* Tea. **Adm £4, chd free.
Sun 17 May, Sun 5 July (11-4.30).**
Award-winning 1-acre country
garden. 3 S-facing levels, hidden
corners and surprise views. Formal
topiary, relaxed perennial planting.
Dramatic specimen yew. Ornamental
ponds, summerhouse overlooking
gravel, rock and stream gardens,
large natural pond with ducks.
Marginal planting incl bamboo.
Woodland area. Large rambling
roses. Unusual ceramics.

43 NEW 2 HOLLIN CLOSE

Rossington, nr Doncaster
DN11 0XX. Mrs Helen Hann. *5m S
of Doncaster. on A638 after Hare and
Tortoise PH turn R (Littleworth Lane)
5m N of Bawtry after T-lights signed
Airport take next L (Littleworth Lane).*

Hollin Close is 2nd R. Home-made
teas. **Adm £3, chd free. Sun 28
June (11-5). Also open Tamarind,
2 Whin Hill Road, Bessacarr.**
⅓ acre terraced garden designed and
maintained by owners with four
themes on three levels. Cottage style
herbaceous planting surrounds a
circular lawn alongside a tranquil
oriental garden. Steps lead to the
greenhouse and Mediterranean gravel
garden with sun-loving plants for bees
and butterflies. Below lies a wildlife
friendly small woodland glade with bug
hotel, stumpery, fruit and ferns. Winner
Doncaster in Bloom - Best Garden.

44 54 HOLLYM ROAD

Withernsea HU19 2PJ. Mr Matthew
Pottage. *23m E of Hull, 16m S of
Hornsea. Enter Withernsea from
A1033 onto Hollym Rd. From
Hornsea, B1242 through town onto
Hollym Rd.* Light refreshments.
Gluten free cake available. **Adm £3,
chd free. Sun 5 July (12-6).**
The family home of Matthew Pottage,
Garden Manager at RHS Garden
Wisley, this treasure is bursting with
colourful, choice and exotic plants.
You'll be shocked to see what can
grow in grotty clay soil on the
Yorkshire coast as well as finding
something to take home for your own
garden from the selection of plants on
sale. The Pottage family look forward
to welcoming you! Excellent
'plantsmans' display of plants.
Featured in Dr. John Grimshaws Diary:
johngrimshawsgardendiary.blogspot.
co.uk/2013/07/a-gardeners-
garden.html. Unsuitable for
wheelchairs after severe wet weather
as most of the garden is accessed via
the lawn.

45 HOLMFIELD

Fridaythorpe YO25 9RZ. Susan &
Robert Nichols, 01377 236627,
susan.nichols@which.net. *9m W of
Driffield. From York A166 through
Fridaythorpe. 1m turn R signed
Holmfield. 1st house on lane.* Home-
made teas. **Adm £4, chd free. Sat
20, Sun 21 June (11-5). Visitors
also welcome by arrangement May
to July groups of 10+.**
Informal 2-acre country garden on
gentle S-facing slope. Developed
from a field over last 25yrs. Large
mixed borders, octagonal gazebo.
Vegetable, orchard and fruit areas.
Cut flower garden. Collection of
phlomis. Family friendly garden with

sunken trampoline, large lawn, tennis
court and hidden paths for hide and
seek. Display of wire sculptures. Bee
friendly planting. Some gravel areas,
sloping lawns.

46 HOTHAM HALL

Hotham YO43 4UA. Stephen &
Carolyn Martin, 01430 422054,
carolynandstephenmartin@btintern
et.com. *15m W of Hull. J38 of M62
turn towards North Cave Wetlands, &
at sharp corner go straight on to
Hotham. Turn R & R again through
Hall gates.* Light refreshments. - incl
in the ticket. **Adm £5, chd £2.50.
Thur 2, Thur 9 Apr (11-3). Visitors
also welcome by arrangement Apr
to June.**
C18 Grade II house (not open), stable
block and clock tower in mature
parkland setting with established
gardens. Lake with bridge over to
island walk (arboretum). Garden with
Victorian pond and mixed borders.
Many spring flowering bulbs. INCL IN
TICKET children's play area, garden
games. Easter Treasure Hunt. Easter
decoration making, light refreshments
and children's picnic basket. Pea
gravel pathways.

47 HUNMANBY GRANGE

Wold Newton YO25 3HS. Tom &
Gill Mellor. *12½ m SE of
Scarborough. Hunmanby Grange
home of Wold Top Brewery, between
Wold Newton & Hunmanby on rd
from Burton Fleming to Fordon.*
Home-made teas in Wold Top
Brewery bar area. **Adm £4, chd free.
Sat 6, Sun 7 June (11-5).**
3-acre garden created over the last
30 yrs from exposed open field, on
top of Yorkshire Wolds nr coast.
Hedges and fences now provide
shelter from wind, making series of
gardens with yr-round interest and
seasonal highlights. Wold Top
Brewery open with garden. Picnics
welcome so bring your Teddy Bears
down to our woodland area. Steps
can be avoided by using grass paths
and lawns. Pond garden not
completely accessible to wheelchairs
but can be viewed from gateway.

48 ◆ JACKSON'S WOLD

Sherburn, Malton YO17 8QJ.
Mr & Mrs Richard Cundall,
07966 531995,
www.jacksonswoldgarden.com.
11m E of Malton, 10m SW of

Scarborough. T-lights take the Weaverthorpe rd after 100 metres R fork to Helperthorpe & Luttons. 1m to top of hill, turn L at garden sign. Home-made teas. **Adm £3, chd free.** For NGS: **Sun 19 Apr, Sun 21 June (1-5). For other opening times and information, please phone or see garden website.**

2-acre garden with stunning views of the Vale of Pickering. Walled garden with mixed borders, numerous old shrub roses underplanted with unusual perennials. Woodland paths lead to further shrub and perennial borders. Lime avenue with wild flower meadow. Traditional vegetable garden with roses, flowers and box edging framed by Victorian greenhouse. Adjoining nursery. Tours by arrangement. Featured in Good Garden's Guide and Country Life.

49 THE JUNGLE GARDEN

76 Gledhow Wood Avenue, Roundhay, Leeds LS8 1NX. Nick & Gill Wilson, 0113 266 5196, nick.wilson@software4hr.co.uk. *4m NE of Leeds. A58 from Leeds for 3¹/₂ m to Oakwood. Turn L onto Gledhow Lane & follow NGS signs.* **Adm £3, chd free.** Sun 26 July **(11-5). Visitors also welcome by arrangement July to Aug for groups of 10 to 30.**

Multi level garden with jungle style planting and accents of hot tropical colour. Boardwalks and bark paths. Crown lifted trees create overhead canopy. Walk under mad, huge Gunnera leaves. 2 ponds, walkway over lower pond and raised deck with seating overlooks upper pond. Elevated 'Jungle Lodge' and aerial walkway with views over the garden. Tea room at Tropical World at Roundhay Park (1m). Featured in Yorkshire Ridings Magazine, Amateur Gardening Magazine and BBC Great British Garden Revival.

50 ◆ LAND FARM

Edge Lane, Colden, nr Hebden Bridge HX7 7PJ. Mr J Williams, 01422 842260, www.landfarmgardens.co.uk. *8m W of Halifax. At Hebden Bridge (A646) after 2 sets of T-lights take turning circle to Heptonstall & Colden. After 2³/₄ m in Colden village turn R at Edge Lane 'no through rd'.* **For opening times and information, please phone or see garden website.**

An intriguing 6 acre upland garden within a sheltered valley, created entirely by the present owner over a period of 40 years. In that time the valley has been planted with 20,000 trees by friends, neighbours and myself, which has encouraged a habitat rich in bird and wildlife. Within the garden, vistas have been created around thought provoking sculptures. Meconopsis and cardiocrinum lilies. Open weekends and Bank Hol Mons May to end Aug. Partial wheelchair access, please telephone.

Colourful borders
and rose beds with
beautiful views over
the parkland down
to the river . . .

51 LANGTON FARM

Great Langton, Northallerton DL7 0TA. Richard & Annabel Fife, 01609 748446, annabelfife@fsmail.net. *5m W of Northallerton. B6271 in Great Langton between Northallerton & Scotch Corner.* Home-made teas. **Adm £4, chd free.** Sun 26 Apr **(12-6). Visitors also welcome by arrangement Apr to Sept for groups of 10+.**

Riverside garden comprising formal and informal gravel areas, nuttery, romantic flower garden with mixed borders and pebble pool. Double Helix of Narcissus Actea through Pear Walk. Many other bulbs and much blossom. Organic. Featured in The English Garden.

52 NEW LANGTON HALL

Little Langton, Northallerton DL7 0PX. Mr & Mrs J A Fife. *NB SatNav not reliable. B6271 to Great Langton between A1 & Northallerton. In village from W take L turn, or E take L turn & continue for 1m. Entrance gates on R topped by stone balls.* Cream teas. **Adm £5, chd free.** Sat 13 June **(2-4.30).**

Set in stunning rural surroundings perched above the R Swale and surrounded by wonderful old parkland. Large lawned garden with wonderful views, colourful borders and rose beds with beautiful views

over the parkland down to the river. The wild flowers on the drive are spectacular in early summer. Access through green garden door off main drive.

53 LINDEN LODGE

Newbridge Lane, nr Wilberfoss, York YO41 5RB. Robert Scott & Jarrod Marsden, 07900 003538, rdsjsm@gmail.com. *10m E of York. Do not enter the village of Wilberfoss from the A1079, take the turning signed Bolton village.* Cream teas in the marquee. **Adm £4, chd free.** Sun 3, Mon 4 May, Sat 12, Sun 13 Sept **(1-5). Visitors also welcome by arrangement May to Sept min 15 people.**

6 acres in total. A 1 acre garden, owner-designed and constructed since 2000, with many choice, unusual plants and trees. Gravel paths edged with box and lavender lead to herbaceous/mixed borders, wildlife pond and summerhouse. Kitchen garden, glasshouse, orchard and woodland area and formal garden with pond and water feature. 5 acres of developing meadow, trees, pathways and Shetland sheep. Plants and local craft stalls. Featured in 100 Inspirational Gardens of England, The Yorkshire Post, Amateur Gardening and Yorkshire Life. Gravel paths and shallow steps.

54 LITTLE EDEN

Lancaster Street, Castleford WF10 2NP. Melvyn & Linda Moran, 01977 514275, melvynmoran609@btinternet.com, NGS Little Eden on Facebook. *2¹/₂ m NW of M62 J32. A639 (Castleford) 1st r'about 2nd exit B6136. At hill top turn L at T-lights, next r'about straight on, then 3rd R (Elizabeth Drive) then 2nd L, then 3rd L.* Home-made teas. **Adm £3, chd free.** Sun 21 June, Sun 23 Aug **(10-4.30). Visitors also welcome by arrangement June to Sept.**

Plant lovers' small hidden oasis of unusual, tender, exotic and tropical plants in the midst of large housing estate. Trellis and archway festooned with climbers, colourful pots and hanging baskets. Herbaceous perennials, succulents, tree ferns, palms, bananas, pond and a decorative summerhouse. Featured on BBC Gardeners World and in Yorkshire Ridings magazine.

GROUP OPENING

55 LITTLETHORPE GARDENS
nr Ripon HG4 3LS. *1½ m SE of Ripon. Off A61 bypass follow signs to Littlethorpe. Turn R at church. From Bishop Monkton follow signs to Ripon (Knaresborough Rd), turn R to Littlethorpe. The gardens are approx ½ m apart.* Home-made teas at Greencroft. **Combined adm £4.50, chd free. Sun 2 Aug (12-5).**

GREENCROFT
David & Sally Walden
Visitors also welcome by arrangement 1 July to 10 Aug.
01765 602487
s.walden@talk21.com

KIRKELLA
Pottery Lane. Jacky Barber

Littlethorpe is a small village characterised by houses interspersed with fields. Greencroft is a ½ acre informal garden made by the owners. Special ornamental features incl gazebo, temple pavilions, formal pool, stone wall with mullions, and gate to rose pergola leading to a cascade water feature. Long herbaceous borders packed with colourful late flowering perennials, annuals and exotics culminate in circular garden with views through to large wildlife pond and surrounding countryside. Kirkella is a small garden recently created by plantswoman and flower arranger to give constant interest. Gravel garden to the front with Mediterranean feel. Densely planted hidden paved rear garden with decorative summerhouse; hostas, half-hardy perennials, salvias, succulents, desirable small shrubs, many in pots and containers. A willow hedge conceals a small productive vegetable plot.

❀ ☕

56 LITTLETHORPE MANOR
Littlethorpe Road, Littlethorpe, Ripon HG4 3LG. Mr & Mrs J P Thackray, thackray@littlethorpemanor.com, www.littlethorpemanor.com. *Outskirts of Ripon nr racecourse. Ripon bypass A61. Follow Littlethorpe Rd from Dallamires Lane r'about to stable block with clock tower. Map supplied on application.* Light refreshments. Tea, coffee, biscuits, £1.50 + cake £2.50 served in marquee. **Adm £8, chd free.**
Visitors welcome by arrangement

May to Oct incls guided tour. 11 acres. Walled garden based on cycle of seasons with box, herbaceous, roses, gazebo. Sunken garden with white rose parterre and herbs. Brick pergola with white wisteria, blue and yellow borders. Terraces with ornamental pots. Formal lawns with fountain pool, hornbeam towers and yew hedging. Box headed hornbeam drive with Aqualens water feature. Extensive perennial borders. Parkland with lake, late summer plantings and classical pavilion. Cut flower garden. Spring bulbs and winter garden. Gravel paths, some steep steps.

♿ ❀ 🚐 ☕

GROUP OPENING

57 LOCKINGTON GARDENS
Driffield YO25 9SR. *7m N of Beverley. Lockington Gardens are situated on Thorpe between A164 & B1248. Park in church car park and follow signs to gardens.* Home-made teas at Penny Cottage. **Combined adm £4, chd free. Sun 7 June (1-6).**

PENNY COTTAGE
42 Thorpe. Sue & John Rowson

THORPE LODGE
Dead Lane. Mrs Jane Warburton

Two small gardens in the village of Lockington. Penny Cottage is a small, well-maintained garden on different levels with conifers, selection of herbaceous perennials and climbers. Small raised vegetable plot. Thorpe Lodge a cottage garden on the site of an old orchard. Interesting shrubs and trees creating contrast and shade. Wildlife pond, summer house and vegetable patch.

🐾 ☕

58 LOW HALL
Dacre Banks, Nidderdale HG3 4AA. Mrs P A Holliday, 01423 780230, pamela@pamelaholliday.co.uk. *10m NW of Harrogate. On B6451 between Dacre Banks & Darley.* Home-made teas. **Adm £3.50, chd free. Sun 10 May (1-5).** Also open with Dacre Banks & Summerbridge Gardens, 5 July, and Woodlands Cottage 10 May. Visitors also welcome by arrangement May to Sept.
Romantic walled garden set on differing levels designed to

complement historic C17 family home (not open). Spring bulbs, rhododendrons; azaleas round tranquil water garden. Asymmetric rose pergola underplanted with auriculas and lithodora links orchard to the garden. Extensive herbaceous borders, shrubs and climbing roses give later interest.

🐾 ❀ 🚐 🛏 ☕

Streamside garden and adjoining wild flower meadow. Organic with abundant wildlife . . .

59 LOW SUTTON
Sutton Lane, Masham HG4 4PB. Steve & Judi Smith, 01765 688565, info@lowsutton.co.uk, www.lowsutton.co.uk. *1½ m W of Masham. From Masham towards Leyburn (A6108). L into Sutton Lane, single track tarmac rd. Low Sutton ¼ m on L.* Home-made teas. **Combined adm with Sutton Grange £5, chd free. Sun 21 June (12-5).** Developing since 2007 a fresh approach to cottage gardening. Concentric circular floral colour wheel surrounded by scented roses and clematis. Abundant variety of fruit and vegetables decoratively grown in raised beds, fruit cage, greenhouse and coldframe. Perennial border, grasses, fernery and courtyard surround the house, all set within 6-acre smallholding.

🐾 ❀ 🛏 ☕

60 LOWER HEUGH COTTAGE GARDEN
14 Kirk Lane, Eastby, nr Skipton BD23 6SH. Trevor & Marian Nash, 01756 793702, mnash862@gmail.com. *2½ m NE of Skipton (Do not use satnav). Follow A59/65 N ringroad around Skipton, turn at sign for Skipton, Embsay (railway) and Eastby. In Embsay turn to Eastby & Barden (Kirk Lane).* **Adm £7, chd free. Visitors welcome by arrangement** only, tour is followed by appropriate refreshment incl in adm.
Japanese Kaiyushiki stroll garden. Uniquely, this little piece of the Orient,

high in the Yorkshire Dales is all Japanese in style. Its many gardens are explained during the 90 minute conducted tour enhancing the understanding of the history, religion, philosophy and concepts behind Japanese garden design. Hosting Professor Fukuhara, one of the world's leading Japanese garden designers for a workshop led by him in late 2011, was a privilege. His Emperor Garden design for the outer Roji extension within this one acre stroll garden has proved inspirational for the many visitors during 2012/13. This all year round garden, created and maintained by the owners, is perhaps best seen from March to October yet can be spectacular in the winter. Limited wheelchair access.

61 ▶ MAIDENS FOLLY
Youlton, Nr Easingwold YO61 1QL. **Mr Henry Dean.** *11m NW of York. From A1(M) and W, 2m NE of Aldwark toll bridge (40p). 4m SW of Easingwold. Off A19 from Tollerton follow Helperby Rd, turn L at Alne Xrds. Car parking in adjacent paddock.* Home-made teas. **Adm £3.50, chd free.** Sun 21 June (1-5). Large cottage garden comprising 4 different themes: double herbaceous borders bounded by beech hedges and divided by stone pathway; enclosed white garden with central feature inspired by Gertrude Jekyll surrounded by flower beds, arches and trellis festooned with climbers; walled area with lavender walk, rose and penstemon border; attractive courtyard garden.

62 ▶ MANOR FARM
Thixendale, Malton YO17 9TG. **Charles & Gilda Brader, 01377 288315, manorfarmthixendale@hotmail. com.** *10m SE of Malton. Unclassified rd through Birdsall, 1/2m up hill, turn L at Xrds for Thixendale - 3m, 1st farm on R. 17m E of York, turn off A166 rd at top of Garrowby Hill, follow signs for Thixendale, 4m turn into village, drive through to end, farm on L. Yellow signs will be on route.* Home-made teas. **Adm £4, chd free.** Sun 6 Sept (12-5). Main lawn surrounded by shrub and herbaceous borders. Ruined shed, small knot garden, little arbour, running water and rocks. Topiary and pots throughout garden. Central pergola to new bespoke

The Jungle Garden

summerhouse, formal pool with sphere, set in stone flagged trellised area. Through curved pergola to alpines planted among farm stones, small courtyard, into garden room overflowing with plants.

63 ▶ NEW ▶ THE MANOR HOUSE
Main Street, Heslington, York YO10 5EA. **George Smith & Brian Withill, www.georgesmithflowers.com.** *2m S York City Centre.* Tea. **Pre-booking essential please contact NGS 01483 211535 www.ngs.org.uk. Adm £15, chd free (incl tea). Sun 14 June (2-5).** Home of the world renowned flower arranger George Smith, this 3 acre garden reflects his painterly style of planting. Sub-divided by mellow walls it abounds with many surprises as each area is colour themed featuring herbaceous perennials, especially hostas and ferns. Exotic sheltered corners, ponds and a shaded woodland create a wildlife haven. The eye of the artist abounds and the effect is of a living flower arrangement with careful attention to plant associations. Refreshments with George Smith will be served in the tiled rustic loggia beneath his Old Granary Studio. House not open.

Featured in 'Britain's Best Gardens' with Alan Titchmarsh. Numerous national and overseas publications.

64 ▶ MANSION COTTAGE
8 Gillus Lane, Bempton, Bridlington YO15 1HW. **Polly & Chris Myers, 01262 851404, chrismyers0807@gmail.com.** *2m NE of Bridlington. From Bridlington take B1255 to Flamborough. 1st L at T lights - Bempton Lane, turn 1st R into Short Lane then L at end. Continue - L fork at Church.* Light refreshments. **Adm £3, chd free. Sun 14 June, Sat 8, Sun 9 Aug (10-4). Visitors also welcome by arrangement July to Aug, garden/ art groups of 15+ adm incl tea.** Exuberant, lush, vibrant perennial planting highlighted with grasses and features offering many views and features. Visitors book comments 'A truly lovely garden and a great lunch', 'The garden is inspirational, a veritable oasis!' June features mass Allium planting. Delicious home-made lunches August only. Produce stalls incl jams, chutneys, pickles and hand-made soaps. Access into the house involves steep steps.

65 MARSTON GRANGE

Tockwith Road, Long Marston, York YO26 7PL. David & Joanne Smakman, 0741 9764813, info@marstongrange.co.uk, www.marstongrange.co.uk. *5m W of York 5m E of Wetherby. From B1224 in Long Marston turn towards Tockwith. ³/₄ m after battlefield monument turn R down single track lane.* Home-made teas and sandwiches served throughout the day. **Adm £5, chd free. Sun 7 June (11-4).**

2 acre garden, with views over the Battlefield of Marston Moor, designed to blend into the arable landscape and planted with many native and wild flower species. Traditional ha-ha, pond and small walled garden. Summerhouse and mature trees, orchard with vegetables and cutting garden. Walks through and around a large perennial wild flower meadow. Bees. Guided battlefield walk at 2pm. Battle of Marston Moor 1644.

❀ 🚐 🛏 ☕

66 MASPIN HOUSE

Hillam Common Lane, Hillam, Monk Fryston, nr Leeds LS25 5HU. Howard & Susan Ferguson, 01977 684922, ferguson@maspin-house.co.uk, www.maspin-house.co.uk. *7m W of Selby. 4m E of A1 on A63. Turn R after leaving Monk Fryston signed Birkin & Beal, L at T-junction. House 1m on L.* Tea. **Adm £4, chd free. Sun 4, Sun 11 Oct (12-4). Visitors also welcome by arrangement 4 to 11 Oct.**

Don't expect miracles, it is October, but if the weather is kind this 2 acre garden will have dramatic colour from salvias, asters and other daisies plus shape and form from many different grasses. Featuring 2 ponds, a rill, hot border, small woodland, pergolas and a summerhouse with seating areas in each part of the garden. Gravel drive.

♿ 🚐 ☕

67 MERE'STEAD

28 Kelmscott Garth, Manston Crossgates, Leeds LS15 8LB. Mr Roberto Renzi. *6m E of Leeds. 1m from M1 J46 follow A63 towards Leeds.Take ring rd A6120 then follow signs to Barwick-in-Elmet. At 2nd T-lights turn R to Pendas Way, then 1st L. No parking in cul-de-sac. Car park signed.* Light refreshments, wine and pizza. **Evening Opening £3, chd free, wine, Fri 24 July (5-8).**

A small enclosed English town garden with an Italian twist lovingly developed and cared for by owners. Mature trees, magnolia and cedar deodara, underplanted with interesting perennials and bulbs giving colour and foliage interest throughout the year. Arches festooned with climbers, small wildlife pond, pots with succulents, colourful summer bulbs and alpine troughs. Winner of Leeds in Bloom for past 10yrs.

❀ ☕

Visit a garden and support hospice care

68 MILLGATE HOUSE

Millgate, Richmond DL10 4JN. Tim Culkin & Austin Lynch, 01748 823571, oztim@millgatehouse.demon.co.uk, www.millgatehouse.com. *Centre of Richmond. House located at bottom of Market Place opp Barclays Bank. Just off corner of Market Place.* **Adm £3.50, chd free. Sun 14, Sun 28 June (8-8). Also open Swale Cottage, 14 June.**

SE walled town garden overlooking R Swale. Although small, the garden is full of character, enchantingly secluded with plants and shrubs. Foliage plants incl ferns and hostas. Old roses, interesting selection of clematis, small trees and shrubs. RHS associate garden. Immensely stylish, national award-winning garden. Featured in GGG and on BBC Gardeners' World.

🛏

69 MILLRACE NURSERY

84 Selby Road, Garforth, Leeds LS25 1LP. Mr & Mrs Carthy, 0113 2869233, carol@millrace-plants.co.uk, www.millrace-plants.co.uk. *5m E of Leeds. On A63 in Garforth. 1m from M1 J46, 3m from A1.* Home-made teas. **Adm £4, chd free. Sun 31 May, Sun 2 Aug (1-5). Visitors also welcome by arrangement Apr to Sept.**

Overlooking a secluded valley, garden

incl large herbaceous borders containing over 3000 varieties of perennials, shrubs and trees, many of which are unusual and drought tolerant. Ornamental pond, vegetable garden and walled terraces leading to wild flower meadow, small woodland, bog garden and wildlife lakes. 2 Aug seed collecting opportunity. Art exhibition, specialist nursery.

♿ 🐕 ❀ 🚐 ☕

70 NEW 23 MOLESCROFT ROAD

Beverley HU17 7DX. Mr & Mrs D Bowden. *Located ¹/₂ m N of the North Bar, Beverley.* Tea. **Adm £3, chd free. Sun 7 June (12-5).**

A suburban garden facing south west bordered by mature trees. Mixed borders and old herbaceous favorites. Several climbers, incl roses. The garden is terraced, on three different levels with lawns and seating areas providing different aspects of the garden. A paved patio area with three steps leads up to the lawn. The attractive summer house in one corner, enjoys views of the garden. A small productive area with fruit cage and greenhouse is screened from the rest of the garden. The lower area around the house has a paved area with rhododendrons and camellias. Sorry there is no wheelchair access also note that the garden has steps which some visitors may find difficult.

☕

71 NEAKINS HOUSE

North Leys Road, Hollym, Withernsea HU19 2QN. David & Trish Smith. *2m S of Withernsea. Enter Hollym on A1033 Hull to Withernsea Rd. Turn E at Xrds. Garden on R after double bend. Strictly no roadside parking, please park in grounds.* Home-made teas. **Adm £3, chd free. Sun 28 June (11-5).**

Quiet country garden with shrubs and choice herbaceous plantings. Specimen evergreens complement formal box topiary and hedging. Enter log arch to shady hosta walk and emerge through rose arch. Gravelled area with seating overlooks large wildlife pond. Folly wall, clothed in clematis, features iron gate leading on to bee and butterfly border. 2015 see's a new additional garden. Classic cars on display. Hosta walk too narrow for wheelchairs but can be viewed from entrance.

♿ 🐕 ❀ ☕

72 **NESS HALL**
Ness, Nunnington YO62 5XD. Mr
Richard & the Hon Mrs Murray
Wells, 01439 748223,
harriettemw@gmail.com. *6m E of
Helmsley, 22m N of York. From
B1257 Helmsley-Malton rd turn L at
Slingsby signed Kirkbymoorside, 3m
to Ness*. Home-made teas. **Adm £5,
chd free.** Sun 28 June (11-4).
**Visitors also welcome by
arrangement Apr to Oct for groups
of 10+.**
Ness is a romantic English flower
garden created by three generations
of keen gardeners. Surrounded by
park land it has views to the North
Yorkshire Moors. Large walled garden
with mixed and herbaceous borders
as well as self seeding beds, and a
water garden, rockery, rose garden
and orchard. There are steps and
slopes in the walled garden but part
of the garden is accessible for
wheelchairs.

The garden is full
of character,
enchantingly
secluded with plants
and shrubs . . .

73 **◆ NEWBY HALL &
GARDENS**
Ripon HG4 5AE. Mr R C Compton,
01423 322583,
www.newbyhall.com. *4m SE of
Ripon. (HG4 5AJ for Sat Nav)*. Follow
brown tourist signs from A1 & Ripon
town centre. Licensed restaurant.
**For opening times and information,
please phone or see garden
website.**
40 acres of extensive gardens and
woodland laid out in 1920s. Full of
rare and beautiful plants. Formal
seasonal gardens, stunning double
herbaceous borders to R Ure and
National Collection of - Cornus.
Miniature railway and adventure
gardens for children. Contemporary
sculpture exhibition (open June -
Sept). Wheelchair map available.

74 **2 NEWLAY GROVE**
Horsforth, Leeds LS18 4LH. Mrs
Kate van Heel. *4m NW Leeds city
centre. From A65 turn down Newlay
Lane then 2nd R onto Newlay Grove.*

*House is 25 metres on L, limited
parking near house.* Light
refreshments. **Adm £3, chd free.**
Wed 12 Aug (1-5).
Large rear family garden within third
acre plot in quiet conservation area
close to R Aire. Landscaped over
past 20 years, featuring late summer
perennials, shrubs, pond and shade
loving plants. Steps and slopes link
lawns and paved terracing. Various
seating areas allow viewing from
different perspectives.

75 **◆ NORTON CONYERS**
Wath, nr Ripon HG4 5EQ.
Sir James & Lady Graham,
01765 640333,
www.weddingsatnortonconyers.
co.uk. *4m N of Ripon. Take
Melmerby & Wath sign off A61 Ripon-
Thirsk. Go through both villages to
boundary wall. Signed entry 300
metres on R*. Tea. Teas provided by
owners. **Adm £6, chd free.** For
NGS: Sun 14 June (2-5). **For other
opening times and information,
please phone or see garden
website.**
Large C18 walled garden of interest
to garden historians. Interesting iron
entrance gate; herbaceous borders,
yew hedges and Orangery with an
attractive pond. Small sales area
specialising in unusual hardy plants.
House, long closed for major repairs,
won the Historic Houses Association-
Sotheby's Restoration Award 2014. It
will re-open in July. The garden
retains the essential features of its
original 18th century design,
combined with sympathetic
replanting in the English style. There
are borders of gold and silver plants,
of old-fashioned peonies, and irises in
season. Visitors frequently comment
on its tranquil atmosphere. Most
areas wheelchair accessible along
gravel paths.

76 **THE NURSERY**
15 Knapton Lane, Acomb, York
YO26 5PX. Tony Chalcraft & Jane
Thurlow, 01904 781691. *2¹/₂ m W of
York. From A1237 take B1224
direction Acomb. At r'about turn L
(Beckfield Ln.), after 150 metres Turn
L*. Home-made teas. **Adm £3, chd
free.** Sun 19 July (1-5); Wed 22
July (2-8).
Hidden attractive and productive
1-acre organic garden behind
suburban house (not open). Wide
range of top and soft fruit with over
100 fruit trees, many in trained form.

Many different vegetables grown both
outside and under cover incl a large
20m greenhouse. Productive areas
interspersed with informal ornamental
plantings providing colour and habitat
for wildlife. Tomato tasting on Wed
opening if there is enough ripe fruit!

GROUP OPENING

77 **NUTKINS & NEW HOUSE,
HORNSEA**
Hornsea HU18 1UR. *12 NE of
Beverley. On B1242 S-side of
Hornsea between Freeport & golf
course. Directions to New House
from Nutkins signed*. Tea at Nutkins.
Combined adm £5, chd free.
Sun 31 May (11-4).

NEW HOUSE
Mrs Kate Willans.
*N end of Cliff Rd, opp bus
garage. Garden is halfway down
L fork*
**Visitors also welcome by
arrangement May to July will
open alone or combined with
'Nutkins'.**
01964 534502
kwkatewillans32@gmail.com

NUTKINS
Alan & Janet Stirling
**Visitors also welcome by
arrangement May to July.**
01964 533721
ashornsea@aol.com

Two gardens set in the popular
seaside town. One large garden
divided into different areas with a
sense of fun, and a smaller garden,
a real gem with plants for the
enthusiast. Hornsea has seaside
attractions, as well as the Mere,
Museum, Freeport and Honeysuckle
Farm nearby. Nutkins covers ³/₄ acre
with herbaceous borders, bog
garden, streamside walk and
woodland garden with pergolas and
gazebo. Plenty of seating to linger
and enjoy different views of the
garden and see light play on many
pieces of stained glass. New House
is a compact plant enthusiasts
garden, close to the sea with island
beds and borders containing hardy
and tender herbaceous and shrubs,
some unusual, wildlife ponds,
greenhouse with a succulent
collection and a seating area. Vertical
'growing wall', new last year.
Wheelchair access at Nutkins.

© Harpur GL

Linden Lodge

78 NEW OAKLEY GARTH

Sneaton Lane, Ruswarp, Whitby
YO22 5HN. Mr & Mrs Michael
Holliday. *2m W of Whitby on edge of
Ruswarp village. From Whitby, follow
B1416 signed Ruswarp & Sneaton.
Pass through Ruswarp village, over
river bridge, bear R, car park 200m
on L, opp auction mart. Footpath to
gardens 50m.* Light refreshments,
home baking. **Combined adm with
Rosebank £4, chd free.** Sun 17
May, Sun 21 June (12-5).
Developed by owners to give year
round interest and colour, on west
facing slope of 2/3 acre. Mature trees
and shrubs, terrace, gravel garden,
water features, large variety of
perennials, raised vegetable beds,
streamside garden and adjoining wild
flower meadow. Organic with
abundant wildlife.

79 OATMILL COTTAGE

Lealholm, nr Whitby YO21 2AG.
Sue Morgan,
jpm.oatmill@btinternet.com. *9m W
of Whitby. Turn from A171 to
Lealholm. Parking in centre of village
or by station. Garden just below
station across railway line.* Home-
made teas. **Adm £3.50, chd free.**
Sun 19 July (11-4.30). Visitors also
welcome by arrangement June to
Aug groups of 10+.
Cottage-style garden with a variety of
herbaceous borders with drought-
tolerant plants, terrace, range of
mature trees and shrubs set on the
hillside overlooking the picturesque
village of Lealholm. Features incl

sculpture, fountain, bog garden and
summerhouse. Plant sales in village
nursery adjacent to the garden and at
the garden. Art Exhibition of garden-
inspired sculpture and painting.
Featured in Amateur Gardening
Magazine.

80 OLD SLENINGFORD HALL

Mickley, nr Ripon HG4 3JD. Jane &
Tom Ramsden. *5m NW of Ripon. Off
A6108. After N Stainley turn L, follow
signs to Mickley. Gates on R after
1½ m opp cottage.* Home-made
teas. **Adm £5, chd free.** Sat 30,
Sun 31 May (12-4).
A large English country garden and
developing 'Forest Garden'. Early
C19 house (not open) and garden
with original layout; wonderful mature
trees, woodland walk and Victorian
fernery; romantic lake with islands,
watermill, walled kitchen garden;
beautiful long herbaceous border,
yew and huge beech hedges. Award
winning permaculture forest garden.
Several plant stalls. Picnics very
welcome. Reasonable wheelchair
access to most parts of garden.
Disabled WC at Old Sleningford Farm
next to the garden.

81 OMEGA

79 Magdalen Lane, Hedon
HU12 8LA. Mr & Mrs D Rosindale,
01482 897370,
mavirosi@hotmail.co.uk. *6m E of
Hull. Through to E Hull onto A1033.
L into St Augustine's Gate through
Market Place, immed R to Magdalen

Gate, ahead to Magdalen Lane.*
Cream teas. **Adm £3, chd free.**
Sat 20, Sun 21 June (12-5.30).
Visitors also welcome by
arrangement June to July groups
min 20, adm incls cream tea.
Front garden has box hedging and
densely planted borders. Small side
garden acers, ferns and planted
troughs. The patio has planted
containers. The back has herbaceous
borders and a shady area. An arch
leads to a small border, greenhouses
and a young orchard. The wild
garden will become a mini-meadow.
Cream Teas, beverages and cakes
available. Afternoon Tea can be
booked in advance by telephone.
Large range of perennial plants for
sale incl hostas, succulents and some
bedding plants.

82 THE ORCHARD

4a Blackwood Rise, Cookridge,
Leeds LS16 7BG. Carol & Michael
Abbott, 0113 2676764,
michael.john.abbott@hotmail.co.uk.
*5m N of Leeds centre. Off A660
(Leeds-Otley) N of A6120 Ring Rd.
Turn L up Otley Old Rd. At top of hill
turn L at T-lights (Tinshill Lane).
Please park in Tinshill Lane.* Home-
made teas. Light Lunches. **Adm £3,
chd free.** Sun 28 June (12.30-5.30).
Visitors also welcome by
arrangement May to July groups of
10+.
A hidden oasis of peace and
tranquillity. Differing levels made by
owners using stone, found on site,
planted for yr-round interest.
Extensive rockery, unusual fruit tree
arbour, sheltered oriental style seated
area linked by grass paths lawns and
steps. Mixed perennials, shrubs,
bulbs and pots amongst paved and
pebbled areas. Best in area award
Leeds in Bloom.

83 ORCHARD HOUSE

Sandholme Lane, Leven
HU17 5LW. Mrs Frances Cooper,
01964 542359,
franciscooper1@gmail.com. *In
Leven turn between Hare & Hounds
PH & PO. Continue for 400yds then
onto Carr Lane picking up yellow
signs to Orchard House.* Light
refreshments. **Adm £5, chd free.**
Visitors welcome by
arrangement Mar to Sept for
groups of 2-30, adm incl
refreshments.
A peaceful verdant refuge, full of

birds, many trees with secluded walkways opening into calm spaces with happy plants and a magical ambience.

84 ◆ PARCEVALL HALL GARDENS

Skyreholme, nr Skipton BD23 6DE. Walsingham College, www.parcevallhallgardens.co.uk. *9m N of Skipton. Signs from B6160 Bolton Abbey-Burnsall rd or off B6265 Grassington-Pateley Bridge.* Light refreshments. **Adm £6, chd free. For NGS: Wed 20 May (10-5).** For other opening times and information, please phone or see garden website.
The only garden open daily in the Yorkshire Dales National Park. 24 acres in Wharfedale sheltered by mixed woodland; terrace garden, rose garden, rock garden, fish ponds. Mixed borders, spring bulbs, tender shrubs (desfontainea, crinodendron, camellias); autumn colour. Bird watching, old apple orchard for picnics. Café.

85 NEW PENNY PIECE COTTAGES

Penny Piece, 41/43 Piercy End, Kirkbymoorside, York YO62 6DQ. Mick & Ann Potter, 01751 430933, skimmers@gmail.com. *Follow A170 to Kirkbymoorside at r'about turn up into Kirkby Main St approx 300yds on R. Some street parking plus council car park at top of Main St.* Home-made teas. **Adm £3.50, chd free. Sun 14 June (12-5).** Visitors also welcome by arrangement Apr to Sept groups 10+.
Hidden away off the main street in Kirkbymoorside is a romantic cottage garden. Now fully matured it offers a sunny circular gravel garden incl lawns with island beds and mixed shrub and herbaceous borders. Gravel pathway leads to a brick garden, informal pond, bog garden and colourful herbaceous border. A rose arbour leads through to a wildlife pond and flower meadow.

86 NEW ◆ PICTORIAL MEADOWS

Sheffield Manor Lodge, 389 Manor Lane, Sheffield S2 1UL. Green Estate Ltd, www.pictorialmeadows.co.uk. *1m Sheffield City Centre. M1 J33/34 Sheffield Parkway A57 to city centre.*

Follow B6070 from Park Square. Manor Oaks Entrance of Sheffield Manor Lodge. Light refreshments in Rhubarb Shed Café. **Adm by donation. For NGS: Fri 3, Sat 4 July (10-4.30).** For other opening times and information, please see garden website.
A chance to get 'behind the scenes' of Pictorial Meadows. Public access to the research beds and new seed production nursery. 12pm on both days there will be a 30 minute introduction to the science and botany of meadows and staff and volunteers will be on hand to answer questions. Lots more to see and do on site as part of the general garden offer incl the fabulous Lavender Labyrinth. Disabled WC is available on site. Paths are mostly grass and the land is sloping but access to most areas with a helper is possible.

87 PILMOOR COTTAGES

Pilmoor, nr Helperby YO61 2QQ. Wendy & Chris Jakeman, 01845 501848, cnjakeman@aol.com. *20m N of York. From A1M J48. N end B'bridge follow rd towards Easingwold. From A19 follow signs to Hutton Sessay then Helperby. Garden next to mainline railway.* Light refreshments. **Adm £3.50, chd free. Wed 10, Wed 17 June, Sun 30 Aug (12-5).** Visitors also welcome by arrangement June to Sept.
2-acre garden round C19 cottages. Developed by 2 avid garden visitors unable to visit a garden without buying a new plant, leading to an informal cottage style, but always with something to look at from bulbs in spring to colchicum and cyclamen in autumn. Clock-golf putting green. 71/4' Gauge railway around the garden, ponds and rockery.

88 THE PRIORY, NUN MONKTON & VILLAGE GARDENS

nr York YO26 8ES. Mr & Mrs R Harpin. *9m W of York, 12 E of Harrogate. E of A1M J47 off A59 signed Nun Monkton.* Light refreshments and home-made teas. **Adm £6, chd free. Sun 21 June (12-5).**
Large country garden at the confluence of the rivers Nidd and Ouse surrounding a William and Mary house (not open). Formal rose garden. Old walls support climbers and give a backdrop to long mixed borders, mature species trees and

clipped yew walk leads to informal parkland with beck. Kitchen garden, greenhouse and glasshouse for ornamentals. Adjacent is St Mary's Church with Burne-Jones stained glass windows and also open some village gardens around quintessential English village green with maypole, PH and duck pond. Gravel paths.

> Plants propagated by enthusiastic knowledgeable owners . . .

ALLOTMENTS

89 QUEENSGATE & KITCHEN LANE ALLOTMENTS

Beverley HU17 8NN. Beverley Town Council. *Outskirts of Beverley Town Centre. On A164 towards Cottingham, allotment site is before Victoria Rd, after double mini r'about & opp Beverley Grammar School.* Tea. **Adm £2.50, chd free. Sun 26 July (12-4).**
Varied allotment site of 85 plots, plus another 35 on Kitchen Lane, growing a wide variety of fruit, vegetables and flowers. Some allotment holders will be present to discuss their plots. Wide grass path for easy viewing and plots either side. Dogs on leads.

90 THE RED HOUSE

17 Whin Hill Road, Bessacarr, Doncaster DN4 7AF. Rosie Hamlin, www.pyjamagardenersyorks.com. *2m S of Doncaster. A638 South, L at T-lights for B1396, Whin Hill Rd is 2nd R. A638 North, R signed Branton B1396 onto Whin Hill.* Home-made teas. **Adm £3.50, chd free. Sat 16, Sun 17 May (2-5).**
Mature 2/3 acre garden. Dry shade a challenge but acid loving plants a joy. Fine acers, camellia, daphne, rhododendrons, kalmia and eucryphia. Terrace and rockery stepping stones lead past and through new wave and cloud pruned shrubs to lawn with modern orb-shaped rotating summerhouse and young trees. White border conceals pond, compost and hens.

PARKINSON'S^{UK}

Thank you to the NGS for supporting Parkinson's nurses

91 REWELA COTTAGE

Skewsby YO61 4SG. John Plant & Daphne Ellis, 01347 888125, plantjohnsgarden@btinternet.com. *4m N of Sheriff Hutton, 15m N of York. After Sheriff Hutton, towards Terrington, turn L towards Whenby & Brandsby. Turn R just past Whenby to Skewsby. Turn L into village. 400yds on R.* Home-made teas. Great cakes & scones, soft drinks. Plus BBQ serving Burgers & Sausages. WC. Adm £3.50, chd free. Sun 3 May, Sun 26 July (11-5). Visitors also welcome by arrangement May to July excl June, min 10 adm £6.
³/₄-acre ornamental garden, designed by current owner, featuring unusual trees, shrubs, and architectural plants. Pond, pergola, natural stone sunken garden, breeze house, vegetable garden/nursery and new outdoor kitchen. Specialist grower of heuchera, hosta and penstemon. Many varieties also for sale. A very friendly welcome. Lovely surroundings for lunch. All unusual trees and shrubs have labels giving full descriptions, picture, and any cultivation notes incl propagation. Plant sales are specimens from garden. Many varieties of Heuchera, Heucherella and Tiarellas, Penstemon, Hostas and herbs for sale. Featured in Garden Answers. Plenty of seats.

♿ 🐕 ✿ 🚐 ☕

92 ◆ RHS GARDEN HARLOW CARR

Crag Lane, Harrogate HG3 1QB. Royal Horticultural Society, 01423 565418, www.rhs.org.uk/harlowcarr. *1½ m W of Harrogate town centre. On B6162 (Harrogate - Otley).* Adm £8.95, chd £4.50. For NGS: Sun 26 Apr (9.30-5). For other opening times and information, please phone or see garden website.
One of Yorkshire's most relaxing yet inspiring locations! Highlights incl spectacular herbaceous borders, streamside garden, alpines, scented and kitchen gardens. 'Gardens Through Time', woodland and wild flower meadows. Betty's Tearoom, gift shop, plant centre and childrens play area incl tree house and log maze. Wheelchairs and mobility scooters available, advanced booking recommended.

♿ ✿ 🚐 ☕

93 THE RIDINGS

South Street, Burton Fleming, Driffield YO25 3PE. Roy & Ruth Allerston, 01262 470489. *11m NE of Driffield. 11m SW of Scarborough. 7m NW of Bridlington. From Driffield B1249, before Foxholes turn R to Burton Fleming. From Scarborough A165 turn R to Burton Fleming.* Home-made teas. Adm £3, chd free. Sun 24 May, Sun 5 July (1-5). Combined adm with Rustic Cottage £5, 5 July. Visitors also welcome by arrangement Apr to Sept.
Tranquil cottage garden designed by owners in 2001 on reclaimed site. Brick pergola and arches covered with climbers lead to secret garden with lavender and box edged beds. Colour-themed mixed borders with old English roses. Paved terrace with water feature and farming bygones, small potager; summerhouse and greenhouse.

🐕 ✿ 🚐 ☕

94 NEW ROSEBANK

Sneaton Lane, Ruswarp, Whitby YO22 5JA. Elaine Hoyle. *2m W of Whitby on edge of Ruswarp village. From Whitby follow B1416 signed Ruswarp & Sneaton. Pass through Ruswarp over river bridge, car park 200m on L. Footpath to gardens, 50 metres.* Light refreshments. Home-made refreshments. Combined adm with Oakley Garth £4, chd free. Sun 17 May, Sun 21 June (12-5).
A plantswoman's garden with a huge range of plants (many unusual,some rare) grown in a variety of situations linked by paths and steps which lead you around the garden. Trees, shrubs, perennials, roses, bulbs and ferns provide a tapestry of colour, texture and scent for year round interest. The ²/₃ acre sloping site (steep in places) is a haven for wildlife.

✿ ☕

95 RUSTIC COTTAGE

Front Street, Wold Newton, nr Driffield YO25 3YQ. Jan Joyce, 01262 470710. *13m N of Driffield. From Driffield take B1249 to Foxholes (12m), take R turning signed Wold Newton. Turn L onto Front St, opp village pond, continue up hill, garden on L.* Combined adm with The Ridings £5, chd free. Sun 5 July (1-5). Visitors also welcome by arrangement Apr to Sept max group size 20.
Plantswoman's cottage garden of much interest with many choice and unusual plants. Hellebores and bulbs are treats for colder months. Old-fashioned roses, fragrant perennials, herbs and wild flowers, all grown together provide habitat for birds, bees, butterflies and small mammals. It has been described as 'organised chaos'! The owner's 2nd NGS garden. Small dogs only.

🐕 ✿

96 ◆ SCAMPSTON WALLED GARDEN

Scampston Hall, Scampston, Malton YO17 8NG. The Legard Family, 01944 759111, www.scampston.co.uk/gardens. *5m E of Malton. ¹/₂ m N of A64, nr the village of Rillington & signed Scampston only.* The restaurant, within the Walled Garden, may be visited without paying entry to the garden. For opening times and information, please phone or see garden website.
An exciting modern garden designed by Piet Oudolf. The 4-acre walled garden contains a series of hedged enclosures designed to look good throughout the year. The garden contains many unusual species and is a must for any keen plantsman. The Walled Garden is set within the grounds and parkland surrounding Scampston Hall. The Hall opens to visitors for a short period during the summer months. A newly restored Richardson conservatory at the heart of the Walled Garden is due to re-open as a Heritage and Learning Centre in 2015.

♿ ✿ 🚐 ☕

97 NEW SERENITY

Arkendale Road, Ferrensby, nr Knaresborough HG5 0QA. Mr & Mrs Smith, 01423 340062, geoffsmith269@gmail.com. *3m NE of Knaresborough, 4m SW of Boroughbridge. On A6055 between Boroughbridge & Knaresborough.*

*A1M J47 follow A168 N, after 3m
turn L to Arkendale & Ferrensby.*
Home-made teas. **Adm £3, chd free.
Wed 5, Sun 9 Aug (12-5). Visitors
also welcome by arrangement July
to Aug groups of 20+, tours and
coaches.**
After the complete renovation of a
¼ acre garden by removal of all
conifers and large overgrown
evergreens in 2013 the garden is
now full of colour with wide borders
and circular lawn feature, over
100 clematis and many thousand
herbaceous perennials and annuals
propagated by enthusiastic
knowledgeable owners. Vegetable
garden, patio, terrace, garden
structures, greenhouse and seating
areas.

❀ 🚐 ☕

98 ◆ SHANDY HALL GARDENS
Coxwold YO61 4AD. The Laurence
Sterne Trust, 01347 868465,
www.laurencesternetrust.org.uk/sh
andy-hall-garden.php. *N of York.
From A19, 7m from both Easingwold
& Thirsk, turn E signed Coxwold.* **For
NGS: Evening Openings £3, chd
£1, Fri 5, Fri 19 June, Fri 3 July
(6.30-8). For other opening times
and information, please phone or
see garden website.**
Home of C18 author Laurence
Sterne. 2 walled gardens, 1 acre of
unusual perennials interplanted with
tulips and old roses in low walled
beds. In old quarry, another acre of
trees, shrubs, bulbs, climbers and
wild flowers encouraging wildlife, incl
over 350 recorded species of moths.
Moth trap, identification and release.
Guardian 'Think outside the box' 'The
Writer's Garden' by Jackie Bennett.
Wheelchair access to wild garden by
arrangement.

♿ 🏠 ❀ 🛏

GROUP OPENING

**99 SHIPTONTHORPE
GARDENS**
York YO43 3PQ. *2m NW of Market
Weighton. From Market Weighton on
A1079, take 2nd turn off to
Shiptonthorpe Cairngorm on R is
start point with car parking opp. Tea
at Cairngorm.* **Combined adm £5,
chd free. Sat 6, Sun 7 June (11-5).**

    6 ALL SAINTS
    Station Rd. Di Thompson

    CAIRNGORM
    Station Road. Peter & Ann
    Almond

    EAST VIEW
    Town Street. Maureen Almond

    FIELD VIEW,
    Mrs L Wollaston
    Visitors also welcome by
    arrangement Mar to Sept for
    groups 4+.
    7950079511
    lynnewollaston@hotmail.com

Four contrasting gardens offering
different approaches to gardening
style - a contemporary garden; a
small garden making a big impression
with good use of vertical height; a
more traditional garden with mixed
and evergreen planting; and lastly a
cottage garden, tucked out of sight.
6 All Saints is planned like a maze
with a mixture of contemporary and
cottage garden features; hidden
corners, water features and pond.
Cairngorm has gravelled areas and
paths, conifers, ferns, hostas, a
vegetable plot, log cabin, greenhouse
and new feature for this year.
East View, hidden away, is a long
narrow garden with cottage
herbaceous planting. Hostas and
ferns set off a water feature near the
cottage and a wildlife pond is tucked
peacefully away. Field View is a small
garden intensively planted with a mix
of evergreen and deciduous small
trees, shrubs and herbaceous
perennials. This provides a tranquil,
private space with all-yr-round
interest and colour. Art work on show
at East View from 2014. Wheelchair
access possible with help at 6 All
Saints, but not at other gardens due
to steep driveways/difficult access.

🏠 ❀ 🚐 ☕

100 NEW SION HILL
Kirby Wiske, Thirsk YO7 4EU.
H.W.Mawer Trust, www.sionhillhall.
co.uk. *6m S of Northallerton off A167
4m W of Thirsk, 6m E of A1 via A61.*
Tea. **Adm £5, chd free. Sat 20,
Sun 21 June (11-5).**
The garden surrounds an Arts and
Crafts neo-Georgian house built in
1913,designed by Walter Brierley of
York(not open). Restored and
replanted after years of neglect by
Michael Mallaby. Formal parterre,
Baroque statuary, clipped box and
hornbeam. Long walk, with yews,
shrubs and herbaceous planting.
Kitchen garden. Centenary garden.
Mostly level gravelled paths surround
the parterre. Grassed Long Walk
accessible in dry weather. Steep
slope to Kitchen garden.

♿ 🚐 ☕

101 SKIPWITH HALL
Skipwith, nr Selby YO8 5SQ.
Mr & Mrs C D Forbes Adam,
www.escrick.com/hall-gardens. *9m
S of York, 6m N of Selby. From York
A19 Selby, L in Escrick, 4m to
Skipwith. From Selby A19 York, R
onto A163 to Market Weighton, then
L after 2m to Skipwith.* Home-made
teas. **Adm £5, chd free. Thur 4
June (1-4).**
4-acre walled garden of Queen Anne
house (not open). Ancient mulberry,
extensive mixed borders and walled
areas by renowned designer Cecil
Pinsent. Recreated working kitchen
garden with 15' beech hedge,
pleached fruit walks, herb maze and
pool. Woodland with specimen trees
and shell house. Decorative orchard
with espaliered and fan-trained fruit
on walls. Gravel paths.

♿ ❀ 🚐 ☕

*Trees, shrubs,
perennials, roses,
bulbs and ferns
provide a tapestry
of colour, texture
and scent . . .*

**102 SLEIGHTHOLMEDALE
LODGE**
Fadmoor YO62 7JG. Patrick &
Natasha James, 01751 430955,
patrick.james@landscapeagency.
co.uk. *6m NE of Helmsley. Parking
can be limited in wet weather.
Garden is the first property in
Sleightholmedale, 1m from Fadmoor.*
Tea Sunday only. **Adm £3.50, chd
free. Sat 4, Sun 5 July (2-6).
Visitors also welcome by
arrangement May to Sept.**
Hillside garden, walled rose garden
and herbaceous borders with
delphiniums, roses, verbascums in
July. Species tulips and meconopsis
in early June. Views over peaceful
valley in N.Yorks Moors.

🏠 ☕

Look out for the NGS yellow arrows ...

GROUP OPENING

103 NEW SPOFFORTH GARDENS

Canby Lane, Spofforth, nr Harrogate HG3 1AQ. *6m SE of Harrogate, 3m NW of Wetherby. On A661, turn into village at mini r'about.* Home-made teas at Castle Holt. **Combined adm £5, chd free.** Sun 14 June (12-5).

> **NEW BROOMHILL**
> Canby Lane. Miss Gillian Pepper

> **NEW CASTLE HOLT**
> Castle Street. Mrs Linda Pinder

A charming village, its origins date pre Doomsday, between Wetherby and Harrogate with a historical Castle, ancestral home of the Percy family, and ancient Church. The Harland Cycle Way links Spofforth to Wetherby. The two gardens are in the heart of the old village within easy walking distance. The large mature garden at Castle Holt has lovely open views, long deep sweeping herbaceous borders full of colour, a shade garden for ferns and hostas, alpine garden with natural exposed bedrock, sloping lawns below long terrace with roses and large pots leading to the vegetable garden, greenhouse, paddock and stream. Broomhill is a small pretty cottage garden renovated and replanted in 2010. Gravel paths lead through mixed planting giving successional colour and where there is limited soil depth due to challenging exposed rock many plants for dry places. An archway leads to greenhouse and terrace with steps to circular lawn and borders full of interest. Please park in Castle Street.

GROUP OPENING

104 STAMFORD BRIDGE GARDENS

Grove Lodge, Butts Close, Stamford Bridge YO41 1PD. G & D Tattersall, 01759 373838, dmt9245@hotmail.co.uk. *Stamford Bridge. Approx 7m E of York on the A166 to Bridlington. Please use main car park in village or station car park on Church Rd.* Home-made teas at Daneswell House. **Combined adm £5, chd free.** Sun 2 Aug (12-5). Visitors also welcome by

arrangement for all 3 gardens July to Aug groups of 10+.

> **DANESWELL HOUSE**
> Brian & Pauline Clayton

> **GROVE LODGE**
> Mr & Mrs G Tattersall

> **MILL TIMBER**
> Mr & Mrs K Chapman

Three interesting and contrasting gardens situated in the historic village of Stamford Bridge. Grove Lodge has a large collection of plants grown from seed or propagated from cuttings by the owner. There are small number of vegetables grown in planters, fruit trees and greenhouse containing a variety of salad vegetables. Mill Timber has a good collection of perennials in a large, eye catching, sloping border. The garden is sheltered on one side by mature trees. Patio planters with summer flowers and hanging baskets displaying a kaleidoscope of colour. Daneswell House is a ³⁄₄ -acre terraced garden that sweeps down to the R Derwent. Pond and water feature with walk over bridge. Large lawned area with mixed borders and shrubs. Attracts wildlife.

White border with dovecote and doves; pink-purple hot border . . .

105 ◆ STILLINGFLEET LODGE

Stewart Lane, Stillingfleet, nr York YO19 6HP. Mr & Mrs J Cook, 01904 728506, www.stillingfleetlodgenurseries.co.uk. *6m S of York. From A19 York-Selby take B1222 towards Sherburn in Elmet. In village turn opp church.* Home-made teas. **Adm £5, chd £1.** For NGS: Sun 10 May, Sun 6 Sept (1-5). **For other opening times and information, please phone or see garden website.**
Organic, wildlife garden subdivided into smaller gardens, each based on colour theme with emphasis on use of foliage plants. Wild flower meadow

and natural pond. 55yd double herbaceous borders. Modern rill garden. Rare breeds of poultry wander freely in garden. Adjacent nursery. Telegraph, Country Living, Yorkshire Ridings, Living North. Gravel paths and lawn. Ramp to cafe if needed No disabled wc.

106 SUTTON GRANGE

Masham, Ripon HG4 4PB. Mr & Mrs Robert Jameson. *1¹⁄₂ m W of Masham. From Masham towards Leyburn (A6108) L into Sutton Lane single track tarmac rd, parking & entry at Low Sutton ¹⁄₄ m on L.* **Combined adm with Low Sutton £5, chd free.** Sun 21 June (12-5).
1¹⁄₂ acre established garden and orchard with woodland walk incl greenhouse with tomatoes and fig tree, walled vegetable garden with cutting flower beds and gazebo, summerhouse lawns surround by herbaceous borders with iris, roses, peonies, wisteria, and clematis, laburnum and honeysuckle arches, many places to sit and enjoy the views or have a game of croquet or boules.

107 NEW SUTTON UPON DERWENT SCHOOL

Main Street, Sutton On Derwent, York YO41 4BN. Head - Angela Ekers. Garden - Annette Atkin. *From M Weighton on A1079, pass Pocklington. At Jet garage on R, go L into Sutton Lane. Follow rd to village, L at tennis courts. Blind corner, school on R.* Teas. **Adm £2.50, chd free.** Sat 11 July (10-3). **Also opening, Bugthorpe Gardens, 15 mins away.**
Sutton upon Derwent school is an RHS level 5 school garden. Grounds developed over the past 6yrs, have become the gardens which are now an integral part of school life; encouraging outdoor lessons in all areas of the curriculum. Outdoor learning spaces incl, a sensory garden, wildlife area, extensive vegetable growing areas, greenhouse and poly tunnel. Children's activities.

108 SWALE COTTAGE

Station Road, Richmond DL10 4LU. Julie Martin & Dave Dalton. *Richmond town centre. On foot, facing bottom of Market Place, turn L onto Frenchgate, then R onto Station Rd. House 1st on R.* Home-

made teas. **Adm £3, chd free.**
Sun 14 June (1-5). **Also open**
Millgate House.
$^1/_2$ -acre urban oasis on steep site,
with sweeping views and hidden
corners. Several enclosed garden
rooms on different levels. Mature
herbaceous, rose and shrub garden
with some areas of recent
improvement. Magnificent yew and
cedar. Organic vegetables and soft
fruit and pond. Adjacent orchard and
paddock with sheep and hens. Some
rough paths and inaccessible areas.

109 NEW **TAMARIND**
2 Whin Hill Road, Bessacarr,
Doncaster DN4 7AE. Ken & Carol
Kilvington. *2m S of Doncaster. A638*
S Doncaster-Bawtry. After Lakeside,
straight on at T-lights then 1st L.
A638 N turn R signed Cantley-
Branton (B1396). Light refreshments.
Adm £3, chd free. Sun 28 June
(11-5). Also open 2 Hollin Close,
Rossington.
This $^2/_3$ acre garden is level to the
front with acers and varied planting
round shaped lawn leading to a
steeply terraced rear garden full of
colour and differing styles. White
border with dovecote and doves;
pink-purple hot border; herbaceous
embankment and newly developed
rhododendron garden. Stream with
waterfalls, ponds, rockery and bog
garden, thatched summerhouse,
patio. Steep steps. Front garden, rear
lower patios are accessible to
wheelchairs, from which most of the
rear garden can be viewed. Steps to
the rest of the garden.

110 **TERRINGTON HOUSE**
Terrington YO60 6PU. Mr & Mrs
James Fenwick,
www.lindafenwickshelldesign.com.
15m NE of York. Last house in village
on R if coming from Sheriff Hutton or
1st on L coming from A64 & Castle
Howard rd. Home-made teas. **Adm**
£4, chd free. Sun 10 May (11-4).
Formal garden set in 3 acres with
exquisite Shell House and mixed
borders. Spring: mixed beds of
brunnera, narcissi, tulips, azaleas,
daffodils, bluebells, rhododendrons,
roses, box hedges, beech hedges,
double blue primroses, philadelphus,
peonies, hostas. Impressive trees
including split-leaf beech,herb garden
parterre and vegetable garden. The
Shell House. Featured in Homes and
Gardens, Period Living, Coast,

Norton Conyers

Yorkshire Post, Daily Telegraph, Nicky
Summer Lifestyle magazine.

111 NEW ◆ **THORNYCROFT**
Rainton, nr Thirsk YO7 3PH. Martin
& Jill Fish, 01845 577157,
www.martinfish.com. *1m E of A1(M)*
between Ripon & Thirsk. Approx 6m
N of Boroughbridge, Access to
Rainton is from J48 or 50 of A1(M) or
from A168 dual carriageway at
Asenby or Topcliffe. Home-made
teas. **Adm £3.50, chd free.** For
NGS: Sun 19 July (11-5). **For other**
opening times and information,
please phone or see garden
website.
A $^3/_4$ acre country garden created
since 2009 comprising lawn areas,
trees, shrubs and perennials and
featuring some unusual plant
specimens. Pergola, summerhouse
and paved courtyard garden with
container plants and raised beds.
Orchard with mixture of heritage and
modern varieties and an ornamental
kitchen garden. Wooden greenhouse
with decorative plants and productive
poly-tunnel. A working garden

featured regularly in Garden News,
Kitchen Garden magazine and the
Harrogate Advertiser series. Martin
Fish is also one of the gardening
experts on BBC Radio York & BBC
Radio Nottingham and will be on
hand to answer garden queries.
Gravel drive leading to main garden.

112 **TICKTON CE PRIMARY**
Main Street, Tickton, Beverley
HU17 9RZ. Miss C Brown, Garden
- Sue McCallum. *E of Beverley.*
Tickton is signed from A1035. Light
refreshments. **Adm £2.50, chd free.**
Fri 19 June (10-3).
At Tickton school we actively
encourage outdoor learning incl
gardening. The aim is to provide a
stimulating environment for play and
educational activities whilst creating
habitats for wildlife. Children will be
involved in a variety of activities to
demonstrate the use of the grounds.
Many of the refreshments will have
been prepared by the children.
Wheelchair access to most of the
garden incl the refreshment area.

Lemon drizzle cake, Victoria sponge … yummy!

113 WARLEY HOUSE GARDEN

Stock Lane, Warley, Halifax HX2 7RU. Dr & Mrs P J Hinton, 01422 831431, warleyhousegardens@outlook.com, www.warleyhousegardens.com. *2m W of Halifax. Take A646 (Burnley) from Halifax. Go through large intersection after approx 1m. Approx 1m further take a R turn up Windle Royd Lane. Signs will direct you from here.* Home-made teas. **Adm £4, chd free.** Sun 10, Wed 13 May (1-5). **Visitors also welcome by arrangement Apr to June we welcome groups of any size (10+) with 4 weeks notice.**

Partly walled 2½ acre garden of demolished C18 House, renovated by the present owners. Rocky paths and Japanese style planting lead to lawns and lovely S-facing views. Alpine ravine planted with ferns and fine trees give structure to the developing woodland area. Drifts of shrubs, herbaceous plantings, wild flowers and heathers maintain constant seasonal interest. WC available to accommodate wheelchairs. Partial wheelchair access to Japanese garden. Disabled parking on site is permitted but limited to perhaps 4 or 5 vehicles.

GROUP OPENING

114 NEW WARLEY VILLAGE

nr Halifax HX2 7RW. *2m W of Halifax. From Halifax take A58 (Rochdale/Burnley). After A58/A646 Junction proceed onto A646. After 1m turn R (Windle Royd Lane) Turn L, park on Stock Lane prior to Village for BOTH gardens.* Cream Teas at Edgeholme, Teas at Green Hill House. **Combined adm £5, chd free.** Sun 12 July (11-5).

  EDGEHOLME
  Stock Lane. Mrs S L Ryan

  NEW **GREEN HILL HOUSE**
  Water Hill Lane. Mrs Pamela
  Berry

This historic hillside village in the Calder Valley boasts rural hostelries, school, children's playground, cricket pitch, unique allotments and also cemetery with outstanding views of the countryside. Leaflet available showing short walks between gardens and these points of interest.The open gardens are a 5 minute walk apart. Edgeholme is a country house garden complementing the 1910 Arts and Crafts house (not open). Colourful mixed herbaceous borders, paths and steps link the upper and lower areas. Natural hillside stream enters via stone trough, flowing into formal and informal ponds and bog garden. Green Hill House garden has been remodelled and renovated in recent years, this ¼ acre family garden has woodland glade, formal lawn, topiary, herbaceous borders and courtyard. I-Spy trail for children. WC. Both gardens have plenty of places to sit and admire the planting and views of the Pennine landscape. Please park as directed due to narrow lanes and steep hills.

We help improve patient care in the community

115 WEATHERVANE HOUSE

Mill Lane, Seaton Ross YO42 4NE. Peter & Julie Williams. *6m S of Pocklington. 15m SE of York & 12m N of Howden.* Home-made teas. **Adm £3, chd free.** Sat 9 May (11-4). Two-acre woodland garden with magnolias, rhododendrons, azaleas, flowering trees and shrubs. A wide range of spring bulbs incl erythroniums and trilliums together with mixed herbaceous borders, lawns and circular meadow. Fruit garden, glasshouse with wide range of hardy and tender plants and large polytunnel with specimen rhododendrons and many other plants. A wide range of interesting and uncommon shrubs and herbaceous perennials for sale that reflect the plants growing in the garden. Examples of plants propagated by cuttings, grafting and raised from seed are available. Artist in the garden. Gravel drive and paths but wheelchair passage possible.

116 THE WHITE HOUSE

Husthwaite YO61 4QA. Mrs A Raper, 01347 868688. *5m S of Thirsk. Turn R off A19 signed Husthwaite. 1½ m to centre of village opp parish church.* Light refreshments. **Adm £5, chd free. Visitors welcome by arrangement any size group.**

Meet an enthusiastic plantswoman. Exchange ideas and visit a 1-acre country garden. Walled garden, conservatory, herbaceous borders, fresh lavender and purple palette in late spring and hot summer border. Unusual plants and shrubs. Collections of pÊonies, clematis and hemerocallis (in season), landscaping, planting and bed of English and shrub roses in the old orchard. A garden for all seasons.

GROUP OPENING

117 WHIXLEY GARDENS

nr York YO26 8AR. *8m W of York, 8m E of Harrogate, 6m N of Wetherby. 3m E of A1(M) off A59 York-Harrogate. Signed Whixley.* Home-made teas at The Old Vicarage. **Combined adm £6, chd free.** Sun 3, Mon 4 May (12-5).

  ASH TREE HOUSE
  High Street. Mr & Mrs E P
  Moffitt

  COBBLE COTTAGE
  John Hawkridge & Barry
  Atkinson
  Visitors also welcome by
  arrangement groups of 10+.
  01423 331419
  johnbarry44@talktalk.net

  NEW **LYDIATE HOUSE**
  Roger & Sheila Lythe.

  THE OLD VICARAGE
  Mr & Mrs Roger Marshall
  Visitors also welcome by
  arrangement May to July
  groups of 10+.
  biddymarshall@btopenworld.
  com

Attractive rural yet accessible village nestling on the edge of the York Plain with beautiful historic church and Queen Anne Hall (not open). The gardens are spread throughout the village with good footpaths. A plantsman's and flower arranger's garden at Cobble Cottage has views to the Hambleton Hills. Further towards the village centre are two

small well designed gardens on sloping sites. Ash tree House with extensive rock garden and borders full of established herbaceous plants, shrubs and roses creating a tapestry of soft colour and textures achieving a cottage garden effect and Lydiate House, recently redesigned, with sloping alpine rockeries, naturalistic borders, foliage plants and unusual perennials. Close to the church, The Old Vicarage, with a ³/₄ - acre walled flower garden, overlooks the old deer park. The walls, house and various structures are festooned with climbers. Gravel and old brick paths lead to hidden seating areas creating the atmosphere of a romantic English garden.

118 NEW WHYNCREST
Bridlington Road, Hunmanby, Filey YO14 9RS. Mrs Lieke Swann, 01723 890923, lieke@whyncrest.wanadoo.co.uk. *Between Hunmanby & Reighton Nursery off A165 between Hunmanby Gap & Reighton. Exit A165, junction signed Reigthon Nurseries & Hunmanby, follow this rd for 200 yds, Whyncrest is on R. Parking on grass verge outside.* Tea. **Adm £4, chd free. Sat 11, Sun 12 July (11-4). Visitors also welcome by arrangement May to Sept.**
Elevated garden with fabulous views across Filey Bay and beyond. The garden has been carefully designed, creating micro climate 'rooms' taking you from jungle garden to a pond garden with tropical planting and a huge waterfall, herbaceous borders and topiary shrubs. The collection of plants is varied, giving an all year interest from early spring with all its bulbs all the way into late autumn.

119 WOODLANDS COTTAGE
Summerbridge, Nidderdale HG3 4BT. Mr & Mrs Stark, 01423 780765, www.woodlandscottagegarden. co.uk. *10m NW of Harrogate. On the B6165 W of Summerbridge.* Home-made teas. **Adm £3.50, chd free. Sun 10 May (2-5). Also open with Dacre Banks & Summerbridge Gardens, 5 July, and Low Hall 10 May. Visitors also welcome by arrangement May to Aug.**
A one-acre country garden created by its owners and making full use of its setting, which includes natural

woodland with wild bluebells and gritstone boulders. There are several gardens within the garden, from a wild flower meadow and woodland rock-garden to a formal herb garden and herbaceous areas; also a productive fruit and vegetable garden. Gravel paths with some slopes.

Elevated garden with fabulous views across Filey Bay and beyond . . .

120 ◆ YORK GATE
Back Church Lane, Adel, Leeds LS16 8DW. Perennial, 0113 2678240, www.yorkgate.org.uk. *5m N of Leeds. N of Leeds 2¹/₄ m SE of Bramhope, signed from A660. Park in Church Lane in lay-by opp church &take public footpath through churchyard to garden.* Light refreshments are available in our newly refurbished tea rooms. **For opening times and information, please phone or see garden website.**
One-acre masterpiece and outstanding example of late C20 garden design. A series of smaller gardens with different themes and in contrasting styles are linked by a succession of delightful vistas. Striking architectural features play a key role throughout the garden which is also noted for its exquisite detailing, For opening times and information, please phone or see the garden website. White and Silver borders, 'Pigmy' pinetum, dell, Kitchen and cutting garden, Herb garden, Nut Walk, Quaint potting shed, succulent house, paved garden, scree garden, and canal. Featured in The English Garden, and on BBC1 Glorious Gardens from above.

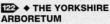

121 ◆ YORKE HOUSE
Dacre Banks, Nidderdale HG3 4EW. Tony & Pat Hutchinson, 01423 780456, pat@yorkehouse.co.uk, www.yorkehouse.co.uk. *4m SE of Pateley Bridge, 10m NW of*

Harrogate, 10m N of Otley. On B6451 near centre of Dacre Banks. Car park. Cream teas. **Adm £4, chd free. Sat 20, Sun 21 June (11-5). Also open with Dacre Banks & Summerbridge Gardens 5 July. Visitors also welcome by arrangement June to July for groups of 10 min.**
Award-winning flower arranger's 2-acre garden with colour-themed borders full of flowering and foliage plants. Water feature incl large ornamental ponds and stream with attractive waterside plantings. Other features incl nut walk, rose walk, patios, gazebo, millennium garden and wildlife areas. Large collection of hostas. The garden enjoys beautiful views across Nidderdale. Orchard picnic area. 'Art in the Garden' event featuring exhibition of watercolour paintings by local artists and Land Art sculpture trail. Winner Harrogate's Glorious Gardens. Harrogate Advertiser. All main features accessible to wheelchair users.

122 ◆ THE YORKSHIRE ARBORETUM
Castle Howard, York YO60 7BY. The Castle Howard Arboretum Trust, 01653 648598, www.yorkshirearboretum.org. *15m NE of York. Off A64. Follow brown signs to Castle Howard then look for Yorkshire Arboretum signs at the obelisk r'about.* The Arboretum Café enjoys an enviable reputation for its delicious food and drink, prepared on-site using the very best in seasonal, local produce. **Adm £6, chd free. For NGS: Sat 30 May (10-6). For other opening times and information, please phone or see garden website.**
A glorious, 120 acre garden of trees from around the world set in a stunning landscape of parkland, lakes and ponds. With walks and lakeside trails, tours, family activities, a woodland playground, café and gift shop we welcome visitors of all ages wanting to enjoy the space, serenity and beauty of this sheltered valley as well as those interested in our extensive collection of trees and shrubs. Internationally renowned collection of trees in a beautiful setting, accompanied by a diversity of wild flowers, birds, insects and other wildlife. Not suitable for wheelchairs. Motorised buggies available on loan, please book 24hrs in advance.

Delacorse, Carmarthenshire & Pembrokeshire

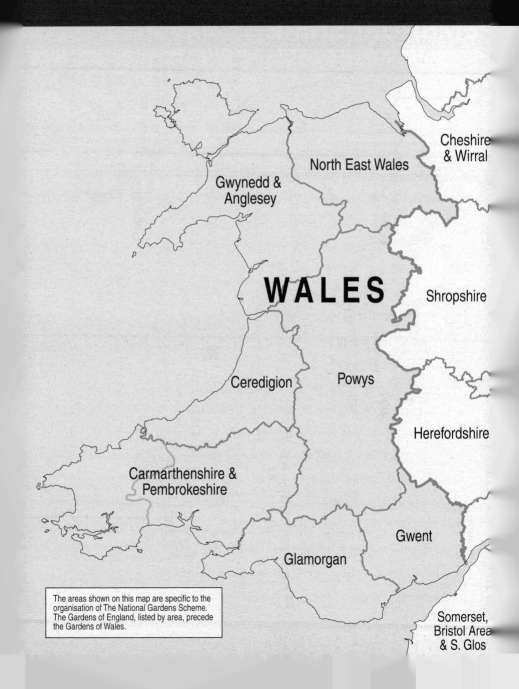

Cheshire
& Wirral

North East Wales

Gwynedd &
Anglesey

WALES

Shropshire

Ceredigion

Powys

Herefordshire

Carmarthenshire &
Pembrokeshire

Gwent

Glamorgan

Somerset,
Bristol Area
& S. Glos

The areas shown on this map are specific to the
organisation of The National Gardens Scheme.
The Gardens of England, listed by area, precede
the Gardens of Wales.

CARMARTHENSHIRE & PEMBROKESHIRE

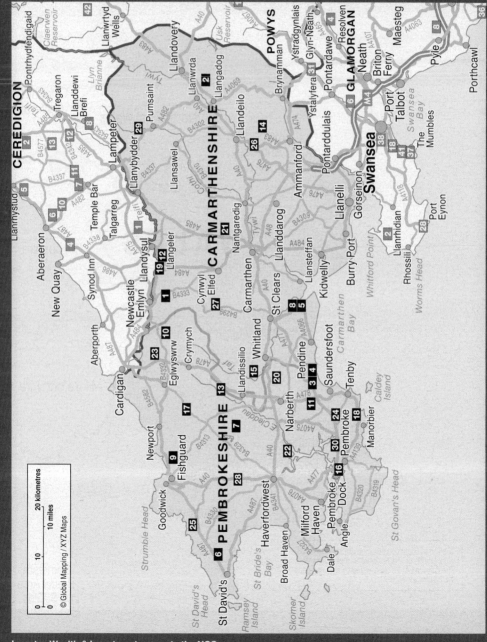

Carmarthenshire & Pembrokeshire

From the rugged western coast, bathed in mild weather thanks to the Gulf Stream, to the foothills of the Black Mountains, Carmarthenshire and Pembrokeshire offer a wide range of gardens to enjoy in countryside untroubled by the traffic jams of more populated areas.

A special feature of many of our gardens is the benefit of superb borrowed landscapes, where the extensive rural views emphasize the overall effect of an uncluttered environment.

Visitors to the area will know the delightful seaside town of Tenby, but may not be acquainted with the opportunities to visit the less well-known gems to be found in The Yellow Book. Even if you do not manage to reach a garden on its specific open day, garden owners who open by arrangement are genuinely delighted to welcome you: just ring to arrange when to visit.

Gardeners in Wales are often also known for their tempting home-baking, which visitors can enjoy as a finale to a stroll in a beautiful garden.

Carmarthenshire & Pembrokeshire Volunteers

County Organiser
Jane Stokes
01558 823233
jane.h.stokes@btinternet.com

County Treasurer
Christine Blower
01267 253334
cheahnwood@toucansurf.com

Publicity
Liz and Paul O'Neill
01949 240717
lizpaulfarm@yahoo.co.uk

Jane Stokes
(as above)

Booklet Coordinator
Jane Stokes
(as above)

Assistant County Organisers
Jackie Batty
01437 741115
bathole2000@aol.com

Paul O'Neill
(as above)

Ivor Stokes
01558 823233
ivor.t.stokes@btopenworld.com

Left: Cilgwyn Lodge © Rowan Isaac

Since our foundation we have donated more than £42.5 million to charity

Opening Dates

All entries subject to change.
For latest information check www.ngs.org.uk

April

- **6** The Crystal Garden (every day until Apr 15)

May

- **6** The Crystal Garden (every day until May 15)
- **17** Moorland Cottage Plants (every day except Wednesday from May 9)

Sunday 3
- **15** Llwyngarreg
- **28** Treffgarne Hall

Sunday 10
- **10** Ffynone

Saturday 16
- **3** NEW Colby Lodge (Private Garden)
- **4** Colby Woodland Garden
- **13** Glyn Bach

Sunday 17
- **3** NEW Colby Lodge (Private Garden)
- **4** Colby Woodland Garden
- **9** Dyffryn Fernant
- **13** Glyn Bach

Sunday 24
- **15** Llwyngarreg

- **20** Panteg
- **22** Picton Castle & Gardens
- **26** Talardd

June

- **6** The Crystal Garden (every day until June 15)
- **17** Moorland Cottage Plants (every day except Wednesday)

Festival Weekend

Saturday 6
- **12** Glandwr

Sunday 7
- **1** Blaenfforest
- **12** Glandwr

Saturday 20
- **13** Glyn Bach

Sunday 21
- **13** Glyn Bach
- **30** Upton Castle Gardens

Sunday 28
- **11** Foxways
- **27** Tradewinds

July

- **6** The Crystal Garden (every day until July 15)
- **17** Moorland Cottage Plants (every day except Wednesday)

Sunday 5
- **15** Llwyngarreg
- **21** NEW Pentresite

Sunday 12
- **28** Treffgarne Hall

Saturday 18
- **13** Glyn Bach

Sunday 19
- **13** Glyn Bach
- **24** Rosewood

Friday 24
- **16** Mead Lodge

Saturday 25
- **16** Mead Lodge

Sunday 26
- **16** Mead Lodge

Monday 27
- **16** Mead Lodge

August

- **6** The Crystal Garden (every day until Aug 15)
- **17** Moorland Cottage Plants (every day except Wednesday)

Sunday 2
- **9** Dyffryn Fernant
- **29** Ty'r Maes

Sunday 9
- **27** Tradewinds

Saturday 22
- **13** Glyn Bach

Sunday 23
- **13** Glyn Bach

September

- **6** The Crystal Garden (every day until Sep 15)
- **17** Moorland Cottage Plants (every day except Wednesday)

Sunday 6
- **9** Dyffryn Fernant
- **15** Llwyngarreg

Gardens open to the public

- **4** Colby Woodland Garden
- **9** Dyffryn Fernant
- **22** Picton Castle & Gardens
- **30** Upton Castle Gardens

By arrangement only

- **2** Cilgwyn Lodge
- **5** The Cors
- **7** Cwm Pibau
- **8** Delacorse
- **14** Llwyn Cyll
- **18** Norchard
- **19** The Old Vicarage
- **23** Rhosygilwen Mansion
- **25** NEW Stable Cottage

Also open by arrangement

- **1** Blaenfforest
- **6** The Crystal Garden
- **12** Glandwr
- **13** Glyn Bach
- **16** Mead Lodge
- **17** Moorland Cottage Plants
- **20** Panteg
- **24** Rosewood
- **26** Talardd
- **28** Treffgarne Hall
- **29** Ty'r Maes

The Gardens

1 BLAENFFOREST

Newcastle Emlyn, Carmarthenshire SA38 9JD. Sally & Russell Jones, 01559 371264, enquiries@blaenfforest.co.uk, www.cottageholidayswales.com. *2m S of Newcastle Emlyn. From Newcastle Emlyn take A484 to Carmarthen, Turn R on B4333. From Carmarthen take A484 to Cardigan, L on B4333 at Cynwil Elfed.* Home-made teas. Adm £3.50, chd free. **Sun 7 June (11.30-4). Visitors also welcome by arrangement May to Sept please arrange refreshments when booking.**
Relaxed and tranquil gardens incl

stunning views from the patio, lush planting by the wildlife ponds, interesting, tucked away corners, bees in the orchard and Woodland Walk, deep in the valley of the R Arad. Peacocks roam freely. Children to be supervised. A place to write poetry! Partial wheelchair access to some parts of gardens.

 ♿ 🚲 ❀ 🛏 ☕

2 CILGWYN LODGE

Llangadog, Carmarthenshire SA19 9LH. Keith Brown & Moira Thomas, 01550 777452, keith@cilgwynlodge.co.uk, www.cilgwynlodge.co.uk. *3m NE of Llangadog village. Turn off A40 into Llangadog. Bear L in front of village*

shop then 1st R to Myddfai. After 2½ m pass Cilgwyn Manor on L then 1st L. Garden ¼ m on L. Adm £4, chd free. **Visitors welcome by arrangement June to Aug. Teas available on request for 14 max.**
A well established and much admired 1 acre garden with something for everyone. Wide variety of plants displayed in extensive colour themed borders, large collection of hostas, many herbaceous perennials, hardy and tender, common, rare or unusual. Traditional vegetable and fruit garden and large waterlily pond and Koi Pond. A Welsh Wonderland. Featured on S4C TV programme Prynhawn Da. Partial wheelchair access.

 ♿ ❀ 🚲 ☕

3 NEW COLBY LODGE (PRIVATE GARDEN)
Nr Amroth, Narberth SA67 8PP.
Anthony Scourfield Lewis. *Access through National Trust entrance to Colby Woodland Garden (use NT car park).* Refreshments at Colby Woodland Garden Tea Rooms. **Combined adm £8.50, chd £3. Sat 16, Sun 17 May (10-5). Combined with the National Trust Colby Woodland Garden.**
An elegant and artistic garden of some 1³/₄ acres surrounding the listed house (not open), lovingly created since 1985: improving the layout and implementing thoughtful new planting throughout. The more formal garden to the south leads to a spring garden overlooking the meadow and streamside gardens to the west.

4 ◆ COLBY WOODLAND GARDEN
Nr Amroth, Narberth SA67 8PP.
National Trust, 01834 811885, www.nationaltrust.org.uk. *6m N of Tenby. 5m SE of Narberth. Follow brown tourist signs on coast rd & A477.* Tea. **Combined adm £8.50, chd £3. For NGS: Sat 16, Sun 17 May (10-5). For other opening times and information, please phone or see garden website.**
8 acre woodland garden in a secluded valley with fine collection of rhododendrons and azaleas. Wildflower meadow and stream with rope swings and stepping stones for children to explore and play. Ornamental walled garden incl unusual gazebo, designed by Wyn Jones, with internal tromp l'oeil. Incl in the *Register of Historic Parks and Gardens: Pembrokeshire.* Extensive play area for children incl den building and log climbing. Free family activities incl duck racing, pond dipping, campfire lighting etc. Children under 5, free entry. Partial access for wheelchair users.

5 THE CORS
Newbridge Road, Laugharne, Carmarthenshire SA33 4SH. Nick Priestland, 01994 427219, nickpriestland@hotmail.com, www.thecors.co.uk. *12m SW of Carmarthen. From Carmarthen, turn R in centre of Laugharne at The Mariners PH. At bottom of Newbridge Rd on R. Please use public car parks, 5 mins walk.* Light refreshments. **Adm £3.50, chd free. Visitors welcome by arrangement Apr to Sept.**

Blaenfforest

Refreshments available on request. Approx 2¹/₂ acres set in beautiful wooded valley bordering river. Large bog garden with ponds, *Gunnera*, bamboos and tree ferns. Exceptional, elegant plantsman's garden with unusual architectural and exotic planting incl *Tetrapanax papyrifer*, *Blechnum chilense*chusan palms and sculptures. Wheelchair access to garden dependant on weather conditions.

6 THE CRYSTAL GARDEN
Golwg yr Ynys, Carnhedryn, St Davids, Pembrokeshire SA62 6XT. Mrs Sue Clark, 01437 721082, sueclark132@gmail.com, www.golwgyrynys.com. *4m E of St Davids, 11m SW of Fishguard, 2m N of Solva. Village of Carnhedryn, off A487 between Fishguard & St Davids.* Tea. **Adm £3, chd free. Daily: 1 Apr to 15 Apr, 1 May to 15 May, 1 June to 15 June, 1 July to 15 July, 1 Aug to 15 Aug, 1 Sept to 15 Sept (1-5.30). Visitors also welcome by arrangement Mar to Oct.**
A ³/₄ acre garden for plantaholics with yr-round floral colour and foliage

interest. Intriguing layout of sheltered rooms full of surprises packed with unusual shrubs, perennials and garden favourites. Ever changing outer garden. The garden never stands still. Specialities incl hebes and hydrangeas. A warm welcome awaits. Art wall, glazed visitor room.

7 CWM PIBAU
New Moat, Haverfordwest, Pembrokeshire SA63 4RE. Mrs Duncan Drew, 01437 532454. *10m NE of Haverfordwest. 3m SW of Maenclochog. Off A40, take B4313 to Maenclochog, follow signs to New Moat, pass church, then 2nd concealed drive on L, ¹/₂ m rural drive.* **Adm £3, chd free. Visitors welcome by arrangement, please telephone first to ensure a welcome.**
5 acre woodland garden surrounded by old deciduous woodland and streams. Created in 1978, contains many mature, unusual shrubs and trees from Chile, New Zealand and Europe, set on S facing hill. More conventional planting nearer house.

WE ARE MACMILLAN. CANCER SUPPORT

The NGS has funded 147 different Macmillan projects

8 DELACORSE

Laugharne, Carmarthenshire SA33 4QP. Annie Hart, 01994 427728, annie.hart@ymail.com, www.buntysblog.co.uk. *13m SW of Carmarthen. A4066 from St Clears 1st L after Cross Inn at 'No Footway' sign. At bend ($\frac{1}{2}$ m) straight down farm track. On foot, riverside path from Dylan Thomas Museum (20mins).* **Adm £4, chd free. Visitors welcome by arrangement Apr to Oct discount for groups 10+.**

3 acre garden beside Taf Estuary in peaceful, beautiful landscape with fine views. Scented walled garden with chamomile lawn; sheltered courtyard; fernery; mixed borders with all-yr interest; living willow work; lawns; specimen trees; millpond; orchard. Carefully managed informal areas merging into woodland, reed beds and salt marsh. Extensive organic kitchen garden. Comprehensive information available on how to grow fruit, vegetable and herbs. Managed 6 acre woodland providing fuel for biomass/solar heating installation. Featured in Carmarthen Journal. Wheelchair access to all of garden except millpond and orchard.

9 ◆ DYFFRYN FERNANT

Llanychaer, Fishguard, Pembrokeshire SA65 9SP. Christina Shand & David Allum, 01348 811282, www.dyffrynfernant.co.uk. *3m E of Fishguard, then $\frac{1}{2}$ m inland. Off A487 towards Llanychaer.* Home-made teas. **Adm £6, chd free. For NGS: Sun 17 May, Sun 2 Aug, Sun**

6 Sept (11-6). For other opening times and information, please phone or see garden website. 'The gardens ambitions are many: to be colourful at all seasons, to provide a fascinating journey through a score of different spaces and atmospheres, to create some rich and surprising planting' Stephen Anderton. 6 acres incl ornamental grasses, marsh packed with wild flowers, wide views of the Preseli landscape, many highly cultivated areas. 'With a drama and flair rarely seen' Noel Kingsbury. Workshops and Guided Talks. Featured on BBC Gardeners World (TV and Magazine), Gardens Illustrated, Country Living Magazine, Cambria Magazine, BBC Radio Wales,Tivy-Side.

10 FFYNONE

Newchapel, Boncath, Pembrokeshire SA37 0HQ. The Hon Robert Lloyd George, 01239 841610, www.ffynone.org. *9m SE of Cardigan. 7m W of Newcastle Emlyn. From Newcastle Emlyn take A484 to Cenarth, turn L on B4332, turn L again at Xrds just before Newchapel.* Light refreshments. **Adm £3.50, chd free. Sun 10 May (1-4.30).**

Large woodland garden designated Grade I on Cadw Register of Historic Parks and Gardens in Wales. Lovely views, fine mature specimen trees; formal garden nr house with massive yew topiary; rhododendrons, azaleas, woodland walks and bluebells. House (also Grade I) by John Nash (1793). Later additions and garden terraces by F Inigo Thomas c1904. House (with garden) open for guided tours on other days. Please see website for details and booking. On site parking. Partial wheelchair access. Some steep paths and steps.

11 FOXWAYS

Thomas Chapel, Begelly, Kilgetty, Pembrokeshire SA68 0XH. Roy & Angela Weston. *From S A478 to Narberth. L after 1m by Regent Garage. Cont 1m & round R bend (ignore SatNav). Foxways 2nd on R. Parking past house to 1st lane on R.* Home-made teas. **Adm £3, chd free. Sun 28 June (1-5).**

Recently developed the 3 acre garden has a wide range of plants from dry shade, cottage garden beds to sunny bog gardens. There are waterfalls and wildlife and ornamental ponds. The garden is for fun and

relaxation so seats abound, as do hidden corners to get the most from our plants and their peace and quiet. The planting is textural to complement leaf colour, size and forms for all season enjoyment. Partial wheelchair access.

12 GLANDWR

Pentrecwrt, Llandysul, Carmarthenshire SA44 5DA. Mrs Jo Hicks, 01559 363729, leehicks@btinternet.com. *15m N of Carmarthen, 2m S of Llandysul, 7m E of Newcastle Emlyn. On A486. At Pentrecwrt village, take minor rd opp Black Horse PH. After bridge keep L for $\frac{1}{4}$ m. Glandwr is on R.* Home-made teas. **Adm £3, chd free. Sat 6, Sun 7 June (11-5). Visitors also welcome by arrangement May to Aug, please phone first.**

Delightful easily accessed 1 acre cottage garden, bordered by a natural stream. Incl a rockery and colour themed beds. Enter the mature woodland, now transformed into an adventurous wander with plenty of shade loving plants, ground covers, interesting trees, shrubs and many surprises.

13 GLYN BACH

Efailwen, Clunderwen, Carmarthenshire SA66 7JP. Peter & Carole Whittaker, 01994 419104, carole.whittaker7@btinternet.com, www.glynbachgardens.co.uk. *Efailwen 8m N of Narberth, 15m S of Cardigan. W off A487 at Glandy Cross garage, follow signs for 1m towards Llangolman.* Home-made teas. **Adm £3, chd free. Sats & Suns 16, 17 May, 20, 21 June, 18, 19 July, 22, 23 Aug (11-5). Visitors also welcome by arrangement May to Sept. Please arrange teas when booking.**

2 acres of garden with numerous perennial borders, alpine walls, tropical border, large pond, bog garden, rose garden, grass beds, raised vegetable beds, cottage garden, polytunnel, greenhouse and *Monarda* collection. Emphasis on nectar rich plants for pollinators. Surrounded by 4 acres of mixed woodland and grassland; woodland walk with bluebells and wildflowers in Spring. Wheelchair access on grass pathways.

14 LLWYN CYLL
Llandeilo, Trap, Carmarthenshire SA19 6TR. Liz & John Smith, 01558 822398. *3m SE of Llandeilo. In Trap turn towards Glanaman & Llandybie (at The Cennen Arms). Llwyn Cyll is ½ m on L adjoining Llwyn Onn. Coach parking nearby.* **Adm £3, chd free. Visitors welcome by arrangement Apr to June, home-made teas on request.**
3½ acre country garden of yr-round interest. Abundant, colourful terraced and walled borders, orchard, highly productive vegetable garden. Sun and shade areas with sympathetic planting. An Enthusiast's garden with many rarities and specimen trees. Up to 30 different magnolias in the arboretum, many in flower late Apr to early June. Scenic views. Partial wheelchair access around house.

15 LLWYNGARREG
Llanfallteg, Whitland, Carmarthenshire SA34 0XH. Paul & Liz O'Neill, 01994 240717, lizpaulfarm@yahoo.co.uk, www.llwyngarreg.co.uk. *19m W of Carmarthen. A40 W from Carmarthen, turn R at Llandewi Velfrey, 2½ m to Llanfallteg. Go through village, garden ½ m further on: 2nd farm on R. Disabled car park in bottom yard.* Home-made teas. **Adm £4, chd free. Suns 3, 24 May, 5 July, 6 Sept (1.30-6). Combined with Panteg (Llandewi Velfrey, Sun 24 May), combined adm £6, chd free.**
3 acre plantaholic's haven with yr-round impact, from spring bulbs through to glorious autumn colour; tapestries of colour and texture in the many trees, interspersed with unusual shrubs and perennial underplantings. Willow tunnel welcomes visitors into a maturing shelter belt, beyond which lies the main garden with wide mixed borders. Closely planted areas in front of the house, gravel gardens behind. Woodland garden leads down to the potager. Plantsmen will linger to find many gems. Several deep ponds. Children to be closely supervised. Wildlife ponds, twig piles for overwintering insects, composting, numerous living willow structures. Featured in The Times. Partial wheelchair access.

16 MEAD LODGE
Imble Lane, Pembroke Dock, Pembrokeshire SA72 6PN. John & Eileen Seal, 01646 682504, eileenseal@aol.com. *From A4139 between Pembroke & Pembroke Dock take B4322 signed Pennar & Leisure Centre. After ½ m turn L into Imble Lane. Mead Lodge at end.* Home-made teas. **Adm £3, chd free. Fri 24, Sat 25, Sun 26, Mon 27 July (11-5). Visitors also welcome by arrangement Apr to Sept. Please request teas when booking.**
Unexpected, secluded country garden, a relaxing oasis on S facing slope overlooking the Pembroke River estuary. Varied ¾ acre garden reflects the owners' keen interest in ferns, grasses and herbs. Incl terraces with Chinese and Mediterranean influences, colour themed beds, small arboretum underplanted for spring colour, Fernery, vegetable garden, pond and bog garden.

Wildflower meadow and stream with rope swings and stepping stones for children to explore . . .

17 MOORLAND COTTAGE PLANTS
Rhyd-y-Groes, Brynberian, Pembrokeshire SA41 3TT. Jennifer & Kevin Matthews, 01239 891363, jenny@moorlandcottageplants.co.uk, www.moorlandcottageplants.co.uk. *12m SW of Cardigan. 16m NE of Haverfordwest, on B4329, ¾ m downhill from cattlegrid (from Haverfordwest) & 1m uphill from signpost to Brynberian (from Cardigan).* **Adm £3, chd £1. Share to Paul Sartori Foundation. Open every day (excl Weds) 9 May to 30 Sept (10.30-4). Visitors also welcome by arrangement May to Sept.**
1½ acres at 700ft on NE hillside overlooking a vast wilderness. Exuberant and diverse plantings provide propagating material for the adjacent nursery. Secretive, enclosed areas where carpets of spring flowers give way to jungly perennials, grasses, bamboos and ferns contrast with formal herbaceous borders and extensive shrubberies. Stunning mountain and moorland vistas. Garden entirely organic. Mollusc proof plantings.

18 NORCHARD
The Ridgeway, Manorbier, Tenby, Pembrokeshire SA70 8LD. Ms H E Davies, 01834 871036. *4m W of Tenby. From Tenby, take A4139 for Pembroke. ½ m after Lydstep, take R at Xrds. Proceed down lane for ¾ m. Norchard on R.* Teas. **Adm £4, chd free. Visitors welcome by arrangement April to June and Sept. Please arrange teas when booking.**
Historic gardens at medieval residence. Nestled in tranquil and sheltered location with ancient oak woodland backdrop. Strong structure with formal and informal areas incl early walled gardens with restored Elizabethan parterre and potager. 1½ acre orchard with old (many local) apple varieties. Mill and millpond. Extensive collections of roses, daffodils and tulips. Partial wheelchair access due to gravel paths. Access to potager via steps only.

19 THE OLD VICARAGE
Llangeler, Carmarthenshire SA44 5EU. Mr & Mrs J C Harcourt, 01559 371168. *4m E of Newcastle Emlyn. 15m N of Carmarthen on A484. From N Emlyn turn down lane on L in Llangeler before church.* Tea. **Adm £2.50, chd free. Visitors welcome by arrangement May to Aug, please request teas when booking.**
A garden gem created since 1993. Less than 1 acre divided into 3 areas of roses, shrubs and a semi formal pool with an interesting collection of unusual herbaceous plants. Ever changing scene. Recent bad winters have taken their toll so some reinvention has been needed. Optimum colour, mid June onwards. Gravel yard, temporary ramp available.

Dyffryn Fernant

20 PANTEG

Llanddewi Velfrey, Narberth, Pembrokeshire SA67 8UU. Mr & Mrs D Pryse Lloyd, 01834 860081, d.pryselloyd@btinternet.com. *Situated off main A40 in village of Llanddewi Velfrey. A40 from Carmarthen, after garage take 1st L. At next T-junction turn L. On R gateway with stone gate pillars which is ¹/₂ m drive to Panteg.* **Combined adm £6, chd free. Sun 24 May (1.30-6). Combined with Llwyngarreg (Llanfallteg). Visitors also welcome by arrangement Mar to Sept, please telephone first. Adm £3, chd free.**
Approached down a woodland drive, this tranquil, S facing, large garden, surrounding a Georgian house (not open), has been developed since early 1990s. A Plantsman's garden set off by lawns on different levels. Walled garden, wisteria covered pergola. Vegetable garden, camellia and azalea bank, wild flower woodland. Many rare shrubs and plants incl, *Embothrium, Eucryphia* and *Hoheria.*

21 NEW PENTRESITE

Rhydargaeau Road, Carmarthen, Carmarthenshire SA32 7AJ. Gayle & Ron Mounsey. *4m N of Carmarthen. Take A485 heading N out of Carmarthen, once out of village of Peniel take 1st R to Horeb & cont for 1m. Turn R at NGS sign, 2nd house down lane.* Home-made teas. **Adm £3.50, chd free. Sun 5 July (2-5).**
1¹/₄ acre garden developed over the last 7yrs with extensive herbaceous and mixed borders, on several levels.

A bog garden and magnificent views of the surrounding countryside. South facing, catching the south westerly winds. Steep in places but possible for wheelchairs.

22 ◆ PICTON CASTLE & GARDENS

The Rhos, Haverfordwest, Pembrokeshire SA62 4AS. Picton Castle Trust, 01437 751326, info@pictoncastle.com, www.pictoncastle.co.uk. *3m E of Haverfordwest. On A40 to Carmarthen, signed off main rd.* Light refreshments. **Adm £6.50, chd £4. For NGS: Sun 24 May (10.30-5). For other opening times and information, please phone or see garden website.**
Mature 40 acre woodland garden with unique collection of rhododendrons and azaleas, many bred over 42yrs, producing hybrids of great merit and beauty; rare and tender shrubs and trees incl *Magnolia,* myrtle, *Embothrium* and *Eucryphia.* Wild flowers abound. Walled garden with roses; fernery; herbaceous and climbing plants and large clearly labelled collection of herbs. Exciting art exhibitions and a wide range of seasonal events. Some woodland walks unsuitable for wheelchair users.

23 RHOSYGILWEN MANSION

Rhoshill, Cilgerran, Cardigan, Pembrokeshire SA43 2TW. Glen Peters & Brenda Squires, 01239 841387, enquiries@retreat.co.uk, www.rhosygilwen.co.uk. *6m S of*

Cardigan. From Cardigan follow A478 signed Tenby. After 6m turn L at Rhoshill towards Cilgerran. After ¹/₄ m turn R signed Rhosygilwen. Mansion gates ¹/₂ m. Light refreshments. **Adm £3, chd free. Visitors welcome by arrangement Apr to Sept. Light refreshments on request when booking.**
20 acres of garden in 55 acre estate. Pretty ¹/₂ m drive through woodland planting. Spacious lightly wooded grounds for leisurely rambling, superb 1 acre walled garden fully productive of fruit, vegetables and flowers; authentically restored Edwardian greenhouses, many old and new trees, small formal garden. Children must be supervised please. Gravel paths around garden. Full disabled facilities.

24 ROSEWOOD

Redberth, nr Tenby, Pembrokeshire SA70 8SA. Jan & Keith Treadaway, 01646 651405, janatredberth@btinternet.com. *3m SW of Kilgetty. On W side of village on old A477, now bypassed. Parking in field opp if dry, or on verge by side of rd if wet.* Home-made teas. **Adm £3.50, chd free. Sun 19 July (1-5). Visitors also welcome by arrangement Apr to Sept groups of 15+. Please request teas when booking.**
Intimate well maintained ¹/₄ acre garden, cleverly designed in different areas with long season of interest. Abundant colourful mixed plantings with many exotic species and a collection of clematis in bloom all yr, but especially in summer. There is a

new pergola with clematis and other climbers, as well as a growing collection of *Hemerocallis*, grasses and ferns. Featured in Tenby Observer and Pembrokeshire Life. Partial wheelchair access.

25 NEW STABLE COTTAGE
Rhoslanog Fawr, Mathry, Haverfordwest, Pembrokeshire SA62 5HG. Mr & Mrs Michael & Jane Bayliss, 01348 837712, michaelandjane1954@michaeland jane.plus.com. *Rhoslanog, nr Mathry. Between Fishguard & St David's. Head W on A487 turn R at Square & Compass sign. 1/2 m, past Chris Neale gallery, at hairpin take track L. Stable Cottage on L with block paved drive.* **Adm £2.50, chd free. Visitors welcome by arrangement Apr to Oct. Very limited parking. Refreshments available.**
Garden extends to approx 1/3 of an acre. It is divided into several smaller garden types, with a seaside garden, small orchard and wildlife area, scented garden, small vegetable/kitchen garden, and two Japanese areas.

26 TALARDD
Golden Grove, Carmarthen, Carmarthenshire SA32 8NN. Mr Steve Bryan, 01558 822418, steve@stevebryan.org.uk, www.talardd-cottages.co.uk. *Off A476 between Crosshands & Llandeilo. R 6m N of Crosshands, L 1 1/2 m S of Llandeilo on A476 nr Z bends. Lane marked by Renault garage sign. Turn L at T junction follow signs to Talardd.* Tea. **Adm £4, chd free. Share to Robert Dickie Charitable Trust. Sun 24 May (2-6). Visitors also welcome by arrangement Apr to Oct, please request teas when booking.**
The historic house is set above the stream with its banks of primulas, astilbes, *Gunnera* and diverse bog garden plants. Nearby is the productive walled kitchen garden, surrounded by beds of herbaceous plants and grasses. Elsewhere, extensive grassed areas are planted with unusual trees, shrubs and spring bulbs. There is also a riverside walk and boules court! The garden covers some 5 acres. Guided tours on request. Wheelchair access to kitchen garden and part of woodland areas on bound gravel paths.

27 TRADEWINDS
Ffynnonwen, Pen-y-Bont, nr Trelech, Carmarthen SA33 6PX. Stuart & Eve Kemp-Gee. *10m NW of Carmarthen. From A40 W of Carmarthen, take B4298 to Meidrim, then R onto B4299 towards Trelech. After 5m turn R at Tradewinds sign.* Home-made teas. **Adm £3, chd free. Sun 28 June, Sun 9 Aug (11-6).**
2 1/2 acre plantsman's garden with abundance of herbaceous perennials, shrubs and trees giving yr-round interest. Mixed borders, natural streams and pond. Picturesque garden in tranquil setting. 100ft grass, 100ft herbaceous and 80ft conifer borders. The arboretum incl *Quercus cerris* 'Argenteovariegata', *Salix fargesii Catalpa, Decaisnea* plus numerous rhododendrons, azaleas and Hydrangeas. Stream banks planted with many moisture loving plants. Many rare and unusual plants to be seen.

28 TREFFGARNE HALL
Treffgarne, Haverfordwest, Pembrokeshire SA62 5PJ. Martin & Jackie Batty, 01437 741115, bathole2000@aol.com. *7m N of Haverfordwest, signed off A40. Proceed up through village & follow rd round sharply to L, Hall 1/4 m further on L.* Home-made teas. **Adm £3.50, chd free. Sun 3 May, Sun 12 July (1-5). Visitors also welcome by arrangement, teas on request.**
Stunning hilltop location with panoramic views: handsome Grade II listed Georgian house (not open) provides formal backdrop to garden of four acres with wide lawns and themed beds. A walled garden, with double rill and pergolas, is planted with a multitude of borderline hardy exotics. Also large scale sculptures, summer broadwalk, meadow patch, gravel garden, heather bed and stumpery. Planted for yr-round interest. The planting schemes are the owner's, and seek to challenge the boundaries of what can be grown in Pembrokeshire.

29 TY'R MAES
Ffarmers, Carmarthenshire SA19 8JP. John & Helen Brooks, 01558 650541, johnhelen@greystones140. freeserve.co.uk. *7m SE of Lampeter. 8m NW of Llanwrda. 1 1/2 m N of Pumsaint on A482, opp turn to*

Ffarmers. Home-made teas. **Adm £3, chd free. Sun 2 Aug (1-5). Visitors also welcome by arrangement Mar to Oct, please request teas when booking.**
4 acre garden with splendid views. Herbaceous and shrub beds - formal design, exuberantly informal planting, full of cottage garden favourites and many unusual plants. Burgeoning arboretum (200+ types of tree); wildlife and lily ponds, pergola, gazebos, post and rope arcade covered in climbers. Gloriously colourful; spring (rhododendrons, azaleas, primulas, 1000's bulbs); late summer (tapestry of annuals/perennials). Craft, produce, books and jewellery stalls. Some gravel paths.

Many rare and unusual plants to be seen . . .

---

30 ◆ UPTON CASTLE GARDENS
Cosheston, Pembroke Dock SA72 4SE. Prue & Stephen Barlow, 01646 689996, info@uptoncastle.com, www.uptoncastlegardens.com. *4m E of Pembroke Dock. 2m N of A477 between Carew & Pembroke Dock. Follow brown signs to Upton Castle Gardens through Cosheston.* Light refreshments. **Adm £4, chd free. For NGS: Sun 21 June (10-4.30). For other opening times and information, please phone or see garden website.**
Lovely location in a tranquil valley leading to the upper reaches of the Cleddau estuary. 35 acres of mature gardens and arboretum; many rare trees and shrubs surrounding the C13 castle (not open) and C12 chapel. Formal rose gardens, herbaceous borders, productive walled kitchen garden, wild flower meadow, woodland walks to estuary. Walk on the Wild Side: Woodland walks funded by Countryside Council for Wales and Welsh Assembly Government. Partial wheelchair access.

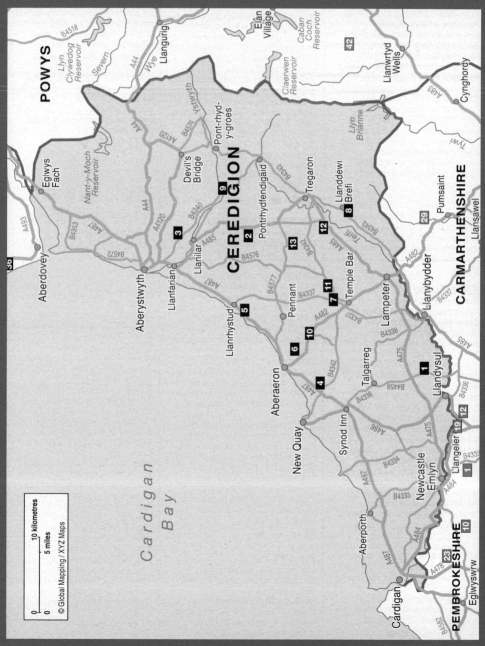

CEREDIGION

Cardigan Bay

POWYS

CEREDIGION

CARMARTHENSHIRE

PEMBROKESHIRE

10 kilometres
5 miles
© Global Mapping / XYZ Maps

Ceredigion

Ceredigion is essentially a rural county, and is the second most sparsely populated in Wales.

There are steep-sided wooded valleys, fast-flowing rivers and streams, acres of moorland and sandy beaches on the coast. Everywhere in the county offers breathtaking views of the Cambrian Mountains, and there are often glimpses of the sea in Cardigan Bay.

The gardens in Ceredigion sit comfortably in the dramatic scenery. There are gardens that have been created with great imagination and enterprise from the barren water-soaked moorland; others have sensitively enhanced and embellished stony hillsides. Rhododendrons and azaleas thrive in the acid soil, and from April till June the gardens are awash with their bright jewel-like blossoms.

Two of our gardens are of historic interest: Llanllyr, which is on the site of a medieval nunnery, and Alltyrodyn Mansion which has a rare stone gothic bath house in the grounds. Both Bwlch y Geuffordd and Ty Glyn Walled Garden provide children with hours of fun and adventure.

In one small, hilly, rock-strewn county, it is surprising how different the gardens are from each other, yet one thing they have in common: they are all created and tended with love, care and imagination.

Ceredigion Volunteers

County Organiser
Pat Causton
01974 272619
pat.causton30@gmail.com

County Treasurer
Steve Yeomans
01974 299370
s.j.yeomans@btinternet.com

Assistant County Organisers
Gay Acres
01974 251559
gayacres@aol.com

Lisa Raw-Rees
01545 570107
hywelrawrees@hotmail.com

Below: Winllan Wildlife Garden

Currently the NGS donates around £2.5 million every year

Opening Dates

All entries subject to change.
For latest information check www.ngs.org.uk

May

Sunday 17
3 Bwlch y Geuffordd

Saturday 23
9 Penybont

Sunday 24
9 Penybont

June

Festival Weekend

Sunday 7
8 Pantyfod

Thursday 18
6 Llanerchaeron (Evening)

Sunday 21
7 Llanllyr

Sunday 28
13 Ysgoldy'r Cwrt

July

Sunday 5
8 Pantyfod

Saturday 18
9 Penybont

Sunday 19
9 Penybont
12 Yr Efail

August

Sunday 2
10 Ty Glyn Walled Garden

Gardens open to the public

6 Llanerchaeron
10 Ty Glyn Walled Garden

By arrangement only

1 Alltyrodyn Mansion
2 Bwlch y Geuffordd Gardens
4 Castell Pigyn
5 Gwynfryn
11 Winllan Wildlife Garden

Also open by arrangement

7 Llanllyr
9 Penybont
12 Yr Efail
13 Ysgoldy'r Cwrt

Wildlife ponds with frogs, newts and dragonflies . . .

The Gardens

1 **ALLTYRODYN MANSION**
Capel Dewi SA44 4PS. Mr & Mrs Donald Usher, 01545 590206. *8m W of Lampeter, off A475. Take B4459 at Rhydowen to Capel Dewi. Entrance on R by South Lodge.* Cream teas. **Adm £4, chd free. Share to Capel Dewi Village Church. Visitors welcome by arrangement** May to Sept.
Early C19 garden. Approx 8 acres, mostly mature woodland with many fine trees. Rare stone built gothic cold bathhouse. Early C20 lake, Dutch garden and rhododendron plantings. Garden is best in spring when rhododendrons and azaleas are in bloom. Large and interesting plant stall. A garden with interesting walks. Partial wheelchair access due to slopes and steps.
♿ 🏵 ❀ ☕

2 **BWLCH Y GEUFFORDD GARDENS**
Bronant, Aberystwyth SY23 4JD. Mr & Mrs J Acres, 01974 251559, gayacres@aol.com. *12m SE of Aberystwyth, 6m NW of Tregaron off A485. Take turning opp Bronant school for 1¹/₂ m then L up ¹/₂ m track.* Tea. **Adm £3.50, chd 50p. Visitors welcome by arrangement** any time, but advisable to phone first.
1000ft high, 3 acre, constantly evolving wildlife garden featuring a lake and several pools. A number of themed gardens, incl Mediterranean, cottage garden, woodland, oriental, memorial and jungle. Plenty of seating. Unique garden sculptures and buildings, incl a cave, gazebo and jungle hut. Developing as a healing garden for those dealing with cancer. Pond dipping, treasure hunt and play area available for children. Unique garden art and buildings. Please contact for information on wheelchair access.
🏵 ❀ 🚐 ☕

3 **BWLCH Y GEUFFORDD**
New Cross, Aberystwyth SY23 4LY. Manuel & Elaine Grande. *4¹/₂ m SE of Aberystwyth. Off A487, onto A4120 Devil's Bridge Rd & immed R on B4340 Trawsgoed rd. Garden 3m on R at bottom of small dip. Park in lay-bys.* Home-made teas. **Adm £3.50, chd free. Sun 17 May (10.30-5).**
An ever evolving 1 acre country garden set on a steep slope with lovely views of the surrounding countryside. Mixed borders with a large variety of plants for yr-round interest. Banks of rhododendrons, azaleas and bluebells. Unusual shade loving plants, acers and ferns merging into carefully managed informal areas. Fish ponds, bog gardens, climbing roses, many cacti and plenty of seating. Wheelchair access to some parts of garden, some steps and steep paths.
🏵 ❀ ☕

4 **CASTELL PIGYN**
Llanarth SA47 0PT. Wendy & Steve Thacker, 01545 580014. *1m N of Llanarth, 3m S of Aberaeron. On A487 midway Cardigan-Aberystwyth. White cottage close to rd, on L when travelling N. Parking for max 4 vehicles on hard standing & drive.* Home-made teas. **Adm £3.50, chd free. Visitors welcome by arrangement** Apr to Aug 16 max. 11am - dusk most days, please ring first.
Knowledgable plantswoman's garden developed from old orchard. Paths wind through herbaceous borders full of hardy geraniums, roses, shrubs and trees. Many varieties of clematis and hellebores. Bog garden, incl gunnera. Fernery, dry river bed, grasses, hostas. 4 wildlife ponds with frogs, newts and dragonflies. Old apple varieties. Seating.
❀ ☕

5 **GWYNFRYN**
Llanrhystud SY23 5BY. Sue Pester, 01974 200948, sueruffles123@gmail.com. *Between Llanrhystud & Llanon, on A487. 1m S of Llanrhystud, after Hidden Dip rd sign. Entrance to garden where rd sign indicates L turn.* Home-made teas. **Adm £3.50, chd free. Visitors welcome by arrangement** June to Oct.
Large garden of 11 acres with woodland, incl over 20 varieties of cherries, paddocks, large vegetable and soft fruit areas. Lawns, herbaceous borders, pond, fuchsia hedges, poultry and other livestock. Stunning views over Cardigan Bay. Level garden, but with gravel and grass paths.
♿ ☕

Llanerchaeron

6 ◆ **LLANERCHAERON**
Ciliau Aeron, Lampeter SA48 8DG.
National Trust, 01545 573029,
www.nationaltrust.org.uk. *2¹/₂ m E
of Aberaeron. On A482 Lampeter to
Aberaeron. Brown sign to
Llanerchaeron gardens from
Aberaeron & opp turning off A487.*
**For NGS: Evening Opening £3.50,
chd free, Light refreshments, Thur
18 June (6-9). For other opening
times and information, please
phone or see garden website.**
Llanerchaeron is a small C18 Welsh
gentry estate set in the beautiful
Dyffryn Aeron. The estate survived
virtually unaltered into the C20. 2

extensive restored walled gardens
produce home grown vegetables,
fruit and herbs for sale. The kitchen
garden sits at the core of the estate
with a John Nash villa built in 1795
and home farm, all virtually unaltered
since its construction. Music,
refreshments, plant and produce
sales.

7 **LLANLLYR**
Talsarn, Lampeter SA48 8QB. Mr &
Mrs Robert Gee, 01570 470900,
lgllanllyr@aol.com. *6m NW of
Lampeter. On B4337 to Llanrhystud.*
Home-made teas. **Adm £4, chd free.
Sun 21 June (2-6). Visitors also
welcome by arrangement Apr to
Oct.**
Large early C19 garden on site of
medieval nunnery, renovated and
replanted since 1989. Large pool,
bog garden, formal water garden,
rose and shrub borders, gravel
gardens, laburnum arbour, allegorical
labyrinth and mount, all exhibiting fine
plantsmanship. Yr-round appeal,
interesting and unusual plants.
Specialist plant fair by Ceredigion
Growers Association.

Find a garden near you – download our free Android app

8 ▶ PANTYFOD

Llanddewi Brefi, Tregaron
SY25 6PE. David & Susan Rowe,
www.pantyfodgarden.co.uk. *About
3m S of Tregaron. From Llanddewi
Brefi village square, take R fork past
Community Centre. Go up hill, past
Ffarmers turning, cont for approx
³/₄ m. Pantyfod is on R.* Home-made
teas. Authentic Italian pizza's cooked
to order in woodfired oven (Sun 5
July). **Adm £3.50, chd free. Sun 7
June, Sun 5 July (12-5.30).**
Peaceful well established 3¹/₂ acre
garden with lots of pathways through
a wide variety of perennials, trees and
shrubs, many unusual. Varying
habitats incl terraces, woodland,
mature trees, natural ponds. Hardy
geraniums, candelabra primulas, Iris
sibirica, grasses, rugosa roses.
Wildlife friendly. Stunning, panoramic
views of the Teifi Valley and
mountains beyond.

9 ▶ PENYBONT

Llanafan, Aberystwyth SY23 4BJ.
Norman & Brenda Jones, 01974
261737,
blakeley@graphics.wanadoo.co.uk.
*9m SW of Aberystwyth. In Ystwyth
valley off B4340. From Aberystwyth,
stay on B4340 for 9m via Trawscoed.
R over stone bridge. ¹/₄ m up hill, turn
R past row of cream houses.* Light
refreshments. **Adm £3.50, chd free.
Sat 23, Sun 24 May, Sat 18, Sun 19
July (11-6). Visitors also welcome
by arrangement May to Aug.**
Starting with a clean sheet and
maturing fast. Penybont shows what
can be achieved from a green field
sloping site in just a few yrs. This
exciting and beautifully planted
garden has been designed to
compliment the modern building, its
forest backdrop and panoramic
views. Country location with stunning
views of the Ystwyth valley. Sloping
ground, good paths and lawn, but
parts of garden not accessible to
wheelchairs.

**10 ◆ TY GLYN WALLED
GARDEN**

Ciliau Aeron, Lampeter SA48 8DE.
Ty Glyn Davis Trust, 01970 832268,
www.tyglyndavistrust.co.uk. *3m SE
of Aberaeron. Turn off A482
Aberaeron to Lampeter at Ciliau
Aeron signed to Pennant. Entrance
700 metres on L.* Home-made teas.
**Adm £3.50, chd free. For NGS: Sun
2 Aug (2-5.30).** For other opening

times and information, please
phone or see garden website.
Secluded walled garden in beautiful
woodland setting alongside R Aeron,
developed specifically for special
needs children. Terraced kitchen
garden overlooks herbaceous
borders, orchard and ponds with
child orientated features and
surprises amidst unusual shrubs and
perennials. Planted fruit trees
selected from former gardener's
notebook of C19. Access paths and
lower garden are accessible to
wheelchairs.

Starting with
a clean
sheet and
maturing fast . . .

**11 ▶ WINLLAN WILDLIFE
GARDEN**

Talsarn, Lampeter SA48 8QE. Joy
Silvester & Martin Gillard, 015704
72936, joyfulsilvester@yahoo.com.
*8m NNW of Lampeter. On B4342,
Talsarn - Llangeitho, 1m E of Talsarn.*
Tea. **Adm £3.50, chd free. Visitors
welcome by arrangement May to
June.**
A 6 acre wildlife garden with 4 acre
hay meadow, over 10,000 wild
orchids incl the rare Greater Butterfly
Orchid. The meadows are subject to
SSSI status and in 2013 was
designated as a Coronation Meadow
to celebrate the Queen's jubilee. The
gardens incl a riverbank walk, a small
wood, and formal area with large
pond. Uneven and sloping ground.

12 ▶ YR EFAIL

Llanio Road, Tregaron SY25 6PU.
Mrs Shelagh Yeomans, 01974
299370, shelaghyeo@hotmail.com.
*3m SW of Tregaron. Lampeter: A485
- Tregaron. L at Llanio to B4578,
Aberystwyth: A487, A485 - Tregaron.
At Tyncelyn B4578, 4m on R.* Home-

made teas. **Adm £3.50, chd free.
Sun 19 July (11-5.30).** Visitors also
welcome by arrangement Mar to
Sept.
A vegetable growers paradise, with
newly developed beds growing a
wide variety of hardy vegetables in
addition to glasshouse and poly
tunnels full of tender crops and fruit
garden. Established ornamental area
with large pond, herbaceous borders,
bog and gravel gardens and shaded
areas. Quiz sheet for children. Garden
vegetables for sale. Home grown
vegetables and fruit used in sweet
and savoury refreshments. Gravelled
paths accessible to wheelchairs but
grass paths difficult when wet.

13 ▶ YSGOLDY'R CWRT

Llangeitho, Tregaron SY25 6QJ.
Mrs Brenda Woodley, 01974
821542. *1¹/₂ m N of Llangeitho.
Llangeitho, turn L at school signed
Penuwch. Garden 1¹/₂ m on R. From
Cross Inn take B4577 past Penuwch
Inn, R after brown sculptures in field.
Garden ³/₄ m on L.* Home-made teas.
**Adm £3.50, chd free. Sun 28 June
(11-5).** Visitors also welcome by
arrangement May to Aug (no WC
available for visitor use at garden).
1 acre hillside garden, with 4 natural
ponds which are a magnet for wildlife.
Areas of wild flower meadow, bog,
dry and woodland gardens. Newly
established rose walk. Rare trees,
large herbaceous beds, Acer
collection, bounded by a mountain
stream, with 2 natural cascades, and
magnificent views. Brand new shade
bed for 2015. Children must be
supervised because of steeply
sloping ground.

Penybont

Visit a garden in your own time – look for by arrangement gardens

GLAMORGAN

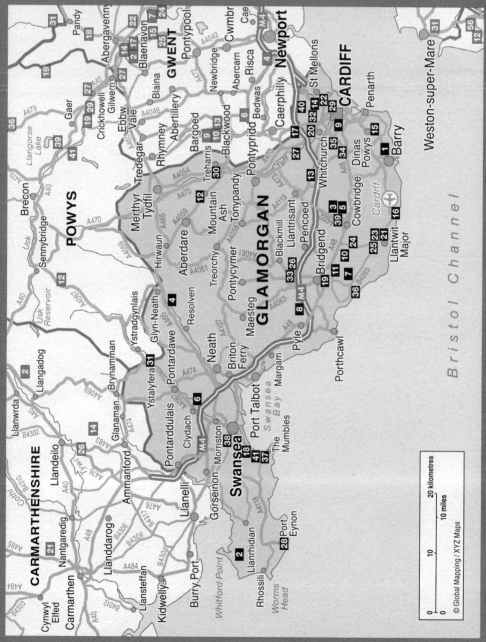

Glamorgan

Glamorgan is a large county stretching from the Brecon Beacons in the north to the Bristol Channel in the south, and from the city of Cardiff in the east to the Gower Peninsula in the west. The area has a natural divide where the hills rise from the vale in a clear line of demarcation.

There are gardens opening for the NGS throughout the county, and in recent years the number of community openings has greatly increased and have been very successful.

A number of gardens open in villages or suburbs, often within walking distance of each other, providing a very pleasant afternoon for the visitors. Each garden has its own distinct character and the locality is full of hospitality and friendliness.

Gardens range from Mediterranean-style to gardens designed to encourage wildlife. Views from our coastal gardens are truly spectacular.

Our openings start around Easter with a woodland and spring bulbs garden and continue through to mid-September.

So just jump in the car – Yellow Book in hand – and head west on the M4. The gardens in Wales are waiting for you!

Glamorgan Volunteers

County Organiser
Rosamund Davies
01656 880048
ros@sladewoodgarden.plus.com

County Treasurer
Trevor Humby
02920 512709
humbyt@cardiff.ac.uk

Publicity
Sara Bentley
02920 512709
sarajanebentley@googlemail.com

Rosamund Davies
(as above)

Booklet Coordinators
Rosamund Davies
(as above)

Jackie Simpson
01446 796630
jackieasimpson@gmail.com

Assistant County Organisers
Sol Blytt Jordens
01792 391676
solinge22@yahoo.co.uk

Melanie Hurst
01446 773659
melanie@hurstcreative.co.uk

Ceri Macfarlane
01792 404906
ceri@mikegravenor.plus.com

Left: Slade

Since our foundation we have donated more than £42.5 million to charity

Opening Dates

All entries subject to change.
For latest information check www.ngs.org.uk

April

Saturday 25
36 Slade

Sunday 26
36 Slade

May

Sunday 3
23 Llanmaes Gardens

Monday 4
39 Trerhyngyll Gardens

Sunday 10
21 Knightsbridge
40 Ty'n Y Berllan
41 NEW 9 Willowbrook Gardens

Saturday 16
25 NEW Lougher Moor

Sunday 17
20 Japanese Garden
25 NEW Lougher Moor

Wednesday 27
3 Bordervale Plants

Saturday 30
30 Pontygwaith Farm

Sunday 31
16 Gileston Manor
30 Pontygwaith Farm
38 Tony Ridlers Garden

June

Festival Weekend

Saturday 6
27 The Old Post Office

Sunday 7
5 Bryn-y-Ddafad
27 The Old Post Office

Saturday 13
31 Rhos y Bedw

Sunday 14
2 Big House Farm
24 Llysworney Gardens
31 Rhos y Bedw
38 Tony Ridlers Garden

Wednesday 17
4 Brynheulog

Saturday 20
17 Hafod y Milgi

Sunday 21
7 Castle Upon Alun House
8 Cefn Cribwr Garden Club
17 Hafod y Milgi
19 Heronsbridge School
28 Overton and Port Eynon Gardens

Tuesday 23
3 Bordervale Plants

Sunday 28
10 Colwinston Village Gardens
22 NEW Llanedeyrn Primary School

32 NEW Rhydypenau Group
33 Rose Cottage
34 St. Fagans Church Primary School

July

Saturday 4
15 Dinas Powys

Sunday 5
14 Cyncoed Gardens
15 Dinas Powys
26 Maes-y-Wertha Farm

Saturday 11
6 Brynyrenfys

Sunday 12
29 Penylan Gardens

Saturday 18
35 St. Peter's Community Garden

Sunday 19
1 Barry Gardens
13 Creigiau Village Gardens
35 St. Peter's Community Garden

Tuesday 21
3 Bordervale Plants

Sunday 26
11 NEW Corntown Gardens
18 16 Hendy Close

August

Sunday 2
21 Knightsbridge

Sunday 9
37 19 Slade Gardens

Tuesday 11
3 Bordervale Plants

September

Tuesday 1
3 Bordervale Plants

Saturday 5
9 Chapter Community Garden

Gardens open to the public

3 Bordervale Plants

By arrangement only

12 The Cottage

Also open by arrangement

1 47 Aneurin Road, Barry Gardens
1 Barry Gardens
2 Big House Farm
4 Brynheulog
5 Bryn-y-Ddafad
6 Brynyrenfys
19 Heronsbridge School
21 Knightsbridge
29 7 Cressy Road, Penylan Gardens
30 Pontygwaith Farm
41 NEW 9 Willowbrook Gardens

The Gardens

GROUP OPENING

1 BARRY GARDENS

Barry CF63 4PP. *Barry Town. 47 Aneurin Rd - head for Police Station on Gladstone rd then follow yellow signs. 11 Arno Rd - head to Waitrose on Palmerston Rd then follow yellow signs.* Light refreshments. **Combined adm £3.50, chd free. Sun 19 July (12-5.30).**

47 ANEURIN ROAD
Dave Bryant
Visitors also welcome by arrangement June to Aug, weekends (12-5) and Weekdays (5pm onwards).
07894 339821
bryantdj@outlook.com

11 ARNO ROAD
Debbie Palmer

2 town gardens. 47 Aneurin Rd is an ever changing small vertical garden with a collection of over 30 clematis, fuchsias and Cranesbill Geraniums. 11 Arno Rd is a redesigned plant lover's small garden with a new front garden with unusual shrubs and shade loving plants.

2 BIG HOUSE FARM

Llanmadoc, Gower, Swansea SA3 1DE. Mark & Sheryl Mead, 07831 725753, sherylandmark@tiscali.co.uk. *15m W of Swansea. M4 J47, L A483 for Llanelli 3rd r'about L, B4296 Gowerton T-lights, R B4295, pass Bury Green R to Llanmadoc. Please*

park in public car park at Port Eynon. Home-made teas. **Adm £4, chd free. Sun 14 June (1-6). Visitors also welcome by arrangement June to Sept for groups 10+.**
Award winning inspirational garden of just under an acre combines colour form and texture in this beautiful much loved Gower village, described by one visitor as 'the best I've seen this season'. Large variety of interesting plants and shrubs, with ambient cottage garden feel, Mediterranean garden, kitchen garden, beautiful views. Located on the Gower Peninsular, Britain's first designated Area of Outstanding Natural Beauty. Featured on TV, in Garden News and The Evening Post. Most of garden is accessible to wheelchairs.

3 ◆ **BORDERVALE PLANTS**
Sandy Lane, Ystradowen,
Cowbridge CF71 7SX. Mrs Claire
Jenkins, 01446 774036,
www.bordervale.co.uk. *8m W of
Cardiff. 10 mins from M4 or take
A4222 from Cowbridge. Turn at
Ystradowen postbox, then 3rd L &
proceed ¹/₂ m, follow brown signs.
Garden on R. Parking in rd.* **Adm £3,
chd free. For NGS: Wed 27 May,
Tues 23 June, 21 July, 11 Aug, 1
Sept (10-5). For other opening
times and information, please
phone or see garden website.**
Within mature woodland valley (semi
tamed), with stream and bog garden,
extensive mixed borders; mini wild
flower meadow, providing diverse
wildlife habitats. Children must be
supervised. The Nursery specialises
in unusual perennials and cottage
garden plants. Nursery open: Fri -
Sun (10-5), (and often open Mon -
Thurs) Mar - Sept, when garden is
also open mid May - Sept. Not for
NGS. Awarded Silver Medal (for
category) RHS Flower Show Cardiff.
Wheelchair access to top third of
garden as well as Nursery.

&♿ ❀

4 ▶ **BRYNHEULOG**
45 Heol y Graig, Cwmgwrach,
Neath SA11 5TW. Lorraine Rudd,
01639 722593,
lorrainejrudd@sky.com. *8m W of
Neath. Turn off A465 at McDonalds
r'about & take exit for Cwmgwrach.
(Yellow NGS sign visible on main
r'about). Turn R at mini r'about.*
Home-made teas. **Adm £3.50, chd
free. Wed 17 June (2-5). Visitors
also welcome by arrangement May
to Aug. Garden clubs very
welcome.**
This keen plantswoman's hillside
garden perfectly reflects the dramatic
setting and surrounding natural
beauty. ³/₄ acre plot on many levels
with cottage style planting, tropical
greenhouse, 2 other greenhouses
showing begonias and carnations,
wildflower areas, large rockery and
ponds. Polytunnel houses all yr-round
vegetables. Lots of scent and colour
with roses and lilies.

❀ ☕

5 ▶ **BRYN-Y-DDAFAD**
Welsh St Donats, Cowbridge
CF71 7ST. Glyn & June Jenkins,
01446 774451,
junejenkins@bydd.co.uk,
www.bydd.co.uk/home/garden/.
10m W of Cardiff. 3m E of

5 Southcourt Road, Penylan Gardens

*Cowbridge. From A48 follow signs to
Welsh St Donats village (for SatNav
use CF71 7SS). Follow brown tourist
signs from Xrds, Bryn-y-Ddafad is
approx 1m from here.* Teas and home
made-cakes. **Adm £4, chd free. Sun
7 June (1-5). Visitors also welcome
by arrangement Apr to Sept,
groups 10+.**
This plant woman's garden has areas
of unusual plantings giving interest
through the seasons. Terraced rear
garden, mature trees, flowering
shrubs, Lily pond, pergola of clematis
and wisteria, rose garden leading to a
bridge crossing the natural stream
and bog garden, areas of grasses,
candelabra primulas, rhododendrons
and azaleas. Attractive raised
courtyard garden planted in pastel
shades. Most of the garden is
accessible by wheelchair.

&♿ ❀ 🛏 ☕

6 ▶ **BRYNYRENFYS**
30 Cefn Road, Glais, Swansea
SA7 9EZ. Edith & Roy Morgan,
01792 842777,
edith.morgan@tiscali.co.uk. *8m N
of Swansea. M4 J45, take A4067 R
at 2nd r'about, then 1st R & follow
yellow signs.* Home-made teas.
**Adm £3.50, chd free. Sat 11 July
(12.30-5). Visitors also welcome by
arrangement May to July for
groups 10 +.**
If you love plants you'll be at home
here. A small surprising garden full of
interest. Unusual trees, shrubs and
perennials vie for attention with the
panoramic view. Wildlife and weed
friendly with no bedding! Seating on
different levels, so stay a while,
unwind and be welcome. Croeso i
bawb. Rare and unusual plants for
sale. Featured on S4C.

❀ 🚐 ☕

7 CASTLE UPON ALUN HOUSE
St Brides Major, Bridgend
CF32 0TN. Lady Inkin. *7m W of Cowbridge. Take B4265 to St. Brides Major. Opp pond & next to Farmers Arms, take rd to Castle Upon Alun, then follow NGS signs.* Home-made teas. **Adm £5, chd free. Sun 21 June (2-6).**
Grade ll listed enclave incl 2 acre walled garden which was redesigned and replanted from 1998. Rose walks, pleached lime walk herbaceous borders, extensive lawns and an ornamental pond garden. Shrubs and roses along tree lined drive not to be missed, with good view over garden. Roses a speciality.

GROUP OPENING

8 CEFN CRIBWR GARDEN CLUB
Cefn Cribwr, Bridgend CF32 0AP. *5m W of Bridgend. Cefn Cribwr is located 5m W of Bridgend on B4281.* Tea at Green Hall Community Centre. **Combined adm £4, chd free. Sun 21 June (11-5).**

6 BEDFORD ROAD
Carole & John Mason

NEW **13 BEDFORD ROAD**
Mr John Loveluck

2 BRYN TERRACE
Alan & Tracy Birch

CEFN CRIBWR PRIMARY SCHOOL & ALLOTMENTS

NEW **CEFN METHODIST CHURCH**

77 CEFN ROAD
Peter & Veronica Davies & Mr Fai Lee

25 EAST AVENUE
Mr & Mrs D Colbridge

15 GREEN MEADOW
Thomas Noble

HILL TOP
Mr & Mrs W G Hodges

6 TAI THORN
Mr Kevin Burnell

21 WEST AVENUE
Mr Martin Morgan

Cefn Cribwr gardening club is the heart of a friendly community. The 11 diverse gardens vary from the local school allotments, an exposed mature garden, a recycled garden, a garden that has its own composting system, a children's garden, a rustic garden, an artists' garden, a productive vegetable garden, a quaint chapel garden, a water garden and lastly a small fascinating garden. Just about something for everyone. Craft stalls, games, raffles, teas, plant stall, local school competition and table top sale, all in Green Hall Community Centre.

Enjoy a warm welcome, home-made teas . . .

9 CHAPTER COMMUNITY GARDEN
Market Road, Canton, Cardiff CF5 1QE. Mr Roger Phillips (Coordinator), www.cantoncommunitygardens.co.uk. *At the front of Chapter Arts Centre. Chapter is situated in Canton, behind Cowbridge Rd East (A4161), between Llandaff Rd (B4267) & Market Rd.* Light refreshments. Adm incl tea/coffee and a cake.
Adm £2.50, chd free. Sat 5 Sept (11.30-3).
Canton Community Gardens was established in July 2009, with the intention of bringing local people together for a range of gardening, recycling and environmental projects in the area. The Chapter Community Garden is an ongoing project involving members and volunteers of Canton Community Gardens. The project was awarded £36,000 in the Big Lottery's People's Millions in November 2001, and was shortlisted for a Big Lunch award organised by the Eden Project for Chapter's Big Lunch in 2012. Featured on S4C's Byw yn yr Ardd, BBC Radio Cymru, and in the South Wales Echo. Flat site with excellent wheelchair access.

GROUP OPENING

10 COLWINSTON VILLAGE GARDENS
Colwinston, Cowbridge CF71 7NE. *Off A48 3m W of Cowbridge. 1st turning L after Pentre Meyrick. 3m E of Bridgend from Waterton r'about, turn R on Crack Hill.* Home-made teas at Village Hall. **Combined adm £5, chd free. Share to St Michael & All Angels Church. Sun 28 June (2-6).**

CHAPEL COTTAGE
Mrs Carole Billett

NEW **THE OLD PARSONAGE**
Stuart & Clare Hutton

OLD SCHOOL HOUSE
Pamela Haines

SYCAMORE HILL
Terry & Liz Morgan

VILLAGE FARMHOUSE
Andrew & Heather Maclehose

Colwinston is a rural village of mixed developments with its beautiful C12 church at its centre. Visit 5 contrasting village gardens from formal to cottage gardens and productive vegetable gardens. Several of the gardens have delightful S facing views over the surrounding countryside. Chapel Cottage - has wonderful terraces of roses geraniums and lavender. Sycamore Hill's - mature garden has extensive views. Village Farmhouse - Well laid out cottage style garden with vegetable plot, pond and boules area. The Old Parsonage consists of herbaceous borders and a vegetable plot. Old School House is a mixed cottage garden with mature shrubs. Plant sale.

GROUP OPENING

11 NEW CORNTOWN GARDENS
Corntown, Bridgend CF35 5BB. *Take B4265 from Bridgend to Ewenny. Take L in Ewenny on B4525 to Corntown follow yellow NGS signs. From A48 take B4525 to Corntown.* Home-made teas. **Combined adm £3.50, chd free. Sun 26 July (11-4).**

NEW **RHOS GELER**
Bob Priddle

NEW **Y BWTHYN**
Mrs Joyce Pegg

Y Bwythyn has had over 30yrs of hard labour, some guesswork and considerable good luck resulting in a delightful garden. The area at the front of the house is a mixture of hot colour combinations whilst at the rear of this modest sized garden the themes are of a more traditional cottage garden style which incl colour themed borders as well as soft fruit,

herbs and vegetables. Rhos Geler's garden has a lavender hedge at the front and subjects to attract butterflies. The main garden area at the back of the house is a long narrow garden that is in a series of themed areas. These incl an herbaceous border, shade loving plants, an Elizabethan style knot garden and a Japanese influenced area. Containers hold a range of subjects incl a collection of sempervivums.

12 THE COTTAGE

Cwmpennar, Mountain Ash CF45 4DB. Helen & Hugh Jones, 01443 472784, hhjones1966@yahoo.co.uk. *18m N of Cardiff. A470 from N or S. Then follow B4059 to Mountain Ash. Follow signs for Cefnpennar then turn R before bus shelter into village of Cwpennar.* Home-made teas. **Adm £3.50, chd free. Visitors welcome by arrangement** Apr to July. **Groups 12 max.**
4 acres and 35yrs of amateur muddling have produced this enchanting garden incl bluebell wood, rhododendron and camellia shrubbery, herbaceous borders, rose garden, small arboretum, many uncommon trees and shrubs. Garden slopes NE/SW. Formerly featured on TV but most recently in South Wales Echo - My Garden.

GROUP OPENING

13 CREIGIAU VILLAGE GARDENS

Maes Y Nant, Creigiau CF15 9EJ. *W of Cardiff (J34 M4). From M4 J34 follow A4119 to T-lights, turn R by Castell Mynach PH, pass through Groes Faen & turn L to Creigiau. Follow NGS signs.* Home-made teas at 28 Maes-y-Nant & Waunwyllt. **Combined adm £5, chd free.** Sun 19 July (10-5).

28 MAES Y NANT
Mike & Lesley Sherwood

31 MAES Y NANT
Frances Bowyer

WAUNWYLLT
John Hughes & Richard Shaw

On the NW side of Cardiff and with easy access from the M3 J34, the village of Creigiau conceals a

wonderful surprise in this trio of vibrant and innovative small gardens. Each quite different, they combine some of the best characteristics of design and planting for modern town gardens with the naturalism of old fashioned cottage gardens. Each has its own forte; at Waunwyllt it is what has been achieved over 4yrs and the coloured themed rooms. At 28 Maes y Nant, cottage garden pastoralism reigns. This is in complete contrast to the strong architecture of 31 Maes y Nant, where the design coordinates water, the garden room and planting, incl a small scale prairie. Anyone looking for ideas for a garden in an urban setting will not go away disappointed; enjoy a warm welcome, home-made teas and plant sales. Creigiau Village Gardens featured in the Daily Telegraph Gardening section.

hospiceUK

The NGS funds vital hospice care projects

GROUP OPENING

14 CYNCOED GARDENS

Cyncoed, Cardiff CF23 6SW. *From Hollybush Rd follow yellow NGS signs to Cyncoed Crescent & Danycoed Rd.* Home-made teas. **Combined adm £3, chd free.** Sun 5 July (12-6).

8 CYNCOED CRESCENT
Alistair & Teresa Pattillo

22 DAN Y COED ROAD
Alan & Miranda Workman

KINSLEY
Ms Jill Davey

This is a group of three, 1930's suburban gardens. Each one has its own individual style. They have been designed by the owner and are continually evolving to create an eclectic collection of climber, perennials and shrubs that reflect the interests of these gardeners. Garden structures and summerhouses are used to add interest and to create

different viewpoints over the gardens. All are within walking distance from each other. Partial wheelchair access only.

GROUP OPENING

15 DINAS POWYS

Dinas Powys CF64 4TL. *Dinas Powys is approx 6m SW of cardiff. Exit M4 at J33, follow A4232 to Leckwith, onto B4267& follow to Merry Harrier T-lights. Turn R & enter Dinas Powys. Follow yellow NGS signs.* Home-made teas. Gluten free also available. **Combined adm £4, chd free.** Share to Local charities. Sat 4, Sun 5 July (12-5.30).

1 ASHGROVE
Sara Bentley

BROOKLEIGH
Mr Duncan & Melanie Syme

NEW THE HUNTSMAN RESTAURANT
Hilary & Peter Rice.
Open Sunday only

32 LONGMEADOW DRIVE
Julie Barnes.
Open Sunday only

30 MILLBROOK ROAD
Mr & Mrs R Golding

32 MILLBROOK ROAD
Mr & Mrs G Marsh

NEW THE POUND
Helen & David Parsons

NEW WEST CLIFF
Jackie Hurley & Alan Blakoe

An inspiring and eclectic group of eight gardens in this small friendly village, all with something different to offer. Attractions incl a garden based on permaculture principles, using perennials, shrubs and edibles together. There are ponds of all sizes and styles, planting in shade and sun, boggy areas, pergolas, child friendly attractions, a caravan and summerhouse, mature shrubs and trees, vegetables and fruit, challenging terraced designs and wild areas. Lovely home-made teas will be served and there are many restful and beautiful areas to sit and relax. Plants sales are also an attraction. Good wheelchair access at 30 and 32 Millbrook Rd. Partial access elsewhere.

11 Arno Road, Barry Gardens

16 **GILESTON MANOR**
Gileston, Barry CF62 4HX. Joshua Llewellyn & Lorraine Garrad-Jones, www.gilestoncoachhouse.co.uk. *From Cardiff airport take B4265 to Llantwit Major. After 3m turn L at petrol station. Go under bridge, turn R follow yellow NGS signs. No turning at Cenotaph.* Home-made teas. **Adm £5, chd free.** Sun 31 May (1-5). C19 kitchen garden and woodland/herbaceous borders in restoration. Lawns and views across the Bristol Channel. Gardens surround the Grade II* listed manor house C18 walled garden with summer house and kitchen garden under new layout work in progress. Secret walled garden and kitchen garden - not yet ready. Walled garden under construction rockery Herbaceous borders Woodland. Walled garden has flat gravel paths, gravel drive.

17 **HAFOD Y MILGI**
Heol y Wenallt, Thornhill CF83 1ND. Eric & Angharad Roberts. *4m from Cardiff centre. From Cardiff take A469 to Caerffili, past Thornhill crematorium. House at junction with Wenallt Rd opp Travellers Rest PH. From Caerffili A470 signed.* Home-made teas. **Adm £3, chd free.** Sat 20, Sun 21 June (2-5).
We love our garden and have enjoyed finding plants that survive in this elevated and sometimes windy position. The aim has been to create sheltered places to sit and enjoy the pond, flowers and views of Nofydd Valley and Garth Mountain. Come and enjoy our ever changing garden. Short ramp, some sloping paths in addition to flat patio.

Every garden visit makes a difference

18 16 HENDY CLOSE

Derwen Fawr, Swansea SA2 8BB. Peter & Wendy Robinson. *Approx 3m W of Swansea. A4067 Mumbles Rd follow sign for Singleton Hospital. Then R onto Sketty Lane at mini r'about, turn L then 2nd R onto Saunders Way. Follow yellow signs. Please park on Saunders Way if possible.* Home-made teas. **Adm £3.50, chd free. Sun 26 July (2.30-5.30).**

New garden which is 4yrs old. Originally the garden was covered with 40ft conifers. Cottage style, some unusual and mainly perennial plants which provide colour in Spring, Summer and Autumn. Hopefully the garden is an example of how to plan for all seasons. Visitors say it is like a secret garden because there are a number of hidden places. Not quite the garden you would expect to see.

☕

19 HERONSBRIDGE SCHOOL

Ewenny Road, Bridgend CF31 3HT. Heronsbridge School, 01446 710423, broadclose1@btinternet.com. *In Bridgend, from A48 turn R onto B4265 Ewenny Rd. School on R.* Home-made teas. **Adm £3, chd free. Sun 21 June (1-4).** Visitors also welcome by arrangement Mar to Oct for any size group.

The special needs school which won Silver at Chelsea 2011 and Gold and Best in Show in RHS Cardiff 2013. You are welcome to visit our sensory kitchen and formal gardens and our heritage orchard, with swings and a willow tunnel. Fantastic home-made cakes made by our children, display of slides from our sister schools in Botswana and Tanzania; imaginative projects for the gardens. Home grown plants for sale. Playground with swings. Beehives, chickens, wild areas, willow tunnel to play in. Disability friendly, as almost all our gardens are purpose built for the disabled. Full access to our afternoon teas and WC.

♿ ✿ ☕

20 JAPANESE GARDEN

Cardiff CF14 6EE. Mr B A Harding. *Rhiwbina garden village. 1st L after Rhiwbina village shops, on L almost to end of Lon Isa.* **Adm £4, chd free. Sun 17 May (11-6).**

Typical Japanese style garden with undulating ground, small stream, pond and tea house. Seeks to evoke and imitate nature with the elements being tranquillity, simplicity and harmony. Maples and pine trees shaped in Japanese traditional way, azaleas clipped in cloud formation and a Japanese tea house. A garden full of tranquility a place to find an inner peace. Featured on A Little Piece of Paradise - HTV Wales.

21 KNIGHTSBRIDGE

21 Monmouth Way, Boverton, Llantwit Major CF61 2GT. Don & Ann Knight, 01446 794529, anncknight@hotmail.co.uk. *At Llanmaes rd T-lights turn onto Eagleswell Rd, next L into Monmouth Way, garden halfway down on R.* Home-made teas. **Adm £3, chd free. Sun 10 May, Sun 2 Aug (11-5).** Visitors also welcome by arrangement Apr to Sept.

Japanese garden with a Zen gate, Torri gate and Japanese lanterns featuring a large collection of Japanese style trees, which incl an English elm, oak, larch etc., a pagoda and two water features. Wheelchair access via rear garden.

♿ ☕

22 NEW LLANEDEYRN PRIMARY SCHOOL

Wellwood, Llanedeyrn, Cardiff CF23 9JN. Mr I James (Headteacher). *Follow directions to Llanedeyrn from A48M. From Circle Way take 2nd turning off r'about onto Llanedeyrn Drive & take 1st right. Llanedeyrn Primary School is on the R.* Home-made teas. **Adm £3, chd free. Sun 28 June (1-4).**

Our school garden has developed recently and we were delighted to win 1st prize in Cardiff in Bloom. Features incl vegetable and flower beds, a pond, a bumble bee garden, forest school and a chicken run. Come and listen to our range of experts who will give talks and advice on the above. There will be lots of activities for young and old to do.

♿ ✿ ☕

Lovely home-made teas will be served and there are many restful and beautiful areas to sit and relax . . . .

GROUP OPENING

23 LLANMAES GARDENS

Llanmaes, Llantwit Major CF61 2XR. *5m S of Cowbridge. From Mehefin & West Winds travel to Church via Gadlys Farm House & Church Cottage on to Brown Lion House & cont down lane for 1m to Old Froglands.* Home-made teas at Old Froglands & Mehefin. **Combined adm £5, chd free. Sun 3 May (1-6).**

BROWN LION HOUSE
Mrs Wendy Hewitt-Sayer

NEW CHURCH COTTAGE
Mrs Claire Sutcliffe

GADLYS FARM HOUSE
Dot Williams

MEHEFIN 🛏
Mrs Alison Morgan
01446 793427,
bb@mehefin.com,
www.mehefin.com

OLD FROGLANDS
Dorne & David Harris

WEST WINDS
Jackie Simpson

Llanmaes, 1m from Llantwit Major, is a pretty village with attractive village green, stream running through and C13 church. Old Froglands is an historic farmhouse with streams and woodland areas linked by bridges. Ducks swim and chickens roam free. The vegetable plot is now productive. Plantings are varied with interesting foliage. West Winds is a work in progress. It was a beautiful and much loved garden that sadly became overgrown and is now being reclaimed. Pathways weave through terraces with balustrades, wooded areas and lawns with views over the village and open fields. The garden has a full range of aspects from deep shade to full sun, and is shared and enjoyed with a diverse collection of wildlife. Church Cottage has a pretty cottage garden and has seen significant work over the past 2yrs. Brown Lion House is a newly renovated garden around mature trees and shrubs with patios and pathways. Gadlys Farm House is 1 acre of informal family garden surrounding a C17 farmhouse. Various sitting areas to relax amongst mature trees, herbaceous borders, summerhouse water feature and courtyard with planters. Mehefin is an enchanting garden with bursts of colour.

♿ ✿ ☕

GROUP OPENING

24 LLYSWORNEY GARDENS
Llysworney, Cowbridge CF71 7NQ. *2m SW of Cowbridge. W along A48 passing Cowbridge. Turn L at Pentre Meyrick on B4268 signed Llysworney & Llantwit Major (CF717NQ).* Home-made teas. **Combined adm £5, chd free. Sun 14 June (2-6).**

BROCTON HOUSE
Peter & Colette Evans

NEW GREAT HOUSE
Mr David Scott-Coombes

NEW SYDNEY HOUSE FARM
Mrs Liz Rees

WOLF HOUSE
Martyn & Melanie Hurst

Llysworney is a charming small rural village with church, duck pond children's play area and friendly people! Four gardens will be open together with St Tydfil's Church which dates back to C13. Wolf House has a walled cottage garden on two levels with a variety of perennials and roses. African summer house offers a quiet place to sit and ponder! Great House is C16 grade II listed with terraced garden and a variety of trees, shrubs and perennials. Brocton House has a pretty terraced garden and large vegetable/fruit garden overlooking farmland with barn and wild flower area. Sydney House Farm is a wildlife friendly garden in over ¹/₂ acre bordering countryside. The garden is planted to encourage lots of wildlife.
❀ ☕

25 NEW LOUGHER MOOR
Morfa Lane, Llantwit Major CF61 2YT. Mr Gordon Baston, www.loughermoor.co.uk. *Follow brown tourist signs from Wick Rd.* Home-made teas, freshly baked scones and cakes. **Adm £3.50, chd free. Sat 16 May (2-5); Sun 17 May (2-5.30).**
More by accident rather than design.This is very much a wildlife garden comprising ponds and woodlands, 30yrs in the making every tree and shrub planted by the owners. The natural habitat created out of what was a field of rye grass, is now home to a variety of bird life flora and fauna. Some steps. Wet conditions will restrict wheelchair access.
♿ ❀ 🛏 ☕

26 MAES-Y-WERTHA FARM
Bryncethin CF32 9YJ. Stella & Tony Leyshon. *3m N of Bridgend. Follow sign for Bryncethin, turn R at Masons Arms. Follow sign for Heol-y-Cyw garden about 1m outside Bryncethin on R.* Home-made teas. **Adm £4.50, chd free. Sun 5 July (1-5).**
A 3 acre garden. Informal mixed beds with large selection of perennial plants, shrubs, conifers and trees. Water garden fed by natural spring. Large grass area under new planting. Mural in the summerhouse by Daniel Llewelyn Hall contemporary artist. His work is represented in the Royal Collection and House of Lords.
♿ 🐕 ❀ ☕

27 THE OLD POST OFFICE
Main Road, Gwaelod-Y-Garth, Cardiff CF15 9HJ. Ms Christine Myant. *N of Cardiff nr Radyr & Pentyrch. Garden on L of rd, 4 houses pass PH. Parking in school car park further down hill.* Home-made teas. **Adm £3, chd free. Sat 6, Sun 7 June (11-5).**
Situated in the popular village of Gwaelod-y-Garth on the northern edge of Cardiff this informal terraced garden provides some splendid views of the green valley and hills opposite.
❀ ☕

Marie Curie Cancer Care

Our nurses work in communities covering 95% of the UK

GROUP OPENING

28 OVERTON AND PORT EYNON GARDENS
Overton Lane, Port Eynon, Swansea SA3 1NR. *16.8m W of Swansea on Gower Peninsula. From Swansea follow A 4118 to Port Eynon. Parking in public car park in Port Eynon. Yellow signs showing* gardens. Maps of gardens locations available at all gardens on entry. Home-made teas at The Bays Farm. **Combined adm £4, chd free. Sun 21 June (2-5.30).**

THE BAYS FARM D
Sol Blytt Jordens

6 THE BOARLANDS
Robert & Annette Dyer

BOX BOAT COTTAGE
Ms Christine Williams

OLD FORT FARM
Mr Dick Metcalfe

TY'R GWYNT
Mr & Mrs Richard Morris

WESTCLIFFE HOUSE
David Carlsen-Browne

On the beautiful Gower Peninsula all very different gardens. There is a flat cottage garden, one a steep sloping garden, one a plantsman's garden, and one a garden created from a deeply excavated site. The last a 4yr old garden in progress. Enjoy views over The Bristol Channel while having teas at The Bays Farm.
❀ ☕

GROUP OPENING

29 PENYLAN GARDENS
Penylan, Cardiff CF23 5BY. *1¹/₂ m NE of Cardiff city centre. M4 J29, Cardiff E A48, then Llanedeyrn/Docks junction, towards Cyncoed. L down Penylan Rd. Marlborough is L at T-lights at bottom of hill.* Delicious home-made cakes. **Combined adm £3, chd free. Sun 12 July (2-6).**

7 CRESSY ROAD
Victoria Thornton
Visitors also welcome by arrangement July to Aug for individuals or groups 10 max. 02920 311215 thornton.victoria@me.com

NEW PALAS Y LURCHER
Mrs Rebecca Remigio

5 SOUTHCOURT ROAD
Pat & Mel Griffiths

Set in the Victorian suburb of Penylan, 3 gardens that demonstrate in a variety of ways how to add interest and individuality to a small space. Palas y Lurcher is less than 12 months old and beautifully illustrates what can be done in a short time, in a small city space. Characterised by ornate ornamental structures and

romantic, nectar rich, organic planting. At 5 Southcourt Road enjoy the fragrance and colour combinations of this beautiful garden. Follow the path under the wisteria and clematis laden arches to the summerhouse. Plentiful seating away from the elements. Awarded Gold Best Senior Citizen Gardener (Penylan area) and 2nd place in same category for City of Cardiff as a whole. 7 Cressy Road, a small subtropical garden, creating an illusion of a much larger space. Lush tropical planting, alive with colour and texture. Nectar rich planting, barrel frog pond. 10 mins walk to Southcourt Rd. Wheelchair access at Palas yr Lurcher.

🌼 ☕

30▶ PONTYGWAITH FARM

Edwardsville, nr Treharris CF46 5PD. Mrs D Cann, 07784 871502, diana.cann@btinternet.com. *2m NW of Treharris. N from Cardiff on A470. At r'about take A4054 N towards Aberfan. 1m after Edwardsville turn sharp L by black bus shelter. Garden at bottom of hill.* Tea. **Adm £3.50, chd free. Sat 30, Sun 31 May (10-5). Visitors also welcome by arrangement May to Aug for max 10 visitors.**
4½ acre garden surrounding C17 farmhouse adjacent to Trevithick's Tramway. Situated in picturesque wooded valley. Fish pond, lawns, perennial borders, new lakeside walk, rose garden, Japanese garden. Grade II listed humpback packhorse bridge in garden, spanning R Taff. A lovely day out for all the family. Welcome to visitors on the Taff Trail (April - Sept, 10am - 5pm). Partial wheelchair access due to steep slope to river, gravel paths.

& 🚻 🌼 ☕

31▶ RHOS Y BEDW

4 Pen y Wern Rd, Ystalyfera, Swansea SA9 2NH. Robert & Helen Davies. *13m N of Swansea. M4 J45 take A4067. Follow signs for Dan yr Ogof caves across 5 r'abouts. After T-lights follow yellow NGS signs. Parking above house on rd off to R.* Home-made teas. Gluten free also available. **Adm £2.50, chd free. Sat 13, Sun 14 June (12-5).**
This constantly evolving garden provides a haven of peace and tranquility with spectacular views. Wander through this glorious

compact garden with its array of planting areas. Perennial, herb, bog, vegetable and knot garden are sure to provide inspiration. A garden to be savoured slowly, relax and enjoy.

🚻 🌼 ☕

GROUP OPENING

32▶ NEW▶ RHYDYPENAU GROUP

Fidlas Avenue, Cardiff CF14 0NX. *From Junction 32 of M4, take A470 S signed Cardiff. After 2m, turn L at T-lights onto Birchgrove Rd then cont ahead looking for yellow NGS signs. Gardens are within 10-15 mins walk of each other.* Home-made teas. **Combined adm £3, chd free. Sun 28 June (12-6).**

NEW▶ RHYDYPENAU ALLOTMENTS
City of Cardiff Council

RHYDYPENAU PRIMARY SCHOOL
Mr Richard Melhuish

Extensive school gardens which attract visiting educators from both home and abroad, this year we are combining with our local allotment association, a large productive area which provides an inner city haven for people and wildlife. Mostly level access, paths uneven in places.

& 🌼 ☕

33▶ ROSE COTTAGE

32 Blackmill Road, Bryncethin, Bridgend CF32 9YN. Maria & Anne Lalic, www.cobwebs.uk.net/ simplecountryfolk. *1m N of M4 J36 on A4061. Follow A4061 to Bryncethin. Straight on at mini r'about for approx 400metres. Just past Used Car Garage, turn R onto side rd at grassed area.* Home-made teas. **Adm £3.50, chd free. Sun 28 June (12-5).**
Rose Cottage has been a working cottage garden for 250yrs. We borrow ideas from Permaculture and No Dig methods, mix with companion planting and old fashioned gardening to give us vegetables all yr-round and fit our simple, nearly self sufficient lifestyle. Bentwood fences and reclaimed Victorian bricks edge paths and flower beds. A separate herb garden provides plants for hedgerow medicine. A raised terrace area alongside the conservatory allows viewing of the field where the goats,

chickens and ducks graze. Rock Bottom Cottage will be creating a vintage tea room for afternoon refreshments incl lovely home-made cakes served on china. Main paths and gateways suitable for wheelchairs. Narrower, bark chip paths around vegetable beds and polytunnel interior are not.

& 🌼 ☕

34▶ ST. FAGANS CHURCH PRIMARY SCHOOL

Drope Road, Cardiff CF5 4SZ. Alison Price, www.stfaganscwprimary.com. *1m from A4232 at Culverhouse Cross r'about, West Cardiff. At r'about, take A48 towards Cardiff & Ely. Turn L at T- lights into Michaelston Rd & L at PH into Drope Rd. Parking available on site.* Home-made teas. **Adm £3, chd free. Sun 28 June (1-5).**
Pupils, parents and staff have worked together to develop The Secret Garden from a piece of wasteland to a stimulating learning environment and beautiful garden. Features incl vegetable beds, a wildlife pond, log circle, woodland area and a fruit forest garden. Tours of the garden by the children will be on offer. The School has received a special award from Cardiff Healthy Schools for the development of the garden.

☕

Spring bulbs, primula and stream give natural informality to sit and dream as well as a courtyard garden and pool . . .

35 ST. PETER'S COMMUNITY GARDEN

St Fagans Road, Cardiff CF5 3DW. Father Colin Sutton, www.stpeterschurchfairwater. org.uk. *A48 to Culverhousecross r'bout take A48 Cowbridge Rd West to Ely r'bout 1st L. At T-lights go L B4488 to Fairwater Green, follow yellow NGS signs*. Light refreshments. **Adm £3, chd free. Sat 18, Sun 19 July (10-5).** Secret Garden in city suburb. Unusual combination of flower beds, raised vegetable beds and nature reserve, all created by volunteers. Features incl a large natural pond surrounded by wild plants, Welsh heritage apple trees, long herb border and wild flower meadow. Planted to encourage birds, butterflies and bees. Home-made refreshments available all day. Also Fairtrade food and wine tastings. Featured in South Wales Echo, Croeso, Community magazine and The Grapvine. Community Centre came 2nd in Cardiff in Bloom for the Community Hall Garden category. Full wheelchair access and disabled WC.

This constantly evolving garden provides a haven of peace and tranquility . . .

36 SLADE

Southerndown CF32 0RP. Rosamund & Peter Davies, 01656 880048, ros@sladewoodgarden.plus.com, www.sladeholidaycottages.co.uk. *5m S of Bridgend. M4 J35 Follow A473 to Bridgend. Take B4265 to St. Brides Major. Turn R in St. Brides Major for Southerndown, then follow yellow NGS signs*. Home-made teas. **Adm £4, chd free. Sat 25, Sun 26 Apr (2-5).** Set in 8 acres, Slade garden is an unexpected gem with established drifts of spring bulbs and a woodland

plant collection. The terraced lawns, mature specimen trees, living willow arbours, rose and clematis pergola, orchard and herbaceous borders, create a very natural garden. Husband's new passion auriculas and alpines!! Extensive views over the Bristol Channel. Heritage Coast wardens will give guided tours of adjacent Dunraven Gardens with slide shows every hour from 2pm. Partial wheelchair access.

37 19 SLADE GARDENS

West Cross, Swansea SA3 5QP. Norma & Peter Stephen. *5m SW of Swansea. At mini r'about on Mumbles Rd A4067 take 2nd exit (Fairwood Rd), 1st L onto West Cross Lane & follow yellow NGS signs*. Light refreshments. **Adm £3, chd free. Sun 9 Aug (2-5).** A small enclosed front and rear garden designed to lead you around its informal planting of over 200 species. Somewhere to sit and relax. Narrow paths and steps make access difficult for less mobile visitors.

38 TONY RIDLERS GARDEN

7 St Peter's Terrace, Cockett, Swansea SA2 0FW. Tony & Caroline Ridler, www.tonyridlersgarden.co.uk. *3m W of Swansea. From M4 J47 take A483 towards Swansea. At Fforestfach Cross T-lights turn R on Station Rd, A4216 at next T-lights turn L onto St Peter's Terrace*. Home-made teas. **Adm £4. Sun 31 May, Sun 14 June (2-5).** 'One of Britain's most compelling modern formal gardens, a delightful essay in the subtle use of balance, form and structure, and all in a third of an acre. Don't expect masses of flowers but be ready to learn many a lesson in how to design a garden' - Stephen Anderton. Regret, garden not suitable for children. Featured in House & Garden magazine.

GROUP OPENING

39 TRERHYNGYLL GARDENS

Trerhyngyll, Cowbridge CF71 7TN. *2m N of Cowbridge on A4222. 15m W of Cardiff via A48 turn L to Cowbridge. Take R turn at next T-lights & cont 2m along A4222 to Trerhyngyll, signed on L*. Home-made

teas. **Combined adm £5, chd free. Mon 4 May (2-6).**

 BIRCHBROOK
Mrs Janice Whiteley

GWDI-HW COTTAGE
Pat & Gerry Long

NEW **WHISPERING WINDS**
Mrs Philippa Walsh

Trerhyngyll is a peaceful countryside hamlet of some 60 dwellings, nestling in the gently folding hills of the Vale of Glamorgan. The 3 gardens are typical of the hamlet.

40 TY'N Y BERLLAN

Graig Llwyn Road, Lisvane, Cardiff CF14 0RP. Jeffrey Morgan. *1m NE Lisvane village. From Lisvane Village take Rudry Rd. After M/W bridge turn R into Graig Llwyn Rd & follow yellow NGS signs*. Home-made teas. **Adm £4, chd free. Sun 10 May (1-6).** A 2 acre garden set around an ancient farmhouse. Beds of azaleas, rhododendrons, camellia and mixed shrubs, set in undulating lawns designed to blend with the fields and woodlands around. The lawns are planted with trees such as oak, beech, hornbeam, ginkgo and tulip which provide interest and yr-round colour, together with stream, pond and new Mediterranean garden. Spring bulbs, primula and stream give natural informality to sit and dream as well as a courtyard garden and pool, Wollemi pine.

41 NEW 9 WILLOWBROOK GARDENS

Mayals, Swansea SA3 5EB. Gislinde Macphereson, 01792 403268, gislinde@willowgardens.idps.co.uk. *Nr Clyne Gardens. Go along Mumbles Rd to Blackpill. Turn R at Texaco garage up Mayals Rd. 1st R along top of Clyne Park, at mini r'about into Westport Ave. 1st L into Willowbrook gardens*. Home-made teas. **Adm £4, chd free. Sun 10 May (1.30-5).** Visitors also welcome by arrangement Apr to June. Informal $1/2$ acre mature garden on acid soil, designed to give natural effect with balance of form and colour between various areas linked by lawns; unusual trees suited to small suburban garden, especially conifers and maples; rock and water garden.

77 Cefn Road, Cefn Cribwr Garden Club

Lemon drizzle cake, Victoria sponge … yummy! ☕

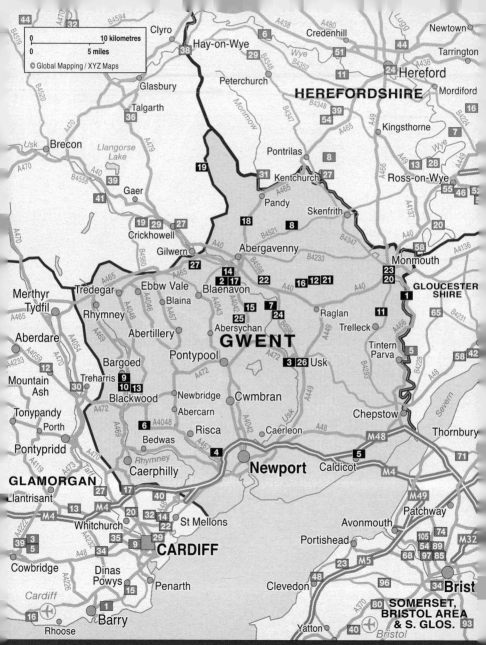

Gwent

Gwent is a county of contrasts with the lush agricultural valley of the River Usk, a handful of stunning border castles, the wild Black Mountains and some of the old industrial heartlands of the South Wales Valleys.

The small town of Usk sits on either side of the river overlooked by the ruins of Usk Castle. The gardens of the castle gatehouse are partly in these romantic ruins opening with the Usk Open Gardens weekend and by arrangement. Occasionally a cannon is discharged from the ramparts by the owners.

The Black Mountains are wild, sheep farming country with mountain ponies grazing on the tops and small stone farmhouses nestling in the shelter of the valleys.

The landscape of the South Wales Valleys has abundant evidence of the industrial past, and Big Pit National Coal Museum and ironworks in Blaenavon are working examples of this.

History, beauty, wilderness and water are all alive in Gwent.

Gwent Volunteers

County Organiser
Joanna Kerr
01873 840422
Joanna@amknet.com

County Treasurer
Position Vacant

Publicity
Joanna Kerr
(as above)

Booklet Coordinator
Joanna Kerr
(as above)

Assistant County Organiser
Sue Torkington
01873 890045
sue@torkington.myzen.co.uk

Below: Croesllanfro Farm

Currently the NGS donates around £2.5 million every year

Opening Dates

All entries subject to change.
For latest information check www.ngs.org.uk

March

Sunday 29
- **15** Llanover

April

Thursday 9
- **6** Forest House

Sunday 12
- **5** Dewstow Gardens & Grottoes

May

Sunday 3
- **12** High House
- **21** The Old Vicarage

Sunday 10
- **11** High Glanau Manor
- **19** Nant y Bedd

Saturday 16
- **22** Penpergwm Lodge

Sunday 17
- **22** Penpergwm Lodge

Saturday 23
- **13** Hillcrest

Sunday 24
- **13** Hillcrest
- **23** **NEW** Rockfield Park

Monday 25
- **13** Hillcrest

Saturday 30
- **24** Trostrey Lodge

Sunday 31
- **2** Castell Cwrt
- **17** Middle Ninfa Farm & Bunkhouse
- **20** The Nelson Garden
- **24** Trostrey Lodge

June

Thursday 4
- **6** Forest House

Festival Weekend

Saturday 6
- **16** Longhouse Farm

Sunday 7
- **16** Longhouse Farm

Sunday 14
- **14** Llanfoist Village Gardens

Friday 19
- **18** Mione

Saturday 20
- **25** Ty Boda

Sunday 21
- **25** Ty Boda
- **27** Wenallt Isaf

Friday 26
- **18** Mione

Saturday 27
- **26** Usk Open Gardens

Sunday 28
- **8** Glen Trothy
- **26** Usk Open Gardens

July

Friday 3
- **18** Mione

Saturday 4
- **7** Glebe House
- **9** 10 Gwerthonor Lane
- **10** 14 Gwerthonor Lane

Sunday 5
- **7** Glebe House
- **9** 10 Gwerthonor Lane
- **10** 14 Gwerthonor Lane

Friday 10
- **18** Mione

Sunday 12
- **1** Birch Tree Well

Sunday 19
- **19** Nant y Bedd

August

Saturday 1
- **13** Hillcrest

Sunday 2
- **13** Hillcrest

Sunday 16
- **4** Croesllanfro Farm

September

Sunday 13
- **5** Dewstow Gardens & Grottoes
- **19** Nant y Bedd

October

Sunday 4
- **2** Castell Cwrt

Gardens open to the public

- **5** Dewstow Gardens & Grottoes

By arrangement only

- **3** Castle House

Also open by arrangement

- **1** Birch Tree Well
- **4** Croesllanfro Farm
- **6** Forest House
- **7** Glebe House
- **13** Hillcrest
- **15** Llanover
- **19** Nant y Bedd
- **22** Penpergwm Lodge

The Gardens

1 BIRCH TREE WELL
Upper Ferry Road, Penallt, Monmouth NP25 4AN. Jill Bourchier,
gillian.bourchier@btinternet.com. *4m SW of Monmouth. Approx 1m from Monmouth on B4293, turn L for Penallt & Trelleck. After 2m turn L to Penallt. On entering village turn L at Xrds.* Cream teas. **Adm £3.50, chd free. Sun 12 July (2-6). Visitors also welcome by arrangement Apr to Sept. Groups welcome but restricted parking.**
Situated in the heart of the Lower Wye Valley this garden is gradually evolving amongst the ancient habitat of woodland, rocks and streams. 3 acres shared with deer, badger and fox so careful planting is constantly under review. A woodland setting with streams and boulders which can be viewed from a look out tower.

Mixed planting incl some wonderful hydrangeas. A look out tower, boulders and streams so children are very welcome - under supervision!
❀ ☕

2 CASTELL CWRT
Llanelen, Abergavenny NP7 9LE. Lorna & John McGlynn. *1m S of Abergavenny. From Abergavenny/Llanfoist take B4269 signed Llanelen. Pass Grove Farm turn R up single track rd. Approx 500yds past canal, garden entrance 2nd on L. Disabled parking. On combined opening day (May) main parking at Castell Cwrt. Limited mobility parking at Middle Ninfa.* Home-made teas. **Adm £3 (Oct), chd free. Sun 31 May (1-6); Sun 4 Oct (2-5). Combined with Middle Ninfa Farm (May), combined adm £4, chd free.**
Large informal wildlife friendly, family garden on 10 acre small holding with fine views overlooking Abergavenny.

Lawns with established trees, shrubs and perennial borders. Organic soft fruit and vegetable gardens. Woodland and haymeadow walks, chickens and geese, livestock in fields and family pets. Children very welcome, animals to see and space to let off steam. Woodland walk to Middle Ninfa. Hay meadow in full bloom. Some gravel paths.
♿ ❀ ☕

Visit a garden on National Gardens Festival Weekend 6 & 7 June

Rockfield Park

3 ▶ CASTLE HOUSE

Castle Parade, Usk NP15 1SD. Mr & Mrs J H L Humphreys, 01291 672563, www.uskcastle.com. *200yds NE from Usk centre. Footpath access signed to Usk Castle 300yds E from town square. Vehicles 400yds (next L) on Castle Parade in Usk.* **Adm £4, chd free. Visitors welcome by arrangement all year. Refreshments for groups on request.**
Overlooked by the romantic ruins of Usk Castle, the gardens date from early C20, with yew hedges and topiary, long herbaceous border, croquet lawn and pond. The herb garden has plants that would have been used when the castle was last lived in c.1469. Most areas easily accessible to wheelchair users.

4 ▶ CROESLLANFRO FARM

Groes Road, Rogerstone, Newport NP10 9GP. Barry & Liz Davies, 01633 894057, lizplants@gmail.com. *3m W of Newport. From M4 J27 take B4591 towards Risca. Take 3rd R, Cefn Walk (also signed 14 Locks Canal Centre). Proceed over bridge, cont ½ m.* Home-made teas. **Adm £4.50, chd free. Sun 16 Aug (1.30-5). Visitors also welcome by arrangement May to Sept for any size group.**

Surrounding a Welsh long house (not open) this 2 acre garden is full of surprises around every corner. Informal, mass planted, perennial borders concentrating on late summer colour incl many unusual plants. The site is dominated by the tithe barn (open) standing in a large, formal courtyard, designed on 6 different levels. A garden for all moods. Let the children try the quiz! Owner co-author of Designing Gardens on Slopes. Some gravel paths and shallow steps to main area of garden.

5 ▶ ◆ DEWSTOW GARDENS & GROTTOES

Caerwent, Monmouthshire NP26 5AH. John Harris, 01291 431020, www.dewstowgardens.co.uk. *Dewstow House, 6m W of Chepstow - 8m E of Newport. A48 Newport to Chepstow rd, drive into village of Caerwent. Follow brown tourist daisy signs to Gardens. (1½ m from Caerwent Village).* Light refreshments. **Adm £6, chd free. For NGS: Sun 12 Apr, Sun 13 Sept (10-4). For other opening times and information, please phone or see garden website.**
5 acre Grade I listed unique garden which was buried and forgotten after World War II and rediscovered in 2000. Created around 1895 by James Pulham & Sons, the garden cont underground grottoes, tunnels and ferneries and above ground stunning water features. You will not be disappointed. Various events throughout the season. No wheelchair access to underground areas. Partial access elsewhere.

6 ▶ FOREST HOUSE

Commercial Street, Ynysddu NP11 7JN. Mrs Joy Beacham, 01495 200333, clivebeacham315@btinternet.com. *9m N of J28, M4. At J28 follow A467 for Brynmawr, then B4251 via Wattsville. At Xrds in Ynysddu turn R then R again. 2m S of Blackwood on B4251, L at Xrds then R.* Home-made teas. **Adm £3.50, chd free. Thur 9 Apr, Thur 4 June (1-5). Visitors also welcome by arrangement Apr to July for max 10 visitors.**
Informal, pretty country garden, with borders overflowing with colour. Gravel garden and mixed borders to the front. Sloping back garden with terraces leading to small waterfall, shady areas and wildlife pond. Small lawn and borders with seating to rest awhile. Productive vegetable plot, fruit cage and cold frames.

Birch Tree Well

7 GLEBE HOUSE

Llanvair Kilgeddin NP7 9BE. Mr & Mrs Murray Kerr, 01873 840422, joanna@amknet.com. *Midway between Abergavenny (5m) & Usk (5m) on B4598.* Home-made teas. Adm £4, chd free. Sat 4, Sun 5 July (2-6). Visitors also welcome by arrangement Apr to Sept.

Borders bursting with colour with some formal hedging and topiary in 1½ acre garden in picturesque Usk Valley. S facing terrace with climbers, ornamental vegetable garden and orchard. Old Rectory of St Mary's Llanvair Kilgeddin with famous Victorian Scraffito Murals which will also be open. Some gravel and gently sloping lawns.

 ❀ ☕

8 GLEN TROTHY

Llanvetherine, Abergavenny NP7 8RB. Mr & Mrs Ben Herbert. *5m NE of Abergavenny. 6m from Abergavenny off B4521 (Old Ross Rd).* Home-made teas. Adm £4, chd free. Sun 28 June (2-6).

Victorian house (not open) in the Scottish Baronial style, set in mature parkland with a small pinetum and arboretum. The walled garden has been renovated over the past 6yrs, incorporating blue and white herbaceous borders, a rose garden and ornamental vegetable garden with pear tunnel as well as an Italianate loggia.

❀ ☕

9 10 GWERTHONOR LANE

Gilfach, Bargoed CF81 8JT. Mr Paul Spearman. *8m N of Caerphilly. A469 to Bargoed. Through T-lights next to school, then L filter lane at next T-lights to turn onto Cardiff Rd. Follow yellow NGS signs.* Light refreshments. Combined adm £4, chd free. Sat 4, Sun 5 July (11-6). Combined with 14 Gwerthonor Lane.

A Japanese garden with over 80 mature bonsai trees, alpines and stone garden features.

♿ ❀ ☕

10 14 GWERTHONOR LANE

Gilfach, Bargoed CF81 8JT. Suzanne & Philip George. *8m N of Caerphilly. A469 to Bargoed. Through T-lights next to School, then L filter lane at next T-lights to turn onto Cardiff Rd. Follow yellow NGS signs.* Light refreshments. Combined adm £4, chd free. Sat 4, Sun 5 July (11-6). Combined with 10 Gwerthonor Lane.

The garden has a beautiful panoramic view of the Rhymney Valley and is in a semi rural setting. It is a real plantswoman's garden with over 400 varieties of trees, shrubs, perenials, bulbs and annuals. There are numerous rare and unusual plants (many available for sale) combined with more traditional and well loved favourites. A pond with a small waterfall adds to the tranquil feel of the garden.

❀ ☕

11 HIGH GLANAU MANOR

Lydart, Monmouth NP25 4AD. Mr & Mrs Hilary Gerrish. *4m SW of Monmouth. Situated on B4293 between Monmouth & Chepstow. Turn R into Private Rd, ¼ m after Craig-y-Dorth turn on B4293.* Home-made teas. Adm £5, chd free. Sun 10 May (2-6).

Listed Arts and Crafts garden laid out by H Avray Tipping in 1922. Original features incl impressive stone terraces with far reaching views over the Vale of Usk to Blorenge, Skirrid, Sugar Loaf and Brecon Beacons. Pergola, herbaceous borders, Edwardian glasshouse, rhododendrons, azaleas, tulips, orchard with wild flowers and woodland walks. Owners book, Edwardian Country Life - the story of H Avray Tipping by Helena Gerrish available to purchase. Featured in Country Life and on Gardeners World.

❀ ☕

12 HIGH HOUSE

Penrhos NP15 2DJ. Mr & Mrs R Cleeve. *4m N of Raglan. From r'about on A40 at Raglan take exit to Clytha. After 50yds turn R at Llantilo Crosseny. Follow garden open signs - 10mins through lanes.* Home-made teas. Combined adm £6.50, chd free. Sun 3 May (2-6). Combined with The Old Vicarage.

3 acres of spacious lawns and trees surrounding C16 house (not open) in a beautiful, hidden part of Monmouthshire. Large extended

pond, orchard with chickens and ducks. S facing terrace and extensive bed of old roses. Swathes of grass with tulips, camassias, wild flowers and far reaching views. Espaliered cherries, pears and scented evergreens in courtyard. Gently sloping lawns.

♿ ❀ ☕

13 HILLCREST

Waunborfa Road, Cefn Fforest, Blackwood NP12 3LB. Mr M O'Leary & Mr B Price, 01443 837029, bev.price@mclweb.net. *3m W of Blackwood town centre or A469 to Pengam (Glan-y-Nant) T-lights, then NGS signs.* Cream teas. **Adm £4, chd free. Sat 23, Sun 24, Mon 25 May, Sat 1, Sun 2 Aug (11-6). Visitors also welcome by arrangement Apr to Sept for groups 30 max. Refreshments on request.**
A cascade of secluded gardens of distinct character, all within 1½ acres. Magnificent, unusual trees with interesting shrubs and perennials. With choices at every turn, visitors exploring the gardens are well rewarded as hidden delights and surprises are revealed. Well placed seats encourage a relaxed pace to fully appreciate the garden's treasures. Delicious cream teas to be enjoyed. Parts of lower garden not accessible to wheelchairs.

♿ 🐇 ☕

14 LLANFOIST VILLAGE GARDENS

Llanfoist, Abergavenny NP7 9NF. *1m SW of Abergavenny on B4246. Map provided with ticket. Most gardens within easy walking distance of village centre. Free minibus to others.* Scrumptious home-made teas in village hall. **Combined adm £5, chd free. Sun 14 June (10.30-5.30).**
Make this a great day out. Visit around 15 exciting and contrasting village gardens, both large and small, set just below the Blorenge Mountain on the edge of the Black Mountains. A number of new gardens opening along with many regulars. This is our 13th annual event. Fantastic lunches and homemade cakes not to be missed. Canal boat trips. Featured in local press. Wheelchair access not available at all gardens.

♿ ❀ ☕

15 LLANOVER

nr Abergavenny NP7 9EF. Mr & Mrs M R Murray, 07753 423635, www.llanovergarden.co.uk. *4m S of Abergavenny, 15m N of Newport, 20m SW Hereford. On A4042 Abergavenny - Pontypool rd, in village of Llanover.* Delicious home-made teas. **Adm £5, chd free. Sun 29 Mar (2-5). Visitors also welcome by arrangement Mar to Oct. Min group 15 for conducted tours.**
15 acre listed garden and arboretum with lovely water features and a circular walled garden. The Rhyd-y-meirch stream tumbles into ponds, down cascades and beneath flagstone bridges suitable for playing poo sticks. Lawns for children to run on or play hide and seek. Given a fine March, many of the spring bulbs and 30+ Magnolias will be in flower. Home of the Llanover Garden School. The House (not open) is the birthplace of Augusta Waddington, Lady Llanover, C19 patriot and supporter of the Welsh Language Descendants. The flock of Welsh Black Mountain Sheep which she introduced, can be seen grazing in the park. Gravel and grass paths and lawns.

♿ 🐇 ❀ ☕

16 LONGHOUSE FARM

Penrhos, Raglan NP15 2DE. Mr & Mrs M H C Anderson. *Midway between Monmouth & Abergavenny. 4m from Raglan. Off Old Raglan/Abergavenny rd signed Clytha. At Bryngwyn/Great Oak Xrds turn towards Great Oak - follow yellow NGS signs from red river box down narrow lane.* Tea. **Adm £4, chd free. Sat 6, Sun 7 June (2-6).**
21yrs (ongoing) of developing this hidden 2 acre garden with a south facing terrace, millrace wall, pond, spacious lawns. Colourful and unusual plants varying from blossom, irises, summer bulbs, roses, vegetables to asters, grasses and a malus avenue of autumn colour. Unspoilt vistas of Monmouthshire. Possible to push wheelchairs around garden and into barn for tea.

❀ ☕

17 MIDDLE NINFA FARM & BUNKHOUSE

Llanelen, Abergavenny NP7 9LE. Richard Lewis, www.middleninfa.co.uk. *2½ m SSW Abergavenny. At A465/ B4246 Junction, S for Llanfoist, L at mini r'about, B4269 towards Llanelen, ½ m R turn up steep lane, over canal. ¾ m to Middle Ninfa on R. Main parking at Castell Cwrt.* Home-made teas. **Combined adm £4, chd free. Sun 31 May (1-6). Combined with Castel Cwrt.**
Large terraced eco-garden on east slopes of the Blorenge mountain. Vegetable beds, polytunnel, 3 greenhouses, orchard, flower borders, wild flowers. Great views, woodland walks, cascading water and ponds. Paths steep in places, unsuitable for less able. Campsite and small bunkhouse on farm. 5 mins walk uphill to scenic Punchbowl Lake and walks on the Blorenge.

🐇 ❀ 🛌 ☕

> Well placed seats encourage a relaxed pace to fully appreciate the garden's treasures . . .

18 MIONE

Old Hereford Road, Llanvihangel Crucorney, Abergaveny NP7 7LB. Yvonne & John O'Neil. *5m N of Abergavenny. From Abergaveny take A465 to Hereford. After 4.8m turn L - signed Pantigelli. Mione is ½ m on L.* Home-made teas. **Adm £3, chd free. Fris 19, 26 June, 3, 10 July (11-7).**
Beautiful garden with a wide variety of established plants, many rare and unusual. Pergola with climbing roses and clematis. Wildlife pond with many newts, insects and frogs. Numerous containers with diverse range of planting. Several seating areas, each with a different atmosphere. Summerhouse.

❀ ☕

19 NANT Y BEDD

Grwyne Fawr, Fforest Coal Pit, Abergavenny NP7 7LY. Sue & Ian Mabberley, 01873 890219, ian.mabberley@btconnect.com, www.nantybedd.com. *In Grwyne Fawr valley. From A465 Llanv Crucorney, direction Llanthony, then L to Fforest Coal Pit. At grey telephone box cont for 4¹/₂ m towards Grwyne Fawr Reservoir.* **Adm £4, chd free. Sun 10 May, Sun 19 July, Sun 13 Sept (11-5). Visitors also welcome by arrangement May to Sept, Fri - Sun. Conducted tours for groups 10+.**

Inspiring 6¹/₂ acre garden, forest and river that blends into surrounding landscape. Organic fruit and vegetables, mature trees, wildlife friendly planting, stone and timber features, livestock and much more. River and forest walk. Tulips and Bluebells in May, but come and come again for the full experience. Enjoy it slowly. Something for everyone. Plants, some garden accessories, made on the premises, available for sale. Shepherd's Hut and natural swimming pond. See garden website for details. Featured in SAGA magazine.

20 THE NELSON GARDEN

Monnow Street, Monmouth NP25 3EE. Penny Thomas (Convenor of U3A Practical Gardening Group). *Garden accessed via Blestium St, follow yellow NGS signs. Also tourist signs indicating the Nelson Garden.* Home-made teas. **Adm £4, chd free. Sun 31 May (2-5).**

This ancient town garden was the site of a real tennis court in C17 and a bowling green by 1718. Roman and Norman remains lie deep beneath the lawn. Admiral Lord Nelson and his entourage took tea here on 19th August 1802. Planting throughout the garden is designed around species that would have been popular in informal gardens of the late C18, early C19.

21 THE OLD VICARAGE

Penrhos, Raglan, Nr Usk NP15 2LE. Professor & Mrs Luke Herrmann. *3m N of Raglan. From A449 take Raglan exit, join A40 & move immed into R lane & turn R across dual carriageway. Follow yellow NGS signs.* Home-made teas at High House. **Combined adm £6.50, chd free. Sun 3 May (2-6). Combined with High House.**

The Old Vicarage has a series of skilfully crafted gardens surrounding a beautiful Victorian Gothic house which invite you to explore as the eye is drawn from one garden into the next. With sweeping lawns, a summer house and formal garden, two charming ponds and immaculate kitchen garden all enhanced by imaginatively placed pots, this gem is not one to be rushed. It gets better each yr. Plant stall.

22 PENPERGWM LODGE

Nr Abergavenny NP7 9AS. Mr & Mrs Simon Boyle, 01873 840208, boyle@penpergwm.co.uk, www.penplants.com. *3m SE of Abergavenny, 5m W of Raglan. On B4598. Turn opp King of Prussia Inn. Entrance 150yds on L.* Home-made teas. **Adm £4.50, chd free. Sat 16, Sun 17 May (2-6). Visitors also welcome by arrangement Apr to Sept.**

3 acre garden with Jubilee tower overlooking terraced ornamental garden containing canal, cascading water and new loggia at head of canal. South facing terraces planted with rich profusion and vibrant colours all surrounded by spacious lawns and mature trees. Brick waisted tower built 2011. Some gravel paths.

23 NEW ROCKFIELD PARK

Rockfield, Monmouth NP25 3BQ. Mark & Melanie Molyneux. *On arriving in Rockfield village from Monmouth, turn R by phone box. After approx. 400yds, church on L. Entrance to Rockfield Park on R, opp church, via private bridge over river.* Home-made teas. **Adm £4.50, chd free. Sun 24 May (12-6).**

Rockfield Park dates from C17 and is situated in the heart of the Monmouthshire countryside on the banks of the R Monnow. The extensive grounds comprise formal gardens, meadows and orchard, complemented by riverside and woodland walks. Main part of gardens can be accessed by wheelchair but not steep garden leading down to river.

24 TROSTREY LODGE

Bettws Newydd, Usk NP15 1JT. Roger & Frances Pemberton. *4m W of Raglan. 7m E of Abergavenny. Off old A40 (unnumbered) Abergavenny - Raglan. 1m S of Clytha Gates & 1¹/₂ m N of Bettws Newydd.* Home-made teas. **Adm £4, chd free. Sat 30, Sun 31 May (2-6).**

Come over the ha-ha to be greeted by a tall Tulip tree. Inside the walled garden you will find colourful, fragrant flowers and herbs, with ribbons of honeysuckle and climbing roses - for bees, butterflies and birds. Also an orchard. Good range of home grown plants and packets of Trostrey poppy seeds to buy to help bees in need.

25 TY BODA

Upper Llanover, Nr Abergavenny NP7 9EP. Mike Shooter. *Off A4042. Follow directions to Upper Llanover (coming from Abergavenny) or Pencroesoped (coming from Cwmbran), narrow lanes. Watch out for signs to Goose & Cuckoo PH. If you get there, you've past us!* Home-made teas. **Adm £5, chd free. Sat 20, Sun 21 June (10-6).**

A 4 acre hillside garden with stunning views out over the Vale of Usk. Wildlife pond, stream and winding paths through a meadow newly planted with fifteen hundred native trees. Medieval style medicinal herb garden, potager, fernery, orchard, rope swing, stone circle and roses, roses everywhere. Steep slopes and slippery steps, so come prepared! Scrumptious home-made cakes and tea.

26 USK OPEN GARDENS

Monmouth Road, Usk NP15 1SD, www.uskopengardens.com. *From M4 J24 take A449, proceed 8m N to Usk exit. Good free parking in town. Blue badge car parking in main car parks & at Usk Castle. Map of gardens provided with ticket.* Light refreshments. **Combined adm £7.50, chd free. Sat 27, Sun 28 June (10-5).**

Proud winner of Wales in Bloom for over 30yrs, with colourful hanging baskets and boxes - a sight not to be missed! The town is a wonderful backdrop to the 20+ gardens from small cottages packed with colourful and unusual plants to large gardens with brimming herbaceous borders. Wonderful romantic garden around the ramparts of Usk Castle. Gardeners' Market with wide selection of interesting plants. Wonderful day out for all the family with lots of places to eat and drink incl picnic places down by the R Usk. Various cafes, PH and restaurants available for refreshments, and many volunteer groups offering teas and cakes. Unmissable. Not all gardens are wheelchair accessible.

♿ ❀ 🚐 🛏 ☕

27 WENALLT ISAF

Twyn Wenallt, Gilwern, Abergavenny NP7 0HP. Tim & Debbie Field. *3m W of Abergavenny. From Gilwern r'about follow A465 towards Merthyr Tydfil take 1st L & follow signs.* Home-made teas. **Adm £4, chd free. Sun 21 June (2-6).** 2½ acre garden 650ft up on a N facing hillside with magnificent views of the Black Mountains. Mature trees, flowering shrubs, borders, productive vegetable garden, small polytunnel, orchard, pigs, chickens, and plenty of space to run about.

☕

Glen Trothy

Treat yourself to a plant from the plant stall ❀

GWYNEDD & ANGLESEY

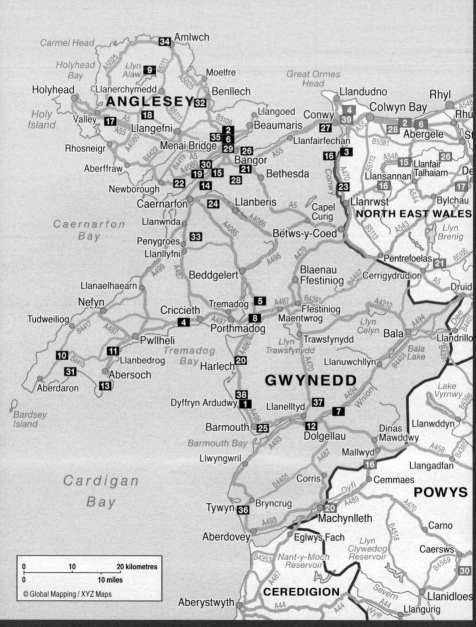

Gwynedd & Anglesey

Gwynedd is a county rich in history and outstanding natural beauty. Bordered by the Irish Sea and home to Snowdonia National Park, Gwynedd can boast some of the most impressive landscapes in the UK.

The mountains in Gwynedd are world-famous, and have attracted visitors for hundreds of years – the most famous perhaps, was Charles Darwin in 1831. As well as enjoying the tallest peaks in the UK, Gwynedd has fine woodland – from hanging oak forests in the mountains to lush, riverside woods.

Holiday-makers flock to Gwynedd to take advantage of the sandy beaches, and many can enjoy sightings of dolphins and porpoises off the coast.

The gardens of Gwynedd are just as appealing an attraction for visitors. A variety of gardens open for Gwynedd NGS, ranging from superbly beautiful Maenan Hall with dramatic views of Snowdonia and set among mature hardwoods, to the sloping 2 acre garden of Bryn Gwern which sits in the hills overlooking the market town of Dolgellau.

So why not escape from the hustle and bustle of everyday life and relax in a beautiful Gwynedd garden? You will be assured of a warm welcome at every garden gate.

Gwynedd & Anglesey Volunteers

North Gwynedd & Anglesey

County Organiser
Grace Meirion-Jones
01286 831195

County Treasurer
Nigel Bond
01407 831354
nigel@cae-newydd.co.uk

Assistant County Organisers
Hazel Bond
01407 831354
nigel@cae-newydd.co.uk

Janet Jones
01758 740296
janetcoron@hotmail.co.uk

South Gwynedd

County Organiser
Hilary Nurse
01341 450255
antique_pete@btinternet.com

County Treasurer
Michael Bishton
01654 710882
m.bishton@btopenworld.com

Below: Maenan Hall

Currently the NGS donates around £2.5 million every year

Opening Dates

All entries subject to change.
For latest information
check www.ngs.org.uk

February

Sunday 8
31 Plas Yn Rhiw

Saturday 14
26 Penrhyn Castle

April

Friday 3
20 Llyn Rhaeadr

Saturday 4
20 Llyn Rhaeadr

Sunday 5
4 Bont Fechan Farm
20 Llyn Rhaeadr

Monday 6
4 Bont Fechan Farm
20 Llyn Rhaeadr

Sunday 12
8 Bwlch y Fedwen

Saturday 25
19 Llanidan Hall

Wednesday 29
29 Plas Cadnant Hidden Gardens

May

Saturday 2
20 Llyn Rhaeadr

Sunday 3
16 Gilfach
20 Llyn Rhaeadr
25 Pen y Bryn
34 Sunningdale

Monday 4
20 Llyn Rhaeadr

Sunday 10
12 Craig y Ffynnon
15 Foxbrush
23 Maenan Hall

Wednesday 13
34 Sunningdale

Saturday 16
11 Coron

Sunday 17
7 Bryn Gwern
11 Coron
21 Llys-y-Gwynt

Wednesday 20
5 Brondanw Gardens

Saturday 23
20 Llyn Rhaeadr

Sunday 24
4 Bont Fechan Farm
20 Llyn Rhaeadr

Monday 25
4 Bont Fechan Farm
20 Llyn Rhaeadr

Tuesday 26
20 Llyn Rhaeadr

Wednesday 27
5 Brondanw Gardens

Friday 29
30 Plas Newydd Country House & Gardens

Sunday 31
8 Bwlch y Fedwen

June

9 **Cae Newydd** (every Thursday)

Festival Weekend

Saturday 6
14 Crûg Farm

Sunday 7
1 An Artist's Garden
9 Cae Newydd
27 Pensychnant

Wednesday 10
34 Sunningdale

Saturday 13
22 Maen Hir

Sunday 14
4 Bont Fechan Farm (Evening)
16 Gilfach
22 Maen Hir
35 Treffos School
36 Ty Cadfan Sant

Saturday 20
13 Crowrach Isaf
19 Llanidan Hall

Sunday 21
13 Crowrach Isaf
32 NEW Rhosbach Cottage

Saturday 27
28 Pentir Gardens

Sunday 28
18 Gwyndy Bach
34 Sunningdale

July

9 **Cae Newydd** (every Thursday)

Saturday 4
17 Gwaelod Mawr
19 Llanidan Hall

Sunday 5
17 Gwaelod Mawr
21 Llys-y-Gwynt
27 Pensychnant

Saturday 11
3 Bodnant Garden

Saturday 18
24 Pant Ifan

Sunday 19
2 Arcady
6 NEW 1 Bryn Eglwys

Saturday 25
33 St John the Baptist & St George

Sunday 26
7 Bryn Gwern

August

Sunday 9
39 41 Victoria Drive

Sunday 16
23 Maenan Hall

Saturday 29
20 Llyn Rhaeadr

Sunday 30
20 Llyn Rhaeadr

Monday 31
20 Llyn Rhaeadr

Plas Cadnant Hidden Gardens

© Joe Wainwright

Visit a garden on National Gardens Festival Weekend 6 & 7 June

September

Sunday 6
1 An Artist's Garden

February 2016

Sunday 7
31 Plas Yn Rhiw

Saturday 13
26 Penrhyn Castle

Gardens open to the public

3 Bodnant Garden
5 Brondanw Gardens
14 Crûg Farm
26 Penrhyn Castle
27 Pensychnant
30 Plas Newydd Country House & Gardens
31 Plas Yn Rhiw

By arrangement only

10 Coed Ty Mawr
37 Ty Capel Ffrwd
38 Ty Newydd

Also open by arrangement

1 An Artist's Garden
4 Bont Fechan Farm

7 Bryn Gwern
13 Crowrach Isaf
15 Foxbrush
16 Gilfach
17 Gwaelod Mawr
18 Gwyndy Bach
19 Llanidan Hall
20 Llyn Rhaeadr
21 Llys-y-Gwynt
23 Maenan Hall
34 Sunningdale
36 Ty Cadfan Sant

The Gardens

1 AN ARTIST'S GARDEN

Ty Llwyd, Dyffryn Ardudwy LL44 2EP. Karen Hall, 01341 242623, karen.artistsgarden@gmail.com, www.artistsgarden.co.uk. *5m N of Barmouth on A496. From Barmouth garden on L, after 20mph sign. From Harlech drive through Dyffryn Ardudwy, garden on R after 20mph sign.* Home-made teas. **Adm £3, chd free. Sun 7 June (11-5.30); Sun 6 Sept (11-5). Visitors also welcome by arrangement May to Sept (48hrs notice required).**
A 140ft village garden. In June roses and peonies feature amongst interesting and unusual perennial plants. In September ornamental grasses and colourful late season perennials take centre stage. Paths meander through abundant planting, with seating areas, 2 ponds, cutting garden polytunnel and greenhouses. Textile studio at the bottom of the garden will be open for visitors to browse. The propagating area will be accesible to view and the plant sales area will be open.

2 ARCADY

Llansadwrn, Menai Bridge LL59 5SE. James Weisters & Liz Mangham. *3m N of Menai Bridge. A5025 Amlwch/Benllech exit from Britannia Bridge. Approx 3m turn R to Llansadwrn (1m after Pentraeth Motors). 1m Arcady on L. Parking in adjoining level field.* Cream teas. **Combined adm £6, chd free. Sun 19 July (11-4.30). Combined with 1 Bryn Eglys.**
Surrounded by farmland and with views of Snowdon range. Approx 1 acre of quirky, structured garden - originally laid out by the artist Ed Povey - pagoda and meditation garden, laburnum walk, small orchard, lawn, ponds and hidden places. Gravel paths with steps. Featured in Amateur gardening.

3 ◆ BODNANT GARDEN

Tal-y-Cafn, nr Colwyn Bay LL28 5RE. National Trust, 01492 650460, www.nationaltrust.org.uk. *8m S of Llandudno. From A55 exit at J19. Follow brown signs to garden. Just off A470 on B rd to Eglwysbach.* Light refreshments. **Adm £11.55, chd £5.78. For NGS: Sat 11 July (10-5). For other opening times and information, please phone or see garden website.**
Among the finest gardens in the country with rhododendrons, magnolias, camellias and the famous laburnum arch. Summer colours incl roses, water lilies, herbaceous borders and hydrangeas. Superb autumn colours in October and the Winter Garden is a delight from November to February. Formal Italianate style terraces contrast with steeply sided shrub borders and the dell. Dogs welcome on short leads Thurs - Sat from Nov - Feb and from 5pm on Weds evenings May - Aug. Garden is steep in places with many steps. Please ensure motorised wheelchairs have fully charged battery.
NCH

4 BONT FECHAN FARM

Llanystumdwy LL52 0LS. Mr & Mrs J D Bean, 01766 522604, Bontfechanfarm.co.uk. *2m W of Criccieth. On A497 to Pwllheli on L of main rd.* Light refreshments. **Adm £2.50, chd free. Sun 5, Mon 6 Apr, Sun 24, Mon 25 May (11-5). Evening Opening, Sun 14 June (6.30-8.30). Visitors also welcome by arrangement Mar to Aug. Visits must be booked in advance.**
Cottage garden with rockery, fish pond, herbaceous border, steps to river. Large variety of plants. Nicely planted tubs; good vegetable garden and poultry. Rhododendrons and azaleas. Music, cheese and wine at our evening opening (Sun 14 June). Wheelchair access to most of garden.

5 ◆ BRONDANW GARDENS

Llanfrothen LL48 6SW. Brondanw Estates, 01766 772772, www.brondanw.org.uk. *5m E of Porthmadog on A4085. Off A498 Caernarfon, Beddgelert Rd, R on the B4410 following Osprey signs until Garreg on A4085. L then R at Gate House. Car Park on L.* Light refreshments. **Adm £4, chd £1, under 12s free. For NGS: Wed 20, Wed 27 May (12-4). For other opening times and information, please phone or see garden website.**
Plas Brondanw is amongst Clough Williams Ellis' best example of his talent for creative landscape design. The main features were laid down during the early part of the C20 before he began Portmeirion. Over 70yrs Sir Clough created a unique and characteristic, romantic landscape. One of the truly great Welsh gardens. Freshly made cakes in the café daily, all local produce used. Slate paths, slopes on some lawns.

6 NEW **1 BRYN EGLWYS**
Llansadwrn, Menai Bridge
LL59 5SE. Mr & Mrs Keith
Williamson. *3m N of Menai Bridge. Follow signs for Amlwch/ Benllech A5025 from either bridge onto Anglesey. Approx 3m turn R to Llansadwrn (pink cottage), Arcady 1m from junction. Please park & pay at Arcady.* **Combined adm £6, chd free. Sun 19 July (11-4.30). Combined with Arcady.**
With panoramic view of Snowdonia range overlooking fields, a garden of characters and character! Small orchards, topiary, lawn, slate obelisk, natural well, many unusual features, incl range of shrubs from Bonsai to Leylandii. Small but full of surprises. With Arcady, 2 gardens unique in their own ways both of artistic quality and variety. Mysteries to be seen! Featured in Daily Mail. Disabled parking for 4 cars to rear.

7 **BRYN GWERN**
Llanfachreth, Dolgellau, Gwynedd
LL40 2DH. H O & P D Nurse, 01341 450255,
antique_pete@btinternet.com. *5m NE of Dolgellau. Do not go to Llanfachreth village, stay on A494 Bala-Dolgellau rd: 13m from Bala. Take 1st R Llanfachreth. From Dolgellau 4m Llanfachreth turn L, follow signs. No coach parking.* Cream teas. **Adm £3.50, chd free. Sun 17 May, Sun 26 July (10-5). Visitors also welcome by arrangement Feb to Oct.**
Sloping 2 acre garden in the hills overlooking Dolgellau with views to Cader Idris, originally wooded but redesigned to enhance its natural features with streams, ponds and imaginative and extensive planting and vibrant colour. The garden is now a haven for wildlife with hedgehogs and 27 species of birds feeding last winter as well as being home to ducks, dogs and cats. Wheelchair access to main area of garden.

8 **BWLCH Y FEDWEN**
Penrhyndeudraeth LL48 6BT.
David & Gillian Surman. *22m N of Dolgellau, 3m E of Porthmadog, 2m E of Portmeirion. Opp Griffin PH, take A4085 along High St to village car park. Walking from there, follow signs to garden approx 150yds.* Home-made teas. **Adm £3.50, chd free. Sun 12 Apr, Sun 31 May (11-4).**
With views towards the Rhinogs,

Moelwyns and the Dwyryd estuary ³/₄ acre of neglected, rocky hillside has been transformed, providing terraced gardens with inter twining paths, many steps with handrails, seating, planted pots, baskets and alpine sinks. Spring bulbs, hellebores, roses, clematis and trees incl embothrium, halesia, koelreuteria, camellias, azaleas, magnolias provide yr-round interest. The owners have a passion for terracotta pots of all shapes and sizes and quirky structures.

9 **CAE NEWYDD**
Rhosgoch, Anglesey LL66 0BG.
Hazel & Nigel Bond, 01407 831354,
nigel@cae-newydd.co.uk. *3m SW of Amlwch. A5025 from Benllech to Amlwch, follow signs for leisure centre & Lastra Farm. Follow yellow NGS signs (approx 3m), car park on L.* Light refreshments. **Adm £3.50, chd free. Every Thur 4 June to 30 July (1-4). Sun 7 June (11-4.30).**
A maturing country garden of 2¹/₂ acres which blends seamlessly into the open landscape with stunning views of Snowdonia and Llyn Alaw. Good variety of shrubs and trees, large wildlife pond, meadow areas, polytunnel, greenhouse, vegetable garden and chicken run. Adjacent sheltered paddock garden. Formal pond and patio area, raised beds. Rose garden with aquilegias, dianthus and lavender. Hay meadow best seen in June. Lots of seating throughout the garden, visitors are welcome to bring a picnic. Thurs - serve yourself tea and coffee; Sun 7 June - Sandwiches available. Garden area closest to house suitable for wheelchairs.

10 **COED TY MAWR**
Ty Mawr, Bryncroes, Pwllheli
LL53 8EH. Nonni & David Goadby,
01758 730359, nonni@goadby.net,
www.coed-tymawr.co.uk. *12m W of Pwllheli. Take B4413 Llanbedrog to Aberdaron. 1³/₄ m past Sarn Meyllteyrn. Turn R at Penygroeslon sign. From Nefyn take B4417, at Xrds with B4413 turn L.* Home-made teas. **Adm £4, chd free. Visitors welcome by arrangement Apr to Oct.**
Outstanding 5 acre woodland garden created from wilderness and situated among some of the most beautiful scenery of Wales. Over 3,000 trees and shrubs incl growing collections of

magnolia, rhododendron, hydrangea and cornus. Also large pond, orchard, fernery, vegetable, oriental and sea view gardens. Plenty of seating. Sit on the raised deck, take in the sea views and enjoy a homemade tea. Grass paths.

11 **CORON**
Llanbedrog LL53 7NN. Mr & Mrs B M Jones. *3m SW of Pwllheli. Turn R off A499 opp Llanbedrog Village sign, before garage, up private drive.* Cream teas. **Adm £4, chd free. Sat 16, Sun 17 May (10.30-5).**
6 acre mature garden featuring Davidia involucrata, overlooking Cardigan Bay. Pathways leading through extensively planted areas with rhododendrons, embothrium, azaleas, camellias, bluebell walks, wooded slopes and rock outcrops providing shelter for tender plants. Lakes and bog gardens; orchards, walled vegetable and formal garden.

12 **CRAIG Y FFYNNON**
Ffordd y Gader, Dolgellau
LL40 1RU. Jon & Sh,n Lea. *Take Tywyn rd from Dolgellau main sq. Park on rd by Penbryn Garage. Walk up rd signed Cader Idris. Garden entrance on L 50yds from junction.* Home-made teas. **Adm £4, chd free. Share to Bumblebee Conservation Trust. Sun 10 May (10-4.30).**
N facing 2 acre Victorian garden set out in 1870s. Planted with mature specimen trees, rhododendrons and azaleas. Formal herbaceous borders and greenhouse enclosed by box hedges. Wildlife pond; bees and call ducks; unusual shade loving plants and ferns. Trad's Diary 'exquisite precision whether formal in box hedges or where azaleas and alpines cohabit under splendid old trees with moss and ferns'. Treasure Hunt for children (and adults).

Llyn Rhaeadr

© Fiona Lea

13 CROWRACH ISAF
Bwlchtocyn LL53 7BY. Margaret & Graham Cook, 01758 712860, crowrach_isaf@hotmail.com. *1½ m SW of Abersoch. Follow rd through Abersoch & Sarn Bach, L at sign for Bwlchtocyn for ½ m until junction & no-through rd - TG Holiday Complex. Turn R, parking 50 metres on R.* Cream teas. **Adm £3.50, chd free. Sat 20, Sun 21 June (1-5). Visitors also welcome by arrangement May to Aug.**
2 acre plot incl 1 acre fenced against rabbits, developed from 2000, incl island beds, windbreak hedges, vegetable garden, wild flower area and wide range of geraniums, shrubs and herbaceous perennials. Views over Cardigan Bay and Snowdonia. Grass and gravel paths, some gentle slopes.

14 ◆ CRÛG FARM
Griffiths Crossing, Caernarfon LL55 1TU. Mr & Mrs B Wynn-Jones, 01248 670232, www.crug-farm.co.uk. *2m NE of Caernarfon. ¼ m off main A487 Caernarfon to Bangor rd. Follow signs from r'about.* Home-made teas. **Adm £3.50, chd free. For NGS: Sat 6 June (9.30-4.30). For other opening times and information, please phone or see garden website.**

3 acres; grounds to old country house (not open). Gardens filled with choice, unusual plants collected by the Wynn-Jones. Woodland garden with shade loving plants, many not seen in cultivation before. Walled garden with more wonderful collections growing. Chelsea Gold Medallists and winners of the President's Award among other many prestigious awards. Partial wheelchair access.

   NCH

15 FOXBRUSH
Aber Pwll, Port Dinorwic, Gwynedd LL56 4JZ. Mr & Mrs B S Osborne, 01248 670463, foxbrush@btinternet.com. *Between Bangor & Caernarfon. On Bangor to Caernarfon rd, entering village on L before Y Felinheli signpost.* Tea. **Adm £3, chd free. Sun 10 May (10-4). Visitors also welcome by arrangement Mar to July. Refreshments must be booked in advance.**
Fascinating large country garden, 33rd NGS yr, created and maintained solely by Jenny. Rare and interesting plant collections incl rhododendrons, ferns, hydrangea, clematis and roses, 45ft long pergola. Fan shaped knot garden, river, new plantings despite floods. Wildlife mill pond with amphibians and wild ducks, heron,

bats, wildflowers abound. Garden changes yr on yr, new wet weather attraction. Very relaxed wildlife garden, densely planted. Private cottage museum offers bad weather shelter.

16 GILFACH
Rowen, Conwy LL32 8TS. James & Isoline Greenhalgh, 01492 650216, isolinegreenhalgh@btinternet.com. *4m S of Conwy. At Xrds 100yds E of Rowen S towards Llanrwst, past Rowen School on L, turn up 2nd drive on L.* Home-made teas. **Adm £3, chd free. Sun 3 May, Sun 14 June (2-5.30). Visitors also welcome by arrangement May to Aug, coffee/biscuits (am), tea/cake (pm).**
1 acre country garden on S facing slope with magnificent views of the R Conwy and mountains; set in 35 acres of farm and woodland. Collection of mature shrubs is added to yearly; woodland garden, herbaceous border and small pool. Spectacular panoramic view of the Conwy Valley and the mountain range of the Carneddau. Classic cars. Large coaches can park at bottom of steep drive, disabled visitors can be driven to garden by the owner.

17 GWAELOD MAWR

Caergeiliog, Anglesey LL65 3YL. John & Tricia Coates, 01407 740080, patriciacoates36@gmail.com. *6m E of Holyhead. ¹/₂ m E of Caergeiliog. From A55 J4. r'about 2nd exit signed Caergeiliog. 300yds, Gwaelod Mawr is 1st house on L.* Home-made teas. **Adm £3.50, chd free. Sat 4, Sun 5 July (11-5). Visitors also welcome by arrangement May to Aug.**
2¹/₂ acre garden created by owners over 20yrs with lake, large rock outcrops and palm tree area. Spanish style patio and laburnum arch lead to sunken garden and wooden bridge over lily pond with fountain and waterfall. Peaceful Chinese orientated garden offering contemplation. Separate Koi carp pond. Abundant seating throughout. Mainly flat, with gravel and stone paths, no wheelchair access to sunken lily pond area.

&.

18 GWYNDY BACH

Tynlon, Llandrygarn LL65 3AJ. Keith & Rosa Andrew, 01407 720651, keithandrew.art@gmail.com. *5m W of Llangefni. From Llangefni take B5109 towards Bodedern, cottage exactly 5m out on L. Postcode good for SatNav.* Home-made teas. **Adm £3, chd free. Sun 28 June (11-4.30). Visitors also welcome by arrangement May to July.**
³/₄ acre artist's garden, set amidst rugged Anglesey landscape. Romantically planted in informal intimate rooms with interesting rare plants and shrubs, box and yew topiary, old roses and Japanese garden with large Koi pond (deep water, children must be supervised). National Collection of Rhapis miniature Japanese palms. Studio attached. Gravel entrance to garden.

&.

19 LLANIDAN HALL

Brynsiencyn LL61 6HJ. Mr J W Beverley (Head Gardener), 07759 305085, beverley.family@btinternet.com. *5m E of Llanfair Pwll. From Llanfair PG follow A4080 towards Brynsiencyn for 4m. After Hooton's farm shop on R take next L, follow lane to gardens.* Tea. **Adm £3.50, chd free. Share to CAFOD. Sat 25 Apr, Sat 20 June, Sat 4 July (10-4). Visitors also welcome by** arrangement Apr to July (daytime visits only).
Walled garden of 1³/₄ acres. Physic and herb gardens, ornamental vegetable garden, herbaceous borders, water features and many varieties of old roses. Sheep, rabbits and hens to see. Children must be kept under supervision. Llanidan Church will be open for viewing. New this yr, walled garden will be open early in the season for viewing of the spring bulbs. New lambs in the stable in April. Hard gravel paths, gentle slopes.

&.

20 LLYN RHAEADR

Parc Bron-y-Graig, Centre of Harlech LL46 2SR. Mr D R Hewitt & Miss J Sharp, 01766 780224. *Centre of Harlech. From A496 take B4573 into Harlech, take turning to main car parks S of town, L past overspill car park, garden 75yds on R.* **Adm £3, chd free. Share to WWF UK. Fri 3, Sat 4, Sun 5, Mon 6 Apr, Sat 2, Sun 3, Mon 4, Sat 23, Sun 24, Mon 25, Tue 26 May, Sat 29, Sun 30, Mon 31 Aug (2-5). Visitors also welcome by arrangement Mar to Oct most days (2-5).**
Hillside garden blending natural wildlife areas with garden plants, shrubs, vegetables and fruit. Small lake with 20 species of waterfowl, fish and wildlife ponds, waterfalls, woodland, rockeries, lawns, borders, snowdrops, daffodils, heathers, bluebells, ferns, camellias, azaleas, rhododendrons, wild flowers, views of Tremadog Bay, Lleyn Peninsula. Good paths and seating with gazebos. Waterfowl collection.

21 LLYS-Y-GWYNT

Pentir Road, Llandygai, Bangor LL57 4BG. Jennifer Rickards & John Evans, 01248 353863. *3m S of Bangor. 300yds from Llandygai r'about at J11, A5 & A55, just off A4244. Follow signs for services (Gwasanaethau). No through rd sign, 50yds beyond. Do not use SatNav.* Cream teas. **Adm £3, chd free. Sun 17 May, Sun 5 July (11-4). Visitors also welcome by arrangement.**
Interesting, harmonious and very varied 2 acre garden incl magnificent views of Snowdonia. An exposed site incl Bronze Age burial cairn. Winding paths and varied levels planted to create shelter, yr-round interest, microclimates and varied rooms. Ponds, waterfall, bridge and other features use local materials and craftspeople. Wild life encouraged, well organised compost. Good family garden.

&.

22 MAEN HIR

Dwyran, Anglesey LL61 6UY. Mr & Mrs K T Evans. *6m SE of Llanfairpwll. From Llanfair P.G (Anglesey) follow A4080 through village Brynsiencyn. Cont on this rd for approx 2m. Maen Hir on R.* Home-made teas. **Adm £3.50, chd free. Sat 13, Sun 14 June (11-5).**
Set in 7 acres incl beautiful walled garden with gazebo, old roses and mixed herbaceous borders replanted 2007. Courtyard, outer garden, woodland walks, greenhouse, potting shed, cutting patch and hay meadow. Maen Hir enjoys magnificent views of Snowdonia range. Refreshments served on the front lawn.

&.

> A maturing country garden of which blends seamlessly into the open landscape . . .

23 MAENAN HALL

Maenan, Llanrwst LL26 0UL. The Hon Mr & Mrs Christopher Mclaren, 01492 640441, cmmclaren@gmail.com. *2m N of Llanrwst. On E side of A470, ¹/₄ m S of Maenan Abbey Hotel.* Home-made teas. **Adm £4, chd free. Share to Wales Air Ambulance. Sun 10 May, Sun 16 Aug (10.30-4.30). Visitors also welcome by arrangement Apr to Sept for groups 8+.**
Superbly beautiful garden (about 4 hectares) on the slopes of the Conwy Valley, with dramatic views of Snowdonia, set amongst mature hardwoods. Both upper part, with sweeping lawns, ornamental ponds and retaining walls, and bluebell carpeted woodland dell contain copious specimen shrubs and trees, many originating at Bodnant. In spring magnolias, rhododendrons, camellias, pieris and cherries amongst many others make a

breathtaking display. Treasure Hunt (£1) on both open days. Upper part of garden accessible but with fairly steep slopes.

24 PANT IFAN
Ceunant, LLanrug, Caernarfon LL55 4HX. Mrs Delia Lanceley. *2m E of Caernarfon. From Llanrug take rd opp PO between Premier Store & Monumental Mason. Straight across at next Xrds. Then 3rd turn on L at Xrds. Pant Ifan 2nd house on L.* Home-made teas. **Adm £3.50, chd free. Sat 18 July (11-5).**
2 acre mix of formal and wildlife garden set around farmhouse and yard. Herbaceous borders, shrubs, vegetables, fruit, ponds and recently planted woodland. Field walks, sitting areas in the sun or shade. Poultry, ducks, geese, donkeys, horse and greenhouses. Deep water, children must be supervised at all times.

25 PEN Y BRYN
Glandwr, Barmouth LL42 1TG. Phil & Jenny Martin. *2m E of Barmouth. On A496 7m W of Dolgellau, 2m E of Barmouth, situated on N side of Mawddach Estuary. Park in or nr layby & walk L up narrow lane.* Cream teas. **Adm £3.50, chd free. Share to Gwynedd Hospice at Home. Sun 3 May (11-5).**
A glorious hillside garden with panoramic views of The Mawddoch Estuary. Woodland walks awash with Bluebells in the spring. Lawns on different levels with vibrant rhododendrons and azaleas, arches of clematis, honeysuckle and roses. Heather filled natural rocks, unusual conifer feature, a rock cannon and a pond for wildlife.

26 ◆ PENRHYN CASTLE
Bangor LL57 4HN. National Trust, 01248 353084, www.nationaltrust.org.uk. *3m E of Bangor. On A5122. Buses from Llandudno, Caernarfon, Betws-y-Coed; alight: Grand Lodge Gate. J11 A55, signed from thereon. For SatNav use LL57 4HT.* Light refreshments. **Adm £7.99, chd £3.99. For NGS: Sat 14 Feb (12-3), Sat 13 Feb 2016. For other opening times and information, please phone or see garden website.**
Large grounds incl Victorian walled garden; fine trees, shrubs, wild garden, good views, snowdrop walks. Coffee shop open. Gravelled and grassed paths, some steps, exposed tree roots, some surfaces bark and chippings.

27 ◆ PENSYCHNANT
Sychnant Pass, nr Conwy LL32 8BJ. Pensychnant Foundation; Wardens Julian Thompson & Anne Mynott, 01492 592595, www.pensychnant.co.uk. *2½ m W of Conwy at top of Sychnant Pass. From Conwy: L into Upper Gate St; after 2½ m Pensychnant's drive signed on R. From Penmaenmawr: fork R, up pass, after walls U turn L into drive.* Home-made teas. **Adm £3.50, chd free. For NGS: Sun 7 June, Sun 5 July (11-5). For other opening times and information, please phone or see garden website.**
Wildlife Garden. Diverse herbaceous cottage garden borders surrounded by mature shrubs, banks of rhododendrons, ancient and Victorian woodlands. 12 acre woodland walks with views of Conwy Mountain and Sychnant. Woodland birds. Picnic tables, archaeological trail on mountain. A peaceful little gem. Large Victorian Arts and Crafts house (open) with art exhibition. Feature in Daily Post. Partial wheelchair access, please phone for advice.

GROUP OPENING

28 PENTIR GARDENS
Pentir, Bangor LL57 4YA. *Take A4244 from J11 of A55/A5. cont for 3m to Pentir. Turn R signed Caerhun/Vaynol PH, into Pentir Square.* Home-made teas at Bryn Meddyg. **Combined adm £5, chd free. Sat 27 June (12-5).**

2 RHYD Y GROES
Mr & Mrs IwanThomas

TAN RALLT
John Lewis & Gary Carvalho

TAN Y BRYN
Mrs Eliz Battle

TY UCHAF
Sian Lewis

Ty Uchaf is a small densely packed garden with a wide variety of cottage favourites, plus unusual planting schemes. It enjoys a romantic feel, prioritizing colour and texture. A secret gate takes visitors to neighbouring Bryn Meddyg, serving refreshments. 10 mins walk takes you to Tan y Bryn, a garden with mature shrubs, a lawned area with herbaceous planting. There is also a vegetable plot, paddock with stunning views, pond and a dwarf conifer collection. Continue along to the secluded garden, 2 Rhyd y Groes to enjoy views of Moel y Ci and Menai Strait. This immaculate garden has a a number of rooms with a variety of planted areas, seating, pond and summerhouse and sculptures. Further along the lane, a 5 mins walk to Tan Rallt, backing onto Moel y Ci, the 0.8 acre garden incl a range of mature trees and shrubs, vegetable and soft fruit, herbaceous borders and areas of lawn. A diversely planted pond with tree ferns, bog plants and giant gunnera.

On summer days, scented plants infuse the air . . .

29 PLAS CADNANT HIDDEN GARDENS
Cadnant Road, Menai Bridge, Anglesey LL59 5NH. Mr Anthony Tavernor, 01248 717174, plascadnantgardens@gmail.com, www.plascadnantgardens.co.uk. *½ m E of Menai Bridge. Take A545 & leave Menai Bridge heading for Beaumaris, then follow brown tourist information signs.* Home-made teas in traditional Tea Room. **Adm £6.50, chd free. Share to Wales Air Ambulance; Anglesey Red Squirrel Trust; Menai Bridge Community Heritage Trust. Wed 29 Apr (12-5).**
Early C19 Picturesque garden undergoing restoration since 1996. Valley gardens with waterfalls, large ornamental walled garden, woodland and early pit house. Serving delicious quiches, soup, freshly made sandwiches, home-made scones and cakes. Visitor centre open. Partial wheelchair access to parts of gardens. Some steps, gravel paths, slopes. Access statement available. Accessible Tea Room and WC.

Treat yourself to a plant from the plant stall

Sunningdale

© Joe Wainwright

30 ◆ **PLAS NEWYDD COUNTRY HOUSE & GARDENS**
Llanfairpwll, Anglesey LL61 6DQ.
National Trust, 01248 714795,
www.nationaltrust.org.uk. *2m S of Llanfairpwll on A4080. A55 J7 & J8 on A4080.* Light refreshments in the Old Dairy Tea Room. **Adm £9.35, chd £4.70. For NGS: Fri 29 May (10.30-5.30).** For other opening times and information, please phone or see garden website.
Plas Newydd is a beautiful C18 country house with spectacular panoramic views across the Menai Strait to Snowdonia. Set in beautiful gardens, there are tranquil walks, an Australasian arboretum and a pretty Italianate Terrace Garden. The house (not open on NGS day), is the family home of the Marquess of Anglesey. Hot food served between 12 noon

and 3pm, snacks, home-made cakes and drinks available all day. Some slopes and gravel paths.

  🔿 ♻ 🚐 ☕

31 ◆ **PLAS YN RHIW**
Rhiw, Pwllheli LL53 8AB. National Trust, 01758 780219,
www.nationaltrust.org.uk. *4m E of Aberdaron. 12m from Pwllheli, signed from B4413 to Aberdaron.* Tea. **Adm £3, chd free. For NGS: Sun 8 Feb (11-3); Sun 7 Feb 2016.** For other opening times and information, please phone or see garden website.
Essentially a cottage garden of ¾ acre laid out around C17 manor house (not open) overlooking Porth Neigwl. Flowering shrubs and trees flourish in compartments framed by formal box hedges and paths. On

summer days, scented plants infuse the air. A place of romance and charm. Snowdrops in spring.

  ♻ ☕

32 **NEW** **RHOSBACH COTTAGE**
Brynteg LL78 8JY. Ena & Bryan Green. *Brynteg, Anglesey. 1.4m W of Benllech. Take B5108 to Brynteg. Follow NGS signs to limited parking on lane on L, extra parking approx 50 metres further along rd on R at Storws Wen Golf Club.* Light refreshments. **Adm £3, chd free. Sun 21 June (1-5).**
Situated close to Cors Goch Nature Reserve, a recently rejuvenated garden full of country charm, a blend of mature trees, shrubs and wide, mixed borders planted to attract wildlife. Entered through a large

gravel area, the garden gently slopes with some steps, seating areas, pond and a new pergola planned for 2015. Winner of North Wales Wildlife Garden, Best Small/Medium Private Garden.

WE ARE MACMILLAN.
CANCER SUPPORT

2015 sees the NGS total to Macmillan pass £15 million

33 ST JOHN THE BAPTIST & ST GEORGE
Lon Batus, Carmel LL54 7AR. Bishop Abbot Demetrius. *7m SE of Caernarfon. On A487 Porthmadog Rd, at Dinas r'about exit 1st L to Groeslon, turn L at PO for 1¹/₂ m. At village centre turn L & L again at Xrds.* Home-made teas. **Adm £2.50, chd free. Sat 25 July (2-4).**
Holy community in the making under the authority of The Orthodox Catholic and Holy Synod of Milan. This is not a garden in the traditional sense but it and the monastery are a spiritual retreat from the stresses and strains of modern life, surrounded on all sides by space and rural tranquillity. We are privileged to share a glimpse of a more contemplative life. Antique collection and Chapel open.

34 SUNNINGDALE
Bull Bay Road, Bull Bay, Amlwch LL68 9SD. Michael Cross & Gill Boniface, 01407 830753, mikeatbb@aol.com. *1¹/₂ m NW of Amlwch. On A5025 through Amlwch towards Cemaes. No parking at house but parking will be signed.* Home-made teas. (Weds pm). **Adm £3.50, chd free. Sun 3 May (11-5); Wed 13 May, Wed 10 June (2-5); Sun 28 June (11-5). Visitors also welcome by arrangement May to July for groups 8+.**
An evolving seaside garden. Headland has cliffs, steps, wild

flowers and seating, spectacular views and sheer drops! Front garden has raised pond and planting to cope with hostile weather. The relatively sheltered rear garden is cottage style; no large lawn here! Lots of different plants, paths, seats, pots and raised bed vegetable area. Star is the 50yr old laburnum. Mentioned in the Mail Saturday supplement and featured in WI Life. Wheelchair access to front garden only.

35 TREFFOS SCHOOL
Llansadwrn, Anglesey LL59 5SD. Stuart & Joyce Humphreys. *2¹/₂ m N of Menai Bridge. A5025 Amlwch/Benllech exit from Britannia Bridge onto Anglesey. Approx 3m turn R towards Llansadwrn. Entrance to Treffos School 200yds on L.* Cream teas. **Adm £3, chd free. Sun 14 June (12-3).**
7 acres, child friendly garden, in rural location, surrounding C17 house now run as school. Garden consists of mature woodland, underplanted with spring flowering bulbs and rhododendrons, ancient beech avenue leading down to rockery, herbaceous borders and courtyards. Art and Craft activities for children. Also face painting.

36 TY CADFAN SANT
National Street, Tywyn LL36 9DD. Mrs Katie Pearce, 01654 712188, Katie@tycadfansant.co.uk. *A493 going S & W. L into one way, garden ahead. Bear R, parking 2nd L. A493 going N, 1st R in 30mph zone, L at bottom by garden, parking 2nd L.* Cream teas and home baked cakes, special diets also catered for. **Adm £3.50, chd free. Sun 14 June (11-5). Visitors also welcome by arrangement May to Sept.**
Large eco friendly garden. In the front, shrubbery, mixed flower beds and roses surround a mature copper beech. Up six steps the largely productive back garden has chickens in the orchard, fruit, vegetables, flowers and a poly tunnel. Crafts, seasonal produce. Partial wheelchair access due to steps to rear garden.

37 TY CAPEL FFRWD
Llanfachreth, nr Dolgellau LL40 2NR. Revs Mary & George Bolt, 01341 422006, georgebolt@talktalk.net. *4m NE of Dolgellau, 18m SW of Bala. From*

Dolgellau 4m up hill to Llanfachreth. Turn L at War Memorial. Follow lane ¹/₂ m to chapel on R. Park & walk down lane past chapel to cottage. Cream teas. **Adm £3, chd free. Visitors welcome by arrangement May to Sept, groups 10 max. Art groups and gardening clubs welcome.**
True cottage garden in Welsh mountains. Azaleas, rhododendrons, acers; large collection of aquilegia. Many different hostas give added strength to spring bulbs and corms. Stream flowing through the garden, 10ft waterfall and on through a small woodland bluebell carpet. For summer visitor's there is a continuous show of colour with herbaceous plants, roses, clematis and lilies, incl cardiocrinum giganteum.

38 TY NEWYDD
Ffordd Clwt Glas, Dyffryn Ardudwy LL44 2DB. Guy & Margaret Lloyd, 01341 247357, guylloyd@btinternet.com. *5¹/₂ m N of Barmouth, 4¹/₂ m S of Harlech. Situated just off A496 Barmouth to Harlech rd ¹/₂ m N of Dyffryn village centre.* Home-made teas. **Adm £3, chd free. Visitors welcome by arrangement Feb to Oct.**
3¹/₂ acre maritime garden diversley planted with trees and shrubs to provide yr-round interest through contrasting foliage colours and forms as well as floral displays. Plants incl a number of more tender subjects such as echium, grevillea and pittosporum. Areas devoted to fruit and vegetable growing and the so called Diamond apple tree. Partial wheelchair access, uneven surfaces, granite chip driveway.

39 41 VICTORIA DRIVE
Llandudno Junction LL31 9PF. Allan Evans. *Llandudno Junction. A55 J18. From Bangor 1st exit, from Colwyn Bay 2nd exit, A546 to Conwy. Next r'about 3rd exit then 1st L.* Home-made teas. **Adm £3, chd free. Sun 9 Aug (1-4.30).**
A very interesting small urban garden, offering so much in creative ideas incl growing exhibition sweet peas and dahlias and colourful bedding and other shrubs and herbaceous plants. Featured on Radio Cymru, in the Daily Post and North Wales Weekly News.

NORTH EAST WALES

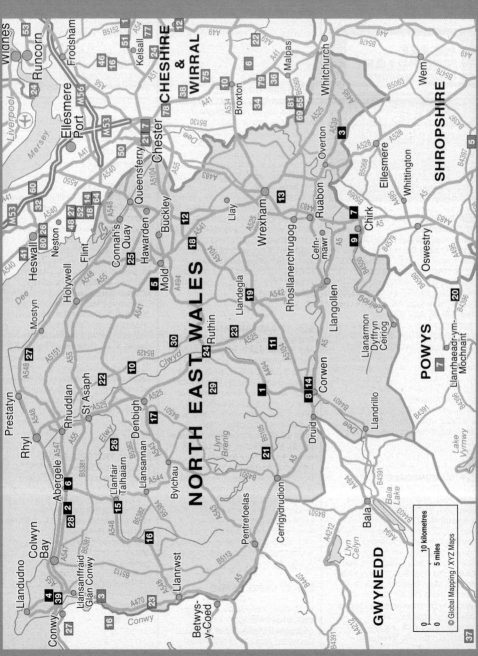

North East Wales

With its diversity of countryside from magnificent hills, seaside vistas and rolling farmland, North East Wales offers a wide range of gardening experiences.

Our gardens offer visitors a wealth of gardening designs, and come in all shapes and sizes; visitors can enjoy an evening opening in the late-summer garden of Bryn Bellan, 11 acres of manicured gardens at Tree Tops Caravan Park, and a charming group of gardens in the picturesque village of Llandegla.

The majority of our gardens are within easy reach of North West England, and being a popular tourist destination make an excellent day out for all the family.

Come and enjoy the beauty and the variety of the gardens of North East Wales with the added bonus of a delicious cup of tea and a slice of cake. Our garden owners await your visit.

North East Wales Volunteers

County Organiser
Jane Moore
01745 890475
jemoore01@live.com

County Treasurers
Elizabeth Sasse
01745 710174
elizabeth.sasse246@btinternet.com

Wendy Sime
01948 830126
sjsime@hotmail.com

Publicity
Jane Moore
(as above)

Booklet Coordinator
Roy Hambleton
01352 740206
royhambleton@btinternet.com

Assistant County Organisers
Fiona Bell
07813 087797
bell_fab@hotmail.com

Ruth Davies
01978 790475
arfrynpentrecelyn@btinternet.com

Ann Knowlson
01745 832002
apk@slaters.com

Ann Rathbone
01244 532948
rathbone.ann@gmail.com

Anne Saxon
01352 771222
annemsaxon@yahoo.co.uk

Susan Watson
01745 710232
clwydfryn@btinternet.com

Above: Tal-y-Bryn Farm

Currently the NGS donates around £2.5 million every year

Opening Dates

All entries subject to change.
For latest information check www.ngs.org.uk

February

Wednesday 11
10 Clwydfryn

March

Wednesday 11
10 Clwydfryn

April

Wednesday 1
1 Aberclwyd Manor
Wednesday 8
10 Clwydfryn
Wednesday 15
1 Aberclwyd Manor

May

Saturday 2
11 Dibleys Nurseries
Sunday 3
11 Dibleys Nurseries
13 Erddig Hall
Monday 4
11 Dibleys Nurseries
Wednesday 6
1 Aberclwyd Manor
Sunday 10
21 The Old Rectory, Llanfihangel Glyn Myfyr
Wednesday 13
10 Clwydfryn

Wednesday 20
1 Aberclwyd Manor
Thursday 21
7 NEW Brynkinalt Hall
Saturday 23
13 Erddig Hall
Sunday 24
8 Caereuni
14 NEW Ffridd-y-Gog
Monday 25
8 Caereuni
14 NEW Ffridd-y-Gog
Saturday 30
25 90 St Peters Park

June

Wednesday 3
1 Aberclwyd Manor

Festival Weekend

Saturday 6
13 Erddig Hall
Wednesday 10
10 Clwydfryn
Saturday 13
9 Chirk Castle
Wednesday 17
1 Aberclwyd Manor
Sunday 21
17 Gwaenynog
20 Llangedwyn Hall
Tuesday 23
4 Bodysgallen Hall & Spa
Saturday 27
3 NEW The Beeches
28 Tudor Cottage
Sunday 28
24 Ruthin Town Gardens
28 Tudor Cottage

July

Wednesday 1
1 Aberclwyd Manor
7 NEW Brynkinalt Hall
Saturday 4
6 33 Bryn Twr and Lynton
Sunday 5
6 33 Bryn Twr and Lynton
23 Penllwyn
27 Tree Tops Caravan Park
Monday 6
27 Tree Tops Caravan Park
Wednesday 8
10 Clwydfryn
Wednesday 15
1 Aberclwyd Manor
Sunday 19
2 Ael y Grug
Sunday 26
19 Llandegla Village Gardens

August

Sunday 2
12 Dove Cottage
Wednesday 5
1 Aberclwyd Manor
Wednesday 12
10 Clwydfryn
Friday 14
5 Bryn Bellan (Evening)
Wednesday 19
1 Aberclwyd Manor

September

Wednesday 2
1 Aberclwyd Manor

February 2016

Thursday 18
16 Glog Ddu
Thursday 25
16 Glog Ddu

Gardens open to the public

9 Chirk Castle
13 Erddig Hall

By arrangement only

15 Garthewin
18 Leeswood Green Farm
22 Pen Y Graig Bach
26 Tal-y-Bryn Farm
29 Tyddyn Bach
30 Wylan

Also open by arrangement

1 Aberclwyd Manor
5 Bryn Bellan
6 33 Bryn Twr and Lynton
7 NEW Brynkinalt Hall
19 Plas Yn Coed, Llandegla Village Gardens
19 Swn y Gwynt, Llandegla Village Gardens
24 46 Mwrog Street, Ruthin Town Gardens
27 Tree Tops Caravan Park
28 Tudor Cottage

The Gardens

1 **ABERCLWYD MANOR**
Derwen, Corwen, Clwyd LL21 9SF.
Miss Irene Brown & Mr G Sparvoli,
01824 750431,
irene662010@live.com. *7m from Ruthin. Travelling on A494 from Ruthin to Corwen. At Bryn S.M service station turn R, follow sign to Derwen. Aberclwyd gates on L before Derwen.* Tea. **Adm £3.50, chd free.**
Weds 1, 15 Apr, 6, 20 May, 3, 17 June, 1, 15 July, 5, 19 Aug, 2 Sept (11-4). Visitors also welcome by arrangement Feb to Sept for groups 10+ daytime or evenings.

A 4 acre garden on a sloping hillside overlooking the Upper Clwyd Valley. The garden has many mature trees underplanted with snowdrops, fritillaries and cyclamen. An Italianate garden of box hedging lies below the house and shrubs, ponds, perennials, roses and an orchard are also to be enjoyed within this cleverly structured area. Mostly flat with some steps and slopes.

2 **AEL Y GRUG**
Rhyd y Foel Road, Llanddulas,
Abergele, Denbighshire
LL22 8EG. Mr Neville McClellan.
From Abergele, go W on Market St (A547) towards Llanddulas. After 2m turn L at Rhydyfoel Rd. Turn R into New Rd, park there then walk up towards Rhydyfoel. Tea. **Adm £3.50, chd free.** Sun 19 July (1-5).

A hillside garden, on several levels, with steep entry, set in 1/2 acre. Mixed herbaceous borders, connected by paths taking you through areas of mature shrubs and perennial flower beds. Beautiful valley views to the Irish sea in the distance.

Visit a garden on National Gardens Festival Weekend 6 & 7 June

Gwaenynog

 NEW **THE BEECHES**
Vicarage Lane, Penley, Wrexham
LL13 0NH. **Stuart & Sue Hamon.**
*Western edge of village. From
Overton turn 1st L after 30mph sign.
From Whitchurch go through village &
turn R just after church, signed to
Adrefelyn. N.B. SatNavs may show
Vicarage Lane as Hollybush Lane.*
Home-made teas. **Adm £3.50, chd
free. Sat 27 June (1-5).**
The garden surrounds an 1841
former vicarage and extends to
3½ acres and has been redesigned
to create an attractive open garden
laid mainly to lawn with a mixture of
mature and younger specimen
trees and shrubs. There are newly
planted shrub, rose and herbaceous
beds together with a productive
vegetable and fruit area. The walled
courtyard garden has more tender
plants incl many agapanthus. A
mostly flat garden with gravelled
paths.

♿ 🐕 🌸 ☕

4 **BODYSGALLEN HALL &
SPA**
The Royal Welsh Way, nr
Llandudno LL30 1RS. **The National
Trust,** 01492 584466,
www.bodysgallen.com. *2m from
Llandudno. Take A55 to its
intersection with A470 (The Royal
Welsh Way) towards Llandudno.
Proceed 1m, hotel is 1m on R.*
Home-made teas in The Upper Wynn

Room. **Adm £4.50, chd £3.50. Tue
23 June (1-4.30).**
Garden is well known for C17 box
hedged parterre. Stone walls
surround lower gardens with rose
gardens and herbaceous borders.
Outside walled garden is cascade
over rocks. Enclosed working fruit
and vegetable garden with espalier-
trained fruit trees, hedging area for
cut flowers with walls covered in
wineberry and Chinese gooseberry.
Restored Victorian woodland, walks
with stunning views of Conwy and
Snowdonia. Gravel paths in places
and steep slopes.

♿ 🌸 🛏 ☕

5 **BRYN BELLAN**
Bryn Road, Gwernaffield CH7 5DE.
**Gabrielle Armstrong & Trevor
Ruddle,** 01352 741806,
trevor@indigoawnings.co.uk. *2m W
of Mold. Leave A541 at Mold on
Gwernaffield rd (Dreflan), ½ m after
Mold derestriction signs turn R to
Rhydymwyn & Llynypandy. After
200yds park in field on R.* **Evening
Opening £6, chd free, wine, Fri 14
Aug (5-8). Visitors also welcome by
arrangement May to Sept for
groups 10+.**
This late summer tranquil and elegant
garden is perfect for a relaxing
evening visit. The garden has been
designed on two levels, a partly
walled upper garden with circular
sunken lawn, featuring a Wellingtonia

and structured borders of a green
and white colour scheme with striking
hydrangeas. The lower garden,
mainly lawn, has an ornamental
cutting and vegetable garden with
bijou potting shed. Some gravel
paths.

♿ 🌸 ☕

6 **33 BRYN TWR AND
LYNTON**
Lynton, Highfield Park, Abergele
LL22 7AU. **Mr & Mrs Colin
Knowlson & Bryn Roberts & Emma
Knowlson-Roberts,** 01745 832002,
apk@slaters.com. *Abergele. From
A55 head W take slip rd into Abergele
town centre. Turn L at 2nd set of T-
lights signed Llanfair TH, 3rd rd on L.
For SatNav use LL22 8DD.* Home-
made teas. **Adm £4, chd free. Share
to Ty Croeso (Dawn Elizabeth
House & Glan Clwyd Hospital). Sat
4, Sun 5 July (1-5). Visitors also
welcome by arrangement any size
group.**
More changes have been made to
the gardens for 2015, mixed
herbaceous and shrub borders, some
trees plus many unusual plants. Lawn
at Lynton replaced with slate chips
and more planting. Garage with
interesting fire engine, cars and
memorabilia, greenhouse over water
capture system, the surrounding
planting coming along nicely. Partial
wheelchair access.

♿ 🐕 🌸 🚐 ☕

7 NEW ▶ BRYNKINALT HALL
Brynkinalt, Chirk, Wrexham
LL14 5NS. Iain & Kate Hill-Trevor,
01691 773425,
info@brynkinalt.co.uk,
www.brynkinalt.co.uk. *6m N of
Oswestry, 10m S of Wrexham. Turn
into Trevor Rd (beside St Mary's
Church). Cont past houses on R. Turn
R on bend into Estate Gates. Over 2
bridges. St on at fork. N.B. Do not
use postcode with SatNav (uses tiny
lane). Home-made teas.* **Adm £4,
chd free. Thur 21 May, Wed 1 July
(2-5).** Visitors also welcome by
arrangement May to Sept for
groups 15+. Refreshments
available.
2 acre garden beside Grade II* house
(see website for opening), with
modern rose and formal beds, deep
herbaceous borders, pond with
shrub/mixed beds, pleached limes
and hedge parterres. Also 5 acre
ornamental woodland shrubbery,
overgrown until recently, now cleared
and replanted, rhododendron walk,
historic ponds, well, grottos, ha-ha
and battlements, new stumpery,
ancient redwoods and yews. Home
of the first Duke of Wellington 's
grandmother. Partial wheelchair
access. Gravel paths in West Garden
and grass paths and slopes in
Shrubbery.

8 ▶ CAEREUNI
Ffordd Ty Cerrig, Godre'r Gaer, nr
Corwen LL21 9YA. Mr S Williams,
www.plantationcaereunigarden.co.
uk. *1m N of Corwen. A5 Corwen to
Bala rd, turn R at T-lights onto A494
to Chester. 1st R after lay by. House
1/4 m on L.* **Combined adm £5, chd
free. Sun 24, Mon 25 May (2-5.30).**
Combined with Ffridd-y-Gog.
Plantsman's collection of rare trees,
shrubs, plants, containers of tender
plants and topiary set in a quirky
themed garden. This 0.3 acre garden
incls Japanese smoke water garden,
old ruin, Spanish courtyard, Welsh
gold mine, Chinese peace garden,
Mexican chapel, 1950s petrol garage,
woodman's lodge and jungle.

☕

9 ◆ CHIRK CASTLE
Chirk, nr Wrexham LL14 5AF.
National Trust, 01691 777701,
www.nationaltrust.org.uk. *7m S of
Wrexham, 2m W of Chirk Village.
Follow brown signs from A483 to
Chirk Village. 2m W on minor rds.*
Home-made teas. **Adm £12, chd £6.**

For NGS: Sat 13 June (10-6). **For
other opening times and
information, please phone or see
garden website.**
5½ acre hilltop garden with good
views over Shropshire and Cheshire.
Often thought to be at its peak at this
time of yr. Formal garden with
outstanding yew topiary, rose garden,
herbaceous borders, rare trees and
shrubs, pond, thatched Hawk House,
Ha-Ha with Terrace and Pavilion.
Newly opened vegetable garden.
Most of garden accessible for
wheelchairs.

♿ 🐕 🚌 🛏 ☕

**WE ARE
MACMILLAN.
CANCER SUPPORT**

**2015 sees the
NGS total to
Macmillan pass
£15 million**

10 ▶ CLWYDFRYN
Bodfari LL16 4HU. Keith & Susan
Watson. *5m outside Denbigh.
Halfway between Bodfari &
Llandyrnog on B5429.* Home-made
teas. **Adm £3.50, chd free. Weds 11
Feb, 11 Mar, 8 Apr, 13 May, 10
June, 8 July, 12 Aug (11-4).**
3/4 acre plantswoman's garden, well
worth a visit any time of the yr.
Collection of epimediums, hellebores
and daffodils in spring. Many unusual
spring shade loving plants and
perennial borders in summer. Grass
border, orchard and colourful cottage
garden potager. Garden access up a
slope from parking area to main
garden.

♿ ☕

11 ▶ DIBLEYS NURSERIES
Llanelidan, Cefn Rhydd LL15 2LG.
Mr & Mrs R Dibley,
www.dibleys.com. *7m S of Ruthin.
Follow brown signs off A525 nr
Llysfasi College.* Tea. **Adm £4, chd
free. Sat 2, Sun 3, Mon 4 May
(10-5).**
8 acre arboretum with wide selection
of rare and unusual trees. There will
be a lovely display of rhododendrons,
magnolias, cherries and camellias.

Ride through the garden on a
miniature railway. 3/4 acre of
glasshouses are open to show a
spectacular display of streptocarpus
and other house plants. National
Collection of *Streptocarpus.* Partial
wheelchair access to glasshouses,
uneven ground in arboretum and
elsewhere.

♿ 🐕 🚌 **NCH** ☕

12 ▶ DOVE COTTAGE
Rhos Road, Penyffordd, nr Chester
CH4 0JR. Chris & Denise Wallis.
*6m SW of Chester. Leave A55 at J35
take A550 to Wrexham. Drive 2m,
turn R onto A5104. From A541
Wrexham/Mold Rd in Pontblyddyn
take A5104 to Chester. Garden opp
train stn.* Tea. **Adm £3.50, chd free.
Sun 2 Aug (2-5).**
Approx 1½ acre garden, shrubs and
herbaceous plants set informally
around lawns. Established vegetable
area, 2 ponds (1 wildlife),
summerhouse and woodland planted
area. Gravel paths.

♿ 🐕 🛏 ☕

13 ◆ ERDDIG HALL
nr Wrexham LL13 0YT. National
Trust, 01978 355314,
www.nationaltrust.org.uk. *2m S of
Wrexham. Signed from A483/A5125
Oswestry rd; also from A525
Whitchurch rd.* Light refreshments.
Adm £7.40, chd £3.70. **For NGS:
Sun 3, Sat 23 May, Sat 6 June
(11-4).** **For other opening times and
information, please phone or see
garden website.**
Important, listed Grade I, historic
garden. Formal C18 and later
Victorian design elements incl
pleached lime tree avenues, trained
fruit trees, wall plants and climbers,
herbaceous borders, roses, herb
border, annual bedding, restored
glasshouse and vine house. National
Collection of Hedera. Free garden
tours at set times during the day.
Guide dogs permitted. Refreshments
in Restaurant, Parlour or Tea Garden.
All areas of the garden accessible to
wheelchairs. Gravelled paths, two
steps which can be avoided and
some short sloping sections.

♿ 🐕 🚌 **NCH** ☕

14 NEW ▶ FFRIDD-Y-GOG
Ffordd Ty Cerrig, Corwen
LL21 9YE. Mr & Mrs D Watkins. *1m
out of Corwen. From A5 to Bala rd
turn R at T-lights onto A494 to
Chester, 1st R after lay by. Ist L into
Ffridd-y-Gog. Park on Est Rd except*

for disabled. Turn L then R into drive. Home-made teas. **Combined adm £5, chd free. Sun 24, Mon 25 May (2-5.30). Combined with Caereuni.** Old Welsh farmhouse set in ³/₄ acre of grounds. Organic kitchen garden growing fruit, vegetables and herbs. Greenhouse and polytunnel. Ornamental gardens with particular emphasis on perennials and alpines. Many container grown plants, mostly propagated and grown by the owners. A haven for wildlife and a peaceful and tranquil space to just sit and enjoy. Whole garden accessible by wheelchair.

&. 🐕 ✿ ☕

The bakers of
the village supply
tasty cakes for
visitors to buy
and enjoy . . .

15 GARTHEWIN
Llanfair T.H LL22 8YR. Mr Michael Grime, 01745 720288, michaelgrime12@btinternet.com. *6m S of Abergele & A55. From Abergele take A548 to Llanfair TH & Llanrwst. Entrance to Garthewin 300yds W of Llanfair TH on A548 to Llanrwst. SatNav misleading.* **Adm £4, chd free. Visitors welcome by arrangement Apr to July max 30 people, no coaches.**
Valley garden with ponds and woodland areas. Much of the 8 acres have been reclaimed and redesigned providing a younger garden with a great variety of azaleas, rhododendrons and young trees, all within a framework of mature shrubs and trees.

🐕

16 GLOG DDU
Llangernyw, Abergele LL22 8PS. Pamela & Anthony Harris, 01745 860611. *1m S of Llangernyw. Llangernyw is halfway between Abergele & Llanrwst on A548. Do not use SatNav. Turn up Uwch Afon Rd*

on Llanrwst side of village & at grass triangle follow direction of yellow sign. Light refreshments. **Adm £5 incl soup and a roll, chd free. Thur 18, Thur 25 Feb 2016 (12-3).**
Approx 2 acres consisting of snowdrops, rhododendrons, herbaceous borders, rare trees and shrubs, many grown from seed. Over 300 different varieties of snowdrops, many hard to find, available for sale. Featured as Garden of the Week in Garden News.

✿ ☕

17 GWAENYNOG
Denbigh LL16 5NU. Major & Mrs Tom Smith. *1m W of Denbigh. On A543, Lodge on L, ¹/₄ m drive.* Cream teas. **Adm £3.50, chd free. Share to St James Church, Nantglyn. Sun 21 June (2-5.30).**
2 acres incl the restored walled garden where Beatrix Potter wrote and illustrated the 'Tale of the Flopsy Bunnies'. Also a small exhibition of some of her work. C16 house (not open) visited by Dr Samuel Johnson during his Tour of Wales. Herbaceous borders some recently replanted, espalier fruit trees, rose pergola and vegetable area.

&. ✿ ☕

18 LEESWOOD GREEN FARM
Leeswood CH7 4SQ. Anne Saxon & John Glenn, 01352 771222, annemsaxon@yahoo.co.uk. *3m SE of Mold. 9m NW of Wrexham. From Wrexham turn L after garage into Dingle rd, at T-junc turn L, after 50yds turn R down country track.* **Adm £4, chd free. Visitors welcome by arrangement Apr to June. Limited parking, no space for coaches.**
Plantswoman's garden surrounding C15 farmhouse in lovely rural location. Many unusual trees, shrubs, perennials and bulbs set around lawns. Ornamental vegetable garden, orchard and paved areas with some unusual features. Meadow with wild flowers and seating to enjoy the vistas. Gravel area near house. Lawned areas, slight incline.

&. 🐕 ✿ ☕

GROUP OPENING

19 LLANDEGLA VILLAGE GARDENS
Llandegla LL11 3AP. *10m W of Wrexham. Off A525 at Llandegla Memorial Hall. Parking & minibus*

from hall. Please park in centre of village as parking is difficult for some gardens. Home-made teas in Plas yn Coed, Glan-yr-Afon and The Gate House. **Combined adm £6, chd free. Sun 26 July (2-6).**

ERW LLAN
Mr & Mrs Keith Jackson

THE GATE HOUSE, RUTHIN ROAD
Rod & Shelagh Williams

GLAN-YR-AFON
Mr & Mrs D C Ion

11 MAES TEG
Mr & Mrs L Evans

13 MAES TEG
Phil & Joan Crawshaw

PLAS YN COED
Fraser & Helen Robertson
Visitors also welcome by arrangement Aug for groups 10+.
01978 790666
www.plasyncoed.me

NEW **THE RECTORY**
The Ven & Mrs R H Griffiths
Robert Griffiths

SWN Y GWYNT
Phil Clark
Visitors also welcome by arrangement July to Aug.
01978 790344

18 TREM Y GRUG
Nick & Ella Cartwright

TY PENDLE
Matt Ellis & Sandra Rogers

TY SIONED
Mr & Mrs Muia

Llandegla Village offers the visitor a truly old fashioned village welcome in the most picturesque area of the county. Every part of the community appears to enjoy the busy atmosphere of the day when the gardens attract so many visitors to raise funds for the NGS charity. The garden owners work hard to get their gardens looking their best, the bakers of the village supply tasty cakes for visitors to buy and enjoy in three of the venues, plants are for sale on the hall yard and the local publican spends his time ferrying visitors back and forth from an out of the village garden with very little parking. Perfect!. Some gardens may be difficult for wheelchair users.

&. 🐕 ✿ ☕

Nantclwyd y Dre, Ruthin Town Gardens

20 LLANGEDWYN HALL

Llangedwyn, Oswestry SY10 9JW.
Mr & Mrs T M Bell. *8m W of
Oswestry. On B4396 to Llanrhaeadr-
ym-Mochnant about 5m W of
Llynclys Xrds.* Home-made teas.
**Adm £4, chd free. Sun 21 June
(12-5).**
Approx 4 acre formal terraced garden
on 3 levels, designed and laid out in
late C17 and early C18. Unusual
herbaceous plants, sunken rose
garden, small water garden, walled
kitchen garden and woodland walk.

21 THE OLD RECTORY, LLANFIHANGEL GLYN MYFYR

Corwen LL21 9UN. Mr & Mrs E T
Hughes. *2¹/₂ m NE of Cerrigydrudion.
From Ruthin take B5105 SW for 12m
to Llanfihangel Glyn Myfyr. Turn R just
after Crown PH (follow signs).
Proceed for ¹/₃ m, garden on L.*
Home-made teas. **Adm £3.50, chd
free. Share to Cancer Research
U.K. Sun 10 May (2-5).**
Garden of approx 1 acre set in
beautiful, tranquil, sheltered valley. A
garden for all seasons; hellebores;
abundance of spring flowers; mixed

borders; water, bog, and gravel
gardens; walled garden with old
roses, pergola, bower and garden of
meditation. Also hardy orchids,
gentians, daffodils, rhododendrons
and acers. Partial wheelchair access
in places.

22 PEN Y GRAIG BACH

Tremeirchion, St Asaph LL17 0UR.
Roger Pawling & Christine Hoyle,
07875 642270,
rogerpawling@gmail.com. *4m SE of
St Asaph. Off A55 take J28/29/30 to
Tremeirchion, then B5429 to Bodfari,
go 0.7m (wide verge), turn L up hill, L
at fork, cont to rd end. From Bodfari
take B5429 take 2nd R (after 1¹/₄ m).*
Tea and biscuits. **Adm £3, chd free.
Visitors welcome by arrangement
Apr to Oct.**
¹/₂ acre wildlife friendly rural cottage
garden. Box hedges and fruit trees
enclose 5 plots of herbaceous
perennials, unusual climbers,
flowering shrubs, soft fruit and
vegetables. Over 200 native and
ornamental trees. Succession of
colour throughout the yr. 4 ponds and
2 acres of paddocks which are
managed organically for wild flowers

and hay. Beehives. Stunning views
from sea to mountains. Partial
wheelchair access, gravel paths
between box hedges and grass
paths.

23 PENLLWYN

Penllwyn, Graigfechan, Ruthin
LL15 2EU. Malcolm & Ann Ingham.
*4m S of Ruthin. From Ruthin take
A525 to Llanfair D.C. then L opp
village School, turn R onto B5429 to
Graigfechan & the Three Pigeons Inn
car park. Walk back through village to
Penllwyn.* **Adm £3.50, chd free. Sun
5 July (12-4).**
1 acre of terraced garden and
woodland managed for wildlife with
spectacular views over the Vale of
Clwyd. Sloping lawns, flower beds,
vegetables, water feature, ponds and
area of woodland all accessed by
meandering paths and steps. Uneven
paths and steep steps. Various bird
and bat boxes and bird feeding
station plus 2 Austin Seven cars and
a 1950 Series 1 Land Rover all add
interest to the visit.

GROUP OPENING

24 RUTHIN TOWN GARDENS

Ruthin LL16 4HP. *Tickets & maps
available at 46 Mwrog St on A494 &
Ruthin Castle in centre of town. Park
at one of the many car parks &
maybe move car to street parking for
153 Mwrog St.* Teas at Nantclwyd y
Dre. **Combined adm £5, chd free.**
Sun 28 June (11-5).

BERWYN
Susan Evans

14 CAE SEREN
Mrs Angela Carrington-Roberts

46 MWROG STREET
Glenna & David Toyne
Visitors also welcome by
arrangement June and July.
01824 707470

153 MWROG STREET
Mrs Hazel Moseley

NANTCLWYD Y DRE
Denbighshire County Council

NEW **6 PARK ROAD**
Mr & Mrs Glyn Jones

RUTHIN CASTLE
Ruthin Castle Ltd
01824 702664
reservations@ruthincastle.co.uk

The beautiful medieval town of Ruthin offers 7 contrasting gardens, ranging from the large garden of Ruthin Castle, surrounded by ancient walls and picturesque grounds, to the tiny town garden at Berwyn, created exclusively with the clever use of a large variety of potted shrubs and plants. Between these two gardens is Nantclwyd y Dre, one of the oldest timbered town house in Wales where teas are available and the restoration of the Lords garden may be seen. 14 Cae Seren behind the Fire Station, is small town garden which is full of plants, trees, vegetables and even a small pond to encourage frogs. 6 Park Rd is a new garden which can be found along the entry by the Chinese takeaway on Denbigh Rd. There are two gardens on Mwrog St. Be amazed by No 46 which has been created by a real plantswoman behind her terraced cottage and further out is 153 Mwrog St, a mature cottage garden with good views over Ruthin Town where many plants have been home propagated.

25 90 ST PETERS PARK

Northop CH7 6YU. Mr P Hunt. *3m N of Mold, 3m S of Flint. Leave A55 at Northop exit J33. Opp cricket ground, turn R. Take 5th turning on R. Garden on R.* Home-made teas. **Adm £3, chd free. Sat 30 May (2-5).**
Garden planted by professional botanist and horticulturalist, Custos Hortorum at Chester Cathedral and creator of Cloister Garth, Cheshire Garden of Distinction. A plantsman's garden with exotic and rare species of trees and ornamental plants. Unique garden cruck house with sedum roof, beamed ceilings, stained glass windows and inglenook fireplace. Other interesting timber framed structures.

26 TAL-Y-BRYN FARM

Llannefydd, Denbigh LL16 5DR. Mr & Mrs Gareth Roberts, 01745 540256, llaeth@villagedairy.co.uk, www.villagedairy.co.uk. *3m W of Henllan. From Henllan take rd signed Llannefydd. After 2¹/₂ m turn R signed Bont Newydd. Garden ¹/₂ m on L.* Tea. **Adm £4, chd free. Share to Elderly Committee of Llannefydd.**
Visitors welcome by arrangement Apr to Sept. Tours of the yoghurt dairy may also be booked.
Medium sized working farmhouse

cottage garden. Ancient farm machinery. Incorporating ancient privy festooned with honeysuckle, clematis and roses. Terraced arches, sunken garden pool and bog garden, fountains and old water pumps. Herb wheels, shrubs and other interesting features. Lovely views of the Clwydian range. Water feature, new rose tunnel, vegetable tunnel and small garden summer house.

We're not the average caravan park and we are sure you will be pleasantly surprised . . .

27 TREE TOPS CARAVAN PARK

Tanlan Hill, Tanlan, Ffynnongroyw, Holywell CH8 9JP. Andrew Walker, 01745 560279, www.treetopscaravanpark.co.uk. *300yds off A548 main coast rd between Flint & Prestatyn.* Light refreshments. **Adm £5, chd free. Sun 5, Mon 6 July (11-5.30).**
Visitors also welcome by arrangement.
We have 11 acres of manicured gardens, each yr we plant around 15,000 bedding plants, many of which we grow on in our own greenhouses. In addition to the bedding plants we have tens of thousands of trees and shrubs. Our gardens have won Wales in Bloom for the last 21yrs. We're not the average caravan park and we are sure you will be pleasantly surprised. We are on a sloping site, but much of the park is accessible to wheelchairs.

28 TUDOR COTTAGE

Isallt Road, Llysfaen, Colwyn Bay LL29 8LJ. Mr & Mrs C Manifold, 01492 518510. *1¹/₂ m SE of Old Colwyn. Turn S off A547 between*

Llandulas & Old Colwyn. Up Highlands Rd for ¹/₂ m, R onto Tan-y-Graig, ignore SatNav, ³/₄ m to swings. Take Isallt Rd on far R. Home-made teas. **Adm £4, chd free. Sat 27, Sun 28 June (2-5). Visitors also welcome by arrangement. Refreshments by request only when booking.**
³/₄ acre garden on different levels set amongst natural rock faces. Unusual and varied planting featuring cottage, scree, Japanese, shade and bog gardens. Display bedding, an abundance of colourful pots and baskets, together with quirky statues, ponds, bridges and a folly. Lovely views from upper level. Some uneven paths and steep steps. Care required. Children must be supervised by an adult at all times please.

29 TYDDYN BACH

Bontuchel, Ruthin LL15 2DG. Mr & Mrs L G Starling, 01824 710248, les.starling@boyns.net. *4m W of Ruthin. B5105 from Ruthin. R at Cross Keys PH to Cyffilliog. Through Bontuchel, 400yds, L up hill before chevron signs. White house on L. Limited parking.* **Adm £3, chd free.**
Visitors welcome by arrangement July to Aug for individuals and groups 25 max.
Mainly organic, very pretty cottage garden with prolific vegetable garden. Wildlife friendly with hedges and wood pile. Greenhouse packed with plants for both pots and the garden. Small wildlife pond completed in May 2010 and small stumpery completed 2012. Excellent views of surrounding countryside. Hoping to extend the project by purchasing small part of adjacent field.

30 WYLAN

Llangynhafal, Ruthin LL15 1RU. John & Carol Perkins, 07713 163652. *3m N of Ruthin. Take A494 from Ruthin to Llanbedr then B5429. After ¹/₂ m turn R signed Llangynhafal 1¹/₂ m.* **Adm £3, chd free. Visitors welcome by arrangement** May to July max 20 people.
1 acre garden designed by owners for all parts to be easily accessible. Magnificent panoramic views. Mature shrubs, mixed borders and water features. Pergola leading into sunken patio with colourful containers. Gradual grass slope at end of front garden to access back garden.

Treat yourself to a plant from the plant stall ✿

POWYS

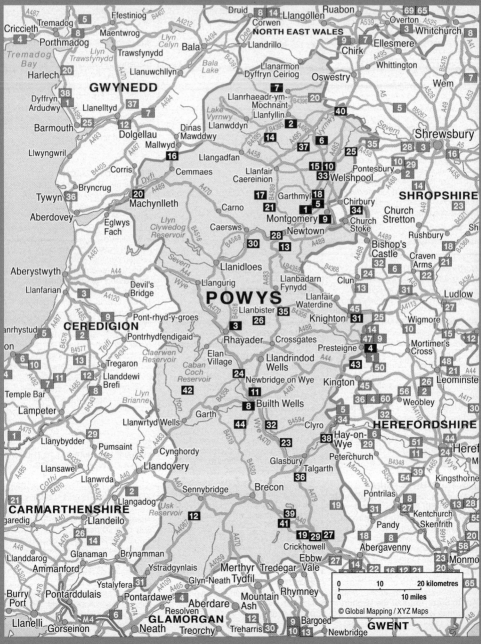

Powys

A three hour drive through Powys takes you through the spectacular and un-spoilt landscape of mid-Wales, from the Berwyn Hills in the north to south of the Brecon Beacons.

Through the valleys and over the hills, beside rippling rivers and wooded ravines, you will see a lot of sheep, pretty market towns, half timbered buildings and houses of stone hewn from the land.

The stunning landscape is home to many of the beautiful NGS gardens of Powys. Some are clustered around the eastern side of the county, where Wales meets the Marches. There are a few in town centres, and the rest, both large and small, are scattered through this agricultural paradise.

Powis Castle, whose 18th century Italian terraces set the gold standard for the other gardens, owes much of its wealth to the farming and mining in the area. The Dingle is world-renowned for the dark, still lake at the centre of fantastic planting.

Here in Powys is the spectacular, the unusual, the peaceful and the enchanting, all opened by generous and welcoming garden owners.

Powys Volunteers

North Powys

County Organiser
Christine Scott
01691 780080
christinemargaretscott@yahoo.com

County Treasurer
Gwyneth Jackson-Jones
01691 648578
gjacksonjones@btinternet.com

Publicity
Group Captain Neil Bale
01691 648451
info@cyfiefarm.co.uk

Booklet Coordinator
Susan Paynton
01686 650531
susanakeen@aol.co.uk

Assistant County Organisers
Penny Davies
01621 828373
digbydavies@aol.com

Susan Paynton
(as above)

South Powys

County Organiser
Katharine Smith
01982 551308
katharinejsmith@hotmail.co.uk

County Treasurer
Steve Carrow
01591 620461
stevetynycwm@hotmail.co.uk

Assistant County Organisers
Christine Carrow
01591 620461
stevetynycwm@hotmail.co.uk

Left: Treberfydd House

Since our foundation we have donated more than £42.5 million to charity

Opening Dates

All entries subject to change.
For latest information check www.ngs.org.uk

March

Sunday 22
21 Gregynog Hall & Garden

April

26 **Mill Cottage (every day)**
Monday 6
43 The Walled Garden
Sunday 12
25 Maesfron Hall and Gardens
Saturday 25
10 1 Church Bank
Sunday 26
10 1 Church Bank
29 Penmyarth House & Glanusk Estate

May

26 **Mill Cottage (every day)**
Saturday 2
37 Tan-y-Llyn
Sunday 3
32 Pontsioni House
37 Tan-y-Llyn
Friday 8
15 Dingle Nurseries & Garden
Saturday 9
15 Dingle Nurseries & Garden
18 Glansevern Hall Gardens
Sunday 10
18 Glansevern Hall Gardens
Saturday 16
34 Priest Weston Gardens
Sunday 17
19 Gliffaes Country House Hotel
34 Priest Weston Gardens

Saturday 23
4 **NEW** Broad Heath House
Sunday 24
8 Caer Beris Manor Hotel
41 Ty Cam
Monday 25
23 Llanstephan House
24 Llysdinam
Wednesday 27
20 Grandma's Garden
Saturday 30
4 **NEW** Broad Heath House
Sunday 31
17 Fraithwen
32 Pontsioni House

June

26 **Mill Cottage (every day)**

Festival Weekend

Saturday 6
4 **NEW** Broad Heath House
37 Tan-y-Llyn
45 **NEW** 1 Ystrad House
Sunday 7
21 Gregynog Hall & Garden
27 The Neuadd
35 The Rock House
37 Tan-y-Llyn
41 Ty Cam
42 Tyn y Cwm
43 The Walled Garden
45 **NEW** 1 Ystrad House
Saturday 13
7 Bryn y Llidiart
10 1 Church Bank
Sunday 14
7 Bryn y Llidiart
10 1 Church Bank
13 Cwm-Weeg
Saturday 20
31 Pont Faen House
34 Priest Weston Gardens
40 **NEW** Tremynfa
Sunday 21
16 Esgair Angell
31 Pont Faen House

33 Powis Castle Garden
34 Priest Weston Gardens
40 **NEW** Tremynfa
Saturday 27
38 Tinto House
Sunday 28
13 Cwm-Weeg
38 Tinto House
39 Treberfydd House

July

26 **Mill Cottage (every day)**
Saturday 4
36 **NEW** Talgarth Mill
37 Tan-y-Llyn
Sunday 5
2 Bachie Uchaf
28 Newtowns Gardens
36 **NEW** Talgarth Mill
37 Tan-y-Llyn
Saturday 18
6 **NEW** Broniarth Hall
Sunday 19
6 **NEW** Broniarth Hall
Saturday 25
44 Welsh Lavender
Sunday 26
13 Cwm-Weeg
17 Fraithwen
44 Welsh Lavender

August

26 **Mill Cottage (every day)**
Sunday 2
3 **NEW** Beili Neuadd
Saturday 8
45 **NEW** 1 Ystrad House
Sunday 9
12 Crai Gardens
42 Tyn y Cwm
45 **NEW** 1 Ystrad House
Saturday 15
37 Tan-y-Llyn (Evening)
Sunday 23
41 Ty Cam (Evening)
Sunday 30
13 Cwm-Weeg

September

26 **Mill Cottage (every day)**

Sunday 6
31 Pont Faen House

October

Saturday 10
15 Dingle Nurseries & Garden
Sunday 11
15 Dingle Nurseries & Garden

Gardens open to the public

15 Dingle Nurseries & Garden
18 Glansevern Hall Gardens
20 Grandma's Garden
21 Gregynog Hall & Garden
33 Powis Castle Garden
44 Welsh Lavender

By arrangement only

1 Abernant
5 Bron Hafren
9 Castell y Gwynt
11 **NEW** The Cider House
14 Cyfie Farm
30 **NEW** Plas Dinam

Also open by arrangement

3 **NEW** Beili Neuadd
4 **NEW** Broad Heath House
7 Bryn y Llidiart
10 1 Church Bank
17 Fraithwen
24 Llysdinam
28 Glynderyn, Newtowns Gardens
34 Chapel House, Priest Weston Gardens
34 Quarry House, Priest Weston Gardens
37 Tan-y-Llyn
38 Tinto House
42 Tyn y Cwm
43 The Walled Garden
45 **NEW** 1 Ystrad House

And to complete your Sunday afternoon, come and enjoy the renowned hospitality of the Crai ladies by sampling their delicious home-made cakes . . .

Over 400 Volunteers help run the NGS – why not become one too?

The Gardens

1 ABERNANT

Garthmyl SY15 6RZ. **J A & B M Gleave, 01686 640494, john.gleave@mac.com.** *On A483 midway between Welshpool & Newtown (both 8m). 1½ m S of Garthmyl. Approached over steep humpback bridge, then straight ahead through gate. No parking for coaches.* Home-made teas. **Adm £3.50, chd free. Visitors welcome by arrangement** Apr to July. Approx 3 acres incl cherry orchard, roses, knot garden, lavender, box hedging, rockery, pond, shrubs, ornamental trees, raised specimen fern beds in natural setting. Examples of archaic sundials, fossilised wood and stone heads. Additional woodland of 9 acres, pond and stream with borrowed views of the Severn Valley. Late April - 90 cherry trees blossom: late June - roses. Picnics welcome.

2 BACHIE UCHAF

Bachie Road, Llanfyllin SY22 5NF. **Glyn & Glenys Lloyd.** *S of Llanfyllin. Going towards Welshpool on A490 turn R onto Bachie Rd after Llanfyllin primary school. Keep straight for 0.8m. Take drive R uphill at cottage on L.* Home-made teas. **Adm £4, chd free. Sun 5 July (2-5).** Inspiring, colourful hillside country garden. Gravel paths meander around extensive planting and over streams cascading down into ponds. Specimen trees, shrubs and vegetable garden. Enjoy the wonderful views from one of the many seats; your senses will be rewarded.

3 NEW BEILI NEUADD

St Harmon, Rhayader LD6 5NS. **Alison Parker, 01597 810211, info@beilineuadd.co.uk, www.beilneuadd.co.uk.** *2m from Rhayader. Rhayader (approx 2m) Take A44 E from clock tower. Leaving Rhayader fork L (Abbey-Cwm-Hir, Brown sign Beili Neuadd). After 1m turn L (brown sign). Beili Neuadd 2nd property on R.* **Adm £3, chd free. Sun 2 Aug (2-5). Visitors also welcome by arrangement May to Aug.** 2 acre garden set within a 6 acre small holding. Established ponds, trees and stunning landscape, set in

1 Church Bank

the foothills of the Cambrian Mountains, provides the framework for an exciting, evolving garden with herbaceous borders, ponds, streams and wooded areas. A haven for birds and wildlife along with our flock of Shetland sheep, rare breed pigs and hens.

4 NEW BROAD HEATH HOUSE

Broadheath, Presteigne LD8 2HG. **Andrea Jude, 07887 556419, apange@aol.com.** *2m E of Presteigne, 4m W of Shobdon on B4362. From W turn R into drive opp middle of common. From E, 30 seconds after sign for Wales turn L into drive.* Home-made teas. **Adm £3.50, chd free. Sat 23, Sat 30 May (10.30-5.30); Sat 6 June (10-1). Visitors also welcome by arrangement May to Aug.** Two acres of formal landscaped gardens, originally designed by Sir Clough Williams Ellis in 1925. Garden divided into distinct rooms: the italianate sunken garden with loggia, rose beds and lilly ponds; the secret garden or well garden with magnolia tree and yew hedging; yew tree walkway with summerhouse and formal kitchen garden with orchard and peach house. Featured in Mid Wales Journal. Refreshments on the loggia overlooking sunken garden. Some steps into sunken garden but can be fully enjoyed from the loggia.

5 BRON HAFREN

Garthmyl, Montgomery SY15 6RT. **John & Marilyn, 01686 640106, mbedworth@googlemail.com.** *By Caerhowel bridge over R Severn, A483 between Welshpool & Newtown. Opp Nags Head turn onto B4835 to Montgomery. 700 metres park in paddock opp turn to Argae Hall Caravan Park. Enter garden through paddock gate.* Cream teas in timber barn. **Adm £4, chd free. Visitors welcome by arrangement Apr to Sept for small or large groups.** 1½ acre mature garden on banks of R Severn. Access from the lawn to further ¾ acre riverside woodland area (uneven) with view of ornate bridge. Surrounding the Victorian house is an orchard, mixed borders, shrubbery, spinney and large redwood. Gravelled area with chicken enclosure, raised vegetable beds, fruit cage, polytunnel, greenhouse, potting shed and outbuildings incl original Ty Bach. Uneven surface in paddock parking area. Wheelchair access to refreshments over gravel.

6 NEW BRONIARTH HALL

Pentrebeirdd, Guilsfield, Welshpool SY21 9DW. Mrs Janet Powell. *From Londis petrol station, Guilsfield, take A490 towards Llanfyllin for just over 2m. Take R towards Sarnau. After 1m turn R for Broniarth Hall.* Home-made teas. **Adm £3.50, chd free. Sat 18 July (2-6); Sun 19 July (2-5).** Broniarth Hall is a C17 farm house (not open) SE facing cottage style garden with 2 small ponds, aviary and perennial filled beds. Unique and quirky features and containers incl a collection of approx 70 heucheras. Stunning views to be appreciated from patio areas with summer bedding and foliage plants.

7 BRYN Y LLIDIART

Cefn Coch, Llanrhaeadr ym Mochnant, Oswestry SY10 0BP. Dr John & Mrs Christine Scott, 01691 780080, christinemargaretscott@yahoo. com. *2m W of Llanrhaeadr. From Llanrhaeadr take rd W uphill towards Penybontfawr, 1/2 m turn R at Bitfel, onto single track rd, follow yellow NGS signs for 1m.* Home-made teas. **Adm £4, chd free. Sat 13, Sun 14 June (2-5).** Visitors also welcome by arrangement May to Aug. Exposed hillside garden in S facing lee of the Berwyns with breathtaking views. Lush planting around the longhouse and contemporary extension merges into wildflower meadows. Dry stone walls, slate, shale and large erratic boulders reflect the landscape beyond. Meander mown paths to view a biodiverse roof, sitouterie, bog garden, new pond, welsh fruit orchard and vegetable garden in unique surroundings. Good footwear required. Partial wheelchair access, shale and rough grass paths, some steps.

8 CAER BERIS MANOR HOTEL

Builth Wells LD2 3NP. Mr Peter & Mrs Katharine Smith, 01982 552601, caerberis@btconnect.com, www.caerberis.com. *W edge Builth Wells. From Builth Wells town centre take A483 signed Llandovery. Caer Beris Manor is on L as you leave Builth.* Home-made teas. **Adm £3.50, chd free. Sun 24 May (11-5).** An original 1927 NGS pioneer garden. 27 acres of mature parklands, with the R Irfon bordering

the property. The grounds were planted early C20 by the Vivien family who were plant hunters. Many varied specimen trees form an Arboretum. Large displays of rhododendrons at time of opening. An Edwardian Rose archway has been recently replanted with David Austin roses. Concert by Builth Wells Ladies Voice Choir. Sunday lunches and afternoon teas available. Lower parkland can be accessed by car or wheelchair.

Parkinson's UK are proud to be the NGS guest charity

9 CASTELL Y GWYNT

Llandyssil, Montgomery SY15 6HR. John & Jacqui Wynn-Jones, 01686 668569, jacquiwj@btinternet.com. *2m out of Montgomery on the Sarn Rd, 1st R, 1st R.* Home-made teas. **Adm £5, chd free.** Visitors welcome by arrangement May to July prior booking necessary as parking limited. 1½ acre garden at 900ft, set within 6 acres of land managed for wildlife. Native woodland corridors with mown rides surround hayfield/wild flower meadow and pool with turf roofed summerhouse. Enclosed kitchen garden with boxed beds of vegetables, fruit and cutting flowers, greenhouse and orchard. Shrubberies, deep mixed borders and more formal areas close to house. Outstanding views of Welsh mountains. Circular path around the whole property which gives unique views of the house, garden and surrounding countryside. Bring good footwear and enjoy the walk.

10 1 CHURCH BANK

Welshpool SY21 7DR. Mel & Heather Parkes, 01938 559112, melandheather@live.co.uk. *Centre of Welshpool. Church Bank leads onto Salop Rd from Church St.*

Follow one way system & use Main Car Park then short walk - follow yellow NGS signs. Home-made teas. **Adm £3, chd free. Sat 25, Sun 26 Apr, Sat 13, Sun 14 June (12-5).** Visitors also welcome by arrangement Apr to Sept min group 6. A jewel in the town, Gothic arch over a zig zag path leads to exotic arbours in the intimate rear garden of an old town house. Sounds of water fill the air and interesting plants fill the outdoor space. Inside garden room well established with mystic pool with smoking dragons. Shell grotto with water feature and sitting area. Children's garden quiz. Featured in Garden News.

11 NEW THE CIDER HOUSE

Llanelwedd, Builth Wells LD2 3TF. Pippa Tee, 07546 888406, pippatee@hotmail.com, www.pencerrigplants.com. *3m NW of Builth Wells. NW, A470, towards Rhayader. R at Cwmbach sign. R just before railway bridge. 1st R up No Through Rd. Follow track to end, The Cider House is on the R.* Home-made teas. **Adm £2, chd 50p.** Visitors welcome by arrangement Apr to Oct. Limited parking at garden. 1½ acres of rocky, wooded hillside, terraces, bog gardens and ponds. There are about 1000 different plant species with everything from mature trees to unusual shrubs and perennials, and masses of wildflowers in Spring. The garden has been created single handedly over the last 7yrs, and work is ongoing. Please note that the slopes are fairly steep with many steps! Fantastic views of the Welsh countryside and hills (weather permitting). Formerly part of the Pencerrig estate, built and owned by Thomas Jones (Welsh artist) in the1700's. Choice of teas, coffee, home-made cold drinks, cake or biscuits.

12 CRAI GARDENS

Crai LD3 8YP. *13m SW of Brecon. Turn W off A4067 signed Crai. Village hall is 50yds straight ahead; park here for admission & information about gardens.* Home-made teas in village hall. **Combined adm £5, chd free. Sun 9 Aug (2-6).** Set against the backdrop of Fan Gyhirych and Fan Brycheiniog, at 1000ft above sea level the Crai valley is a hidden gem, off the beaten track

between Brecon and Swansea. Those in the know have long enjoyed visiting our serene valley, with its easy access to the hills and its fabulous views. In difficult climatic conditions, the Crai Gardens reflect a true passion for gardening. The gardens come in a wide variety of size, purpose and design, and incl: a range of shrubs, perennials and annuals; organically grown vegetables and fruits; raised beds; polytunnels; water features; prolific hanging baskets, patio containers and window boxes. Not to forget the chickens and ducks. And to complete your Sunday afternoon, come and enjoy the renowned hospitality of the Crai ladies by sampling their delicious home-made cakes in the village hall.

13 CWM-WEEG
Dolfor, Newtown SY16 4AT. Dr W Schaefer & Mr K D George. *4½ m SE of Newtown. Take A489 E from Newtown for 1½ m, turn R towards Dolfor. After 2m turn L down farm track, signed at entrance. N.B. Do not rely on SatNav. Also signed from Dolfor.* Home-made teas. **Adm £4, chd free. Suns 14, 28 June, 26 July, 30 Aug (1-5).**
2½ acre garden set within 24 acres of wild flower meadows and bluebell woodland with stream centred around C15 farmhouse (open by prior arrangement). Formal garden in English landscape tradition with vistas, grottos, lawns and extensive borders terraced with stone walls, translates older garden vocabulary into an innovative C21 concept. Under cover area for refreshments if wet. Often featured in press and on TV. Partial wheelchair access.

14 CYFIE FARM
Llanfihangel, Llanfyllin SY22 5JE. Group Captain Neil & Mrs Claire Bale, 01691 648451, info@cyfiefarm.co.uk, www.cyfiefarm.co.uk. *6m SE of Lake Vyrnwy. ½ m N Llanfyllin on B490 turn L B4393 towards L Vrynwy. 4m turn L B4382 signed Llanfihangel go straight through, 1½ m, 1st L, 3rd on L.* Tea. **Adm £4, chd free. Visitors welcome by arrangement Mar to Oct. Min 48hrs notice normally required. Nibbles, wine, tea or coffee on request.**
Beautiful 1 acre hillside garden with spectacular views of Vyrnwy valley

and Welsh hills. Linger over the roses or wander through the woodland garden with rhododendrons and bluebell banks. Many places to sit and contemplate the stunning views. Wild flower meadow and garden sculptures. Unusual garden statues. Spectacular Views, Peaceful setting. Partial wheelchair access.

Linger over the roses or wander through the woodland garden . . .

15 ◆ DINGLE NURSERIES & GARDEN
Welshpool SY21 9JD. Mr & Mrs D Hamer, 01938 555145, www.dinglenurseries.co.uk. *2m NW of Welshpool. Take A490 towards Llanfyllin & Guilsfield. After 1m turn L at sign for Dingle Nurseries & Garden.* **Adm £3.50, chd free. For NGS: Fri 8, Sat 9 May, Sat 10, Sun 11 Oct (9-5). For other opening times and information, please phone or see garden website.**
RHS recommended 4½ acre garden on S facing site, sloping down to lakes surrounded by yr-round interest. Beds mostly colour themed with a huge variety of rare and unusual trees, ornamental shrubs and herbaceous plants. Set in hills of mid Wales this beautiful and well known garden attracts visitors from Britain and abroad. Open all yr except 24 Dec - 2 Jan.

16 ESGAIR ANGELL
Aberangell, Machynlleth SY20 9QJ. Carole Jones, www.upperbarncottage.co.uk. *Midway between Dogellau & Machynlleth. Turn off A470 towards village of Aberangell, then signed.* Home-made teas. **Adm £4, chd free. Sun 21 June (11-5).**
The garden extends to over 2 acres just above the R Angell, within the

Dovey Forest and Snowdonia National Park. Around the central lake, which supports an abundance of plant and animal life, is a small wood, a wildlife meadow, vegetable garden and the aviaries that house our families of owls. New for 2015 - a second lake and a circular walk through the neighbouring fields with spectacular views. Partial wheelchair access, mainly laid to lawn. Access on gravelled area above lake affording excellent views.

17 FRAITHWEN
Tregynon SY16 3EW. Sydney Thomas, 01686 650307. *6m N of Newtown. On B4389 midway between villages of Bettws Cedewain & Tregynon.* Home-made teas. **Adm £3, chd free. Sun 31 May, Sun 26 July (2-6). Visitors also welcome by arrangement Feb to Oct.**
1½ acre established garden with herbaceous borders, rockeries and ponds. Planted with rare plants for yr-round interest. Newly established vegetable plot. Plants in flower every day of the year - spring bulbs and alpines - Alstroemaria collection. Lilies in garden not pots. Partial wheelchair access. Some steps, gravel and slopes.

18 ◆ GLANSEVERN HALL GARDENS
Berriew, Welshpool SY21 8AH. The Owen Family, 01686 640644, www.glansevern.co.uk. *5m SW of Welshpool. On A483 towards Newtown, clearly marked on Brown tourist signs.* Light refreshments. **Adm £7, chd £3.50. For NGS: Sat 9, Sun 10 May (10.30-5). For other opening times and information, please phone or see garden website.**
Beautiful Greek revival house (not open) set in mature parkland with rare and ancient trees. 25 acres of gardens incl walled garden of rooms, vegetable garden, original potting shed, Victorian grotto and orangery. Wysteria scented fountain walk, 4 acre lake with shady seating areas, folly island and wildfowl. Birdhide on banks of R Severn & R Rhiw. The Potting Shed Cafe and Chic Shed Shop open 10.30am - 5pm. Tues - Sat and BH Mons. Steep bridge at end of lake inaccessible for wheelchairs.

Glansevern Hall Gardens

19 ▸ GLIFFAES COUNTRY HOUSE HOTEL

Gliffaes Rd, Crickhowell NP8 1RH. Mrs N Brabner and Mr & Mrs J C Suter, 01874 730 371, calls@gliffaeshotel.com, www.gliffaes.com. *3¹/₂ m W of Crickhowell. 1m off A40, 2¹/₂ m W of Crickhowell.* Cream teas. **Adm £4, chd free. Sun 17 May (2-6).**
The Gliffaes gardens lie in a dream position on a plateau 120ft above the spectacular fast flowing R Usk. As well as breath taking views of the Brecon Beacons and 33 acres of parkland and lawns there are ancient and ornamental trees, fine maples, new tree plantings, spring bulbs, rhododendrons, azaleas, many shrubs and an ornamental pond. Gliffaes is a country house hotel and is open for lunch, bar snacks, afternoon tea and dinner to non residents and garden visitors. Wheelchair ramp at entrance of hotel. In dry weather main lawns accessible, but more difficult if wet.

20 ▸ ◆ GRANDMA'S GARDEN

Dolguog Estates, Felingerrig, Machynlleth SY20 8UJ. Diana & Richard Rhodes, 01654 702244, info@plasdolguog.co.uk, www.plasdolguog.co.uk/grandmasgarden.htm. *1¹/₂ m E of Machynlleth. Turn L off A489 Machynlleth to Newtown rd. Follow brown tourist signs to Plas Dolguog Hotel.* Cream teas. **Adm £4, chd £1.50. For NGS: Wed 27 May (10.30-4.30). For other opening times and information, please phone or see garden website.**
Inspiration for the senses, unique, fascinating, educational and fun. Strategic seating, continuous new attractions, wildlife abundant, 9 acres of peace. Sculptures, poetry arboretum. Seven sensory gardens, wildlife pond, riverside boardwalk, stone circle, labyrinth. Azaleas and bluebells in May. Children welcome. Open every Sun & Wed (10.30-4.30). Plas Dolguog Hotel open their café in the conservatory - the hotel is the admission point - serving inside and out on patio overlooking gardens.

21 ▸ ◆ GREGYNOG HALL & GARDEN

Tregynon, Newtown SY16 3PW. Gregynog, 01686 650224, www.gregynog.org. *5m N of Newtown. From main A483, take turning for Berriew. In Berriew follow sign for Bettws then for Tregynon (£2.50 car parking charge applies).* Home-made teas at Courtyard Cafe. **Adm £3, chd £1. For NGS: Sun 22 Mar, Sun 7 June (11-4). For other opening times and information, please phone or see garden website.**
Grade I listed garden set within 750 acres of Gregynog Estate which was designated a National Nature Reserve in 2013. Fountains, lily lake and water garden. A mass display of rhododendrons and yew hedge create a spectacular backdrop to the sunken lawns. Thousands of daffodils in Spring. Courtyard café serving morning coffee, light lunches and Welsh afternoon teas. Some gravel paths.

23 ▸ LLANSTEPHAN HOUSE

Llanstephan, nr Llyswen, Powys LD3 0YR. Lord & Lady Milford. *10m SW of Builth Wells. Leave A470 at Llyswen onto B4350. 1st L after crossing river in Boughrood. From Builth Wells leave A470, Erwood Bridge, 1st L. Follow signs.* Home-made teas. **Adm £3, chd free. Mon 25 May (1-5).**
Large garden with rhododendrons, azaleas, shrubs, water garden, shrub roses, walled kitchen garden, greenhouses and very fine specimen trees. Beautiful views of Wye Valley and Black Mountains.

24 LLYSDINAM

Newbridge-on-Wye LD1 6NB. Sir John & Lady Venables-Llewelyn & Llysdinam Charitable Trust, 01597 860190, elster@f2s.com. *5m SW of Llandrindod Wells. Turn W off A470 at Newbridge-on-Wye; turn R immed after crossing R Wye; entrance up hill.* Cream teas. **Adm £3, chd free. Mon 25 May (2-5).** Visitors also welcome by arrangement.
Llysdinam Gardens are among the loveliest in Mid Wales, especially noted for a magnificent display of rhododendrons and azaleas in May. Covering some 6 acres in all, they command sweeping views down the Wye Valley. Successive family members have developed the gardens over the last 150yrs to incl woodland with specimen trees, large herbaceous and shrub borders and a water garden, all of which provide varied and colourful planting throughout the yr. The Victorian walled kitchen garden and extensive greenhouses grow a wide variety of vegetables, hothouse fruit, and exotic plants. Gravel paths.
♿ 🏋 ❉ 🚐 ☕

An exciting walk through the jungle in Newtown . . . !

25 MAESFRON HALL AND GARDENS

Trewern, Welshpool SY21 8EA. Dr & Mrs TD Owen, www.maesfron.co.uk. *4m E of Welshpool. On N side of A458 Welshpool to Shrewsbury Rd.* Tea. **Adm £4, chd free. Sun 12 Apr (2-5).**
Georgian house (partly open) built in Italian villa style set in 4 acres of S facing gardens on lower slopes of Moel-y-Golfa with panoramic views of The Long Mountain. Terraces, walled kitchen garden, tropical garden, restored Victorian conservatories, tower and shell grotto. Woodland and parkland walks with wide variety of trees. Some gravel, steps and slopes.
♿ 🏋 ☕

26 MILL COTTAGE

Abbeycwmhir LD1 6PH. Mr & Mrs B D Parfitt, 01597 851935, nkmillcottage@yahoo.co.uk, www.abbeycwmhir.co.uk. *8m N of Llandrindod Wells. Turn L off A483 1m N of Crossgates r'about, then 3½m on L, signed Abbeycwmhir. Limited parking.* Tea. **Adm £3, chd free. Daily Wed 1 Apr to Wed 30 Sept (12-6).**
⅓ acre stream side garden in spectacular valley setting on the Glyndwr Way, consisting mainly of mature, rare and unusual trees and shrubs, particularly interesting to the plantsman. Rockery with numerous ericaceous plants and interesting water feature. Beautiful church and Abbey ruins nearby on a national trail - Glyndwr's Way.
❉ 🛌 ☕

27 THE NEUADD

Llanbedr, Nr Crickhowell NP8 1SP. Robin & Philippa Herbert. *1m NE of Crickhowell. Leave Crickhowell by Llanbedr Rd. At junction with Great Oak Rd bear L, cont up hill for approx 1m, garden on L. Ample parking.* Home-made teas. **Adm £4.50, chd free. Sun 7 June (2-6).**
Robin and Philippa Herbert have worked on the restoration of the garden at The Neuadd since 1999 and have planted a wide range of unusual trees and shrubs in the dramatic setting of the Brecon Beacons National Park. One of the major features is the walled garden, which has both traditional and decorative planting of fruit, vegetables and flowers. There is also a woodland walk with ponds, streams and a formal garden with flowering terraces. Water and spectacular views. The owner uses a wheelchair and most of the garden is accessible, but some steep paths.
♿ 🏋 ❉ ☕

GROUP OPENING

28 NEWTOWNS GARDENS

Newtown SY16 3HD. *½ m W of Newtown. Glynderyn: on B4568 Newtown to Aberhafesp rd, 1st gate past Dolerw Park Drive. Bryn Teg: Lane on L before hosp on Llanfair Rd towards Bettws Cedewain.* Home-made teas at Glynderyn. **Combined adm £4, chd free. Sun 5 July (2-5).**

NEW ▶ **BRYN TEG**
Dolly Childs

GLYNDERYN
Janet & Frank Podmore
Visitors also welcome by arrangement Apr to Sept max group 20. Refreshments by request.
01686 626745

Glynderyn: Lovingly restored ¼ acre garden complements 1965 bungalow featuring curved pergola for wisterias. Perennials, alpines and shrubs in geometric beds begin the journey around the garden. Seating areas to appreciate the views across the valley. The plant enthusiast is rewarded by interesting plants in diverse areas including a pond. Bryn Teg: An exciting walk through the jungle in Newtown! High above the head are banana leaves and colourful climbers. An exotic garden planted to remind me of my childhood. A winding path from the front door around the side of the house to the back door takes you on a journey to another land. Wheelchair access and plants for sale at Glynderyn only.
♿ ❉ ☕

29 PENMYARTH HOUSE & GLANUSK ESTATE

The Glanusk Estate, Crickhowell NP8 1LP. Mrs Harry Legge-Bourke, 01873 810414, Robyn@glanuskestate.com, www.glanuskestate.com. *2m NW of Crickhowell. Please access open garden via main estate entrance off A40 & follow signs to car park.* Home-made teas. **Adm £6, chd free. Sun 26 Apr (11-4).**
The garden is adorned with many established plant species such as rhododendrons, azaleas, acers, camelias, magnolia, prunus and dogwood giving a vast array of colour in the spring and summer months. There will be exhibits of works for sale from some of the artists and craftsmen who live and work on the estate. These will incl bespoke furniture, hand turned wooden garden items, Welsh slateware, delicious preserves, home grown plants and architectural salvage items. There will also be a presentation of slides from the private archives in the family Rod Room throughout the day and the chapel will be open. (For more information on the garden please see our extended description or visit our website).
🏋 ❉ 🚐 🛌 ☕

30 NEW PLAS DINAM

Llandinam SY17 5DQ. Eldrydd Lamp, 07415 503554, eldrydd@plasdinam.co.uk, www.plasdinamcountryhouse.co.uk. *7¹/₂ m SW Newtown. On A470.* **Adm £4, chd free.** Visitors welcome by arrangement Mar to Oct for groups 10+ (ex school holidays).

12 acres of fabulous gardens, lawns and woodland set at the foot of glorious rolling hills with spectacular views across the Severn Valley. Parkland setting. Spring - lots of daffodils. May to July - wild flower meadows with wild orchids. Autumn - glorious colour. Until recently the home of Lord and Lady Davies and his predecessors since 1884 (not open).

31 PONT FAEN HOUSE

Farrington Lane, Knighton LD7 1LA. Mr John & Mrs Brenda Morgan. *S of Knighton off Ludlow Rd. W from Ludlow on A4113 into Knighton. 1st L after 20mph sign before school.* Home-made teas. **Adm £3.50, chd free. Sat 20, Sun 21 June, Sun 6 Sept (1-4.30).** Colourful ¹/₂ acre garden, full of flowers, surrounds house on edge of town. Paths through floriferous arches and gazebos lead from shady, ferny corners to deep borders filled with a large range of colourful perennials, annuals, 40 varieties of roses, rhododendrons, azaleas and hydrangeas. Water features and a fish pond. Enjoy the views of the hills

beyond from many seats in this flat garden. Featured Mid Wales Journal.

32 PONTSIONI HOUSE

Aberedw, Builth Wells LD2 3SQ. Mr & Mrs Jonathan Reeves. *5m SE of Builth Wells. On B4567 between Erwood Bridge & Aberedw on Radnorshire side of R Wye.* Home-made teas. **Adm £3, chd free. Sun 3, Sun 31 May (2.30-6).** With a background of old ruins and steep rocky woodland, this Wye Valley garden has been created mainly over the last 12yrs. Herbaceous and shrub borders, terraces and natural rockery merge with lawns, bluebell and young rhododendron bank. Walks through wildflower meadow along a mile of old railway line with bluebell woods and walks up to the Abeeredw Rocks. Spectacular rocky and woody situation. Extensive bluebells.

33 ◆ POWIS CASTLE GARDEN

Welshpool SY21 8RF. National Trust, 01938 551929, www.nationaltrust.org.uk. *1m S of Welshpool. From Welshpool take A490 S towards Newtown. After ³/₄ m turn R into Red Lane. Cont up lane for ¹/₄ m & turn R into property.* **Adm £9.60, chd £4.80. For NGS: Sun 21 June (10-4).** For other opening times and information, please phone or see garden website. Laid out in early C18 the garden features the finest remaining examples of Italian terraces in Britain.

Richly planted herbaceous borders; enormous yew hedges; lead statuary, Orangery and large wild flower areas. One of the NT's finest gardens. National Collection of *Laburnum.* Short introduction talks run throughout the day. Step free route around the garden, gravel paths, due to steep slopes only 4 wheeled PMV's permitted.

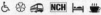

GROUP OPENING

34 PRIEST WESTON GARDENS

Priest Weston, Montgomery SY15 6DF. *Approx 4m E Montgomery. Follow signs to Priest Weston out of Churchstoke or Chirbury.* Home-made teas at Quarry House. **Combined adm £4.50, chd free. Sat 16, Sun 17 May, Sat 20, Sun 21 June (11-4.30).**

CHAPEL HOUSE
Mr & Mrs Andrew Craig
Visitors also welcome by arrangement Apr to Sept.
01938 561336
jaycraig@priestweston.com

QUARRY HOUSE ⊨
Roger & Christine Dixon
Visitors also welcome by arrangement May to Sept for groups 10 max (evenings preferred).
01938 561397
chris.rog.dixon@hotmail.co.uk

Quarry House stands in an elevated position with stunning views south

Welsh Lavender

towards the Kerry Ridgeway and west towards Snowdonia. The garden has evolved over 18yrs into a series of herbaceous borders, accessed by steep zigzagged grass paths and steps. A lower lawn is bordered by lilac trees. Higher up there is a wild flower meadow (harebells, lady's bedstraw) where you may picnic. Chapel House is an essentially wild cottage garden of approx 1 acre on a steep hillside. Several different terraces each with its own character incl kitchen garden, orchard, gravel garden, woodland area and meadow, gravel garden, cliff, borders and lawns. Spectacular views across valley to Montgomery and beyond. These gardens are not suitable for people who are unsure of foot. Featured in Shropshire Magazine.

35 THE ROCK HOUSE

Llanbister LD1 6TN. Jude Boutle & Sue Cox. *10m N of Llandrindod Wells. Off B4356 just above Llanbister village*. Home-made teas. Adm £4, chd free. Sun 7 June (2-5).

An acre of informal hillside garden at 1000ft, with sweeping views over Radnorshire Hills, managed using organic principles. The garden features hardy perennials and shrubs, raised beds, a walkway over a bog garden, dry shady border, fish and wildlife ponds, grazed bluebell meadow and a laburnum arch. Children's quiz to keep small people busy in the garden and meadow.

36 NEW TALGARTH MILL

The Square, Talgarth, Brecon LD3 0BW, www.talgarthmill.com. *In centre of Talgarth. Park in large free car park opp rugby club, turn L out of car park entrance, follow high st to end, cross bridge, the Mill is on your R.* Light refreshments. Adm £5, chd free. Sat 4, Sun 5 July (10-4).

A pretty riverside garden, maintained by volunteers. Along the riverside there is mixed herbaceous planting, a shady area, and steps up to a productive garden with espalier fruit trees, vegetables, soft fruits and a wildlife area. Places to sit and watch the river and its bird life (dippers, wagtails, kingfishers, herons) and the mill wheel turning. Garden is part of a working water mill. Tour explaining how we use water power to mill our

wide range of flours. Award winning café and bakery which champions local, seasonal produce, gourmet coffee and tea. Open 10am - 4pm. (Sorry, no credit/debit cards, cash only). Garden can be accessed by lift. Wide, flat paths for wheelchair access.

37 TAN-Y-LLYN

Meifod SY22 6YB. Callum Johnston & Brenda Moor, 01938 500370, admin@tanyllyn-nurseries.co.uk, www.tanyllyn-nursery.co.uk. *1m SE of Meifod. From Oswestry on A495 turn L in village, cross R Vyrnwy & climb hill for 1/2 m. From Welshpool on A490 look for Meifod sign on L just past Groesllwyd.* Home-made teas. Adm £3.50, chd free. Share to Meifod Eisteddfod Committee. Sat 2, Sun 3 May, Sat 6, Sun 7 June, Sat 4, Sun 5 July (2-5). Evening Opening £3.50, chd free, Light refreshments, Sat 15 Aug (6.30-8.30). Visitors also welcome by arrangement Apr to Oct.

The garden sits on the side of Broniarth Hill above the Vyrnwy Valley. Shrubs and perennials border the grass paths running along the contours: wild hedges are punctuated with porthole views before merging into the surrounding woodland. The garden hovers between clipped control and barely tamed nature. It is 550ft up, south facing and sheltered; the soil is well drained, slightly acid clay loam. 20yrs of summer events will be celebrated with an exhibition of Leafworks by Jennie Ashmore, acappella music by Nostalgia, and an Emporium and Gallery showcasing the works of past exhibitors. The season will culminate in an evening of words and music with the Rosemont Players and guests.

38 TINTO HOUSE

13 Broad Street, Hay-on-Wye HR3 5DB. John & Karen Clare, 01497 821556, tintohouse13@gmail.com, www.tinto-house.co.uk. *Tinto House faces the clocktower in the centre of Hay-on-Wye. Entrance to garden through the coach arch.* Home-made teas. Adm £3.50, chd free. Sat 27, Sun 28 June (2-6). Visitors also welcome by arrangement Apr to Sept.

Tinto House is a hidden treasure in Hay. Beyond the Georgian

townhouse lies an extensive traditional English garden overlooking the R Wye. It is divided into different rooms, each with its own character, featuring a wide range of plants incl climbing and shrub roses, clematis, hardy perennials and annuals. The vegetable garden is stocked with a wide range of soft fruit and vegetables. Art gallery. Home-made afternoon tea served in the garden. Wheelchair users may require some assistance as entrance is via a cobble courtyard.

Award winning café and bakery which champions local, seasonal produce . . .

39 TREBERFYDD HOUSE

Llangasty, Bwlch, Brecon LD3 7PX. David Raikes & Carla Rapoport, www.treberfydd.com. *6 1/2 m E of Brecon. From Abergavenny on A40, turn R in Bwlch on B5460. Take 1st turning L towards Pennorth & cont 2m along lane. From Brecon, turn L off A40 towards Pennorth in Llanhamlach.* Home-made teas. Adm £3.50, chd free. Sun 28 June (1-5.30).

Grade 1 listed Victorian Gothic house with 10 acres of grounds designed by W A Nesfield. Magnificent Cedar of Lebanon, avenue of mature Beech, towering Atlantic Cedars, Victorian rockery, herbaceous border and manicured lawns ideal for a picnic. Wonderful views of the Black Mountains. Plants available from Commercial Nursery in grounds - Walled Garden Treberfydd. House tours every half hour (additional £2), last tour 4pm.

Penmyarth House & Glanusk Estate

Join us on Facebook and spread the word

40 NEW TREMYNFA
Carreghofa Lane, Llanymynech
SY22 6LA. Jon & Gillian Fynes.
Edge of Llanymynech village. From N leave Oswestry on A483 to Welshpool. In Llanymynech turn R at Xrds (car wash on corner). Take 2nd R then follow NGS signs. House 300 metres, park on approach, limited disabled parking nr garden. Home-made teas. **Adm £4, chd free. Sat 20, Sun 21 June (10-4).**
S facing 1 acre garden developed over 8yrs. Old railway cottage set in herbaceous and raised borders, patio with many pots of colourful and unusual plants. Garden slopes down to productive fruit and vegetable area, ponds, spinney, wild areas and peat bog. Patio and seats to enjoy extensive views incl Llanymynech rocks and surrounding farmland. Pet ducks on site. Montgomery canal close by.

41 TY CAM
Talybont-on-Usk LD3 7JD. Harry & Ceri Chapman, 01874 676458, hcwoodturn@hotmail.com. *7m E of Brecon off A40. Garden next door to the White Hart PH! Also look out for mushrooms.* **Adm £2, chd free. Sun 24 May, Sun 7 June (2-6). Evening Opening £2, chd free, Sun 23 Aug (6-10).**
Small garden of secret surprises imaginatively created on three levels with steps built into an old railway embankment. Attractive features incl patios, decks, pergola, pond and waterfalls. Many choice herbaceous plants, trees and shrubs. Woodturning workshop, craft gallery and chickens!

42 TYN Y CWM
Beulah, Llanwrtyd Wells LD5 4TS. Steve & Christine Carrow, 01591 620461, stevetynycwm@hotmail.co.uk. *10m W of Builth Wells. On A483 at Beulah take rd towards Abergwesyn for 2m. Drive drops down to L.* Home-made teas. **Adm £3.50, chd free. Sun 7 June, Sun 9 Aug (2-5.30). Visitors also welcome by arrangement Apr to Sept.**
Garden mainly started 13yrs ago, lower garden has spring/woodland area, raised beds mixed with vegetables, fruit trees, fruit and flowers. Perennial borders, summer house gravel paths through rose and clematis pergola. Upper garden, partly sloped, incl bog, winter, water

gardens and perennial beds with unusual slate steps. Beautiful views. Property bounded by small river. Craft Stall. Lower garden has wide gravel mainly level paths. Upper garden is grassed with slopes and not suitable for wheelchairs.

43 THE WALLED GARDEN
Knill, nr Presteigne LD8 2PR. Dame Margaret Anstee, 01544 267411, agapanthus1@btinternet.com. *3m SW of Presteigne. B4362 Walton-Presteigne rd. In Knill village turn R over cattle grid, keep R down drive. SatNav stops short of property. Coaches park up hill by church.* Home-made teas in neighbouring garden, The Rose Garden. **Adm £3.50, chd free. Mon 6 Apr, Sun 7 June (2-5). Visitors also welcome by arrangement Jan to Oct. Refreshments by prior arrangement only.**
4 acres: walled garden; river, bog garden and small grotto; primulas; over 100 varieties of roses, shrub, modern and climbing; peonies; mixed and herbaceous borders; many varieties of shrubs and mature trees; lovely spring garden. Nr C13 church in beautiful valley. Most of main garden accessible to wheelchairs.

44 ◆ WELSH LAVENDER
Cefnperfedd Uchaf, Maesmynis, Builth Wells LD2 3HU. Nancy Durham & Bill Newton-Smith, 01982 552467, www.welshlavender.com. *Approx 4½ m S of Builth Wells & 12m from Brecon Cathedral off B4520.* Tea. **Adm £3.50, chd free. For NGS: Sat 25, Sun 26 July (10-7).** For other opening times and information, please phone or see garden website.
Our 10,000 lavenders grow high in the hills of mid Wales. Two varieties are purely decorative. A third, Grosso, is distilled on the farm to produce essential oil. At 1100 feet our growing season is short and challenging. Flower beds around the house are colourful and unpredictable. Spectacular views in all directions. Visitors are welcome to roam the lavender fields, see how the distillation process works, and visit the farm shop to try the body creams made with lavender oil distilled on the farm. 10% of sales go to the NGS. Coffee, tea, wine and light refreshments available. Featured in

House & Garden Magazine, Country Living, Country Homes and Interiors, Mail on Sunday You Magazine, Cambria, ITV's Countrywise with Ben Fogle, on BBC Radio and S4C. Partial wheelchair access. Large paved area adjacent to tea and shop area easy to negotiate.

45 NEW 1 YSTRAD HOUSE
1 Church Road, Knighton LD7 1EB. John & Margaret Davis, 01547 528 154, jamdavis@ystradhouse.plus.com. *At the junction of Church Road & Station Road. 225yds along Station Rd (488 Clun) opp Knighton Hotel. Yellow Hse at junction with Church Rd.* Home-made teas. **Adm £3.50, chd free. Sat 6, Sun 7 June, Sat 8, Sun 9 Aug (2-5.30). Visitors also welcome by arrangement Mar to Sept maximum 30.**
An unsuspected town garden hidden behind Ystrad House, a Regency villa of earlier origins. Developed over the last ten years with an emphasis on tranquillity and timelessness: having broad lawns and wide borders, mature trees and more intimate features adding interest and surprise. The formal areas merge with wooded glades leading to a riverside walk alongside the Teme. Lawns and gravelled paths mostly flat except access to riverside walk.

Early Openings 2016
Plan your garden visiting well ahead – put these dates in your 2016 diary!

Gardens across the country open from early January onwards – before the new Yellow Book is published – with glorious displays of colour including hellebores, aconites, snowdrops and carpets of spring bulbs.

Bedfordshire

Sun 31 January (2-4)
King's Arms Garden

Buckinghamshire

Sun 21 February (12-4)
Quainton Gardens

Cambridgeshire

Sun 28 February (11-4)
6 Robins Wood

Cumbria

Sun 21 February (11.30-4)
Summerdale House

Devon

Sun 7, Fri 19 February (2-5)
Cherubeer Gardens

Sat 6, Sun 7, Sat 13, Sun 14 February (12-3.30)
Little Cumbre

Essex

Sun 21 February (10-3)
Writtle College

Gloucestershire

Sun 31 January, Sun 14 February (11-3)
Home Farm

Sun 14, Sun 28 February (2-5)
Kempsford Manor

Sat 13, Sun 14 February (2-4)
Snowshill Manor & Garden

Sun 14, Sun 21 February (11-5)
Trench Hill

Gwynedd

Sat 13 February (12-3)
Penrhyn Castle

Sun 7 February (11-3)
Plas Yn Rhiw

Herefordshire

Thurs 4, 11, 18, 25 February (9-4)
Ivy Croft

Kent

Sun 14 February (12-4)
Copton Ash

Sun 7, Sun 21 February (11-3)
Knowle Hill Farm

Sun 21, Sun 28 February (2-5)
Mere House

By arrangement in February
The Old Rectory

Sun 28 February (12-5)
Yew Tree Cottage

Lancashire, Merseyside & Greater Manchester

Suns 14, 21, 28 February (12-4)
Weeping Ash Garden

Lincolnshire

Sat 27 February (11-4), Sun 28 February (11-6)
21 Chapel Street

Sat 13, Sun 14 February (11-4)
Little Ponton Hall

North East Wales

Thur 18, Thur 25 February (12-3)
Glog Ddu

Northamptonshire

Sun 28 February (12-4)
Jericho

Oxfordshire

Sun 14 February (1.30-4)
14 Chawley Lane

Sun 21 February (1.30-4)
Hollyhocks

Somerset, Bristol & South Gloucestershire

Sun 7 February (10-5)
East Lambrook Manor Gardens

Sun 7, Sun 14 February (11-4)
Rock House

Sun 14, Mon 15 February (11-4)
Sherborne Garden

Suffolk

Sun 14 February (11-4)
Gable House

Surrey

Sun 14 February (11-4)
Gatton Park

Wiltshire

Wed 24, Sat 27 February (10.30-5.30)
Lacock Abbey Gardens

Yorkshire

Wed 24 February (12-4)
Austwick Hall

By arrangement 15 to 22 February
3 Bainton Close

Sun 21 February (11-4.30)
Devonshire Mill

Garden Index

This index lists gardens alphabetically and gives the page number on which they are to be found.

Look out for exciting Designer Gardens **D**

Lemon drizzle cake, Victoria sponge … yummy! ☕

Llys-y-Gwynt, Gwynedd

Accommodation available at NGS Gardens

We feature here a list of NGS gardens offering accommodation, listed by Yellow Book county. You will find contact details in the garden listing.

We are happy to provide this list to help you find accommodation, however please note:

The NGS has no statutory control over the establishments or their methods of operating. The NGS cannot become involved in legal or contractual matters and cannot get involved in seeking financial recompense. All liability for loss, disappointment, negligence or other damage is hereby excluded.

Bedfordshire
Luton Hoo Hotel Golf & Spa

Berkshire
Field Farm Cottage
Littlecote House Hotel
Rookwood Farm House
Sunningdale Park
Whitehouse Farm Cottage

Buckinghamshire
9 Brookside, Lillingstone Lovell Gardens
Danesfield House
Glebe Farm, Lillingstone Lovell Gardens
Grange Drive Wooburn
Magnolia House, Grange Drive Wooburn
Nether Winchendon House
Westend House

Cambridgeshire
Chequer Cottage, Streetly End Gardens
39 Foster Road
Kenilworth Smallholding
Madingley Hall

Carmarthenshire & Pembrokeshire
Blaenfforest
The Cors
Dyffryn Fernant
Ffynone
The Old Vicarage
Picton Castle & Gardens
Rhosygilwen Mansion
Talardd
Upton Castle Gardens

Cheshire & Wirral
Tatton Park

Cornwall
The Barn House
Benallack Barn
Boconnoc
Bonython Manor
Carminowe Valley Garden
Cosawes Barton
Eden Project
Glendurgan
Hidden Valley Gardens
The Homestead Woodland Garden
Tregoose
Trelissick
Trerice
Trerose Manor
Trevoole Farm

Cumbria
Askham Hall
Braeside
Eller How House
Lakeside Hotel & Rocky Bank
Langholme Mill
Matson Ground
Rydal Hall
Swarthmoor Hall
Windy Hall

Derbyshire
Cascades Gardens
Clovermead
Tissington Hall

Devon
Avenue Cottage
Durcombe Water
Fursdon
Goren Farm
Hotel Endsleigh
Langtrees
Regency House
Shapcott Barton Estate
South Worden
Southcombe Gardens
West Down House
Whitstone Bluebells
Whitstone Farm

Dorset
Deans Court
Domineys Yard
Farrs
Marren
Old Down House
Queen Ann House
The Secret Garden

Essex
Horkesley Hall
Rookwoods

Glamorgan
Bryn-y-Ddafad
Gileston Manor
Lougher Moor
Mehefin, Llanmaes Gardens
Slade

Gloucestershire
Aylworth Manor
Barnsley House
Berrys Place Farm
Kempsford Manor
Matara Gardens of Wellbeing
Snugborough Mill, Blockley Gardens
Wells Cottage

Gwent

Castle House
Middle Ninfa Farm & Bunkhouse
Penpergwm Lodge
Usk Open Gardens

Gwynedd

Plas Cadnant Hidden Gardens

Hampshire

12 Christchurch Road
Durmast House
Four Seasons Hotel
The Mill at Gordleton
Tylney Hall Hotel

Herefordshire

Brobury House Gardens
Caves Folly Nurseries
Cloister Garden
Kentchurch Court, Kentchurch
  Gardens
Lawless Hill
Little Llanavon
Midland Farm
Montpelier Cottage
The Old Rectory, Thruxton
Perrycroft
Rhodds Farm
Wolferlow House

Isle of Wight

Clatterford House
Northcourt Manor Gardens

Kent

Boldshaves
Canterbury Cathedral Gardens
Port Lympne, The Aspinall
  Foundation
Rock Farm
The Secret Gardens of Sandwich
  at The Salutation
Sissinghurst Castle
Thatched Cottage

Lancashire, Merseyside & Greater Manchester

Arevinti, The Stubbins Gardens
Mill Barn
The Ridges
Sefton Villa, Sefton Park Gardens
Thie Shey, Port Erin Group

Leicestershire & Rutland

Hill Top Farm, Braunston Gardens
Tresillian House

Lincolnshire

Doddington Hall Gardens
Goltho House
Gunby Hall & Gardens
Hall Farm
Hope House
Manor House
Marigold Cottage
Willow Cottage

London

6 Cornford Grove
58A Teignmouth Road
West Lodge Park

Norfolk

Bagthorpe Hall
Chaucer Barn
Hindringham Hall
Manor House Farm, Wellingham
Narborough Hall
The Old Rectory, Ridlington
Severals Grange

North East

Bitchfield Tower
Fallodon Hall
Gibside
Loughbrow House
Stobgreen House
Thornley House
Whalton Manor Gardens

North East Wales

Aberclwyd Manor
Bodysgallen Hall & Spa
Chirk Castle
Dove Cottage
Ruthin Castle, Ruthin Town
  Gardens
Tal-y-Bryn Farm

Northamptonshire

Dale House, Spratton Gardens

Nottinghamshire

Hodsock Priory Gardens
Patchings Art Centre
The Summer House, Gringley
  Gardens

Oxfordshire

Buttslade House, Sibford Gower
  Gardens
Gowers Close, Sibford Gower
  Gardens
Old Swan & Minster Mill
Ruskin College, Headington
  Gardens
South Newington House

Powys

Beili Neuadd
Caer Beris Manor Hotel
Cyfie Farm
Esgair Angell
Gliffaes Country House Hotel
Grandma's Garden
Gregynog Hall & Garden
Mill Cottage
Penmyarth House & Glanusk
  Estate
Powis Castle Garden
Quarry House, Priest Weston
  Gardens
Tinto House
Tyn y Cwm
1 Ystrad House

Shropshire

Brownhill House
The Citadel
Edge Villa
Goldstone Hall Gardens
Sambrook Manor
Shoothill House
Upper Shelderton House
Walcot Hall
Wollaston Lodge

Somerset, Bristol & South Gloucestershire

Cherry Bolberry Farm
Church Farm House
Hangeridge Farmhouse
Hartwood House
Honeyhurst Farm
Jacob's Loft, Glastonbury Secret
  Gardens
Sole Retreat
Stoberry Garden
Ston Easton Park

Staffordshire, Birmingham & West Midlands

Badger Hill
Colour Mill
The Trentham Estate
Woodbrooke Quaker Study Centre

Suffolk

Bays Farm
Drinkstone Park
The Lucy Redman Garden
Rosemary

Surrey

Barnett Hill
Coverwood Lakes

Sussex

Ashdown Park Hotel
Butlers Farmhouse
Copyhold Hollow
Follers Manor
Holly House
King John's Lodge
Lordington House
The Middle House, Mayfield
  Gardens
Newtimber Place

Ocklynge Manor
South Grange
West Dean Gardens

Warwickshire

The Granary
Springfield House, Warmington
  Village Gardens

Wiltshire

Broomsgrove Lodge
Dauntsey Park, Dauntsey Gardens
The Mill House
The Pound House
Stourhead Garden

Worcestershire

Brook Farm
Chasewood, Hanley Swan NGS
  Gardens
Nafford House, Eckington Gardens

Yorkshire

Austwick Hall
Basin Howe Farm
Devonshire Mill
Dowthorpe Hall & Horse Pasture
  Cottage
Fawley House
Four Gables
Goldsborough Hall
Low Hall, Dacre Banks &
  Summerbridge Gardens
Low Sutton
Lower Heugh Cottage Garden
Manor Farm
Marston Grange
Millgate House
Shandy Hall Gardens
Thornycroft

Gregynog Hall & Garden, Powys

Take your Group to an NGS garden

Garden Visiting Around the World

The National Gardens Scheme is without doubt the largest and oldest of its type in the world but there are others in existence. So if you are heading off on holiday and a passionate garden visitor here are the details of other schemes that you can support.

America

GARDEN CONSERVANCY
W www.gardenconservancy.org
Visit America's very best rarely seen private gardens. Open Days is a national program of The Garden Conservancy, a non-profit organisation that saves and shares outstanding American gardens for the education and inspiration of the public.

VIRGINIA'S HISTORIC GARDEN WEEK
April 18-25 2015
W www.vagardenweek.org
House & Garden Tours offered statewide
Each spring visitors are welcomed to over 250 of Virginia's most beautiful gardens, homes and historic landmarks during "America's Largest Open House." This 8-day statewide event provides visitors a unique opportunity to see unforgettable gardens at the peak of Virginia's springtime colour, as well as beautiful houses sparkling with over 2,000 flower arrangements created by Garden Club of Virginia members. Tour proceeds fund the restoration and preservation of Virginia's historic gardens, and provide graduate level research fellowships for building comprehensive and ongoing records of historic gardens and landscapes in the Commonwealth, and support the mission of the Garden Club of Virginia.

Belgium

Publication Catalogue of private Belgian Open Gardens, published annually in March Contact Dominique Petit-Heymans
E info@jardinsouverts.be
W www.jardinsouverts.be
A non-profit organization founded in 1994. Over 200 remarkable private gardens throughout Belgium open to members. Membership (for two people) of €25 entitles you to the full-colour yearly agenda, comprising photographs, descriptions, opening dates and access plans of the gardens. Most of the proceeds from entry fees support charities chosen by garden owners.
The philosophy of the gardens owners is to invite visitors to discover gardens of quality, of all kinds and sizes.

France

JARDINS ET SANTE
E contact@jardins-sante.org
W www.jardins-sante.org
Founded in 2004, Jardins et Santé is a charitable voluntary association with humanitarian aims. Increasing numbers of gardens open each year across many regions of France. Entry often includes guided tours, exhibitions and concerts. Funds raised from visitor entry fees help finance scientific research in the field of mental illness and also contribute to developing the therapeutic role of the garden, particularly in hospitals and care centres. Every two years the Charity receives appeals from over 140 establishments seeking assistance for the creation of healing gardens. We are happy to be able to contribute towards many of these projects. Our role as information hub for the growing interest, research and activities in the field of hortitherapy is rapidly gaining momentum. Our 4th Symposium held under the patronage of the French Ministry of Environment, took place in Paris in November 2014. Further details can be found on our website.

Japan

THE N.G.S. JAPAN
Contact Tamie Taniguchi
E tamieta@syd.odn.ne.jp
W www.ngs-jp.org
The N.G.S. Japan was founded in 2001. Most of the proceeds from the entry fees support children's and welfare charities as nominated by owners and Japanese garden conservation. It has run a series of lectures entitled 'Lifestyle & Gardening with Charity' since 2004.

Netherlands

Publication Open Tuingids, published annually in March
E info@tuinenstichting.nl
W www.tuinenstichting.nl
Nearly 300 selected private gardens from all over Holland open on behalf of the Dutch Garden Society. This is a not-for profit organisation which was founded in 1980 to protect and restore Dutch gardening heritage consisting of gardens, public parks, urban spaces and cemeteries.

New Zealand

E valeside@xtra.co.nz
W www.gardenstovisit.co.nz
Welcome to Gardens to Visit in New Zealand.
A site that lists private/public and International Gardens along with garden events. If you have a garden or an event that you would like to list please contact me. This site lists formal gardens, tropical gardens, vegetable gardens, and 'many other garden designs and venues for Weddings, Accommodation, Plant sales, Other (gifts, garden art) sales, Cafe/Restaurant and Functions.

Scotland

SCOTLAND'S GARDENS
Publication Scotland's Gardens Guide
Contact Paddy Scott
T 0131 226 3714
E info@scotlandsgardens.org
W www.scotlandsgardens.org
Founded in 1931 Scotland's Gardens facilitates the opening of Scotland's finest gardens of all sizes and kinds to the public as a means of raising money for charity. 40% of the funds raised goes to charities nominated by each garden owner whilst 60% net goes to the Scotland's Gardens beneficiaries: Maggie's Cancer Caring Centres, The Queen's Nursing Institute Scotland, The Gardens Fund of The National Trust for Scotland and Perennial.

Plant Heritage
National Council for the Conservation of Plants & Gardens

Over 70 gardens that open for The National Gardens Scheme are guardians of a Plant Heritage National Plant Collection®, although this may not always be noted in the garden description. These gardens carry the **NCH** symbol.

The county that appears after the garden name indicates the section of The Yellow Book where the entry can be found.

Plant Heritage 12 Home Farm, Loseley Park, Guildford, Surrey GU3 1HS. Tel: 01483 447540 Website: www.plantheritage.com

ACER (EXCL. PALMATUM CVS.)
Blagdon
North East

AGAPANTHUS - FAIRWEATHER NURSERY TRIALS COLLECTION (HORTICULTURAL)
Fairweather's Nursery
Hampshire

AKEBIA
190 Barnet Road
London

ALNUS
Blagdon
North East

ANEMONE (JAPANESE)
Broadview Gardens
Kent

ANEMONE NEMOROSA
Avondale Nursery
Warwickshire

ANEMONE NEMOROSA CVS.
Kingston Lacy
Dorset

ARALIACEAE
Meon Orchard
Hampshire

ARBUTUS
Barton House
Warwickshire

ASPLENIUM SCOLOPENDRIUM
Sizergh Castle
Cumbria

ASTER AUTUMN FLOWERING
The Picton Garden
Herefordshire

ASTER NOVAE-ANGLIAE
Avondale Nursery
Warwickshire

ASTILBE
Holehird Gardens
Cumbria
Marwood Hill
Devon

BRUNNERA
Hearns House
Oxfordshire

BUDDLEJA DAVIDII CVS. & HYBRIDS
Shapcott Barton Estate
Devon

CAMELLIAS & RHODODENDRONS INTRODUCED TO HELIGAN PRE-1920
The Lost Gardens of Heligan
Cornwall

CARPINUS BETULUS CVS.
West Lodge Park
London

CATALPA
Barton House
Warwickshire

CEANOTHUS
Eccleston Square
London

CERCIDIPHYLLUM
Hodnet Hall Gardens
Shropshire

CLEMATIS VITICELLA
Longstock Park
Hampshire

CLEMATIS VITICELLA CVS.
Roseland House
Cornwall

CODONOPSIS
Woodlands
Lincolnshire

CONVALLARIA
Kingston Lacy
Dorset

CORIARIA
Crûg Farm
Gwynedd

CORNUS (EXCL. C. FLORIDA CVS.)
Newby Hall & Gardens
Yorkshire

COTINUS
Bath Priory Hotel
Somerset, Bristol & South Gloucestershire

CYCLAMEN (EXCL. PERSICUM CVS.)
Higher Cherubeer, Cherubeer Gardens
Devon

CYDONIA OBLONGA
Norton Priory Museum & Gardens
Cheshire & Wirral

CYSTOPTERIS
Sizergh Castle
Cumbria

DIGITALIS
The Harris Garden
Berkshire

DRYOPTERIS
Sizergh Castle
Cumbria

EMBOTHRIUM
Bodnant Garden
Gwynedd

EUCALYPTUS
Meon Orchard
Hampshire

EUCALYPTUS SPP.
The World Garden at Lullingstone
Castle
Kent

EUCRYPHIA
Whitstone Farm
Devon

EUCRYPHIA
Bodnant Garden
Gwynedd

EUONYMUS (DECIDUOUS)
East Bergholt Place - The Place for
Plants
Suffolk

EUPHORBIA
University of Oxford Botanic Garden
Oxfordshire

EUPHORBIA (HARDY)
Firvale Allotment Garden
Yorkshire

**GERANIUM SYLVATICUM &
RENARDII - FORMS, CVS. &
HYBRIDS**
Wren's Nest
Cheshire & Wirral

GEUM
1 Brickwall Cottages
Kent

GUNNERA
The Mowle
Norfolk

HEDERA
Erddig Hall
North East Wales

HELIOTROPIUM
Hampton Court Palace
London

**HELIOTROPIUM
ARBORESCENS CVS.**
The Homestead
Leicestershire & Rutland

HELLEBORUS
Broadview Gardens
Kent

**HEPATICA SPP. & CVS.
(EXCL. H NOBILIS VAR.
JAPONICA CVS.)**
Hazelwood Farm
Cumbria

HOHERIA
Abbotsbury Gardens
Dorset

**HOSTA (EUROPEAN AND
ASIATIC)**
Hanging Hosta Garden
Hampshire

HOSTA (MODERN HYBRIDS)
Cleave House
Devon

IRIS ENSATA
Marwood Hill
Devon

JUGLANS
Upton Wold
Gloucestershire

**JUGLANS (INCL REGIA
CVS.)**
Wimpole Estate
Cambridgeshire

LABURNUM
Powis Castle Garden
Powys

LANTANA
Hampton Court Palace
London

**LAPAGERIA ROSEA (&
NAMED CVS)**
Roseland House
Cornwall

**LEUCANTHEMUM X
SUPERBUM
(CHRYSANTHEMUM
MAXIMUM)**
Shapcott Barton Estate
Devon

LEWISIA
'John's Garden' at Ashwood
Nurseries
Staffordshire, Birmingham & West
Midlands

MAGNOLIA SPP.
Bodnant Garden
Gwynedd

**MALUS (CVS. FROM NOTTS
& DERBY, LINCS, LEICS &
YORKS)**
Clumber Park Walled Kitchen Garden
Nottinghamshire

MALUS (ORNAMENTAL)
Barnards Farm
Essex

**MECONOPSIS (LARGE
PERENNIAL SPP. &
HYBRIDS)**
Holehird Gardens
Cumbria

**MENTHA - UK CULTIVATED
MINTS IN POTS**
Canalia, Adderbury Gardens
Oxfordshire

MONARDA
Glyn Bach
Carmarthenshire & Pembrokeshire

MUSCARI
16 Witton Lane
Norfolk

NERINE SARNIENSIS CVS.
Bickham Cottage
Devon

OMPHALODES
Hearns House
Oxfordshire

OSMUNDA
Sizergh Castle
Cumbria

PARIS
Crûg Farm
Gwynedd

PATRINIA
The Hyde
Hampshire

PENNISETUM
Knoll Gardens
Dorset

PENSTEMON
Froggery Cottage
Northamptonshire

PENSTEMON CVS.
Kingston Maurward Gardens and
Animal Park
Dorset

PHLOMIS
Foamlea
Devon

PINUS SPP.
The Lovell Quinta Arboretum
Cheshire & Wirral

POLYGONATUM
Crûg Farm
Gwynedd

POLYSTICHUM
Holehird Gardens
Cumbria

PTEROCARYA
Upton Wold
Gloucestershire

**QUEEN MARY II EXOTICKS
COLLECTION**
Hampton Court Palace
London

QUERCUS
Chevithorne Barton
Devon

RHAPIS SPP. & CVS.
Gwyndy Bach
Gwynedd

RHEUM (CULINARY CVS.)
Clumber Park Walled Kitchen Garden
Nottinghamshire

RHODODENDRON (GHENT AZALEAS)
Sheffield Park and Garden
Sussex

RHODODENDRON FORRESTII
Bodnant Garden
Gwynedd

ROSA (RAMBLING)
Moor Wood
Gloucestershire

SALVIA (TENDER)
Kingston Maurward Gardens and Animal Park
Dorset

SALVIA SPP.
2 Hillside Cottages
Hampshire

SANGUISORBA
Avondale Nursery
Warwickshire

SAXIFRAGA SECT. LIGULATAE: SPP. & CVS.
Waterperry Gardens
Oxfordshire

SAXIFRAGA SUBSECT. KABSCHIA & ENGLERIA
Waterperry Gardens
Oxfordshire

SIBERIAN IRIS CVS: BRITISH, AWARD WINNERS & HISTORICALLY SIGNIFICANT
Aulden Farm
Herefordshire

SORBUS
Ness Botanic Gardens
Cheshire & Wirral
Blagdon
North East

STERN, SIR F (PLANTS SELECTED BY)
Highdown Gardens
Sussex

STEWARTIA - ASIAN SPP.
High Beeches Woodland and Water Garden
Sussex

STREPTOCARPUS
Dibleys Nurseries
North East Wales

STYRACACEAE (INCL HALESIA, PTEROSTYRAX, STYRAX, SINOJACKIA)
Holker Hall Gardens
Cumbria

TAXODIUM SPP. & CVS.
West Lodge Park
London

TULBAGHIA SPP. & SUBSP.
Marwood Hill
Devon

YUCCA
Renishaw Hall & Gardens
Derbyshire

Aulden Farm, Herefordshire

Find a garden near you – download our free iOS app

Acknowledgements

Each year the NGS receives fantastic support from the community of garden photographers who donate and make available images of gardens for use in The Yellow Book and NGS publicity material. The NGS would like to thank them for their generous donations.

We also thank the garden owners who have kindly submitted images of their gardens.

Unless otherwise stated, photographs are kindly supplied by permission of the garden owner.

The Yellow Book 2015 Production Team: Elna Broe, Linda Ellis, Rosalind Ellis, Louise Grainger, Rachel Hick, Kali Masure, Chris Morley, Azam Parkar, George Plumptre, Jane Sennett, Georgina Waters, Debbie Wilson. With special thanks to our NGS County Volunteers.

CONSTABLE
First published in Great Britain in 2015 by Constable
Copyright © The National Gardens Scheme 2015

The moral right of the author has been asserted.

A CIP catalogue record for this book is available from the British Library.
ISBN 978-1-472120-87-8
ISSN 1365-0572
EAN 9 781905 942008

Designed by Level Partnership Ltd
Maps by Global Mapping © The XYZ Digital Map Co
Typeset in Helvetica Neue by Chat Noir Design
Printed and bound in Italy by Rotolito Lombard

Constable
is an imprint of
Constable & Robinson Ltd
100 Victoria Embankment
London EC4Y 0DY

An Hachette UK Company
www.hachette.co.uk
www.constablerobinson.com

If you require this information in alternative formats, please telephone 01483 211535 or email ngs@ngs.org.uk

The Society of Garden Designers

Members of The Society of Garden Designers participating in the NGS in 2015.

Fellow of the Society of Garden Designers (FSGD) is awarded to Members for exceptional contributions to the Society or to the profession

Rosemary Alexander FSGD
Sally Court FSGD
Roderick Griffin FSGD
Lucy Huntington FSGD
Ian Kitson FSGD
Robin Templar-Williams FSGD
Julie Toll FSGD

Member of the Society of Garden Designers (MSGD) is awarded after passing adjudication

Sol Blytt-Jordens MSGD
Timothy Carless MSGD
Mhairi Clutson MSGD
Rosemary Coldstream MSGD
Chris Eves MSGD
Jill Fenwick MSGD
Paul Gazerwitz MSGD
Dawn Isaac MSGD
Arabella Lennox-Boyd MSGD
Dan Pearson MSGD
Emma Plunket MSGD
Debbie Roberts MSGD
Charles Rutherfoord MSGD
Ian Smith MSGD
Tom Stuart-Smith MSGD
Sue Townsend MSGD
Cleve West MSGD
Barbara Hunt MSGD (retired)

Pre-Registered Member is a member working towards gaining Registered Membership

Joanne Bernstein
Selina Botham
Judy Bryant
Fiona Cadwallader
Wendy Cartwright
Anna Dargavel
Louise Hardwick
Guy Petheram
Kate Smart
Susan Summers
Helen Thomas
Virginia von Celsing
Jo Ward-Ellison
Julia Whiteaway

Student
Cate Caldwell

From tiny back plots to country estates …